2019 EDITION

Best Colleges

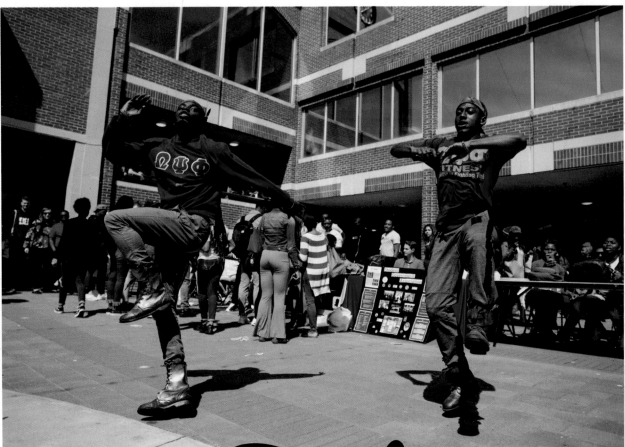

HOW TO ORDER: Additional copies of U.S. News & World Report's Best Colleges 2019 guidebook are available for purchase at usnews.com/collegeguide or by calling (800) 836-6397. To order custom reprints, please call (877) 652-5295 or email usnews@wrightsmedia.com. For permission to republish articles, data or other content from this book, email permissions@usnews.com.

FLORIDA STATE UNIVERSITY

BRETT ZIEGLER FOR USN&WR

CONTENTS

42

52

CLOCKWISE FROM TOP LEFT: GETTY IMAGES, ILLUSTRATION BY SHAW NIELSEN FOR USN&WR, GETTY IMAGES, BRETT ZIEGLER FOR USN&WR

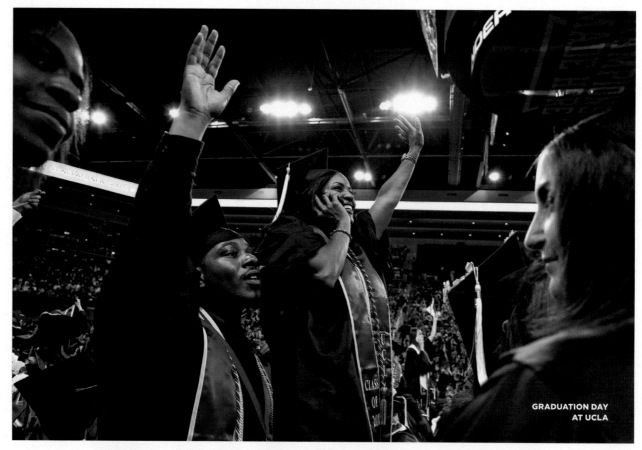

GRADUATION DAY AT UCLA

The U.S. News Rankings

TROY HARVEY FOR USN&WR, GETTY IMAGES

CONTENTS

CHAPTER 4

Getting In

CHAPTER 5

Finding the Money

134

DEANNA DENT FOR USN&WR, GETTY IMAGES (2)

@usnews.com

YOUR COLLEGE GAME PLAN

Insider Advice

If you're looking for college advice, you've come to the right place. We provide expert tips to help families research, apply to and pay for college. Our articles and slideshows feature college admissions and financial aid officers, counselors, current students, graduates, parents and more, who all share their insights to help demystify the process.
usnews.com/collegeadvice

GETTING IN

College Admissions Playbook

Get tips from Varsity Tutors, an academic tutoring and test-prep provider. This blog offers advice on mastering the SAT and ACT as well as the college application process.
usnews.com/collegeplaybook

COLLEGE VISITS

Take a Road Trip

We've gone on numerous trips to visit campuses in case you can't. Check out our compendium of more than 30 different trips to 100-plus schools.
usnews.com/roadtrips

RANKINGS INSIGHT

Morse Code Blog

Get the inside scoop on the rankings – and the commentary and controversy surrounding them – from U.S. News' Bob Morse, the mastermind behind our education rankings projects.
usnews.com/morsecode

IN-DEPTH DATA

College Compass

Gain access to the U.S. News College Compass, which offers comprehensive searchable data and tools for high school students starting down the path to campus. To get a 25 percent discount, subscribe at **usnews.com/compassoffer**

PAYING FOR COLLEGE

Researching Aid

Visit our guide to all your possible sources of college funds. Learn about your savings options and which schools meet students' full need.
usnews.com/payforcollege

The Student Loan Ranger

Don't fall into the trap of taking on too much debt. Bloggers from the National Foundation for Credit Counseling provide guidance if you must turn to loans to pay for college.
usnews.com/studentloanranger

DISTANCE LEARNING

Online Education

Do you need to balance school with work or other obligations? Consult our rankings of the best online degree programs for leads on how to get your diploma without leaving home.
usnews.com/online

FOR SCHOOLS ONLY

Academic Insights

U.S. News Academic Insights is an analytics dashboard intended for use by institutions that comprises all of the undergraduate and graduate historical rankings data we've collected. The dashboard allows for peer group comparisons and includes easy-to-understand visualizations.
ai.usnews.com

BEST COLLEGES
2019 EDITION

Executive Committee Chairman and Editor-in-Chief Mortimer B. Zuckerman
Chairman Eric Gertler
Editor and Chief Content Officer Brian Kelly
Executive Editor Anne McGrath
Deputy Editor Michael Morella
Chief Data Strategist Robert J. Morse
Senior Data Analyst Eric Brooks
Data Collection Manager Matthew Mason
Art Director Rebecca Pajak
Director of Photography Avi Gupta
Contributing Editors Elizabeth Whitehead, Lindsay Lyon
Associate Editor Lindsay Cates
Photography Editor Brett Ziegler
Assistant Photo Editor Lydia Chebbine
Contributors Ann Claire Carnahan, Stacey Colino, Elizabeth Gardner, Mariya Greeley, Katherine Hobson, Beth Howard, Ned Johnson, Margaret Loftus, Alison Murtagh, Courtney Rubin, Barbara Sadick, William Stixrud, Arlene Weintraub
Research Manager Myke Freeman
Directory Janie S. Price

USNEWS.COM/EDUCATION
Executive Editor Kimberly Castro
Managing Editors Anita Narayan, Liz Opsitnik, Katy Marquardt
Assistant Managing Editor Nathan Hellman
Senior Editors Autumn Arnett, Dennis Kelly, Liz Weiss
Editor Whitney Wyckoff
Associate Editors Ray Frager, Ali Follman
Reporters Ilana Kowarski, Farran Powell
Senior Digital Producers Briana Boyington, Nancy Pham
Digital Producer Melissa Shin
Vice President and General Manager Michael Nolan
Senior Product Manager Amanda Grace Johnson
Product Manager Amanda Gustafson
SEO Analyst Jeff Budd

ACADEMIC INSIGHTS
Vice President and General Manager, Healthcare & Insights Evan Jones
Senior Product Manager Cale Gosnell
Account Manager Gaetana DiRoberto
Marketing Manager, Insights Taylor Suggs

INFORMATION SERVICES
Vice President, Data and Information Strategy Stephanie Salmon
Data Analysts Alexis Krivian, Kenneth Hines, Elizabeth Martin
Data Collection Kaylah Denis, Keke Ellis, Eric Newsom

TECHNOLOGY
Senior Director of Engineering Matt Kupferman
Senior Directors of Software Development Dan Brown, Jerome Gipe
Senior Systems Manager Cathy Cacho
Software Technical Lead Ben Gmurczyk, David Jessup
Developers Alex Blum, Nick Doty, William Garcia, Erik Gartz, Brian Stewart, David Kaminsky, Jonathan Kvicky
Project Manager Sangeetha Sharma
Quality Assurance Sandy Sathyanarayanan
Digital Production Michael A. Brooks (Manager); Michael Fingerhuth

President and Chief Executive Officer William D. Holiber

ADVERTISING AND MARKETING
Vice President, Advertising Linda Brancato
Vice President, Marketing and Advertising Strategy Alexandra Kalaf
Vice President, Pharmaceutical and Life Sciences Sales Josh Kramon
Director, Integrated Media Solutions Peter Bowes
New York Advertising Director Heather Levine
Pacific Northwest Advertising Director Peter Teese
Health Care Advertising Director Colin Hamilton
Director of Education Advertising Shannon Tkach
Senior Account Executive Ivy Zenati
Account Executives Julie Izzo, Eddie Kelly, Spencer Vastoler
Managing Editor, BrandFuse Jada Graves
Web Designer, BrandFuse Sara Hampt
Programmatic Account Manager Hector Guerra
Senior Manager of Ad Technology and Platforms Teron Samuel
Director of Marketing and Sales Strategy Tina Lopez
Manager, Sales Strategy Gary DeNardis
Sales Planners Gina DeNatale, Jade-Ashley Thomas, Michael Zee
Director of Advertising Operations Cory Nesser
Senior Manager, Client Success Katina Sangare
Account Managers James Adeleye, Katie Harper, Niani Patterson
Manager, Ad Operations Tessa Gluck
Ad Operations Trafficker Lauren Sousa
Senior Manager of Audience Development, Social Media Greg Hicks
Audience Development Specialists, Social Media David Oliver, Darian Somers, Megan Trimble
Director of Advertising Services Phyllis Panza
Business Operations Karolee Jarnecki
Administration Judy David, Anny Lasso, Carmen Caraballo
Vice President, Specialty Marketing Mark W. White
Director of Specialty Marketing Abbe Weintraub

Chief Operating Officer Karen S. Chevalier
Chief Product Officer Chad Smolinski
Chief Financial Officer Neil Maheshwari
Senior Vice President, Education, News, Money Chris DiCosmo
Senior Vice President, Strategic Development and General Counsel Peter M. Dwoskin
Senior Vice President, Technology Yingjie Shu

Additional copies of **U.S. News & World Report's Best Colleges 2019** guidebook are available for purchase at (800) 836-6397 or online at **usnews.com/collegeguide.** To order custom reprints, call (877) 652-5295 or email **usnews@wrightsmedia.com.** For all other permissions, email **permissions@usnews.com.**

Paying for college is one of the biggest risks families face – AXA Achievement℠ can help.

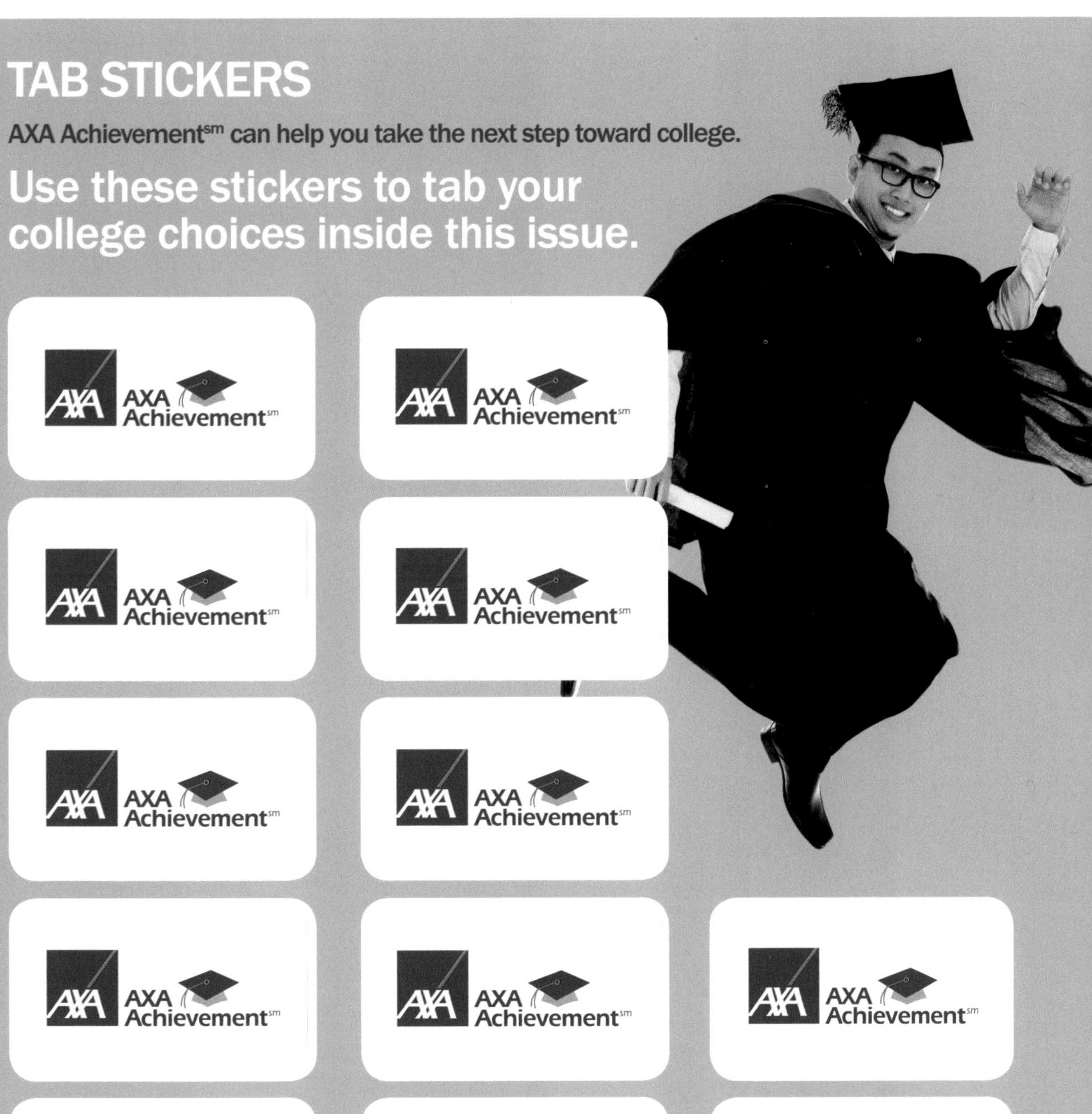

Next steps toward college

Taking the right small steps today can help eliminate the risk of not being able to afford a college education

Filling out the FAFSA helps you minimize borrowing. It's a misconception that filling out the Free Application for Federal Student Aid (FAFSA) is the fast track to student loan debt. You risk losing need-based grants and scholarships from the university. The reason? The universities you selected on the FAFSA to receive your information use it to evaluate your financial aid eligibility.

To avoid losing need-based aid you might qualify for:

1. **Fill out the FAFSA as early as possible.** Some need-based aid is limited in numbers and available on a first-come first-served basis for those who qualify. Universities have a limited amount of grant aid. Applying late could mean you miss out.

2. **Select schools.** Always select schools that are being considered on the form. Otherwise, the information won't arrive at the colleges that need it. Amend the FAFSA form online if school choices change.

3. **Fill out the special circumstances forms when needed.** Whether you're applying for next year or are already in college, you need to fill out a special circumstances form if your income changes due to a number of reasons, such as a medical situation, a layoff, or a salary reduction.

4. **Practice filling out the FAFSA on the FAFSA4caster site from the Department of Education as early as middle school.** It's designed to roughly estimate financial aid years in advance.

5. **Follow up with schools to make sure information is received and to check on financial aid availability.** Bonus: you may find out about a scholarship you previously didn't know about during the phone call.

Choosing universities with the lowest listed tuition prices can sometimes cost you more money. A private school with "sticker price" that is four times more than that of a state school may offer scholarships and grants that make it the cheaper alternative. Find out which schools offer the best financial aid packages before applying. Net price calculators available on most college websites are one way to estimate what you would pay based on individual circumstances.

To better understand the relative costs of higher education:

1. **Narrow college choices down to ten using factors such as majors, campus size and internship placement.** Talk with your high school counselor early to start the process of college selection and career exploration.

2. **Request information from each school on what's important to you.** For instance, call the career center to ask about graduate employment rates.

3. **Visit the websites of your top ten college choices.** Find the net price calculator on their website by entering "net price calculator" into the search box on the school's home page. Enter information such as family income and number of children in college.

4. **Call financial aid offices at your top five choices to see if there are any changes in grant awards for the year you will be attending.** Available funds change, so you want to make sure you factor in the most recent information into your family's application decisions.

5. **Use the net price calculator as a baseline.** You may also qualify for merit-based aid.

To learn more and apply, visit www.axa.com/achievers

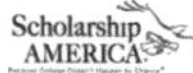

From the Editor's Desk

by **Brian Kelly**

This college search thing can be a little intimidating, especially if you're going through it for the first time. This is our 34th go-round at U.S. News, so we feel like we've got some experience worth sharing.

Over the years, we've improved our information and sharpened our focus, with our primary objective being to help students and their parents make one of life's most important – and costliest – decisions. Prospective students and their parents need objective measures that allow them to evaluate and compare schools. The U.S. News rankings are one tool to help them make choices, along with all the other insights and guidance contained in these pages. This sort of assistance is more relevant than ever, with some private colleges now costing over $250,000 for a bachelor's degree. At the same time, many public high schools have greatly reduced their college counseling resources, leaving students and parents to educate themselves about the search and admissions process.

Of course, we have adjusted our rankings methodology over the years to reflect changes in the world of higher education, and we make it clear that we are not doing peer-reviewed social science research, although we do maintain very high survey and data standards. We have always been open and transparent. We have always said that the rankings are not perfect. The first were based solely on schools' academic reputation among leaders at peer institutions; we later developed a formula in which the opinions of experts and peers account for 20 percent of a school's score and important quantitative measures such as graduation and retention rates, class size and student-faculty ratios account for the rest. Over time, we have shifted weight from inputs (indicators of the quality of students and resources) to outputs (success in graduating students). We operate under this guiding principle: The methodology is altered only if a change will better aid our readers and web audience in comparing schools. This year, we've incorporated a way to assess schools' commitment to promoting social mobility; we measure how good a job they're doing graduating students who have received Pell Grants. And we've removed colleges' acceptance rates as an indicator of student excellence.

A starting point. It has helped us a great deal to have these principles to focus on as we have faced the inevitable criticisms from academia about our rankings' growing influence. One main critique remains: that it is impossible to reduce the complexities of a college's offerings and attributes to a single number. It's important to keep in mind that our information is a starting point. The next steps in a college search should include detailed research on a smaller list of choices, campus visits, and conversations with students, faculty and alumni wherever you can find them. Feedback from academia has helped improve the rankings over time. We meet with our critics, listen to their points of view, debate them on the merits of what we do, and make appropriate changes.

U.S. News is keenly aware that the higher education community is also a major audience for our rankings. We understand how seriously academics, college presidents, trustees and governing boards take our data. They study, analyze and use them in various ways, including benchmarking against peers, alumni fundraising, and advertising to attract students.

BEST COLLEGES U.S.News & WORLD REPORT 2019

What does all of this mean in today's global information marketplace? U.S. News has become a respected, unbiased resource that higher education administrators and policymakers and the college-bound public worldwide turn to for reliable guidance. In fact, the Best Colleges rankings have become a key part of the evolving higher education accountability movement. Universities are increasingly being held responsible for their policies, how their funds are spent, the level of student engagement, and how much graduates have learned. The U.S. News rankings have become the annual public benchmark to measure the academic performance of the country's colleges and universities.

We know our role has limits. The rankings should only be used as one factor in the college search – we've long said that there is no single "best college." There is only the best college for you or, more likely, a handful of good options. Our website, usnews.com, features thousands of pages of rankings, research, sortable data, information on getting in and getting financial aid, and a personalized tool called College Compass.

We know the process of choosing a college is not simple. But our experience tells us the hard work is worth it in the end. ◆

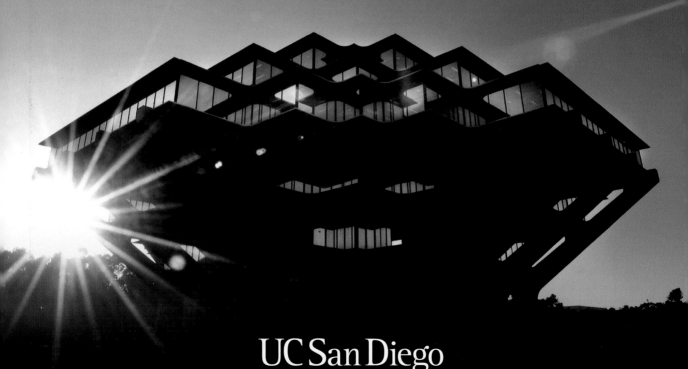

Here at the University of California San Diego, we have a history of pursuing the greater good in a most unconventional fashion. How? By approaching complex issues with wholly unexpected solutions. Like using cell phone records to predict and prevent global conflict. And developing clean-burning cookstoves as a means of reversing global warming trends. Established in 1960, our academic community has been shaped by exceptional scholars who aren't afraid to push boundaries, challenge the status quo, and redefine conventional wisdom. You could even say our most cherished tradition is never blindly following tradition—something that comes in handy when you want to change the world. So, if this unconventional courage to look at the world differently is in your DNA, then you might just be one of us.

Apply at ucsd.edu.

Transforming Lives and Shaping Futures

The ***2nd*** *best college in the nation* for quality of education, timely graduation, affordability, and alumni success, UC San Diego is setting students on the path of upward mobility. (*Money*, 2018)

Unconventional Solutions Drive the Health Care Revolution

Our Department of Bioengineering, ranked ***2nd*** *in the nation for biomedical/bioengineering,* is solving complex biological and medical problems with the principles and tools of engineering. (*U.S. News & World Report*, 2018)

Cultivating Innovative Artists Who Reimagine Our World

UC San Diego was ranked one of the ***TOP 5*** *undergraduate acting schools in the nation,* preparing the next generation of artists and scholars to redefine the way we interpret our world through the performing arts. (*The Hollywood Reporter*, 2018)

Fostering Community and Inclusion

One of the ***TOP 10*** *public universities in the nation for LGBTQ+ students,* UC San Diego was recognized for our commitment to LGBTQ+ inclusion, intersectional learning opportunities, and the critical gender studies major. (*College Choice*, 2017)

CHAPTER

Study th

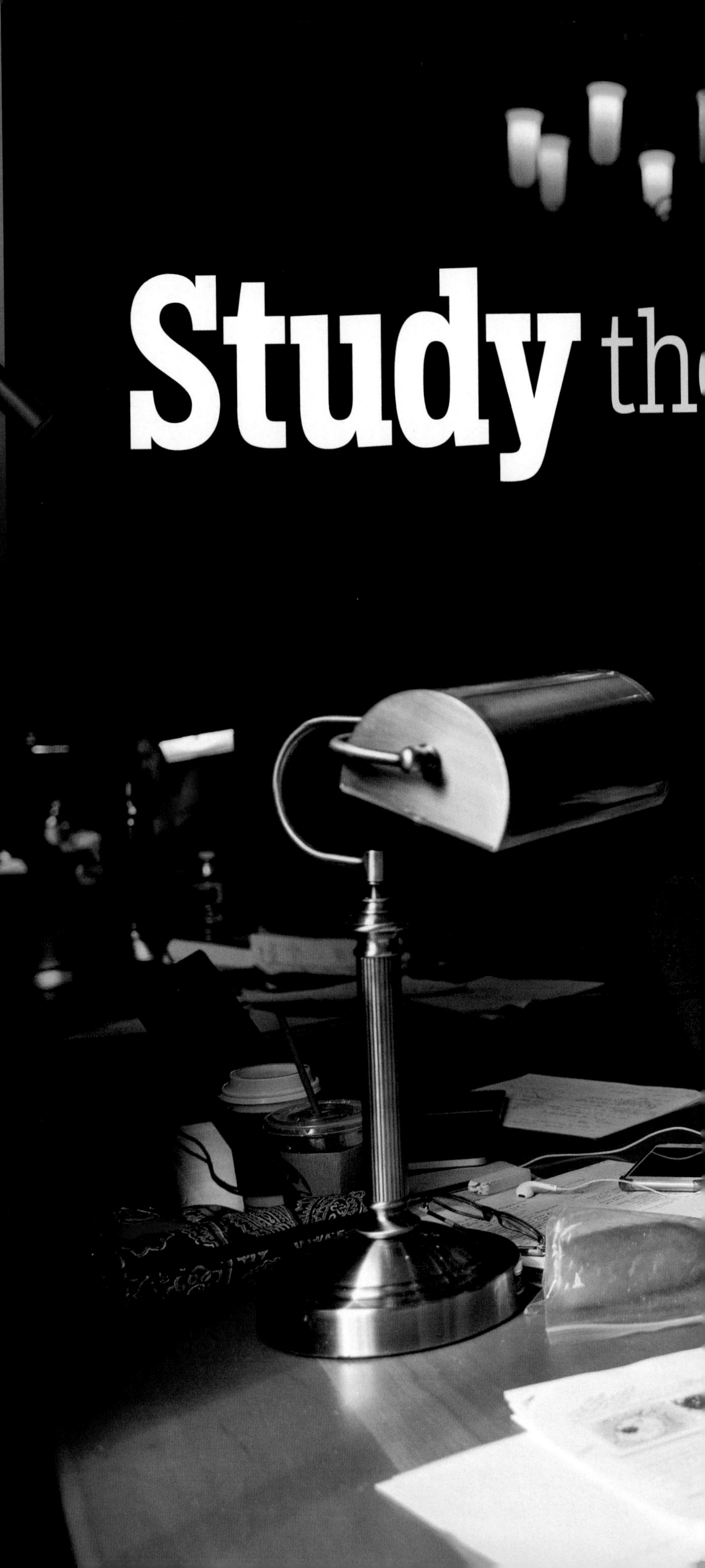

THE UNIVERSITY OF ILLINOIS–URBANA-CHAMPAIGN

BRETT ZIEGLER FOR USN&WR

Schools

Political Science &
nternational Relations

Your Goal: Success!

When choosing a school, look for programs that will help you thrive

by **Katherine Hobson**

When Destiny Caldwell started at Agnes Scott College near Atlanta in 2016, she planned to study nursing. Then, in the spring of her first year, she traveled to central Europe with a group of classmates as part of the school's required Global Journeys course, which is designed to develop international awareness and involves a weeklong immersion trip. Her course and trip focused on the region's changing politics, but Caldwell found herself thinking a lot about why it was safe to drink the water in only some of the countries she visited. After the students returned to campus, they reflected on their experiences. "We asked ourselves questions like 'How do you want to change things?' and 'How do you want to change yourself?'" she recalls. Caldwell's own answers led her in a new direction: She switched her major to public health, hoping to explore some of the economic, social and political dimensions of health in addition to the clinical ones.

UNDERGRADS SHOW OFF RESEARCH AND CREATIVE WORK AT SUNY-GENESEO.

Agnes Scott is one of many schools across the country that are increasingly turning to more in-depth, experiential forms of learning and other

RACHEL JEROME FERRARO FOR USN&WR

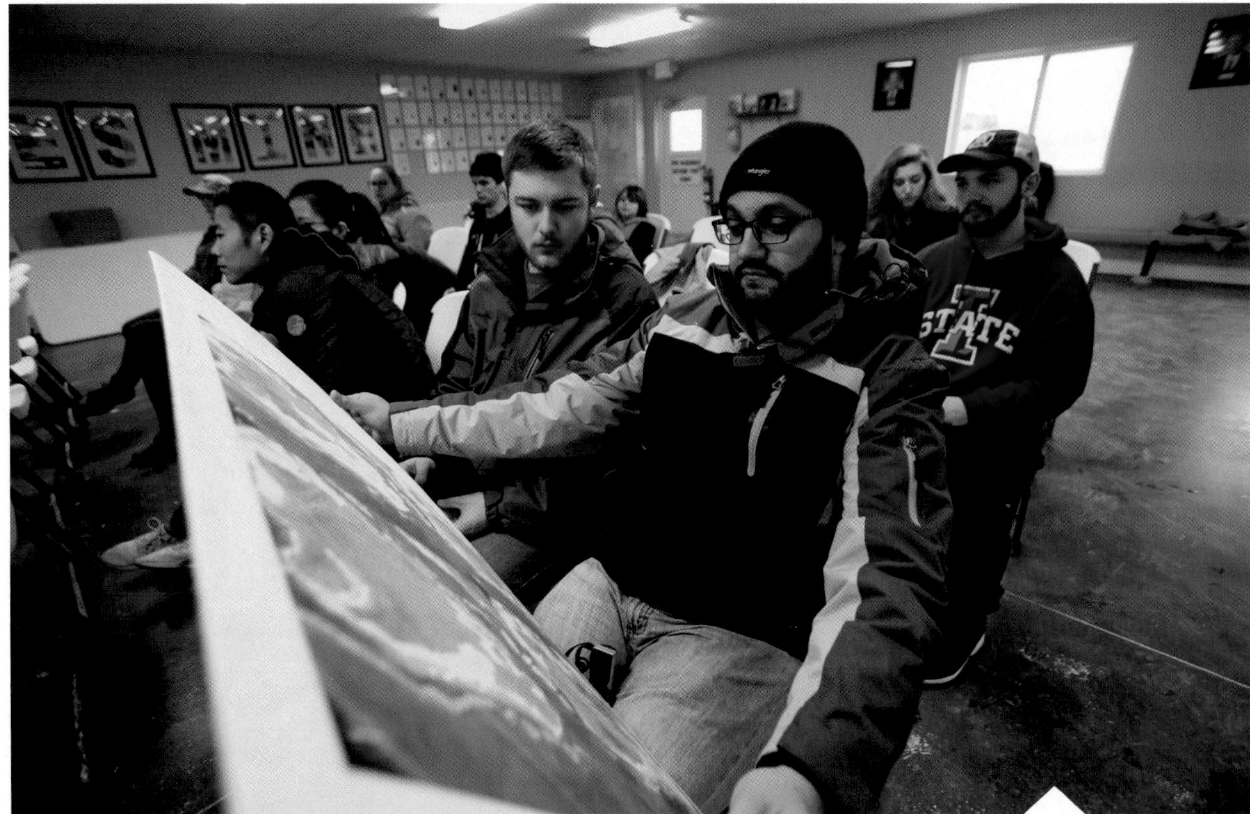

STUDENTS IN IOWA STATE'S EARTH, WIND AND FIRE LEARNING COMMUNITY PREPARE TO TOUR A MINE.

"high-impact practices" aimed at helping students feel intellectually engaged and connected to their college from the minute they set foot on campus. These opportunities, worth looking for during a college search, include first-year seminars, learning communities (in which small groups of students take a class or classes together, for example), undergraduate research, service learning (part of the course syllabus involves service out in the community) and studying abroad. All can "pay dividends in a number of ways," says Alexander McCormick, associate professor of educational leadership and policy studies at Indiana University and director of the annual National Survey of Student Engagement, which asks students about their participation in activities linked to learning and personal development.

Research suggests participation in high-impact practices is tied to greater engagement, perceived gains in learning and overall satisfaction, as well as a higher likelihood of sticking with a school beyond the first year. And these experiences also are preparation for postgraduate life in a way that traditional classes alone are not. "If done well, they speak to real concerns in the real world," says Debra Humphreys, vice president of strategic engagement at the Lumina Foundation, a private organization that aims to widen post-high school learning for students of all backgrounds.

The 2018 NSSE survey of more than 275,000 college freshmen and seniors at nearly 500 schools in the U.S. showed that 60 percent of seniors had participated in at least two high-impact practices. That's McCormick's recommendation: one experience in the first year and at least one more tied to a student's major, such as a senior capstone project.

Easing the transition. Many schools focus on freshman year, which can be a big adjustment both academically and socially for incoming students. First-year experiences might include intensive orientation programs, short bonding trips with a small group of peers, and freshman seminars or other academic expe-

First-Year Experience

U.S. News asked college officials in 2018 to nominate up to 15 schools with strong first-year experience programs that help students form close relationships and transition to college. These schools (listed alphabetically) got the most votes. See more at **usnews.com.**

Abilene Christian University (TX)
Agnes Scott College (GA)
Alverno College (WI)
Amherst College (MA)
Appalachian State University (NC)*
Bard College (NY)
Bates College (ME)
Belmont University (TN)
Berea College (KY)
Bowdoin College (ME)
Dartmouth College (NH)
Elon University (NC)
Georgia State University*
Princeton University (NJ)
University of South Carolina*

(*Public)

REBECCA F. MILLER FOR USN&WR

riences intended to accustom new students to more rigorous classes than they had in high school. At Butler University in Indianapolis, all 1,000-plus incoming freshmen take a two-semester seminar with the same cohort (usually capped at 18 students) to sharpen their speaking, reading and writing skills within the context of a cross-disciplinary topic like "Gettysburg in History and Memory" or "Classical Music and the Self."

"It's a way to get students to engage in critical thinking with a group of peers they're comfortable with," says Angela Hofstetter, co-director of Butler's first-year seminar program. "We place them together during the Welcome Week, so from the moment that class begins, students have formed a bond." SJ Baker, a junior at Butler majoring in economics and history, says her first-year seminar, "Identity, Community and Social Justice," helped her learn to interact with students with diverse viewpoints, a skill she says she's already used in and out of the classroom. "It's not only about standing up for your opinions, but considering the possibility that you're wrong, or that your thoughts aren't complete," she says.

Learning communities, another common first-year approach, can also help build bonds between students, typically through a common group of classes and sometimes shared housing. At Iowa State University, there are some 90 learning community options primarily for first-year students, organized by academic topic or other affinities. Possibilities include International Leadership and Women in Science and Engineering.

Emily Gilbertson, a sophomore from Cedar Rapids, Iowa, considering a food science major, was attracted to her freshman Food Science and Human Nutrition community because it "would make a big school smaller." She took a handful of core classes with about a dozen people from the group, some of whom became close friends; around Thanksgiving last year, the community gathered to cook dinner with their professors.

Not all learning communities operate the same way, and they're not all limited to first years. At Evergreen State College in Washington state, most of the school's 3,400-plus undergrads take a

Learning Communities

In these programs, students typically take courses as a group to build common bonds. Some are also residential. These schools (arranged alphabetically) got the most mentions in U.S. News' 2018 survey. See others at **usnews.com.**

Agnes Scott College (GA)
Amherst College (MA)
Belmont University (TN)
Bucknell University (PA)
Dartmouth College (NH)
Elon University (NC)
Evergreen State College (WA)*
Indiana U.-Purdue U.-Indianapolis*
Michigan State University*
University of Maryland-College Park*
University of Michigan-Ann Arbor*
University of South Carolina*
University of Washington*
University of Wisconsin-Madison*
Vanderbilt University (TN)
Yale University (CT)

(*Public)

Keeping on Track

As colleges work to help students succeed – and graduate on time – some schools, such as Georgia State University in Atlanta and Temple University in Philadelphia, have turned to predictive systems that crunch huge amounts of data to identify students who show warning signs, such as getting a C on a test in a key prerequisite course or enrolling in a class that they mistakenly think will count toward their major. "We had a large subset of students who were dropping out, but who weren't raising their hands and saying they had trouble or going to a faculty member or the registrar's office," says Timothy Renick, senior vice president for student success at Georgia State.

First launched at the beginning of the 2012-13 school year, the university's GPS Advising system now tracks some 800 academic risk factors for all 25,000-plus of its undergraduates daily. Students who show potential signs of trouble – such as dropping a course in the middle of the semester – are flagged for one-on-one meetings with their academic adviser and can get tutoring or supplemental instruction, if needed.

Rising rates. Since GPS was launched, six-year graduation rates for full-time students have risen from 48 to 55 percent – approaching the national average of 60 percent. The system has particularly helped part-time and transfer students, Renick says, and those most at risk, including African-American, Latino and low-income students.

Georgia State isn't alone. Arizona State University has integrated streams of information about housing, academic success and finances into a portal that every student's academic adviser can consult before reaching out to students who need help. The University of Texas–Austin has seen its four-year graduation rate climb from 52 to 66 percent since 2012 using student success initiatives, including predictive analytics that incorporate academic and demographic data. Students who aren't doing well in certain major-specific STEM classes can get linked up with tutoring or even switch majors early on to stay on track. Says Carolyn Connerat, associate vice provost for enrollment management at UT–Austin: "We want to open a conversation and tell them, 'You have the potential to succeed, and we're here to help you.'" *–K.H.*

single cross-disciplinary "program" each academic quarter. Earth Dynamics, for example, could encompass courses in economics, geology and world history. Students have the same classmates for the entire program, so "you have this network of friendships that tie you to the experience, which assures you that you can get through difficult moments, stay here, and graduate," says George Bridges, president of the college. Some schools, including Iowa State, Carnegie Mellon University in Pittsburgh and the University of Wisconsin–Madison, include common housing in some of their communities.

At Vanderbilt University in Nashville, all 1,600 freshmen live in one of 10 houses of the Martha Rivers Ingram Commons, a first-year residential college system. That's where students have their first meetings with faculty, who help them understand academic expectations. The idea is to have easy access to resources that help with the transition to college, says Vanessa Beasley, associate provost and dean of residential faculty, as well as an associate professor of communication studies. Ten faculty "heads of house" live in the residences alongside students. Vanderbilt is expanding the system to upperclassmen. Yale, the University of Southern California and Case Western Reserve University in Cleveland are among those that also have residential college systems.

Service Learning

In the latest U.S. News survey, these schools were recognized for having strong service-learning offerings, where volunteer work in the community is an instructional strategy. See more at **usnews.com.**

- **Abilene Christian University** (TX)
- **Agnes Scott College** (GA)
- **Bates College** (ME)
- **Belmont University** (TN)
- **Berea College** (KY)
- **Boston College**
- **Brown University** (RI)
- **Duke University** (NC)
- **Elon University** (NC)
- **Georgetown University** (DC)
- **Michigan State University***
- **Portland State University** (OR)*
- **Stanford University** (CA)
- **Tulane University** (LA)
- **University of Notre Dame** (IN)

(*Public)

Breaking the campus bubble. While study abroad programs have been around for years, these days there's no longer an assumption that constructive learning will happen automatically. As a result, more schools have tweaked their approach so that "there's more intentionality in what students are learning while abroad," says Joy Phaphouvaninh, director of Illinois Abroad & Global Exchange at the University of Illinois–Urbana-Champaign. That means plenty of time for reflection and identifying learning outcomes, she says. And the trip itself may come in the context of a larger required course on global education, a semester-length study abroad program or, as with Agnes Scott, both.

Going beyond the classroom to learn in the real world also happens closer to home. Service learning, which integrates community field work into the academic curriculum, is the most popular of the high-impact practices, with 62 percent of seniors reporting participation, according to the NSSE data. The University of North Carolina–Chapel Hill, for instance, offers 80-plus service-learning courses, covering topics like local journalism and integrating philosophy into primary and secondary schools. "We want students to be thinking deeply about what it means to be part of a community of people who were here before they came and will be here after," says Ryan Nilsen, a program officer with UNC's Carolina Center for Public Service.

For UNC senior Justin Williford that meant a three-credit class combined with a paid internship at Chapel Hill-based Theater Delta, which uses interactive theater to promote social change in communities around the world. "It gives you space to apply whatever you learn," says Williford, a math and statistics major, who did quantitative analysis for the group.

Hands on. Internships and co-op programs continue to be popular with undergrads, who see them as a way to build skills and on-the-job experience at a real company or organization – and maybe even help land them a job. At the Georgia Institute of Technology, 60 to 75 percent of students do either a paid, part-time internship or a full-fledged co-op, which consists of three semesters of paid, full-time work, says Michelle Tullier, executive director of the school's Center for Career Discovery and Development. (Co-op students typically take five years to get a degree but don't pay tuition during their work periods.) On average, students who participate have a GPA that is 15 percent higher than those who don't, she says. At Northeastern University in Boston, the entire curriculum is built around the co-op approach. Starting in their second year, students alternate periods of academic study with six months of full-time employment at organizations in about 40 states and more than 130 countries.

At Kettering University in Michigan, students similarly alternate terms in class and in a professional setting, for a total of two and a half years of workplace experience. "It creates this wonderful virtuous

Undergraduate Research / Creative Projects

Independently or in small teams, students do intensive research or creative work, with faculty mentoring. In the most recent U.S. News survey, these schools (listed here in alphabetical order) got the most votes for their offerings. Find out more at **usnews.com.**

- **Amherst College** (MA)
- **California Institute of Technology**
- **Carleton College** (MN)
- **Carnegie Mellon University** (PA)
- **College of Wooster** (OH)
- **Cornell University** (NY)
- **Duke University** (NC)
- **Elon University** (NC)
- **Harvard University** (MA)
- **Harvey Mudd College** (CA)
- **Massachusetts Institute of Technology**
- **Princeton University** (NJ)
- **Rice University** (TX)
- **Stanford University** (CA)
- **University of Michigan-Ann Arbor***
- **University of North Carolina-Chapel Hill***

(*Public)

KETTERING UNDERGRADS WORK TOGETHER AS PART OF A CO-OP EXPERIENCE.

circle between what they're learning in the classroom and applying in the field," says Robert McMahan, Kettering's president. Plus, many students get postgrad job offers in their junior year, he says.

Alyssa Gilliland interviewed for her first co-op, at Dow Automotive Systems in Auburn Hills, Michigan, even before she arrived at Kettering, as a high school senior. She stayed with the company through all eight of her co-op terms at the university, where she majored in chemical engineering. "The transition was really refreshing," she says. "Just when you started feeling drained from school, you were back to work." She learned how to interact and collaborate with her co-workers, who she says helped her sharpen her résumé and other skills. After graduating in 2017, Gilliland took a job as an analyzer systems engineer with the Dow Chemical Company in Freeport, Texas.

Opportunities for undergrads to pursue their own research are also expanding. At the State University of New York at Geneseo, 40 percent of students work with faculty on research; classes are canceled for one day each spring to give those who have done substantial creative or scientific inquiry the chance to make presentations and exhibit their work. School data suggests that those who participate have a higher GPA and graduate in a more timely manner, says Stacey Robertson, provost and vice president for academic affairs. Jimmy Feng, a 2018 grad in geography, credits the research he did on anti-Chinese prejudice in Australia and public access to transportation in Shenzhen, China, with preparing him for the Ph.D. program in geography he is starting at the University of Tennessee in Knoxville. "It was something I was fully invested in, rather than a topic assigned by a professor," he says.

Many schools are also working to open and encourage research for students pursuing nonscientific fields. At Clemson University in South Carolina, the Creative Inquiry program attracts plenty of students in the humanities, social sciences and education, as well as the sciences, engineering and agriculture, says Barbara Speziale, director of the program.

Hannah Cupp, who is completing a fine arts bachelor's at Clemson, says that the school's Community Supported Art Creative Inquiry taught her about the business of art (acquisition, sales, promotion and more) in a way she otherwise wouldn't have learned at school. She says her newfound marketing skills have given her the confidence that she can sell the work that she creates. ◆

Internships

U.S. News asked college officials in 2018 to nominate up to 15 schools with standout internship programs, practicums or co-op offerings, in which a period of study typically alternates with one of work. The following (listed alphabetically) were named the most. See more at **usnews.com.**

American University (DC)
Belmont University (TN)
Berea College (KY)
Claremont McKenna College (CA)
Cornell University (NY)
Drexel University (PA)
Elon University (NC)
Embry-Riddle Aeronautical U. (FL)
Georgia Institute of Technology*
Kettering University (MI)
Massachusetts Institute of Technology
Northeastern University (MA)
Purdue University-West Lafayette (IN)*
Rochester Institute of Technology (NY)
University of Cincinnati*
Worcester Polytechnic Institute (MA)

(*Public)

RACHEL WOOLF FOR USN&WR

STUDY THE SCHOOLS

Programs are pushing creativity and communication skills alongside technical abilities

The Art of Business & Engineering

by **Elizabeth Gardner**

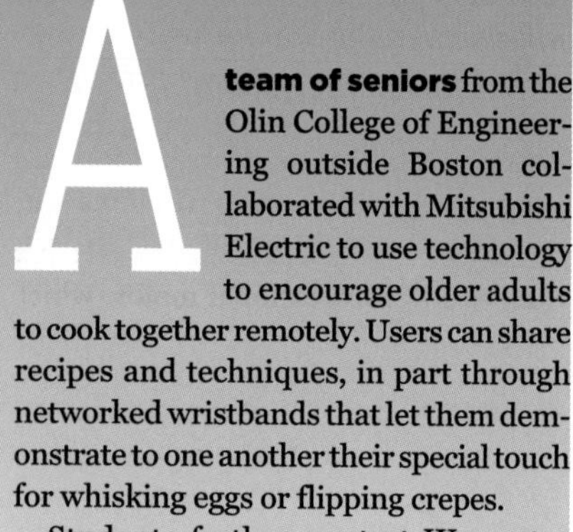

A **team of seniors** from the Olin College of Engineering outside Boston collaborated with Mitsubishi Electric to use technology to encourage older adults to cook together remotely. Users can share recipes and techniques, in part through networked wristbands that let them demonstrate to one another their special touch for whisking eggs or flipping crepes.

Students farther west at Worcester Polytechnic Institute have helped an Australian not-for-profit collect data on microplastic pollution in the ocean, which lawmakers can use to help create policy for a cleanup effort.

And undergraduate business students at Bucknell University in central Pennsylvania have designed play areas for a local children's museum that teach about concepts like air and gravity, which they have presented to the museum's board.

What do all of these activities have in common? Each is a class or project incorporating two key elements that many undergraduate institutions are increasingly building into their engineering and business curricula: First, the work combines technical study in preprofessional fields with approaches often associated with the liberal arts, such as nurturing big-picture thinking and developing analytical and writing skills. In addition, colleges are asking students to apply their efforts to real-world needs, working in teams and with actual clients just as they will after they graduate.

Engineering and business are common "get-a-job" college program choices, with about 1 in 5 college graduates in 2016 majoring in business and 5 percent earning degrees in engineering, according to federal data. The fields also command some of the highest average starting salaries, according to the National Association of Colleges and Employers. But many such programs have traditionally centered around teaching the technical nuts and bolts of business and engineering. Now, as automation, new technology and other forces transform the global workforce, many schools are responding to the demands of employers who are putting a premium on graduates who have both technical know-how and creative and communication skills.

Emily Gross, a 2018 Bucknell grad who was part of the children's museum play-area design project, says it helped her break out of her comfort zone and gain confidence in her creative abili-

MADISON HEALEY (LEFT) WORKS WITH AN ENGINEERING CLASSMATE AT WPI.

ties. She worked closely with the museum's board and staff, and had to juggle conflicting feedback – giving her a taste of real business settings. "Even if you have the most beautiful design and model, your idea won't be chosen unless you can communicate clearly and persuasively to your client," she says.

Madison Healey, a senior mechanical engineering major at WPI who was in the group that went to Australia to study microplastic pollution, also found the project sharpened her communication skills and ignited her passion to pursue a career in environmental sustainability. Healey was expecting primarily to solve math problems in her college program, just as she had in high school, so she was a little surprised that most of her engineering courses have included writing reports and making presentations. "Professors are always saying how the industry values writing and people skills as much as the technical skills we are learning," she says. Plus, emerging evidence shows that integrating the STEM fields of science, technology, engineering and math (plus medicine) with the arts and humanities at the higher ed level can improve problem-solving, communication and teamwork skills, according to a report released in May from the National Academies of Sciences, Engineering, and Medicine.

Indeed, through partnerships with and feedback from employers, many schools are increasingly recognizing that, while narrowly focused technical curricula may help students get that first job, they will need broader skills to move up, to start their own businesses, or to blaze an unconventional career path. At Franklin and Marshall College, a liberal arts institution in Pennsylvania, business is approached more as a cross-disciplinary social science than as a preprofessional major, which helps to develop students' big-picture thinking, says Bryan Stinchfield, associate professor of organization studies and former chair of the school's Business, Organizations and Society department.

"Students want a program that's going to allow them to blend their intellectual curiosities with their passions, and business education at a liberal arts school really allows that," he says. (Stinchfield worked as a consultant earlier in his career and recalls being mortified at the quality of the correspondence produced by one of the salespeople, who had a bachelor's in business but did not attend a lib-

ELLEN WEBBER FOR USN&WR

eral arts college.) Every course in the department, even statistics, involves plenty of writing, and class sizes are capped at 16 to 25 to allow faculty time to provide feedback and individualized help.

Bucknell's management majors take the same core liberal arts classes as English majors, and they also must complete at least three writing-intensive courses in the management school or elsewhere in the university, says Raquel Alexander, dean of Bucknell's Freeman College of Management.

Innovative engineering programs often encourage students to apply their skills as they acquire them instead of making them achieve a certain level of overall mastery before they're let loose in the lab or the workshop. "Students are tired of the math-science death march: two years of courses when what they really want to do is make stuff," says Khanjan Mehta, vice provost for creative inquiry at Lehigh University in Pennsylvania, which offers a variety of ways to pursue integrated studies among its three undergraduate colleges: arts and sciences, business and engineering. The overall objective is to steep students in ideas like design thinking, global citizenship and evidence-based problem-solving. "These are all going to be helpful no matter what they do," Mehta says.

Lehigh's Mountaintop Initiative has repurposed a former Bethlehem Steel research facility into a 120,000-square-foot space where students can pursue such cross-disciplinary projects as making and testing 3D printed concrete or developing a Facebook widget that measures the political polarization of a user's news feed. One recent group of undergrads invented a method to convert waste drywall into fertilizer, which led them to co-author several published research papers and to see their names on patents. "When you work on real projects and see why your knowledge is relevant, it makes you learn your math and science better," Mehta says.

More than three dozen schools, including Bucknell, Lehigh, Franklin and Marshall, San Francisco State University and the University of Wisconsin–Madison, participate in the Aspen Undergraduate Consortium, a program of the nonprofit Aspen Institute that focuses on how to integrate liberal arts and business curricula. The consortium sponsors an annual meeting and a faculty workshop where schools explore points of intersection between business and other disciplines, discuss integrated teaching techniques that develop leadership, and present their curriculum innovations to their peers.

Many engineering programs, including Olin, WPI and Rochester Institute of Technology in New York, are taking their cues from the National Academy of Engineering's Grand Challenges Scholars Program, a combined curricular and co-curricular effort designed to prepare students to address 14 global issues for the field, such as securing cyberspace, making solar energy economical, and developing better medicines. More than 50 undergraduate engineering schools have a program approved by the NAE, and dozens more are in development. They're allowed to execute in any way they see fit – as long as the work is multidisciplinary, multicultural and designed to promote creativity, original research, social consciousness and entrepreneurship.

The multidisciplinary component is especially key, says Karen Oates, a professor of biology and immediate past dean of arts and sciences at WPI. "None of these problems will be solved just by an engineer, so we are interested in combining the very best of engineering and the very best of liberal arts and science." Rather than creating new interdisciplinary courses as some institutions do, WPI incorporates social context directly into its existing engineering curriculum, and pairs engineering and other faculty – for example, a biomedical engineer and a political scientist – to participate in one another's courses. Their joint course might cover the technical aspects of producing large amounts of a vaccine and a device for dispensing it, but also the social implications of getting it out to the populations that need it and providing it at a reasonable cost.

STUDENTS OUTSIDE THE OLD MAIN BUILDING AT FRANKLIN AND MARSHALL COLLEGE

DEB GROVE – FRANKLIN & MARSHALL COLLEGE

Olin's size (about 350 undergrads) and newness (it was established in 1997) in some ways give it an edge in cross-disciplinary training in that the school doesn't have to overcome decades (or centuries) of tradition, says Robert Martello, associate dean for curriculum and academic programs, as well as the school's only history professor. "Our experiment is to look at engineering in a new way, as a people-to-people process," he says. "We want our engineers to look at how their solutions are going to change society."

Martello estimates that roughly 15 to 25 percent of Olin classes combine liberal arts with technology in some form. "Engineering for Humanity," co-taught by an engineer and an anthropologist, has students devise solutions for the challenges of specific people: for example, designing measuring cups and a cutting board for use by a woman with macular degeneration who has lost the center of her field of vision, or creating videos and learning aids for new immigrants learning English.

Mary Martin, a 2018 Olin grad who was part of the remote cooking capstone project, was attracted to the school's holistic approach and the freedom it offered to design her own education. That led her to projects like creating a laser maze that players had to navigate without breaking the beams and setting off an alarm. The exercise gave her five-person team a technical workout and tested their design and budgeting skills. "It's been a great conversation starter at networking events," says Martin, who joins Bose Corp.'s new business development lab this fall as a mechanical engineer.

RIT has 30 students involved in the first year of its NAE Grand Challenges Scholars Program, and the school is providing funding to help them cover the costs of design projects and international trips. Among the ways that RIT has integrated the liberal arts is a general education course for incoming freshmen that links engineering and other disciplines. The current iteration is called "Clean Water," and it brings together engineering and philosophy faculty to explore water management – both the technical (such as removing salt from ocean water) and the ethical (how to address the lead-tainted water system in Flint, Michigan, or allocate scarce water in the American Southwest).

Such courses are just the start of a multiyear, cross-disciplinary curriculum that culminates in senior design projects like medical centrifuges for places without electricity or 3D printing of prosthetics. Twenty years ago, a senior project might have consisted of "a limited scope engineering project like making a new shock absorber or a control system," says Doreen Edwards, dean of RIT's Kate Gleason College of Engineering. "Today, our design projects are scoped much more broadly. How is it impacting people?"

Even many large public universities, where students sometimes have to apply to be a part of business or engineering majors, are looking to broaden their preprofessional programs to include the development of critical thinking and writing. San Francisco State is working to increase the breadth of its business offerings and researching a minor in sustainability to complement current undergrad business electives, says Denise Kleinrichert, director of the university's Center for Ethical and Sustainable Business.

The University of Wisconsin is exploring ways to incorporate cross-disciplinary content across a school of about 31,000 undergrads, says Suzanne Dove, assistant dean for academic innovations at the university's Wisconsin School of Business. Recently the B-school used the common text from a universitywide reading program – the book "Just Mercy" by Equal Justice Initiative executive director Bryan Stevenson – to spark first-year business undergrads to create visual representations of some of its civil rights and justice themes. "One of our students said, 'Gosh, I thought I was going to have to give up my artistic side when I went to be a business major!'" Dove says. "It was great news for the students to know that we value all of these aspects of their personalities and want them to bring those out." ◆

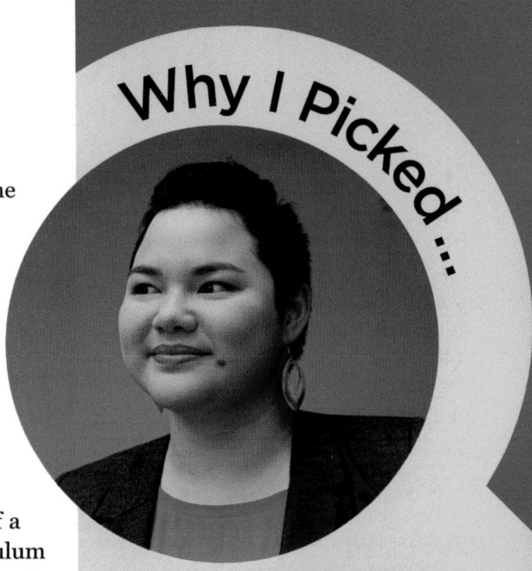

Why I Picked...

Scripps College

CLAREMONT, CALIFORNIA

Madeline Sy, '18

▶ **Scripps has given me rich, diverse learning experiences and access to a wide network of peers, as the college is part of a five-school undergraduate consortium. Every student must complete a senior thesis, and Scripps provides funding to tap resources outside the college. For my thesis on Sylvia Plath's poetry, I received funding to travel to the Plath archives in Northampton, Massachusetts. Seeing actual drafts of Plath's poems inspired me to tackle a topic little explored by previous Plath scholars: motherhood.**

Opportunities at Scripps are often hands-on, a quality also reflected in campus organizations. I learned finance (something I value as an English major!) as a part of the Student Investment Fund, and last year we distributed over $15,000 in stock earnings to campus clubs. Through the consortium, I also learned how to ride with the coed Claremont Equestrian Team. Scripps gives me the best of both worlds: the supportiveness of a small women's college and the resources of a midsized university.

JACKIE LEGAZCUE

Business Programs

Each year, U.S. News ranks undergraduate business programs accredited by the Association to Advance Collegiate Schools of Business; the results are based solely on surveys of B-school deans and senior faculty. Participants were asked to rate the quality of business programs with which they're familiar on a scale of 1 (marginal) to 5 (distinguished); 43.7 percent of those canvassed responded to the most recent survey conducted in the spring of 2018. Two years of data were used to calculate the peer assessment score. Deans and faculty members also were asked to nominate up to 15 programs they consider best in a number of specialty areas; the five schools receiving the most mentions in the 2018 survey appear on page 31.

Top Programs

Rank	School (State) (*Public)	Peer assessment score (5.0=highest)
1.	**University of Pennsylvania** (Wharton)	4.8
2.	**Massachusetts Inst. of Technology** (Sloan)	4.6
2.	**University of California–Berkeley** (Haas)*	4.6
4.	**University of Michigan–Ann Arbor** (Ross)*	4.5
5.	**New York University** (Stern)	4.4
6.	**Carnegie Mellon University** (Tepper) (PA)	4.3
6.	**University of Texas–Austin** (McCombs)*	4.3
8.	**U. of N. Carolina–Chapel Hill** (Kenan-Flagler)*	4.2
8.	**University of Virginia** (McIntire)*	4.2
10.	**Cornell University** (Dyson) (NY)	4.1
10.	**Indiana University–Bloomington** (Kelley)*	4.1
10.	**University of Notre Dame** (Mendoza) (IN)	4.1
10.	**University of Southern California** (Marshall)	4.1
14.	**Washington University in St. Louis** (Olin)	4.0
15.	**Emory University** (Goizueta) (GA)	3.9
15.	**Georgetown University** (McDonough) (DC)	3.9
15.	**Ohio State University–Columbus** (Fisher)*	3.9
18.	**University of Illinois–Urbana-Champaign***	3.8
18.	**U. of Minnesota–Twin Cities** (Carlson)*	3.8
18.	**Univ. of Wisconsin–Madison***	3.8
21.	**Boston College** (Carroll)	3.7
21.	**Georgia Institute of Technology** (Scheller)*	3.7
21.	**Michigan State University** (Broad)*	3.7
21.	**Pennsylvania State U.–Univ. Park** (Smeal)*	3.7
21.	**Purdue U.–West Lafayette** (Krannert) (IN)*	3.7
21.	**University of Arizona** (Eller)*	3.7
21.	**University of Georgia** (Terry)*	3.7
21.	**Univ. of Maryland–College Park***	3.7
21.	**University of Washington** (Foster)*	3.7
30.	**Arizona State University–Tempe** (Carey)*	3.6
30.	**Babson College** (MA)	3.6
30.	**Johns Hopkins University** (MD)	3.6
30.	**Texas A&M U.–College Station** (Mays)*	3.6
30.	**University of Florida** (Warrington)*	3.6
35.	**Brigham Young Univ.–Provo** (Marriott) (UT)	3.5
35.	**Case Western Reserve U.** (Weatherhead) (OH)	3.5
35.	**University of California–Irvine** (Merage)*	3.5
35.	**University of Colorado–Boulder** (Leeds)*	3.5
35.	**University of Iowa** (Tippie)*	3.5
35.	**University of Pittsburgh***	3.5
35.	**Wake Forest University** (NC)	3.5
42.	**Boston University**	3.4
42.	**George Washington University** (DC)	3.4
44.	**College of William & Mary** (Mason) (VA)*	3.3
44.	**Florida State University***	3.3
44.	**Georgia State University** (Robinson)*	3.3
44.	**Pepperdine University** (CA)	3.3
44.	**Southern Methodist University** (Cox) (TX)	3.3
44.	**Syracuse University** (Whitman) (NY)	3.3
44.	**Tulane University** (Freeman) (LA)	3.3
44.	**United States Air Force Academy** (CO)*	3.3
44.	**University of Alabama** (Culverhouse)*	3.3
44.	**University of Arkansas** (Walton)*	3.3
44.	**University of California–San Diego** (Rady)*	3.3
44.	**Univ. of Massachusetts–Amherst** (Isenberg)*	3.3
44.	**Univ. of Nebraska–Lincoln***	3.3
44.	**University of Oregon** (Lundquist)*	3.3
44.	**Univ. of South Carolina** (Moore)*	3.3
44.	**University of Utah** (Eccles)*	3.3
44.	**Villanova University** (PA)	3.3
44.	**Virginia Tech** (Pamplin)*	3.3
62.	**Auburn University** (Harbert) (AL)*	3.2
62.	**Baylor University** (Hankamer) (TX)	3.2
62.	**Bentley University** (MA)	3.2
62.	**CUNY–Baruch College** (Zicklin)*	3.2
62.	**Fordham University** (Gabelli) (NY)	3.2
62.	**Miami University–Oxford** (Farmer) (OH)*	3.2
62.	**Northeastern U.** (D'Amore-McKim) (MA)	3.2
62.	**Rochester Inst. of Technology** (Saunders) (NY)	3.2
62.	**Santa Clara University** (Leavey) (CA)	3.2
62.	**Temple University** (Fox) (PA)*	3.2
62.	**University of Connecticut***	3.2
62.	**University of Kansas***	3.2
62.	**University of Kentucky** (Gatton)*	3.2
62.	**University of Miami** (FL)	3.2
62.	**University of Oklahoma** (Price)*	3.2
62.	**University of Tennessee** (Haslam)*	3.2
62.	**University of Texas–Dallas** (Jindal)*	3.2
79.	**Clemson University** (SC)*	3.1
79.	**Iowa State University***	3.1
79.	**Loyola Marymount University** (CA)	3.1
79.	**Loyola University Chicago** (Quinlan)	3.1
79.	**Rensselaer Polytechnic Inst.** (Lally) (NY)	3.1
79.	**Rutgers University–New Brunswick** (NJ)*	3.1
79.	**Texas Christian University** (Neeley)	3.1
79.	**Univ. of Missouri** (Trulaske)*	3.1
87.	**American University** (Kogod) (DC)	3.0
87.	**Brandeis University** (MA)	3.0
87.	**Colorado State University***	3.0
87.	**Creighton University** (NE)	3.0
87.	**DePaul University** (Driehaus) (IL)	3.0
87.	**George Mason University** (VA)*	3.0
87.	**Lehigh University** (PA)	3.0
87.	**Marquette University** (WI)	3.0
87.	**North Carolina State U.–Raleigh** (Poole)*	3.0
87.	**Oklahoma State University** (Spears)*	3.0
87.	**Saint Louis University** (Cook)	3.0
87.	**San Diego State University***	3.0
87.	**University at Buffalo–SUNY***	3.0
87.	**University of California–Riverside***	3.0
87.	**University of Cincinnati** (Lindner)*	3.0
87.	**University of Delaware** (Lerner)*	3.0
87.	**University of Denver** (Daniels)	3.0
87.	**University of Houston** (Bauer)*	3.0
87.	**University of Illinois–Chicago***	3.0
87.	**University of Richmond** (Robins) (VA)	3.0
87.	**Washington State University** (Carson)*	3.0
108.	**Binghamton University–SUNY***	2.9
108.	**Cal. Poly. State U.–San Luis Obispo** (Orfalea)*	2.9
108.	**Drexel University** (LeBow) (PA)	2.9
108.	**Gonzaga University** (WA)	2.9
108.	**James Madison University** (VA)*	2.9
108.	**Kansas State University***	2.9
108.	**Louisiana State U.–Baton Rouge** (Ourso)*	2.9
108.	**Loyola University Maryland** (Sellinger)	2.9
108.	**Oregon State University***	2.9
108.	**Rutgers University–Newark** (NJ)*	2.9
108.	**Seton Hall University** (Stillman) (NJ)	2.9
108.	**Texas Tech University** (Rawls)*	2.9
108.	**United States Coast Guard Academy** (CT)*	2.9
108.	**University of Hawaii–Manoa** (Shidler)*	2.9
108.	**University of Louisville** (KY)*	2.9
108.	**University of Mississippi***	2.9
108.	**University of San Diego**	2.9
108.	**University of San Francisco**	2.9
108.	**Xavier University** (Williams) (OH)	2.9
127.	**Bucknell University** (PA)	2.8
127.	**Butler University** (IN)	2.8
127.	**California State University–Los Angeles***	2.8
127.	**Elon University** (Love) (NC)	2.8
127.	**Florida International University***	2.8
127.	**Hofstra University** (Zarb) (NY)	2.8
127.	**Howard University** (DC)	2.8
127.	**Ohio University***	2.8
127.	**Seattle University** (Albers)	2.8
127.	**St. Joseph's University** (Haub) (PA)	2.8
127.	**University at Albany–SUNY***	2.8
127.	**University of Alabama–Birmingham** (Collat)*	2.8
127.	**University of Central Florida***	2.8
127.	**University of Colorado–Denver***	2.8
127.	**University of Montana***	2.8
127.	**University of New Mexico** (Anderson)*	2.8
127.	**U. of North Carolina–Charlotte** (Belk)*	2.8
127.	**University of Texas–Arlington***	2.8
127.	**Univ. of Wisconsin–Milwaukee** (Lubar)*	2.8
127.	**Washington and Lee U.** (Williams) (VA)	2.8
147.	**Ball State University** (Miller) (IN)*	2.7
147.	**California State Polytechnic U.–Pomona***	2.7
147.	**The Citadel** (SC)*	2.7
147.	**Kennesaw State University** (Coles) (GA)*	2.7
147.	**Mississippi State University***	2.7
147.	**Quinnipiac University** (CT)	2.7
147.	**Rutgers University–Camden** (NJ)*	2.7

Rank	School (State) (*Public)	Peer assessment score (5.0=highest)
147.	**San Jose State University** (Lucas) (CA)*	2.7
147.	**Univ. of Colo.–Colorado Springs***	2.7
147.	**Univ. of Massachusetts–Boston***	2.7
147.	**University of Memphis** (Fogelman)*	2.7
147.	**University of Minnesota–Duluth** (Labovitz)*	2.7
147.	**Univ. of Missouri–Kansas City** (Bloch)*	2.7
147.	**Univ. of Missouri–St. Louis***	2.7
147.	**University of Nevada–Las Vegas** (Lee)*	2.7
147.	**University of New Hampshire** (Paul)*	2.7
147.	**U. of North Carolina–Greensboro** (Bryan)*	2.7
147.	**University of Rhode Island***	2.7
147.	**University of South Florida** (Muma)*	2.7
147.	**University of St. Thomas** (Opus) (MN)	2.7
147.	**University of Vermont***	2.7
147.	**Utah State University** (Huntsman)*	2.7
147.	**Virginia Commonwealth University***	2.7
147.	**West Virginia University***	2.7
147.	**Worcester Polytechnic Inst.** (MA)	2.7
172.	**Boise State University** (ID)*	2.6
172.	**Bradley University** (Foster) (IL)	2.6
172.	**California State U.–Fullerton** (Mihaylo)*	2.6
172.	**Chapman University** (Argyros) (CA)	2.6
172.	**Drake University** (IA)	2.6
172.	**Duquesne University** (Palumbo) (PA)	2.6
172.	**Fairfield University** (Dolan) (CT)	2.6
172.	**John Carroll University** (Boler) (OH)	2.6
172.	**Kent State University** (OH)*	2.6
172.	**Northern Illinois University***	2.6
172.	**Pace University** (Lubin) (NY)	2.6
172.	**Purdue University–Northwest** (IN)*	2.6
172.	**Rollins College** (FL)	2.6
172.	**San Francisco State University***	2.6
172.	**Stevens Institute of Technology** (NJ)	2.6
172.	**St. John's University** (Tobin) (NY)	2.6
172.	**University of Alabama–Huntsville***	2.6
172.	**University of Arkansas–Little Rock***	2.6
172.	**University of Dayton** (OH)	2.6
172.	**University of Evansville** (Schroeder) (IN)	2.6
172.	**University of Idaho***	2.6
172.	**University of Maine***	2.6
172.	**U. of Massachusetts–Dartmouth** (Charlton)*	2.6
172.	**University of Nebraska–Omaha***	2.6
172.	**University of Portland** (Pamplin) (OR)	2.6
172.	**University of Wyoming***	2.6
172.	**Valparaiso University** (IN)	2.6
199.	**Bowling Green State University** (OH)*	2.5
199.	**Bryant University** (RI)	2.5
199.	**California State University–Long Beach***	2.5
199.	**California State University–Northridge***	2.5
199.	**Clarkson University** (NY)	2.5
199.	**Clark University** (MA)	2.5
199.	**Florida Atlantic University***	2.5
199.	**Illinois Institute of Technology** (Stuart)	2.5
199.	**Illinois State University***	2.5
199.	**Indiana State University***	2.5
199.	**Ithaca College** (NY)	2.5
199.	**Loyola University New Orleans**	2.5
199.	**Morehouse College** (GA)	2.5
199.	**New Jersey Inst. of Technology***	2.5
199.	**New Mexico State University***	2.5
199.	**Northern Arizona University** (Franke)*	2.5
199.	**Old Dominion University** (Strome) (VA)*	2.5
199.	**Portland State University** (OR)*	2.5
199.	**Providence College** (RI)	2.5
199.	**Purdue University–Fort Wayne** (Doermer)*	2.5
199.	**Southern Illinois University–Carbondale***	2.5
199.	**Trinity University** (TX)	2.5
199.	**University of Dallas** (Gupta)	2.5
199.	**University of Hartford** (Barney) (CT)	2.5
199.	**Univ. of Massachusetts–Lowell** (Manning)*	2.5
199.	**University of Michigan–Dearborn***	2.5
199.	**U. of N. Carolina–Wilmington** (Cameron)*	2.5
199.	**University of North Texas***	2.5
199.	**University of Scranton** (Kania) (PA)	2.5
199.	**University of South Dakota** (Beacom)*	2.5
199.	**University of Tampa** (Sykes) (FL)	2.5
199.	**Univ. of Tennessee–Chattanooga***	2.5
199.	**University of Texas–San Antonio***	2.5
199.	**University of Tulsa** (Collins) (OK)	2.5
199.	**Wayne State University** (MI)*	2.5
199.	**Western Michigan University** (Haworth)*	2.5

Note: Peer assessment surveys in 2018 conducted by U.S. News. To be ranked in a specialty, an undergraduate business school may have either a program or course offerings in that subject area. Extended undergraduate business rankings can be found at usnews.com/bestcolleges.

Best in the Specialties (*Public)

ACCOUNTING
1. **University of Texas–Austin** (McCombs)*
2. **Brigham Young Univ.–Provo** (Marriott) (UT)
2. **University of Illinois–Urbana-Champaign***
4. **University of Michigan–Ann Arbor** (Ross)*
5. **University of Pennsylvania** (Wharton)

ENTREPRENEURSHIP
1. **Babson College** (MA)
2. **Massachusetts Institute of Technology** (Sloan)
3. **Indiana University–Bloomington** (Kelley)*
4. **University of California–Berkeley** (Haas)*
4. **University of Michigan–Ann Arbor** (Ross)*
4. **U. of North Carolina–Chapel Hill** (Kenan-Flagler)*

FINANCE
1. **University of Pennsylvania** (Wharton)
2. **New York University** (Stern)
3. **Massachusetts Institute of Technology** (Sloan)
4. **University of Michigan–Ann Arbor** (Ross)*
5. **University of Texas–Austin** (McCombs)*

INSURANCE/RISK MANAGEMENT
1. **University of Georgia** (Terry)*
2. **Univ. of Wisconsin–Madison***
3. **Georgia State University** (Robinson)*
4. **Temple University** (Fox) (PA)*
5. **Florida State University***
5. **University of Pennsylvania** (Wharton)

INTERNATIONAL BUSINESS
1. **Univ. of South Carolina** (Moore)*
2. **New York University** (Stern)
3. **Georgetown University** (McDonough) (DC)
4. **University of California–Berkeley** (Haas)*
5. **University of Pennsylvania** (Wharton)

MANAGEMENT
1. **University of Michigan–Ann Arbor** (Ross)*
2. **University of Pennsylvania** (Wharton)
3. **University of California–Berkeley** (Haas)*
4. **U. of North Carolina–Chapel Hill** (Kenan-Flagler)*
5. **University of Virginia** (McIntire)*

MANAGEMENT INFORMATION SYSTEMS
1. **Massachusetts Institute of Technology** (Sloan)
2. **Carnegie Mellon University** (Tepper) (PA)
3. **University of Arizona** (Eller)*
4. **University of Texas–Austin** (McCombs)*
5. **University of Minnesota–Twin Cities** (Carlson)*

MARKETING
1. **University of Michigan–Ann Arbor** (Ross)*
2. **University of Pennsylvania** (Wharton)
3. **New York University** (Stern)
4. **University of Texas–Austin** (McCombs)*
5. **U. of North Carolina–Chapel Hill** (Kenan-Flagler)*

PRODUCTION/OPERATIONS MANAGEMENT
1. **Massachusetts Institute of Technology** (Sloan)
2. **University of Michigan–Ann Arbor** (Ross)*
3. **University of Pennsylvania** (Wharton)
4. **Purdue University–West Lafayette** (Krannert) (IN)*
5. **Carnegie Mellon University** (Tepper) (PA)

QUANTITATIVE ANALYSIS/METHODS
1. **Massachusetts Institute of Technology** (Sloan)
2. **Carnegie Mellon University** (Tepper) (PA)
3. **University of Pennsylvania** (Wharton)
4. **New York University** (Stern)
5. **University of Texas–Austin** (McCombs)*

REAL ESTATE
1. **University of Pennsylvania** (Wharton)
2. **Univ. of Wisconsin–Madison***
3. **University of California–Berkeley** (Haas)*
4. **New York University** (Stern)
5. **University of Georgia** (Terry)*

SUPPLY CHAIN MANAGEMENT/LOGISTICS
1. **Michigan State University** (Broad)*
2. **Arizona State University–Tempe** (Carey)*
3. **Massachusetts Institute of Technology** (Sloan)
4. **Pennsylvania State U.–Univ. Park** (Smeal)*
5. **Ohio State University–Columbus** (Fisher)*

Engineering Programs

On these pages, U.S. News ranks undergraduate engineering programs accredited by ABET. The rankings are based solely on surveys of engineering deans and senior faculty at accredited programs. Participants were asked to rate programs with which they're familiar on a scale from 1 (marginal) to 5 (distinguished); the two most recent years' survey results were used to calculate the peer assessment score. Students who prefer a program that focuses on its undergrads can use the list of top institutions whose terminal engineering degree is a bachelor's or master's; universities that grant doctorates in engineering, whose programs are ranked separately, may boast a wider range of offerings at the undergraduate level. For the spring 2018 surveys, 33 percent of those canvassed returned ratings of the group below; 58 percent did so for the doctorate group. Respondents were also asked to name up to 15 top programs in specialty areas; those mentioned most often in the 2018 survey alone appear here.

Top Programs ▶ AT ENGINEERING SCHOOLS WHOSE HIGHEST DEGREE IS A BACHELOR'S OR MASTER'S

Rank	School (State) (*Public)	Peer assessment score (5.0=highest)
1.	**Harvey Mudd College** (CA)	4.6
1.	**Rose-Hulman Institute of Technology** (IN)	4.6
3.	**Franklin W. Olin Col. of Engineering** (MA)	4.4
4.	**United States Military Academy** (NY)*	4.2
4.	**United States Naval Academy** (MD)*	4.2
6.	**Bucknell University** (PA)	4.1
6.	**United States Air Force Academy** (CO)*	4.1
8.	**Cal. Poly. State U.–San Luis Obispo***	4.0
9.	**Cooper Union** (NY)	3.8
9.	**Milwaukee School of Engineering**	3.8
11.	**Cal. State Polytechnic U.–Pomona***	3.6
11.	**Lafayette College** (PA)	3.6
11.	**United States Coast Guard Academy** (CT)*	3.6
11.	**University of San Diego**	3.6
15.	**Embry-Riddle Aeronautical U.–Prescott** (AZ)	3.5
15.	**Kettering University** (MI)	3.5
15.	**Smith College** (MA)	3.5
18.	**Gonzaga University** (WA)	3.4
18.	**Loyola Marymount University** (CA)	3.4
18.	**San Jose State University** (CA)*	3.4
18.	**Swarthmore College** (PA)	3.4
18.	**Valparaiso University** (IN)	3.4
23.	**The Citadel** (SC)*	3.3
23.	**Rowan University** (NJ)*	3.3
23.	**U.S. Merchant Marine Acad.** (NY)*	3.3
26.	**Bradley University** (IL)	3.2
26.	**Seattle University**	3.2
26.	**University of Portland** (OR)	3.2
26.	**Virginia Military Institute***	3.2
30.	**James Madison University** (VA)*	3.1
30.	**Mercer University** (GA)	3.1
30.	**Miami University–Oxford** (OH)*	3.1
30.	**Ohio Northern University**	3.1
30.	**Union College** (NY)	3.1
35.	**Brigham Young University–Idaho**	3.0
35.	**California State University–Northridge***	3.0
35.	**Hofstra University** (NY)	3.0
35.	**Manhattan College** (NY)	3.0
35.	**New York Inst. of Technology**	3.0
35.	**Oregon Inst. of Technology***	3.0
35.	**Penn State Univ.–Erie, Behrend Col.***	3.0
35.	**Purdue University–Northwest** (IN)*	3.0
35.	**Univ. of Wisconsin–Platteville***	3.0
35.	**Wentworth Inst. of Technology** (MA)	3.0
45.	**California State University–Fullerton***	2.9
45.	**California State University–Los Angeles***	2.9
45.	**Grand Valley State University** (MI)*	2.9
45.	**LeTourneau University** (TX)	2.9
45.	**Northern Arizona University***	2.9
45.	**Northern Illinois University***	2.9
45.	**Purdue University–Fort Wayne***	2.9
45.	**Trinity College** (CT)	2.9
45.	**Trinity University** (TX)	2.9
45.	**University of Minnesota–Duluth***	2.9
45.	**University of St. Thomas** (MN)	2.9
45.	**University of the Pacific** (CA)	2.9
57.	**California State U.–Maritime Academy***	2.8
57.	**California State University–Sacramento***	2.8
57.	**Cedarville University** (OH)	2.8
57.	**College of New Jersey***	2.8
57.	**Humboldt State University** (CA)*	2.8
57.	**Loyola University Maryland**	2.8
57.	**Massachusetts Maritime Academy***	2.8
57.	**Seattle Pacific University**	2.8
57.	**Southern Illinois University–Edwardsville***	2.8
57.	**SUNY Polytechnic Institute–Albany/Utica***	2.8
57.	**Texas Christian University**	2.8
57.	**University of Alaska–Anchorage***	2.8
57.	**University of Hartford** (CT)	2.8
57.	**Western New England Univ.** (MA)	2.8

Best in the Specialties ▶

(*Public)

AEROSPACE/AERONAUTICAL/ASTRONAUTICAL

1. **Embry-Riddle Aeronautical U.–Prescott** (AZ)
2. **California Polytechnic State University–San Luis Obispo***
4. **Bucknell University** (PA)
5. **California State Polytechnic University–Pomona***
5. **Harvey Mudd College** (CA)

BIOMEDICAL/BIOMEDICAL ENGINEERING

1. **Bucknell University** (PA)

CHEMICAL

1. **Bucknell University** (PA)
2. **Rose-Hulman Institute of Technology** (IN)

CIVIL

1. **Rose-Hulman Institute of Technology** (IN)
2. **United States Military Academy** (NY)*
3. **California Polytechnic State University–San Luis Obispo***

COMPUTER ENGINEERING

1. **California Polytechnic State University–San Luis Obispo***
1. **Rose-Hulman Institute of Technology** (IN)
3. **Bucknell University** (PA)
4. **Milwaukee School of Engineering**
5. **California State Polytechnic University–Pomona***
5. **Harvey Mudd College** (CA)

ELECTRICAL/ELECTRONIC/COMMUNICATIONS

1. **Rose-Hulman Institute of Technology** (IN)
2. **California Polytechnic State University–San Luis Obispo***
3. **Bucknell University** (PA)
4. **Harvey Mudd College** (CA)
5. **California State Polytechnic University–Pomona***
5. **Milwaukee School of Engineering**

INDUSTRIAL/MANUFACTURING

1. **California Polytechnic State University–San Luis Obispo***

MECHANICAL

1. **Rose-Hulman Institute of Technology** (IN)
2. **California Polytechnic State University–San Luis Obispo***
3. **Bucknell University** (PA)
4. **Franklin W. Olin College of Engineering** (MA)
5. **Kettering University** (MI)
5. **United States Naval Academy** (MD)*

Top Programs ▶ AT ENGINEERING SCHOOLS WHOSE HIGHEST DEGREE IS A DOCTORATE

Rank	School (State) (*Public)	Peer assessment score (5.0=highest)
1.	Massachusetts Institute of Technology	4.9
2.	Stanford University (CA)	4.8
3.	University of California–Berkeley*	4.7
4.	California Institute of Technology	4.6
4.	Georgia Institute of Technology*	4.6
6.	Carnegie Mellon University (PA)	4.4
6.	University of Illinois–Urbana-Champaign*	4.4
6.	University of Michigan–Ann Arbor*	4.4
9.	Cornell University (NY)	4.2
9.	Purdue University–West Lafayette (IN)*	4.2
9.	University of Texas–Austin*	4.2
12.	Princeton University (NJ)	4.1
13.	Virginia Tech*	4.0
14.	Johns Hopkins University (MD)	3.9
14.	Northwestern University (IL)	3.9
14.	Texas A&M University–College Station*	3.9
14.	Univ. of Wisconsin–Madison*	3.9
18.	Columbia University (NY)	3.8
18.	Duke University (NC)	3.8
18.	Rice University (TX)	3.8
18.	University of California–Los Angeles*	3.8
18.	University of California–San Diego*	3.8
18.	University of Washington*	3.8
24.	Harvard University (MA)	3.7
24.	Pennsylvania State U.–Univ. Park*	3.7
24.	Univ. of Maryland–College Park*	3.7
24.	University of Minnesota–Twin Cities*	3.7
24.	University of Pennsylvania	3.7
24.	University of Southern California	3.7
30.	Ohio State University–Columbus*	3.6
30.	Rensselaer Polytechnic Inst. (NY)	3.6
32.	North Carolina State U.–Raleigh*	3.5
32.	University of California–Davis*	3.5
32.	University of California–Santa Barbara*	3.5
32.	University of Colorado–Boulder*	3.5
32.	University of Florida*	3.5
32.	Yale University (CT)	3.5
38.	Arizona State University–Tempe*	3.4
38.	Brown University (RI)	3.4
38.	University of Virginia*	3.4
38.	Vanderbilt University (TN)	3.4
38.	Washington University in St. Louis	3.4
43.	Case Western Reserve Univ. (OH)	3.3
43.	Colorado School of Mines*	3.3
43.	Iowa State University*	3.3
43.	University of California–Irvine*	3.3
43.	University of Notre Dame (IN)	3.3
48.	Boston University	3.2
48.	Dartmouth College (NH)	3.2
48.	Lehigh University (PA)	3.2
48.	Michigan State University*	3.2
48.	Northeastern University (MA)	3.2
48.	Rutgers University–New Brunswick (NJ)*	3.2
48.	University of Pittsburgh*	3.2
55.	Clemson University (SC)*	3.1
55.	Drexel University (PA)	3.1
55.	University of Arizona*	3.1
55.	University of Delaware*	3.1
59.	Auburn University (AL)*	3.0
59.	Rochester Inst. of Technology (NY)	3.0
59.	Tufts University (MA)	3.0
59.	Univ. of Massachusetts–Amherst*	3.0
59.	U. of North Carolina–Chapel Hill*	3.0
59.	University of Tennessee*	3.0
59.	University of Utah*	3.0
59.	Worcester Polytechnic Inst. (MA)	3.0

Best in the Specialties ▶

(*Public)

AEROSPACE/AERONAUTICAL/ASTRONAUTICAL
1. Massachusetts Institute of Technology
2. Georgia Institute of Technology*
3. California Institute of Technology
4. University of Michigan–Ann Arbor*
5. Purdue University–West Lafayette (IN)*

BIOLOGICAL/AGRICULTURAL
1. Purdue University–West Lafayette (IN)*
2. Texas A&M University–College Station*
3. Iowa State University*
4. University of California–Davis*
5. Cornell University (NY)
5. University of Illinois–Urbana-Champaign*

BIOMEDICAL/BIOMEDICAL ENGINEERING
1. Johns Hopkins University (MD)
2. Massachusetts Institute of Technology
3. Georgia Institute of Technology*
4. Duke University (NC)
5. Stanford University (CA)

CHEMICAL
1. Massachusetts Institute of Technology
2. Georgia Institute of Technology*
3. University of California–Berkeley*
4. University of Texas–Austin*
5. California Institute of Technology

CIVIL
1. University of California–Berkeley*
2. Georgia Institute of Technology*
3. University of Illinois–Urbana-Champaign*
4. University of Texas–Austin*
5. Purdue University–West Lafayette (IN)*

COMPUTER ENGINEERING
1. Carnegie Mellon University (PA)
2. Massachusetts Institute of Technology
3. Stanford University (CA)
4. University of California–Berkeley*
5. Georgia Institute of Technology*

ELECTRICAL/ELECTRONIC/COMMUNICATIONS
1. Massachusetts Institute of Technology
2. University of California–Berkeley*
3. Stanford University (CA)
4. Georgia Institute of Technology*
5. University of Illinois–Urbana-Champaign*

ENVIRONMENTAL/ENVIRONMENTAL HEALTH
1. Stanford University (CA)
1. University of California–Berkeley*
3. University of Illinois–Urbana-Champaign*
4. Georgia Institute of Technology*
5. University of Texas–Austin*

INDUSTRIAL/MANUFACTURING
1. Georgia Institute of Technology*
2. University of Michigan–Ann Arbor*
3. Purdue University–West Lafayette (IN)*
4. University of California–Berkeley*
5. Stanford University (CA)

MATERIALS
1. Massachusetts Institute of Technology
2. University of Michigan–Ann Arbor*
3. Georgia Institute of Technology*
4. Stanford University (CA)
5. Northwestern University (IL)
5. University of Illinois–Urbana-Champaign*

MECHANICAL
1. Massachusetts Institute of Technology
2. Georgia Institute of Technology*
3. Stanford University (CA)
4. University of California–Berkeley*
5. University of Michigan–Ann Arbor*

PETROLEUM
1. University of Texas–Austin*
2. Texas A&M University–College Station*
3. Pennsylvania State U.–Univ. Park*

Note: Peer assessment survey in 2018 conducted by U.S. News. To be ranked in a specialty, a school may have either a program or course offerings in that subject area; ABET accreditation of that program is not needed. Extended rankings can be found at usnews.com/bestcolleges.

Dealing With Distress

Colleges are expanding services for students battling anxiety, depression and other challenges

by **Barbara Sadick**

Evelyn Wallace was just 3 years old when she was mauled at the playground by a pit bull, a trauma that has led to crippling bouts of "life dread" in situations that make her feel insecure. Experiences, for example, like adjusting to freshman year at the University of Michigan – and a housing situation that wasn't ideal for her. Wallace says that she and her roommate barely spoke, and that she eventually felt so uncomfortable in her room that she rarely spent time there. Thinking about returning to school after spring break filled her with apprehension.

But she did return, and then found the help she needed to finish out the year – and stay. The therapist Wallace began seeing every other week at Michigan's Counseling and Psychological Services center helped her discuss her daily struggles and begin to cope better. Then, sophomore year, she discovered the Wolverine Support Network, a student-led organization launched in 2014 that aims to address and promote mental health and well-being by engaging peers from across campus in small, diverse discussion groups. The focus is on members' personal experiences, including social and academic life and body image. "I've found a place on campus where people not only know my whole story, but are looking out for me and empowering me

to pursue what I really care about while at the same time helping me feel appreciated even on the days when I have difficulty getting myself to class," says Wallace.

As at Michigan, colleges and universities across the country are ramping up their services for undergrads in distress – and there's increasing demand. A 2017 survey by the American College Health Association revealed that about 61 percent of students had experienced "overwhelming anxiety" within the previous year, up from 51 percent in 2011. According to Pennsylvania State University's Center for Collegiate Mental Health, campus counseling centers saw an average 30 percent jump in the number of students seeking help between 2009 and 2015. During that same period, the total number of students enrolled rose by about 5 percent. A 2017 analysis by the center found that roughly half of students who sought counseling in the previous year had some symptoms of depression. Anxiety concerns had affected 62 percent. More than one-third of those seeking help had contemplated suicide at some point in their lifetime. Micky Sharma, director of the Office of Student Life Counseling and Consultation Service at Ohio State University, thinks the numbers can be partly explained by the fact that many students who previously would not have attended college are now doing so, thanks to better treatments. In addition, he speculates, "this generation's constant connection to technology may be inhibiting their coping and problem-solving skills."

One priority has been to make access to crisis care easier and quicker while handling noncritical and long-term needs as expeditiously as possible or making referrals. At Ohio State, phone triage screening gets students who call for help a roughly 15-minute conversation with a counselor within a day to determine how quickly they need to be seen and either schedule an appointment with a campus therapist or provide a referral to another service. Those who are high priority get an individual counseling session within the week. Students who call up in crisis after hours can connect to ProtoCall, a phone counseling service operating all day every day. Those in crisis at the University of Southern California, who account for about half of the more than 2,000 students seen each year, are helped immediately during and after hours by crisis counselors and are provided care until they're stable. Those not in acute need can wait up to four weeks during busy times for an appointment at the counseling center or be referred to someone in the community.

At Michigan and the University of Texas–Austin, counselors have been embedded across campus. "This model incorporates the best of both worlds – a coherent centralized approach to student mental health on a large campus with localized delivery and expertise," says Todd Sevig, director of Counseling and Psychological Services at Michigan, which can now be accessed in 12 of the university's schools and colleges. Staff members get to know the culture of the school, the professors and the issues that are of concern to those specific students.

Technology is expanding the mental health armamentarium. Hamilton College in New York, for example, is exploring an initiative that will connect students in need of counseling with online psychologists and psychiatrists. Students at Penn

ILLUSTRATION BY PUSHART FOR USN&WR

State can tap web-based tools that help them determine whether they're anxious or depressed and try an online five- or six-week treatment module using cognitive behavioral therapy before opting for counseling. The school's 24-hour crisis line provides immediate access to support.

Workshops, group support and wellness programs are springing up, too. USC's new Office of Campus Wellness and Crisis Intervention offers a mindfulness program and is developing what will be a required course for first-year students focused on flourishing, healthy relationships, emotional intelligence, self-care and lifestyle design. At Duke University in North Carolina, support services include, for example, groups to help students build relationships and resilience and regulate emotions. Carleton College in Minnesota runs expressive arts therapy groups to help undergrads with depression and anxiety get in touch with their feelings and bond through drawing, painting, writing and discussion.

Twenty-eight peer groups meet regularly every week for an entire semester at Michigan. Student facilitators are trained in how to ask open-ended questions and guide group discussions on topics like recognizing and coping with depression and understanding eating disorders. Sam Orley, a 2018 graduate and former executive director of WSN, who was inspired to become involved with mental illness initiatives following his brother's suicide, believes that students are the most potent source of influence on other students. He notes that the WSN model is now being replicated at the University of Cincinnati and Michigan State, with 30 other colleges showing interest in adopting it.

At Ohio State, drop-in workshops led by campus clinicians are available to students every day on subjects ranging from how to set realistic goals to how to beat anxiety. As at many colleges, yoga and mindfulness sessions are ongoing, and the school offers 30 options for group therapy that include Everyday Mindfulness, Surviving to Thriving, and Bringing Back Balance.

In some cases, wellness topics are even being addressed in class. At UT-Austin, a curriculum expert works with faculty across campus to figure out ways to acknowledge the importance of student well-being by beginning class with a mindfulness exercise, say, or by promoting group activities and closer social connections. In the first year of a three-year grant, some early successes include stronger ties between faculty and students, says Chris Brownson, director of the Counseling and Mental Health Center.

A number of schools offer the THRIVE program developed by Philadelphia-area therapist Christie Versagli to teach students evidence-based skills for increasing their well-being and life satisfaction. The program, which delves into how to manage thoughts, health, relationships, impact, vision and emotions, has been presented by Johns Hopkins University in Baltimore, Hamilton, and Franklin and Marshall in Pennsylvania. According to Terry Martinez, vice president and dean of students at Hamilton, undergrads have praised THRIVE for equipping them with insights and skills that help them feel fulfilled, empowered and prepared to deal with daily challenges.

Because entering college is such a big transition, prospective students and parents should know what to expect from health services on and off campus. For those who have been receiving ongoing care, it's important to know what long-term services are available. Schools in large cities may have mental health support readily available nearby for when the limit on college counseling is reached or when a more specialized therapy is needed.

Parents also need to understand that while they might like to be in the loop and able to speak with their child's mental health providers, these professionals are legally and ethically bound to uphold confidentiality and cannot give out information to anybody without a student's permission. Exceptions may be made only if a student is a threat to himself or others or if the protection of children and minors makes it necessary. In other circumstances, students must sign a consent form to allow such communication.

Most college counseling centers welcome requests from families about their services and advise against assuming that every school can meet every mental health need. It's best not to "make assumptions about what might be available," cautions Ben Locke, senior director for Counseling and Psychological Services at Penn State and the founding director of the university's Center for Collegiate Mental Health. "And everyone needs to understand the difference between mental health challenges that can be worked on, what can be done to feel well in the world, and what is beyond the scope" of a college counseling program. ◆

Mind Your Health

Consider these possible resources to help maintain good mental health on campus:

ULifeline
Operated by the nonprofit Jed Foundation, this site offers general info and school-specific support from a searchable database of more than 1,500 college campuses that are in the ULifeline network. A self-evaluator tool can also help you learn more about your own mental health.
ulifeline.org

MentalHealth.gov
In addition to facts and data related to mental health, find details about care available close to home or school.
mentalhealth.gov

24-Hour Hotlines
The National Suicide Prevention Lifeline (**1-800-273-8255** or **suicidepreventionlifeline.org**) and the National Sexual Assault Hotline (**1-800-656-4673** or **online.rainn.org**) offer round-the-clock help.

Active Minds
Founded in 2003 by a college student, this nonprofit group works to build awareness and advocacy around student mental health. Find online support or link up with one of the organization's 450-plus chapters nationwide.
activeminds.org

National Alliance on Mental Illness
This national grassroots advocacy organization offers educational resources, information about local chapters and support, and online discussion groups, which can be anonymous.
nami.org

SAVANNAH LUSK
BS '18, Exercise Physiology
Hometown: Covel, WV
2014 Foundation Scholar
2018 Fulbright Scholar
Plans to start a nonprofit or become Surgeon General.
OFFERING MORE SCHOLARSHIPS
to more students like you.
We believe in grit and determination, not just test scores. That's why 93% of our new undergraduate students receive aid, often in the form of scholarships and grants. And we're expanding our scholarship tiers to offer even more students the chance to follow their passions — wherever they lead.
WestVirginiaUniversity.
go.wvu.edu/usnews
MOUNTAINEERS GO FIRST.

STUDY THE SCHOOLS

A Safer Campus Culture

Schools aim to prevent sexual assault while protecting the rights of victims and the accused

by **Beth Howard**

In a class called "Flip the Script," designed to help women avoid a sexual assault, Abigail Brickley practiced martial arts-like self-defense maneuvers and learned to identify potential perpetrators, such as men who try to isolate women from a group or insist that they have another drink even after they've refused it. The for-credit class also focused on "getting the narrative of weakness out of our heads and promoting confidence in ourselves," says Brickley, a junior at the University of Iowa.

The new elective is among the myriad ways that colleges and universities have doubled down to combat sexual violence on campus since 2011, when the Department of Education put schools on notice that they needed to do a better job of protecting students or else they would risk losing federal funding. During the Obama administration, the DOE launched more than 300 investigations into schools' handling of complaints, as potential violations of Title IX, the landmark legislation guaranteeing women equal rights to education.

Some critics have said the new rules don't adequately protect accused students – and Secretary of Education Betsy DeVos has taken steps to address that criticism. Meanwhile, many schools remain committed to reforming campus culture and educating all students about healthy relationships and anti-violence measures. These initiatives are now taking place against the backdrop of the #MeToo movement, which has rocked so many sectors of society, including academia.

A key component of reducing incidents of sexual assault is to assess how pervasive it is and what circumstances contribute to it. The Sexual Health Initiative to Foster Transformation, a research project completed at Columbia University and

A THEATER WORKSHOP AT THE UNIVERSITY OF OREGON HIGHLIGHTING THE IMPORTANCE OF CONSENT

Barnard College in New York, revealed that, in 2016, 22 percent of students who participated in the survey reported experiencing some sort of unwanted sexual contact. This figure is consistent with studies from other universities, noted SHIFT's two lead researchers, Claude Ann Mellins, a professor of clinical psychology at the New York State Psychiatric Institute and Columbia, and Jennifer S. Hirsch, a professor at the Columbia Mailman School of Public Health.

The results showed that heterosexual women experienced the greatest number of incidents, while the rates were highest among LGBT and other students representing sexual minorities. The data also found that more than 12 percent of men studied had experienced sexual assault. The researchers examined not just experiences of sexual assault, but the social circumstances in which they're most likely to occur.

Increasingly, schools are drawing on research like that from SHIFT to help craft effective prevention strategies. One approach – something every new college student will likely encounter during orientation or early first semester – is mandatory school-sponsored training on avoiding or preventing situations that can lead to sexual assault. Definitions of consent are apt to be covered, too, particularly as some states have passed or are considering laws that define consent as a voluntary, affirmative and mutual agreement. Called affirmative consent, or "yes means yes," such policies sharply depart from past practices where the absence of a "no" counted as consent, whether or not a student was inebriated or passed out. Along with California and New York, a number of schools have affirmative consent policies, including the University of Minnesota, Texas A&M, the University of Virginia, Indiana University and the University of New Hampshire, according to End Rape on Campus, a victim advocacy group.

How this information is conveyed varies. At the University of Oregon, for example, all freshmen are required to view the "It Can't Be Rape" theater production, which "details an experience of sexual assault and the impact it has on the survivor, the perpetrator and their friends," says Abigail Leeder, director of the university's Experiential Education and Prevention Initiatives. The production touches on issues of alcohol use and sexual identity, and it defines sexual assault and consent.

NATALIE BEHRING FOR USN&WR

At the play's end, students get handouts that cover campus resources when they break into smaller groups to debrief.

Incoming students at the University of Wisconsin–Madison and Carnegie Mellon University in Pittsburgh must complete an online module on sexual violence before school starts and then undergo in-person training when they get to campus. The University of Maryland–College Park is working to implement sexual violence prevention programming in all four years of undergraduate student life.

Schools are also getting better at supporting victims by offering counseling and survivor support groups like those at the University of Florida and the University of Michigan. And more campus health centers are staffed with Sexual Assault Nurse Examiners trained to provide specialized care to victims, conduct forensic exams and give expert testimony if a case goes to trial. Likewise, colleges nationwide are expanding the ranks of Title IX coordinators and other professionals tasked with handling complaints of sexual violence, and otherwise keeping the school in line with federal requirements, such as promptly investigating all complaints filed and protecting victims' confidentiality.

Whether many of these new initiatives are paying off is still being determined in many cases, so schools are expanding their data collection with campus culture surveys and are investing in programs that do have clear track records. One encouraging approach: tapping the power of other students to reduce campus assaults. Under the 2013 Campus Sexual Violence Elimination Act, bystander programs that teach those who see trouble brewing how to intervene effectively are now required at U.S. colleges.

"Engaging bystanders is the most promising way to mobilize a community around this issue and help people build skills they need to contribute to a solution," says Lea Hegge, vice president of program development at Alteristic, the nonprofit that licenses the Green Dot bystander program. Green Dot has been implemented at more than 100 U.S. colleges. A 2016 study supported by the University of Kentucky and the National Institutes of Health showed that students who participated in Green Dot training had a 17 percent lower risk of interpersonal violence. And, says Bob Ritter, head football coach at Middlebury College in Vermont, who provides the training to athletic teams at the school, "This approach resonates with our guys more than anything else that was tried in the past. It allows them to speak up about assault in ways that they wouldn't have known about beforehand."

Both Green Dot and another proven program – Bringing in the Bystander, which originated at UNH – help members of the campus community quickly recognize situations that might be concerning and come up with strategies to safely avert an incident, from confronting a potential perpetrator in a sketchy situation to turning up the lights or turning off the music at a party where things are getting out of hand. For instance, one student started a conga line when she saw how uncomfortable her roommate looked when a guy wedged close to her on a couch.

> **"Schools are also getting better at addressing the needs of victims."**

"It's easy for some students to put on their superhero cape and be direct in stopping something that doesn't look right. But most aren't comfortable with that," says Sharyn Potter, a sociology professor at UNH and executive director of research for the university's Prevention Innovations Research Center, which also pioneered the related social marketing campaign Know Your Power. Bringing in the Bystander is now in place at some 600 colleges and universities across the U.S. and Canada, including Georgetown University in Washington, D.C., and the University of Kansas.

Yet bystanders are present in less than 20 percent of sexual assault situations, so colleges need to employ multiple tools to spark real change. That's why new approaches are being developed, such as "Flip the Script," which originated in Canada and is formally known as the Enhanced Assess, Acknowledge, Act Sexual Assault Resistance education program. The initiative is now available at the University of Iowa and other U.S. colleges and universities.

The program emphasizes that "sexual assaults are most commonly perpetrated by someone you know and should be able to trust," says Charlene Senn, professor of psychology and Women's and Gender Studies at Ontario's University of Windsor, who developed it. "And they occur most often in social situations that people don't consider dangerous."

The workshop features role-playing scenarios that often precede sexual misconduct and allows participants to practice various strategies to foil an assault. It also indirectly addresses self-blame. "When women blame themselves or feel guilty for what's happening, they're actually less likely to resist," says Sarah Deatherage-Rauzin, a health promotion coordinator at Florida Atlantic University, which offers the program. "Flip the Script" was found to cut the number of rapes experienced by women who participated nearly in half and the number of attempted rapes by a remarkable 63 percent, compared with a group of women who didn't attend the classes, according to tracking surveys for up to two years after the training.

Schools are also revamping their adjudication processes, which some believe have been historically stacked against victims. In the past, students complained that colleges allowed those found responsible for an assault to remain on campus or blamed victims for their own attacks. While some have called for campus sexual assault cases to be turned over to local po-

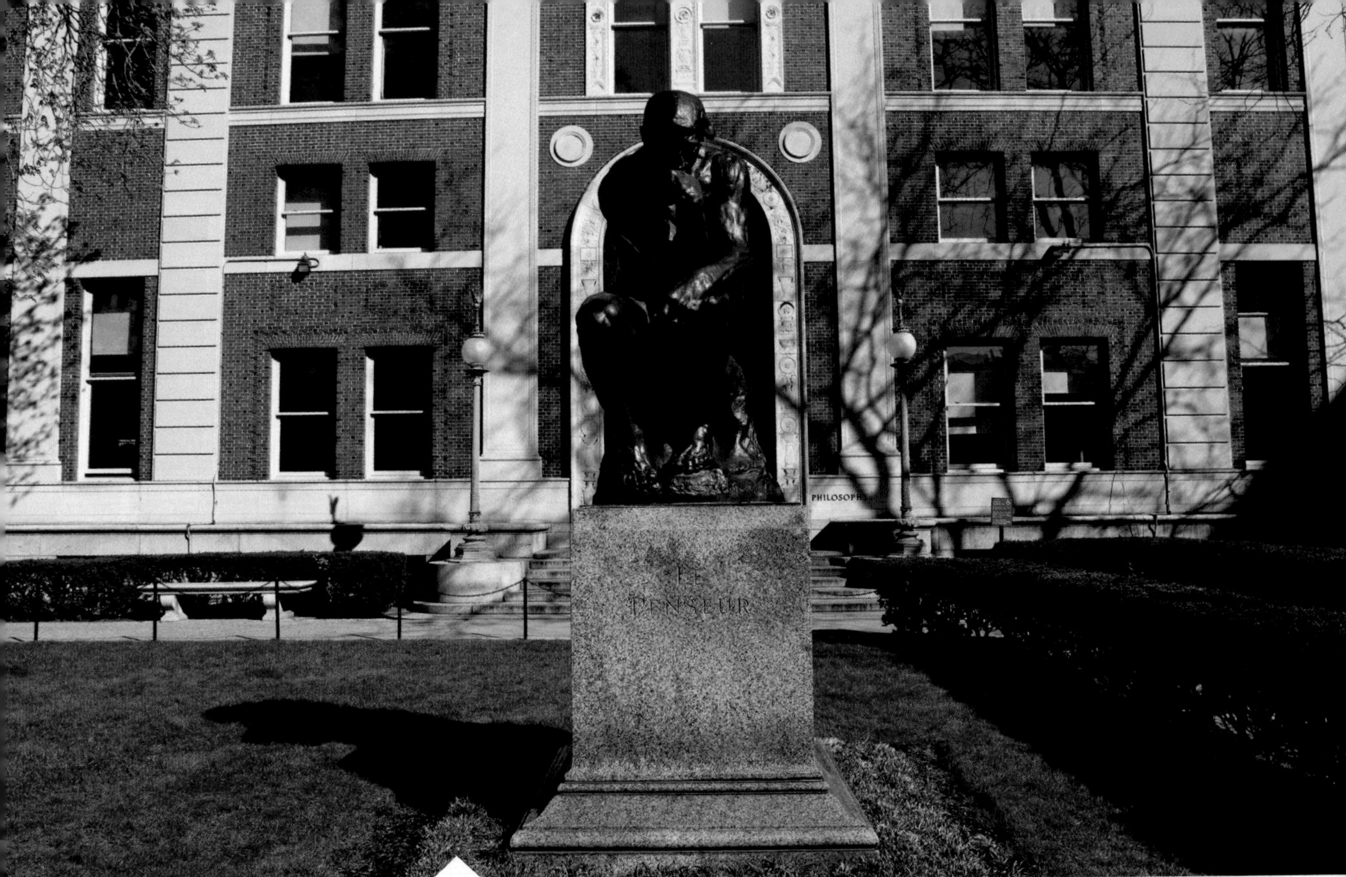

AT COLUMBIA UNIVERSITY, WHERE RESEARCHERS ARE STUDYING SEXUAL ASSAULT

lice, the idea is controversial.

Advocates for victims say many do not want to file criminal charges against their alleged attackers. According to the Rape, Abuse & Incest National Network, an anti-sexual violence organization, less than 4 percent of rapes reported to police end up being referred to prosecutors, and less than two-thirds of those few cases result in felony convictions. (By contrast, schools must adjudicate all cases brought before them.) Court records are also public, and victims may fear retaliation – or at least a protraction of their trauma.

While most colleges have been using "preponderance of the evidence" – a civil court standard – to determine responsibility, this has raised concerns about whether the accused are being treated fairly. A slew of lawsuits directed at colleges in the past few years by accused students have claimed violations of due process. Some see these suits as a needed correction to colleges' swinging too far to protect accusers' rights. Others view them as a defense attorney tactic "to silence survivors and exhaust their financial resources," says Carly N. Mee, the interim executive director of SurvJustice, a not-for-profit organization that offers legal assistance to sexual violence survivors.

At press time, news reports suggested that the DOE was drafting new rules governing how schools handle sexual assault cases. According to The New York Times, these potential changes include providing more protections for the accused and narrowing the liability of colleges to assaults that are committed on campus and reported to designated authorities. Earlier guidance from the DOE gave colleges the choice of using either the preponderance of the evidence standard or the stricter "clear and convincing" evidence standard. (The latter is still a lower threshold than the "beyond a reasonable doubt" bar that must be reached in criminal court.) The DOE called the reports "premature and speculative" and declined, through a spokesperson, to comment.

Recent cases suggest that, at least under current rules, some victims are prevailing against their attackers. Like other schools, the University of Notre Dame has increased its prevention efforts and protections for victims of sexual assault through programs like Green Dot and by requiring mandatory training for students, faculty and staff. When a Notre Dame student told a friend that she'd been sexually assaulted by another student in December of 2016, the friend convinced her to go to the hospital and have evidence collected. She struggled with depression and thought about dropping out of college before she finally reported the assault to the university the following spring. "I had heard that the process was brutal," she says. "But I knew what had happened was wrong."

She and the accused student made statements to the school's investigators, and at a hearing that July, members of a three-person panel drawn from the school's administration asked them questions and heard witness testimony. She informed U.S. News that in August 2017, she received a letter from Notre Dame advising her that the accused had been found responsible for the assault and expelled from the university.

Notre Dame declined to comment as per policy on any student case. However, in the formal adjudication letter the young woman provided to U.S. News, university officials confirmed that the accused was "more likely than not responsible" for violating four of the school's Standards of Conduct, including those related to sexual assault and harassment. "I finally feel safe on campus again," the young woman says.

That's the ultimate goal, says Barbara Scales, director of Middle Tennessee State University's June Anderson Center for Women & Nontraditional Students. "We can't afford to go backwards," she says. ◆

RAYMOND BOYD–GETTY IMAGES

STUDY THE SCHOOLS

8 Hot Majors With a Bright Future

You can hit the sweet spot between pursuing your passions and having great job prospects

by **Stacey Colino**

When **the time** comes to choose a major, many college students are torn between going with a subject they're most interested in and choosing a field that will set them up for a plum job after graduation. The good news is that it's often possible to do both. In fact, 4 in 5 undergraduates choose a major that is connected to strong job prospects, according to a 2015 report by the Georgetown University Center on Education and the Workforce. For instance, big data is having an impact in many fields, from health care to human resources, so the range of majors connected to data science and analytics have a bright job outlook. Here are eight hot areas you may want to consider:

1 Mechatronics Engineering

Standing at the juncture between mechanical and electrical engineering, mechatronics is an interdisciplinary field that teaches students how to build and control mechanical devices like motors and robots and how to take sensor data and turn it into commands. "The mechanical engineering major is changing a lot," says Jonathan Rogers, an associate professor in the department at Georgia Institute of Technology in Atlanta who specializes in automation and mechatronics. "Mechatronics is a huge growth area for modern technology, especially robotics and autonomous driving."

Purdue University in Indiana and Middle Tennessee State University are among what is for now a small handful of institutions offering a dedicated mechatronics major; most undergrads specializing in the field do so under the umbrella of mechanical engineering. They typically take courses in 3D modeling, dynamics and control systems.

In general, engineering grads have the highest average starting salary – roughly $66,500 – according to a 2018 survey by the National Association of Colleges and Employers. Other engineering fields with strong earnings potential include petroleum engineering, mining and mineral engineering, and chemical engineering, according to the Georgetown report. Regardless of their specialty or career path, "engineers create solutions to address the needs of society and improve humanity," says Harriet Nembhard,

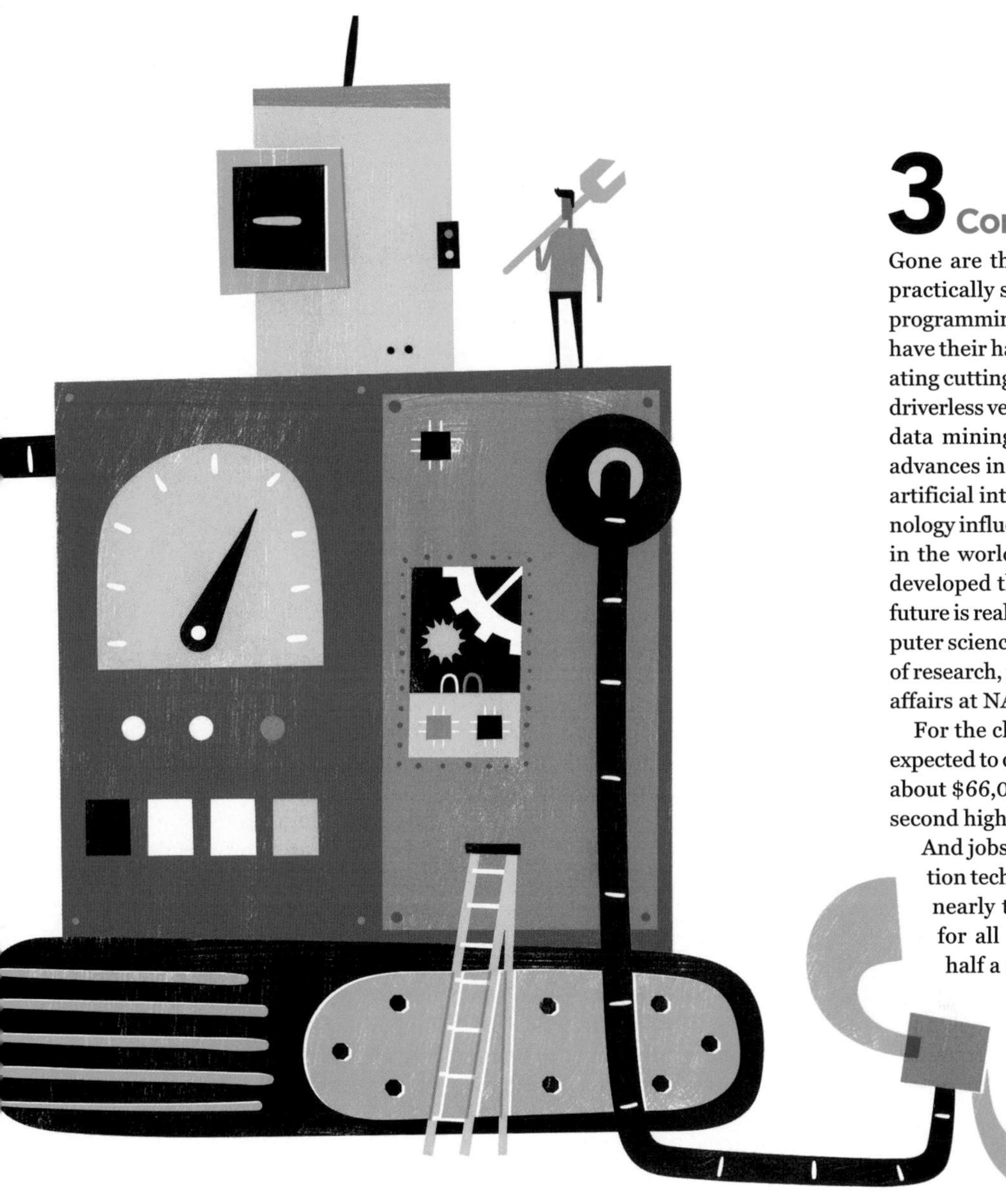

3 Computer Science

Gone are the days when the field was practically synonymous with computer programming. Now, computer scientists have their hands in everything from creating cutting-edge educational tools and driverless vehicles to doing sophisticated data mining in health care to making advances in cybersecurity, robotics and artificial intelligence. With digital technology influencing just about everything in the world and "new products being developed that are digitally driven, the future is really about creativity with computer science," says Edwin Koc, director of research, public policy, and legislative affairs at NACE.

For the class of 2018, CS degrees are expected to command a starting salary of about $66,000, according to NACE, the second highest figure after engineering. And jobs in computing and information technology are expected to grow nearly twice as fast as the average for all careers, adding more than half a million new jobs from 2016 to 2026, according to the Bureau of Labor Statistics. The discipline's reach is widespread; its influence is felt in fields from the arts and politics to medicine. "For example, in health care, research at Carnegie Mellon is changing how kidney donors and patients are matched and, in public policy, our researchers are exploring techniques to address the difficult problem of eliminating gerrymandering in the drawing of political boundaries," says Srinivasan Seshan, professor of computer science and the head of the department at Carnegie Mellon University in Pittsburgh. The goal is to train a future generation of computer scientists to create innovative designs for new algorithms, languages, applications and systems that will enhance productivity.

Strong undergraduate programs in computer science include those at the University of Texas–Austin, Stanford, Massachusetts Institute of Technology, Pomona College in California, Carleton

head of the school of mechanical, industrial and manufacturing engineering at Oregon State University.

2 Business

Besides taking courses in accounting, finance, marketing, business law and management, business majors often work on team projects involving real-world case studies and participate in internships or hands-on experiences, including working with industry partners. It's one of the most popular areas – and for good reason. At the bachelor's level, eight of the 10 top majors that are in demand by employers are in the business category, such as accounting or sales, according to NACE. "We've seen a growth in new business practices, which involves managing more complicated work spaces and processes and juggling telecommuters and interconnectivity with global economies," says Jeff Strohl, director of research at Georgetown's Center on Education and the Workforce.

International business and finance majors have the highest combination of midcareer median pay ($112,200) and annual job growth (10 percent), according to PayScale, a compensation software and data company. The reason: "More companies are going global, especially as it's easier to do so through technology," says Lydia Frank, vice president of content strategy at PayScale. "It's important to have someone who can navigate the standard business practices and customs in different locations."

ILLUSTRATIONS BY SHAW NIELSEN FOR USN&WR

College in Minnesota, Swarthmore College in Pennsylvania and the University of Southern California.

4 Data Science

"Data runs the world now," Koc says. Indeed, by the year 2020, the number of positions for data and analytics experts in the U.S. is expected to increase by 364,000 to a total of more than 2.7 million, according to a 2017 report from Burning Glass Technologies, a labor market analytics company. Those steeped in the subject are at the forefront of predictive analytics – helping companies like Google and Yahoo improve their search engine functionality, or giving doctors and clinicians the tools to more effectively customize medical treatment to individual patients based on specific data points. Data scientists also play an important role in risk assessment within the credit card industry and in allocation and optimization of resources in environmental science and public policy.

"We're in an era where data is readily available, easy to collect, and people appreciate the value of making decisions based on empirical data," says Daniel Gillen, professor and chair of the department of statistics at the University of California–Irvine, which launched a new bachelor's in data science degree in 2015. The first incoming class had five students; the following year, 68 students enrolled. Other colleges with data science/analytics programs for undergrads include the University of Rochester in New York, Denison University in Ohio and Pennsylvania State University.

A data science major will typically learn a combination of statistics, mathematics, computer science, computer programming and database systems, plus how to think critically about complex information and how to communicate it.

5 Cognitive Science

The phrase cognitive science may be a bit of a head-scratcher, but it describes a relatively new interdisciplinary field that blends elements of psychology, computer science, philosophy, neuroscience and linguistics. In other words, it studies the mind, its processes and the nature of intelligence. "It's really about how people think in mental terms and neural terms," says Michael McCloskey, professor of cognitive science at Johns Hopkins University in Baltimore, where the number of students choosing the major has doubled in the last five years. There's an emphasis on how to think critically and engage in constructive problem-solving. Cognitive science majors go on to work in health care settings (in hospital administration or as research coordinators in labs, for instance), neuropsychological testing centers, business-related careers such as marketing, and the technology sector, among others. The major can also be good training for medical school, law school and business school, McCloskey notes. Schools with dedicated programs include Tufts University in Massachusetts, the University of California–Berkeley, the University of California–San Diego, Rice University in Houston, and the University of Pennsylvania.

6 Nursing

Want practically guaranteed employment? The nursing field is projected to add more than 64,000 jobs between 2016 and 2026, according to the BLS, a 31 percent increase. "Health care is one of the fastest-growing sectors of the economy, and our research has shown it has a large skills gap, with 1.7 openings per worker for advanced clinical care roles like nurse practitioners," notes Matt Sigelman, CEO of Burning Glass Technologies.

Explaining the growing need for nurses are an aging population and the fact that an increasing number of people have multiple chronic health conditions, says Patricia M. Davidson, dean and professor at the Johns Hopkins School of Nursing. "Studies have shown that nursing is one of the few occupations not decreasing due to technological innovation."

As part of their undergraduate education, nursing majors take classes in pharmacology, biostatistics, pathophysiology, chronic health assessment and health promotion. Students also participate in clinical rotations working with real patients alongside physicians and other health professionals, as well as "simulation labs, which offer a safe environment for students to practice hands-on skills and procedures," Davidson says. Strong undergraduate nursing programs are offered at Georgetown, Case Western Reserve University in Cleveland, UCLA, the University of Washington and Emory University in Atlanta. The Commission on Collegiate Nursing Education offers a list of accredited bachelor's programs online.

7 Pharmaceutical Sciences

For similar reasons, plus the diversification of health care and the growth of the pharmaceutical industry, there's a bright future for pharmaceutical science majors. "This is an area where the human touch is going to remain strong," Strohl says. "People like to talk to their pharmacist."

Undergrad programs aim to prepare students for technical positions in the development, production or sales divisions of drug companies or for a career as a pharmacist or pharmaceutical researcher. With a B.S. in pharmaceutical sciences but not a doctorate degree, you can work as a pharmacy assistant or technician or in sales for drug companies. With a median annual salary of $113,000, those who major in pharmacy, pharmaceutical sciences or pharmaceutical administration have the only nonengineering major among the top 10 ranked by wages, according to Georgetown's research.

After gaining a foundation with courses in math and science, pharmacy majors progress to advanced coursework in drug design, mechanisms of drug action, toxicology, quality assurance, regulatory compliance and other issues. For instance, at the University of Michigan's College of Pharmacy, which offers a bachelor's in pharm sciences (and revamped it in 2016), majors study the chemistry of medicines and drug delivery systems, regulatory issues and ethical concerns related to drug discovery.

8 Human Resources

Even in an increasingly automated world, there's no taking the "human" out of human resources – these are the professionals who handle hiring, training and other employee relations tasks for companies or organizations. "Going into the future, human resources looks to have more demand than supply," Koc says. The field is another one that is transforming because of data.

"Two important trends in HR are the increasing use of people analytics to drive HR decisions and the expansion of the scope of employee assistance programs offered by employers," says Peter Madsen, associate professor of organizational behavior and human resources in the Brigham Young University Marriott School of Business in Utah. Among the school's 2017 class of 40 HR management majors, 97 percent of those seeking jobs had positions within three months of graduating.

Usually under the umbrella of a business program, an HR major typically includes coursework in organizational behavior, applied social psychology, talent management, labor relations and employment law, plus business fundamentals. "The power of this major is its utility across industries, sectors and locations," says Erin Bass, an associate professor of management at the University of Nebraska–Omaha. "Any organization that employs people needs HR majors to help recruit, retain and engage its employees." ◆

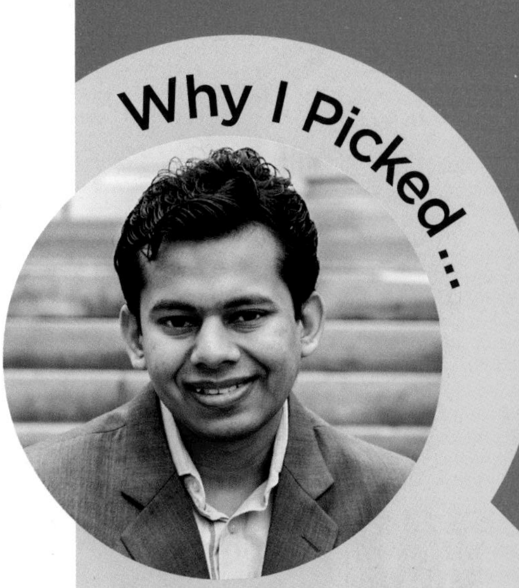

Lafayette College

EASTON, PENNSYLVANIA

Ali Ehsan, '20

▶ Coming from Bangladesh, I wanted to find an entrepreneurial and intellectually stimulating environment, and Lafayette offered just that – along with generous financial aid. In high school, I started two businesses, and with the help of my college economics professor, I developed a new investment model for the education sector. Lafayette paid for me to present my research at the global Social Business Academia Conference in Paris. My trip was also sponsored by the school's Dyer Center for Innovation and Entrepreneurship, which teaches critical skills like design thinking, product/idea prototyping, and marketing – paradise for people like me who talk, eat and sleep entrepreneurship.

I am also currently a board member of the Lafayette College International Students Association, which organizes events to celebrate the heritage of international students. I made my first American friend through an ISA event, an experience that was reflective of Lafayette's welcoming atmosphere for everyone.

CLAY WEGRZYNOWICZ

STUDY THE SCHOOLS

What's the Alternative?

Students who don't follow the standard four-year path have ever more appealing options

by **Mariya Greeley**

In 2013, 20-YEAR-OLD Carmel Wright, who had worked as a nanny and tutor after graduating from high school, was ready to consider college. Then she mysteriously lost the use of her right leg. What turned out to be an unusual muscle-bone condition set her on a yearlong path of treatment in Sacramento, California, where she eventually received the surgery that enabled her to walk again. Throughout her treatment she remembers thinking, "I have to recover because I've got to go to school."

Because she had missed the application deadline for the nearby University of California–Davis, Wright registered at Sacramento City College. She earned two associate degrees in two years there – one in political science and one in behavioral science – and was accepted to UCLA as a junior and awarded a full-ride scholarship. Wright had taken a specific set of classes at SCC that were guaranteed to fulfill first- and second-year general education requirements for many majors at schools in the University of California and California State University systems. Community college "allowed me to pursue education in a cost-efficient and manageable way," Wright says.

For some 5.6 million students in 2017, roughly 30 percent of all undergrads, enrolling at a two-year public college was their chosen option, according to data from the National Student Clearinghouse Research Center. Students choosing this route can save significant money, considering that the average yearly tuition at community colleges is about $3,570 compared to roughly $10,000 for in-state public universities and nearly $35,000 for private four-year schools.

States from California to Florida to Massachusetts have created "articulation agreements" to clarify requirements for those hoping to transfer to four-year institutions, such as what course credits will be accepted and minimum GPAs – issues that have often tripped up students. Some articulation agreements even promise applicants admission to institutions like the University of Virginia, Arizona State University and six of the UC schools if they meet certain guidelines.

Still, a successful leap is not guaranteed. While more than 80 percent of students enter community colleges with the intent to transfer and earn a bachelor's degree, only about 25 percent end up moving to a four-year school within five years, according to the Community College Research Center at Columbia University's Teachers College. Wright boosted her odds by regularly visiting advisers to cross-check information and plot her course schedule. Playing tennis

on the intercollegiate team at SCC also helped earn her priority registration for the classes she needed.

On the other hand, there's no question that an associate degree on its own can open the door to a range of well-paying, so-called middle-skill jobs ranging from web developer to registered nurse with median salaries around $70,000, according to the Bureau of Labor Statistics. Still, data from the Georgetown University Center on Education and the Workforce suggest that continuing on to secure that bachelor's will yield the biggest payoff: Lifetime earnings for someone with a four-year degree are $2.3 million compared to $1.7 million for an associate degree.

A virtual option. For many who are trying to get their bachelor's around work or family responsibilities, trekking to campus several times a week is not an option. Distance-learning programs can offer these students the flexibility to hold on to their job and their salary. David Taranto, 25, for example, is a clinical microbiologist in Needham, Massachusetts, who is simultaneously earning a fully online bachelor's in medical laboratory science from George Washington University in Washington, D.C. (The program includes several in-person clinical practicums at an approved lab of the student's choice.) Taranto's classes include "a little bit of everything," he says. They might be available live or be posted on a class website depending on the professor. Students generally have discussions and ask questions through online blogs and video threads. They also do group projects, give presentations via video, and take exams in 24-hour windows using a virtual proctoring service.

"I really wanted to get my bachelor's so I could grow my career, get new jobs, move up, become a lead tech or a supervisor," Taranto says. He was able to transfer many of the credits he earned from his associate degree in clinical laboratory science to GW and expects to graduate after about a year and a half. Taranto's employer pays for roughly a fourth of the program cost, which can run about $35,000 depending on the amount of

FOR CARMEL WRIGHT, COMMUNITY COLLEGE OFFERED THE BEST PATH TO HER BACHELOR'S DEGREE.

JENNA SCHOENEFELD FOR USN&WR

credits students are able to transfer. He's able to cover the rest with his salary. For comparison, full-time, on-campus tuition at GW is more than $55,000 a year.

Over 2.1 million undergraduates were enrolled exclusively in online courses in the fall of 2016, according to the National Center for Education Statistics. While many distance-degree programs are fully online, others blend online and on-campus learning. Students in the bachelor's in rehabilitation sciences program at New England Institute of Technology, for example, meet for class at the school's Rhode Island campus once every other week. Other schools, such as Harvard Extension School (part of Harvard University), require students to complete a certain number of credits on campus. At Harvard, weekend or three-week intensive courses are options. Online coursework tends to be as rigorous as the on-campus programs, so don't expect an easier path to a degree.

While students can lose some networking advantages by studying remotely, many college career centers are narrowing that gap by connecting students with job listings, career exploration tools and even one-on-one coaching to help them refine résumés and interview skills. Certain schools invite online students to campus for career fairs and some, like Arizona State, offer virtual job fairs where students can have one-on-one, text-based chats with employers.

When assessing different online programs, students should look at the distinctive elements of each to find the best fit. While earning a bachelor's online is often less expensive than doing so on campus, this is not uniformly true, so you'll want to compare tuition costs. Consider, too, issues such as whether you will be taught by full-time or adjunct faculty. You'll also want to make sure you can get 24/7 technical support and reach faculty as needed. In GW's program "you get quite a bit of access to professors," Taranto says. This access came in handy when his internet crashed on a Saturday night while he was taking an exam. He was able to email his professor and reschedule within 24 hours. Many schools now offer online degrees, including the University of Georgia, West Texas A&M University and Washington State University.

Companies were initially skeptical about online degrees, but they are now more accepting. These days "employers are looking at individuals holistically," says Paul McDonald, senior executive director at global staffing company Robert Half. Someone who gets an online bachelor's in computer science while working in IT, say, is "a very employable person," he notes. Soft skills like teamwork and public speaking are increasingly important to employers, McDonald adds, so online students should ensure that they can show those abilities through work or other activities.

"Online coursework tends to be as rigorous as that in on-campus programs."

Emphasizing mastery. Competency-based programs, a fairly new concept in higher education, are popping up as an alternative model to the traditional credit-hour system. They are designed primarily for those with some college credit or on-the-job experience, and students progress through these typically online programs at whatever rate they are able to prove they've mastered each concept or skill. Students pay a flat fee to enroll for a certain time frame – a cost-effective model if you're able to move through coursework steadily to your degree.

Western Governors University, an online school with over 60 competency-based degree programs, including bachelor's degrees in healthcare management, accounting and software development, was created over 20 years ago by a group of state governors. WGU students pay a bit over $3,000 at the start of each six-month term, an "all-you-can-learn" model during which they complete as many of their courses as possible. On average, students take two and a half years to finish a bachelor's program, for a total of around $15,000.

Students move through lessons at their own pace and meet with subject experts individually or in groups as needed. Each student also has an assigned mentor throughout the program who helps him or her map out a course plan and stay on track with weekly check-ins. Assessments, which students can take whenever they feel ready, could be tests, projects, papers or presentations. Purdue University in Indiana, the University of Wisconsin system, and Southern New Hampshire University's College for America all offer competency-based bachelor's degrees.

Remember, though, that if you don't finish your coursework within the set time frame, you can't defer it or get your money back. Also, many schools may not accept credits from competency-based programs should you try to transfer to a traditional college, so it's important to research your options carefully.

So, will a competency-based degree help in the job market? Many employers are still learning about them. A 2015 survey by the American Enterprise Institute found that fewer than 10 percent of employers reported a "strong understanding" of competency-based education. But after reading a description, about 85 percent reported being either interested or very interested in hiring those with CBE degrees.

Bottom line: Students can feel reassured that they now have multiple paths to a bachelor's. Wright graduated from college this past spring and plans to eventually get a joint J.D. and master's in education administration with hopes of helping reduce racial and economic disparities in K-12 education. "Don't be afraid," she says, "to have a different journey." ◆

Learning for the Future

Working across disciplines and taking a hands-on approach are key to success in the automation age

Artificial intelligence and automation promise to transform the way people live and work, in everything from health care to manufacturing to ordering groceries. What does this mean for college-bound students? For insights, **U.S. News** spoke with **Joseph Aoun**, president of Northeastern University in Boston and author of the 2017 book "Robot-Proof: Higher Education in the Age of Artificial Intelligence." Edited excerpts:

There's a lot of concern about AI's impact. What's your take?

Automation, AI and robotics are already taking away jobs and creating new jobs as we speak. This is a phenomenon that is already with us. What is key is how education can prepare people for this new world. I think that's what parents and students need to concentrate on.

What key skills should young people develop?

I believe that the mission of education is to help students become robot-proof for life. The way to do that is to integrate three literacies – this is what I call "the humanics." Every learner nowadays should understand how computers work and how to interact with computers. That's tech literacy. The second is data literacy – namely, every learner should understand the sea of information that is being generated and how to navigate it. The third is human literacy. We should focus on doing what machines in the foreseeable future cannot do or duplicate: being creative, being innovative, being empathetic with other people. Every learner should master the three literacies, but in an integrated way. So, for instance, when you are working on the environment, you have to focus on the scientific perspective, but in order to really understand how the environment is impacted, you need to also bring in the human aspects, the policy aspects.

How else can one can make oneself "robot-proof"?

This is where experiential education comes into play. It's the integration of classroom experience with work experience. It means partaking in real, long-term experiences – internships, co-ops, etc. – that will allow you to discover what you're good at, what you're not good at. It will allow you to work with other people, and it will allow you to move from one context to another. That's the first step in your robot-proof journey.

Describe Northeastern's co-ops, which alternate semesters of class with full-time work.

We work with 3,000 employers in over 140 countries. Before students apply, we work with them to make them realize why they are seeking this particular opportunity. After they come back, we integrate the experience into the classroom.

So what should someone look for in a college?

If it doesn't offer you a full-fledged humanics curriculum, the college should allow you the flexibility and opportunity to put your own curriculum together. For instance, that could include combining majors in very different disciplines. If you're in computer science and you're interested in, let's say, cybersecurity, are you able also to have some courses that will allow you to integrate discussions about privacy, about ethics, about behavioral psychology? See whether the college is going to provide opportunities to have an experiential dimension.

Should students be gravitating toward the STEM fields instead of, say, the liberal arts?

Technical skills are going to evolve and are going to become obsolete. What is going to allow you to master the subjects and the fields you're working on is precisely this integration of the human skills with the technical skills. We have created this false dichotomy between going into STEM fields or going into a liberal arts field. Integration is key.

What other advice would you share?

Our education system has been siloed. Go beyond the silos. Go beyond the disciplines and integrate them. If a college doesn't have the flexibility or doesn't provide you with an opportunity to do that, take notice. ◆

DANIEL REICHERT PHOTOGRAPHY

2

CHAPTER

Take a Road Trip

64 ILLINOIS

Northwestern University
University of Chicago
Knox College
University of Illinois—Urbana-Champaign

FOOTBALL PRACTICE AT MIDDLEBURY

BRETT ZIEGLER FOR USN&WR

TAKE A ROAD TRIP

FLORIDA

by **Lindsay Cates**

Attending school in the Sunshine State means that students are likely to enjoy a good bit of time at the beach along with strong academics and plenty of opportunities for hands-on learning. U.S. News visited the University of Miami, Rollins College, and two public institutions (and fierce rivals), the University of Florida and Florida State University.

Florida State University
Tallahassee

University of Florida
Gainesville

Rollins College
Winter Park

University of Miami
Coral Gables

University of Miami

CORAL GABLES

D**otted with palm trees** and surrounding scenic Lake Osceola, the University of Miami's campus is something of a south Florida oasis for academics, athletics and community, students say. Year-round sunshine and ample outdoor study spots are conducive to bringing people together, and with around 10,220 undergraduates, the university is "small enough to recognize familiar faces, yet big enough to meet new people every day," says Millie Chokshi, a junior from Orlando, Florida, majoring in public health and Spanish.

Founded nearly 100 years ago, UM brings together students from all 50 states and 120 countries, with more than half of undergrads coming from outside Florida. About 1 in 4 students are Hispanic or Latino, 9 percent are black, and 15 percent come from outside the U.S.

UM has nine colleges offering more than 180 undergraduate majors and programs. Another 6,000 or so grad students also attend. A flexible curriculum makes it easy, and common, to take classes across multiple schools, although switching majors requires careful planning, since different prerequisites can be required in each college. Students need to complete classes in each of three broad thematic "cognates" – science, technology, engineering and mathematics; arts and humanities; and people and society. (The third category might include courses like "The Business of Advertising" or "Gender and Politics," for example.) Additionally, undergrads take a writing course and a math or quantitative skills course.

Andrea Trespalacios, a senior from Miami, appreciated how easy UM made it to pursue her interests: two majors (English and international studies), plus minors in philosophy and ecosystem science and policy. She even found the time to study abroad in Prague, one of more than 60 international opportunities.

UM's Coral Gables campus is located about 7 miles southwest of downtown Miami. Each day, at least a handful of the school's 300-plus clubs set up tables throughout the Student Center Complex and along the lakeside patio to try to promote their events or recruit new members. Scuba Club is one of the largest (you can learn skills in the pool on campus), and other options include CaneStage

PHOTOGRAPHY BY **BRETT ZIEGLER** FOR USN&WR

DIVING PRACTICE AT THE UNIVERSITY OF MIAMI'S CAMPUS IN CORAL GABLES

Theatre Company, beach volleyball and a number of multicultural organizations. About one-fifth of students join a fraternity or sorority.

Athletics are a big draw, and all events are free for UM students – including football games, which are played at Hard Rock Stadium, also home to the NFL's Miami Dolphins. A weekly farmers market on campus and Thursday music performances that echo off the lake add to the lively vibe. Homecoming weekend, with its sporting events, returning alumni, parade and fireworks, is a highlight of the year.

UNDERGRADUATES
Full-time: 10,216

TOTAL COST*
$64,334

U.S. NEWS RANKING
National Universities: #53

*Tuition, fees and room & board for 2018-19

All nonlocal first-year students are required to live on campus, where they join one of several residential colleges. Each has a live-in faculty member, plus resident assistants and first-year fellows who serve as academic mentors to help new students get acquainted with all that the university has to offer. Half of all undergraduate classes have 16 or fewer students, and since you're typically not in a large lecture hall, professors will recognize your face and know your name, says Adrian Nuñez, a 2018 management and political science grad from Miami. A new housing option for upperclassmen, currently under construction, will consist of about two dozen interconnected buildings on the edge of the lake, with residences, outdoor patios, study spaces, an auditorium and more.

For those looking to venture beyond campus, a nearby Metrorail stop can get students to downtown Miami in about 15 minutes. There, they can find plenty of options for food, sports, entertainment, internships and service projects, or just otherwise explore the city's sights and distinctive neighborhoods. The nearest beaches are about 20 minutes away by car. "Miami is a place where if you dive in," says Nuñez, "you can do anything." ◆

Rollins College

WINTER PARK

Rollins' nearly 2,000 undergraduates spend a good bit of time away from their sunny suburban campus in central Florida. All told, 75 percent of them study abroad, and in keeping with the college's mission of promoting civic engagement and global awareness, every year Rollins coordinates off-campus "Immersion" trips, where students complete community service and social entrepreneurship projects for a week or weekend at a time.

UNDERGRADUATES
Full-time: 1,977

TOTAL COST*
$64,230

U.S. NEWS RANKING
Regional Universities (South): #2

*Tuition, fees and room & board for 2018-19

The experiences really help you "find your anchor" and embrace "what interests and engages you," says Ailin McCullough, a 2018 political science and environmental studies grad from Gainesville, Florida. He completed seven Immersions. One took him to Tanzania, where he helped build an ecolodge in the foothills of Mount Kilimanjaro. In another, he traveled to Utah to tackle conservation and wildlife habitat restoration projects.

For many, community engagement starts at the annual SPARC (for Service, Passion, Action, Rollins College) Day, held just before fall classes start. All freshmen participate in a day of volunteer work in the local community, usually with the professor who will teach their required first-year seminar (called a Rollins College Conference) and their classmates in the course. First-years also live in the same residence halls as their RCC classmates, which helps them form close connections.

Undergraduates can major in fields like international relations, social innovation and marine biology, or they might pursue an accelerated bachelor's and MBA program offered in conjunction with the Crummer Graduate School of Business. The college also enrolls some 600 grad students. In addition to their major requirements, everyone takes courses in writing, a foreign language, math, ethics, and health and wellness.

Students also complete a set of five Foundations seminars, which cover science, the arts, the humanities and the social sciences, and are organized around a common theme. "It creates more meaning in your classes, rather than just checking off a requirement," says Mollie Thibodeau, a 2018 communications grad from Cape Elizabeth, Maine. Her "Mysteries and Marvels" themed classes focused on asking questions about big puzzles in science, religion, culture and so on.

The college's 10:1 student-faculty ratio and average class size of 17 allow for strong connections with professors – and provide ample opportunity for one-on-one research. Recent anthropology grad SaraJane Renfroe of Gulf Breeze, Florida, traveled to Barcelona, Spain, with a professor as part of a research project on migrant women in Spain and Florida. She is now pursuing a master's degree in human rights studies at Columbia University.

Rollins' campus is full of Spanish-Mediterranean-style architecture, and its location on the edge of Lake Virginia provides easy access to water skiing, sailing or just enjoying the views from a gazebo overlooking the water. Every spring, students wait for a random day dubbed "Fox Day" that the president deems "too pretty to have class." Everyone is treated to food and activities instead.

CLASSES AT ROLLINS AVERAGE ABOUT 17 UNDERGRADS, HELPING THEM FORM TIGHT BONDS.

The Tars compete in a range of men's and women's varsity sports, including rowing, water skiing and sailing. There are over 100 student organizations, and some 40 percent of students get involved in Greek life. The Center for Leadership & Community Engagement helps connect undergrads with service opportunities and other activities at local organizations in Winter Park and the surrounding area, such as Habitat for Humanity and the Mead Botanical Garden.

Just steps off campus is Park Avenue, home to shops, dining options and a shared outdoor space. Central Florida's cultural institutions, gardens and theme parks – including Disney World and Universal Studios – are all nearby, and students can get discounted tickets. The SunRail commuter rail system, which stops on Park Avenue, can get to downtown Orlando in about 15 minutes.

Karina Barbesino, a senior international relations and Asian studies major from Croatia, came to Rollins knowing about its intense focus on global engagement. When she couldn't find a study abroad option for exactly what she wanted, she worked with the college to create one and ended up spending nine months in China studying business, culture and language. "If you set your mind to something, Rollins will help you as much as possible," says Barbesino, who hopes to either study or teach in Taiwan after she graduates and eventually work for the government. ◆

University of Florida

GAINESVILLE

Growing up in Ocala, Mario Agosto owned a Florida Gators hoodie and hat and was certainly familiar with the public university about 40 miles from home. But in terms of all that makes the place special, "I never understood it until I got here," he says. Before graduating in the spring with a bachelor's degree in criminology and law, Agosto presented criminology research he assisted on at an academic conference, served as student body vice president, and traveled to both the state's and the nation's capitals to meet with lawmakers and advocate for making college more accessible. He's now sticking around to earn a master's degree in real estate at the university. "UF is synonymous with opportunity," he says.

Indeed, a wealth of options – and a strong Gator spirit – characterize UF, whose 2,000-acre main campus is home to more than 31,000 full-time undergrads. From academics to athletics to extracurricular activities, "there's an involvement culture," says Brendon Jonassaint of Okeechobee, Florida, a 2017 health science grad now earning a master's degree at UF in health administration. He found his community on campus in part through intramural sports, his fraternity, and the dean of students' office. About 20 percent of students join sororities and fraternities, which often host events on campus. Hundreds of undergrads get involved with planning for an annual dance marathon in the spring that raises money for Children's Miracle Network Hospitals. Every fall, Gator Growl brings

UNDERGRADUATES
Full-time: 31,384

TOTAL COST*
In-State: $16,501
Out-of-State: $38,778

U.S. NEWS RANKING
National Universities: #35

*Tuition, fees and room & board for 2018-19

students together with food, a festival, a pep rally and a concert. (Snoop Dogg was a headliner in 2017.)

On the academic side, larger classes are more common until you move higher up in your major. But small-group sessions led by teaching assistants ensure you are grasping the concepts. UF offers a range of resources to assist those who take advantage, including a central Office of Academic Support, peer tutoring and frequent group study sessions for certain difficult courses, such as chemistry and calculus. The University Minority Mentor Program pairs students from diverse backgrounds with a faculty or staff member for one-on-one mentoring to help them transition to college. Roughly 1 in 4 students identify as belonging to a traditionally underrepresented minority group. The honors program, which enrolls about 10 percent of undergrads, offers smaller courses, advising and scholarship opportunities.

More than 90 percent of students come from within the Sunshine State, and most undergrads say that the UF community is friendly and caring. "People you don't know say hello," says Jackie Phillips, a recent grad in family, youth and community sciences from Jacksonville, Florida. There are opportunities to get to know professors, too, such as through undergraduate research. "UF has so many different programs that give you funding," says Jessica Valdes Garcia, a 2018 grad in political science and Portuguese from Miami, who got involved in research with a faculty member in African-American studies beginning in her sophomore year. She also went on to do other research on child abuse prevention in Brazil and the representation of women throughout history in Cuba.

Three-quarters of freshmen live on campus, where there are 26 residences and some 45 dining options. A favorite is the vegetarian and vegan Krishna Lunch served outside every weekday on the Plaza of the Americas, a central hub of student activity.

The Division I Gators sports teams compete in the Southeastern Conference, and the highly anticipated football games at Ben Hill Griffin Stadium – known as The Swamp – draw upwards of 90,000 fans, typically decked out in the school's distinctive blue and orange. A season ticket for students is $140.

Gainesville is a quintessential college town with many shops and restaurants. Nearby attractions include Ichetucknee River (for outdoor activities like kayaking, canoeing and tubing) and Devil's Den Spring, a popular spot for snorkeling. Orlando and the St. Augustine beaches to the east are each about a 90-minute drive. ◆

MEMBERS OF THE DELTA SIGMA THETA SORORITY AT UF, WHICH HAS MORE THAN 1,000 STUDENT ORGANIZATIONS

STUDENTS INSIDE FSU'S STOCK EXCHANGE-STYLE TRADING ROOM

Florida State University

TALLAHASSEE

With over 29,000 full-time undergrads and a 485-acre main campus, Florida State's size attracts students looking for a wide array of academic and research opportunities, Division I athletics, and a contagious Seminole pride. Even with its large scope, students say the university still finds ways to retain an intimate feel. And for those who take the initiative, "I've never met a professor that won't go the extra mile," says Stacey Pierre, a senior biology major from Miramar, Florida.

FSU makes a big effort to help students find their place, says Joe O'Shea, the school's assistant provost. When they arrive on campus, all first-years have access to a student success team, which can include a college life coach and both an academic and a career adviser. Incoming students can join a freshman interest group focused on a topic that excites them, such as STEM, business or communications. Undergrads in a FIG take several foundation courses together and connect with a cohort of 20 or so peers. Students can take that manner of bonding even further by applying to be part of a living-learning community, where they not only take classes together but live in residence halls alongside others interested in health professions, say, or global and public affairs.

Student success resources extend to every population across campus. The Center for Global Engagement brings together FSU's international student community (roughly 3 percent of undergrads) and hosts activities and events open to all. The Center for Academic Retention & Enhancement offers a range of resources geared toward helping minority, first-generation and other traditionally underrepresented students succeed. Roughly 81 percent of students come from within the Sunshine State, although FSU enrolls undergrads from all 50 states and more than 100 countries.

While students can expect some bigger classes, about 84 percent have fewer than 50 undergrads, and roughly 2 out of 5 enroll fewer than 20. Even with the university's 7,860 graduate students, proactive undergrads can find ways to get involved with research, often through the Center for Undergraduate Research and Academic Engagement.

Undergraduates can choose from more than 100 majors and programs. Certain so-called limited access majors, such as business and nursing, require that students apply directly for admittance as sophomores. Music, theater and dance also require an extra application for entrance the first year. The university's new entrepreneurship school offers majors in commercial, social and retail entrepreneurship. In a 14,000-square-foot innovation hub on campus, students from a wide range of disciplines can take advantage of cutting-edge tech equipment like 3D printers and virtual reality.

The school's 700-plus clubs and activities provide ample opportunities to "create your own version of normal," says Inam Sakinah, a 2018 graduate in interdisciplinary social science from Jacksonville, Florida. The student-run Union Productions group plans and hosts more than 150 concerts and special events per year. There are nearly 50 fraternities and sororities, which count about one-fifth of undergrads as members. Athletic events from FSU's 18 varsity sports teams, which compete in the Atlantic Coast Conference, are another way that students showcase their intense Seminole spirit. Football, in particular, tends to attract many fans and brings "a unifying force to the community," says Pierre.

FSU is 25 miles north of the Gulf Coast, and students make occasional beach visits around the area. Four miles away, the FSU Reservation on Lake Bradford offers outdoor activities like volleyball, climbing and kayaking. The university's proximity to downtown Tallahassee offers easy access to museums, government agencies and the state capitol building. ◆

UNDERGRADUATES
Full-time: 29,286

TOTAL COST*
In-State: $16,965
Out-of-State: $32,131

U.S. NEWS RANKING
National Universities: #70

*Tuition, fees and room & board for 2018-19

TAKE A ROAD TRIP

VERMONT

by **Lindsay Cates**

Winters in the Green Mountain State attract plenty of skiers, snowboarders and other outdoor adventurers, but these four schools have lots of other attributes that make them distinctive. U.S. News visited Bennington and Middlebury, two liberal arts colleges, before venturing north to the University of Vermont and St. Michael's College near scenic Lake Champlain.

St. Michael's College
Colchester

University of Vermont
Burlington

Middlebury College
Middlebury

Bennington College
Bennington

Bennington College

BENNINGTON

With just over 700 undergraduates and a rural setting in southern Vermont, Bennington might seem to have the makeup of a sleepy college. But an intense spirit of creativity and doing things differently gives the campus a buzz. In many ways, Bennington offers an unconventional college experience. There are no majors, and instead students design their own four-year course of study with a faculty adviser (and oversight from a faculty committee) to help focus their interests on a specific track, called a Plan.

A student could focus on environmental studies, for instance, and organize his or her Plan around the question, "How does understanding human perception of the environment help shift policy?" He or she might take classes in environmental studies, literature, Earth science and politics.

Students must complete a number of writing assignments as part of their Plan process. And every winter, each must find a way to get practical experience for the seven-week Field Work Term between semesters. Ronan Canty, a senior from Hyde Park, Massachusetts, spent Field Work Terms studying architecture in Rome, examining the design of a psychiatric hospital in Vermont, and helping with clinical care at a hospital in Maine.

"I came to Bennington wanting to study in an interdisciplinary way," says Canty, who credits the Plan process for allowing him to fully explore his dual interests and to take classes in both psychology and architecture. His thesis will focus on how the layout of therapists' offices impacts patients and the professionals themselves. Canty has his sights set on working in a hospital as a psychologist or therapist after finishing school.

About 90 percent of classes at Bennington enroll fewer than 20 undergrads, and the college's 10:1 student-faculty ratio means it's easy to form strong bonds with professors and peers. Many faculty members also remain active practitioners in their fields and serve as mentors to students. The academic environment can be intense, some say, with many students adopting a grad school-like focus on their work, but there are plenty of extracurricular outlets.

Dance, drama, music and the arts are popular areas of study, with the Visual and Performing Arts Center,

PHOTOGRAPHY BY **BRETT ZIEGLER** FOR USN&WR, EUGENE SERGEEV – GETTY IMAGES

BENNINGTON'S 10:1 STUDENT-FACULTY RATIO MAKES FOR A CLOSE-KNIT COMMUNITY.

known as VAPA, becoming a second home to many, says senior Julia Granillo Tostado, a Mexico City native studying animation, dance and art history. Some art students get their own studio space to complete projects, and at times it seems that "everyone is very dedicated and wants to create something" in their free time, says Granillo Tostado.

Chloe Amos, a 2017 grad who studied dance and environmental studies, designed a museum and a mock exhibit that would highlight overlooked stories of her native Hawaii as part of her work with the Center for the Advancement of Public Action. About 80 percent of the most recent graduating class took at least one CAPA course, which could involve responding to urgent local, national and global problems like researching contaminated water sources in the region or supporting the rights of refugees in crisis.

UNDERGRADUATES
Full-time: 724
TOTAL COST*
$69,470
U.S. NEWS RANKING
National Liberal Arts: #95
*Tuition, fees and room & board for 2018-19

Bennington offers a variety of housing options, but most students live in one of 18 coed houses, each with about 30 to 40 undergrads. The vibrant campus hosts many concerts, shows and readings on a daily basis. The college doesn't have its own varsity sports teams, but students can participate in several club sports including Ultimate Frisbee, soccer and basketball.

Shuttles are available to take students the 4 miles to downtown Bennington, which boasts museums, a farmers market, shops, restaurants and other cultural attractions. For those wanting to explore further off campus, the outdoor recreation program offers regular trips for white-water rafting and cross-country skiing. The Blue Trail, a popular route for hiking and biking, winds through campus and connects to other regional trails. ◆

Middlebury College

MIDDLEBURY

Set in Vermont's Champlain Valley, complete with scenic views of the surrounding Green Mountains and the Adirondacks, Middlebury College's 350-acre campus fosters a close-knit environment for the school's 2,500-plus undergraduates. Much of that starts with the college's honor code. Students pledge not to lie or cheat, which means there is zero tolerance for plagiarism and that undergrads can often take exams without proctors. The whole thing helps develop "a community of respect," says Jin-Mi Sohn, a 2018 international and global studies grad from Holbrook, New York.

UNDERGRADUATES
Full-time: 2,531

TOTAL COST*
$69,980

U.S. NEWS RANKING
National Liberal Arts: #5

*Tuition, fees and room & board for 2018-19

With more than 45 majors, a dozen language programs and a large emphasis on writing and rhetoric, Middlebury's academic and extracurricular offerings are especially robust for a small liberal arts college. Popular majors include economics, political science, computer science and environmental studies. Academics are rigorous, students say, but the atmosphere is more collaborative than competitive. The average class size of 18 and the 8:1 student-faculty ratio also help undergrads get plenty of individual attention from professors, says Mehek Naqvi, a senior psychology and religion major from Trenton, New Jersey.

Ample research opportunities are available in all disciplines. Maddie Morgan, a 2018 grad in molecular biology and biochemistry from Atherton, California, spent about 12 hours per week working with premedical sciences professor Grace Spatafora studying a specific strand of bacteria that causes dental cavities. Andrew Plotch, a senior international politics and economics major from Fair Lawn, New Jersey, traveled to campaign rallies all over New Hampshire leading up to the 2016 presidential primary there as part of a project with a political science professor on voter psychology. "It was a great way to experience politics [through] an academic lens," says Plotch. About 60 percent of undergrads study abroad.

Bonding with classmates happens quickly for incoming freshmen, who choose a required first-year seminar (2018 options include "The Women of Game of Thrones" and "The Philosophy of Human Rights") that is capped at 15 students. That group makes up one's neighbors in the residential Commons. As living-learning communities, the five Commons (each housing about 500 students) host events like dinners with visiting speakers and community meals, and each has a faculty head who lives nearby. They also compete with each other in activities like the Commons Olympics. Students generally live in the Commons for two years before they can move to other residence halls, on-campus apartments, houses or themed living spaces.

INSIDE THE ANDERSON FREEMAN RESOURCE CENTER AT MIDDLEBURY

In between the fall and spring semesters, Middlebury offers a monthlong winter term in January, during which students take a single class that might cover a topic that's "off the beaten path," says Clayton Read, a junior international politics and economics major from San Francisco. Students must complete at least two winter terms, and many find that taking one class at a time allows for "time to ski and build relationships," says Read, who chose a winter term course on protest music and another on welfare economics that took a deep dive into health, education and child care systems in different countries.

For many, winter is also a time for celebration. The closest ski mountain is about 20 minutes away, and Middlebury's annual Winter Carnival features NCAA ski races, along with a bonfire, a figure skating show and a ball. Each February, the school also welcomes about 100 incoming first-year students called "Febs" who took time off after high school for other experiences. (Plotch, for instance, taught English to kids in Ecuador before he enrolled in February 2015.) Four years later, at their own February graduation celebration, the Febs ski down the trails at Middlebury's Snow Bowl in their caps and gowns.

There is no Greek life, though undergrads can join coed social houses. Students may also get involved with more than 150 campus organizations, frequent cultural programs and events, and about 30 varsity sports teams. Athletic facilities include an ice arena and golf course, and many also take advantage of nearby forests, lakes and other outdoor retreats to hike, bike, camp, fish and more. Just up the road, the town of Middlebury (population: about 8,500) draws students to its stores, art gallery, restaurants and other businesses. ◆

University of Vermont

BURLINGTON

At nearly 10,200 full-time undergraduates, the University of Vermont is "a happy medium" in terms of its size and scope, says Julia Campanella, a 2018 grad from Manchester, Vermont, who majored in business administration with a minor in studio art. UVM has many of the same academic options (100-plus majors) and research opportunities (40 percent of undergrads get involved) available at large research universities, yet with class sizes averaging 33 students, it fosters close student-teacher connections and a small-town feel. "You have a chance to find your niche, whatever that may be," says Campanella.

Unlike at many large state schools, the student-faculty ratio is 16:1, and 98 percent of classes are taught by faculty rather than teaching assistants from among the university's 1,500 grad students. "Students sense the enthusiasm from professors who are engaged with their work" as both teachers and scholars, says Kathy Fox, associate dean of the College of Arts and Sciences and a sociology professor. Fox has taught a justice studies class based on her research on reintegrating prisoners into society to UVM undergrads and women from the nearby Chittenden Regional Correctional Facility.

Teaching extends beyond the classroom in a number of ways. Students can participate in hands-on learning

UNDERGRADUATES
Full-time: 10,183

TOTAL COST*
In-State: $30,738
Out-of-State: $54,978

U.S. NEWS RANKING
National Universities: #96

*Tuition, fees and room & board for 2018-19

experiences on the peak of nearby Mount Mansfield or UVM's aquatic research vessel Melosira. Undergrads might take a class on the opioid epidemic taught by medical school faculty, and an intensive Wall Street seminar concludes with a trip to New York City to give a presentation to executives at Morgan Stanley. The way that UVM allows students to pursue "a malleable education" attracted JD Kelly, a 2018 grad in economics and finance from Westfield, New Jersey, who participated in the Wall Street seminar and got a postgrad job at a commercial real estate firm in New York.

Contrary to popular belief, "you don't have to ski to come here," says Rosie Steinberg, a 2018 math and economics grad from Natick, Massachusetts. But winter sports enthusiasts have easy access to several popular mountains. Students in the Ski & Snowboard Club get discounted passes and free transportation to the peaks, and the Outing Club takes frequent trips open to all.

All told, students can participate in 200-plus clubs, and many enjoy watching the Division I Catamounts sports teams compete. Rugby, crew, football and more are offered at the club level, and intramurals include some quirky options like canoe battleship and broomball, a twist on ice hockey. Less than 10 percent of students join a fraternity or sorority.

UNDERGRADS EXPLORING A GREENHOUSE ON THE UNIVERSITY OF VERMONT CAMPUS

In general, students can't say enough good things about the school's location in Burlington – although it requires enduring some cold winters. The city of about 42,000 is located on the eastern shore of Lake Champlain, roughly 50 miles from the Canadian border. There are a range of options for enjoying live music, eating out and shopping along the pedestrian-only Church Street Marketplace, as well as a bike path along the lake. Ice cream fans can take note that Ben & Jerry's was founded in Burlington, and its headquarters is nearby.

Undergraduates must live on campus for two years, and nearly all student housing is grouped by common interest. The themes include Sustainability, Innovation and Entrepreneurship, and the Wellness Environment, an initiative that has gained national recognition for encouraging healthy behavior. ◆

St. Michael's College

COLCHESTER

Lindsey Rogers of Park Ridge, New Jersey, had never been rock climbing before she came to St. Mike's in northwestern Vermont. By the time she graduated in 2018, the neuroscience major had logged dozens of trips across New England as an assistant instructor for the college's Adventure Sports Center. In addition to its hands-on learning and ample outdoor recreational options, the private liberal arts college's small class sizes (average: 18 students) attracted Rogers, as did the general sense of community among the school's roughly 1,800 undergraduates. "There's a ton of opportunities, and they make it all really accessible," says Rogers.

Founded in 1904 by the Society of Saint Edmund, a Catholic group, St. Michael's infuses its campus culture with a spirit of serving others. Some 70 percent of students participate in giving back, and options include organic gardening, afterschool tutoring, caring for animals and baking for hungry families. The Mobilization of Volunteer Efforts program is a one-stop shop for getting involved in service. Leah Seften, a 2018 neuroscience grad from Bolton, Connecticut, volunteered for one of several St. Mike's mentorship programs where she led one-on-one trips, games and special events for area middle schoolers. Outside of the local area, MOVE sends more than 135 students each year to 12 other states and two international sites – in the Dominican Republic and either India or Guatemala – over school breaks.

Although religion is the backbone

VOLUNTEERS ARE ON CALL 24/7 WITH THE STUDENT-RUN ST. MICHAEL'S COLLEGE FIRE AND RESCUE.

of the school, for many "it has only a subtle presence on campus," says recent grad Kerra Photiades, from Bedford, New Hampshire, who double-majored in education and English. More than half of students identify as Catholic, and another 25 percent or so note another religious preference. As part of the curriculum, students must complete two courses focused on Christian and Catholic intellectual traditions.

Rounding out the core curriculum are requirements in philosophy, arts and literature, history and society, scientific inquiry, quantitative reasoning, global issues and languages. Undergrads are introduced to the school's small classes and writing-intensive coursework in a first-year seminar. The college's honors program includes a set of specialized seminars (capped at 15), a senior capstone project, and a colloquium course through which students attend community events and discuss them. About 30 percent of undergrads study abroad in more than 100 locations around the world, and many work in one-on-one research projects with faculty. Senior Mia DelleBovi, an elementary education and American studies major from Buffalo, New York, worked with an education professor to modify toy cars so children with mobility challenges could ride in them.

The college's 440-acre campus features a number of stately, red brick buildings, an astronomer's observatory and nature trails. Some students can enjoy mountain views from their dorm rooms, and 98 percent of undergrads live on campus all four years. Furthering the feeling of camaraderie, faculty are known to turn up at sporting events, meet students for coffee, and attend fundraisers for the 40-plus campus organizations. With a 13:1 student-faculty ratio, the professors know you, "so you can't just be a ski bum and not show up to class," says Sarah Kelly, vice president for enrollment and marketing. Burlington is just a few minutes away, while Montreal is two hours by car.

Outside the classroom, the Adventure Sports Center hosts outings for all students interested in hiking, mountain biking and climbing. Students can also participate in frequent low-cost trips to try snowshoeing, ice climbing or kayaking, as well as workshops and lessons to build skills in emergency medicine, decision-making and teamwork. Free buses head to the slopes every weekend.

The school fields 21 NCAA Division II athletic teams, with club and intramural options, too. And at the student-run St. Michael's College Fire and Rescue, undergrads are on call 24/7 to provide fire and emergency medical services to Colchester and the surrounding area. The school is also home to a professional performing arts playhouse where some students sharpen their skills over the summer in theater and music, which are among the roughly 38 majors offered at the college. ◆

UNDERGRADUATES
Full-time: 1,766

TOTAL COST*
$57,595

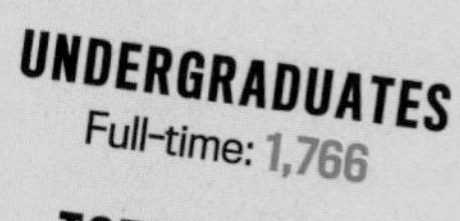

U.S. NEWS RANKING
National Liberal Arts: #116

*Tuition, fees and room & board for 2018-19

TAKE A ROAD TRIP

ILLINOIS

by **Mariya Greeley**

U.S. News visited universities big, small and in between across the Prairie State, making stops at Northwestern and the University of Chicago around the Windy City, liberal arts institution Knox College, and the University of Illinois–Urbana-Champaign. Follow along for a sense of how these Midwest schools stand out and measure up.

Northwestern University

EVANSTON

Starting the winter of his freshman year, Matthew Xu would travel from Northwestern's campus in Evanston to Chicago several times a week to work in a research lab affiliated with Ann and Robert H. Lurie Children's Hospital. There, the 2018 grad from Portland, Oregon, who completed the school's integrated science program, examined potential ways of regulating a gene that is associated with the severity of cystic fibrosis alongside a faculty member and a graduate student mentor. "My professor would advise me," he says, "but I was getting to really dictate the scope of my research" and "where I wanted to take my questions."

Northwestern offers a wide range of hands-on learning opportunities for its 8,100-plus full-time undergrads, from cutting-edge research across disciplines to internships, which about 80 percent of students complete before they graduate. Undergrads can enroll in nine of the university's schools and choose from about 100 majors and 90 minors and certificate programs. More than 12,000 graduate and professional students also attend.

Each school has its own set of graduation requirements, and many encourage experiential learning. Lyndsey Armacost, a 2018 grad in journalism and history from North Reading, Massachusetts, interned at NBC Sports covering the 2018 Winter Olympics in Pyeongchang, South Korea. In the engineering school, first-years take a course in which teams of students partner with local organizations to help them solve real-world challenges. Betty Bu, who is completing a joint biomedical engineering bachelor's and master's program, worked with the Rehabilitation Institute of Chicago to create a camera accessory to help an aspiring photographer who'd lost the ability to move part of his body. In addition to sharpening her math and science skills, Bu, a Chicago native, appreciated how the work helped her learn "how to connect with the humans that are actually using the product."

Academics can be rigorous, students say, but the environment is "not cutthroat to the point where you're going to fail no matter how hard you work," says Carolyne Guo, a 2018 grad in chemistry and economics from Niskayuna, New York. Plus, first-year students are set up with a faculty adviser, a peer adviser and other support. More than three-

PHOTOGRAPHY BY BRETT ZIEGLER FOR USN&WR, GETTY IMAGES

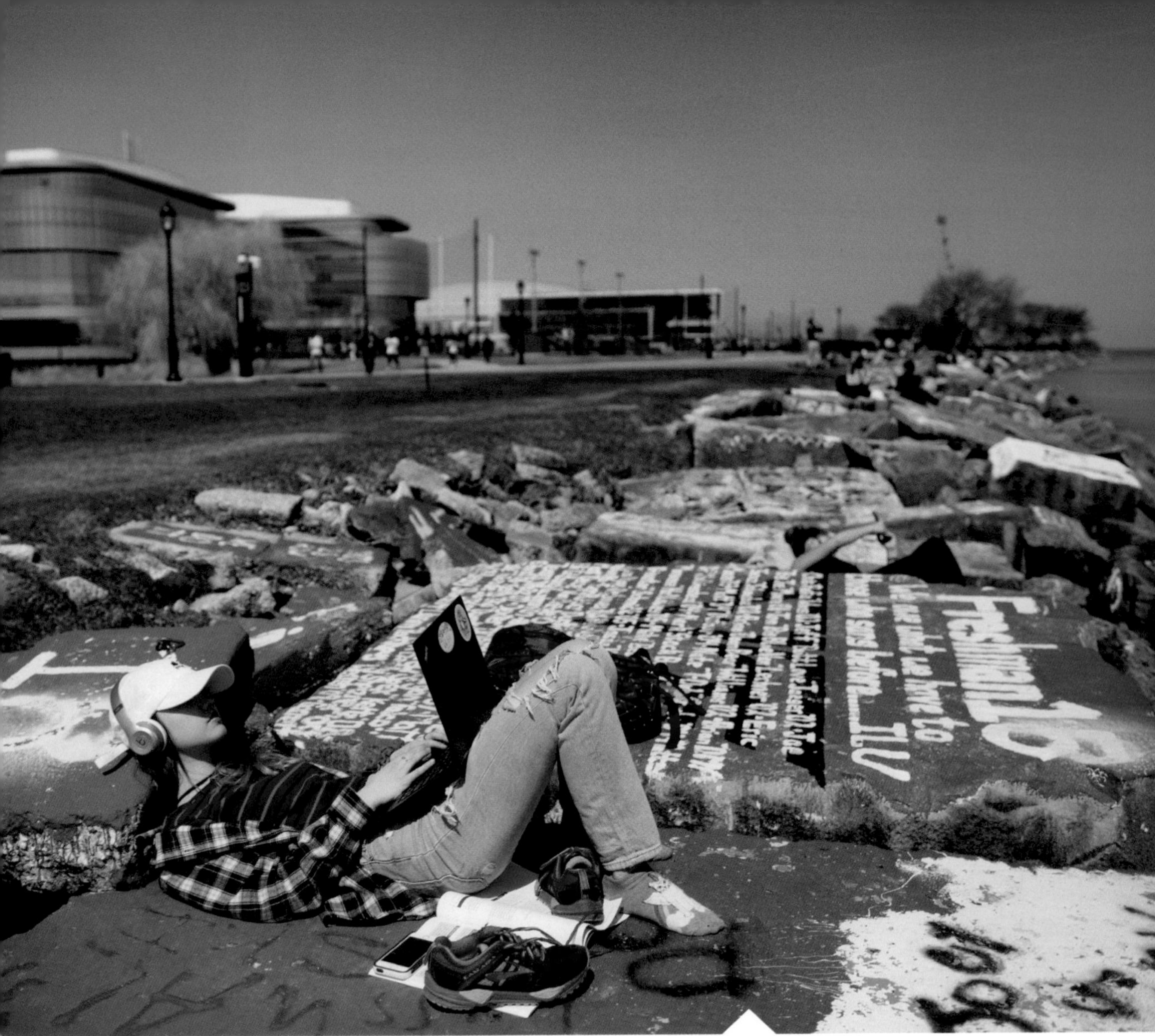

NORTHWESTERN STUDENTS OFTEN PAINT THE ROCKS ON CAMPUS ALONG LAKE MICHIGAN.

quarters of classes enroll fewer than 20 undergrads, and students say that professors, even in larger courses, are generally accessible.

Northwestern's 240-acre campus on the western shore of Lake Michigan boasts scenic views of the Chicago skyline on a clear day. The city is reachable by train, bus and a free shuttle. Closer to campus, downtown Evanston, just a few blocks away, is also home to many restaurants, cafes and shops. Undergrads often hang out or do homework on the lawn by the lake or rent a boat from the school's sailing center. Students frequently paint the large rocks that line the lakefront with elaborate designs and messages. Each spring, people gather there for Dillo Day, a music festival with food and other activities.

Students who live on campus can choose to live in one of 10 residential colleges or four residential communities, each with dedicated professors, staff and graduate students who plan activities, such as fireside chats with esteemed faculty and excursions for students. Some residential colleges have subject themes that steer the programming – international studies, for example, or science and engineering. (Residential communities also have live-in faculty.)

More than 2 in 5 undergrads are affiliated with a Greek organization, involvement that is often "supplementary to everything else they're doing," says Armacost, who was president of her sorority, Alpha Phi. As a producer and sports director for the university's sports broadcasting television program, she covered the Division I Wildcats, who compete in the Big Ten Conference. With 500-plus student organizations and activities, "there are so many different pockets and communities at Northwestern that you can participate in," she says. ◆

UNDERGRADUATES
Full-time: 8,117

TOTAL COST*
$71,193

U.S. NEWS RANKING
National Universities: #10

*Tuition, fees and room & board for 2018-19

University of Chicago

CHICAGO

UNDERGRADUATES
Full-time: 6,242

TOTAL COST*
$73,356

U.S. NEWS RANKING
National Universities: #3

*Tuition, fees and room & board for 2018-19

Some 6,200 undergraduates attend the University of Chicago, located about 8 miles south of downtown in Hyde Park. Students have access to big city resources and activities, but the campus retains a residential feel. One of the most selective schools in the country, UChicago admitted about 7.3 percent of applicants to the latest first-year class. Students are high achievers, and the university prides itself on its commitment to "complete freedom of speech on all subjects," in the words of its first president, William Rainey Harper.

Undergrads can pursue about 50 majors, plus a range of minors and preprofessional programs. The academic calendar is arranged in quarters, so students typically take three or four courses each term. Many appreciate the pace and flexibility, but "it definitely does get easy to fall behind," says Afreen Ahmed, a senior economics major from Chicago.

To help, everyone is assigned an academic adviser as soon as they enroll. "She knows me more than I know myself I feel like most of the time," says Christian Porras, a third-year biological sciences major from Cooper City, Florida. More than 3 out of 4 classes have fewer than 20 undergrads, so you can expect individual attention from professors across the board.

About a third of one's classes are part of the core curriculum, which includes requirements in the humanities, science, math, the social sciences, civilization studies and the arts. Many elect to complete their civilization studies requirement on a quarterlong immersion trip abroad, where about 25 students take classes and go on educational excursions with UChicago faculty.

In addition, more than 4 in 5 undergrads participate in research, in part through the 160-plus research institutions and groups across campus. At times, it can seem like there are "more research opportunities than students to fill them," says Emily Shen, a senior from Taiwan studying neuroscience and biological sciences. She has worked with a professor to investigate the impact of oral health on the overall wellness of patients at the university's medical center. The work inspired her to start a student-run organization that provides oral health education in nearby elementary schools and day cares and to pursue a career in dentistry and health policy.

The Office of Civic Engagement helps connect undergrads with service options in the community, while the Office of Career Advancement links them with internships, job shadowing and short "treks" around the world to explore career paths in a particular field.

There are about 420 student organizations and 20 Division III varsity sports teams. Student IDs double as city passes, giving undergrads free or discounted access to more than 70 cultural institutions around the area. Public buses and trains are also free or discounted to students during the school year. The campus Department of Safety and Security maintains a

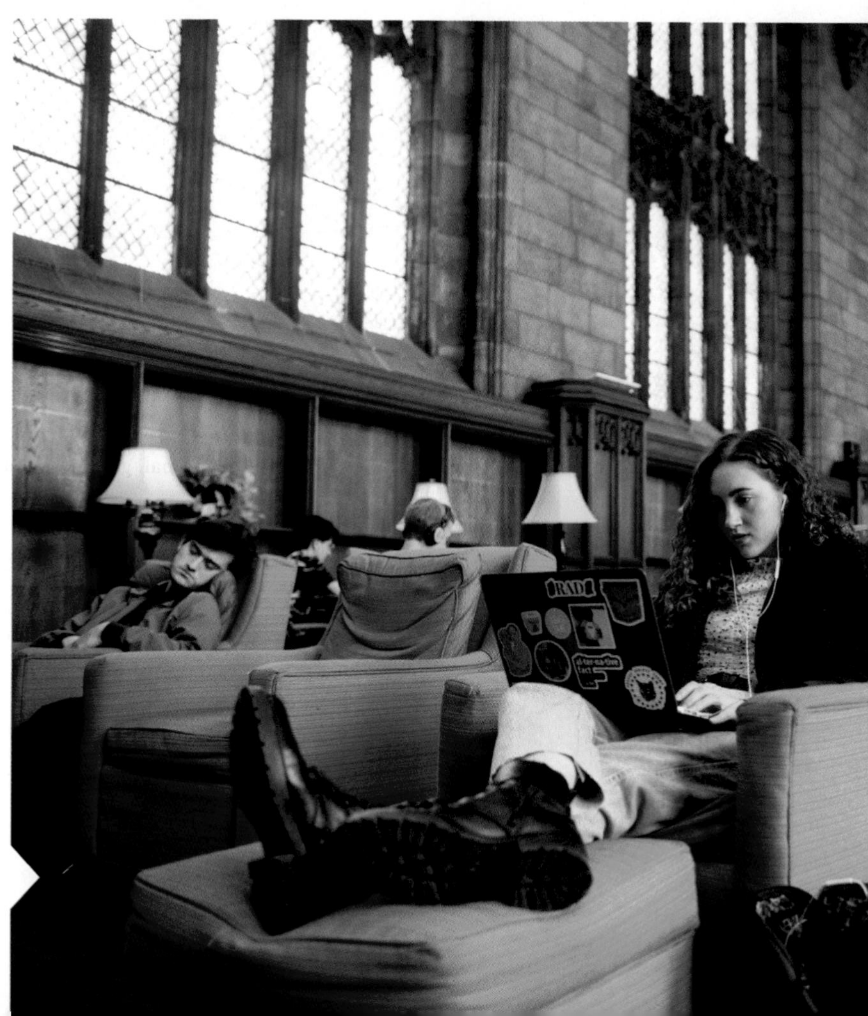

STUDENTS RELAX AND STUDY INSIDE THE ARLEY D. CATHEY LEARNING CENTER ON UCHICAGO'S CAMPUS.

visible presence, and on the whole, "the university really makes an effort for students to feel safe," says Meera Dhodapkar, a senior studying public policy and biological sciences from New Haven, Connecticut.

All first-years live on campus as a member of one of nearly 40 college houses. Each community serves as home base to about 80 students, plus resident assistants and a resident head (a grad student or university staff or faculty member). In each of the main residence halls, a resident dean (a senior faculty member who helps organize outings and events), also lives alongside undergrads. The houses give everyone the opportunity "to form close-knit relationships," says Darien Dey, a recent sociology grad from Guyana. Each house has a distinct personality and traditions, such as bad movie nights or teaming up for the annual UChicago scavenger hunt. ◆

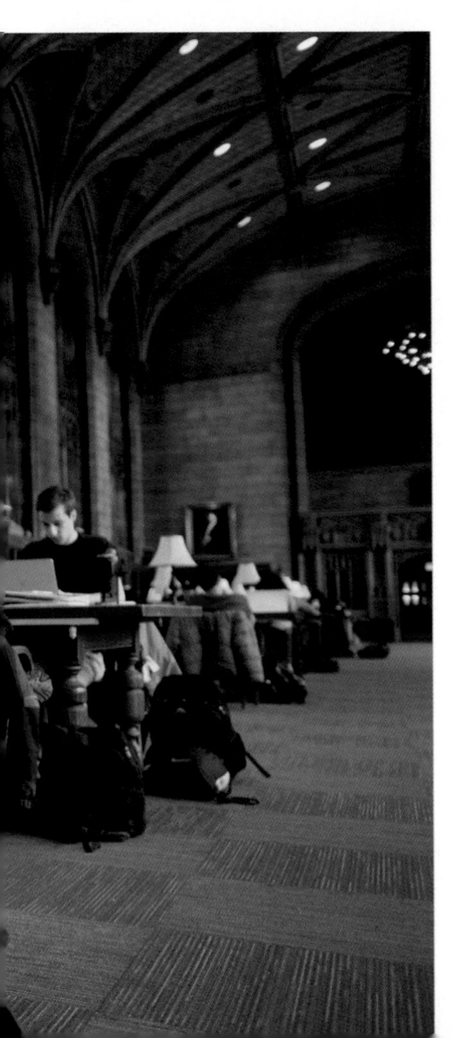

Knox College

GALESBURG

Located in western Illinois, about 200 miles from Chicago, Knox College is rich with history and community. Old Main, a collegiate Gothic building at the heart of campus, was the site of one of Abraham Lincoln's famous 1858 senatorial debates with Stephen A. Douglas. The old Knox County jail has been refurbished to hold classrooms, offices and a student-run bike repair shop.

Knox was founded more than two decades before the Civil War by anti-slavery advocates. Today, just over a third of the college's 1,300 or so undergrads are people of color, and international students make up 17 percent of the population.

The diverse mix of students forms a close-knit campus, in part thanks to an 11:1 student-faculty ratio and classes that average 14 undergrads. "You're able to have a personal connection with professors," says Jordan Anderson, a senior from Paxton, Illinois, studying sports management and communication, who says his academic adviser frequently texts him good luck before or congratulations after his varsity football games. Faculty also frequently collaborate with undergrads on research. (There are no grad students.) During Pumphandle, on the day before classes begin in the fall, students, faculty and staff gather on the lawn near Old Main in winding lines to shake hands and greet each other one by one.

Knox's academic calendar is broken into three 10-week trimesters, and students take three classes at a time. Everyone must complete one of the college's 40-plus majors and a minor (or a second major). Preceptorial is an interdisciplinary class required of all first-year students that aims to prepare them to think critically and see diverse perspectives around topics like "The American Dream" or "The Challenge of Sustainability." From there, undergrads fulfill requirements in the arts, humanities, the sciences, writing and more.

UNDERGRADUATES
Full-time: 1,334

TOTAL COST*
$56,424

U.S. NEWS RANKING
National Liberal Arts: #68

*Tuition, fees and room & board for 2018-19

Students also complete at least one experiential learning opportunity with a beyond-the-classroom component. Options include internships, study abroad experiences and community service. Sam Tatum, a 2018 psychology graduate from Atlanta, interned at Tri States Public Radio, an NPR affiliate near campus. Atithya Ghai, a 2018 grad in education and economics from India, worked as a student teacher at a local elementary school. In 2017, Knox also began offering every incoming student a $2,000 Power of Experience grant to fund a learning experience during their junior or senior year.

One can also opt to take an immersion term, during which an entire trimester focuses on one field of study. Those interested in entrepreneurship, say, can enroll in StartUp Term, where small teams work with faculty mentors to develop a business plan and pitch their ideas to a panel of alumni and local business leaders. In Green Oaks Term, students do field work and take cross-disciplinary classes at the Green Oaks Biological Field Station, a 700-acre nature preserve about 20 miles from campus.

Knox is located in the center of Galesburg, a city of about 30,000, where students speak highly of the locals' Midwestern hospitality and several downtown spots. "There's a

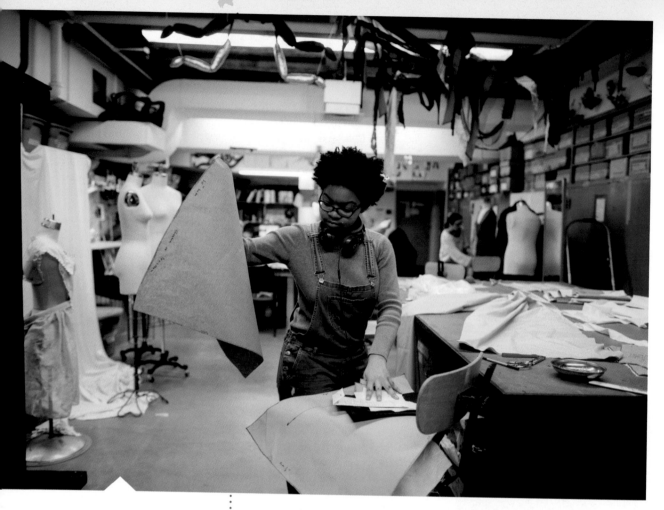

INSIDE THE COSTUME SHOP AT KNOX COLLEGE, WHICH ENROLLS SOME 1,300 UNDERGRADS

lot to do in Galesburg if you're willing to break out of the Knox bubble," says Tatum. The area also offers many opportunities to camp, fish, hike or otherwise enjoy the outdoors.

On campus, there are more than 100 registered student clubs, including several fraternities and sororities, which count about 30 percent of students as members. There are 20 NCAA Division III varsity sports teams, plus club and intramural options. About 90 percent of students live on campus all four years, another means of fostering community. "I can't walk two minutes here without seeing a person that I know," says Kelsie Pos, a 2018 biology grad from Salt Lake City. "You really feel like you belong here." ◆

University of Illinois–Urbana-Champaign

CHAMPAIGN

Since its founding as Illinois Industrial University in 1867, the University of Illinois–Urbana-Champaign has encouraged innovation. The first shared computer-based education system and the foundation for the medical MRI are among the technologies developed at the state's flagship university, which is home to about 32,000 full-time undergraduates and 14,000 grad students.

Today, close to 70 percent of undergrads participate in some form of research. Lauren Sargeant, a recent bioengineering grad from Park Ridge, Illinois, worked in a research lab exploring the causes of liver cancer for three and a half years (including three summers), which earned her a co-author credit on a published scientific paper and helped her develop close relationships with a graduate student and a professor who were "in my corner," she says. Some students can also get hands-on experience by seeking out jobs and internships at the university's research park, a cluster of startups and R&D operations for major companies like Capital One, Caterpillar and State Farm.

Despite its size, about 80 percent of classes have fewer than 50 students. Larger lecture classes break out into lab or discussion sections of 20 to 30 students that are led by a teaching assistant who can provide more personalized attention. Still, "you have to take the initiative to do well," Sargeant says. "Your professors aren't necessarily going to reach out to you if you're falling behind." The university does offer a range of academic support systems, such as advising, tutoring and mentoring, to help along the way.

Undergrads can choose from more than 150 majors across 10 colleges. Everyone must complete courses in the humanities and the arts, the social and natural sciences, cultural studies, and several other categories. There are ample opportunities for cross-disciplinary study, such as with the programs in agricultural and consumer economics or interdisciplinary health sciences. In a recently developed set of degrees called CS + X, students explore computer science through the lens of another subject, such as chemistry, linguistics or music. The undergraduate business (see Page 30) and engineering programs (see Page 32) each are ranked among the top 20 in the country by U.S. News.

UIUC's Division I sports teams compete in the Big Ten Conference, and students typically pack the stands to cheer on the Fighting Illini, especially during football and basketball seasons. "We could be down by 40 points, and everybody is still into the game and excited to be there," says Ryan Salzeider, a senior English major from Pawnee, Illinois, who is a member of Orange Krush, the official basketball cheering section, which also raises money for local and national charities. About 90 percent of undergrads from the U.S. come from within the Prairie State.

UNDERGRADUATES
Full-time: 32,613

TOTAL COST*
In-State: $27,306
Out-of-State: $43,876

U.S. NEWS RANKING
National Universities: #46

*Tuition, fees and room & board for 2018-19

Roughly 1 in 4 students join one of the nearly 90 fraternities and sororities on campus. Undergrads can also get involved with any of UIUC's 1,000-plus student organizations, which include intramural sports teams, arts-related groups and cultural associations.

About half of undergrads live on campus, which spans nearly 10 square miles across Urbana and Champaign, a pair of cities about 140 miles south of Chicago. Main Quad, at the center of campus, provides an expansive green space where people study, play Frisbee and just hang out. On one side of the quad, an ever-burning oil lamp used to promise couples who kissed beneath it eternal love. (The electric light there now tends to flicker, so students joke that the result will be an on-again, off-again relationship.) One can take in a show at the Krannert Center for the Performing Arts, go bowling or play arcade games in the student union, or visit Japan House for a tea ceremony or calligraphy workshop.

Students can use the free bus system to get around campus and downtown or opt to bring a car or bike. In "Campustown," an Illini-themed area located around Green Street near the middle of campus, undergrads can enjoy a variety of restaurants, bars, boutiques and events. ◆

NEARLY 70 PERCENT OF UNIVERSITY OF ILLINOIS UNDERGRADS GET INVOLVED WITH RESEARCH.

CHAPTER

GRADUATION DAY AT UCLA

TROY HARVEY FOR USN&WR

The U.S. News

Rankings

How We Rank Colleges

Collegebound students can make good use of our statistics

by **Robert J. Morse** *and* **Eric M. Brooks**

Deciding where to go to school is tough. But the U.S. News Best Colleges rankings, now in their 34th year, are an excellent resource to tap as you begin your search. They can help you compare the academic quality of institutions you're considering based on such widely accepted indicators of excellence as graduation rates and the strength of the faculty. As you learn about colleges already on your shortlist, you may narrow your list even further or discover unfamiliar new options. Yes, many factors other than those spotlighted here will figure in your decision, including location and the feel of campus life; the range of academic offerings and activities; and the cost. But combined with campus visits, interviews and attention to your own intuition, our rankings can be a powerful tool in your quest for the best fit.

How does the methodology work? The U.S. News ranking system rests on two pillars. The formula uses quantitative and qualitative statistical measures that education experts have proposed as reliable indicators of academic quality, and is based on our researched view of what matters in education.

First, we categorize regionally accredited institutions by their mission, to establish valid comparisons: National Universities, National Liberal Arts Colleges, Regional Universities and Regional Colleges. The national universities offer a full range of undergraduate majors plus master's and Ph.D. programs and emphasize faculty research (Page 76). The national liberal arts colleges focus almost exclusively on undergraduate education (Page 84). They award at least 50 percent of their degrees in the arts and sciences.

The regional universities (Page 90) offer a broad scope of undergraduate degrees and some master's degree programs but few, if any, doctoral programs. The regional colleges (Page 106) focus on undergraduate education but grant fewer than 50 percent of their degrees in liberal arts disciplines; this category also includes schools that have small bachelor's degree programs but primarily grant two-year associate degrees. The regional universities and regional colleges are further divided and ranked in four geographical groups: North, South, Midwest and West.

The framework used to group schools is derived from the 2015 Update of the Carnegie Classification of Institutions of Higher Education's Basic Classification. The Carnegie classification is used extensively by higher education researchers; the U.S. Department of Education and many higher education associations use the system to organize their data and to determine colleges' eligibility for grant money, for example.

Next, we gather data from each college on up to 16 indicators of academic excellence. Each factor is

BRETT ZIEGLER FOR USN&WR

AN ENGINEERING CLASS AT NORTHWESTERN UNIVERSITY IN ILLINOIS

assigned a weight that reflects our research about how much a measure matters. Finally, the colleges and universities in each category are ranked against their peers using their overall scores, which are calculated from the sum of their indicators.

Some schools are not ranked and thus do not appear in the tables. The most common reason is that the school does not use ACT or SAT test scores in admissions decisions for first-time, first-year, degree-seeking applicants. (Schools with test-optional and test-flexible admission policies are included because they do consider ACT or SAT scores when provided.) In fewer cases, colleges are not ranked because they received too few ratings in the peer assessment survey, had a total enrollment of fewer than 200 students, had a large proportion of nontraditional students, or had no first-year students (as is the situation at upper-division schools). As a result of these standards, many for-profit institutions are not ranked. We also did not rank highly specialized schools in the arts, business and engineering, although eligible specialized schools are included in our separate rankings of business and engineering programs.

Colleges report most of the data themselves, via the annual U.S. News statistical survey. This year, 92 percent of the 1,397 ranked colleges and universities returned their statistical information during our 2018 data collection period. To ensure the highest possible quality of data, U.S. News compared schools' survey responses to their earlier cohorts' statistics, third-party data, and data reported by other schools. Schools were instructed to review, revise and verify the accuracy of their data, particularly any flagged by U.S. News as requiring a second look. For eligible colleges that declined to complete our survey (identified as nonresponders), we made extensive use of data they reported to the National Center for Education Statistics and other organizations. Estimates were used in the calculations when schools failed to report data not available from other sources, although missing data are reported in the tables as N/A.

The indicators we use to capture academic quality, described below, include input measures that reflect schools' student bodies, faculties and resources as well as outcome measures that signal how well institutions are engaging and educating their students. Outcome measures, the most heavily weighted, account for 35 percent of the overall score. A more detailed explanation of the methodology, which underwent several significant changes this year, can be found at usnews.com/collegemeth.

Outcomes (weighted at 35 percent, up from 30 percent previously): The higher the proportion of first-year students who return to campus for sophomore year and eventually graduate, the better a school most likely is at offering the classes and services that students need to succeed. More than one-third of a school's rank reflects its success at retaining and graduating students within six years.

This measure has several components: six-year graduation and first-year retention rates (together 22 percent of the outcomes score); graduation rate performance, or how well a school performs at graduating students

Weighing What's Important

The U.S. News rankings are based on several categories of quality indicators, listed below. Scores for each group are weighted as shown to arrive at a final overall score. In the case of the national universities and national liberal arts colleges, the assessment figure represents input from both academic peers (15 percent) and high school guidance counselors (5 percent); for regional universities and colleges, it reflects peer opinion only.

The Scoring Breakdown

Outcomes*	35%
Expert Opinion	20%
Faculty Resources	20%
Financial Resources	10%
Student Excellence	10%
Alumni Giving	5%

*Graduation, retention, graduation rate performance, social mobility.

compared to a predicted graduation rate based on student and school characteristics (8 percent); and the school's record on promoting social mobility by graduating low-income students who received federal Pell Grants. The social mobility measure, new this year, accounts for 5 percent of the outcomes score. It considers both a school's six-year graduation rate among students entering in the fall of 2011 who received Pell Grants and how that performance compares with the graduation rate of all other students.

This metric assesses each school's performance at supporting students from underserved backgrounds relative to all of its other students. Scores were then adjusted by the proportion of the entering class that was awarded Pell Grants, because achieving a higher graduation rate among low-income students is more challenging with a larger proportion of low-income students.

The average six-year graduation rate (of students entering in fall 2008 through fall 2011) was weighted at 17.6 percent of the outcomes indicator, down from 18 percent previously. Average first-year retention rate (of fall 2013 through fall 2016 entrants) was weighted at 4.4 percent, down from 4.5 percent.

A school's graduation rate performance shows the effect of programs and policies on the graduation rate when controlling for other factors that might influence it. These include spending per student, admissions selectivity, the proportion of undergraduates receiving Pell Grants, and – for national universities only – the proportion of undergrad degrees awarded in science, technology, engineering and mathematics disciplines. We compare a school's six-year graduation rate for the class that entered in 2011 to the graduation rate we predicted for that class. If the actual graduation rate is higher than the predicted rate, then the college is enhancing achievement. This factor's 8 percent weighting is up from 7.5 percent last year.

Faculty Resources (20 percent): Research shows that the greater access students have to quality instructors, the more engaged they will be in class, the more they will learn, and the more likely they are to graduate. U.S. News uses five factors from the 2017-2018 academic year to assess commitment to instruction: class size, faculty salary, faculty with the highest degree in their field, student-faculty ratio and proportion of faculty who are full time.

Class size is the most heavily weighted, at 8 percent of the faculty resources score. Schools receive the most credit for the proportion of their fall 2017 classes with fewer than 20 students. Classes with 20 to 29 students score second highest, and so forth. Classes that have 50 or more students receive no credit.

Faculty salary (7 percent) reflects average pay plus benefits during the 2016-2017 and 2017-2018 academic years, adjusted for regional differences in the cost of living using indexes from the consulting firm Runzheimer International. The other factors are weighted as follows: proportion of full-time professors with the highest degree in their field (3 percent), student-faculty ratio (1 percent), and proportion of faculty who are full time (1 percent).

Expert Opinion (20 percent, down from 22.5 percent): We survey presidents, provosts and deans of admissions, asking them to rate the academic quality of peer institutions with which they are familiar on a scale of 1 (marginal) to 5 (distinguished). To get another set of important opinions about the national universities and national liberal arts colleges, U.S. News also surveyed nearly 24,400 counselors at public, private and parochial high schools from all 50 states and Washington, D.C. Academic reputation matters because it can account for attributes that cannot easily be captured elsewhere. For example, an institution known for having innovative approaches to teaching may perform especially well on this indicator, whereas a school

USNEWS.COM/BESTCOLLEGES

Visit **usnews.com** regularly while conducting your research, as U.S. News frequently adds content aimed at helping collegebound students find the best fit, impress admissions, and figure out how to finance their studies. We also occasionally make updates when new data become available or new information changes the data.

IN DANCE CLASS AT BENNINGTON COLLEGE

for 1.25 percent of the overall score in last year's ranking) entirely as a ranking factor. Also, we reduced the weight of the two remaining student excellence factors, standardized tests and high school class standing. The test scores for the fall 2017 entering class used in this year's rankings were weighted at 7.75 percent, down from 8.125 percent. High school class standing was weighted at 2.25 percent, down from 3.125.

Schools sometimes fail to report SAT and ACT scores for athletes, international students, minority students, legacies, those admitted by special arrangement and those who started in the summer. For any school that did not report all scores (or declined to say whether all scores were reported), U.S. News discounted its test-score value by 15 percent. Additionally, if test scores reported represented less than 75 percent of students entering, the value was discounted by 15 percent.

As for high school class standing, U.S. News incorporates the proportion of first-year students at national universities and national liberal arts colleges who graduated in the top 10 percent of their high school classes. For regional universities and regional colleges, we used the proportion of those who graduated in the top quarter of their high school classes.

struggling to keep its accreditation will likely perform poorly.

The peer assessment score is derived from averaging survey results from spring 2017 and 2018. In the case of the national universities and liberal arts colleges, it is weighted at 15 percent of the expert opinion score; the high school counselor assessment is weighted at 5 percent in these categories, for a total of 20 percent. The peer assessment alone is weighted at 20 percent for regional universities and regional colleges. The high school counselor assessment score is an average of survey results from spring 2016, 2017 and 2018. Approximately half of the counselors (12,200) were asked to rate the schools in the national universities category and the other half were asked to rate the national liberal arts colleges.

Financial Resources (10 percent): Generous per-student spending indicates that a college can offer a wide variety of programs and services. U.S. News measures financial resources by using the average spending per student on instruction, research, student services and related educational expenditures in the 2016 and 2017 fiscal years. Spending on sports, dorms and hospitals does not count.

Student Excellence (10 percent, down from 12.5 percent in 2018): A school's academic atmosphere is influenced by the selectivity of its admissions. Simply put, students who achieved strong grades and test scores during high school have the highest probability of succeeding at college-level coursework, enabling instructors to design classes that have great rigor.

Still, in adding social mobility as an outcomes indicator, we lessened the weight given to this input and removed acceptance rate (which accounted

Alumni Giving (5 percent): This is the average percentage of living alumni with bachelor's degrees who gave to their school during 2015-2016 and 2016-2017. Giving measures student satisfaction and postgraduate engagement.

To arrive at a school's rank, we calculated the weighted sum of its standardized scores. The scores were rescaled so the top college or university in each category received a value of 100 and the other schools' weighted scores were calculated as a proportion of the top score. Final scores were rounded to the nearest whole number and ranked in descending order. Tied schools appear in alphabetical order.

As you mine the tables that follow for insights (a sense of which schools might be impressed enough by your ACT or SAT scores to offer some merit aid, for example, or where you will be apt to get the most attention from professors), keep in mind that the rankings provide a launching pad for more research, not an easy answer. ◆

BRETT ZIEGLER FOR USN&WR

Best National Uni

Rank	School (State) (*Public)	Overall score	Peer assessment score (5.0=highest)	High school counselor assessment score	Graduation and retention rank	Average first-year student retention rate	2017 graduation rate: Predicted	2017 graduation rate: Actual	2017 graduation rate: Over-performance (+) Under-performance (-)
1.	**Princeton University** (NJ)	100	4.9	4.9	5	98%	96%	97%	+1
2.	**Harvard University** (MA)	96	4.9	4.9	3	97%	96%	96%	None
3.	**Columbia University** (NY)	94	4.7	4.8	3	99%	94%	96%	+2
3.	**Massachusetts Institute of Technology**	94	4.9	4.9	21	99%	93%	94%	+1
3.	**University of Chicago**	94	4.6	4.7	26	99%	95%	93%	-2
3.	**Yale University** (CT)	94	4.8	4.9	7	99%	96%	97%	+1
7.	**Stanford University** (CA)	93	4.9	4.9	13	98%	94%	94%	None
8.	**Duke University** (NC)	92	4.5	4.7	13	97%	94%	95%	+1
8.	**University of Pennsylvania**	92	4.5	4.8	7	98%	96%	96%	None
10.	**Johns Hopkins University** (MD)	90	4.6	4.8	21	97%	94%	94%	None
10.	**Northwestern University** (IL)	90	4.4	4.7	19	98%	95%	94%	-1
12.	**California Institute of Technology**	88	4.7	4.7	37	98%	95%	89%	-6
12.	**Dartmouth College** (NH)	88	4.3	4.8	13	98%	95%	96%	+1
14.	**Brown University** (RI)	85	4.4	4.8	7	98%	94%	95%	+1
14.	**Vanderbilt University** (TN)	85	4.2	4.7	26	97%	94%	92%	-2
16.	**Cornell University** (NY)	84	4.6	4.8	13	97%	93%	93%	None
16.	**Rice University** (TX)	84	4.1	4.6	26	97%	93%	91%	-2
18.	**University of Notre Dame** (IN)	83	4.1	4.7	19	98%	95%	95%	None
19.	**University of California–Los Angeles***	82	4.3	4.5	1	97%	87%	91%	+4
19.	**Washington University in St. Louis**	82	4.1	4.6	37	97%	97%	94%	-3
21.	**Emory University** (GA)	79	4.1	4.5	34	94%	90%	91%	+1
22.	**Georgetown University** (DC)	78	4.1	4.7	13	96%	95%	95%	None
22.	**University of California–Berkeley***	78	4.7	4.7	7	97%	90%	91%	+1
22.	**University of Southern California**	78	4.0	4.5	13	96%	93%	92%	-1
25.	**Carnegie Mellon University** (PA)	74	4.3	4.7	37	97%	90%	89%	-1
25.	**University of Virginia***	74	4.2	4.5	26	97%	94%	95%	+1
27.	**Tufts University** (MA)	72	3.7	4.5	31	97%	95%	93%	-2
27.	**University of Michigan–Ann Arbor***	72	4.4	4.5	31	97%	94%	92%	-2
27.	**Wake Forest University** (NC)	72	3.6	4.2	55	94%	94%	88%	-6
30.	**New York University**	71	3.9	4.5	42	93%	85%	84%	-1
30.	**University of California–Santa Barbara***	71	3.6	4.0	21	93%	84%	86%	+2
30.	**U. of North Carolina–Chapel Hill***	71	4.1	4.5	21	97%	89%	91%	+2
33.	**University of California–Irvine***	70	3.7	4.1	2	93%	81%	85%	+4
33.	**University of Rochester** (NY)	70	3.4	4.1	34	97%	88%	85%	-3
35.	**Brandeis University** (MA)	69	3.6	4.1	21	93%	85%	90%	+5
35.	**Georgia Institute of Technology***	69	4.3	4.5	37	97%	89%	85%	-4
35.	**University of Florida***	69	3.7	4.1	7	96%	82%	88%	+6
38.	**Boston College**	68	3.6	4.4	34	95%	93%	92%	-1
38.	**College of William & Mary** (VA)*	68	3.8	4.4	42	95%	93%	92%	-1
38.	**University of California–Davis***	68	3.9	4.2	12	93%	82%	85%	+3
41.	**University of California–San Diego***	67	3.8	4.2	5	95%	82%	84%	+2
42.	**Boston University**	66	3.6	4.4	60	93%	83%	87%	+4
42.	**Case Western Reserve Univ.** (OH)	66	3.7	4.2	66	93%	83%	83%	None
44.	**Northeastern University** (MA)	65	3.4	4.3	50	97%	85%	87%	+2
44.	**Tulane University** (LA)	65	3.5	4.2	74	92%	85%	83%	-2
46.	**Pepperdine University** (CA)	64	3.3	4.2	37	92%	76%	85%	+9
46.	**University of Georgia***	64	3.6	4.1	42	95%	76%	85%	+9
46.	**University of Illinois–Urbana-Champaign***	64	3.9	4.1	50	93%	80%	85%	+5
49.	**Rensselaer Polytechnic Inst.** (NY)	63	3.5	4.3	62	93%	84%	83%	-1
49.	**University of Texas–Austin***	63	4.1	4.3	50	95%	83%	83%	None
49.	**Univ. of Wisconsin–Madison***	63	4.0	4.2	55	95%	84%	87%	+3
49.	**Villanova University** (PA)	63	3.2	4.2	31	95%	87%	90%	+3

Note: Key to footnotes, Page 83

versities

…f …es …20 …)	% of classes of 50 or more ('17)	Student/ faculty ratio ('17)	Selectivity rank	SAT/ACT 25th-75th percentile** ('17)	Freshmen in top 10% of HS class ('17)	Acceptance rate ('17)	Financial resources rank	Alumni giving rank	Average alumni giving rate
%	10%	5/1	10	1430-1570	91%[5]	6%	10	1	59%
%	11%	6/1	5	1460-1590	95%[5]	5%	7	9	33%
%	9%	6/1	5	32-35	96%[5]	6%	13	15	30%
%	11%	3/1	1	1490-1570	98%[5]	7%	1	8	34%
%	6%	5/1	1	32-35	99%	9%	7	5	40%
%	9%	6/1	5	1420-1590	94%[5]	7%	1	18	28%
%	12%	4/1	10	1390-1540	94%[5]	5%	5	12	32%
%	7%	6/1	16	31-35	90%[5]	10%	15	9	33%
%	11%	6/1	5	32-35	96%[5]	9%	14	7	37%
%	10%	7/1	3	33-35	94%[5]	12%	4	6	38%
%	6%	6/1	10	32-35	91%[5]	9%	9	16	30%
%	10%	3/1	3	1530-1590	93%	8%	1	22	26%
%	7%	7/1	10	1430-1560	93%[5]	10%	16	2	44%
%	11%	7/1	5	31-35	94%[5]	9%	24	13	32%
%	8%	7/1	10	32-35	90%[5]	11%	12	24	25%
%	18%	9/1	19	1390-1550	86%[5]	13%	17	21	26%
%	9%	6/1	10	33-35	89%[5]	16%	20	11	33%
%	10%	10/1	16	32-34	91%[5]	19%	25	3	41%
%	19%	18/1	27	1240-1500	97%	16%	19	122	8%
%	11%	8/1	16	32-34	87%[5]	16%	6	24	24%
%	12%	9/1	24	30-33	83%[5]	22%	17	32	21%
%	6%	11/1	19	1350-1520	90%[5]	16%	32	13	31%
%	19%	18/1	19	1300-1530	98%	17%	36	87	12%
%	12%	8/1	34	30-34	88%[5]	16%	20	3	42%
%	13%	13/1	24	1430-1560	74%[5]	22%	36	57	15%
%	15%	14/1	26	1310-1500	89%[5]	27%	50	34	20%
%	7%	9/1	19	31-34	80%[5]	15%	30	31	21%
%	18%	15/1	39	30-33	77%[5]	27%	40	47	17%
%	1%	11/1	39	28-32[2]	77%[5]	28%	10	24	24%
%	10%	9/1	32	1290-1490[2]	72%[5]	28%	32	87	11%
%	20%	17/1	27	1240-1470	100%	33%	70	50	16%
%	13%	13/1	34	27-32	78%	24%	30	47	17%
%	22%	18/1	53	1170-1410	98%	37%	56	168	6%
%	11%	10/1	46	1300-1490[2]	66%[5]	34%	20	27	23%
%	9%	10/1	39	29-33	65%[5]	34%	47	35	19%
%	26%	22/1	19	1370-1520	88%[5]	23%	61	32	21%
%	16%	19/1	39	1240-1400	77%	42%	44	75	13%
%	7%	12/1	27	1320-1490	78%[5]	32%	63	23	25%
%	7%	11/1	31	1300-1480	81%[5]	36%	109	17	29%
%	28%	20/1	57	1120-1360	100%[5]	44%	28	154	7%
%	35%	19/1	46	1140-1380	100%	34%	23	209	4%
%	13%	10/1	45	1300-1480[2]	62%[5]	25%	53	105	10%
%	13%	11/1	32	30-33	70%[5]	33%	36	39	19%
%	6%	14/1	27	32-34	75%[5]	27%	79	87	11%
%	6%	8/1	34	30-33	62%[5]	21%	42	50	16%
%	2%	13/1	73	1200-1390	49%[5]	40%	65	122	9%
%	11%	17/1	66	26-31	54%	54%	123	62	14%
%	19%	20/1	57	26-32	50%[5]	62%	56	147	7%
%	12%	13/1	39	1320-1500	63%[5]	43%	65	96	11%
%	26%	18/1	46	1230-1460	74%	36%	77	96	11%
%	22%	18/1	57	27-31	52%[5]	54%	61	75	13%
%	2%	11/1	38	30-33	65%[5]	36%	109	19	27%

What Is a National University?

To assess more than 1,600 of the country's four-year colleges and universities, U.S. News first assigns each to a group of its peers, based on the categories of higher education institutions developed by the Carnegie Foundation for the Advancement of Teaching. The National Universities category consists of 312 institutions (191 public, 114 private and seven for-profit) that offer a wide range of undergraduate majors as well as master's and doctoral degrees; some institutions emphasize research. A list of the top 30 public national universities appears on Page 83.

Data on up to 16 indicators of academic quality are gathered from each institution and tabulated. Schools are ranked by total weighted score; those tied at the same rank are listed alphabetically. For a description of the methodology, see Page 72. For more on a college, turn to the directory at the back of the book.

BEST NATIONAL UNIVERSITIES

Rank	School (State) (*Public)	Overall score	Peer assessment score (5.0=highest)	High school counselor assessment score	Average first-year student retention rate	2017 graduation rate: Predicted	2017 graduation rate: Actual	% of classes under 20 ('17)	% of classes of 50 or more ('17)	SAT/ACT 25th-75th percentile** ('17)	Freshmen in top 10% of HS class ('17)	Acceptance rate ('17)	Average alumni giving rate
53.	**Lehigh University** (PA)	62	3.3	4.0	96%	94%	86%	45%	12%	1270-1430	63%[5]	25%	19%
53.	**Syracuse University** (NY)	62	3.3	4.0	91%	69%	83%	59%	9%	1160-1350	36%[5]	47%	13%
53.	**University of Miami** (FL)	62	3.4	4.1	92%	88%	84%	54%	8%	28-32	46%[5]	36%	14%
56.	**Ohio State University–Columbus***	61	3.8	4.1	94%	79%	83%	31%	22%	27-31	64%[5]	48%	15%
56.	**Purdue University–West Lafayette** (IN)*	61	3.8	4.2	93%	72%	79%	38%	18%	1150-1380	44%[5]	57%	19%
56.	**Rutgers University–New Brunswick** (NJ)*	61	3.4	4.0	93%	68%	80%	39%	21%	1190-1400	40%[5]	58%	8%
59.	**Pennsylvania State U.–Univ. Park***	60	3.7	4.0	93%	75%	85%	30%	18%	1160-1340	35%[5]	50%	14%
59.	**Southern Methodist University** (TX)	60	3.2	3.9	90%	80%	81%	59%	9%	28-32	52%[5]	49%	22%
59.	**University of Washington***	60	3.9	4.1	94%	88%	84%	31%	24%	1190-1420	63%[5]	46%	13%
59.	**Worcester Polytechnic Inst.** (MA)	60	3.0	3.9	96%	83%	89%	65%	11%	1280-1440[2]	68%[5]	48%	10%
63.	**George Washington University** (DC)	59	3.5	4.3	92%	85%	81%	52%	10%	1280-1440[2]	61%[5]	41%	9%
63.	**University of Connecticut***	59	3.3	3.9	93%	75%	83%	53%	16%	1210-1390	54%[5]	48%	10%
63.	**Univ. of Maryland–College Park***	59	3.7	4.0	96%	85%	85%	46%	17%	1290-1470	72%[5]	44%	7%
66.	**Brigham Young Univ.–Provo** (UT)	58	3.1	3.8	88%	75%	83%	45%	12%	27-32	54%	52%	14%
66.	**Clark University** (MA)	58	2.9	3.7	87%	71%	83%	58%	5%	1180-1380[2]	37%[5]	56%	19%
66.	**Clemson University** (SC)*	58	3.3	4.1	93%	78%	82%	53%	15%	27-31	62%	47%	23%
66.	**Texas A&M University–College Station***	58	3.6	4.1	91%	76%	82%	23%	25%	1140-1360	60%	70%	16%
70.	**Florida State University***	57	3.2	3.8	93%	70%	80%	40%	16%	26-30	41%	49%	19%
70.	**Fordham University** (NY)	57	3.1	4.0	91%	76%	79%	52%	1%	1230-1410	48%[5]	46%	16%
70.	**Stevens Institute of Technology** (NJ)	57	2.8	4.0	94%	80%	83%	38%	9%	1320-1470[2]	72%[5]	44%	16%
70.	**University of California–Santa Cruz***	57	3.1	3.8	90%	80%	80%	43%	28%	1160-1370	96%	51%	4%
70.	**Univ. of Massachusetts–Amherst***	57	3.4	3.9	91%	66%	77%	48%	18%	1180-1360	34%[5]	57%	9%
70.	**University of Pittsburgh***	57	3.5	3.9	93%	81%	82%	43%	19%	1240-1420	53%[5]	60%	9%
76.	**University of Minnesota–Twin Cities***	56	3.7	3.8	93%	77%	80%	37%	20%	26-31	50%	50%	8%
76.	**Virginia Tech***	56	3.5	4.2	93%	74%	84%	27%	22%	1180-1360	38%[5]	70%	11%
78.	**American University** (DC)	55	3.2	4.0	89%	80%	79%	50%	2%	1180-1350[2]	31%[5]	29%	6%
78.	**Baylor University** (TX)	55	3.1	3.9	89%	74%	77%	52%	10%	26-31	44%	39%	16%
80.	**Binghamton University–SUNY***	54	3.0	3.7	91%	76%	82%	48%	13%	1290-1431	49%[5]	40%	7%
80.	**Colorado School of Mines***	54	3.4	4.3	93%	78%	78%	27%	20%	28-32	49%[5]	56%	10%
80.	**North Carolina State U.–Raleigh***	54	3.2	3.7	94%	72%	79%	36%	16%	27-31	46%	51%	10%
80.	**Stony Brook–SUNY***	54	3.3	3.7	90%	67%	72%	43%	24%	1210-1410	48%[5]	42%	8%
80.	**Texas Christian University**	54	2.8	3.8	91%	75%	83%	44%	5%	25-30	48%[5]	41%	18%
80.	**Yeshiva University** (NY)	54	2.8	3.3	90%	78%	82%	59%	1%	1160-1420	N/A	63%	18%
85.	**Michigan State University***	53	3.5	3.9	92%	69%	79%	25%	24%	1100-1320	30%[5]	72%	9%
85.	**University of California–Riverside***	53	3.1	3.6	90%	70%	75%	23%	30%	1090-1300	94%	57%	3%
85.	**University of San Diego**	53	2.9	3.8	89%	78%	82%	38%	0.1%	26-30	40%[5]	50%	12%
89.	**Howard University** (DC)	52	3.0	4.0	89%	55%	63%	55%	5%	1090-1290[3]	25%[5]	41%	11%
89.	**Indiana University–Bloomington***	52	3.6	3.9	90%	73%	77%	36%	18%	25-31	36%[5]	76%	12%
89.	**Loyola University Chicago**	52	3.0	3.9	84%	69%	77%	42%	6%	24-29	37%[5]	71%	6%
89.	**Marquette University** (WI)	52	3.0	4.0	89%	74%	80%	45%	10%	24-29	34%[5]	89%	14%
89.	**University at Buffalo–SUNY***	52	3.0	3.6	87%	65%	75%	29%	23%	1140-1310	38%[5]	57%	8%
89.	**University of Delaware***	52	3.2	3.8	92%	78%	83%	34%	16%	1150-1330	32%[5]	60%	8%
89.	**University of Iowa***	52	3.5	3.8	86%	70%	74%	51%	13%	23-28	30%	86%	10%
96.	**Illinois Institute of Technology**	51	2.8	3.6	92%	71%	72%	50%	9%	25-31	55%[5]	54%	8%
96.	**Miami University–Oxford** (OH)*	51	3.2	3.9	91%	73%	79%	34%	11%	26-31	34%[5]	68%	19%
96.	**University of Colorado–Boulder***	51	3.6	3.9	86%	70%	69%	49%	15%	25-30	29%[5]	80%	6%
96.	**University of Denver**	51	2.9	3.7	87%	78%	75%	57%	5%	25-30	38%[5]	58%	9%
96.	**University of San Francisco**	51	2.9	3.8	85%	63%	77%	47%	2%	1100-1290	24%[5]	66%	7%
96.	**University of Vermont***	51	3.0	3.7	86%	69%	75%	49%	15%	1180-1350	38%[5]	67%	10%
102.	**Clarkson University** (NY)	50	2.7	3.5	90%	65%	74%	52%	18%	1143-1330	37%	66%	16%
102.	**Drexel University** (PA)	50	3.1	3.8	87%	72%	71%	55%	9%	1155-1360	36%[5]	79%	7%
102.	**Rochester Inst. of Technology** (NY)	50	3.3	4.1	88%	67%	70%	47%	5%	1190-1380	40%	57%	6%
102.	**University of Oregon***	50	3.3	3.9	87%	63%	72%	38%	21%	1080-1270	20%[5]	83%	8%
106.	**New Jersey Inst. of Technology***	49	2.7	3.4	87%	57%	64%	33%	5%	1190-1370	37%[5]	61%	8%
106.	**Saint Louis University**	49	2.9	3.8	90%	79%	77%	43%	9%	25-31	50%[5]	64%	11%
106.	**SUNY Col. of Envir. Sci. and Forestry***	49	2.6	3.5	84%	71%	78%	44%	10%	1150-1300	32%	52%	18%
106.	**Temple University** (PA)*	49	3.0	3.6	90%	58%	71%	38%	9%	1130-1310[2]	21%[5]	57%	6%
106.	**University of Arizona***	49	3.6	3.7	81%	62%	63%	43%	17%	21-28[2]	34%[5]	84%	8%

Note: Key to footnotes, Page 83

ank	School (State) (*Public)	Overall score	Peer assessment score (5.0=highest)	High school counselor assessment score	Average first-year student retention rate	2017 graduation rate: Predicted	2017 graduation rate: Actual	% of classes under 20 ('17)	% of classes of 50 or more ('17)	SAT/ACT 25th-75th percentile** ('17)	Freshmen in top 10% of HS class ('17)	Acceptance rate ('17)	Average alumni giving rate
06.	**University of New Hampshire***	49	2.9	3.6	86%	63%	77%	43%	12%	1080-1260	20%	77%	7%
06.	**Univ. of South Carolina***	49	3.1	3.8	88%	68%	75%	38%	16%	25-30	29%	72%	14%
06.	**University of the Pacific** (CA)	49	2.6	3.5	85%	64%	66%	57%	5%	1070-1330	34%[5]	65%	6%
06.	**University of Tulsa** (OK)	49	2.7	3.5	90%	87%	69%	61%	4%	25-32	70%[5]	39%	19%
15.	**Arizona State University–Tempe***	48	3.4	3.7	86%	59%	63%	41%	18%	22-29[2]	34%	84%	11%
15.	**Auburn University** (AL)*	48	3.3	3.8	91%	78%	77%	33%	16%	24-30	31%[5]	84%	13%
15.	**Rutgers University–Newark** (NJ)*	48	2.7	3.8	85%	54%	68%	27%	14%	1010-1170	22%	64%	5%
15.	**University of Tennessee***	48	3.2	3.7	86%	73%	70%	30%	14%	24-30	N/A	77%	11%
19.	**DePaul University** (IL)	47	2.9	3.8	85%	62%	71%	41%	1%	22-28[2]	23%[4]	72%	6%
19.	**Duquesne University** (PA)	47	2.6	3.7	87%	68%	79%	42%	8%	1120-1270[2]	25%	72%	7%
19.	**Iowa State University***	47	3.3	3.7	87%	67%	73%	29%	25%	22-28	25%	89%	11%
19.	**Seton Hall University** (NJ)	47	2.9	3.8	85%	61%	67%	48%	3%	1140-1280	32%[5]	73%	8%
19.	**University of Utah***	47	3.1	3.5	90%	63%	67%	39%	18%	22-29	39%[5]	66%	10%
24.	**University of Oklahoma***	46	3.1	3.7	88%	71%	67%	46%	11%	23-29	36%	69%	14%
24.	**University of South Florida***	46	2.8	3.5	89%	62%	71%	30%	16%	1150-1310	37%	44%	12%
24.	**University of St. Thomas** (MN)	46	2.4	3.4	88%	71%	77%	39%	1%	24-29	23%[5]	84%	14%
27.	**San Diego State University***	45	2.9	3.8	89%	54%	75%	26%	24%	1090-1290	31%[5]	35%	6%
27.	**University of Dayton** (OH)	45	2.6	3.6	90%	72%	79%	36%	3%	24-29[3]	29%[5]	72%	13%
29.	**The Catholic University of America** (DC)	44	2.7	3.7	85%	66%	71%	56%	4%	1120-1320[2]	N/A	83%	9%
29.	**University of Alabama***	44	3.2	3.8	87%	75%	68%	32%	22%	23-32	39%	56%	27%
29.	**University of Illinois–Chicago***	44	3.0	3.6	80%	57%	57%	37%	19%	20-26	25%[5]	77%	2%
29.	**University of Kansas***	44	3.3	3.8	81%	69%	63%	47%	12%	23-28	26%	93%	13%
29.	**Univ. of Missouri***	44	3.2	3.7	87%	69%	68%	38%	17%	23-29	29%	78%	13%
29.	**Univ. of Nebraska–Lincoln***	44	3.1	3.7	83%	68%	68%	35%	18%	22-29	26%	64%	18%

BRETT ZIEGLER FOR USN&WR

GEORGETOWN UNIVERSITY, TIED AT NO. 22

Rank	School (State) (*Public)	Overall score	Peer assessment score (5.0=highest)	High school counselor assessment score	Average first-year student retention rate	2017 graduation rate Predicted	Actual	% of classes under 20 ('17)	% of classes of 50 or more ('17)	SAT/ACT 25th-75th percentile** ('17)	Freshmen in top 10% of HS class ('17)	Acceptance rate ('17)	Average alumni giving rate
129.	University of Texas–Dallas*	44	2.8	3.8	87%	67%	70%	24%	22%	1220-1430	36%	76%	3%
136.	George Mason University (VA)*	43	3.1	3.9	88%	63%	71%	31%	14%	1100-1290[2]	17%[5]	81%	3%
136.	Michigan Technological University*	43	2.7	3.9	85%	67%	67%	46%	13%	1160-1340	32%	74%	8%
136.	University of California–Merced*	43	2.7	3.5	84%	48%	64%	25%	28%	910-1120[3]	N/A	69%	11%
136.	University of La Verne (CA)	43	2.0	3.1	85%	53%	67%	69%	0.2%	1030-1195	20%[5]	48%	5%
140.	Colorado State University*	42	3.0	3.7	86%	63%	69%	27%	24%	22-28	20%	83%	11%
140.	Hofstra University (NY)	42	2.8	3.6	81%	67%	63%	50%	3%	1130-1310[2]	28%[5]	64%	11%
140.	Louisiana State University–Baton Rouge*	42	2.9	3.6	84%	69%	67%	41%	18%	23-28	23%	74%	12%
140.	Mercer University (GA)	42	2.4	3.6	85%	66%	64%	57%	4%	25-30	36%	73%	11%
140.	Oregon State University*	42	3.0	3.6	84%	60%	65%	29%	20%	1070-1300	26%	79%	9%
140.	University at Albany–SUNY*	42	2.8	3.6	83%	57%	65%	33%	16%	1000-1190	16%[5]	54%	7%
140.	Washington State University*	42	3.0	3.6	80%	59%	62%	35%	20%	1020-1220	38%	73%	12%
147.	Adelphi University (NY)	41	2.3	3.1	83%	61%	68%	48%	2%	1060-1240[9]	26%[5]	73%	9%
147.	Kansas State University*	41	3.0	3.6	84%	64%	63%	47%	12%	22-28	25%[5]	95%	19%
147.	The New School (NY)	41	2.8	3.7	82%	63%	68%	91%	1%	1100-1310[9]	17%[5]	70%	2%
147.	University of Cincinnati*	41	2.8	3.4	87%	65%	69%	37%	17%	23-28	22%	76%	10%
147.	University of Kentucky*	41	3.1	3.7	83%	70%	61%	32%	15%	22-28	29%[5]	96%	12%
152.	St. John Fisher College (NY)	40	2.2	3.1	86%	60%	71%	41%	1%	1060-1230	16%	65%	8%
152.	St. John's University (NY)	40	2.8	3.6	82%	54%	58%	32%	5%	1060-1250[2]	16%[5]	68%	4%
152.	Union University (TN)	40	1.9	2.9	86%	73%	75%	78%	0%	23-29	35%	60%	3%
152.	University of Arkansas*	40	2.9	3.4	82%	70%	62%	48%	18%	23-29	26%	66%	22%
152.	University of Mississippi*	40	2.9	3.6	86%	63%	60%	45%	16%	22-29[2]	26%	84%	13%
157.	Biola University (CA)	39	1.9	3.1	86%	65%	73%	51%	5%	1050-1260	28%[5]	72%	6%
157.	Missouri Univ. of Science & Tech.*	39	2.7	3.8	84%	70%	64%	28%	23%	25-31	39%	84%	12%
157.	Oklahoma State University*	39	2.8	3.6	81%	64%	63%	35%	15%	22-28	27%	74%	11%
157.	University of Alabama–Birmingham*	39	2.8	3.5	82%	61%	53%	39%	17%	21-28	28%	92%	8%
157.	University of Hawaii–Manoa*	39	2.7	3.4	78%	62%	60%	53%	13%	1050-1240	26%	83%	5%
157.	Univ. of Massachusetts–Lowell*	39	2.5	3.2	85%	58%	60%	50%	7%	1130-1310[2]	21%[5]	69%	12%
157.	University of Rhode Island*	39	2.8	3.5	84%	59%	66%	42%	10%	1080-1250[3]	17%	69%	6%
157.	Virginia Commonwealth University*	39	2.8	3.6	86%	59%	63%	33%	18%	1076-1292[2]	17%	77%	5%
165.	Edgewood College (WI)	38	1.7	3.0	80%	54%	61%	84%	0%	21-25	17%	71%	7%
165.	University of Central Florida*	38	2.7	3.4	89%	66%	70%	26%	25%	1150-1320	31%	50%	5%
165.	University of Idaho*	38	2.7	3.4	79%	54%	55%	55%	8%	1010-1230	20%	73%	10%
165.	Univ. of Maryland–Baltimore County*	38	2.8	3.5	88%	65%	63%	35%	13%	1140-1360	25%	60%	4%
169.	Montclair State University (NJ)*	37	2.2	3.2	82%	50%	65%	34%	2%	990-1150[2]	10%	71%	4%
169.	Seattle Pacific University	37	2.3	3.4	83%	64%	69%	53%	3%	990-1230	N/A	91%	5%
171.	Ball State University (IN)*	36	2.6	3.3	81%	57%	61%	41%	6%	1080-1240[2]	18%	62%	9%
171.	Illinois State University*	36	2.5	3.3	81%	62%	69%	33%	11%	21-26	N/A	89%	7%
171.	Ohio University*	36	2.9	3.6	80%	63%	64%	32%	17%	22-26	18%	74%	4%
171.	Rowan University (NJ)*	36	2.3	3.1	86%	60%	69%	32%	1%	1040-1250	N/A	59%	3%
171.	University of Houston*	36	2.8	3.5	86%	60%	54%	27%	24%	1110-1280	32%	61%	13%
171.	University of Louisville (KY)*	36	2.8	3.5	80%	65%	54%	38%	9%	22-29[3]	28%[5]	76%	8%
177.	Florida Institute of Technology	35	2.4	3.4	80%	61%	60%	43%	7%	1130-1320	28%[5]	63%	6%
177.	Maryville Univ. of St. Louis	35	1.9	3.1	86%	64%	72%	72%	0%	21-27[2]	21%[5]	92%	7%
177.	Mississippi State University*	35	2.6	3.5	80%	62%	58%	37%	15%	21-28	25%	73%	15%
177.	Pace University (NY)	35	2.5	3.3	78%	56%	53%	51%	2%	1040-1220[2]	16%[5]	80%	4%
177.	Suffolk University (MA)	35	2.3	3.2	76%	57%	60%	46%	0%	1000-1180	12%[5]	83%	5%
177.	University of Maine*	35	2.7	3.5	76%	57%	58%	41%	16%	1050-1250	18%	92%	7%
183.	Immaculata University (PA)	34	1.9	3.0	80%	55%	62%	85%	0.2%	950-1170[2]	13%	83%	7%
183.	Lesley University (MA)	34	2.1	3.1	79%	58%	60%	62%	0%	1020-1210	N/A	73%	4%[4]
183.	Robert Morris University (PA)	34	2.2	3.0	82%	54%	61%	41%	4%	1020-1200	18%	83%	6%
183.	University of Wyoming*	34	2.6	3.4	76%	65%	58%	41%	12%	22-27	24%[5]	97%	13%[7]
187.	Florida International University*	33	2.4	3.0	87%	48%	56%	21%	26%	1100-1260	25%[5]	51%	4%
187.	Georgia State University*	33	2.7	3.5	81%	49%	54%	25%	15%	970-1170[3]	17%[5]	52%	4%
187.	Texas Tech University*	33	2.8	3.7	84%	61%	59%	24%	21%	1070-1240	19%	69%	11%
187.	University of New Mexico*	33	2.8	3.5	79%	56%	48%	54%	10%	19-25[3]	N/A	49%	N/A
191.	Kent State University (OH)*	32	2.6	3.3	81%	54%	57%	53%	8%	21-25	15%	88%	4%
191.	Nova Southeastern University (FL)	32	2.0	3.2	77%	50%	52%	72%	2%	1080-1280	39%[5]	58%	1%

Note: Key to footnotes, Page 8

Rank	School (State) (*Public)	Overall score	Peer assessment score (5.0=highest)	High school counselor assessment score	Average first-year student retention rate	2017 graduation rate: Predicted	2017 graduation rate: Actual	% of classes under 20 ('17)	% of classes of 50 or more ('17)	SAT/ACT 25th-75th percentile** ('17)	Freshmen in top 10% of HS class ('17)	Acceptance rate ('17)	Average alumni giving rate
191.	**Univ. of Massachusetts–Boston***	32	2.6	3.4	79%	50%	48%	36%	7%	1000-1200[2]	15%[5]	75%	5%
194.	**Andrews University** (MI)	31	1.8	2.8	83%	57%	55%	75%	4%	21-29	19%	58%	4%
194.	**East Carolina University** (NC)*	31	2.3	3.2	82%	55%	61%	32%	18%	20-24	13%	79%	3%
194.	**Indiana University-Purdue U.–Indianapolis***	31	2.9	3.7	74%	52%	45%	35%	11%	1000-1190	15%	80%	7%
194.	**Lipscomb University** (TN)	31	2.0	3.1	82%	65%	59%	57%	7%	23-29	29%[5]	60%	12%
194.	**University of Hartford** (CT)	31	2.5	3.3	75%	55%	58%	73%	0.1%	1030-1230	N/A	81%	3%
194.	**U. of North Carolina–Charlotte***	31	2.7	3.7	83%	54%	54%	26%	25%	22-26	17%[5]	66%	3%
194.	**Widener University** (PA)	31	2.1	3.1	79%	53%	57%	56%	2%	1020-1180	9%[4]	65%	3%
201.	**Regent University** (VA)	30	1.8	2.8	78%	45%	61%	66%	0.4%	960-1180	13%[5]	81%	2%
201.	**University of Montana***	30	2.6	3.4	71%	54%	50%	47%	11%	21-26	14%	93%	9%
201.	**University of Nevada–Reno***	30	2.4	3.0	81%	59%	55%	39%	20%	21-26	25%	88%	8%
201.	**U. of North Carolina–Greensboro***	30	2.6	3.4	77%	51%	55%	24%	23%	1030-1180	13%	78%	6%
205.	**Azusa Pacific University** (CA)	29	2.1	3.0	86%[8]	65%	68%[8]	54%	2%	990-1220	N/A	60%	5%
205.	**California State University–Fresno***	29	2.4	3.3	82%	43%	56%	17%	10%	890-1110	15%	59%	3%
205.	**Central Michigan University***	29	2.3	3.2	77%	51%	58%	28%	8%	1010-1200	17%[5]	68%	5%
205.	**Montana State University***	29	2.5	3.3	77%	57%	52%	43%	14%	21-28	20%	83%	8%
205.	**University of Colorado–Denver***	29	2.8	3.4	70%	61%	45%	34%	9%	21-27	18%[5]	65%	3%
205.	**University of North Dakota***	29	2.5	3.3	81%	62%	54%	39%	10%	21-26	17%	83%	7%
205.	**Utah State University***	29	2.6	3.3	71%	60%	48%	49%	13%	21-27	20%	89%	5%
205.	**Wayne State University** (MI)*	29	2.5	3.3	79%	52%	47%	50%	8%	1000-1210	19%[5]	67%	5%
205.	**Western Michigan University***	29	2.4	3.2	79%	53%	51%	39%	11%	960-1190	11%	82%	4%
205.	**West Virginia University***	29	2.7	3.4	78%	61%	57%	31%	21%	21-27	20%	72%	10%
215.	**Bowling Green State University** (OH)*	28	2.5	3.2	77%	54%	52%	41%	10%	20-25	12%	68%	6%
215.	**North Dakota State University***	28	2.5	3.3	79%	64%	58%	32%	25%	21-26	16%	92%	6%
215.	**Old Dominion University** (VA)*	28	2.5	3.4	80%	53%	54%	37%	10%	980-1200[2]	9%	86%	5%
215.	**Shenandoah University** (VA)	28	1.9	2.8	79%	61%	62%	63%	1%	1010-1200	16%	83%	5%
215.	**University of Alaska–Fairbanks***	28	2.5	3.1	76%	60%	39%	70%	3%	17-25	21%[5]	77%	4%[4]
215.	**Univ. of Massachusetts–Dartmouth***	28	2.5	3.4	75%	53%	48%	42%	9%	1000-1190	N/A	84%	2%
221.	**Benedictine University** (IL)	27	2.0	3.0	70%	53%	50%	67%	0.4%	20-25	12%	62%	N/A
221.	**California State University–Fullerton***	27	2.5	3.4	88%	52%	54%	22%	9%	1020-1180	22%	59%	2%[7]
221.	**Dallas Baptist University**	27	1.9	2.9	73%	63%	58%	68%	3%	19-24	21%	39%	1%
221.	**New Mexico State University***	27	2.5	3.4	74%	51%	46%	49%	10%	18-23	22%	64%	6%
221.	**University of Texas–Arlington***	27	2.6	3.5	70%	57%	50%	34%	26%	1060-1270	31%	71%	2%
226.	**South Dakota State University***	26	2.5	3.3	77%	58%	56%[8]	30%	19%	20-26	14%	91%	7%
226.	**Southern Illinois University–Carbondale***	26	2.3	3.1	67%	50%	40%	57%	5%	20-26	13%	76%	5%
226.	**Univ. of Missouri–St. Louis***	26	2.4	3.2	77%	65%	56%	55%	7%	22-27	27%	76%	4%
226.	**University of South Dakota***	26	2.5	3.3	75%	59%	57%	44%	12%	20-25	14%	87%	6%

School (State) (*Public)	Peer assessment score (5.0=highest)	High school counselor assessment score	Average first-year student retention rate	2017 graduation rate: Predicted	2017 graduation rate: Actual	% of classes under 20 ('17)	% of classes of 50 or more ('17)	SAT/ACT 25th-75th percentile** ('17)	Freshmen in top 10% of HS class ('17)	Acceptance rate ('17)	Average alumni giving rate
SCHOOLS RANKED 230 THROUGH 301 ARE LISTED HERE ALPHABETICALLY											
American International College (MA)	1.7	2.6	67%[8]	38%	41%	52%	4%	902-1090[2]	N/A	72%	4%
Ashland University (OH)	1.7	2.9	77%	57%	55%	53%	1%	20-25	15%[4]	74%	5%
Augusta University (GA)*	2.0	3.1	73%	64%	27%	N/A	N/A	20-26[3]	N/A	76%	2%
Barry University (FL)	1.9	2.8	64%[8]	41%	35%	72%	0%	850-1020	N/A	85%	2%
Boise State University (ID)*	2.6	3.4	77%	51%	43%	34%	11%	940-1160[2]	15%	84%	7%
Cardinal Stritch University (WI)	1.8	2.9	73%	52%	42%	71%	0%	18-23[2]	21%[5]	78%	3%
Clark Atlanta University	2.2	3.0	66%	33%	40%	31%	7%	17-22	12%	58%	2%[4]
Cleveland State University*	2.2	3.0	71%	46%	43%	34%	11%	19-25	16%	90%	4%
Eastern Michigan University*	2.3	3.1	73%	49%	40%	39%	4%	840-1310	14%	73%	2%
East Tennessee State University*	2.0	2.9	72%	52%	41%	43%	9%	19-26	20%[4]	85%	3%[4]
Florida A&M University*	2.2	3.3	83%	38%	40%[8]	31%	14%	18-22	12%[5]	46%	5%
Florida Atlantic University*	2.3	3.1	77%	53%	51%	29%	18%	1060-1220	14%	60%	3%
Gardner-Webb University (NC)	1.9	2.9	73%	59%	49%	73%	0%	1000-1200	22%	53%	4%
Georgia Southern University*	2.3	3.4	81%	56%	50%	26%	10%	1100-1230	19%	68%	5%
Grand Canyon University[1] (AZ)	1.7	2.7	65%[8]	44%	35%[6]	N/A	N/A	N/A[2]	N/A	57%[4]	N/A

School (State) (*Public)	Peer assessment score (5.0=highest)	High school counselor assessment score	Average first-year student retention rate	2017 graduation rate Predicted	Actual	% of classes under 20 ('17)	% of classes of 50 or more ('17)	SAT/ACT 25th-75th percentile** ('17)	Freshmen in top 10% of HS class ('17)	Acceptance rate ('17)	Average alumni giving rate
CONTINUED (SCHOOLS RANKED 230 THROUGH 301 ARE LISTED HERE ALPHABETICALLY)											
Indiana State University*	2.5	3.3	65%	44%	39%	27%	10%	900-1110	10%	85%	5%
Indiana Univ. of Pennsylvania*	2.1	2.7	74%	48%	56%	35%	12%	910-1100[3]	8%	91%	5%
Jackson State University (MS)*	1.9	2.9	70%[8]	31%	40%[6]	39%	10%	17-21	N/A	72%	N/A
Kennesaw State University (GA)*	2.3	3.0	79%	52%	42%	31%	12%	21-26	21%[5]	61%	3%
Lamar University (TX)*	1.9	3.0	62%	46%	30%	33%	9%	950-1140[3]	15%	82%	2%
Liberty University (VA)	1.7	2.9	81%	50%	52%	33%	4%	1040-1240[3]	20%[5]	30%	1%
Lindenwood University (MO)	1.7	3.1	70%	54%	50%	68%	0.1%	20-25[2]	18%[4]	74%	4%
Louisiana Tech University*	2.4	3.3	81%	63%	54%	45%	10%	22-27	20%	65%	8%
Middle Tennessee State Univ.*	2.1	3.2	74%	52%	44%	46%	7%	20-25	18%[5]	59%	3%
Morgan State University (MD)*	2.1	2.9	75%	34%	38%	47%	2%	900-1070	7%[5]	64%	15%
National Louis University (IL)	1.9	2.8	68%[8]	36%	50%	81%	0%	N/A[2]	N/A	86%	N/A
North Carolina A&T State Univ.*	2.1	3.1	77%	36%	44%	27%	11%	930-1090	10%	62%	8%
Northern Arizona University*	2.4	3.3	75%	54%	55%	30%	16%	20-25[2]	21%	81%	3%
Northern Illinois University*	2.3	3.2	72%	51%	45%	49%	8%	19-24	13%	53%	4%
Oakland University (MI)*	2.1	3.4	77%	59%	46%	38%	13%	1010-1230	20%	84%	4%
Portland State University (OR)*	2.6	3.4	72%	50%	49%	32%	14%	19-25[2]	15%	92%	2%
Prairie View A&M University (TX)*	1.9	2.8	68%	29%	35%	16%	8%	870-1050	6%	79%	N/A
Sam Houston State University (TX)*	2.2	3.3	78%	51%	51%	26%	13%	1000-1140	19%	75%	8%
San Francisco State University*	2.6	3.4	81%	49%	54%	24%	14%	950-1150	N/A	70%	1%
Spalding University[1] (KY)	1.7	3.0	75%[8]	41%	42%[6]	N/A	N/A	18-23[4]	N/A	50%[4]	N/A
Tennessee State University*	2.0	3.0	47%[8]	32%	31%	57%	2%	16-20[4]	N/A	48%	N/A
Tennessee Technological Univ.*	2.1	3.2	77%	58%	49%	44%	11%	21-28	25%	66%	6%
Texas A&M University–Commerce*	2.2	3.4	68%	45%	42%	34%	4%	960-1150	15%	34%	2%
Texas A&M University–Corpus Christi*	2.2	3.4	56%	46%	35%	19%	22%	870-1080	7%	86%	2%[4]
Texas A&M Univ.–Kingsville*	2.1	3.3	68%	40%	35%	37%	5%	17-22	15%	84%	1%
Texas Southern University*	2.1	3.1	52%	27%	23%	34%	18%	717-912	4%	67%	3%
Texas State University*	2.2	3.2	77%	53%	54%	27%	17%	1020-1200	14%	73%	4%
Texas Woman's University*	2.3	3.3	77%	43%	36%	37%	9%	890-1080[2]	15%	86%	3%
Trevecca Nazarene University (TN)	1.6	2.8	79%	58%	54%	62%	3%	19-26	N/A	70%	5%
Trinity International University (IL)	1.8	2.8	69%	48%	52%	70%	0%	20-27	N/A	75%	N/A
University of Akron (OH)*	2.2	3.1	74%	48%	43%	42%	7%	19-26	24%[5]	93%	3%
University of Alabama–Huntsville*	2.4	3.3	81%	65%	49%	28%	21%	25-31	38%[5]	81%	3%
University of Arkansas–Little Rock*	2.3	3.0	70%	50%	33%	59%[4]	2%[4]	19-25	14%[4]	75%	3%[7]
University of Louisiana–Lafayette*	2.2	3.2	75%	56%	44%	34%	9%	21-26	21%	51%	6%
University of Louisiana–Monroe*	2.1	3.1	73%	53%	42%	39%	12%	20-25	20%	72%	4%
Univ. of Maryland–Eastern Shore*	2.1	3.0	66%	34%	38%	59%	3%	860-1040	N/A	39%	3%
University of Memphis*	2.5	3.2	75%	50%	44%	45%	10%	19-25	15%	85%	6%
Univ. of Missouri–Kansas City[1]*	2.5	3.2	74%[8]	66%	49%[6]	56%[4]	10%[4]	21-28[4]	31%[4]	62%[4]	6%[4]
University of Nebraska–Omaha*	2.5	3.5	77%	58%	48%	47%	7%	19-26	14%	87%	5%
University of Nevada–Las Vegas*	2.5	3.3	76%	56%	42%	30%	16%	18-25	23%	81%	4%
University of New Orleans*	2.1	3.0	64%	55%	32%	41%	10%	20-25	15%	57%	4%
University of Northern Colorado*	2.3	3.2	70%	60%	48%	34%	11%	19-25	13%	89%	3%
University of North Texas*	2.5	3.3	79%	57%	55%	25%	23%	1060-1260[3]	20%	72%	4%
University of South Alabama*	2.0	3.0	74%	53%	40%	44%	8%	20-26[2]	N/A	81%	N/A
Univ. of Southern Mississippi*	2.2	3.1	73%	51%	47%	41%	12%	19-26	N/A	98%	8%
University of Texas–El Paso*	2.4	3.1	72%	38%	39%[8]	33%	14%	920-1130[2]	17%	100%	4%[4]
University of Texas–Rio Grande Valley*	2.1	3.1	79%[8]	37%	41%[6]	24%	16%	17-22	21%	80%	0.3%[7]
University of Texas–San Antonio*	2.5	3.4	69%	50%	37%	15%	33%	1030-1210	17%	79%	6%
University of the Cumberlands (KY)	1.7	3.4	65%[8]	52%	39%[8]	59%[4]	1%[4]	19-25	11%	74%	3%[4]
University of Toledo (OH)*	2.4	3.1	73%	53%	42%	37%	15%	20-26	17%	94%	5%
University of West Florida*	2.0	3.0	74%	54%	44%	34%	8%	22-27	15%	50%	3%
University of West Georgia*	2.0	3.0	73%	45%	40%	32%	9%	920-1070	N/A	59%	2%
Univ. of Wisconsin–Milwaukee*	2.7	3.5	72%	52%	41%	42%	13%	20-25[2]	10%	72%	3%
Valdosta State University (GA)*	2.0	3.0	70%	46%	37%	50%	5%	980-1130	N/A	74%	2%[4]
Wichita State University (KS)*	2.4	3.3	72%	58%	47%	47%	11%	20-27[2]	20%	97%	7%
Wilmington University (DE)	2.1	3.1	60%[8]	59%	18%	82%	0%	N/A[2]	N/A	100%	N/A
Wright State University (OH)*	2.2	3.0	66%	50%	36%	27%[4]	29%[4]	19-25	18%	97%	4%[4]

BRETT ZIEGLER FOR USN&WR

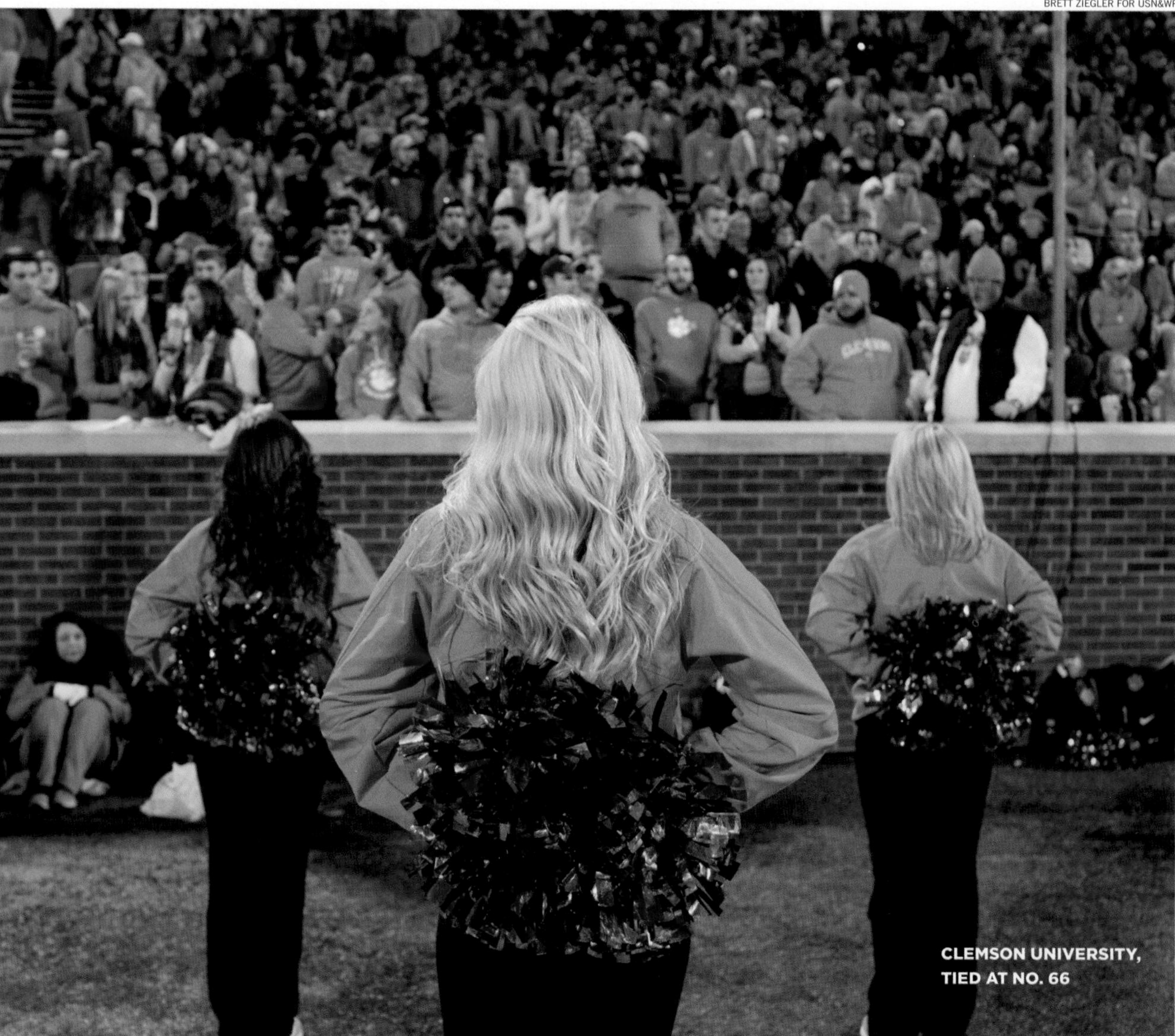

CLEMSON UNIVERSITY, TIED AT NO. 66

The Top 30 Public National Universities

Rank	School (State)
1.	University of California–Los Angeles
2.	University of California–Berkeley
3.	University of Virginia
4.	University of Michigan–Ann Arbor
5.	U. of California–Santa Barbara
5.	U. of North Carolina–Chapel Hill
7.	University of California–Irvine
8.	Georgia Institute of Technology
8.	University of Florida
10.	College of William & Mary (VA)
10.	University of California–Davis
12.	University of California–San Diego
13.	University of Georgia
13.	U. of Illinois–Urbana-Champaign
15.	University of Texas–Austin
15.	Univ. of Wisconsin–Madison
17.	Ohio State University–Columbus
17.	Purdue U.–West Lafayette (IN)
17.	Rutgers U.–New Brunswick (NJ)
20.	Pennsylvania State U.–Univ. Park
20.	University of Washington
22.	University of Connecticut
22.	Univ. of Maryland–College Park
24.	Clemson University (SC)
24.	Texas A&M University–College Station
26.	Florida State University
26.	University of California–Santa Cruz
26.	Univ. of Massachusetts–Amherst
26.	University of Pittsburgh
30.	University of Minnesota–Twin Cities
30.	Virginia Tech

Footnotes:
1. School refused to fill out U.S. News statistical survey. Data that appear are from school in previous years or from another source such as the National Center for Education Statistics.
2. SAT and/or ACT not required by school for some or all applicants.
3. In reporting SAT/ACT scores, the school did not include all students for whom it had scores or refused to tell U.S. News whether all students with scores had been included.
4. Data reported to U.S. News in previous years
5. Data based on fewer than 51 percent of enrolled freshmen.
6. Some or all data reported to the National Center for Education Statistics.
7. Data reported to the Council for Aid to Education.
8. This rate, normally based on four years of data, is given here for fewer than four years because school didn't report rate for the most recent year or years to U.S. News.
9. SAT and/or ACT may not be required by school for some or all applicants, and in reporting SAT/ACT scores, the school did not include all students for whom it had scores or refused to tell U.S. News whether all students with scores had been included.
**The SAT scores used in the rankings and published in this guidebook are for the "new" SAT test taken starting March 2016.
N/A means not available.

Best National Libera

Rank School (State) (*Public)	Overall score	Peer assessment score (5.0=highest)	High school counselor assessment score	Graduation and retention rank	Average first-year student retention rate	2017 graduation rate: Predicted	2017 graduation rate: Actual	2017 graduation rate: Over-performance (+) Under-performance (-)	Fa res r
1. **Williams College** (MA)	100	4.7	4.6	2	98%	95%	94%	-1	
2. **Amherst College** (MA)	96	4.7	4.6	2	97%	93%	95%	+2	
3. **Swarthmore College** (PA)	93	4.6	4.6	8	97%	95%	94%	-1	
3. **Wellesley College** (MA)	93	4.5	4.5	13	95%	92%	89%	-3	
5. **Bowdoin College** (ME)	91	4.4	4.6	13	96%	94%	95%	+1	
5. **Carleton College** (MN)	91	4.3	4.4	13	96%	92%	94%	+2	
5. **Middlebury College** (VT)	91	4.3	4.5	17	96%	96%	95%	-1	
5. **Pomona College** (CA)	91	4.4	4.5	4	98%	95%	93%	-2	
9. **Claremont McKenna College** (CA)	90	4.3	4.5	25	95%	92%	90%	-2	
10. **Davidson College** (NC)	89	4.3	4.4	13	95%	92%	91%	-1	
11. **Grinnell College** (IA)	88	4.2	4.3	11	94%	85%	87%	+2	
11. **Haverford College** (PA)	88	4.1	4.3	17	97%	95%	93%	-2	
11. **Smith College** (MA)	88	4.3	4.5	21	93%	85%	88%	+3	
11. **Vassar College** (NY)	88	4.2	4.5	4	95%	90%	90%	None	
11. **Washington and Lee University** (VA)	88	3.8	4.2	29	96%	94%	92%	-2	
16. **Colgate University** (NY)	87	4.1	4.4	29	95%	90%	91%	+1	
16. **Hamilton College** (NY)	87	3.9	4.2	17	95%	92%	94%	+2	
18. **Colby College** (ME)	86	4.0	4.4	34	93%	90%	92%	+2	
18. **Harvey Mudd College** (CA)	86	4.4	4.6	11	98%	96%	96%	None	
18. **United States Military Academy** (NY)*	86	4.2	4.8	21	95%	86%	85%	-1	
18. **Wesleyan University** (CT)	86	4.1	4.4	6	95%	87%	90%	+3	
22. **Bates College** (ME)	85	4.1	4.4	21	95%	88%	92%	+4	
22. **Soka University of America** (CA)	85	2.6	3.2	1	94%	81%	94%	+13	
22. **United States Naval Academy** (MD)*	85	4.3	4.9	6	97%	87%	91%	+4	
25. **Barnard College** (NY)	83	4.0	4.5	8	95%	88%	93%	+5	
25. **University of Richmond** (VA)	83	3.9	4.2	34	93%	86%	88%	+2	
27. **Bryn Mawr College** (PA)	82	4.1	4.3	29	93%	87%	83%	-4	
27. **Colorado College**	82	3.9	4.2	49	95%	90%	88%	-2	
27. **Macalester College** (MN)	82	4.0	4.4	25	94%	88%	87%	-1	
30. **Kenyon College** (OH)	80	3.9	4.2	41	94%	89%	91%	+2	
30. **Mount Holyoke College** (MA)	80	4.0	4.1	49	91%	83%	86%	+3	
30. **Oberlin College** (OH)	80	4.1	4.4	58	91%	90%	86%	-4	
30. **Scripps College** (CA)	80	3.9	4.4	41	93%	93%	88%	-5	
30. **United States Air Force Academy** (CO)*	80	4.1	4.7	29	94%	88%	79%	-9	1
35. **College of the Holy Cross** (MA)	79	3.6	4.2	8	95%	85%	92%	+7	
36. **Bucknell University** (PA)	77	3.9	4.4	41	93%	88%	90%	+2	1
36. **Franklin and Marshall College** (PA)	77	3.6	4.1	41	92%	87%	85%	-2	
36. **Lafayette College** (PA)	77	3.6	4.1	29	94%	88%	90%	+2	
39. **Occidental College** (CA)	76	3.9	4.2	38	92%	82%	84%	+2	
39. **Union College** (NY)	76	3.4	4.0	41	92%	84%	85%	+1	
41. **Pitzer College** (CA)	75	3.7	4.3	49	94%	85%	83%	-2	
41. **Skidmore College** (NY)	75	3.6	4.1	38	93%	81%	87%	+6	
43. **Denison University** (OH)	74	3.5	4.0	49	89%	80%	86%	+6	
43. **Thomas Aquinas College** (CA)	74	2.8	3.4	21	93%	69%	79%	+10	
43. **Whitman College** (WA)	74	3.5	4.1	61	94%	88%	88%	None	
46. **Centre College** (KY)	73	3.5	4.1	41	91%	82%	82%	None	
46. **Connecticut College**	73	3.5	4.0	49	90%	86%	85%	-1	
46. **Trinity College** (CT)	73	3.6	4.1	64	89%	83%	81%	-2	
49. **Gettysburg College** (PA)	72	3.5	4.0	64	90%	87%	84%	-3	
49. **Sewanee–University of the South** (TN)	72	3.6	4.1	89	88%	81%	77%	-4	

Note: Key to footnotes, Page 89.

Arts Colleges

…f …es …20	% of classes of 50 or more ('17)	Student/ faculty ratio ('17)	Selectivity rank	SAT/ACT 25th-75th percentile** ('17)	Freshmen in top 10% of HS class ('17)	Acceptance rate ('17)	Financial resources rank	Alumni giving rank	Average alumni giving rate
%	2%	7/1	3	31-35	88%[5]	15%	4	2	51%
%	3%	8/1	6	32-34	83%[5]	13%	8	5	47%
%	3%	8/1	3	31-34	91%[5]	11%	8	20	37%
%	0.2%	7/1	9	30-33	81%[5]	22%	6	3	49%
%	2%	9/1	9	1290-1510[2]	86%[5]	14%	12	3	49%
%	1%	9/1	6	31-34	86%[5]	21%	29	6	47%
%	1%	8/1	8	30-34	85%[5]	17%	5	18	39%
%	1%	8/1	3	30-34	94%[5]	8%	6	55	26%
%	2%	8/1	21	30-34	82%[5]	10%	15	26	34%
%	1%	9/1	15	30-33	76%[5]	20%	29	12	42%
%	0.2%	9/1	17	30-34	69%[5]	29%	22	19	37%
%	1%	9/1	1	1390-1530	96%[5]	20%	15	16	40%
%	4%	9/1	17	1290-1490[2]	72%[5]	32%	15	37	31%
%	0.3%	8/1	17	1370-1510	65%	24%	15	51	26%
%	0%	8/1	9	31-33	81%[5]	22%	27	9	45%
%	1%	9/1	12	31-33	77%[5]	28%	29	10	45%
%	0.4%	9/1	12	31-33	77%[5]	24%	22	17	39%
%	2%	10/1	12	31-33[2]	78%[5]	16%	19	11	43%
%	4%	8/1	1	1470-1570	90%[5]	15%	14	55	25%
%	0%	7/1	71	1185-1400	46%	10%	8	33	32%
%	3%	8/1	21	29-33[2]	60%[5]	16%	43	22	37%
%	1%	10/1	28	1270-1450[2]	63%[5]	22%	43	14	41%
%	0%	8/1	47	1200-1390	50%[5]	37%	1	61	25%
%	0%	8/1	100	1150-1370	57%	8%	2	156	14%
%	7%	10/1	21	30-33	84%[5]	15%	50	72	23%
%	0.2%	8/1	25	29-32	62%[5]	33%	26	72	24%
%	3%	8/1	17	1310-1500[2]	68%[5]	38%	19	28	34%
%	0%	10/1	16	29-33[2]	70%[5]	15%	22	76	23%
%	1%	10/1	24	29-32	67%[5]	41%	50	22	36%
%	1%	9/1	28	29-33	63%[5]	34%	41	33	32%
%	1%	9/1	28	1270-1463[2]	54%[5]	51%	41	30	32%
%	2%	9/1	28	28-33	58%[5]	34%	36	48	27%
%	0%	10/1	25	29-33	73%[5]	33%	29	48	27%
%	0.1%	9/1	38	29-33	52%	12%	2	167	14%
%	2%	10/1	62	1270-1410[2]	57%[5]	40%	50	7	46%
%	2%	9/1	34	1250-1420	60%[5]	31%	36	45	28%
%	1%	9/1	25	1260-1420[2]	68%[5]	34%	34	61	25%
%	1%	10/1	38	28-31	58%[5]	31%	36	44	29%
%	0%	9/1	28	1280-1440	62%[5]	42%	58	126	17%
%	0.3%	10/1	28	1270-1430[2]	63%[5]	37%	48	37	31%
%	0%	11/1	67	29-32[2]	63%[5]	16%	34	67	24%
%	0.4%	8/1	53	1205-1400[2]	29%[5]	25%	48	88	21%
%	0%	9/1	41	28-31[2]	65%[5]	37%	61	96	19%
%	0%	11/1	49	1200-1380	54%[5]	72%	88	1	59%
%	0%	9/1	34	26-31[2]	59%[5]	52%	56	41	31%
%	0%	10/1	34	26-31	64%[5]	76%	78	12	43%
%	1%	9/1	78	1270-1400[2]	44%[5]	38%	36	51	26%
%	0.4%	9/1	71	28-32[2]	49%[5]	34%	27	48	27%
%	0.2%	9/1	38	1270-1410	65%[5]	46%	56	72	24%
%	1%	10/1	53	27-30[2]	36%[5]	47%	50	30	32%

What Is a National Liberal Arts College?

The country's 233 liberal arts colleges emphasize undergraduate education and award at least half of their degrees in the arts and sciences, which include such disciplines as English, the biological and physical sciences, history, foreign languages, and the visual and performing arts but exclude professional disciplines such as business, education and nursing. There are 213 private and 20 public liberal arts colleges; none are for-profit. The top public colleges appear below.

The Top 10 Public Colleges

Rank School (State)

1. **United States Military Academy** (NY)
2. **United States Naval Academy** (MD)
3. **United States Air Force Academy** (CO)
4. **Virginia Military Institute**
5. **New College of Florida**
6. **St. Mary's College of Maryland**
7. **U. of North Carolina–Asheville**
8. **University of Minnesota–Morris**
9. **Massachusetts Col. of Liberal Arts**
10. **Purchase College–SUNY**

BEST NATIONAL LIBERAL ARTS COLLEGES

Rank	School (State) (*Public)	Overall score	Peer assessment score (5.0=highest)	High school counselor assessment score	Average first-year student retention rate	2017 graduation rate: Predicted	2017 graduation rate: Actual	% of classes under 20 ('17)	% of classes of 50 or more ('17)	SAT/ACT 25th-75th percentile** ('17)	Freshmen in top 10% of HS class ('17)	Acceptance rate ('17)	Average alumni giving rate
51.	**Agnes Scott College** (GA)	71	3.3	3.9	85%	69%	67%	78%	0%	1110-1300[2]	30%	66%	35%
51.	**Dickinson College** (PA)	71	3.5	4.0	91%	84%	83%	75%	0%	1230-1420[2]	48%[5]	49%	25%
51.	**Furman University** (SC)	71	3.6	4.1	90%	82%	81%	60%	0%	26-31[2]	38%[5]	61%	22%
51.	**Rhodes College** (TN)	71	3.5	4.1	91%	80%	83%	69%	0%	27-32	50%[5]	51%	34%
51.	**Spelman College** (GA)	71	3.6	4.0	90%	58%	75%	60%	1%	1070-1215	26%[5]	40%	32%
56.	**Bard College** (NY)	70	3.5	4.0	85%	89%	74%	80%	0%	1220-1400[2]	41%[5]	58%	30%
56.	**DePauw University** (IN)	70	3.5	3.9	92%	80%	81%	70%	0%	24-29	40%[5]	67%	25%
56.	**Lawrence University** (WI)	70	3.3	3.9	90%	79%	80%	81%	2%	25-32[2]	38%[5]	61%	31%
56.	**St. Lawrence University** (NY)	70	3.3	3.8	90%	78%	85%	64%	1%	1170-1355[2]	46%[5]	48%	24%
56.	**Wabash College** (IN)	70	3.4	3.6	88%	74%	77%	77%	1%	1070-1280	27%	64%	40%
61.	**Berea College** (KY)	69	3.5	4.0	84%	53%	66%	76%	0.4%	22-27	24%	35%	16%
61.	**St. John's College** (MD)	69	3.4	4.1	83%	71%	67%	98%	1%	1220-1430[2]	36%[5]	55%	21%
61.	**St. Olaf College** (MN)	69	3.7	4.1	93%	83%	88%	54%	3%	25-31	45%[5]	43%	22%
61.	**Wheaton College** (IL)	69	3.1	3.9	94%	80%	89%	65%	2%	27-32	47%[5]	85%	20%
65.	**Kalamazoo College** (MI)	68	3.4	4.0	91%	80%	86%	63%	1%	26-30[2]	50%[5]	73%	25%
65.	**Sarah Lawrence College** (NY)	68	3.4	4.1	85%	82%	79%	93%	1%	1240-1410[2]	25%[5]	53%	18%
67.	**College of Wooster** (OH)	67	3.4	3.9	88%	77%	76%	75%	1%	24-30	45%	56%	19%
68.	**Beloit College** (WI)	66	3.3	3.8	86%	77%	86%	68%	0%	24-30[2]	30%[5]	54%	20%
68.	**Hobart & William Smith Colleges** (NY)	66	3.2	3.8	86%	76%	81%	66%	0%	1210-1360[2]	33%[5]	61%	28%
68.	**Knox College** (IL)	66	3.2	3.7	86%	72%	76%	77%	1%	23-30[2]	34%[5]	72%	33%
68.	**Lewis & Clark College** (OR)	66	3.4	4.0	84%	77%	80%	67%	2%	27-31[2]	35%[5]	71%	17%
72.	**Illinois Wesleyan University**	65	3.1	3.7	92%	79%	78%	71%	1%	24-29	39%[5]	61%	20%
72.	**St. John's College** (NM)	65	3.2	3.9	80%	72%	65%	100%	0%	1120-1410[2]	47%[5]	63%	15%
72.	**University of Puget Sound** (WA)	65	3.3	3.9	86%	75%	78%	62%	0.2%	25-31[2]	34%[5]	84%	14%
72.	**Wofford College** (SC)	65	3.2	3.9	89%	78%	81%	65%	0%	24-30[2]	43%	69%	22%
76.	**Allegheny College** (PA)	64	3.2	3.6	83%	73%	75%	73%	0.2%	1140-1320[2]	33%	68%	22%
76.	**Hendrix College** (AR)	64	3.4	4.0	84%	81%	75%	73%	0%	24-29	60%	80%	25%
76.	**Hillsdale College** (MI)	64	2.5	3.7	94%	84%	85%	69%	0.2%	28-32	N/A	41%	14%
76.	**Transylvania University** (KY)	64	3.0	3.6	84%	75%	75%	78%	0%	25-30[2]	34%	95%	31%
76.	**Willamette University** (OR)	64	3.2	3.9	86%	74%	73%	66%	0%	1120-1340[2]	47%[5]	89%	12%
81.	**Cornell College** (IA)	63	3.1	3.8	81%	68%	71%	77%	0%	26-29[2]	19%[4]	65%	18%
81.	**Earlham College** (IN)	63	3.4	3.9	83%	70%	68%	76%	2%	25-30[2]	29%[5]	52%	22%
81.	**Muhlenberg College** (PA)	63	3.0	3.8	91%	80%	86%	70%	1%	1140-1340[2]	31%[5]	48%	18%
81.	**Principia College** (IL)	63	2.4	2.7	89%	67%	84%	97%	0%	1033-1293	44%[5]	91%	24%
81.	**Virginia Military Institute***	63	3.1	4.0	88%	70%	77%	76%	0.1%	1100-1280[3]	15%	53%	28%
86.	**College of St. Benedict** (MN)	62	3.1	3.7	87%	73%	82%	57%	1%	22-28	32%	81%	17%
86.	**Juniata College** (PA)	62	2.8	3.7	85%	72%	84%	70%	2%	1080-1290[2]	31%	71%	24%
86.	**Wheaton College** (MA)	62	3.3	4.0	86%	77%	78%	65%	1%	1150-1350[2]	26%[5]	48%	18%
89.	**Luther College** (IA)	61	3.1	3.7	84%	72%	80%	61%	1%	23-28	26%	65%	25%
90.	**Gustavus Adolphus College** (MN)	60	3.2	3.8	89%	74%	80%	61%	0%	24-30[2]	33%	68%	18%
90.	**New College of Florida***	60	3.1	4.0	81%	74%	65%	71%	1%	1190-1380	38%	69%	17%
90.	**Reed College**[1] (OR)	60	3.8	4.3	88%[8]	69%	80%[6]	N/A	N/A	1280-1480[4]	N/A	31%[4]	N/A
90.	**Southwestern University** (TX)	60	3.0	4.0	85%	76%	74%	63%	0.3%	1110-1320	37%	43%	26%
90.	**Ursinus College** (PA)	60	2.9	3.6	87%	72%	77%	68%	0.2%	1110-1310[2]	25%[5]	78%	18%
95.	**Augustana College** (IL)	59	3.1	3.6	86%	72%	75%	69%	0.2%	23-28[2]	36%[5]	59%	19%
95.	**Bennington College** (VT)	59	3.0	3.7	81%	78%	67%	89%	0.4%	1210-1390[2]	N/A	57%	21%
95.	**College of the Atlantic** (ME)	59	2.7	3.6	80%	70%	66%	94%	0%	1190-1350[2]	22%[5]	68%	32%
95.	**Ohio Wesleyan University**	59	3.1	4.0	79%	73%	70%	76%	0.2%	22-28[2]	22%	71%	22%
95.	**St. Anselm College** (NH)	59	2.7	3.6	89%	67%	80%	67%	2%	1140-1300[2]	24%[5]	76%	17%
95.	**St. John's University** (MN)	59	3.2	3.8	88%	72%	74%	57%	1%	22-27	15%[5]	80%	23%
95.	**St. Mary's College** (IN)	59	2.9	3.7	87%	71%	80%	50%	0.3%	23-29	28%[5]	78%	31%
95.	**St. Mary's College of Maryland***	59	3.0	3.7	87%	73%	78%	74%	0%	1070-1280	8%	82%	12%
103.	**Austin College** (TX)	58	3.0	3.8	83%	73%	68%	62%	1%	1160-1360[2]	41%[5]	52%	19%[4]
103.	**Hollins University** (VA)	58	2.8	3.3	77%	64%	62%	88%	0%	1110-1300	29%	48%	21%
103.	**Hope College** (MI)	58	3.0	3.7	89%	70%	80%	59%	2%	24-29	32%	74%	19%
103.	**Lake Forest College** (IL)	58	3.0	3.5	85%	69%	72%	62%	0.3%	24-29[2]	38%[5]	53%	24%
103.	**Washington and Jefferson Col.** (PA)	58	3.0	3.7	82%	70%	70%	67%	0%	1120-1290[2]	34%	48%	15%
108.	**Linfield College** (OR)	57	2.7	3.6	85%	67%	78%	75%	0.2%	1020-1210	30%	81%	13%
108.	**Millsaps College** (MS)	57	3.0	3.7	79%	75%	67%	79%	0%	22-28	100%[4]	49%	18%
108.	**Washington College** (MD)	57	2.9	3.6	85%	75%	76%	74%	2%	1090-1300	38%[5]	48%	19%
108.	**Westmont College** (CA)	57	2.8	3.5	83%	73%	75%	64%	2%	1130-1380	40%[5]	85%	15%

Note: Key to footnotes, Page 89.

HAVERFORD COLLEGE, TIED AT NO. 11

BRETT ZIEGLER FOR USN&WR

BEST NATIONAL LIBERAL ARTS COLLEGES

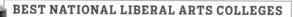

Rank	School (State) (*Public)	Overall score	Peer assessment score (5.0=highest)	High school counselor assessment score	Average first-year student retention rate	2017 graduation rate: Predicted	2017 graduation rate: Actual	% of classes under 20 ('17)	% of classes of 50 or more ('17)	SAT/ACT 25th-75th percentile** ('17)	Freshmen in top 10% of HS class ('17)	Acceptance rate ('17)	Average alumni giving rate
108.	**Whittier College** (CA)	57	3.1	3.6	80%	57%	69%	58%	1%	1010-1220[2]	21%	74%	20%
113.	**Elizabethtown College** (PA)	56	2.7	3.4	84%	67%	75%	68%	0%	1070-1280	30%	74%	18%
113.	**Hampden-Sydney College** (VA)	56	2.9	3.6	83%	67%	63%	73%	0%	1050-1265	13%	55%	26%
113.	**Hanover College** (IN)	56	2.8	3.7	81%	68%	71%	71%	0%	22-27[2]	32%	84%	16%
116.	**Drew University** (NJ)	55	2.8	3.5	85%	70%	62%	70%	1%	1100-1300[2]	24%[5]	63%	20%
116.	**Goucher College** (MD)	55	3.1	3.9	79%	69%	66%	73%	0.3%	1050-1260[2]	28%[5]	79%	19%
116.	**Marlboro College** (VT)	55	2.3	3.3	72%[8]	59%	50%	100%	0%	1150-1340[2]	N/A	97%	22%
116.	**St. Michael's College** (VT)	55	2.8	3.5	87%	72%	78%	61%	0%	1150-1310[2]	25%	85%	19%
120.	**Grove City College** (PA)	54	2.5	3.4	91%	74%	83%	54%	4%	1071-1349	35%	80%	19%
120.	**Randolph-Macon College** (VA)	54	2.9	3.3	81%	63%	66%	69%	0%	1050-1233	19%	62%	36%
120.	**Ripon College** (WI)	54	2.7	3.3	80%	65%	68%	65%	3%	20-26[2]	16%	68%	25%
120.	**Westminster College** (PA)	54	2.7	3.5	80%	60%	70%	66%	1%	940-1200	22%	72%	15%
124.	**Coe College** (IA)	53	3.0	3.7	78%	69%	68%	73%	1%	22-28	27%	56%	16%
124.	**McDaniel College** (MD)	53	2.7	3.6	80%	59%	68%	67%	0%	1060-1230	26%	85%	13%
124.	**Stonehill College** (MA)	53	2.8	3.7	89%	77%	80%	49%	0.1%	1080-1270[2]	22%	72%	15%
127.	**Concordia College–Moorhead** (MN)	52	2.8	3.5	83%	70%	70%	56%	1%	22-28	27%	62%	16%
127.	**Presbyterian College** (SC)	52	2.8	3.7	81%	68%	68%	66%	0.3%	21-27[2]	25%	63%	18%
127.	**St. Norbert College** (WI)	52	2.7	3.4	84%	70%	73%	49%	1%	22-27	20%	79%	16%
127.	**Sweet Briar College** (VA)	52	2.1	3.3	58%	68%	54%	98%	0%	993-1180[2]	17%	93%	37%
131.	**Birmingham-Southern College** (AL)	51	2.8	3.7	82%	73%	66%	63%	0.3%	23-29[2]	54%	62%	16%
131.	**College of Idaho**	51	2.6	3.3	79%	64%	67%	68%	0.4%	21-27[2]	24%	76%	30%
131.	**Lycoming College** (PA)	51	2.5	3.2	80%	56%	67%	69%	1%	988-1200[2]	14%	64%	18%
131.	**Salem College**[1] (NC)	51	2.3	3.4	80%[8]	46%	61%[6]	87%[4]	0%[4]	21-27[4]	40%[4]	57%[4]	23%[4]
135.	**Eckerd College** (FL)	50	2.9	3.7	81%	67%	70%	50%	0%	23-29	N/A	73%	N/A
135.	**Monmouth College** (IL)	50	2.7	3.4	74%	55%	60%	79%	0%	20-25	17%	67%	19%
135.	**Roanoke College** (VA)	50	2.9	3.4	82%	64%	67%	55%	0%	1040-1230	16%	67%	19%
135.	**Siena College** (NY)	50	2.7	3.6	89%	67%	78%	37%	0%	1060-1250[2]	22%	65%	13%
135.	**Simpson College** (IA)	50	2.6	3.3	80%	61%	68%	79%	1%	21-27	23%	84%	14%
135.	**Susquehanna University** (PA)	50	3.0	3.5	85%	67%	71%	54%	0.2%	1070-1240[2]	26%	68%	11%
141.	**Central College**[1] (IA)	49	2.7	3.3	79%[8]	65%	67%[8]	70%[4]	1%[4]	21-26[4]	23%[4]	73%[4]	11%[4]
141.	**Randolph College** (VA)	49	2.6	3.2	73%	66%	59%	86%	0%	950-1190	15%	86%	20%
143.	**Alma College** (MI)	48	2.6	3.7	80%	66%	68%	67%	1%	1030-1230	18%	64%	18%
143.	**Franklin College** (IN)	48	2.6	3.4	77%	55%	62%	69%	0%	1010-1200	18%	78%	19%
143.	**Houghton College** (NY)	48	2.5	3.3	86%[8]	64%	73%[6]	67%	2%	1060-1320[2]	26%	91%	16%
143.	**Illinois College**	48	2.6	3.2	78%	62%	60%	68%	1%	19-25[2]	14%	55%	21%
143.	**Morehouse College** (GA)	48	3.3	3.9	82%	55%	55%	53%	0.2%	950-1160	12%	74%	14%
143.	**U. of North Carolina–Asheville***	48	3.0	3.8	77%	61%	62%	50%	1%	22-27	15%	81%	7%
143.	**Warren Wilson College** (NC)	48	2.6	3.5	63%	65%	53%	90%	0%	25-29[2]	15%[5]	79%	14%
143.	**Wartburg College** (IA)	48	2.7	3.5	78%	65%	66%	52%	1%	21-27	27%	77%	21%
143.	**Wesleyan College** (GA)	48	2.7	3.7	74%	61%	56%	85%	0%	1020-1190	28%	47%	25%
152.	**Albion College** (MI)	47	2.8	3.5	81%	67%	57%	59%	0%	1010-1200	N/A	71%	13%
152.	**Fisk University** (TN)	47	2.8	3.6	81%	48%	53%	73%	0%	16-22	11%	45%	25%
152.	**Saint Vincent College** (PA)	47	2.4	3.5	85%	63%	69%	50%	0%	1020-1210	13%	62%	20%
155.	**Doane University** (NE)	46	2.3	3.3	73%	57%	63%	80%	1%	20-25[3]	15%	65%	13%
155.	**Elmira College** (NY)	46	2.5	3.3	76%	62%	60%	81%	0.3%	1040-1200[2]	20%[4]	85%	14%
155.	**Hiram College** (OH)	46	2.5	3.4	69%	51%	56%	82%	0%	18-24[2]	11%	64%	11%
155.	**Moravian College** (PA)	46	2.6	3.2	80%	59%	63%	62%	2%	1010-1210[3]	18%	76%	18%
155.	**University of Minnesota–Morris***	46	2.7	3.5	79%	65%	59%	72%	2%	22-28	24%	64%	11%
155.	**Westminster College** (MO)	46	2.6	3.3	78%	64%	64%	79%	0%	21-26	13%	90%	15%
155.	**William Jewell College** (MO)	46	2.6	3.2	79%	69%	59%	75%	0%	23-28[2]	26%	46%	9%
162.	**Claflin University** (SC)	45	2.1	3.0	76%	30%	53%	64%	1%	18-20	11%	41%	46%
162.	**Emory and Henry College** (VA)	45	2.7	3.5	73%	54%	52%	74%	1%	988-1170	20%	72%	21%
162.	**Gordon College** (MA)	45	2.4	3.2	84%	66%	70%	63%	4%	1050-1290[3]	28%[5]	89%	10%
162.	**Massachusetts Col. of Liberal Arts***	45	2.5	3.2	76%	49%	54%	66%	0%	970-1190	10%[5]	77%	7%
162.	**Meredith College** (NC)	45	2.4	3.6	79%	57%	63%	65%	0%	20-25	17%	69%	20%
162.	**Northland College** (WI)	45	2.3	3.4	72%	60%	64%	68%	0%	20-26[2]	16%	61%	13%
168.	**Centenary College of Louisiana**	44	2.4	3.3	76%	62%	48%	76%	0%	22-28	29%	62%	12%
168.	**Covenant College** (GA)	44	2.3	2.9	86%	65%	69%	58%	2%	24-30	31%[5]	95%	12%
168.	**Guilford College** (NC)	44	3.0	3.8	70%	52%	53%	65%	0%	19-25[2]	13%	91%	12%
168.	**Wittenberg University** (OH)	44	2.7	3.7	76%	70%	67%	52%	1%	22-28[2]	14%	72%	17%
172.	**Purchase College–SUNY***	43	2.6	3.4	81%	57%	68%	61%	3%	1020-1200[2]	N/A	74%	4%

School (State) (*Public)	Peer assessment score (5.0=highest)	High school counselor assessment score	Average first-year student retention rate	2017 graduation rate: Predicted	2017 graduation rate: Actual	% of classes under 20 ('17)	% of classes of 50 or more ('17)	SAT/ACT 25th-75th percentile** ('17)	Freshmen in top 10% of HS class ('17)	Acceptance rate ('17)	Average alumni giving rate
SCHOOLS RANKED 173 THROUGH 229 ARE LISTED HERE ALPHABETICALLY											
Albright College (PA)	2.5	3.2	74%	54%	53%	67%	0%	990-1170[2]	15%	50%	9%
Allen University[1] (SC)	1.8	2.4	53%[8]	23%	22%[6]	N/A	N/A	N/A[2]	N/A	N/A	N/A
American Jewish University[1] (CA)	2.2	2.5	69%[8]	64%	56%[6]	N/A	N/A	N/A[2]	N/A	60%[4]	N/A
Ave Maria University[1] (FL)	2.1	2.9	73%[8]	61%	52%[6]	N/A	N/A	21-27[4]	N/A	40%[4]	N/A
Bard College at Simon's Rock (MA)	3.0	3.7	78%	77%	28%	94%	0%	1240-1440[9]	56%[5]	55%	14%
Bethany College (WV)	2.3	3.2	66%	46%	46%	86%	1%	850-1110	10%	94%	15%
Bethany Lutheran College (MN)	2.1	3.2	77%	58%	52%	77%	0.4%	20-25	17%	79%	15%
Bethel College (KS)	2.4	3.3	63%	58%	42%	74%	2%	18-24	16%	56%	16%
Bethune-Cookman University (FL)	2.2	3.1	65%	21%	37%	43%	3%	15-19	2%	54%	6%
Bloomfield College (NJ)	2.0	2.9	68%	32%	32%	80%	0%	840-1040[2]	10%	64%	7%
Bridgewater College (VA)	2.4	3.1	76%	56%	61%	52%	0%	970-1170	15%	52%	14%
Bryn Athyn Col. of New Church[1] (PA)	1.9	2.6	67%[8]	63%	55%[6]	72%[4]	0%[4]	N/A	N/A	82%[4]	N/A
Carthage College (WI)	2.7	3.3	79%	63%	60%	57%	0.3%	21-27[2]	22%	68%	14%
Cheyney U. of Pennsylvania*	1.8	2.7	54%[8]	27%	20%[6]	N/A	N/A	650-860[4]	N/A	39%	N/A
Davis and Elkins College[1] (WV)	2.3	2.9	67%[8]	37%	43%[6]	N/A	N/A	17-23[4]	N/A	50%[4]	N/A
Dillard University (LA)	2.5	3.5	73%	36%	40%	52%	1%	18-21	12%[5]	41%	18%
East-West University[1] (IL)	1.6	1.6	38%[8]	26%	10%[6]	N/A	N/A	N/A	N/A	N/A	N/A
Emmanuel College (MA)	2.4	3.4	78%	62%	66%	39%	0%	1090-1250[9]	13%	73%	16%
Erskine College (SC)	2.3	3.4	65%	56%	60%	78%	0%	19-24[3]	17%	55%	18%
Fort Lewis College (CO)*	2.5	3.1	62%	50%	40%	52%	2%	20-25	13%	83%	3%
Georgetown College (KY)	2.5	3.7	69%	64%	54%	66%	0%	20-25	23%	67%	19%
Hartwick College (NY)	2.5	3.2	74%	63%	53%	74%	0.3%	920-1100[2]	8%	89%	12%
Holy Cross College (IN)	2.6	3.7	62%	49%	40%	60%	1%	1020-1320	N/A	82%	11%
Johnson C. Smith University (NC)	2.1	2.8	67%	34%	44%	76%	0%	748-960	5%[4]	38%	15%
Judson College[1] (AL)	2.1	3.1	65%[8]	49%	39%[6]	N/A	N/A	19-24[4]	N/A	58%[4]	N/A
The King's College (NY)	2.5	3.2	71%[8]	66%	51%	41%	4%	24-29	N/A	41%	3%
LaGrange College (GA)	2.4	2.9	65%	54%	41%	71%	0%	20-24	18%[5]	57%	13%
Louisiana State University–Alexandria*	2.1	3.1	59%	45%	24%[6]	51%	4%	18-22	8%	31%	4%
Lyon College (AR)	2.5	3.3	67%	64%	53%	63%	1%	22-28	27%	64%	11%
Marymount Manhattan College (NY)	2.4	3.3	74%	58%	49%	71%	0%	980-1200	N/A	79%	7%
Maryville College (TN)	2.5	3.2	72%	63%	57%	57%	1%	20-27	21%	49%	21%
Oglethorpe University (GA)	2.8	3.6	74%	59%	47%	51%	0%	1110-1310	26%	58%	10%
Ouachita Baptist University (AR)	2.2	3.3	78%	65%	64%	60%	1%	21-28	36%	71%	16%
Pacific Union College (CA)	2.5	3.3	75%	51%	48%	71%	3%	950-1150	N/A	50%	5%
Paine College[1] (GA)	1.8	2.6	41%[8]	22%	20%[6]	N/A	N/A	14-17[4]	N/A	25%[4]	N/A
Philander Smith College (AR)	1.9	2.7	68%	33%	30%	73%	0%	15-19	15%	24%	6%
Pine Manor College (MA)	1.9	2.3	56%	32%	26%	81%	0%	740-915[2]	N/A	14%	4%
Providence Christian College[1] (CA)	2.0	2.6	68%[8]	57%	63%[6]	N/A	N/A	N/A[2]	N/A	64%[4]	N/A
Schreiner University (TX)	2.4	3.2	69%	50%	48%	66%	0%	960-1140[3]	14%	92%	6%
Shepherd University (WV)*	2.2	3.3	65%	47%	42%	60%	1%	19-24	N/A	89%	7%
Southern Virginia University[1]	2.0	3.0	71%[8]	46%	31%[6]	N/A	N/A	16-26[4]	N/A	45%[4]	N/A
Spring Hill College (AL)	2.3	3.6	77%	62%	53%	60%	0.2%	21-26	15%[5]	46%	17%
Stillman College (AL)	2.4	3.2	64%[8]	30%	20%[6]	N/A	N/A	N/A	N/A	N/A	15%
Thiel College (PA)	2.1	3.3	68%	43%	40%[8]	N/A	N/A	860-1110[3]	5%	N/A	14%[4]
Thomas More Col. of Lib. Arts[1] (NH)	2.3	2.9	93%[8]	52%	59%[6]	N/A	N/A	N/A[2]	N/A	100%[4]	N/A
Tougaloo College (MS)	2.3	2.9	73%	33%	50%	67%	0.4%	16-24	25%	75%	24%
University of Maine–Machias[1]*	2.1	3.0	68%[8]	44%	29%[6]	N/A	N/A	N/A	N/A	N/A	N/A
University of Pikeville (KY)	2.0	2.8	57%	44%	31%	64%	1%	18-23	15%	100%	4%
Univ. of Science and Arts of Okla.*	2.4	3.3	77%[8]	53%	42%[6]	73%[4]	4%[4]	19-24[2]	17%	48%	N/A
University of Virginia–Wise*	2.6	3.4	67%	46%	45%	74%	1%	940-1118	18%	78%	8%
Univ. of Wisconsin–Parkside*	2.1	3.4	73%	45%	34%	41%	7%	18-23[2]	14%	80%	1%
Virginia Union University	2.2	2.9	56%	24%	27%	47%	2%	780-980[2]	2%[5]	50%	9%
Virginia Wesleyan University	2.4	3.4	64%	51%	52%	78%	0.4%	952-1160	15%	71%	6%
Wells College (NY)	2.6	3.5	72%[8]	54%	46%	82%	0%	17-27[2]	14%	80%	N/A
West Virginia State University*	2.1	3.5	59%	46%	26%	58%	2%	17-22	N/A	98%	4%
William Peace University[1] (NC)	2.1	2.9	63%[8]	48%	40%[6]	N/A	N/A	16-22[4]	N/A	63%[4]	N/A
Young Harris College (GA)	2.2	2.9	67%	55%	34%	70%	0%	910-1078	10%	56%	9%

Footnotes:
1. School refused to fill out U.S. News statistical survey. Data that appear are from school in previous years or from another source such as the National Center for Education Statistics.
2. SAT and/or ACT not required by school for some or all applicants.
3. In reporting SAT/ACT scores, the school did not include all students for whom it had scores or refused to tell U.S. News whether all students with scores had been included.
4. Data reported to U.S. News in previous years.
5. Data based on fewer than 51 percent of enrolled freshmen.
6. Some or all data reported to the National Center for Education Statistics.
7. Data reported to the Council for Aid to Education.
8. This rate, normally based on four years of data, is given here for fewer than four years because school didn't report rate for the most recent year or years to U.S. News.
9. SAT and/or ACT may not be required by school for some or all applicants, and in reporting SAT/ACT scores, the school did not include all students for whom it had scores or refused to tell U.S. News whether all students with scores had been included.

**The SAT scores used in the rankings and published in this guidebook are for the "new" SAT taken starting March 2016.
N/A means not available.

Best Regional Universities

What Is a Regional University?

Like the national universities, the institutions that appear here provide a full range of undergraduate majors and master's programs; the difference is that they offer few, if any, doctoral programs. The 656 universities in this category are not ranked nationally but rather against their peer group in one of four regions – North, South, Midwest and West – because in general they tend to draw students most heavily from surrounding states.

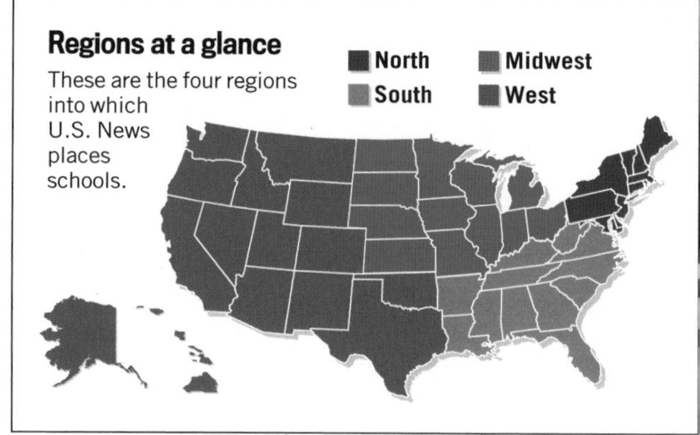

Regions at a glance
These are the four regions into which U.S. News places schools.
North
Midwest
South
West

NORTH ▶

Rank	School (State) (*Public)	Overall score	Peer assessment score (5.0=highest)	Average first-year student retention rate	2017 graduation rate Predicted	2017 graduation rate Actual	% of classes under 20 ('17)	% of classes of 50 or more ('17)	Student/ faculty ratio ('17)	SAT/ACT 25th-75th percentile** ('17)	Freshmen in top 25% of HS class ('17)	Acceptance rate ('17)	Average alumni giving rate
1.	Fairfield University (CT)	100	3.6	89%	82%	81%	44%	1%	12/1	1180-1320[2]	79%[5]	61%	17%
2.	Providence College (RI)	99	3.7	92%	78%	84%	54%	3%	12/1	1160-1330[2]	65%[5]	52%	17%
3.	Bentley University (MA)	98	3.5	94%	83%	91%	19%	0%	11/1	1210-1380	74%[5]	44%	6%
4.	College of New Jersey*	95	3.4	94%	82%	87%	44%	0.3%	13/1	1170-1330	73%[5]	48%	7%
5.	Loyola University Maryland	94	3.6	87%	80%	81%	47%	0.4%	11/1	1140-1310[2]	68%[5]	75%	11%
6.	Emerson College (MA)	90	3.4	88%	79%	81%	67%	1%	13/1	1200-1360[2]	71%[5]	46%	5%
6.	University of Scranton (PA)	90	3.3	88%	70%	77%	53%	0.1%	12/1	1080-1280	63%[5]	75%	11%
8.	Marist College (NY)	89	3.4	90%	76%	83%	43%	0%	16/1	1120-1320[2]	53%[5]	43%	11%
9.	Ithaca College (NY)	88	3.5	85%	74%	76%	61%	3%	10/1	1150-1330[2]	55%[5]	71%	7%
10.	Bryant University (RI)	87	3.1	89%	71%	79%	22%	0%	13/1	1120-1280[2]	52%[5]	73%	9%
11.	Simmons College (MA)	84	3.0	85%	70%	73%	69%	3%	12/1	1130-1310	70%	60%	15%
12.	St. Joseph's University (PA)	83	3.2	90%	73%	82%	41%	1%	11/1	1110-1290[2]	51%[5]	77%	11%
13.	Quinnipiac University (CT)	80	3.4	87%	76%	75%	43%	3%	16/1	1080-1260[2]	51%	74%	3%
14.	SUNY–Geneseo*	79	3.5	88%	78%	77%	24%	10%	19/1	1120-1300	64%[5]	72%	9%
15.	Manhattan College (NY)	78	2.9	86%	63%	75%	45%	0.1%	13/1	1050-1243[3]	54%[5]	75%	16%
15.	Thomas Jefferson University (PA)	78	2.9	82%	66%	66%	70%	4%	18/1	1030-1210	42%	60%	4%
17.	Le Moyne College (NY)	77	2.9	86%	62%	74%	43%	1%	13/1	1080-1240[2]	51%	64%	17%
18.	SUNY Polytechnic Inst.–Albany/Utica*	76	2.7	77%	57%	52%	54%	1%	13/1	1000-1290[3]	66%[5]	62%	4%
19.	Massachusetts Maritime Academy*	75	3.0	89%	59%	75%	38%	2%	16/1	1040-1200	N/A	83%	14%
20.	CUNY–Baruch College*	74	3.0	91%	59%	70%	20%	17%	19/1	1190-1350	75%	29%	3%
20.	Gallaudet University (DC)	74	3.3	69%	61%	53%	97%	0%	7/1	15-19[2]	N/A	59%	N/A
22.	St. Bonaventure University (NY)	73	2.9	84%	59%	69%	54%	0%	12/1	1020-1220	47%[5]	71%	18%
23.	Canisius College (NY)	72	2.7	85%	65%	69%	55%	0%	11/1	1040-1260	49%	78%	12%
24.	Lebanon Valley College (PA)	71	2.6	83%	72%	73%	62%	2%	10/1	1063-1250[2]	55%	73%	14%
25.	CUNY–Hunter College*	70	3.2	84%	58%	52%	38%	7%	14/1	1070-1260	57%	40%	11%
25.	Endicott College (MA)	70	2.7	85%	60%	75%	61%	0%	14/1	1050-1210[2]	44%[5]	81%	13%
25.	Molloy College (NY)	70	2.3	88%	64%	72%	67%	3%	10/1	1020-1200	54%[5]	76%	10%
28.	Assumption College (MA)	69	2.7	83%	64%	71%	50%	0%	11/1	1070-1250[2]	41%[5]	79%	13%
28.	Monmouth University (NJ)	69	2.9	81%	65%	70%	40%	0.1%	13/1	970-1190	37%[5]	74%	4%
28.	Ramapo College of New Jersey*	69	2.7	87%	63%	74%	39%	0%	18/1	1050-1230	41%[5]	57%	4%
28.	Rutgers University–Camden (NJ)*	69	3.0	86%	56%	58%	44%	10%	12/1	1000-1180	37%	69%	3%
28.	Salve Regina University (RI)	69	2.8	84%	63%	71%	39%	0.2%	14/1	1080-1230[2]	42%[5]	72%	16%
28.	Springfield College (MA)	69	2.8	85%	60%	74%	45%	2%	12/1	1020-1220	44%	70%	9%
28.	St. Francis University (PA)	69	2.6	87%	63%	62%	66%	0%	14/1	1030-1230	57%	76%	21%
35.	La Salle University (PA)	68	2.9	78%	55%	67%	46%	1%	11/1	970-1160	36%	79%	10%
35.	Misericordia University (PA)	68	2.5	83%	63%	76%	48%	0%	12/1	1030-1205	51%	79%	14%
35.	Nazareth College (NY)	68	2.6	83%	67%	67%	52%	0%	9/1	1070-1250[2]	60%	63%	10%
35.	Rider University (NJ)	68	2.8	80%	63%	62%	47%	1%	11/1	990-1190	43%[5]	67%	8%

Note: Key to footnotes Page 105.

NORTH ▶

Rank	School (State) (*Public)	Overall score	Peer assessment score (5.0=highest)	Average first-year student retention rate	2017 graduation rate: Predicted	2017 graduation rate: Actual	% of classes under 20 ('17)	% of classes of 50 or more ('17)	Student/faculty ratio ('17)	SAT/ACT 25th-75th percentile** ('17)	Freshmen in top 25% of HS class ('17)	Acceptance rate ('17)	Average alumni giving rate
35.	Sacred Heart University (CT)	68	3.1	83%	66%	72%	41%	1%	14/1	1060-1200[2]	29%	60%	8%
35.	Stockton University (NJ)*	68	2.7	87%	58%	73%	27%	2%	17/1	1010-1200	47%	82%	2%
41.	Mount St. Mary's University (MD)	67	2.9	76%	61%	63%	55%	0%	13/1	970-1190	30%	64%	16%
41.	SUNY–New Paltz*	67	2.9	88%	64%	72%	25%	4%	16/1	1100-1260	69%[5]	44%	2%
43.	Hood College (MD)	66	2.8	78%	60%	61%	72%	0%	10/1	980-1220[2]	34%	81%	15%
43.	Marywood University (PA)	66	2.5	83%	59%	69%	57%	0.4%	12/1	1000-1190	47%	75%	12%
43.	Niagara University (NY)	66	2.7	84%	57%	68%	57%	1%	11/1	1020-1200	47%	84%	8%
43.	Roger Williams University (RI)	66	2.9	81%	66%	64%	48%	1%	14/1	1090-1250[2]	N/A	82%	5%
43.	Wagner College (NY)	66	2.7	85%	75%	70%	66%	2%	13/1	1070-1250[2]	50%[5]	70%	7%
48.	Gannon University (PA)	65	2.6	83%	58%	68%	53%	0.3%	13/1	990-1220	53%[5]	80%	8%
48.	SUNY–Oswego*	65	2.9	80%	57%	66%	55%	5%	17/1	1075-1225[3]	52%	54%	6%
50.	Merrimack College (MA)	64	2.8	82%	59%	68%	38%	1%	14/1	1020-1190[2]	24%	82%	8%
50.	New York Inst. of Technology	64	2.8	75%	62%	50%	65%	1%	12/1	1040-1230	52%[4]	77%	8%
50.	Seton Hill University (PA)	64	2.7	81%	56%	58%	62%	1%	14/1	1020-1220[2]	47%	74%	16%
50.	SUNY–Fredonia*	64	2.7	79%	55%	63%	58%	5%	14/1	980-1190	35%	65%	4%
50.	Towson University (MD)*	64	3.1	85%	61%	72%	28%	3%	17/1	1055-1210	41%[5]	77%	5%
55.	Arcadia University (PA)	63	2.5	79%	64%	66%	66%	6%	11/1	1060-1240	55%	62%	10%
55.	CUNY–City College*	63	2.8	86%	48%	50%	32%	4%	15/1	980-1190	N/A	41%	15%
55.	CUNY–Queens College*	63	2.8	85%	58%	54%	34%	8%	15/1	1060-1220	N/A	43%	18%
55.	DeSales University (PA)	63	2.5	81%	61%	70%	57%	2%	12/1	1010-1230	52%[5]	74%	8%
55.	King's College (PA)	63	2.5	74%	57%	67%	55%	0%	13/1	980-1190[2]	42%	71%	14%
55.	SUNY College–Oneonta*	63	2.8	85%	58%	71%	34%	4%	17/1	1040-1190	39%[5]	60%	N/A
55.	University of St. Joseph (CT)	63	2.4	75%	62%	68%	77%	0.4%	9/1	970-1160[2]	54%	90%	14%
62.	Alfred University (NY)	62	2.7	74%	58%	53%	67%	3%	11/1	990-1210	41%	63%	8%
62.	Chatham University (PA)	62	2.4	80%	60%	63%	65%	2%	10/1	1050-1240[2]	51%	55%	12%
62.	Fairleigh Dickinson Univ. (NJ)	62	3.0	77%	60%	52%	71%	1%	14/1	1020-1210	49%	86%	3%
62.	St. Joseph's College New York	62	2.4	84%	57%	72%	67%	0%	13/1	1000-1170	N/A	69%	4%
62.	Wentworth Inst. of Technology (MA)	62	2.8	84%	58%	67%	37%	2%	18/1	1080-1270	41%[5]	92%	6%
67.	Geneva College (PA)	61	2.3	82%	43%	69%	67%	3%	12/1	950-1210	42%	69%	9%
68.	Iona College (NY)	60	2.7	78%	57%	64%	32%	0.2%	15/1	980-1180	21%[5]	92%	8%
68.	Mercyhurst University (PA)	60	2.5	80%	59%	68%	55%	0.3%	15/1	1000-1190[2]	29%[4]	70%	11%
68.	SUNY College–Cortland*	60	2.7	79%	57%	71%	30%	6%	16/1	1050-1200[9]	42%[5]	48%	7%
68.	West Chester Univ. of Pennsylvania*	60	2.8	87%	58%	73%	26%	6%	19/1	1040-1210	32%	69%	5%
68.	Western New England Univ. (MA)	60	2.7	77%	63%	59%	58%	0.1%	12/1	980-1180[2]	40%[5]	81%	4%
68.	Wilkes University (PA)	60	2.5	77%	60%	60%	55%	5%	13/1	1040-1220	51%	75%	13%
74.	Caldwell University (NJ)	58	2.3	80%	49%	66%	64%	1%	12/1	930-1150[3]	32%[5]	64%	11%
74.	CUNY–Brooklyn College*	58	2.8	82%	53%	58%	31%	4%	17/1	1030-1190	N/A	40%	6%
74.	Eastern University (PA)	58	2.3	76%	54%	66%	88%	0.2%	10/1	1000-1200[2]	N/A	66%	10%
74.	Johnson & Wales University (RI)	58	2.9	78%	55%	60%	48%	0%	19/1	980-1170[2]	N/A	88%	N/A
74.	Norwich University (VT)	58	2.8	76%	62%	60%	36%	4%	13/1	20-26[2]	34%[5]	65%	14%
74.	SUNY Maritime College*	58	2.9	86%	57%	62%	40%	2%	15/1	1100-1253[3]	33%[5]	69%	5%
74.	University of New England (ME)	58	2.7	79%	61%	60%	54%	6%	13/1	1030-1210	N/A	81%	7%
81.	Champlain College (VT)	57	2.6	80%	59%	60%	63%	0%	14/1	1090-1300[2]	42%[5]	75%	4%
81.	Keene State College (NH)*	57	2.7	74%	53%	62%	54%	1%	15/1	930-1140[2]	21%[5]	83%	4%
81.	Notre Dame of Maryland University	57	2.7	79%	64%	43%	90%	0%	7/1	870-1110[2]	69%[4]	71%	7%
81.	Saint Peter's University (NJ)	57	2.5	82%	47%	54%	57%	0%	13/1	930-1110[2]	43%[5]	71%	9%
81.	Stevenson University (MD)	57	2.7	79%	56%	54%	61%	0.1%	16/1	1010-1190	45%	61%	5%
81.	Waynesburg University (PA)	57	2.3	79%	56%	66%	69%	1%	13/1	980-1160	36%	95%	8%
87.	Salisbury University (MD)*	56	2.7	83%	64%	70%	33%	3%	16/1	1100-1260[9]	50%[5]	65%	6%
87.	SUNY College–Potsdam*	56	2.5	76%	48%	53%	71%	2%	11/1	1000-1190[2]	35%[5]	67%	7%
87.	SUNY–Plattsburgh*	56	2.5	82%	55%	63%	39%	4%	16/1	1050-1190[3]	47%[5]	53%	6%
90.	College at Brockport–SUNY*	55	2.5	81%	53%	66%	29%	7%	17/1	1000-1180	34%	53%	3%
90.	Monroe College (NY)	55	1.9	77%	28%	74%	50%	0%	17/1	744-1053[2]	N/A	52%	3%
90.	Slippery Rock U. of Pennsylvania*	55	2.7	82%	54%	66%	16%	10%	21/1	1000-1160	36%	71%	5%
93.	Eastern Connecticut State University*	54	2.6	76%	54%	55%	34%	0%	15/1	1000-1180[9]	36%	62%	8%
93.	Roberts Wesleyan College (NY)	54	2.3	79%	56%	60%	69%	2%	12/1	1040-1230	48%	69%	9%
93.	The Sage Colleges (NY)	54	2.3	79%	49%	56%	67%	0%	11/1	980-1170[2]	50%	56%	9%
93.	University of New Haven (CT)	54	2.6	80%	62%	60%	43%	3%	16/1	1010-1210	39%	88%	7%
93.	William Paterson Univ. of N.J.*	54	2.5	76%	49%	55%	52%	1%	14/1	930-1120	N/A	92%	4%
93.	York College of Pennsylvania	54	2.4	79%	58%	56%	52%	0%	15/1	1000-1190	34%	70%	7%
99.	Albertus Magnus College (CT)	53	2.3	73%	40%	57%	91%	0%	13/1	810-1050	N/A	64%	8%

Note: Key to footnotes Page 105.

Rank	School (State) (*Public)	Overall score	Peer assessment score (5.0=highest)	Average first-year student retention rate	2017 graduation rate: Predicted	2017 graduation rate: Actual	% of classes under 20 ('17)	% of classes of 50 or more ('17)	Student/faculty ratio ('17)	SAT/ACT 25th-75th percentile** ('17)	Freshmen in top 25% of HS class ('17)	Acceptance rate ('17)	Average alumni giving rate
99.	**College of Our Lady of the Elms** (MA)	53	2.0	83%	43%	57%	77%	0%	12/1	930-1130	N/A	79%	11%
99.	**College of Saint Rose** (NY)	53	2.3	77%	56%	59%	68%	0.1%	14/1	970-1142[9]	24%[5]	83%	12%
99.	**Manhattanville College** (NY)	53	2.5	78%	59%	55%	71%	0.2%	11/1	940-1160[2]	27%[5]	82%	10%
103.	**Millersville U. of Pennsylvania***	52	2.5	77%	56%	62%	32%	6%	18/1	970-1160	28%	79%	4%
103.	**SUNY Buffalo State***	52	2.7	70%	46%	50%	47%	4%	15/1	870-1070	30%[4]	58%	3%
105.	**Alvernia University** (PA)	51	2.4	78%	50%	60%	64%	2%	13/1	950-1148	32%[4]	71%	8%
105.	**Bay Path University** (MA)	51	2.2	75%	42%	58%	88%	0%	13/1	970-1190[2]	47%	63%	5%
105.	**Carlow University** (PA)	51	2.2	77%	46%	57%	72%	0.3%	12/1	900-1070	41%	92%	8%
105.	**Central Connecticut State University***	51	2.5	78%	50%	52%	40%	3%	16/1	980-1160	26%	67%	4%
105.	**Chestnut Hill College** (PA)	51	2.2	76%	41%	55%	85%	0%	10/1	960-1150	21%	96%	14%
105.	**Point Park University** (PA)	51	2.3	77%	49%	55%	74%	0.4%	13/1	980-1190	38%	65%	3%
105.	**Wheelock College**[1] (MA)	51	2.3	71%[8]	58%	60%[8]	60%[4]	0%[4]	9/1[4]	800-1015[4]	10%[4]	84%[4]	12%[4]
112.	**College of Mount St. Vincent** (NY)	50	2.2	75%	39%	54%	52%	0%	13/1	880-1060	17%[5]	91%	14%
112.	**Keuka College** (NY)	50	2.3	71%	52%	57%	77%	1%	8/1	980-1140[2]	33%[4]	87%	11%
112.	**Shippensburg U. of Pennsylvania***	50	2.6	72%	49%	52%	35%	3%	19/1	960-1140	25%	84%	10%
112.	**Southern New Hampshire University**	50	2.7	73%	49%	55%[6]	70%	0%	14/1	990-1160[2]	27%	95%	1%
112.	**Westfield State University** (MA)*	50	2.3	78%	51%	65%	38%	1%	16/1	970-1150	20%[5]	85%	3%
117.	**Bloomsburg U. of Pennsylvania***	49	2.5	77%	51%	58%	27%	5%	19/1	970-1150	29%	73%	5%
117.	**Bridgewater State University** (MA)*	49	2.5	79%	53%	59%	42%	0%	19/1	980-1160[2]	N/A	80%	5%
117.	**Worcester State University** (MA)*	49	2.5	80%	53%	55%	53%	0.2%	17/1	980-1170[2]	N/A	76%	7%
120.	**CUNY–Lehman College***	48	2.7	84%	43%	46%	46%	1%	17/1	970-1100	N/A	35%	3%
120.	**LIU Post** (NY)	48	2.3	75%	57%	48%	72%	1%	14/1	1055-1240	33%[5]	83%	3%
120.	**Utica College** (NY)	48	2.4	73%	50%	49%	62%	0%	13/1	980-1180[2]	33%	84%	7%
123.	**Framingham State University** (MA)*	47	2.5	75%	53%	54%	47%	1%	14/1	950-1130	21%[5]	68%	5%
123.	**Mansfield Univ. of Pennsylvania***	47	2.2	74%	46%	57%	50%	3%	15/1	950-1130[2]	29%	68%	N/A
123.	**Mount St. Mary College** (NY)	47	2.2	77%	53%	54%	55%	1%	13/1	1000-1160	29%	93%	7%
126.	**Cairn University** (PA)	46	1.9	73%	50%	58%	70%	2%	12/1	880-1125	36%[5]	99%	5%
126.	**Frostburg State University** (MD)*	46	2.5	76%	48%	49%	53%	2%	15/1	920-1110	29%	72%	5%
126.	**Lasell College** (MA)	46	2.2	76%	47%	54%	69%	0%	13/1	980-1160[2]	17%[5]	81%	9%
126.	**Lock Haven U. of Pennsylvania***	46	2.3	70%	46%	55%	40%	6%	17/1	910-1110	27%	89%	5%
126.	**Rosemont College** (PA)	46	2.2	68%	48%	61%	74%	0%	11/1	910-1110	N/A	70%	11%[4]
126.	**St. Thomas Aquinas College** (NY)	46	2.4	77%	54%	54%	71%	0%	12/1	880-1110[3]	23%[5]	78%	7%
132.	**Cabrini University** (PA)	45	2.3	73%	55%	55%[8]	78%	0.4%	13/1[4]	990-1160[9]	N/A	73%	9%[4]
132.	**Daemen College** (NY)	45	2.1	79%	56%	55%	61%	1%	12/1	1040-1220[2]	58%	49%	3%
132.	**Delaware Valley University** (PA)	45	2.3	70%	60%	56%	57%	2%	14/1	960-1165	23%[5]	66%	6%
132.	**Plymouth State University** (NH)*	45	2.5	72%	48%	57%	52%	1%	17/1	890-1130[2]	18%	79%	4%
132.	**Southern Connecticut State U.**[1]*	45	2.4	76%[8]	43%	52%[8]	43%[4]	1%[4]	14/1[4]	830-1030[4]	8%[4]	64%[4]	4%[4]
137.	**Fitchburg State University** (MA)*	44	2.4	77%	53%	60%	42%	1%	14/1	970-1140[2]	N/A	80%	3%
137.	**Kutztown Univ. of Pennsylvania***	44	2.5	73%	49%	53%	24%	8%	18/1	970-1140	24%	74%	5%
139.	**CUNY–John Jay Col. of Crim. Justice***	43	3.0	78%	40%	43%[8]	28%	1%	18/1	920-1060	N/A	34%[4]	1%[7]
139.	**Georgian Court University** (NJ)	43	2.1	76%	49%	48%	77%	0%	12/1	910-1120	28%	69%	6%
139.	**Kean University** (NJ)*	43	2.4	75%	46%	49%	37%	0%	17/1	880-1070	N/A	83%	3%

School (State) (*Public)	Peer assessment score (5.0=highest)	Average first-year student retention rate	2017 graduation rate: Predicted	2017 graduation rate: Actual	% of classes under 20 ('17)	% of classes of 50 or more ('17)	Student/faculty ratio ('17)	SAT/ACT 25th-75th percentile** ('17)	Freshmen in top 25% of HS class ('17)	Acceptance rate ('17)	Average alumni giving rate
SCHOOLS RANKED 142 THROUGH 187 ARE LISTED HERE ALPHABETICALLY											
Anna Maria College (MA)	1.9	67%	44%	42%	78%	0%	12/1	910-1110[2]	16%	79%	6%
Bowie State University (MD)*	2.3	74%	44%	37%[6]	46%	2%	16/1	860-1040	N/A	41%[4]	6%
California U. of Pennsylvania*	2.2	74%	48%	55%	32%	11%	20/1	930-1140	23%	94%	3%
Centenary University[1] (NJ)	2.1	80%[8]	51%	59%[8]	N/A	N/A	10/1[4]	830-1050[4]	N/A	88%[4]	N/A
Clarion U. of Pennsylvania*	2.2	74%	47%	52%	28%	6%	18/1	920-1120	27%	95%	2%
College of New Rochelle[1] (NY)	1.9	75%[8]	29%	31%[6]	71%[4]	1%[4]	14/1[4]	840-1020[4]	53%[4]	43%[4]	16%[4]
College of St. Elizabeth (NJ)	2.2	66%	52%	41%	83%[4]	0%[4]	10/1[4]	800-1000	N/A	64%	N/A
Coppin State University (MD)*	2.2	67%	31%	25%	N/A	N/A	14/1	850-1010[3]	N/A	N/A	N/A
CUNY–College of Staten Island*	2.5	80%	46%	48%	22%	6%	18/1	990-1160	N/A	100%	2%
Curry College (MA)	2.2	70%	53%	52%	58%	0%	13/1	930-1100[2]	16%[5]	90%	4%
Delaware State University*	2.5	71%	43%	37%	45%	4%	15/1	820-990	25%	45%	10%
Dominican College (NY)	2.1	72%	44%	43%	66%	0%	15/1	880-1080[2]	N/A	46%	N/A

NORTH ▶

School (State) (*Public)	Peer assessment score (5.0=highest)	Average first-year student retention rate	2017 graduation rate Predicted	Actual	% of classes under 20 ('17)	% of classes of 50 or more ('17)	Student/ faculty ratio ('17)	SAT/ACT 25th-75th percentile** ('17)	Freshmen in top 25% of HS class ('17)	Accept-ance rate ('17)	Average alumni giving rate
CONTINUED (SCHOOLS RANKED 142 THROUGH 187 ARE LISTED HERE ALPHABETICALLY)											
D'Youville College (NY)	2.0	79%	57%	53%	64%	1%	9/1	710-930	50%[5]	97%	13%
Eastern Nazarene College (MA)	2.0	70%	45%	49%	N/A	N/A	8/1[4]	940-1160	34%[4]	68%	N/A
East Stroudsburg Univ. of Pa.*	2.5	72%	51%	49%	41%	8%	19/1	910-1090[2]	23%	79%	4%
Edinboro Univ. of Pennsylvania[1]*	2.2	70%[8]	40%	49%[6]	N/A	N/A	18/1[4]	830-1070[4]	N/A	95%[4]	N/A
Felician University (NJ)	2.1	81%	49%	47%	68%	0.4%	14/1	900-1080	23%	79%	3%
Franklin Pierce University (NH)	2.3	67%	53%	49%	60%	2%	14/1	940-1160[2]	20%	76%	5%
Green Mountain College (VT)	2.0	66%	54%	51%	75%	0%	14/1	925-1175[2]	N/A	78%	9%
Gwynedd Mercy University (PA)	2.3	80%	48%	58%	59%	8%	11/1	930-1110	21%	94%	4%
Harrisburg Univ. of Science and Tech. (PA)	2.2	55%	51%	32%	N/A	N/A	32/1[4]	N/A[2]	N/A	N/A	N/A
Holy Family University (PA)	2.1	76%	52%	55%	62%	0%	15/1	920-1090	28%	71%	4%
Husson University (ME)	2.2	76%	44%	54%	53%	0.2%	15/1	950-1130	37%	86%	4%
Johnson State College[1] (VT)*	2.1	69%[8]	41%	35%[6]	N/A	N/A	13/1[4]	783-1058[4]	N/A	95%[4]	N/A
Lincoln University (PA)*	2.0	73%	39%	46%	22%	0%	15/1	870-1070	34%[5]	80%	13%
Medaille College[1] (NY)	1.9	64%[8]	44%	42%[6]	N/A	N/A	16/1[4]	780-990[4]	N/A	69%[4]	N/A
Metropolitan College of New York	1.8	45%	29%	15%	94%	0%	11/1	N/A[2]	N/A	91%	N/A
Neumann University (PA)	2.2	72%	53%	57%	59%	2%	15/1	890-1080	N/A	96%	8%
New England College (NH)	2.3	58%	39%	43%	80%	0%	15/1	870-1080[2]	30%[5]	100%	5%
New Jersey City University*	2.1	76%	36%	25%	45%	1%	15/1	870-1080[3]	28%	91%	2%
Nyack College (NY)	2.0	66%	36%	46%	81%	1%	12/1	860-1110[2]	16%[5]	98%	5%
Post University (CT)	2.1	41%	42%	27%	68%	0%	23/1	850-850[9]	N/A	61%	N/A
Rhode Island College*	2.5	76%	49%	46%	50%	1%	14/1	880-1090	39%	74%	3%
Rivier University[1] (NH)	2.1	76%[8]	51%	49%[6]	N/A	N/A	15/1[4]	N/A[2]	N/A	71%[4]	N/A
Salem State University (MA)*	2.4	79%	52%	52%	46%	0.4%	14/1	980-1150[2]	N/A	82%	4%
St. Joseph's College[1] (ME)	2.4	81%[8]	54%	57%[6]	N/A	N/A	12/1[4]	810-1020[4]	N/A	78%[4]	N/A
SUNY College–Old Westbury*	2.3	82%	45%	47%	24%	1%	17/1	950-1100[3]	N/A	78%	N/A
Thomas College[1] (ME)	2.1	69%[8]	38%	45%[6]	N/A	N/A	18/1[4]	N/A[2]	N/A	N/A	N/A
Touro College (NY)	1.9	67%	55%	49%	86%	0.4%	11/1	1010-1300[2]	N/A	74%	N/A
Trinity Washington University[1] (DC)	2.6	65%[8]	32%	43%[6]	N/A	N/A	12/1[4]	N/A[2]	N/A	89%[4]	N/A
University of Baltimore*	2.5	73%	45%	33%	41%	0%	14/1	900-1110	N/A	81%	4%
University of Bridgeport (CT)	2.1	65%	44%	42%	72%	1%	17/1	860-1050	31%[5]	54%	4%
University of Southern Maine*	2.5	65%	46%	33%	54%	3%	14/1	950-1160	37%	83%	2%
Univ. of the District of Columbia*	1.8	63%	57%	44%	79%	4%	N/A	700-910[4]	N/A	39%	0.4%[4]
Washington Adventist University (MD)	1.9	71%	38%	37%	89%	0%	9/1	800-1000[2]	N/A	62%	1%
Western Connecticut State University*	2.4	75%	51%	44%	41%	2%	13/1	910-1150[2]	24%	71%	2%

SOUTH ▶

Rank	School (State) (*Public)	Overall score	Peer assessment score (5.0=highest)	Average first-year student retention rate	2017 graduation rate Predicted	Actual	% of classes under 20 ('17)	% of classes of 50 or more ('17)	Student/ faculty ratio ('17)	SAT/ACT 25th-75th percentile** ('17)	Freshmen in top 25% of HS class ('17)	Accept-ance rate ('17)	Average alumni giving rate
1.	**Elon University** (NC)	100	4.1	90%	80%	84%	51%	0%	12/1	1140-1330	54%[5]	67%	22%
2.	**Rollins College** (FL)	98	3.8	85%	77%	75%	75%	0%	10/1	1195-1350[2]	58%[5]	64%	7%
3.	**The Citadel** (SC)*	91	3.9	86%	61%	73%	41%	1%	12/1	20-25	30%	81%	25%
4.	**Samford University** (AL)	90	3.9	88%	76%	76%	66%	3%	12/1	23-29	58%[5]	83%	9%
5.	**Stetson University** (FL)	87	3.6	78%	65%	62%	60%	0.2%	13/1	1110-1290[2]	50%	68%	9%
6.	**Belmont University** (TN)	84	3.8	84%	71%	70%	43%	1%	13/1	24-29	56%[5]	81%	8%
6.	**James Madison University** (VA)*	84	4.0	87%	72%	83%	34%	13%	16/1	1100-1260[2]	51%	75%	7%
8.	**Appalachian State University** (NC)*	83	3.7	87%	61%	74%	33%	8%	16/1	24-27	57%	70%	7%
9.	**Berry College** (GA)	82	3.3	81%	75%	64%	56%	0%	11/1	24-29[3]	66%	62%	15%
10.	**Christopher Newport Univ.** (VA)*	81	3.3	87%	66%	75%	59%	3%	15/1	1110-1270[2]	50%	72%	20%
11.	**College of Charleston** (SC)*	79	3.8	79%	67%	69%	41%	5%	15/1	22-27	53%	80%	5%
12.	**Loyola University New Orleans**	77	3.4	79%	68%	56%	53%	1%	11/1	22-28	60%[5]	69%	6%
13.	**John Brown University** (AR)	76	3.0	83%	68%	73%	52%	0%	14/1	24-29[2]	58%[5]	76%	11%
14.	**Asbury University** (KY)	75	3.0	82%	62%	69%	69%	0.3%	12/1	21-28	66%[5]	70%	17%
15.	**Embry-Riddle Aeronautical U.** (FL)	73	3.7	79%	71%	59%	21%	2%	17/1	1080-1320[2]	50%	75%	2%
15.	**Univ. of North Carolina–Wilmington***	73	3.4	85%	64%	72%	28%	10%	18/1	23-27	62%	67%	5%
17.	**Bellarmine University** (KY)	72	3.0	78%	68%	65%	58%	0%	12/1	22-27	52%[4]	89%	12%
18.	**Queens University of Charlotte** (NC)	71	3.1	76%	59%	54%	64%	0%	10/1	1010-1198	42%	79%	21%
19.	**Univ. of Mary Washington** (VA)*	70	3.3	82%	66%	71%	48%	4%	14/1	1080-1260[2]	46%	73%	12%
20.	**Florida Southern College**	69	2.9	81%	62%	63%	60%	0%	15/1	23-28	60%[5]	51%	9%

Note: Key to footnotes Page 105.

SOUTH ▶

Rank	School (State) (*Public)	Overall score	Peer assessment score (5.0=highest)	Average first-year student retention rate	2017 graduation rate: Predicted	2017 graduation rate: Actual	% of classes under 20 ('17)	% of classes of 50 or more ('17)	Student/faculty ratio ('17)	SAT/ACT 25th-75th percentile** ('17)	Freshmen in top 25% of HS class ('17)	Acceptance rate ('17)	Average alumni giving rate
20.	Harding University (AR)	69	3.0	83%	64%	67%	54%	7%	14/1	22-28	51%	74%	10%
20.	University of Tampa (FL)	69	3.3	75%	59%	60%	34%	3%	18/1	1070-1230	46%[5]	53%	18%
23.	Converse College (SC)	68	2.7	70%	59%	72%	86%	1%	14/1	20-26	50%	71%	11%
23.	Milligan College (TN)	68	2.7	78%	61%	64%	74%	3%	9/1	23-27	65%[4]	67%	18%
25.	Longwood University (VA)*	67	3.0	80%	57%	68%	54%	1%	14/1	960-1140	29%	92%	11%
25.	Winthrop University (SC)*	67	3.3	76%	55%	57%	49%	2%	14/1	19-25	51%	73%	7%
27.	Hampton University (VA)	66	3.0	78%	56%	55%	54%	6%	13/1	20-24[2]	35%	36%	17%
28.	Georgia College & State University*	65	3.3	85%	64%	66%	38%	4%	17/1	23-27	N/A	79%	3%
28.	Xavier University of Louisiana	65	3.2	72%	49%	44%	55%	3%	14/1	20-25	54%	64%	17%
30.	Campbell University (NC)	64	3.1	73%	58%	50%	58%	7%	15/1	20-25	60%	81%	7%
31.	Mary Baldwin University (VA)	63	2.9	66%	43%	45%	81%	0.4%	9/1	950-1200	55%	95%	14%
32.	Mississippi College	62	3.1	77%	56%	59%	55%	5%	14/1	22-29[3]	63%	39%	5%
32.	University of Lynchburg (VA)	62	2.7	75%	57%	59%	64%	1%	11/1	1000-1180	17%	75%	14%
34.	Bob Jones University (SC)	61	2.1	81%	47%	69%	65%	8%	12/1	24-27	35%[5]	86%	8%
34.	Murray State University (KY)*	61	3.1	73%	55%	49%	58%	3%	15/1	21-27	52%	87%	6%
34.	Western Carolina University (NC)*	61	3.1	79%	51%	59%	27%	5%	17/1	20-24	38%	39%	5%
34.	Western Kentucky University*	61	3.2	72%	51%	51%	48%	6%	18/1	19-27	46%	95%	7%
38.	Wheeling Jesuit University (WV)	60	2.5	70%	63%	63%	64%	3%	13/1	19-24	38%	51%	8%
39.	Christian Brothers University (TN)	59	2.8	81%	55%	44%	66%	0%	13/1	21-27	56%	53%	16%
39.	Freed-Hardeman University (TN)	59	2.5	77%	57%	55%	62%	4%	13/1	22-28	58%	95%	10%
39.	William Carey University (MS)	59	2.6	80%	37%	57%	71%	1%	15/1	21-28[3]	54%	49%	4%
42.	Marshall University (WV)*	58	3.4	73%	52%	49%	45%	5%	19/1	19-25	N/A	90%	4%
42.	University of Montevallo (AL)*	58	3.0	77%	56%	50%	48%	1%	14/1	20-26	N/A	67%	8%
42.	University of North Florida*	58	3.0	81%	59%	57%	30%	11%	18/1	1090-1280	43%	59%	4%
42.	University of Tennessee–Martin*	58	2.8	74%	50%	50%	60%	3%	15/1	20-25	44%	62%	6%
46.	Radford University (VA)*	57	3.1	75%	48%	55%	35%	9%	16/1	940-1120[2]	21%	74%	3%
47.	Brenau University (GA)	56	2.8	66%	44%	48%	72%	2%	9/1	880-1090[2]	37%	69%	4%
47.	Columbia International Univ. (SC)	56	2.3	74%	51%	66%	73%	7%	15/1	840-1070	25%	28%	8%
47.	Eastern Mennonite University (VA)	56	2.4	75%	63%	63%	72%	1%	9/1	990-1170	N/A	54%	N/A
47.	Lee University (TN)	56	2.9	79%	55%	52%	55%	6%	16/1	21-28	50%	85%	8%
47.	Saint Leo University (FL)	56	2.7	71%	40%	45%	44%	0%	14/1	970-1140[2]	30%	88%	5%
52.	Coastal Carolina University (SC)*	55	3.0	67%	48%	42%	38%	2%	17/1	19-24	36%	61%	11%
52.	Columbia College (SC)	55	2.5	72%	43%	49%	70%	0%	15/1	17-21[2]	34%	87%	10%
52.	Palm Beach Atlantic University (FL)	55	2.7	75%	56%	54%	63%	2%	12/1	980-1200	44%	97%	2%
52.	Wingate University (NC)	55	2.9	74%	55%	53%	41%	1%	16/1	18-23	32%	93%	10%
56.	Jacksonville University (FL)	54	2.8	70%	58%	43%	71%	1%	11/1	21-27[2]	N/A	87%	5%
56.	Keiser University (FL)	54	1.9	85%	34%	55%	95%	3%	12/1	N/A[2]	N/A	N/A	1%
58.	Lincoln Memorial University (TN)	53	2.6	69%	48%	53%	63%	2%	14/1	19-25[9]	N/A	61%	5%
58.	Marymount University (VA)	53	2.8	78%	54%	53%	54%	0.2%	13/1	960-1140[2]	26%[5]	92%	4%
58.	Mississippi Univ. for Women*	53	3.0	66%	48%	44%	57%	7%	14/1	18-23	48%	98%	11%
58.	University of North Georgia*	53	3.1	81%	54%	54%	33%	3%	19/1	1030-1180	62%[5]	65%	7%
58.	West Virginia Wesleyan College	53	2.6	72%	55%	50%	64%	0.3%	13/1	19-25	49%	71%	16%
63.	Piedmont College (GA)	52	2.5	68%	45%	49%	72%	0%	10/1	950-1130[3]	28%	60%	5%
64.	North Carolina Central Univ.*	51	2.5	79%	35%	44%	38%	5%	16/1	890-1030	22%	83%	11%
65.	Anderson University (SC)	50	2.8	76%	55%	57%	42%	7%	16/1	1000-1190	58%	79%	5%
65.	Belhaven University (MS)	50	2.7	66%	43%	51%	83%	1%	11/1	22-25	27%[5]	59%	3%
65.	Morehead State University (KY)*	50	2.8	70%	54%	42%	51%	4%	18/1	20-26	51%	80%	9%
65.	Southern Adventist University (TN)	50	2.3	77%	49%	50%	65%	7%	14/1	20-27	N/A	95%	12%
65.	Univ. of Tennessee–Chattanooga*	50	3.1	72%	55%	45%	40%	9%	19/1	21-26	N/A	83%	4%
70.	U. of South Florida–St. Petersburg*	49	2.9	71%	50%	36%	24%	10%	19/1	1080-1230	46%	40%	16%
71.	Bryan College (TN)	48	2.4	68%	56%	47%	70%	3%	15/1	20-26[2]	44%[5]	54%	7%
71.	Elizabeth City State Univ. (NC)*	48	2.1	71%	27%	37%	74%	0%	14/1	860-990[3]	3%	60%	N/A
71.	King University (TN)	48	2.3	72%	46%	52%	78%	1%	13/1	18-28[2]	50%	59%	6%
71.	Lenoir-Rhyne University (NC)	48	2.6	71%	51%	43%	56%	0%	13/1	870-1090[4]	N/A	74%	12%
71.	University of Central Arkansas*	48	2.8	72%	52%	41%	50%	2%	16/1	21-27	49%	90%	7%
76.	Carson-Newman University (TN)	47	2.8	69%	54%	46%	57%	0.2%	13/1	20-26	N/A	67%	6%
76.	Eastern Kentucky University*	47	2.9	73%	51%	49%	37%	6%	16/1	20-25	42%	87%	4%
78.	Florida Gulf Coast University*	46	2.9	79%	50%	48%	16%	15%	22/1	21-25	36%	64%	3%
78.	Francis Marion University (SC)*	46	2.6	68%	43%	37%	59%	4%	14/1	17-22	46%	60%	6%
78.	North Greenville University (SC)	46	2.3	73%	50%	51%	74%	0.2%	14/1	19-28[3]	38%	60%	2%[4]
78.	Pfeiffer University (NC)	46	2.4	64%	44%	42%	79%	0.1%	11/1	16-22[2]	28%	66%	9%

Note: Key to footnotes Page 105.

Rank	School (State) (*Public)	Overall score	Peer assessment score (5.0=highest)	Average first-year student retention rate	2017 graduation rate: Predicted	2017 graduation rate: Actual	% of classes under 20 ('17)	% of classes of 50 or more ('17)	Student/ faculty ratio ('17)	SAT/ACT 25th-75th percentile** ('17)	Freshmen in top 25% of HS class ('17)	Accept- ance rate ('17)	Average alumni giving rate
78.	University of North Alabama*	46	2.8	75%	52%	44%	47%	4%	19/1	19-25	N/A	70%	5%
78.	Virginia State University*	46	2.4	70%	28%	43%	N/A	N/A	15/1	820-1010[3]	18%[5]	91%	5%
84.	Northern Kentucky University*	45	2.9	71%	50%	40%	35%	4%	19/1	20-26	34%	90%	4%
85.	Austin Peay State University (TN)*	44	3.0	69%	42%	36%	50%	5%	18/1	19-24[2]	35%	90%	3%
85.	St. Thomas University (FL)	44	2.5	67%	42%	44%	61%	0%	11/1	860-1080	40%[5]	49%	2%
87.	Methodist University (NC)	43	2.4	62%	43%	41%	65%[4]	0%[4]	11/1	18-23	37%	57%	11%
87.	Thomas More College (KY)	43	2.5	69%	57%	44%	66%	1%	16/1	19-24	N/A	91%	9%
89.	Alcorn State University (MS)*	42	2.4	75%	30%	33%	48%	2%	19/1	16-21	N/A	83%	8%
89.	Charleston Southern University (SC)	42	2.7	67%	46%	34%	52%	1%	14/1	20-22	52%	56%	21%
91.	Henderson State University (AR)*	41	2.6	61%	42%	32%	67%	1%	13/1	19-25	37%	80%	4%
91.	Louisiana College	41	2.2	55%	35%	43%	69%	2%	12/1	19-24	30%[5]	72%	1%
91.	Norfolk State University (VA)*	41	2.4	74%	32%	39%	57%	2%	17/1	840-1040	15%	90%	N/A
91.	University of Charleston (WV)	41	2.9	63%	54%	49%	57%	1%	15/1	18-22[3]	N/A	64%	6%
95.	Arkansas State University[1]*	40	2.9	75%[8]	49%	40%[6]	N/A	N/A	18/1[4]	21-26[4]	N/A	70%[4]	8%[7]
95.	Auburn University–Montgomery (AL)*	40	3.0	66%	50%	28%	47%	3%	16/1	19-24	43%	83%	3%
95.	Fayetteville State University (NC)*	40	2.3	75%	29%	33%	42%	1%	15/1	870-1020	24%	68%	2%
95.	Montreat College (NC)	40	2.2	60%	38%	32%	84%	0%	9/1	920-1150	28%	65%	N/A
95.	Tuskegee University[1] (AL)	40	3.0	72%[8]	53%	46%[6]	N/A	N/A	14/1[4]	21-22[4]	N/A	50%[4]	N/A
100.	Lynn University (FL)	39	2.5	70%	56%	51%	54%	0.2%	17/1	958-1130[2]	14%[4]	85%	3%
100.	Nicholls State University (LA)*	39	2.6	69%	51%	47%	39%	10%	19/1	20-24	40%	94%	6%
102.	Arkansas Tech University*	38	2.6	70%	42%	41%	45%	5%	19/1	19-25	36%	95%	3%
102.	Columbus State University (GA)*	38	2.7	74%	42%	33%	52%	5%	17/1	870-1070	37%	53%	3%
102.	Southern Wesleyan University[1] (SC)	38	2.3	71%[8]	40%	53%[6]	N/A	N/A	18/1[4]	N/A[2]	N/A	55%[4]	N/A
102.	Tusculum University (TN)	38	2.5	63%	36%	33%	67%	0.2%	17/1	17-24	N/A	89%	19%
102.	U. of North Carolina–Pembroke*	38	2.5	68%	40%	38%	51%	3%	16/1	18-21	32%	81%	4%

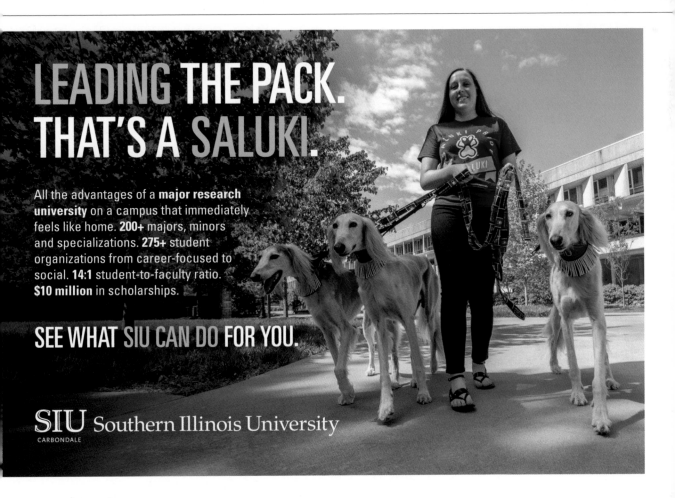

SOUTH ▶

School (State) (*Public)	Peer assessment score (5.0=highest)	Average first-year student retention rate	2017 graduation rate Predicted	2017 graduation rate Actual	% of classes under 20 ('17)	% of classes of 50 or more ('17)	Student/faculty ratio ('17)	SAT/ACT 25th-75th percentile** ('17)	Freshmen in top 25% of HS class ('17)	Acceptance rate ('17)	Average alumni giving rate
SCHOOLS RANKED 107 THROUGH 141 ARE LISTED HERE ALPHABETICALLY											
Alabama Agricultural and Mechanical University*	2.4	59%[8]	35%	24%	41%	3%	18/1	16-19[3]	N/A	90%	11%
Alabama State University*	2.3	59%	32%	28%	49%	0.3%	15/1	16-19	34%[5]	98%	4%
Albany State University (GA)*	2.2	69%	28%	34%	42%	1%	15/1	740-900	24%[5]	97%	7%[4]
Amridge University (AL)	1.8	N/A	30%	26%[6]	N/A	N/A	N/A	N/A	N/A	N/A	N/A
Bethel University (TN)	2.4	58%[8]	35%	27%	77%	1%	20/1	16-21[2]	23%	94%	N/A
Campbellsville University (KY)	2.6	61%	47%	34%	70%	0.2%	13/1	18-24	33%	69%	7%
Clayton State University (GA)*	2.3	69%	40%	31%	42%	3%	18/1	860-1020	N/A	42%	2%
Concord University (WV)*	2.2	66%	43%	35%	70%	1%	15/1	18-23	42%	90%	4%
Cumberland University (TN)	2.4	67%	53%	50%	53%	3%	17/1	19-23	8%[5]	52%	5%
Delta State University[1] (MS)*	2.4	65%[8]	43%	34%[6]	N/A	N/A	14/1[4]	19-25[4]	N/A	89%[4]	N/A
Fairmont State University (WV)*	2.3	66%	43%	36%	59%	3%	15/1	18-23	33%	71%	1%
Faulkner University (AL)	2.5	57%	31%	28%	70%	2%	12/1	18-22	60%[4]	52%	2%
Fort Valley State University (GA)*	2.2	71%	30%	27%	52%	4%	17/1	820-910	16%	41%	9%
Georgia Southwestern State University*	2.3	70%	43%	25%	49%	3%	18/1	960-1110	36%	67%	2%
Grambling State University (LA)*	2.3	66%	28%	39%	36%	8%	26/1	16-20	15%	43%	4%
Jacksonville State University (AL)*	2.7	75%	46%	37%	42%	5%	19/1	19-26[3]	45%	54%	8%[4]
Lindsey Wilson College (KY)	2.3	61%	35%	33%	60%	0%	13/1	19-24[2]	36%	94%	11%
Louisiana State University–Shreveport[1]*	2.5	65%[8]	53%	34%[6]	56%[4]	4%[4]	20/1[4]	N/A	N/A	89%[4]	N/A
McNeese State University (LA)*	2.6	68%	50%	41%	45%	7%	21/1	20-25	45%	62%	4%
Midway University[1] (KY)	2.1	79%[8]	37%	45%[6]	N/A	N/A	14/1[4]	18-23[4]	49%[4]	60%[4]	N/A
Mississippi Valley State Univ.*	2.2	63%	22%	30%	60%	1%	15/1	16-19	N/A	86%	N/A
Northwestern State University of Louisiana*	2.5	71%	48%	37%	48%	6%	19/1	19-24	40%	80%	N/A
Savannah State University (GA)*	2.3	60%[8]	30%	28%	32%	0.1%	17/1	860-1010[3]	N/A	52%	5%
South Carolina State University*	2.1	65%	33%	36%	54%	2%	17/1	15-18	27%	78%	7%
Southeastern Louisiana University*	2.4	64%	47%	41%	34%	6%	19/1	20-24	37%	88%	4%
Southeastern University (FL)	2.4	68%	42%	40%	60%	4%	20/1	19-24[3]	28%	54%	4%
Southern Arkansas University*	2.2	64%	43%	35%	44%	5%	18/1	19-25	40%	69%	6%
Southern Univ. and A&M College (LA)*	2.2	65%	25%	29%	38%	8%	16/1	16-20	7%[4]	34%	14%
Southern University–New Orleans*	2.1	53%	26%	20%	46%	0.3%	20/1	15-18	24%[5]	25%	1%
South University[1] (GA)	1.8	43%[8]	22%	9%[6]	N/A	N/A	11/1[4]	N/A[2]	N/A	N/A	N/A
Thomas University (GA)	1.9	63%[8]	39%	27%[6]	N/A	N/A	N/A	N/A[2]	N/A	23%	N/A
Troy University (AL)*	3.0	67%[8]	49%	41%	20%	50%	15/1	18-25	N/A	88%	N/A
Union College[1] (KY)	2.4	61%[8]	43%	30%[6]	N/A	N/A	16/1[4]	18-22[4]	N/A	67%[4]	N/A
University of West Alabama*	2.5	65%	38%	32%	58%	8%	13/1	18-23	N/A	28%	3%
Winston-Salem State Univ.[1] (NC)*	2.6	77%[8]	38%	46%[6]	N/A	N/A	14/1[4]	800-940[4]	N/A	63%[4]	N/A

MIDWEST ▶

Rank	School (State) (*Public)	Overall score	Peer assessment score (5.0=highest)	Average first-year student retention rate	2017 graduation rate Predicted	2017 graduation rate Actual	% of classes under 20 ('17)	% of classes of 50 or more ('17)	Student/faculty ratio ('17)	SAT/ACT 25th-75th percentile** ('17)	Freshmen in top 25% of HS class ('17)	Acceptance rate ('17)	Average alumni giving rate
1.	**Butler University** (IN)	100	4.0	90%	82%	79%	52%	3%	11/1	25-30	76%[5]	65%	22%
1.	**Creighton University** (NE)	100	4.2	90%	83%	81%	46%	7%	11/1	25-30	69%[5]	72%	12%
3.	**Drake University** (IA)	93	3.9	88%	80%	79%	55%	5%	11/1	24-30[2]	66%	69%	11%
4.	**John Carroll University** (OH)	87	3.5	85%	63%	78%	54%	0.3%	12/1	22-27	57%[5]	85%	14%
5.	**Valparaiso University** (IN)	85	3.8	84%	70%	72%	46%	4%	11/1	23-29	63%	84%	16%
6.	**Bradley University** (IL)	83	3.6	87%	70%	72%	56%	2%	12/1	22-28	60%	71%	9%
7.	**University of Evansville** (IN)	80	3.3	85%	72%	73%	68%	1%	11/1	22-29[2]	67%	70%	12%
8.	**Xavier University** (OH)	79	3.7	85%	70%	69%	42%	1%	12/1	22-28[3]	45%[5]	74%	14%
9.	**Truman State University** (MO)*	78	3.7	88%	76%	75%	46%	2%	16/1	24-30	83%	67%	7%
10.	**Milwaukee School of Engineering**	72	3.4	84%	74%	67%	43%	0.2%	16/1	25-30	N/A	63%	7%
11.	**Dominican University** (IL)	71	2.9	78%	54%	62%	64%	0.1%	11/1	20-25	55%	65%	15%
11.	**Franciscan Univ. of Steubenville** (OH)	71	2.6	86%	65%	78%	55%	1%	14/1	23-28	55%[5]	84%	12%
13.	**Baldwin Wallace University** (OH)	70	3.1	81%	64%	67%	63%	1%	11/1	21-27[2]	48%	78%	7%
13.	**Hamline University** (MN)	70	3.3	81%	60%	67%	47%	1%	13/1	20-26	43%	69%	10%
13.	**North Central College** (IL)	70	3.1	79%	67%	68%	41%	0.2%	14/1	22-27	55%[5]	54%	17%
13.	**St. Catherine University** (MN)	70	3.3	82%	61%	58%	65%	2%	10/1	21-26	62%	70%	13%
17.	**Bethel University** (MN)	69	3.0	85%	66%	70%	56%	3%	11/1	21-27	52%	83%	8%
17.	**Nebraska Wesleyan University**	69	3.1	78%	69%	64%	72%	1%	11/1	22-28	51%	71%	15%
17.	**Otterbein University** (OH)	69	3.3	81%	64%	64%	63%	2%	11/1	21-27	55%	76%	11%
20.	**Augsburg University** (MN)	68	3.2	77%	51%	63%	63%	0%	13/1	19-24	N/A	45%	8%
20.	**Elmhurst College** (IL)	68	3.3	80%	60%	64%	55%	1%	14/1	20-26	49%[5]	71%	9%

Note: Key to footnotes Page 105.

MIDWEST ▶

Rank School (State) (*Public)	Overall score	Peer assessment score (5.0=highest)	Average first-year student retention rate	2017 graduation rate Predicted	Actual	% of classes under 20 ('17)	% of classes of 50 or more ('17)	Student/faculty ratio ('17)	SAT/ACT 25th-75th percentile** ('17)	Freshmen in top 25% of HS class ('17)	Acceptance rate ('17)	Average alumni giving rate
20. Lewis University (IL)	68	2.9	82%	58%	67%	64%	0.4%	13/1	21-26	49%	54%	7%
23. Rockhurst University (MO)	67	3.1	86%	72%	75%	41%	1%	13/1	22-27	56%	72%	13%
23. Webster University (MO)	67	2.8	77%	61%	64%	90%	0%	9/1	21-26	37%	47%	3%
25. Kettering University (MI)	65	3.0	93%	77%	62%	49%	1%	15/1	1190-1350	60%	70%	8%
25. University of Detroit Mercy	65	2.9	84%	70%	62%	47%	5%	10/1	1040-1230	54%	65%	9%
25. University of Northern Iowa*	65	3.3	83%	62%	67%	29%	8%	18/1	21-26	46%	81%	8%
28. University of St. Francis (IL)	63	2.8	80%	60%	63%	67%	0.3%	12/1	20-25	41%[5]	52%	8%
29. Bethel College (IN)	61	2.7	78%	48%	64%	68%	3%	12/1	950-1160	41%	90%	9%
29. Drury University (MO)	61	2.9	81%	60%	55%	57%	0.2%	13/1	23-28	66%	72%	12%
29. Grand Valley State University (MI)*	61	3.1	84%	58%	65%	25%	6%	17/1	1060-1230	45%	81%	5%
32. Indiana Wesleyan University	60	2.9	82%	60%	63%	66%	2%	14/1	21-26	57%	72%	7%
32. Robert Morris University (IL)	60	2.5	49%	38%	76%	51%	1%	21/1	16-20[2]	10%	67%	1%
32. Univ. of Wisconsin–La Crosse*	60	3.2	85%	68%	71%	27%	12%	19/1	22-26	58%	81%	3%
35. Capital University (OH)	58	2.7	76%	62%	59%	64%	1%	11/1	22-27[3]	48%	69%	8%
35. Concordia University (NE)	58	2.7	76%	62%	67%	53%	2%	14/1	21-26	43%	75%	20%
37. University of Findlay (OH)	57	2.8	80%	65%	61%	58%	1%	16/1	21-27	56%	75%	9%
38. Aquinas College (MI)	56	2.8	78%	58%	59%	67%	0%	11/1	1020-1220	N/A	75%	13%
38. Eastern Illinois University*	56	2.6	74%	51%	56%	53%	2%	14/1	18-23	33%	52%	3%
38. Marian University (IN)	56	2.8	77%	55%	52%	67%	1%	14/1	1000-1200	44%	59%	15%
38. St. Ambrose University (IA)	56	2.9	78%	58%	63%	46%	0.3%	12/1	21-26[3]	42%[5]	61%	6%
38. University of Indianapolis	56	3.1	75%	57%	56%	55%	1%	13/1	990-1180	47%	86%	11%
38. University of Michigan–Dearborn*	56	2.8	81%	59%	58%	30%	9%	17/1	1060-1290	55%	64%	8%
38. Univ. of Wisconsin–Eau Claire*	56	3.1	83%	62%	67%	21%	16%	22/1	21-26	48%	86%	7%
45. University of Minnesota–Duluth*	55	3.0	77%	60%	59%	37%	16%	18/1	22-26	48%	77%	6%
45. Ursuline College (OH)	55	2.6	68%	50%	53%	89%	0%	8/1	18-24	50%	93%	13%
47. Alverno College (WI)	54	3.1	72%	38%	45%	81%	0%	10/1	17-22	38%[4]	78%	9%
47. Anderson University (IN)	54	2.8	75%	57%	57%	70%	2%	10/1	910-1110	43%	65%	10%
47. College of St. Scholastica (MN)	54	2.9	83%	60%	67%	48%	5%	14/1	19-27	55%	68%	5%
50. Baker University (KS)	53	2.6	76%	59%	57%	72%	0%	13/1	21-25	48%	86%	9%
50. St. Mary's Univ. of Minnesota	53	2.8	77%	57%	58%	73%	0%	18/1	20-25	38%[4]	64%	8%
50. Univ. of Illinois–Springfield*	53	2.9	77%	61%	50%	57%	1%	13/1	20-27	54%	52%	5%
53. Carroll University (WI)	52	2.9	80%	60%	66%	55%	4%	16/1	21-26	47%	71%	9%
53. Olivet Nazarene University (IL)	52	2.7	77%	60%	66%	43%	9%	17/1	20-26	47%	66%	13%
53. Spring Arbor University (MI)	52	2.6	79%	50%	60%	66%	1%	13/1	1000-1205	48%	67%	9%
53. Univ. of Nebraska–Kearney*	52	2.8	81%	54%	61%	51%	2%	14/1	19-25	44%	82%	7%
53. Western Illinois University*	52	2.6	69%	49%	50%	55%	3%	14/1	18-23	30%	60%	4%
58. Heidelberg University (OH)	51	2.8	69%	50%	49%	64%	0%	14/1	20-26	N/A	76%	17%
58. Mount Mercy University (IA)	51	2.5	76%	54%	58%	58%	1%	15/1	19-24	44%	57%	11%
58. Univ. of Northwestern–St. Paul (MN)	51	2.6	83%[8]	63%	62%	56%	4%	18/1	21-27	50%	93%	5%
58. Walsh University (OH)	51	2.5	78%	53%	61%	74%	0.1%	13/1	20-26[2]	40%[4]	79%	10%
62. Lawrence Technological Univ. (MI)	50	2.8	82%	71%	48%	75%	0.3%	11/1	1060-1280	54%[5]	60%	4%
62. Morningside College (IA)	50	2.4	72%	55%	56%	63%	0%	14/1	20-25	38%	55%	20%
62. Muskingum University (OH)	50	2.6	72%	51%	48%	69%	1%	12/1	18-24	40%	74%	13%
65. Madonna University (MI)	49	2.4	79%	54%	70%	70%	2%	13/1	19-24	30%	74%	2%
65. McKendree University (IL)	49	2.6	75%	54%	51%	69%	0%	14/1	19-25[2]	39%	62%	8%
65. North Park University (IL)	49	2.8	76%	55%	59%	60%	1%	10/1	19-24	N/A	54%	N/A
65. Univ. of Wisconsin–Stevens Point*	49	2.9	75%	57%	65%	34%	10%	19/1	20-25[9]	33%	91%	4%
65. Univ. of Wisconsin–Whitewater*	49	2.9	80%	51%	62%	30%	5%	20/1	20-24	30%	83%	7%
70. Concordia University Wisconsin	48	2.7	76%	52%	54%	57%	2%	11/1	20-26[3]	51%	63%	3%
70. Grace College and Seminary (IN)	48	2.3	81%	55%	62%	52%	3%	20/1	990-1220	45%	82%	14%
72. College of St. Mary (NE)	47	2.6	79%	49%	48%	65%	0%	11/1	18-24	40%	56%	11%
72. Concordia University Chicago	47	2.6	65%	46%	48%	80%	0.3%	10/1	20-24	45%[5]	75%	7%
72. Fontbonne University (MO)	47	2.5	77%	53%	50%	86%	0%	10/1	20-26	N/A	92%	5%
72. Southern Illinois U.–Edwardsville*	47	2.9	73%	56%	48%	43%	10%	19/1	20-26	43%	90%	3%
72. Stephens College (MO)	47	2.5	66%	55%	60%	84%	1%	8/1	19-25	40%	53%	8%[4]
72. St. Xavier University (IL)	47	2.9	73%	53%	53%	45%	1%	14/1	19-23	51%	75%	5%
72. University of Saint Francis (IN)	47	2.8	71%	50%	56%	64%	1%	10/1	960-1140	40%	99%	4%
72. Winona State University (MN)*	47	2.8	78%	54%	61%	31%	7%	18/1	20-25	31%	66%	5%
80. University of Wisconsin–Stout*	46	2.9	74%	52%	54%	31%	1%	20/1	19-25	31%	86%	2%
81. Malone University (OH)	45	2.4	72%	52%	49%	64%	0.3%	12/1	19-24	33%	66%	8%
81. Northern Michigan University*	45	3.0	75%	45%	53%	40%	8%	20/1	940-1150[3]	N/A	74%	4%
81. University of Central Missouri*	45	2.8	71%	49%	48%	47%	5%	18/1	19-25[2]	34%	84%	N/A

MIDWEST

Rank	School (State) (*Public)	Overall score	Peer assessment score (5.0=highest)	Average first-year student retention rate	2017 graduation rate: Predicted	2017 graduation rate: Actual	% of classes under 20 ('17)	% of classes of 50 or more ('17)	Student/faculty ratio ('17)	SAT/ACT 25th-75th percentile** ('17)	Freshmen in top 25% of HS class ('17)	Acceptance rate ('17)	Average alumni giving rate
84.	**Mount St. Joseph University** (OH)	44	2.3	70%	51%	61%	65%	1%	11/1	20-24	36%	57%	8%
84.	**Mount Vernon Nazarene U.** (OH)	44	2.3	80%	55%	62%	65%	2%	15/1	19-28	44%	77%	5%
86.	**Judson University** (IL)	43	2.4	73%	50%	54%	67%	1%	9/1	19-25	10%[5]	71%	4%
86.	**Northwest Missouri State Univ.***	43	2.7	72%	51%	49%	43%	7%	21/1	18-25	41%	74%	10%
88.	**MidAmerica Nazarene U.** (KS)	42	2.2	68%	41%	54%	67%	5%	7/1	18-24[2]	36%	66%	8%
88.	**Roosevelt University** (IL)	42	2.5	65%	46%	40%	64%	1%	11/1	20-25	46%[5]	70%	5%
90.	**Ohio Dominican University**	41	2.6	68%	53%	47%	53%	0%	14/1	19-24[2]	43%	77%	5%
90.	**Southeast Missouri State Univ.***	41	2.7	74%	53%	52%	45%	5%	20/1	20-26[3]	42%	85%	4%
90.	**Wayne State College** (NE)*	41	2.4	69%	46%	51%	45%	2%	19/1	18-25[2]	30%	100%	10%
90.	**William Woods University** (MO)	41	2.6	75%	54%	56%	85%	0%	11/1	20-26	37%[5]	75%	6%
94.	**Bemidji State University** (MN)*	40	2.7	68%	47%	47%	40%	9%	21/1	20-24	30%	66%	5%
94.	**Concordia University–St. Paul** (MN)	40	2.7	70%	48%	55%	69%	0%	18/1	18-24[3]	27%[4]	55%	4%
94.	**Ferris State University** (MI)*	40	2.8	77%	53%	50%	53%	2%	16/1	940-1170[9]	N/A	74%	2%
94.	**Quincy University** (IL)	40	2.5	69%[8]	48%	46%	70%	0.4%	15/1	19-24	31%	67%	12%
94.	**University of Sioux Falls** (SD)	40	2.6	70%	63%	49%	63%	2%	12/1	20-25	35%	92%	4%
94.	**Univ. of Wisconsin–Green Bay***	40	2.9	75%	57%	51%	30%	9%	23/1	20-25	N/A	95%	4%
94.	**Univ. of Wisconsin–Oshkosh***	40	2.8	77%	54%	52%	42%	8%	20/1	20-24[3]	33%	64%	3%
101.	**Minnesota State Univ.–Moorhead***	39	2.6	74%	49%	46%	43%	7%	19/1	20-25	30%	60%	5%
101.	**Mount Marty College** (SD)	39	2.2	71%	49%	56%	76%	0%	11/1	19-24	N/A	67%	8%
101.	**Northern State University** (SD)*	39	2.4	71%	53%	50%	64%	2%	19/1	19-24	24%	88%	11%
101.	**Pittsburg State University** (KS)*	39	2.6	74%	47%	47%	52%	6%	18/1	19-25	55%	87%	6%
101.	**Rockford University** (IL)	39	2.3	66%	47%	41%	81%	0%	10/1	19-23	N/A	47%	8%
106.	**Cornerstone University** (MI)	38	2.3	78%	56%	53%	54%	2%	15/1	920-1160	43%	67%	3%
106.	**Emporia State University** (KS)*	38	2.7	72%	47%	45%	52%	5%	17/1	19-25[9]	38%	83%	9%
106.	**University of Dubuque** (IA)	38	2.7	64%	45%	43%	72%	1%	16/1	16-22[3]	20%	74%	8%
106.	**Univ. of Wisconsin–River Falls***	38	2.7	75%	51%	53%	42%	8%	18/1	20-25	34%	75%	6%[4]
106.	**Washburn University** (KS)*	38	2.9	70%	50%	37%	48%	2%	14/1	18-25	34%	100%	10%
111.	**Minnesota State Univ.–Mankato***	37	2.8	74%	50%	47%	36%	9%	23/1	20-24	27%	61%	4%
111.	**Missouri State Univ.***	37	2.8	77%[8]	56%	55%	26%	14%	21/1	21-26	49%	84%	N/A
111.	**University of Mary**[1] (ND)	37	2.6	77%[8]	54%	53%[6]	67%[4]	5%[4]	15/1[4]	20-26[4]	51%[4]	84%[4]	1%[4]
111.	**Univ. of Wisconsin–Platteville***	37	2.8	77%	49%	51%	25%	5%	21/1	20-25	28%	79%	N/A
115.	**Graceland University** (IA)	36	2.2	62%	55%	49%	65%	1%	17/1	18-23	23%	56%	16%
115.	**Siena Heights University**[1] (MI)	36	2.6	69%[8]	49%	45%[8]	80%[4]	0%[4]	13/1[4]	19-22[4]	29%[4]	72%[4]	N/A
115.	**University of Michigan–Flint***	36	2.5	72%	52%	44%	54%	2%	13/1	950-1200	43%	65%	1%
118.	**Dakota State University** (SD)*	35	2.5	71%	54%	35%	53%	1%	17/1	19-26	25%	84%	7%
118.	**Greenville University** (IL)	35	2.2	69%	49%	39%	61%	1%	13/1	19-25	38%[4]	66%	15%
118.	**Marian University** (WI)	35	2.4	70%	50%	48%	74%	0.4%	12/1	17-22	25%	68%	6%
118.	**St. Cloud State University** (MN)*	35	2.8	70%	48%	44%	43%	4%	21/1	18-24	27%	86%	3%[4]
122.	**Mount Mary University** (WI)	34	2.4	76%	47%	39%	86%	0%	11/1	17-21	44%	56%	N/A
123.	**Aurora University**[1] (IL)	33	2.5	70%[8]	47%	57%[6]	N/A	N/A	17/1[4]	19-24[4]	N/A	88%[4]	6%[7]
124.	**Friends University** (KS)	32	2.3	68%	45%	35%	76%	1%	10/1	19-25	48%	48%	9%
124.	**Southwest Baptist University** (MO)	32	2.2	66%[8]	46%	46%	81%	2%	12/1	20-26[3]	49%	73%	5%
124.	**Southwestern College** (KS)	32	2.2	64%	55%	41%	72%	2%	10/1	18-23	33%	97%	4%
124.	**Viterbo University**[1] (WI)	32	2.7	76%[8]	50%	49%[6]	N/A	N/A	12/1[4]	20-26[4]	N/A	63%[4]	N/A

School (State) (*Public)	Peer assessment score (5.0=highest)	Average first-year student retention rate	2017 graduation rate: Predicted	2017 graduation rate: Actual	% of classes under 20 ('17)	% of classes of 50 or more ('17)	Student/faculty ratio ('17)	SAT/ACT 25th-75th percentile** ('17)	Freshmen in top 25% of HS class ('17)	Acceptance rate ('17)	Average alumni giving rate
SCHOOLS RANKED 128 THROUGH 165 ARE LISTED HERE ALPHABETICALLY											
Avila University[1] (MO)	2.5	70%[8]	46%	50%[6]	N/A	N/A	12/1[4]	19-23[4]	N/A	56%[4]	N/A
Black Hills State University (SD)*	2.6	66%[8]	46%	34%[6]	N/A	N/A	20/1[4]	19-24[4]	9%[4]	87%	N/A
Calumet College of St. Joseph (IN)	2.2	53%	40%	28%	80%	2%	10/1	860-1033[2]	18%	33%	2%
Chicago State University*	1.8	57%[8]	33%	12%	76%	0%	10/1	17-21	N/A	78%	N/A
Columbia College Chicago[1]	2.6	70%[8]	52%	43%[6]	N/A	N/A	13/1[4]	N/A[2]	N/A	88%[4]	N/A
Davenport University (MI)	2.2	69%	40%	47%	65%	0%	13/1	950-1160[2]	N/A	82%	1%
DeVry University[1] (IL)	1.5	N/A	27%	28%[8]	91%[4]	0%[4]	17/1[4]	N/A[2]	N/A	N/A	N/A
Evangel University (MO)	2.2	75%[8]	49%	51%[6]	N/A	N/A	14/1	19-25[3]	N/A	94%	N/A
Fort Hays State University (KS)*	2.5	70%[8]	50%	39%[8]	49%	4%	17/1	18-24[2]	31%	89%	10%
Governors State University (IL)*	2.2	54%[8]	N/A	N/A	60%	0.1%	12/1	17-20	33%	43%	N/A
Herzing University[1] (WI)	1.7	32%[8]	28%	33%[6]	N/A	N/A	16/1[4]	N/A[2]	N/A	84%[4]	N/A
Indiana University East*	2.3	65%	42%	36%	64%	1%	14/1	940-1118	30%	70%	5%

Note: Key to footnotes Page 105.

GONZAGA UNIVERSITY,
NO. 4 IN THE WEST

BRETT ZIEGLER FOR USN&WR

MIDWEST ▶

School (State) (*Public)	Peer assessment score (5.0=highest)	Average first-year student retention rate	2017 graduation rate: Predicted	2017 graduation rate: Actual	% of classes under 20 ('17)	% of classes of 50 or more ('17)	Student/faculty ratio ('17)	SAT/ACT 25th-75th percentile** ('17)	Freshmen in top 25% of HS class ('17)	Acceptance rate ('17)	Average alumni giving rate
CONTINUED (SCHOOLS RANKED 128 THROUGH 165 ARE LISTED HERE ALPHABETICALLY)											
Indiana University Northwest*	2.5	67%	43%	28%	49%	5%	14/1	890-1093	32%	74%	5%
Indiana University–South Bend*	2.6	66%	45%	30%	42%	3%	13/1	930-1120	25%	78%	6%
Indiana University Southeast*	2.4	61%	46%	32%	47%	1%	14/1	17-22	32%	83%	6%
Lake Erie College (OH)	2.1	67%	52%	46%	76%	0.3%	14/1	18-23[2]	29%	60%	6%
Lakeland University[1] (WI)	2.1	70%[8]	47%	53%[6]	N/A	N/A	12/1[4]	16-22[4]	N/A	55%[4]	N/A
Lincoln University (MO)*	2.0	52%	40%	14%	46%	2%	17/1	14-19	15%	52%	9%[4]
Lourdes University (OH)	2.2	66%	37%	34%	63%	0%	13/1	18-24	28%	97%	5%[4]
Marygrove College[1] (MI)	2.2	42%[8]	26%	24%[6]	N/A	N/A	6/1[4]	15-20[4]	N/A	41%[4]	N/A
Metropolitan State University[1] (MN)*	2.2	71%[8]	46%	35%[6]	N/A	N/A	17/1[4]	N/A[2]	N/A	100%[4]	N/A
Minot State University (ND)*	2.4	70%	53%	38%	N/A	N/A	12/1	19-24	20%	69%	3%
Missouri Baptist University[1]	2.1	61%[8]	50%	39%[6]	N/A	N/A	19/1[4]	18-23[4]	N/A	51%[4]	N/A
Newman University (KS)	2.5	74%	58%	53%	63%	1%	11/1	19-25[9]	48%	64%	5%
Northeastern Illinois University*	2.4	56%	46%	23%	52%	0.3%	16/1	15-19	14%	69%	2%
Notre Dame College of Ohio[1]	2.3	63%[8]	47%	37%[6]	N/A	N/A	14/1[4]	18-22[4]	N/A	90%[4]	N/A
Park University (MO)	2.4	58%	56%	24%	77%	0%	15/1	17-22[2]	N/A	67%	1%
Purdue University–Fort Wayne*	2.9	63%	52%	30%	54%	4%	14/1	970-1170	34%	94%	3%
Purdue University–Northwest (IN)*	2.8	66%	48%	34%	46%	3%	16/1	970-1160	37%	92%	N/A
Saginaw Valley State Univ. (MI)*	2.6	71%	48%	40%	37%	2%	17/1	990-1190	45%	74%	N/A
Silver Lake College[1] (WI)	2.0	72%[8]	43%	41%[8]	N/A	N/A	8/1[4]	14-22[4]	N/A	55%[4]	N/A
Southwest Minnesota State University*	2.4	66%	53%	46%	43%[4]	3%[4]	16/1	18-24	20%	62%	9%
Tiffin University (OH)	2.5	63%	25%	33%	44%	0%	12/1	17-22[9]	42%[5]	69%	4%
University of Southern Indiana*	2.6	71%	45%	40%	38%	4%	17/1	970-1170	37%	94%	3%
University of St. Mary (KS)	2.4	70%	43%	44%	74%	0.4%	9/1	19-24	8%	49%	N/A
Upper Iowa University[1]	2.1	57%[8]	51%	41%[8]	89%[4]	0%[4]	17/1[4]	17-24[4]	27%[4]	94%[4]	3%[4]
William Penn University[1] (IA)	2.1	56%[8]	37%	30%[6]	N/A	N/A	16/1[4]	17-21[4]	N/A	59%[4]	N/A
Youngstown State University (OH)*	2.5	74%	38%	35%	39%	6%	17/1	19-25	34%	65%	5%

WEST ▶

Rank	School (State) (*Public)	Overall score	Peer assessment score (5.0=highest)	Average first-year student retention rate	2017 graduation rate: Predicted	2017 graduation rate: Actual	% of classes under 20 ('17)	% of classes of 50 or more ('17)	Student/faculty ratio ('17)	SAT/ACT 25th-75th percentile** ('17)	Freshmen in top 25% of HS class ('17)	Acceptance rate ('17)	Average alumni giving rate
1.	**Santa Clara University** (CA)	100	4.1	95%	84%	90%	47%	1%	11/1	28-32	87%[5]	54%	19%
2.	**Trinity University** (TX)	99	4.1	89%	88%	80%	57%	1%	9/1	27-32	76%	38%	14%
3.	**Loyola Marymount University** (CA)	92	3.9	90%	77%	79%	53%	1%	10/1	1180-1360	75%[5]	52%	20%
4.	**Gonzaga University** (WA)	89	4.0	93%	76%	87%	33%	2%	12/1	1180-1350	75%[5]	65%	15%
5.	**Chapman University** (CA)	83	3.8	90%	82%	79%	45%	4%	14/1	25-30	78%[5]	57%	8%
6.	**University of Portland** (OR)	81	3.7	90%	76%	82%	32%	1%	12/1	1140-1320	83%[5]	70%	11%
7.	**Mills College** (CA)	79	3.3	77%	70%	70%	70%	0.4%	10/1	1030-1290[2]	55%[5]	87%	17%
8.	**Seattle University**	78	3.7	86%	73%	74%	55%	1%	11/1	1130-1330	68%[5]	74%	6%
8.	**St. Mary's College of California**	78	3.4	87%	68%	76%	62%	0.1%	11/1	1060-1240[3]	N/A	82%	8%
8.	**Whitworth University** (WA)	78	3.7	85%	73%	75%	63%	1%	11/1	1090-1310[2]	70%[5]	89%	13%
11.	**University of Redlands** (CA)	74	3.3	85%	70%	72%[8]	68%[4]	0.1%[4]	13/1[4]	1070-1250	55%[4]	75%	12%[4]
12.	**Calif. Poly. State U.-San Luis Obispo***	73	4.0	94%	75%	82%	16%	13%	19/1	1220-1400[3]	86%[5]	35%	4%
12.	**St. Edward's University** (TX)	73	3.5	82%	64%	64%	57%	0.1%	13/1	1080-1250	58%	84%	10%
14.	**University of Dallas**	72	3.5	82%	74%	68%	61%	3%	11/1	1140-1370[3]	71%[5]	47%	15%
15.	**California Lutheran University**	71	3.3	84%	69%	71%	56%	0.3%	16/1	1060-1230	66%[5]	73%	13%
15.	**St. Mary's Univ. of San Antonio**	71	3.2	76%	55%	63%	59%	0%	11/1	1040-1230	58%	80%	10%
17.	**Point Loma Nazarene University** (CA)	69	3.3	86%	69%	74%	40%	2%	14/1	1100-1290	71%[5]	76%	7%
18.	**Mount Saint Mary's University** (CA)	68	3.1	78%	50%	70%	72%	0.1%	11/1	920-1120[2]	43%[5]	81%	12%
19.	**Western Washington University***	66	3.5	82%	61%	69%	42%	14%	18/1	1080-1280	53%[5]	85%	4%
20.	**Westminster College** (UT)	65	3.1	78%	66%	62%	73%	0%	9/1	21-28	53%	93%	12%
21.	**Abilene Christian University** (TX)	64	3.4	77%	68%	61%	44%	9%	14/1	21-26	54%	61%	10%
21.	**Pacific University** (OR)	64	3.1	80%	67%	64%	61%	3%	10/1	1070-1260	N/A	84%	10%
23.	**Pacific Lutheran University** (WA)	63	3.3	82%	70%	68%	51%	2%	15/1	1040-1270	85%[4]	75%	9%
24.	**George Fox University** (OR)	62	3.3	82%	65%	71%	49%	3%	14/1	1030-1240	60%[5]	82%	5%
25.	**Dominican University of California**	59	2.8	84%	65%	72%	64%	0%	9/1	1040-1215	57%	76%	N/A
26.	**California State U.–Long Beach***	58	3.3	89%	58%	71%	23%	8%	24/1	1020-1230	N/A	29%	3%
26.	**Regis University** (CO)	58	3.2	79%	65%	71%	58%	1%	13/1	20-26	55%[5]	60%	4%
28.	**Calif. State Polytechnic U.–Pomona***	57	3.6	89%	43%	66%	12%	14%	25/1	1010-1240[3]	N/A	58%	2%
28.	**LeTourneau University** (TX)	57	2.9	78%	62%	59%	69%	1%	15/1	1060-1310[2]	52%	47%	7%
28.	**Oklahoma City University**	57	3.0	82%	74%	63%	75%	2%	11/1	23-28[3]	61%	72%	5%

Note: Key to footnotes Page 105.

WEST ▶

Rank	School (State) (*Public)	Overall score	Peer assessment score (5.0=highest)	Average first-year student retention rate	2017 graduation rate: Predicted	2017 graduation rate: Actual	% of classes under 20 ('17)	% of classes of 50 or more ('17)	Student/faculty ratio ('17)	SAT/ACT 25th-75th percentile** ('17)	Freshmen in top 25% of HS class ('17)	Acceptance rate ('17)	Average alumni giving rate
28.	University of St. Thomas (TX)	57	3.0	85%	65%	57%	58%	0%	11/1	1070-1235	29%	81%	9%
32.	California Baptist University	56	3.0	78%	48%	59%	55%	5%	17/1	980-1190	46%[5]	77%	2%
33.	San Jose State University (CA)*	54	3.3	87%	48%	57%	23%	10%	26/1	1030-1230[3]	N/A	67%	2%
34.	California State U.–Monterey Bay*	53	2.9	81%	50%	60%	19%	6%	26/1	970-1170	48%	53%	2%
35.	Evergreen State College (WA)*	52	3.2	66%	48%	57%	46%	9%	21/1	960-1190	32%[5]	96%	2%
35.	N.M. Inst. of Mining and Tech.*	52	3.1	76%	79%	47%	60%	8%	11/1	23-29	68%	22%	N/A
37.	Concordia University (CA)	51	2.9	76%	52%	65%	56%	0%	16/1	1010-1200	36%[5]	58%	5%
37.	Saint Martin's University (WA)	51	2.8	79%	54%	59%	64%	0.3%	11/1	980-1190[2]	52%	98%	3%
39.	Fresno Pacific University (CA)	50	2.5	78%	44%	63%	72%	1%	13/1	915-1090	63%	95%	N/A
39.	Univ. of the Incarnate Word (TX)	50	2.9	76%	50%	53%	63%	2%	13/1	940-1120	40%	94%	4%
41.	California State University–Chico*	49	2.9	86%[8]	59%	64%[8]	25%[4]	14%[4]	23/1	990-1170	76%[4]	69%	4%[7]
41.	Hardin-Simmons University (TX)	49	2.8	70%	57%	51%	64%	2%	12/1	18-24[3]	44%	82%	8%
41.	Oral Roberts University (OK)	49	2.6	81%	53%	57%	55%	7%	14/1	20-26	46%[5]	93%	11%
44.	Chaminade University of Honolulu	48	2.7	76%	49%	53%	55%	0.4%	11/1	970-1180	46%	91%	2%
44.	Walla Walla University (WA)	48	2.8	82%[8]	62%	64%	61%	6%	14/1	1020-1240	N/A	65%	N/A
46.	The Master's U. and Seminary (CA)	47	2.4	86%	65%	50%	69%	6%	12/1	1030-1240	69%[5]	66%	10%
46.	Northwest University (WA)	47	2.5	78%	45%	59%	61%	4%	12/1	1005-1240	N/A	97%	7%
48.	California State U.–Stanislaus*	46	2.7	83%	38%	52%	23%	6%	23/1	910-1100[2]	N/A	77%	1%[4]
48.	Central Washington University*	46	2.9	77%	49%	60%	41%	5%	19/1	960-1160[3]	N/A	86%	2%
48.	Notre Dame de Namur University (CA)	46	2.6	74%	51%	44%	68%	0%	12/1	910-1110	27%[5]	94%	10%
48.	Univ. of Colo.–Colorado Springs*	46	3.2	67%	53%	43%	40%	7%	19/1	21-26	38%	93%	5%
52.	California State U.–Los Angeles*	45	3.0	82%	25%	47%	20%	8%	24/1	890-1080[2]	5%[5]	46%	2%
52.	Northwest Nazarene University (ID)	45	2.6	76%	58%	56%	62%	5%	16/1	1030-1240	51%	96%	10%
54.	California State U.–San Bernardino*	44	2.7	86%	35%	54%	23%	20%	28/1	910-1090[2]	N/A	57%	2%
54.	Humboldt State University (CA)*	44	2.8	72%	48%	47%	30%	11%	22/1	960-1170[2]	46%	81%	4%
54.	La Sierra University (CA)	44	2.5	76%[8]	49%	53%	61%	4%	14/1	845-1100	36%	48%	N/A
54.	Univ. of Mary Hardin-Baylor (TX)	44	2.9	70%	52%	48%	48%	4%	18/1	1020-1200[3]	45%	79%	5%
54.	Vanguard U. of Southern California	44	2.4	75%	53%	61%	61%	5%	14/1	930-1120	42%	48%	8%
59.	Texas A&M International University*	43	3.0	81%	42%	44%	30%	17%	22/1	930-1100	52%	51%	2%
59.	Woodbury University (CA)	43	2.2	79%	42%	52%	78%	0%	9/1	955-1188[2]	N/A	62%	3%
61.	Holy Names University (CA)	42	2.3	74%	48%	43%	68%	0%	8/1	730-870	23%[5]	53%	8%
61.	University of Houston–Clear Lake*	42	2.9	74%[8]	N/A	N/A	33%	5%	15/1	1020-1190	43%	73%	5%[4]
63.	Western Oregon University*	41	2.8	71%	41%	44%	50%	5%	15/1	16-25[2]	35%[4]	81%	3%
64.	Alaska Pacific University	40	2.2	60%[8]	67%	55%[6]	96%[4]	0%[4]	8/1[4]	21-26[4]	N/A	55%[4]	N/A
64.	Corban University (OR)	40	2.3	79%	61%	49%	53%	1%	14/1	1040-1230	60%[5]	33%	2%
64.	Oklahoma Christian U.	40	2.8	79%	62%	52%	58%	7%	14/1	20-27[3]	52%	63%	10%
64.	Sonoma State University (CA)*	40	2.9	79%	55%	58%	24%	22%	23/1	980-1170	N/A	82%	1%
64.	Texas Wesleyan University	40	2.8	52%	47%	36%	66%	0%	14/1	930-1100	38%	34%	7%
69.	California State U.–Sacramento*	39	3.0	82%[8]	40%	50%	23%	15%	25/1	940-1140	N/A	68%	3%
69.	Hawaii Pacific University	39	2.8	68%	62%	44%	60%	0.4%	12/1	1000-1198	47%	75%	1%
69.	Houston Baptist University	39	2.7	69%	54%	48%	51%	1%	14/1	1030-1190	51%	69%	3%
69.	Our Lady of the Lake University (TX)	39	2.6	60%	42%	38%	57%	0%	9/1	930-1080	36%	91%	13%
73.	California State U.–Channel Islands[1]*	38	2.8	79%[8]	45%	59%[6]	N/A	N/A	22/1[4]	N/A[2]	N/A	74%[4]	N/A
73.	California State U.–Northridge*	38	3.2	78%	38%	49%[8]	14%	13%	27/1	1010-1120	N/A	58%	4%[7]
75.	Northwest Christian University (OR)	36	2.2	70%	53%	53%	73%	2%	15/1	943-1118	16%	69%	4%
75.	Stephen F. Austin State Univ. (TX)*	36	3.0	71%	46%	44%	30%	9%	19/1	990-1180	43%	65%	3%
77.	Eastern Washington University*	35	2.7	77%[8]	45%	52%	39%	11%	21/1	870-1090	N/A	96%	N/A
77.	Hope International University (CA)	35	2.2	75%	36%	48%	65%	0%	13/1	910-1100	35%	28%	7%
77.	University of Central Oklahoma*	35	3.0	63%	49%	37%	39%	2%	18/1	19-24	37%	81%	1%
77.	Western State Colorado University*	35	2.5	68%	48%	41%	62%	0%	18/1	20-25	25%	86%	N/A
81.	Southern Utah University*	34	2.6	68%	52%	37%	42%	8%	19/1	20-27	44%	76%	4%
81.	University of Alaska–Anchorage*	34	2.9	71%	58%	25%	57%	4%	12/1	18-24[2]	35%	83%	3%
81.	University of Texas–Tyler*	34	2.8	61%	54%	42%	32%	12%	19/1	1070-1240	47%[5]	65%	N/A
81.	West Texas A&M University*	34	2.8	65%	51%	41%	37%	10%	20/1	19-23	43%	61%	3%
85.	California State Univ.–San Marcos*	33	2.8	82%[8]	46%	53%	14%	7%	26/1	18-23	N/A	77%	1%[7]
85.	Lubbock Christian University (TX)	33	2.4	70%	51%	47%	65%	2%	13/1	19-25[3]	39%	94%	5%
85.	Oklahoma Wesleyan University	33	2.4	55%	50%	34%	77%	3%	14/1	18-24	4%	62%	16%[4]
88.	California State U.–Dominguez Hills*	32	2.6	80%	32%	43%	22%	9%	21/1	16-20[2]	N/A	77%	2%
88.	Southern Oregon University*	32	2.7	71%	49%	38%	46%	5%	21/1	870-1120	N/A	78%	1%
88.	U. of Texas of the Permian Basin*	32	2.5	69%	54%	43%	31%	12%	27/1	900-1120	56%	82%	6%
91.	Prescott College[1] (AZ)	31	2.6	71%[8]	49%	32%[6]	99%[4]	1%[4]	9/1[4]	920-1200[4]	N/A	68%[4]	N/A
91.	Simpson University[1] (CA)	31	2.3	76%[8]	49%	49%[8]	74%[4]	2%[4]	11/1[4]	860-1105[4]	51%[4]	52%[4]	3%[4]
91.	Tarleton State University (TX)*	31	2.5	68%	42%	46%	32%	9%	19/1	960-1130	29%	74%	2%[7]
94.	California State Univ.–Bakersfield*	30	2.6	73%	33%	40%	30%	9%	25/1	810-1050[2]	N/A	100%	N/A
94.	Midwestern State University (TX)*	30	2.4	69%[8]	52%	45%	42%	11%	18/1	930-1120	35%	81%	4%

School (State) (*Public)	Peer assessment score (5.0=highest)	Average first-year student retention rate	2017 graduation rate Predicted	2017 graduation rate Actual	% of classes under 20 ('17)	% of classes of 50 or more ('17)	Student/faculty ratio ('17)	SAT/ACT 25th-75th percentile** ('17)	Freshmen in top 25% of HS class ('17)	Acceptance rate ('17)	Average alumni giving rate
SCHOOLS RANKED 96 THROUGH 127 ARE LISTED HERE ALPHABETICALLY											
Adams State University[1] (CO)*	2.4	57%[8]	37%	27%[6]	N/A	N/A	16/1[4]	17-22[4]	N/A	99%[4]	N/A
Angelo State University (TX)*	2.3	64%[8]	46%	37%	29%	8%	19/1	17-22	33%	74%	2%
California State University–East Bay*	2.7	78%	43%	42%	14%	18%	24/1	890-1090[2]	N/A	74%	N/A
Cameron University (OK)*	2.3	64%	37%	23%	50%	1%	20/1	16-21[2]	14%	100%	3%
Colorado Christian University[1]	2.5	76%[8]	47%	46%[6]	N/A	N/A	16/1[4]	N/A[2]	N/A	N/A	N/A
Colorado State University–Pueblo*	2.8	64%	37%	35%	53%	6%	14/1	18-23	36%	95%	2%
Concordia University Texas[1]	2.4	67%[8]	52%	36%[6]	N/A	N/A	13/1[4]	880-1080[4]	N/A	83%[4]	N/A
East Central University (OK)*	2.3	57%	41%	33%	45%	1%	18/1	18-23	N/A	25%	N/A
Eastern New Mexico University*	2.6	60%	42%	32%	67%	2%	17/1	16-22	30%	60%	2%
Eastern Oregon University*	2.4	64%	41%	30%	65%	4%	17/1	18-23	39%	98%	1%
Langston University (OK)*	2.0	61%[8]	35%	15%[6]	50%	7%	17/1	17-26[3]	N/A	43%	N/A
Metropolitan State University of Denver*	2.8	65%	39%	28%	38%	1%	17/1	17-22[3]	14%	64%	N/A
Montana State Univ.–Billings*	2.8	55%	45%	28%	55%	3%	14/1	18-23[2]	26%	100%	N/A
New Mexico Highlands University[1]*	2.1	48%[8]	37%	19%[6]	77%[4]	1%[4]	N/A	15-20[4]	17%[4]	100%[4]	N/A
Northeastern State University (OK)*	2.5	63%	45%	31%	51%	3%	18/1	19-24[3]	51%	90%	5%
Northwestern Oklahoma State U.*	2.3	55%	42%	28%	60%	0.4%	13/1	17-23	29%	83%	5%
Sierra Nevada College (NV)	2.2	65%[8]	48%	41%[6]	88%	0%	10/1	910-1140[3]	20%	69%	N/A
Southeastern Oklahoma State U.*	2.3	61%	43%	28%	53%	3%	18/1	18-23	45%	72%	2%
Southern Nazarene University[1] (OK)	2.6	64%[8]	41%	42%[6]	N/A	N/A	14/1[4]	N/A	N/A	N/A	N/A
Southwestern Assemblies of God University[1] (TX)	2.3	75%[8]	41%	43%[6]	N/A	N/A	16/1[4]	19-25[4]	N/A	23%[4]	N/A
Southwestern Oklahoma State U.*	2.5	67%	49%	34%	45%	5%	21/1	18-24[2]	48%	92%	N/A
Sul Ross State University[1] (TX)*	2.2	57%[8]	36%	20%[6]	N/A	N/A	12/1[4]	730-949[4]	N/A	92%[4]	N/A
Texas A&M University–Texarkana*	2.7	55%[8]	47%	30%	55%	0%	15/1	19-23[2]	30%	93%	N/A
University of Alaska–Southeast[1]*	2.3	60%[8]	61%	19%[6]	N/A	N/A	9/1[4]	N/A[2]	N/A	49%[4]	N/A
University of Hawaii–Hilo[1]*	2.9	67%[8]	54%	37%[6]	N/A	N/A	13/1[4]	18-24[4]	N/A	69%[4]	2%[7]
University of Houston–Downtown*	2.8	68%	34%	21%	32%	3%	19/1	920-1078	32%	84%	1%
University of Houston–Victoria[1]*	2.7	50%[8]	40%	18%[8]	43%[4]	7%[4]	18/1[4]	780-1000[4]	18%[4]	53%[4]	N/A
University of North Texas–Dallas*	2.8	71%[8]	29%	33%[6]	36%	0.2%	17/1	820-990	33%[5]	74%	N/A
University of the Southwest[1] (NM)	2.1	55%[8]	40%	12%[6]	N/A	N/A	13/1[4]	15-21[4]	N/A	66%[4]	N/A
Utah Valley University*	2.3	62%	40%	26%	40%	6%	25/1	18-25[2]	27%	88%	N/A
Wayland Baptist University (TX)	2.2	48%	52%	19%	82%	0%	8/1	17-23	21%	98%	1%
Weber State University (UT)*	3.0	65%	53%	33%	47%	7%	21/1	18-24[2]	26%	100%	2%

The Top Public Regional Universities

NORTH

Rank	School (State)
1.	**College of New Jersey**
2.	**SUNY–Geneseo**
3.	**SUNY Polytechnic Institute–Albany/Utica**
4.	**Massachusetts Maritime Academy**
5.	**CUNY–Baruch College**
6.	**CUNY–Hunter College**
7.	**Ramapo College of New Jersey**
7.	**Rutgers University–Camden** (NJ)
9.	**Stockton University** (NJ)
10.	**SUNY–New Paltz**
11.	**SUNY–Oswego**
12.	**SUNY–Fredonia**
12.	**Towson University** (MD)
14.	**CUNY–City College**
14.	**CUNY–Queens College**
14.	**SUNY College–Oneonta**

SOUTH

Rank	School (State)
1.	**The Citadel** (SC)
2.	**James Madison University** (VA)
3.	**Appalachian State University** (NC)
4.	**Christopher Newport Univ.** (VA)
5.	**College of Charleston** (SC)
6.	**U. of North Carolina–Wilmington**
7.	**U. of Mary Washington** (VA)
8.	**Longwood University** (VA)
8.	**Winthrop University** (SC)
10.	**Georgia College & State U.**
11.	**Murray State University** (KY)
11.	**Western Carolina University** (NC)
11.	**Western Kentucky University**
14.	**Marshall University** (WV)
14.	**University of Montevallo** (AL)
14.	**University of North Florida**
14.	**University of Tennessee–Martin**

MIDWEST

Rank	School (State)
1.	**Truman State University** (MO)
2.	**University of Northern Iowa**
3.	**Grand Valley State University** (MI)
4.	**University of Wisconsin–La Crosse**
5.	**Eastern Illinois University**
5.	**University of Michigan–Dearborn**
5.	**U. of Wisconsin–Eau Claire**
8.	**University of Minnesota–Duluth**
9.	**University of Illinois–Springfield**
10.	**University of Nebraska–Kearney**
10.	**Western Illinois University**
12.	**U. of Wisconsin–Stevens Point**
12.	**U. of Wisconsin–Whitewater**
14.	**Southern Illinois University–Edwardsville**
14.	**Winona State University** (MN)

WEST

Rank	School (State)
1.	**California Polytechnic State University–San Luis Obispo**
2.	**Western Washington University**
3.	**California State U.–Long Beach**
4.	**California State Polytechnic University–Pomona**
5.	**San Jose State University** (CA)
6.	**California State U.–Monterey Bay**
7.	**Evergreen State College** (WA)
7.	**N.M. Inst. of Mining and Tech.**
9.	**California State University–Chico**
10.	**California State U.–Stanislaus**
10.	**Central Washington University**
10.	**U. of Colorado–Colorado Springs**
13.	**California State U.–Los Angeles**
14.	**Calif. State U.–San Bernardino**
14.	**Humboldt State University** (CA)

Footnotes:

1. School refused to fill out U.S. News statistical survey. Data that appear are from school in previous years or from another source such as the National Center for Education Statistics.
2. SAT and/or ACT not required by school for some or all applicants.
3. In reporting SAT/ACT scores, the school did not include all students for whom it had scores or refused to tell U.S. News whether all students with scores had been included.
4. Data reported to U.S. News in previous years.
5. Data based on fewer than 51 percent of enrolled freshmen.
6. Some or all data reported to the National Center for Education Statistics.
7. Data reported to the Council for Aid to Education.
8. This rate, normally based on four years of data, is given here for fewer than four years because school didn't report rate for the most recent year or years to U.S. News.
9. SAT and/or ACT may not be required by school for some or all applicants, and in reporting SAT/ACT scores, the school did not include all students for whom it had scores or refused to tell U.S. News whether all students with scores had been included.
**The SAT scores used in the rankings and published in this guidebook are for the "new" SAT test taken starting March 2016.
N/A means not available.

What Is a Regional College?

These schools focus almost entirely on the undergraduate experience and offer a broad range of programs in the liberal arts (which account for fewer than half of bachelor's degrees granted) and in fields such as business, nursing and education. They grant few graduate degrees. Because most of the 322 colleges in the category draw heavily from nearby states, they are ranked by region: North, South, Midwest, West.

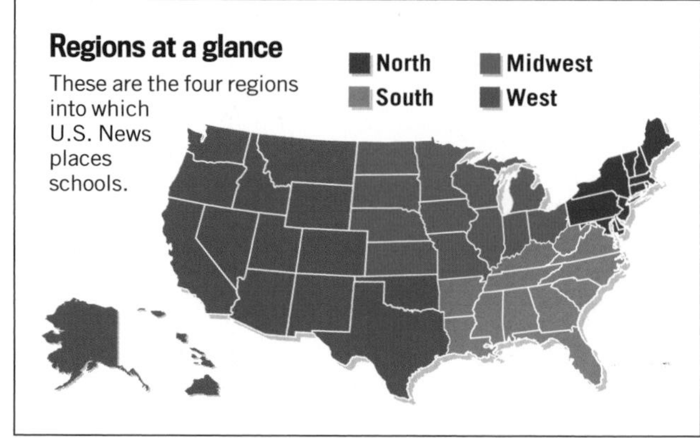

NORTH ▶

Rank	School (State) (*Public)	Overall score	Peer assessment score (5.0=highest)	Average first-year student retention rate	2017 graduation rate: Predicted	2017 graduation rate: Actual	% of classes under 20 ('17)	% of classes of 50 or more ('17)	Student/faculty ratio ('17)	SAT/ACT 25th-75th percentile** ('17)	Freshmen in top 25% of HS class ('17)	Acceptance rate ('17)	Average alumni giving rate
1.	**Cooper Union** (NY)	100	4.2	96%	90%	83%	73%	1%	7/1	1310-1530	85%[5]	13%	22%
2.	**U.S. Coast Guard Academy** (CT)*	90	4.3	93%	82%	81%	56%	0%	7/1	1180-1343[3]	75%	21%	N/A
3.	**U.S. Merchant Marine Acad.** (NY)*	83	3.9	91%[8]	81%	77%	45%[4]	0.3%[4]	13/1	25-29	64%	15%	N/A
4.	**Maine Maritime Academy***	70	3.6	81%	53%	68%	51%	0%	10/1	990-1180	57%	80%	18%
5.	**Messiah College** (PA)	68	3.1	87%	68%	81%	48%	2%	12/1	1100-1310	63%	77%	11%
6.	**Cedar Crest College** (PA)	54	3.0	77%	50%	50%	76%	2%	10/1	940-1170	44%	63%	12%
7.	**Colby-Sawyer College** (NH)	53	3.1	76%[8]	45%	56%	67%	1%	13/1	1030-1210[2]	N/A	87%	10%
8.	**Vaughn Col. of Aeron. and Tech.** (NY)	50	3.2	74%	43%	52%	72%	0%	15/1	921-1100[3]	N/A	90%	5%
9.	**University of Maine–Farmington***	46	2.9	74%	41%	51%	64%	1%	13/1	970-1075[2]	42%	83%	3%
10.	**St. Francis College** (NY)	45	2.7	77%	39%	51%	61%	0%	14/1	950-1120	N/A	63%	10%
11.	**Cazenovia College** (NY)	40	2.7	71%	46%	54%	86%	0%	10/1	923-1098[2]	23%	92%	6%
12.	**Pennsylvania College of Technology***	39	2.9	77%	50%	45%	63%	0%	14/1	950-1140[2]	25%	59%	1%
12.	**SUNY College of Technology–Alfred***	39	2.9	77%	40%	50%	47%	2%	18/1	940-1130[2]	N/A	68%	2%
14.	**Paul Smith's College** (NY)	37	3.0	72%	41%	52%	59%	3%	13/1	860-1100[4]	14%	81%	10%
14.	**SUNY College of A&T–Cobleskill***	37	2.8	74%	38%	52%	46%	4%	16/1	17-22[2]	21%[5]	94%	3%
16.	**Unity College** (ME)	36	2.6	69%	46%	65%	47%	0%	15/1	990-1240[2]	35%[5]	89%	2%
16.	**Wilson College** (PA)	36	2.5	73%	57%	51%	81%	1%	10/1	940-1120[2]	38%	59%	15%
18.	**SUNY College of Technology–Delhi***	35	2.9	70%	38%	57%	43%	3%	16/1	900-1120	17%[5]	63%	3%
19.	**Farmingdale State College–SUNY***	33	2.9	81%	49%	53%	23%	1%	20/1	980-1140	30%[5]	59%	0.4%
19.	**Vermont Technical College***	33	2.7	76%	51%	44%	75%	0%	12/1	20-23[2]	25%[5]	63%	1%
21.	**Fisher College** (MA)	32	2.5	60%	26%	53%	74%	0%	16/1	800-1040[2]	N/A	66%	N/A
22.	**Concordia College** (NY)	31	2.8	75%	36%	46%	N/A	N/A	11/1	930-1140[2]	38%[5]	76%	7%
23.	**Dean College** (MA)	30	2.8	72%	40%	47%	49%	0.3%	17/1	880-1080[2]	N/A	66%	6%
23.	**La Roche College** (PA)	30	2.3	72%	38%	51%	67%	0%	12/1	950-1140	17%	97%	5%
25.	**Southern Vermont College**	29	2.7	66%	36%	51%	56%	0%	11/1	920-1080[2]	24%	90%	N/A
26.	**SUNY Col. of Technology–Canton***	25	2.8	77%	31%	37%	42%	3%	17/1	880-1080[2]	20%	79%	2%
26.	**SUNY–Morrisville** (NY)*	25	2.7	66%	32%	33%	52%	3%	15/1	910-1100[2]	16%[5]	72%	3%
26.	**University of Valley Forge** (PA)	25	2.3	71%	36%	49%	78%	2%	12/1	918-1150[2]	11%	53%	3%
29.	**Keystone College** (PA)	24	2.6	67%	32%	39%	73%	0%	13/1	780-970[4]	N/A	94%	4%[4]
30.	**Castleton University**[1] (VT)*	23	2.8	73%[8]	43%	48%[6]	N/A	N/A	12/1[4]	860-1068[4]	N/A	95%[4]	N/A
31.	**Newbury College** (MA)	22	2.5	60%[8]	36%	39%	74%	0%	12/1	870-1110[2]	N/A	75%	1%
31.	**University of Maine–Presque Isle***	22	2.7	61%	48%	26%	76%	0%	15/1	910-1130[2]	25%	95%	0.4%
33.	**Mount Aloysius College**[1] (PA)	18	2.5	N/A	35%	37%[6]	78%[4]	0%[4]	11/1[4]	870-1030[4]	N/A	N/A	N/A
34.	**CUNY–York College***	17	2.7	73%[8]	32%	29%	28%	8%	18/1	860-1020	N/A	65%	N/A
34.	**University of Maine–Fort Kent***	17	2.5	68%	37%	33%	50%	6%	14/1	860-1110[2]	11%	97%	4%

Note: Key to footnotes, Page 113.

NORTH

School (State) (*Public)	Peer assessment score (5.0=highest)	Average first-year student retention rate	2017 graduation rate: Predicted	2017 graduation rate: Actual	% of classes under 20 ('17)	% of classes of 50 or more ('17)	Student/faculty ratio ('17)	SAT/ACT 25th-75th percentile** ('17)	Freshmen in top 25% of HS class ('17)	Acceptance rate ('17)	Average alumni giving rate
SCHOOLS RANKED 36 THROUGH 47 ARE LISTED HERE ALPHABETICALLY											
Bay State College (MA)	2.1	N/A	37%	33%[6]	N/A	N/A	15/1	N/A[2]	N/A	44%	N/A
Becker College[1] (MA)	2.5	70%[8]	38%	31%[6]	N/A	N/A	17/1[4]	920-1130[4]	N/A	65%[4]	N/A
Central Penn College	2.3	56%	34%	34%	68%	0%	10/1	660-910[4]	N/A	79%	1%
College of St. Joseph[1] (VT)	2.7	65%[8]	36%	26%[6]	N/A	N/A	10/1[4]	N/A[2]	N/A	58%[4]	N/A
CUNY–Medgar Evers College*	2.6	66%	30%	20%	6%	2%	18/1	730-910[9]	N/A	100%	N/A
CUNY–New York City Col. of Tech.*	2.9	77%	25%	25%[8]	27%	0%	16/1[4]	740-940[4]	N/A	77%	1%
Five Towns College[1] (NY)	2.1	69%[8]	37%	33%[6]	N/A	N/A	15/1[4]	N/A[2]	N/A	55%[4]	N/A
Lyndon State College[1] (VT)*	2.7	66%[8]	37%	37%[6]	N/A	N/A	14/1[4]	840-1060[4]	N/A	98%[4]	N/A
Mitchell College[1] (CT)	2.4	69%[8]	44%	43%[6]	N/A	N/A	13/1[4]	N/A[2]	N/A	88%[4]	N/A
New England Institute of Technology[1] (RI)	2.5	N/A	N/A	N/A	N/A	N/A	13/1[4]	N/A[2]	N/A	N/A	N/A
University of Maine–Augusta*	2.8	54%	30%	15%	65%	5%	15/1	N/A[2]	N/A	97%	0.4%
Wesley College[1] (DE)	3.0	51%[8]	34%	21%[6]	N/A	N/A	15/1[4]	740-930[4]	16%[4]	60%[4]	N/A

SOUTH

Rank	School (State) (*Public)	Overall score	Peer assessment score (5.0=highest)	Average first-year student retention rate	2017 graduation rate: Predicted	2017 graduation rate: Actual	% of classes under 20 ('17)	% of classes of 50 or more ('17)	Student/faculty ratio ('17)	SAT/ACT 25th-75th percentile** ('17)	Freshmen in top 25% of HS class ('17)	Acceptance rate ('17)	Average alumni giving rate
1.	**High Point University** (NC)	100	3.8	80%	62%	63%	50%	1%	14/1	1050-1240[9]	47%[5]	81%	10%
2.	**Flagler College** (FL)	87	3.6	71%	54%	55%	54%	0%	16/1	950-1160	N/A	57%	14%
3.	**University of the Ozarks** (AR)	80	3.5	68%[8]	59%	51%	54%	0%	14/1	18-23[2]	30%	89%	13%
4.	**Catawba College** (NC)	77	3.2	73%	44%	45%	73%	0.2%	12/1	18-23[9]	44%	42%	12%
5.	**Barton College** (NC)	75	2.8	69%	38%	53%	73%	0.4%	10/1	950-1140	39%	39%	8%
5.	**Coker College** (SC)	75	3.1	65%	40%	47%	82%	0%	13/1	17-21	22%	62%	7%
5.	**University of Mobile** (AL)	75	3.4	73%	45%	46%	74%	0.3%	13/1	20-25	62%	47%	2%
8.	**Blue Mountain College** (MS)	71	2.8	69%	42%	61%	70%	1%	14/1	18-24	40%	100%	6%
8.	**Univ. of South Carolina–Aiken***	71	3.3	69%	43%	41%	55%	1%	15/1	18-23	42%	53%	5%
10.	**U. of South Carolina–Upstate***	70	3.2	71%	39%	44%	55%	1%	13/1	17-22	32%	52%	2%
11.	**Huntingdon College** (AL)	69	3.1	66%	47%	37%	59%	1%	15/1	19-24	27%	56%	28%
12.	**Newberry College** (SC)	67	2.8	68%	43%	52%	57%	1%	14/1	17-22	30%	58%	16%
13.	**Averett University** (VA)	66	3.0	61%	42%	40%	79%	0%	12/1	830-1020	24%	62%	4%
13.	**Kentucky Wesleyan College**	66	3.1	66%	48%	32%	78%	0.4%	13/1	19-26	N/A	58%	11%
13.	**Welch College** (TN)	66	2.7	72%	52%	48%	90%	1%	9/1	21-26	66%[5]	46%	15%
16.	**Alice Lloyd College** (KY)	65	3.1	63%	40%	29%	47%	5%	16/1	18-23	40%	26%	45%
16.	**Tennessee Wesleyan University**	65	3.0	68%[8]	42%	39%	66%	2%	12/1	19-25	36%[5]	60%	6%
18.	**Belmont Abbey College** (NC)	64	3.1	62%	41%	43%	65%	0.2%	15/1	980-1120[2]	N/A	99%	6%
19.	**Greensboro College** (NC)	63	2.8	59%	34%	42%	86%	0.3%	11/1	17-22	24%	41%	14%
20.	**Florida Memorial University**[1]	61	2.7	68%[8]	13%	38%[6]	N/A	N/A	16/1[4]	16-19[4]	N/A	23%[4]	N/A
21.	**Lander University** (SC)*	60	2.9	68%	35%	42%	45%	3%	16/1	940-1120	35%	48%	7%
22.	**Mars Hill University** (NC)	59	2.9	58%	34%	31%	76%	0.2%	11/1	17-22	26%	60%	13%
22.	**Toccoa Falls College** (GA)	59	2.5	69%	38%	53%	64%	1%	15/1	920-1150	40%[5]	59%	2%
22.	**University of Holy Cross** (LA)	59	3.0	68%[8]	41%	52%	76%	1%	11/1	18-23[2]	N/A	46%	1%
25.	**Reinhardt University** (GA)	57	2.9	59%	36%	40%	72%	0%	12/1	18-23	25%	89%	5%
25.	**University of Mount Olive** (NC)	57	2.7	64%	34%	43%	67%	0%	14/1	870-1066[2]	N/A	49%	3%[7]
27.	**Lees-McRae College** (NC)	55	2.9	63%	35%	32%	82%	0%	12/1	18-23[2]	27%[4]	71%	8%
27.	**Shorter University** (GA)	55	3.0	60%[8]	47%	43%[6]	N/A	N/A	14/1	17-24[3]	34%	53%	N/A
27.	**Williams Baptist University** (AR)	55	2.7	60%	42%	42%	67%	0%	13/1	18-22	29%	57%	3%
30.	**Alderson Broaddus University** (WV)	54	2.6	56%	49%	47%	70%	4%	16/1	18-23	24%	41%	6%
30.	**Brescia University** (KY)	54	2.8	63%	46%	39%	89%	0%	11/1	19-23	N/A	43%	10%
30.	**Kentucky State University***	54	2.7	58%	39%	21%	65%	2%	11/1	16-21	26%[4]	45%	N/A
33.	**South Florida State College***	53	2.7	61%	42%	40%	69%	0%	11/1	N/A[2]	N/A	100%	N/A
34.	**Bennett College** (NC)	52	2.3	49%	31%	37%	72%	1%	10/1	780-930	18%	89%	19%
34.	**Emmanuel College** (GA)	52	2.6	60%	37%	46%	61%	0%	15/1	950-1110	N/A	43%	7%
36.	**Ferrum College** (VA)	51	2.8	52%	27%	35%	70%	0%	14/1	850-1078[2]	12%	72%	6%
37.	**Martin Methodist College** (TN)	49	2.7	54%	33%	33%	60%	0%	15/1	18-23	N/A	99%	14%
37.	**North Carolina Wesleyan College**	49	2.7	56%	28%	31%	79%	0%	17/1	870-1060[2]	23%	53%	3%
37.	**West Liberty University** (WV)*	49	2.6	70%	38%	43%[8]	66%	0.4%	15/1	17-23	34%	72%	2%
40.	**Brevard College**[1] (NC)	48	3.1	55%[8]	42%	42%[6]	N/A	N/A	11/1[4]	N/A[2]	N/A	42%[4]	N/A
40.	**Oakwood University** (AL)	48	2.9	73%[8]	37%	44%[6]	N/A	N/A	N/A	N/A	N/A	N/A	N/A
42.	**Talladega College** (AL)	47	2.6	56%	38%	41%[8]	66%	2%	16/1	N/A	N/A	47%	13%
43.	**Bluefield College** (VA)	46	2.8	57%	35%	21%	71%	0%	14/1	870-1085	25%	91%	7%
43.	**Ohio Valley University** (WV)	46	2.4	54%	43%	31%	69%	0%	11/1	18-23[2]	26%	49%	8%

Note: Key to footnotes, Page 113.

GRADUATION DAY AT THE
U.S. COAST GUARD ACADEMY

JESSICA HILL—AP

BEST REGIONAL COLLEGES

SOUTH ▶

Rank	School (State) (*Public)	Overall score	Peer assessment score (5.0=highest)	Average first-year student retention rate	2017 graduation rate: Predicted	2017 graduation rate: Actual	% of classes under 20 ('17)	% of classes of 50 or more ('17)	Student/ faculty ratio ('17)	SAT/ACT 25th-75th percentile** ('17)	Freshmen in top 25% of HS class ('17)	Accept- ance rate ('17)	Average alumni giving rate
45.	**Gordon State College** (GA)*	45	2.6	55%[8]	26%	50%[6]	N/A	N/A	20/1	840-1030	N/A	84%	1%
45.	**Limestone College** (SC)	45	2.5	55%	37%	26%	67%	0%	13/1[4]	17-22[2]	19%[4]	52%[4]	N/A
45.	**Point University** (GA)	45	2.6	57%	34%	27%	69%	1%	15/1	16-21[2]	27%[5]	35%	N/A
45.	**University of Arkansas–Pine Bluff***	45	2.7	68%	31%	29%	52%	2%	15/1	16-20	33%	47%	7%
49.	**Univ. of South Carolina–Beaufort***	44	2.9	56%	38%	24%[8]	57%	3%	15/1	930-1090	34%	64%	N/A
50.	**Chowan University** (NC)	43	2.8	48%	23%	26%	48%	0.2%	16/1	780-950	25%	63%	18%
51.	**Truett McConnell University** (GA)	42	2.6	65%	33%	38%	60%	6%	19/1	920-1120	28%	95%	1%
52.	**Everglades University**[1] (FL)	41	2.4	53%[8]	28%	45%[6]	88%[4]	0%[4]	13/1[4]	N/A[2]	N/A	74%[4]	0%[4]
52.	**Georgia Gwinnett College***	41	3.1	68%	29%	15%	37%	0%	18/1	910-1110	15%	88%	4%
52.	**Glenville State College** (WV)*	41	2.4	66%	36%	43%	60%	1%	18/1	16-21	23%	54%	3%
55.	**Central Baptist College** (AR)	40	2.5	66%	37%	24%	73%	0%	12/1	18-22	25%	68%	7%
55.	**Middle Georgia State University***	40	2.7	66%	29%	33%[8]	52%	1%	20/1	820-1020	N/A	59%	1%
55.	**Warner University** (FL)	40	2.6	63%	32%	33%	57%	1%	13/1	16-20[2]	2%[5]	41%	3%
58.	**Bluefield State College** (WV)*	39	2.5	63%	30%	25%	86%	0%	13/1	17-21	56%[5]	91%	5%
58.	**Pensacola State College** (FL)*	39	2.9	74%	38%	22%	85%	0.1%	21/1	17-22[2]	N/A	100%	8%
60.	**Kentucky Christian University**[1]	38	2.7	59%[8]	40%	35%[6]	N/A	N/A	11/1[4]	18-23[4]	N/A	39%[4]	N/A
61.	**College of Coastal Georgia***	36	2.8	61%	24%	23%	41%	2%	20/1	890-1090	N/A	95%	1%[4]
61.	**St. Augustine's University** (NC)	36	2.3	45%[8]	28%	30%[6]	64%	1%	12/1	760-950	N/A	76%	7%
61.	**Voorhees College** (SC)	36	2.3	52%[8]	20%	31%	61%	2%	17/1	800-940[2]	8%	53%	5%
64.	**Webber International University** (FL)	35	2.6	53%	34%	30%	49%	0%	21/1	17-20[2]	19%	49%	N/A

School (State) (*Public)	Peer assessment score (5.0=highest)	Average first-year student retention rate	2017 graduation rate: Predicted	2017 graduation rate: Actual	% of classes under 20 ('17)	% of classes of 50 or more ('17)	Student/ faculty ratio ('17)	SAT/ACT 25th-75th percentile** ('17)	Freshmen in top 25% of HS class ('17)	Accept- ance rate ('17)	Average alumni giving rate
SCHOOLS RANKED 65 THROUGH 85 ARE LISTED HERE ALPHABETICALLY											
Abraham Baldwin Agricultural College[1] (GA)*	2.5	61%[8]	33%	21%[6]	N/A	N/A	22/1[4]	820-1048[4]	N/A	66%[4]	N/A
Arkansas Baptist College[1]	2.1	47%[8]	20%	5%[6]	57%[4]	0%[4]	22/1[4]	17-19[4]	N/A	28%[4]	N/A
Atlanta Metropolitan State College[1] (GA)*	2.1	60%[8]	N/A	N/A	N/A	N/A	17/1[4]	17-21[4]	N/A	19%[4]	1%[4]
Benedict College[1] (SC)	2.3	59%[8]	19%	27%[6]	N/A	N/A	18/1[4]	N/A[2]	N/A	N/A	N/A
Brewton-Parker College[1] (GA)	2.4	40%[8]	34%	19%[6]	N/A	N/A	14/1[4]	N/A[2]	N/A	N/A	N/A
Broward College (FL)*	2.8	N/A	N/A	N/A	35%	0.2%	25/1	N/A[2]	4%	100%	0.2%
Chipola College[1] (FL)*	2.7	N/A	N/A	N/A	N/A	N/A	16/1[4]	N/A[2]	N/A	N/A	N/A
Crowley's Ridge College[1] (AR)	2.4	58%[8]	32%	29%[6]	N/A	N/A	10/1[4]	N/A[2]	N/A	N/A	N/A
East Georgia State College[1]*	2.4	N/A	N/A	N/A	N/A	N/A	24/1[4]	N/A[2]	N/A	N/A	N/A
ECPI University (VA)	2.1	52%	42%	36%	86%	0%	12/1	N/A[2]	N/A	71%	0%[4]
Edward Waters College[1] (FL)	2.3	49%[8]	18%	22%[6]	N/A	N/A	22/1[4]	15-18[4]	N/A	58%[4]	N/A
Florida College	2.5	N/A	47%	20%[6]	61%	7%	13/1	20-26[4]	N/A	79%	N/A
Georgia Highlands College[1]*	2.9	N/A	N/A	N/A	N/A	N/A	21/1[4]	N/A[2]	N/A	N/A	N/A
Indian River State College (FL)*	2.9	N/A	N/A	N/A	33%	1%	N/A	N/A[2]	N/A	100%	N/A
Lane College[1] (TN)	2.5	55%[8]	17%	25%[6]	N/A	N/A	19/1[4]	14-16[4]	N/A	50%[4]	N/A
LeMoyne-Owen College (TN)	2.5	48%[8]	25%	14%	77%	0%	13/1	14-17	N/A	100%	N/A
Livingstone College (NC)	2.3	51%	20%	26%	56%	1%	16/1	755-920[3]	8%	37%	10%
Morris College (SC)	2.2	49%[8]	17%	29%[6]	N/A	N/A	N/A	N/A	N/A	79%	N/A
Rust College[1] (MS)	2.4	51%[8]	24%	28%[6]	N/A	N/A	21/1[4]	13-17[4]	N/A	N/A	N/A
Shaw University (NC)	2.2	44%[8]	22%	18%	45%	0%	17/1	763-935	5%	53%	N/A
University of Arkansas–Fort Smith[1]*	2.8	65%[8]	39%	26%[6]	N/A	N/A	18/1[4]	N/A	N/A	N/A	N/A

MIDWEST ▶

Rank	School (State) (*Public)	Overall score	Peer assessment score (5.0=highest)	Average first-year student retention rate	2017 graduation rate: Predicted	2017 graduation rate: Actual	% of classes under 20 ('17)	% of classes of 50 or more ('17)	Student/ faculty ratio ('17)	SAT/ACT 25th-75th percentile** ('17)	Freshmen in top 25% of HS class ('17)	Accept- ance rate ('17)	Average alumni giving rate
1.	**Calvin College** (MI)	100	4.1	86%	72%	72%	30%	1%	13/1	23-30[2]	57%[5]	83%	20%
1.	**Taylor University** (IN)	100	4.0	88%	74%	79%	58%	5%	13/1	22-29	63%[5]	87%	19%
3.	**College of the Ozarks** (MO)	94	3.7	77%	48%	72%	55%	1%	14/1	21-26[3]	62%	16%	20%
4.	**Augustana University** (SD)	92	3.7	84%	70%	71%	51%	3%	12/1	23-29	64%	68%	11%
4.	**Ohio Northern University**	92	3.5	86%	74%	73%	63%	1%	11/1	22-28	55%	66%	11%
6.	**Dordt College** (IA)	91	3.5	84%	61%	64%	64%	5%	12/1	22-28[2]	43%	72%	21%
7.	**Northwestern College** (IA)	86	3.4	80%	61%	68%	68%	1%	11/1	21-27	59%	68%	18%
7.	**University of Mount Union** (OH)	86	3.6	78%	52%	62%	55%	0.2%	13/1	20-25	45%	81%	17%
9.	**Cottey College** (MO)	83	2.9	74%	56%	57%	96%	0%	6/1	19-23	39%	75%	6%
9.	**Goshen College** (IN)	83	3.4	79%	61%	72%	63%	1%	11/1	980-1238	46%	65%	20%

Note: Key to footnotes, Page 113.

MIDWEST ▶

Rank	School (State) (*Public)	Overall score	Peer assessment score (5.0=highest)	Average first-year student retention rate	2017 graduation rate: Predicted	2017 graduation rate: Actual	% of classes under 20 ('17)	% of classes of 50 or more ('17)	Student/ faculty ratio ('17)	SAT/ACT 25th-75th percentile** ('17)	Freshmen in top 25% of HS class ('17)	Accept-ance rate ('17)	Average alumni giving rate
9.	**Millikin University** (IL)	83	3.6	76%	56%	61%	72%	1%	10/1	19-26	38%	65%	11%
12.	**Cedarville University** (OH)	80	3.3	86%	71%	72%	60%	6%	14/1	23-29	62%[5]	71%	10%
13.	**Benedictine College** (KS)	79	3.5	78%	55%	64%	60%	1%	13/1	22-28	48%[5]	97%	22%
13.	**Loras College** (IA)	79	3.3	79%	64%	68%	46%	0%	12/1	20-26	46%	95%	19%
13.	**Marietta College** (OH)	79	3.2	69%	65%	49%	83%	0.2%	9/1	20-25	41%	68%	16%
16.	**Clarke University** (IA)	75	3.1	74%	52%	64%[6]	75%	0.4%	8/1	20-25	47%	63%	13%
16.	**Wisconsin Lutheran College**	75	3.0	75%	63%	67%	71%	0.3%	10/1	20-26	35%	90%	16%
18.	**Buena Vista University** (IA)	73	3.1	75%	62%	60%	73%	0.4%	9/1	19-24	38%	64%	6%
19.	**Adrian College** (MI)	72	3.2	66%	51%	52%	69%	1%	13/1	950-1148	52%	60%	10%
20.	**Huntington University** (IN)	71	3.3	81%	53%	57%	71%	1%	13/1	950-1170	49%	81%	16%
21.	**Saint Mary-of-the-Woods College** (IN)	69	3.1	74%	46%	57%	91%	0%	7/1	890-1070	N/A	75%	23%
21.	**Trinity Christian College** (IL)	69	2.8	84%	57%	68%	59%	0.4%	10/1	19-26	24%[5]	83%	11%
23.	**Hastings College** (NE)	68	3.2	70%	59%	54%	67%	2%	14/1	20-25[3]	45%	68%	18%
24.	**Central Methodist University** (MO)	65	2.8	66%	55%	52%	66%	2%	12/1	20-25	42%	63%	10%
24.	**Trine University** (IN)	65	3.3	74%	59%	55%	46%	2%	16/1	970-1160	51%	70%	9%
26.	**Manchester University** (IN)	62	3.2	68%	52%	57%	54%	1%	14/1	850-1100[2]	39%	62%	18%
27.	**Union College** (NE)	61	2.8	77%	50%	54%	70%	1%	9/1	19-26	N/A	60%	16%
28.	**Dakota Wesleyan University** (SD)	60	3.1	70%	40%	48%	66%	1%	11/1	20-24	36%	76%	8%
29.	**University of Jamestown** (ND)	59	3.2	73%	49%	53%	57%	2%	12/1	19-24[3]	37%	65%	15%
30.	**Blackburn College** (IL)	58	2.6	62%	46%	49%	78%	0%	12/1	18-23	35%	60%	14%
30.	**Bluffton University** (OH)	58	2.8	68%	51%	51%	68%	0%	11/1	18-24	34%	49%	8%
30.	**Dunwoody College of Tech.** (MN)	58	2.4	66%	40%	67%	84%	0%	10/1	N/A[2]	30%	81%	3%
33.	**Defiance College** (OH)	55	2.8	57%	44%	44%[8]	100%	0%	11/1	18-22[3]	23%	56%	8%
33.	**Eureka College** (IL)	55	2.7	72%	52%	44%	71%	0%	13/1	19-24	33%	62%	15%
35.	**Univ. of Wisconsin–Superior***	54	3.0	70%	52%	44%	62%	2%	16/1	19-23	26%	72%	5%

MIDWEST ▶

Rank School (State) (*Public)	Overall score	Peer assessment score (5.0=highest)	Average first-year student retention rate	2017 graduation rate: Predicted	2017 graduation rate: Actual	% of classes under 20 ('17)	% of classes of 50 or more ('17)	Student/faculty ratio ('17)	SAT/ACT 25th-75th percentile** ('17)	Freshmen in top 25% of HS class ('17)	Acceptance rate ('17)	Average alumni giving rate
36. **Briar Cliff University** (IA)	53	2.7	65%	49%	42%	72%	1%	12/1	19-24	30%	52%	11%
36. **McPherson College** (KS)	53	2.8	62%	46%	35%	76%	0%	13/1	19-22[2]	21%	69%	8%
36. **University of Minnesota–Crookston***	53	2.7	68%	50%	54%	71%	0.4%	16/1	19-24[3]	34%	69%	1%
39. **Culver-Stockton College** (MO)	52	2.8	69%	46%	47%	60%	0%	15/1	18-23	28%	55%	19%
39. **Grand View University** (IA)	52	2.7	70%	42%	50%	70%	0%	13/1	18-23	36%	93%	3%
39. **Oakland City University** (IN)	52	2.2	70%	43%	57%	83%	0%	11/1	950-1150[2]	19%[5]	72%	3%
42. **Valley City State University** (ND)*	51	2.9	71%	48%	35%	73%	3%	13/1	18-23	N/A	99%	9%
43. **Mayville State University** (ND)*	50	2.6	55%	44%	34%	86%	1%	14/1	18-23	N/A	48%	16%
44. **Lake Superior State University** (MI)*	48	2.8	69%	47%	44%	54%	6%	17/1	990-1180[2]	37%	56%	2%
44. **Ottawa University** (KS)	48	2.7	62%	50%	47%	65%	1%	12/1	18-22[2]	30%	22%	11%
46. **Crown College** (MN)	46	2.4	69%	50%	66%	70%	2%	19/1	18-25	17%[5]	51%	2%
46. **Wilmington College**[1] (OH)	46	2.9	67%[8]	40%	52%[6]	N/A	N/A	15/1[4]	18-23[4]	N/A	87%[4]	N/A
48. **Bethany College** (KS)	44	2.5	57%	45%	47%	65%	2%	14/1	18-23	25%	70%	11%[4]
48. **Maranatha Baptist University** (WI)	44	2.2	69%	44%	49%	80%	3%	11/1	20-25	37%[5]	73%	N/A
48. **Olivet College** (MI)	44	2.7	63%	40%	51%	55%	3%	17/1	18-23[4]	N/A	70%	7%[4]
51. **Tabor College** (KS)	43	2.6	60%	49%	38%	68%	1%	10/1	18-24	33%	52%	7%
52. **Dickinson State University** (ND)*	41	2.7	58%	49%	30%	78%	1%	10/1	18-23[9]	N/A	99%	1%
52. **Kansas Wesleyan University**	41	2.6	60%	43%	32%	70%	1%	13/1	19-24	34%	53%	8%
54. **Kuyper College**[1] (MI)	39	2.1	64%[8]	42%	56%[6]	N/A	N/A	9/1[4]	19-28[4]	N/A	73%[4]	N/A
54. **York College** (NE)	39	2.5	62%	44%	47%[6]	42%	1%	12/1	18-23	20%	25%	N/A
56. **Midland University**[1] (NE)	38	2.8	62%[8]	47%	46%[6]	N/A	N/A	16/1[4]	19-24[4]	N/A	61%[4]	N/A
57. **North Central University** (MN)	37	2.4	73%	41%	38%	54%	9%	16/1	18-25	45%	65%	4%
58. **Grace Christian University** (MI)	36	2.1	62%[8]	28%	41%	78%	1%	21/1	17-23[4]	25%	55%	8%
59. **MacMurray College**[1] (IL)	34	2.2	70%[8]	40%	28%[8]	70%[4]	1%[4]	12/1[4]	18-22[4]	31%[4]	57%[4]	13%[4]
59. **Rochester College** (MI)	34	2.6	63%[8]	41%	33%[6]	77%	1%	12/1	16-23	N/A	100%	N/A

School (State) (*Public)	Peer assessment score (5.0=highest)	Average first-year student retention rate	2017 graduation rate: Predicted	2017 graduation rate: Actual	% of classes under 20 ('17)	% of classes of 50 or more ('17)	Student/faculty ratio ('17)	SAT/ACT 25th-75th percentile** ('17)	Freshmen in top 25% of HS class ('17)	Acceptance rate ('17)	Average alumni giving rate
SCHOOLS RANKED 61 THROUGH 79 ARE LISTED HERE ALPHABETICALLY											
Bismarck State College[1] (ND)*	2.5	N/A	N/A	N/A	N/A	N/A	14/1[4]	17-22[4]	15%[4]	100%[4]	2%[4]
Central Christian College (KS)	2.0	59%	29%	37%	87%	1%	14/1	17-22[9]	N/A	35%	11%
Central State University (OH)*	1.8	48%	27%	20%	57%	1%	13/1	15-18[2]	26%	48%	31%
Finlandia University[1] (MI)	2.2	54%[8]	29%	28%[6]	N/A	N/A	9/1[4]	16-21[4]	N/A	46%[4]	N/A
Hannibal-LaGrange University (MO)	2.5	57%	44%	40%[6]	81%	1%	14/1	N/A	N/A	55%	4%
Harris-Stowe State University (MO)*	2.0	50%	27%	7%	N/A	N/A	16/1	16-19[3]	15%[4]	40%	N/A
Indiana University–Kokomo*	2.5	63%	37%	39%	46%	2%	16/1	950-1120	28%	70%	6%
Iowa Wesleyan University	2.4	53%	35%	27%	72%	0%	10/1	18-22[3]	9%	48%	6%
Kendall College[1] (IL)	2.4	63%[8]	37%	19%[8]	72%[4]	1%[4]	9/1[4]	18-21[4]	N/A	84%[4]	N/A
Lincoln College[1] (IL)	2.2	44%[8]	25%	8%[6]	N/A	N/A	18/1[4]	15-19[4]	N/A	62%[4]	N/A
Missouri Southern State University*	2.5	64%	29%	33%	42%	1%	19/1	19-24	N/A	95%	N/A
Missouri Valley College[1]	2.2	43%[8]	34%	27%[6]	N/A	N/A	14/1[4]	N/A	N/A	46%[4]	N/A
Missouri Western State University[1]*	2.6	65%[8]	39%	31%[6]	N/A	N/A	16/1[4]	N/A[2]	N/A	N/A	5%[7]
Ohio Christian University	2.6	64%[8]	31%	33%[6]	N/A	N/A	11/1	N/A[2]	N/A	N/A	N/A
Shawnee State University (OH)*	2.1	65%	36%	24%	47%	20%	15/1	19-24[2]	8%[5]	70%	N/A
Sterling College[1] (KS)	2.4	70%[8]	46%	42%[6]	N/A	N/A	12/1[4]	18-23[4]	N/A	37%[4]	N/A
Urbana University[1] (OH)	2.3	49%[8]	37%	35%[6]	N/A	N/A	19/1[4]	17-21[4]	N/A	92%[4]	N/A
Waldorf University[1] (IA)	2.1	56%[8]	34%	28%[6]	N/A	N/A	21/1[4]	18-23[4]	N/A	67%[4]	N/A
Wilberforce University[1] (OH)	2.2	51%[8]	20%	26%[6]	N/A	N/A	9/1[4]	15-19[4]	N/A	38%[4]	N/A

WEST ▶

Rank School (State) (*Public)	Overall score	Peer assessment score (5.0=highest)	Average first-year student retention rate	2017 graduation rate: Predicted	2017 graduation rate: Actual	% of classes under 20 ('17)	% of classes of 50 or more ('17)	Student/faculty ratio ('17)	SAT/ACT 25th-75th percentile** ('17)	Freshmen in top 25% of HS class ('17)	Acceptance rate ('17)	Average alumni giving rate
1. **Carroll College** (MT)	100	3.6	81%	62%	71%	62%	2%	11/1	22-28	64%[5]	78%	14%
2. **William Jessup University** (CA)	90	3.5	75%	50%	64%	73%	1%	12/1	1000-1215	43%[5]	66%	5%
3. **California State U.–Maritime Academy***	89	3.3	81%	58%	64%	25%	2%	14/1	1070-1250	N/A	67%	6%
4. **Texas Lutheran University**	87	3.5	71%	53%	52%	57%	0.2%	14/1	970-1150	44%	49%	14%
5. **Montana Tech of the Univ. of Mont.***	83	3.7	74%	62%	44%	59%	5%	13/1	22-27	56%	92%	13%
5. **Oregon Inst. of Technology***	83	3.6	77%	48%	44%	59%	3%	15/1	1040-1230	57%	61%	5%
7. **Oklahoma Baptist University**	82	3.5	75%	60%	52%	70%	3%	12/1	20-26	56%	65%	6%

WEST ▶

Rank	School (State) (*Public)	Overall score	Peer assessment score (5.0=highest)	Average first-year student retention rate	2017 graduation rate Predicted	Actual	% of classes under 20 ('17)	% of classes of 50 or more ('17)	Student/ faculty ratio ('17)	SAT/ACT 25th-75th percentile** ('17)	Freshmen in top 25% of HS class ('17)	Accept-ance rate ('17)	Average alumni giving rate
8.	**Rocky Mountain College** (MT)	78	3.3	70%	53%	52%	75%	1%	11/1	20-25	43%	64%	9%
9.	**University of Montana–Western***	77	3.4	70%	37%	50%	64%	0%	17/1	16-22[3]	18%	61%	3%
10.	**Warner Pacific College** (OR)	76	3.2	65%	47%	39%	82%	1%	9/1	880-1100	34%	95%	4%
11.	**San Diego Christian College**	73	3.1	70%	39%	57%	86%	0%	14/1	850-980[2]	28%	62%	N/A
12.	**John Paul the Great Catholic U.** (CA)	72	3.2	74%	57%	61%	55%	9%	15/1	1020-1190	35%[5]	95%	6%
13.	**Southwestern Adventist Univ.** (TX)	71	2.9	74%	40%	37%	73%	1%	12/1	900-1140	30%[5]	62%	5%
14.	**Howard Payne University** (TX)	67	3.1	54%	47%	41%	84%	0%	10/1	19-22[3]	28%	59%	7%
15.	**Marymount California University**	65	3.6	64%	51%	35%	61%	0.3%	16/1	860-1040[2]	N/A	83%	0.4%
16.	**McMurry University** (TX)	64	3.1	57%	41%	36%	74%	1%	11/1	17-22	33%	43%	9%
17.	**Brigham Young University–Hawaii**[1]	58	3.3	62%[8]	49%	47%[6]	N/A	N/A	16/1[4]	22-26[4]	N/A	27%[4]	N/A
17.	**Brigham Young University–Idaho**[1]	58	3.3	69%[8]	43%	48%[6]	N/A	N/A	23/1[4]	20-25[4]	N/A	96%[4]	N/A
17.	**East Texas Baptist University**	58	3.2	59%	42%	31%	50%	1%	15/1	18-23	38%	54%	3%
20.	**University of Providence** (MT)	54	3.0	64%[8]	44%	45%	68%	0%	10/1	17-24[3]	N/A	76%	N/A
21.	**University of Hawaii–West Oahu***	53	3.0	66%	53%	39%	47%	0%	24/1	16-20[2]	45%	78%	3%
22.	**Arizona Christian University** (AZ)	51	3.0	62%[8]	50%	47%	N/A	N/A	16/1	N/A	N/A	64%	N/A
22.	**Cogswell Polytechnical College** (CA)	51	2.8	79%	50%	37%	80%	0%	11/1	1070-1270[2]	N/A	65%	N/A
24.	**Southwestern Christian U.** (OK)	45	2.9	53%	32%	26%	87%	0%	10/1	6-22[3]	N/A	47%	N/A
25.	**Colorado Mesa University***	40	2.9	71%	36%	33%	51%	8%	21/1	18-24	29%	82%	2%
26.	**Dixie State University** (UT)*	39	2.8	56%	40%	20%	42%	5%	22/1	17-23[2]	29%	100%	23%
27.	**Okla. State U. Inst. of Tech.–Okmulgee***	37	2.9	59%	40%	32%	76%	0%	15/1	16-21	22%	29%	1%

School (State) (*Public)	Peer assessment score (5.0=highest)	Average first-year student retention rate	2017 graduation rate Predicted	Actual	% of classes under 20 ('17)	% of classes of 50 or more ('17)	Student/ faculty ratio ('17)	SAT/ACT 25th-75th percentile** ('17)	Freshmen in top 25% of HS class ('17)	Accept-ance rate ('17)	Average alumni giving rate
SCHOOLS RANKED 28 THROUGH 36 ARE LISTED HERE ALPHABETICALLY											
Bacone College[1] (OK)	1.9	36%[8]	26%	9%[6]	N/A	N/A	21/1[4]	15-19[4]	N/A	50%[4]	N/A
Huston-Tillotson University[1] (TX)	2.7	57%[8]	36%	25%[8]	N/A	N/A	N/A	690-920[4]	N/A	36%[4]	N/A
Jarvis Christian College (TX)	2.2	50%	21%	21%	56%	4%	20/1	750-930	10%[4]	11%	5%
Lewis-Clark State College (ID)*	3.1	59%[8]	35%	15%	59%	1%	13/1	930-1100[9]	24%	100%	N/A
Montana State Univ.–Northern[1]*	2.8	60%[8]	37%	23%[6]	N/A	N/A	16/1[4]	16-22[4]	N/A	100%[4]	N/A
Nevada State College[1]*	2.5	70%[8]	49%	14%[6]	N/A	N/A	16/1[4]	N/A[2]	N/A	76%[4]	N/A
Oklahoma Panhandle State Univ.*	2.4	59%[8]	38%	32%[6]	N/A	N/A	14/1[4]	N/A[2]	N/A	N/A	N/A
Rogers State University (OK)*	2.7	66%	37%	25%	59%	2%	18/1	18-19	19%	83%	N/A
Wiley College[1] (TX)	2.2	58%[8]	21%	19%[6]	N/A	N/A	18/1[4]	N/A[2]	N/A	N/A	N/A

The Top Public Regional Colleges ▶

NORTH

Rank School (State)

1. **U.S. Coast Guard Academy** (CT)
2. **U.S. Merchant Marine Acad.** (NY)
3. **Maine Maritime Academy**
4. **University of Maine–Farmington**
5. **Pennsylvania Col. of Technology**
5. **SUNY College of Technology–Alfred**

SOUTH

Rank School (State)

1. **University of South Carolina–Aiken**
2. **University of South Carolina–Upstate**
3. **Lander University** (SC)
4. **Kentucky State University**
5. **South Florida State College**

MIDWEST

Rank School (State)

1. **University of Wisconsin–Superior**
2. **University of Minnesota–Crookston**
3. **Valley City State University** (ND)
4. **Mayville State University** (ND)
5. **Lake Superior State University** (MI)

WEST

Rank School (State)

1. **California State University–Maritime Academy**
2. **Montana Tech of the U. of Mont.**
2. **Oregon Inst. of Technology**
4. **University of Montana–Western**
5. **University of Hawaii–West Oahu**

Footnotes:

1. School refused to fill out U.S. News statistical survey. Data that appear are from school in previous years or from another source such as the National Center for Education Statistics.
2. SAT and/or ACT not required by school for some or all applicants.
3. In reporting SAT/ACT scores, the school did not include all students for whom it had scores or refused to tell U.S. News whether all students with scores had been included.
4. Data reported to U.S. News in previous years.
5. Data based on fewer than 51 percent of enrolled freshmen.
6. Some or all data reported to the National Center for Education Statistics.
7. Data reported to the Council for Aid to Education.
8. This rate, normally based on four years of data, is given here for fewer than four years because school didn't report rate for the most recent year or years to U.S. News.
9. SAT and/or ACT may not be required by school for some or all applicants, and in reporting SAT/ACT scores, the school did not include all students for whom it had scores, or refused to tell U.S. News whether all students with scores had been included.
**The SAT scores used in the rankings and published in this guidebook are for the "new" SAT test taken starting March 2016.
N/A means not available.

Best Historically Black Colleges

Increasingly, the nation's top historically black colleges and universities are an appealing option for applicants of all races; many HBCUs, in fact, now actively recruit Hispanic, international and white students in addition to African-American high school graduates. Which schools offer the best undergraduate education? U.S. News each year surveys administrators at the HBCUs, asking the president, provost and admissions dean at each to rate the academic quality of all other HBCUs with which they are familiar.

In addition to the two most recent years of survey results reflected in the peer assessment score, the rankings below are based on nearly all the same ranking indicators (although weighted slightly differently) as those used in ranking the regional universities. These include graduation and retention rates, social mobility, high school class standing, admission test scores, and the strength of the faculty, among others.

To be part of the universe, a school must be designated by the Department of Education as an HBCU, be a baccalaureate-granting institution that enrolls primarily first-year, first-time students, and have been part of this year's Best Colleges survey and ranking process. If an HBCU is unranked in the 2019 Best Colleges rankings, it is also unranked here; reasons that schools are not ranked vary, but include a school's policy not to use test scores in admissions decisions.

There are 80 HBCUs, and 76 were ranked. HBCUs in the top three-quarters are numerically ranked, and those in the bottom quarter are listed alphabetically. For more detail and an explanation of the methodology changes U.S. News made for this ranking, visit **usnews.com/hbcu.**

Key Measures

Outcomes	**30%**
Expert Opinion	**25%**
Faculty Resources	**20%**
Financial Resources	**10%**
Student Excellence	**10%**
Alumni Giving	**5%**

Rank	School (State) (*Public)	Overall score	Peer assessment score (5.0=highest)	Average first-year student retention rate	Average graduation rate	% of classes under 20 ('17)	% of classes of 50 or more ('17)	Student/faculty ratio ('17)	% of faculty who are full time ('17)	SAT/ACT 25th-75th percentile** ('17)	Freshmen in top 25% of HS class ('17)	Acceptance rate ('17)	Average alumni giving rate
1.	**Spelman College** (GA)	100	4.6	90%	76%	60%	1%	11/1	88%	1070-1215	53%[5]	40%	32%
2.	**Howard University** (DC)	93	4.5	89%	61%	55%	5%	8/1	89%	1090-1290[3]	58%[5]	41%	11%
3.	**Hampton University** (VA)	74	4.3	78%	60%[6]	54%	6%	13/1	92%	20-24[2]	35%	36%	17%
3.	**Morehouse College** (GA)	74	4.2	82%	52%	53%	0.2%	12/1	91%	950-1160	36%	74%	14%
5.	**Xavier University of Louisiana**	72	4.3	72%	42%	55%	3%	14/1	97%	20-25	54%	64%	17%
6.	**Fisk University** (TN)	63	3.5	81%	45%[6]	73%	0%	10/1	81%	16-22	26%	45%	25%
7.	**Claflin University** (SC)	62	3.9	76%	44%[6]	64%	1%	13/1	86%	18-20	30%	41%	46%
7.	**North Carolina A&T State Univ.***	62	4.2	77%	45%[6]	27%	11%	18/1	87%	930-1090	33%	62%	8%
9.	**Florida A&M University***	60	3.8	83%	40%[8]	31%	14%	16/1	93%	18-22	27%[5]	46%	5%
10.	**North Carolina Central Univ.***	59	3.9	79%	44%	38%	5%	16/1	87%	890-1030	22%	83%	11%
11.	**Dillard University** (LA)	57	3.6	73%	38%[6]	52%	1%	14/1	80%	18-21	38%[5]	41%	18%
12.	**Delaware State University***	53	3.6	71%	41%	45%	4%	15/1	85%	820-990	25%	45%	10%
12.	**Tougaloo College** (MS)	53	3.2	73%	47%[6]	67%	0.4%	9/1	92%	16-24	51%	75%	24%
14.	**Morgan State University** (MD)*	51	3.7	75%	33%[6]	47%	2%	13/1	86%	900-1070	25%[5]	64%	15%
15.	**Clark Atlanta University**	48	3.5	66%	39%[6]	31%	7%	20/1	84%	17-22	28%	58%	2%
15.	**Tuskegee University**[1] (AL)	48	4.0	72%[8]	46%[6]	N/A	N/A	14/1[4]	100%[4]	21-22[4]	N/A	50%[4]	N/A
17.	**Jackson State University** (MS)*	47	3.6	70%[8]	40%[6]	39%	10%	17/1	84%	17-21	N/A	72%	N/A
17.	**Univ. of Maryland–Eastern Shore***	47	3.3	66%	36%	59%	3%	13/1	87%	860-1040	N/A	39%	3%
19.	**Virginia State University***	46	3.4	70%	45%[6]	N/A	N/A	15/1	91%	820-1010[3]	18%[5]	91%	5%
20.	**Prairie View A&M University** (TX)*	44	3.5	68%	34%[6]	16%	8%	20/1	92%	870-1050	19%	79%	N/A
21.	**Alcorn State University** (MS)*	43	3.1	75%	34%[6]	48%	2%	19/1	89%	16-21	N/A	83%	8%
22.	**Fayetteville State University** (NC)*	42	3.1	75%	33%	42%	1%	15/1	92%	870-1020	24%	68%	2%
22.	**Johnson C. Smith University** (NC)	42	3.2	67%	46%	76%	0%	12/1	78%	748-960	20%[4]	38%	15%
22.	**Kentucky State University***	42	2.8	58%	21%	65%	2%	11/1	93%	16-21	26%[4]	45%	N/A
22.	**Norfolk State University** (VA)*	42	3.4	74%	36%	57%	2%	17/1	87%	840-1040	15%	90%	N/A
26.	**Alabama Agricultural & Mechanical U.***	41	3.5	59%[8]	29%[6]	41%	3%	18/1	87%	16-19[3]	N/A	90%	11%
27.	**Bowie State University** (MD)*	40	3.3	74%	37%[6]	46%	2%	16/1	77%	860-1040	N/A	41%[4]	6%
27.	**Lincoln University** (PA)*	40	2.9	73%	43%[6]	22%	0%	15/1	73%	870-1070	34%[5]	80%	13%
29.	**Bethune-Cookman University** (FL)	37	3.3	65%	38%	43%	3%	16/1	77%	15-19	10%	54%	6%

Note: Key to footnotes, Page 105

Rank	School (State) (*Public)	Overall score	Peer assessment score (5.0=highest)	Average first-year student retention rate	Average graduation rate	% of classes under 20 ('17)	% of classes of 50 or more ('17)	Student/ faculty ratio ('17)	% of faculty who are full time ('17)	SAT/ACT 25th-75th percentile** ('17)	Freshmen in top 25% of HS class ('17)	Accept-ance rate ('17)	Average alumni giving rate
29.	**Elizabeth City State Univ.** (NC)*	37	2.6	71%	38%	74%	0%	14/1	N/A	860-990[3]	3%	60%	N/A
31.	**Alabama State University***	36	3.1	59%	26%[6]	49%	0.3%	15/1	76%	16-19	34%[5]	98%	4%
31.	**Fort Valley State University** (GA)*	36	2.9	71%	28%[6]	52%	4%	17/1	91%	820-910	16%	41%	9%
31.	**Southern U. and A&M College** (LA)*	36	3.1	65%	31%	38%	8%	16/1	88%	16-20	7%[4]	34%	14%
34.	**Tennessee State University***	35	3.4	47%[8]	38%[6]	57%	2%	14/1[4]	78%	16-20[4]	N/A	48%	N/A
34.	**University of Arkansas–Pine Bluff***	35	3.1	68%	26%	52%	2%	15/1	93%	16-20	33%	47%	7%
36.	**Bennett College** (NC)	34	2.8	49%	42%	72%	1%	10/1	82%	780-930	18%	89%	19%
36.	**Mississippi Valley State Univ.***	34	2.9	63%	28%[6]	60%	1%	15/1	86%	16-19	N/A	86%	N/A
36.	**West Virginia State University***	34	3.0	59%	27%	58%	2%	13/1	79%	17-22	N/A	98%	4%
36.	**Winston-Salem State Univ.**[1] (NC)*	34	3.3	77%[8]	46%[6]	N/A	N/A	14/1[4]	88%[4]	800-940[4]	N/A	63%[4]	N/A
40.	**Albany State University** (GA)*	32	2.9	69%	34%[6]	42%	1%	15/1	88%	740-900	24%[5]	97%	7%[4]
40.	**Central State University** (OH)*	32	2.9	48%	22%	57%	1%	13/1	72%	15-18[2]	26%	48%	31%
40.	**Florida Memorial University**[1]	32	2.9	68%[8]	38%[6]	N/A	N/A	16/1[4]	90%[4]	16-19[4]	N/A	23%[4]	N/A
40.	**South Carolina State University***	32	2.8	65%	37%	54%	2%	17/1	84%	15-18	27%	78%	7%
44.	**Philander Smith College** (AR)	31	2.8	68%	37%[6]	73%	0%	15/1	75%	15-19	29%	24%	6%
45.	**Grambling State University** (LA)*	30	3.0	66%	35%[6]	36%	8%	26/1	97%	16-20	15%	43%	4%
45.	**Oakwood University** (AL)	30	3.3	73%[8]	44%[6]	N/A	N/A	N/A	N/A	N/A	N/A	N/A	N/A
45.	**Texas Southern University***	30	3.2	52%	19%[6]	34%	18%	19/1	79%	717-912	16%	67%	3%
48.	**Talladega College** (AL)	29	2.9	56%	41%[8]	66%	2%	16/1	82%	N/A	N/A	47%	13%
48.	**Univ. of the District of Columbia***	29	2.9	63%	32%	79%	4%	N/A	61%[4]	700-910[4]	N/A	39%	0.4%[4]
50.	**Bluefield State College** (WV)*	26	2.8	63%	23%[6]	86%	0%	13/1	81%	17-21	56%[5]	91%	5%
50.	**Lincoln University** (MO)*	26	2.8	52%	20%	46%	2%	17/1	87%	14-19	15%	52%	9%[4]
50.	**Virginia Union University**	26	3.0	56%	30%	47%	2%	16/1	90%	780-980[2]	12%[5]	50%	9%
53.	**Coppin State University** (MD)*	24	2.8	67%	20%[6]	N/A	N/A	14/1	74%	850-1010[3]	N/A	N/A	N/A
54.	**Savannah State University** (GA)*	23	2.9	60%[8]	28%	32%	0.1%	17/1	93%	860-1010[3]	N/A	52%	5%
55.	**Southern University–New Orleans***	21	2.7	53%	15%[6]	46%	0.3%	20/1	87%	15-18	24%[5]	25%	1%
55.	**St. Augustine's University** (NC)	21	2.6	45%[8]	30%[6]	64%	1%	12/1	81%	760-950	N/A	76%	7%
55.	**Voorhees College** (SC)	21	2.7	52%[8]	31%[6]	61%	2%	17/1	91%	800-940[2]	8%	53%	5%

School (State) (*Public)	Peer assessment score (5.0=highest)	Average first-year student retention rate	Average graduation rate	% of classes under 20 ('17)	% of classes of 50 or more ('17)	Student/ faculty ratio ('17)	% of faculty who are full time ('17)	SAT/ACT 25th-75th percentile** ('17)	Freshmen in top 25% of HS class ('17)	Accept-ance rate ('17)	Average alumni giving rate
SCHOOLS RANKED 58 THROUGH 76 ARE LISTED HERE ALPHABETICALLY											
Allen University[1] (SC)	2.4	53%[8]	22%[6]	N/A	N/A	15/1[4]	100%[4]	N/A[2]	N/A	N/A	N/A
Arkansas Baptist College[1]	2.4	47%[8]	5%[6]	57%[4]	0%[4]	22/1[4]	71%[4]	17-19[4]	N/A	28%[4]	N/A
Benedict College[1] (SC)	2.9	59%[8]	27%[6]	N/A	N/A	18/1[4]	87%[4]	N/A[2]	N/A	N/A	N/A
Cheyney U. of Pennsylvania*	2.4	54%[8]	20%[6]	N/A	N/A	N/A	75%[4]	650-860[4]	N/A	39%	N/A
Edward Waters College[1] (FL)	2.4	49%[8]	22%[6]	N/A	N/A	22/1[4]	82%[4]	15-18[4]	N/A	58%[4]	N/A
Harris-Stowe State University (MO)*	2.7	50%	7%	N/A	N/A	16/1	38%	16-19[3]	15%[4]	40%	N/A
Huston-Tillotson University[1] (TX)	2.7	57%[8]	25%[8]	N/A	N/A	N/A	N/A	690-920[4]	N/A	36%[4]	N/A
Jarvis Christian College (TX)	2.6	50%	17%[6]	56%	4%	20/1	74%	750-930	10%[4]	11%	5%
Lane College[1] (TN)	2.6	55%[8]	25%[6]	N/A	N/A	19/1[4]	95%[4]	14-16[4]	N/A	50%[4]	N/A
Langston University (OK)*	2.8	61%[8]	15%[6]	50%	7%	17/1	92%	17-26[3]	N/A	43%	N/A
LeMoyne-Owen College (TN)	2.5	48%[8]	15%[6]	77%	0%	13/1	70%	14-17	N/A	100%	N/A
Livingstone College (NC)	2.5	51%	25%	56%	1%	16/1	94%	755-920[3]	8%	37%	10%
Morris College (SC)	2.7	49%[8]	29%[6]	N/A	N/A	N/A	N/A	N/A	N/A	79%	N/A
Paine College[1] (GA)	2.2	41%[8]	20%[6]	N/A	N/A	10/1[4]	81%[4]	14-17[4]	N/A	25%[4]	N/A
Rust College[1] (MS)	2.8	51%[8]	28%[6]	N/A	N/A	21/1[4]	98%[4]	13-17[4]	N/A	N/A	N/A
Shaw University (NC)	2.8	44%[8]	23%[6]	45%	0%	17/1	79%	763-935	5%	53%	N/A
Stillman College (AL)	2.6	64%[8]	20%[6]	N/A	N/A	14/1	79%	N/A	N/A	N/A	15%
Wilberforce University[1] (OH)	2.5	51%[8]	26%[6]	N/A	N/A	9/1[4]	60%[4]	15-19[4]	N/A	38%[4]	N/A
Wiley College[1] (TX)	2.8	58%[8]	19%[6]	N/A	N/A	18/1[4]	83%[4]	N/A[2]	N/A	N/A	N/A

Sources: Statistical data from the schools. The spring 2018 peer assessment data was collected by U.S. News.

Best Online Degree Programs

When we surveyed colleges in 2017 about their online options, more than 350 schools reported having bachelor's programs that can be completed without showing up in person for class (though attendance may be required for testing, orientations or support services). These offerings, typically degree-completion programs aimed at working adults and community college grads, were evaluated on their success at engaging students, the credentials of their faculty, and the services and technologies made available remotely. The table below features some of the most significant ranking factors, such as the prevalence of faculty holding a Ph.D. or other terminal degree, class size, the percentages of new entrants who stayed enrolled and later graduated, and the debt load of recent graduates. The top half of programs are listed here. Ranks are determined by the institutions' rounded overall program scores, displayed below. To see the rest of the ranked online bachelor's programs and to read the full methodology, visit usnews.com/online. You'll also find detail-rich profile pages for each of the schools and (in case you want to plan ahead) rankings of online MBA programs and graduate programs in engineering, nursing, education and more.

(*Public, **For profit)

Rank	School	Overall program score	Average peer assessment score (5.0=highest)	'17 total program enrollment	'17 - '18 tuition[1]	'17 full-time faculty with Ph.D.	'17 average class size	'17 retention rate	'17 graduation rate[2]	% graduates with debt ('17)	Average debt of graduates ('17)
1.	Ohio State University–Columbus*	100	3.5	266	$387	59%	27	94%	91%	40%	$13,789
2.	Embry-Riddle Aeronautical University (FL)	98	3.6	15,257	$375	64%	16	80%	26%	14%	$7,982
2.	Temple University* (PA)	98	3.7	247	$595	66%	17	100%	N/A	62%	$19,919
4.	Arizona State University*	95	3.8	29,621	$510	69%	42	89%	66%	63%	$20,081
5.	Utah State University*	94	3.6	1,599	$325	59%	54	66%	58%	59%	$18,716
6.	Oregon State University*	93	3.8	5,424	$208	66%	34	82%	41%	64%	$25,700
7.	Pennsylvania State University–World Campus*	92	4.2	8,415	$555	61%	27	80%	38%	73%	$37,229
7.	University of North Carolina–Wilmington*	92	3.2	1,139	$668	90%	32	98%	N/A	39%	$15,988
9.	Colorado State University–Global Campus*	91	3.4	11,779	$350	100%	14	69%	48%	61%	$24,605
9.	University of Oklahoma*	91	3.5	1,234	$672	90%	17	79%	40%	55%	$22,507
9.	West Texas A&M University*	91	2.8	1,260	$295	76%	36	86%	77%	56%	$10,100
12.	University of Florida*	90	3.6	2,530	$500	76%	70	88%	66%	53%	$18,223
12.	Western Kentucky University*	90	3.1	3,775	$510	60%	19	83%	52%	44%	$15,895
14.	Loyola University Chicago (IL)	89	3.4	403	$655	85%	13	82%	N/A	53%	$24,731
15.	University of Illinois–Chicago*	88	3.3	286	$537	26%	22	94%	48%	60%	$15,390
16.	CUNY School of Professional Studies*	87	3.1	1,865	$285	75%	17	59%	39%	58%	$6,779
16.	New England Institute of Technology (RI)	87	3.1	131	$230	81%	13	83%	N/A	96%	$29,780
16.	University of Arkansas*	87	3.3	799	$246	57%	30	89%	66%	47%	$24,893
16.	University of Central Florida*	87	3.7	11,273	$300	70%	73	83%	68%	60%	$21,238
16.	University of Massachusetts–Amherst*	87	3.6	1,659	$390	61%	27	74%	70%	62%	$23,333
16.	University of Nebraska–Omaha*	87	3.4	175	$442	76%	24	83%	68%	57%	$30,785
22.	University of Massachusetts–Lowell*	86	3.5	2,084	$375	83%	25	84%	40%	54%	$28,566
23.	California Baptist University	85	3.1	2,235	$566	74%	20	85%	N/A	88%	$34,001
23.	Colorado State University*	85	3.5	578	$462	69%	13	78%	50%	71%	$25,729
23.	Daytona State College* (FL)	85	2.4	1,451	$550	56%	24	79%	61%	40%	$23,115
23.	George Washington University (DC)	85	3.6	422	$580	40%	18	67%	57%	31%	$20,452
23.	Robert Morris University (PA)	85	2.7	451	$745	85%	14	65%	88%	51%	$33,235
23.	Siena Heights University (MI)	85	N/A	1,403	$510	64%	16	87%	79%	68%	$19,745
23.	University of Missouri–St. Louis*	85	3.2	25	$452	60%	25	100%	77%	47%	$5,862
23.	Washington State University*	85	3.6	2,154	$569	75%	31	71%	50%	56%	$21,980
31.	City University of Seattle (WA)	84	3.0	2,515	$414	12%	10	65%	48%	21%	$9,702
31.	Creighton University (NE)	84	3.4	147	$445	100%	12	77%	N/A	65%	$24,933
31.	University of Georgia*	84	3.6	113	$562	100%	18	72%	N/A	59%	$17,102
31.	University of North Florida*	84	3.0	236	$285	94%	30	82%	N/A	32%	$7,330
35.	Ball State University* (IN)	83	3.4	1,136	$501	65%	28	86%	41%	70%	$26,752
35.	Charleston Southern University (SC)	83	2.9	295	$490	81%	13	55%	53%	73%	$29,245
35.	Fort Hays State University* (KS)	83	3.0	7,928	$213	57%	24	90%	70%	28%	$23,881
35.	Regent University (VA)	83	2.8	4,392	$395	76%	17	76%	32%	67%	$30,578
35.	University of Cincinnati* (OH)	83	3.1	2,272	$1,098	56%	30	64%	79%	68%	$24,733
35.	University of Nebraska–Lincoln*	83	3.5	25	$551	95%	30	77%	N/A	46%	$29,889
41.	Indiana University– Online*	82	3.3	2,304	$315	65%	23	86%	63%	78%	$26,426
41.	Marist College (NY)	82	2.9	150	$675	67%	15	94%	54%	85%	$26,255

N/A=Data were not provided by the school. **1.** Tuition is reported on a per-credit-hour basis. Out-of-state tuition is listed for public institutions.
2. Displayed here for standardization are six-year graduation rates.

(*Public, **For profit)

Rank	School	Overall program score	Average peer assessment score (5.0=highest)	'17 total program enrollment	'17 - '18 tuition[1]	'17 full-time faculty with Ph.D.	'17 average class size	'17 retention rate	'17 graduation rate[2]	% graduates with debt ('17)	Average debt of graduates ('17)
41.	**Pace University** (NY)	82	2.8	352	$555	94%	10	69%	57%	47%	$36,050
41.	**Sacred Heart University** (CT)	82	2.6	305	$575	75%	16	87%	67%	71%	$26,707
41.	**Savannah College of Art and Design** (GA)	82	3.2	764	$798	28%	19	79%	45%	71%	$42,424
41.	**University of Illinois–Springfield***	82	3.5	1,091	$359	79%	21	78%	47%	61%	$23,317
47.	**Northern Arizona University***	81	3.4	4,599	$425	59%	32	88%	56%	66%	$20,303
47.	**Sam Houston State University*** (TX)	81	2.7	2,181	$228	95%	37	79%	N/A	63%	$24,065
47.	**Southeast Missouri State University***	81	3.0	858	$273	97%	30	72%	38%	71%	N/A
47.	**University of Denver** (CO)	81	3.3	103	$623	100%	7	85%	42%	65%	$40,676
47.	**University of North Carolina–Charlotte***	81	3.5	589	$583	70%	26	91%	79%	33%	$15,650
47.	**University of North Texas***	81	3.2	1,400	$695	77%	40	80%	N/A	60%	$20,126
47.	**University of the Incarnate Word** (TX)	81	2.3	1,470	$530	100%	18	71%	65%	67%	$21,397
47.	**Western Carolina University*** (NC)	81	3.0	1,223	$485	N/A	22	80%	62%	47%	$16,214
47.	**Westfield State University*** (MA)	81	2.4	188	$306	92%	19	88%	47%	70%	$18,412
56.	**Dakota Wesleyan University** (SD)	80	2.4	170	$375	38%	14	89%	N/A	62%	$30,705
56.	**Lee University** (TN)	80	3.0	927	$214	85%	9	87%	N/A	66%	$24,151
56.	**University of Arizona***	80	3.1	792	$490	73%	26	81%	N/A	65%	$21,299
56.	**University of Wisconsin–Whitewater***	80	3.4	230	$389	67%	25	84%	58%	60%	N/A
60.	**Florida International University***	79	3.1	4,405	$247	75%	49	87%	31%	62%	$10,784
60.	**SUNY College of Technology–Delhi***	79	3.0	930	$333	44%	18	69%	50%	50%	$17,333
60.	**University at Buffalo–SUNY***	79	3.5	125	$333	100%	36	84%	N/A	N/A	N/A
60.	**University of Bridgeport** (CT)	79	2.7	1,258	$525	92%	15	87%	70%	N/A	N/A
60.	**University of Massachusetts–Boston***	79	3.4	440	$410	74%	28	73%	59%	55%	$19,524
60.	**Western Illinois University***	79	N/A	668	$285	76%	23	78%	42%	44%	$8,014
66.	**Central Michigan University***	78	3.3	1,441	$417	77%	20	62%	29%	67%	$13,620
66.	**Clarion University of Pennsylvania***	78	2.3	612	$337	85%	25	82%	60%	71%	$23,935
66.	**Old Dominion University*** (VA)	78	3.1	6,369	$369	68%	42	83%	59%	N/A	N/A
66.	**University of North Dakota***	78	3.4	423	$300	71%	19	58%	42%	62%	$27,945
66.	**Utica College** (NY)	78	3.0	1,021	$400	59%	15	83%	52%	51%	$10,576
71.	**College of Coastal Georgia***	77	2.5	164	$136	68%	26	61%	N/A	80%	$6,209
71.	**Granite State College*** (NH)	77	N/A	2,091	$345	33%	13	78%	48%	66%	$16,705
71.	**North Carolina State University–Raleigh***	77	3.3	69	$742	100%	19	83%	73%	45%	$14,703
71.	**Southwestern College** (KS)	77	2.6	1,499	$478	100%	11	76%	48%	24%	$23,596
71.	**Texas A&M University–Commerce***	77	3.2	1,863	$670	71%	22	79%	58%	56%	$20,506
71.	**University of La Verne** (CA)	77	2.7	326	$625	84%	19	79%	51%	78%	$30,216
77.	**Bowling Green State University*** (OH)	76	3.2	353	$397	76%	19	87%	39%	63%	$29,970
77.	**California State University–Dominguez Hills***	76	2.6	542	$670	89%	21	86%	59%	30%	$18,639
77.	**California University of Pennsylvania***	76	2.6	1,474	$319	58%	49	84%	54%	73%	$24,478
77.	**Illinois State University***	76	2.9	40	$741	N/A	25	90%	4%	62%	$14,174
77.	**Lamar University*** (TX)	76	2.4	2,080	$248	68%	32	74%	72%	7%	$26,390
77.	**Maranatha Baptist University** (WI)	76	N/A	69	$404	43%	9	93%	N/A	53%	$12,369
77.	**University of Alabama–Birmingham***	76	3.1	1,247	$793	80%	39	73%	N/A	66%	$20,312
77.	**University of Northern Colorado***	76	3.0	494	$410	N/A	13	81%	65%	56%	$14,693
77.	**University of St. Francis** (IL)	76	N/A	313	$620	90%	13	66%	57%	59%	$26,386
77.	**University of Wisconsin–Superior***	76	3.1	588	$305	25%	11	81%	36%	74%	$27,479
77.	**Wayne State University*** (MI)	76	3.1	43	$444	67%	20	85%	N/A	85%	$32,277
88.	**New England Col. of Business and Finance**** (MA)	75	2.4	832	$485	50%	19	89%	42%	59%	$37,900
88.	**SUNY College of Technology–Canton***	75	3.0	1,063	$333	60%	19	74%	55%	75%	$28,395
88.	**Saint Leo University** (FL)	75	2.7	4,274	$360	61%	16	72%	23%	64%	$34,956
88.	**Texas A&M University–College Station***	75	3.5	67	$731	38%	18	94%	N/A	N/A	N/A
88.	**University of North Alabama***	75	N/A	339	$554	91%	17	81%	50%	56%	$16,666
88.	**University of the Cumberlands** (KY)	75	2.6	813	$199	49%	13	81%	N/A	61%	$21,149
94.	**American Public University System**** (WV)	74	2.4	53,796	$270	55%	18	54%	34%	32%	$28,614
94.	**Brandman University** (CA)	74	2.5	1,319	$500	88%	24	70%	54%	73%	$31,841
94.	**ECPI University** (VA)	74	N/A	2,920	$490	56%	16	8%	30%	68%	$32,925
94.	**Eastern Oregon University***	74	2.5	1,270	$232	60%	18	89%	52%	68%	$25,576
94.	**Florida State University***	74	3.5	512	$776	37%	30	N/A	N/A	N/A	N/A
94.	**Herzing University** (WI)	74	2.1	1,285	$570	38%	16	86%	29%	81%	$21,330
94.	**Kansas State University***	74	3.6	327	$433	67%	24	88%	N/A	75%	$33,283
94.	**Palm Beach Atlantic University** (FL)	74	3.1	47	$475	71%	10	59%	38%	87%	$32,729
94.	**Union Institute and University** (OH)	74	N/A	1,391	$530	50%	8	73%	98%	53%	$38,060
94.	**University of Louisiana–Lafayette***	74	3.1	1,556	$316	44%	32	68%	N/A	N/A	N/A
94.	**University of Maine–Augusta***	74	2.9	3,268	$285	61%	28	79%	22%	74%	$27,451
94.	**University of South Carolina–Aiken***	74	2.5	216	$849	71%	20	85%	74%	70%	$24,567
94.	**University of Wisconsin–Milwaukee***	74	3.3	3,186	$337	87%	30	83%	28%	73%	$29,226
107.	**Concordia University Chicago** (IL)	73	2.1	145	$505	43%	7	44%	N/A	88%	$23,482

(*Public, **For profit)

Rank	School	Overall program score	Average peer assessment score (5.0=highest)	'17 total program enrollment	'17 - '18 tuition[1]	'17 full-time faculty with Ph.D.	'17 average class size	'17 retention rate	'17 graduation rate[2]	% graduates with debt ('17)	Average debt of graduates ('17)
107.	**Drexel University** (PA)	73	3.4	2,007	$585	7%	22	81%	35%	62%	$29,072
107.	**Ferris State University*** (MI)	73	2.9	992	$429	49%	20	76%	53%	53%	$17,700
107.	**New England College** (NH)	73	2.3	1,286	$405	63%	18	50%	N/A	78%	$18,480
107.	**Stevenson University** (MD)	73	2.9	509	$450	100%	14	82%	56%	47%	$23,782
107.	**United States Sports Academy** (AL)	73	2.9	279	$407	100%	4	51%	35%	73%	$24,783
107.	**Upper Iowa University**	73	2.9	2,503	$441	38%	14	86%	47%	87%	$28,618
107.	**Valdosta State University*** (GA)	73	2.8	861	$250	68%	15	70%	N/A	50%	$29,878
115.	**Chatham University** (PA)	72	2.5	109	$854	78%	9	75%	70%	43%	$15,942
115.	**Colorado Technical University****	72	2.7	28,163	$325	100%	31	89%	28%	79%	$22,499
115.	**Duquesne University** (PA)	72	3.0	153	$878	77%	16	N/A	N/A	42%	$31,664
115.	**Eastern Kentucky University***	72	2.9	2,215	$409	74%	17	80%	38%	90%	$35,051
115.	**Florida Institute of Technology**	72	3.1	2,335	$510	77%	18	72%	10%	80%	$40,181
115.	**Georgia Southern University***	72	2.7	747	$204	89%	38	78%	N/A	76%	$25,709
115.	**Kentucky Wesleyan College**	72	2.4	40	$425	50%	9	N/A	N/A	80%	$25,920
115.	**Lindenwood University** (MO)	72	2.4	243	$460	70%	16	77%	N/A	60%	$10,127
115.	**Missouri State University***	72	3.1	495	$285	67%	18	N/A	N/A	N/A	N/A
115.	**Southwestern Oklahoma State University***	72	2.4	567	$582	40%	19	89%	67%	53%	$14,497
125.	**Berkeley College**** (NY)	71	N/A	1,681	$825	58%	20	74%	35%	81%	$30,424
125.	**Cornerstone University** (MI)	71	2.7	213	$410	75%	10	92%	47%	82%	$24,907
125.	**McKendree University** (IL)	71	N/A	381	$380	78%	14	90%	N/A	77%	$17,069
125.	**Southern Illinois University–Edwardsville***	71	3.0	659	$292	30%	19	93%	N/A	32%	$14,002
125.	**University of Memphis*** (TN)	71	3.0	1,516	$480	73%	30	77%	43%	75%	$25,232
125.	**University of Toledo*** (OH)	71	2.8	1,927	$774	69%	19	68%	33%	77%	$17,535
131.	**Columbia College** (MO)	70	2.8	14,680	$305	77%	18	67%	8%	62%	$30,766
131.	**Concordia University–St. Paul** (MN)	70	2.3	1,370	$420	53%	12	76%	62%	77%	$23,873
131.	**Friends University** (KS)	70	N/A	302	$430	82%	15	68%	N/A	87%	$26,150
131.	**Frostburg State University*** (MD)	70	N/A	561	$556	50%	18	76%	100%	12%	$3,745
131.	**National University** (CA)	70	2.1	9,243	$362	79%	17	64%	33%	60%	$18,712
131.	**North Carolina Central University***	70	2.6	128	$555	56%	37	1%	20%	68%	$6,348
131.	**St. Joseph's University** (PA)	70	3.0	115	$584	81%	13	85%	50%	96%	$26,995
138.	**Northeastern State University*** (OK)	69	2.8	1,063	$430	45%	20	83%	35%	N/A	N/A
138.	**Rutgers University–New Brunswick*** (NJ)	69	N/A	235	$550	100%	34	N/A	N/A	73%	$29,502
138.	**St. Joseph's College New York**	69	2.9	184	$520	79%	13	51%	21%	56%	$22,590
138.	**University of Missouri***	69	3.3	358	$362	68%	23	64%	N/A	59%	$16,103
138.	**Valley City State University*** (ND)	69	2.6	168	$177	58%	14	N/A	N/A	19%	$15,545

GETTY IMAGES

Note: Key to footnotes, Page 116.

(*Public, **For profit)

Rank	School	Overall program score	Average peer assessment score (5.0=highest)	'17 total program enrollment	'17 - '18 tuition[1]	'17 full-time faculty with Ph.D.	'17 average class size	'17 retention rate	'17 graduation rate[2]	% graduates with debt ('17)	Average debt of graduates ('17)
143.	Anderson University (SC)	68	N/A	N/A	N/A	70%	13	2%	28%	N/A	N/A
143.	East Carolina University* (NC)	68	3.1	10,128	$700	71%	25	N/A	N/A	61%	$23,623
143.	Indiana University-Purdue U.–Fort Wayne*	68	3.3	483	$372	64%	22	50%	N/A	91%	$28,991
143.	Johnson & Wales University (RI)	68	3.1	802	$330	N/A	19	58%	N/A	86%	N/A
143.	La Salle University (PA)	68	N/A	26	$400	50%	10	N/A	62%	57%	$17,911
143.	Linfield College (OR)	68	2.4	407	$495	79%	12	80%	73%	68%	$23,238
143.	Slippery Rock University of Pennsylvania*	68	2.6	264	$319	80%	23	76%	51%	37%	$7,942
143.	Texas Tech University*	68	3.4	570	$250	27%	35	N/A	N/A	N/A	N/A
143.	University of Massachusetts–Dartmouth*	68	3.4	348	$322	83%	15	65%	N/A	N/A	N/A
143.	University of Missouri–Kansas City*	68	3.3	107	$871	N/A	20	88%	N/A	N/A	N/A
153.	Ashland University (OH)	67	2.2	186	$417	73%	16	47%	N/A	60%	$21,616
153.	Bellevue University (NE)	67	2.4	5,789	$410	83%	13	92%	N/A	74%	$19,714
153.	Bluefield College (VA)	67	N/A	563	$365	65%	14	64%	N/A	77%	$19,760
153.	Champlain College (VT)	67	2.6	2,080	$640	33%	14	81%	N/A	54%	$30,046
153.	Columbia College (SC)	67	N/A	765	$395	93%	16	57%	N/A	80%	$17,316
153.	Concordia University Wisconsin	67	2.5	229	$483	N/A	7	N/A	N/A	65%	$6,593
153.	Loyola University New Orleans (LA)	67	3.2	14	$325	100%	8	N/A	N/A	N/A	N/A
153.	Marian University (IN)	67	N/A	509	$795	39%	25	91%	89%	89%	$51,779
153.	Oakland University* (MI)	67	2.7	226	$796	73%	25	71%	54%	N/A	N/A
153.	University of Wisconsin–Stout*	67	3.3	2,476	$334	59%	25	N/A	54%	82%	$21,193
153.	Warner University (FL)	67	N/A	N/A	$438	45%	11	85%	56%	79%	$29,054
153.	Wright State University* (OH)	67	N/A	125	$803	100%	16	81%	N/A	52%	$20,368
165.	Appalachian State University* (NC)	66	2.9	451	$643	79%	24	92%	33%	37%	$12,357
165.	Campbellsville University (KY)	66	N/A	378	$399	61%	18	84%	N/A	N/A	N/A
165.	Northwestern College (IA)	66	3.2	21	$325	N/A	12	77%	N/A	100%	$13,501
165.	Peirce College (PA)	66	2.1	1,100	$600	69%	15	68%	35%	N/A	N/A
165.	Post University** (CT)	66	2.0	10,104	$570	33%	15	63%	29%	58%	$32,433
165.	University of Louisville* (KY)	66	N/A	395	$497	61%	25	68%	N/A	58%	$23,445
165.	University of North Carolina–Greensboro*	66	N/A	1,534	$662	81%	32	73%	47%	63%	$20,032
165.	University of Wisconsin–Green Bay*	66	3.2	1,733	$590	83%	25	74%	62%	67%	$25,000
165.	University of Wisconsin–Platteville*	66	3.4	404	$370	N/A	15	68%	65%	N/A	N/A

Best Online Bachelor's Programs For Veterans

Which programs offer military veterans and active-duty service members the best distance education? To ensure academic quality, all schools included in this ranking had to first qualify for a spot by being in the top half of the Best Online Degree Programs ranking, above. They had to be housed in a regionally accredited institution and were judged on a multitude of factors, including program reputation, faculty credentials, student graduation rate and graduate debt load. Secondly, because veterans and active-duty members often wish to take full advantage of federal benefits designed to make their coursework less expensive, programs also had to be certified for the GI Bill and participate in the Yellow Ribbon Program or charge in-state tuition that can be fully covered by the GI Bill to veterans from out of state. A third criterion for being ranked is that a program must have enrolled a critical mass of students with military backgrounds. The undergraduate-level rankings require a total of 25 veterans and active-duty service members to be included. Qualifying programs were ranked in descending order based on their spot in the overall ranking.

Rank	School (State)
1.	Embry-Riddle Aeronautical University (FL)
1.	Temple University* (PA)
3.	Arizona State University*
4.	Utah State University*
5.	Oregon State University*
6.	Pennsylvania State University–World Campus*
6.	University of North Carolina–Wilmington*
8.	Colorado State University–Global Campus*
8.	University of Oklahoma*
8.	West Texas A&M University*
11.	University of Florida*
11.	Western Kentucky University*
13.	CUNY School of Professional Studies*
13.	University of Arkansas*
13.	University of Central Florida*
13.	University of Massachusetts–Amherst*
13.	University of Nebraska–Omaha*
18.	University of Massachusetts–Lowell*
19.	California Baptist University
19.	Colorado State University*
19.	Daytona State College* (FL)
19.	George Washington University (DC)
19.	Robert Morris University (PA)
19.	Siena Heights University (MI)
19.	Washington State University*
26.	City University of Seattle (WA)
27.	Charleston Southern University (SC)
27.	Fort Hays State University* (KS)
27.	Regent University (VA)
30.	Indiana University– Online*
30.	University of Illinois–Springfield*
32.	Northern Arizona University*
32.	Sam Houston State University* (TX)
32.	Southeast Missouri State University*
32.	University of the Incarnate Word (TX)
36.	University of Arizona*
36.	U. of Wisconsin–Whitewater*
38.	Florida International University*
38.	Western Illinois University*
40.	Central Michigan University*
40.	Old Dominion University* (VA)
40.	University of North Dakota*
40.	Utica College (NY)
44.	Granite State College* (NH)
44.	Southwestern College (KS)
44.	University of La Verne (CA)
47.	Bowling Green State University* (OH)
47.	California University of Pennsylvania*
47.	University of Alabama–Birmingham*
47.	University of Wisconsin–Superior*

CHAPTER

Get

ting In

INSIDE AN ART STUDIO AT THE UNIVERSITY OF FLORIDA

BRETT ZIEGLER FOR USN&WR

Make Your

Application Sing

Students and admissions pros share their tips for standing out from the pack

by **Margaret Loftus**

JACK MALONEY (RIGHT) IN REHEARSAL AT OXBRIDGE ACADEMY

NEWS YOU CAN USE

Ever since Jack Maloney played the Artful Dodger in a local children's theater production of the musical "Oliver!" when he was 6, he knew he wanted to be a professional actor. The theater program at his school, Oxbridge Academy in West Palm Beach, Florida, was still finding its footing during his early years there, so Maloney took it upon himself to create and stage productions, including a concert of songs from the musical "Rent" and a full production of "Urinetown" that he developed out of an honors performance class. He also helped get the course into the curriculum by writing a proposal in collaboration with his theater teacher and lobbying administrators.

Now a freshman at Pennsylvania State University studying musical theater, Maloney believes that his resourcefulness – and highlighting that in his college essays – was a big factor in getting into his three top choices. (The others were Northwestern in Illinois and the University of Michigan.) He also elaborated on his experiences in interviews whenever he got the chance. "I wrote my own story," he says, "and it was much more compelling in the end."

College counselors have long urged high school students to find and focus on their passion. But developing it to create new opportunities for yourself and others can really grab the attention of admissions officers. For many of them, there's a certain sameness to the applications they read, so when prospective students carve out their own opportunities, colleges notice, says Maria Laskaris, former dean of admissions and financial aid at Dartmouth College and now a senior private counselor at Top Tier Admissions, a company focused on helping applicants navigate the admissions process. "We tell students to push beyond what the school offers," Laskaris says.

These days, with the sheer volume of applications growing, aspiring college students need to use every edge they can muster. According to the latest State of College Admission report from the National Association for College Admission Counseling, the overall number of applications from first-time freshmen inched up 7 percent between fall 2015 and fall 2016. Distinguishing yourself from the crowd has become more important than ever. But remember, even though many coveted schools are growing more and more selective, overall colleges accept an average of two-thirds of first-time freshman applicants, according to NACAC. U.S. News talked to experts to find out how to make your application stand out.

Build on your academic strengths. While the weight that admissions officers give each component of your application varies from school to school, academics is always the heaviest. After all, schools are looking for students who have not only done well but who have also challenged themselves, as they are more likely to succeed in college-level courses. Of course, reviewers also take into account the level of rigor available at a particular school. The key is to plan ahead and start in eighth or ninth

NICK DONNER FOR USN&WR

grade to build a foundation that will open doors to advanced coursework later on. For instance, being ready to get advanced algebra out of the way sophomore year puts you on track to take calculus before earning that high school diploma, which might set you up better should you apply to a program that requires it, such as engineering. The bottom line: "Position yourself to keep your options open," Laskaris says.

Tackling honors, Advanced Placement or International Baccalaureate classes (if they're available) shows that you're up for the rigors of college, even if you don't ace them. "We'd prefer to see students challenge themselves to get a B in AP or honors courses rather than an A in a standard-level course," says David Kaiser, the director of undergraduate enrollment management at Temple University's Fox School of Business in Philadelphia. This shows someone who "isn't afraid of hard work," Kaiser says, and "it's a better indicator of the student's ability to perform." That

Two Essays That Worked

What makes a college admissions essay successful? Below are two submissions that helped students get into **Johns Hopkins University** in Baltimore, plus commentary from **Ellen Kim,** dean of undergraduate admissions, about what these applicants did right. Remember, Kim advises, that "what works in these essays works because of who the student is" and how it fits into the rest of the application. In other words, you'll want to apply these principles to a topic that reveals something intriguing about you.

"This title is interesting," Kim says. "But it's up to students to decide whether they want to title an essay." If nothing brilliant comes to mind, then you can skip.

More Than Thick Eyebrows

By Caroline

The author takes a straightforward approach to starting, Kim says. "But you can tell you are going to get to know her."

Rarely have I studied a topic that flows from my ears to my brain to my tongue as easily as the Italian language. The Italian blood that runs through me is more than the genetics that gave me my dark hair and thick eyebrows. It is the work of the generation that traveled from Istria in the north and Sicilia in the south, meeting through friends in Chicago, and encouraging their children to study hard and make a living for their future families. In time, that influence would be passed on to me; finding my grandfather's meticulously-written electricity notes circa 1935 – filled with drawings and words I did not yet understand – inspired me to take Italian at my own high school.

Many personal statements include short scenes, Kim notes. But the strongest essays are the ones that put those anecdotes toward a larger purpose, as the author does here. "She is helping us understand where she is in her journey with Italian," Kim says. "It's not just being descriptive for the sake of being descriptive."

The moment I realized that my Italian heritage was wholly a part of me was a rather insignificant one, yet to me is one of the most remarkable realizations of my life. The summer after my second year of Italian study, I was driving in my car, listening to a young trio of Italian teenagers, *Il Volo*, meaning "The Flight." As one of the tenors sang a solo, *Ti voglio tanto bene*, I realized that I could understand every word he was singing. Though it was a simple declaration of love and devotion in a beautiful tune, what mattered was that I was not just listening to three cute teenagers sing a song. I was fully engaged with the words and could finally sing along.

The author chose to write about something very accessible and approachable, Kim notes. "Everyone can relate to family heritage," she says. "It would have been very easy to talk about the members of the family, but she does a good job of making it say something about herself," which is the goal.

After that moment, I sought out all the Italian I could get my hands on: watching *Cinema Paradis* and *La Dolce Vita*, absorbing phrases of the language I felt I could now call my own. Even better, that I felt confident enough in my skill that I could use it with my closest living Italian relative, m father's mother, *la mia nonna*. More than speaking the language, I discovered my family's past. I conversing with her and my father, I discovered that I will be only the third person in my paternal grandparents' family to attend college, that my grandmother had only a sixth-grade education, that my grandfather, despite never holding a degree in mathematics or physics, wor for three decades on CTA train cars as an electrician. The marriage of my grandparents in 1952 represented a synthesis of the culture of northern and southern Italy and America.

In this paragraph, Kim says, "We learn not just about her intellectual appetite for something, but also about what she does when she is passionate."

Having now studied three full years of this language, I only want to consume more of it. I want to read Dante's *Divina Commedia* in its original vernacular, to watch my favorite Italian films without the subtitles, to sing every Italian refrain with fluid understanding of what the melody means, and to finally – finally! – visit my grandparents' childhood homes: the town of Trapan in Sicilia and the Istrian peninsula on the Adriatic coast. To me, the Italian language holds an essential connection to my past, but also a constant goal for the future. It is likely that I will never fully master the vernacular and colloquialisms, yet learning this language will stimulate me intellectually and culturally for life. I believe I can claim Italian as mine now, but there is still so much more to learn. Italian is a gift that I will hold dear forever, and I am glad that I received it so early in life.

"This is a good way to close the essay, by describing why this matters to who she is as a person," Kim says.

said, it's also important to consider carefully which advanced courses will build on your strengths – and don't overdo it. Taking every AP option available may backfire for those who don't excel in a particular subject, for instance, and they could see their overall GPA drop as a result.

Remember: Once you've been accepted, don't slack on your studies. "Grades throughout the senior year are critical to demonstrate continued growth," says Laskaris. "The worst students can do is take their foot off the gas."

Get a handle on the tests. Of course, colleges have long relied on standardized tests to help them differentiate between students in a way that grades alone cannot. Increasingly, applicants are choosing to take both the SAT and the ACT. Christoph Guttentag, dean of undergraduate admissions at Duke University in North Carolina, suggests doing just that to

String Theory

By Joanna

If string theory is really true, then the entire world is made up of strings, and I cannot tie a single one. This past summer, I applied for my very first job at a small, busy bakery and café in my neighborhood. I knew that if I were hired there, I would learn how to use a cash register, prepare sandwiches, and take cake orders. I imagined that my biggest struggle would be catering to demanding New Yorkers, but I never thought that it would be the benign act of tying a box that would become both my biggest obstacle and greatest teacher.

On my first day of work in late August, one of the bakery's employees hastily explained the procedure. It seemed simple: wrap the string around your hand, then wrap it three times around the box both ways, and knot it. I recited the anthem in my head, "three times, turn it, three times, knot" until it became my mantra. After observing multiple employees, it was clear that anyone tying the box could complete it in a matter of seconds. For weeks, I labored endlessly, only to watch the strong and small pieces of my pride unravel each time I tried.

As I rushed to discreetly shove half-tied cake boxes into plastic bags, I could not help but wonder what was wrong with me. I have learned Mozart arias, memorized the functional groups in organic chemistry, and calculated the anti-derivatives of functions that I will probably never use in real life – all with a modest amount of energy. For some reason though, after a month's effort, tying string around a cake box still left me in a quandary.

As the weeks progressed, my skills slowly began to improve. Of course there were days when I just wanted to throw all of the string in the trash and use Scotch tape; this sense of defeat was neither welcome nor wanted, but remarks like "Oh, you must be new" from snarky customers catapulted my determination to greater heights.

It should be more difficult to develop an internal pulse and sense of legato in a piece of music than it is to find the necessary rhythm required to tie a box, but this seemingly trivial task has clearly proven not to be trivial at all. The difficulties that I encountered trying to keep a single knot intact are proof of this. The lack of cooperation between my coordination and my understanding left me frazzled, but the satisfaction I felt when I successfully tied my first box was almost as great as any I had felt before.

Scientists developing string theory say that string can exist in a straight line, but it can also bend, oscillate, or break apart. I am thankful that the string I work with is not quite as temperamental, but still cringe when someone asks for a chocolate mandel bread. Supposedly, the string suggested in ring theory is responsible for unifying general relativity with quantum physics. The only thing I am sponsible for when I use string is delivering someone's pie to them without the box falling apart. ing a cake box may not be quantum physics, but it is just as crucial to holding together what matters.

n beginning to realize that I should not be ashamed if it takes me longer to learn. I persist, I continue to tie boxes every weekend at work. Even though I occasionally backslide into feelings asperation, I always rewrap the string around my hand and start over because I have learned he most gratifying victories come from tenacity. If the universe really is comprised of strings, I nfident that I will be able to tie them together, even if I do have to keep my fingers crossed that ots hold up.

Students should try to grab the reader's attention at the first sentence. "Her opening paragraph is interesting," says Kim. "You read it, and you aren't sure what the essay is going to be about. It makes you curious about what she is going to tell you."

"A lot of times students feel like they need to write an essay about a life accomplishment or a life-changing event or something really extraordinary," Kim says. "But it's also possible to write a very effective personal statement about an ordinary thing. It's not the topic that has to be unique. It's what you say that has to be unique."

The author does a good job of providing a window into her thought process, Kim notes. "You also see how she responds to a challenge in a very approachable way."

In this instance, dropping in some academic references works with the theme of the essay, but students shouldn't think they have to follow suit, Kim cautions. It only works if it reinforces your central point.

This essay, like all strong essays, was well-written, clear and error-free, Kim notes. The writing felt natural - not as though the author was reaching for a thesaurus. "This should sound like you," she says.

Personal statements are called "personal" for a reason, Kim observes. They should tell the admissions committee something about the student. This essay does a good job of wrapping up the piece on a personal note.

determine which test better suits your test-taking style. You might opt to sit for your preferred test again, but twice should be the limit, he says. Duke, for example, accepts scores for both tests, but check with your prospective schools on their policies and whether you should submit scores for both tests. At Duke, admissions officers consider scores of individual sections from both tests, but they'll use the highest composite score in their admissions rubric. And what about the optional SAT essay section? While many places don't require it, some do, and that may change year to year. Again, it's best to consult a school's individual policies.

More and more schools – including Bennington College in Vermont, Ohio Wesleyan University, Arizona State University and, as of this summer, the University of Chicago – are going test-optional, meaning certain applicants can choose not to submit standardized-test scores for review in admissions decisions. You can find a comprehensive list of test-optional schools at fairtest.org, operated by the National Center for Fair and Open Testing. When in doubt, check with the school's admissions office.

Laskaris cautions students and parents to take "test-optional" with a grain of salt. "Just because those colleges are not requiring [scores] from everyone doesn't mean 80 percent of them don't take them," she says. "It still does matter for many top institutions."

Think outside your school's extracurriculars. While Santa Monica, California, native Brendan Terry's interest in environmental and social justice issues was first sparked in middle school, he found most of the opportunities to nurture his activist spirit off campus. Terry interned at an educational nonprofit as a summer camp counselor for local children from low-income families and Chinese exchange students, volunteered at a community health clinic, and served as the "educational ambassador" for the 5 Gyres Institute, a Los Angeles-based nonprofit that focuses on reducing global plastic pollution, among other activities.

Now a junior majoring in chemistry at Pomona College in California, Terry is well aware of the impact of his community work on his college apps. "It was huge," he says. "Schools always brought it up." Terry wrote about his activism in the majority of his essays, as well as the "activities" and "additional information" sections of the Common Application. "I used part of it to provide background on each organization that I worked with, and to provide links for clippings about activist work I had done," he says. " His recommendations – one from a teacher and the other from one of the directors at 5 Gyres – reinforced his work as an activist.

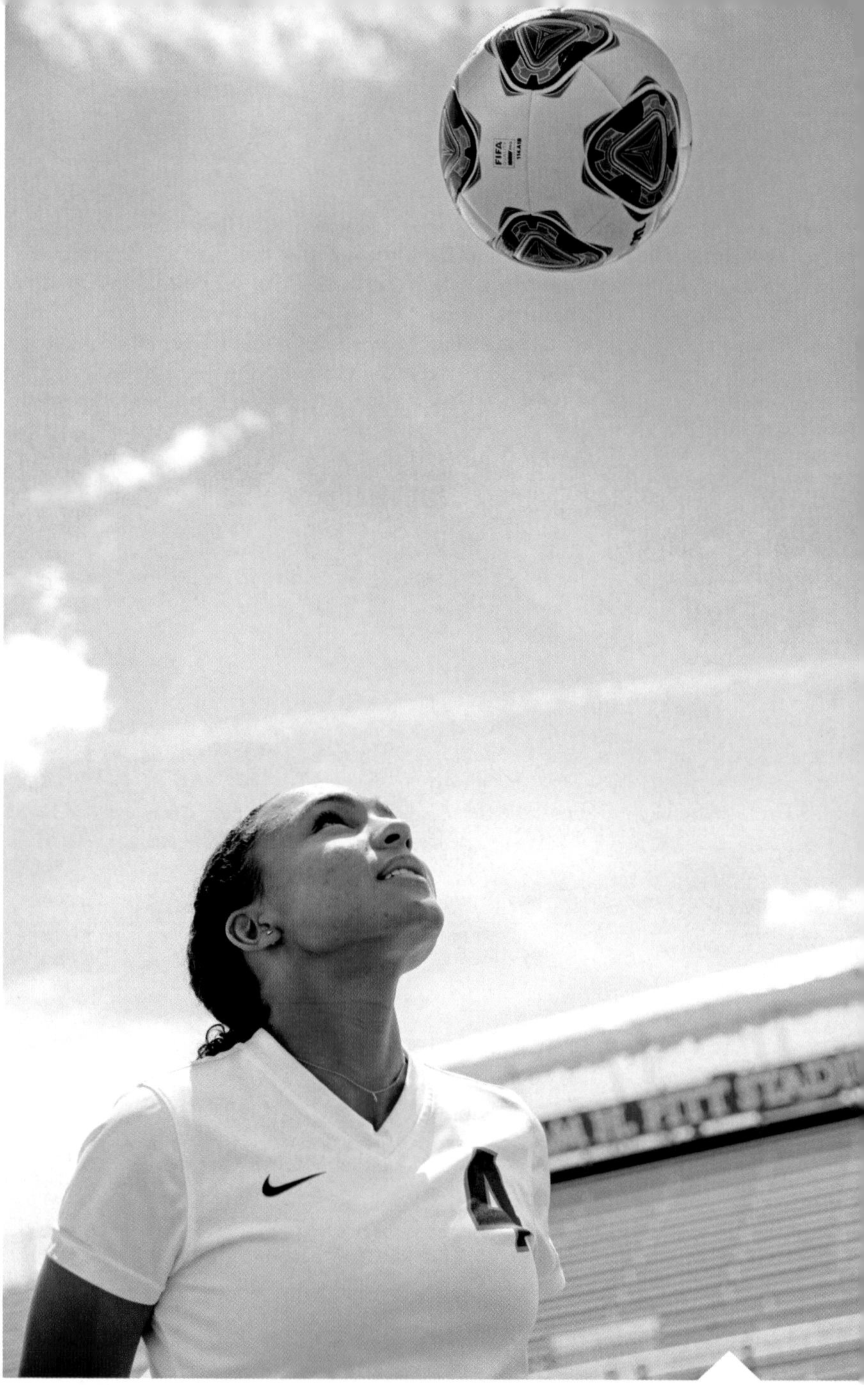

ARIANNA HILLIARD ENJOYED SOCCER IN HIGH SCHOOL AND WILL PLAY ON AT VASSAR.

No matter what your interests are, find ways to use them to make a contribution to your school or local community. If math is your thing, for example, think about how you can tap your skills to get other kids interested in the subject. Arianna Hilliard, a classmate of Maloney's at Oxbridge Academy who is now in her first year at Vassar College in New York, was vice president of a club at her school called Race Alliance in which members met weekly to discuss the topic of race in popular culture.

Whatever you do, use your time outside of schoolwork wisely. For instance, three-season athletes who know they're not going to be recruited for sports might consider skipping one or two seasons to focus on other interests. Think depth instead of

NICK DONNER FOR USN&WR

breadth, says Seth Allen, vice president and dean of admissions and financial aid at Pomona. "We're looking for students who have decided to go down a particular path with as much enthusiasm as they can muster," he says.

To be sure, some students are too busy with a part-time job or, say, babysitting younger siblings to devote themselves to even one season of sports, much less an activity or a cause. But employment and child care are responsibilities that you can learn from, too. "Colleges look at extracurriculars in the context of a student's environment," says Craig Meister, director of college counseling at Oxbridge Academy and founder of college consulting firm Admissions Intel. He urges his students to list those experiences on their apps. "It's a combination of what you can afford and what you're passionate about," he says.

Consider recommendations carefully. "Always give great consideration to the people you ask to write a recommendation," says Susan Schaurer, associate vice president for strategic enrollment management and marketing at Miami University in Ohio. Colleges vary on their preferences and typically spell that out in their application instructions. For instance, Miami asks for letters from a high school counselor or academic teacher, Schaurer says. "Preferably someone who's had close academic encounters with you," she says. "Ask someone who can really provide insight."

The ideal scenario is when you can ask an instructor who taught you more than once – such as during freshman year and again later on – because then they can speak to your growth and how you might have overcome any particular challenges. Duke, meanwhile, prefers letters from two teachers and a guidance counselor. "We find counselor recommendations so valuable in understanding the student as a member of a community," says Guttentag.

Do a social media check. Meister implores his ninth and 10th graders to not put anything on social media or online that could be questionable. Nonetheless, he says, when looking at their info, "nine times out of 10 I find something they should take down." And while it's true admissions officers don't have time to scroll through your entire Instagram feed, they may stumble upon social media info if searching online to verify a part of your app. What's more, it's not unusual for schools to be alerted by alumni, community members or others to social media that paints a student in an unflattering light. "We can't ignore what may be brought to our attention," says Schaurer, even after acceptance. "Most institutions put a disclaimer in acceptance letters that stipulates good behavior," she says, or they reserve the right to withdraw the offer of admission.

Meister advises students to always use appropriate language online and to scrub their social media to the extent they can of anything that doesn't reflect the image projected in their applications. "Admission officers are savvier than ever in comparing your application persona versus your recommender's impression of your persona versus your online persona to see if they all match up," he says. A good rule of thumb: "I tell them that if they wouldn't want an admissions officer to see it, nobody else should see it online either," Meister adds.

Show up (to the extent you're able). Time was, if you had your heart set on a particular school, counselors advised you to visit the campus to show the admissions office that you'd be likely to attend if accepted (which is music to their ears). Showing up is still a great way to reveal what schools refer to as "demonstrated interest," a factor that some 70 percent of colleges say plays at least some role in their admissions decisions, according to NACAC. At the same time, "most schools are attuned to resources," Schaurer says, and "they don't want to put students at risk who can't afford to come for a visit."

Indeed, making a trip to campus isn't the only way to let your interest be known, especially in the digital age. "We count any way students engage with us," she notes, which includes opening a college's emails or clicking on a link in a particular message, participating in a webinar or Facebook Live event, and more. Schaurer encourages applicants to ask colleges if they consider demonstrated interest – and how. And be sure to introduce yourself to recruiters during visits to your high school or at local college fairs, Schaurer advises. "You can show interest without leaving home." ◆

Why I Picked...

Butler University

INDIANAPOLIS

Riley Schmidt, '18

▶ **Butler has a warm, intimate environment. Most students are friendly and involved in campus groups, like Butler University Dance Marathon, College Mentors for Kids, and intramural volleyball, which I joined. Professors are really supportive, too – fortunately, as it took me three years to settle on my major.**

Sophomore year I wanted to switch from a pre-med track to a new major that would steer me towards physical therapy. I was worried, though, that the course changes might prevent my taking advantage of Butler's robust study abroad program (40 percent of students participate). But my professors helped me plot out a new schedule that enabled me to spend a wonderful semester in Sydney. Ironically, I got sick near the end and was hospitalized. That experience made me realize I wanted to be a nurse. My understanding professors and pre-health adviser again worked with me to change my major. Thanks to Butler, I'm now headed to nursing school and planning to become a nurse practitioner.

R. BRENT SMITH

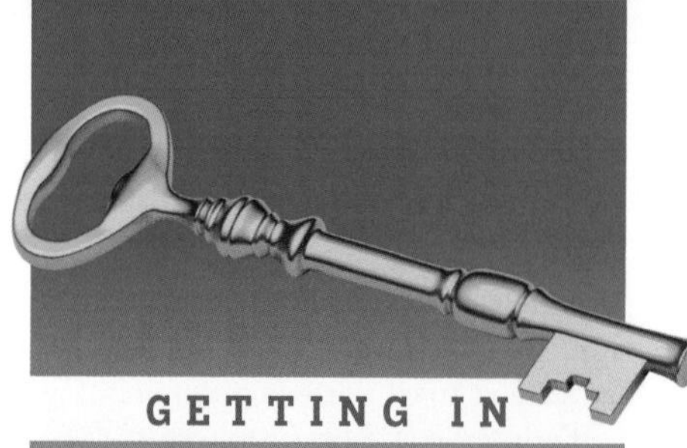

The Early Edge

Applying ahead of the regular decision deadline requires careful planning, but it can have its perks

by Courtney Rubin

Once upon a time there were only two kinds of "early" options when it came to applying to college, and each school offered only one (if any): early decision, where students applied to one school in November, got a reply by mid-December, and were obligated to attend if they were accepted; and early action, where one also applied in November and also got an answer in December, but there was no binding commitment to attend.

But in the past decade, the options have multiplied. Now, they include everything from two rounds of early decision at a single school (such as at Bates College in Maine and Emory University in Atlanta); universities offering both early decision and early action (Tulane in New Orleans and Fordham in New York, for example); and places that have multiple rounds of early routes (the University of Chicago and Pace University in New York). A number of schools even offer a hybrid called restrictive early action, where students can typically only apply early to one school – not send out materials to a bunch of early action programs, say – without having to commit.

Even some college deans struggle to keep everything straight. "What used to be very clear terminology is no longer," says Nancy Meislahn, dean of admission and financial aid at Wesleyan University in Connecticut, which offers two rounds of binding early decision with deadlines of Nov. 15 and Jan. 1. (Results come in mid-December and mid-February.) Because many schools have their own rules, she recommends checking the fine print for every single school.

What is clear is that early applications have been rising steadily over the past 15 years. Between fall 2015 and fall 2016, colleges reported a 5 percent increase in early decision applicants and a 6 percent increase in early decision admits, according to a 2017 report from the National Association for College Admission Counseling. Applications through early action were up 15 percent, and admits had risen 16 percent.

About a third of colleges say they offer an early action program, according to the NACAC report, compared to just 8 percent who reported so in 2005. In the case of binding early decision, the advantage to the school is clear: locking down great candidates. But colleges with programs that don't lock you in say the early deadline allows them more time to review all applications, since students usually apply at the last minute.

With many more schools adopting nonbinding early action programs, students seem to face "no downside to applying," says Michael Carter, director of college counseling at St. Stephen's and St. Agnes School in Alexandria, Virginia. There, some 80 percent of the 110-member senior class files an early application, Carter says. The Common Application and other online application portals, which make it easier both to apply early and to try for more schools, have also boosted numbers.

But perhaps the biggest driver of early applications is the widespread notion that applying by Nov. 15 to a highly selective college makes it easier to get in. Many college admissions deans dispute the notion that it's quite that simple. "There's no Rumpelstiltskin-like effect to applying early," says Meislahn. "It doesn't spin straw into gold. You need to be squarely in the school's profile." That said, Wesleyan admitted roughly half its incoming fall 2018 freshman class in its two binding early decision rounds; acceptance rates for ED were close to 40 percent, compared to about 17 percent in the regular round.

At Duke University in North Carolina, just over 21 percent of early decision applicants for the undergraduate class of 2022 were admitted, compared to about 6.7 percent of those in the regular pool. Fewer students applied early (roughly 4,070 to 33,200 regular), but "I'm not

AT ST. STEPHEN'S AND ST. AGNES, WHERE ABOUT 4 IN 5 SENIORS APPLY EARLY TO COLLEGE

sure I would see any meaningful difference between students admitted early decision and students admitted regular decision," says Christoph Guttentag, Duke's dean of undergraduate admissions. But while applying early is not the surefire way to get into a school that's a serious reach, it can send a clear signal to admissions officers that a particular school is your top choice. Eric Eng, an independent admissions counselor and founder of Ivy College Admit based in Cupertino, California, sometimes suggests that certain students (particularly those with competitive credentials) use early deadlines to test the waters about the strength of their application essay, for instance, and recalibrate for regular decision if needed.

No matter a school's approach, applying early can also have an impact on financial aid. Some schools say a student receives the same financial aid package no matter when they apply. "Ours is need-based, so you get the same package you'd get in March," says Meislahn. But Mark Montgomery, a Denver-based college admissions consultant, cautions that many schools have little incentive to offer their most attractive financial aid packages to students who apply early and are anything less than "rock stars."

In general, it pays to confirm the details – and to be familiar with each individual school's policy. Most schools with binding early offers of admission only offer an escape clause if financial aid does not meet need. At the University of Arkansas, for instance, about 80 percent of merit-based scholarships are awarded to those who apply by the school's Nov. 1 nonbinding "priority application deadline." Prospective students should keep a record of how financial aid deadlines compare to those for applications. When in doubt, ask the schools for clarity.

Keep in mind that applying early means accelerating the process, though that could also give you a head start before January, when many regular decision apps are due. Going into her final semester of high school, "it was nice to know I already had options," says Shannon Chen of Saratoga, California, now a sophomore at Princeton, who was accepted early action there and at the University of Michigan. But remember, Chen and others advise, if you do apply early be sure you know you'd like to attend that school if the process is binding. That way, if you're admitted, you can head off to a place that wants you as much as you want it. ◆

WYATT REID WESTLUND FOR USN&WR

A+ Schools for B Students

So you're a scholar with lots to offer and the GPA of a B student, and your heart is set on going to a great college. No problem. U.S. News has screened the universe of colleges and universities to identify those where nonsuperstars have a decent shot at being accepted and thriving – where spirit and hard work could make all the difference to the admissions office. To make this list, which is presented alphabetically, schools had to admit a meaningful proportion of applicants whose test scores and class standing put them in non-A territory (methodology, Page 133). Since many truly seek a broad and engaged student body, be sure to display your individuality and seriousness of purpose as you apply.

▶ National Universities

School (State) (*Public)	SAT/ACT 25th-75th percentile** ('17)	Average high school GPA ('17)	Freshmen in top 25% of class ('17)
Adelphi University (NY)	1060-1240[9]	3.5	58%[5]
American University (DC)	1180-1350[2]	3.6	66%[5]
Andrews University (MI)	21-29	3.6	42%
Arizona State University–Tempe*	22-29[2]	3.5	64%
Auburn University (AL)*	24-30	3.9	63%[5]
Ball State University (IN)*	1080-1240[2]	3.5	48%
Biola University (CA)	1050-1260	3.6	55%[5]
California State University–Fullerton*	1020-1180	3.6	68%
Clarkson University (NY)	1143-1330	3.6	74%
Colorado State University*	22-28	3.6	47%
Duquesne University (PA)	1120-1270[2]	3.7	56%
Edgewood College (WI)	21-25	3.5	46%
Florida Institute of Technology	1130-1320	3.7	60%[5]
Florida International University*	1100-1260	4.0	58%[5]
George Mason University (VA)*	1100-1290[2]	3.7	51%[5]
Hofstra University (NY)	1130-1310[2]	3.6	62%[5]
Howard University (DC)	1090-1290[3]	3.5	58%[5]
Iowa State University*	22-28	3.5	57%
Kansas State University*	22-28	3.5	51%[5]
Lipscomb University (TN)	23-29	3.5	54%[5]
Louisiana State University–Baton Rouge*	23-28	3.4	48%
Loyola University Chicago	24-29	3.7	70%[5]
Marquette University (WI)	24-29	N/A	64%[5]
Maryville University of St. Louis	21-27[2]	3.6	56%[5]
Mercer University (GA)	25-30	3.9	71%
Michigan State University*	1100-1320	3.7	67%[5]
Michigan Technological University*	1160-1340	3.7	65%
Mississippi State University*	21-28	3.4	54%
Montana State University*	21-28	3.4	44%
The New School (NY)	1100-1310[9]	3.4	47%[5]
North Dakota State University*	21-26	3.5	41%
Nova Southeastern University (FL)	1080-1280	4.0	55%[5]
Ohio University*	22-26	3.5	46%
Oklahoma State University*	22-28	3.7	54%
Oregon State University*	1070-1300	3.6	58%
Pace University (NY)	1040-1220[2]	3.3	42%[5]
Pennsylvania State U.–University Park*	1160-1340	3.6	73%[5]
Robert Morris University (PA)	1020-1200	3.5	42%
Rutgers University–Newark (NJ)*	1010-1170	N/A	54%
San Diego State University*	1090-1290	3.7	70%[5]
Seton Hall University (NJ)	1140-1280	3.5	61%[5]
St. John Fisher College (NY)	1060-1230	3.5	52%
St. John's University (NY)	1060-1250[2]	3.5	43%[5]
SUNY Col. of Environmental Sci. and Forestry*	1150-1300	3.7	62%
Syracuse University (NY)	1160-1350	3.6	69%[5]
Temple University (PA)*	1130-1310[2]	3.5	55%[5]
Texas Christian University	25-30	N/A	77%[5]
Texas Tech University*	1070-1240	3.6	50%
Union University (TN)	23-29	3.7	62%
University at Albany–SUNY*	1000-1190	3.2	48%[5]
University at Buffalo–SUNY*	1140-1310	3.6	73%[5]
University of Alabama–Birmingham*	21-28	3.7	52%
University of Arizona*	21-28[2]	3.3	61%[5]
University of Arkansas*	23-29	3.7	54%
University of Central Florida*	1150-1320	3.9	70%
University of Cincinnati*	23-28	3.6	48%
University of Colorado–Boulder*	25-30	3.7	59%[5]
University of Dayton (OH)	24-29[3]	3.7	61%[5]
University of Delaware*	1150-1330	3.7	66%[5]
University of Denver	25-30	3.7	73%[5]
University of Hawaii–Manoa*	1050-1240	3.5	55%
University of Houston*	1110-1280	N/A	65%
University of Idaho*	1010-1230	3.4	42%
University of Illinois–Chicago*	20-26	3.3	58%[5]
University of Iowa*	23-28	3.7	61%
University of Kansas*	23-28	3.6	57%
University of Kentucky*	22-28	N/A	58%[5]
University of La Verne (CA)	1030-1195	3.4	49%[5]
University of Louisville (KY)*	22-29[3]	3.6	56%[5]
University of Maine*	1050-1250	3.3	44%
University of Massachusetts–Boston*	1000-1200[2]	3.3	43%[5]
University of Massachusetts–Lowell*	1130-1310[2]	3.6	52%[5]
University of Mississippi*	22-29[2]	3.6	52%
University of Missouri*	23-29	N/A	60%
University of Missouri–St. Louis*	22-27	3.5	58%
University of Nebraska–Lincoln*	22-29	3.6	53%
University of Nevada–Reno*	21-26	3.4	54%
University of New Hampshire*	1080-1260	3.5	49%
University of North Carolina–Charlotte*	22-26	3.4	50%[5]
University of North Dakota*	21-26	3.4	43%
University of Oklahoma*	23-29	3.6	65%
University of Oregon*	1080-1270	3.5	56%[5]
University of Rhode Island*	1080-1250[3]	3.5	48%
University of San Diego	26-30	3.9	75%[5]
University of San Francisco	1100-1290	3.4	63%[5]
University of South Carolina*	25-30	4.0	61%
University of South Florida*	1150-1310	3.9	71%
University of St. Thomas (MN)	24-29	3.6	55%[5]
University of the Pacific (CA)	1070-1330	3.5	68%[5]
University of Utah*	22-29	3.6	71%[5]
University of Vermont*	1180-1350	3.7	76%[5]
University of Wyoming*	22-27	3.5	51%[5]

Note: Key to footnotes, Page 83.

School (State) (*Public)	SAT/ACT 25th-75th percentile** ('17)	Average high school GPA ('17)	Freshmen in top 25% of class ('17)
Virginia Commonwealth University*	1076-1292[2]	3.6	46%
Washington State University*	1020-1220	3.4	61%
Wayne State University (MI)*	1000-1210	3.4	47%[5]
West Virginia University*	21-27	3.5	44%

National Liberal Arts Colleges

School (State) (*Public)	SAT/ACT 25th-75th percentile** ('17)	Average high school GPA ('17)	Freshmen in top 25% of class ('17)
Agnes Scott College (GA)	1110-1300[2]	3.8	65%
Allegheny College (PA)	1140-1320[2]	3.5	65%
Augustana College (IL)	23-28[2]	3.3	64%[5]
Beloit College (WI)	24-30[2]	3.3	57%[5]
Berea College (KY)	22-27	3.5	64%
Centenary College of Louisiana	22-28	3.5	54%
Coe College (IA)	22-28	3.6	54%
College of St. Benedict (MN)	22-28	3.7	66%
College of the Atlantic (ME)	1190-1350[2]	3.7	50%[5]
College of Wooster (OH)	24-30	3.7	75%
Concordia College–Moorhead (MN)	22-28	3.6	55%
Covenant College (GA)	24-30	3.6	61%[5]
DePauw University (IN)	24-29	3.8	70%[5]
Drew University (NJ)	1100-1300[2]	3.5	60%[5]
Earlham College (IN)	25-30[2]	3.7	64%[5]
Elizabethtown College (PA)	1070-1280	N/A	60%
Franklin College (IN)	1010-1200	3.5	48%
Gordon College (MA)	1050-1290[3]	3.6	53%[5]
Goucher College (MD)	1050-1260[2]	3.1	54%[5]
Gustavus Adolphus College (MN)	24-30[2]	3.6	65%
Hanover College (IN)	22-27[2]	3.6	60%
Hollins University (VA)	1110-1300	3.8	66%
Hope College (MI)	24-29	3.9	66%
Houghton College (NY)	1060-1320[2]	3.5	54%
Illinois Wesleyan University	24-29	3.7	72%[5]
Juniata College (PA)	1080-1290[2]	3.7	64%
Knox College (IL)	23-30[2]	3.4	66%[5]
Lake Forest College (IL)	24-29[2]	3.6	67%[5]
Linfield College (OR)	1020-1210	3.6	67%
Luther College (IA)	23-28	3.7	54%
McDaniel College (MD)	1060-1230	3.5	51%
Meredith College (NC)	20-25	3.4	45%
Moravian College (PA)	1010-1210[3]	3.5	48%
Muhlenberg College (PA)	1140-1340[2]	3.3	61%[5]
Ohio Wesleyan University	22-28[2]	3.4	47%
Presbyterian College (SC)	21-27[2]	3.3	62%
Principia College (IL)	1033-1293	3.4	50%[5]
Randolph-Macon College (VA)	1050-1233	3.7	56%
Ripon College (WI)	20-26[2]	3.4	43%
Sewanee–University of the South (TN)	27-30[2]	N/A	61%[5]
Siena College (NY)	1060-1250[2]	3.5	49%
Simpson College (IA)	21-27	3.6	58%
Southwestern University (TX)	1110-1320	N/A	73%
Spelman College (GA)	1070-1215	3.6	53%[5]
St. Anselm College (NH)	1140-1300[2]	3.3	55%[5]
St. John's University (MN)	22-27	3.5	43%[5]
St. Mary's College (IN)	23-29	3.8	64%[5]
St. Michael's College (VT)	1150-1310[2]	N/A	48%
St. Norbert College (WI)	22-27	3.5	51%
Stonehill College (MA)	1080-1270[2]	3.3	51%
Susquehanna University (PA)	1070-1240[2]	3.5	57%
Transylvania University (KY)	25-30[2]	3.7	65%
University of Minnesota–Morris*	22-28	3.6	49%
University of North Carolina–Asheville*	22-27	3.4	44%
Ursinus College (PA)	1110-1310[2]	3.3	53%[5]
Virginia Military Institute*	1100-1280[3]	3.7	45%
Wabash College (IN)	1070-1280	3.7	57%
Wartburg College (IA)	21-27	3.6	53%
Washington and Jefferson College (PA)	1120-1290[2]	3.7	62%
Washington College (MD)	1090-1300	3.7	70%[5]
Wheaton College (MA)	1150-1350[2]	3.4	55%[5]
Willamette University (OR)	1120-1340[2]	3.8	75%[5]
William Jewell College (MO)	23-28[2]	3.7	57%
Wofford College (SC)	24-30[2]	3.7	76%

Regional Universities

School (State) (*Public)	SAT/ACT 25th-75th percentile** ('17)	Average high school GPA ('17)	Freshmen in top 25% of class ('17)
NORTH			
Arcadia University (PA)	1060-1240	3.6	55%
Assumption College (MA)	1070-1250[2]	3.3	41%[5]
Bryant University (RI)	1120-1280[2]	3.4	52%[5]
Canisius College (NY)	1040-1260	3.5	49%
Champlain College (VT)	1090-1300[2]	3.2	42%[5]
Chatham University (PA)	1050-1240[2]	3.7	51%
College of New Jersey*	1170-1330	N/A	73%[5]
CUNY–Baruch College*	1190-1350	3.3	75%
CUNY–Hunter College*	1070-1260	3.4	57%
Daemen College (NY)	1040-1220[2]	3.6	58%
DeSales University (PA)	1010-1230	3.2	52%[5]
Endicott College (MA)	1050-1210[2]	3.3	44%[5]
Fairfield University (CT)	1180-1320[2]	3.5	79%[5]
Fairleigh Dickinson University (NJ)	1020-1210	3.4	49%
Gannon University (PA)	990-1220	3.5	53%[5]
Ithaca College (NY)	1150-1330[2]	N/A	55%[5]
Lebanon Valley College (PA)	1063-1250[2]	3.7	55%
Le Moyne College (NY)	1080-1240[2]	3.5	51%
Loyola University Maryland	1140-1310[2]	3.5	68%[5]
Manhattan College (NY)	1050-1243[3]	3.3	54%[5]
Marist College (NY)	1120-1320[2]	3.3	53%[5]
Marywood University (PA)	1000-1190	3.4	47%
Misericordia University (PA)	1030-1205	3.4	51%
Molloy College (NY)	1020-1200	3.0	54%[5]
Nazareth College (NY)	1070-1250[2]	3.5	60%
Niagara University (NY)	1020-1200	3.4	47%
Providence College (RI)	1160-1330[2]	3.4	65%[5]
Quinnipiac University (CT)	1080-1260[2]	3.4	51%
Ramapo College of New Jersey*	1050-1230	3.4	41%[5]
Rider University (NJ)	990-1190	3.3	43%[5]
Roberts Wesleyan College (NY)	1040-1230	3.5	48%
The Sage Colleges (NY)	980-1170[2]	3.2	50%
Salisbury University (MD)*	1100-1260[9]	3.6	50%[5]
Salve Regina University (RI)	1080-1230[2]	N/A	42%[5]
Seton Hill University (PA)	1020-1220[2]	3.6	47%
Simmons College (MA)	1130-1310	3.4	70%
Springfield College (MA)	1020-1220	3.4	44%

▶ Regional Universities (continued)

School (State) (*Public)	SAT/ACT 25th-75th percentile** ('17)	Average high school GPA ('17)	Freshmen in top 25% of class ('17)
St. Bonaventure University (NY)	1020-1220	3.4	47%[5]
Stevenson University (MD)	1010-1190	3.1	45%
St. Francis University (PA)	1030-1230	3.6	57%
St. Joseph's University (PA)	1110-1290[2]	3.6	51%[5]
Stockton University (NJ)*	1010-1200	N/A	47%
SUNY College–Cortland*	1050-1200[9]	3.4	42%[5]
SUNY–Geneseo*	1120-1300	3.6	64%[5]
SUNY–New Paltz*	1100-1260	3.6	69%[5]
SUNY–Oswego*	1075-1225[3]	3.5	52%
SUNY–Plattsburgh*	1050-1190[3]	3.3	47%[5]
SUNY Polytechnic Inst.–Albany/Utica*	1000-1290[3]	3.7	66%[5]
Thomas Jefferson University (PA)	1030-1210	3.5	42%
Towson University (MD)*	1055-1210	3.6	41%[5]
University of Scranton (PA)	1080-1280	3.5	63%[5]
Wagner College (NY)	1070-1250[2]	3.5	50%[5]
Wentworth Inst. of Technology (MA)	1080-1270	3.0	41%[5]
Western New England University (MA)	980-1180[2]	3.4	40%[5]
Wilkes University (PA)	1040-1220	3.5	51%

SOUTH

School (State) (*Public)	SAT/ACT 25th-75th percentile** ('17)	Average high school GPA ('17)	Freshmen in top 25% of class ('17)
Anderson University (SC)	1000-1190	3.6	58%
Appalachian State University (NC)*	24-27	3.5	57%
Asbury University (KY)	21-28	N/A	66%[5]
Belmont University (TN)	24-29	3.7	56%[5]
Berry College (GA)	24-29[3]	3.7	66%
Christian Brothers University (TN)	21-27	3.7	56%
Christopher Newport University (VA)*	1110-1270[2]	3.8	50%
College of Charleston (SC)*	22-27	3.9	53%
Elon University (NC)	1140-1330	4.0	54%[5]
Embry-Riddle Aeronautical U. (FL)	1080-1320[2]	3.7	50%
Florida Southern College	23-28	3.7	60%[5]
Freed-Hardeman University (TN)	22-28	3.7	58%
Harding University (AR)	22-28	3.7	51%
James Madison University (VA)*	1100-1260[2]	N/A	51%
John Brown University (AR)	24-29[2]	3.7	58%[5]
Lee University (TN)	21-28	3.6	50%
Loyola University New Orleans	22-28	3.6	60%[5]
Mississippi College	22-29[3]	3.6	63%
Palm Beach Atlantic University (FL)	980-1200	N/A	44%
Queens University of Charlotte (NC)	1010-1198	N/A	42%
Rollins College (FL)	1195-1350[2]	3.3	58%[5]
Samford University (AL)	23-29	3.7	58%[5]
Stetson University (FL)	1110-1290[2]	3.8	50%
University of Mary Washington (VA)*	1080-1260[2]	3.6	46%
U. of North Carolina–Wilmington*	23-27	4.0	62%
University of North Florida*	1090-1280	3.8	43%
University of North Georgia*	1030-1180	3.6	62%[5]
University of Tampa (FL)	1070-1230	3.4	46%[5]
William Carey University (MS)	21-28[3]	3.5	54%

MIDWEST

School (State) (*Public)	SAT/ACT 25th-75th percentile** ('17)	Average high school GPA ('17)	Freshmen in top 25% of class ('17)
Baker University (KS)	21-25	3.5	48%
Baldwin Wallace University (OH)	21-27[2]	N/A	48%
Bethel University (MN)	21-27	3.5	52%
Bradley University (IL)	22-28	3.6	60%
Butler University (IN)	25-30	3.8	76%[5]

BRETT ZIEGLER FOR USN&WR

THE UNIVERSITY OF DENVER

School (State) (*Public)	SAT/ACT 25th-75th percentile** ('17)	Average high school GPA ('17)	Freshmen in top 25% of class ('17)
Capital University (OH)	22-27[3]	3.5	48%
Carroll University (WI)	21-26	N/A	47%
Concordia University (NE)	21-26	3.5	43%
Concordia University Wisconsin	20-26[3]	3.5	51%
Creighton University (NE)	25-30	3.8	69%[5]
Dominican University (IL)	20-25	3.7	55%
Drake University (IA)	24-30[2]	3.7	66%
Drury University (MO)	23-28	3.8	66%
Elmhurst College (IL)	20-26	3.5	49%[5]
Franciscan U. of Steubenville (OH)	23-28	3.8	55%[5]
Grace College and Seminary (IN)	990-1220	3.5	45%
Grand Valley State University (MI)*	1060-1230	3.6	45%
Hamline University (MN)	20-26	3.4	43%
Indiana Wesleyan University	21-26	3.6	57%
John Carroll University (OH)	22-27	3.5	57%[5]
Kettering University (MI)	1190-1350	3.7	60%
Lawrence Technological U. (MI)	1060-1280	3.5	54%[5]
Lewis University (IL)	21-26	3.5	49%
Marian University (IN)	1000-1200	3.5	44%
Missouri State University*	21-26	3.6	49%
Nebraska Wesleyan University	22-28	3.7	51%
North Central College (IL)	22-27	3.7	55%[5]
Olivet Nazarene University (IL)	20-26	3.6	47%
Otterbein University (OH)	21-27	3.6	55%
Rockhurst University (MO)	22-27	3.6	56%
Spring Arbor University (MI)	1000-1205	3.5	48%
St. Ambrose University (IA)	21-26[3]	3.2	42%[5]
St. Catherine University (MN)	21-26	3.6	62%
University of Detroit Mercy	1040-1230	3.6	54%
University of Evansville (IN)	22-29[2]	3.7	67%
University of Findlay (OH)	21-27	3.6	56%
University of Illinois–Springfield*	20-27	3.6	54%
University of Indianapolis	990-1180	3.5	47%
University of Michigan–Dearborn*	1060-1290	3.6	55%
University of Minnesota–Duluth*	22-26	3.5	48%
University of Northern Iowa*	21-26	3.5	46%
U. of Northwestern–St. Paul (MN)	21-27	3.5	50%
University of St. Francis (IL)	20-25	3.5	41%[5]
University of Wisconsin–Eau Claire*	21-26	N/A	48%
University of Wisconsin–La Crosse*	22-26	N/A	58%
Valparaiso University (IN)	23-29	3.6	63%
Xavier University (OH)	22-28[3]	3.6	45%[5]
WEST			
Abilene Christian University (TX)	21-26	3.6	54%
California Baptist University	980-1190	3.6	46%[5]
California Lutheran University	1060-1230	3.7	66%[5]
California State University–Chico*	990-1170	3.3	76%[4]
Chapman University (CA)	25-30	3.7	78%[5]
Corban University (OR)	1040-1230	3.6	60%[5]
Dominican University of California	1040-1215	3.7	57%
George Fox University (OR)	1030-1240	3.6	60%[5]
Gonzaga University (WA)	1180-1350	3.7	75%[5]
LeTourneau University (TX)	1060-1310[2]	3.6	52%
The Master's U. and Seminary (CA)	1030-1240	3.7	69%[5]
Mills College (CA)	1030-1290[2]	3.5	55%[5]
New Mexico Inst. of Mining and Tech.*	23-29	3.6	68%
Northwest Nazarene University (ID)	1030-1240	3.6	51%
Oklahoma Christian University	20-27[3]	3.5	52%
Oklahoma City University	23-28[3]	3.8	61%
Oral Roberts University (OK)	20-26	3.6	46%[5]
Point Loma Nazarene University (CA)	1100-1290	3.8	71%[5]
Regis University (CO)	20-26	3.5	55%[5]
Saint Martin's University (WA)	980-1190[2]	3.4	52%
Seattle University	1130-1330	3.6	68%[5]
St. Edward's University (TX)	1080-1250	N/A	58%
St. Mary's University of San Antonio	1040-1230	3.5	58%
Western Washington University*	1080-1280	3.4	53%[5]
Westminster College (UT)	21-28	3.5	53%
Whitworth University (WA)	1090-1310[2]	3.6	70%[5]

▶ Regional Colleges

School (State) (*Public)	SAT/ACT 25th-75th percentile** ('17)	Average high school GPA ('17)	Freshmen in top 25% of class ('17)
NORTH			
Maine Maritime Academy*	990-1180	3.1	57%
Messiah College (PA)	1100-1310	3.8	63%
U.S. Coast Guard Academy (CT)*	1180-1343[3]	3.7	75%
U.S. Merchant Marine Academy (NY)*	25-29	N/A	64%
SOUTH			
High Point University (NC)	1050-1240[9]	3.3	47%[5]
MIDWEST			
Augustana University (SD)	23-29	3.7	64%
Benedictine College (KS)	22-28	3.5	48%[5]
Calvin College (MI)	23-30[2]	3.7	57%[5]
Cedarville University (OH)	23-29	3.7	62%[5]
College of the Ozarks (MO)	21-26[3]	3.6	62%
Dordt College (IA)	22-28[2]	3.6	43%
Goshen College (IN)	980-1238	3.5	46%
Loras College (IA)	20-26	3.4	46%
Northwestern College (IA)	21-27	3.6	59%
Ohio Northern University	22-28	3.7	55%
Taylor University (IN)	22-29	3.8	63%[5]
University of Mount Union (OH)	20-25	3.4	45%
WEST			
Carroll College (MT)	22-28	3.6	64%[5]
Oregon Institute of Technology*	1040-1230	3.5	57%
William Jessup University (CA)	1000-1215	3.4	43%[5]

Methodology: To be eligible, national universities, liberal arts colleges, regional universities and regional colleges all had to be numerically ranked among the top three-quarters of their peer groups in the 2019 Best Colleges rankings. They had to admit a meaningful proportion of non-A students, as indicated by fall 2017 admissions data on SAT Evidence-based Reading and Writing and Math scores or Composite ACT scores and high school class standing. The cutoffs were: The 75th percentile for the SAT had to be less than or equal to 1,350; the 25th percentile, greater than or equal to 980. The ACT composite range: less than or equal to 30 and greater than or equal to 20. The proportion of freshmen from the top 10 percent of their high school class had to be less than or equal to 50 percent (for national universities and liberal arts colleges only); for all schools, the proportion of freshmen from the top 25 percent of their high school class had to be less than or equal to 80 percent, and greater than or equal to 40 percent. Average freshman retention rates for all schools had to be greater than or equal to 75 percent. Average high school GPA itself was not used in the calculations identifying the A-plus schools. N/A means not available.

Note: Key to footnotes, Page 83.

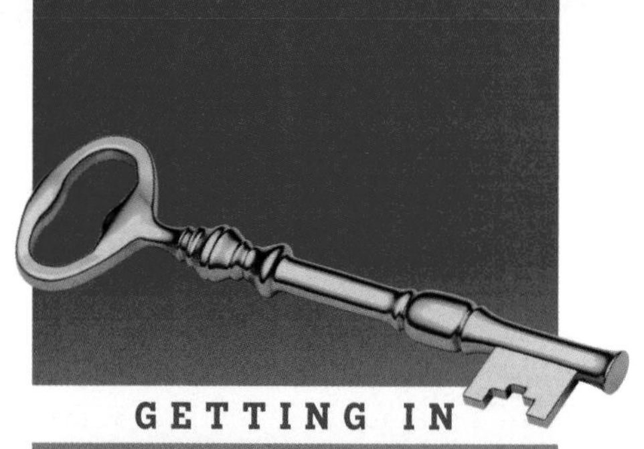

GETTING IN

We Did It!

How eight Arizona high school seniors got accepted

by **Lindsay Cates**

Applying to college is a daunting task for even the most accomplished students. From acing the SAT or ACT and writing a flawless essay (or four) to touring campuses and figuring out how to pay for it all, applicants have a lot to consider – on top of juggling their homework, sports and extracurriculars. U.S. News visited Catalina Foothills High School in Tucson, Arizona, in early May to see how eight seniors managed it all and found the right college fit.

Some opted for in-state choices at the University of Arizona (just a 20-minute drive from CFHS) and Arizona State University in Tempe, while others are headed across the country and even the globe. Among the public high school's roughly 1,800 students, 60 percent are white, 27 percent are Hispanic, 7 percent are Asian/Pacific Islander, and 2 percent are African-American. CFHS's suburban, cactus-dotted campus in the shadow of the Santa Catalina Mountains offers 20 Advanced Placement courses, and 90 percent of grads go on to pursue higher education. Hear from several newly minted grads who share their admission struggles, triumphs and lessons learned:

PHOTOGRAPHY BY **DEANNA DENT** FOR USN&WR

Sarah Cho

The daughter of missionaries, Cho attended an international school in China for 10 years before moving to Tucson in ninth grade. An avid researcher, she familiarized herself with the college application process and focused on city schools with public health programs. She started by consulting the U.S. News college rankings and followed up by scouring school websites to check their programs and individual requirements.

"Things started coming together," she says, when early in her junior year she stumbled upon QuestBridge, a national nonprofit that matches highly qualified applicants with need to top schools across the country. After receiving the news in November that she was a QuestBridge finalist, she had only two weeks to get applications submitted to seven partner schools, which included Dartmouth, Brown, the University of Pennsylvania, and Emory University in Atlanta. She wasn't "matched" to any of the schools (a binding decision that comes with a full-ride scholarship), so she quickly submitted an application to Northwestern University near Chicago, but she was denied.

Undeterred, over winter break she got together 10 regular decision apps and was accepted at George Washington University in the District of Columbia, the University of Arizona, the University of California–Irvine, the University of California–San Diego, Drexel University in Philadelphia and Wheaton College in Illinois. She was rejected at Boston University and waitlisted at New York University, UCLA, and the University of California–Berkeley. Her choice came down to financial aid and a visit to GW, where the location and the open-minded people she met impressed her. She'll study international affairs with a concentration in global health.

GPA: 3.94

SAT/ACT: 660 math; 750 evidence-based reading and writing / 32

Extracurriculars: Secretary of National Honor Society, president of HOSA–Future Health Professionals, speech and debate club, church youth group leader

Essay: She adapted her QuestBridge personal statement – the prompt was "share your story" – and described the struggle of living in a two-bedroom apartment with four other family members. But she thinks it may have been too broad for the Common Application, and she wishes she had spent more time improving the focus.

Helpful tip: Get admissions counselors on the phone. Calling was the easiest way to get a straight answer.

Stressor: With parents who don't speak English, Cho was largely on her own to figure out financial documents. Finding supportive friends and counselors to help her along the way was critical.

Cost: Financial aid from GW is covering 90 percent of the $55,140 annual tuition. She'll take out $5,500 in loans each year, and the rest will be covered by scholarships and her parents.

Fly-ins: For students with financial need, visiting schools can be tough. She applied to several fly-in programs, which arrange college visits for underrepresented students, and she went on two to Tufts near Boston and GW.

Advice: "Enjoy your time in high school and don't do things just for college apps."

Be prepared. The process can be unexpected.

Have a focused plan each year.

Inge Pham-Swann

Undecided on a major, musically talented Pham-Swann – she sings and plays the piano, violin and ukulele – wanted a change of scenery. She even thought about going abroad for college, but decided she didn't want to be that far from family or complicate the already stressful application process. Ultimately, she focused on schools in the Northeast and Midwest mostly based on rankings and what she had heard about them. In early fall, she applied early decision to Brown but was denied. "By that point I was OK with it," she says. "You can't get in everywhere."

She forged ahead and scored acceptances to Northeastern University in Boston, Oberlin College in Ohio, Macalester College in Minnesota, and Arizona

Sarah Cho (left) and Inge Pham-Swann

State University. She was denied at Tufts, Cornell and Northwestern, and she was wait-listed at Boston University. The combination of Macalester's small size (about 2,100 undergraduates) and urban feel, plus a generous financial aid package, sealed the deal. Planning to minor in music, Pham-Swann also wants to learn French and interpretive dance and generally "try new things."
GPA: 3.8
SAT/ACT: 710 math; 690 evidence-based reading and writing / 32
Extracurriculars: President of concert choir, member of Tucson Girls Chorus, orchestra, HOSA–Future Health Professionals, tutored middle schoolers in algebra I, and taught music lessons to kids
Essay: Being cast as the lead in the musical "Xanadu" despite having had no previous musical theater experience. "I learned what I was, and what I was not," she says. She formatted her essay like a script, describing her experience through numbered acts.
Focus: She made sure to block out time on busy days of schoolwork and choir to focus on apps.
Cost: Financial aid and scholarships are covering $45,000 of the $66,500 total cost of attendance each year. She'll also have a work-study job and will take out loans.
Surprisingly helpful: Brown's early application had several short-answer questions, and writing them out helped her formulate a plan for the rest of her apps.
Advice: "Give yourself more time than you think you will need."

Deevany Tirado Flores

Tirado Flores grew up surrounded by animals. Her dad's family owns two farms that raise cattle and pigs, and watching the TV show "Fetch the Vet" as a toddler sparked her interest in becoming a veterinarian. When it came time to apply to college, Tirado Flores targeted top veterinary science programs. She thinks her dedication to extracurriculars, strong grades, and Hispanic heritage helped her land acceptances to every school she applied to: the University of Washington, Oregon State University, the University of Arizona, Northern Arizona University, the University of Iowa, and Iowa State University.

If you want to apply to a school, don't let anything stop you.

During a visit to Iowa State in the winter of her senior year, she says, "the snow captivated my heart." A careful planner, she cut down her list – eliminating schools that were too expensive or too selective – to make sure she had time to focus on applications during a busy fall schedule of schoolwork and marching band.
GPA: 3.63
ACT: 24
Extracurriculars: Concert band (French horn), marching band, National Honor Society, junior varsity basketball, Link Crew (a club that helps freshmen get acclimated to high school); volunteer for the AIDS Foundation, the Ronald McDonald House and Tucson Wildlife Center
Essay: She wrote several versions to address the specific prompts for each school, but all centered around a personal battle. One recounted her experience undergoing a half dozen surgeries to treat heart conditions, and how her time in the hospital has brought her family closer. Another explained how losing her grandfather when she was 16 "was the hardest thing I've ever experienced."
Big help: Her high school field science teacher encouraged her to pursue the sciences and gave her a list of schools to check out.
Cost: Financial aid, a work-study position and scholarships are covering most of Iowa State's $35,600 annual total expected cost of attendance. Her parents will pitch in for the rest.
Advice: Start going on visits early. Tirado Flores didn't make her first trip until senior year, and she wishes she had had time for more.

Deevany Tirado Flores

Nolan Mac Ban

Nolan was looking for a school that had it all: sports, diverse academic offerings, and a lively social scene. He and his twin brother, Shay (older by one minute), navigated the college search at the same time, but after years of what felt like living in his sibling's shadow, Nolan faced a tough decision when they both found the University of Southern California appealing. He thought UCLA might give him more freedom, but he was "shocked" on his USC visit to discover he loved the school.

In addition to those two Los Angeles universities, Nolan gained acceptances to Texas Christian University, Baylor University (also in Texas), the University of Washington, the University of Kansas, Arizona State and the University of Arizona. He was denied by UC–Berkeley and the University of North Carolina–Chapel Hill. He's looking forward to classes in USC's business program and plans to minor in communications with the hope of becoming an athletic director or working in sports broadcasting.
GPA: 4.0
SAT: 720 math; 650

Current students will always tell you the good and the bad.

Put your hat in the ring and put yourself out there.

evidence-based reading and writing
Extracurriculars: Student council (sophomore year vice president, junior year president), National Honor Society, Assisteens community service group, varsity basketball, varsity soccer, Young Life (a Christian ministry group)
Essay: Often compared to his twin, he wrote about how it felt like "struggling through quicksand" to find his own footing. Student council brought him his own opportunity to shine, and he planned the most successful prom in CFHS's history – raking in a $20,000 profit.
Plan: Knowing that some California schools required four essays each, he got other apps out of the way early.
Helpful sources: He talked to friends who attended his top choices to get an inside perspective.
Advice: "Go with your gut." It's not all about prestige, but about where you feel you fit.

Shay Mac Ban

With family on the East Coast, Shay always thought he would end up near them. But after tearing his ACL late junior year, he postponed taking the SAT and didn't start on applications until he was fully recovered, causing him to miss the early decision deadline for Duke in North Carolina. "I had to cut down my list a bit," he says. Even then, looking for a large school with a balance of academics, clubs and sports, he sent apps to 10 schools; his top four were USC, the University of Virginia, UCLA, and Duke. He got accepted at USC, UCLA, the University of Washington, UC-Davis, UC-San Diego, and UC-Santa Barbara, plus the honors colleges at the University of Arizona and Arizona State. He was denied at Duke and UVA. Ultimately, he chose USC for its highly ranked undergraduate business program, large alumni network, and internship opportunities across Los Angeles, plus what he saw as a beautiful campus.
GPA: 4.0
SAT: 730 math; 670 evidence-based reading and writing
Extracurriculars: Student body president, president of Arizona Association of Student Councils (a state network of student government clubs), chairman of Assisteens service group, captain of varsity volleyball team, Catalina Foothills Site Council member
Essay: Be fearless. After the ACL injury and another accident in which he was hit in the face with a golf club, he wrote about "living life with reckless abandonment" and how he's ready to face college with no fear.
Smart move: "Google Calendar is a remarkable thing and

Nolan (left) and Shay Mac Ban

really saved my behind."
Costly mistake: Missing USC's Dec. 1 deadline for merit scholarships. He's taking out loans and planning to sell his car.
Regret: Not answering optional essay questions. If they're there, it's probably for a reason, he says, so you should do them.

Find friends that lift you up. Competition is miserable.

Rohan Bakshi

Although excited to start classes at the University of Arizona's Honors College, Bakshi says he has "a lot of regrets" about his college application process. In high school he didn't always try for the best grades (often settling for a B+), and he admits to procrastinating by submitting his applications only a day or two before the deadlines. But impressive test scores earned him acceptances to the honors colleges at UA and Arizona State. He was denied at USC, UCLA, UC–Berkeley and Duke. Ultimately, he was sold on UA's management information systems major, where he'll take classes on using cutting-edge technology to solve real-world business problems. The business curriculum is flexible enough that he could try classes outside of the major to graduate with "a unique perspective."
GPA: 3.73
SAT/ACT: 770 math; 710 evidence-based reading and writing / 33
Extracurriculars: Varsity basketball, varsity volleyball, saxophone and steel drums in band, student council vice president
Essay: He "laid out his personality" by writing a direct dialogue with each school. Pinpointing specific activities he wanted to be involved with at each place, he showed his interests and what he would be bringing to campus. He also addressed his shortcomings head on, writing that "mediocrity is not an option" and assuring admissions counselors that he had ambitious goals for himself in college and beyond.
Cost: He received UA's Wildcat Excellence Tuition Award, which will cover $10,000 of the $12,400 in-state annual tuition per year. His parents will shoulder the costs of room and board.
Lifeline: Talking with teachers and supportive friends throughout the process. "Having peers doing it

Get the hard wor done earl then ride t wave to the end.

Rohan Bakshi (left) and Jorge Garavito

with you makes the process much less stressful."
Regrets: He wishes he had tried harder in classes and in finding an activity that interested him – and sticking with it – instead of prioritizing hanging out with friends.

Jorge Garavito

Garavito started playing soccer at age 4 and practically never stopped. His talent and dedication on the field earned him the title of captain for both his club and school varsity teams, but he says he never considered himself a leader until he had to write about it for his college applications. Growing up in Nogales, a small Arizona city on the border with Mexico, Garavito thought he would finish up at CFHS and help run his family's small insurance business. Now he's planning on a biology major and going pre-med. His leadership, solid grades and extracurricular involvement got him accepted to all four schools he applied to: Pepperdine University in California, the University of San Diego, the University of Arizona, and Arizona State. At the latter's honors college, Garavito found a community and challenging classes within a big university that has Division I sports, Greek life, and a large alumni network.
GPA: 3.89
SAT/ACT: 620 math; 600 evidence-based reading and writing / 25
Extracurriculars: President of Spirit Club, captain of varsity soccer team and a club soccer team, student council, Link Crew, Young Life
Essay: Based on the quote "You get the heart of your father and the brain of your mother." Growing up without a father, he had to grow a "synthetic heart" through his activities and accomplishments – with a college acceptance being the final step.
Influencer: His mom didn't attend college in the U.S. and couldn't give much hands-on help, but "her moral support, trust and proudness" kept him going.
Good move: Diligent in his planning, Garavito put together a detailed spreadsheet with essay prompts, due dates and recommendation letter deadlines. He also finished all essays weeks early to leave plenty of time to edit.
Proudest achievement: Being the guy who takes initiative. As founder of the Spirit Club, he organized school pride activities and was always "the guy screaming his head off" at athletic events.
Option: He considered trying to play soccer for a Division III school like Haverford College near Philadelphia or Johns Hopkins in Baltimore, but he felt those schools were a bit too small.
College visits: Generous financial aid and a strong biology program made USD tempting, but after a trip to campus, Garavito felt the place wasn't the right fit. "Don't believe it until you see it," he says.

Don't stress. It will all come together.

Talya Rezetko

Talya Rezetko

Rezetko's family moved around a lot when she was growing up – spending time in Mexico (where her mother's family resides) and then the Netherlands and Scotland (for her dad's work as a professor) – before ending up in Arizona to be with family on both sides. Still, she didn't consider heading abroad for college until December of her senior year. The more she pictured what she wanted her life to be like, the more her thoughts drifted back to her time in Edinburgh and the possibility of being near friends and family there.

From the start, though, she knew she wanted a school in a midsized city where she could study both business and psychology. She cast a wide net: In the U.S., she was accepted at the University of Arizona, Arizona State, and Northern Arizona University; she was denied at the University of Minnesota–Twin Cities, the University of Massachusetts, and Temple University in Philadelphia. In Great Britain, she received conditional offers (meaning she still had to show strong grades in her final semester) to the University of Aberdeen, the University of Stirling, the University of Glasgow, and the University of Strathclyde, all in Scotland, as well as the University of Sussex in England. Her decision was made after hearing advice from her older sister, who attended school in England and had good insights on UK schools. She gave Aberdeen a strong review.
GPA: 3.34
SAT/ACT: 540 math; 520 evidence-based reading and writing / 20
Extracurriculars: Varsity tennis and cross country
Essay: Her experience living among different cultures, each with its own "levels of freedom." In Holland, she could explore on her bike wherever she wanted, whereas in Mexico she restricted her schedule to home, school and sports.
Research: Rankings mattered to her with schools in the UK. For U.S. schools, she was more concerned with location, preferring something in between a big city and a small town.
Bonus: Her dad is a writer and editor, and he went through her essays closely with her.
Biggest strength: Being independent. Her twin sister is attending Northern Arizona University, and Rezetko thinks heading abroad will help her continue to be her own person. She is "excited to start something new." ◆

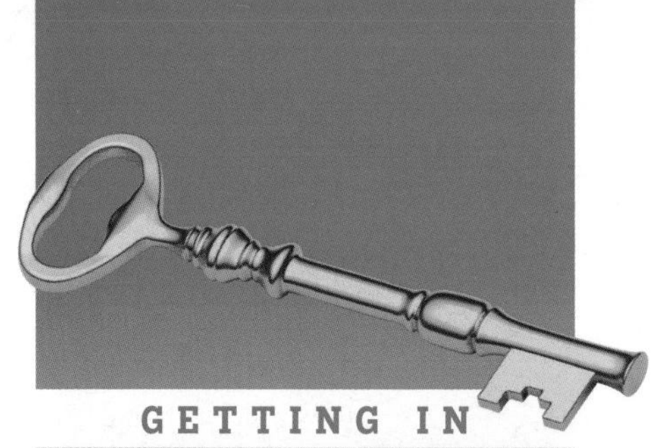

GETTING IN

Your College Search: A To-Do List

by **Ned Johnson**

Prepare for a great high school *experience. You'll have opportunities to grow inside and outside the classroom, while making sure that you're well prepared to apply to college in three short years. Use this calendar to guide your experience. Careful planning and good choices over time make for strong options later. Ready, set, go!*

Freshman Year

☐ **Listen and observe.** Faced with more challenging high school classwork, you'll want to pay attention to what your new teachers expect from you and look for ways to work harder and smarter. Grades are important in ninth grade, but seek balance so that you are challenged but not overwhelmed. Ask for help if you run into trouble and treat a low grade as constructive feedback to help you become a better learner.

☐ **Get involved.** High school is not simply a four-year audition for college but a critical period to develop yourself. Grades are important, but so, too, are your social connections and extracurriculars. Use part-time jobs, clubs, community service, arts and music, photography, cheer squad, robotics club, and so on to pursue your passions. It will also give you an energy boost to push you through the less exciting parts of school life.

☐ **Read voraciously.** Dive into books, newspapers, magazines and blogs. Explore subjects that engage you. Additionally, check out TED Talks, YouTube videos and other free learning opportunities such as the massive open online courses known as MOOCs.

☐ **Find mentors.** Look for knowledgeable people who can offer helpful advice over time: teachers, coaches, counselors and friends. These relationships can pay off in other ways, too: People like to help students they know!

☐ **Schedule downtime.** That means turning off electronic devices. No phones. No screens. We all need time to daydream and think about ourselves and our place in the world.

Sophomore Year

Focus on evolving as a learner *while developing your understanding of your strengths and passions.*

☐ **Challenge yourself (wisely).** Strive for strong grades and take on new challenges, but ask for help when needed and avoid overtaxing yourself. Balance is your goal.

☐ **Speak up in class.** Share and discuss your ideas with others. Colleges look for students who contribute and elevate class discussions. Additionally, down the road, you'll request letters of recommendation, and teachers won't know you without hearing your thoughts.

☐ **Sleep.** The typical 15-year-old brain needs eight to 10 hours of sleep to function at 100 percent, so that should be your goal.

☐ **Refine your route.** Look ahead to the 11th- and 12th-grade courses you might be interested in taking and plan to work into

ILLUSTRATIONS BY ANDREA COBB FOR USN&WR

your schedule any prerequisites. Take advantage of special courses, particularly rigorous ones that are in line with your academic interests.

☐ **Learn from the masters.** As you take inventory of your own interests, find people who work in related areas. Listen to their stories and consider opportunities for gaining firsthand experience of your own. A 20-minute conversation with a professional could even turn into a fruitful internship opportunity.

☐ **Put together an activities list.** Start jotting down your hobbies, jobs and extracurricular activities to keep track of what you have accomplished. This document will form the basis of your résumé and will be essential in preparing for college interviews and applications, in addition to possible jobs, internships and summer programs.

☐ **Make your summer matter.** Work, volunteer, play sports, travel or take a class. Research summer programs and internships to give yourself the chance to move beyond the scope of your regular high school courses. Plunge into an activity that excites you or one that builds on a special interest.

☐ **Settle on a testing strategy.** Use your PSAT scores and other practice tests to help you identify the right test for you (i.e., SAT vs. ACT). Set up a test-prep plan.

Junior Year

Essays and testing and APs. Oh my!

Your grades, test scores and activities this year form a large part of what colleges consider for admission, so prepare for your exams and do your best in class.

☐ **Plot out your calendar.** Talk with your parents and guidance counselor about which exams to take and when. If your 10th-grade PSAT scores put you in reach of a National Merit Scholarship, concentrated prep time might be worth it. Then, take the SAT or ACT in winter or early spring. In May or June, the SAT Subject Tests (required by some colleges) are also an option in areas where you shine or in subjects you covered this year. If you're enrolled in an AP or honors course now, consider taking one of the College Board's practice AP tests.

☐ **Immerse yourself in activities.** Look for extracurriculars, both in and out of school, that you enjoy and that show you are dedicated, play well with others and can assume leadership roles. High school is not simply a four-year audition for college. Rather, it's a time to discover what you like, to develop, and to sharpen skills you'll use after high school.

☐ **Build your college list in the spring.** Once you get your test scores, talk to a counselor and put together a list of target, reach and likely schools. Use apps to aid your research. Explore college websites and resources such as ed.gov/finaid and usnews.com/bestcolleges. And clean up your social media (e.g., Instagram, Facebook, Twitter) since college admissions folks may see them.

☐ **Visit schools.** Spring break and summer vacation are ideal times to check out a few campuses. Attend college fairs and talk with the people behind the tables who can provide information and may serve as future contacts.

☐ **Get recommendations.** Right after spring break, ask two teachers with different perspectives on your performance if they will write letters for you. Choose teachers with whom you have a good relationship and who will effectively communicate your academic and personal qualities.

☐ **Write.** Reflect on your experiences and highlight your strengths. Procrastination causes stress, so aim to have first drafts done by Labor Day of senior year. Share them with an English teacher, parent or counselor.

Senior Year

☐ **Don't slack off.** Colleges look at senior-year transcripts, so keep working hard in your classes.

☐ **Finish testing.** If necessary, you can retake the SAT, ACT or SAT Subject Tests. The early fall test dates give you time to apply early. Check deadlines and the admissions testing policies of your schools. Are they test optional or do they require the SAT or ACT? If so, do you also need the optional written essays for either test? What about the SAT Subject Tests?

☐ **Know your deadlines.** Many colleges have multiple deadline options. Consider the implications of early decision, early action, rolling, regular and other deadlines and plan accordingly (related story, Page 128).

☐ **Apply.** Craft your essays with a well-thought-out narrative. Fill out applications carefully. Review a copy of your transcript. Have you displayed an upward trend that should be discussed? Does an anomaly need context? Discuss with your counselor. Leave yourself time to reread essays to clean up any errors.

☐ **Follow up.** Check that your colleges have received records and recs from your high school and your SAT or ACT scores from the testing organization. A month after you submit your application, call the college and confirm that your file is complete.

☐ **Confirm aid rules.** Check with each college for specific financial aid application requirements. Dates and forms may vary.

☐ **Make a choice.** Try to visit or even revisit the colleges where you've been accepted before committing. Talk with alumni; attend an accepted-student reception. Then, make your college choice official by sending in your deposit. Congrats! ◆

Ned Johnson is founder of and tutor-geek at PrepMatters (prepmatters.com) where, along with colleagues, he torments teens with test prep, educational counseling and general attempts to help them thrive. He is also co-author of the 2018 book "The Self-Driven Child: The Science and Sense of Giving Your Kids More Control Over Their Lives."

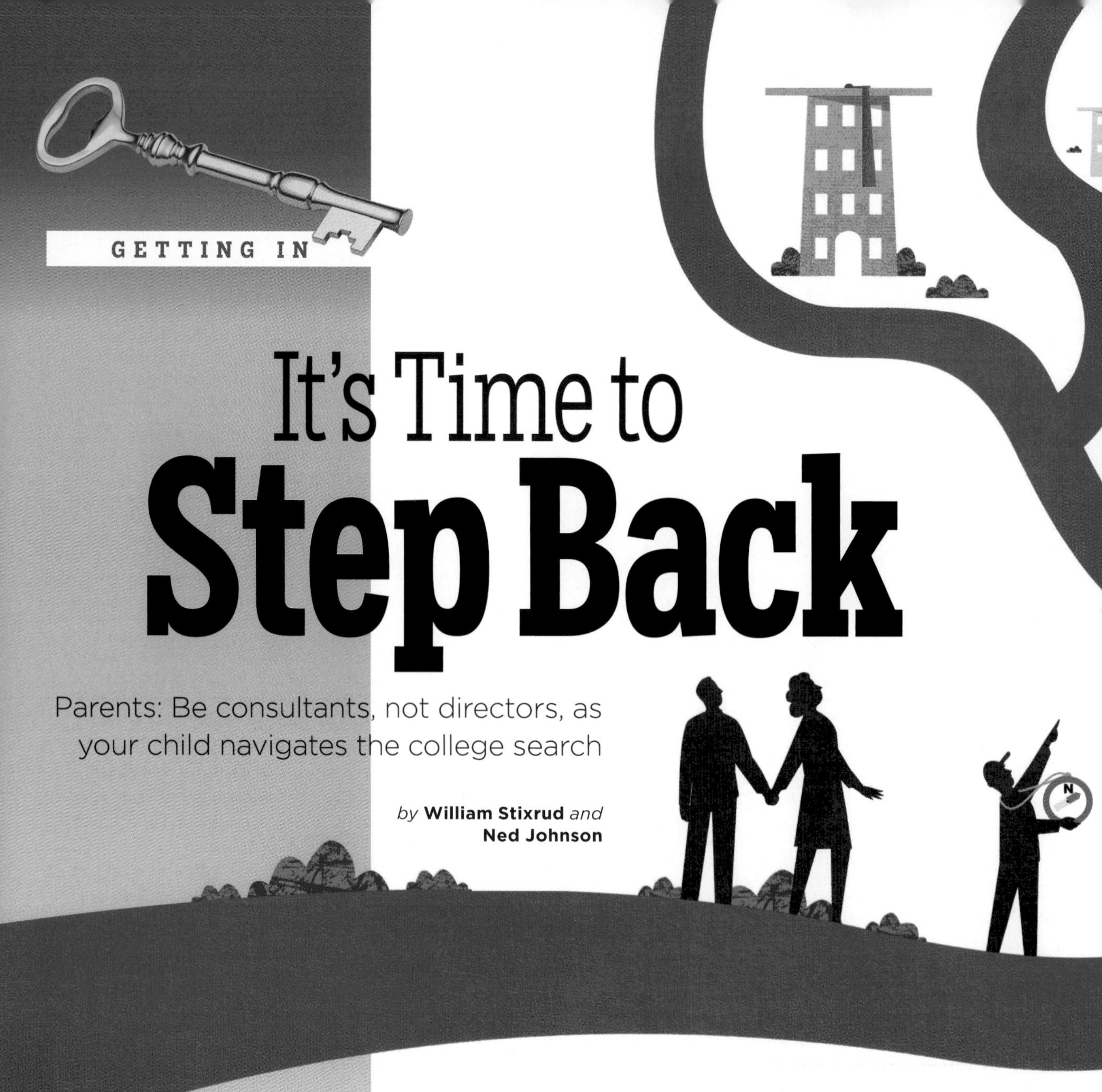

GETTING IN

It's Time to Step Back

Parents: Be consultants, not directors, as your child navigates the college search

by **William Stixrud** *and* **Ned Johnson**

Every year, we see kids who struggle to make it through their first year of college. In most cases, they also had difficulties with the college search and admissions process, which was often driven by their parents. This is a familiar scenario. Parents want their kids to succeed in school and to be able to plan their own academic paths, but this can only happen if they resist the urge to micromanage. The best way for parents to help kids succeed during their college search is for them to act less like directors and more like consultants – advising, but not controlling.

After all, if a teen can't handle being in control of the admissions process, then she will likely struggle when navigating college. Ideally, kids should get plenty of experience running their own lives before they leap into a new environment that may be academically and emotionally challenging. We think this is particularly important, given the growing mental health crisis on college campuses, where increasing numbers of students report feeling stress and anxiety (related story, Page 34).

Of course, that doesn't mean handing over the reins is easy. Parents need to talk to their child before the college search process begins. Assure her that you are not going to try to talk her into any one school or out of another. You might say, "There are thousands of colleges out there. Ultimately, nobody can make a better decision than you about what will suit you best." And remind her (and yourself) that she is the person who is going to work hard there for four years, not you.

Set boundaries. Be clear about what you will or won't do, just as a consultant would. Explain that you won't do the research on programs or write admissions essays for your child, but that you will be there as a sounding board to help him think through every angle and find the best fit. Brain science tells us that when kids have a sense of control over their lives in this manner, they operate more out of their prefrontal cortex, the area of the brain that controls executive functioning

(problem-solving, planning and decision-making, for instance), rather than from a place of fear or self-defense. And since the brain develops according to how it's used, the more time spent exercising this part of it, the better it is for overall development.

Choosing a school is a process in which kids can really learn to better understand themselves – and get valuable practice in making important decisions on their own. As a parent, you send a powerful message when you let your child know that you trust him to make good choices. It encourages him to think honestly about himself and to seek advice from other knowledgeable people. Plus, you can still find ways to help him make an informed decision. You might say, "There are going to be places you like and places you hate, and I'm going to ask you annoying questions to help you figure out why."

Standardized tests represent another opportunity to put on your consultant hat. Parents constantly ask us if they should make their kid take a particular test or how much exam prep he needs, but these are the wrong questions. Don't make the decisions for him. Instead, help him gather information about the tests and what colleges require, and then let him decide – and do the work.

Try asking questions: "Do you want to take a class? Prep by yourself or with a tutor? Do you want to take the ACT or SAT one more time?" Supporting his decision-making is good for your relationship; it teaches problem-solving, and it encourages autonomy. Plus, if you push too hard, you may actually harm his score.

Years of neuroscience research have shown that, just as a healthy sense of control allows the brain to function optimally, a low sense of control is extremely stressful and impairs one's learning ability, judgment and emotional well-being. The less kids feel in control of their lives and the more pressure they feel, the less likely they are to perform well. They'll also be less motivated. Everyone has a sweet spot of performance, one where they are challenged but not overly stressed. The more your child understands where this place is, the better he will do in positioning himself for success.

When the time comes to start applying to schools, you might ask, "Do you want help with organizing the process?" or "Can I help you find time to work on this?" If she is feeling motivated but overloaded, then she might appreciate the help. But if she doesn't want it, don't push. Remember: She may not be comfortable with the timetable that you prefer. She needs to wrestle with that on her own, just as she'll eventually have to grapple with deadlines for college papers and projects by herself.

Research has demonstrated that you cannot force someone else to feel motivated. The best thing to do is to start early to encourage your child to pursue activities about which he is enthusiastic. The more time he spends deeply engrossed in activities he loves, the more self-directed his brain will be overall, and that success can carry over to the college search process.

At the end of the day, if you are working harder than your kid to get him into college, then that's a clear indicator that he probably isn't ready – and that readiness won't magically appear at freshman orientation. In that case, it might be worth considering another option, such as a gap year. Although letting go can be tough, remember that what all parents ultimately want for their kids is the ability to make good decisions for themselves. ◆

William Stixrud, Ph.D., *is a clinical neuropsychologist and a faculty member at George Washington University's medical school and Children's National Medical Center in Washington, D.C.*

Ned Johnson *is the founder of and tutor-geek at PrepMatters, a tutoring and educational advising company in Washington, D.C.*

Stixrud and Johnson *co-authored the 2018 book "The Self-Driven Child: The Science and Sense of Giving Your Kids More Control Over Their Lives."*

ILLUSTRATION BY MIKE AUSTIN FOR USN&WR

5

CHAPTER

Finding

THE UNIVERSITY OF VERMONT

BRETT ZIEGLER FOR USN&WR

the Money

Cracking the Financial Aid Code

Understanding the way the aid process works will help you land the most generous package

by **Arlene Weintraub**

One big consideration in choosing a college, at least for most people, is how brutal a blow the bills will deal to the family finances. By following a smart strategy in applying for financial aid, you may encounter some pleasant surprises – like an offer from that pricey private college at the top of your wish list so generous that the school ends up being more of a bargain than the local state university. Read on for the intel you will need to get the best possible deal.

Your first move in tapping Uncle Sam's rich resources is to fill out the Free Application for Federal Student Aid – better known as the FAFSA – as early as possible. The deadline for the 2019-2020 school year is June 30, but you can file the form as early as Oct. 1 of senior year. Colleges use the form to allocate their own money, too, and

RACHEL WOOLF FOR USN&WR

Jessie Baren
University of Michigan

ONE STUDENT'S STRATEGY:
Sell apparel for campus eve

◆ **When the Alpha Phi** sorority at the University of Michigan needed personalized T-shirts for a St. Patri Day party in 2018, they zapped a te message with their order to Jessie Baren, the campus rep for Fresh Prints, a national custom-apparel company started by college student

JESSIE BAREN ON MICHIGAN'S CAMPUS IN ANN ARBOR

in 2009. Baren, who graduated in the spring of 2018, started working for the business second semester freshman year, and over time built his customer base from five campus clubs to 100, helping design and order apparel for events ranging from dance marathons to tailgate parties at sporting events.

Baren, who took about a 7 percent cut of each order, earned almost $100,000. As a result, and with his parents' help, he made his way through Michigan – his total cost per year as an out-of-stater from Los Angeles ran north of $65,000 – without needing financial aid. And he had enough left over to seed a Roth IRA.

A communications major who hopes to work in the music industry, Baren says fostering contacts at campus clubs was the key to maximizing his Fresh Prints returns. "It's all about building customer relationships," he says. He got into a routine of predicting which groups would want custom apparel for certain events, and then reached out to his contacts a month in advance with offers to help design and order the clothing. In addition to a cut of every sale, Fresh Prints gave him a 3 percent bonus each semester for hitting predetermined sales goals.

It was Baren's cousin, who attended the University of Pennsylvania with one of the company's founders, who first made him aware of Fresh Prints. While he spent his summers doing odd jobs to bring in more cash, Baren says he was earning enough from the Fresh Prints gig to also accept some nonpaying internships – doing marketing for record labels, for example – to help him toward his career goals. *–A.W.*

each school you're applying to could have a different deadline, so it's important to make sure you're on top of the key dates.

The FAFSA crunches your family financial data and arrives at an amount it determines you can afford to pay. But multiple factors will come into play as schools assemble their aid packages and offer letters. First, it's helpful to know whether they are "need aware" or "need blind." Admissions officers at need-blind colleges don't have access to applicants' financial data, meaning they're making admission decisions based entirely on a student's academic and other credentials. Schools that are need aware, on the other hand, may consider a family's need for financial assistance in weighing candidates.

> "Once you have a **pile of offers** in hand, it's important to scour them carefully."

"Among the many things our admissions office takes into consideration when they're determining the admissibility of a student is how much that student would cost us," says Sean Martin, director of financial aid services at Connecticut College. Part of the reason is that the school also commits to meeting every student's full demonstrated need, meaning the gap between how much the FAFSA form says is your "expected family contribution" and the total cost of attending. Not all schools do so. Many resort to "gapping," meaning they offer a package that falls short of the full need of some applicants, perhaps those who are not in their top tier. Other colleges sometimes "admit-deny," which means they're glad to accept a qualified applicant but don't come close to offering sufficient money.

Still, students who need financial aid shouldn't assume that will work against them, Martin says. "They may bring other things to the table that outweigh cost," such as geographic diversity, academic strength in a particular subject, or a strong interest in music or political action, say. A good tactic is to apply to at least some colleges where you beat the average performance of previously admitted students on typical measures like GPA and standardized-test scores. Many schools release these statistics on their websites.

After students are admitted, universities get to work packaging together what is typically a mix of federal grants and loans and scholarships from the school itself based not on need but on academic merit or special talents. Some students will also receive work-study jobs as part of their federal package. A growing number of schools are moving toward no-loan

Chardonnay Hightower-Collins

Mills College

ONE STUDENT'S STRATEGY: Assemble multiple sources of financial aid

◆ **When Chardonnay** Hightower-Collins was in eighth grade, she joined College Track, a program based in her hometown of Oakland, California, that helps students from underserved communities along the path to college completion. The program assists those with limited resources by providing tutoring, counseling, standardized-test preparation and other services, as well as financial rewards for academic performance that they can apply toward college costs. She knew she would have to finance her education herself. With the help of College Track's counselors, she put together a multifaceted plan to pay the roughly $30,000-per-year tuition plus other costs to attend Mills College in Oakland.

Mills gave Hightower-Collins a renewable merit-based scholarship of $17,500 per semester, and she qualified for work-study, taking a position as an administrative assistant in the office of residential life for three of her four years at Mills. She also nabbed a $4,000-per-year scholarship from the East Bay College Fund and applied for several off-the-radar private award

Going all in. "I only went for the scholarships I thought I could get. But I applied to as many as possible, both in high school and in college," Hightowe Collins says. During her sophomore year at Mills, for example, her grandfather received a letter from his labor union alerting him to a scholarship application, which he passed along to Hightower-Collins. She received $1,500 from the union.

Still, each year Hightower-Collins had a $5,000 to $10,000 gap between her scholarship aid and the

DAVID BUTOW – REDUX FOR USN&WR

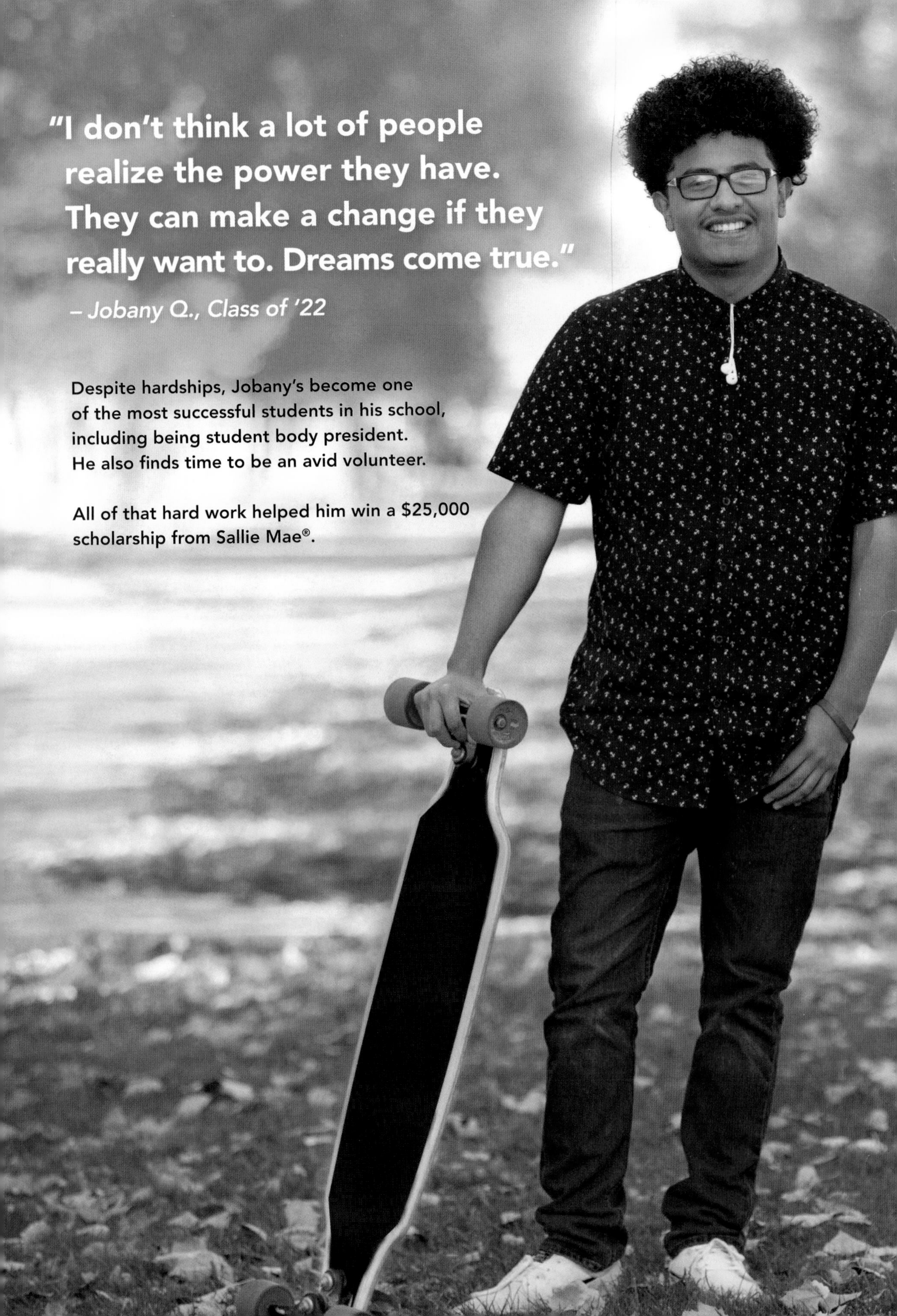
"I don't think a lot of people realize the power they have. They can make a change if they really want to. Dreams come true."
– Jobany Q., Class of '22
Despite hardships, Jobany's become one of the most successful students in his school, including being student body president. He also finds time to be an avid volunteer.
All of that hard work helped him win a $25,000 scholarship from Sallie Mae®.

recalls a conversation with parents who whipped out an offer letter from a college they thought was being much more generous than Richmond was. "The dollar value looked higher than our offer," says Deffenbaugh. But the competing offer included a Parent PLUS loan, an optional loan offered by the federal government.

She explained that Richmond provides information about Parent PLUS loans but doesn't count the potential value in the package. To "compare apples to apples, take the cost of each school and subtract the grants and scholarships," Deffenbaugh says. "What's left is the amount you'll pay out of pocket," which may or may not include loans. (For more on smart borrowing, see Page 156.)

It's also important to consider how your burden will change in subsequent years. Some scholarships and grants will automatically renew, while others may be one-time awards or require that the student maintain a certain GPA. If those details are not in the offer letter, be sure to ask the financial aid office to clarify.

The tuition factor. You'll also want to be prepared for any changes in tuition in years two, three and four. "Some schools will tell you the tuition will stay flat for all four years, but they may still increase their fees" for using scientific labs or counseling centers, say, notes Robert Durkle, associate vice president and dean of admission and financial aid at the University of Dayton in Ohio. Dayton is one of several colleges with a so-called fixed-price tuition plan promising accepted students that their net tuition will stay flat for four years. (Scholarships and grants will increase to offset any rise in tuition.) The school doesn't charge fees, he adds, and it offers up to $500 per semester toward textbooks to families who file the FAFSA.

Student borrowing at Dayton for the class of 2017 (whose tuition was $41,750) dropped 22 percent compared to 2013, when the fixed-price policy was adopted. The average total debt is $18,000, significantly lower than the $30,000 national average. Other colleges with fixed-price plans include Ohio University and George Washington University in the District of Columbia.

Another good way to reduce your loan burden is to apply for private scholarships.

A Stake in Your Future Income

With **the amount of student debt** soaring, some schools are offering a new financing option: an income-share agreement. Investors or college endowments pay part of a student's tuition in exchange for a fixed percentage of his or her future income for a specified number of years (say eight to 10).

Purdue University in Indiana, Point Loma Nazarene University in San Diego, Clarkson University in New York, and Lackawanna College in Pennsylvania have offered the agreements, and others are exploring the possibility. "The main advantage is that an ISA provides an assurance of a manageable payback amount that will never be higher than the agreed-upon portion of the borrower's income," says Brian Edelman, president of the Purdue Research Foundation, which manages the program. "It shifts the risk of any unanticipated career shortcoming or change in career path from the student to the investor."

The gamble. If a graduate does well financially, the investor can make more than the face value of the award. For example, if two students who receive $10,000 agree to pay 5 percent of their income for five years and one lands a job paying double what the other earns, that student will pay back twice as much. On the other hand, if graduates end up with low-paying jobs or are unemployed for a period, investors could lose money.

Purdue sets a minimum income threshold and a payment cap. So students won't pay anything if they don't make the minimum income ($20,000), and those earning a high salary won't pay more than 2.5 times the initial funding. Clarkson offers $10,000 per year up to a total of $40,000, with a payback rate of 6.2 percent of earned income for 10 years.

ISAs aren't without critics. "The most generous terms and conditions are being offered to students who look like they are low risk, based on their household income," says Jessica Thompson, policy and research director of the Institute for College Access & Success, a nonprofit that aims to make higher education available to all. "The idea that a private entity is going to offer a high-risk, low-income student a cheaper product than the federal government is beyond believability." She also objects to "disingenuous marketing" of ISAs. "It's a financial obligation even if it's not called debt or loan," she says. So borrowers should still beware. *–Stacey Colino*

GETTY IMAGES

emainder of her costs. She took out $21,000 n loans, mostly subsidized Stafford loans, neaning the federal government covered the nterest prior to graduation. About $1,000 of that total was an unsubsidized loan she ealized she would need junior year shortly fter turning it down; she walked into the inancial aid office and negotiated to get it back. "I had multiple talks with my financial id counselor" to explain the situation, says Hightower-Collins, who graduated with a sociology degree in May of 2017 and went on o work as an operations manager at College Track before taking a job as a college coach at a different organization in Oakland. She now has a monthly loan payment of about $250.

As a junior, Hightower-Collins found another way to cut costs while embarking on an adventure that expanded her horizons: She took advantage of a semester-abroad program in Havana. The Cuban experience not only gave her a taste of the challenges of living in a developing country but also allowed her to save $15,000 in tuition that semester. "I had a good time," she says of the experience. "And it was cost-effective." *–A.W.*

CHARDONNAY HIGHTOWER-COLLINS AT COLLEGE TRACK'S OAKLAND SITE

packages, meaning they offer private grants in lieu of federal loans. Some 50 schools follow this practice for low-income families, and 16 have extended it to all families, including Brown, Princeton and Vanderbilt University in Nashville.

Many colleges – particularly those that commit to meeting every student's full need – will expect you to file a supplemental form known as the CSS Profile. The form, which you fill out at the College Board website, goes into far more detail than the FAFSA form does, collecting data about the amount of equity your family has in your home, for example, and how much income comes in from a family-held business. If the student's parents are divorced or separated, financial information about both may be needed – and new spouses, if applicable. The FAFSA only considers the income and assets of the custodial parent (and that parent's spouse, if remarried).

Apples to apples. Once you (with luck) have a pile of offers in hand, scour them carefully. Though the bottom lines may be equivalent, one package may be more heavily tilted toward loans than another; colleges often are more generous in giving outright grants to students they really want. Cindy Deffenbaugh, assistant vice president and director of financial aid at the University of Richmond in Virginia,

The amounts may seem small, and many are one-time awards, which may cause your school to adjust your package downward accordingly. But most colleges use outside scholarships to offset what they would otherwise offer in loans or work-study funding.

"Start early, in your junior or sophomore year," advises Shivraj "Sunny" Sandhu, a junior at Princeton who stacked up $600,000 in scholarships and needed no financial aid. He started by downloading Scholly, a smartphone app that matches students with scholarships based on their GPAs, hometowns and unique demographic characteristics. "The app streamlined all the scholarships that were applicable to me and gave me the due dates," Sandhu says. He applied to more than 25 and pulled in money from organizations like the Bill & Melinda Gates Foundation, Coca-Cola and Burger King. After he applied for a small scholarship from his local Elks Club in Wilson, North Carolina, he was entered into a national competition that netted him $40,000. He also nabbed $25,000 from Foot Locker, which he qualified for by playing on his high school's soccer and tennis teams. "It takes a lot of research time, but it's worth it," says Sandhu.

The art of the deal. If an offer arrives that's far better than the one your dream college has made, is it OK to negotiate? In the right circumstances, most schools will likely be open to an appeal – for example, if your financial situation has changed since you submitted the FAFSA. A divorce, unexpected medical bills, natural disasters – such circumstances can resonate with financial aid officers, says Brooke Fincke, the director of college counseling at Chapel Hill-Chauncy Hall, a private high school in Waltham, Massachusetts. Fincke recommends creating a spreadsheet of all your monthly expenditures, not counting college costs, and being prepared to include it as part of your appeal.

Otherwise, experts don't advise pitting one school against another unless you're certain your chosen college will consider appeals from students whose financial situation hasn't changed. Students who bring sought-after skills to the table can come out of negotiations with a better package, but they'll have to reveal what the competing school is and how much it is offering. Specialty colleges might also be open to negotiations. "If a competitor is offering more money, we ask them to send us that award letter," says Kathleen Gailor, director of student financial planning at the Culinary Institute of America. "We ask them to write a short essay about what they did to prepare to come to school here and what's going to make them successful in the food world."

> "Most schools will be open to an appeal if your **financial situation** has changed."

If you do appeal, make your case with facts and be as personable as possible with financial aid officers, suggests Charlie Javice, founder and CEO of Frank, an online tool designed to help college students with the financial aid process. "Share your story in a compelling but succinct way," she suggests.

That strategy worked for Javice, who successfully negotiated for an increase in her aid package in all of her three years at the University of Pennsylvania. "There was a lot of back-and-forth with the financial aid office," recalls Javice, who graduated in 2013. "But schools will work with you." They're reluctant, she says, to lose out on good students once they've made the offer. ◆

Southern Methodist U.

DALLAS

Greg Guggenmos, '18

▶ **SMU provides students incredible opportunities to apply what they're learning. I was accepted to the Dedman College Scholars honors program, and I've gotten great mentoring and support. After I became interested in the criminal justice system from a history class, my honors mentor helped me secure a two-week, all-expenses-paid fellowship to New York to research how accused nonviolent offenders (often later acquitted) become stuck in pretrial detention when they can't make bail. That experience led me to start a community bail fund in Dallas providing small grants to low-level defendants.**

SMU also encourages students to see the world with wonderful travel courses. I did archival research on the Supreme Court at the Library of Congress in Washington. I took an arts course in New York and history courses in Rome and Paris. SMU has shown me exciting new directions to steer my career. I plan to earn my master's in applied statistics and data analytics and work in the nonprofit sector.

HILLSMAN JACKSON – SOUTHERN METHODIST UNIVERSITY

FINDING THE MONEY

Get the Scoop on Scholarships

There's no shortage of options to help you trim the college tab

by **Alison Murtagh**

Roughly 2 out of 3 undergrads use grants and scholarships to help them pay for college, according to the most recent federal data. But finding the best options can be a daunting task. Websites like Fastweb (fastweb.com) and Cappex (cappex.com/scholarships) allow you to create a free profile, research what's available and end up with personalized matches based on a variety of criteria, such as ethnicity, location, activities, academic interests and honors. Scholly (myscholly.com), another scholarship matching system accessible on the web or through a mobile app, allows users to see choices, track deadlines and follow the status of their submissions for a $2.99 monthly fee. Through such platforms, applicants and students might find some ultraspecific awards that they might qualify for, such as the Travers Tool Metalworking Student Scholarship (for students interested in that particular craft) or the BMI Foundation's John Lennon Scholarships (for undergrad songwriters and composers of contemporary music).

The U.S. Department of Education also offers a range of resources at studentaid.ed.gov for exploring grants from a variety of sources, including all 50 states and federal agencies like the Department of Labor and the Department of Health and Human Services. It's also a good idea to check with individual colleges to see what awards they might have available and whether they require an extra application.

Whether you're looking for a scholarship based on your background, academic credentials, potential major(s) or other attributes, here's a sampling of possibilities to consider:

- **The Gates Scholarship.** Awarded to 300 minority high school seniors every year who exhibit strong leadership skills and academic records and who demonstrate great financial need. Funds cover the remaining cost of attendance after expected family contribution and other awards. **thegatesscholarship.org**
- **National Merit Scholarship Program.** Approximately 7,500 high school seniors a year receive some level of an award based on PSAT/NMSQT scores and other criteria. **nationalmerit.org**
- **Coca-Cola Scholars Program.** Each year, scholarships of $20,000 per person are awarded to 150 students based on their academic merits, leadership skills and service. Smaller awards are also available. **coca-colascholarsfoundation.org**

Other major corporations with scholarship options include Microsoft, Burger King and Dunkin' Donuts.

• **Society of Women Engineers Scholarships.** A range of awards are given to support women interested in careers in engineering, computer science and engineering technology.
societyofwomenengineers.swe.org/scholarships

• **Google Scholarships.** Google offers a variety of specific scholarships for women, underrepresented minority students, and those with disabilities looking to study computer science.
buildyourfuture.withgoogle.com/scholarships

• **Dell Scholars Program.** Recipients get $20,000, a laptop and credits for textbooks. The award is directed toward low-income students who have overcome challenges and "are better than their numbers indicate," according to the scholarship foundation's website.
dellscholars.org

• **UNCF Scholarships.** More than 10,000 African-American students receive some form of aid each year through several scholarship options, such as those for people pursuing the STEM fields or aspiring entrepreneurs.
uncf.org/scholarships

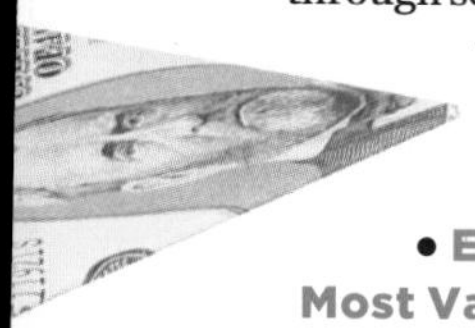

• **Elks National Foundation Most Valuable Student Scholarship.** Four-year scholarships are awarded to 500 high school seniors based on academics, leadership and financial need. Most receive $4,000 each, while 20 finalists receive between $20,000 and $50,000 total.
elks.org/scholars

• **Boren Scholarships.** Students planning to pursue a job in national security and study what the National Security Education Program refers to as a "less commonly taught" language, such as Arabic, Swahili or Hebrew, are awarded $8,000 to $20,000 to study abroad for a summer, semester or six- to 12-month stint.
borenawards.org

• **Cooke College Scholarship Program.** Scholarships of up to $40,000 per year are awarded to high-achieving high school students with financial need as selected by the education-focused Jack Kent Cooke Foundation.
jkcf.org

• **James Beard Foundation National Scholars Program.** Ten candidates receive $20,000 apiece to pursue a variety of food-related subjects, such as culinary arts, agriculture and sustainability. Other smaller awards are also available.
jamesbeard.org/scholarships

Find more on scholarships and financing a degree at **usnews.com/payingforcollege**

GETTY IMAGES

FINDING THE MONEY

A Smarter Way to Borrow

Weighing all your loan options and crunching the numbers in advance can be key to keeping debt down

by **Alison Murtagh**

Hailey Weiman will graduate from the University of Northern Colorado next spring with a degree in recreation, tourism and hospitality and about $30,000 in student loan debt. To help save on costs, Weiman opted to attend college in her home state, where tuition runs about $10,000 a year compared to almost $22,000 annually for nonresidents. She also has a work-study job in the financial aid office, which gives her some added money for expenses and an extra window into savvy payment strategies. "Overall, I found it's a great investment in my future," says Weiman. But she advises students to try not to take on more debt than needed. When in doubt, applicants should talk to their own financial aid offices and "ask all the questions they have," she says.

Weiman is one of the many college students who borrow to help finance a bachelor's degree. While the average college grad has close to $30,000 in debt, the total outstanding student loan burden among all those who have borrowed has now topped $1.5 trillion. (The eye-popping debt loads have inspired

BRITTANY MCDONALD FOR USN&WR

HAILEY WEIMAN AT THE UNIVERSITY OF NORTHERN COLORADO

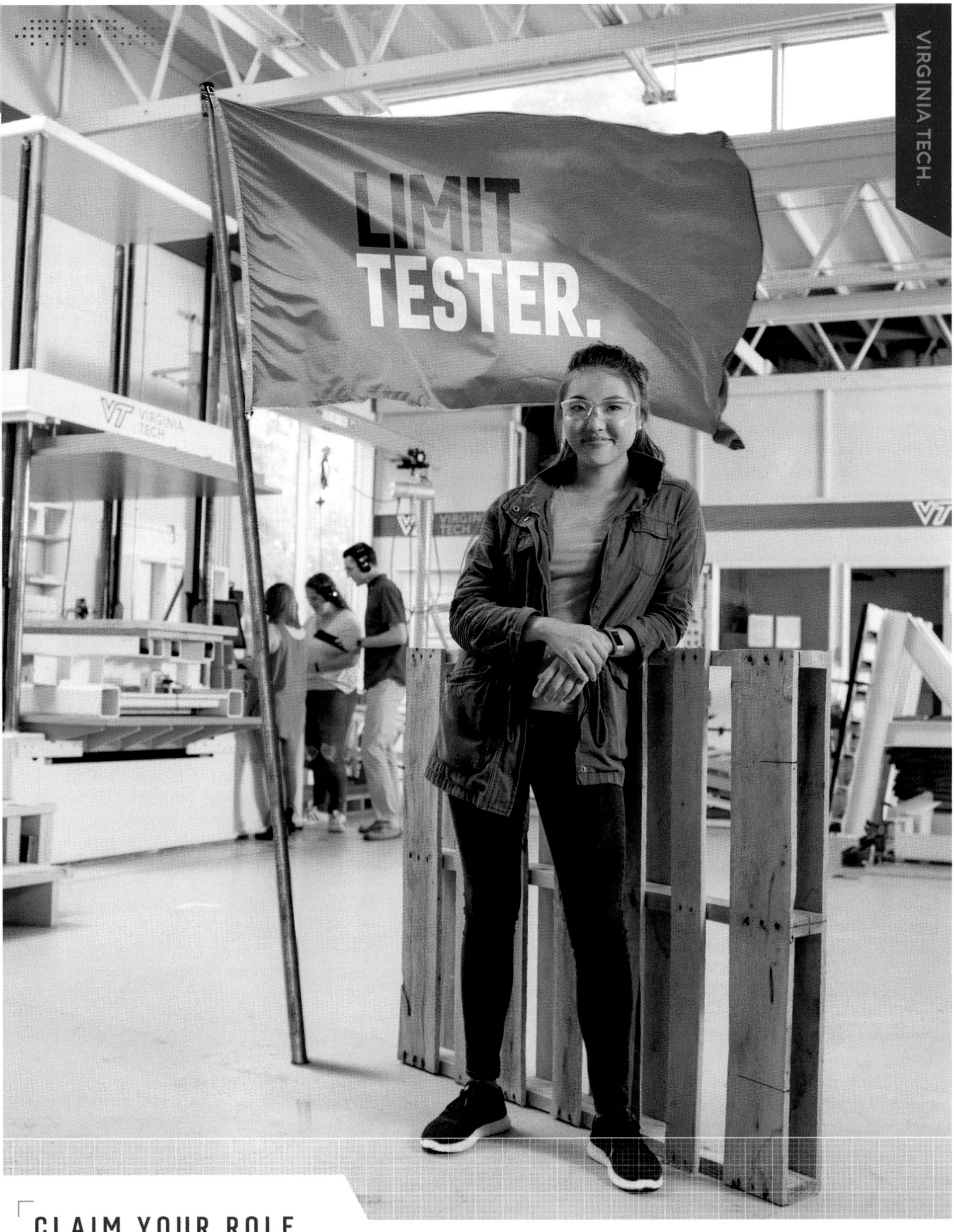

channel truTV to create a new game show called "Paid Off," where young people compete to answer trivia questions in exchange for money toward their loans.) To help avoid taking on massive debt, students should start early and plan carefully. "Think hard about what your alternatives are and whether it makes sense" to borrow, says Sandy Baum, a fellow at the Urban Institute who has written widely on college finance and student debt.

In general, advisers suggest that prospective borrowers consider their future career path and potential earnings. "The rule of thumb is usually borrow, in total, the amount that you expect to earn in a first-year-out-of-school salary," advises Gail Holt, dean of financial aid at Amherst College in Massachusetts. Using an online student loan repayment calculator can give you a sense of the potential monthly tab, plus how much of the total burden will be from interest (box). Doing some advance planning is key, because debt "can really hamper students' plans after college" when it comes to buying a car or a house, for instance, says Andrew Belasco, chief executive officer of College Transitions, an admissions consulting company.

To start, once you exhaust any savings and scholarships, advisers recommend exploring your federal loan options. The Free Application for Federal Student Aid (available at fafsa.gov) determines how much a family is expected to pay toward a child's college expenses, as well as how much government aid one will be eligible for (related story, Page 146). Schools use the form to calculate their aid awards, and some private lenders also look at the FAFSA when determining loan eligibility.

From there, undergrads might explore direct loans (also commonly known as Stafford loans), which allow dependent students to borrow up to $5,500 for their first year, $6,500 for year two, and $7,500 for their third year and beyond, up to a limit of $31,000 for all of college. These loans can either be subsidized (meaning that for those with financial need the government pays interest during school) or unsubsidized (interest starts accruing right away and the borrower is responsible for paying it). For 2018-19, direct loans for undergrads have an interest rate of 5.05 percent; the rate for any future loans is readjusted each summer.

If direct loans don't cover the bill, parents can apply for federal Parent PLUS loans up to the full cost of attendance (after other aid) as determined by the school. PLUS loans currently carry an interest rate of 7.6 percent and are also readjusted each summer for future borrowers.

In addition to locking in fixed interest rates, federal loans carry a number of repayment benefits, such as a six-month grace period after graduation before one has to start paying off debt. One can also choose from a variety of repayment plans. Under income-driven repayment, for instance, borrowers can adjust their monthly bills to a percentage of their discretionary income. You can find additional details at studentaid.ed.gov.

Students working full time in a qualifying public sector job – for the government or a nonprofit, say – can apply to have their direct loans "forgiven" (or erased) after 10 years of steady monthly payments. Those interested in this option should submit the Department of Education's employment certification form each year to be sure their job qualifies. Borrowers should also pay attention to future news about the program, as some policymakers have proposed doing away with it.

After federal loans, experts suggest exploring private loans, which offer a range of interest rates and repayment options. Discover, for instance, offers a 1 percent cash reward per loan for those who maintain a GPA of at least 3.0. Wells Fargo gives a discount to those who have an account with the bank. Some private loans offer their own grace periods before first payments are due.

These days, many private loans offer both fixed interest rates and variable ones, which might swing based on market conditions and other factors. For example, Sallie Mae currently offers fixed-rate loans between about 5.74 and 11.85 percent and variable ones from 4.12 to 10.98 percent. Securing the lowest options typically depends on one's credit, and some private lenders require a co-signer (usually a parent or guardian). With a wide range in variable rates, recent grads could see their bills fluctuate toward a much higher rate than when they took out a loan. Although protections vary by lender, private loans do not generally have the same safeguards as federal ones, advisers say.

Like any investment, one should fully consider all options before signing on the dotted line. "Sometimes it's worth it," says Stephen Payne, assistant director of federal relations at the National Association of Student Financial Aid Administrators, but "sometimes it's a decision that I think some students and families might wish that they had back." ◆

Do the Math

▶ To get a sense of some different repayment plans, try an online loan calculator such as those at finaid.org/calculators/loanpayments.phtml or nerdwallet.com/blog/loans/student-loans/student-loan-calculator.

For instance, **say you were to borrow $20,000 at 5 percent interest.** Here's what your monthly bill might be – as well as the total interest you would pay over the life of the loan – if your repayment period were:

10 YEARS

Monthly payment: $212

Total interest: $5,456

20 YEARS

Monthly payment: $132

Total interest: $11,678

25 YEARS

Monthly payment: $117

Total interest: $15,076

FINDING THE MONEY

Great Schools, Great Prices

Which colleges and universities offer students the best value? The calculation used here takes into account a school's academic quality based on its U.S. News Best Colleges ranking and the 2017-18 net cost of attendance for a student who received the average level of need-based financial aid. The higher the quality of the program and the lower the cost, the better the deal. Only schools in the top half of their U.S. News ranking categories are included because U.S. News considers the most significant values to be among colleges that perform well academically.

▸ National Universities

Rank	School (State) (*Public)	% receiving grants based on need ('17)	Average cost after receiving grants based on need ('17)	Average discount from total cost ('17)
1.	**Princeton University** (NJ)	60%	$15,585	77%
2.	**Harvard University** (MA)	55%	$15,996	77%
3.	**Massachusetts Institute of Technology**	60%	$19,540	71%
4.	**Yale University** (CT)	50%	$18,928	74%
5.	**Stanford University** (CA)	47%	$19,309	72%
6.	**Columbia University** (NY)	50%	$20,294	73%
7.	**Vanderbilt University** (TN)	49%	$20,098	70%
8.	**U. of North Carolina–Chapel Hill***	41%	$17,377	66%
9.	**California Institute of Technology**	52%	$23,104	66%
10.	**Dartmouth College** (NH)	48%	$23,245	68%
11.	**Brigham Young Univ.–Provo** (UT)	38%	$13,353	27%
12.	**University of Pennsylvania**	46%	$26,407	64%
13.	**Duke University** (NC)	41%	$25,814	65%
14.	**Rice University** (TX)	38%	$23,173	63%
15.	**Northwestern University** (IL)	44%	$27,160	63%
16.	**University of Chicago**	42%	$28,066	62%
17.	**Brown University** (RI)	41%	$25,886	64%
18.	**Johns Hopkins University** (MD)	48%	$30,887	56%
19.	**Emory University** (GA)	43%	$27,379	59%
20.	**Washington University in St. Louis**	41%	$28,231	61%
21.	**Cornell University** (NY)	46%	$29,831	58%
22.	**University of Notre Dame** (IN)	47%	$30,474	56%
23.	**University of Rochester** (NY)	53%	$28,002	60%
24.	**Wake Forest University** (NC)	30%	$26,220	63%
25.	**Georgetown University** (DC)	35%	$29,924	59%
26.	**Tufts University** (MA)	35%	$28,037	60%
27.	**Lehigh University** (PA)	39%	$25,453	61%
28.	**University of Virginia***	30%	$28,001	55%
29.	**Brandeis University** (MA)	45%	$30,554	57%
30.	**Illinois Institute of Technology**	62%	$28,182	55%
31.	**Clarkson University** (NY)	80%	$34,351	48%
32.	**Clark University** (MA)	54%	$28,322	49%
33.	**Boston College**	37%	$30,145	57%
34.	**Carnegie Mellon University** (PA)	38%	$33,035	53%
35.	**Mercer University** (GA)	70%	$27,072	48%
36.	**Saint Louis University**	53%	$26,304	54%
37.	**University of Southern California**	33%	$33,615	53%
38.	**SUNY Col. of Envir. Sci. and Forestry***	76%	$28,195	21%
39.	**Pepperdine University** (CA)	52%	$34,151	52%
40.	**Duquesne University** (PA)	66%	$29,364	44%
41.	**Rensselaer Polytechnic Inst.** (NY)	58%	$36,819	49%
42.	**Case Western Reserve Univ.** (OH)	49%	$34,671	47%
43.	**Rochester Inst. of Technology** (NY)	71%	$33,458	39%
44.	**Texas A&M University–College Station***	43%	$27,629	42%
45.	**University of the Pacific** (CA)	69%	$36,662	43%
46.	**Boston University**	39%	$34,247	51%
47.	**University of Michigan–Ann Arbor***	27%	$32,147	48%
48.	**Villanova University** (PA)	45%	$35,023	49%
49.	**Marquette University** (WI)	58%	$32,712	41%
50.	**University of La Verne** (CA)	83%	$39,757	33%

▸ National Liberal Arts Colleges

Rank	School (State) (*Public)	% receiving grants based on need ('17)	Average cost after receiving grants based on need ('17)	Average discount from total cost ('17)
1.	**Williams College** (MA)	51%	$18,877	73%
2.	**Pomona College** (CA)	57%	$18,011	74%
3.	**Amherst College** (MA)	57%	$20,109	72%
4.	**Swarthmore College** (PA)	56%	$20,165	71%
5.	**Principia College** (IL)	72%	$15,249	65%
6.	**Wellesley College** (MA)	58%	$22,659	68%
7.	**Vassar College** (NY)	62%	$22,706	68%
8.	**Davidson College** (NC)	50%	$22,244	67%
9.	**Middlebury College** (VT)	44%	$22,225	68%
10.	**Smith College** (MA)	61%	$23,744	66%
11.	**Soka University of America** (CA)	85%	$24,622	50%
12.	**Grinnell College** (IA)	65%	$24,220	63%
13.	**College of the Atlantic** (ME)	83%	$18,898	66%
14.	**Earlham College** (IN)	88%	$20,804	65%
15.	**Haverford College** (PA)	47%	$22,701	68%
16.	**Washington and Lee University** (VA)	43%	$22,004	67%
17.	**Bowdoin College** (ME)	46%	$23,246	66%
18.	**Colgate University** (NY)	36%	$21,491	69%
19.	**Colby College** (ME)	42%	$22,257	68%
20.	**Wesleyan University** (CT)	41%	$23,839	66%
21.	**Hamilton College** (NY)	51%	$25,202	63%
22.	**University of Richmond** (VA)	41%	$22,999	65%
23.	**Agnes Scott College** (GA)	76%	$24,043	56%
24.	**Macalester College** (MN)	69%	$27,603	59%
25.	**Claremont McKenna College** (CA)	40%	$25,421	65%
26.	**St. John's College** (MD)	77%	$25,474	61%
27.	**Hollins University** (VA)	80%	$21,828	60%
28.	**Franklin and Marshall College** (PA)	54%	$24,428	65%
29.	**Carleton College** (MN)	55%	$28,160	59%
30.	**Wabash College** (IN)	75%	$25,227	54%
31.	**Centre College** (KY)	59%	$23,423	57%
32.	**St. Olaf College** (MN)	74%	$25,227	57%
33.	**Bates College** (ME)	43%	$25,966	62%
34.	**Bryn Mawr College** (PA)	52%	$26,616	61%
35.	**Thomas Aquinas College** (CA)	60%	$22,153	38%
36.	**Colorado College**	31%	$23,785	66%
37.	**Wofford College** (SC)	63%	$23,218	58%
38.	**Trinity College** (CT)	48%	$24,314	66%
39.	**Lawrence University** (WI)	60%	$24,537	58%
40.	**Mount Holyoke College** (MA)	65%	$28,833	55%

Methodology: The rankings were based on the following three variables: **1.** Ratio of quality to price: a school's overall score in the latest Best Colleges rankings divided by the net cost to a student receiving the average need-based scholarship or grant. The higher the ratio of rank to the discounted cost (tuition, fees, room and board, and other expenses less average need-based scholarship or grant), the better the value. **2.** Percentage of all undergrads receiving need-based scholarships or grants during the 2017-18 school year. **3.** Average discount: percentage of a school's total costs for 2017-18 school year covered by the average need-based scholarship or grant to undergrads. For public institutions, 2017-18 out-of-state tuition and percentage of out-of-state students receiving need-based scholarships or grants were used. Only those schools ranked in the top half of their U.S. News ranking categories were considered. Ranks were determined by standardizing scores achieved by every school in each of the three variables and weighting those scores. Ratio of quality to price accounted for 60 percent of the overall score; percentage of undergrads receiving need-based grants, for 25 percent; and average discount, for 15 percent. The school with the most total weighted points became No. 1 in its category.

Regional Universities

Rank	School (State) (*Public)	% receiving grants based on need ('17)	Average cost after receiving grants based on need ('17)	Average discount from total cost ('17)
NORTH				
1.	**Gallaudet University** (DC)	85%	$17,480	54%
2.	**St. Bonaventure University** (NY)	74%	$23,214	51%
3.	**Geneva College** (PA)	82%	$21,768	44%
4.	**Simmons College** (MA)	76%	$29,891	49%
5.	**Le Moyne College** (NY)	83%	$27,764	44%
6.	**Waynesburg University** (PA)	79%	$20,815	42%
7.	**Bentley University** (MA)	43%	$33,233	50%
8.	**SUNY–Oswego***	63%	$22,258	34%
9.	**Gannon University** (PA)	76%	$25,126	46%
10.	**Canisius College** (NY)	75%	$27,831	47%
11.	**SUNY Polytechnic Inst.–Albany/Utica***	1%	$22,727	35%
12.	**Niagara University** (NY)	70%	$25,154	47%
12.	**Saint Peter's University** (NJ)	91%	$24,183	55%
14.	**Ithaca College** (NY)	67%	$33,717	45%
15.	**Lebanon Valley College** (PA)	85%	$29,717	48%
SOUTH				
1.	**Lincoln Memorial University** (TN)	83%	$14,352	51%
2.	**Coastal Carolina University** (SC)*	21%	$13,477	66%
3.	**William Carey University** (MS)	95%	$16,405	37%
4.	**Bob Jones University** (SC)	73%	$16,638	39%
5.	**Berry College** (GA)	71%	$25,683	49%
6.	**Milligan College** (TN)	82%	$22,397	48%
7.	**Mary Baldwin University** (VA)	93%	$21,749	50%
8.	**Harding University** (AR)	58%	$19,989	33%
9.	**Converse College** (SC)	86%	$22,109	36%
10.	**Freed-Hardeman University** (TN)	77%	$19,999	43%
11.	**The Citadel** (SC)*	41%	$28,073	46%
12.	**Loyola University New Orleans**	75%	$27,428	52%
13.	**John Brown University** (AR)	60%	$24,520	37%
14.	**Saint Leo University** (FL)	73%	$19,581	46%
15.	**West Virginia Wesleyan College**	80%	$19,991	56%
MIDWEST				
1.	**Valparaiso University** (IN)	76%	$22,880	57%
2.	**Truman State University** (MO)*	40%	$21,226	24%
3.	**Dominican University** (IL)	85%	$24,663	46%
4.	**Creighton University** (NE)	52%	$31,817	40%
5.	**Bradley University** (IL)	66%	$27,701	41%
6.	**Baldwin Wallace University** (OH)	79%	$25,128	45%
7.	**University of Evansville** (IN)	62%	$27,304	46%
8.	**John Carroll University** (OH)	70%	$30,621	45%
9.	**Milwaukee School of Engineering**	77%	$26,791	48%
10.	**Augsburg University** (MN)	80%	$25,769	50%
11.	**Aquinas College** (MI)	77%	$21,254	50%
12.	**Concordia University** (NE)	76%	$21,936	48%
13.	**University of St. Francis** (IL)	82%	$24,499	45%
14.	**Grand Valley State University** (MI)*	4%	$18,044	38%
15.	**Franciscan Univ. of Steubenville** (OH)	64%	$25,356	34%
WEST				
1.	**Trinity University** (TX)	46%	$25,506	55%
2.	**St. Mary's Univ. of San Antonio**	75%	$22,428	48%
3.	**Mills College** (CA)	79%	$26,225	59%
4.	**University of Dallas**	63%	$26,556	52%
5.	**Whitworth University** (WA)	69%	$29,997	48%
6.	**Gonzaga University** (WA)	53%	$33,600	41%
7.	**Westminster College** (UT)	60%	$26,095	44%
8.	**Pacific Lutheran University** (WA)	74%	$28,029	49%
9.	**University of St. Thomas** (TX)	67%	$24,756	47%
10.	**Abilene Christian University** (TX)	67%	$27,698	43%
11.	**California Lutheran University**	70%	$32,277	46%
12.	**LeTourneau University** (TX)	69%	$25,582	41%
13.	**Oral Roberts University** (OK)	70%	$23,303	43%
14.	**Saint Martin's University** (WA)	83%	$26,625	47%
15.	**Santa Clara University** (CA)	32%	$40,466	42%

Regional Colleges

Rank	School (State) (*Public)	% receiving grants based on need ('17)	Average cost after receiving grants based on need ('17)	Average discount from total cost ('17)
NORTH				
1.	**Cooper Union** (NY)	54%	$19,459	70%
2.	**Cazenovia College** (NY)	92%	$20,538	59%
3.	**Cedar Crest College** (PA)	93%	$26,638	49%
4.	**Messiah College** (PA)	72%	$29,369	39%
5.	**Colby-Sawyer College** (NH)	79%	$28,344	51%
6.	**Paul Smith's College** (NY)	90%	$24,189	44%
7.	**SUNY College of Technology–Alfred***	61%	$21,000	23%
8.	**Unity College** (ME)	84%	$26,342	34%
9.	**Wilson College** (PA)	83%	$27,159	30%
10.	**University of Maine–Farmington***	12%	$21,748	32%
SOUTH				
1.	**Blue Mountain College** (MS)	83%	$12,401	45%
2.	**Alice Lloyd College** (KY)	92%	$15,585	39%
3.	**Newberry College** (SC)	92%	$19,623	51%
4.	**Averett University** (VA)	86%	$23,494	49%
5.	**Flagler College** (FL)	63%	$24,383	27%
6.	**Huntingdon College** (AL)	77%	$22,642	41%
7.	**Barton College** (NC)	86%	$26,472	42%
8.	**Tennessee Wesleyan University**	52%	$19,454	45%
9.	**Emmanuel College** (GA)	77%	$18,335	41%
10.	**Alderson Broaddus University** (WV)	87%	$21,372	45%
MIDWEST				
1.	**Cottey College** (MO)	72%	$14,214	54%
2.	**College of the Ozarks** (MO)	90%	$18,740	37%
3.	**Ohio Northern University**	81%	$22,719	51%
4.	**Augustana University** (SD)	62%	$22,421	51%
5.	**University of Mount Union** (OH)	79%	$23,751	44%
6.	**Goshen College** (IN)	74%	$22,951	51%
7.	**Buena Vista University** (IA)	83%	$21,985	52%
8.	**Manchester University** (IN)	86%	$19,716	55%
9.	**Loras College** (IA)	75%	$22,581	48%
10.	**Clarke University** (IA)	87%	$23,909	48%
WEST				
1.	**Texas Lutheran University**	81%	$21,438	50%
2.	**Rocky Mountain College** (MT)	76%	$20,651	49%
3.	**Carroll College** (MT)	64%	$27,339	44%
4.	**William Jessup University** (CA)	80%	$26,459	43%
5.	**Southwestern Adventist Univ.** (TX)	61%	$21,108	34%
6.	**Howard Payne University** (TX)	84%	$22,766	43%
7.	**McMurry University** (TX)	81%	$23,641	42%
8.	**Warner Pacific College** (OR)	64%	$30,334	19%
9.	**Oklahoma Baptist University**	55%	$33,146	17%
10.	**Montana Tech of the Univ. of Mont.***	23%	$29,864	17%

The Payback Picture

With tuition rising and financial aid budgets shrinking, many undergrads have to borrow their way to a degree. U.S. News has compiled a list of the schools whose class of 2017 graduated with the heaviest and lightest debt loads. The data include loans taken out by students from their colleges, from private financial institutions, and from federal, state and local governments. Loans directly to parents are not included. The first data column indicates what percentage of the class graduated owing money and, by extrapolation, what percentage graduated debt-free. "Average amount of debt" refers to the cumulative amount borrowed by students who incurred debt; it's not an average for all students.

MOST DEBT

National Universities

School (State) (*Public)	% of grads with debt	Average amount of debt
Baylor University (TX)	52%	$44,859
Duquesne University (PA)	61%	$43,637
Texas Christian University	36%	$42,212
University of St. Thomas (MN)	64%	$40,983
New Jersey Inst. of Technology*	62%	$40,979
Boston University	48%	$40,089
Indiana Univ. of Pennsylvania*	83%	$39,929
Robert Morris University (PA)	76%	$39,856
Pace University (NY)	69%	$39,752
Rochester Inst. of Technology (NY)	76%	$38,927
Syracuse University (NY)	59%	$38,918
St. John Fisher College (NY)	79%	$38,639
Stevens Institute of Technology (NJ)	69%	$38,402
University of Pittsburgh*	62%	$38,322
Barry University (FL)	70%	$38,176

Regional Universities

School (State) (*Public)	% of grads with debt	Average amount of debt
NORTH		
Bryant University (RI)	71%	$52,949
University of New Haven (CT)	79%	$49,941
Quinnipiac University (CT)	68%	$48,894
Wilkes University (PA)	83%	$47,907
Misericordia University (PA)	84%	$47,764
SOUTH		
Grambling State University (LA)*	92%	$47,162
Northwestern State University of Louisiana*	69%	$42,399
Saint Leo University (FL)	73%	$40,359
Eastern Mennonite University (VA)	72%	$39,845
Winthrop University (SC)*	74%	$36,147
MIDWEST		
University of Saint Francis (IN)	81%	$41,481
College of St. Scholastica (MN)	77%	$41,133
Xavier University (OH)	53%	$40,868
Butler University (IN)	61%	$40,393
St. Mary's Univ. of Minnesota	78%	$39,917
WEST		
Univ. of Mary Hardin-Baylor (TX)	76%	$43,344
Trinity University (TX)	44%	$40,800
Prescott College (AZ)	63%	$39,720
California Baptist University	78%	$38,324
St. Mary's Univ. of San Antonio	77%	$37,866

National Liberal Arts Colleges

School (State) (*Public)	% of grads with debt	Average amount of debt
Washington and Jefferson Col. (PA)	77%	$54,184
Carthage College (WI)	80%	$52,145
Saint Vincent College (PA)	82%	$46,794
Holy Cross College (IN)	70%	$46,000
Albion College (MI)	64%	$44,140
Westminster College (PA)	85%	$43,241
Hartwick College (NY)	82%	$43,187
College of St. Benedict (MN)	74%	$42,833
Elizabethtown College (PA)	77%	$42,316
St. John's University (MN)	72%	$41,698
Roanoke College (VA)	76%	$41,187
Grove City College (PA)	59%	$40,747
Bethune-Cookman University (FL)	92%	$40,601
St. Michael's College (VT)	77%	$40,009
Alma College (MI)	80%	$39,264

Regional Colleges

School (State) (*Public)	% of grads with debt	Average amount of debt
NORTH		
Maine Maritime Academy*	95%	$52,580
Southern Vermont College	87%	$48,822
Dean College (MA)	83%	$48,728
Cedar Crest College (PA)	92%	$44,031
Wilson College (PA)	84%	$38,217
SOUTH		
University of Holy Cross (LA)	95%	$49,798
Chowan University (NC)	94%	$43,064
Warner University (FL)	81%	$41,805
Livingstone College (NC)	98%	$39,231
High Point University (NC)	50%	$35,934
MIDWEST		
Central State University (OH)*	88%	$45,561
Bethany College (KS)	89%	$45,416
Adrian College (MI)	82%	$41,262
Clarke University (IA)	84%	$39,907
University of Mount Union (OH)	82%	$38,692
WEST		
McMurry University (TX)	86%	$40,390
East Texas Baptist University	83%	$33,823
Howard Payne University (TX)	69%	$33,810
Texas Lutheran University	78%	$32,437
University of Providence (MT)	70%	$31,642

Note: Student debt data are as of August 24, 2018.

LEAST DEBT

National Universities

School (State) (*Public)	% of grads with debt	Average amount of debt
Princeton University (NJ)	17%	$9,005
Yale University (CT)	16%	$13,050
Brigham Young Univ.–Provo (UT)	26%	$14,998
Harvard University (MA)	19%	$15,114
California Institute of Technology	34%	$16,777
University of California–Berkeley*	35%	$18,197
California State University–Fresno*	47%	$18,308
New Mexico State University*	50%	$19,109
University of California–Davis*	49%	$19,124
San Francisco State University*	45%	$19,347
University of California–Merced*	70%	$19,551
Dartmouth College (NH)	52%	$19,571
San Diego State University*	47%	$19,633
Northwestern University (IL)	37%	$19,718
University of California–Irvine*	55%	$19,745
University of Washington*	35%	$19,880
Florida International University*	47%	$20,022
Massachusetts Inst. of Technology	29%	$20,048
Stanford University (CA)	18%	$20,205
University of California–Santa Barbara*	51%	$20,665
University of New Orleans*	48%	$20,723
Boston College	47%	$20,915
University of Colorado–Denver*	52%	$20,941
University of New Mexico*	45%	$20,979
University of California–Riverside*	66%	$21,104

National Liberal Arts Colleges

School (State) (*Public)	% of grads with debt	Average amount of debt
Berea College (KY)	25%	$7,468
Haverford College (PA)	23%	$15,000
Williams College (MA)	35%	$16,230
New College of Florida*	34%	$16,297
Bard College at Simon's Rock (MA)	38%	$16,700
Pomona College (CA)	31%	$17,408
Principia College (IL)	65%	$18,335
Wellesley College (MA)	49%	$18,370
Amherst College (MA)	29%	$19,075
Hamilton College (NY)	43%	$19,281
Thomas Aquinas College (CA)	87%	$19,319
Middlebury College (VT)	46%	$19,382
Grinnell College (IA)	55%	$19,392
Vassar College (NY)	45%	$19,439
Scripps College (CA)	41%	$19,639
Swarthmore College (PA)	27%	$20,209
Bates College (ME)	42%	$20,715
Pitzer College (CA)	32%	$20,947
Fort Lewis College (CO)*	57%	$20,988
Carleton College (MN)	44%	$21,035
University of Virginia–Wise*	58%	$21,389
Claremont McKenna College (CA)	31%	$21,421
St. Mary's College of Maryland*	51%	$21,925
Kenyon College (OH)	40%	$22,025
Univ. of Science and Arts of Okla.*	69%	$22,351

Regional Universities

School (State) (*Public)	% of grads with debt	Average amount of debt
NORTH		
CUNY–Brooklyn College*	15%	$11,550
CUNY–Hunter College*	15%	$12,122
CUNY–Baruch College*	22%	$12,500
CUNY–Lehman College*	29%	$12,736
CUNY–Queens College*	15%	$14,738
SOUTH		
University of North Georgia*	53%	$12,345
Western Carolina University (NC)*	61%	$15,669
Lincoln Memorial University (TN)	75%	$18,038
University of North Florida*	49%	$18,787
William Carey University (MS)	80%	$19,500
MIDWEST		
Northeastern Illinois University*	53%	$15,819
Univ. of Nebraska–Kearney*	53%	$19,538
Purdue University–Northwest (IN)*	67%	$20,962
Indiana University East*	74%	$22,392
Muskingum University (OH)	79%	$22,413
WEST		
Univ. of the Incarnate Word (TX)	68%	$13,106
Western Washington University*	51%	$15,663
Texas A&M International University*	79%	$15,932
Southeastern Oklahoma State U.*	61%	$16,542
Southern Utah University*	52%	$16,824

Regional Colleges

School (State) (*Public)	% of grads with debt	Average amount of debt
NORTH		
U.S. Merchant Marine Acad. (NY)*	25%	$3,852
University of Valley Forge (PA)	57%	$17,181
Cooper Union (NY)	17%	$18,373
Farmingdale State College–SUNY*	50%	$22,105
University of Maine–Presque Isle*	74%	$23,574
SOUTH		
Pensacola State College (FL)*	61%	$3,239
Alice Lloyd College (KY)	66%	$9,828
Ohio Valley University (WV)	64%	$14,296
Blue Mountain College (MS)	49%	$19,084
Central Baptist College (AR)	76%	$21,714
MIDWEST		
Dickinson State University (ND)*	64%	$18,834
Central Christian College (KS)	89%	$22,489
Cottey College (MO)	27%	$23,533
Indiana University–Kokomo*	73%	$23,664
Iowa Wesleyan University	83%	$24,398
WEST		
Dixie State University (UT)*	86%	$12,201
University of Hawaii–West Oahu*	46%	$18,492
Jarvis Christian College (TX)	95%	$25,225
Oklahoma Baptist University	63%	$25,262
Lewis-Clark State College (ID)*	69%	$25,547

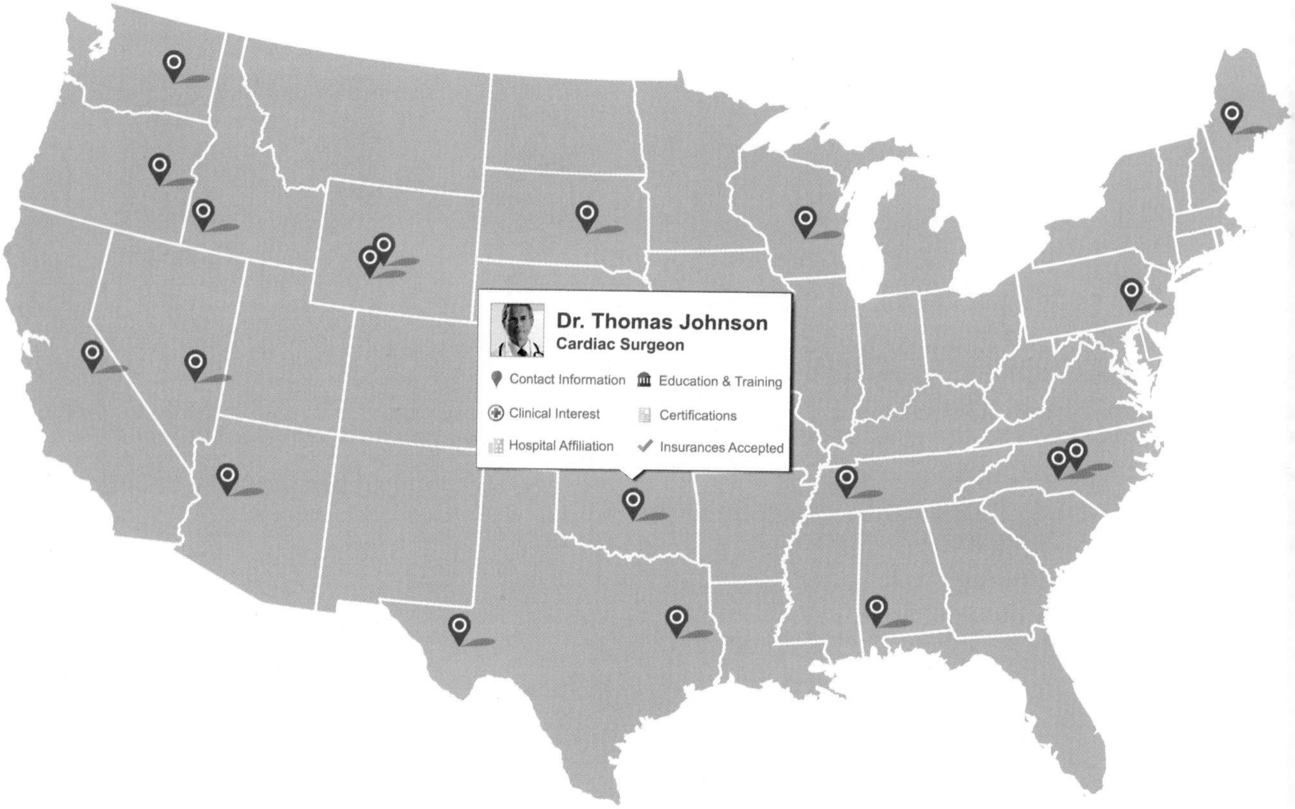

2019 EDITION

DIRECTORY OF COLLEGES AND UNIVERSITIES

INSIDE

The latest facts and figures on over 1,600 American colleges and universities, including schools' U.S. News rankings

New data on tuition, admissions, the makeup of the undergraduate student body, popular majors and financial aid

Statistical profiles of freshman classes, including entrance exam scores and high school class standing

Using the Directory

How to interpret the statistics in the following entries on more than 1,600 American colleges and universities – and how to get the most out of them

The snapshots of colleges and universities presented here, alphabetized by state, contain a wealth of helpful information on everything from the most popular majors offered to the stats on the freshman class that arrived in the fall of 2017. The statistics were collected in the spring and summer of 2018 and are as of Aug. 30, 2018; they are explained in detail below. A school whose name has been footnoted did not return the U.S. News statistical questionnaire, so limited data appear. If a college did not reply to a particular question, you'll see N/A, for "not available." By tapping our online directory at usnews.com/collegesearch, you can experiment with a customized search of our database that allows you to pick schools based on major, location and other criteria. To find a school of interest in the rankings tables, consult the index at the back of the book.

EXAMPLE

Fairfield University

Fairfield CT
1—(203) 254-4100
2—**U.S. News ranking:** Reg. U. (N), No. 1
3—**Website:** www.fairfield.edu
4—**Admissions email:** admis@fairfield.edu
5—**Private;** founded 1942
Affiliation: Roman Catholic
6—**Freshman admissions:** more selective; 2017-2018: 11,218 applied, 6,794 accepted. Neither SAT nor ACT required. SAT 25/75 percentile: 1180-1320. High school rank: 41% in top tenth, 79% in top quarter, 98% in top half
7—**Early decision deadline:** 11/15, notification date: 12/15
Early action deadline: 11/1, notification date: 12/20
8—**Application deadline (fall):** 1/15
9—**Undergraduate student body:** 3,879 full time, 234 part time; 40% male, 60% female; 0% American Indian, 2% Asian, 2% black, 8% Hispanic, 2% multiracial, 0% Pacific Islander, 78% white, 3% international; 29% from in state; 71% live on campus; N/A of students in fraternities, N/A in sororities
10—**Most popular majors:** 41% Business, Management, Marketing, and Related Support Services, 12% Health Professions and Related Programs, 10% Communication, Journalism, and Related Programs, 7% Social Sciences, 6% Psychology
11—**Expenses:** 2018-2019: $48,350; room/board: $14,710
12—**Financial aid:** (203) 254-4000; 45% of undergrads determined to have financial need; average aid package $34,731

1. TELEPHONE NUMBER

This number reaches the admissions office.

2. U.S. NEWS RANKING

The abbreviation indicates which category of institution the school falls into: National Universities (Nat. U.), National Liberal Arts Colleges (Nat. Lib. Arts), Regional Universities (Reg. U.), or Regional Colleges (Reg. Coll.). The regional universities and regional colleges are further divided by region: North (N), South (S), Midwest (Mid. W), and West (W). "Business" refers to business specialty schools, and "Engineering" refers to engineering specialty schools. "Arts" refers to schools devoted to the fine and performing arts.

Next, you'll find the school's 2019 rank within its category. Schools falling in the top three-fourths of their categories are ranked numerically. (Those ranked in the bottom 25 percent of their category are listed alphabetically in the ranking tables.) You cannot compare ranks of schools in different categories; U.S. News ranks schools only against their peers. Specialty schools that focus on business, engineering and the arts aren't ranked. Also unranked are schools with fewer than 200 students, with a high percentage of older or part-time students, that don't use SAT or ACT test scores for admission decisions, or that have received a very small number of peer assessment votes in a survey conducted in spring 2018.

3. WEBSITE

Visit the school's website to research programs, take a virtual tour, or submit an application.

4. ADMISSIONS EMAIL

You can use this email address to request information or to submit an application.

5. TYPE/AFFILIATION

Is the school public, private or for-profit? Affiliated with a religious denomination?

6. FRESHMAN ADMISSIONS

How competitive is the admissions process at this institution? Schools are designated "most selective," "more selective," "selective," "less selective" or "least selective." The more selective a school, the harder it will probably be to get in. All of the admissions statistics reported are for the class that entered in the fall of 2017. The 25/75 percentiles for the SAT Evidence-Based Reading and Writing and Math or ACT Composite scores show the range in which half the students scored: 25 percent of students scored at or below the lower end, and 75 percent scored at or below the upper end. If a school reported the averages and not the 25/75 percentiles, the average score is listed. The test score that is published represents the test that the greatest percentage of entering students took. The SAT scores used in the rankings and published in this book are for the new test administered starting in March 2016.

7. EARLY DECISION/ EARLY ACTION DEADLINES

Applicants who plan to take the early decision route to fall 2019 enrollment will have to meet the deadline listed for the school. If the school offers an early action option, the application deadline and notification date are also shown.

8. APPLICATION DEADLINE

The date shown is the regular admission deadline for the academic year starting in the fall of 2019. "Rolling" means the school makes admissions decisions as applications come in until the class is filled.

9. UNDERGRADUATE STUDENT BODY

This section gives the breakdown of full-time vs. part-time students and male and female enrollment, the ethnic makeup of the student body, proportions of in-state and out-of-state students, percentage living on campus, and percentage in fraternities and sororities. Figures are for 2017-2018.

10. MOST POPULAR MAJORS

The five most popular majors appear, along with the percentage majoring in each among 2017 graduates with a bachelor's degree.

11. EXPENSES

The first figure represents tuition (including required fees); next is total room and board. Figures are for the 2018-2019 academic year; if data are not available, we use figures for the 2017-2018 academic year. For public schools, we list both in-state and out-of-state tuition.

12. FINANCIAL AID

The percentage of undergrads determined to have financial need and the amount of the average package (grants, loans and jobs) in 2017-2018. We also provide the phone number of the financial aid office.

ALABAMA

Alabama Agricultural and Mechanical University

Normal AL
(256) 372-5245
U.S. News ranking: Reg. U. (S), second tier
Website: www.aamu.edu/admissions/undergraduateadmissions/pages/default.aspx
Admissions email: admissions@aamu.edu
Public; founded 1875
Freshman admissions: least selective; 2017-2018: 8,610 applied, 7,772 accepted. Either SAT or ACT required. ACT 25/75 percentile: 16-19. High school rank: N/A
Early decision deadline: N/A, notification date: N/A
Early action deadline: N/A, notification date: N/A
Application deadline (fall): 7/15
Undergraduate student body: 4,714 full time, 324 part time; 42% male, 58% female; N/A American Indian, N/A Asian, N/A black, N/A Hispanic, N/A multiracial, N/A Pacific Islander, N/A white, N/A international
Most popular majors: Information not available
Expenses: 2017-2018: $9,857 in state, $18,236 out of state; room/board: $9,020
Financial aid: (256) 372-5400

Alabama State University

Montgomery AL
(334) 229-4291
U.S. News ranking: Reg. U. (S), second tier
Website: www.alasu.edu
Admissions email: admissions@alasu.edu
Public; founded 1887
Freshman admissions: less selective; 2017-2018: 6,842 applied, 6,696 accepted. Either SAT or ACT required. ACT 25/75 percentile: 16-19. High school rank: 18% in top tenth, 34% in top quarter, 65% in top half
Early decision deadline: 3/5, notification date: 5/29
Early action deadline: N/A, notification date: N/A
Application deadline (fall): 7/30
Undergraduate student body: 3,866 full time, 342 part time; 38% male, 62% female; 0% American Indian, 0% Asian, 94% black, 1% Hispanic, 1% multiracial, 0% Pacific Islander, 1% white, 1% international; 65% from in state; 51% live on campus; 4% of students in fraternities, 5% in sororities
Most popular majors: 18% Health Information/Medical Records Administration/Administrator, 13% Elementary Education and Teaching, 11% Business Administration and Management, General, 9% Speech Communication and Rhetoric, 8% Biology/Biological Sciences, General
Expenses: 2018-2019: $11,068 in state, $19,396 out of state; room/board: $5,422
Financial aid: (334) 229-4712; 94% of undergrads determined to have financial need; average aid package $16,124

Amridge University

Montgomery AL
(888) 790-8080
U.S. News ranking: Reg. U. (S), second tier
Website: www.amridgeuniversity.edu
Admissions email: admissions@amridgeuniversity.edu
Private; founded 1967
Freshman admissions: less selective; 2017-2018: N/A applied, N/A accepted. Either SAT or ACT required. SAT 25/75 percentile: N/A. High school rank: N/A
Early decision deadline: N/A, notification date: N/A
Early action deadline: N/A, notification date: N/A
Application deadline (fall): rolling
Undergraduate student body: 150 full time, 180 part time; 36% male, 64% female; 0% American Indian, 1% Asian, 65% black, 13% Hispanic, 0% multiracial, 0% Pacific Islander, 19% white, 0% international
Most popular majors: 41% Bible/Biblical Studies, 22% Business Administration and Management, General, 20% Criminal Justice/Safety Studies, 10% Human Development and Family Studies, General, 7% Human Resources Management/Personnel Administration, General
Expenses: 2018-2019: $9,900; room/board: N/A
Financial aid: (334) 387-7523; 98% of undergrads determined to have financial need; average aid package $7,710

Athens State University

Athens AL
(256) 233-8217
U.S. News ranking: Reg. Coll. (S), unranked
Website: www.athens.edu/
Admissions email: N/A
Public; founded 1822
Freshman admissions: least selective; 2017-2018: 0 applied, 0 accepted. Neither SAT nor ACT required. SAT 25/75 percentile: N/A. High school rank: N/A
Early decision deadline: N/A, notification date: N/A
Early action deadline: N/A, notification date: N/A
Application deadline (fall): N/A
Undergraduate student body: 1,210 full time, 1,757 part time; 33% male, 67% female; 2% American Indian, 1% Asian, 13% black, 3% Hispanic, 2% multiracial, 0% Pacific Islander, 77% white, 0% international; 96% from in state; N/A live on campus; N/A of students in fraternities, N/A in sororities
Most popular majors: 38% Business, Management, Marketing, and Related Support Services, 31% Education, 4% English Language and Literature/Letters, 4% Liberal Arts and Sciences, General Studies and Humanities, 3% Multi/Interdisciplinary Studies
Expenses: 2018-2019: $6,810 in state, $12,870 out of state; room/board: $0
Financial aid: (256) 233-8161; 75% of undergrads determined to have financial need; average aid package $10,201

Auburn University

Auburn AL
(334) 844-6425
U.S. News ranking: Nat. U., No. 115
Website: www.auburn.edu
Admissions email: admissions@auburn.edu
Public; founded 1856
Freshman admissions: more selective; 2017-2018: 18,072 applied, 15,168 accepted. Either SAT or ACT required. ACT 25/75 percentile: 24-30. High school rank: 31% in top tenth, 63% in top quarter, 91% in top half
Early decision deadline: N/A, notification date: N/A
Early action deadline: 2/1, notification date: 10/1
Application deadline (fall): 6/1
Undergraduate student body: 21,762 full time, 2,202 part time; 51% male, 49% female; 0% American Indian, 2% Asian, 6% black, 3% Hispanic, 2% multiracial, 0% Pacific Islander, 82% white, 3% international; 65% from in state; 19% live on campus; 25% of students in fraternities, 44% in sororities
Most popular majors: 24% Business, Management, Marketing, and Related Support Services, 18% Engineering, 12% Biological and Biomedical Sciences, 6% Communication, Journalism, and Related Programs, 6% Health Professions and Related Programs
Expenses: 2018-2019: $11,276 in state, $30,524 out of state; room/board: $13,332
Financial aid: (334) 844-4634; 36% of undergrads determined to have financial need; average aid package $10,829

Auburn University–Montgomery

Montgomery AL
(334) 244-3615
U.S. News ranking: Reg. U. (S), No. 95
Website: www.aum.edu
Admissions email: admissions@aum.edu
Public; founded 1967
Freshman admissions: selective; 2017-2018: 2,474 applied, 2,042 accepted. Either SAT or ACT required. ACT 25/75 percentile: 19-24. High school rank: 16% in top tenth, 43% in top quarter, 75% in top half
Early decision deadline: N/A, notification date: N/A
Early action deadline: N/A, notification date: N/A
Application deadline (fall): 8/15
Undergraduate student body: 3,239 full time, 1,074 part time; 36% male, 64% female; 0% American Indian, 3% Asian, 38% black, 1% Hispanic, 3% multiracial, 0% Pacific Islander, 50% white, 4% international; 94% from in state; 23% live on campus; N/A of students in fraternities, N/A in sororities
Most popular majors: 24% Health Professions and Related Programs, 20% Business, Management, Marketing, and Related Support Services, 8% Education, 6% Computer and Information Sciences and Support Services, 6% Psychology
Expenses: 2018-2019: $8,404 in state, $17,862 out of state; room/board: $6,980
Financial aid: (334) 244-3571; 68% of undergrads determined to have financial need; average aid package $8,780

Birmingham-Southern College

Birmingham AL
(205) 226-4696
U.S. News ranking: Nat. Lib. Arts, No. 131
Website: www.bsc.edu/index.html
Admissions email: admission@bsc.edu
Private; founded 1856
Affiliation: United Methodist
Freshman admissions: more selective; 2017-2018: 2,559 applied, 1,583 accepted. Neither SAT nor ACT required. ACT 25/75 percentile: 23-29. High school rank: 54% in top tenth, 54% in top quarter, 82% in top half
Early decision deadline: 11/1, notification date: 12/1
Early action deadline: 11/15, notification date: 12/15
Application deadline (fall): rolling
Undergraduate student body: 1,272 full time, 11 part time; 48% male, 52% female; 1% American Indian, 5% Asian, 12% black, 2% Hispanic, 1% multiracial, 0% Pacific Islander, 79% white, 0% international; 58% from in state; 84% live on campus; 19% of students in fraternities, 28% in sororities
Most popular majors: 23% Business Administration and Management, General, 14% Biology/Biological Sciences, General, 11% Psychology, General, 8% Mathematics, General, 6% Teacher Education, Multiple Levels
Expenses: 2018-2019: $17,650; room/board: $12,050
Financial aid: (205) 226-4688; 59% of undergrads determined to have financial need; average aid package $32,882

Concordia College[1]

Selma AL
(334) 874-5700
U.S. News ranking: Reg. Coll. (S), unranked
Website: www.ccal.edu/
Admissions email: admission@ccal.edu
Private; founded 1922
Application deadline (fall): N/A
Undergraduate student body: N/A full time, N/A part time
Expenses: 2017-2018: $10,320; room/board: $5,700
Financial aid: (334) 874-5700

Faulkner University

Montgomery AL
(334) 386-7200
U.S. News ranking: Reg. U. (S), second tier
Website: www.faulkner.edu
Admissions email: admissions@faulkner.edu
Private; founded 1942
Affiliation: Churches of Christ
Freshman admissions: selective; 2017-2018: 2,184 applied, 1,143 accepted. Either SAT or ACT required. ACT 25/75 percentile: 18-22. High school rank: N/A
Early decision deadline: N/A, notification date: N/A
Early action deadline: N/A, notification date: N/A
Application deadline (fall): 8/1
Undergraduate student body: 1,744 full time, 928 part time; 40% male, 60% female; 0% American Indian, 0% Asian, 50% black, 2% Hispanic, 2% multiracial, 0% Pacific Islander, 41% white, 2% international; 85% from in state; 28% live on campus; 7% of students in fraternities, 8% in sororities
Most popular majors: 33% Business Administration and Management, General, 17% Criminal Justice/Safety Studies, 13% Business/Commerce, General, 12% Human Resources Management/Personnel Administration, General, 4% Elementary Education and Teaching
Expenses: 2018-2019: $21,690; room/board: $7,550
Financial aid: (334) 386-7195

Huntingdon College

Montgomery AL
(334) 833-4497
U.S. News ranking: Reg. Coll. (S), No. 11
Website: www.huntingdon.edu
Admissions email: admiss@hawks.huntingdon.edu
Private; founded 1854
Affiliation: United Methodist
Freshman admissions: selective; 2017-2018: 2,074 applied, 1,161 accepted. Either SAT or ACT required. ACT 25/75 percentile: 19-24. High school rank: 13% in top tenth, 27% in top quarter, 69% in top half
Early decision deadline: N/A, notification date: N/A
Early action deadline: N/A, notification date: N/A
Application deadline (fall): rolling
Undergraduate student body: 878 full time, 224 part time; 48% male, 52% female; 1% American Indian, 0% Asian, 21% black, 6% Hispanic, 5% multiracial, 0% Pacific Islander, 64% white, 0% international; 70% from in state; 68% live on campus; 18% of students in fraternities, 43% in sororities
Most popular majors: 45% Business, Management, Marketing, and Related Support Services, 13% Parks, Recreation, Leisure, and Fitness Studies, 9% Biological and Biomedical Sciences, 7% Education, 5% Communication, Journalism, and Related Programs

Expenses: 2018-2019: $27,400; room/board: $9,750
Financial aid: (334) 833-4428; 77% of undergrads determined to have financial need; average aid package $19,156

Jacksonville State University

Jacksonville AL
(256) 782-5268
U.S. News ranking: Reg. U. (S), second tier
Website: www.jsu.edu
Admissions email: info@jsu.edu
Public; founded 1883
Freshman admissions: selective; 2017-2018: 6,005 applied, 3,244 accepted. Either SAT or ACT required. ACT 25/75 percentile: 19-26. High school rank: 20% in top tenth, 45% in top quarter, 77% in top half
Early decision deadline: N/A, notification date: N/A
Early action deadline: N/A, notification date: N/A
Application deadline (fall): rolling
Undergraduate student body: 5,523 full time, 1,968 part time; 43% male, 57% female; 1% American Indian, 1% Asian, 19% black, 1% Hispanic, 0% multiracial, 0% Pacific Islander, 72% white, 2% international; 84% from in state; 18% live on campus; 15% of students in fraternities, 18% in sororities
Most popular majors: 17% Registered Nursing/Registered Nurse, 5% Business Administration and Management, General, 5% Elementary Education and Teaching, 4% Criminal Justice/Safety Studies, 4% Liberal Arts and Sciences/ Liberal Studies
Expenses: 2018-2019: $10,020 in state, $19,290 out of state; room/board: $7,898
Financial aid: (256) 782-5006; 88% of undergrads determined to have financial need; average aid package $9,800

Judson College[1]

Marion AL
(800) 447-9472
U.S. News ranking: Nat. Lib. Arts, second tier
Website: www.judson.edu/
Admissions email: admissions@judson.edu
Private
Application deadline (fall): N/A
Undergraduate student body: N/A full time, N/A part time
Expenses: 2017-2018: $17,896; room/board: $10,276
Financial aid: N/A

Miles College[1]

Birmingham AL
(205) 929-1000
U.S. News ranking: Reg. Coll. (S), unranked
Website: www.miles.edu
Admissions email: admissions@mail.miles.edu
Private
Application deadline (fall): N/A
Undergraduate student body: N/A full time, N/A part time
Expenses: 2017-2018: $11,794; room/board: $7,254
Financial aid: N/A

Oakwood University

Huntsville AL
(256) 726-7356
U.S. News ranking: Reg. Coll. (S), No. 40
Website: www.oakwood.edu
Admissions email: admissions@oakwood.edu
Private; founded 1896
Affiliation: Seventh Day Adventist
Freshman admissions: less selective; 2017-2018: N/A applied, N/A accepted. Either SAT or ACT required. SAT 25/75 percentile: N/A. High school rank: N/A
Early decision deadline: N/A, notification date: N/A
Early action deadline: N/A, notification date: N/A
Application deadline (fall): N/A
Undergraduate student body: 1,521 full time, 135 part time; 42% male, 58% female; N/A American Indian, N/A Asian, N/A black, N/A Hispanic, N/A multiracial, N/A Pacific Islander, N/A white, N/A international
Most popular majors: Information not available
Expenses: 2017-2018: $16,720; room/board: $9,700
Financial aid: N/A

Samford University

Birmingham AL
(800) 888-7218
U.S. News ranking: Reg. U. (S), No. 4
Website: www.samford.edu
Admissions email: admission@samford.edu
Private; founded 1841
Affiliation: Baptist
Freshman admissions: more selective; 2017-2018: 3,808 applied, 3,168 accepted. Either SAT or ACT required. ACT 25/75 percentile: 23-29. High school rank: 28% in top tenth, 58% in top quarter, 86% in top half
Early decision deadline: N/A, notification date: N/A
Early action deadline: N/A, notification date: N/A
Application deadline (fall): 5/1
Undergraduate student body: 3,266 full time, 107 part time; 34% male, 66% female; 0% American Indian, 1% Asian, 7% black, 3% Hispanic, 2% multiracial, 0% Pacific Islander, 84% white, 2% international; 33% from in state; 68% live on campus; 36% of students in fraternities, 56% in sororities
Most popular majors: 30% Health Professions and Related Programs, 21% Business, Management, Marketing, and Related Support Services, 7% Communication, Journalism, and Related Programs, 6% Education, 6% Visual and Performing Arts
Expenses: 2018-2019: $31,650; room/board: $10,550
Financial aid: (205) 726-2905; 42% of undergrads determined to have financial need; average aid package $20,201

Spring Hill College

Mobile AL
(251) 380-3030
U.S. News ranking: Nat. Lib. Arts, second tier
Website: www.shc.edu
Admissions email: admit@shc.edu
Private; founded 1830
Freshman admissions: selective; 2017-2018: 8,544 applied, 3,903 accepted. Either SAT or ACT required. ACT 25/75 percentile: 21-26. High school rank: 15% in top tenth, 50% in top quarter, 85% in top half
Early decision deadline: N/A, notification date: N/A
Early action deadline: N/A, notification date: N/A
Application deadline (fall): 7/15
Undergraduate student body: 1,379 full time, 14 part time; 37% male, 63% female; 1% American Indian, 1% Asian, 16% black, 2% Hispanic, 5% multiracial, 0% Pacific Islander, 68% white, 4% international; 42% from in state; 71% live on campus; 26% of students in fraternities, 28% in sororities
Most popular majors: 19% Business, Management, Marketing, and Related Support Services, 14% Education, 12% Psychology, 9% Biological and Biomedical Sciences, 9% Health Professions and Related Programs
Expenses: 2018-2019: $39,464; room/board: $13,462
Financial aid: (800) 548-7886; 69% of undergrads determined to have financial need; average aid package $33,589

Stillman College

Tuscaloosa AL
(205) 366-8817
U.S. News ranking: Nat. Lib. Arts, second tier
Website: www.stillman.edu
Admissions email: admissions@stillman.edu
Private; founded 1876
Affiliation: Interdenominational
Freshman admissions: less selective; 2017-2018: N/A applied, N/A accepted. Either SAT or ACT required. SAT 25/75 percentile: N/A. High school rank: N/A
Early decision deadline: N/A, notification date: N/A
Early action deadline: N/A, notification date: N/A
Application deadline (fall): rolling
Undergraduate student body: 559 full time, 135 part time; 45% male, 55% female; 0% American Indian, 0% Asian, 88% black, 1% Hispanic, 0% multiracial, 0% Pacific Islander, 6% white, 0% international; 71% from in state; 45% live on campus; 10% of students in fraternities, 20% in sororities
Most popular majors: Biological and Biomedical Sciences, Business, Management, Marketing, and Related Support Services, Communication, Journalism, and Related Programs, Psychology, Theology and Religious Vocations
Expenses: 2018-2019: $11,992; room/board: $8,394
Financial aid: (205) 247-8071; 94% of undergrads determined to have financial need

Talladega College

Talladega AL
(256) 761-6235
U.S. News ranking: Reg. Coll. (S), No. 42
Website: www.talladega.edu
Admissions email: admissions@talladega.edu
Private; founded 1867
Affiliation: United Church of Christ
Freshman admissions: less selective; 2017-2018: 5,681 applied, 2,682 accepted. Either SAT or ACT required. SAT 25/75 percentile: N/A. High school rank: N/A
Early decision deadline: N/A, notification date: N/A
Early action deadline: N/A, notification date: N/A
Application deadline (fall): N/A
Undergraduate student body: 762 full time, 20 part time; 53% male, 47% female; 0% American Indian, 0% Asian, 87% black, 5% Hispanic, 2% multiracial, 0% Pacific Islander, 2% white, 2% international; N/A from in state; 81% live on campus; 2% of students in fraternities, 6% in sororities
Most popular majors: 23% Business Administration and Management, General, 12% Social Work, 11% Psychology, General, 10% Computer and Information Sciences, General, 9% Biology/ Biological Sciences, General
Expenses: 2018-2019: $12,340; room/board: $6,504
Financial aid: (256) 761-6237

Troy University

Troy AL
(334) 670-3179
U.S. News ranking: Reg. U. (S), second tier
Website: www.troy.edu/
Admissions email: admit@troy.edu
Public; founded 1887
Freshman admissions: selective; 2017-2018: 7,367 applied, 6,492 accepted. Either SAT or ACT required. ACT 25/75 percentile: 18-25. High school rank: N/A
Early decision deadline: N/A, notification date: N/A
Early action deadline: N/A, notification date: N/A
Application deadline (fall): rolling
Undergraduate student body: 9,491 full time, 4,509 part time; 40% male, 60% female; 0% American Indian, 1% Asian, 30% black, 4% Hispanic, 3% multiracial, 0% Pacific Islander, 53% white, 5% international
Most popular majors: 16% Business, Management, Marketing, and Related Support Services, 14% Psychology, 13% Homeland Security, Law Enforcement, Firefighting and Related Protective Services, 9% Social Sciences, 8% Education
Expenses: 2017-2018: $12,155 in state, $22,267 out of state; room/board: $7,946
Financial aid: (334) 670-3182; 68% of undergrads determined to have financial need; average aid package $4,356

Tuskegee University[1]

Tuskegee AL
(334) 727-8500
U.S. News ranking: Reg. U. (S), No. 95
Website: www.tuskegee.edu
Admissions email: admiweb@tusk.edu
Private; founded 1881
Application deadline (fall): rolling
Undergraduate student body: N/A full time, N/A part time
Expenses: 2018-2019: $22,235; room/board: $9,650
Financial aid: (334) 727-8088; 80% of undergrads determined to have financial need; average aid package $19,900

University of Alabama

Tuscaloosa AL
(205) 348-5666
U.S. News ranking: Nat. U., No. 129
Website: www.ua.edu
Admissions email: admissions@ua.edu
Public; founded 1831
Freshman admissions: more selective; 2017-2018: 38,129 applied, 21,344 accepted. Either SAT or ACT required. ACT 25/75 percentile: 23-32. High school rank: 39% in top tenth, 60% in top quarter, 83% in top half
Early decision deadline: N/A, notification date: N/A
Early action deadline: N/A, notification date: N/A
Application deadline (fall): rolling
Undergraduate student body: 29,923 full time, 3,382 part time; 44% male, 56% female; 0% American Indian, 1% Asian, 10% black, 5% Hispanic, 3% multiracial, 0% Pacific Islander, 78% white, 2% international; 40% from in state; 24% live on campus; 28% of students in fraternities, 44% in sororities
Most popular majors: 31% Business, Management, Marketing, and Related Support Services, 10% Communication, Journalism, and Related Programs, 10% Engineering, 10% Health Professions and Related Programs, 7% Family and Consumer Sciences/Human Sciences
Expenses: 2018-2019: $10,780 in state, $29,230 out of state; room/board: $10,102
Financial aid: (205) 348-6756; 44% of undergrads determined to have financial need; average aid package $16,985

University of Alabama–Birmingham

Birmingham AL
(205) 934-8221
U.S. News ranking: Nat. U., No. 157
Website: www.uab.edu
Admissions email: chooseuab@uab.edu
Public; founded 1969
Freshman admissions: more selective; 2017-2018: 7,555 applied, 6,936 accepted. Either

AT or ACT required. ACT 25/75 ercentile: 21-28. High school ank: 28% in top tenth, 52% in p quarter, 82% in top half
arly decision deadline: N/A, otification date: N/A
arly action deadline: N/A, otification date: N/A
pplication deadline (fall): rolling
ndergraduate student body: 9,677 ll time, 3,457 part time; 41% ale, 59% female; 0% American ndian, 6% Asian, 26% black, % Hispanic, 4% multiracial, % Pacific Islander, 58% white, % international; 89% from in ate; 23% live on campus; 7% students in fraternities, 10% sororities
ost popular majors: 23% Health rofessions and Related Programs, 0% Business, Management, larketing, and Related Support ervices, 8% Biological and iomedical Sciences, 8% ducation, 7% Engineering
xpenses: 2018-2019: $10,710 state, $24,630 out of state; om/board: $11,682
inancial aid: (205) 934-8223; 1% of undergrads determined to ave financial need; average aid ackage $10,787

niversity of labama–Huntsville

untsville AL
256) 824-6070
.S. News ranking: Nat. U., econd tier
ebsite: www.uah.edu/
dmissions email: dmissions@uah.edu
ublic; founded 1950
eshman admissions: more elective; 2017-2018: 4,454 pplied, 3,618 accepted. Either AT or ACT required. ACT 25/75 ercentile: 25-31. High school ank: 38% in top tenth, 66% in p quarter, 89% in top half
arly decision deadline: N/A, otification date: N/A
arly action deadline: N/A, otification date: N/A
pplication deadline (fall): 8/17
ndergraduate student body: 5,903 ll time, 1,187 part time; 58% ale, 42% female; 1% American ndian, 4% Asian, 11% black, % Hispanic, 3% multiracial, % Pacific Islander, 74% white, % international; 88% from in ate; 27% live on campus; 7% students in fraternities, 8% in prorities
ost popular majors: 29% ngineering, 23% Business, lanagement, Marketing, and elated Support Services, 10% ealth Professions and Related rograms, 8% Computer and formation Sciences and Support ervices, 6% Biological and iomedical Sciences
xpenses: 2018-2019: $10,313 state, $21,504 out of state; om/board: $10,015
nancial aid: (256) 824-6650; 3% of undergrads determined to ave financial need; average aid ackage $10,367

University of Mobile

Mobile AL
(251) 442-2222
U.S. News ranking: Reg. Coll. (S), No. 5
Website: www.umobile.edu
Admissions email: umenrollment@umobile.edu
Private; founded 1961
Affiliation: Baptist
Freshman admissions: selective; 2017-2018: 1,493 applied, 702 accepted. Either SAT or ACT required. ACT 25/75 percentile: 20-25. High school rank: 38% in top tenth, 62% in top quarter, 81% in top half
Early decision deadline: N/A, notification date: N/A
Early action deadline: N/A, notification date: N/A
Application deadline (fall): rolling
Undergraduate student body: 1,152 full time, 291 part time; 36% male, 64% female; 1% American Indian, 1% Asian, 18% black, 2% Hispanic, 3% multiracial, 0% Pacific Islander, 54% white, 3% international; 77% from in state; 45% live on campus; N/A of students in fraternities, N/A in sororities
Most popular majors: 21% Business, Management, Marketing, and Related Support Services, 17% Education, 14% Health Professions and Related Programs, 7% Theology and Religious Vocations, 6% Psychology
Expenses: 2018-2019: $22,590; room/board: $9,666
Financial aid: (251) 442-2222; 72% of undergrads determined to have financial need; average aid package $19,822

University of Montevallo

Montevallo AL
(205) 665-6030
U.S. News ranking: Reg. U. (S), No. 42
Website: www.montevallo.edu
Admissions email: admissions@montevallo.edu
Public; founded 1896
Freshman admissions: selective; 2017-2018: 1,868 applied, 1,245 accepted. Either SAT or ACT required. ACT 25/75 percentile: 20-26. High school rank: N/A
Early decision deadline: N/A, notification date: N/A
Early action deadline: N/A, notification date: N/A
Application deadline (fall): 8/15
Undergraduate student body: 2,101 full time, 245 part time; 33% male, 67% female; 0% American Indian, 1% Asian, 16% black, 5% Hispanic, 3% multiracial, 0% Pacific Islander, 69% white, 2% international; 88% from in state; N/A live on campus; 18% of students in fraternities, 21% in sororities
Most popular majors: Information not available
Expenses: 2018-2019: $12,760 in state, $25,780 out of state; room/board: $9,330
Financial aid: (205) 665-6050; 68% of undergrads determined to have financial need; average aid package $12,058

University of North Alabama

Florence AL
(256) 765-4608
U.S. News ranking: Reg. U. (S), No. 78
Website: www.una.edu
Admissions email: admissions@una.edu
Public; founded 1830
Freshman admissions: selective; 2017-2018: 3,969 applied, 2,787 accepted. Either SAT or ACT required. ACT 25/75 percentile: 19-25. High school rank: N/A
Early decision deadline: N/A, notification date: N/A
Early action deadline: N/A, notification date: N/A
Application deadline (fall): rolling
Undergraduate student body: 5,150 full time, 1,071 part time; 41% male, 59% female; 1% American Indian, 1% Asian, 15% black, 3% Hispanic, 3% multiracial, 0% Pacific Islander, 73% white, 3% international; 83% from in state; 26% live on campus; 12% of students in fraternities, 19% in sororities
Most popular majors: 21% Business, Management, Marketing, and Related Support Services, 13% Health Professions and Related Programs, 10% Education, 6% Parks, Recreation, Leisure, and Fitness Studies, 6% Social Sciences
Expenses: 2018-2019: $10,370 in state, $18,680 out of state; room/board: $4,650
Financial aid: (256) 765-4278; 77% of undergrads determined to have financial need; average aid package $8,629

University of South Alabama

Mobile AL
(251) 460-6141
U.S. News ranking: Nat. U., second tier
Website: www.southalabama.edu
Admissions email: recruitment@southalabama.edu
Public; founded 1963
Freshman admissions: selective; 2017-2018: 6,035 applied, 4,911 accepted. Neither SAT nor ACT required. ACT 25/75 percentile: 20-26. High school rank: N/A
Early decision deadline: N/A, notification date: N/A
Early action deadline: N/A, notification date: N/A
Application deadline (fall): 7/15
Undergraduate student body: 9,090 full time, 1,898 part time; 43% male, 57% female; 1% American Indian, 3% Asian, 23% black, 3% Hispanic, 3% multiracial, 0% Pacific Islander, 59% white, 6% international; 82% from in state; 29% live on campus; N/A of students in fraternities, N/A in sororities
Most popular majors: 14% Registered Nursing/Registered Nurse, 6% Elementary Education and Teaching, 6% Health/Medical Preparatory Programs, Other, 5% Biology/Biological Sciences, General, 5% Multi/Interdisciplinary Studies
Expenses: 2018-2019: $10,376 in state, $20,328 out of state; room/board: $8,512
Financial aid: (251) 460-6231

University of West Alabama

Livingston AL
(205) 652-3578
U.S. News ranking: Reg. U. (S), second tier
Website: www.uwa.edu
Admissions email: admissions@uwa.edu
Public; founded 1835
Freshman admissions: selective; 2017-2018: 7,388 applied, 2,084 accepted. Either SAT or ACT required. ACT 25/75 percentile: 18-23. High school rank: N/A
Early decision deadline: N/A, notification date: N/A
Early action deadline: N/A, notification date: N/A
Application deadline (fall): rolling
Undergraduate student body: 1,843 full time, 268 part time; 45% male, 55% female; 0% American Indian, 0% Asian, 44% black, 2% Hispanic, 3% multiracial, 0% Pacific Islander, 42% white, 5% international; 80% from in state; 43% live on campus; 9% of students in fraternities, 12% in sororities
Most popular majors: 19% Multi-/Interdisciplinary Studies, Other, 12% Kinesiology and Exercise Science, 7% Biology/Biological Sciences, General, 7% Physical Education Teaching and Coaching, 6% Communication and Media Studies, Other
Expenses: 2018-2019: $9,204 in state, $16,818 out of state; room/board: $7,080
Financial aid: (205) 652-3576; 75% of undergrads determined to have financial need; average aid package $10,427

ALASKA

Alaska Pacific University

Anchorage AK
(800) 252-7528
U.S. News ranking: Reg. U. (W), No. 64
Website: www.alaskapacific.edu
Admissions email: admissions@alaskapacific.edu
Private; founded 1957
Freshman admissions: selective; 2017-2018: N/A applied, N/A accepted. Neither SAT nor ACT required. ACT 25/75 percentile: 21-26. High school rank: N/A
Early decision deadline: N/A, notification date: N/A
Early action deadline: N/A, notification date: N/A
Application deadline (fall): rolling
Undergraduate student body: 203 full time, 93 part time; 35% male, 65% female; N/A American Indian, N/A Asian, N/A black, N/A Hispanic, N/A multiracial, N/A Pacific Islander, N/A white, N/A international
Most popular majors: Information not available
Expenses: 2017-2018: $20,760; room/board: $7,900
Financial aid: (907) 564-8342

University of Alaska–Anchorage

Anchorage AK
(907) 786-1480
U.S. News ranking: Reg. U. (W), No. 81
Website: www.uaa.alaska.edu
Admissions email: admissions@alaska.edu
Public; founded 1954
Freshman admissions: selective; 2017-2018: 3,716 applied, 3,078 accepted. Neither SAT nor ACT required. ACT 25/75 percentile: 18-24. High school rank: 14% in top tenth, 35% in top quarter, 63% in top half
Early decision deadline: N/A, notification date: N/A
Early action deadline: N/A, notification date: N/A
Application deadline (fall): 8/15
Undergraduate student body: 6,975 full time, 8,115 part time; 43% male, 57% female; 6% American Indian, 9% Asian, 3% black, 8% Hispanic, 12% multiracial, 1% Pacific Islander, 56% white, 2% international
Most popular majors: 19% Business, Management, Marketing, and Related Support Services, 16% Health Professions and Related Programs, 9% Engineering, 6% Social Sciences, 5% Psychology
Expenses: 2018-2019: $7,688 in state, $23,858 out of state; room/board: $12,200
Financial aid: (907) 786-1517; 56% of undergrads determined to have financial need; average aid package $9,779

University of Alaska–Fairbanks

Fairbanks AK
(800) 478-1823
U.S. News ranking: Nat. U., No. 215
Website: www.uaf.edu
Admissions email: admissions@uaf.edu
Public; founded 1917
Freshman admissions: selective; 2017-2018: 1,631 applied, 1,251 accepted. Either SAT or ACT required. ACT 25/75 percentile: 17-25. High school rank: 21% in top tenth, 49% in top quarter, 73% in top half
Early decision deadline: N/A, notification date: N/A
Early action deadline: N/A, notification date: N/A
Application deadline (fall): 6/15
Undergraduate student body: 3,022 full time, 3,696 part time; 42% male, 58% female; 14% American Indian, 2% Asian, 3% black, 7% Hispanic, 8% multiracial, 0% Pacific Islander, 49% white, 1% international; 86% from in state; 36% live on campus; 0% of students in fraternities, 0% in sororities
Most popular majors: 19% Engineering, 12% Business, Management, Marketing, and Related Support Services, 10% Homeland Security, Law Enforcement, Firefighting and

Related Protective Services, 9% Biological and Biomedical Sciences, 5% Natural Resources and Conservation
Expenses: 2018-2019: $8,800 in state, $24,970 out of state; room/board: $8,930
Financial aid: (907) 474-7256; 54% of undergrads determined to have financial need; average aid package $8,233

University of Alaska–Southeast[1]

Juneau AK
(907) 465-6457
U.S. News ranking: Reg. U. (W), second tier
Website: www.uas.alaska.edu
Admissions email: admissions@uas.alaska.edu
Public
Application deadline (fall): N/A
Undergraduate student body: N/A full time, N/A part time
Expenses: 2017-2018: $6,828 in state, $19,533 out of state; room/board: $9,200
Financial aid: N/A

ARIZONA

Arizona Christian University

Phoenix AZ
(602) 386-4100
U.S. News ranking: Reg. Coll. (W), No. 22
Website: arizonachristian.edu/
Admissions email: admissions@arizonachristian.edu
Private; founded 1960
Affiliation: Undenominational
Freshman admissions: less selective; 2017-2018: 599 applied, 386 accepted. Either SAT or ACT required. SAT 25/75 percentile: N/A. High school rank: N/A
Early decision deadline: N/A, notification date: N/A
Early action deadline: 11/1, notification date: 11/5
Application deadline (fall): 8/15
Undergraduate student body: 646 full time, 141 part time; 63% male, 37% female; 1% American Indian, 1% Asian, 15% black, 22% Hispanic, 6% multiracial, 0% Pacific Islander, 48% white, 4% international; 71% from in state; 32% live on campus; 0% of students in fraternities, 0% in sororities
Most popular majors: 32% Business, Management, Marketing, and Related Support Services, 19% Education, 14% Psychology, 10% Theology and Religious Vocations, 7% Biological and Biomedical Sciences
Expenses: 2018-2019: $26,796; room/board: $10,674
Financial aid: (602) 386-4115; 77% of undergrads determined to have financial need; average aid package $17,558

Arizona State University–Tempe

Tempe AZ
(480) 965-7788
U.S. News ranking: Nat. U., No. 115
Website: www.asu.edu
Admissions email: admissions@asu.edu
Public; founded 1885
Freshman admissions: more selective; 2017-2018: 24,127 applied, 20,302 accepted. Neither SAT nor ACT required. ACT 25/75 percentile: 22-29. High school rank: 34% in top tenth, 64% in top quarter, 90% in top half
Early decision deadline: N/A, notification date: N/A
Early action deadline: N/A, notification date: N/A
Application deadline (fall): rolling
Undergraduate student body: 38,814 full time, 3,613 part time; 57% male, 43% female; 1% American Indian, 7% Asian, 4% black, 21% Hispanic, 4% multiracial, 0% Pacific Islander, 50% white, 12% international; 75% from in state; 22% live on campus; 10% of students in fraternities, 17% in sororities
Most popular majors: 26% Business, Management, Marketing, and Related Support Services, 12% Engineering, 9% Social Sciences, 8% Biological and Biomedical Sciences, 7% Visual and Performing Arts
Expenses: 2018-2019: $10,822 in state, $28,336 out of state; room/board: $12,648
Financial aid: (855) 278-5080; 54% of undergrads determined to have financial need; average aid package $15,993

Grand Canyon University[1]

Phoenix AZ
(800) 800-9776
U.S. News ranking: Nat. U., second tier
Website: apply.gcu.edu
Admissions email: golopes@gcu.edu
For-profit; founded 1949
Application deadline (fall): rolling
Undergraduate student body: N/A full time, N/A part time
Expenses: 2017-2018: $17,050; room/board: $8,550
Financial aid: (602) 639-6600

Northcentral University

San Diego AZ
(888) 327-2877
U.S. News ranking: Nat. U., unranked
Website: www.ncu.edu
Admissions email: admissions@ncu.edu
For-profit; founded 1996
Affiliation: Other
Freshman admissions: least selective; 2017-2018: N/A applied, N/A accepted. Neither SAT nor ACT required. SAT 25/75 percentile: N/A. High school rank: N/A
Early decision deadline: N/A, notification date: N/A
Early action deadline: N/A, notification date: N/A
Application deadline (fall): rolling
Undergraduate student body: 14 full time, 75 part time; 28% male, 72% female; 1% American Indian, 2% Asian, 21% black, 9% Hispanic, 3% multiracial, 0% Pacific Islander, 28% white, 0% international
Most popular majors: Information not available
Expenses: 2018-2019: $14,055; room/board: N/A
Financial aid: (888) 896-5112

Northern Arizona University

Flagstaff AZ
(928) 523-5511
U.S. News ranking: Nat. U., second tier
Website: www.nau.edu
Admissions email: admissions@nau.edu
Public; founded 1899
Freshman admissions: selective; 2017-2018: 36,875 applied, 29,812 accepted. Neither SAT nor ACT required. ACT 25/75 percentile: 20-25. High school rank: 21% in top tenth, 51% in top quarter, 82% in top half
Early decision deadline: N/A, notification date: N/A
Early action deadline: N/A, notification date: N/A
Application deadline (fall): rolling
Undergraduate student body: 21,990 full time, 5,096 part time; 40% male, 60% female; 2% American Indian, 2% Asian, 3% black, 24% Hispanic, 6% multiracial, 0% Pacific Islander, 57% white, 4% international; 71% from in state; 35% live on campus; 3% of students in fraternities, 4% in sororities
Most popular majors: 20% Business, Management, Marketing, and Related Support Services, 13% Health Professions and Related Programs, 10% Liberal Arts and Sciences, General Studies and Humanities, 9% Education, 8% Social Sciences
Expenses: 2018-2019: $11,564 in state, $25,828 out of state; room/board: $10,282
Financial aid: (928) 523-4951; 61% of undergrads determined to have financial need; average aid package $12,003

Prescott College[1]

Prescott AZ
(877) 350-2100
U.S. News ranking: Reg. U. (W), No. 91
Website: www.prescott.edu/
Admissions email: admissions@prescott.edu
Private; founded 1966
Application deadline (fall): 8/15
Undergraduate student body: N/A full time, N/A part time
Expenses: 2018-2019: $31,485; room/board: $7,700
Financial aid: (928) 350-1104; 72% of undergrads determined to have financial need; average aid package $21,680

The School of Architecture at Taliesin[1]

Scottsdale AZ
(480) 627-5345
U.S. News ranking: Arts, unranked
Website: www.taliesin.edu/
Admissions email: admissions@taliesin.edu
Private; founded 1932
Application deadline (fall): 4/1
Undergraduate student body: N/A full time, N/A part time
Expenses: N/A
Financial aid: N/A

Southwest University of Visual Arts[1]

Tucson AZ
(520) 325-0123
U.S. News ranking: Arts, unranked
Website: www.suva.edu/
Admissions email: N/A
For-profit
Application deadline (fall): N/A
Undergraduate student body: N/A full time, N/A part time
Expenses: N/A
Financial aid: N/A

University of Arizona

Tucson AZ
(520) 621-3237
U.S. News ranking: Nat. U., No. 106
Website: www.arizona.edu
Admissions email: admissions@arizona.edu
Public; founded 1885
Freshman admissions: more selective; 2017-2018: 33,608 applied, 28,089 accepted. Neither SAT nor ACT required. ACT 25/75 percentile: 21-28. High school rank: 34% in top tenth, 61% in top quarter, 85% in top half
Early decision deadline: N/A, notification date: N/A
Early action deadline: N/A, notification date: N/A
Application deadline (fall): 5/1
Undergraduate student body: 29,783 full time, 5,340 part time; 48% male, 52% female; 1% American Indian, 5% Asian, 4% black, 27% Hispanic, 5% multiracial, 0% Pacific Islander, 50% white, 7% international; 69% from in state; 19% live on campus; N/A of students in fraternities, N/A in sororities
Most popular majors: 15% Business, Management, Marketing, and Related Support Services, 10% Biological and Biomedical Sciences, 8% Health Professions and Related Programs, 8% Multi/Interdisciplinary Studies, 8% Social Sciences
Expenses: 2017-2018: $11,644 in state, $32,449 out of state; room/board: $11,300
Financial aid: (520) 621-1858; 51% of undergrads determined to have financial need; average aid package $13,288

University of Phoenix[1]

Phoenix AZ
(866) 766-0766
U.S. News ranking: Nat. U., unranked
Website: www.phoenix.edu
Admissions email: N/A
For-profit
Application deadline (fall): N/A
Undergraduate student body: N/A full time, N/A part time
Expenses: N/A
Financial aid: N/A

ARKANSAS

Arkansas Baptist College[1]

Little Rock AR
(501) 420-1234
U.S. News ranking: Reg. Coll. (S), second tier
Website: www.arkansasbaptist.edu
Admissions email: admissions@arkansasbaptist.edu
Private; founded 1884
Affiliation: Baptist
Application deadline (fall): rolling
Undergraduate student body: N/A full time, N/A part time
Expenses: 2017-2018: $8,760; room/board: $4,412
Financial aid: (501) 420-1223

Arkansas State University[1]

State University AR
(870) 972-3024
U.S. News ranking: Reg. U. (S), No. 95
Website: www.astate.edu
Admissions email: admissions@astate.edu
Public; founded 1909
Application deadline (fall): 8/22
Undergraduate student body: N/A full time, N/A part time
Expenses: 2017-2018: $8,478 in state, $14,778 out of state; room/board: $8,740
Financial aid: (870) 972-2310

Arkansas Tech University

Russellville AR
(479) 968-0343
U.S. News ranking: Reg. U. (S), No. 102
Website: www.atu.edu
Admissions email: tech.enroll@atu.edu
Public; founded 1909
Freshman admissions: selective; 2017-2018: 5,006 applied, 4,743 accepted. Either SAT or ACT required. ACT 25/75 percentile: 19-25. High school rank: 14% in top tenth, 36% in top quarter, 66% in top half
Early decision deadline: N/A, notification date: N/A
Early action deadline: N/A, notification date: N/A
Application deadline (fall): rolling
Undergraduate student body: 6,729 full time, 4,052 part time; 46% male, 54% female; 1% American Indian, 1% Asian, 8% black, 7% Hispanic, 3% multiracial, 0% Pacific Islander, 75% white, 4% international; 96% from in state; 31% live on campus; 8% of students in fraternities, 8% in sororities
Most popular majors: 17% Multi/Interdisciplinary Studies, 15% Education, 14% Health Professions and Related Programs 13% Business, Management, Marketing, and Related Support Services, 6% Engineering

More @ usnews.com/bestcolleges

Expenses: 2018-2019: $9,068 in state, $15,848 out of state; room/board: $7,870
Financial aid: (479) 968-0399; 69% of undergrads determined to have financial need; average aid package $9,538

Central Baptist College

Conway AR
(501) 329-6873
U.S. News ranking: Reg. Coll. (S), No. 55
Website: www.cbc.edu
Admissions email: admissions@cbc.edu
Private; founded 1952
Affiliation: Baptist
Freshman admissions: selective; 2017-2018: 375 applied, 256 accepted. Either SAT or ACT required. ACT 25/75 percentile: 18-22. High school rank: 6% in top tenth, 25% in top quarter, 56% in top half
Early decision deadline: N/A, notification date: N/A
Early action deadline: N/A, notification date: N/A
Application deadline (fall): 8/10
Undergraduate student body: 599 full time, 146 part time; 57% male, 43% female; 1% American Indian, 1% Asian, 23% black, 4% Hispanic, 0% multiracial, 0% Pacific Islander, 66% white, 3% international; 78% from in state; 25% live on campus; 0% of students in fraternities, 0% in sororities
Most popular majors: 12% Business, Management, Marketing, and Related Support Services, Other, 8% Bible/Biblical Studies, 8% Organizational Behavior Studies, 6% Kinesiology and Exercise Science, 6% Psychology, General
Expenses: 2018-2019: $16,200; room/board: $7,500
Financial aid: (501) 205-8809; 82% of undergrads determined to have financial need; average aid package $12,006

Crowley's Ridge College[1]

Paragould AR
U.S. News ranking: Reg. Coll. (S), second tier
Admissions email: N/A
Private
Application deadline (fall): N/A
Undergraduate student body: N/A full time, N/A part time
Expenses: 2017-2018: $12,250; room/board: $6,350
Financial aid: N/A

Harding University

Searcy AR
(800) 477-4407
U.S. News ranking: Reg. U. (S), No. 20
Website: www.harding.edu
Admissions email: admissions@harding.edu
Private; founded 1924
Affiliation: Churches of Christ
Freshman admissions: more selective; 2017-2018: 2,023 applied, 1,491 accepted. Either SAT or ACT required. ACT 25/75 percentile: 22-28. High school rank: 25% in top tenth, 51% in top quarter, 77% in top half
Early decision deadline: N/A, notification date: N/A
Early action deadline: N/A, notification date: N/A
Application deadline (fall): rolling
Undergraduate student body: 3,945 full time, 239 part time; 45% male, 55% female; 0% American Indian, 1% Asian, 4% black, 3% Hispanic, 3% multiracial, 0% Pacific Islander, 82% white, 6% international; 29% from in state; 88% live on campus; 0% of students in fraternities, 0% in sororities
Most popular majors: 17% Business, Management, Marketing, and Related Support Services, 14% Education, 12% Health Professions and Related Programs, 7% Liberal Arts and Sciences, General Studies and Humanities, 6% Communication, Journalism, and Related Programs
Expenses: 2018-2019: $19,640; room/board: $7,004
Financial aid: (501) 279-4257; 62% of undergrads determined to have financial need; average aid package $13,044

Henderson State University

Arkadelphia AR
(870) 230-5028
U.S. News ranking: Reg. U. (S), No. 91
Website: www.hsu.edu/admissions
Admissions email: admissions@hsu.edu
Public; founded 1890
Freshman admissions: selective; 2017-2018: 2,367 applied, 1,886 accepted. Either SAT or ACT required. ACT 25/75 percentile: 19-25. High school rank: 17% in top tenth, 37% in top quarter, 68% in top half
Early decision deadline: N/A, notification date: N/A
Early action deadline: N/A, notification date: N/A
Application deadline (fall): rolling
Undergraduate student body: 2,565 full time, 267 part time; 44% male, 56% female; 0% American Indian, 1% Asian, 22% black, 5% Hispanic, 3% multiracial, 0% Pacific Islander, 66% white, 1% international; 86% from in state; 51% live on campus; N/A of students in fraternities, N/A in sororities
Most popular majors: 16% Education, 14% Business, Management, Marketing, and Related Support Services, 13% Liberal Arts and Sciences, General Studies and Humanities, 8% Health Professions and Related Programs, 8% Psychology
Expenses: 2018-2019: $8,436 in state, $10,086 out of state; room/board: $7,640
Financial aid: (870) 230-5148; 75% of undergrads determined to have financial need; average aid package $10,091

Hendrix College

Conway AR
(800) 277-9017
U.S. News ranking: Nat. Lib. Arts, No. 76
Website: www.hendrix.edu
Admissions email: adm@hendrix.edu
Private; founded 1876
Freshman admissions: more selective; 2017-2018: 1,465 applied, 1,169 accepted. Either SAT or ACT required. ACT 25/75 percentile: 24-29. High school rank: 60% in top tenth, 81% in top quarter, 96% in top half
Early decision deadline: N/A, notification date: N/A
Early action deadline: 11/15, notification date: 12/15
Application deadline (fall): 6/1
Undergraduate student body: 1,228 full time, 10 part time; 48% male, 52% female; 1% American Indian, 5% Asian, 7% black, 6% Hispanic, 4% multiracial, 0% Pacific Islander, 70% white, 2% international
Most popular majors: 24% Social Sciences, 20% Biological and Biomedical Sciences, 10% Psychology, 7% Physical Sciences, 6% Health Professions and Related Programs
Expenses: 2018-2019: $45,790; room/board: $12,284
Financial aid: (501) 450-1368; 72% of undergrads determined to have financial need; average aid package $38,736

John Brown University

Siloam Springs AR
(479) 524-9500
U.S. News ranking: Reg. U. (S), No. 13
Website: www.jbu.edu
Admissions email: jbuinfo@jbu.edu
Private; founded 1919
Freshman admissions: more selective; 2017-2018: 1,198 applied, 908 accepted. Neither SAT nor ACT required. ACT 25/75 percentile: 24-29. High school rank: 29% in top tenth, 58% in top quarter, 83% in top half
Early decision deadline: N/A, notification date: N/A
Early action deadline: N/A, notification date: N/A
Application deadline (fall): rolling
Undergraduate student body: 1,490 full time, 482 part time; 43% male, 57% female; 2% American Indian, 1% Asian, 2% black, 6% Hispanic, 4% multiracial, 0% Pacific Islander, 74% white, 6% international; 51% from in state; 58% live on campus; N/A of students in fraternities, N/A in sororities
Most popular majors: 47% Business, Management, Marketing, and Related Support Services, 12% Visual and Performing Arts, 10% Engineering, 5% Family and Consumer Sciences/Human Sciences, 4% Education
Expenses: 2018-2019: $26,928; room/board: $9,224
Financial aid: (479) 524-7427; 70% of undergrads determined to have financial need; average aid package $18,117

Lyon College

Batesville AR
(800) 423-2542
U.S. News ranking: Nat. Lib. Arts, second tier
Website: www.lyon.edu
Admissions email: admissions@lyon.edu
Private; founded 1872
Affiliation: Presbyterian Church (USA)
Freshman admissions: more selective; 2017-2018: 1,774 applied, 1,142 accepted. Either SAT or ACT required. ACT 25/75 percentile: 22-28. High school rank: 27% in top tenth, 49% in top quarter, 82% in top half
Early decision deadline: N/A, notification date: N/A
Early action deadline: 1/15, notification date: 3/15
Application deadline (fall): rolling
Undergraduate student body: 652 full time, 20 part time; 55% male, 45% female; 2% American Indian, 3% Asian, 7% black, 8% Hispanic, 0% multiracial, 0% Pacific Islander, 70% white, 4% international; 68% from in state; 70% live on campus; 22% of students in fraternities, 27% in sororities
Most popular majors: 24% Psychology, 21% Biological and Biomedical Sciences, 12% Business, Management, Marketing, and Related Support Services, 9% English Language and Literature/Letters, 9% Social Sciences
Expenses: 2018-2019: $28,790; room/board: $9,130
Financial aid: (870) 307-7250; 74% of undergrads determined to have financial need; average aid package $22,842

Ouachita Baptist University

Arkadelphia AR
(870) 245-5110
U.S. News ranking: Nat. Lib. Arts, second tier
Website: www.obu.edu
Admissions email: admissions@obu.edu
Private; founded 1886
Affiliation: Southern Baptist
Freshman admissions: more selective; 2017-2018: 1,786 applied, 1,267 accepted. Either SAT or ACT required. ACT 25/75 percentile: 21-28. High school rank: 36% in top tenth, 64% in top quarter, 86% in top half
Early decision deadline: N/A, notification date: N/A
Early action deadline: N/A, notification date: N/A
Application deadline (fall): rolling
Undergraduate student body: 1,500 full time, 45 part time; 45% male, 55% female; 0% American Indian, 0% Asian, 8% black, 5% Hispanic, 2% multiracial, 0% Pacific Islander, 82% white, 2% international; 68% from in state; 96% live on campus; 32% of students in fraternities, 49% in sororities
Most popular majors: 17% Business, Management, Marketing, and Related Support Services, 15% Biological and Biomedical Sciences, 10% Education, 10% Theology and Religious Vocations, 9% Visual and Performing Arts
Expenses: 2018-2019: $26,790; room/board: $7,880
Financial aid: (870) 245-5316; 67% of undergrads determined to have financial need; average aid package $23,850

Philander Smith College

Little Rock AR
(501) 370-5221
U.S. News ranking: Nat. Lib. Arts, second tier
Website: www.philander.edu
Admissions email: admissions@philander.edu
Private; founded 1877
Affiliation: United Methodist
Freshman admissions: less selective; 2017-2018: 4,449 applied, 1,050 accepted. Either SAT or ACT required. ACT 25/75 percentile: 15-19. High school rank: 15% in top tenth, 29% in top quarter, 51% in top half
Early decision deadline: N/A, notification date: N/A
Early action deadline: N/A, notification date: N/A
Application deadline (fall): rolling
Undergraduate student body: 840 full time, 51 part time; 38% male, 62% female; 0% American Indian, 0% Asian, 94% black, 1% Hispanic, 2% multiracial, 0% Pacific Islander, 1% white, 2% international; 52% from in state; N/A live on campus; N/A of students in fraternities, N/A in sororities
Most popular majors: 41% Business Administration and Management, General, 15% Biology/Biological Sciences, General, 11% Psychology, General, 8% Computer Science, 7% Social Work
Expenses: 2017-2018: $12,714; room/board: $8,250
Financial aid: (501) 370-5380

Southern Arkansas University

Magnolia AR
(870) 235-4040
U.S. News ranking: Reg. U. (S), second tier
Website: www.saumag.edu
Admissions email: muleriders@saumag.edu
Public; founded 1909
Freshman admissions: selective; 2017-2018: 3,604 applied, 2,503 accepted. Either SAT or ACT required. ACT 25/75 percentile: 19-25. High school rank: 15% in top tenth, 40% in top quarter, 72% in top half
Early decision deadline: N/A, notification date: N/A
Early action deadline: N/A, notification date: N/A
Application deadline (fall): 8/27
Undergraduate student body: 2,924 full time, 551 part time; 45% male, 55% female; 1% American Indian, 1% Asian, 27% black, 4% Hispanic, 0% multiracial, 0% Pacific Islander, 65% white, 2% international; 77% from in state; 52% live on campus; 1% of students in fraternities, 1% in sororities

Most popular majors: 19% Business, Management, Marketing, and Related Support Services, 13% Health Professions and Related Programs, 10% Education, 8% Biological and Biomedical Sciences, 8% Physical Sciences
Expenses: 2018-2019: $8,676 in state, $12,786 out of state; room/board: $6,140
Financial aid: (870) 235-4023; 80% of undergrads determined to have financial need; average aid package $12,305

University of Arkansas

Fayetteville AR
(800) 377-8632
U.S. News ranking: Nat. U., No. 152
Website: www.uark.edu
Admissions email: uofa@uark.edu
Public; founded 1871
Freshman admissions: more selective; 2017-2018: 21,715 applied, 14,324 accepted. Either SAT or ACT required. ACT 25/75 percentile: 23-29. High school rank: 26% in top tenth, 54% in top quarter, 86% in top half
Early decision deadline: N/A, notification date: N/A
Early action deadline: 11/1, notification date: 12/15
Application deadline (fall): 8/1
Undergraduate student body: 20,464 full time, 2,580 part time; 47% male, 53% female; 1% American Indian, 2% Asian, 4% black, 9% Hispanic, 4% multiracial, 0% Pacific Islander, 76% white, 3% international; 55% from in state; 25% live on campus; 21% of students in fraternities, 38% in sororities
Most popular majors: 27% Business, Management, Marketing, and Related Support Services, 10% Engineering, 9% Health Professions and Related Programs, 6% Communication, Journalism, and Related Programs, 6% Parks, Recreation, Leisure, and Fitness Studies
Expenses: 2018-2019: $9,130 in state, $25,168 out of state; room/board: $11,020
Financial aid: (479) 575-3806; 43% of undergrads determined to have financial need; average aid package $9,830

University of Arkansas–Fort Smith[1]

Fort Smith AR
(479) 788-7120
U.S. News ranking: Reg. Coll. (S), second tier
Website: www.uafortsmith.edu/Home/Index
Admissions email: N/A
Public; founded 1928
Application deadline (fall): rolling
Undergraduate student body: N/A full time, N/A part time
Expenses: 2017-2018: $5,577 in state, $12,650 out of state; room/board: $8,426
Financial aid: N/A

University of Arkansas–Little Rock

Little Rock AR
(501) 569-3127
U.S. News ranking: Nat. U., second tier
Website: www.ualr.edu/
Admissions email: admissions@ualr.edu
Public; founded 1927
Freshman admissions: selective; 2017-2018: 2,109 applied, 1,574 accepted. Either SAT or ACT required. ACT 25/75 percentile: 19-25. High school rank: N/A
Early decision deadline: N/A, notification date: N/A
Early action deadline: N/A, notification date: N/A
Application deadline (fall): 8/5
Undergraduate student body: 4,672 full time, 4,652 part time; 39% male, 61% female; 0% American Indian, 2% Asian, 28% black, 4% Hispanic, 10% multiracial, 0% Pacific Islander, 52% white, 4% international; 91% from in state; N/A live on campus; N/A of students in fraternities, N/A in sororities
Most popular majors: 20% Health Professions and Related Programs, 16% Business, Management, Marketing, and Related Support Services, 8% Homeland Security, Law Enforcement, Firefighting and Related Protective Services, 6% Psychology, 5% Communication, Journalism, and Related Programs
Expenses: 2017-2018: $8,401 in state, $19,797 out of state; room/board: $9,218
Financial aid: (501) 569-3035

University of Arkansas–Monticello[1]

Monticello AR
(870) 367-6811
U.S. News ranking: Reg. U. (S), unranked
Website: www.uamont.edu
Admissions email: admissions@uamont.edu
Public
Application deadline (fall): N/A
Undergraduate student body: N/A full time, N/A part time
Expenses: 2017-2018: $7,462 in state, $13,312 out of state; room/board: $6,550
Financial aid: N/A

University of Arkansas–Pine Bluff

Pine Bluff AR
(870) 575-8492
U.S. News ranking: Reg. Coll. (S), No. 45
Website: www.uapb.edu/
Admissions email: owasoyop@uapb.edu
Public; founded 1873
Freshman admissions: less selective; 2017-2018: 4,393 applied, 2,051 accepted. Either SAT or ACT required. ACT 25/75 percentile: 16-20. High school rank: 13% in top tenth, 33% in top quarter, 63% in top half
Early decision deadline: N/A, notification date: N/A
Early action deadline: N/A, notification date: N/A
Application deadline (fall): rolling
Undergraduate student body: 2,341 full time, 176 part time; 41% male, 59% female; 0% American Indian, 0% Asian, 92% black, 2% Hispanic, 1% multiracial, 0% Pacific Islander, 3% white, 1% international
Most popular majors: 15% Biology/Biological Sciences, General, 8% Business Administration and Management, General, 8% General Studies, 7% Criminal Justice/Safety Studies, 7% Family and Consumer Sciences/Human Sciences, General
Expenses: 2018-2019: $7,944 in state, $14,304 out of state; room/board: $8,281
Financial aid: (870) 575-8302; 88% of undergrads determined to have financial need; average aid package $12,593

University of Central Arkansas

Conway AR
(501) 450-3128
U.S. News ranking: Reg. U. (S), No. 71
Website: www.uca.edu
Admissions email: admissions@uca.edu
Public; founded 1907
Freshman admissions: selective; 2017-2018: 5,362 applied, 4,823 accepted. Either SAT or ACT required. ACT 25/75 percentile: 21-27. High school rank: 21% in top tenth, 49% in top quarter, 79% in top half
Early decision deadline: N/A, notification date: N/A
Early action deadline: N/A, notification date: N/A
Application deadline (fall): rolling
Undergraduate student body: 8,064 full time, 1,478 part time; 41% male, 59% female; 1% American Indian, 2% Asian, 17% black, 5% Hispanic, 4% multiracial, 0% Pacific Islander, 66% white, 5% international; 91% from in state; 50% live on campus; 14% of students in fraternities, 17% in sororities
Most popular majors: 22% Health Professions and Related Programs, 18% Business, Management, Marketing, and Related Support Services, 9% Education, 8% Visual and Performing Arts, 6% Psychology
Expenses: 2018-2019: $8,751 in state, $15,274 out of state; room/board: $6,854
Financial aid: (501) 450-3140

University of the Ozarks

Clarksville AR
(479) 979-1227
U.S. News ranking: Reg. Coll. (S), No. 3
Website: www.ozarks.edu
Admissions email: admiss@ozarks.edu
Private; founded 1834
Affiliation: Presbyterian Church (USA)
Freshman admissions: selective; 2017-2018: 995 applied, 887 accepted. Neither SAT nor ACT required. ACT 25/75 percentile: 18-23. High school rank: 6% in top tenth, 30% in top quarter, 67% in top half
Early decision deadline: N/A, notification date: N/A
Early action deadline: N/A, notification date: N/A
Application deadline (fall): rolling
Undergraduate student body: 747 full time, 8 part time; 50% male, 50% female; 1% American Indian, 1% Asian, 8% black, 10% Hispanic, 4% multiracial, 0% Pacific Islander, 53% white, 19% international; 47% from in state; 70% live on campus; 0% of students in fraternities, 0% in sororities
Most popular majors: 11% Biology/Biological Sciences, General, 11% Public Health Education and Promotion, 8% Public Relations, Advertising, and Applied Communication, Other, 7% Physical Education Teaching and Coaching, 7% Political Science and Government, General
Expenses: 2018-2019: $24,230; room/board: $7,400
Financial aid: (479) 979-1447; 68% of undergrads determined to have financial need; average aid package $22,322

Williams Baptist University

Walnut Ridge AR
(800) 722-4434
U.S. News ranking: Reg. Coll. (S), No. 27
Website: www.williamsbaptistcollege.com
Admissions email: admissions@wbcoll.edu
Private; founded 1941
Affiliation: Southern Baptist
Freshman admissions: selective; 2017-2018: 764 applied, 433 accepted. Either SAT or ACT required. ACT 25/75 percentile: 18-22. High school rank: 10% in top tenth, 29% in top quarter, 53% in top half
Early decision deadline: N/A, notification date: N/A
Early action deadline: N/A, notification date: N/A
Application deadline (fall): rolling
Undergraduate student body: 446 full time, 47 part time; 57% male, 43% female; 0% American Indian, 0% Asian, 13% black, 6% Hispanic, 3% multiracial, 0% Pacific Islander, 72% white, 5% international
Most popular majors: 22% Psychology, General, 17% General Studies, 14% Biology, General, 11% Business Administration and Management, General, 8% Elementary Education and Teaching
Expenses: 2018-2019: $17,320; room/board: $7,800
Financial aid: (870) 759-4112; 68% of undergrads determined to have financial need; average aid package $17,498

CALIFORNIA

Academy of Art University

San Francisco CA
(800) 544-2787
U.S. News ranking: Arts, unranked
Website: www.academyart.edu/
Admissions email: admissions@academyart.edu
For-profit; founded 1929
Freshman admissions: least selective; 2017-2018: 2,529 applied, 2,529 accepted. Neither SAT nor ACT required. SAT 25/75 percentile: N/A. High school rank: N/A
Early decision deadline: N/A, notification date: N/A
Early action deadline: N/A, notification date: N/A
Application deadline (fall): rolling
Undergraduate student body: 4,422 full time, 3,230 part time; 43% male, 57% female; 0% American Indian, 6% Asian, 7% black, 11% Hispanic, 3% multiracial, 1% Pacific Islander, 18% white, 29% international; 56% from in state; 15% live on campus; N/A of students in fraternities, N/A in sororities
Most popular majors: 45% Visual and Performing Arts, 20% Computer and Information Sciences and Support Services, 15% Engineering Technologies and Engineering-Related Fields, 11% Communications Technologies/Technicians and Support Services, 4% Communication, Journalism, and Related Programs
Expenses: 2018-2019: $27,810; room/board: $16,648
Financial aid: (415) 618-6190; 41% of undergrads determined to have financial need; average aid package $12,614

Alliant International University

San Diego CA
(858) 635-4772
U.S. News ranking: Nat. U., unranked
Website: www.alliant.edu
Admissions email: admissions@alliant.edu
Private; founded 1969
Freshman admissions: least selective; 2017-2018: 36 applied, 35 accepted. Neither SAT nor ACT required. SAT 25/75 percentile: N/A. High school rank: N/A
Early decision deadline: N/A, notification date: N/A
Early action deadline: N/A, notification date: N/A
Application deadline (fall): rolling
Undergraduate student body: 110 full time, 1,223 part time; 41% male, 59% female; N/A American Indian, N/A Asian, N/A black, N/A Hispanic, N/A multiracial, N/A Pacific Islander, N/A white, N/A international
Most popular majors: 52% Business Administration and Management, General, 37% Psychology, General
Expenses: 2018-2019: $18,060; room/board: N/A

More @ usnews.com/bestcolleges

Financial aid: (858) 635-4700; 41% of undergrads determined to have financial need

American Jewish University[1]

Bel-Air CA
(310) 440-1247
U.S. News ranking: Nat. Lib. Arts, second tier
Website: www.aju.edu
Admissions email: admissions@aju.edu
Private; founded 1947
Application deadline (fall): rolling
Undergraduate student body: N/A full time, N/A part time
Expenses: 2018-2019: $31,946; room/board: $16,956
Financial aid: (310) 476-9777

Argosy University[1]

Orange CA
U.S. News ranking: Nat. U., unranked
Website: www.argosy.edu/
Admissions email: N/A
For-profit
Application deadline (fall): N/A
Undergraduate student body: N/A full time, N/A part time
Expenses: 2017-2018: $13,438; room/board: N/A
Financial aid: N/A

ArtCenter College of Design

Pasadena CA
(626) 396-2373
U.S. News ranking: Arts, unranked
Website: www.artcenter.edu
Admissions email: admissions@artcenter.edu
Private; founded 1930
Freshman admissions: least selective; 2017-2018: N/A applied, N/A accepted. Neither SAT nor ACT required. SAT 25/75 percentile: N/A. High school rank: N/A
Early decision deadline: N/A, notification date: N/A
Early action deadline: N/A, notification date: N/A
Application deadline (fall): rolling
Undergraduate student body: 1,717 full time, 288 part time; 46% male, 54% female; 0% American Indian, 33% Asian, 1% black, 13% Hispanic, 4% multiracial, 0% Pacific Islander, 16% white, 31% international
Most popular majors: 28% Illustration, 18% Graphic Design, 10% Engineering-Related Fields, Other, 9% Automotive Engineering Technology/Technician, 8% Cinematography and Film/Video Production
Expenses: 2017-2018: $42,008; room/board: N/A
Financial aid: (626) 396-2215

Ashford University[1]

San Diego CA
(866) 711-1700
U.S. News ranking: Reg. U. (W), unranked
Website: www.ashford.edu
Admissions email: admissions@ashford.edu
For-profit
Application deadline (fall): N/A
Undergraduate student body: N/A full time, N/A part time
Expenses: 2017-2018: $11,248; room/board: N/A
Financial aid: N/A

Azusa Pacific University

Azusa CA
(800) 825-5278
U.S. News ranking: Nat. U., No. 205
Website: www.apu.edu
Admissions email: admissions@apu.edu
Private; founded 1899
Affiliation: Evangelical Christian
Freshman admissions: selective; 2017-2018: 8,939 applied, 5,374 accepted. Either SAT or ACT required. SAT 25/75 percentile: 990-1220. High school rank: N/A
Early decision deadline: N/A, notification date: N/A
Early action deadline: 11/15, notification date: 1/15
Application deadline (fall): 6/1
Undergraduate student body: 5,075 full time, 596 part time; 34% male, 66% female; 0% American Indian, 9% Asian, 5% black, 32% Hispanic, 8% multiracial, 1% Pacific Islander, 39% white, 3% international; 80% from in state; 68% live on campus; 0% of students in fraternities, 0% in sororities
Most popular majors: 31% Health Professions and Related Programs, 14% Business, Management, Marketing, and Related Support Services, 12% Psychology, 8% Visual and Performing Arts, 6% Education
Expenses: 2018-2019: $37,506; room/board: $9,794
Financial aid: (800) 825-5278; 74% of undergrads determined to have financial need; average aid package $24,503

Biola University

La Mirada CA
(562) 903-4752
U.S. News ranking: Nat. U., No. 157
Website: www.biola.edu
Admissions email: admissions@biola.edu
Private; founded 1908
Affiliation: Multiple Protestant Denomination
Freshman admissions: more selective; 2017-2018: 3,926 applied, 2,826 accepted. Either SAT or ACT required. SAT 25/75 percentile: 1050-1260. High school rank: 28% in top tenth, 55% in top quarter, 86% in top half
Early decision deadline: 11/15, notification date: 1/15
Early action deadline: 11/15, notification date: 1/15
Application deadline (fall): rolling
Undergraduate student body: 3,883 full time, 165 part time; 36% male, 64% female; 0% American Indian, 18% Asian, 2% black, 21% Hispanic, 6% multiracial, 0% Pacific Islander, 46% white, 3% international; 77% from in state; 65% live on campus; 0% of students in fraternities, 0% in sororities
Most popular majors: Information not available
Expenses: 2018-2019: $40,488; room/board: $11,312
Financial aid: (562) 903-4742; 68% of undergrads determined to have financial need; average aid package $21,694

Brandman University[1]

Irvine CA
(800) 746-0082
U.S. News ranking: Reg. U. (W), unranked
Website: www.brandman.edu
Admissions email: apply@brandman.edu
Private; founded 1958
Affiliation: Other
Application deadline (fall): rolling
Undergraduate student body: N/A full time, N/A part time
Expenses: 2017-2018: $15,540; room/board: N/A
Financial aid: (800) 746-0082

California Baptist University

Riverside CA
(877) 228-8866
U.S. News ranking: Reg. U. (W), No. 32
Website: www.calbaptist.edu
Admissions email: admissions@calbaptist.edu
Private; founded 1950
Affiliation: Southern Baptist
Freshman admissions: selective; 2017-2018: 5,039 applied, 3,884 accepted. Either SAT or ACT required. SAT 25/75 percentile: 980-1190. High school rank: 18% in top tenth, 46% in top quarter, 79% in top half
Early decision deadline: N/A, notification date: N/A
Early action deadline: 12/15, notification date: 1/31
Application deadline (fall): rolling
Undergraduate student body: 6,367 full time, 1,047 part time; 37% male, 63% female; 1% American Indian, 5% Asian, 7% black, 36% Hispanic, 6% multiracial, 1% Pacific Islander, 39% white, 2% international; 92% from in state; 40% live on campus; N/A of students in fraternities, N/A in sororities
Most popular majors: 13% Business/Commerce, General, 13% Registered Nursing/Registered Nurse, 10% Psychology, General, 7% Kinesiology and Exercise Science, 5% Liberal Arts and Sciences/Liberal Studies
Expenses: 2018-2019: $33,478; room/board: $9,060
Financial aid: (951) 343-4235; 82% of undergrads determined to have financial need; average aid package $20,693

California College of the Arts

San Francisco CA
(800) 447-1278
U.S. News ranking: Arts, unranked
Website: www.cca.edu
Admissions email: enroll@cca.edu
Private; founded 1907
Freshman admissions: less selective; 2017-2018: 2,005 applied, 1,277 accepted. Neither SAT nor ACT required. SAT 25/75 percentile: 895-1200. High school rank: N/A
Early decision deadline: N/A, notification date: N/A
Early action deadline: N/A, notification date: N/A
Application deadline (fall): rolling
Undergraduate student body: 1,408 full time, 78 part time; 36% male, 64% female; 0% American Indian, 17% Asian, 5% black, 13% Hispanic, 0% multiracial, 1% Pacific Islander, 23% white, 37% international; 62% from in state; 30% live on campus; 1% of students in fraternities, 1% in sororities
Most popular majors: 77% Visual and Performing Arts, 9% Communications Technologies/Technicians and Support Services, 6% Architecture and Related Services, 1% English Language and Literature/Letters, 1% Precision Production
Expenses: 2018-2019: $49,148; room/board: $12,986
Financial aid: (415) 703-9573; 47% of undergrads determined to have financial need; average aid package $32,759

California Institute of Integral Studies[1]

San Francisco CA
(415) 575-6100
U.S. News ranking: Nat. U., unranked
Website: www.ciis.edu
Admissions email: N/A
Private; founded 1968
Application deadline (fall): N/A
Undergraduate student body: N/A full time, N/A part time
Expenses: N/A
Financial aid: N/A

California Institute of Technology

Pasadena CA
(626) 395-6341
U.S. News ranking: Nat. U., No. 12
Website: www.caltech.edu
Admissions email: ugadmissions@caltech.edu
Private; founded 1891
Freshman admissions: most selective; 2017-2018: 7,339 applied, 568 accepted. Either SAT or ACT required. SAT 25/75 percentile: 1530-1590. High school rank: 93% in top tenth, 100% in top quarter, 100% in top half
Early decision deadline: N/A, notification date: N/A
Early action deadline: 11/1, notification date: 12/15
Application deadline (fall): 1/3
Undergraduate student body: 961 full time, 0 part time; 55% male, 45% female; 0% American Indian, 43% Asian, 1% black, 12% Hispanic, 7% multiracial, 0% Pacific Islander, 28% white, 9% international; 34% from in state; 85% live on campus; 0% of students in fraternities, 0% in sororities
Most popular majors: 36% Engineering, 26% Computer and Information Sciences and Support Services, 20% Physical Sciences, 11% Mathematics and Statistics, 5% Biological and Biomedical Sciences
Expenses: 2018-2019: $52,362; room/board: $15,525
Financial aid: (626) 395-6280; 52% of undergrads determined to have financial need; average aid package $49,951

California Institute of the Arts

Valencia CA
(661) 255-1050
U.S. News ranking: Arts, unranked
Website: www.calarts.edu
Admissions email: admissions@calarts.edu
Private; founded 1961
Freshman admissions: least selective; 2017-2018: 2,237 applied, 535 accepted. Neither SAT nor ACT required. SAT 25/75 percentile: N/A. High school rank: N/A
Early decision deadline: N/A, notification date: N/A
Early action deadline: N/A, notification date: N/A
Application deadline (fall): N/A
Undergraduate student body: 959 full time, 25 part time; 43% male, 57% female; N/A American Indian, N/A Asian, N/A black, N/A Hispanic, N/A multiracial, N/A Pacific Islander, N/A white, N/A international
Most popular majors: Information not available
Expenses: N/A
Financial aid: (661) 253-7869

California Lutheran University

Thousand Oaks CA
(877) 258-3678
U.S. News ranking: Reg. U. (W), No. 15
Website: www.callutheran.edu
Admissions email: admissions@callutheran.edu
Private; founded 1959
Affiliation: Evangelical Lutheran Church
Freshman admissions: selective; 2017-2018: 5,251 applied, 3,820 accepted. Either SAT or ACT required. SAT 25/75 percentile: 1060-1230. High school rank: 28% in top tenth, 66% in top quarter, 96% in top half
Early decision deadline: N/A, notification date: N/A
Early action deadline: 11/1, notification date: 1/15
Application deadline (fall): N/A
Undergraduate student body: 2,858 full time, 105 part time; 43% male, 57% female; 0% American Indian, 5% Asian, 4% black, 32% Hispanic, 8% multiracial, 0% Pacific Islander, 45% white, 3% international
Most popular majors: 13% Business Administration and Management, General, 12% Psychology, General, 11% Speech Communication and Rhetoric, 5% Biology/Biological Sciences, General, 5% Kinesiology and Exercise Science
Expenses: 2018-2019: $42,693; room/board: $13,650

Financial aid: (805) 493-3139; 72% of undergrads determined to have financial need; average aid package $36,600

California Polytechnic State University–San Luis Obispo

San Luis Obispo CA
(805) 756-2311
U.S. News ranking: Reg. U. (W), No. 12
Website: www.calpoly.edu/
Admissions email: admissions@calpoly.edu
Public; founded 1901
Freshman admissions: more selective; 2017-2018: 48,588 applied, 16,817 accepted. Either SAT or ACT required. SAT 25/75 percentile: 1220-1400. High school rank: 55% in top tenth, 86% in top quarter, 98% in top half
Early decision deadline: N/A, notification date: N/A
Early action deadline: N/A, notification date: N/A
Application deadline (fall): 11/30
Undergraduate student body: 20,530 full time, 767 part time; 52% male, 48% female; 0% American Indian, 13% Asian, 1% black, 17% Hispanic, 8% multiracial, 0% Pacific Islander, 55% white, 2% international; 86% from in state; 36% live on campus; 7% of students in fraternities, 11% in sororities
Most popular majors: 26% Engineering, 15% Business, Management, Marketing, and Related Support Services, 11% Agriculture, Agriculture Operations, and Related Sciences, 6% Biological and Biomedical Sciences, 5% Social Sciences
Expenses: 2018-2019: $9,789 in state, $21,669 out of state; room/board: $13,796
Financial aid: (805) 756-2927; 40% of undergrads determined to have financial need; average aid package $10,456

California State Polytechnic University–Pomona

Pomona CA
(909) 869-5299
U.S. News ranking: Reg. U. (W), No. 28
Website: www.cpp.edu
Admissions email: admissions@cpp.edu
Public; founded 1938
Freshman admissions: selective; 2017-2018: 34,919 applied, 20,194 accepted. Either SAT or ACT required. SAT 25/75 percentile: 1010-1240. High school rank: N/A
Early decision deadline: N/A, notification date: N/A
Early action deadline: N/A, notification date: N/A
Application deadline (fall): 11/30
Undergraduate student body: 21,668 full time, 2,651 part time; 54% male, 46% female; 0% American Indian, 22% Asian, 3% black, 43% Hispanic, 4% multiracial, 0% Pacific Islander, 17% white, 7% international; 99% from in state; 10% live on campus; 2% of students in fraternities, 1% in sororities
Most popular majors: 25% Business Administration and Management, General, 7% Hospitality Administration/Management, General, 4% Computer Science, 4% Mechanical Engineering, 3% Civil Engineering, General
Expenses: 2018-2019: $7,297 in state, $19,177 out of state; room/board: $14,514
Financial aid: (909) 869-3700; 69% of undergrads determined to have financial need; average aid package $10,911

California State University–Bakersfield

Bakersfield CA
(661) 654-3036
U.S. News ranking: Reg. U. (W), No. 94
Website: www.csub.edu
Admissions email: admissions@csub.edu
Public
Freshman admissions: less selective; 2017-2018: 5,429 applied, 5,429 accepted. Neither SAT nor ACT required. SAT 25/75 percentile: 810-1050. High school rank: N/A
Early decision deadline: N/A, notification date: N/A
Early action deadline: 11/30, notification date: 3/1
Application deadline (fall): 3/1
Undergraduate student body: 7,521 full time, 1,106 part time; 39% male, 61% female; 1% American Indian, 7% Asian, 6% black, 57% Hispanic, 3% multiracial, 0% Pacific Islander, 17% white, 6% international; 99% from in state; 4% live on campus; 3% of students in fraternities, 3% in sororities
Most popular majors: 29% Liberal Arts and Sciences, General Studies and Humanities, 12% Social Sciences, 11% Education, 8% History, 7% Psychology
Expenses: 2018-2019: $7,146 in state, $19,224 out of state; room/board: $13,230
Financial aid: (661) 654-3016; 80% of undergrads determined to have financial need; average aid package $11,346

California State University–Channel Islands[1]

Camarillo CA
(805) 437-8500
U.S. News ranking: Reg. U. (W), No. 73
Website: www.csuci.edu
Admissions email: N/A
Public
Application deadline (fall): N/A
Undergraduate student body: N/A full time, N/A part time
Expenses: 2017-2018: $6,817 in state, $18,697 out of state; room/board: $16,954
Financial aid: N/A

California State University–Chico

Chico CA
(530) 898-4428
U.S. News ranking: Reg. U. (W), No. 41
Website: www.csuchico.edu
Admissions email: info@csuchico.edu
Public; founded 1887
Freshman admissions: selective; 2017-2018: 22,853 applied, 15,796 accepted. Either SAT or ACT required. SAT 25/75 percentile: 990-1170. High school rank: 35% in top tenth, 76% in top quarter, 100% in top half
Early decision deadline: N/A, notification date: N/A
Early action deadline: N/A, notification date: N/A
Application deadline (fall): 11/30
Undergraduate student body: 15,048 full time, 1,622 part time; 47% male, 53% female; 1% American Indian, 5% Asian, 3% black, 33% Hispanic, 5% multiracial, 0% Pacific Islander, 42% white, 3% international
Most popular majors: 17% Business, Management, Marketing, and Related Support Services, 10% Health Professions and Related Programs, 9% Social Sciences, 8% Parks, Recreation, Leisure, and Fitness Studies, 6% Psychology
Expenses: 2018-2019: $7,078 in state, $20,834 out of state; room/board: $12,712
Financial aid: (530) 898-6451; 68% of undergrads determined to have financial need; average aid package $13,962

California State University–Dominguez Hills

Carson CA
(310) 243-3300
U.S. News ranking: Reg. U. (W), No. 88
Website: www.csudh.edu
Admissions email: info@csudh.edu
Public; founded 1960
Freshman admissions: least selective; 2017-2018: 12,094 applied, 9,333 accepted. Neither SAT nor ACT required. ACT 25/75 percentile: 16-20. High school rank: N/A
Early decision deadline: N/A, notification date: N/A
Early action deadline: N/A, notification date: N/A
Application deadline (fall): rolling
Undergraduate student body: 10,043 full time, 3,073 part time; 37% male, 63% female; 0% American Indian, 9% Asian, 12% black, 62% Hispanic, 3% multiracial, 0% Pacific Islander, 6% white, 5% international; 100% from in state; 5% live on campus; 1% of students in fraternities, 1% in sororities
Most popular majors: 17% Business, Management, Marketing, and Related Support Services, 13% Health Professions and Related Programs, 11% Psychology, 10% Social Sciences, 8% Homeland Security, Law Enforcement, Firefighting and Related Protective Services
Expenses: 2018-2019: $8,132 in state, $17,636 out of state; room/board: $12,540
Financial aid: (310) 243-3189; 74% of undergrads determined to have financial need; average aid package $6,247

California State University–East Bay

Hayward CA
(510) 885-3500
U.S. News ranking: Reg. U. (W), second tier
Website: www.csueastbay.edu
Admissions email: admissions@csueastbay.edu
Public; founded 1957
Freshman admissions: less selective; 2017-2018: 15,963 applied, 11,824 accepted. Neither SAT nor ACT required. SAT 25/75 percentile: 890-1090. High school rank: N/A
Early decision deadline: N/A, notification date: N/A
Early action deadline: N/A, notification date: N/A
Application deadline (fall): 11/30
Undergraduate student body: 11,306 full time, 1,692 part time; 38% male, 62% female; 0% American Indian, 24% Asian, 10% black, 35% Hispanic, 6% multiracial, 1% Pacific Islander, 15% white, 6% international; 99% from in state; N/A live on campus; 0% of students in fraternities, 0% in sororities
Most popular majors: 21% Business Administration and Management, General, 11% Health Professions and Related Programs, 8% Psychology, General, 6% Criminal Justice/Safety Studies, 6% Sociology
Expenses: 2017-2018: $6,834 in state, $18,714 out of state; room/board: $14,184
Financial aid: (510) 885-2784

California State University–Fresno

Fresno CA
(559) 278-2191
U.S. News ranking: Nat. U., No. 205
Website: www.csufresno.edu
Admissions email: lyager@csufresno.edu
Public; founded 1911
Freshman admissions: selective; 2017-2018: 17,920 applied, 10,646 accepted. Either SAT or ACT required. SAT 25/75 percentile: 890-1110. High school rank: 15% in top tenth, 80% in top quarter, 100% in top half
Early decision deadline: N/A, notification date: N/A
Early action deadline: N/A, notification date: N/A
Application deadline (fall): 11/30
Undergraduate student body: 18,793 full time, 3,428 part time; 42% male, 58% female; 0% American Indian, 14% Asian, 3% black, 52% Hispanic, 3% multiracial, 0% Pacific Islander, 18% white, 6% international; 99% from in state; 4% live on campus; 7% of students in fraternities, 4% in sororities
Most popular majors: 14% Business, Management, Marketing, and Related Support Services, 12% Health Professions and Related Programs, 8% Homeland Security, Law Enforcement, Firefighting and Related Protective Services, 7% Agriculture, Agriculture Operations, and Related Sciences, 7% Liberal Arts and Sciences, General Studies and Humanities
Expenses: 2018-2019: $6,585 in state, $12,723 out of state; room/board: $10,587
Financial aid: (559) 278-2182; 76% of undergrads determined to have financial need; average aid package $13,051

California State University–Fullerton

Fullerton CA
(657) 278-7788
U.S. News ranking: Nat. U., No. 221
Website: www.fullerton.edu
Admissions email: admissions@fullerton.edu
Public; founded 1957
Freshman admissions: selective; 2017-2018: 35,768 applied, 20,943 accepted. Either SAT or ACT required. SAT 25/75 percentile: 1020-1180. High school rank: 22% in top tenth, 68% in top quarter, 96% in top half
Early decision deadline: N/A, notification date: N/A
Early action deadline: N/A, notification date: N/A
Application deadline (fall): 11/30
Undergraduate student body: 28,462 full time, 6,458 part time; 44% male, 56% female; 0% American Indian, 21% Asian, 2% black, 43% Hispanic, 4% multiracial, 0% Pacific Islander, 19% white, 6% international; 99% from in state; 1% live on campus; N/A of students in fraternities, 3% in sororities
Most popular majors: 25% Business, Management, Marketing, and Related Support Services, 13% Communication, Journalism, and Related Programs, 10% Health Professions and Related Programs, 7% Psychology, 5% Social Sciences
Expenses: 2018-2019: $6,870 in state, $16,374 out of state; room/board: $15,898
Financial aid: (657) 278-5254; 73% of undergrads determined to have financial need; average aid package $10,107

California State University–Long Beach

Long Beach CA
(562) 985-5471
U.S. News ranking: Reg. U. (W), No. 26
Website: www.csulb.edu
Admissions email: eslb@csulb.edu
Public; founded 1949
Freshman admissions: selective; 2017-2018: 61,806 applied, 17,650 accepted. Either SAT or ACT required. SAT 25/75 percentile: 1020-1230. High school rank: N/A
Early decision deadline: N/A, notification date: N/A

More @ usnews.com/bestcolleges

Early action deadline: N/A, notification date: N/A
Application deadline (fall): rolling
Undergraduate student body: 26,688 full time, 4,663 part time; 43% male, 57% female; 0% American Indian, 22% Asian, 4% black, 42% Hispanic, 5% multiracial, 0% Pacific Islander, 17% white, 7% international; 99% from in state; 20% live on campus; 1% of students in fraternities, 1% in sororities
Most popular majors: 18% Business, Management, Marketing, and Related Support Services, 11% Health Professions and Related Programs, 11% Social Sciences, 10% Family and Consumer Sciences/Human Sciences, 9% Communication, Journalism, and Related Programs
Expenses: 2018-2019: $6,798 in state, $17,094 out of state; room/ board: $12,720
Financial aid: (562) 985-8403; 76% of undergrads determined to have financial need; average aid package $13,720

California State University–Los Angeles

Los Angeles CA
(323) 343-3901
U.S. News ranking: Reg. U. (W), No. 52
Website: www.calstatela.edu
Admissions email: admission@calstatela.edu
Public; founded 1947
Freshman admissions: less selective; 2017-2018: 37,396 applied, 17,369 accepted. Neither SAT nor ACT required. SAT 25/75 percentile: 890-1080. High school rank: 2% in top tenth, 5% in top quarter, 90% in top half
Early decision deadline: N/A, notification date: N/A
Early action deadline: N/A, notification date: N/A
Application deadline (fall): 11/30
Undergraduate student body: 20,881 full time, 3,748 part time; 43% male, 57% female; 0% American Indian, 14% Asian, 4% black, 66% Hispanic, 2% multiracial, 0% Pacific Islander, 6% white, 7% international; 100% from in state; 4% live on campus; 2% of students in fraternities, 3% in sororities
Most popular majors: 9% Sociology, 6% Business Administration and Management, General, 6% Psychology, General, 5% Early Childhood Education and Teaching, 4% Communication and Media Studies
Expenses: 2018-2019: $6,745 in state, $17,249 out of state; room/ board: $11,723
Financial aid: (323) 343-6260; 89% of undergrads determined to have financial need; average aid package $11,993

California State University–Maritime Academy

Vallejo CA
(707) 654-1330
U.S. News ranking: Reg. Coll. (W), No. 3
Website: www.csum.edu
Admissions email: admission@csum.edu
Public; founded 1929
Freshman admissions: selective; 2017-2018: 1,155 applied, 769 accepted. Either SAT or ACT required. SAT 25/75 percentile: 1070-1250. High school rank: N/A
Early decision deadline: N/A, notification date: N/A
Early action deadline: 10/31, notification date: 12/15
Application deadline (fall): 11/30
Undergraduate student body: 1,007 full time, 43 part time; 82% male, 18% female; 0% American Indian, 9% Asian, 2% black, 20% Hispanic, 12% multiracial, 1% Pacific Islander, 48% white, 1% international
Most popular majors: Information not available
Expenses: 2017-2018: $7,056 in state, $18,936 out of state; room/ board: $12,807
Financial aid: N/A

California State University–Monterey Bay

Seaside CA
(831) 582-3783
U.S. News ranking: Reg. U. (W), No. 34
Website: www.csumb.edu
Admissions email: admissions@csumb.edu
Public; founded 1994
Freshman admissions: selective; 2017-2018: 13,112 applied, 6,976 accepted. Either SAT or ACT required. SAT 25/75 percentile: 970-1170. High school rank: 14% in top tenth, 48% in top quarter, 89% in top half
Early decision deadline: N/A, notification date: N/A
Early action deadline: N/A, notification date: N/A
Application deadline (fall): 11/30
Undergraduate student body: 6,111 full time, 660 part time; 37% male, 63% female; 1% American Indian, 6% Asian, 5% black, 40% Hispanic, 8% multiracial, 1% Pacific Islander, 29% white, 5% international; 98% from in state; N/A live on campus; 4% of students in fraternities, 5% in sororities
Most popular majors: 15% Business, Management, Marketing, and Related Support Services, 14% Liberal Arts and Sciences, General Studies and Humanities, 14% Psychology, 11% Parks, Recreation, Leisure, and Fitness Studies, 7% Public Administration and Social Service Professions
Expenses: 2018-2019: $6,873 in state, $19,023 out of state; room/ board: N/A
Financial aid: (831) 582-4136; 71% of undergrads determined to have financial need; average aid package $11,621

California State University–Northridge

Northridge CA
(818) 677-3700
U.S. News ranking: Reg. U. (W), No. 73
Website: www.csun.edu
Admissions email: admissions.records@csun.edu
Public; founded 1958
Freshman admissions: less selective; 2017-2018: 30,165 applied, 17,391 accepted. Either SAT or ACT required. SAT 25/75 percentile: 1010-1120. High school rank: N/A
Early decision deadline: N/A, notification date: N/A
Early action deadline: N/A, notification date: N/A
Application deadline (fall): 11/30
Undergraduate student body: 29,690 full time, 5,919 part time; 46% male, 54% female; 0% American Indian, 10% Asian, 5% black, 48% Hispanic, 3% multiracial, 0% Pacific Islander, 21% white, 9% international; 97% from in state; N/A live on campus; N/A of students in fraternities, N/A in sororities
Most popular majors: 18% Business, Management, Marketing, and Related Support Services, 13% Social Sciences, 10% Psychology, 8% Communication, Journalism, and Related Programs, 8% Health Professions and Related Programs
Expenses: 2018-2019: $6,875 in state, $18,755 out of state; room/ board: $10,402
Financial aid: N/A; 78% of undergrads determined to have financial need; average aid package $18,771

California State University–Sacramento

Sacramento CA
(916) 278-3901
U.S. News ranking: Reg. U. (W), No. 69
Website: www.csus.edu
Admissions email: outreach@csus.edu
Public; founded 1947
Freshman admissions: less selective; 2017-2018: 24,137 applied, 16,351 accepted. Either SAT or ACT required. SAT 25/75 percentile: 940-1140. High school rank: N/A
Early decision deadline: N/A, notification date: N/A
Early action deadline: N/A, notification date: 12/1
Application deadline (fall): 11/30
Undergraduate student body: 22,829 full time, 5,235 part time; 44% male, 56% female; 0% American Indian, 21% Asian, 6% black, 31% Hispanic, 6% multiracial, 1% Pacific Islander, 26% white, 3% international; 99% from in state; 7% live on campus; N/A of students in fraternities, N/A in sororities
Most popular majors: 11% Business, Management, Marketing, and Related Support Services, 9% Education, 9% Social Sciences, 8% Public Administration and Social Service Professions, 7% Parks, Recreation, Leisure, and Fitness Studies
Expenses: 2018-2019: $7,204 in state, $19,084 out of state; room/ board: $14,396
Financial aid: (916) 278-1000; 77% of undergrads determined to have financial need; average aid package $10,572

California State University–San Bernardino

San Bernardino CA
(909) 537-5188
U.S. News ranking: Reg. U. (W), No. 54
Website: www.csusb.edu
Admissions email: moreinfo@csusb.edu
Public; founded 1962
Freshman admissions: less selective; 2017-2018: 15,637 applied, 8,934 accepted. Neither SAT nor ACT required. SAT 25/75 percentile: 910-1090. High school rank: N/A
Early decision deadline: N/A, notification date: N/A
Early action deadline: N/A, notification date: 5/1
Application deadline (fall): rolling
Undergraduate student body: 16,341 full time, 1,902 part time; 40% male, 60% female; 0% American Indian, 5% Asian, 5% black, 64% Hispanic, 3% multiracial, 0% Pacific Islander, 12% white, 7% international; 100% from in state; 7% live on campus; 4% of students in fraternities, 4% in sororities
Most popular majors: 23% Business, Management, Marketing, and Related Support Services, 14% Psychology, 10% Social Sciences, 8% Health Professions and Related Programs, 6% Parks, Recreation, Leisure, and Fitness Studies
Expenses: 2018-2019: $6,926 in state, $13,064 out of state; room/ board: $12,711
Financial aid: (909) 537-5227; 85% of undergrads determined to have financial need; average aid package $9,586

California State University–San Marcos

San Marcos CA
(760) 750-4848
U.S. News ranking: Reg. U. (W), No. 85
Website: www.csusm.edu
Admissions email: apply@csusm.edu
Public; founded 1989
Freshman admissions: less selective; 2017-2018: 14,129 applied, 10,864 accepted. Either SAT or ACT required. ACT 25/75 percentile: 18-23. High school rank: N/A
Early decision deadline: N/A, notification date: N/A
Early action deadline: N/A, notification date: N/A
Application deadline (fall): 11/30
Undergraduate student body: 11,079 full time, 2,237 part time; 39% male, 61% female; 0% American Indian, 9% Asian, 3% black, 45% Hispanic, 5% multiracial, 0% Pacific Islander, 26% white, 5% international; 98% from in state; N/A live on campus; N/A of students in fraternities, N/A in sororities
Most popular majors: 17% Social Sciences, 14% Business, Management, Marketing, and Related Support Services, 11% Health Professions and Related Programs, 10% Family and Consumer Sciences/Human Sciences, 8% Communication, Journalism, and Related Programs
Expenses: 2018-2019: $7,648 in state, $16,576 out of state; room/ board: $13,227
Financial aid: (760) 750-4881

California State University–Stanislaus

Turlock CA
(209) 667-3070
U.S. News ranking: Reg. U. (W), No. 48
Website: www.csustan.edu
Admissions email: Outreach_Help_Desk@csustan.edu
Public; founded 1957
Freshman admissions: less selective; 2017-2018: 8,069 applied, 6,218 accepted. Neither SAT nor ACT required. SAT 25/75 percentile: 910-1100. High school rank: N/A
Early decision deadline: N/A, notification date: N/A
Early action deadline: N/A, notification date: N/A
Application deadline (fall): 11/30
Undergraduate student body: 7,460 full time, 1,431 part time; 35% male, 65% female; 0% American Indian, 10% Asian, 2% black, 53% Hispanic, 4% multiracial, 1% Pacific Islander, 22% white, 4% international; 99% from in state; 8% live on campus; 5% of students in fraternities, 6% in sororities
Most popular majors: 20% Business Administration and Management, General, 14% Psychology, General, 11% Sociology, 10% Liberal Arts and Sciences/Liberal Studies, 9% Criminal Justice/Safety Studies
Expenses: 2018-2019: $7,038 in state, $18,918 out of state; room/ board: $8,670
Financial aid: (209) 667-3337; 77% of undergrads determined to have financial need; average aid package $17,144

Chapman University

Orange CA
(888) 282-7759
U.S. News ranking: Reg. U. (W), No. 5
Website: www.chapman.edu
Admissions email: admit@chapman.edu
Private; founded 1861
Affiliation: Christian Church (Disciples of Christ)

Freshman admissions: more selective; 2017-2018: 13,170 applied, 7,539 accepted. Either SAT or ACT required. ACT 25/75 percentile: 25-30. High school rank: 37% in top tenth, 78% in top quarter, 95% in top half
Early decision deadline: 11/1, notification date: N/A
Early action deadline: 11/1, notification date: 1/10
Application deadline (fall): 1/15
Undergraduate student body: 6,515 full time, 505 part time; 40% male, 60% female; 0% American Indian, 12% Asian, 2% black, 15% Hispanic, 7% multiracial, 0% Pacific Islander, 55% white, 4% international; 69% from in state; 33% live on campus; 25% of students in fraternities, 48% in sororities
Most popular majors: 20% Business Administration and Management, General, 10% Cinematography and Film/Video Production, 7% Business/Corporate Communications, 5% Psychology, General, 5% Speech Communication and Rhetoric
Expenses: 2018-2019: $52,724; room/board: $15,828
Financial aid: (714) 997-6741; 57% of undergrads determined to have financial need; average aid package $34,858

Claremont McKenna College

Claremont CA
(909) 621-8088
U.S. News ranking: Nat. Lib. Arts, No. 9
Website: www.claremontmckenna.edu
Admissions email: admission@cmc.edu
Private; founded 1946
Freshman admissions: most selective; 2017-2018: 6,349 applied, 658 accepted. Either SAT or ACT required. ACT 25/75 percentile: 30-34. High school rank: 82% in top tenth, 96% in top quarter, 100% in top half
Early decision deadline: 11/1, notification date: 12/15
Early action deadline: N/A, notification date: N/A
Application deadline (fall): 1/5
Undergraduate student body: 1,337 full time, 1 part time; 52% male, 48% female; 0% American Indian, 11% Asian, 4% black, 15% Hispanic, 6% multiracial, 0% Pacific Islander, 41% white, 17% international; 45% from in state; 97% live on campus; N/A of students in fraternities, N/A in sororities
Most popular majors: 32% Econometrics and Quantitative Economics, 15% Political Science and Government, General, 10% International Relations and Affairs, 9% Experimental Psychology, 7% Accounting
Expenses: 2018-2019: $54,405; room/board: $16,705
Financial aid: (909) 621-8356; 41% of undergrads determined to have financial need; average aid package $49,848

Cogswell Polytechnical College

San Jose CA
(408) 498-5160
U.S. News ranking: Reg. Coll. (W), No. 22
Website: www. cogswell.edu
Admissions email: admissions@cogswell.edu
Private; founded 1887
Freshman admissions: selective; 2017-2018: 231 applied, 149 accepted. Neither SAT nor ACT required. SAT 25/75 percentile: 1070-1270. High school rank: N/A
Early decision deadline: N/A, notification date: N/A
Early action deadline: 12/1, notification date: 12/1
Application deadline (fall): rolling
Undergraduate student body: 436 full time, 172 part time; 71% male, 29% female; 1% American Indian, 22% Asian, 5% black, 20% Hispanic, 7% multiracial, 1% Pacific Islander, 35% white, 2% international; 93% from in state; 30% live on campus; 0% of students in fraternities, 0% in sororities
Most popular majors: 57% Animation, Interactive Technology, Video Graphics and Special Effects, 14% Music Technology, 11% Game and Interactive Media Design, 7% Computer Programming/Programmer, General, 7% Modeling, Virtual Environments and Simulation
Expenses: 2018-2019: $20,440; room/board: N/A
Financial aid: (408) 541-0100

Concordia University

Irvine CA
(949) 214-3010
U.S. News ranking: Reg. U. (W), No. 37
Website: www.cui.edu
Admissions email: admission@cui.edu
Private; founded 1972
Affiliation: Lutheran Church–Missouri Synod
Freshman admissions: selective; 2017-2018: 4,979 applied, 2,910 accepted. Either SAT or ACT required. SAT 25/75 percentile: 1010-1200. High school rank: 18% in top tenth, 36% in top quarter, 75% in top half
Early decision deadline: N/A, notification date: N/A
Early action deadline: 12/1, notification date: 12/15
Application deadline (fall): 8/1
Undergraduate student body: 1,645 full time, 208 part time; 38% male, 62% female; 0% American Indian, 8% Asian, 5% black, 23% Hispanic, 7% multiracial, 0% Pacific Islander, 51% white, 5% international; 82% from in state; 49% live on campus; N/A of students in fraternities, N/A in sororities
Most popular majors: 24% Health Professions and Related Programs, 20% Business, Management, Marketing, and Related Support Services, 9% Psychology, 8% Liberal Arts and Sciences, General Studies and Humanities, 7% Parks, Recreation, Leisure, and Fitness Studies
Expenses: 2018-2019: $35,400; room/board: $11,300
Financial aid: (949) 214-3066; 70% of undergrads determined to have financial need; average aid package $22,186

Dominican University of California

San Rafael CA
(415) 485-3204
U.S. News ranking: Reg. U. (W), No. 25
Website: www.dominican.edu
Admissions email: enroll@dominican.edu
Private; founded 1890
Freshman admissions: selective; 2017-2018: 1,867 applied, 1,410 accepted. Either SAT or ACT required. SAT 25/75 percentile: 1040-1215. High school rank: 20% in top tenth, 57% in top quarter, 89% in top half
Early decision deadline: N/A, notification date: N/A
Early action deadline: N/A, notification date: N/A
Application deadline (fall): rolling
Undergraduate student body: 1,135 full time, 167 part time; 26% male, 74% female; 1% American Indian, 26% Asian, 5% black, 21% Hispanic, 8% multiracial, 1% Pacific Islander, 32% white, 1% international; 91% from in state; 39% live on campus; N/A of students in fraternities, N/A in sororities
Most popular majors: 41% Health Professions and Related Programs, 15% Business, Management, Marketing, and Related Support Services, 10% Biological and Biomedical Sciences, 9% Psychology, 7% Social Sciences
Expenses: 2018-2019: $45,850; room/board: $14,810
Financial aid: (415) 257-1350; 79% of undergrads determined to have financial need; average aid package $38,214

Fashion Institute of Design & Merchandising

Los Angeles CA
(800) 624-1200
U.S. News ranking: Arts, unranked
Website: fidm.edu/
Admissions email: admissions@fidm.edu
Private; founded 1969
Freshman admissions: least selective; 2017-2018: 1,973 applied, 802 accepted. Neither SAT nor ACT required. SAT 25/75 percentile: N/A. High school rank: N/A
Early decision deadline: N/A, notification date: N/A
Early action deadline: 6/30, notification date: 8/1
Application deadline (fall): rolling
Undergraduate student body: 2,470 full time, 313 part time; 12% male, 88% female; 1% American Indian, 10% Asian, 6% black, 22% Hispanic, 4% multiracial, 1% Pacific Islander, 35% white, 15% international
Most popular majors: 92% Business, Management, Marketing, and Related Support Services, Other, 4% Fashion/Apparel Design, 3% Marketing/Marketing Management, General, 1% Apparel and Textile Marketing Management, 1% Drama and Dramatics/Theatre Arts, General
Expenses: N/A
Financial aid: N/A

Fresno Pacific University

Fresno CA
(559) 453-2039
U.S. News ranking: Reg. U. (W), No. 39
Website: www.fresno.edu
Admissions email: ugadmis@fresno.edu
Private; founded 1944
Affiliation: Mennonite Brethren Church
Freshman admissions: selective; 2017-2018: 623 applied, 593 accepted. Either SAT or ACT required. SAT 25/75 percentile: 915-1090. High school rank: 22% in top tenth, 63% in top quarter, 89% in top half
Early decision deadline: N/A, notification date: N/A
Early action deadline: N/A, notification date: N/A
Application deadline (fall): 7/31
Undergraduate student body: 2,211 full time, 574 part time; 32% male, 68% female; 1% American Indian, 4% Asian, 5% black, 49% Hispanic, 1% multiracial, 1% Pacific Islander, 29% white, 2% international; 98% from in state; 17% live on campus; N/A of students in fraternities, N/A in sororities
Most popular majors: 4% Psychology, 3% Homeland Security, Law Enforcement, Firefighting and Related Protective Services, 2% Business, Management, Marketing, and Related Support Services, 2% Liberal Arts and Sciences, General Studies and Humanities, 2% Parks, Recreation, Leisure, and Fitness Studies
Expenses: 2018-2019: $31,452; room/board: $8,676
Financial aid: (559) 453-7137; 88% of undergrads determined to have financial need; average aid package $20,340

Golden Gate University

San Francisco CA
(415) 442-7800
U.S. News ranking: Reg. U. (W), unranked
Website: www.ggu.edu/apply
Admissions email: maguilar@ggu.edu
Private; founded 1901
Affiliation: Other
Freshman admissions: least selective; 2017-2018: N/A applied, N/A accepted. Neither SAT nor ACT required. SAT 25/75 percentile: N/A. High school rank: N/A
Early decision deadline: N/A, notification date: N/A
Early action deadline: N/A, notification date: N/A
Application deadline (fall): N/A
Undergraduate student body: 229 full time, 241 part time; 56% male, 44% female; 1% American Indian, 12% Asian, 12% black, 17% Hispanic, 4% multiracial, 2% Pacific Islander, 26% white, 2% international
Most popular majors: 96% Business Administration and Management, General, 2% Accounting, 1% International Business/Trade/Commerce, 1% Liberal Arts and Sciences/Liberal Studies
Expenses: 2018-2019: $16,095; room/board: N/A
Financial aid: (415) 442-6632; 58% of undergrads determined to have financial need; average aid package $7,870

Harvey Mudd College

Claremont CA
(909) 621-8011
U.S. News ranking: Nat. Lib. Arts, No. 18
Website: www.hmc.edu
Admissions email: admission@hmc.edu
Private; founded 1955
Freshman admissions: most selective; 2017-2018: 4,078 applied, 629 accepted. Either SAT or ACT required. SAT 25/75 percentile: 1470-1570. High school rank: 90% in top tenth, 100% in top quarter, 100% in top half
Early decision deadline: N/A, notification date: N/A
Early action deadline: N/A, notification date: N/A
Application deadline (fall): N/A
Undergraduate student body: 844 full time, 0 part time; 52% male, 48% female; 0% American Indian, 17% Asian, 4% black, 18% Hispanic, 11% multiracial, 0% Pacific Islander, 34% white, 10% international; 43% from in state; 98% live on campus; 0% of students in fraternities, 0% in sororities
Most popular majors: 38% Engineering, 14% Computer and Information Sciences and Support Services, 13% Physical Sciences, 12% Multi/Interdisciplinary Studies, 11% Mathematics and Statistics
Expenses: 2018-2019: $56,876; room/board: $18,127
Financial aid: (909) 621-8055; 50% of undergrads determined to have financial need; average aid package $43,248

Holy Names University

Oakland CA
(510) 436-1351
U.S. News ranking: Reg. U. (W), No. 61
Website: www.hnu.edu
Admissions email: admissions@hnu.edu
Private; founded 1868
Affiliation: Roman Catholic
Freshman admissions: least selective; 2017-2018: 2,713 applied, 1,426 accepted. Either SAT or ACT required. SAT 25/75 percentile: 730-870. High school rank: 8% in top tenth, 23% in top quarter, 51% in top half

Early decision deadline: N/A, notification date: N/A
Early action deadline: N/A, notification date: N/A
Application deadline (fall): rolling
Undergraduate student body: 543 full time, 48 part time; 36% male, 64% female; 0% American Indian, 9% Asian, 19% black, 43% Hispanic, 3% multiracial, 2% Pacific Islander, 18% white, 3% international
Most popular majors: Information not available
Expenses: 2018-2019: $39,316; room/board: $13,190
Financial aid: (510) 436-1348; 88% of undergrads determined to have financial need; average aid package $34,078

Hope International University

Fullerton CA
(888) 352-4673
U.S. News ranking: Reg. U. (W), No. 77
Website: www.hiu.edu
Admissions email: admissions@hiu.edu
Private; founded 1928
Affiliation: Christian Churches and Churches of Christ
Freshman admissions: selective; 2017-2018: 786 applied, 223 accepted. Either SAT or ACT required. SAT 25/75 percentile: 910-1100. High school rank: 10% in top tenth, 35% in top quarter, 61% in top half
Early decision deadline: N/A, notification date: N/A
Early action deadline: N/A, notification date: N/A
Application deadline (fall): rolling
Undergraduate student body: 581 full time, 146 part time; 43% male, 57% female; 1% American Indian, 4% Asian, 8% black, 29% Hispanic, 13% multiracial, 1% Pacific Islander, 38% white, 2% international; 93% from in state; 48% live on campus; N/A of students in fraternities, N/A in sororities
Most popular majors: 23% Liberal Arts and Sciences/Liberal Studies, 19% Human Development and Family Studies, General, 14% Business Administration and Management, General, 14% Theological and Ministerial Studies, Other, 11% Social Sciences, General
Expenses: 2018-2019: $33,400; room/board: $10,200
Financial aid: (714) 879-3901; 66% of undergrads determined to have financial need; average aid package $21,348

Hult International Business School

San Francisco CA
(415) 869-2900
U.S. News ranking: Business, unranked
Website: www.hult.edu
Admissions email: undergraduate.info@hult.edu
Private; founded 1964
Freshman admissions: least selective; 2017-2018: 3,372 applied, 1,580 accepted. Neither SAT nor ACT required. Average composite ACT score: N/A. High school rank: N/A
Early decision deadline: 11/1, notification date: 12/15
Early action deadline: N/A, notification date: N/A
Application deadline (fall): rolling
Undergraduate student body: 1,266 full time, 0 part time; 63% male, 37% female; 0% American Indian, 0% Asian, 0% black, 0% Hispanic, 0% multiracial, 0% Pacific Islander, 0% white, 99% international
Most popular majors: Information not available
Expenses: 2018-2019: $41,250; room/board: $15,000
Financial aid: N/A; 69% of undergrads determined to have financial need; average aid package $12,180

Humboldt State University

Arcata CA
(707) 826-4402
U.S. News ranking: Reg. U. (W), No. 54
Website: www.humboldt.edu
Admissions email: hsuinfo@humboldt.edu
Public; founded 1913
Freshman admissions: selective; 2017-2018: 11,453 applied, 9,321 accepted. Neither SAT nor ACT required. SAT 25/75 percentile: 960-1170. High school rank: 13% in top tenth, 46% in top quarter, 80% in top half
Early decision deadline: N/A, notification date: N/A
Early action deadline: N/A, notification date: N/A
Application deadline (fall): 11/30
Undergraduate student body: 7,236 full time, 538 part time; 43% male, 57% female; 1% American Indian, 3% Asian, 4% black, 35% Hispanic, 7% multiracial, 0% Pacific Islander, 42% white, 1% international; 95% from in state; 26% live on campus; 2% of students in fraternities, 2% in sororities
Most popular majors: 17% Natural Resources/Conservation, General, 11% Biology/Biological Sciences, General, 10% Psychology, General, 10% Social Sciences, General, 8% Business/Commerce, General
Expenses: 2018-2019: $7,492 in state, $19,372 out of state; room/board: $13,342
Financial aid: (707) 826-4321; 80% of undergrads determined to have financial need; average aid package $14,037

Humphreys College[1]

Stockton CA
(209) 478-0800
U.S. News ranking: Reg. Coll. (W), unranked
Website: www.humphreys.edu
Admissions email: ugadmission@humphreys.edu
Private
Application deadline (fall): N/A
Undergraduate student body: N/A full time, N/A part time
Expenses: 2017-2018: $14,004; room/board: N/A
Financial aid: N/A

John F. Kennedy University[1]

Pleasant Hill CA
(925) 969-3300
U.S. News ranking: Reg. U. (W), unranked
Website: www.jfku.edu
Admissions email: proginfo@jfku.edu
Private; founded 1964
Application deadline (fall): N/A
Undergraduate student body: N/A full time, N/A part time
Expenses: N/A
Financial aid: N/A

John Paul the Great Catholic University

Escondido CA
(858) 653-6740
U.S. News ranking: Reg. Coll. (W), No. 12
Website: jpcatholic.edu/
Admissions email: N/A
For-profit; founded 2006
Affiliation: Roman Catholic
Freshman admissions: selective; 2017-2018: 201 applied, 191 accepted. Either SAT or ACT required. SAT 25/75 percentile: 1020-1190. High school rank: 9% in top tenth, 35% in top quarter, 57% in top half
Early decision deadline: N/A, notification date: N/A
Early action deadline: N/A, notification date: N/A
Application deadline (fall): rolling
Undergraduate student body: 247 full time, 13 part time; 52% male, 48% female; 0% American Indian, 3% Asian, 1% black, 24% Hispanic, 3% multiracial, 0% Pacific Islander, 51% white, 2% international; 48% from in state; 77% live on campus; N/A of students in fraternities, N/A in sororities
Most popular majors: 74% Visual and Performing Arts, 26% Business, Management, Marketing, and Related Support Services
Expenses: 2018-2019: $26,100; room/board: $7,650
Financial aid: (858) 653-6740

Laguna College of Art and Design

Laguna Beach CA
(949) 376-6000
U.S. News ranking: Arts, unranked
Website: www.lcad.edu/
Admissions email: admissions@lcad.edu
Private; founded 1961
Freshman admissions: least selective; 2017-2018: 770 applied, 257 accepted. Neither SAT nor ACT required. SAT 25/75 percentile: N/A. High school rank: N/A
Early decision deadline: N/A, notification date: N/A
Early action deadline: 2/1, notification date: N/A
Application deadline (fall): 8/1
Undergraduate student body: 562 full time, 74 part time; 32% male, 68% female; 1% American Indian, 19% Asian, 2% black, 19% Hispanic, 3% multiracial, 0% Pacific Islander, 48% white, 5% international
Most popular majors: Animation, Interactive Technology, Video Graphics and Special Effects, Fine/Studio Arts, General, Game and Interactive Media Design, Graphic Design, Illustration
Expenses: 2018-2019: $30,700; room/board: $10,000
Financial aid: (949) 376-6000

La Sierra University

Riverside CA
(951) 785-2176
U.S. News ranking: Reg. U. (W), No. 54
Website: lasierra.edu/about/
Admissions email: Admissions@lasierra.edu
Private; founded 1922
Freshman admissions: less selective; 2017-2018: 4,117 applied, 1,984 accepted. Either SAT or ACT required. SAT 25/75 percentile: 845-1100. High school rank: 12% in top tenth, 36% in top quarter, 72% in top half
Early decision deadline: N/A, notification date: N/A
Early action deadline: N/A, notification date: N/A
Application deadline (fall): 7/15
Undergraduate student body: 1,704 full time, 267 part time; 40% male, 60% female; 0% American Indian, 15% Asian, 7% black, 49% Hispanic, 4% multiracial, 2% Pacific Islander, 13% white, 10% international; 86% from in state; 28% live on campus; 0% of students in fraternities, 0% in sororities
Most popular majors: 16% Criminal Justice/Safety Studies, 8% Biomedical Sciences, General, 7% Pre-Medicine/Pre-Medical Studies, 6% Business Administration and Management, General, 6% Kinesiology and Exercise Science
Expenses: 2018-2019: $32,778; room/board: $8,415
Financial aid: (951) 785-2175; 77% of undergrads determined to have financial need; average aid package $22,896

Loyola Marymount University

Los Angeles CA
(310) 338-2750
U.S. News ranking: Reg. U. (W), No. 3
Website: www.lmu.edu
Admissions email: admission@lmu.edu
Private; founded 1911
Affiliation: Roman Catholic
Freshman admissions: more selective; 2017-2018: 15,381 applied, 8,072 accepted. Either SAT or ACT required. SAT 25/75 percentile: 1180-1360. High school rank: 41% in top tenth, 75% in top quarter, 95% in top half
Early decision deadline: 11/1, notification date: 12/1
Early action deadline: 11/1, notification date: 12/20
Application deadline (fall): 1/15
Undergraduate student body: 6,164 full time, 227 part time; 44% male, 56% female; 0% American Indian, 10% Asian, 7% black, 21% Hispanic, 7% multiracial, 0% Pacific Islander, 44% white, 10% international; 71% from in state; 53% live on campus; 17% of students in fraternities, 29% in sororities
Most popular majors: 25% Business, Management, Marketing, and Related Support Services, 15% Social Sciences, 15% Visual and Performing Arts, 9% Communication, Journalism, and Related Programs, 7% Psychology
Expenses: 2018-2019: $48,172; room/board: $15,185
Financial aid: (310) 338-2753; 53% of undergrads determined to have financial need; average aid package $29,906

Marymount California University

Rancho Palos Verdes CA
(310) 303-7311
U.S. News ranking: Reg. Coll. (W), No. 15
Website: www.marymountcalifornia.edu
Admissions email: admissions@marymountcalifornia.edu
Private; founded 1933
Affiliation: Roman Catholic
Freshman admissions: less selective; 2017-2018: 1,683 applied, 1,391 accepted. Neither SAT nor ACT required. SAT 25/75 percentile: 860-1040. High school rank: N/A
Early decision deadline: N/A, notification date: N/A
Early action deadline: N/A, notification date: N/A
Application deadline (fall): rolling
Undergraduate student body: 892 full time, 43 part time; 50% male, 50% female; 0% American Indian, 5% Asian, 8% black, 41% Hispanic, 2% multiracial, 0% Pacific Islander, 20% white, 17% international; 91% from in state; 36% live on campus; 0% of students in fraternities, 0% in sororities
Most popular majors: 42% Business Administration, Management and Operations, 24% Liberal Arts and Sciences, General Studies and Humanities, 22% Psychology, General, 9% Business/Commerce, General, 3% Criminal Justice and Corrections
Expenses: 2017-2018: $35,884; room/board: $14,412
Financial aid: (310) 303-7217

The Master's University and Seminary

Santa Clarita CA
(800) 568-6248
U.S. News ranking: Reg. U. (W), No. 46
Website: www.masters.edu
Admissions email: admissions@masters.edu
Private; founded 1927
Affiliation: Other
Freshman admissions: selective; 2017-2018: 617 applied, 406 accepted. Either SAT or ACT required. SAT 25/75 percentile: 1030-1240. High school rank: 31% in top tenth, 69% in top quarter, 90% in top half
Early decision deadline: N/A, notification date: N/A

Early action deadline: 11/15, notification date: 12/22
Application deadline (fall): rolling
Undergraduate student body: 975 full time, 365 part time; 54% male, 46% female; 0% American Indian, 5% Asian, 2% black, 11% Hispanic, 6% multiracial, 0% Pacific Islander, 65% white, 4% international; 64% from in state; 74% live on campus; 0% of students in fraternities, 0% in sororities
Most popular majors: 20% Business, Management, Marketing, and Related Support Services, 20% Theology and Religious Vocations, 13% Liberal Arts and Sciences, General Studies and Humanities, 12% Communication, Journalism, and Related Programs, 7% Biological and Biomedical Sciences
Expenses: 2018-2019: $25,390; room/board: $11,200
Financial aid: (661) 362-2290; 83% of undergrads determined to have financial need; average aid package $23,050

Menlo College

Atherton CA
(800) 556-3656
U.S. News ranking: Business, unranked
Website: www.menlo.edu
Admissions email: admissions@menlo.edu
Private; founded 1927
Freshman admissions: selective; 2017-2018: 2,490 applied, 1,085 accepted. Neither SAT nor ACT required. SAT 25/75 percentile: 1008-1165. High school rank: N/A
Early decision deadline: N/A, notification date: N/A
Early action deadline: 11/15, notification date: 1/15
Application deadline (fall): 4/1
Undergraduate student body: 727 full time, 18 part time; 56% male, 44% female; 0% American Indian, 9% Asian, 8% black, 25% Hispanic, 9% multiracial, 3% Pacific Islander, 24% white, 14% international
Most popular majors: Information not available
Expenses: 2018-2019: $42,800; room/board: $14,225
Financial aid: N/A; 64% of undergrads determined to have financial need; average aid package $33,775

Mills College

Oakland CA
(510) 430-2135
U.S. News ranking: Reg. U. (W), No. 7
Website: www.mills.edu
Admissions email: admission@mills.edu
Private; founded 1852
Freshman admissions: selective; 2017-2018: 965 applied, 837 accepted. Neither SAT nor ACT required. SAT 25/75 percentile: 1030-1290. High school rank: 25% in top tenth, 55% in top quarter, 90% in top half
Early decision deadline: N/A, notification date: N/A
Early action deadline: 11/15, notification date: 12/1
Application deadline (fall): 1/15
Undergraduate student body: 739 full time, 22 part time; 0% male, 100% female; 0% American Indian, 10% Asian, 9% black, 28% Hispanic, 9% multiracial, 0% Pacific Islander, 41% white, 1% international; N/A from in state; 64% live on campus; 0% of students in fraternities, 0% in sororities
Most popular majors: 15% Psychology, General, 14% English Language and Literature, General, 8% Biology/Biological Sciences, General, 7% Economics, General, 6% Sociology
Expenses: 2018-2019: $30,257; room/board: $13,448
Financial aid: (510) 430-2039; 86% of undergrads determined to have financial need; average aid package $43,117

Minerva Schools at Keck Graduate Institute[1]

San Francisco CA
U.S. News ranking: Reg. Coll. (W), unranked
Admissions email: admissions@minerva.kgi.edu
Private
Application deadline (fall): N/A
Undergraduate student body: N/A full time, N/A part time
Expenses: 2017-2018: $13,150; room/board: $10,000
Financial aid: N/A

Mount Saint Mary's University

Los Angeles CA
(310) 954-4250
U.S. News ranking: Reg. U. (W), No. 18
Website: www.msmu.edu
Admissions email: admissions@msmu.edu
Private; founded 1925
Affiliation: Roman Catholic
Freshman admissions: less selective; 2017-2018: 2,352 applied, 1,910 accepted. Neither SAT nor ACT required. SAT 25/75 percentile: 920-1120. High school rank: 9% in top tenth, 43% in top quarter, 78% in top half
Early decision deadline: N/A, notification date: N/A
Early action deadline: 12/1, notification date: 1/30
Application deadline (fall): 8/1
Undergraduate student body: 2,054 full time, 547 part time; 6% male, 94% female; N/A American Indian, N/A Asian, N/A black, N/A Hispanic, N/A multiracial, N/A Pacific Islander, N/A white, N/A international; 97% from in state; 24% live on campus; N/A of students in fraternities, N/A in sororities
Most popular majors: 33% Health Professions and Related Programs, 13% Business, Management, Marketing, and Related Support Services, 13% Social Sciences, 12% Psychology, 6% Public Administration and Social Service Professions
Expenses: 2018-2019: $41,170; room/board: $12,235
Financial aid: (310) 954-4190; 90% of undergrads determined to have financial need; average aid package $27,877

National University[1]

La Jolla CA
(855) 355-6288
U.S. News ranking: Reg. U. (W), unranked
Website: www.nu.edu
Admissions email: advisor@nu.edu
Private; founded 1971
Application deadline (fall): rolling
Undergraduate student body: N/A full time, N/A part time
Expenses: 2018-2019: $13,320; room/board: N/A
Financial aid: N/A

NewSchool of Architecture and Design

San Diego CA
(619) 684-8828
U.S. News ranking: Arts, unranked
Website: newschoolarch.edu/
Admissions email: fguidali@newschoolarch.edu
For-profit; founded 1980
Freshman admissions: least selective; 2017-2018: N/A applied, N/A accepted. Neither SAT nor ACT required. SAT 25/75 percentile: N/A. High school rank: N/A
Early decision deadline: N/A, notification date: N/A
Early action deadline: N/A, notification date: N/A
Application deadline (fall): rolling
Undergraduate student body: 403 full time, 29 part time; 65% male, 35% female; N/A American Indian, N/A Asian, N/A black, N/A Hispanic, N/A multiracial, N/A Pacific Islander, N/A white, N/A international
Most popular majors: Animation, Interactive Technology, Video Graphics and Special Effects, Architecture, Construction Management, Industrial and Product Design, Interior Design
Expenses: N/A
Financial aid: (619) 684-8803

Notre Dame de Namur University

Belmont CA
(650) 508-3600
U.S. News ranking: Reg. U. (W), No. 48
Website: www.ndnu.edu
Admissions email: admissions@ndnu.edu
Private; founded 1851
Affiliation: Roman Catholic
Freshman admissions: less selective; 2017-2018: 1,759 applied, 1,647 accepted. Either SAT or ACT required. SAT 25/75 percentile: 910-1110. High school rank: 8% in top tenth, 27% in top quarter, 60% in top half
Early decision deadline: N/A, notification date: N/A
Early action deadline: 12/1, notification date: 12/15
Application deadline (fall): rolling
Undergraduate student body: 718 full time, 206 part time; 33% male, 67% female; 0% American Indian, 11% Asian, 6% black, 43% Hispanic, 5% multiracial, 2% Pacific Islander, 22% white, 6% international; 89% from in state; 55% live on campus; 0% of students in fraternities, 0% in sororities
Most popular majors: 22% Business Administration and Management, General, 15% Psychology, General, 10% Public Administration and Social Service Professions, 9% Speech Communication and Rhetoric, 7% Exercise Physiology
Expenses: 2018-2019: $35,350; room/board: $14,494
Financial aid: (650) 508-3741; 82% of undergrads determined to have financial need; average aid package $28,382

Occidental College

Los Angeles CA
(323) 259-2700
U.S. News ranking: Nat. Lib. Arts, No. 39
Website: www.oxy.edu
Admissions email: admission@oxy.edu
Private; founded 1887
Freshman admissions: more selective; 2017-2018: 6,775 applied, 2,831 accepted. Either SAT or ACT required. SAT 25/75 percentile: 1280-1440. High school rank: 62% in top tenth, 86% in top quarter, 99% in top half
Early decision deadline: 11/15, notification date: 12/15
Early action deadline: N/A, notification date: N/A
Application deadline (fall): 1/15
Undergraduate student body: 2,035 full time, 20 part time; 42% male, 58% female; 0% American Indian, 14% Asian, 5% black, 14% Hispanic, 8% multiracial, 0% Pacific Islander, 51% white, 6% international; 49% from in state; 81% live on campus; 16% of students in fraternities, 22% in sororities
Most popular majors: 13% Economics, General, 10% Biology/Biological Sciences, General, 8% Psychology, General, 7% International Relations and Affairs, 6% Cognitive Science
Expenses: 2018-2019: $54,686; room/board: $15,496
Financial aid: (323) 259-2548; 57% of undergrads determined to have financial need; average aid package $49,013

Otis College of Art and Design[1]

Los Angeles CA
(310) 665-6800
U.S. News ranking: Arts, unranked
Website: www.otis.edu
Admissions email: admissions@otis.edu
Private; founded 1918
Application deadline (fall): N/A
Undergraduate student body: N/A full time, N/A part time
Expenses: N/A
Financial aid: (310) 665-6898

Pacific Union College

Angwin CA
(707) 965-6336
U.S. News ranking: Nat. Lib. Arts, second tier
Website: www.puc.edu
Admissions email: enroll@puc.edu
Private; founded 1882
Affiliation: Seventh Day Adventist
Freshman admissions: selective; 2017-2018: 1,904 applied, 956 accepted. Either SAT or ACT required. SAT 25/75 percentile: 950-1150. High school rank: N/A
Early decision deadline: N/A, notification date: N/A
Early action deadline: N/A, notification date: N/A
Application deadline (fall): 9/15
Undergraduate student body: 1,077 full time, 149 part time; 38% male, 62% female; 1% American Indian, 19% Asian, 8% black, 26% Hispanic, 8% multiracial, 1% Pacific Islander, 22% white, 3% international
Most popular majors: 29% Registered Nursing/Registered Nurse, 14% Business/Commerce, General, 6% Biology/Biological Sciences, General, 5% Biochemistry, 5% Psychology, General
Expenses: 2018-2019: $30,060; room/board: $8,310
Financial aid: (707) 965-7200; 78% of undergrads determined to have financial need; average aid package $25,116

Pepperdine University

Malibu CA
(310) 506-4392
U.S. News ranking: Nat. U., No. 46
Website: www.pepperdine.edu
Admissions email: admission-seaver@pepperdine.edu
Private; founded 1937
Affiliation: Churches of Christ
Freshman admissions: more selective; 2017-2018: 11,704 applied, 4,664 accepted. Either SAT or ACT required. SAT 25/75 percentile: 1200-1390. High school rank: 49% in top tenth, 80% in top quarter, 97% in top half
Early decision deadline: N/A, notification date: N/A
Early action deadline: N/A, notification date: N/A
Application deadline (fall): 1/5
Undergraduate student body: 3,300 full time, 304 part time; 41% male, 59% female; 0% American Indian, 10% Asian, 4% black, 14% Hispanic, 6% multiracial, 0% Pacific Islander, 51% white, 11% international; 55% from in state; 52% live on campus; 23% of students in fraternities, 32% in sororities
Most popular majors: 20% Business, Management, Marketing, and Related Support Services, 10% Psychology, 6% Parks, Recreation, Leisure, and Fitness Studies, 5% Social Sciences, 4% Communication, Journalism, and Related Programs
Expenses: 2018-2019: $53,932; room/board: $15,320

More @ usnews.com/bestcolleges

Financial aid: (310) 506-4301; 52% of undergrads determined to have financial need; average aid package $40,728

Pitzer College

Claremont CA
(909) 621-8129
U.S. News ranking: Nat. Lib. Arts, No. 41
Website: www.pitzer.edu
Admissions email: admission@pitzer.edu
Private; founded 1963
Freshman admissions: more selective; 2017-2018: 3,753 applied, 608 accepted. Neither SAT nor ACT required. ACT 25/75 percentile: 29-32. High school rank: 63% in top tenth, 88% in top quarter, 100% in top half
Early decision deadline: 11/15, notification date: 12/18
Early action deadline: N/A, notification date: N/A
Application deadline (fall): 1/1
Undergraduate student body: 1,074 full time, 38 part time; 46% male, 54% female; 0% American Indian, 10% Asian, 6% black, 15% Hispanic, 7% multiracial, 0% Pacific Islander, 47% white, 9% international; 45% from in state; 72% live on campus; 0% of students in fraternities, 0% in sororities
Most popular majors: 22% Social Sciences, 10% Communication, Journalism, and Related Programs, 9% Multi/Interdisciplinary Studies, 9% Psychology, 8% Natural Resources and Conservation
Expenses: 2017-2018: $52,236; room/board: $16,264
Financial aid: (909) 621-8208; 42% of undergrads determined to have financial need; average aid package $48,929

Point Loma Nazarene University

San Diego CA
(619) 849-2273
U.S. News ranking: Reg. U. (W), No. 17
Website: www.pointloma.edu
Admissions email: admissions@pointloma.edu
Private; founded 1902
Affiliation: Church of the Nazarene
Freshman admissions: more selective; 2017-2018: 3,007 applied, 2,294 accepted. Either SAT or ACT required. SAT 25/75 percentile: 1100-1290. High school rank: 31% in top tenth, 71% in top quarter, 92% in top half
Early decision deadline: N/A, notification date: N/A
Early action deadline: 11/15, notification date: 12/21
Application deadline (fall): 2/15
Undergraduate student body: 2,621 full time, 529 part time; 35% male, 65% female; 0% American Indian, 7% Asian, 2% black, 26% Hispanic, 8% multiracial, 1% Pacific Islander, 53% white, 1% international; 83% from in state; 56% live on campus; N/A of students in fraternities, N/A in sororities
Most popular majors: 27% Health Professions and Related Programs, 25% Business, Management, Marketing, and Related Support Services, 7% Biological and Biomedical Sciences, 7% Psychology, 4% Education
Expenses: 2018-2019: $35,700; room/board: $10,450
Financial aid: (619) 849-2538; 65% of undergrads determined to have financial need; average aid package $22,975

Pomona College

Claremont CA
(909) 621-8134
U.S. News ranking: Nat. Lib. Arts, No. 5
Website: www.pomona.edu
Admissions email: admissions@pomona.edu
Private; founded 1887
Freshman admissions: most selective; 2017-2018: 9,045 applied, 756 accepted. Either SAT or ACT required. ACT 25/75 percentile: 30-34. High school rank: 94% in top tenth, 100% in top quarter, 100% in top half
Early decision deadline: 11/1, notification date: 12/15
Early action deadline: N/A, notification date: N/A
Application deadline (fall): 1/1
Undergraduate student body: 1,682 full time, 21 part time; 50% male, 50% female; 0% American Indian, 15% Asian, 9% black, 16% Hispanic, 7% multiracial, 0% Pacific Islander, 36% white, 11% international; 26% from in state; 98% live on campus; 5% of students in fraternities, 0% in sororities
Most popular majors: 25% Social Sciences, 12% Biological and Biomedical Sciences, 9% Computer and Information Sciences and Support Services, 8% Mathematics and Statistics, 6% Physical Sciences
Expenses: 2018-2019: $52,780; room/board: $16,716
Financial aid: (909) 621-8205; 57% of undergrads determined to have financial need; average aid package $55,114

Providence Christian College[1]

Pasadena CA
(866) 323-0233
U.S. News ranking: Nat. Lib. Arts, second tier
Website: www.providencecc.net/
Admissions email: N/A
Private; founded 2003
Application deadline (fall): rolling
Undergraduate student body: N/A full time, N/A part time
Expenses: 2017-2018: $29,372; room/board: $8,568
Financial aid: N/A

San Diego Christian College

Santee CA
(800) 676-2242
U.S. News ranking: Reg. Coll. (W), No. 11
Website: www.sdcc.edu/
Admissions email: admissions@sdcc.edu
Private; founded 1970
Affiliation: Undenominational
Freshman admissions: less selective; 2017-2018: 409 applied, 255 accepted. Neither SAT nor ACT required. SAT 25/75 percentile: 850-980. High school rank: 13% in top tenth, 28% in top quarter, 48% in top half
Early decision deadline: N/A, notification date: N/A
Early action deadline: 12/1, notification date: 1/15
Application deadline (fall): rolling
Undergraduate student body: 504 full time, 154 part time; 49% male, 51% female; 1% American Indian, 3% Asian, 11% black, 29% Hispanic, 7% multiracial, 2% Pacific Islander, 40% white, 1% international
Most popular majors: 20% Business Administration and Management, General, 16% Human Development and Family Studies, General, 13% Theological and Ministerial Studies, Other, 9% Kinesiology and Exercise Science, 9% Psychology, General
Expenses: 2017-2018: $30,438; room/board: $11,300
Financial aid: N/A

San Diego State University

San Diego CA
(619) 594-6336
U.S. News ranking: Nat. U., No. 127
Website: www.sdsu.edu
Admissions email: admissions@sdsu.edu
Public; founded 1897
Freshman admissions: more selective; 2017-2018: 60,697 applied, 21,379 accepted. Either SAT or ACT required. SAT 25/75 percentile: 1090-1290. High school rank: 31% in top tenth, 70% in top quarter, 95% in top half
Early decision deadline: N/A, notification date: N/A
Early action deadline: N/A, notification date: N/A
Application deadline (fall): 11/30
Undergraduate student body: 27,028 full time, 3,137 part time; 46% male, 54% female; 0% American Indian, 13% Asian, 4% black, 31% Hispanic, 7% multiracial, 0% Pacific Islander, 33% white, 7% international; 90% from in state; 14% live on campus; 11% of students in fraternities, 13% in sororities
Most popular majors: 21% Business, Management, Marketing, and Related Support Services, 11% Social Sciences, 8% Health Professions and Related Programs, 8% Psychology, 7% Engineering
Expenses: 2018-2019: $7,488 in state, $19,368 out of state; room/board: $16,735
Financial aid: (619) 594-6323; 54% of undergrads determined to have financial need; average aid package $9,700

San Francisco Art Institute

San Francisco CA
(800) 345-7324
U.S. News ranking: Arts, unranked
Website: www.sfai.edu
Admissions email: admissions@sfai.edu
Private; founded 1871
Freshman admissions: selective; 2017-2018: 451 applied, 337 accepted. Neither SAT nor ACT required. SAT 25/75 percentile: 1020-1290. High school rank: N/A
Early decision deadline: N/A, notification date: N/A
Early action deadline: 11/15, notification date: 12/12
Application deadline (fall): rolling
Undergraduate student body: 279 full time, 20 part time; 37% male, 63% female; 0% American Indian, 8% Asian, 2% black, 15% Hispanic, 8% multiracial, 0% Pacific Islander, 41% white, 21% international; 56% from in state; 36% live on campus; N/A of students in fraternities, N/A in sororities
Most popular majors: 28% Painting, 24% Photography, 13% Printmaking, 9% Sculpture, 7% Visual and Performing Arts, Other
Expenses: 2018-2019: $46,534; room/board: $11,650
Financial aid: (415) 749-4520; 57% of undergrads determined to have financial need; average aid package $16,140

San Francisco Conservatory of Music

San Francisco CA
(800) 899-7326
U.S. News ranking: Arts, unranked
Website: www.sfcm.edu
Admissions email: admit@sfcm.edu
Private; founded 1917
Affiliation: Other
Freshman admissions: least selective; 2017-2018: 429 applied, 182 accepted. Neither SAT nor ACT required. SAT 25/75 percentile: N/A. High school rank: N/A
Early decision deadline: N/A, notification date: N/A
Early action deadline: N/A, notification date: N/A
Application deadline (fall): 12/1
Undergraduate student body: 204 full time, 1 part time; 57% male, 43% female; 1% American Indian, 8% Asian, 6% black, 6% Hispanic, 9% multiracial, 0% Pacific Islander, 34% white, 30% international; 45% from in state; 64% live on campus; 0% of students in fraternities, 0% in sororities
Most popular majors: 38% Stringed Instruments, 29% Voice and Opera, 9% Brass Instruments, 9% Keyboard Instruments, 9% Woodwind Instruments
Expenses: 2018-2019: $46,110; room/board: $14,510
Financial aid: (415) 503-6214; 83% of undergrads determined to have financial need; average aid package $35,000

San Francisco State University

San Francisco CA
(415) 338-6486
U.S. News ranking: Nat. U., second tier
Website: www.sfsu.edu
Admissions email: ugadmit@sfsu.edu
Public; founded 1899
Freshman admissions: selective; 2017-2018: 34,524 applied, 24,327 accepted. Either SAT or ACT required. SAT 25/75 percentile: 950-1150. High school rank: N/A
Early decision deadline: N/A, notification date: N/A
Early action deadline: N/A, notification date: N/A
Application deadline (fall): 11/30
Undergraduate student body: 22,200 full time, 4,417 part time; 44% male, 56% female; 0% American Indian, 26% Asian, 5% black, 33% Hispanic, 6% multiracial, 0% Pacific Islander, 18% white, 6% international; 99% from in state; 15% live on campus; N/A of students in fraternities, N/A in sororities
Most popular majors: 25% Business, Management, Marketing, and Related Support Services, 9% Communication, Journalism, and Related Programs, 8% Social Sciences, 8% Visual and Performing Arts, 6% Biological and Biomedical Sciences
Expenses: 2018-2019: $7,260 in state, $19,140 out of state; room/board: $13,462
Financial aid: (415) 338-7000; 72% of undergrads determined to have financial need; average aid package $15,520

San Jose State University

San Jose CA
(408) 283-7500
U.S. News ranking: Reg. U. (W), No. 33
Website: www.sjsu.edu/Admissions/
Admissions email: admissions@sjsu.edu
Public; founded 1857
Freshman admissions: selective; 2017-2018: 31,909 applied, 21,340 accepted. Either SAT or ACT required. SAT 25/75 percentile: 1030-1230. High school rank: N/A
Early decision deadline: N/A, notification date: N/A
Early action deadline: N/A, notification date: N/A
Application deadline (fall): 11/30
Undergraduate student body: 23,097 full time, 4,681 part time; 52% male, 48% female; 0% American Indian, 36% Asian, 3% black, 28% Hispanic, 5% multiracial, 0% Pacific Islander, 16% white, 8% international; N/A from in state; 15% live on campus; N/A of students in fraternities, N/A in sororities
Most popular majors: 22% Business, Management, Marketing, and Related Support Services, 12% Engineering, 8% Visual and Performing Arts, 7% Computer and Information Sciences and Support Services, 7% Health Professions and Related Programs
Expenses: 2018-2019: $9,850 in state, $9,850 out of state; room/board: $16,442
Financial aid: (408) 924-6086; 67% of undergrads determined to have financial need; average aid package $18,791

Santa Clara University
Santa Clara CA
(408) 554-4700
U.S. News ranking: Reg. U. (W), No. 1
Website: www.scu.edu
Admissions email: Admission@scu.edu
Private; founded 1851
Affiliation: Roman Catholic
Freshman admissions: more selective; 2017-2018: 15,061 applied, 8,067 accepted. Either SAT or ACT required. ACT 25/75 percentile: 28-32. High school rank: 57% in top tenth, 87% in top quarter, 99% in top half
Early decision deadline: 11/1, notification date: 12/31
Early action deadline: 11/1, notification date: 12/31
Application deadline (fall): 1/7
Undergraduate student body: 5,411 full time, 88 part time; 50% male, 50% female; 0% American Indian, 16% Asian, 3% black, 18% Hispanic, 7% multiracial, 0% Pacific Islander, 50% white, 4% international; 71% from in state; 56% live on campus; 0% of students in fraternities, 0% in sororities
Most popular majors: 22% Business, Management, Marketing, and Related Support Services, 15% Engineering, 14% Social Sciences, 8% Communication, Journalism, and Related Programs, 8% Psychology
Expenses: 2018-2019: $51,711; room/board: $14,910
Financial aid: (408) 551-1000; 44% of undergrads determined to have financial need; average aid package $37,051

Scripps College
Claremont CA
(909) 621-8149
U.S. News ranking: Nat. Lib. Arts, No. 30
Website: www.scrippscollege.edu/
Admissions email: admission@scrippscollege.edu
Private; founded 1926
Freshman admissions: more selective; 2017-2018: 2,841 applied, 948 accepted. Either SAT or ACT required. ACT 25/75 percentile: 29-33. High school rank: 73% in top tenth, 94% in top quarter, 98% in top half
Early decision deadline: 11/15, notification date: 12/15
Early action deadline: N/A, notification date: N/A
Application deadline (fall): 1/1
Undergraduate student body: 1,056 full time, 3 part time; 0% male, 100% female; 0% American Indian, 16% Asian, 4% black, 13% Hispanic, 4% multiracial, 0% Pacific Islander, 53% white, 5% international; 49% from in state; 100% live on campus; N/A of students in fraternities, N/A in sororities
Most popular majors: 19% Biological and Biomedical Sciences, 13% Social Sciences, 10% Psychology, 8% Area, Ethnic, Cultural, Gender, and Group Studies, 8% Visual and Performing Arts
Expenses: 2018-2019: $55,024; room/board: $16,932
Financial aid: (909) 621-8275; 38% of undergrads determined to have financial need; average aid package $44,090

Simpson University[1]
Redding CA
(530) 226-4606
U.S. News ranking: Reg. U. (W), No. 91
Website: www.simpsonu.edu
Admissions email: admissions@simpsonu.edu
Private; founded 1921
Affiliation: Christ and Missionary Alliance Church
Application deadline (fall): 8/1
Undergraduate student body: N/A full time, N/A part time
Expenses: 2017-2018: $27,700; room/board: $8,350
Financial aid: (530) 226-4621

Soka University of America
Aliso Viejo CA
(888) 600-7652
U.S. News ranking: Nat. Lib. Arts, No. 22
Website: www.soka.edu
Admissions email: admission@soka.edu
Private; founded 1987
Freshman admissions: more selective; 2017-2018: 489 applied, 182 accepted. Either SAT or ACT required. SAT 25/75 percentile: 1200-1390. High school rank: 50% in top tenth, 90% in top quarter, 100% in top half
Early decision deadline: N/A, notification date: N/A
Early action deadline: 11/1, notification date: 12/1
Application deadline (fall): 1/15
Undergraduate student body: 411 full time, 1 part time; 38% male, 62% female; 0% American Indian, 13% Asian, 4% black, 10% Hispanic, 7% multiracial, 0% Pacific Islander, 20% white, 43% international; 54% from in state; 99% live on campus; 0% of students in fraternities, 0% in sororities
Most popular majors: 100% Liberal Arts and Sciences/Liberal Studies
Expenses: 2018-2019: $33,146; room/board: $12,530
Financial aid: (949) 480-4000; 85% of undergrads determined to have financial need; average aid package $36,220

Sonoma State University
Rohnert Park CA
(707) 664-2778
U.S. News ranking: Reg. U. (W), No. 64
Website: www.sonoma.edu
Admissions email: student.outreach@sonoma.edu
Public; founded 1960
Freshman admissions: selective; 2017-2018: 15,711 applied, 12,888 accepted. Either SAT or ACT required. SAT 25/75 percentile: 980-1170. High school rank: N/A
Early decision deadline: N/A, notification date: N/A
Early action deadline: N/A, notification date: N/A
Application deadline (fall): 11/30
Undergraduate student body: 7,857 full time, 694 part time; 38% male, 62% female; 0% American Indian, 5% Asian, 2% black, 33% Hispanic, 7% multiracial, 0% Pacific Islander, 44% white, 2% international
Most popular majors: 19% Business Administration and Management, General, 14% Sociology, 9% Psychology, General, 7% Liberal Arts and Sciences/Liberal Studies, 5% Early Childhood Education and Teaching
Expenses: 2018-2019: $7,798 in state, $19,678 out of state; room/board: $13,960
Financial aid: (707) 664-2389; 60% of undergrads determined to have financial need; average aid package $10,616

Southern California Institute of Architecture[1]
Los Angeles CA
(213) 613-2200
U.S. News ranking: Arts, unranked
Website: www.sciarc.edu
Admissions email: admissions@sciarc.edu
Private
Application deadline (fall): N/A
Undergraduate student body: N/A full time, N/A part time
Expenses: N/A
Financial aid: N/A

Stanford University
Stanford CA
(650) 723-2091
U.S. News ranking: Nat. U., No. 7
Website: www.stanford.edu
Admissions email: admission@stanford.edu
Private; founded 1885
Freshman admissions: most selective; 2017-2018: 44,073 applied, 2,085 accepted. Either SAT or ACT required. SAT 25/75 percentile: 1390-1540. High school rank: 94% in top tenth, 99% in top quarter, 100% in top half
Early decision deadline: N/A, notification date: N/A
Early action deadline: 11/1, notification date: 12/15
Application deadline (fall): 1/2
Undergraduate student body: 7,061 full time, 1 part time; 50% male, 50% female; 1% American Indian, 22% Asian, 7% black, 16% Hispanic, 10% multiracial, 0% Pacific Islander, 36% white, 9% international; 41% from in state; 93% live on campus; 19% of students in fraternities, 27% in sororities
Most popular majors: 20% Engineering, 16% Computer and Information Sciences and Support Services, 16% Multi/Interdisciplinary Studies, 13% Social Sciences, 4% Biological and Biomedical Sciences
Expenses: 2018-2019: $51,354; room/board: $15,763
Financial aid: (650) 723-3058; 49% of undergrads determined to have financial need; average aid package $53,500

St. Mary's College of California
Moraga CA
(925) 631-4224
U.S. News ranking: Reg. U. (W), No. 8
Website: www.stmarys-ca.edu
Admissions email: smcadmit@stmarys-ca.edu
Private; founded 1863
Affiliation: Roman Catholic
Freshman admissions: selective; 2017-2018: 4,676 applied, 3,815 accepted. Either SAT or ACT required. SAT 25/75 percentile: 1060-1240. High school rank: N/A
Early decision deadline: N/A, notification date: N/A
Early action deadline: 11/15, notification date: 1/15
Application deadline (fall): 2/1
Undergraduate student body: 2,614 full time, 44 part time; 41% male, 59% female; 0% American Indian, 15% Asian, 4% black, 28% Hispanic, 3% multiracial, 2% Pacific Islander, 44% white, 3% international; 88% from in state; 60% live on campus; 0% of students in fraternities, 0% in sororities
Most popular majors: 32% Business, Management, Marketing, and Related Support Services, 11% Social Sciences, 8% Liberal Arts and Sciences, General Studies and Humanities, 8% Psychology, 6% Biological and Biomedical Sciences
Expenses: 2018-2019: $47,280; room/board: $15,370
Financial aid: (925) 631-4370; 69% of undergrads determined to have financial need; average aid package $31,609

Thomas Aquinas College
Santa Paula CA
(800) 634-9797
U.S. News ranking: Nat. Lib. Arts, No. 43
Website: www.thomasaquinas.edu
Admissions email: admissions@thomasaquinas.edu
Private; founded 1971
Affiliation: Roman Catholic
Freshman admissions: more selective; 2017-2018: 192 applied, 138 accepted. Either SAT or ACT required. SAT 25/75 percentile: 1200-1380. High school rank: 54% in top tenth, 72% in top quarter, 91% in top half
Early decision deadline: N/A, notification date: N/A
Early action deadline: N/A, notification date: N/A
Application deadline (fall): rolling
Undergraduate student body: 370 full time, 0 part time; 48% male, 52% female; 1% American Indian, 2% Asian, 1% black, 16% Hispanic, 5% multiracial, 0% Pacific Islander, 72% white, 2% international; 40% from in state; 100% live on campus; N/A of students in fraternities, N/A in sororities
Most popular majors: Information not available
Expenses: 2018-2019: $25,000; room/board: $8,400
Financial aid: (805) 421-5936; 70% of undergrads determined to have financial need; average aid package $20,095

Trident University International[1]
Cypress CA
(800) 375-9878
U.S. News ranking: Nat. U., unranked
Website: www.trident.edu
Admissions email: N/A
For-profit
Application deadline (fall): N/A
Undergraduate student body: N/A full time, N/A part time
Expenses: 2017-2018: $9,240; room/board: N/A
Financial aid: N/A

United States University[1]
Chula Vista CA
U.S. News ranking: Reg. Coll. (W), unranked
Admissions email: N/A
For-profit
Application deadline (fall): N/A
Undergraduate student body: N/A full time, N/A part time
Expenses: 2017-2018: $12,020; room/board: N/A
Financial aid: N/A

University of California–Berkeley
Berkeley CA
(510) 642-3175
U.S. News ranking: Nat. U., No. 22
Website: www.berkeley.edu
Admissions email: N/A
Public; founded 1868
Freshman admissions: most selective; 2017-2018: 85,057 applied, 14,552 accepted. Either SAT or ACT required. SAT 25/75 percentile: 1300-1530. High school rank: 98% in top tenth, 100% in top quarter, 100% in top half
Early decision deadline: N/A, notification date: N/A
Early action deadline: N/A, notification date: N/A
Application deadline (fall): 11/30
Undergraduate student body: 29,351 full time, 1,223 part time; 47% male, 53% female; 0% American Indian, 35% Asian, 2% black, 15% Hispanic, 6% multiracial, 0% Pacific Islander, 26% white, 12% international; 84% from in state; 25% live on campus; 10% of students in fraternities, 10% in sororities
Most popular majors: 18% Social Sciences, 12% Engineering, 11% Biological and Biomedical Sciences, 7% Multi/Interdisciplinary Studies, 6% Computer and Information Sciences and Support Services
Expenses: 2018-2019: $14,240 in state, $43,232 out of state; room/board: $17,764

More @ usnews.com/bestcolleges

Financial aid: (510) 642-7117; 48% of undergrads determined to have financial need; average aid package $24,048

University of California–Davis

Davis CA
(530) 752-2971
U.S. News ranking: Nat. U., No. 38
Website: www.ucdavis.edu
Admissions email: undergraduateadmissions@ucdavis.edu
Public; founded 1905
Freshman admissions: more selective; 2017-2018: 70,214 applied, 30,573 accepted. Either SAT or ACT required. SAT 25/75 percentile: 1120-1360. High school rank: 100% in top tenth, 100% in top quarter, 100% in top half
Early decision deadline: N/A, notification date: N/A
Early action deadline: N/A, notification date: N/A
Application deadline (fall): 11/30
Undergraduate student body: 29,362 full time, 783 part time; 40% male, 60% female; 0% American Indian, 28% Asian, 2% black, 21% Hispanic, 5% multiracial, 0% Pacific Islander, 25% white, 16% international
Most popular majors: Information not available
Expenses: 2018-2019: $14,463 in state, $43,458 out of state; room/board: $15,765
Financial aid: (530) 752-2396; 60% of undergrads determined to have financial need; average aid package $21,951

University of California–Irvine

Irvine CA
(949) 824-6703
U.S. News ranking: Nat. U., No. 33
Website: www.uci.edu
Admissions email: admissions@uci.edu
Public; founded 1965
Freshman admissions: more selective; 2017-2018: 85,102 applied, 31,063 accepted. Either SAT or ACT required. SAT 25/75 percentile: 1170-1410. High school rank: 98% in top tenth, 100% in top quarter, 100% in top half
Early decision deadline: N/A, notification date: N/A
Early action deadline: N/A, notification date: N/A
Application deadline (fall): 11/30
Undergraduate student body: 28,851 full time, 456 part time; 47% male, 53% female; 0% American Indian, 36% Asian, 2% black, 26% Hispanic, 4% multiracial, 0% Pacific Islander, 14% white, 17% international; 97% from in state; 61% live on campus; 8% of students in fraternities, 9% in sororities
Most popular majors: 9% Social Psychology, 8% Public Health, Other, 7% Biology/Biological Sciences, General, 7% Business/Managerial Economics, 6% Computer Science
Expenses: 2017-2018: $15,516 in state, $43,530 out of state; room/board: $14,829
Financial aid: (949) 824-5337; 64% of undergrads determined to have financial need; average aid package $23,438

University of California–Los Angeles

Los Angeles CA
(310) 825-3101
U.S. News ranking: Nat. U., No. 19
Website: www.ucla.edu/
Admissions email: ugadm@saonet.ucla.edu
Public; founded 1919
Freshman admissions: most selective; 2017-2018: 102,242 applied, 16,456 accepted. Either SAT or ACT required. SAT 25/75 percentile: 1240-1500. High school rank: 97% in top tenth, 100% in top quarter, 100% in top half
Early decision deadline: N/A, notification date: N/A
Early action deadline: N/A, notification date: N/A
Application deadline (fall): 11/30
Undergraduate student body: 30,458 full time, 544 part time; 43% male, 57% female; 0% American Indian, 28% Asian, 3% black, 22% Hispanic, 5% multiracial, 0% Pacific Islander, 27% white, 12% international; 88% from in state; 48% live on campus; 11% of students in fraternities, 13% in sororities
Most popular majors: 26% Social Sciences, 13% Biological and Biomedical Sciences, 11% Psychology, 7% Engineering, 7% Multi/Interdisciplinary Studies
Expenses: 2018-2019: $13,280 in state, $41,294 out of state; room/board: $15,991
Financial aid: (310) 206-0401; 54% of undergrads determined to have financial need; average aid package $23,980

University of California–Merced

Merced CA
(866) 270-7301
U.S. News ranking: Nat. U., No. 136
Website: www.ucmerced.edu
Admissions email: admissions@ucmerced.edu
Public; founded 2005
Freshman admissions: less selective; 2017-2018: 22,574 applied, 15,619 accepted. Either SAT or ACT required. SAT 25/75 percentile: 910-1120. High school rank: 21% in top tenth, N/A in top quarter, N/A in top half
Early decision deadline: N/A, notification date: N/A
Early action deadline: N/A, notification date: N/A
Application deadline (fall): 11/30
Undergraduate student body: 7,297 full time, 78 part time; 49% male, 51% female; 0% American Indian, 20% Asian, 5% black, 53% Hispanic, 3% multiracial, 1% Pacific Islander, 10% white, 7% international; 100% from in state; 38% live on campus; N/A of students in fraternities, N/A in sororities
Most popular majors: 23% Biological and Biomedical Sciences, 18% Engineering, 17% Psychology, 15% Social Sciences, 11% Business, Management, Marketing, and Related Support Services
Expenses: 2018-2019: $13,627 in state, $41,641 out of state; room/board: $16,454
Financial aid: (209) 228-7178; 90% of undergrads determined to have financial need; average aid package $25,198

University of California–Riverside

Riverside CA
(951) 827-3411
U.S. News ranking: Nat. U., No. 85
Website: www.ucr.edu
Admissions email: admissions@ucr.edu
Public; founded 1954
Freshman admissions: more selective; 2017-2018: 43,682 applied, 25,001 accepted. Either SAT or ACT required. SAT 25/75 percentile: 1090-1300. High school rank: 94% in top tenth, 100% in top quarter, 100% in top half
Early decision deadline: N/A, notification date: N/A
Early action deadline: N/A, notification date: N/A
Application deadline (fall): 11/30
Undergraduate student body: 19,716 full time, 353 part time; 46% male, 54% female; 0% American Indian, 34% Asian, 3% black, 41% Hispanic, 6% multiracial, 0% Pacific Islander, 11% white, 3% international; 99% from in state; 31% live on campus; 4% of students in fraternities, 7% in sororities
Most popular majors: 21% Social Sciences, 18% Business, Management, Marketing, and Related Support Services, 14% Biological and Biomedical Sciences, 10% Psychology, 9% Engineering
Expenses: 2018-2019: $13,887 in state, $42,879 out of state; room/board: $16,000
Financial aid: (951) 827-7249; 78% of undergrads determined to have financial need; average aid package $23,586

University of California–San Diego

La Jolla CA
(858) 534-4831
U.S. News ranking: Nat. U., No. 41
Website: www.ucsd.edu/
Admissions email: admissionsinfo@ucsd.edu
Public; founded 1960
Freshman admissions: most selective; 2017-2018: 88,428 applied, 30,212 accepted. Either SAT or ACT required. SAT 25/75 percentile: 1140-1380. High school rank: 100% in top tenth, 100% in top quarter, 100% in top half
Early decision deadline: N/A, notification date: N/A
Early action deadline: N/A, notification date: N/A
Application deadline (fall): 11/30
Undergraduate student body: 28,159 full time, 428 part time; 51% male, 49% female; 0% American Indian, 38% Asian, 2% black, 18% Hispanic, 0% multiracial, 0% Pacific Islander, 19% white, 20% international; 94% from in state; 40% live on campus; 12% of students in fraternities, 12% in sororities
Most popular majors: 21% Biology, General, 12% Economics, 10% Computer Engineering, 5% Psychology, General, 4% Electrical, Electronics and Communications Engineering
Expenses: 2018-2019: $14,060 in state, $42,074 out of state; room/board: $13,733
Financial aid: (858) 534-4480; 57% of undergrads determined to have financial need; average aid package $24,288

University of California–Santa Barbara

Santa Barbara CA
(805) 893-2881
U.S. News ranking: Nat. U., No. 30
Website: www.ucsb.edu/
Admissions email: admissions@sa.ucsb.edu
Public; founded 1909
Freshman admissions: most selective; 2017-2018: 80,319 applied, 26,295 accepted. Either SAT or ACT required. SAT 25/75 percentile: 1240-1470. High school rank: 100% in top tenth, 100% in top quarter, 100% in top half
Early decision deadline: N/A, notification date: N/A
Early action deadline: N/A, notification date: N/A
Application deadline (fall): 11/30
Undergraduate student body: 21,776 full time, 410 part time; 46% male, 54% female; 0% American Indian, 20% Asian, 2% black, 27% Hispanic, 6% multiracial, 0% Pacific Islander, 33% white, 10% international; 96% from in state; 38% live on campus; 4% of students in fraternities, 8% in sororities
Most popular majors: 25% Social Sciences, 10% Biological and Biomedical Sciences, 9% Multi/Interdisciplinary Studies, 9% Psychology, 7% Communication, Journalism, and Related Programs
Expenses: 2018-2019: $14,472 in state, $42,486 out of state; room/board: $15,673
Financial aid: (805) 893-2432; 59% of undergrads determined to have financial need; average aid package $23,771

University of California–Santa Cruz

Santa Cruz CA
(831) 459-4008
U.S. News ranking: Nat. U., No. 70
Website: www.ucsc.edu
Admissions email: admissions@ucsc.edu
Public; founded 1965
Freshman admissions: more selective; 2017-2018: 52,975 applied, 27,235 accepted. Either SAT or ACT required. SAT 25/75 percentile: 1160-1370. High school rank: 96% in top tenth, 100% in top quarter, 100% in top half
Early decision deadline: N/A, notification date: N/A
Early action deadline: N/A, notification date: N/A
Application deadline (fall): 11/30
Undergraduate student body: 17,082 full time, 495 part time; 50% male, 50% female; 0% American Indian, 22% Asian, 2% black, 28% Hispanic, 8% multiracial, 0% Pacific Islander, 31% white, 6% international; 96% from in state; 52% live on campus; 6% of students in fraternities, 8% in sororities
Most popular majors: 10% Psychology, General, 6% Business/Managerial Economics, 6% Computer and Information Sciences, General, 6% Sociology, 5% Cell/Cellular and Molecular Biology
Expenses: 2018-2019: $13,949 in state, $41,963 out of state; room/board: $16,407
Financial aid: (831) 459-2963; 63% of undergrads determined to have financial need; average aid package $25,754

University of La Verne

La Verne CA
(800) 876-4858
U.S. News ranking: Nat. U., No. 136
Website: www.laverne.edu
Admissions email: admission@laverne.edu
Private; founded 1891
Freshman admissions: selective; 2017-2018: 8,012 applied, 3,809 accepted. Either SAT or ACT required. SAT 25/75 percentile: 1030-1195. High school rank: 20% in top tenth, 49% in top quarter, 84% in top half
Early decision deadline: N/A, notification date: N/A
Early action deadline: N/A, notification date: N/A
Application deadline (fall): rolling
Undergraduate student body: 2,673 full time, 80 part time; 42% male, 58% female; 0% American Indian, 6% Asian, 5% black, 57% Hispanic, 5% multiracial, 1% Pacific Islander, 19% white, 6% international; 96% from in state; 30% live on campus; 3% of students in fraternities, 6% in sororities
Most popular majors: 25% Business, Management, Marketing, and Related Support Services, 15% Psychology, 11% Education, 10% Social Sciences, 9% Biological and Biomedical Sciences
Expenses: 2018-2019: $43,050; room/board: $12,850
Financial aid: (800) 649-0160; 84% of undergrads determined to have financial need; average aid package $32,166

University of Redlands

Redlands CA
(800) 455-5064
U.S. News ranking: Reg. U. (W), No. 11
Website: www.redlands.edu
Admissions email: admissions@redlands.edu
Private; founded 1907
Freshman admissions: selective; 2017-2018: 4,776 applied, 3,580 accepted. Either SAT or ACT required. SAT 25/75 percentile: 1070-1250. High school rank: N/A
Early decision deadline: N/A, notification date: N/A
Early action deadline: 11/15, notification date: 1/15
Application deadline (fall): 1/15
Undergraduate student body: 2,518 full time, 613 part time; 43% male, 57% female; N/A American Indian, N/A Asian, N/A black, N/A Hispanic, N/A multiracial, N/A Pacific Islander, N/A white, N/A international
Most popular majors: Information not available
Expenses: 2017-2018: $48,072; room/board: $13,862
Financial aid: (909) 748-8266

University of San Diego

San Diego CA
(619) 260-4506
U.S. News ranking: Nat. U., No. 85
Website: www.SanDiego.edu
Admissions email: admissions@SanDiego.edu
Private; founded 1949
Affiliation: Roman Catholic
Freshman admissions: more selective; 2017-2018: 14,739 applied, 7,339 accepted. Either SAT or ACT required. ACT 25/75 percentile: 26-30. High school rank: 40% in top tenth, 75% in top quarter, 96% in top half
Early decision deadline: N/A, notification date: N/A
Early action deadline: N/A, notification date: N/A
Application deadline (fall): 12/15
Undergraduate student body: 5,605 full time, 169 part time; 46% male, 54% female; 0% American Indian, 8% Asian, 4% black, 20% Hispanic, 6% multiracial, 0% Pacific Islander, 52% white, 8% international; 62% from in state; 46% live on campus; 23% of students in fraternities, 31% in sororities
Most popular majors: 44% Business, Management, Marketing, and Related Support Services, 12% Biological and Biomedical Sciences, 12% Social Sciences, 8% Communication, Journalism, and Related Programs, 6% Engineering
Expenses: 2018-2019: $49,358; room/board: $12,980
Financial aid: (619) 260-2700; 52% of undergrads determined to have financial need; average aid package $35,580

University of San Francisco

San Francisco CA
(415) 422-6563
U.S. News ranking: Nat. U., No. 96
Website: www.usfca.edu
Admissions email: admission@usfca.edu
Private; founded 1855
Affiliation: Roman Catholic
Freshman admissions: more selective; 2017-2018: 16,313 applied, 10,707 accepted. Either SAT or ACT required. SAT 25/75 percentile: 1100-1290. High school rank: 24% in top tenth, 63% in top quarter, 93% in top half
Early decision deadline: 11/1, notification date: 12/1
Early action deadline: 11/1, notification date: 12/14
Application deadline (fall): 1/15
Undergraduate student body: 6,586 full time, 261 part time; 38% male, 62% female; 0% American Indian, 22% Asian, 4% black, 22% Hispanic, 7% multiracial, 1% Pacific Islander, 26% white, 17% international; 82% from in state; 21% live on campus; 3% of students in fraternities, 11% in sororities
Most popular majors: 13% Business Administration and Management, General, 12% Registered Nursing/Registered Nurse, 8% Finance, General, 8% Psychology, General, 6% Business Administration and Management, General
Expenses: 2018-2019: $48,066; room/board: $14,830
Financial aid: (415) 422-2020; 57% of undergrads determined to have financial need; average aid package $35,212

University of Southern California

Los Angeles CA
(213) 740-1111
U.S. News ranking: Nat. U., No. 22
Website: www.usc.edu/
Admissions email: admitusc@usc.edu
Private; founded 1880
Freshman admissions: most selective; 2017-2018: 56,676 applied, 9,042 accepted. Either SAT or ACT required. ACT 25/75 percentile: 30-34. High school rank: 88% in top tenth, 96% in top quarter, 100% in top half
Early decision deadline: N/A, notification date: N/A
Early action deadline: N/A, notification date: N/A
Application deadline (fall): 1/15
Undergraduate student body: 18,631 full time, 539 part time; 48% male, 52% female; 0% American Indian, 21% Asian, 5% black, 14% Hispanic, 6% multiracial, 0% Pacific Islander, 40% white, 13% international; 65% from in state; 30% live on campus; 26% of students in fraternities, 27% in sororities
Most popular majors: 24% Business, Management, Marketing, and Related Support Services, 12% Social Sciences, 12% Visual and Performing Arts, 10% Engineering, 9% Communication, Journalism, and Related Programs
Expenses: 2018-2019: $56,225; room/board: $15,400
Financial aid: (213) 740-4444; 38% of undergrads determined to have financial need; average aid package $51,509

University of the Antelope Valley[1]

Lancaster CA
U.S. News ranking: Reg. Coll. (W), unranked
Website: www.uav.edu
Admissions email: N/A
Public
Application deadline (fall): N/A
Undergraduate student body: N/A full time, N/A part time
Expenses: N/A
Financial aid: N/A

University of the Pacific

Stockton CA
(209) 946-2011
U.S. News ranking: Nat. U., No. 106
Website: www.pacific.edu
Admissions email: admissions@pacific.edu
Private; founded 1851
Freshman admissions: more selective; 2017-2018: 13,064 applied, 8,475 accepted. Either SAT or ACT required. SAT 25/75 percentile: 1070-1330. High school rank: 34% in top tenth, 68% in top quarter, 94% in top half
Early decision deadline: N/A, notification date: N/A
Early action deadline: 11/15, notification date: 1/15
Application deadline (fall): 1/15
Undergraduate student body: 3,452 full time, 96 part time; 46% male, 54% female; 0% American Indian, 36% Asian, 3% black, 20% Hispanic, 7% multiracial, 0% Pacific Islander, 23% white, 6% international; 93% from in state; 44% live on campus; 4% of students in fraternities, 6% in sororities
Most popular majors: Information not available
Expenses: 2018-2019: $48,040; room/board: $13,650
Financial aid: (209) 946-2421; 71% of undergrads determined to have financial need; average aid package $34,876

University of the West[1]

Rosemead CA
(855) 468-9378
U.S. News ranking: Reg. Coll. (W), unranked
Website: www.uwest.edu
Admissions email: admission@uwest.edu
Private; founded 1991
Application deadline (fall): 5/1
Undergraduate student body: N/A full time, N/A part time
Expenses: 2017-2018: $11,990; room/board: $7,514
Financial aid: (626) 571-8811

Vanguard University of Southern California

Costa Mesa CA
(714) 966-5496
U.S. News ranking: Reg. U. (W), No. 54
Website: www.vanguard.edu
Admissions email: admissions@vanguard.edu
Private; founded 1920
Affiliation: Assemblies of God Church
Freshman admissions: selective; 2017-2018: 3,352 applied, 1,621 accepted. Either SAT or ACT required. SAT 25/75 percentile: 930-1120. High school rank: 14% in top tenth, 42% in top quarter, 74% in top half
Early decision deadline: N/A, notification date: N/A
Early action deadline: 12/1, notification date: 1/15
Application deadline (fall): 8/1
Undergraduate student body: 1,511 full time, 294 part time; 35% male, 65% female; 0% American Indian, 3% Asian, 5% black, 40% Hispanic, 4% multiracial, 1% Pacific Islander, 40% white, 1% international; 89% from in state; 50% live on campus; 0% of students in fraternities, 0% in sororities
Most popular majors: 23% Business Administration and Management, General, 16% Psychology, General, 14% Speech Communication and Rhetoric, 12% Kinesiology and Exercise Science, 6% Education, General
Expenses: 2018-2019: $33,720; room/board: $9,980
Financial aid: (714) 966-5490; 87% of undergrads determined to have financial need; average aid package $14,614

Westmont College

Santa Barbara CA
(805) 565-6000
U.S. News ranking: Nat. Lib. Arts, No. 108
Website: www.westmont.edu
Admissions email: admissions@westmont.edu
Private; founded 1937
Freshman admissions: more selective; 2017-2018: 1,826 applied, 1,546 accepted. Either SAT or ACT required. SAT 25/75 percentile: 1130-1380. High school rank: 40% in top tenth, 64% in top quarter, 91% in top half
Early decision deadline: N/A, notification date: N/A
Early action deadline: 11/15, notification date: 12/1
Application deadline (fall): rolling
Undergraduate student body: 1,298 full time, 5 part time; 39% male, 61% female; 0% American Indian, 7% Asian, 2% black, 18% Hispanic, 6% multiracial, 0% Pacific Islander, 62% white, 1% international; 73% from in state; 85% live on campus; N/A of students in fraternities, N/A in sororities
Most popular majors: 17% Business, Management, Marketing, and Related Support Services, 15% Parks, Recreation, Leisure, and Fitness Studies, 10% Biological and Biomedical Sciences, 8% Social Sciences, 8% Visual and Performing Arts
Expenses: 2018-2019: $45,304; room/board: $14,296
Financial aid: (805) 565-6063; 69% of undergrads determined to have financial need; average aid package $33,174

Whittier College

Whittier CA
(562) 907-4238
U.S. News ranking: Nat. Lib. Arts, No. 108
Website: www.whittier.edu
Admissions email: admission@whittier.edu
Private; founded 1887
Freshman admissions: selective; 2017-2018: 5,773 applied, 4,277 accepted. Neither SAT nor ACT required. SAT 25/75 percentile: 1010-1220. High school rank: 21% in top tenth, 33% in top quarter, 92% in top half
Early decision deadline: N/A, notification date: N/A
Early action deadline: 11/15, notification date: 12/30
Application deadline (fall): rolling
Undergraduate student body: 1,640 full time, 41 part time; 43% male, 57% female; 0% American Indian, 7% Asian, 5% black, 50% Hispanic, 7% multiracial, 0% Pacific Islander, 27% white, 3% international; N/A from in state; 50% live on campus; 2% of students in fraternities, 3% in sororities
Most popular majors: 22% Social Sciences, 18% Business, Management, Marketing, and Related Support Services, 10% Parks, Recreation, Leisure, and Fitness Studies, 8% Psychology, 7% Biological and Biomedical Sciences
Expenses: 2018-2019: $47,886; room/board: $13,742
Financial aid: (562) 907-4285; 78% of undergrads determined to have financial need; average aid package $37,931

William Jessup University

Rocklin CA
(916) 577-2222
U.S. News ranking: Reg. Coll. (W), No. 2
Website: www.jessup.edu
Admissions email: admissions@jessup.edu
Private; founded 1939
Freshman admissions: selective; 2017-2018: 816 applied, 539 accepted. Either SAT or ACT required. SAT 25/75 percentile: 1000-1215. High school rank: 24% in top tenth, 43% in top quarter, 84% in top half
Early decision deadline: N/A, notification date: N/A
Early action deadline: N/A, notification date: N/A
Application deadline (fall): 8/18
Undergraduate student body: 987 full time, 217 part time; 41% male, 59% female; 2% American Indian, 5% Asian, 6% black, 20% Hispanic, 1% multiracial, 1% Pacific Islander, 60% white,

More @ usnews.com/bestcolleges

3% international; 93% from in state; 53% live on campus; 0% of students in fraternities, 0% in sororities
Most popular majors: 25% Psychology, 22% Business, Management, Marketing, and Related Support Services, 13% Theology and Religious Vocations, 10% Education, 6% Visual and Performing Arts
Expenses: 2018-2019: $33,550; room/board: $11,320
Financial aid: (916) 577-2232; 81% of undergrads determined to have financial need; average aid package $23,400

Woodbury University

Burbank CA
(818) 252-5221
U.S. News ranking: Reg. U. (W), No. 59
Website: woodbury.edu/
Admissions email: info@woodbury.edu
Private; founded 1884
Freshman admissions: selective; 2017-2018: 1,327 applied, 818 accepted. Neither SAT nor ACT required. SAT 25/75 percentile: 955-1188. High school rank: N/A
Early decision deadline: N/A, notification date: N/A
Early action deadline: N/A, notification date: N/A
Application deadline (fall): rolling
Undergraduate student body: 923 full time, 101 part time; 50% male, 50% female; 0% American Indian, 9% Asian, 3% black, 31% Hispanic, 3% multiracial, 0% Pacific Islander, 32% white, 21% international; 85% from in state; 18% live on campus; N/A of students in fraternities, N/A in sororities
Most popular majors: Information not available
Expenses: 2018-2019: $39,780; room/board: $11,920
Financial aid: (818) 252-5273; 66% of undergrads determined to have financial need; average aid package $23,281

COLORADO

Adams State University[1]

Alamosa CO
(800) 824-6494
U.S. News ranking: Reg. U. (W), second tier
Website: www.adams.edu
Admissions email: ascadmit@adams.edu
Public
Application deadline (fall): N/A
Undergraduate student body: N/A full time, N/A part time
Expenses: 2017-2018: $9,440 in state, $20,456 out of state; room/board: $8,630
Financial aid: N/A

Art Institute of Colorado[1]

Denver CO
(303) 837-0825
U.S. News ranking: Arts, unranked
Website: www.artinstitutes.edu/denver/
Admissions email: N/A
For-profit
Application deadline (fall): N/A
Undergraduate student body: N/A full time, N/A part time
Expenses: N/A
Financial aid: N/A

Colorado Christian University[1]

Lakewood CO
(303) 963-3200
U.S. News ranking: Reg. U. (W), second tier
Website: www.ccu.edu
Admissions email: admission@ccu.edu
Private
Application deadline (fall): N/A
Undergraduate student body: N/A full time, N/A part time
Expenses: 2017-2018: $30,370; room/board: $10,516
Financial aid: N/A

Colorado College

Colorado Springs CO
(719) 389-6344
U.S. News ranking: Nat. Lib. Arts, No. 27
Website: www.ColoradoCollege.edu
Admissions email: admission@ColoradoCollege.edu
Private; founded 1874
Freshman admissions: most selective; 2017-2018: 8,223 applied, 1,244 accepted. Neither SAT nor ACT required. ACT 25/75 percentile: 29-33. High school rank: 70% in top tenth, 94% in top quarter, 99% in top half
Early decision deadline: 11/10, notification date: 12/15
Early action deadline: 11/10, notification date: 12/20
Application deadline (fall): 1/15
Undergraduate student body: 2,091 full time, 16 part time; 46% male, 54% female; 1% American Indian, 4% Asian, 3% black, 9% Hispanic, 9% multiracial, 0% Pacific Islander, 66% white, 8% international; 17% from in state; 78% live on campus; N/A of students in fraternities, N/A in sororities
Most popular majors: 8% Economics, General, 6% Political Science and Government, General, 6% Sociology, 5% Cell/Cellular and Molecular Biology, 5% Environmental Science
Expenses: 2018-2019: $55,470; room/board: $12,512
Financial aid: (719) 389-6651; 32% of undergrads determined to have financial need; average aid package $48,900

Colorado Mesa University

Grand Junction CO
(970) 248-1875
U.S. News ranking: Reg. Coll. (W), No. 25
Website: www.coloradomesa.edu/
Admissions email: admissions@coloradomesa.edu
Public; founded 1925
Freshman admissions: selective; 2017-2018: 6,982 applied, 5,702 accepted. Either SAT or ACT required. ACT 25/75 percentile: 18-24. High school rank: 10% in top tenth, 29% in top quarter, 59% in top half
Early decision deadline: N/A, notification date: N/A
Early action deadline: N/A, notification date: N/A
Application deadline (fall): rolling
Undergraduate student body: 7,145 full time, 2,314 part time; 47% male, 53% female; 1% American Indian, 2% Asian, 2% black, 19% Hispanic, 4% multiracial, 1% Pacific Islander, 69% white, 1% international; 86% from in state; 23% live on campus; N/A of students in fraternities, N/A in sororities
Most popular majors: 17% Business/Commerce, General, 12% Kinesiology and Exercise Science, 10% Registered Nursing/Registered Nurse, 7% Biology/Biological Sciences, General, 6% Criminal Justice/Safety Studies
Expenses: 2018-2019: $9,243 in state, $22,440 out of state; room/board: $10,925
Financial aid: (970) 248-1396; 65% of undergrads determined to have financial need; average aid package $9,301

Colorado Mountain College[1]

Glenwood Springs CO
(970) 945-8691
U.S. News ranking: Reg. Coll. (W), unranked
Admissions email: joinus@coloradomtn.edu
Public; founded 1967
Application deadline (fall): rolling
Undergraduate student body: N/A full time, N/A part time
Expenses: 2017-2018: $6,360 in state, $13,200 out of state; room/board: $9,280
Financial aid: N/A

Colorado School of Mines

Golden CO
(303) 273-3220
U.S. News ranking: Nat. U., No. 80
Website: www.mines.edu
Admissions email: admissions@mines.edu
Public; founded 1874
Freshman admissions: more selective; 2017-2018: 10,619 applied, 5,916 accepted. Either SAT or ACT required. ACT 25/75 percentile: 28-32. High school rank: 49% in top tenth, 87% in top quarter, 99% in top half
Early decision deadline: N/A, notification date: N/A
Early action deadline: N/A, notification date: N/A
Application deadline (fall): 5/1
Undergraduate student body: 4,546 full time, 248 part time; 71% male, 29% female; 0% American Indian, 5% Asian, 1% black, 8% Hispanic, 5% multiracial, 0% Pacific Islander, 73% white, 6% international; 61% from in state; 11% live on campus; 12% of students in fraternities, 24% in sororities
Most popular majors: 89% Engineering, 6% Computer and Information Sciences and Support Services, 2% Mathematics and Statistics, 2% Physical Sciences, 1% Social Sciences
Expenses: 2018-2019: $18,964 in state, $38,584 out of state; room/board: $13,169
Financial aid: (303) 273-3301; 45% of undergrads determined to have financial need; average aid package $13,912

Colorado State University

Fort Collins CO
(970) 491-6909
U.S. News ranking: Nat. U., No. 140
Website: www.colostate.edu
Admissions email: admissions@colostate.edu
Public; founded 1870
Freshman admissions: selective; 2017-2018: 23,137 applied, 19,116 accepted. Either SAT or ACT required. ACT 25/75 percentile: 22-28. High school rank: 20% in top tenth, 47% in top quarter, 82% in top half
Early decision deadline: N/A, notification date: N/A
Early action deadline: 12/1, notification date: 2/1
Application deadline (fall): 8/1
Undergraduate student body: 21,969 full time, 3,934 part time; 48% male, 52% female; 0% American Indian, 3% Asian, 2% black, 13% Hispanic, 4% multiracial, 0% Pacific Islander, 72% white, 4% international; 76% from in state; 26% live on campus; 5% of students in fraternities, 7% in sororities
Most popular majors: 14% Business, Management, Marketing, and Related Support Services, 11% Biological and Biomedical Sciences, 9% Engineering, 9% Social Sciences, 7% Parks, Recreation, Leisure, and Fitness Studies
Expenses: 2018-2019: $11,982 in state, $29,884 out of state; room/board: $12,566
Financial aid: (970) 491-6321; 51% of undergrads determined to have financial need; average aid package $11,635

Colorado State University–Pueblo

Pueblo CO
(719) 549-2461
U.S. News ranking: Reg. U. (W), second tier
Website: www.csupueblo.edu
Admissions email: info@colostate-pueblo.edu
Public; founded 1933
Freshman admissions: less selective; 2017-2018: 5,899 applied, 5,624 accepted. Either SAT or ACT required. ACT 25/75 percentile: 18-23. High school rank: 13% in top tenth, 36% in top quarter, 68% in top half
Early decision deadline: N/A, notification date: N/A
Early action deadline: N/A, notification date: N/A
Application deadline (fall): 8/1
Undergraduate student body: 3,292 full time, 1,329 part time; 48% male, 52% female; 1% American Indian, 1% Asian, 7% black, 34% Hispanic, 5% multiracial, 0% Pacific Islander, 48% white, 2% international; 86% from in state; 22% live on campus; 1% of students in fraternities, 1% in sororities
Most popular majors: 12% Registered Nursing/Registered Nurse, 11% Business/Commerce, General, 11% Sociology, 8% Kinesiology and Exercise Science, 6% Mass Communication/Media Studies
Expenses: 2018-2019: $12,867 in state, $28,787 out of state; room/board: $10,068
Financial aid: (719) 549-2753; 78% of undergrads determined to have financial need; average aid package $12,173

Colorado Technical University[1]

Colorado Springs CO
(888) 404-7555
U.S. News ranking: Reg. U. (W), unranked
Website: www.coloradotech.edu
Admissions email: info@ctuonline.edu
For-profit
Application deadline (fall): N/A
Undergraduate student body: N/A full time, N/A part time
Expenses: 2017-2018: $11,689; room/board: N/A
Financial aid: N/A

Fort Lewis College

Durango CO
(970) 247-7184
U.S. News ranking: Nat. Lib. Arts, second tier
Website: www.fortlewis.edu
Admissions email: admission@fortlewis.edu
Public; founded 1911
Freshman admissions: selective; 2017-2018: 4,473 applied, 3,722 accepted. Either SAT or ACT required. ACT 25/75 percentile: 20-25. High school rank: 13% in top tenth, 21% in top quarter, 73% in top half
Early decision deadline: N/A, notification date: N/A
Early action deadline: N/A, notification date: N/A
Application deadline (fall): 8/1
Undergraduate student body: 2,921 full time, 378 part time; 48% male, 52% female; 26% American Indian, 1% Asian, 1% black, 11% Hispanic, 9% multiracial, 0% Pacific Islander, 48% white, 0% international; 48% from in state; 42% live on campus; 0% of students in fraternities, 0% in sororities
Most popular majors: 20% Business, Management, Marketing, and Related Support Services, 12% Social Sciences, 10% Parks, Recreation, Leisure, and Fitness Studies, 8% Visual and Performing Arts, 7% Physical Sciences
Expenses: 2018-2019: $9,040 in state, $19,696 out of state; room/board: $9,878
Financial aid: (970) 247-7142; 56% of undergrads determined to have financial need; average aid package $17,537

Metropolitan State University of Denver
Denver CO
(303) 556-3058
U.S. News ranking: Reg. U. (W), second tier
Website: www.msudenver.edu
Admissions email: askmetro@msudenver.edu
Public; founded 1963
Freshman admissions: less selective; 2017-2018: 11,435 applied, 7,348 accepted. Either SAT or ACT required. ACT 25/75 percentile: 17-22. High school rank: 2% in top tenth, 14% in top quarter, 49% in top half
Early decision deadline: N/A, notification date: N/A
Early action deadline: N/A, notification date: N/A
Application deadline (fall): 7/1
Undergraduate student body: 12,759 full time, 6,907 part time; 47% male, 53% female; 1% American Indian, 4% Asian, 6% black, 27% Hispanic, 5% multiracial, 0% Pacific Islander, 54% white, 1% international
Most popular majors: 6% Biology/Biological Sciences, General, 6% Psychology, General, 5% Business Administration and Management, General, 5% Criminal Justice/Safety Studies, 4% Accounting
Expenses: 2017-2018: $7,352 in state, $20,149 out of state; room/board: N/A
Financial aid: (303) 605-5504; 66% of undergrads determined to have financial need; average aid package $9,130

Naropa University
Boulder CO
(303) 546-3572
U.S. News ranking: Reg. U. (W), unranked
Website: www.naropa.edu
Admissions email: admissions@naropa.edu
Private; founded 1974
Freshman admissions: least selective; 2017-2018: 105 applied, 105 accepted. Neither SAT nor ACT required. SAT 25/75 percentile: N/A. High school rank: N/A
Early decision deadline: N/A, notification date: N/A
Early action deadline: N/A, notification date: N/A
Application deadline (fall): rolling
Undergraduate student body: 368 full time, 29 part time; 35% male, 65% female; 0% American Indian, 1% Asian, 1% black, 11% Hispanic, 10% multiracial, 0% Pacific Islander, 62% white, 3% international; 37% from in state; 18% live on campus; 0% of students in fraternities, 0% in sororities
Most popular majors: 33% Psychology, General, 15% Multi-/Interdisciplinary Studies, Other, 12% Environmental Studies, 12% Health and Physical Education/Fitness, Other, 9% English Language and Literature, General
Expenses: 2018-2019: $31,790; room/board: $12,849
Financial aid: (303) 546-3509; 74% of undergrads determined to have financial need; average aid package $36,786

Regis University
Denver CO
(303) 458-4900
U.S. News ranking: Reg. U. (W), No. 26
Website: www.regis.edu
Admissions email: ruadmissions@regis.edu
Private; founded 1877
Affiliation: Roman Catholic
Freshman admissions: more selective; 2017-2018: 7,388 applied, 4,427 accepted. Either SAT or ACT required. ACT 25/75 percentile: 20-26. High school rank: 33% in top tenth, 55% in top quarter, 81% in top half
Early decision deadline: N/A, notification date: N/A
Early action deadline: N/A, notification date: N/A
Application deadline (fall): 8/1
Undergraduate student body: 2,378 full time, 1,496 part time; 39% male, 61% female; 0% American Indian, 5% Asian, 4% black, 21% Hispanic, 4% multiracial, 0% Pacific Islander, 56% white, 1% international; 62% from in state; N/A live on campus; 0% of students in fraternities, 0% in sororities
Most popular majors: 33% Health Professions and Related Programs, 26% Business, Management, Marketing, and Related Support Services, 6% Computer and Information Sciences and Support Services, 5% Biological and Biomedical Sciences, 5% Psychology
Expenses: 2018-2019: $36,810; room/board: $11,560
Financial aid: (303) 964-4162; 67% of undergrads determined to have financial need; average aid package $28,259

Rocky Mountain College of Art and Design[1]
Lakewood CO
(303) 753-6046
U.S. News ranking: Arts, unranked
Website: www.rmcad.edu/
Admissions email: admissions@rmcad.edu
For-profit; founded 1963
Application deadline (fall): N/A
Undergraduate student body: N/A full time, N/A part time
Expenses: N/A
Financial aid: (303) 225-8551

United States Air Force Academy
USAF Academy CO
(800) 443-9266
U.S. News ranking: Nat. Lib. Arts, No. 30
Website: academyadmissions.com
Admissions email: rr_webmail@usafa.edu
Public; founded 1954
Freshman admissions: more selective; 2017-2018: 10,202 applied, 1,180 accepted. Either SAT or ACT required. ACT 25/75 percentile: 29-33. High school rank: 52% in top tenth, 81% in top quarter, 95% in top half
Early decision deadline: N/A, notification date: N/A
Early action deadline: N/A, notification date: N/A
Application deadline (fall): 12/31
Undergraduate student body: 4,276 full time, 0 part time; 74% male, 26% female; 0% American Indian, 5% Asian, 6% black, 11% Hispanic, 7% multiracial, 1% Pacific Islander, 63% white, 1% international; 15% from in state; 100% live on campus; 0% of students in fraternities, 0% in sororities
Most popular majors: 25% Engineering, 21% Business, Management, Marketing, and Related Support Services, 18% Social Sciences, 8% Biological and Biomedical Sciences, 8% Multi/Interdisciplinary Studies
Expenses: N/A
Financial aid: N/A

University of Colorado–Boulder
Boulder CO
(303) 492-6301
U.S. News ranking: Nat. U., No. 96
Website: www.colorado.edu
Admissions email: apply@colorado.edu
Public; founded 1876
Freshman admissions: more selective; 2017-2018: 36,149 applied, 28,861 accepted. Either SAT or ACT required. ACT 25/75 percentile: 25-30. High school rank: 29% in top tenth, 59% in top quarter, 90% in top half
Early decision deadline: N/A, notification date: N/A
Early action deadline: 11/15, notification date: 2/1
Application deadline (fall): 1/15
Undergraduate student body: 26,917 full time, 2,174 part time; 56% male, 44% female; 0% American Indian, 6% Asian, 2% black, 12% Hispanic, 5% multiracial, 0% Pacific Islander, 68% white, 7% international; 58% from in state; 28% live on campus; 12% of students in fraternities, 21% in sororities
Most popular majors: 14% Biological and Biomedical Sciences, 13% Business, Management, Marketing, and Related Support Services, 13% Engineering, 12% Social Sciences, 10% Communication, Journalism, and Related Programs
Expenses: 2018-2019: $12,534 in state, $37,288 out of state; room/board: $14,418
Financial aid: (303) 492-5091; 36% of undergrads determined to have financial need; average aid package $16,699

University of Colorado–Colorado Springs
Colorado Springs CO
(719) 255-3383
U.S. News ranking: Reg. U. (W), No. 48
Website: www.uccs.edu
Admissions email: admrecor@uccs.edu
Public; founded 1965
Freshman admissions: selective; 2017-2018: 9,909 applied, 9,197 accepted. Either SAT or ACT required. ACT 25/75 percentile: 21-26. High school rank: 14% in top tenth, 38% in top quarter, 74% in top half
Early decision deadline: N/A, notification date: N/A
Early action deadline: N/A, notification date: N/A
Application deadline (fall): rolling
Undergraduate student body: 8,200 full time, 2,418 part time; 48% male, 52% female; 0% American Indian, 3% Asian, 4% black, 18% Hispanic, 8% multiracial, 0% Pacific Islander, 64% white, 1% international; 87% from in state; 16% live on campus; N/A of students in fraternities, N/A in sororities
Most popular majors: 21% Business, Management, Marketing, and Related Support Services, 16% Health Professions and Related Programs, 9% Biological and Biomedical Sciences, 9% Social Sciences, 8% Engineering
Expenses: 2018-2019: $8,507 in state, $20,051 out of state; room/board: $9,800
Financial aid: (719) 255-3460; 62% of undergrads determined to have financial need; average aid package $8,705

University of Colorado–Denver
Denver CO
(303) 556-2704
U.S. News ranking: Nat. U., No. 205
Website: www.ucdenver.edu
Admissions email: admissions@ucdenver.edu
Public; founded 1912
Freshman admissions: selective; 2017-2018: 11,362 applied, 7,416 accepted. Either SAT or ACT required. ACT 25/75 percentile: 21-27. High school rank: 18% in top tenth, 50% in top quarter, 81% in top half
Early decision deadline: N/A, notification date: N/A
Early action deadline: N/A, notification date: N/A
Application deadline (fall): rolling
Undergraduate student body: 8,671 full time, 6,915 part time; 45% male, 55% female; 0% American Indian, 10% Asian, 5% black, 21% Hispanic, 6% multiracial, 0% Pacific Islander, 48% white, 8% international; 91% from in state; 0% live on campus; N/A of students in fraternities, N/A in sororities
Most popular majors: 17% Business, Management, Marketing, and Related Support Services, 15% Health Professions and Related Programs, 13% Social Sciences, 10% Biological and Biomedical Sciences, 8% Visual and Performing Arts
Expenses: 2018-2019: $11,395 in state, $32,005 out of state; room/board: $11,547
Financial aid: (303) 315-1850; 61% of undergrads determined to have financial need; average aid package $10,169

University of Denver
Denver CO
(303) 871-2036
U.S. News ranking: Nat. U., No. 96
Website: www.du.edu
Admissions email: admission@du.edu
Private; founded 1864
Freshman admissions: more selective; 2017-2018: 19,904 applied, 11,554 accepted. Either SAT or ACT required. ACT 25/75 percentile: 25-30. High school rank: 38% in top tenth, 73% in top quarter, 95% in top half
Early decision deadline: 11/1, notification date: 12/15
Early action deadline: 11/1, notification date: 1/15
Application deadline (fall): 1/15
Undergraduate student body: 5,494 full time, 271 part time; 47% male, 53% female; 0% American Indian, 4% Asian, 2% black, 11% Hispanic, 4% multiracial, 0% Pacific Islander, 69% white, 7% international; 38% from in state; 50% live on campus; 25% of students in fraternities, 30% in sororities
Most popular majors: 31% Business, Management, Marketing, and Related Support Services, 18% Social Sciences, 9% Psychology, 8% Biological and Biomedical Sciences, 7% Communication, Journalism, and Related Programs
Expenses: 2018-2019: $50,556; room/board: $13,005
Financial aid: (303) 871-4020; 43% of undergrads determined to have financial need; average aid package $40,587

University of Northern Colorado
Greeley CO
(970) 351-2881
U.S. News ranking: Nat. U., second tier
Website: www.unco.edu
Admissions email: admissions@unco.edu
Public; founded 1890
Freshman admissions: selective; 2017-2018: 7,481 applied, 6,665 accepted. Either SAT or ACT required. ACT 25/75 percentile: 19-25. High school rank: 13% in top tenth, 36% in top quarter, 74% in top half
Early decision deadline: N/A, notification date: N/A
Early action deadline: N/A, notification date: N/A
Application deadline (fall): 8/1
Undergraduate student body: 8,319 full time, 1,658 part time; 35% male, 65% female; 0% American Indian, 2% Asian, 5% black, 21% Hispanic, 5% multiracial, 0% Pacific Islander, 61% white, 1% international; 84% from in state; 36% live on campus; 7% of students in fraternities, 5% in sororities
Most popular majors: 17% Health Professions and Related Programs, 11% Business, Management, Marketing, and Related Support Services, 10% Education, 9% Parks, Recreation, Leisure, and Fitness Studies, 8% Multi/Interdisciplinary Studies

More @ usnews.com/bestcolleges

Expenses: 2018-2019: $9,545 in state, $21,131 out of state; room/board: $10,982
Financial aid: (970) 351-2502; 64% of undergrads determined to have financial need; average aid package $13,815

Western State Colorado University

Gunnison CO
(800) 876-5309
U.S. News ranking: Reg. U. (W), No. 77
Website: www.western.edu
Admissions email: discover@western.edu
Public; founded 1901
Freshman admissions: selective; 2017-2018: 1,955 applied, 1,681 accepted. Either SAT or ACT required. ACT 25/75 percentile: 20-25. High school rank: 8% in top tenth, 25% in top quarter, 49% in top half
Early decision deadline: N/A, notification date: N/A
Early action deadline: N/A, notification date: N/A
Application deadline (fall): rolling
Undergraduate student body: 1,832 full time, 597 part time; 57% male, 43% female; 1% American Indian, 1% Asian, 3% black, 11% Hispanic, 4% multiracial, 0% Pacific Islander, 71% white, 0% international; 30% from in state; 37% live on campus; N/A of students in fraternities, N/A in sororities
Most popular majors: 24% Business, Management, Marketing, and Related Support Services, 15% Parks, Recreation, Leisure, and Fitness Studies, 10% Biological and Biomedical Sciences, 10% Social Sciences, 7% Visual and Performing Arts
Expenses: 2018-2019: $10,114 in state, $21,586 out of state; room/board: $9,635
Financial aid: (970) 943-7015; 57% of undergrads determined to have financial need; average aid package $11,207

CONNECTICUT

Albertus Magnus College

New Haven CT
(800) 578-9160
U.S. News ranking: Reg. U. (N), No. 99
Website: www.albertus.edu
Admissions email: admissions@albertus.edu
Private; founded 1925
Freshman admissions: least selective; 2017-2018: 933 applied, 596 accepted. Either SAT or ACT required. SAT 25/75 percentile: 810-1050. High school rank: N/A
Early decision deadline: N/A, notification date: N/A
Early action deadline: N/A, notification date: N/A
Application deadline (fall): rolling
Undergraduate student body: 1,012 full time, 116 part time; 33% male, 67% female; 0% American Indian, 1% Asian, 35% black, 19% Hispanic, 1% multiracial, 0% Pacific Islander, 33% white, 1% international; 94% from in state; 17% live on campus; 0% of students in fraternities, 0% in sororities
Most popular majors: 53% Business, Management, Marketing, and Related Support Services, 9% Psychology, 7% Homeland Security, Law Enforcement, Firefighting and Related Protective Services, 7% Social Sciences
Expenses: 2018-2019: $32,060; room/board: $13,400
Financial aid: (203) 773-8508; 88% of undergrads determined to have financial need; average aid package $17,021

Central Connecticut State University

New Britain CT
(860) 832-2278
U.S. News ranking: Reg. U. (N), No. 105
Website: www.ccsu.edu
Admissions email: admissions@ccsu.edu
Public; founded 1849
Freshman admissions: selective; 2017-2018: 7,870 applied, 5,254 accepted. Either SAT or ACT required. SAT 25/75 percentile: 980-1160. High school rank: 8% in top tenth, 26% in top quarter, 65% in top half
Early decision deadline: N/A, notification date: N/A
Early action deadline: N/A, notification date: N/A
Application deadline (fall): 5/1
Undergraduate student body: 7,605 full time, 1,949 part time; 53% male, 47% female; 0% American Indian, 4% Asian, 13% black, 15% Hispanic, 3% multiracial, 0% Pacific Islander, 61% white, 1% international; 97% from in state; 24% live on campus; N/A of students in fraternities, N/A in sororities
Most popular majors: 26% Business, Management, Marketing, and Related Support Services, 13% Social Sciences, 8% Psychology, 7% Communication, Journalism, and Related Programs, 6% Biological and Biomedical Sciences
Expenses: 2018-2019: $10,616 in state, $21,856 out of state; room/board: $12,179
Financial aid: (860) 832-2203; 79% of undergrads determined to have financial need; average aid package $10,230

Charter Oak State College

New Britain CT
(860) 515-3701
U.S. News ranking: Nat. Lib. Arts, unranked
Website: www.charteroak.edu
Admissions email: admissions@charteroak.edu
Public; founded 1973
Freshman admissions: least selective; 2017-2018: N/A applied, N/A accepted. Neither SAT nor ACT required. SAT 25/75 percentile: N/A. High school rank: N/A
Early decision deadline: N/A, notification date: N/A
Early action deadline: N/A, notification date: N/A
Application deadline (fall): rolling
Undergraduate student body: 290 full time, 1,126 part time; 32% male, 68% female; 0% American Indian, 2% Asian, 17% black, 16% Hispanic, 3% multiracial, 0% Pacific Islander, 56% white, 1% international; 81% from in state; N/A live on campus; N/A of students in fraternities, N/A in sororities
Most popular majors: 70% Liberal Arts and Sciences/Liberal Studies, 14% Business Administration and Management, General, 9% Health/Health Care Administration/Management, 6% Psychology, General, 1% Computer and Information Systems Security/Information Assurance
Expenses: 2018-2019: $10,161 in state, $13,101 out of state; room/board: N/A
Financial aid: (860) 515-3703

Connecticut College

New London CT
(860) 439-2200
U.S. News ranking: Nat. Lib. Arts, No. 46
Website: www.conncoll.edu
Admissions email: admission@conncoll.edu
Private; founded 1911
Freshman admissions: more selective; 2017-2018: 5,434 applied, 2,063 accepted. Neither SAT nor ACT required. SAT 25/75 percentile: 1270-1400. High school rank: 44% in top tenth, 78% in top quarter, 96% in top half
Early decision deadline: 11/15, notification date: 12/15
Early action deadline: N/A, notification date: N/A
Application deadline (fall): 1/1
Undergraduate student body: 1,766 full time, 51 part time; 37% male, 63% female; 0% American Indian, 4% Asian, 4% black, 8% Hispanic, 3% multiracial, 0% Pacific Islander, 71% white, 8% international; 18% from in state; 99% live on campus; 0% of students in fraternities, 0% in sororities
Most popular majors: 18% Economics, General, 11% Psychology, General, 8% Neuroscience, 7% Computer Science, 6% Political Science and Government, General
Expenses: 2018-2019: $54,820; room/board: $15,150
Financial aid: N/A; 58% of undergrads determined to have financial need; average aid package $42,988

Eastern Connecticut State University

Willimantic CT
(860) 465-5286
U.S. News ranking: Reg. U. (N), No. 93
Website: www.easternct.edu
Admissions email: admissions@easternct.edu
Public; founded 1889
Freshman admissions: selective; 2017-2018: 5,817 applied, 3,590 accepted. Neither SAT nor ACT required. SAT 25/75 percentile: 1000-1180. High school rank: 10% in top tenth, 36% in top quarter, 76% in top half
Early decision deadline: N/A, notification date: N/A
Early action deadline: N/A, notification date: N/A
Application deadline (fall): rolling
Undergraduate student body: 4,210 full time, 863 part time; 43% male, 57% female; 0% American Indian, 3% Asian, 9% black, 11% Hispanic, 3% multiracial, 0% Pacific Islander, 67% white, 1% international
Most popular majors: 10% Business, Management, Marketing, and Related Support Services, 10% Liberal Arts and Sciences, General Studies and Humanities, 9% Communication, Journalism, and Related Programs, 9% Psychology, 7% Social Sciences
Expenses: 2018-2019: $11,356 in state, $22,596 out of state; room/board: $13,520
Financial aid: (860) 465-5775; 67% of undergrads determined to have financial need; average aid package $13,868

Fairfield University

Fairfield CT
(203) 254-4100
U.S. News ranking: Reg. U. (N), No. 1
Website: www.fairfield.edu
Admissions email: admis@fairfield.edu
Private; founded 1942
Affiliation: Roman Catholic
Freshman admissions: more selective; 2017-2018: 11,218 applied, 6,794 accepted. Neither SAT nor ACT required. SAT 25/75 percentile: 1180-1320. High school rank: 41% in top tenth, 79% in top quarter, 98% in top half
Early decision deadline: 11/15, notification date: 12/15
Early action deadline: 11/1, notification date: 12/20
Application deadline (fall): 1/15
Undergraduate student body: 3,879 full time, 234 part time; 40% male, 60% female; 0% American Indian, 2% Asian, 2% black, 8% Hispanic, 2% multiracial, 0% Pacific Islander, 78% white, 3% international; 29% from in state; 71% live on campus; N/A of students in fraternities, N/A in sororities
Most popular majors: 41% Business, Management, Marketing, and Related Support Services, 12% Health Professions and Related Programs, 10% Communication, Journalism, and Related Programs, 7% Social Sciences, 6% Psychology
Expenses: 2018-2019: $48,350; room/board: $14,710
Financial aid: (203) 254-4000; 45% of undergrads determined to have financial need; average aid package $34,731

Lincoln College of New England–Southington[1]

Southington CT
U.S. News ranking: Reg. Coll. (N), unranked
Admissions email: N/A
For-profit
Application deadline (fall): N/A
Undergraduate student body: N/A full time, N/A part time
Expenses: 2017-2018: $20,050; room/board: $11,300
Financial aid: N/A

Mitchell College[1]

New London CT
(860) 701-5000
U.S. News ranking: Reg. Coll. (N), second tier
Website: www.mitchell.edu
Admissions email: admissions@mitchell.edu
Private
Application deadline (fall): N/A
Undergraduate student body: N/A full time, N/A part time
Expenses: 2017-2018: $32,442; room/board: $12,750
Financial aid: N/A

Post University

Waterbury CT
(800) 660-6615
U.S. News ranking: Reg. U. (N), second tier
Website: www.post.edu
Admissions email: admissions@post.edu
For-profit; founded 1890
Freshman admissions: least selective; 2017-2018: 4,068 applied, 2,483 accepted. Neither SAT nor ACT required. SAT 25/75 percentile: 850-850. High school rank: N/A
Early decision deadline: N/A, notification date: N/A
Early action deadline: N/A, notification date: N/A
Application deadline (fall): rolling
Undergraduate student body: 2,617 full time, 5,227 part time; 35% male, 65% female; 1% American Indian, 1% Asian, 25% black, 7% Hispanic, 5% multiracial, 0% Pacific Islander, 41% white, 1% international; 25% from in state; 10% live on campus; 0% of students in fraternities, 0% in sororities
Most popular majors: 42% Business Administration and Management, General, 11% Criminal Justice/Safety Studies, 8% Accounting, 7% Management Information Systems, General, 7% Public Administration and Social Service Professions
Expenses: 2018-2019: $17,810; room/board: $11,600
Financial aid: (800) 345-2562; 82% of undergrads determined to have financial need; average aid package $12,261

Quinnipiac University

Hamden CT
(203) 582-8600
U.S. News ranking: Reg. U. (N), No. 13
Website: www.qu.edu
Admissions email: admissions@qu.edu

Private; founded 1929
Affiliation: Undenominational
Freshman admissions: selective; 2017-2018: 22,048 applied, 16,304 accepted. Neither SAT nor ACT required. SAT 25/75 percentile: 1080-1260. High school rank: 22% in top tenth, 51% in top quarter, 91% in top half
Early decision deadline: 11/1, notification date: 12/1
Early action deadline: N/A, notification date: N/A
Application deadline (fall): 2/1
Undergraduate student body: 6,959 full time, 402 part time; 39% male, 61% female; 0% American Indian, 3% Asian, 4% black, 9% Hispanic, 3% multiracial, 0% Pacific Islander, 76% white, 2% international; 29% from in state; 75% live on campus; 24% of students in fraternities, 30% in sororities
Most popular majors: 36% Health Professions and Related Programs, 23% Business, Management, Marketing, and Related Support Services, 11% Communication, Journalism, and Related Programs, 6% Psychology, 5% Biological and Biomedical Sciences
Expenses: 2018-2019: $47,960; room/board: $14,540
Financial aid: (203) 582-8750; 64% of undergrads determined to have financial need; average aid package $28,707

Sacred Heart University

Fairfield CT
(203) 371-7880
U.S. News ranking: Reg. U. (N), No. 35
Website: www.sacredheart.edu
Admissions email: enroll@sacredheart.edu
Private; founded 1963
Affiliation: Roman Catholic
Freshman admissions: selective; 2017-2018: 9,992 applied, 6,023 accepted. Neither SAT nor ACT required. SAT 25/75 percentile: 1060-1200. High school rank: 10% in top tenth, 29% in top quarter, 68% in top half
Early decision deadline: 12/1, notification date: 12/15
Early action deadline: 12/15, notification date: 1/31
Application deadline (fall): rolling
Undergraduate student body: 4,982 full time, 621 part time; 36% male, 64% female; 0% American Indian, 2% Asian, 5% black, 11% Hispanic, 2% multiracial, 0% Pacific Islander, 74% white, 1% international; 35% from in state; 52% live on campus; 16% of students in fraternities, 37% in sororities
Most popular majors: 32% Health Professions and Related Programs, 26% Business, Management, Marketing, and Related Support Services, 10% Psychology, 6% Communication, Journalism, and Related Programs, 5% Homeland Security, Law Enforcement, Firefighting and Related Protective Services
Expenses: 2018-2019: $41,420; room/board: $15,310
Financial aid: (203) 371-7980; 67% of undergrads determined to have financial need; average aid package $20,729

Southern Connecticut State University[1]

New Haven CT
(203) 392-5644
U.S. News ranking: Reg. U. (N), No. 132
Website: www.southernct.edu/
Admissions email: information@southernct.edu
Public; founded 1893
Application deadline (fall): rolling
Undergraduate student body: N/A full time, N/A part time
Expenses: 2017-2018: $10,537 in state, $21,995 out of state; room/board: $11,975
Financial aid: (203) 392-5222

Trinity College

Hartford CT
(860) 297-2180
U.S. News ranking: Nat. Lib. Arts, No. 46
Website: www.trincoll.edu
Admissions email: admissions.office@trincoll.edu
Private; founded 1823
Affiliation: Undenominational
Freshman admissions: more selective; 2017-2018: 6,085 applied, 2,061 accepted. Neither SAT nor ACT required. ACT 25/75 percentile: 28-32. High school rank: 49% in top tenth, 81% in top quarter, 95% in top half
Early decision deadline: 11/15, notification date: 12/15
Early action deadline: N/A, notification date: N/A
Application deadline (fall): 1/15
Undergraduate student body: 2,117 full time, 104 part time; 49% male, 51% female; 0% American Indian, 4% Asian, 6% black, 8% Hispanic, 3% multiracial, 0% Pacific Islander, 65% white, 12% international; 19% from in state; 90% live on campus; 29% of students in fraternities, 17% in sororities
Most popular majors: 27% Social Sciences, 12% Biological and Biomedical Sciences, 8% Psychology, 7% Area, Ethnic, Cultural, Gender, and Group Studies, 7% Foreign Languages, Literatures, and Linguistics
Expenses: 2018-2019: $56,910; room/board: $14,750
Financial aid: (860) 297-2048; 49% of undergrads determined to have financial need; average aid package $50,520

United States Coast Guard Academy

New London CT
(800) 883-8724
U.S. News ranking: Reg. Coll. (N), No. 2
Website: www.uscga.edu
Admissions email: admissions@uscga.edu
Public; founded 1932
Freshman admissions: more selective; 2017-2018: 2,021 applied, 433 accepted. Either SAT or ACT required. SAT 25/75 percentile: 1180-1343. High school rank: 39% in top tenth, 75% in top quarter, 98% in top half
Early decision deadline: N/A, notification date: N/A
Early action deadline: 10/15, notification date: 2/1
Application deadline (fall): 1/15
Undergraduate student body: 1,045 full time, 0 part time; 65% male, 35% female; 0% American Indian, 7% Asian, 6% black, 9% Hispanic, 9% multiracial, 0% Pacific Islander, 65% white, 3% international; 5% from in state; 100% live on campus; N/A of students in fraternities, N/A in sororities
Most popular majors: 47% Engineering, 20% Business, Management, Marketing, and Related Support Services, 12% Biological and Biomedical Sciences, 12% Social Sciences, 10% Computer and Information Sciences and Support Services
Expenses: 2018-2019: $1,056 in state, $1,056 out of state; room/board: N/A
Financial aid: N/A

University of Bridgeport

Bridgeport CT
(203) 576-4552
U.S. News ranking: Reg. U. (N), second tier
Website: www.bridgeport.edu
Admissions email: admit@bridgeport.edu
Private; founded 1927
Freshman admissions: less selective; 2017-2018: 7,947 applied, 4,283 accepted. Either SAT or ACT required. SAT 25/75 percentile: 860-1050. High school rank: 8% in top tenth, 31% in top quarter, 64% in top half
Early decision deadline: N/A, notification date: N/A
Early action deadline: N/A, notification date: N/A
Application deadline (fall): rolling
Undergraduate student body: 2,300 full time, 829 part time; 36% male, 64% female; 1% American Indian, 4% Asian, 34% black, 22% Hispanic, 2% multiracial, 0% Pacific Islander, 24% white, 13% international; 68% from in state; 37% live on campus; 2% of students in fraternities, 2% in sororities
Most popular majors: 12% Psychology, General, 10% General Studies, 8% Dental Hygiene/Hygienist, 7% Public Administration and Social Service Professions, 6% Finance, General
Expenses: 2018-2019: $32,850; room/board: $13,860
Financial aid: (203) 576-4568; 82% of undergrads determined to have financial need; average aid package $28,677

University of Connecticut

Storrs CT
(860) 486-3137
U.S. News ranking: Nat. U., No. 63
Website: www.uconn.edu
Admissions email: beahusky@uconn.edu
Public; founded 1881
Freshman admissions: more selective; 2017-2018: 34,198 applied, 16,360 accepted. Either SAT or ACT required. SAT 25/75 percentile: 1210-1390. High school rank: 54% in top tenth, 88% in top quarter, 98% in top half
Early decision deadline: N/A, notification date: N/A
Early action deadline: N/A, notification date: N/A
Application deadline (fall): 1/15
Undergraduate student body: 18,555 full time, 686 part time; 50% male, 50% female; 0% American Indian, 11% Asian, 6% black, 10% Hispanic, 3% multiracial, 0% Pacific Islander, 59% white, 8% international; 78% from in state; 66% live on campus; 11% of students in fraternities, 14% in sororities
Most popular majors: 7% Economics, General, 7% Psychology, General, 5% Allied Health and Medical Assisting Services, Other, 5% Speech Communication and Rhetoric, 4% Registered Nursing/Registered Nurse
Expenses: 2018-2019: $15,730 in state, $38,098 out of state; room/board: $12,874
Financial aid: (860) 486-2819; 54% of undergrads determined to have financial need; average aid package $14,884

University of Hartford

West Hartford CT
(860) 768-4296
U.S. News ranking: Nat. U., No. 194
Website: www.hartford.edu
Admissions email: admission@hartford.edu
Private; founded 1877
Freshman admissions: selective; 2017-2018: 14,043 applied, 11,360 accepted. Either SAT or ACT required. SAT 25/75 percentile: 1030-1230. High school rank: N/A
Early decision deadline: N/A, notification date: N/A
Early action deadline: 11/15, notification date: 12/1
Application deadline (fall): rolling
Undergraduate student body: 4,460 full time, 609 part time; 49% male, 51% female; 0% American Indian, 4% Asian, 15% black, 13% Hispanic, 4% multiracial, 0% Pacific Islander, 55% white, 6% international; 55% from in state; 61% live on campus; N/A of students in fraternities, N/A in sororities
Most popular majors: 16% Visual and Performing Arts, 14% Business, Management, Marketing, and Related Support Services, 14% Health Professions and Related Programs, 13% Engineering, 7% Psychology
Expenses: 2018-2019: $40,694; room/board: $12,476
Financial aid: (860) 768-4296; 73% of undergrads determined to have financial need; average aid package $27,599

University of New Haven

West Haven CT
(203) 932-7319
U.S. News ranking: Reg. U. (N), No. 93
Website: www.newhaven.edu
Admissions email: admissions@newhaven.edu
Private; founded 1920
Freshman admissions: selective; 2017-2018: 9,953 applied, 8,735 accepted. Either SAT or ACT required. SAT 25/75 percentile: 1010-1210. High school rank: 15% in top tenth, 39% in top quarter, 75% in top half
Early decision deadline: 12/1, notification date: 12/15
Early action deadline: 12/15, notification date: 1/15
Application deadline (fall): rolling
Undergraduate student body: 4,831 full time, 385 part time; 47% male, 53% female; 0% American Indian, 3% Asian, 12% black, 12% Hispanic, 1% multiracial, 0% Pacific Islander, 61% white, 6% international; 44% from in state; 52% live on campus; N/A of students in fraternities, N/A in sororities
Most popular majors: 42% Homeland Security, Law Enforcement, Firefighting and Related Protective Services, 11% Business, Management, Marketing, and Related Support Services, 11% Engineering, 8% Visual and Performing Arts, 7% Psychology
Expenses: 2018-2019: $39,270; room/board: $15,900
Financial aid: (203) 932-7315; 77% of undergrads determined to have financial need; average aid package $23,082

University of St. Joseph

West Hartford CT
(860) 231-5216
U.S. News ranking: Reg. U. (N), No. 55
Website: www.usj.edu
Admissions email: admissions@usj.edu
Private; founded 1932
Affiliation: Roman Catholic
Freshman admissions: selective; 2017-2018: 649 applied, 586 accepted. Neither SAT nor ACT required. SAT 25/75 percentile: 970-1160. High school rank: 31% in top tenth, 54% in top quarter, 84% in top half
Early decision deadline: N/A, notification date: N/A
Early action deadline: N/A, notification date: N/A
Application deadline (fall): rolling
Undergraduate student body: 654 full time, 156 part time; 2% male, 98% female; 0% American Indian, 5% Asian, 15% black, 16% Hispanic, 1% multiracial, 0% Pacific Islander, 55% white, 1% international; 95% from in state; 25% live on campus; N/A of students in fraternities, N/A in sororities

More @ usnews.com/bestcolleges

Most popular majors: 43% Health Professions and Related Programs, 14% Public Administration and Social Service Professions, 13% Family and Consumer Sciences/Human Sciences, 10% Biological and Biomedical Sciences, 6% Psychology
Expenses: 2018-2019: $39,173; room/board: $11,428
Financial aid: (860) 231-5223; 93% of undergrads determined to have financial need; average aid package $27,986

Wesleyan University

Middletown CT
(860) 685-3000
U.S. News ranking: Nat. Lib. Arts, No. 18
Website: www.wesleyan.edu
Admissions email: admissions@wesleyan.edu
Private; founded 1831
Freshman admissions: most selective; 2017-2018: 12,360 applied, 2,013 accepted. Neither SAT nor ACT required. ACT 25/75 percentile: 29-33. High school rank: 60% in top tenth, 92% in top quarter, 98% in top half
Early decision deadline: 11/15, notification date: 12/15
Early action deadline: N/A, notification date: N/A
Application deadline (fall): 1/1
Undergraduate student body: 2,896 full time, 80 part time; 46% male, 54% female; 0% American Indian, 8% Asian, 6% black, 11% Hispanic, 5% multiracial, 0% Pacific Islander, 54% white, 12% international; 8% from in state; 100% live on campus; 4% of students in fraternities, 1% in sororities
Most popular majors: Information not available
Expenses: 2018-2019: $54,614; room/board: $16,090
Financial aid: (860) 685-2800; 44% of undergrads determined to have financial need; average aid package $51,397

Western Connecticut State University

Danbury CT
(203) 837-9000
U.S. News ranking: Reg. U. (N), second tier
Website: www.wcsu.edu
Admissions email: admissions@wcsu.edu
Public; founded 1903
Freshman admissions: selective; 2017-2018: 5,671 applied, 4,017 accepted. Neither SAT nor ACT required. SAT 25/75 percentile: 910-1150. High school rank: 6% in top tenth, 24% in top quarter, 66% in top half
Early decision deadline: N/A, notification date: N/A
Early action deadline: N/A, notification date: N/A
Application deadline (fall): rolling
Undergraduate student body: 4,089 full time, 993 part time; 48% male, 52% female; 0% American Indian, 4% Asian, 11% black, 18% Hispanic, 3% multiracial, 0% Pacific Islander, 61% white, 0% international
Most popular majors: 24% Business, Management, Marketing, and Related Support Services, 13% Health Professions and Related Programs, 12% Homeland Security, Law Enforcement, Firefighting and Related Protective Services, 9% Psychology, 8% Communication, Journalism, and Related Programs
Expenses: 2018-2019: $10,819 in state, $22,059 out of state; room/board: $13,072
Financial aid: (203) 837-8580

Yale University

New Haven CT
(203) 432-9300
U.S. News ranking: Nat. U., No. 3
Website: www.yale.edu/
Admissions email: student.questions@yale.edu
Private; founded 1701
Freshman admissions: most selective; 2017-2018: 32,879 applied, 2,277 accepted. Either SAT or ACT required. SAT 25/75 percentile: 1420-1590. High school rank: 94% in top tenth, 93% in top quarter, 99% in top half
Early decision deadline: N/A, notification date: N/A
Early action deadline: 11/1, notification date: 12/15
Application deadline (fall): 1/1
Undergraduate student body: 5,743 full time, 3 part time; 50% male, 50% female; 1% American Indian, 18% Asian, 7% black, 13% Hispanic, 6% multiracial, 0% Pacific Islander, 45% white, 11% international
Most popular majors: 26% Social Sciences, 8% History, 7% Multi/Interdisciplinary Studies, 6% Area, Ethnic, Cultural, Gender, and Group Studies, 6% Engineering
Expenses: 2018-2019: $53,430; room/board: $16,000
Financial aid: (203) 432-2700; 50% of undergrads determined to have financial need; average aid package $55,828

DELAWARE

Delaware State University

Dover DE
(302) 857-6353
U.S. News ranking: Reg. U. (N), second tier
Website: www.desu.edu
Admissions email: admissions@desu.edu
Public; founded 1891
Freshman admissions: less selective; 2017-2018: 7,636 applied, 3,450 accepted. Either SAT or ACT required. SAT 25/75 percentile: 820-990. High school rank: 7% in top tenth, 25% in top quarter, 62% in top half
Early decision deadline: N/A, notification date: N/A
Early action deadline: N/A, notification date: N/A
Application deadline (fall): rolling
Undergraduate student body: 3,571 full time, 479 part time; 35% male, 65% female; 0% American Indian, 0% Asian, 75% black, 7% Hispanic, 5% multiracial, 0% Pacific Islander, 9% white, 3% international; 49% from in state; 58% live on campus; 3% of students in fraternities, 3% in sororities
Most popular majors: 13% Communication, Journalism, and Related Programs, 13% Social Sciences, 11% Business, Management, Marketing, and Related Support Services, 11% Parks, Recreation, Leisure, and Fitness Studies, 9% Psychology
Expenses: 2018-2019: $7,868 in state, $16,904 out of state; room/board: $11,054
Financial aid: (302) 857-6250; 82% of undergrads determined to have financial need; average aid package $21,122

Goldey-Beacom College[1]

Wilmington DE
(302) 998-8814
U.S. News ranking: Business, unranked
Website: www.gbc.edu
Admissions email: admissions@gbc.edu
Private; founded 1886
Application deadline (fall): N/A
Undergraduate student body: N/A full time, N/A part time
Expenses: N/A
Financial aid: (302) 225-6265

University of Delaware

Newark DE
(302) 831-8123
U.S. News ranking: Nat. U., No. 89
Website: www.udel.edu/
Admissions email: admissions@udel.edu
Public; founded 1743
Freshman admissions: more selective; 2017-2018: 27,803 applied, 16,648 accepted. Either SAT or ACT required. SAT 25/75 percentile: 1150-1330. High school rank: 32% in top tenth, 66% in top quarter, 93% in top half
Early decision deadline: N/A, notification date: N/A
Early action deadline: N/A, notification date: N/A
Application deadline (fall): 1/15
Undergraduate student body: 17,432 full time, 1,514 part time; 43% male, 57% female; 0% American Indian, 5% Asian, 5% black, 8% Hispanic, 3% multiracial, 0% Pacific Islander, 72% white, 5% international; 38% from in state; 40% live on campus; 18% of students in fraternities, 23% in sororities
Most popular majors: 20% Business, Management, Marketing, and Related Support Services, 12% Health Professions and Related Programs, 11% Social Sciences, 10% Engineering, 6% Biological and Biomedical Sciences
Expenses: 2018-2019: $13,680 in state, $34,310 out of state; room/board: $12,864
Financial aid: (302) 831-0520; 49% of undergrads determined to have financial need; average aid package $13,017

Wesley College[1]

Dover DE
(302) 736-2400
U.S. News ranking: Reg. Coll. (N), second tier
Website: www.wesley.edu
Admissions email: admissions@wesley.edu
Private; founded 1873
Affiliation: United Methodist
Application deadline (fall): 4/30
Undergraduate student body: N/A full time, N/A part time
Expenses: 2017-2018: $26,406; room/board: $11,442
Financial aid: (302) 736-2483

Wilmington University

New Castle DE
(302) 328-9407
U.S. News ranking: Nat. U., second tier
Website: www.wilmu.edu
Admissions email: undergradadmissions@wilmu.edu
Private; founded 1968
Freshman admissions: less selective; 2017-2018: 1,953 applied, 1,953 accepted. Neither SAT nor ACT required. SAT 25/75 percentile: N/A. High school rank: N/A
Early decision deadline: N/A, notification date: N/A
Early action deadline: N/A, notification date: N/A
Application deadline (fall): rolling
Undergraduate student body: 3,039 full time, 5,421 part time; 35% male, 65% female; 1% American Indian, 2% Asian, 21% black, 2% Hispanic, 6% multiracial, 0% Pacific Islander, 42% white, 2% international; 70% from in state; 0% live on campus; 0% of students in fraternities, 0% in sororities
Most popular majors: 23% Nursing Practice, 11% Behavioral Sciences, 9% Business Administration and Management, General, 7% Criminal Justice/Law Enforcement Administration, 6% Organizational Behavior Studies
Expenses: 2018-2019: $11,210; room/board: N/A
Financial aid: (302) 356-4636

DISTRICT OF COLUMBIA

American University

Washington DC
(202) 885-6000
U.S. News ranking: Nat. U., No. 78
Website: www.american.edu
Admissions email: admissions@american.edu
Private; founded 1893
Affiliation: United Methodist
Freshman admissions: more selective; 2017-2018: 18,699 applied, 5,498 accepted. Neither SAT nor ACT required. SAT 25/75 percentile: 1180-1350. High school rank: 31% in top tenth, 66% in top quarter, 94% in top half
Early decision deadline: 11/15, notification date: 12/31
Early action deadline: N/A, notification date: N/A
Application deadline (fall): 1/15
Undergraduate student body: 7,764 full time, 359 part time; 38% male, 62% female; 0% American Indian, 7% Asian, 7% black, 14% Hispanic, 4% multiracial, 0% Pacific Islander, 57% white, 8% international; 18% from in state; N/A live on campus; 9% of students in fraternities, 11% in sororities
Most popular majors: 38% Social Sciences, 17% Business, Management, Marketing, and Related Support Services, 9% Communication, Journalism, and Related Programs, 6% Visual and Performing Arts, 5% Multi/Interdisciplinary Studies
Expenses: 2018-2019: $48,459; room/board: $14,880
Financial aid: (202) 885-6500; 54% of undergrads determined to have financial need; average aid package $33,279

The Catholic University of America

Washington DC
(800) 673-2772
U.S. News ranking: Nat. U., No. 129
Website: www.catholic.edu/
Admissions email: cua-admissions@cua.edu
Private; founded 1887
Affiliation: Roman Catholic
Freshman admissions: selective; 2017-2018: 6,073 applied, 5,015 accepted. Neither SAT nor ACT required. SAT 25/75 percentile: 1120-1320. High school rank: N/A
Early decision deadline: 11/15, notification date: 12/20
Early action deadline: 11/1, notification date: 12/20
Application deadline (fall): 1/15
Undergraduate student body: 3,194 full time, 121 part time; 46% male, 54% female; 0% American Indian, 4% Asian, 5% black, 13% Hispanic, 5% multiracial, 0% Pacific Islander, 65% white, 6% international; 3% from in state; 58% live on campus; 1% of students in fraternities, 1% in sororities
Most popular majors: 11% Registered Nursing/Registered Nurse, 9% Political Science and Government, General, 9% Psychology, General, 6% Architecture, 6% Mechanical Engineering
Expenses: 2018-2019: $45,804; room/board: $14,650
Financial aid: (202) 319-5307; 58% of undergrads determined to have financial need; average aid package $30,182

Gallaudet University

Washington DC
(202) 651-5750
U.S. News ranking: Reg. U. (N), No. 20
Website: www.gallaudet.edu
Admissions email: admissions.office@gallaudet.edu
Private; founded 1864

Freshman admissions: less selective; 2017-2018: 588 applied, 345 accepted. Neither SAT nor ACT required. ACT 25/75 percentile: 15-19. High school rank: N/A
Early decision deadline: N/A, notification date: N/A
Early action deadline: N/A, notification date: N/A
Undergraduate student body: 1,074 full time, 55 part time; 44% male, 56% female; 1% American Indian, 4% Asian, 16% black, 9% Hispanic, 4% multiracial, 1% Pacific Islander, 51% white, 5% international; 3% from in state; 86% live on campus; 6% of students in fraternities, 7% in sororities
Most popular majors: 16% Communication, Journalism, and Related Programs, 11% Foreign Languages, Literatures, and Linguistics, 10% Area, Ethnic, Cultural, Gender, and Group Studies, 8% Parks, Recreation, Leisure, and Fitness Studies, 8% Public Administration and Social Service Professions
Expenses: 2018-2019: $17,038; room/board: $14,100
Financial aid: (202) 651-5290; 87% of undergrads determined to have financial need; average aid package $23,059

Georgetown University

Washington DC
(202) 687-3600
U.S. News ranking: Nat. U., No. 22
Website: www.georgetown.edu
Admissions email: guadmiss@georgetown.edu
Private; founded 1789
Affiliation: Roman Catholic
Freshman admissions: most selective; 2017-2018: 21,462 applied, 3,365 accepted. Either SAT or ACT required. SAT 25/75 percentile: 1350-1520. High school rank: 90% in top tenth, 97% in top quarter, 100% in top half
Early decision deadline: N/A, notification date: N/A
Early action deadline: 11/1, notification date: 12/15
Application deadline (fall): 1/10
Undergraduate student body: 6,987 full time, 476 part time; 44% male, 56% female; 0% American Indian, 10% Asian, 6% black, 10% Hispanic, 5% multiracial, 0% Pacific Islander, 54% white, 13% international; 2% from in state; 78% live on campus; N/A of students in fraternities, N/A in sororities
Most popular majors: 34% Social Sciences, 26% Business, Management, Marketing, and Related Support Services, 6% Multi/Interdisciplinary Studies, 5% Biological and Biomedical Sciences, 5% Foreign Languages, Literatures, and Linguistics
Expenses: 2018-2019: $54,104; room/board: $16,418
Financial aid: (202) 687-4547; 37% of undergrads determined to have financial need; average aid package $46,571

George Washington University

Washington DC
(202) 994-6040
U.S. News ranking: Nat. U., No. 63
Website: www.gwu.edu
Admissions email: gwadm@gwu.edu
Private; founded 1821
Freshman admissions: more selective; 2017-2018: 26,987 applied, 11,059 accepted. Neither SAT nor ACT required. SAT 25/75 percentile: 1280-1440. High school rank: 61% in top tenth, 88% in top quarter, 99% in top half
Early decision deadline: 11/1, notification date: 12/15
Early action deadline: N/A, notification date: N/A
Application deadline (fall): 1/1
Undergraduate student body: 10,893 full time, 1,106 part time; 40% male, 60% female; 0% American Indian, 10% Asian, 7% black, 10% Hispanic, 4% multiracial, 0% Pacific Islander, 53% white, 11% international; 3% from in state; 61% live on campus; 15% of students in fraternities, 19% in sororities
Most popular majors: 34% Social Sciences, 17% Business, Management, Marketing, and Related Support Services, 11% Health Professions and Related Programs, 6% Communication, Journalism, and Related Programs, 6% Engineering
Expenses: 2018-2019: $55,230; room/board: $13,850
Financial aid: (202) 994-6620; 47% of undergrads determined to have financial need; average aid package $46,444

Howard University

Washington DC
(202) 806-2755
U.S. News ranking: Nat. U., No. 89
Website: www.howard.edu
Admissions email: admission@howard.edu
Private; founded 1867
Freshman admissions: selective; 2017-2018: 16,815 applied, 6,964 accepted. Either SAT or ACT required. SAT 25/75 percentile: 1090-1290. High school rank: 25% in top tenth, 58% in top quarter, 88% in top half
Early decision deadline: N/A, notification date: N/A
Early action deadline: 11/1, notification date: 12/20
Application deadline (fall): 2/15
Undergraduate student body: 6,090 full time, 264 part time; 31% male, 69% female; 0% American Indian, 1% Asian, 90% black, 1% Hispanic, 0% multiracial, 0% Pacific Islander, 1% white, 7% international; 6% from in state; 62% live on campus; 3% of students in fraternities, 5% in sororities
Most popular majors: 15% Communication, Journalism, and Related Programs, 15% Physical Sciences, 14% Business, Management, Marketing, and Related Support Services, 12% Biological and Biomedical Sciences, 11% Social Sciences
Expenses: 2018-2019: $26,756; room/board: $13,895
Financial aid: (202) 806-2820; 80% of undergrads determined to have financial need; average aid package $15,264

Strayer University[1]

Washington DC
(202) 408-2400
U.S. News ranking: Reg. U. (N), unranked
Website: www.strayer.edu
Admissions email: mzm@strayer.edu
For-profit; founded 1892
Application deadline (fall): N/A
Undergraduate student body: N/A full time, N/A part time
Expenses: 2017-2018: $13,857; room/board: N/A
Financial aid: N/A

Trinity Washington University[1]

Washington DC
(202) 884-9400
U.S. News ranking: Reg. U. (N), second tier
Website: www.trinitydc.edu
Admissions email: admissions@trinitydc.edu
Private
Application deadline (fall): N/A
Undergraduate student body: N/A full time, N/A part time
Expenses: 2017-2018: $23,690; room/board: $10,490
Financial aid: N/A

University of the District of Columbia

Washington DC
(202) 274-5010
U.S. News ranking: Reg. U. (N), second tier
Website: www.udc.edu/
Admissions email: N/A
Public; founded 1976
Freshman admissions: least selective; 2017-2018: 4,807 applied, 1,882 accepted. Either SAT or ACT required. SAT 25/75 percentile: 700-910. High school rank: N/A
Early decision deadline: N/A, notification date: N/A
Early action deadline: N/A, notification date: N/A
Application deadline (fall): rolling
Undergraduate student body: 1,830 full time, 2,029 part time; 43% male, 57% female; 0% American Indian, 2% Asian, 59% black, 11% Hispanic, 0% multiracial, 0% Pacific Islander, 4% white, 12% international
Most popular majors: 18% Business Administration, Management and Operations, 9% Legal Professions and Studies, 7% Accounting and Related Services, 7% Political Science and Government, 5% Health Professions and Related Programs
Expenses: 2018-2019: $5,888 in state, $12,416 out of state; room/board: $17,183
Financial aid: (202) 274-6053; 59% of undergrads determined to have financial need; average aid package $9,136

University of the Potomac[1]

Washington DC
(202) 274-2303
U.S. News ranking: Business, unranked
Website: www.potomac.edu
Admissions email: admissions@potomac.edu
For-profit; founded 1991
Application deadline (fall): rolling
Undergraduate student body: N/A full time, N/A part time
Expenses: N/A
Financial aid: N/A

FLORIDA

Ave Maria University[1]

Ave Maria FL
(877) 283-8648
U.S. News ranking: Nat. Lib. Arts, second tier
Website: www.avemaria.edu
Admissions email: N/A
Private; founded 2003
Application deadline (fall): rolling
Undergraduate student body: N/A full time, N/A part time
Expenses: 2017-2018: $19,970; room/board: $10,955
Financial aid: (239) 280-2423

Barry University

Miami Shores FL
(305) 899-3100
U.S. News ranking: Nat. U., second tier
Website: www.barry.edu
Admissions email: admissions@barry.edu
Private; founded 1940
Affiliation: Roman Catholic
Freshman admissions: less selective; 2017-2018: 5,110 applied, 4,350 accepted. Either SAT or ACT required. SAT 25/75 percentile: 850-1020. High school rank: N/A
Early decision deadline: N/A, notification date: N/A
Early action deadline: N/A, notification date: N/A
Application deadline (fall): rolling
Undergraduate student body: 2,991 full time, 514 part time; 40% male, 60% female; 0% American Indian, 1% Asian, 34% black, 34% Hispanic, 1% multiracial, 0% Pacific Islander, 19% white, 8% international; 80% from in state; 30% live on campus; N/A of students in fraternities, N/A in sororities
Most popular majors: 29% Business, Management, Marketing, and Related Support Services, 21% Health Professions and Related Programs, 9% Public Administration and Social Service Professions, 8% Biological and Biomedical Sciences, 5% Computer and Information Sciences and Support Services
Expenses: 2018-2019: $29,850; room/board: $11,100
Financial aid: (305) 899-3673; 75% of undergrads determined to have financial need; average aid package $22,133

Beacon College[1]

Leesburg FL
(352) 787-7660
U.S. News ranking: Reg. Coll. (S), unranked
Website: www.beaconcollege.edu/
Admissions email: admissions@beaconcollege.edu
Private
Application deadline (fall): N/A
Undergraduate student body: N/A full time, N/A part time
Expenses: 2017-2018: $37,788; room/board: $11,090
Financial aid: N/A

Bethune-Cookman University

Daytona Beach FL
(800) 448-0228
U.S. News ranking: Nat. Lib. Arts, second tier
Website: www.bethune.cookman.edu
Admissions email: admissions@cookman.edu
Private; founded 1904
Freshman admissions: least selective; 2017-2018: 12,786 applied, 6,967 accepted. Either SAT or ACT required. ACT 25/75 percentile: 15-19. High school rank: 2% in top tenth, 10% in top quarter, 53% in top half
Early decision deadline: N/A, notification date: N/A
Early action deadline: N/A, notification date: N/A
Application deadline (fall): rolling
Undergraduate student body: 3,755 full time, 237 part time; 38% male, 62% female; 0% American Indian, 0% Asian, 79% black, 3% Hispanic, 2% multiracial, 0% Pacific Islander, 1% white, 2% international; 73% from in state; 63% live on campus; 1% of students in fraternities, 3% in sororities
Most popular majors: 19% Liberal Arts and Sciences/Liberal Studies, 13% Corrections and Criminal Justice, Other, 10% Business Administration and Management, General, 10% Psychology, General, 6% Gerontology
Expenses: 2018-2019: $14,814; room/board: $9,412
Financial aid: (386) 481-2620; 95% of undergrads determined to have financial need; average aid package $14,838

Broward College

Fort Lauderdale FL
(954) 201-7350
U.S. News ranking: Reg. Coll. (S), second tier
Website: www.broward.edu
Admissions email: N/A
Public; founded 1960
Freshman admissions: least selective; 2017-2018: 5,566 applied, 5,566 accepted. Neither SAT nor ACT required. SAT 25/75 percentile: N/A. High school rank: 1% in top tenth, 4% in top quarter, N/A in top half

More @ usnews.com/bestcolleges

Early decision deadline: N/A, notification date: N/A
Early action deadline: N/A, notification date: N/A
Application deadline (fall): rolling
Undergraduate student body: 12,037 full time, 28,717 part time; 40% male, 60% female; 33% American Indian, 0% Asian, 9% black, 37% Hispanic, 3% multiracial, 17% Pacific Islander, 3% white, 4% international; 99% from in state; 0% live on campus; 0% of students in fraternities, 0% in sororities
Most popular majors: 39% Business Administration, Management and Operations, Other, 17% Registered Nursing/Registered Nurse, 16% Information Technology, 12% Special Education and Teaching, General, 6% Computer/Information Technology Services Administration and Management, Other
Expenses: 2018-2019: $3,537 in state, $10,779 out of state; room/board: N/A
Financial aid: (954) 201-2330; 53% of undergrads determined to have financial need; average aid package $8,027

Chipola College[1]

Marianna FL
(850) 718-2211
U.S. News ranking: Reg. Coll. (S), second tier
Website: www.chipola.edu
Admissions email: N/A
Public
Application deadline (fall): N/A
Undergraduate student body: N/A full time, N/A part time
Expenses: 2018-2019: $8,308 in state, $19,526 out of state; room/board: N/A
Financial aid: N/A; 74% of undergrads determined to have financial need

College of Central Florida[1]

Ocala FL
(352) 854-2322
U.S. News ranking: Reg. Coll. (S), unranked
Website: www.cf.edu
Admissions email: admissions@cf.edu
Public; founded 1957
Application deadline (fall): 8/12
Undergraduate student body: N/A full time, N/A part time
Expenses: 2017-2018: $3,210 in state, $12,660 out of state; room/board: N/A.
Financial aid: (352) 854-2322

Daytona State College[1]

Daytona Beach FL
(386) 506-3000
U.S. News ranking: Reg. Coll. (S), unranked
Website: www.daytonastate.edu
Admissions email: N/A
Public; founded 1957
Application deadline (fall): N/A
Undergraduate student body: N/A full time, N/A part time
Expenses: 2017-2018: $3,109 in state, $11,998 out of state; room/board: N/A
Financial aid: N/A

Eastern Florida State College[1]

Cocoa FL
(321) 633-1111
U.S. News ranking: Reg. Coll. (S), unranked
Website: www.easternflorida.edu
Admissions email: N/A
Public; founded 1960
Application deadline (fall): rolling
Undergraduate student body: N/A full time, N/A part time
Expenses: 2017-2018: $2,496 in state, $9,739 out of state; room/board: N/A
Financial aid: N/A

Eckerd College

St. Petersburg FL
(727) 864-8331
U.S. News ranking: Nat. Lib. Arts, No. 135
Website: www.eckerd.edu
Admissions email: admissions@eckerd.edu
Private
Freshman admissions: selective; 2017-2018: 4,525 applied, 3,291 accepted. Either SAT or ACT required. ACT 25/75 percentile: 23-29. High school rank: N/A
Early decision deadline: N/A, notification date: N/A
Early action deadline: 11/15, notification date: 12/15
Application deadline (fall): rolling
Undergraduate student body: 1,909 full time, 48 part time; 34% male, 66% female; 0% American Indian, 2% Asian, 3% black, 9% Hispanic, 3% multiracial, 0% Pacific Islander, 78% white, 4% international; 22% from in state; 87% live on campus; 0% of students in fraternities, 0% in sororities
Most popular majors: 18% Environmental Studies, 15% Marine Biology and Biological Oceanography, 13% Biology/Biological Sciences, General, 11% Psychology, General, 8% International Business/Trade/Commerce
Expenses: 2018-2019: $44,540; room/board: $12,588
Financial aid: (727) 864-8334; 61% of undergrads determined to have financial need; average aid package $36,810

Edward Waters College[1]

Jacksonville FL
(904) 470-8200
U.S. News ranking: Reg. Coll. (S), second tier
Website: www.ewc.edu
Admissions email: admissions@ewc.edu
Private
Application deadline (fall): N/A
Undergraduate student body: N/A full time, N/A part time
Expenses: 2017-2018: $13,525; room/board: $7,282
Financial aid: N/A

Embry-Riddle Aeronautical University

Daytona Beach FL
(800) 862-2416
U.S. News ranking: Reg. U. (S), No. 15
Website: www.embryriddle.edu
Admissions email: dbadmit@erau.edu
Private; founded 1926
Freshman admissions: more selective; 2017-2018: 4,564 applied, 3,419 accepted. Neither SAT nor ACT required. SAT 25/75 percentile: 1080-1320. High school rank: 23% in top tenth, 50% in top quarter, 83% in top half
Early decision deadline: N/A, notification date: N/A
Early action deadline: N/A, notification date: N/A
Application deadline (fall): rolling
Undergraduate student body: 5,378 full time, 351 part time; 78% male, 22% female; 0% American Indian, 5% Asian, 5% black, 7% Hispanic, 7% multiracial, 0% Pacific Islander, 56% white, 12% international; 36% from in state; 40% live on campus; N/A of students in fraternities, N/A in sororities
Most popular majors: 45% Transportation and Materials Moving, 30% Engineering, 7% Business, Management, Marketing, and Related Support Services, 6% Homeland Security, Law Enforcement, Firefighting and Related Protective Services, 4% Psychology
Expenses: 2018-2019: $35,714; room/board: $11,438
Financial aid: (386) 226-6300; 57% of undergrads determined to have financial need; average aid package $16,996

Everglades University[1]

Boca Raton FL
(888) 772-6077
U.S. News ranking: Reg. Coll. (S), No. 52
Website: www.evergladesuniversity.edu
Admissions email: N/A
Private; founded 2002
Application deadline (fall): rolling
Undergraduate student body: N/A full time, N/A part time
Expenses: 2017-2018: $17,000; room/board: N/A
Financial aid: (561) 912-1211

Flagler College

St. Augustine FL
(800) 304-4208
U.S. News ranking: Reg. Coll. (S), No. 2
Website: www.flagler.edu
Admissions email: admissions@flagler.edu
Private; founded 1968
Freshman admissions: selective; 2017-2018: 4,921 applied, 2,785 accepted. Either SAT or ACT required. SAT 25/75 percentile: 950-1160. High school rank: N/A
Early decision deadline: 11/1, notification date: 11/15
Early action deadline: N/A, notification date: N/A
Application deadline (fall): 3/1
Undergraduate student body: 2,591 full time, 85 part time; 35% male, 65% female; 0% American Indian, 1% Asian, 4% black, 6% Hispanic, 3% multiracial, 0% Pacific Islander, 77% white, 4% international; 57% from in state; 44% live on campus; 0% of students in fraternities, 0% in sororities
Most popular majors: 19% Business, Management, Marketing, and Related Support Services, 12% Communication, Journalism, and Related Programs, 12% Social Sciences, 12% Visual and Performing Arts, 11% Psychology
Expenses: 2018-2019: $18,700; room/board: $11,340
Financial aid: (904) 819-6225; 64% of undergrads determined to have financial need; average aid package $12,755

Florida A&M University

Tallahassee FL
(850) 599-3796
U.S. News ranking: Nat. U., second tier
Website: www.famu.edu
Admissions email: ugradmissions@famu.edu
Public; founded 1887
Freshman admissions: selective; 2017-2018: 7,533 applied, 3,437 accepted. Either SAT or ACT required. ACT 25/75 percentile: 18-22. High school rank: 12% in top tenth, 27% in top quarter, 79% in top half
Early decision deadline: N/A, notification date: N/A
Early action deadline: N/A, notification date: N/A
Application deadline (fall): 5/15
Undergraduate student body: 6,875 full time, 1,149 part time; 35% male, 65% female; 0% American Indian, 0% Asian, 89% black, 3% Hispanic, 3% multiracial, 0% Pacific Islander, 3% white, 1% international
Most popular majors: 21% Health Professions and Related Programs, 20% Multi/Interdisciplinary Studies, 10% Business, Management, Marketing, and Related Support Services, 6% Homeland Security, Law Enforcement, Firefighting and Related Protective Services, 6% Psychology
Expenses: 2018-2019: $5,785 in state, $17,725 out of state; room/board: $10,058
Financial aid: (850) 599-3730; 85% of undergrads determined to have financial need; average aid package $13,408

Florida Atlantic University

Boca Raton FL
(561) 297-3040
U.S. News ranking: Nat. U., second tier
Website: www.fau.edu
Admissions email: Admissions@fau.edu
Public; founded 1961
Freshman admissions: selective; 2017-2018: 15,176 applied, 9,107 accepted. Either SAT or ACT required. SAT 25/75 percentile: 1060-1220. High school rank: 14% in top tenth, 45% in top quarter, 84% in top half
Early decision deadline: N/A, notification date: N/A
Early action deadline: N/A, notification date: N/A
Application deadline (fall): 5/1
Undergraduate student body: 16,325 full time, 8,700 part time; 44% male, 56% female; 0% American Indian, 4% Asian, 20% black, 27% Hispanic, 4% multiracial, 0% Pacific Islander, 41% white, 3% international; 95% from in state; 17% live on campus; 6% of students in fraternities, 6% in sororities
Most popular majors: 20% Business, Management, Marketing, and Related Support Services, 8% Multi/Interdisciplinary Studies, 8% Psychology, 7% Health Professions and Related Programs, 7% Homeland Security, Law Enforcement, Firefighting and Related Protective Services
Expenses: 2018-2019: $6,039 in state, $21,595 out of state; room/board: $11,896
Financial aid: (561) 297-3531; 61% of undergrads determined to have financial need; average aid package $13,750

Florida College

Temple Terrace FL
(800) 326-7655
U.S. News ranking: Reg. Coll. (S), second tier
Website: www.floridacollege.edu/
Admissions email: N/A
Private; founded 1946
Freshman admissions: less selective; 2017-2018: 284 applied, 223 accepted. Either SAT or ACT required. ACT 25/75 percentile: 20-26. High school rank: N/A
Early decision deadline: N/A, notification date: N/A
Early action deadline: N/A, notification date: N/A
Application deadline (fall): 8/25
Undergraduate student body: 490 full time, 18 part time; 48% male, 52% female; 1% American Indian, 0% Asian, 6% black, 9% Hispanic, 4% multiracial, 0% Pacific Islander, 74% white, 3% international; 51% from in state; 82% live on campus; N/A of students in fraternities, N/A in sororities
Most popular majors: Information not available
Expenses: 2017-2018: $17,042; room/board: $8,420
Financial aid: (813) 988-5131

Florida Gateway College[1]
Lake City FL
U.S. News ranking: Reg. Coll. (S), unranked
Admissions email: N/A
Public
Application deadline (fall): N/A
Undergraduate student body: N/A full time, N/A part time
Expenses: 2017-2018: $3,100 in state, $11,747 out of state; room/board: N/A
Financial aid: N/A

Florida Gulf Coast University
Fort Myers FL
(239) 590-7878
U.S. News ranking: Reg. U. (S), No. 78
Website: www.fgcu.edu
Admissions email: admissions@fgcu.edu
Public; founded 1991
Freshman admissions: selective; 2017-2018: 13,832 applied, 8,889 accepted. Either SAT or ACT required. ACT 25/75 percentile: 21-25. High school rank: 13% in top tenth, 36% in top quarter, 75% in top half
Early decision deadline: N/A, notification date: N/A
Early action deadline: N/A, notification date: N/A
Application deadline (fall): 5/1
Undergraduate student body: 10,947 full time, 2,873 part time; 44% male, 56% female; 0% American Indian, 2% Asian, 7% black, 21% Hispanic, 3% multiracial, 0% Pacific Islander, 64% white, 2% international; 93% from in state; 34% live on campus; 6% of students in fraternities, 10% in sororities
Most popular majors: 10% Speech Communication and Rhetoric, 8% Business Administration and Management, General, 8% Resort Management, 6% Criminal Justice/Safety Studies, 6% Psychology, General
Expenses: 2018-2019: $6,118 in state, $24,255 out of state; room/board: $9,672
Financial aid: (239) 590-1210; 44% of undergrads determined to have financial need; average aid package $10,560

Florida Institute of Technology
Melbourne FL
(800) 888-4348
U.S. News ranking: Nat. U., No. 177
Website: www.fit.edu
Admissions email: admission@fit.edu
Private; founded 1958
Freshman admissions: more selective; 2017-2018: 8,898 applied, 5,647 accepted. Either SAT or ACT required. SAT 25/75 percentile: 1130-1320. High school rank: 28% in top tenth, 60% in top quarter, 87% in top half
Early decision deadline: N/A, notification date: N/A
Early action deadline: N/A, notification date: N/A
Application deadline (fall): rolling
Undergraduate student body: 3,269 full time, 366 part time; 71% male, 29% female; 0% American Indian, 3% Asian, 6% black, 9% Hispanic, 2% multiracial, 0% Pacific Islander, 45% white, 32% international; 50% from in state; 41% live on campus; 3% of students in fraternities, 3% in sororities
Most popular majors: 13% Mechanical Engineering, 8% Aerospace, Aeronautical and Astronautical/Space Engineering, 7% Aviation/Airway Management and Operations, 6% Chemical Engineering, 4% Electrical and Electronics Engineering
Expenses: 2018-2019: $41,850; room/board: $12,880
Financial aid: (321) 674-8070; 52% of undergrads determined to have financial need; average aid package $37,796

Florida International University
Miami FL
(305) 348-2363
U.S. News ranking: Nat. U., No. 187
Website: www.fiu.edu
Admissions email: admiss@fiu.edu
Public; founded 1972
Freshman admissions: selective; 2017-2018: 14,861 applied, 7,596 accepted. Either SAT or ACT required. SAT 25/75 percentile: 1100-1260. High school rank: 25% in top tenth, 58% in top quarter, 90% in top half
Early decision deadline: N/A, notification date: N/A
Early action deadline: N/A, notification date: N/A
Undergraduate student body: 26,697 full time, 20,889 part time; 43% male, 57% female; 0% American Indian, 2% Asian, 12% black, 67% Hispanic, 3% multiracial, 0% Pacific Islander, 9% white, 6% international; 96% from in state; 7% live on campus; N/A of students in fraternities, N/A in sororities
Most popular majors: 29% Business, Management, Marketing, and Related Support Services, 12% Psychology, 7% Communication, Journalism, and Related Programs, 7% Health Professions and Related Programs, 7% Social Sciences
Expenses: 2018-2019: $6,558 in state, $18,956 out of state; room/board: $10,882
Financial aid: (305) 348-2333; 93% of undergrads determined to have financial need; average aid package $7,885

Florida Memorial University[1]
Miami FL
(305) 626-3750
U.S. News ranking: Reg. Coll. (S), No. 20
Website: www.fmuniv.edu/
Admissions email: admit@fmuniv.edu
Private; founded 1879
Affiliation: Baptist
Application deadline (fall): rolling
Undergraduate student body: N/A full time, N/A part time
Expenses: 2017-2018: $15,536; room/board: $6,734
Financial aid: (305) 626-3745

Florida National University–Main Campus
Hialeah FL
(305) 821-3333
U.S. News ranking: Reg. Coll. (S), unranked
Website: www.fnu.edu/
Admissions email: rlopez@fnu.edu
For-profit; founded 1988
Freshman admissions: least selective; 2017-2018: 1,785 applied, 1,687 accepted. Neither SAT nor ACT required. SAT 25/75 percentile: N/A. High school rank: N/A
Early decision deadline: N/A, notification date: N/A
Early action deadline: N/A, notification date: N/A
Application deadline (fall): N/A
Undergraduate student body: 2,899 full time, 1,124 part time; 29% male, 71% female; 0% American Indian, 0% Asian, 3% black, 81% Hispanic, 1% multiracial, 0% Pacific Islander, 1% white, 13% international; 99% from in state; 0% live on campus; 0% of students in fraternities, 0% in sororities
Most popular majors: 58% Registered Nursing/Registered Nurse, 18% Health Services Administration, 10% Business Administration and Management, General, 7% Accounting, 6% Criminal Justice/Law Enforcement Administration
Expenses: 2018-2019: $13,250; room/board: N/A
Financial aid: (305) 821-3333; 90% of undergrads determined to have financial need

Florida Southern College
Lakeland FL
(863) 680-4131
U.S. News ranking: Reg. U. (S), No. 20
Website: www.flsouthern.edu
Admissions email: fscadm@flsouthern.edu
Private; founded 1883
Freshman admissions: more selective; 2017-2018: 5,983 applied, 3,062 accepted. Either SAT or ACT required. ACT 25/75 percentile: 23-28. High school rank: 31% in top tenth, 60% in top quarter, 80% in top half
Early decision deadline: 11/1, notification date: 12/1
Early action deadline: N/A, notification date: N/A
Application deadline (fall): rolling
Undergraduate student body: 2,364 full time, 269 part time; 35% male, 65% female; 1% American Indian, 3% Asian, 5% black, 10% Hispanic, 1% multiracial, 0% Pacific Islander, 75% white, 4% international; 62% from in state; 92% live on campus; 30% of students in fraternities, 33% in sororities
Most popular majors: 27% Business Administration, Management and Operations, 13% Biological and Biomedical Sciences, 12% Health Professions and Related Programs, 8% Communication, Journalism, and Related Programs, 8% Education
Expenses: 2018-2019: $36,348; room/board: $11,670
Financial aid: (863) 680-4140; 67% of undergrads determined to have financial need; average aid package $28,756

Florida SouthWestern State College
Fort Myers FL
(239) 489-9094
U.S. News ranking: Reg. Coll. (S), unranked
Website: www.fsw.edu
Admissions email: admissions@fsw.edu
Public; founded 1962
Freshman admissions: least selective; 2017-2018: 5,852 applied, 4,731 accepted. Neither SAT nor ACT required. SAT 25/75 percentile: N/A. High school rank: N/A
Early decision deadline: N/A, notification date: N/A
Early action deadline: N/A, notification date: N/A
Application deadline (fall): 8/17
Undergraduate student body: 6,104 full time, 10,726 part time; 41% male, 59% female; 0% American Indian, 2% Asian, 11% black, 31% Hispanic, 2% multiracial, 0% Pacific Islander, 46% white, 2% international
Most popular majors: 36% Business, Management, Marketing, and Related Support Services, 29% Health Professions and Related Programs, 27% Education, 7% Homeland Security, Law Enforcement, Firefighting and Related Protective Services
Expenses: 2018-2019: $3,400 in state, $12,978 out of state; room/board: $8,000
Financial aid: (239) 489-9336

Florida State College–Jacksonville[1]
Jacksonville FL
(904) 359-5433
U.S. News ranking: Reg. Coll. (S), unranked
Website: www.fscj.edu
Admissions email: N/A
Public
Application deadline (fall): N/A
Undergraduate student body: N/A full time, N/A part time
Expenses: 2017-2018: $2,878 in state, $9,992 out of state; room/board: N/A
Financial aid: N/A

Florida State University
Tallahassee FL
(850) 644-6200
U.S. News ranking: Nat. U., No. 70
Website: www.fsu.edu
Admissions email: admissions@admin.fsu.edu
Public; founded 1851
Freshman admissions: more selective; 2017-2018: 35,334 applied, 17,381 accepted. Either SAT or ACT required. ACT 25/75 percentile: 26-30. High school rank: 41% in top tenth, 83% in top quarter, 99% in top half
Early decision deadline: N/A, notification date: N/A
Early action deadline: N/A, notification date: N/A
Application deadline (fall): 2/7
Undergraduate student body: 29,286 full time, 3,722 part time; 44% male, 56% female; 0% American Indian, 2% Asian, 8% black, 20% Hispanic, 4% multiracial, 0% Pacific Islander, 62% white, 2% international; 89% from in state; 20% live on campus; 19% of students in fraternities, 24% in sororities
Most popular majors: 7% Psychology, General, 6% Finance, General, 5% Criminal Justice/Safety Studies, 5% English Language and Literature, General, 5% Marketing/Marketing Management, General
Expenses: 2018-2019: $6,507 in state, $21,673 out of state; room/board: $10,458
Financial aid: (850) 644-5716; 48% of undergrads determined to have financial need; average aid package $15,040

Gulf Coast State College[1]
Panama City FL
U.S. News ranking: Reg. Coll. (S), unranked
Admissions email: N/A
Public
Application deadline (fall): N/A
Undergraduate student body: N/A full time, N/A part time
Expenses: 2018-2019: $2,370 in state, $7,685 out of state; room/board: N/A
Financial aid: (850) 873-3543

Hodges University[1]
Naples FL
(239) 513-1122
U.S. News ranking: Reg. U. (S), unranked
Website: www.hodges.edu
Admissions email: admit@hodges.edu
Private; founded 1990
Application deadline (fall): rolling
Undergraduate student body: N/A full time, N/A part time
Expenses: 2017-2018: $13,940; room/board: N/A
Financial aid: (239) 938-7765

Indian River State College
Fort Pierce FL
(772) 462-7460
U.S. News ranking: Reg. Coll. (S), second tier
Website: www.irsc.edu
Admissions email: N/A
Public
Freshman admissions: less selective; 2017-2018: 1,659 applied, 1,659 accepted. Neither SAT nor ACT required. SAT 25/75 percentile: N/A. High school rank: N/A

More @ usnews.com/bestcolleges

Early decision deadline: N/A, notification date: N/A
Early action deadline: N/A, notification date: N/A
Application deadline (fall): rolling
Undergraduate student body: 5,827 full time, 11,771 part time; 40% male, 60% female; 0% American Indian, 2% Asian, 17% black, 23% Hispanic, 3% multiracial, 0% Pacific Islander, 51% white, 1% international
Most popular majors: Information not available
Expenses: 2018-2019: $2,640 in state, $9,890 out of state; room/board: $5,700
Financial aid: (772) 462-7450; 62% of undergrads determined to have financial need; average aid package $5,209

Jacksonville University

Jacksonville FL
(800) 225-2027
U.S. News ranking: Reg. U. (S), No. 56
Website: www.ju.edu/index.php
Admissions email: admiss@ju.edu
Private; founded 1934
Freshman admissions: selective; 2017-2018: 3,192 applied, 2,773 accepted. Neither SAT nor ACT required. ACT 25/75 percentile: 21-27. High school rank: N/A
Early decision deadline: N/A, notification date: N/A
Early action deadline: N/A, notification date: N/A
Application deadline (fall): 7/1
Undergraduate student body: 2,180 full time, 697 part time; 39% male, 61% female; 0% American Indian, 2% Asian, 19% black, 11% Hispanic, 3% multiracial, 0% Pacific Islander, 57% white, 7% international; 67% from in state; 41% live on campus; 1% of students in fraternities, 3% in sororities
Most popular majors: 53% Health Professions and Related Programs, 14% Business, Management, Marketing, and Related Support Services, 7% Social Sciences, 5% Visual and Performing Arts, 4% Parks, Recreation, Leisure, and Fitness Studies
Expenses: 2018-2019: $36,670; room/board: $14,080
Financial aid: (904) 256-7062; 75% of undergrads determined to have financial need; average aid package $26,187

Keiser University

Ft. Lauderdale FL
(954) 776-4456
U.S. News ranking: Reg. U. (S), No. 56
Website: www.keiseruniversity.edu/admissions/
Admissions email: N/A
Private; founded 1977
Freshman admissions: less selective; 2017-2018: N/A applied, N/A accepted. Neither SAT nor ACT required. SAT 25/75 percentile: N/A. High school rank: N/A
Early decision deadline: N/A, notification date: N/A
Early action deadline: N/A, notification date: N/A
Application deadline (fall): rolling
Undergraduate student body: 10,275 full time, 6,485 part time; 30% male, 70% female; 1% American Indian, 2% Asian, 22% black, 33% Hispanic, 3% multiracial, 0% Pacific Islander, 36% white, 1% international
Most popular majors: 20% Business Administration and Management, General, 11% Multi/Interdisciplinary Studies, 8% Health Services Administration, 8% Psychology, General, 7% Criminal Justice/Law Enforcement Administration
Expenses: 2018-2019: $29,920; room/board: N/A
Financial aid: (954) 776-4476; 84% of undergrads determined to have financial need; average aid package $6,219

Lake-Sumter State College

Leesburg FL
(352) 323-3665
U.S. News ranking: Reg. Coll. (S), unranked
Website: www.lssc.edu/admissions
Admissions email: AdmissionsOffice@lssc.edu
Public; founded 1962
Freshman admissions: least selective; 2017-2018: 1,504 applied, 1,504 accepted. Neither SAT nor ACT required. SAT 25/75 percentile: N/A. High school rank: N/A
Early decision deadline: N/A, notification date: N/A
Early action deadline: N/A, notification date: N/A
Application deadline (fall): 8/6
Undergraduate student body: 1,534 full time, 3,347 part time; 40% male, 60% female; 0% American Indian, 4% Asian, 10% black, 21% Hispanic, 3% multiracial, 0% Pacific Islander, 57% white, 1% international
Most popular majors: 70% Liberal Arts and Sciences/Liberal Studies, 18% Massage Therapy/Therapeutic Massage, 3% Information Technology, 2% Office Management and Supervision, 1% Business Administration and Management, General
Expenses: 2017-2018: $3,172 in state, $13,276 out of state; room/board: N/A
Financial aid: (352) 365-3567

Lynn University

Boca Raton FL
(561) 237-7900
U.S. News ranking: Reg. U. (S), No. 100
Website: www.lynn.edu
Admissions email: admission@lynn.edu
Private; founded 1962
Freshman admissions: less selective; 2017-2018: 3,003 applied, 2,541 accepted. Neither SAT nor ACT required. SAT 25/75 percentile: 958-1130. High school rank: N/A
Early decision deadline: N/A, notification date: N/A
Early action deadline: 11/15, notification date: 12/15
Application deadline (fall): 3/1
Undergraduate student body: 1,826 full time, 378 part time; 52% male, 48% female; 0% American Indian, 1% Asian, 11% black, 15% Hispanic, 1% multiracial, 0% Pacific Islander, 44% white, 17% international; 59% from in state; 46% live on campus; 5% of students in fraternities, 4% in sororities
Most popular majors: 48% Business, Management, Marketing, and Related Support Services, 13% Communication, Journalism, and Related Programs, 8% Homeland Security, Law Enforcement, Firefighting and Related Protective Services, 6% Parks, Recreation, Leisure, and Fitness Studies, 6% Psychology
Expenses: 2018-2019: $38,210; room/board: $12,170
Financial aid: (561) 237-7973; 41% of undergrads determined to have financial need; average aid package $22,741

Miami Dade College[1]

Miami FL
(305) 237-8888
U.S. News ranking: Reg. Coll. (S), unranked
Website: www.mdc.edu/
Admissions email: mdcinfo@mdc.edu
Public
Application deadline (fall): N/A
Undergraduate student body: N/A full time, N/A part time
Expenses: 2017-2018: $2,838 in state, $9,661 out of state; room/board: N/A
Financial aid: N/A

Miami International University of Art & Design[1]

Miami FL
(305) 428-5700
U.S. News ranking: Arts, unranked
Website: www.aimiu.aii.edu/
Admissions email: N/A
For-profit
Application deadline (fall): 9/14
Undergraduate student body: N/A full time, N/A part time
Expenses: N/A
Financial aid: N/A

New College of Florida

Sarasota FL
(941) 487-5000
U.S. News ranking: Nat. Lib. Arts, No. 90
Website: www.ncf.edu
Admissions email: admissions@ncf.edu
Public; founded 1960
Freshman admissions: more selective; 2017-2018: 1,353 applied, 933 accepted. Either SAT or ACT required. SAT 25/75 percentile: 1190-1380. High school rank: 38% in top tenth, 71% in top quarter, 95% in top half
Early decision deadline: 11/1, notification date: 12/15
Early action deadline: N/A, notification date: N/A
Application deadline (fall): 4/15
Undergraduate student body: 835 full time, 0 part time; 37% male, 63% female; 0% American Indian, 3% Asian, 3% black, 18% Hispanic, 3% multiracial, 0% Pacific Islander, 69% white, 2% international; 82% from in state; 79% live on campus; 0% of students in fraternities, 0% in sororities
Most popular majors: 49% Liberal Arts and Sciences, General Studies and Humanities, Other, 34% Biological and Physical Sciences, 7% Environmental Studies, 6% Foreign Languages and Literatures, General, 4% International/Global Studies
Expenses: 2018-2019: $6,916 in state, $29,944 out of state; room/board: $9,370
Financial aid: (941) 487-5000; 57% of undergrads determined to have financial need; average aid package $14,822

Northwest Florida State College[1]

Niceville FL
(850) 678-5111
U.S. News ranking: Reg. Coll. (S), unranked
Website: www.owcc.cc.fl.us/
Admissions email: N/A
Public
Application deadline (fall): rolling
Undergraduate student body: N/A full time, N/A part time
Expenses: 2017-2018: $3,133 in state, $11,940 out of state; room/board: N/A
Financial aid: (850) 729-5370

Nova Southeastern University

Ft. Lauderdale FL
(954) 262-8000
U.S. News ranking: Nat. U., No. 191
Website: www.nova.edu
Admissions email: admissions@nova.edu
Private; founded 1964
Freshman admissions: more selective; 2017-2018: 7,779 applied, 4,525 accepted. Either SAT or ACT required. SAT 25/75 percentile: 1080-1280. High school rank: 39% in top tenth, 55% in top quarter, 88% in top half
Early decision deadline: 11/1, notification date: N/A
Early action deadline: 11/1, notification date: N/A
Application deadline (fall): 2/12
Undergraduate student body: 3,154 full time, 1,343 part time; 29% male, 71% female; 0% American Indian, 10% Asian, 15% black, 27% Hispanic, 3% multiracial, 0% Pacific Islander, 34% white, 6% international; 78% from in state; 29% live on campus; 8% of students in fraternities, 7% in sororities
Most popular majors: 40% Health Professions and Related Programs, 24% Biological and Biomedical Sciences, 13% Business, Management, Marketing, and Related Support Services, 5% Psychology, 2% Education
Expenses: 2018-2019: $30,900; room/board: $12,040
Financial aid: (800) 806-3680; 71% of undergrads determined to have financial need; average aid package $30,300

Palm Beach Atlantic University

West Palm Beach FL
(888) 468-6722
U.S. News ranking: Reg. U. (S), No. 52
Website: www.pba.edu
Admissions email: admit@pba.edu
Private; founded 1968
Affiliation: Interdenominational
Freshman admissions: selective; 2017-2018: 1,380 applied, 1,344 accepted. Either SAT or ACT required. SAT 25/75 percentile: 980-1200. High school rank: 16% in top tenth, 44% in top quarter, 73% in top half
Early decision deadline: N/A, notification date: N/A
Early action deadline: 5/1, notification date: 6/1
Application deadline (fall): rolling
Undergraduate student body: 2,350 full time, 653 part time; 37% male, 63% female; 0% American Indian, 2% Asian, 11% black, 16% Hispanic, 3% multiracial, 0% Pacific Islander, 63% white, 3% international; 66% from in state; 50% live on campus; N/A of students in fraternities, N/A in sororities
Most popular majors: 26% Business, Management, Marketing, and Related Support Services, 13% Psychology, 11% Health Professions and Related Programs, 10% Theology and Religious Vocations, 7% Communication, Journalism, and Related Programs
Expenses: 2018-2019: $31,450; room/board: $10,130
Financial aid: (561) 803-2629; 72% of undergrads determined to have financial need; average aid package $21,938

Palm Beach State College[1]

Lake Worth FL
U.S. News ranking: Reg. Coll. (S), unranked
Admissions email: N/A
Public
Application deadline (fall): N/A
Undergraduate student body: N/A full time, N/A part time
Expenses: 2017-2018: $2,444 in state, $8,732 out of state; room/board: N/A
Financial aid: N/A

Pensacola State College

Pensacola FL
(850) 484-2544
U.S. News ranking: Reg. Coll. (S), No. 58
Website: www.pensacolastate.edu

Admissions email: askus@pensacolastate.edu
Public; founded 1948
Freshman admissions: less selective; 2017-2018: 4,544 applied, 4,544 accepted. Neither SAT nor ACT required. ACT 25/75 percentile: 17-22. High school rank: N/A
Early decision deadline: N/A, notification date: N/A
Early action deadline: N/A, notification date: N/A
Application deadline (fall): rolling
Undergraduate student body: 3,583 full time, 6,072 part time; 39% male, 61% female; 1% American Indian, 3% Asian, 17% black, 7% Hispanic, 6% multiracial, 0% Pacific Islander, 63% white, 0% international; 95% from in state; N/A live on campus; N/A of students in fraternities, N/A in sororities
Most popular majors: 69% Liberal Arts and Sciences, General Studies and Humanities, 18% Health Professions and Related Programs, 4% Business, Management, Marketing, and Related Support Services, 4% Computer and Information Sciences and Support Services, 1% Personal and Culinary Services
Expenses: 2018-2019: $13,393 in state, $20,958 out of state; room/board: N/A
Financial aid: (850) 484-1708; 35% of undergrads determined to have financial need; average aid package $1,590

Polk State College[1]
Winter Haven FL
U.S. News ranking: Reg. Coll. (S), unranked
Admissions email: N/A
Public
Application deadline (fall): N/A
Undergraduate student body: N/A full time, N/A part time
Expenses: 2017-2018: $3,366 in state, $12,272 out of state; room/board: N/A
Financial aid: N/A

Ringling College of Art and Design
Sarasota FL
(800) 255-7695
U.S. News ranking: Arts, unranked
Website: www.ringling.edu
Admissions email: admissions@ringling.edu
Private; founded 1931
Freshman admissions: least selective; 2017-2018: 1,995 applied, 1,275 accepted. Neither SAT nor ACT required. SAT 25/75 percentile: N/A. High school rank: N/A
Early decision deadline: N/A, notification date: N/A
Early action deadline: 11/1, notification date: 12/15
Application deadline (fall): rolling
Undergraduate student body: 1,395 full time, 61 part time; 32% male, 68% female; 0% American Indian, 9% Asian, 4% black, 17% Hispanic, 4% multiracial, 0% Pacific Islander, 48% white, 16% international; 46% from in state; 71% live on campus; 0% of students in fraternities, 0% in sororities
Most popular majors: 35% Illustration, 25% Animation, Interactive Technology, Video Graphics and Special Effects, 11% Game and Interactive Media Design, 9% Cinematography and Film/Video Production, 5% Fine/Studio Arts, General
Expenses: 2018-2019: $46,420; room/board: $15,070
Financial aid: (941) 359-7532; 64% of undergrads determined to have financial need; average aid package $25,765

Rollins College
Winter Park FL
(407) 646-2161
U.S. News ranking: Reg. U. (S), No. 2
Website: www.rollins.edu
Admissions email: admission@rollins.edu
Private; founded 1885
Freshman admissions: more selective; 2017-2018: 5,297 applied, 3,384 accepted. Neither SAT nor ACT required. SAT 25/75 percentile: 1195-1350. High school rank: 31% in top tenth, 58% in top quarter, 91% in top half
Early decision deadline: 11/15, notification date: 12/15
Early action deadline: N/A, notification date: N/A
Application deadline (fall): 2/1
Undergraduate student body: 1,977 full time, 7 part time; 39% male, 61% female; 0% American Indian, 3% Asian, 4% black, 16% Hispanic, 4% multiracial, 0% Pacific Islander, 60% white, 10% international; 59% from in state; 59% live on campus; 33% of students in fraternities, 33% in sororities
Most popular majors: 30% Business, Management, Marketing, and Related Support Services, 16% Social Sciences, 14% Communication, Journalism, and Related Programs, 7% Psychology, 6% Visual and Performing Arts
Expenses: 2018-2019: $49,760; room/board: $14,470
Financial aid: (407) 646-2395; 52% of undergrads determined to have financial need; average aid package $39,094

Saint Johns River State College[1]
Palatka FL
U.S. News ranking: Reg. Coll. (S), unranked
Admissions email: N/A
Public
Application deadline (fall): N/A
Undergraduate student body: N/A full time, N/A part time
Expenses: 2017-2018: $2,839 in state, $10,347 out of state; room/board: N/A
Financial aid: N/A

Saint Leo University
Saint Leo FL
(800) 334-5532
U.S. News ranking: Reg. U. (S), No. 47
Website: www.saintleo.edu
Admissions email: admission@saintleo.edu
Private; founded 1889
Affiliation: Roman Catholic
Freshman admissions: less selective; 2017-2018: 3,320 applied, 2,912 accepted. Neither SAT nor ACT required. SAT 25/75 percentile: 970-1140. High school rank: 12% in top tenth, 30% in top quarter, 62% in top half
Early decision deadline: N/A, notification date: N/A
Early action deadline: N/A, notification date: N/A
Application deadline (fall): N/A
Undergraduate student body: 2,057 full time, 72 part time; 44% male, 56% female; 0% American Indian, 2% Asian, 14% black, 20% Hispanic, 2% multiracial, 0% Pacific Islander, 41% white, 12% international; 71% from in state; 66% live on campus; 16% of students in fraternities, 20% in sororities
Most popular majors: 22% Business, Management, Marketing, and Related Support Services, 12% Computer and Information Sciences and Support Services, 12% Homeland Security, Law Enforcement, Firefighting and Related Protective Services, 9% Biological and Biomedical Sciences, 9% Psychology
Expenses: 2018-2019: $22,770; room/board: $10,920
Financial aid: (800) 240-7658; 73% of undergrads determined to have financial need; average aid package $22,237

Santa Fe College[1]
Gainesville FL
U.S. News ranking: Reg. Coll. (S), unranked
Admissions email: N/A
Public
Application deadline (fall): N/A
Undergraduate student body: N/A full time, N/A part time
Expenses: 2017-2018: $2,563 in state, $9,189 out of state; room/board: N/A
Financial aid: N/A

Seminole State College of Florida[1]
Sanford FL
(407) 708-2380
U.S. News ranking: Reg. Coll. (S), unranked
Website: www.seminolestate.edu
Admissions email: admissions@seminolestate.edu
Public; founded 1965
Application deadline (fall): N/A
Undergraduate student body: N/A full time, N/A part time
Expenses: 2017-2018: $3,131 in state, $11,456 out of state; room/board: N/A
Financial aid: N/A

Southeastern University
Lakeland FL
(800) 500-8760
U.S. News ranking: Reg. U. (S), second tier
Website: www.seu.edu
Admissions email: admission@seu.edu
Private; founded 1935
Affiliation: Assemblies of God Church
Freshman admissions: selective; 2017-2018: 4,038 applied, 2,167 accepted. Either SAT or ACT required. ACT 25/75 percentile: 19-24. High school rank: 10% in top tenth, 28% in top quarter, 57% in top half
Early decision deadline: N/A, notification date: N/A
Early action deadline: N/A, notification date: N/A
Application deadline (fall): 5/1
Undergraduate student body: 4,288 full time, 1,952 part time; 44% male, 56% female; 1% American Indian, 2% Asian, 15% black, 20% Hispanic, 0% multiracial, 1% Pacific Islander, 60% white, 1% international; 53% from in state; 32% live on campus; N/A of students in fraternities, N/A in sororities
Most popular majors: 20% Theology and Religious Vocations, 18% Business, Management, Marketing, and Related Support Services, 8% Education, 6% Communication, Journalism, and Related Programs, 6% Psychology
Expenses: 2018-2019: $25,360; room/board: $9,550
Financial aid: (863) 667-5306; 77% of undergrads determined to have financial need; average aid package $15,554

South Florida State College
Avon Park FL
(863) 453-6661
U.S. News ranking: Reg. Coll. (S), No. 33
Website: www.southflorida.edu
Admissions email: deborah.fuschetti@southflorida.edu
Public; founded 1966
Freshman admissions: less selective; 2017-2018: 371 applied, 371 accepted. Neither SAT nor ACT required. SAT 25/75 percentile: N/A. High school rank: N/A
Early decision deadline: N/A, notification date: N/A
Early action deadline: N/A, notification date: N/A
Application deadline (fall): rolling
Undergraduate student body: 975 full time, 1,910 part time; 36% male, 64% female; 0% American Indian, 2% Asian, 12% black, 37% Hispanic, 2% multiracial, 0% Pacific Islander, 45% white, 2% international
Most popular majors: Information not available
Expenses: 2017-2018: $3,165 in state, $11,859 out of state; room/board: N/A
Financial aid: (863) 784-7108; 45% of undergrads determined to have financial need

State College of Florida–Manatee-Sarasota[1]
Bradenton FL
U.S. News ranking: Reg. Coll. (S), unranked
Admissions email: N/A
Public
Application deadline (fall): N/A
Undergraduate student body: N/A full time, N/A part time
Expenses: 2017-2018: $3,074 in state, $11,606 out of state; room/board: N/A
Financial aid: N/A

Stetson University
DeLand FL
(800) 688-0101
U.S. News ranking: Reg. U. (S), No. 5
Website: www.stetson.edu
Admissions email: admissions@stetson.edu
Private; founded 1883
Freshman admissions: more selective; 2017-2018: 11,732 applied, 7,958 accepted. Neither SAT nor ACT required. SAT 25/75 percentile: 1110-1290. High school rank: 22% in top tenth, 50% in top quarter, 84% in top half
Early decision deadline: N/A, notification date: N/A
Early action deadline: N/A, notification date: N/A
Application deadline (fall): N/A
Undergraduate student body: 3,044 full time, 37 part time; 43% male, 57% female; 0% American Indian, 2% Asian, 8% black, 16% Hispanic, 4% multiracial, 0% Pacific Islander, 61% white, 6% international; 73% from in state; 66% live on campus; 29% of students in fraternities, 32% in sororities
Most popular majors: 30% Business, Management, Marketing, and Related Support Services, 10% Visual and Performing Arts, 9% Psychology, 9% Social Sciences, 8% Biological and Biomedical Sciences
Expenses: 2018-2019: $46,030; room/board: $13,052
Financial aid: (386) 822-7120; 68% of undergrads determined to have financial need; average aid package $36,776

St. Petersburg College[1]
St. Petersburg FL
(727) 341-4772
U.S. News ranking: Reg. Coll. (S), unranked
Website: www.spcollege.edu/
Admissions email: information@spcollege.edu
Public
Application deadline (fall): N/A
Undergraduate student body: N/A full time, N/A part time
Expenses: 2017-2018: $3,352 in state, $11,607 out of state; room/board: N/A
Financial aid: N/A

More @ usnews.com/bestcolleges

t. Thomas University

iami Gardens FL
305) 628-6546
.S. News ranking: Reg. U. (S),
o. 85
ebsite: www.stu.edu
dmissions email: signup@stu.edu
rivate; founded 1961
ffiliation: Roman Catholic
reshman admissions: selective;
017-2018: 2,137 applied,
,041 accepted. Either SAT
r ACT required. SAT 25/75
ercentile: 860-1080. High school
ank: 15% in top tenth, 40% in
op quarter, 90% in top half
arly decision deadline: N/A,
otification date: N/A
arly action deadline: N/A,
otification date: N/A
pplication deadline (fall): rolling
ndergraduate student body: 935
ull time, 1,971 part time; 42%
nale, 58% female; 0% American
ndian, 0% Asian, 26% black,
5% Hispanic, 2% multiracial,
% Pacific Islander, 7% white,
4% international; 89% from in
tate; 40% live on campus; 0%
f students in fraternities, 0% in
ororities
lost popular majors: 16%
)rganizational Leadership, 11%
riminal Justice/Safety Studies,
% Biology/Biological Sciences,
eneral, 8% Psychology, General,
% Business Administration,
lanagement and Operations,
ther
xpenses: 2017-2018: $29,730;
oom/board: $11,700
inancial aid: (305) 474-6960

Jniversity of Central Florida

rlando FL
407) 823-3000
.S. News ranking: Nat. U.,
lo. 165
Vebsite: www.ucf.edu
dmissions email:
dmission@ucf.edu
ublic; founded 1963
reshman admissions: more
elective; 2017-2018: 37,693
pplied, 18,810 accepted. Either
AT or ACT required. SAT 25/75
ercentile: 1150-1320. High
chool rank: 31% in top tenth,
0% in top quarter, 96% in
op half
arly decision deadline: N/A,
otification date: N/A
arly action deadline: N/A,
otification date: N/A
pplication deadline (fall): 5/1
ndergraduate student body:
39,962 full time, 17,010 part
ime; 46% male, 54% female;
% American Indian, 6% Asian,
1% black, 26% Hispanic, 4%
nultiracial, 0% Pacific Islander,
9% white, 2% international;
4% from in state; 18% live
n campus; 6% of students in
raternities, 7% in sororities
lost popular majors: 20%
Business, Management,
Marketing, and Related Support
Services, 17% Health Professions
and Related Programs, 9%
Psychology, 8% Education, 8%
Engineering
Expenses: 2018-2019: $6,368 in state, $22,467 out of state; room/board: $9,617
Financial aid: (407) 823-2827; 63% of undergrads determined to have financial need; average aid package $8,655

University of Florida

Gainesville FL
(352) 392-1365
U.S. News ranking: Nat. U., No. 35
Website: www.ufl.edu
Admissions email: webrequests@admissions.ufl.edu
Public; founded 1853
Freshman admissions: most selective; 2017-2018: 32,747 applied, 13,758 accepted. Either SAT or ACT required. SAT 25/75 percentile: 1240-1400. High school rank: 77% in top tenth, 96% in top quarter, 100% in top half
Early decision deadline: N/A, notification date: N/A
Early action deadline: N/A, notification date: N/A
Application deadline (fall): 3/1
Undergraduate student body: 31,384 full time, 3,863 part time; 44% male, 56% female; 0% American Indian, 8% Asian, 6% black, 22% Hispanic, 3% multiracial, 1% Pacific Islander, 55% white, 2% international; 94% from in state; 22% live on campus; 18% of students in fraternities, 23% in sororities
Most popular majors: 14% Engineering, 12% Business, Management, Marketing, and Related Support Services, 11% Biological and Biomedical Sciences, 11% Social Sciences, 8% Communication, Journalism, and Related Programs
Expenses: 2018-2019: $6,381 in state, $28,658 out of state; room/board: $10,120
Financial aid: (352) 392-1275; 50% of undergrads determined to have financial need; average aid package $15,372

University of Miami

Coral Gables FL
(305) 284-4323
U.S. News ranking: Nat. U., No. 53
Website: www.miami.edu
Admissions email: admission@miami.edu
Private; founded 1925
Freshman admissions: more selective; 2017-2018: 30,634 applied, 10,936 accepted. Either SAT or ACT required. ACT 25/75 percentile: 28-32. High school rank: 46% in top tenth, 77% in top quarter, 94% in top half
Early decision deadline: 11/1, notification date: 12/20
Early action deadline: 11/1, notification date: 1/20
Application deadline (fall): 1/1
Undergraduate student body: 10,216 full time, 616 part time; 48% male, 52% female; 0% American Indian, 5% Asian, 8% black, 23% Hispanic, 3% multiracial, 0% Pacific Islander, 42% white, 15% international; 45% from in state; 39% live on campus; 18% of students in fraternities, 20% in sororities
Most popular majors: 20% Business, Management, Marketing, and Related Support Services, 15% Biological and Biomedical Sciences, 11% Social Sciences, 10% Health Professions and Related Programs, 9% Communication, Journalism, and Related Programs
Expenses: 2018-2019: $50,226; room/board: $14,108
Financial aid: (305) 284-2270; 41% of undergrads determined to have financial need; average aid package $47,896

University of North Florida

Jacksonville FL
(904) 620-2624
U.S. News ranking: Reg. U. (S), No. 42
Website: www.unf.edu
Admissions email: admissions@unf.edu
Public; founded 1965
Freshman admissions: selective; 2017-2018: 14,305 applied, 8,399 accepted. Either SAT or ACT required. SAT 25/75 percentile: 1090-1280. High school rank: 15% in top tenth, 43% in top quarter, 79% in top half
Early decision deadline: N/A, notification date: N/A
Early action deadline: N/A, notification date: N/A
Application deadline (fall): rolling
Undergraduate student body: 10,223 full time, 4,032 part time; 44% male, 56% female; 0% American Indian, 5% Asian, 9% black, 12% Hispanic, 5% multiracial, 0% Pacific Islander, 67% white, 1% international; 96% from in state; 24% live on campus; N/A of students in fraternities, N/A in sororities
Most popular majors: 20% Health Professions and Related Programs, 19% Business, Management, Marketing, and Related Support Services, 9% Psychology, 7% Communication, Journalism, and Related Programs, 6% Social Sciences
Expenses: 2018-2019: $6,394 in state, $20,112 out of state; room/board: $9,772
Financial aid: (904) 620-5555; 42% of undergrads determined to have financial need; average aid package $8,820

University of South Florida

Tampa FL
(813) 974-3350
U.S. News ranking: Nat. U., No. 124
Website: www.usf.edu
Admissions email: admission@admin.usf.edu
Public; founded 1956
Freshman admissions: more selective; 2017-2018: 36,861 applied, 16,055 accepted. Either SAT or ACT required. SAT 25/75 percentile: 1150-1310. High school rank: 37% in top tenth, 71% in top quarter, 93% in top half
Early decision deadline: N/A, notification date: N/A
Early action deadline: N/A, notification date: N/A
Application deadline (fall): 3/15
Undergraduate student body: 24,672 full time, 7,100 part time; 46% male, 54% female; 0% American Indian, 7% Asian, 10% black, 21% Hispanic, 4% multiracial, 0% Pacific Islander, 48% white, 6% international; 94% from in state; 18% live on campus; 6% of students in fraternities, 6% in sororities
Most popular majors: 22% Health Professions and Related Programs, 16% Business, Management, Marketing, and Related Support Services, 12% Biological and Biomedical Sciences, 11% Social Sciences, 6% Engineering
Expenses: 2018-2019: $6,410 in state, $17,324 out of state; room/board: $9,700
Financial aid: (813) 974-4700; 62% of undergrads determined to have financial need; average aid package $11,413

University of South Florida–St. Petersburg

St. Petersburg FL
(727) 873-4142
U.S. News ranking: Reg. U. (S), No. 70
Website: www.usfsp.edu
Admissions email: admissions@usfsp.edu
Public; founded 1965
Freshman admissions: more selective; 2017-2018: 5,575 applied, 2,226 accepted. Either SAT or ACT required. SAT 25/75 percentile: 1080-1230. High school rank: 17% in top tenth, 46% in top quarter, 84% in top half
Early decision deadline: N/A, notification date: N/A
Early action deadline: 11/15, notification date: 12/1
Application deadline (fall): 5/1
Undergraduate student body: 2,845 full time, 1,406 part time; 37% male, 63% female; 0% American Indian, 3% Asian, 8% black, 17% Hispanic, 4% multiracial, 0% Pacific Islander, 63% white, 1% international; 96% from in state; 17% live on campus; N/A of students in fraternities, N/A in sororities
Most popular majors: 32% Business, Management, Marketing, and Related Support Services, 17% Social Sciences, 13% Biological and Biomedical Sciences, 12% Psychology, 7% Education
Expenses: 2018-2019: $5,821 in state, $16,735 out of state; room/board: $10,808
Financial aid: (727) 873-4128; 67% of undergrads determined to have financial need; average aid package $10,570

University of Tampa

Tampa FL
(888) 646-2738
U.S. News ranking: Reg. U. (S), No. 20
Website: www.ut.edu
Admissions email: admissions@ut.edu
Private; founded 1931
Freshman admissions: selective; 2017-2018: 20,495 applied, 10,915 accepted. Either SAT or ACT required. SAT 25/75 percentile: 1070-1230. High school rank: 18% in top tenth, 46% in top quarter, 80% in top half
Early decision deadline: N/A, notification date: N/A
Early action deadline: 11/15, notification date: 12/15
Application deadline (fall): rolling
Undergraduate student body: 7,728 full time, 246 part time; 42% male, 58% female; 0% American Indian, 2% Asian, 5% black, 13% Hispanic, 3% multiracial, 0% Pacific Islander, 61% white, 10% international; 30% from in state; 53% live on campus; 17% of students in fraternities, 22% in sororities
Most popular majors: 7% Business Administration and Management, General, 6% Criminology, 6% Finance, General, 6% Marketing/Marketing Management, General, 5% Accounting
Expenses: 2018-2019: $29,208; room/board: $10,810
Financial aid: (813) 253-6219; 60% of undergrads determined to have financial need; average aid package $17,348

University of West Florida

Pensacola FL
(850) 474-2230
U.S. News ranking: Nat. U., second tier
Website: uwf.edu
Admissions email: admissions@uwf.edu
Public; founded 1963
Freshman admissions: selective; 2017-2018: 5,774 applied, 2,863 accepted. Either SAT or ACT required. ACT 25/75 percentile: 22-27. High school rank: 15% in top tenth, 46% in top quarter, 80% in top half
Early decision deadline: N/A, notification date: N/A
Early action deadline: N/A, notification date: N/A
Application deadline (fall): 6/30
Undergraduate student body: 6,887 full time, 3,122 part time; 43% male, 57% female; 1% American Indian, 3% Asian, 12% black, 9% Hispanic, 5% multiracial, 0% Pacific Islander, 65% white, 2% international; 89% from in state; 14% live on campus; N/A of students in fraternities, N/A in sororities
Most popular majors: 21% Health Professions and Related Programs, 14% Business, Management, Marketing, and Related Support Services, 8% Social Sciences,

6% Communication, Journalism, and Related Programs, 6% Parks, Recreation, Leisure, and Fitness Studies
Expenses: 2018-2019: $6,360 in state, $18,628 out of state; room/board: $9,942
Financial aid: (850) 474-3145; 34% of undergrads determined to have financial need; average aid package $10,166

Valencia College[1]
Orlando FL
U.S. News ranking: Reg. Coll. (S), unranked
Admissions email: N/A
Public
Application deadline (fall): N/A
Undergraduate student body: N/A full time, N/A part time
Expenses: 2017-2018: $2,474 in state, $9,383 out of state; room/board: N/A
Financial aid: N/A

Warner University
Lake Wales FL
(800) 309-9563
U.S. News ranking: Reg. Coll. (S), No. 55
Website: www.warner.edu
Admissions email: admissions@warner.edu
Private; founded 1964
Affiliation: Church of God
Freshman admissions: less selective; 2017-2018: 1,232 applied, 505 accepted. Neither SAT nor ACT required. ACT 25/75 percentile: 16-20. High school rank: 1% in top tenth, 2% in top quarter, 51% in top half
Early decision deadline: N/A, notification date: N/A
Early action deadline: N/A, notification date: N/A
Application deadline (fall): rolling
Undergraduate student body: 869 full time, 133 part time; 54% male, 46% female; 1% American Indian, 0% Asian, 38% black, 11% Hispanic, 2% multiracial, 0% Pacific Islander, 43% white, 4% international; 93% from in state; 43% live on campus; 0% of students in fraternities, 0% in sororities
Most popular majors: 30% Business, Management, Marketing, and Related Support Services, 28% Liberal Arts and Sciences, General Studies and Humanities, 11% Education, 10% Parks, Recreation, Leisure, and Fitness Studies, 8% Theology and Religious Vocations
Expenses: 2018-2019: $21,915; room/board: $8,520
Financial aid: (863) 638-7202; 90% of undergrads determined to have financial need; average aid package $16,278

Webber International University
Babson Park FL
(800) 741-1844
U.S. News ranking: Reg. Coll. (S), No. 64
Website: www.webber.edu
Admissions email: admissions@webber.edu
Private; founded 1927
Freshman admissions: less selective; 2017-2018: 912 applied, 447 accepted. Neither SAT nor ACT required. ACT 25/75 percentile: 17-20. High school rank: 4% in top tenth, 19% in top quarter, 63% in top half
Early decision deadline: N/A, notification date: N/A
Early action deadline: N/A, notification date: N/A
Application deadline (fall): 8/1
Undergraduate student body: 585 full time, 42 part time; 71% male, 29% female; 0% American Indian, 0% Asian, 33% black, 12% Hispanic, 1% multiracial, 1% Pacific Islander, 34% white, 19% international; 83% from in state; 51% live on campus; 0% of students in fraternities, 0% in sororities
Most popular majors: 62% Business, Management, Marketing, and Related Support Services, 21% Parks, Recreation, Leisure, and Fitness Studies, 14% Homeland Security, Law Enforcement, Firefighting and Related Protective Services, 2% Computer and Information Sciences and Support Services, 1% Legal Professions and Studies
Expenses: 2018-2019: $26,116; room/board: $9,150
Financial aid: (863) 638-2930; 74% of undergrads determined to have financial need; average aid package $20,525

GEORGIA

Abraham Baldwin Agricultural College[1]
Tifton GA
(800) 733-3653
U.S. News ranking: Reg. Coll. (S), second tier
Website: www.abac.edu/
Admissions email: N/A
Public; founded 1908
Application deadline (fall): 8/1
Undergraduate student body: N/A full time, N/A part time
Expenses: 2017-2018: $3,503 in state, $10,241 out of state; room/board: $7,518
Financial aid: (229) 391-4985

Agnes Scott College
Decatur GA
(800) 868-8602
U.S. News ranking: Nat. Lib. Arts, No. 51
Website: www.agnesscott.edu
Admissions email: admission@agnesscott.edu
Private; founded 1889
Affiliation: Presbyterian Church (USA)
Freshman admissions: more selective; 2017-2018: 1,534 applied, 1,006 accepted. Neither SAT nor ACT required. SAT 25/75 percentile: 1110-1300. High school rank: 30% in top tenth, 65% in top quarter, 91% in top half
Early decision deadline: 11/1, notification date: 12/1
Early action deadline: 11/15, notification date: 12/15
Application deadline (fall): 5/1
Undergraduate student body: 913 full time, 8 part time; 0% male, 100% female; 0% American Indian, 7% Asian, 30% black, 12% Hispanic, 7% multiracial, 0% Pacific Islander, 35% white, 7% international; 54% from in state; 84% live on campus; N/A of students in fraternities, N/A in sororities
Most popular majors: 12% Public Health, General, 9% Psychology, General, 8% Business Administration and Management, General, 6% Mathematics, General, 5% Economics, General
Expenses: 2018-2019: $41,160; room/board: $12,330
Financial aid: (404) 471-6395; 76% of undergrads determined to have financial need; average aid package $36,231

Albany State University
Albany GA
(229) 430-4646
U.S. News ranking: Reg. U. (S), second tier
Website: www.asurams.edu/
Admissions email: admissions@asurams.edu
Public; founded 1903
Freshman admissions: least selective; 2017-2018: 3,115 applied, 3,026 accepted. Either SAT or ACT required. SAT 25/75 percentile: 740-900. High school rank: 8% in top tenth, 24% in top quarter, 52% in top half
Early decision deadline: N/A, notification date: N/A
Early action deadline: N/A, notification date: N/A
Application deadline (fall): 7/1
Undergraduate student body: 3,927 full time, 2,335 part time; 29% male, 71% female; 0% American Indian, 0% Asian, 71% black, 2% Hispanic, 2% multiracial, 0% Pacific Islander, 20% white, 1% international
Most popular majors: 13% Health Professions and Related Programs, 11% Homeland Security, Law Enforcement, Firefighting and Related Protective Services, 10% Business, Management, Marketing, and Related Support Services, 6% Psychology, 2% Education
Expenses: 2018-2019: $5,675 in state, $16,136 out of state; room/board: $8,820
Financial aid: (855) 211-8543; 87% of undergrads determined to have financial need; average aid package $4,720

Art Institute of Atlanta[1]
Atlanta GA
(770) 394-8300
U.S. News ranking: Arts, unranked
Website: www.artinstitutes.edu/atlanta/
Admissions email: aiaadm@aii.edu
For-profit
Application deadline (fall): N/A
Undergraduate student body: N/A full time, N/A part time
Expenses: N/A
Financial aid: N/A

Atlanta Metropolitan State College[1]
Atlanta GA
(404) 756-4004
U.S. News ranking: Reg. Coll. (S), second tier
Website: www.Atlm.edu
Admissions email: admissions@atlm.edu
Public; founded 1974
Application deadline (fall): rolling
Undergraduate student body: N/A full time, N/A part time
Expenses: 2017-2018: $3,416 in state, $9,880 out of state; room/board: N/A
Financial aid: N/A

Augusta University
Augusta GA
(706) 721-2725
U.S. News ranking: Nat. U., second tier
Website: www.augusta.edu/
Admissions email: admissions@augusta.edu
Public; founded 1828
Freshman admissions: less selective; 2017-2018: 2,584 applied, 1,952 accepted. Either SAT or ACT required. ACT 25/75 percentile: 20-26. High school rank: N/A
Early decision deadline: N/A, notification date: N/A
Early action deadline: N/A, notification date: N/A
Application deadline (fall): N/A
Undergraduate student body: 4,251 full time, 1,040 part time; 35% male, 65% female; N/A American Indian, N/A Asian, N/A black, N/A Hispanic, N/A multiracial, N/A Pacific Islander, N/A white, N/A international; 91% from in state; N/A live on campus; 6% of students in fraternities, 7% in sororities
Most popular majors: 17% Registered Nursing/Registered Nurse, 8% Psychology, General, 7% Kinesiology and Exercise Science, 5% Marketing/Marketing Management, General, 4% Speech Communication and Rhetoric
Expenses: 2017-2018: $8,634 in state, $23,606 out of state; room/board: $14,620
Financial aid: (706) 737-1524

Berry College
Mount Berry GA
(706) 236-2215
U.S. News ranking: Reg. U. (S), No. 9
Website: www.berry.edu
Admissions email: admissions@berry.edu
Private; founded 1902
Freshman admissions: selective; 2017-2018: 3,883 applied, 2,392 accepted. Either SAT or ACT required. ACT 25/75 percentile: 24-29. High school rank: 34% in top tenth, 66% in top quarter, 92% in top half
Early decision deadline: 11/1, notification date: 12/1
Early action deadline: 11/1, notification date: 12/15
Application deadline (fall): 7/20
Undergraduate student body: 1,945 full time, 33 part time; 39% male, 61% female; 0% American Indian, 2% Asian, 5% black, 7% Hispanic, 3% multiracial, 0% Pacific Islander, 80% white, 1% international; 68% from in state; 89% live on campus; N/A of students in fraternities, N/A in sororities
Most popular majors: 20% Biological and Biomedical Sciences, 18% Business, Management, Marketing, and Related Support Services, 9% Psychology, 7% Communication, Journalism, and Related Programs, 7% Parks, Recreation, Leisure, and Fitness Studies
Expenses: 2018-2019: $36,556; room/board: $12,770
Financial aid: (706) 236-1714; 71% of undergrads determined to have financial need; average aid package $29,832

Brenau University
Gainesville GA
(770) 534-6100
U.S. News ranking: Reg. U. (S), No. 47
Website: www.brenau.edu
Admissions email: admissions@brenau.edu
Private; founded 1878
Freshman admissions: less selective; 2017-2018: 1,751 applied, 1,210 accepted. Neither SAT nor ACT required. SAT 25/75 percentile: 880-1090. High school rank: 8% in top tenth, 37% in top quarter, 70% in top half
Early decision deadline: N/A, notification date: N/A
Early action deadline: N/A, notification date: N/A
Application deadline (fall): rolling
Undergraduate student body: 1,080 full time, 656 part time; 9% male, 91% female; 0% American Indian, 2% Asian, 32% black, 8% Hispanic, 3% multiracial, 0% Pacific Islander, 46% white, 4% international; 93% from in state; 27% live on campus; 0% of students in fraternities, 9% in sororities
Most popular majors: 38% Health Professions and Related Programs, 26% Business, Management, Marketing, and Related Support Services, 14% Visual and Performing Arts, 6% Education, 6% Psychology
Expenses: 2018-2019: $29,050; room/board: $12,418
Financial aid: (770) 534-6176; 84% of undergrads determined to have financial need; average aid package $19,551

Brewton-Parker College[1]
Mount Vernon GA
(912) 583-3265
U.S. News ranking: Reg. Coll. (S), second tier
Website: www.bpc.edu
Admissions email: admissions@bpc.edu
Private; founded 1904
Application deadline (fall): rolling
Undergraduate student body: N/A full time, N/A part time

More @ usnews.com/bestcolleges

Expenses: 2017-2018: $17,740; room/board: $8,380
Financial aid: N/A

Clark Atlanta University

Atlanta GA
(800) 688-3228
U.S. News ranking: Nat. U., second tier
Website: www.cau.edu
Admissions email: cauadmissions@cau.edu
Private
Freshman admissions: selective; 2017-2018: 13,940 applied, 3,075 accepted. Either SAT or ACT required. ACT 25/75 percentile: 17-22. High school rank: 12% in top tenth, 28% in top quarter, 70% in top half
Early decision deadline: N/A, notification date: N/A
Early action deadline: N/A, notification date: N/A
Application deadline (fall): 6/1
Undergraduate student body: 3,187 full time, 115 part time; 28% male, 72% female; 0% American Indian, 0% Asian, 85% black, 0% Hispanic, 0% multiracial, 0% Pacific Islander, 0% white, 5% international; 36% from in state; 64% live on campus; 2% of students in fraternities, 3% in sororities
Most popular majors: 25% Business, Management, Marketing, and Related Support Services, 20% Communication, Journalism, and Related Programs, 12% Psychology, 9% Biological and Biomedical Sciences, 7% Construction Trades
Expenses: 2018-2019: $23,438; room/board: $11,156
Financial aid: N/A; 90% of undergrads determined to have financial need; average aid package $7,459

Clayton State University

Morrow GA
(678) 466-4115
U.S. News ranking: Reg. U. (S), second tier
Website: www.clayton.edu
Admissions email: ccsu-info@mail.clayton.edu
Public; founded 1969
Freshman admissions: less selective; 2017-2018: 2,418 applied, 1,011 accepted. Either SAT or ACT required. SAT 25/75 percentile: 860-1020. High school rank: N/A
Early decision deadline: N/A, notification date: N/A
Early action deadline: N/A, notification date: N/A
Application deadline (fall): 7/1
Undergraduate student body: 3,743 full time, 2,812 part time; 31% male, 69% female; 0% American Indian, 5% Asian, 65% black, 6% Hispanic, 3% multiracial, 0% Pacific Islander, 16% white, 1% international; 97% from in state; 16% live on campus; N/A of students in fraternities, N/A in sororities
Most popular majors: 14% Liberal Arts and Sciences/Liberal Studies, 12% Registered Nursing/Registered Nurse, 11% Community Psychology, 9% Hospital and Health Care Facilities Administration/Management, 7% Office Management and Supervision
Expenses: 2018-2019: $6,410 in state, $19,486 out of state; room/board: $10,156
Financial aid: (678) 466-4181; 86% of undergrads determined to have financial need; average aid package $10,557

College of Coastal Georgia

Brunswick GA
(912) 279-5730
U.S. News ranking: Reg. Coll. (S), No. 61
Website: www.ccga.edu
Admissions email: admiss@ccga.edu
Public; founded 1961
Freshman admissions: less selective; 2017-2018: 1,562 applied, 1,479 accepted. Either SAT or ACT required. SAT 25/75 percentile: 890-1090. High school rank: N/A
Early decision deadline: N/A, notification date: N/A
Early action deadline: N/A, notification date: N/A
Application deadline (fall): rolling
Undergraduate student body: 2,217 full time, 1,446 part time; 33% male, 67% female; 0% American Indian, 2% Asian, 21% black, 6% Hispanic, 4% multiracial, 0% Pacific Islander, 64% white, 1% international; 82% from in state; 19% live on campus; N/A of students in fraternities, N/A in sororities
Most popular majors: 19% Registered Nursing/Registered Nurse, 13% Business/Commerce, General, 12% Psychology, General, 11% Early Childhood Education and Teaching, 9% Junior High/Intermediate/Middle School Education and Teaching
Expenses: 2018-2019: $4,696 in state, $13,118 out of state; room/board: $10,036
Financial aid: (912) 279-5726; 49% of undergrads determined to have financial need; average aid package $4,857

Columbus State University

Columbus GA
(706) 507-8800
U.S. News ranking: Reg. U. (S), No. 102
Website: www.columbusstate.edu
Admissions email: admissions@columbusstate.edu
Public; founded 1958
Freshman admissions: selective; 2017-2018: 3,483 applied, 1,860 accepted. Either SAT or ACT required. SAT 25/75 percentile: 870-1070. High school rank: 13% in top tenth, 37% in top quarter, 67% in top half
Early decision deadline: N/A, notification date: N/A
Early action deadline: N/A, notification date: N/A
Application deadline (fall): 6/30
Undergraduate student body: 4,693 full time, 2,105 part time; 41% male, 59% female; 0% American Indian, 2% Asian, 39% black, 6% Hispanic, 2% multiracial, 0% Pacific Islander, 49% white, 1% international; 85% from in state; 20% live on campus; 5% of students in fraternities, 5% in sororities
Most popular majors: 24% Health Professions and Related Programs, 17% Business, Management, Marketing, and Related Support Services, 7% Education, 7% Homeland Security, Law Enforcement, Firefighting and Related Protective Services, 6% Visual and Performing Arts
Expenses: 2018-2019: $7,200 in state, $20,682 out of state; room/board: $9,880
Financial aid: (706) 507-8800; 72% of undergrads determined to have financial need; average aid package $9,917

Covenant College

Lookout Mountain GA
(706) 820-2398
U.S. News ranking: Nat. Lib. Arts, No. 168
Website: www.covenant.edu
Admissions email: admissions@covenant.edu
Private; founded 1955
Affiliation: The Presbyterian Church in America
Freshman admissions: more selective; 2017-2018: 692 applied, 659 accepted. Either SAT or ACT required. ACT 25/75 percentile: 24-30. High school rank: 31% in top tenth, 61% in top quarter, 90% in top half
Early decision deadline: N/A, notification date: N/A
Early action deadline: 11/15, notification date: 12/1
Application deadline (fall): 2/1
Undergraduate student body: 983 full time, 47 part time; 47% male, 53% female; 0% American Indian, 1% Asian, 3% black, 3% Hispanic, 4% multiracial, 0% Pacific Islander, 86% white, 3% international; 30% from in state; 85% live on campus; 0% of students in fraternities, 0% in sororities
Most popular majors: 14% Social Sciences, 10% Biological and Biomedical Sciences, 10% English Language and Literature/Letters, 10% Multi/Interdisciplinary Studies, 8% Psychology
Expenses: 2018-2019: $34,330; room/board: $10,260
Financial aid: (706) 419-1104; 68% of undergrads determined to have financial need; average aid package $28,669

Dalton State College[1]

Dalton GA
(706) 272-4436
U.S. News ranking: Reg. Coll. (S), unranked
Website: www.daltonstate.edu/
Admissions email: N/A
Public
Application deadline (fall): N/A
Undergraduate student body: N/A full time, N/A part time
Expenses: 2017-2018: $4,212 in state, $12,634 out of state; room/board: $8,128
Financial aid: N/A

East Georgia State College[1]

Swainsboro GA
U.S. News ranking: Reg. Coll. (S), second tier
Admissions email: N/A
Public
Application deadline (fall): 8/15
Undergraduate student body: N/A full time, N/A part time
Expenses: 2017-2018: $3,110 in state, $9,307 out of state; room/board: $8,605
Financial aid: N/A

Emmanuel College

Franklin Springs GA
(800) 860-8800
U.S. News ranking: Reg. Coll. (S), No. 34
Website: www.ec.edu
Admissions email: admissions@ec.edu
Private; founded 1919
Affiliation: Pentecostal Holiness Church
Freshman admissions: selective; 2017-2018: 1,119 applied, 482 accepted. Either SAT or ACT required. SAT 25/75 percentile: 950-1110. High school rank: N/A
Early decision deadline: N/A, notification date: N/A
Early action deadline: N/A, notification date: N/A
Application deadline (fall): 8/1
Undergraduate student body: 822 full time, 130 part time; 52% male, 48% female; 0% American Indian, 0% Asian, 15% black, 8% Hispanic, 3% multiracial, 1% Pacific Islander, 65% white, 8% international; 70% from in state; 60% live on campus; N/A of students in fraternities, N/A in sororities
Most popular majors: 23% Parks, Recreation, Leisure, and Fitness Studies, 19% Business, Management, Marketing, and Related Support Services, 16% Education, 9% Psychology, 8% Biological and Biomedical Sciences
Expenses: 2018-2019: $20,292; room/board: $7,994
Financial aid: (706) 245-2844; 78% of undergrads determined to have financial need; average aid package $16,176

Emory University

Atlanta GA
(404) 727-6036
U.S. News ranking: Nat. U., No. 21
Website: www.emory.edu
Admissions email: admission@emory.edu
Private; founded 1836
Affiliation: United Methodist
Freshman admissions: most selective; 2017-2018: 23,747 applied, 5,234 accepted. Either SAT or ACT required. ACT 25/75 percentile: 30-33. High school rank: 83% in top tenth, 97% in top quarter, 100% in top half
Early decision deadline: 11/1, notification date: 12/15
Early action deadline: N/A, notification date: N/A
Application deadline (fall): 1/1
Undergraduate student body: 6,794 full time, 143 part time; 40% male, 60% female; 0% American Indian, 20% Asian, 8% black, 9% Hispanic, 4% multiracial, 0% Pacific Islander, 41% white, 16% international; 21% from in state; 65% live on campus; 26% of students in fraternities, 29% in sororities
Most popular majors: 15% Business Administration and Management, General, 8% Biology/Biological Sciences, General, 8% Registered Nursing/Registered Nurse, 7% Economics, General, 6% Psychology, General
Expenses: 2018-2019: $51,306; room/board: $14,456
Financial aid: (404) 727-6039; 45% of undergrads determined to have financial need; average aid package $43,777

Fort Valley State University

Fort Valley GA
(478) 825-6307
U.S. News ranking: Reg. U. (S), second tier
Website: www.fvsu.edu
Admissions email: admissap@mail.fvsu.edu
Public; founded 1895
Freshman admissions: less selective; 2017-2018: 3,237 applied, 1,337 accepted. Either SAT or ACT required. SAT 25/75 percentile: 820-910. High school rank: 3% in top tenth, 16% in top quarter, 44% in top half
Early decision deadline: N/A, notification date: N/A
Early action deadline: N/A, notification date: N/A
Application deadline (fall): 7/19
Undergraduate student body: 2,115 full time, 229 part time; 41% male, 59% female; 0% American Indian, 0% Asian, 92% black, 1% Hispanic, 2% multiracial, 0% Pacific Islander, 3% white, 0% international
Most popular majors: 41% Psychology, 13% Health Professions and Related Programs, 12% Homeland Security, Law Enforcement, Firefighting and Related Protective Services, 9% Physical Sciences, 7% Biological and Biomedical Sciences
Expenses: 2018-2019: $4,186 in state, $19,744 out of state; room/board: $8,084
Financial aid: (478) 825-6363; 95% of undergrads determined to have financial need; average aid package $7,135

Georgia College & State University

Milledgeville GA
(478) 445-1283
U.S. News ranking: Reg. U. (S), No. 28
Website: www.gcsu.edu

Admissions email: admissions@gcsu.edu
Public; founded 1889
Freshman admissions: selective; 2017-2018: 4,089 applied, 3,230 accepted. Either SAT or ACT required. ACT 25/75 percentile: 23-27. High school rank: N/A
Early decision deadline: N/A, notification date: N/A
Early action deadline: 11/1, notification date: 1/1
Application deadline (fall): 4/1
Undergraduate student body: 5,442 full time, 545 part time; 38% male, 62% female; 0% American Indian, 1% Asian, 5% black, 5% Hispanic, 3% multiracial, 0% Pacific Islander, 84% white, 0% international; 99% from in state; 33% live on campus; 6% of students in fraternities, 12% in sororities
Most popular majors: 9% Registered Nursing/Registered Nurse, 8% Business Administration and Management, General, 8% Marketing/Marketing Management, General, 7% Journalism, 7% Kinesiology and Exercise Science
Expenses: 2018-2019: $9,346 in state, $28,060 out of state; room/board: $12,964
Financial aid: (478) 445-5149; 52% of undergrads determined to have financial need; average aid package $10,745

Georgia Gwinnett College

Lawrenceville GA
(678) 407-5313
U.S. News ranking: Reg. Coll. (S), No. 52
Website: www.ggc.edu
Admissions email: ggcadmissions@ggc.edu
Public; founded 2005
Freshman admissions: less selective; 2017-2018: 4,073 applied, 3,573 accepted. Either SAT or ACT required. SAT 25/75 percentile: 910-1110. High school rank: 3% in top tenth, 15% in top quarter, 43% in top half
Early decision deadline: N/A, notification date: N/A
Early action deadline: N/A, notification date: N/A
Application deadline (fall): 6/1
Undergraduate student body: 8,289 full time, 3,998 part time; 44% male, 56% female; 0% American Indian, 10% Asian, 33% black, 19% Hispanic, 3% multiracial, 0% Pacific Islander, 30% white, 2% international; 99% from in state; 5% live on campus; N/A of students in fraternities, N/A in sororities
Most popular majors: 32% Business/Commerce, General, 12% Information Technology, 11% Psychology, General, 10% Biology/Biological Sciences, General, 8% Early Childhood Education and Teaching
Expenses: 2018-2019: $5,634 in state, $16,348 out of state; room/board: $13,086
Financial aid: (678) 407-5701; 75% of undergrads determined to have financial need; average aid package $15,979

Georgia Highlands College[1]

Rome GA
U.S. News ranking: Reg. Coll. (S), second tier
Admissions email: N/A
Public
Application deadline (fall): N/A
Undergraduate student body: N/A full time, N/A part time
Expenses: 2017-2018: $3,288 in state, $9,485 out of state; room/board: $7,200
Financial aid: N/A

Georgia Institute of Technology

Atlanta GA
(404) 894-4154
U.S. News ranking: Nat. U., No. 35
Website: admission.gatech.edu/information/
Admissions email: admission@gatech.edu
Public; founded 1885
Freshman admissions: most selective; 2017-2018: 31,497 applied, 7,369 accepted. Either SAT or ACT required. SAT 25/75 percentile: 1370-1520. High school rank: 88% in top tenth, 98% in top quarter, 99% in top half
Early decision deadline: N/A, notification date: N/A
Early action deadline: 10/15, notification date: 1/13
Application deadline (fall): 1/1
Undergraduate student body: 13,974 full time, 1,599 part time; 62% male, 38% female; 0% American Indian, 20% Asian, 7% black, 7% Hispanic, 4% multiracial, 0% Pacific Islander, 50% white, 9% international; 67% from in state; 43% live on campus; 26% of students in fraternities, 30% in sororities
Most popular majors: 65% Engineering, 13% Computer and Information Sciences and Support Services, 11% Business, Management, Marketing, and Related Support Services, 4% Biological and Biomedical Sciences, 1% Physical Sciences
Expenses: 2018-2019: $12,424 in state, $33,020 out of state; room/board: $14,596
Financial aid: (404) 894-4160; 42% of undergrads determined to have financial need; average aid package $15,931

Georgia Southern University

Statesboro GA
(912) 478-5391
U.S. News ranking: Nat. U., second tier
Website: www.georgiasouthern.edu/
Admissions email: admissions@georgiasouthern.edu
Public; founded 1906
Freshman admissions: selective; 2017-2018: 9,202 applied, 6,284 accepted. Either SAT or ACT required. SAT 25/75 percentile: 1100-1230. High school rank: 19% in top tenth, 45% in top quarter, 75% in top half
Early decision deadline: N/A, notification date: N/A
Early action deadline: N/A, notification date: N/A
Application deadline (fall): 5/1
Undergraduate student body: 15,755 full time, 2,004 part time; 50% male, 50% female; 0% American Indian, 2% Asian, 24% black, 6% Hispanic, 2% multiracial, 0% Pacific Islander, 63% white, 2% international; 95% from in state; 28% live on campus; 13% of students in fraternities, 20% in sororities
Most popular majors: 21% Business, Management, Marketing, and Related Support Services, 9% Parks, Recreation, Leisure, and Fitness Studies, 6% Engineering, 6% Health Professions and Related Programs, 6% Liberal Arts and Sciences, General Studies and Humanities
Expenses: 2018-2019: $6,890 in state, $19,022 out of state; room/board: $9,650
Financial aid: (912) 478-5413; 63% of undergrads determined to have financial need; average aid package $10,721

Georgia Southwestern State University

Americus GA
(229) 928-1273
U.S. News ranking: Reg. U. (S), second tier
Website: www.gsw.edu
Admissions email: admissions@gsw.edu
Public; founded 1906
Freshman admissions: selective; 2017-2018: 1,279 applied, 863 accepted. Either SAT or ACT required. SAT 25/75 percentile: 960-1110. High school rank: 12% in top tenth, 36% in top quarter, 72% in top half
Early decision deadline: N/A, notification date: N/A
Early action deadline: N/A, notification date: N/A
Application deadline (fall): 7/21
Undergraduate student body: 1,779 full time, 827 part time; 37% male, 63% female; 0% American Indian, 1% Asian, 26% black, 6% Hispanic, 2% multiracial, 0% Pacific Islander, 62% white, 2% international; 96% from in state; 32% live on campus; 10% of students in fraternities, 10% in sororities
Most popular majors: 18% Business Administration and Management, General, 13% Accounting, 12% Registered Nursing/Registered Nurse, 11% Elementary Education and Teaching, 10% Psychology, General
Expenses: 2018-2019: $6,372 in state, $19,448 out of state; room/board: $8,120
Financial aid: (229) 928-1378; 73% of undergrads determined to have financial need; average aid package $9,680

Georgia State University

Atlanta GA
(404) 413-2500
U.S. News ranking: Nat. U., No. 187
Website: www.gsu.edu
Admissions email: admissions@gsu.edu
Public; founded 1913
Freshman admissions: selective; 2017-2018: 18,971 applied, 9,898 accepted. Either SAT or ACT required. SAT 25/75 percentile: 970-1170. High school rank: 17% in top tenth, 49% in top quarter, 87% in top half
Early decision deadline: N/A, notification date: N/A
Early action deadline: 11/15, notification date: 12/15
Application deadline (fall): 3/1
Undergraduate student body: 19,909 full time, 5,881 part time; 41% male, 59% female; 0% American Indian, 14% Asian, 42% black, 11% Hispanic, 6% multiracial, 0% Pacific Islander, 23% white, 2% international; 96% from in state; 22% live on campus; N/A of students in fraternities, N/A in sororities
Most popular majors: 23% Business, Management, Marketing, and Related Support Services, 11% Social Sciences, 10% Psychology, 8% Biological and Biomedical Sciences, 7% Computer and Information Sciences and Support Services
Expenses: 2018-2019: $10,858 in state, $29,432 out of state; room/board: $14,692
Financial aid: (404) 413-2600; 79% of undergrads determined to have financial need; average aid package $11,651

Gordon State College

Barnesville GA
(678) 359-5021
U.S. News ranking: Reg. Coll. (S), No. 45
Website: www.gordonstate.edu/
Admissions email: admissions@gordonstate.edu
Public; founded 1852
Freshman admissions: least selective; 2017-2018: 3,212 applied, 2,689 accepted. Either SAT or ACT required. SAT 25/75 percentile: 840-1030. High school rank: N/A
Early decision deadline: N/A, notification date: N/A
Early action deadline: N/A, notification date: N/A
Application deadline (fall): rolling
Undergraduate student body: 2,686 full time, 1,300 part time; 33% male, 67% female; 0% American Indian, 1% Asian, 42% black, 4% Hispanic, 4% multiracial, 0% Pacific Islander, 49% white, 0% international
Most popular majors: 26% Public Administration and Social Service Professions, 16% Biology/Biological Sciences, General, 16% Elementary Education and Teaching, 12% Health Information/Medical Records Administration/Administrator, 10% Business Administration and Management, General
Expenses: 2018-2019: $4,164 in state, $12,422 out of state; room/board: $8,101
Financial aid: (678) 359-5990

Kennesaw State University

Kennesaw GA
(770) 423-6300
U.S. News ranking: Nat. U., second tier
Website: www.kennesaw.edu
Admissions email: ksuadmit@kennesaw.edu
Public; founded 1963
Freshman admissions: selective; 2017-2018: 13,998 applied, 8,487 accepted. Either SAT or ACT required. ACT 25/75 percentile: 21-26. High school rank: 21% in top tenth, 53% in top quarter, 81% in top half
Early decision deadline: N/A, notification date: N/A
Early action deadline: N/A, notification date: N/A
Application deadline (fall): 4/1
Undergraduate student body: 24,869 full time, 8,076 part time; 52% male, 48% female; 0% American Indian, 5% Asian, 21% black, 10% Hispanic, 5% multiracial, 0% Pacific Islander, 56% white, 2% international; 88% from in state; 15% live on campus; 5% of students in fraternities, 9% in sororities
Most popular majors: 21% Business, Management, Marketing, and Related Support Services, 9% Communication, Journalism, and Related Programs, 8% Computer and Information Sciences and Support Services, 7% Engineering, 6% Psychology
Expenses: 2018-2019: $7,432 in state, $21,158 out of state; room/board: $11,467
Financial aid: (770) 423-6074; 68% of undergrads determined to have financial need; average aid package $9,525

LaGrange College

LaGrange GA
(706) 880-8005
U.S. News ranking: Nat. Lib. Arts, second tier
Website: www.lagrange.edu
Admissions email: admission@lagrange.edu
Private; founded 1831
Affiliation: United Methodist
Freshman admissions: selective; 2017-2018: 1,548 applied, 879 accepted. Either SAT or ACT required. ACT 25/75 percentile: 20-24. High school rank: 18% in top tenth, 43% in top quarter, 82% in top half
Early decision deadline: N/A, notification date: N/A
Early action deadline: N/A, notification date: N/A
Application deadline (fall): rolling
Undergraduate student body: 888 full time, 49 part time; 49% male, 51% female; 0% American Indian, 1% Asian, 22% black, 1% Hispanic, 3% multiracial, 0% Pacific Islander, 73% white, 1% international; 85% from in

More @ usnews.com/bestcolleges

state; 59% live on campus; 21% of students in fraternities, 38% in sororities
Most popular majors: 16% Business Administration and Management, General, 16% Registered Nursing/Registered Nurse, 13% Kinesiology and Exercise Science, 8% Biology/ Biological Sciences, General, 7% Psychology, General
Expenses: 2018-2019: $30,470; room/board: $11,630
Financial aid: (706) 880-8249; 87% of undergrads determined to have financial need; average aid package $26,065

Mercer University

Macon GA
(478) 301-2650
U.S. News ranking: Nat. U., No. 140
Website: www.mercer.edu
Admissions email: admissions@mercer.edu
Private; founded 1833
Freshman admissions: more selective; 2017-2018: 4,749 applied, 3,479 accepted. Either SAT or ACT required. ACT 25/75 percentile: 25-30. High school rank: 36% in top tenth, 71% in top quarter, 93% in top half
Early decision deadline: N/A, notification date: N/A
Early action deadline: N/A, notification date: N/A
Application deadline (fall): 2/1
Undergraduate student body: 4,135 full time, 612 part time; 38% male, 62% female; 0% American Indian, 7% Asian, 29% black, 5% Hispanic, 3% multiracial, 0% Pacific Islander, 48% white, 2% international; 82% from in state; 78% live on campus; 21% of students in fraternities, 28% in sororities
Most popular majors: 20% Business, Management, Marketing, and Related Support Services, 16% Engineering, 15% Biological and Biomedical Sciences, 8% Psychology, 8% Social Sciences
Expenses: 2018-2019: $36,894; room/board: $12,522
Financial aid: (478) 301-2670; 70% of undergrads determined to have financial need; average aid package $35,680

Middle Georgia State University

Macon GA
(877) 238-8664
U.S. News ranking: Reg. Coll. (S), No. 55
Website: www.mga.edu/
Admissions email: admissions@mga.edu
Public; founded 2013
Freshman admissions: less selective; 2017-2018: 3,554 applied, 2,107 accepted. Either SAT or ACT required. SAT 25/75 percentile: 820-1020. High school rank: N/A
Early decision deadline: N/A, notification date: N/A
Early action deadline: N/A, notification date: N/A
Application deadline (fall): rolling
Undergraduate student body: 4,507 full time, 2,714 part time; 42% male, 58% female; 0% American Indian, 3% Asian, 35% black, 5% Hispanic, 4% multiracial, 0% Pacific Islander, 53% white, 1% international
Most popular majors: 17% Business Administration and Management, General, 14% Registered Nursing/Registered Nurse, 10% Computer and Information Sciences, General, 9% Psychology, General, 7% Criminal Justice/Safety Studies
Expenses: 2017-2018: $4,608 in state, $10,242 out of state; room/ board: N/A
Financial aid: N/A

Morehouse College

Atlanta GA
(844) 512-6672
U.S. News ranking: Nat. Lib. Arts, No. 143
Website: www.morehouse.edu
Admissions email: admissions@morehouse.edu
Private; founded 1867
Freshman admissions: selective; 2017-2018: 2,349 applied, 1,748 accepted. Either SAT or ACT required. SAT 25/75 percentile: 950-1160. High school rank: 12% in top tenth, 36% in top quarter, 66% in top half
Early decision deadline: 11/1, notification date: 12/15
Early action deadline: 11/1, notification date: 12/15
Application deadline (fall): 2/15
Undergraduate student body: 2,090 full time, 112 part time; 100% male, 0% female; 0% American Indian, 0% Asian, 94% black, 1% Hispanic, 2% multiracial, 0% Pacific Islander, 0% white, 1% international; 28% from in state; 61% live on campus; 3% of students in fraternities, 0% in sororities
Most popular majors: 22% Social Sciences, 20% Business, Management, Marketing, and Related Support Services, 10% Biological and Biomedical Sciences, 7% Psychology, 7% Visual and Performing Arts
Expenses: 2018-2019: $27,574; room/board: $13,438
Financial aid: (844) 512-6672; 82% of undergrads determined to have financial need; average aid package $23,565

Oglethorpe University

Atlanta GA
(404) 364-8307
U.S. News ranking: Nat. Lib. Arts, second tier
Website: www.oglethorpe.edu
Admissions email: admission@oglethorpe.edu
Private; founded 1835
Freshman admissions: more selective; 2017-2018: 2,159 applied, 1,253 accepted. Either SAT or ACT required. SAT 25/75 percentile: 1110-1310. High school rank: 26% in top tenth, 61% in top quarter, 90% in top half
Early decision deadline: N/A, notification date: N/A
Early action deadline: 11/15, notification date: 8/1
Application deadline (fall): rolling
Undergraduate student body: 1,166 full time, 84 part time; 41% male, 59% female; 1% American Indian, 4% Asian, 24% black, 11% Hispanic, 2% multiracial, 0% Pacific Islander, 38% white, 7% international; 72% from in state; 60% live on campus; 6% of students in fraternities, 15% in sororities
Most popular majors: 21% Business Administration and Management, General, 14% Rhetoric and Composition, 10% Psychology, General, 5% Biology/ Biological Sciences, General, 5% Biopsychology
Expenses: 2018-2019: $38,100; room/board: $13,200
Financial aid: (404) 504-1500; 75% of undergrads determined to have financial need; average aid package $31,801

Paine College[1]

Augusta GA
(706) 821-8320
U.S. News ranking: Nat. Lib. Arts, second tier
Website: www.paine.edu
Admissions email: admissions@paine.edu
Private; founded 1882
Application deadline (fall): 7/15
Undergraduate student body: N/A full time, N/A part time
Expenses: 2017-2018: $14,226; room/board: $6,662
Financial aid: N/A

Piedmont College

Demorest GA
(800) 277-7020
U.S. News ranking: Reg. U. (S), No. 63
Website: www.piedmont.edu
Admissions email: ugrad@piedmont.edu
Private; founded 1897
Affiliation: United Church of Christ
Freshman admissions: less selective; 2017-2018: 1,287 applied, 766 accepted. Either SAT or ACT required. SAT 25/75 percentile: 950-1130. High school rank: 8% in top tenth, 28% in top quarter, 71% in top half
Early decision deadline: N/A, notification date: N/A
Early action deadline: N/A, notification date: N/A
Application deadline (fall): 7/1
Undergraduate student body: 1,160 full time, 121 part time; 34% male, 66% female; 0% American Indian, 1% Asian, 10% black, 8% Hispanic, 0% multiracial, 0% Pacific Islander, 67% white, 0% international; 90% from in state; 72% live on campus; N/A of students in fraternities, N/A in sororities
Most popular majors: 29% Health Professions and Related Programs, 17% Business, Management, Marketing, and Related Support Services, 16% Education, 10% Visual and Performing Arts, 6% Psychology
Expenses: 2018-2019: $25,920; room/board: $10,168
Financial aid: (706) 776-0114; 82% of undergrads determined to have financial need; average aid package $20,522

Point University

West Point GA
(706) 385-1202
U.S. News ranking: Reg. Coll. (S), No. 45
Website: www.point.edu
Admissions email: admissions@point.edu
Private; founded 1937
Affiliation: Christian Churches and Churches of Christ
Freshman admissions: less selective; 2017-2018: 1,406 applied, 493 accepted. Neither SAT nor ACT required. ACT 25/75 percentile: 16-21. High school rank: 12% in top tenth, 27% in top quarter, 60% in top half
Early decision deadline: N/A, notification date: N/A
Early action deadline: N/A, notification date: N/A
Application deadline (fall): 8/1
Undergraduate student body: 1,119 full time, 807 part time; 46% male, 54% female; 0% American Indian, 1% Asian, 37% black, 6% Hispanic, 6% multiracial, 0% Pacific Islander, 42% white, 3% international; 82% from in state; 39% live on campus; N/A of students in fraternities, N/A in sororities
Most popular majors: Information not available
Expenses: 2017-2018: $20,600; room/board: $7,900
Financial aid: (706) 385-1462

Reinhardt University

Waleska GA
(770) 720-5526
U.S. News ranking: Reg. Coll. (S), No. 25
Website: www.reinhardt.edu/
Admissions email: admissions@reinhardt.edu
Private; founded 1883
Affiliation: United Methodist
Freshman admissions: selective; 2017-2018: 1,442 applied, 1,278 accepted. Either SAT or ACT required. ACT 25/75 percentile: 18-23. High school rank: 6% in top tenth, 25% in top quarter, 60% in top half
Early decision deadline: N/A, notification date: N/A
Early action deadline: N/A, notification date: N/A
Application deadline (fall): 8/21
Undergraduate student body: 1,260 full time, 148 part time; 53% male, 47% female; 0% American Indian, 1% Asian, 19% black, 8% Hispanic, 1% multiracial, 0% Pacific Islander, 63% white, 0% international; N/A from in state; N/A live on campus; 0% of students in fraternities, 0% in sororities
Most popular majors: 12% Sport and Fitness Administration/ Management, 11% Business Administration and Management, General, 11% Criminal Justice/ Safety Studies, 10% Organizational Leadership, 7% Biology/ Biological Sciences, General
Expenses: 2018-2019: $23,300; room/board: $10,200
Financial aid: (770) 720-5667; 78% of undergrads determined to have financial need; average aid package $15,606

Savannah College of Art and Design

Savannah GA
(912) 525-5100
U.S. News ranking: Arts, unranked
Website: www.scad.edu
Admissions email: admission@scad.edu
Private; founded 1978
Freshman admissions: selective; 2017-2018: 12,942 applied, 9,381 accepted. Either SAT or ACT required. SAT 25/75 percentile: 1030-1230. High school rank: N/A
Early decision deadline: N/A, notification date: N/A
Early action deadline: N/A, notification date: N/A
Application deadline (fall): rolling
Undergraduate student body: 9,474 full time, 1,850 part time; 33% male, 67% female; 1% American Indian, 5% Asian, 10% black, 8% Hispanic, 0% multiracial, 0% Pacific Islander, 52% white, 21% international; 20% from in state; N/A live on campus; N/A of students in fraternities, N/A in sororities
Most popular majors: 54% Visual and Performing Arts, 18% Communication, Journalism, and Related Programs, 16% Communications Technologies/ Technicians and Support Services, 6% Family and Consumer Sciences/Human Sciences, 3% Architecture and Related Services
Expenses: 2018-2019: $36,630; room/board: $14,550
Financial aid: (912) 525-5100; 50% of undergrads determined to have financial need; average aid package $18,094

Savannah State University

Savannah GA
(912) 358-4338
U.S. News ranking: Reg. U. (S), second tier
Website: www.savannahstate.edu
Admissions email: admissions@ savannahstate.edu
Public; founded 1890
Freshman admissions: least selective; 2017-2018: 4,356 applied, 2,257 accepted. Either SAT or ACT required. SAT 25/75 percentile: 860-1010. High school rank: N/A
Early decision deadline: N/A, notification date: N/A
Early action deadline: N/A, notification date: N/A
Application deadline (fall): 7/15
Undergraduate student body: 3,687 full time, 552 part time; 40% male, 60% female; 0% American Indian, 0% Asian, 84% black,

7% Hispanic, 4% multiracial, 0% Pacific Islander, 3% white, 1% international; 100% from in state; 58% live on campus; 0% of students in fraternities, 0% in sororities
Most popular majors: 22% Homeland Security, Law Enforcement, Firefighting and Related Protective Services, Other, 14% Biology/Biological Sciences, General, 14% Business Administration and Management, General, 13% Journalism, 8% Political Science and Government, General
Expenses: 2017-2018: $3,367 in state, $9,905 out of state; room/board: N/A
Financial aid: (912) 358-4162

Shorter University

Rome GA
(800) 868-6980
U.S. News ranking: Reg. Coll. (S), No. 27
Website: su.shorter.edu
Admissions email: admissions@shorter.edu
Private; founded 1873
Affiliation: Baptist
Freshman admissions: less selective; 2017-2018: 1,722 applied, 919 accepted. Either SAT or ACT required. ACT 25/75 percentile: 17-24. High school rank: 12% in top tenth, 34% in top quarter, 69% in top half
Early decision deadline: N/A, notification date: N/A
Early action deadline: N/A, notification date: N/A
Application deadline (fall): N/A
Undergraduate student body: 1,140 full time, 263 part time; 43% male, 57% female; 0% American Indian, 0% Asian, 28% black, 6% Hispanic, 2% multiracial, 0% Pacific Islander, 60% white, 3% international
Most popular majors: 20% Business Administration and Management, General, 8% Criminal Justice/Safety Studies, 8% Sport and Fitness Administration/Management, 6% Registered Nursing/Registered Nurse, 5% Public Administration and Social Service Professions
Expenses: 2017-2018: $21,730; room/board: $9,400
Financial aid: (706) 233-7227

South Georgia State College[1]

Douglas GA
(912) 260-4206
U.S. News ranking: Reg. Coll. (S), unranked
Website: www.sgsc.edu
Admissions email: admissions@sgsc.edu
Private
Application deadline (fall): rolling
Undergraduate student body: N/A full time, N/A part time
Expenses: 2017-2018: $9,451; room/board: $8,250
Financial aid: N/A

South University[1]

Savannah GA
(912) 201-8000
U.S. News ranking: Reg. U. (S), second tier
Website: www.southuniversity.edu
Admissions email: cshall@southuniversity.edu
Private
Application deadline (fall): N/A
Undergraduate student body: N/A full time, N/A part time
Expenses: 2017-2018: $17,014; room/board: N/A
Financial aid: N/A

Spelman College

Atlanta GA
(800) 982-2411
U.S. News ranking: Nat. Lib. Arts, No. 51
Website: www.spelman.edu
Admissions email: admiss@spelman.edu
Private; founded 1881
Freshman admissions: selective; 2017-2018: 8,344 applied, 3,342 accepted. Either SAT or ACT required. SAT 25/75 percentile: 1070-1215. High school rank: 26% in top tenth, 53% in top quarter, 89% in top half
Early decision deadline: 11/1, notification date: 12/15
Early action deadline: 11/15, notification date: 12/31
Application deadline (fall): 2/1
Undergraduate student body: 2,086 full time, 51 part time; 0% male, 100% female; 2% American Indian, 0% Asian, 97% black, 0% Hispanic, 1% multiracial, 0% Pacific Islander, 0% white, 1% international; 28% from in state; 67% live on campus; N/A of students in fraternities, 6% in sororities
Most popular majors: 18% Psychology, General, 12% Biology/Biological Sciences, General, 10% Economics, General, 10% Political Science and Government, General, 7% International/Global Studies
Expenses: 2018-2019: $29,064; room/board: $13,865
Financial aid: (404) 270-5209; 83% of undergrads determined to have financial need; average aid package $17,443

Thomas University

Thomasville GA
(229) 227-6934
U.S. News ranking: Reg. U. (S), second tier
Website: www.thomasu.edu
Admissions email: rgagliano@thomasu.edu
Private; founded 1950
Freshman admissions: less selective; 2017-2018: 359 applied, 81 accepted. Neither SAT nor ACT required. SAT 25/75 percentile: N/A. High school rank: N/A
Early decision deadline: N/A, notification date: N/A
Early action deadline: N/A, notification date: N/A
Application deadline (fall): rolling
Undergraduate student body: 438 full time, 680 part time; 36% male, 64% female; N/A American Indian, N/A Asian, N/A black, N/A Hispanic, N/A multiracial, N/A Pacific Islander, N/A white, N/A international
Most popular majors: 9% Criminal Justice/Law Enforcement Administration, 8% Registered Nursing, Nursing Administration, Nursing Research and Clinical Nursing, Other, 7% Business Administration and Management, General, 7% Clinical/Medical Laboratory Science and Allied Professions, Other, 7% Social Work
Expenses: 2017-2018: $16,940; room/board: $7,500
Financial aid: (229) 226-1621

Toccoa Falls College

Toccoa Falls GA
(888) 785-5624
U.S. News ranking: Reg. Coll. (S), No. 22
Website: www.tfc.edu
Admissions email: admissions@tfc.edu
Private; founded 1907
Affiliation: Christ and Missionary Alliance Church
Freshman admissions: selective; 2017-2018: 843 applied, 495 accepted. Either SAT or ACT required. SAT 25/75 percentile: 920-1150. High school rank: 12% in top tenth, 40% in top quarter, 71% in top half
Early decision deadline: N/A, notification date: N/A
Early action deadline: N/A, notification date: N/A
Application deadline (fall): rolling
Undergraduate student body: 872 full time, 539 part time; 41% male, 59% female; 0% American Indian, 6% Asian, 8% black, 6% Hispanic, 2% multiracial, 0% Pacific Islander, 75% white, 2% international; 65% from in state; 56% live on campus; 0% of students in fraternities, 0% in sororities
Most popular majors: 17% Counseling Psychology, 12% Missions/Missionary Studies and Missiology, 8% Divinity/Ministry, 6% Bible/Biblical Studies, 6% Religious Education
Expenses: 2018-2019: $22,744; room/board: $8,330
Financial aid: (706) 886-7299; 89% of undergrads determined to have financial need; average aid package $16,922

Truett McConnell University

Cleveland GA
(706) 865-2134
U.S. News ranking: Reg. Coll. (S), No. 51
Website: truett.edu/
Admissions email: admissions@truett.edu
Private; founded 1946
Affiliation: Southern Baptist
Freshman admissions: less selective; 2017-2018: 558 applied, 528 accepted. Either SAT or ACT required. SAT 25/75 percentile: 920-1120. High school rank: 9% in top tenth, 28% in top quarter, 60% in top half
Early decision deadline: N/A, notification date: N/A
Early action deadline: N/A, notification date: N/A
Application deadline (fall): 8/1
Undergraduate student body: 780 full time, 1,793 part time; 44% male, 56% female; 0% American Indian, 0% Asian, 8% black, 5% Hispanic, 0% multiracial, 0% Pacific Islander, 83% white, 2% international
Most popular majors: 22% Health Professions and Related Programs, 21% Theology and Religious Vocations, 17% Business, Management, Marketing, and Related Support Services, 15% Education, 8% Psychology
Expenses: 2018-2019: $20,230; room/board: $7,550
Financial aid: (706) 865-2134; 82% of undergrads determined to have financial need; average aid package $15,836

University of Georgia

Athens GA
(706) 542-8776
U.S. News ranking: Nat. U., No. 46
Website: www.admissions.uga.edu
Admissions email: adm-info@uga.edu
Public; founded 1785
Freshman admissions: more selective; 2017-2018: 24,165 applied, 13,052 accepted. Either SAT or ACT required. ACT 25/75 percentile: 26-31. High school rank: 54% in top tenth, 90% in top quarter, 99% in top half
Early decision deadline: N/A, notification date: N/A
Early action deadline: 10/15, notification date: 12/1
Application deadline (fall): 1/1
Undergraduate student body: 27,142 full time, 1,706 part time; 43% male, 57% female; 0% American Indian, 10% Asian, 8% black, 6% Hispanic, 4% multiracial, 0% Pacific Islander, 69% white, 2% international; 89% from in state; 33% live on campus; 20% of students in fraternities, 31% in sororities
Most popular majors: 8% Finance, General, 6% Biology/Biological Sciences, General, 6% Psychology, General, 5% Marketing/Marketing Management, General, 3% International Relations and Affairs
Expenses: 2018-2019: $11,830 in state, $30,404 out of state; room/board: $10,038
Financial aid: (706) 542-6147; 44% of undergrads determined to have financial need; average aid package $12,182

University of North Georgia

Dahlonega GA
(706) 864-1800
U.S. News ranking: Reg. U. (S), No. 58
Website: ung.edu/
Admissions email: admissions-dah@ung.edu
Public; founded 1873
Freshman admissions: selective; 2017-2018: 4,392 applied, 2,862 accepted. Either SAT or ACT required. SAT 25/75 percentile: 1030-1180. High school rank: 23% in top tenth, 62% in top quarter, 92% in top half
Early decision deadline: N/A, notification date: N/A
Early action deadline: 11/15, notification date: 12/15
Application deadline (fall): 2/15
Undergraduate student body: 12,712 full time, 5,461 part time; 44% male, 56% female; 0% American Indian, 3% Asian, 4% black, 12% Hispanic, 3% multiracial, 0% Pacific Islander, 74% white, 2% international; 96% from in state; 22% live on campus; 6% of students in fraternities, 10% in sororities
Most popular majors: 23% Business, Management, Marketing, and Related Support Services, 20% Education, 10% Health Professions and Related Programs, 7% Homeland Security, Law Enforcement, Firefighting and Related Protective Services, 6% Biological and Biomedical Sciences
Expenses: 2018-2019: $7,336 in state, $21,148 out of state; room/board: $10,800
Financial aid: (706) 864-1412; 61% of undergrads determined to have financial need; average aid package $14,234

University of West Georgia

Carrollton GA
(678) 839-5600
U.S. News ranking: Nat. U., second tier
Website: www.westga.edu
Admissions email: admiss@westga.edu
Public; founded 1906
Freshman admissions: selective; 2017-2018: 7,909 applied, 4,636 accepted. Either SAT or ACT required. SAT 25/75 percentile: 920-1070. High school rank: N/A
Early decision deadline: N/A, notification date: N/A
Early action deadline: N/A, notification date: N/A
Application deadline (fall): 6/1
Undergraduate student body: 8,938 full time, 2,291 part time; 37% male, 63% female; 0% American Indian, 1% Asian, 38% black, 6% Hispanic, 4% multiracial, 0% Pacific Islander, 48% white, 1% international; 94% from in state; 27% live on campus; 2% of students in fraternities, 3% in sororities
Most popular majors: 23% Business, Management, Marketing, and Related Support Services, 17% Social Sciences, 14% Health Professions and Related Programs, 10% Psychology, 7% Education
Expenses: 2018-2019: $7,292 in state, $20,774 out of state; room/board: $10,218
Financial aid: (678) 839-6421; 74% of undergrads determined to have financial need; average aid package $8,828

Valdosta State University

Valdosta GA
(229) 333-5791
U.S. News ranking: Nat. U., second tier
Website: www.valdosta.edu
Admissions email: admissions@valdosta.edu
Public; founded 1906
Freshman admissions: selective; 2017-2018: 5,303 applied, 3,933 accepted. Either SAT or ACT required. SAT 25/75 percentile: 980-1130. High school rank: N/A
Early decision deadline: N/A, notification date: N/A
Early action deadline: N/A, notification date: N/A
Application deadline (fall): 6/15
Undergraduate student body: 7,166 full time, 1,612 part time; 38% male, 62% female; 0% American Indian, 1% Asian, 38% black, 6% Hispanic, 4% multiracial, 0% Pacific Islander, 47% white, 2% international; 86% from in state; 28% live on campus; 3% of students in fraternities, 4% in sororities
Most popular majors: 24% Business, Management, Marketing, and Related Support Services, 12% Health Professions and Related Programs, 9% Education, 8% Communication, Journalism, and Related Programs, 8% Psychology
Expenses: 2018-2019: $6,410 in state, $17,196 out of state; room/board: $7,900
Financial aid: (229) 333-5935; 78% of undergrads determined to have financial need; average aid package $15,750

Wesleyan College

Macon GA
(800) 447-6610
U.S. News ranking: Nat. Lib. Arts, No. 143
Website: www.wesleyancollege.edu
Admissions email: admissions@wesleyancollege.edu
Private; founded 1836
Affiliation: United Methodist
Freshman admissions: selective; 2017-2018: 309 applied, 144 accepted. Either SAT or ACT required. SAT 25/75 percentile: 1020-1190. High school rank: 28% in top tenth, 58% in top quarter, 88% in top half
Early decision deadline: N/A, notification date: N/A
Early action deadline: N/A, notification date: N/A
Application deadline (fall): rolling
Undergraduate student body: 431 full time, 133 part time; 2% male, 98% female; 0% American Indian, 2% Asian, 29% black, 5% Hispanic, 5% multiracial, 0% Pacific Islander, 42% white, 15% international; 90% from in state; 53% live on campus; 0% of students in fraternities, 0% in sororities
Most popular majors: 21% Registered Nursing/Registered Nurse, 19% Business Administration and Management, General, 11% Biology/Biological Sciences, General, 11% Psychology, General, 8% Accounting
Expenses: 2018-2019: $23,000; room/board: $9,860
Financial aid: (478) 757-5146; 65% of undergrads determined to have financial need; average aid package $21,610

Young Harris College

Young Harris GA
(706) 379-3111
U.S. News ranking: Nat. Lib. Arts, second tier
Website: www.yhc.edu
Admissions email: cpdaniels@yhc.edu
Private; founded 1886
Affiliation: United Methodist
Freshman admissions: selective; 2017-2018: 1,584 applied, 884 accepted. Either SAT or ACT required. SAT 25/75 percentile: 910-1078. High school rank: 10% in top tenth, 27% in top quarter, 60% in top half
Early decision deadline: N/A, notification date: N/A
Early action deadline: N/A, notification date: N/A
Application deadline (fall): rolling
Undergraduate student body: 1,014 full time, 188 part time; 41% male, 59% female; 0% American Indian, 1% Asian, 7% black, 4% Hispanic, 4% multiracial, 0% Pacific Islander, 76% white, 7% international; 9% from in state; 72% live on campus; 3% of students in fraternities, 10% in sororities
Most popular majors: 24% Business Administration and Management, General, 12% Communication and Media Studies, 12% Psychology, General, 10% Biology/Biological Sciences, General, 10% Visual and Performing Arts, General
Expenses: 2017-2018: $29,062; room/board: $10,684
Financial aid: N/A

HAWAII

Brigham Young University–Hawaii[1]

Laie Oahu HI
(808) 293-3738
U.S. News ranking: Reg. Coll. (W), No. 17
Website: www.byuh.edu
Admissions email: admissions@byuh.edu
Private
Application deadline (fall): N/A
Undergraduate student body: N/A full time, N/A part time
Expenses: 2017-2018: $5,400; room/board: $6,310
Financial aid: N/A

Chaminade University of Honolulu

Honolulu HI
(808) 735-8340
U.S. News ranking: Reg. U. (W), No. 44
Website: www.chaminade.edu
Admissions email: admissions@chaminade.edu
Private; founded 1955
Affiliation: Roman Catholic
Freshman admissions: selective; 2017-2018: 742 applied, 674 accepted. Either SAT or ACT required. SAT 25/75 percentile: 970-1180. High school rank: 19% in top tenth, 46% in top quarter, 81% in top half
Early decision deadline: N/A, notification date: N/A
Early action deadline: N/A, notification date: N/A
Application deadline (fall): rolling
Undergraduate student body: 1,125 full time, 32 part time; 29% male, 71% female; 0% American Indian, 37% Asian, 3% black, 4% Hispanic, 10% multiracial, 26% Pacific Islander, 14% white, 1% international; 71% from in state; 23% live on campus; N/A of students in fraternities, N/A in sororities
Most popular majors: 20% Criminal Justice/Safety Studies, 17% Registered Nursing/Registered Nurse, 16% Business Administration and Management, General, 11% Psychology, General, 8% Biology/Biological Sciences, General
Expenses: 2018-2019: $25,374; room/board: $13,630
Financial aid: (808) 735-4780; 72% of undergrads determined to have financial need; average aid package $17,701

Hawaii Pacific University

Honolulu HI
(808) 544-0238
U.S. News ranking: Reg. U. (W), No. 69
Website: www.hpu.edu/
Admissions email: admissions@hpu.edu
Private; founded 1965
Freshman admissions: selective; 2017-2018: 6,551 applied, 4,892 accepted. Either SAT or ACT required. SAT 25/75 percentile: 1000-1198. High school rank: 16% in top tenth, 47% in top quarter, 81% in top half
Early decision deadline: N/A, notification date: N/A
Early action deadline: 11/15, notification date: 12/31
Application deadline (fall): 8/15
Undergraduate student body: 2,411 full time, 1,149 part time; 40% male, 60% female; 1% American Indian, 16% Asian, 6% black, 16% Hispanic, 17% multiracial, 2% Pacific Islander, 27% white, 11% international; 58% from in state; 14% live on campus; N/A of students in fraternities, N/A in sororities
Most popular majors: 28% Business, Management, Marketing, and Related Support Services, 21% Health Professions and Related Programs, 11% Biological and Biomedical Sciences, 6% Communication, Journalism, and Related Programs, 6% Psychology
Expenses: 2018-2019: $25,980; room/board: $14,800
Financial aid: (808) 544-0253; 58% of undergrads determined to have financial need; average aid package $14,367

University of Hawaii–Hilo[1]

Hilo HI
(800) 897-4456
U.S. News ranking: Reg. U. (W), second tier
Website: www.uhh.hawaii.edu
Admissions email: uhhadm@hawaii.edu
Public; founded 1947
Application deadline (fall): 7/1
Undergraduate student body: N/A full time, N/A part time
Expenses: 2017-2018: $7,648 in state, $20,608 out of state; room/board: $11,064
Financial aid: (808) 932-7449

University of Hawaii–Manoa

Honolulu HI
(808) 956-8975
U.S. News ranking: Nat. U., No. 157
Website: www.manoa.hawaii.edu/
Admissions email: manoa.admissions@hawaii.edu
Public; founded 1907
Freshman admissions: selective; 2017-2018: 8,523 applied, 7,069 accepted. Either SAT or ACT required. SAT 25/75 percentile: 1050-1240. High school rank: 26% in top tenth, 55% in top quarter, 87% in top half
Early decision deadline: N/A, notification date: N/A
Early action deadline: N/A, notification date: N/A
Application deadline (fall): 3/1
Undergraduate student body: 10,702 full time, 2,179 part time; 44% male, 56% female; 0% American Indian, 40% Asian, 2% black, 2% Hispanic, 16% multiracial, 17% Pacific Islander, 20% white, 3% international; 73% from in state; 24% live on campus; 1% of students in fraternities, 1% in sororities
Most popular majors: 20% Business, Management, Marketing, and Related Support Services, 9% Engineering, 9% Social Sciences, 8% Health Professions and Related Programs, 7% Biological and Biomedical Sciences
Expenses: 2018-2019: $11,970 in state, $34,002 out of state; room/board: $13,689
Financial aid: (808) 956-7251; 56% of undergrads determined to have financial need; average aid package $15,005

University of Hawaii–Maui College[1]

Kahului HI
(808) 984-3267
U.S. News ranking: Reg. Coll. (W), unranked
Website: www.maui.hawaii.edu/
Admissions email: N/A
Public
Application deadline (fall): N/A
Undergraduate student body: N/A full time, N/A part time
Expenses: 2017-2018: $3,158 in state, $8,294 out of state; room/board: N/A
Financial aid: N/A

University of Hawaii–West Oahu

Kapolei HI
(808) 689-2900
U.S. News ranking: Reg. Coll. (W), No. 21
Website: www.uhwo.hawaii.edu
Admissions email: uhwo.admissions@hawaii.edu
Public; founded 1976
Freshman admissions: less selective; 2017-2018: 1,060 applied, 832 accepted. Neither SAT nor ACT required. ACT 25/75 percentile: 16-20. High school rank: 13% in top tenth, 45% in top quarter, 85% in top half
Early decision deadline: N/A, notification date: N/A
Early action deadline: N/A, notification date: N/A
Application deadline (fall): 7/1
Undergraduate student body: 1,611 full time, 1,471 part time; 34% male, 66% female; 0% American Indian, 38% Asian, 2% black, 2% Hispanic, 15% multiracial, 31% Pacific Islander, 11% white, 2% international; 99% from in state; 2% live on campus; 2% of students in fraternities, 2% in sororities
Most popular majors: 38% Business, Management, Marketing, and Related Support Services, 24% Public Administration and Social Service Professions, 21% Social Sciences, 8% Multi/Interdisciplinary Studies, 5% Liberal Arts and Sciences, General Studies and Humanities
Expenses: 2018-2019: $7,512 in state, $20,572 out of state; room/board: N/A
Financial aid: (808) 689-2900; 55% of undergrads determined to have financial need; average aid package $7,097

IDAHO

Boise State University

Boise ID
(208) 426-1156
U.S. News ranking: Nat. U., second tier
Website: www.BoiseState.edu
Admissions email: bsuinfo@boisestate.edu
Public; founded 1932
Freshman admissions: selective; 2017-2018: 8,876 applied, 7,455 accepted. Neither SAT nor ACT required. SAT 25/75 percentile: 940-1160. High school rank: 15% in top tenth, 39% in top quarter, 75% in top half
Early decision deadline: N/A, notification date: N/A
Early action deadline: N/A, notification date: N/A
Undergraduate student body: 12,477 full time, 8,290 part time; 44% male, 56% female; 0% American Indian, 2% Asian, 2% black, 13% Hispanic, 5% multiracial, 0% Pacific Islander, 74% white, 2% international; 69% from in state; 18% live on campus; N/A of students in fraternities, N/A in sororities
Most popular majors: Information not available

Expenses: 2018-2019: $7,693 in state, $23,776 out of state; room/board: $10,692
Financial aid: (208) 426-1664; 59% of undergrads determined to have financial need; average aid package $10,187

Brigham Young University–Idaho[1]

Rexburg ID
(208) 496-1036
U.S. News ranking: Reg. Coll. (W), No. 17
Website: www.byui.edu
Admissions email: admissions@byui.edu
Private
Application deadline (fall): N/A
Undergraduate student body: N/A full time, N/A part time
Expenses: 2017-2018: $4,018; room/board: $4,592
Financial aid: N/A

College of Idaho

Caldwell ID
(800) 224-3246
U.S. News ranking: Nat. Lib. Arts, No. 131
Website: www.collegeofidaho.edu
Admissions email: admissions@collegeofidaho.edu
Private; founded 1891
Freshman admissions: selective; 2017-2018: 1,665 applied, 1,263 accepted. Neither SAT nor ACT required. ACT 25/75 percentile: 21-27. High school rank: 24% in top tenth, 26% in top quarter, 50% in top half
Early decision deadline: N/A, notification date: N/A
Early action deadline: 11/16, notification date: 12/21
Application deadline (fall): 2/16
Undergraduate student body: 896 full time, 47 part time; 50% male, 50% female; 1% American Indian, 2% Asian, 4% black, 14% Hispanic, 4% multiracial, 1% Pacific Islander, 64% white, 6% international; 34% from in state; 68% live on campus; 12% of students in fraternities, 16% in sororities
Most popular majors: 19% Business, Management, Marketing, and Related Support Services, 13% Health Professions and Related Programs, 13% Psychology, 11% Biological and Biomedical Sciences, 10% Social Sciences
Expenses: 2018-2019: $29,825; room/board: $9,697
Financial aid: (208) 459-5307; 65% of undergrads determined to have financial need; average aid package $27,221

Idaho State University[1]

Pocatello ID
(208) 282-0211
U.S. News ranking: Nat. U., unranked
Website: www.isu.edu
Admissions email: info@isu.edu
Public
Application deadline (fall): N/A
Undergraduate student body: N/A full time, N/A part time
Expenses: 2017-2018: $7,166 in state, $21,942 out of state; room/board: $7,024
Financial aid: N/A

Lewis-Clark State College

Lewiston ID
(208) 792-2210
U.S. News ranking: Reg. Coll. (W), second tier
Website: www.lcsc.edu
Admissions email: admissions@lcsc.edu
Public; founded 1893
Freshman admissions: less selective; 2017-2018: 1,760 applied, 1,753 accepted. Neither SAT nor ACT required. SAT 25/75 percentile: 930-1100. High school rank: 8% in top tenth, 24% in top quarter, 32% in top half
Early decision deadline: N/A, notification date: N/A
Early action deadline: N/A, notification date: N/A
Application deadline (fall): 8/8
Undergraduate student body: 2,215 full time, 1,531 part time; 38% male, 62% female; N/A American Indian, N/A Asian, N/A black, N/A Hispanic, N/A multiracial, N/A Pacific Islander, N/A white, N/A international; 78% from in state; 8% live on campus; N/A of students in fraternities, N/A in sororities
Most popular majors: 27% Health Professions and Related Programs, 22% Business, Management, Marketing, and Related Support Services, 9% Parks, Recreation, Leisure, and Fitness Studies, 8% Education, 7% Public Administration and Social Service Professions
Expenses: 2018-2019: $6,618 in state, $19,236 out of state; room/board: $7,580
Financial aid: (208) 792-2224; 70% of undergrads determined to have financial need; average aid package $8,277

Northwest Nazarene University

Nampa ID
(208) 467-8000
U.S. News ranking: Reg. U. (W), No. 52
Website: www.nnu.edu
Admissions email: Admissions@nnu.edu
Private; founded 1913
Freshman admissions: selective; 2017-2018: 818 applied, 783 accepted. Either SAT or ACT required. SAT 25/75 percentile: 1030-1240. High school rank: 24% in top tenth, 51% in top quarter, 80% in top half
Early decision deadline: N/A, notification date: N/A
Early action deadline: 1/15, notification date: 9/15
Application deadline (fall): 8/15
Undergraduate student body: 1,154 full time, 376 part time; 42% male, 58% female; 1% American Indian, 2% Asian, 2% black, 7% Hispanic, 4% multiracial, 0% Pacific Islander, 75% white, 4% international; 58% from in state; 71% live on campus; N/A of students in fraternities, N/A in sororities
Most popular majors: Information not available
Expenses: 2018-2019: $29,800; room/board: $7,400
Financial aid: (208) 467-8347; 78% of undergrads determined to have financial need; average aid package $23,634

University of Idaho

Moscow ID
(888) 884-3246
U.S. News ranking: Nat. U., No. 165
Website: www.uidaho.edu/admissions
Admissions email: admissions@uidaho.edu
Public; founded 1889
Freshman admissions: selective; 2017-2018: 7,087 applied, 5,180 accepted. Either SAT or ACT required. SAT 25/75 percentile: 1010-1230. High school rank: 20% in top tenth, 42% in top quarter, 74% in top half
Early decision deadline: N/A, notification date: N/A
Early action deadline: N/A, notification date: N/A
Application deadline (fall): 8/1
Undergraduate student body: 7,166 full time, 2,719 part time; 50% male, 50% female; 1% American Indian, 1% Asian, 1% black, 11% Hispanic, 4% multiracial, 0% Pacific Islander, 74% white, 5% international; 79% from in state; 36% live on campus; 22% of students in fraternities, 17% in sororities
Most popular majors: 6% Psychology, General, 5% Mechanical Engineering, 4% Finance, General, 4% Marketing/Marketing Management, General, 3% Accounting
Expenses: 2018-2019: $7,864 in state, $25,500 out of state; room/board: $8,880
Financial aid: (208) 885-6312; 64% of undergrads determined to have financial need; average aid package $13,785

ILLINOIS

American Academy of Art[1]

Chicago IL
(312) 461-0600
U.S. News ranking: Arts, unranked
Website: www.aaart.edu
Admissions email: N/A
For-profit
Application deadline (fall): N/A
Undergraduate student body: N/A full time, N/A part time
Expenses: N/A
Financial aid: N/A

American InterContinental University[1]

Hoffman Estates IL
(877) 701-3800
U.S. News ranking: Reg. U. (Mid. W), unranked
Website: www.aiuniv.edu
Admissions email: N/A
For-profit
Application deadline (fall): N/A
Undergraduate student body: N/A full time, N/A part time
Expenses: 2017-2018: $10,992; room/board: N/A
Financial aid: N/A

Augustana College

Rock Island IL
(800) 798-8100
U.S. News ranking: Nat. Lib. Arts, No. 95
Website: www.augustana.edu
Admissions email: admissions@augustana.edu
Private; founded 1860
Affiliation: Evangelical Lutheran Church
Freshman admissions: more selective; 2017-2018: 6,750 applied, 3,980 accepted. Neither SAT nor ACT required. ACT 25/75 percentile: 23-28. High school rank: 36% in top tenth, 64% in top quarter, 90% in top half
Early decision deadline: 11/1, notification date: 11/15
Early action deadline: 11/1, notification date: 12/20
Application deadline (fall): rolling
Undergraduate student body: 2,637 full time, 10 part time; 42% male, 58% female; 0% American Indian, 2% Asian, 4% black, 10% Hispanic, 3% multiracial, 0% Pacific Islander, 72% white, 7% international; 85% from in state; 69% live on campus; 23% of students in fraternities, 39% in sororities
Most popular majors: 17% Business Administration and Management, General, 13% Biology/Biological Sciences, General, 8% Psychology, General, 5% Accounting, 5% Speech Communication and Rhetoric
Expenses: 2018-2019: $42,135; room/board: $10,572
Financial aid: (309) 794-7207; 78% of undergrads determined to have financial need; average aid package $32,384

Aurora University[1]

Aurora IL
(800) 742-5281
U.S. News ranking: Reg. U. (Mid. W), No. 123
Website: www.aurora.edu
Admissions email: admission@aurora.edu
Private
Application deadline (fall): N/A
Undergraduate student body: N/A full time, N/A part time
Expenses: 2017-2018: $23,520; room/board: $9,636
Financial aid: N/A

Benedictine University

Lisle IL
(630) 829-6300
U.S. News ranking: Nat. U., No. 221
Website: www.ben.edu
Admissions email: admissions@ben.edu
Private; founded 1887
Affiliation: Roman Catholic
Freshman admissions: selective; 2017-2018: 5,334 applied, 3,318 accepted. Either SAT or ACT required. ACT 25/75 percentile: 20-25. High school rank: 12% in top tenth, 38% in top quarter, 65% in top half
Early decision deadline: N/A, notification date: N/A
Early action deadline: N/A, notification date: N/A
Application deadline (fall): rolling
Undergraduate student body: 2,473 full time, 412 part time; 52% male, 48% female; 1% American Indian, 15% Asian, 8% black, 17% Hispanic, 0% multiracial, 0% Pacific Islander, 44% white, 1% international; 93% from in state; 22% live on campus; 0% of students in fraternities, 0% in sororities
Most popular majors: 34% Business, Management, Marketing, and Related Support Services, 25% Health Professions and Related Programs, 10% Psychology, 7% Biological and Biomedical Sciences, 5% Family and Consumer Sciences/Human Sciences
Expenses: 2018-2019: $34,290; room/board: $9,480
Financial aid: (630) 829-6100; 80% of undergrads determined to have financial need; average aid package $23,183

Blackburn College

Carlinville IL
(800) 233-3550
U.S. News ranking: Reg. Coll. (Mid. W), No. 30
Website: www.blackburn.edu
Admissions email: justin.norwood@blackburn.edu
Private; founded 1837
Affiliation: Presbyterian Church (USA)
Freshman admissions: selective; 2017-2018: 944 applied, 562 accepted. Either SAT or ACT required. ACT 25/75 percentile: 18-23. High school rank: 9% in top tenth, 35% in top quarter, 66% in top half
Early decision deadline: N/A, notification date: N/A
Early action deadline: N/A, notification date: N/A
Application deadline (fall): rolling
Undergraduate student body: 546 full time, 11 part time; 43% male, 57% female; 0% American Indian, 1% Asian, 11% black, 5% Hispanic, 3% multiracial, 0% Pacific Islander, 76% white, 2% international; 91% from in state; 71% live on campus; 0% of students in fraternities, 0% in sororities
Most popular majors: 22% Business, Management, Marketing, and Related Support Services, 17% Biological and Biomedical Sciences, 10% Homeland Security, Law Enforcement, Firefighting and Related Protective Services, 10% Psychology, 8% Visual and Performing Arts
Expenses: 2018-2019: $22,410; room/board: $8,140
Financial aid: (217) 854-5774; 91% of undergrads determined to have financial need; average aid package $20,810

More @ usnews.com/bestcolleges

Bradley University

Peoria IL
(309) 677-1000
U.S. News ranking: Reg. U. (Mid. W), No. 6
Website: www.bradley.edu
Admissions email: admissions@bradley.edu
Private; founded 1897
Freshman admissions: more selective; 2017-2018: 10,232 applied, 7,303 accepted. Either SAT or ACT required. ACT 25/75 percentile: 22-28. High school rank: 26% in top tenth, 60% in top quarter, 90% in top half
Early decision deadline: N/A, notification date: N/A
Early action deadline: N/A, notification date: N/A
Application deadline (fall): 5/1
Undergraduate student body: 4,512 full time, 137 part time; 49% male, 51% female; 0% American Indian, 4% Asian, 7% black, 10% Hispanic, 2% multiracial, 0% Pacific Islander, 73% white, 2% international; 82% from in state; 62% live on campus; 32% of students in fraternities, 31% in sororities
Most popular majors: 20% Engineering, 19% Business, Management, Marketing, and Related Support Services, 11% Health Professions and Related Programs, 10% Communication, Journalism, and Related Programs, 7% Education
Expenses: 2018-2019: $33,760; room/board: $10,620
Financial aid: (309) 677-3089; 68% of undergrads determined to have financial need; average aid package $23,839

Chicago State University

Chicago IL
(773) 995-2513
U.S. News ranking: Reg. U. (Mid. W), second tier
Website: www.csu.edu
Admissions email: ug-admissions@csu.edu
Public; founded 1867
Freshman admissions: less selective; 2017-2018: 1,396 applied, 1,087 accepted. ACT required. ACT 25/75 percentile: 17-21. High school rank: N/A
Early decision deadline: N/A, notification date: N/A
Early action deadline: N/A, notification date: N/A
Application deadline (fall): rolling
Undergraduate student body: 1,297 full time, 732 part time; 30% male, 70% female; 0% American Indian, 0% Asian, 74% black, 7% Hispanic, 0% multiracial, 0% Pacific Islander, 4% white, 3% international
Most popular majors: 19% Psychology, General, 10% Business Administration and Management, General, 10% Criminal Justice/Safety Studies, 5% Registered Nursing/Registered Nurse, 4% Sociology
Expenses: 2017-2018: $10,252 in state, $17,212 out of state; room/board: $8,724
Financial aid: N/A

Columbia College Chicago[1]

Chicago IL
(312) 344-7130
U.S. News ranking: Reg. U. (Mid. W), second tier
Website: www.colum.edu
Admissions email: admissions@colum.edu
Private
Application deadline (fall): N/A
Undergraduate student body: N/A full time, N/A part time
Expenses: 2017-2018: $26,474; room/board: $13,630
Financial aid: N/A

Concordia University Chicago

River Forest IL
(877) 282-4422
U.S. News ranking: Reg. U. (Mid. W), No. 72
Website: www.cuchicago.edu/
Admissions email: admission@cuchicago.edu
Private; founded 1864
Affiliation: Lutheran Church–Missouri Synod
Freshman admissions: selective; 2017-2018: 4,755 applied, 3,553 accepted. Either SAT or ACT required. ACT 25/75 percentile: 20-24. High school rank: 25% in top tenth, 45% in top quarter, 78% in top half
Early decision deadline: N/A, notification date: N/A
Early action deadline: N/A, notification date: N/A
Application deadline (fall): rolling
Undergraduate student body: 1,299 full time, 112 part time; 41% male, 59% female; 0% American Indian, 3% Asian, 14% black, 30% Hispanic, 3% multiracial, 0% Pacific Islander, 47% white, 2% international; 75% from in state; 36% live on campus; 0% of students in fraternities, 0% in sororities
Most popular majors: 23% Business, Management, Marketing, and Related Support Services, 18% Education, 8% Health Professions and Related Programs, 8% Psychology, 8% Theology and Religious Vocations
Expenses: 2018-2019: $32,078; room/board: $9,748
Financial aid: (708) 209-3113; 86% of undergrads determined to have financial need; average aid package $23,649

DePaul University

Chicago IL
(312) 362-8300
U.S. News ranking: Nat. U., No. 119
Website: www.depaul.edu
Admissions email: admission@depaul.edu
Private; founded 1898
Affiliation: Roman Catholic
Freshman admissions: more selective; 2017-2018: 21,613 applied, 15,506 accepted. Neither SAT nor ACT required. ACT 25/75 percentile: 22-28. High school rank: N/A
Early decision deadline: N/A, notification date: N/A
Early action deadline: 11/15, notification date: 1/15
Application deadline (fall): 2/1
Undergraduate student body: 12,886 full time, 1,930 part time; 48% male, 52% female; 0% American Indian, 9% Asian, 8% black, 19% Hispanic, 4% multiracial, 0% Pacific Islander, 53% white, 3% international; 76% from in state; 18% live on campus; 5% of students in fraternities, 11% in sororities
Most popular majors: 30% Business, Management, Marketing, and Related Support Services, 14% Communication, Journalism, and Related Programs, 9% Liberal Arts and Sciences, General Studies and Humanities, 8% Visual and Performing Arts, 6% Psychology
Expenses: 2018-2019: $39,975; room/board: $14,235
Financial aid: (312) 362-8520; 70% of undergrads determined to have financial need; average aid package $24,298

DeVry University[1]

Downers Grove IL
(630) 515-3000
U.S. News ranking: Reg. U. (Mid. W), second tier
Website: www.devry.edu
Admissions email: N/A
For-profit; founded 1931
Application deadline (fall): rolling
Undergraduate student body: N/A full time, N/A part time
Expenses: N/A
Financial aid: N/A

Dominican University

River Forest IL
(708) 524-6800
U.S. News ranking: Reg. U. (Mid. W), No. 11
Website: www.dom.edu/
Admissions email: domadmis@dom.edu
Private; founded 1901
Affiliation: Roman Catholic
Freshman admissions: selective; 2017-2018: 4,697 applied, 3,052 accepted. Either SAT or ACT required. ACT 25/75 percentile: 20-25. High school rank: 25% in top tenth, 55% in top quarter, 85% in top half
Early decision deadline: N/A, notification date: N/A
Early action deadline: N/A, notification date: N/A
Application deadline (fall): 7/1
Undergraduate student body: 2,014 full time, 157 part time; 33% male, 67% female; 0% American Indian, 3% Asian, 7% black, 51% Hispanic, 1% multiracial, 0% Pacific Islander, 33% white, 2% international; 100% from in state; 26% live on campus; 0% of students in fraternities, 0% in sororities
Most popular majors: 19% Business Administration and Management, General, 16% Social Sciences, General, 11% Nutrition Sciences, 11% Pre-Medicine/Pre-Medical Studies, 8% Psychology, General
Expenses: 2018-2019: $33,434; room/board: $10,241
Financial aid: (708) 524-6950; 86% of undergrads determined to have financial need; average aid package $24,710

Eastern Illinois University

Charleston IL
(877) 581-2348
U.S. News ranking: Reg. U. (Mid. W), No. 38
Website: www.eiu.edu
Admissions email: admissions@eiu.edu
Public; founded 1895
Freshman admissions: selective; 2017-2018: 6,965 applied, 3,588 accepted. Either SAT or ACT required. ACT 25/75 percentile: 18-23. High school rank: 12% in top tenth, 33% in top quarter, 67% in top half
Early decision deadline: N/A, notification date: N/A
Early action deadline: N/A, notification date: N/A
Application deadline (fall): 8/15
Undergraduate student body: 4,319 full time, 1,249 part time; 40% male, 60% female; 0% American Indian, 1% Asian, 21% black, 7% Hispanic, 3% multiracial, 0% Pacific Islander, 63% white, 3% international; 93% from in state; 34% live on campus; 18% of students in fraternities, 15% in sororities
Most popular majors: 14% Education, 12% Business, Management, Marketing, and Related Support Services, 10% Parks, Recreation, Leisure, and Fitness Studies, 9% Communication, Journalism, and Related Programs, 8% Liberal Arts and Sciences, General Studies and Humanities
Expenses: 2018-2019: $11,803 in state, $14,023 out of state; room/board: $9,882
Financial aid: (217) 581-6405; 70% of undergrads determined to have financial need; average aid package $13,067

East-West University[1]

Chicago IL
(312) 939-0111
U.S. News ranking: Nat. Lib. Arts, second tier
Website: www.eastwest.edu
Admissions email: seeyou@eastwest.edu
Private; founded 1980
Application deadline (fall): rolling
Undergraduate student body: N/A full time, N/A part time
Expenses: 2017-2018: $21,450; room/board: N/A
Financial aid: N/A

Elmhurst College

Elmhurst IL
(630) 617-3400
U.S. News ranking: Reg. U. (Mid. W), No. 20
Website: www.elmhurst.edu
Admissions email: admit@elmhurst.edu
Private; founded 1871
Affiliation: United Church of Christ
Freshman admissions: selective; 2017-2018: 3,645 applied, 2,571 accepted. Either SAT or ACT required. ACT 25/75 percentile: 20-26. High school rank: 21% in top tenth, 49% in top quarter, 77% in top half
Early decision deadline: N/A, notification date: N/A
Early action deadline: 11/1, notification date: 12/1
Application deadline (fall): rolling
Undergraduate student body: 2,732 full time, 143 part time; 39% male, 61% female; 0% American Indian, 5% Asian, 5% black, 21% Hispanic, 4% multiracial, 0% Pacific Islander, 63% white, 0% international; 91% from in state; 32% live on campus; 9% of students in fraternities, 14% in sororities
Most popular majors: 21% Business, Management, Marketing, and Related Support Services, 16% Health Professions and Related Programs, 10% Psychology, 8% English Language and Literature/Letters, 7% Education
Expenses: 2018-2019: $37,055; room/board: $10,566
Financial aid: (630) 617-3015; 77% of undergrads determined to have financial need; average aid package $27,497

Eureka College

Eureka IL
(309) 467-6350
U.S. News ranking: Reg. Coll. (Mid. W), No. 33
Website: www.eureka.edu
Admissions email: admissions@eureka.edu
Private; founded 1855
Affiliation: Christian Church (Disciples of Christ)
Freshman admissions: selective; 2017-2018: 771 applied, 478 accepted. Either SAT or ACT required. ACT 25/75 percentile: 19-24. High school rank: 14% in top tenth, 33% in top quarter, 65% in top half
Early decision deadline: N/A, notification date: N/A
Early action deadline: N/A, notification date: N/A
Application deadline (fall): 8/15
Undergraduate student body: 593 full time, 21 part time; 50% male, 50% female; 0% American Indian, 0% Asian, 7% black, 3% Hispanic, 4% multiracial, 0% Pacific Islander, 83% white, 1% international; 94% from in state; 61% live on campus; 31% of students in fraternities, 31% in sororities
Most popular majors: 15% Business Administration and Management, General, 9% Biology/Biological Sciences, General, 9% Corrections and Criminal Justice, Other, 9% Elementary Education and Teaching, 6% English Language and Literature, General
Expenses: 2018-2019: $25,390; room/board: $9,620
Financial aid: (309) 467-6311; 76% of undergrads determined to have financial need; average aid package $16,506

Governors State University

University Park IL
(708) 534-4490
U.S. News ranking: Reg. U. (Mid. W), second tier
Website: www.govst.edu/
Admissions email: admissions@govst.edu
Public; founded 1969
Freshman admissions: less selective; 2017-2018: 1,305 applied, 561 accepted. Either SAT or ACT required. ACT 25/75 percentile: 17-20. High school rank: 8% in top tenth, 33% in top quarter, 67% in top half
Early decision deadline: 11/15, notification date: 12/15
Early action deadline: N/A, notification date: N/A
Application deadline (fall): 4/1
Undergraduate student body: 1,879 full time, 1,447 part time; 37% male, 63% female; 0% American Indian, 2% Asian, 40% black, 13% Hispanic, 3% multiracial, 0% Pacific Islander, 31% white, 1% international; 98% from in state; 7% live on campus; 0% of students in fraternities, 0% in sororities
Most popular majors: 18% Liberal Arts and Sciences, General Studies and Humanities, 17% Business, Management, Marketing, and Related Support Services, 16% Health Professions and Related Programs, 11% Psychology, 9% Homeland Security, Law Enforcement, Firefighting and Related Protective Services
Expenses: 2018-2019: $12,196 in state, $21,586 out of state; room/board: $10,346
Financial aid: N/A; 97% of undergrads determined to have financial need; average aid package $11,536

Greenville University

Greenville IL
(618) 664-7100
U.S. News ranking: Reg. U. (Mid. W), No. 118
Website: www.greenville.edu
Admissions email: admissions@greenville.edu
Private; founded 1892
Affiliation: Free Methodist
Freshman admissions: selective; 2017-2018: 1,287 applied, 852 accepted. Either SAT or ACT required. ACT 25/75 percentile: 19-25. High school rank: N/A
Early decision deadline: N/A, notification date: N/A
Early action deadline: N/A, notification date: N/A
Application deadline (fall): rolling
Undergraduate student body: 887 full time, 98 part time; 51% male, 49% female; 0% American Indian, 1% Asian, 14% black, 6% Hispanic, 2% multiracial, 0% Pacific Islander, 69% white, 4% international; 69% from in state; 82% live on campus; 0% of students in fraternities, 0% in sororities
Most popular majors: 9% Biology/Biological Sciences, General, 9% Elementary Education and Teaching, 7% Business Administration and Management, General, 6% Organizational Behavior Studies, 6% Social Work
Expenses: 2018-2019: $27,152; room/board: $9,048
Financial aid: (618) 664-7108; 83% of undergrads determined to have financial need; average aid package $21,791

Illinois College

Jacksonville IL
(217) 245-3030
U.S. News ranking: Nat. Lib. Arts, No. 143
Website: www.ic.edu
Admissions email: admissions@mail.ic.edu
Private; founded 1829
Freshman admissions: selective; 2017-2018: 4,121 applied, 2,261 accepted. Neither SAT nor ACT required. ACT 25/75 percentile: 19-25. High school rank: 14% in top tenth, 41% in top quarter, 80% in top half
Early decision deadline: N/A, notification date: N/A
Early action deadline: 12/1, notification date: 12/23
Application deadline (fall): rolling
Undergraduate student body: 950 full time, 9 part time; 49% male, 51% female; 0% American Indian, 1% Asian, 11% black, 9% Hispanic, 3% multiracial, 0% Pacific Islander, 71% white, 5% international; 86% from in state; 85% live on campus; 0% of students in fraternities, 0% in sororities
Most popular majors: 17% Biological and Biomedical Sciences, 15% Multi/Interdisciplinary Studies, 15% Psychology, 12% English Language and Literature/Letters, 12% Social Sciences
Expenses: 2018-2019: $33,000; room/board: $9,280
Financial aid: (217) 245-3035; 84% of undergrads determined to have financial need; average aid package $27,382

Illinois Institute of Art–Chicago[1]

Chicago IL
(312) 280-3500
U.S. News ranking: Arts, unranked
Website: www.artinstitutes.edu/chicago/
Admissions email: N/A
For-profit
Application deadline (fall): N/A
Undergraduate student body: N/A full time, N/A part time
Expenses: N/A
Financial aid: N/A

Illinois Institute of Technology

Chicago IL
(800) 448-2329
U.S. News ranking: Nat. U., No. 96
Website: admissions.iit.edu/undergraduate/apply
Admissions email: admission@iit.edu
Private; founded 1890
Freshman admissions: more selective; 2017-2018: 4,708 applied, 2,545 accepted. Either SAT or ACT required. ACT 25/75 percentile: 25-31. High school rank: 55% in top tenth, 83% in top quarter, 99% in top half
Early decision deadline: N/A, notification date: N/A
Early action deadline: N/A, notification date: N/A
Application deadline (fall): 8/1
Undergraduate student body: 2,631 full time, 269 part time; 69% male, 31% female; 0% American Indian, 15% Asian, 6% black, 17% Hispanic, 3% multiracial, 0% Pacific Islander, 35% white, 21% international; 74% from in state; 39% live on campus; 10% of students in fraternities, 13% in sororities
Most popular majors: 47% Engineering, 16% Computer and Information Sciences and Support Services, 15% Architecture and Related Services, 6% Business, Management, Marketing, and Related Support Services, 4% Engineering Technologies and Engineering-Related Fields
Expenses: 2018-2019: $47,646; room/board: $13,192
Financial aid: (312) 567-7219; 62% of undergrads determined to have financial need; average aid package $40,603

Illinois State University

Normal IL
(309) 438-2181
U.S. News ranking: Nat. U., No. 171
Website: illinoisstate.edu/
Admissions email: admissions@ilstu.edu
Public; founded 1857
Freshman admissions: selective; 2017-2018: 11,592 applied, 10,332 accepted. Either SAT or ACT required. ACT 25/75 percentile: 21-26. High school rank: N/A
Early decision deadline: N/A, notification date: N/A
Early action deadline: N/A, notification date: N/A
Application deadline (fall): 4/1
Undergraduate student body: 17,165 full time, 1,165 part time; 45% male, 55% female; 0% American Indian, 2% Asian, 9% black, 10% Hispanic, 3% multiracial, 0% Pacific Islander, 75% white, 0% international; 98% from in state; 31% live on campus; 4% of students in fraternities, 6% in sororities
Most popular majors: 21% Business, Management, Marketing, and Related Support Services, 16% Education, 10% Health Professions and Related Programs, 6% Communication, Journalism, and Related Programs, 5% Social Sciences
Expenses: 2018-2019: $14,490 in state, $26,014 out of state; room/board: $9,948
Financial aid: (309) 438-2231; 60% of undergrads determined to have financial need; average aid package $10,666

Illinois Wesleyan University

Bloomington IL
(800) 332-2498
U.S. News ranking: Nat. Lib. Arts, No. 72
Website: www.iwu.edu
Admissions email: iwuadmit@iwu.edu
Private; founded 1850
Freshman admissions: more selective; 2017-2018: 3,697 applied, 2,250 accepted. Either SAT or ACT required. ACT 25/75 percentile: 24-29. High school rank: 39% in top tenth, 72% in top quarter, 95% in top half
Early decision deadline: N/A, notification date: N/A
Early action deadline: 11/15, notification date: 12/15
Application deadline (fall): rolling
Undergraduate student body: 1,646 full time, 3 part time; 45% male, 55% female; 0% American Indian, 6% Asian, 5% black, 8% Hispanic, 2% multiracial, 0% Pacific Islander, 69% white, 8% international; 86% from in state; 79% live on campus; 32% of students in fraternities, 34% in sororities
Most popular majors: 14% Accounting, 14% Business/Commerce, General, 8% Registered Nursing/Registered Nurse, 7% Biology/Biological Sciences, General, 7% Psychology, General
Expenses: 2018-2019: $47,636; room/board: $10,984
Financial aid: (309) 556-3096; 65% of undergrads determined to have financial need; average aid package $34,735

Judson University

Elgin IL
(847) 628-2510
U.S. News ranking: Reg. U. (Mid. W), No. 86
Website: www.judsonu.edu
Admissions email: admissions@judsonu.edu
Private; founded 1963
Affiliation: American Baptist
Freshman admissions: selective; 2017-2018: 757 applied, 539 accepted. Either SAT or ACT required. ACT 25/75 percentile: 19-25. High school rank: 7% in top tenth, 10% in top quarter, 37% in top half
Early decision deadline: N/A, notification date: N/A
Early action deadline: N/A, notification date: N/A
Application deadline (fall): rolling
Undergraduate student body: 761 full time, 320 part time; 45% male, 55% female; 0% American Indian, 2% Asian, 10% black, 23% Hispanic, 2% multiracial, 0% Pacific Islander, 47% white, 4% international; 78% from in state; 60% live on campus; 0% of students in fraternities, 0% in sororities
Most popular majors: 18% Business Administration, Management and Operations, Other, 10% Psychology, General, 8% Architecture, 8% Public Administration and Social Service Professions, 7% Business Administration and Management, General
Expenses: 2018-2019: $29,860; room/board: $9,988
Financial aid: (847) 628-2531; 76% of undergrads determined to have financial need; average aid package $23,674

Kendall College[1]

Chicago IL
(877) 588-8860
U.S. News ranking: Reg. Coll. (Mid. W), second tier
Website: www.kendall.edu
Admissions email: Kendalladmissions@kendall.edu
For-profit; founded 1934
Application deadline (fall): rolling
Undergraduate student body: N/A full time, N/A part time
Expenses: 2017-2018: $19,828; room/board: N/A
Financial aid: (312) 752-2194

Knox College

Galesburg IL
(800) 678-5669
U.S. News ranking: Nat. Lib. Arts, No. 68
Website: www.knox.edu
Admissions email: admission@knox.edu
Private; founded 1837
Freshman admissions: more selective; 2017-2018: 3,222 applied, 2,305 accepted. Neither SAT nor ACT required. ACT 25/75 percentile: 23-30. High school rank: 34% in top tenth, 66% in top quarter, 94% in top half
Early decision deadline: 11/1, notification date: 11/15
Early action deadline: 12/1, notification date: 1/15
Application deadline (fall): rolling
Undergraduate student body: 1,334 full time, 22 part time; 43% male, 57% female; 0% American Indian, 5% Asian, 8% black, 15% Hispanic, 6% multiracial, 0% Pacific Islander, 47% white, 17% international; 45% from in state; 89% live on campus; 35% of students in fraternities, 28% in sororities
Most popular majors: 12% Creative Writing, 12% Psychology, General, 10% Economics, General, 8% Biology/Biological Sciences, General, 8% Sociology and Anthropology
Expenses: 2018-2019: $46,554; room/board: $9,870
Financial aid: (309) 341-7149; 85% of undergrads determined to have financial need; average aid package $35,746

Lake Forest College

Lake Forest IL
(847) 735-5000
U.S. News ranking: Nat. Lib. Arts, No. 103
Website: www.lakeforest.edu
Admissions email: admissions@lakeforest.edu
Private; founded 1857
Freshman admissions: more selective; 2017-2018: 4,303 applied, 2,280 accepted. Neither SAT nor ACT required. ACT 25/75 percentile: 24-29. High school rank: 38% in top tenth, 67% in top quarter, 93% in top half

More @ usnews.com/bestcolleges

Early decision deadline: 11/1, notification date: 12/15
Early action deadline: 11/1, notification date: 12/15
Application deadline (fall): 2/15
Undergraduate student body: 1,487 full time, 21 part time; 43% male, 57% female; 0% American Indian, 6% Asian, 6% black, 15% Hispanic, 4% multiracial, 0% Pacific Islander, 58% white, 8% international; 62% from in state; 75% live on campus; 17% of students in fraternities, 18% in sororities
Most popular majors: 19% Social Sciences, 18% Business, Management, Marketing, and Related Support Services, 10% Biological and Biomedical Sciences, 7% Psychology, 6% Communication, Journalism, and Related Programs
Expenses: 2018-2019: $47,064; room/board: $10,052
Financial aid: (847) 735-5104; 77% of undergrads determined to have financial need; average aid package $42,300

Lewis University

Romeoville IL
(800) 897-9000
U.S. News ranking: Reg. U. (Mid. W), No. 20
Website: www.lewisu.edu
Admissions email: admissions@lewisu.edu
Private; founded 1932
Affiliation: Roman Catholic
Freshman admissions: selective; 2017-2018: 5,447 applied, 2,932 accepted. Either SAT or ACT required. ACT 25/75 percentile: 21-26. High school rank: 20% in top tenth, 49% in top quarter, 77% in top half
Early decision deadline: N/A, notification date: N/A
Early action deadline: N/A, notification date: N/A
Application deadline (fall): rolling
Undergraduate student body: 3,687 full time, 819 part time; 47% male, 53% female; 0% American Indian, 4% Asian, 5% black, 20% Hispanic, 3% multiracial, 0% Pacific Islander, 59% white, 2% international; 91% from in state; 22% live on campus; 2% of students in fraternities, 4% in sororities
Most popular majors: 15% Registered Nursing/Registered Nurse, 10% Criminal Justice/Safety Studies, 7% Psychology, General, 6% Business Administration and Management, General, 6% Computer Science
Expenses: 2018-2019: $32,450; room/board: $10,578
Financial aid: (815) 836-5263; 76% of undergrads determined to have financial need; average aid package $25,119

Lincoln College[1]

Lincoln IL
(800) 569-0556
U.S. News ranking: Reg. Coll. (Mid. W), second tier
Website: www.lincolncollege.edu
Admissions email: admission@lincolncollege.edu
Private; founded 1865
Application deadline (fall): rolling
Undergraduate student body: N/A full time, N/A part time
Expenses: 2017-2018: $18,100; room/board: $7,400
Financial aid: (217) 732-3155

Loyola University Chicago

Chicago IL
(800) 262-2373
U.S. News ranking: Nat. U., No. 89
Website: www.luc.edu
Admissions email: admission@luc.edu
Private; founded 1870
Affiliation: Roman Catholic
Freshman admissions: more selective; 2017-2018: 23,571 applied, 16,639 accepted. Either SAT or ACT required. ACT 25/75 percentile: 24-29. High school rank: 37% in top tenth, 70% in top quarter, 93% in top half
Early decision deadline: N/A, notification date: N/A
Early action deadline: N/A, notification date: N/A
Application deadline (fall): rolling
Undergraduate student body: 10,681 full time, 739 part time; 34% male, 66% female; 0% American Indian, 12% Asian, 6% black, 16% Hispanic, 4% multiracial, 0% Pacific Islander, 55% white, 5% international; 65% from in state; 40% live on campus; 8% of students in fraternities, 17% in sororities
Most popular majors: 13% Biology/Biological Sciences, General, 11% Registered Nursing/Registered Nurse, 9% Psychology, General, 5% Marketing/Marketing Management, General, 5% Public Relations, Advertising, and Applied Communication, Other
Expenses: 2018-2019: $44,048; room/board: $14,480
Financial aid: (773) 508-7704; 65% of undergrads determined to have financial need; average aid package $34,844

MacMurray College[1]

Jacksonville IL
(217) 479-7056
U.S. News ranking: Reg. Coll. (Mid. W), No. 59
Website: www.mac.edu
Admissions email: admissions@mac.edu
Private; founded 1846
Affiliation: United Methodist
Application deadline (fall): 8/15
Undergraduate student body: N/A full time, N/A part time
Expenses: 2017-2018: $26,100; room/board: $8,925
Financial aid: (217) 479-7041

McKendree University

Lebanon IL
(618) 537-6831
U.S. News ranking: Reg. U. (Mid. W), No. 65
Website: www.mckendree.edu
Admissions email: inquiry@mckendree.edu
Private; founded 1828
Affiliation: United Methodist
Freshman admissions: selective; 2017-2018: 2,206 applied, 1,361 accepted. Neither SAT nor ACT required. ACT 25/75 percentile: 19-25. High school rank: 13% in top tenth, 39% in top quarter, 77% in top half
Early decision deadline: N/A, notification date: N/A
Early action deadline: N/A, notification date: N/A
Application deadline (fall): rolling
Undergraduate student body: 1,692 full time, 412 part time; 46% male, 54% female; 0% American Indian, 1% Asian, 13% black, 4% Hispanic, 3% multiracial, 0% Pacific Islander, 66% white, 3% international; 73% from in state; 77% live on campus; 3% of students in fraternities, 15% in sororities
Most popular majors: 16% Registered Nursing/Registered Nurse, 12% Business Administration and Management, General, 9% Psychology, General, 6% Human Resources Management/Personnel Administration, General, 6% Sociology
Expenses: 2018-2019: $30,520; room/board: $9,920
Financial aid: (618) 537-6532; 79% of undergrads determined to have financial need; average aid package $22,465

Midstate College[1]

Peoria IL
(309) 692-4092
U.S. News ranking: Reg. Coll. (Mid. W), unranked
Website: www.midstate.edu/
Admissions email: dprandle@midstate.edu
For-profit
Application deadline (fall): N/A
Undergraduate student body: N/A full time, N/A part time
Expenses: 2017-2018: $16,230; room/board: N/A
Financial aid: N/A

Millikin University

Decatur IL
(217) 424-6210
U.S. News ranking: Reg. Coll. (Mid. W), No. 9
Website: www.millikin.edu
Admissions email: admis@millikin.edu
Private; founded 1901
Affiliation: Presbyterian
Freshman admissions: selective; 2017-2018: 3,431 applied, 2,216 accepted. Either SAT or ACT required. ACT 25/75 percentile: 19-26. High school rank: 13% in top tenth, 38% in top quarter, 71% in top half
Early decision deadline: N/A, notification date: N/A
Early action deadline: N/A, notification date: N/A
Application deadline (fall): rolling
Undergraduate student body: 1,840 full time, 110 part time; 43% male, 57% female; 0% American Indian, 1% Asian, 15% black, 7% Hispanic, 4% multiracial, 0% Pacific Islander, 69% white, 2% international; 83% from in state; 58% live on campus; 21% of students in fraternities, 28% in sororities
Most popular majors: 21% Business, Management, Marketing, and Related Support Services, 19% Visual and Performing Arts, 14% Health Professions and Related Programs, 11% Education, 6% Parks, Recreation, Leisure, and Fitness Studies
Expenses: 2018-2019: $35,002; room/board: $11,419
Financial aid: (217) 424-6317; 84% of undergrads determined to have financial need; average aid package $25,844

Monmouth College

Monmouth IL
(800) 747-2687
U.S. News ranking: Nat. Lib. Arts, No. 135
Website: www.monmouthcollege.edu/admissions
Admissions email: admissions@monmouthcollege.edu
Private; founded 1853
Freshman admissions: selective; 2017-2018: 2,428 applied, 1,628 accepted. Either SAT or ACT required. ACT 25/75 percentile: 20-25. High school rank: 17% in top tenth, 42% in top quarter, 71% in top half
Early decision deadline: N/A, notification date: N/A
Early action deadline: N/A, notification date: N/A
Application deadline (fall): rolling
Undergraduate student body: 1,016 full time, 17 part time; 49% male, 51% female; 0% American Indian, 1% Asian, 11% black, 10% Hispanic, 3% multiracial, 0% Pacific Islander, 63% white, 7% international; 84% from in state; 91% live on campus; 22% of students in fraternities, 33% in sororities
Most popular majors: 23% Business, Management, Marketing, and Related Support Services, 8% Psychology, 7% Multi/Interdisciplinary Studies, 7% Personal and Culinary Services, 6% Parks, Recreation, Leisure, and Fitness Studies
Expenses: 2018-2019: $37,674; room/board: $8,966
Financial aid: (309) 457-2129; 84% of undergrads determined to have financial need; average aid package $34,091

National Louis University

Chicago IL
(888) 658-8632
U.S. News ranking: Nat. U., second tier
Website: www.nl.edu
Admissions email: nluinfo@nl.edu
Private
Freshman admissions: less selective; 2017-2018: 2,701 applied, 2,310 accepted. Neither SAT nor ACT required. SAT 25/75 percentile: N/A. High school rank: N/A
Early decision deadline: N/A, notification date: N/A
Early action deadline: N/A, notification date: N/A
Application deadline (fall): N/A
Undergraduate student body: 1,250 full time, 633 part time; 27% male, 73% female; 0% American Indian, 2% Asian, 29% black, 47% Hispanic, 1% multiracial, 0% Pacific Islander, 17% white, 1% international
Most popular majors: 33% Multi-/Interdisciplinary Studies, Other, 22% Management Science, 8% Health and Medical Administrative Services, Other, 8% Public Administration and Social Service Professions, Other, 5% Criminology
Expenses: 2017-2018: $10,440; room/board: N/A
Financial aid: N/A

North Central College

Naperville IL
(630) 637-5800
U.S. News ranking: Reg. U. (Mid. W), No. 13
Website: www.northcentralcollege.edu
Admissions email: admissions@noctrl.edu
Private; founded 1861
Affiliation: United Methodist
Freshman admissions: more selective; 2017-2018: 7,220 applied, 3,928 accepted. Either SAT or ACT required. ACT 25/75 percentile: 22-27. High school rank: 28% in top tenth, 55% in top quarter, 85% in top half
Early decision deadline: N/A, notification date: N/A
Early action deadline: N/A, notification date: N/A
Application deadline (fall): rolling
Undergraduate student body: 2,634 full time, 135 part time; 46% male, 54% female; 0% American Indian, 3% Asian, 4% black, 15% Hispanic, 4% multiracial, 0% Pacific Islander, 65% white, 3% international; 93% from in state; 49% live on campus; N/A of students in fraternities, N/A in sororities
Most popular majors: 10% Psychology, General, 8% Marketing/Marketing Management, General, 7% Business Administration, Management and Operations, Other, 7% Kinesiology and Exercise Science, 5% Finance, General
Expenses: 2018-2019: $38,880; room/board: $11,019
Financial aid: (630) 637-5600; 78% of undergrads determined to have financial need; average aid package $27,601

Northeastern Illinois University

Chicago IL
(773) 442-4000
U.S. News ranking: Reg. U. (Mid. W), second tier
Website: www.neiu.edu
Admissions email: admrec@neiu.edu
Public; founded 1867
Affiliation: Other
Freshman admissions: least selective; 2017-2018: 6,788 applied, 4,710 accepted. Either SAT or ACT required. ACT 25/75 percentile: 15-19. High school rank: 3% in top tenth, 14% in top quarter, 45% in top half

Early decision deadline: N/A, notification date: N/A
Early action deadline: N/A, notification date: N/A
Application deadline (fall): 7/1
Undergraduate student body: 4,164 full time, 2,949 part time; 44% male, 56% female; 0% American Indian, 9% Asian, 12% black, 38% Hispanic, 2% multiracial, 0% Pacific Islander, 28% white, 2% international; 99% from in state; 4% live on campus; 1% of students in fraternities, 1% in sororities
Most popular majors: 22% Business, Management, Marketing, and Related Support Services, 12% Liberal Arts and Sciences, General Studies and Humanities, 7% Education, 7% Psychology, 7% Public Administration and Social Service Professions
Expenses: 2018-2019: $11,218 in state, $20,726 out of state; room/board: $13,020
Financial aid: (773) 442-5010; 65% of undergrads determined to have financial need; average aid package $9,950

Northern Illinois University

DeKalb IL
(815) 753-0446
U.S. News ranking: Nat. U., second tier
Website: www.niu.edu/
Admissions email: admissions@niu.edu
Public; founded 1895
Freshman admissions: selective; 2017-2018: 14,640 applied, 7,806 accepted. Either SAT or ACT required. ACT 25/75 percentile: 19-24. High school rank: 13% in top tenth, 37% in top quarter, 73% in top half
Early decision deadline: N/A, notification date: N/A
Early action deadline: N/A, notification date: N/A
Application deadline (fall): 8/1
Undergraduate student body: 11,788 full time, 1,666 part time; 50% male, 50% female; 0% American Indian, 5% Asian, 16% black, 18% Hispanic, 4% multiracial, 0% Pacific Islander, 55% white, 2% international; 97% from in state; 27% live on campus; 4% of students in fraternities, 3% in sororities
Most popular majors: 7% Speech Communication and Rhetoric, 6% Accounting, 6% Psychology, General, 5% Health/Medical Preparatory Programs, Other, 5% Registered Nursing/Registered Nurse
Expenses: 2018-2019: $14,750 in state, $14,750 out of state; room/board: $10,880
Financial aid: (815) 753-1300; 73% of undergrads determined to have financial need; average aid package $12,381

North Park University

Chicago IL
(773) 244-5500
U.S. News ranking: Reg. U. (Mid. W), No. 65
Website: www.northpark.edu
Admissions email: admissions@northpark.edu
Private; founded 1891
Affiliation: Evangelical Covenant Church of America
Freshman admissions: selective; 2017-2018: 4,839 applied, 2,600 accepted. Either SAT or ACT required. ACT 25/75 percentile: 19-24. High school rank: N/A
Early decision deadline: N/A, notification date: N/A
Early action deadline: N/A, notification date: N/A
Application deadline (fall): 7/1
Undergraduate student body: 1,812 full time, 217 part time; 37% male, 63% female; 0% American Indian, 8% Asian, 8% black, 27% Hispanic, 5% multiracial, 2% Pacific Islander, 41% white, 6% international
Most popular majors: Information not available
Expenses: 2017-2018: $28,620; room/board: $9,310
Financial aid: N/A

Northwestern University

Evanston IL
(847) 491-7271
U.S. News ranking: Nat. U., No. 10
Website: www.northwestern.edu
Admissions email: ug-admission@northwestern.edu
Private; founded 1851
Freshman admissions: most selective; 2017-2018: 37,259 applied, 3,442 accepted. Either SAT or ACT required. ACT 25/75 percentile: 32-35. High school rank: 91% in top tenth, 100% in top quarter, 100% in top half
Early decision deadline: 11/1, notification date: 12/15
Early action deadline: N/A, notification date: N/A
Application deadline (fall): 1/1
Undergraduate student body: 8,117 full time, 161 part time; 50% male, 50% female; 0% American Indian, 17% Asian, 6% black, 13% Hispanic, 5% multiracial, 0% Pacific Islander, 46% white, 9% international; 32% from in state; 52% live on campus; 32% of students in fraternities, 40% in sororities
Most popular majors: 14% Economics, General, 6% Journalism, 6% Psychology, General, 5% Political Science and Government, General, 4% Biology/Biological Sciences, General
Expenses: 2018-2019: $54,567; room/board: $16,626
Financial aid: (847) 491-7400; 45% of undergrads determined to have financial need; average aid package $49,030

Olivet Nazarene University

Bourbonnais IL
(815) 939-5011
U.S. News ranking: Reg. U. (Mid. W), No. 53
Website: www.olivet.edu
Admissions email: admissions@olivet.edu
Private; founded 1907
Affiliation: Church of the Nazarene
Freshman admissions: selective; 2017-2018: 3,963 applied, 2,622 accepted. Either SAT or ACT required. ACT 25/75 percentile: 20-26. High school rank: 21% in top tenth, 47% in top quarter, 76% in top half
Early decision deadline: N/A, notification date: N/A
Early action deadline: N/A, notification date: N/A
Application deadline (fall): 8/1
Undergraduate student body: 3,113 full time, 258 part time; 41% male, 59% female; 0% American Indian, 3% Asian, 8% black, 8% Hispanic, 3% multiracial, 0% Pacific Islander, 77% white, 1% international
Most popular majors: 24% Registered Nursing/Registered Nurse, 10% Business Administration and Management, General, 5% Engineering, General, 5% Psychology, General, 4% Elementary Education and Teaching
Expenses: 2018-2019: $36,070; room/board: $7,900
Financial aid: (815) 939-5249; 81% of undergrads determined to have financial need; average aid package $29,045

Principia College

Elsah IL
(618) 374-5181
U.S. News ranking: Nat. Lib. Arts, No. 81
Website: www.principiacollege.edu
Admissions email: collegeadmissions@principia.edu
Private; founded 1910
Affiliation: Other
Freshman admissions: selective; 2017-2018: 134 applied, 122 accepted. Either SAT or ACT required. SAT 25/75 percentile: 1033-1293. High school rank: 44% in top tenth, 50% in top quarter, 61% in top half
Early decision deadline: N/A, notification date: N/A
Early action deadline: N/A, notification date: N/A
Application deadline (fall): 7/25
Undergraduate student body: 441 full time, 14 part time; 51% male, 49% female; 0% American Indian, 2% Asian, 2% black, 2% Hispanic, 1% multiracial, 0% Pacific Islander, 72% white, 18% international
Most popular majors: 16% Business Administration and Management, General, 15% Sociology and Anthropology, 12% Education, Other, 11% Fine/Studio Arts, General, 8% Education, General
Expenses: 2018-2019: $29,470; room/board: $11,610
Financial aid: (618) 374-5187; 72% of undergrads determined to have financial need; average aid package $31,771

Quincy University

Quincy IL
(217) 228-5210
U.S. News ranking: Reg. U. (Mid. W), No. 94
Website: www.quincy.edu
Admissions email: admissions@quincy.edu
Private; founded 1860
Affiliation: Roman Catholic
Freshman admissions: selective; 2017-2018: 1,230 applied, 828 accepted. Either SAT or ACT required. ACT 25/75 percentile: 19-24. High school rank: 10% in top tenth, 31% in top quarter, 72% in top half
Early decision deadline: N/A, notification date: N/A
Early action deadline: N/A, notification date: N/A
Application deadline (fall): rolling
Undergraduate student body: 970 full time, 126 part time; 47% male, 53% female; 0% American Indian, 1% Asian, 11% black, 4% Hispanic, 0% multiracial, 0% Pacific Islander, 70% white, 1% international
Most popular majors: 23% Business, Management, Marketing, and Related Support Services, 19% Health Professions and Related Programs, 11% Biological and Biomedical Sciences, 8% Psychology, 6% Homeland Security, Law Enforcement, Firefighting and Related Protective Services
Expenses: 2018-2019: $27,396; room/board: $10,500
Financial aid: (217) 228-5260; 80% of undergrads determined to have financial need; average aid package $24,846

Robert Morris University

Chicago IL
(800) 762-5960
U.S. News ranking: Reg. U. (Mid. W), No. 32
Website: www.robertmorris.edu/
Admissions email: enroll@robertmorris.edu
Private; founded 1913
Freshman admissions: less selective; 2017-2018: 2,705 applied, 1,809 accepted. Neither SAT nor ACT required. ACT 25/75 percentile: 16-20. High school rank: 3% in top tenth, 10% in top quarter, 40% in top half
Early decision deadline: N/A, notification date: N/A
Early action deadline: N/A, notification date: N/A
Application deadline (fall): rolling
Undergraduate student body: 1,895 full time, 108 part time; 56% male, 44% female; 0% American Indian, 3% Asian, 25% black, 31% Hispanic, 2% multiracial, 0% Pacific Islander, 34% white, 1% international; 87% from in state; 11% live on campus; 0% of students in fraternities, 0% in sororities
Most popular majors: 73% Business, Management, Marketing, and Related Support Services, 18% Multi/Interdisciplinary Studies, 4% Computer and Information Sciences and Support Services, 3% Visual and Performing Arts, 2% Health Professions and Related Programs
Expenses: 2018-2019: $28,530; room/board: $15,915
Financial aid: (312) 935-4077; 92% of undergrads determined to have financial need; average aid package $17,114

Rockford University

Rockford IL
(815) 226-4050
U.S. News ranking: Reg. U. (Mid. W), No. 101
Website: www.rockford.edu
Admissions email: Admissions@Rockford.edu
Private; founded 1847
Freshman admissions: selective; 2017-2018: 2,401 applied, 1,118 accepted. Either SAT or ACT required. ACT 25/75 percentile: 19-23. High school rank: N/A
Early decision deadline: N/A, notification date: N/A
Early action deadline: N/A, notification date: N/A
Application deadline (fall): 8/15
Undergraduate student body: 917 full time, 144 part time; 45% male, 55% female; 0% American Indian, 2% Asian, 10% black, 15% Hispanic, 3% multiracial, 0% Pacific Islander, 62% white, 4% international; 67% from in state; 32% live on campus; 0% of students in fraternities, 0% in sororities
Most popular majors: Information not available
Expenses: 2018-2019: $30,930; room/board: $8,660
Financial aid: (815) 226-3385; 91% of undergrads determined to have financial need; average aid package $21,219

Roosevelt University

Chicago IL
(877) 277-5978
U.S. News ranking: Reg. U. (Mid. W), No. 88
Website: www.roosevelt.edu
Admissions email: admission@roosevelt.edu
Private; founded 1945
Freshman admissions: selective; 2017-2018: 4,018 applied, 2,793 accepted. Either SAT or ACT required. ACT 25/75 percentile: 20-25. High school rank: 8% in top tenth, 46% in top quarter, 62% in top half
Early decision deadline: N/A, notification date: N/A
Early action deadline: N/A, notification date: N/A
Application deadline (fall): rolling
Undergraduate student body: 2,115 full time, 399 part time; 37% male, 63% female; 0% American Indian, 6% Asian, 17% black, 25% Hispanic, 3% multiracial, 0% Pacific Islander, 44% white, 4% international; 83% from in state; 21% live on campus; N/A of students in fraternities, 2% in sororities
Most popular majors: 35% Business, Management, Marketing, and Related Support Services, 13% Psychology, 9% Biological and Biomedical Sciences, 9% Visual and Performing Arts, 7% Education
Expenses: 2018-2019: $29,832; room/board: $13,223
Financial aid: (312) 341-3868; 96% of undergrads determined to have financial need; average aid package $23,112

More @ usnews.com/bestcolleges

School of the Art Institute of Chicago

Chicago IL
(312) 629-6100
U.S. News ranking: Arts, unranked
Website: www.saic.edu
Admissions email: admiss@saic.edu
Private; founded 1866
Freshman admissions: selective; 2017-2018: 5,686 applied, 3,468 accepted. Either SAT or ACT required. ACT 25/75 percentile: 22-30. High school rank: N/A
Early decision deadline: N/A, notification date: N/A
Early action deadline: 11/15, notification date: 12/25
Application deadline (fall): 4/15
Undergraduate student body: 2,735 full time, 154 part time; 25% male, 75% female; 0% American Indian, 10% Asian, 3% black, 11% Hispanic, 3% multiracial, 0% Pacific Islander, 34% white, 33% international
Most popular majors: Information not available
Expenses: 2018-2019: $50,160; room/board: $27,800
Financial aid: N/A

Southern Illinois University–Carbondale

Carbondale IL
(618) 536-4405
U.S. News ranking: Nat. U., No. 226
Website: www.siu.edu
Admissions email: admissions@siu.edu
Public; founded 1869
Freshman admissions: selective; 2017-2018: 7,941 applied, 6,049 accepted. Either SAT or ACT required. ACT 25/75 percentile: 20-26. High school rank: 13% in top tenth, 38% in top quarter, 69% in top half
Early decision deadline: N/A, notification date: N/A
Early action deadline: N/A, notification date: N/A
Application deadline (fall): 5/1
Undergraduate student body: 9,455 full time, 1,532 part time; 54% male, 46% female; 0% American Indian, 2% Asian, 16% black, 9% Hispanic, 4% multiracial, 0% Pacific Islander, 65% white, 4% international; 83% from in state; 22% live on campus; 9% of students in fraternities, 9% in sororities
Most popular majors: 11% Education, 9% Business, Management, Marketing, and Related Support Services, 9% Engineering Technologies and Engineering-Related Fields, 8% Health Professions and Related Programs, 6% Visual and Performing Arts
Expenses: 2018-2019: $14,704 in state, $14,704 out of state; room/board: $10,622
Financial aid: (618) 453-4613; 71% of undergrads determined to have financial need; average aid package $15,046

Southern Illinois University–Edwardsville

Edwardsville IL
(618) 650-3705
U.S. News ranking: Reg. U. (Mid. W), No. 72
Website: www.siue.edu
Admissions email: admissions@siue.edu
Public; founded 1957
Affiliation: Undenominational
Freshman admissions: selective; 2017-2018: 6,273 applied, 5,615 accepted. Either SAT or ACT required. ACT 25/75 percentile: 20-26. High school rank: 17% in top tenth, 43% in top quarter, 76% in top half
Early decision deadline: N/A, notification date: N/A
Early action deadline: N/A, notification date: N/A
Application deadline (fall): 5/1
Undergraduate student body: 9,550 full time, 1,852 part time; 47% male, 53% female; 0% American Indian, 2% Asian, 14% black, 5% Hispanic, 3% multiracial, 0% Pacific Islander, 74% white, 1% international; 88% from in state; 25% live on campus; 4% of students in fraternities, 6% in sororities
Most popular majors: 17% Registered Nursing/Registered Nurse, 11% Business/Commerce, General, 7% Psychology, General, 6% Biology/Biological Sciences, General, 5% Criminal Justice/Safety Studies
Expenses: 2018-2019: $12,132 in state, $12,132 out of state; room/board: $9,761
Financial aid: (618) 650-3880; 66% of undergrads determined to have financial need; average aid package $13,649

St. Augustine College[1]

Chicago IL
(773) 878-8756
U.S. News ranking: Reg. Coll. (Mid. W), unranked
Website: www.staugustinecollege.edu/index.asp
Admissions email: info@staugustine.edu
Private
Application deadline (fall): N/A
Undergraduate student body: N/A full time, N/A part time
Expenses: 2017-2018: $13,200; room/board: N/A
Financial aid: N/A

St. Xavier University

Chicago IL
(773) 298-3050
U.S. News ranking: Reg. U. (Mid. W), No. 72
Website: www.sxu.edu
Admissions email: admission@sxu.edu
Private; founded 1846
Affiliation: Roman Catholic
Freshman admissions: selective; 2017-2018: 7,331 applied, 5,469 accepted. Either SAT or ACT required. ACT 25/75 percentile: 19-23. High school rank: 20% in top tenth, 51% in top quarter, 85% in top half
Early decision deadline: N/A, notification date: N/A
Early action deadline: N/A, notification date: N/A
Application deadline (fall): rolling
Undergraduate student body: 2,638 full time, 304 part time; 36% male, 64% female; 0% American Indian, 3% Asian, 12% black, 38% Hispanic, 3% multiracial, 0% Pacific Islander, 41% white, 0% international; 96% from in state; 16% live on campus; 0% of students in fraternities, 0% in sororities
Most popular majors: 21% Health Professions and Related Programs, 20% Business, Management, Marketing, and Related Support Services, 11% Psychology, 7% Biological and Biomedical Sciences, 5% Education
Expenses: 2018-2019: $33,880; room/board: $11,340
Financial aid: (773) 298-3073; 88% of undergrads determined to have financial need; average aid package $26,801

Trinity Christian College

Palos Heights IL
(800) 748-0085
U.S. News ranking: Reg. Coll. (Mid. W), No. 21
Website: www.trnty.edu
Admissions email: admissions@trnty.edu
Private; founded 1959
Affiliation: Other
Freshman admissions: selective; 2017-2018: 889 applied, 737 accepted. Either SAT or ACT required. ACT 25/75 percentile: 19-26. High school rank: 11% in top tenth, 24% in top quarter, 66% in top half
Early decision deadline: N/A, notification date: N/A
Early action deadline: N/A, notification date: N/A
Application deadline (fall): rolling
Undergraduate student body: 907 full time, 200 part time; 33% male, 67% female; 0% American Indian, 1% Asian, 8% black, 13% Hispanic, 1% multiracial, 0% Pacific Islander, 64% white, 10% international; 69% from in state; 46% live on campus; 0% of students in fraternities, 0% in sororities
Most popular majors: 24% Education, 15% Business, Management, Marketing, and Related Support Services, 10% Health Professions and Related Programs, 9% Psychology, 8% Public Administration and Social Service Professions
Expenses: 2018-2019: $29,950; room/board: $9,790
Financial aid: (708) 239-4872; 80% of undergrads determined to have financial need; average aid package $20,865

Trinity International University

Deerfield IL
(800) 822-3225
U.S. News ranking: Nat. U., second tier
Website: www.tiu.edu
Admissions email: tcadmissions@tiu.edu
Private; founded 1897
Affiliation: Evangelical Free Church of America
Freshman admissions: selective; 2017-2018: 500 applied, 375 accepted. Either SAT or ACT required. ACT 25/75 percentile: 20-27. High school rank: N/A
Early decision deadline: N/A, notification date: N/A
Early action deadline: N/A, notification date: N/A
Application deadline (fall): rolling
Undergraduate student body: 667 full time, 408 part time; 52% male, 48% female; 0% American Indian, 3% Asian, 16% black, 6% Hispanic, 5% multiracial, 0% Pacific Islander, 46% white, 3% international
Most popular majors: 15% Religious Education, 14% Business/Commerce, General, 13% Psychology, General, 8% Mass Communication/Media Studies, 6% Elementary Education and Teaching
Expenses: 2018-2019: $32,370; room/board: $9,600
Financial aid: (847) 317-4200; 79% of undergrads determined to have financial need; average aid package $27,933

University of Chicago

Chicago IL
(773) 702-8650
U.S. News ranking: Nat. U., No. 3
Website: www.uchicago.edu
Admissions email: collegeadmissions@uchicago.edu
Private; founded 1890
Freshman admissions: most selective; 2017-2018: 27,694 applied, 2,419 accepted. Either SAT or ACT required. ACT 25/75 percentile: 32-35. High school rank: 99% in top tenth, 100% in top quarter, 100% in top half
Early decision deadline: 11/1, notification date: 12/18
Early action deadline: 11/1, notification date: 12/18
Application deadline (fall): 1/1
Undergraduate student body: 6,242 full time, 22 part time; 51% male, 49% female; 0% American Indian, 18% Asian, 5% black, 13% Hispanic, 6% multiracial, 0% Pacific Islander, 42% white, 13% international; 18% from in state; 54% live on campus; N/A of students in fraternities, N/A in sororities
Most popular majors: 21% Econometrics and Quantitative Economics, 9% Biology/Biological Sciences, General, 8% Mathematics, General, 7% Political Science and Government, General, 5% Public Policy Analysis, General
Expenses: 2018-2019: $57,006; room/board: $16,350
Financial aid: (773) 702-8666; 42% of undergrads determined to have financial need; average aid package $52,643

University of Illinois–Chicago

Chicago IL
(312) 996-4350
U.S. News ranking: Nat. U., No. 129
Website: www.uic.edu
Admissions email: uicadmit@uic.edu
Public; founded 1965
Freshman admissions: selective; 2017-2018: 18,768 applied, 14,467 accepted. Either SAT or ACT required. ACT 25/75 percentile: 20-26. High school rank: 25% in top tenth, 58% in top quarter, 89% in top half
Early decision deadline: N/A, notification date: N/A
Early action deadline: 11/1, notification date: 12/1
Application deadline (fall): 1/15
Undergraduate student body: 17,961 full time, 1,487 part time; 50% male, 50% female; 0% American Indian, 22% Asian, 8% black, 33% Hispanic, 3% multiracial, 0% Pacific Islander, 30% white, 4% international; 97% from in state; 15% live on campus; 4% of students in fraternities, 5% in sororities
Most popular majors: 15% Business, Management, Marketing, and Related Support Services, 14% Biological and Biomedical Sciences, 13% Engineering, 13% Psychology, 9% Health Professions and Related Programs
Expenses: 2018-2019: $14,816 in state, $27,672 out of state; room/board: $10,882
Financial aid: (312) 996-5563; 76% of undergrads determined to have financial need; average aid package $15,041

University of Illinois–Springfield

Springfield IL
(217) 206-4847
U.S. News ranking: Reg. U. (Mid. W), No. 50
Website: www.uis.edu
Admissions email: admissions@uis.edu
Public; founded 1969
Freshman admissions: selective; 2017-2018: 1,746 applied, 915 accepted. Either SAT or ACT required. ACT 25/75 percentile: 20-27. High school rank: 24% in top tenth, 54% in top quarter, 84% in top half
Early decision deadline: N/A, notification date: N/A
Early action deadline: N/A, notification date: N/A
Application deadline (fall): rolling
Undergraduate student body: 1,903 full time, 1,029 part time; 51% male, 49% female; 0% American Indian, 3% Asian, 14% black, 9% Hispanic, 3% multiracial, 0% Pacific Islander, 66% white, 4% international; 86% from in state; 30% live on campus; 3% of students in fraternities, 2% in sororities
Most popular majors: 19% Business Administration and Management, General, 13% Computer

Science, 10% Psychology, General, 8% Accounting, 7% Communication and Media Studies
Expenses: 2018-2019: $11,823 in state, $20,808 out of state; room/board: $9,760
Financial aid: (217) 206-6724; 68% of undergrads determined to have financial need; average aid package $13,691

University of Illinois–Urbana-Champaign

Champaign IL
(217) 333-0302
U.S. News ranking: Nat. U., No. 46
Website: illinois.edu
Admissions email: ugradadmissions@illinois.edu
Public; founded 1867
Freshman admissions: more selective; 2017-2018: 38,965 applied, 23,974 accepted. Either SAT or ACT required. ACT 25/75 percentile: 26-32. High school rank: 50% in top tenth, 83% in top quarter, 98% in top half
Early decision deadline: N/A, notification date: N/A
Early action deadline: 11/1, notification date: 12/16
Application deadline (fall): 12/1
Undergraduate student body: 32,613 full time, 1,342 part time; 55% male, 45% female; 0% American Indian, 18% Asian, 6% black, 11% Hispanic, 3% multiracial, 0% Pacific Islander, 45% white, 16% international; 90% from in state; 50% live on campus; 21% of students in fraternities, 27% in sororities
Most popular majors: 20% Engineering, 14% Business, Management, Marketing, and Related Support Services, 9% Social Sciences, 7% Communication, Journalism, and Related Programs, 6% Agriculture, Agriculture Operations, and Related Sciences
Expenses: 2018-2019: $15,998 in state, $32,568 out of state; room/board: $11,308
Financial aid: (217) 333-0100; 47% of undergrads determined to have financial need; average aid package $16,997

University of St. Francis

Joliet IL
(800) 735-7500
U.S. News ranking: Reg. U. (Mid. W), No. 28
Website: www.stfrancis.edu
Admissions email: admissions@stfrancis.edu
Private; founded 1920
Affiliation: Roman Catholic
Freshman admissions: selective; 2017-2018: 1,560 applied, 806 accepted. Either SAT or ACT required. ACT 25/75 percentile: 20-25. High school rank: 12% in top tenth, 41% in top quarter, 74% in top half
Early decision deadline: N/A, notification date: N/A
Early action deadline: N/A, notification date: N/A
Application deadline (fall): 8/1
Undergraduate student body: 1,273 full time, 98 part time; 37% male, 63% female; 0% American Indian, 2% Asian, 8% black, 22% Hispanic, 4% multiracial, 0% Pacific Islander, 60% white, 4% international; 95% from in state; 25% live on campus; N/A of students in fraternities, 2% in sororities
Most popular majors: 32% Health Professions and Related Programs, 17% Business, Management, Marketing, and Related Support Services, 8% Education, 7% Biological and Biomedical Sciences, 7% Parks, Recreation, Leisure, and Fitness Studies
Expenses: 2018-2019: $32,320; room/board: $9,544
Financial aid: (815) 740-3403; 83% of undergrads determined to have financial need; average aid package $24,529

VanderCook College of Music

Chicago IL
(312) 225-6288
U.S. News ranking: Arts, unranked
Website: www.vandercook.edu
Admissions email: admissions@vandercook.edu
Private; founded 1909
Freshman admissions: selective; 2017-2018: 38 applied, 38 accepted. Either SAT or ACT required. ACT 25/75 percentile: 21-29. High school rank: 0% in top tenth, 0% in top quarter, 100% in top half
Early decision deadline: N/A, notification date: N/A
Early action deadline: N/A, notification date: N/A
Application deadline (fall): rolling
Undergraduate student body: 88 full time, 34 part time; 56% male, 44% female; 0% American Indian, 1% Asian, 3% black, 23% Hispanic, 3% multiracial, 1% Pacific Islander, 59% white, 2% international; 77% from in state; 14% live on campus; N/A of students in fraternities, N/A in sororities
Most popular majors: 100% Music Teacher Education
Expenses: 2018-2019: $28,434; room/board: $13,192
Financial aid: (312) 788-1146; 68% of undergrads determined to have financial need; average aid package $16,900

Western Illinois University

Macomb IL
(309) 298-3157
U.S. News ranking: Reg. U. (Mid. W), No. 53
Website: www.wiu.edu
Admissions email: admissions@wiu.edu
Public; founded 1899
Freshman admissions: selective; 2017-2018: 9,767 applied, 5,857 accepted. Either SAT or ACT required. ACT 25/75 percentile: 18-23. High school rank: 10% in top tenth, 30% in top quarter, 69% in top half
Early decision deadline: N/A, notification date: N/A
Early action deadline: N/A, notification date: N/A
Application deadline (fall): rolling
Undergraduate student body: 6,668 full time, 931 part time; 49% male, 51% female; 0% American Indian, 1% Asian, 22% black, 12% Hispanic, 3% multiracial, 0% Pacific Islander, 59% white, 1% international; 90% from in state; 44% live on campus; 14% of students in fraternities, 14% in sororities
Most popular majors: 19% Criminal Justice/Law Enforcement Administration, 14% Business Administration and Management, General, 10% Liberal Arts and Sciences, General Studies and Humanities, Other, 6% Parks, Recreation and Leisure Facilities Management, General, 5% Agriculture, Agriculture Operations, and Related Sciences
Expenses: 2018-2019: $11,267 in state, $11,267 out of state; room/board: $9,830
Financial aid: (309) 298-2446; 77% of undergrads determined to have financial need; average aid package $12,356

Wheaton College

Wheaton IL
(800) 222-2419
U.S. News ranking: Nat. Lib. Arts, No. 61
Website: www.wheaton.edu
Admissions email: admissions@wheaton.edu
Private; founded 1860
Affiliation: Protestant, not specified
Freshman admissions: more selective; 2017-2018: 1,693 applied, 1,439 accepted. Either SAT or ACT required. ACT 25/75 percentile: 27-32. High school rank: 47% in top tenth, 73% in top quarter, 93% in top half
Early decision deadline: N/A, notification date: N/A
Early action deadline: 11/1, notification date: 12/31
Application deadline (fall): 1/10
Undergraduate student body: 2,310 full time, 81 part time; 46% male, 54% female; 0% American Indian, 9% Asian, 3% black, 6% Hispanic, 4% multiracial, 0% Pacific Islander, 75% white, 3% international; 28% from in state; 89% live on campus; 0% of students in fraternities, 0% in sororities
Most popular majors: 15% Social Sciences, 9% Business, Management, Marketing, and Related Support Services, 8% English Language and Literature/Letters, 8% Visual and Performing Arts, 7% Theology and Religious Vocations
Expenses: 2018-2019: $36,420; room/board: $10,180
Financial aid: (630) 752-5021; 56% of undergrads determined to have financial need; average aid package $25,883

INDIANA

Anderson University

Anderson IN
(765) 641-4080
U.S. News ranking: Reg. U. (Mid. W), No. 47
Website: www.anderson.edu
Admissions email: info@anderson.edu
Private; founded 1917
Affiliation: Church of God
Freshman admissions: selective; 2017-2018: 2,236 applied, 1,459 accepted. Either SAT or ACT required. SAT 25/75 percentile: 910-1110. High school rank: 18% in top tenth, 43% in top quarter, 70% in top half
Early decision deadline: N/A, notification date: N/A
Early action deadline: N/A, notification date: N/A
Application deadline (fall): rolling
Undergraduate student body: 1,431 full time, 135 part time; 41% male, 59% female; 1% American Indian, 1% Asian, 9% black, 2% Hispanic, 0% multiracial, 0% Pacific Islander, 81% white, 2% international; 76% from in state; 65% live on campus; N/A of students in fraternities, N/A in sororities
Most popular majors: 21% Business, Management, Marketing, and Related Support Services, 13% Education, 12% Health Professions and Related Programs, 9% Visual and Performing Arts, 7% Psychology
Expenses: 2018-2019: $30,450; room/board: $9,890
Financial aid: (765) 641-4180; 84% of undergrads determined to have financial need; average aid package $21,160

Ball State University

Muncie IN
(765) 285-8300
U.S. News ranking: Nat. U., No. 171
Website: www.bsu.edu
Admissions email: askus@bsu.edu
Public; founded 1918
Freshman admissions: selective; 2017-2018: 24,191 applied, 15,017 accepted. Neither SAT nor ACT required. SAT 25/75 percentile: 1080-1240. High school rank: 18% in top tenth, 48% in top quarter, 86% in top half
Early decision deadline: N/A, notification date: N/A
Early action deadline: N/A, notification date: N/A
Application deadline (fall): 8/10
Undergraduate student body: 15,203 full time, 1,801 part time; 40% male, 60% female; 0% American Indian, 1% Asian, 8% black, 5% Hispanic, 3% multiracial, 0% Pacific Islander, 79% white, 1% international; 85% from in state; 44% live on campus; 13% of students in fraternities, 14% in sororities
Most popular majors: 18% Business, Management, Marketing, and Related Support Services, 14% Communication, Journalism, and Related Programs, 10% Health Professions and Related Programs, 9% Education, 7% Liberal Arts and Sciences, General Studies and Humanities
Expenses: 2018-2019: $9,896 in state, $26,468 out of state; room/board: $10,234
Financial aid: (765) 285-5600; 70% of undergrads determined to have financial need; average aid package $13,413

Bethel College

Mishawaka IN
(800) 422-4101
U.S. News ranking: Reg. U. (Mid. W), No. 29
Website: www.bethelcollege.edu
Admissions email: admissions@bethelcollege.edu
Private; founded 1947
Affiliation: Missionary Church Inc
Freshman admissions: selective; 2017-2018: 1,065 applied, 956 accepted. Either SAT or ACT required. SAT 25/75 percentile: 950-1160. High school rank: 14% in top tenth, 41% in top quarter, 72% in top half
Early decision deadline: N/A, notification date: N/A
Early action deadline: N/A, notification date: N/A
Application deadline (fall): rolling
Undergraduate student body: 1,033 full time, 261 part time; 36% male, 64% female; 0% American Indian, 2% Asian, 10% black, 9% Hispanic, 5% multiracial, 0% Pacific Islander, 72% white, 2% international; 73% from in state; 52% live on campus; 0% of students in fraternities, 0% in sororities
Most popular majors: 21% Business, Management, Marketing, and Related Support Services, 14% Health Professions and Related Programs, 10% Education, 8% Parks, Recreation, Leisure, and Fitness Studies, 7% Theology and Religious Vocations
Expenses: 2018-2019: $28,590; room/board: $9,000
Financial aid: (574) 807-7415

Butler University

Indianapolis IN
(317) 940-8150
U.S. News ranking: Reg. U. (Mid. W), No. 1
Website: www.butler.edu
Admissions email: admission@butler.edu
Private; founded 1855
Freshman admissions: more selective; 2017-2018: 14,635 applied, 9,532 accepted. Either SAT or ACT required. ACT 25/75 percentile: 25-30. High school rank: 46% in top tenth, 76% in top quarter, 94% in top half
Early decision deadline: N/A, notification date: N/A
Early action deadline: 11/1, notification date: 12/20
Application deadline (fall): 2/1
Undergraduate student body: 4,179 full time, 50 part time; 40% male, 60% female; 0% American Indian, 3% Asian, 4% black, 4% Hispanic, 3% multiracial, 0% Pacific Islander, 83% white, 1% international; 47% from in

state; 67% live on campus; 22% of students in fraternities, 36% in sororities
Most popular majors: 32% Business, Management, Marketing, and Related Support Services, 9% Communication, Journalism, and Related Programs, 9% Education, 9% Social Sciences, 8% Visual and Performing Arts
Expenses: 2018-2019: $41,120; room/board: $14,690
Financial aid: (317) 940-8200; 59% of undergrads determined to have financial need; average aid package $25,357

Calumet College of St. Joseph

Whiting IN
(219) 473-4295
U.S. News ranking: Reg. U. (Mid. W), second tier
Website: www.ccsj.edu
Admissions email: admissions@ccsj.edu
Private; founded 1951
Freshman admissions: less selective; 2017-2018: 438 applied, 143 accepted. Neither SAT nor ACT required. SAT 25/75 percentile: 860-1033. High school rank: 7% in top tenth, 18% in top quarter, 43% in top half
Early decision deadline: N/A, notification date: N/A
Early action deadline: N/A, notification date: N/A
Application deadline (fall): rolling
Undergraduate student body: 427 full time, 197 part time; 55% male, 45% female; 0% American Indian, 1% Asian, 23% black, 30% Hispanic, 2% multiracial, 0% Pacific Islander, 42% white, 0% international; 51% from in state; 0% live on campus; N/A of students in fraternities, N/A in sororities
Most popular majors: 44% Criminal Justice/Safety Studies, 30% Business Administration and Management, General, 6% Elementary Education and Teaching, 4% Biological and Physical Sciences, 4% Liberal Arts and Sciences, General Studies and Humanities, Other
Expenses: 2018-2019: $19,870; room/board: N/A
Financial aid: (219) 473-4296; 82% of undergrads determined to have financial need; average aid package $13,997

DePauw University

Greencastle IN
(765) 658-4006
U.S. News ranking: Nat. Lib. Arts, No. 56
Website: www.depauw.edu
Admissions email: admission@depauw.edu
Private; founded 1837
Freshman admissions: more selective; 2017-2018: 5,173 applied, 3,479 accepted. Either SAT or ACT required. ACT 25/75 percentile: 24-29. High school rank: 40% in top tenth, 70% in top quarter, 95% in top half
Early decision deadline: 11/1, notification date: 12/1
Early action deadline: 12/1, notification date: 1/15
Application deadline (fall): 2/1
Undergraduate student body: 2,140 full time, 18 part time; 48% male, 52% female; 0% American Indian, 4% Asian, 5% black, 7% Hispanic, 5% multiracial, 0% Pacific Islander, 68% white, 10% international; 39% from in state; 96% live on campus; 71% of students in fraternities, 64% in sororities
Most popular majors: 22% Social Sciences, 12% Communication, Journalism, and Related Programs, 9% Biological and Biomedical Sciences, 9% Computer and Information Sciences and Support Services, 8% English Language and Literature/Letters
Expenses: 2018-2019: $49,704; room/board: $13,020
Financial aid: (765) 658-4030; 59% of undergrads determined to have financial need; average aid package $42,206

Earlham College

Richmond IN
(765) 983-1600
U.S. News ranking: Nat. Lib. Arts, No. 81
Website: www.earlham.edu/admissions
Admissions email: admission@earlham.edu
Private; founded 1847
Affiliation: Friends
Freshman admissions: more selective; 2017-2018: 2,799 applied, 1,452 accepted. Neither SAT nor ACT required. ACT 25/75 percentile: 25-30. High school rank: 29% in top tenth, 64% in top quarter, 92% in top half
Early decision deadline: 11/1, notification date: 12/1
Early action deadline: 1/15, notification date: 2/15
Application deadline (fall): 2/15
Undergraduate student body: 1,051 full time, 9 part time; 45% male, 55% female; 1% American Indian, 6% Asian, 11% black, 7% Hispanic, 0% multiracial, 0% Pacific Islander, 52% white, 22% international; 18% from in state; 92% live on campus; 0% of students in fraternities, 0% in sororities
Most popular majors: 20% Multi/Interdisciplinary Studies, 17% Biological and Biomedical Sciences, 10% Physical Sciences, 8% Psychology, 8% Social Sciences
Expenses: 2018-2019: $46,450; room/board: $10,400
Financial aid: (765) 983-1217; 88% of undergrads determined to have financial need; average aid package $42,386

Franklin College

Franklin IN
(317) 738-8062
U.S. News ranking: Nat. Lib. Arts, No. 143
Website: www.franklincollege.edu
Admissions email: admissions@franklincollege.edu
Private; founded 1834
Affiliation: American Baptist
Freshman admissions: selective; 2017-2018: 1,821 applied, 1,418 accepted. Either SAT or ACT required. SAT 25/75 percentile: 1010-1200. High school rank: 18% in top tenth, 48% in top quarter, 85% in top half
Early decision deadline: N/A, notification date: N/A
Early action deadline: N/A, notification date: N/A
Application deadline (fall): rolling
Undergraduate student body: 962 full time, 54 part time; 48% male, 52% female; 0% American Indian, 1% Asian, 4% black, 3% Hispanic, 4% multiracial, 0% Pacific Islander, 87% white, 0% international; 93% from in state; 69% live on campus; 28% of students in fraternities, 43% in sororities
Most popular majors: 10% Kinesiology and Exercise Science, 9% Elementary Education and Teaching, 8% Biology/Biological Sciences, General, 8% Public Relations/Image Management, 7% Psychology, General
Expenses: 2018-2019: $32,010; room/board: $9,946
Financial aid: (317) 738-8073; 85% of undergrads determined to have financial need; average aid package $24,162

Goshen College

Goshen IN
(574) 535-7535
U.S. News ranking: Reg. Coll. (Mid. W), No. 9
Website: www.goshen.edu
Admissions email: admissions@goshen.edu
Private; founded 1894
Affiliation: Mennonite Church
Freshman admissions: selective; 2017-2018: 1,185 applied, 772 accepted. Either SAT or ACT required. SAT 25/75 percentile: 980-1238. High school rank: 18% in top tenth, 46% in top quarter, 83% in top half
Early decision deadline: N/A, notification date: N/A
Early action deadline: N/A, notification date: N/A
Application deadline (fall): 8/15
Undergraduate student body: 816 full time, 67 part time; 36% male, 64% female; 0% American Indian, 2% Asian, 4% black, 21% Hispanic, 2% multiracial, 0% Pacific Islander, 62% white, 8% international; 42% from in state; 53% live on campus; 0% of students in fraternities, 0% in sororities
Most popular majors: 26% Health Professions and Related Programs, 10% Biological and Biomedical Sciences, 9% Business, Management, Marketing, and Related Support Services, 7% Communication, Journalism, and Related Programs, 7% Visual and Performing Arts
Expenses: 2018-2019: $33,700; room/board: $10,650
Financial aid: (574) 535-7525; 76% of undergrads determined to have financial need; average aid package $27,982

Grace College and Seminary

Winona Lake IN
(574) 372-5100
U.S. News ranking: Reg. U. (Mid. W), No. 70
Website: www.grace.edu
Admissions email: enroll@grace.edu
Private; founded 1948
Affiliation: Other
Freshman admissions: selective; 2017-2018: 4,056 applied, 3,319 accepted. Either SAT or ACT required. SAT 25/75 percentile: 990-1220. High school rank: 20% in top tenth, 45% in top quarter, 79% in top half
Early decision deadline: N/A, notification date: N/A
Early action deadline: 12/1, notification date: 12/20
Application deadline (fall): 3/1
Undergraduate student body: 1,438 full time, 323 part time; 40% male, 60% female; 0% American Indian, 1% Asian, 4% black, 6% Hispanic, 3% multiracial, 0% Pacific Islander, 84% white, 1% international; 64% from in state; 65% live on campus; 0% of students in fraternities, 0% in sororities
Most popular majors: 13% Business Administration and Management, General, 7% Psychology, General, 7% Public Administration and Social Service Professions, Other, 6% General Studies, 5% Clinical, Counseling and Applied Psychology, Other
Expenses: 2018-2019: $24,768; room/board: $9,134
Financial aid: (574) 372-5100; 77% of undergrads determined to have financial need; average aid package $13,603

Hanover College

Hanover IN
(812) 866-7021
U.S. News ranking: Nat. Lib. Arts, No. 113
Website: www.hanover.edu
Admissions email: admission@hanover.edu
Private; founded 1827
Freshman admissions: more selective; 2017-2018: 2,757 applied, 2,310 accepted. Neither SAT nor ACT required. ACT 25/75 percentile: 22-27. High school rank: 32% in top tenth, 60% in top quarter, 90% in top half
Early decision deadline: N/A, notification date: N/A
Early action deadline: 12/1, notification date: 12/1
Application deadline (fall): rolling
Undergraduate student body: 1,081 full time, 8 part time; 46% male, 54% female; 1% American Indian, 1% Asian, 5% black, 3% Hispanic, 2% multiracial, 0% Pacific Islander, 76% white, 2% international; 67% from in state; 94% live on campus; 38% of students in fraternities, 31% in sororities
Most popular majors: 10% Speech Communication and Rhetoric, 8% Kinesiology and Exercise Science, 8% Psychology, General, 7% Economics, General, 6% Biology/Biological Sciences, General
Expenses: 2018-2019: $37,670; room/board: $11,580
Financial aid: (812) 866-7029; 79% of undergrads determined to have financial need; average aid package $31,606

Holy Cross College

Notre Dame IN
(574) 239-8400
U.S. News ranking: Nat. Lib. Arts, second tier
Website: www.hcc-nd.edu/home
Admissions email: admissions@hcc-nd.edu
Private; founded 1966
Affiliation: Roman Catholic
Freshman admissions: selective; 2017-2018: 1,646 applied, 1,354 accepted. Either SAT or ACT required. SAT 25/75 percentile: 1020-1320. High school rank: N/A
Early decision deadline: N/A, notification date: N/A
Early action deadline: N/A, notification date: N/A
Application deadline (fall): 7/28
Undergraduate student body: 526 full time, 31 part time; 61% male, 39% female; 1% American Indian, 3% Asian, 11% black, 13% Hispanic, 4% multiracial, 0% Pacific Islander, 60% white, 3% international; 51% from in state; 63% live on campus; 0% of students in fraternities, 0% in sororities
Most popular majors: 48% Business/Commerce, General, 15% Communication and Media Studies, 11% Psychology, General, 7% Liberal Arts and Sciences/Liberal Studies, 7% Theology/Theological Studies
Expenses: 2018-2019: $30,700; room/board: $11,500
Financial aid: (574) 239-8362; 64% of undergrads determined to have financial need; average aid package $24,300

Huntington University

Huntington IN
(800) 642-6493
U.S. News ranking: Reg. Coll. (Mid. W), No. 20
Website: www.huntington.edu
Admissions email: admissions@huntington.edu
Private; founded 1897
Affiliation: Other
Freshman admissions: selective; 2017-2018: 909 applied, 732 accepted. Either SAT or ACT required. SAT 25/75 percentile: 950-1170. High school rank: 21% in top tenth, 49% in top quarter, 82% in top half
Early decision deadline: N/A, notification date: N/A
Early action deadline: N/A, notification date: N/A
Application deadline (fall): 8/1
Undergraduate student body: 893 full time, 186 part time; 42% male, 58% female; 0% American Indian, 1% Asian, 3% black, 7% Hispanic, 3% multiracial, 0% Pacific Islander, 80% white, 6% international; 67% from in state; 57% live on campus; N/A of students in fraternities, N/A in sororities

Most popular majors: Information not available
Expenses: 2018-2019: $26,180; room/board: $8,668
Financial aid: (800) 642-6493; 64% of undergrads determined to have financial need; average aid package $19,060

Indiana Institute of Technology

Fort Wayne IN
(800) 937-2448
U.S. News ranking: Business, unranked
Website: www.indianatech.edu
Admissions email: admissions@indianatech.edu
Private; founded 1930
Freshman admissions: least selective; 2017-2018: 3,068 applied, 2,144 accepted. Either SAT or ACT required. SAT 25/75 percentile: N/A. High school rank: N/A
Early decision deadline: N/A, notification date: N/A
Early action deadline: N/A, notification date: N/A
Application deadline (fall): 8/1
Undergraduate student body: 1,511 full time, 193 part time; 66% male, 34% female; 0% American Indian, 1% Asian, 18% black, 7% Hispanic, 4% multiracial, 0% Pacific Islander, 46% white, 20% international
Most popular majors: Information not available
Expenses: 2018-2019: $26,900; room/board: $12,660
Financial aid: (260) 422-5561

Indiana State University

Terre Haute IN
(812) 237-2121
U.S. News ranking: Nat. U., second tier
Website: www.indstate.edu/
Admissions email: admissions@indstate.edu
Public; founded 1865
Freshman admissions: less selective; 2017-2018: 11,720 applied, 9,904 accepted. Either SAT or ACT required. SAT 25/75 percentile: 900-1110. High school rank: 10% in top tenth, 28% in top quarter, 63% in top half
Early decision deadline: N/A, notification date: N/A
Early action deadline: N/A, notification date: N/A
Application deadline (fall): 8/15
Undergraduate student body: 9,369 full time, 2,222 part time; 45% male, 55% female; 0% American Indian, 1% Asian, 19% black, 4% Hispanic, 4% multiracial, 0% Pacific Islander, 65% white, 4% international; 80% from in state; 29% live on campus; 13% of students in fraternities, 12% in sororities
Most popular majors: 16% Business, Management, Marketing, and Related Support Services, 15% Health Professions and Related Programs, 11% Engineering Technologies and Engineering-Related Fields, 11% Social Sciences, 7% Education
Expenses: 2018-2019: $9,090 in state, $19,836 out of state; room/board: $10,590
Financial aid: (800) 841-4744; 74% of undergrads determined to have financial need; average aid package $10,965

Indiana University–Bloomington

Bloomington IN
(812) 855-0661
U.S. News ranking: Nat. U., No. 89
Website: www.iub.edu
Admissions email: iuadmit@indiana.edu
Public; founded 1820
Freshman admissions: more selective; 2017-2018: 41,939 applied, 31,878 accepted. Either SAT or ACT required. ACT 25/75 percentile: 25-31. High school rank: 36% in top tenth, 70% in top quarter, 95% in top half
Early decision deadline: N/A, notification date: N/A
Early action deadline: 11/1, notification date: 1/15
Application deadline (fall): rolling
Undergraduate student body: 32,212 full time, 1,217 part time; 51% male, 49% female; 0% American Indian, 5% Asian, 4% black, 6% Hispanic, 4% multiracial, 0% Pacific Islander, 70% white, 10% international; 66% from in state; 36% live on campus; 24% of students in fraternities, 21% in sororities
Most popular majors: 23% Business/Commerce, General, 7% Public Administration, 6% Informatics, 6% Kinesiology and Exercise Science, 4% Psychology, General
Expenses: 2018-2019: $10,681 in state, $35,456 out of state; room/board: $10,465
Financial aid: (812) 855-6500; 41% of undergrads determined to have financial need; average aid package $13,956

Indiana University East

Richmond IN
(765) 973-8208
U.S. News ranking: Reg. U. (Mid. W), second tier
Website: www.iue.edu
Admissions email: applynow@iue.edu
Public; founded 1971
Freshman admissions: selective; 2017-2018: 1,279 applied, 891 accepted. Either SAT or ACT required. SAT 25/75 percentile: 940-1118. High school rank: 8% in top tenth, 30% in top quarter, 71% in top half
Early decision deadline: N/A, notification date: N/A
Early action deadline: N/A, notification date: N/A
Application deadline (fall): rolling
Undergraduate student body: 1,887 full time, 1,405 part time; 36% male, 64% female; 0% American Indian, 1% Asian, 5% black, 4% Hispanic, 3% multiracial, 0% Pacific Islander, 85% white, 1% international; 76% from in state; N/A live on campus; N/A of students in fraternities, N/A in sororities
Most popular majors: 25% Business/Commerce, General, 18% Registered Nursing/Registered Nurse, 11% Psychology, General, 7% Liberal Arts and Sciences, General Studies and Humanities, Other, 6% Criminal Justice/Law Enforcement Administration
Expenses: 2018-2019: $7,344 in state, $19,400 out of state; room/board: N/A
Financial aid: (765) 973-8206; 76% of undergrads determined to have financial need; average aid package $9,118

Indiana University–Kokomo

Kokomo IN
(765) 455-9217
U.S. News ranking: Reg. Coll. (Mid. W), second tier
Website: www.iuk.edu
Admissions email: iuadmiss@iuk.edu
Public; founded 1945
Freshman admissions: selective; 2017-2018: 1,770 applied, 1,244 accepted. Either SAT or ACT required. SAT 25/75 percentile: 950-1120. High school rank: 8% in top tenth, 28% in top quarter, 70% in top half
Early decision deadline: N/A, notification date: N/A
Early action deadline: N/A, notification date: N/A
Application deadline (fall): rolling
Undergraduate student body: 2,215 full time, 661 part time; 36% male, 64% female; 0% American Indian, 1% Asian, 4% black, 6% Hispanic, 3% multiracial, 0% Pacific Islander, 83% white, 1% international; 98% from in state; N/A live on campus; N/A of students in fraternities, N/A in sororities
Most popular majors: 34% Registered Nursing/Registered Nurse, 14% Business/Commerce, General, 11% Liberal Arts and Sciences, General Studies and Humanities, Other, 5% Health and Wellness, General, 4% Criminal Justice/Safety Studies
Expenses: 2018-2019: $7,344 in state, $19,400 out of state; room/board: N/A
Financial aid: (765) 455-9216; 68% of undergrads determined to have financial need; average aid package $8,946

Indiana University Northwest

Gary IN
(219) 980-6991
U.S. News ranking: Reg. U. (Mid. W), second tier
Website: www.iun.edu
Admissions email: admit@iun.edu
Public; founded 1948
Freshman admissions: less selective; 2017-2018: 1,749 applied, 1,302 accepted. Either SAT or ACT required. SAT 25/75 percentile: 890-1093. High school rank: 11% in top tenth, 32% in top quarter, 69% in top half
Early decision deadline: N/A, notification date: N/A
Early action deadline: N/A, notification date: N/A
Application deadline (fall): rolling
Undergraduate student body: 2,608 full time, 1,092 part time; 30% male, 70% female; 0% American Indian, 3% Asian, 17% black, 23% Hispanic, 3% multiracial, 0% Pacific Islander, 53% white, 0% international; 97% from in state; N/A live on campus; N/A of students in fraternities, N/A in sororities
Most popular majors: 12% Registered Nursing/Registered Nurse, 11% Business/Commerce, General, 11% Criminal Justice/Safety Studies, 9% Liberal Arts and Sciences, General Studies and Humanities, Other, 8% Psychology, General
Expenses: 2018-2019: $7,344 in state, $19,400 out of state; room/board: N/A
Financial aid: (219) 980-6778; 70% of undergrads determined to have financial need; average aid package $8,947

Indiana University-Purdue University–Indianapolis

Indianapolis IN
(317) 274-4591
U.S. News ranking: Nat. U., No. 194
Website: www.iupui.edu
Admissions email: apply@iupui.edu
Public; founded 1969
Freshman admissions: selective; 2017-2018: 11,091 applied, 8,834 accepted. Either SAT or ACT required. SAT 25/75 percentile: 1000-1190. High school rank: 15% in top tenth, 43% in top quarter, 84% in top half
Early decision deadline: N/A, notification date: N/A
Early action deadline: N/A, notification date: N/A
Application deadline (fall): 5/1
Undergraduate student body: 17,521 full time, 4,089 part time; 44% male, 56% female; 0% American Indian, 4% Asian, 9% black, 7% Hispanic, 4% multiracial, 0% Pacific Islander, 70% white, 4% international; 96% from in state; 11% live on campus; 3% of students in fraternities, 4% in sororities
Most popular majors: 13% Business/Commerce, General, 10% Registered Nursing/Registered Nurse, 6% Liberal Arts and Sciences, General Studies and Humanities, Other, 5% Psychology, General, 4% Elementary Education and Teaching
Expenses: 2018-2019: $9,465 in state, $29,821 out of state; room/board: $8,924
Financial aid: (311) 274-4162; 67% of undergrads determined to have financial need; average aid package $11,800

Indiana University–South Bend

South Bend IN
(574) 520-4839
U.S. News ranking: Reg. U. (Mid. W), second tier
Website: www.iusb.edu
Admissions email: admissions@iusb.edu
Public; founded 1922
Freshman admissions: less selective; 2017-2018: 2,580 applied, 2,005 accepted. Either SAT or ACT required. SAT 25/75 percentile: 930-1120. High school rank: 7% in top tenth, 25% in top quarter, 66% in top half
Early decision deadline: N/A, notification date: N/A
Early action deadline: N/A, notification date: N/A
Application deadline (fall): rolling
Undergraduate student body: 3,767 full time, 1,109 part time; 38% male, 62% female; 0% American Indian, 2% Asian, 8% black, 11% Hispanic, 4% multiracial, 0% Pacific Islander, 71% white, 3% international; 95% from in state; 8% live on campus; N/A of students in fraternities, N/A in sororities
Most popular majors: 21% Business/Commerce, General, 12% Registered Nursing/Registered Nurse, 11% Liberal Arts and Sciences, General Studies and Humanities, Other, 6% Psychology, General, 6% Social Work
Expenses: 2018-2019: $7,344 in state, $19,400 out of state; room/board: $7,309
Financial aid: (574) 520-4357; 73% of undergrads determined to have financial need; average aid package $9,441

Indiana University Southeast

New Albany IN
(812) 941-2212
U.S. News ranking: Reg. U. (Mid. W), second tier
Website: www.ius.edu
Admissions email: admissions@ius.edu
Public; founded 1941
Freshman admissions: selective; 2017-2018: 2,273 applied, 1,881 accepted. Either SAT or ACT required. ACT 25/75 percentile: 17-22. High school rank: 9% in top tenth, 32% in top quarter, 70% in top half
Early decision deadline: N/A, notification date: N/A
Early action deadline: N/A, notification date: N/A
Application deadline (fall): rolling
Undergraduate student body: 3,218 full time, 1,605 part time; 40% male, 60% female; 0% American Indian, 1% Asian, 7% black, 4% Hispanic, 3% multiracial, 0% Pacific Islander, 83% white, 1% international; 69% from in state; 8% live on campus; 5% of students in fraternities, 5% in sororities
Most popular majors: 21% Business/Commerce, General, 13% Registered Nursing/Registered Nurse, 10% Psychology, General, 8% Liberal Arts

and Sciences, General Studies and Humanities, Other, 7% Criminal Justice/Safety Studies
Expenses: 2018-2019: $7,344 in state, $19,400 out of state; room/board: $6,780
Financial aid: (812) 941-2246; 67% of undergrads determined to have financial need; average aid package $8,797

Indiana Wesleyan University

Marion IN
(866) 468-6498
U.S. News ranking: Reg. U. (Mid. W), No. 32
Website: www.indwes.edu
Admissions email: admissions@indwes.edu
Private; founded 1920
Freshman admissions: selective; 2017-2018: 3,796 applied, 2,734 accepted. Either SAT or ACT required. ACT 25/75 percentile: 21-26. High school rank: 23% in top tenth, 57% in top quarter, 88% in top half
Early decision deadline: N/A, notification date: N/A
Early action deadline: N/A, notification date: N/A
Application deadline (fall): rolling
Undergraduate student body: 2,634 full time, 165 part time; 35% male, 65% female; 0% American Indian, 1% Asian, 4% black, 4% Hispanic, 4% multiracial, 0% Pacific Islander, 84% white, 1% international; 54% from in state; 82% live on campus; 0% of students in fraternities, 0% in sororities
Most popular majors: 26% Health Professions and Related Programs, 12% Business, Management, Marketing, and Related Support Services, 11% Education, 8% Theology and Religious Vocations, 7% Psychology
Expenses: 2018-2019: $25,980; room/board: $8,312
Financial aid: (765) 677-2115; 78% of undergrads determined to have financial need; average aid package $29,681

Manchester University

North Manchester IN
(800) 852-3648
U.S. News ranking: Reg. Coll. (Mid. W), No. 26
Website: www.manchester.edu
Admissions email: admitinfo@manchester.edu
Private; founded 1889
Affiliation: Church of Brethren
Freshman admissions: less selective; 2017-2018: 4,115 applied, 2,541 accepted. Neither SAT nor ACT required. SAT 25/75 percentile: 850-1100. High school rank: 17% in top tenth, 39% in top quarter, 74% in top half
Early decision deadline: N/A, notification date: N/A
Early action deadline: N/A, notification date: N/A
Application deadline (fall): rolling
Undergraduate student body: 1,244 full time, 22 part time; 48% male, 52% female; 0% American Indian, 1% Asian, 7% black, 7% Hispanic, 4% multiracial, 0% Pacific Islander, 74% white, 4% international; 86% from in state; 73% live on campus; 0% of students in fraternities, 0% in sororities
Most popular majors: 27% Business, Management, Marketing, and Related Support Services, 13% Health Professions and Related Programs, 10% Education, 7% Social Sciences, 6% Parks, Recreation, Leisure, and Fitness Studies
Expenses: 2018-2019: $32,758; room/board: $9,580
Financial aid: (260) 982-5237; 86% of undergrads determined to have financial need; average aid package $30,161

Marian University

Indianapolis IN
(317) 955-6300
U.S. News ranking: Reg. U. (Mid. W), No. 38
Website: www.marian.edu
Admissions email: admissions@marian.edu
Private; founded 1851
Affiliation: Roman Catholic
Freshman admissions: selective; 2017-2018: 2,246 applied, 1,320 accepted. Either SAT or ACT required. SAT 25/75 percentile: 1000-1200. High school rank: 18% in top tenth, 44% in top quarter, 80% in top half
Early decision deadline: N/A, notification date: N/A
Early action deadline: N/A, notification date: N/A
Application deadline (fall): 8/1
Undergraduate student body: 1,961 full time, 342 part time; 38% male, 62% female; 0% American Indian, 2% Asian, 11% black, 5% Hispanic, 3% multiracial, 0% Pacific Islander, 74% white, 1% international; 77% from in state; 40% live on campus; N/A of students in fraternities, N/A in sororities
Most popular majors: 43% Health Professions and Related Programs, 25% Business, Management, Marketing, and Related Support Services, 6% Education, 5% Parks, Recreation, Leisure, and Fitness Studies, 4% Biological and Biomedical Sciences
Expenses: 2018-2019: $34,000; room/board: $10,640
Financial aid: (317) 955-6040; 79% of undergrads determined to have financial need; average aid package $27,762

Martin University[1]

Indianapolis IN
(317) 543-3235
U.S. News ranking: Nat. Lib. Arts, unranked
Website: www.martin.edu
Admissions email: admissions@martin.edu
Private
Application deadline (fall): N/A
Undergraduate student body: N/A full time, N/A part time
Expenses: 2017-2018: $13,200; room/board: N/A
Financial aid: N/A

Oakland City University

Oakland City IN
(800) 737-5125
U.S. News ranking: Reg. Coll. (Mid. W), No. 39
Website: www.oak.edu
Admissions email: admission@oak.edu
Private; founded 1885
Affiliation: General Baptist
Freshman admissions: selective; 2017-2018: 547 applied, 395 accepted. Neither SAT nor ACT required. SAT 25/75 percentile: 950-1150. High school rank: 8% in top tenth, 19% in top quarter, 61% in top half
Early decision deadline: N/A, notification date: N/A
Early action deadline: N/A, notification date: N/A
Application deadline (fall): rolling
Undergraduate student body: 572 full time, 541 part time; 44% male, 56% female; 0% American Indian, 0% Asian, 6% black, 2% Hispanic, 1% multiracial, 0% Pacific Islander, 77% white, 3% international; 81% from in state; 35% live on campus; N/A of students in fraternities, N/A in sororities
Most popular majors: 36% Business, Management, Marketing, and Related Support Services, 24% Homeland Security, Law Enforcement, Firefighting and Related Protective Services, 9% Education, 7% Parks, Recreation, Leisure, and Fitness Studies, 6% Psychology
Expenses: 2018-2019: $24,000; room/board: $9,900
Financial aid: (812) 749-1225; 81% of undergrads determined to have financial need; average aid package $21,053

Purdue University–Fort Wayne

Fort Wayne IN
(260) 481-6812
U.S. News ranking: Reg. U. (Mid. W), second tier
Website: www.pfw.edu
Admissions email: ask@pfw.edu
Public; founded 1964
Freshman admissions: selective; 2017-2018: 4,403 applied, 4,157 accepted. Either SAT or ACT required. SAT 25/75 percentile: 970-1170. High school rank: 11% in top tenth, 34% in top quarter, 69% in top half
Early decision deadline: N/A, notification date: N/A
Early action deadline: N/A, notification date: N/A
Application deadline (fall): 8/1
Undergraduate student body: 5,913 full time, 4,044 part time; 44% male, 56% female; 0% American Indian, 3% Asian, 6% black, 7% Hispanic, 4% multiracial, 0% Pacific Islander, 79% white, 2% international; 94% from in state; 10% live on campus; N/A of students in fraternities, 1% in sororities
Most popular majors: 29% Business, Management, Marketing, and Related Support Services, 19% Social Sciences, 18% Health Professions and Related Programs, 18% Multi/Interdisciplinary Studies, 15% Liberal Arts and Sciences, General Studies and Humanities
Expenses: 2018-2019: $9,551 in state, $21,389 out of state; room/board: N/A
Financial aid: (260) 481-6140; 69% of undergrads determined to have financial need; average aid package $9,662

Purdue University–Northwest

Hammond IN
(219) 989-2213
U.S. News ranking: Reg. U. (Mid. W), second tier
Website: www.pnw.edu/
Admissions email: admissons@pnw.edu
Public; founded 2016
Freshman admissions: selective; 2017-2018: 1,984 applied, 1,823 accepted. Either SAT or ACT required. SAT 25/75 percentile: 970-1160. High school rank: 11% in top tenth, 37% in top quarter, 74% in top half
Early decision deadline: N/A, notification date: N/A
Early action deadline: N/A, notification date: N/A
Application deadline (fall): 8/1
Undergraduate student body: 6,172 full time, 4,962 part time; 43% male, 57% female; 0% American Indian, 2% Asian, 10% black, 18% Hispanic, 3% multiracial, 0% Pacific Islander, 61% white, 4% international; 91% from in state; 6% live on campus; N/A of students in fraternities, N/A in sororities
Most popular majors: 41% Health Professions and Related Programs, 16% Business, Management, Marketing, and Related Support Services, 8% Engineering Technologies and Engineering-Related Fields, 6% Engineering, 4% Psychology
Expenses: 2018-2019: $8,439 in state, $18,121 out of state; room/board: $7,640
Financial aid: (855) 608-4600; 68% of undergrads determined to have financial need; average aid package $3,704

Purdue University–West Lafayette

West Lafayette IN
(765) 494-1776
U.S. News ranking: Nat. U., No. 56
Website: www.purdue.edu
Admissions email: admissions@purdue.edu
Public; founded 1869
Freshman admissions: more selective; 2017-2018: 48,912 applied, 28,092 accepted. Either SAT or ACT required. SAT 25/75 percentile: 1150-1380. High school rank: 44% in top tenth, 78% in top quarter, 97% in top half
Early decision deadline: N/A, notification date: N/A
Early action deadline: 11/1, notification date: 12/12
Application deadline (fall): rolling
Undergraduate student body: 29,629 full time, 1,377 part time; 57% male, 43% female; 0% American Indian, 8% Asian, 3% black, 5% Hispanic, 3% multiracial, 0% Pacific Islander, 63% white, 16% international; 63% from in state; 40% live on campus; 21% of students in fraternities, 23% in sororities
Most popular majors: 24% Engineering, 18% Business, Management, Marketing, and Related Support Services, 10% Liberal Arts and Sciences, General Studies and Humanities, 9% Agriculture, Agriculture Operations, and Related Sciences, 6% Engineering Technologies and Engineering-Related Fields
Expenses: 2018-2019: $10,002 in state, $28,804 out of state; room/board: $10,030
Financial aid: (765) 494-5050; 42% of undergrads determined to have financial need; average aid package $13,942

Rose-Hulman Institute of Technology

Terre Haute IN
(812) 877-8213
U.S. News ranking: Engineering, unranked
Website: www.rose-hulman.edu
Admissions email: admissions@rose-hulman.edu
Private; founded 1874
Freshman admissions: more selective; 2017-2018: 4,473 applied, 2,726 accepted. Either SAT or ACT required. ACT 25/75 percentile: 27-32. High school rank: 64% in top tenth, 91% in top quarter, 100% in top half
Early decision deadline: N/A, notification date: N/A
Early action deadline: 11/1, notification date: 12/15
Application deadline (fall): 2/1
Undergraduate student body: 2,147 full time, 21 part time; 75% male, 25% female; 0% American Indian, 5% Asian, 3% black, 5% Hispanic, 5% multiracial, 0% Pacific Islander, 68% white, 15% international; 36% from in state; 58% live on campus; 36% of students in fraternities, 34% in sororities
Most popular majors: 34% Mechanical Engineering, 17% Chemical Engineering, 9% Computer Science, 8% Bioengineering and Biomedical Engineering, 8% Electrical and Electronics Engineering
Expenses: 2018-2019: $47,571; room/board: $14,766
Financial aid: (812) 877-8672; 58% of undergrads determined to have financial need; average aid package $30,070

Saint Mary-of-the-Woods College

St. Mary-of-the-Woods IN
(800) 926-7692
U.S. News ranking: Reg. Coll. (Mid. W), No. 21
Website: www.smwc.edu
Admissions email: admission@smwc.edu
Private; founded 1840

Affiliation: Roman Catholic
Freshman admissions: less selective; 2017-2018: 578 applied, 434 accepted. Either SAT or ACT required. SAT 25/75 percentile: 890-1070. High school rank: N/A
Early decision deadline: N/A, notification date: N/A
Early action deadline: N/A, notification date: N/A
Application deadline (fall): rolling
Undergraduate student body: 397 full time, 359 part time; 10% male, 90% female; 1% American Indian, 1% Asian, 4% black, 2% Hispanic, 2% multiracial, 0% Pacific Islander, 80% white, 1% international; 72% from in state; 42% live on campus; 0% of students in fraternities, 0% in sororities
Most popular majors: 31% Education, 21% Business, Management, Marketing, and Related Support Services, 8% Psychology, 7% Health Professions and Related Programs, 6% Public Administration and Social Service Professions
Expenses: 2018-2019: $29,960; room/board: $10,914
Financial aid: (812) 535-5110; 98% of undergrads determined to have financial need; average aid package $25,390

St. Mary's College

Notre Dame IN
(574) 284-4587
U.S. News ranking: Nat. Lib. Arts, No. 95
Website: www.saintmarys.edu
Admissions email: admission@saintmarys.edu
Private; founded 1844
Affiliation: Roman Catholic
Freshman admissions: more selective; 2017-2018: 1,830 applied, 1,432 accepted. Either SAT or ACT required. ACT 25/75 percentile: 23-29. High school rank: 28% in top tenth, 64% in top quarter, 93% in top half
Early decision deadline: 11/15, notification date: 12/15
Early action deadline: N/A, notification date: N/A
Application deadline (fall): rolling
Undergraduate student body: 1,486 full time, 45 part time; 1% male, 99% female; 0% American Indian, 2% Asian, 2% black, 11% Hispanic, 3% multiracial, 0% Pacific Islander, 78% white, 1% international; 30% from in state; 85% live on campus; 0% of students in fraternities, 0% in sororities
Most popular majors: 11% Registered Nursing/Registered Nurse, 9% Biology/Biological Sciences, General, 9% Business Administration and Management, General, 9% Communication Sciences and Disorders, General, 9% Psychology, General
Expenses: 2018-2019: $42,220; room/board: $12,580
Financial aid: (574) 284-4557; 71% of undergrads determined to have financial need; average aid package $35,934

Taylor University

Upland IN
(765) 998-5134
U.S. News ranking: Reg. Coll. (Mid. W), No. 1
Website: www.taylor.edu
Admissions email: admissions_u@taylor.edu
Private; founded 1846
Affiliation: Interdenominational
Freshman admissions: more selective; 2017-2018: 1,673 applied, 1,452 accepted. Either SAT or ACT required. ACT 25/75 percentile: 22-29. High school rank: 35% in top tenth, 63% in top quarter, 88% in top half
Early decision deadline: N/A, notification date: N/A
Early action deadline: N/A, notification date: N/A
Application deadline (fall): rolling
Undergraduate student body: 1,840 full time, 270 part time; 44% male, 56% female; 1% American Indian, 3% Asian, 4% black, 4% Hispanic, 0% multiracial, 0% Pacific Islander, 83% white, 5% international; 42% from in state; 89% live on campus; N/A of students in fraternities, N/A in sororities
Most popular majors: 18% Business, Management, Marketing, and Related Support Services, 10% Parks, Recreation, Leisure, and Fitness Studies, 9% Education, 9% Psychology, 8% Visual and Performing Arts
Expenses: 2018-2019: $34,114; room/board: $9,614
Financial aid: (765) 998-5358; 62% of undergrads determined to have financial need; average aid package $23,875

Trine University

Angola IN
(260) 665-4100
U.S. News ranking: Reg. Coll. (Mid. W), No. 24
Website: www.trine.edu
Admissions email: admit@trine.edu
Private; founded 1884
Freshman admissions: selective; 2017-2018: 3,502 applied, 2,455 accepted. Either SAT or ACT required. SAT 25/75 percentile: 970-1160. High school rank: 23% in top tenth, 51% in top quarter, 84% in top half
Early decision deadline: N/A, notification date: N/A
Early action deadline: N/A, notification date: N/A
Application deadline (fall): 8/1
Undergraduate student body: 1,920 full time, 2,184 part time; 55% male, 45% female; 0% American Indian, 1% Asian, 3% black, 4% Hispanic, 3% multiracial, 0% Pacific Islander, 81% white, 6% international; 61% from in state; 69% live on campus; 26% of students in fraternities, 19% in sororities
Most popular majors: 37% Engineering, General, 19% Business, Management, Marketing, and Related Support Services, 13% Kinesiology and Exercise Science, 10% CAD/CADD Drafting and/or Design Technology/Technician, 8% Criminal Justice/Law Enforcement Administration
Expenses: 2018-2019: $32,175; room/board: $10,810
Financial aid: (260) 665-4438; 84% of undergrads determined to have financial need; average aid package $27,988

University of Evansville

Evansville IN
(812) 488-2468
U.S. News ranking: Reg. U. (Mid. W), No. 7
Website: www.evansville.edu
Admissions email: admission@evansville.edu
Private; founded 1854
Affiliation: United Methodist
Freshman admissions: more selective; 2017-2018: 3,825 applied, 2,676 accepted. Neither SAT nor ACT required. ACT 25/75 percentile: 22-29. High school rank: 37% in top tenth, 67% in top quarter, 92% in top half
Early decision deadline: N/A, notification date: N/A
Early action deadline: 12/1, notification date: 12/15
Application deadline (fall): rolling
Undergraduate student body: 2,024 full time, 318 part time; 44% male, 56% female; 0% American Indian, 2% Asian, 3% black, 3% Hispanic, 2% multiracial, 0% Pacific Islander, 73% white, 14% international; 65% from in state; 51% live on campus; 25% of students in fraternities, 24% in sororities
Most popular majors: 17% Business, Management, Marketing, and Related Support Services, 14% Health Professions and Related Programs, 12% Engineering, 12% Parks, Recreation, Leisure, and Fitness Studies, 9% Visual and Performing Arts
Expenses: 2018-2019: $36,416; room/board: $12,460
Financial aid: (812) 488-2364; 65% of undergrads determined to have financial need; average aid package $31,270

University of Indianapolis

Indianapolis IN
(317) 788-3216
U.S. News ranking: Reg. U. (Mid. W), No. 38
Website: www.uindy.edu
Admissions email: admissions@uindy.edu
Private; founded 1902
Affiliation: United Methodist
Freshman admissions: selective; 2017-2018: 7,918 applied, 6,830 accepted. Either SAT or ACT required. SAT 25/75 percentile: 990-1180. High school rank: 20% in top tenth, 47% in top quarter, 86% in top half
Early decision deadline: N/A, notification date: N/A
Early action deadline: N/A, notification date: N/A
Application deadline (fall): rolling
Undergraduate student body: 3,828 full time, 660 part time; 36% male, 64% female; 0% American Indian, 2% Asian, 9% black, 6% Hispanic, 3% multiracial, 0% Pacific Islander, 66% white, 7% international; 91% from in state; 41% live on campus; 0% of students in fraternities, 0% in sororities
Most popular majors: 22% Registered Nursing/Registered Nurse, 13% Business Administration and Management, General, 10% Psychology, General, 6% Kinesiology and Exercise Science, 4% Banking and Financial Support Services
Expenses: 2018-2019: $29,688; room/board: $11,240
Financial aid: (317) 788-3217; 76% of undergrads determined to have financial need; average aid package $22,605

University of Notre Dame

Notre Dame IN
(574) 631-7505
U.S. News ranking: Nat. U., No. 18
Website: www.nd.edu
Admissions email: admissions@nd.edu
Private; founded 1842
Affiliation: Roman Catholic
Freshman admissions: most selective; 2017-2018: 19,564 applied, 3,702 accepted. Either SAT or ACT required. ACT 25/75 percentile: 32-34. High school rank: 91% in top tenth, 98% in top quarter, 100% in top half
Early decision deadline: N/A, notification date: N/A
Early action deadline: 11/1, notification date: 12/15
Application deadline (fall): 1/1
Undergraduate student body: 8,557 full time, 19 part time; 53% male, 47% female; 0% American Indian, 5% Asian, 4% black, 11% Hispanic, 5% multiracial, 0% Pacific Islander, 69% white, 6% international; 7% from in state; 79% live on campus; N/A of students in fraternities, N/A in sororities
Most popular majors: 12% Finance, General, 7% Accounting, 6% Economics, General, 6% Political Science and Government, General, 5% Psychology, General
Expenses: 2018-2019: $53,391; room/board: $15,410
Financial aid: (574) 631-6436; 48% of undergrads determined to have financial need; average aid package $49,410

University of Saint Francis

Fort Wayne IN
(260) 399-8000
U.S. News ranking: Reg. U. (Mid. W), No. 72
Website: www.sf.edu
Admissions email: admis@sf.edu
Private; founded 1890
Affiliation: Roman Catholic
Freshman admissions: selective; 2017-2018: 1,249 applied, 1,233 accepted. Either SAT or ACT required. SAT 25/75 percentile: 960-1140. High school rank: 14% in top tenth, 40% in top quarter, 80% in top half
Early decision deadline: N/A, notification date: N/A
Early action deadline: N/A, notification date: N/A
Application deadline (fall): rolling
Undergraduate student body: 1,523 full time, 383 part time; 29% male, 71% female; 0% American Indian, 2% Asian, 7% black, 7% Hispanic, 3% multiracial, 0% Pacific Islander, 79% white, 1% international; 90% from in state; 22% live on campus; N/A of students in fraternities, N/A in sororities
Most popular majors: 44% Health Professions and Related Programs, 13% Business, Management, Marketing, and Related Support Services, 13% Visual and Performing Arts, 6% Biological and Biomedical Sciences, 5% Public Administration and Social Service Professions
Expenses: 2018-2019: $30,430; room/board: $9,840
Financial aid: (260) 399-8003; 88% of undergrads determined to have financial need; average aid package $21,993

University of Southern Indiana

Evansville IN
(812) 464-1765
U.S. News ranking: Reg. U. (Mid. W), second tier
Website: www.usi.edu
Admissions email: enroll@usi.edu
Public; founded 1965
Freshman admissions: selective; 2017-2018: 4,569 applied, 4,277 accepted. Either SAT or ACT required. SAT 25/75 percentile: 970-1170. High school rank: 13% in top tenth, 37% in top quarter, 71% in top half
Early decision deadline: N/A, notification date: N/A
Early action deadline: N/A, notification date: N/A
Application deadline (fall): 8/15
Undergraduate student body: 6,538 full time, 1,168 part time; 38% male, 62% female; 0% American Indian, 1% Asian, 4% black, 3% Hispanic, 2% multiracial, 0% Pacific Islander, 86% white, 2% international; 87% from in state; 32% live on campus; 8% of students in fraternities, 7% in sororities
Most popular majors: 24% Health Professions and Related Programs, 16% Business, Management, Marketing, and Related Support Services, 8% Education, 6% Communication, Journalism, and Related Programs, 6% Parks, Recreation, Leisure, and Fitness Studies
Expenses: 2018-2019: $7,970 in state, $18,626 out of state; room/board: $8,838
Financial aid: (812) 464-1767; 64% of undergrads determined to have financial need; average aid package $9,456

Valparaiso University

Valparaiso IN
(888) 468-2576
U.S. News ranking: Reg. U. (Mid. W), No. 5
Website: www.valpo.edu
Admissions email: undergrad.admission@valpo.edu
Private; founded 1859

More @ usnews.com/bestcolleges

Freshman admissions: more selective; 2017-2018: 7,954 applied, 6,704 accepted. Either SAT or ACT required. ACT 25/75 percentile: 23-29. High school rank: 32% in top tenth, 63% in top quarter, 94% in top half
Early decision deadline: N/A, notification date: N/A
Early action deadline: N/A, notification date: N/A
Application deadline (fall): rolling
Undergraduate student body: 3,180 full time, 71 part time; 45% male, 55% female; 0% American Indian, 2% Asian, 6% black, 10% Hispanic, 3% multiracial, 0% Pacific Islander, 71% white, 4% international; 45% from in state; 64% live on campus; 26% of students in fraternities, 26% in sororities
Most popular majors: 15% Registered Nursing/Registered Nurse, 7% Mechanical Engineering, 5% Finance, General, 4% Business Administration and Management, General, 3% Electrical and Electronics Engineering
Expenses: 2018-2019: $40,260; room/board: $11,860
Financial aid: (219) 464-5015; 76% of undergrads determined to have financial need; average aid package $32,030

Vincennes University[1]

Vincennes IN
(800) 742-9198
U.S. News ranking: Reg. Coll. (Mid. W), unranked
Website: www.vinu.edu
Admissions email: N/A
Public; founded 1801
Application deadline (fall): rolling
Undergraduate student body: N/A full time, N/A part time
Expenses: 2017-2018: $5,737 in state, $13,567 out of state; room/board: $9,702
Financial aid: (812) 888-4361

Wabash College

Crawfordsville IN
(800) 345-5385
U.S. News ranking: Nat. Lib. Arts, No. 56
Website: www.wabash.edu
Admissions email: admissions@wabash.edu
Private; founded 1832
Freshman admissions: more selective; 2017-2018: 1,317 applied, 840 accepted. Either SAT or ACT required. SAT 25/75 percentile: 1070-1280. High school rank: 27% in top tenth, 57% in top quarter, 95% in top half
Early decision deadline: 10/15, notification date: 11/16
Early action deadline: 11/1, notification date: 12/11
Application deadline (fall): 1/15
Undergraduate student body: 864 full time, 0 part time; 100% male, 0% female; 0% American Indian, 1% Asian, 6% black, 8% Hispanic, 3% multiracial, 0% Pacific Islander, 73% white, 7% international; 78% from in state; 97% live on campus; 63% of students in fraternities, 0% in sororities
Most popular majors: 20% Political Science and Government, General, 15% Mathematics, General, 12% English Language and Literature, General, 12% Spanish Language and Literature, 9% Biology/Biological Sciences, General
Expenses: 2018-2019: $43,650; room/board: $10,050
Financial aid: (765) 361-6370; 76% of undergrads determined to have financial need; average aid package $37,666

IOWA

Briar Cliff University

Sioux City IA
(712) 279-5200
U.S. News ranking: Reg. Coll. (Mid. W), No. 36
Website: www.briarcliff.edu
Admissions email: admissions@briarcliff.edu
Private; founded 1930
Affiliation: Roman Catholic
Freshman admissions: selective; 2017-2018: 1,288 applied, 664 accepted. Either SAT or ACT required. ACT 25/75 percentile: 19-24. High school rank: 6% in top tenth, 30% in top quarter, 67% in top half
Early decision deadline: N/A, notification date: N/A
Early action deadline: N/A, notification date: N/A
Application deadline (fall): rolling
Undergraduate student body: 720 full time, 225 part time; 41% male, 59% female; 1% American Indian, 2% Asian, 10% black, 16% Hispanic, 1% multiracial, 0% Pacific Islander, 64% white, 4% international; 44% from in state; 44% live on campus; 0% of students in fraternities, 0% in sororities
Most popular majors: 28% Registered Nursing/Registered Nurse, 14% Business Administration and Management, General, 10% Social Work, 7% Accounting, 7% Kinesiology and Exercise Science
Expenses: 2017-2018: $29,606; room/board: $8,640
Financial aid: N/A

Buena Vista University

Storm Lake IA
(800) 383-9600
U.S. News ranking: Reg. Coll. (Mid. W), No. 18
Website: www.bvu.edu
Admissions email: admissions@bvu.edu
Private; founded 1891
Affiliation: Presbyterian Church (USA)
Freshman admissions: selective; 2017-2018: 1,477 applied, 943 accepted. Either SAT or ACT required. ACT 25/75 percentile: 19-24. High school rank: 14% in top tenth, 38% in top quarter, 77% in top half
Early decision deadline: N/A, notification date: N/A
Early action deadline: N/A, notification date: N/A
Application deadline (fall): rolling
Undergraduate student body: 1,522 full time, 282 part time; 36% male, 64% female; 0% American Indian, 1% Asian, 2% black, 3% Hispanic, 2% multiracial, 0% Pacific Islander, 33% white, 1% international; 74% from in state; 90% live on campus; 0% of students in fraternities, 0% in sororities
Most popular majors: 25% Business, Management, Marketing, and Related Support Services, 18% Education, 12% Parks, Recreation, Leisure, and Fitness Studies, 8% Biological and Biomedical Sciences, 6% Communication, Journalism, and Related Programs
Expenses: 2018-2019: $34,004; room/board: $9,538
Financial aid: (712) 749-2164; 84% of undergrads determined to have financial need; average aid package $29,026

Central College[1]

Pella IA
(641) 628-5286
U.S. News ranking: Nat. Lib. Arts, No. 141
Website: www.central.edu
Admissions email: admission@central.edu
Private; founded 1853
Application deadline (fall): 8/15
Undergraduate student body: N/A full time, N/A part time
Expenses: 2017-2018: $35,930; room/board: $9,980
Financial aid: (641) 628-5336

Clarke University

Dubuque IA
(563) 588-6316
U.S. News ranking: Reg. Coll. (Mid. W), No. 16
Website: www.clarke.edu
Admissions email: admissions@clarke.edu
Private; founded 1843
Affiliation: Roman Catholic
Freshman admissions: selective; 2017-2018: 1,149 applied, 726 accepted. Either SAT or ACT required. ACT 25/75 percentile: 20-25. High school rank: 15% in top tenth, 47% in top quarter, 78% in top half
Early decision deadline: N/A, notification date: N/A
Early action deadline: N/A, notification date: N/A
Application deadline (fall): rolling
Undergraduate student body: 708 full time, 60 part time; 36% male, 64% female; 1% American Indian, 1% Asian, 6% black, 7% Hispanic, 2% multiracial, 1% Pacific Islander, 80% white, 1% international; 50% from in state; 60% live on campus; N/A of students in fraternities, N/A in sororities
Most popular majors: 26% Registered Nursing/Registered Nurse, 18% Psychology, General, 12% Business Administration and Management, General, 11% Elementary Education and Teaching, 5% Social Work
Expenses: 2018-2019: $33,350; room/board: $9,600
Financial aid: (563) 588-6327; 87% of undergrads determined to have financial need; average aid package $27,131

Coe College

Cedar Rapids IA
(319) 399-8500
U.S. News ranking: Nat. Lib. Arts, No. 124
Website: www.coe.edu
Admissions email: admission@coe.edu
Private; founded 1851
Freshman admissions: more selective; 2017-2018: 7,002 applied, 3,937 accepted. Either SAT or ACT required. ACT 25/75 percentile: 22-28. High school rank: 27% in top tenth, 54% in top quarter, 88% in top half
Early decision deadline: N/A, notification date: N/A
Early action deadline: 12/10, notification date: 1/20
Application deadline (fall): 3/1
Undergraduate student body: 1,369 full time, 25 part time; 44% male, 56% female; 0% American Indian, 4% Asian, 8% black, 10% Hispanic, 3% multiracial, 0% Pacific Islander, 68% white, 2% international; 43% from in state; 95% live on campus; 24% of students in fraternities, 24% in sororities
Most popular majors: 15% Business, Management, Marketing, and Related Support Services, 12% Biological and Biomedical Sciences, 12% Psychology, 7% Visual and Performing Arts, 6% Social Sciences
Expenses: 2018-2019: $44,050; room/board: $9,480
Financial aid: (319) 399-8540; 83% of undergrads determined to have financial need; average aid package $35,630

Cornell College

Mount Vernon IA
(800) 747-1112
U.S. News ranking: Nat. Lib. Arts, No. 81
Website: www.cornellcollege.edu
Admissions email: admissions@cornellcollege.edu
Private; founded 1853
Affiliation: United Methodist
Freshman admissions: more selective; 2017-2018: 2,276 applied, 1,480 accepted. Neither SAT nor ACT required. ACT 25/75 percentile: 26-29. High school rank: N/A
Early decision deadline: 11/1, notification date: 12/15
Early action deadline: 12/1, notification date: 2/1
Application deadline (fall): 2/1
Undergraduate student body: 999 full time, 7 part time; 51% male, 49% female; 1% American Indian, 3% Asian, 6% black, 9% Hispanic, 2% multiracial, 0% Pacific Islander, 70% white, 5% international; 19% from in state; 88% live on campus; 21% of students in fraternities, 32% in sororities
Most popular majors: 21% Social Sciences, 11% Biological and Biomedical Sciences, 10% Psychology, 9% Education, 8% Parks, Recreation, Leisure, and Fitness Studies
Expenses: 2018-2019: $42,299; room/board: $9,384
Financial aid: (319) 895-4216; 71% of undergrads determined to have financial need; average aid package $30,999

Dordt College

Sioux Center IA
(800) 343-6738
U.S. News ranking: Reg. Coll. (Mid. W), No. 6
Website: www.dordt.edu
Admissions email: admissions@dordt.edu
Private; founded 1955
Affiliation: Christian Reformed Church
Freshman admissions: selective; 2017-2018: 1,443 applied, 1,040 accepted. Neither SAT nor ACT required. ACT 25/75 percentile: 22-28. High school rank: 18% in top tenth, 43% in top quarter, 73% in top half
Early decision deadline: N/A, notification date: N/A
Early action deadline: N/A, notification date: N/A
Application deadline (fall): 8/16
Undergraduate student body: 1,341 full time, 108 part time; 52% male, 48% female; 0% American Indian, 1% Asian, 1% black, 2% Hispanic, 8% multiracial, 0% Pacific Islander, 78% white, 9% international; 41% from in state; 89% live on campus; 0% of students in fraternities, 0% in sororities
Most popular majors: 20% Business/Commerce, General, 18% Elementary Education and Teaching, 10% Agricultural Business and Management, General, 8% Engineering, General, 6% Chiropractic
Expenses: 2018-2019: $30,870; room/board: $9,590
Financial aid: (712) 722-6082; 67% of undergrads determined to have financial need; average aid package $25,154

Drake University

Des Moines IA
(800) 443-7253
U.S. News ranking: Reg. U. (Mid. W), No. 3
Website: www.drake.edu
Admissions email: admission@drake.edu
Private; founded 1881
Freshman admissions: more selective; 2017-2018: 5,574 applied, 3,835 accepted. Neither SAT nor ACT required. ACT 25/75 percentile: 24-30. High school rank: 38% in top tenth, 66% in top quarter, 94% in top half
Early decision deadline: N/A, notification date: N/A
Early action deadline: N/A, notification date: N/A
Application deadline (fall): rolling
Undergraduate student body: 2,955 full time, 143 part time; 43% male, 57% female; 0% American Indian, 3% Asian, 5% black, 5% Hispanic, 3% multiracial,

0% Pacific Islander, 78% white, 5% international; 31% from in state; 70% live on campus; 36% of students in fraternities, 29% in sororities
Most popular majors: 32% Business, Management, Marketing, and Related Support Services, 13% Communication, Journalism, and Related Programs, 8% Education, 8% Social Sciences, 7% Visual and Performing Arts
Expenses: 2018-2019: $41,396; room/board: $10,528
Financial aid: (515) 271-2905; 61% of undergrads determined to have financial need; average aid package $28,868

Graceland University

Lamoni IA
(866) 472-2352
U.S. News ranking: Reg. U. (Mid. W), No. 115
Website: www.graceland.edu
Admissions email: admissions@graceland.edu
Private; founded 1895
Affiliation: Other
Freshman admissions: selective; 2017-2018: 2,800 applied, 1,572 accepted. Either SAT or ACT required. ACT 25/75 percentile: 18-23. High school rank: 9% in top tenth, 23% in top quarter, 58% in top half
Early decision deadline: N/A, notification date: N/A
Early action deadline: N/A, notification date: N/A
Application deadline (fall): rolling
Undergraduate student body: 1,061 full time, 343 part time; 44% male, 56% female; 0% American Indian, 1% Asian, 11% black, 11% Hispanic, 4% multiracial, 1% Pacific Islander, 62% white, 4% international; 23% from in state; 71% live on campus; N/A of students in fraternities, N/A in sororities
Most popular majors: 29% Health Professions and Related Programs, 15% Business, Management, Marketing, and Related Support Services, 6% Visual and Performing Arts, 5% Biological and Biomedical Sciences, 5% Parks, Recreation, Leisure, and Fitness Studies
Expenses: 2018-2019: $29,240; room/board: $8,760
Financial aid: (641) 784-5117; 82% of undergrads determined to have financial need; average aid package $24,479

Grand View University

Des Moines IA
(515) 263-2810
U.S. News ranking: Reg. Coll. (Mid. W), No. 39
Website: www.grandview.edu
Admissions email: admissions@grandview.edu
Private; founded 1896
Affiliation: Evangelical Lutheran Church
Freshman admissions: selective; 2017-2018: 820 applied, 760 accepted. Either SAT or ACT required. ACT 25/75 percentile: 18-23. High school rank: 15% in top tenth, 36% in top quarter, 69% in top half
Early decision deadline: N/A, notification date: N/A
Early action deadline: N/A, notification date: N/A
Application deadline (fall): 8/15
Undergraduate student body: 1,574 full time, 214 part time; 44% male, 56% female; 0% American Indian, 3% Asian, 7% black, 5% Hispanic, 6% multiracial, 0% Pacific Islander, 68% white, 3% international; 85% from in state; 52% live on campus; 0% of students in fraternities, 0% in sororities
Most popular majors: 29% Business, Management, Marketing, and Related Support Services, 10% Health Professions and Related Programs, 8% Parks, Recreation, Leisure, and Fitness Studies, 7% Psychology, 7% Public Administration and Social Service Professions
Expenses: 2018-2019: $27,518; room/board: $9,178
Financial aid: (515) 263-2853; 82% of undergrads determined to have financial need; average aid package $20,886

Grinnell College

Grinnell IA
(800) 247-0113
U.S. News ranking: Nat. Lib. Arts, No. 11
Website: www.grinnell.edu
Admissions email: admission@grinnell.edu
Private; founded 1846
Freshman admissions: most selective; 2017-2018: 5,850 applied, 1,689 accepted. Either SAT or ACT required. ACT 25/75 percentile: 30-34. High school rank: 69% in top tenth, 91% in top quarter, 99% in top half
Early decision deadline: 11/15, notification date: 12/15
Early action deadline: N/A, notification date: N/A
Application deadline (fall): 1/15
Undergraduate student body: 1,662 full time, 50 part time; 47% male, 53% female; 0% American Indian, 8% Asian, 6% black, 7% Hispanic, 4% multiracial, 0% Pacific Islander, 51% white, 20% international; 8% from in state; 88% live on campus; 0% of students in fraternities, 0% in sororities
Most popular majors: 27% Social Sciences, 13% Biological and Biomedical Sciences, 9% Physical Sciences, 8% Computer and Information Sciences and Support Services, 8% Foreign Languages, Literatures, and Linguistics
Expenses: 2018-2019: $52,392; room/board: $12,810
Financial aid: (641) 269-3250; 65% of undergrads determined to have financial need; average aid package $47,561

Iowa State University

Ames IA
(515) 294-2592
U.S. News ranking: Nat. U., No. 119
Website: www.iastate.edu
Admissions email: admissions@iastate.edu
Public; founded 1858
Freshman admissions: more selective; 2017-2018: 19,262 applied, 17,208 accepted. Either SAT or ACT required. ACT 25/75 percentile: 22-28. High school rank: 25% in top tenth, 57% in top quarter, 92% in top half
Early decision deadline: N/A, notification date: N/A
Early action deadline: N/A, notification date: N/A
Application deadline (fall): rolling
Undergraduate student body: 28,590 full time, 1,816 part time; 58% male, 42% female; 0% American Indian, 3% Asian, 3% black, 5% Hispanic, 2% multiracial, 0% Pacific Islander, 74% white, 7% international; 65% from in state; 41% live on campus; 13% of students in fraternities, 21% in sororities
Most popular majors: 20% Engineering, 17% Business, Management, Marketing, and Related Support Services, 10% Agriculture, Agriculture Operations, and Related Sciences, 6% Biological and Biomedical Sciences, 5% Education
Expenses: 2018-2019: $9,002 in state, $23,392 out of state; room/board: $8,720
Financial aid: (515) 294-2223; 49% of undergrads determined to have financial need; average aid package $12,456

Iowa Wesleyan University

Mount Pleasant IA
(319) 385-6231
U.S. News ranking: Reg. Coll. (Mid. W), second tier
Website: www.iw.edu
Admissions email: admit@iw.edu
Private; founded 1842
Affiliation: United Methodist
Freshman admissions: less selective; 2017-2018: 5,312 applied, 2,554 accepted. Either SAT or ACT required. ACT 25/75 percentile: 18-22. High school rank: 3% in top tenth, 9% in top quarter, 26% in top half
Early decision deadline: N/A, notification date: N/A
Early action deadline: N/A, notification date: N/A
Application deadline (fall): rolling
Undergraduate student body: 539 full time, 34 part time; 48% male, 52% female; 1% American Indian, 1% Asian, 17% black, 7% Hispanic, 5% multiracial, 1% Pacific Islander, 37% white, 17% international; 31% from in state; 72% live on campus; 8% of students in fraternities, 8% in sororities
Most popular majors: 30% Business, Management, Marketing, and Related Support Services, 17% Health Professions and Related Programs, 14% Education, 7% Homeland Security, Law Enforcement, Firefighting and Related Protective Services, 7% Public Administration and Social Service Professions
Expenses: 2018-2019: $30,500; room/board: $10,500
Financial aid: (319) 385-6242; 97% of undergrads determined to have financial need; average aid package $15,398

Loras College

Dubuque IA
(800) 245-6727
U.S. News ranking: Reg. Coll. (Mid. W), No. 13
Website: www.loras.edu
Admissions email: admission@loras.edu
Private; founded 1839
Affiliation: Roman Catholic
Freshman admissions: selective; 2017-2018: 1,159 applied, 1,102 accepted. Either SAT or ACT required. ACT 25/75 percentile: 20-26. High school rank: 17% in top tenth, 46% in top quarter, 73% in top half
Early decision deadline: N/A, notification date: N/A
Early action deadline: N/A, notification date: N/A
Application deadline (fall): rolling
Undergraduate student body: 1,335 full time, 62 part time; 52% male, 48% female; 0% American Indian, 1% Asian, 2% black, 8% Hispanic, 2% multiracial, 0% Pacific Islander, 82% white, 2% international; 42% from in state; 65% live on campus; N/A of students in fraternities, N/A in sororities
Most popular majors: 6% Business Administration and Management, General, 6% Criminal Justice/Safety Studies, 6% Psychology, General, 6% Social Work, 5% Marketing/Marketing Management, General
Expenses: 2018-2019: $34,184; room/board: $8,275
Financial aid: (563) 588-7817; 75% of undergrads determined to have financial need; average aid package $27,733

Luther College

Decorah IA
(563) 387-1287
U.S. News ranking: Nat. Lib. Arts, No. 89
Website: www.luther.edu
Admissions email: admissions@luther.edu
Private; founded 1861
Affiliation: Evangelical Lutheran Church
Freshman admissions: more selective; 2017-2018: 4,288 applied, 2,791 accepted. Either SAT or ACT required. ACT 25/75 percentile: 23-28. High school rank: 26% in top tenth, 54% in top quarter, 86% in top half
Early decision deadline: N/A, notification date: N/A
Early action deadline: N/A, notification date: N/A
Application deadline (fall): rolling
Undergraduate student body: 2,014 full time, 39 part time; 45% male, 55% female; 0% American Indian, 1% Asian, 2% black, 5% Hispanic, 2% multiracial, 0% Pacific Islander, 81% white, 8% international; 29% from in state; 93% live on campus; 1% of students in fraternities, 2% in sororities
Most popular majors: 10% Biology/Biological Sciences, General, 8% Business Administration and Management, General, 7% Music, General, 6% Psychology, General, 4% English Language and Literature, General
Expenses: 2018-2019: $42,290; room/board: $9,460
Financial aid: (563) 387-1018; 79% of undergrads determined to have financial need; average aid package $35,397

Maharishi University of Management[1]

Fairfield IA
(641) 472-7000
U.S. News ranking: Reg. U. (Mid. W), unranked
Website: www.mum.edu
Admissions email: admissions@mum.edu
Private
Application deadline (fall): N/A
Undergraduate student body: N/A full time, N/A part time
Expenses: 2017-2018: $27,530; room/board: $7,400
Financial aid: N/A

Morningside College

Sioux City IA
(712) 274-5111
U.S. News ranking: Reg. U. (Mid. W), No. 62
Website: www.morningside.edu
Admissions email: mscadm@morningside.edu
Private; founded 1894
Affiliation: United Methodist
Freshman admissions: selective; 2017-2018: 4,603 applied, 2,540 accepted. Either SAT or ACT required. ACT 25/75 percentile: 20-25. High school rank: 17% in top tenth, 38% in top quarter, 71% in top half
Early decision deadline: N/A, notification date: N/A
Early action deadline: N/A, notification date: N/A
Application deadline (fall): rolling
Undergraduate student body: 1,252 full time, 70 part time; 47% male, 53% female; 1% American Indian, 1% Asian, 2% black, 8% Hispanic, 3% multiracial, 0% Pacific Islander, 76% white, 5% international; 62% from in state; 46% live on campus; 5% of students in fraternities, 2% in sororities
Most popular majors: 33% Business, Management, Marketing, and Related Support Services, 22% Education, 13% Biological and Biomedical Sciences, 13% Health Professions and Related Programs, 10% Psychology
Expenses: 2018-2019: $31,530; room/board: $9,610
Financial aid: (712) 274-5159; 79% of undergrads determined to have financial need; average aid package $24,135

Mount Mercy University

Cedar Rapids IA
(319) 368-6460
U.S. News ranking: Reg. U. (Mid. W), No. 58
Website: www.mtmercy.edu
Admissions email: admission@mtmercy.edu
Private; founded 1928
Affiliation: Roman Catholic

Freshman admissions: selective; 2017-2018: 1,457 applied, 834 accepted. Either SAT or ACT required. ACT 25/75 percentile: 19-24. High school rank: 17% in top tenth, 44% in top quarter, 82% in top half
Early decision deadline: N/A, notification date: N/A
Early action deadline: N/A, notification date: N/A
Application deadline (fall): rolling
Undergraduate student body: 1,083 full time, 434 part time; 32% male, 68% female; 2% American Indian, 2% Asian, 7% black, 1% Hispanic, 2% multiracial, 0% Pacific Islander, 79% white, 4% international; 88% from in state; 36% live on campus; N/A of students in fraternities, N/A in sororities
Most popular majors: 33% Registered Nursing/Registered Nurse, 11% Business/Commerce, General, 8% Business Administration and Management, General, 7% Criminal Justice/Law Enforcement Administration, 5% Marketing/Marketing Management, General
Expenses: 2018-2019: $31,998; room/board: $9,534
Financial aid: (319) 368-6467; 77% of undergrads determined to have financial need; average aid package $24,022

Northwestern College

Orange City IA
(800) 747-4757
U.S. News ranking: Reg. Coll. (Mid. W), No. 7
Website: www.nwciowa.edu
Admissions email: admissions@nwciowa.edu
Private; founded 1882
Affiliation: Reformed Church in America
Freshman admissions: selective; 2017-2018: 1,955 applied, 1,331 accepted. Either SAT or ACT required. ACT 25/75 percentile: 21-27. High school rank: 25% in top tenth, 59% in top quarter, 83% in top half
Early decision deadline: N/A, notification date: N/A
Early action deadline: N/A, notification date: N/A
Application deadline (fall): rolling
Undergraduate student body: 997 full time, 51 part time; 44% male, 56% female; 0% American Indian, 1% Asian, 1% black, 4% Hispanic, 2% multiracial, 0% Pacific Islander, 83% white, 3% international; 57% from in state; 86% live on campus; 0% of students in fraternities, 0% in sororities
Most popular majors: 18% Business Administration and Management, General, 10% Elementary Education and Teaching, 10% Registered Nursing/Registered Nurse, 5% Biology/Biological Sciences, General, 4% Accounting
Expenses: 2018-2019: $31,100; room/board: $9,200
Financial aid: (712) 707-7131; 74% of undergrads determined to have financial need; average aid package $25,696

Simpson College

Indianola IA
(515) 961-1624
U.S. News ranking: Nat. Lib. Arts, No. 135
Website: www.simpson.edu
Admissions email: admiss@simpson.edu
Private; founded 1860
Affiliation: United Methodist
Freshman admissions: selective; 2017-2018: 1,245 applied, 1,044 accepted. Either SAT or ACT required. ACT 25/75 percentile: 21-27. High school rank: 23% in top tenth, 58% in top quarter, 82% in top half
Early decision deadline: N/A, notification date: N/A
Early action deadline: N/A, notification date: N/A
Application deadline (fall): rolling
Undergraduate student body: 1,280 full time, 152 part time; 45% male, 55% female; 0% American Indian, 2% Asian, 2% black, 4% Hispanic, 2% multiracial, 0% Pacific Islander, 84% white, 1% international; 81% from in state; 77% live on campus; 24% of students in fraternities, 24% in sororities
Most popular majors: 14% Business Administration and Management, General, 8% Criminal Justice/Law Enforcement Administration, 8% Elementary Education and Teaching, 6% Kinesiology and Exercise Science, 6% Psychology, General
Expenses: 2018-2019: $39,144; room/board: $8,380
Financial aid: (515) 961-1596; 83% of undergrads determined to have financial need; average aid package $29,443

St. Ambrose University

Davenport IA
(563) 333-6300
U.S. News ranking: Reg. U. (Mid. W), No. 38
Website: www.sau.edu
Admissions email: admit@sau.edu
Private; founded 1882
Affiliation: Roman Catholic
Freshman admissions: selective; 2017-2018: 5,335 applied, 3,244 accepted. Either SAT or ACT required. ACT 25/75 percentile: 21-26. High school rank: 14% in top tenth, 42% in top quarter, 76% in top half
Early decision deadline: N/A, notification date: N/A
Early action deadline: N/A, notification date: N/A
Application deadline (fall): rolling
Undergraduate student body: 2,215 full time, 155 part time; 44% male, 56% female; 0% American Indian, 1% Asian, 5% black, 8% Hispanic, 3% multiracial, 0% Pacific Islander, 74% white, 5% international; 41% from in state; 66% live on campus; N/A of students in fraternities, N/A in sororities
Most popular majors: 25% Business, Management, Marketing, and Related Support Services, 14% Psychology, 12% Health Professions and Related Programs, 12% Parks, Recreation, Leisure, and Fitness Studies, 6% Education
Expenses: 2018-2019: $30,894; room/board: $10,470
Financial aid: (563) 333-6318; 75% of undergrads determined to have financial need; average aid package $22,886

University of Dubuque

Dubuque IA
(563) 589-3200
U.S. News ranking: Reg. U. (Mid. W), No. 106
Website: www.dbq.edu
Admissions email: admssns@dbq.edu
Private; founded 1852
Affiliation: Presbyterian Church (USA)
Freshman admissions: less selective; 2017-2018: 1,761 applied, 1,306 accepted. Either SAT or ACT required. ACT 25/75 percentile: 16-22. High school rank: 4% in top tenth, 20% in top quarter, 50% in top half
Early decision deadline: N/A, notification date: N/A
Early action deadline: N/A, notification date: N/A
Application deadline (fall): rolling
Undergraduate student body: 1,710 full time, 255 part time; 58% male, 42% female; 0% American Indian, 2% Asian, 15% black, 9% Hispanic, 3% multiracial, 0% Pacific Islander, 61% white, 6% international; 45% from in state; 45% live on campus; 2% of students in fraternities, 5% in sororities
Most popular majors: 33% Business, Management, Marketing, and Related Support Services, 11% Education, 10% Transportation and Materials Moving, 9% Parks, Recreation, Leisure, and Fitness Studies, 7% Health Professions and Related Programs
Expenses: 2018-2019: $34,110; room/board: $9,780
Financial aid: (563) 589-3125; 82% of undergrads determined to have financial need; average aid package $27,850

University of Iowa

Iowa City IA
(319) 335-3847
U.S. News ranking: Nat. U., No. 89
Website: www.uiowa.edu
Admissions email: admissions@uiowa.edu
Public; founded 1847
Freshman admissions: more selective; 2017-2018: 27,734 applied, 23,862 accepted. Either SAT or ACT required. ACT 25/75 percentile: 23-28. High school rank: 30% in top tenth, 61% in top quarter, 91% in top half
Early decision deadline: N/A, notification date: N/A
Early action deadline: N/A, notification date: N/A
Application deadline (fall): 5/1
Undergraduate student body: 21,222 full time, 3,281 part time; 47% male, 53% female; 0% American Indian, 4% Asian, 3% black, 8% Hispanic, 3% multiracial, 0% Pacific Islander, 71% white, 9% international; 63% from in state; 28% live on campus; 13% of students in fraternities, 16% in sororities
Most popular majors: 20% Business, Management, Marketing, and Related Support Services, 12% Parks, Recreation, Leisure, and Fitness Studies, 9% Social Sciences, 8% Engineering, 7% Communication, Journalism, and Related Programs
Expenses: 2018-2019: $8,965 in state, $30,609 out of state; room/board: $10,450
Financial aid: (319) 335-1450; 47% of undergrads determined to have financial need; average aid package $16,084

University of Northern Iowa

Cedar Falls IA
(800) 772-2037
U.S. News ranking: Reg. U. (Mid. W), No. 25
Website: uni.edu/
Admissions email: admissions@uni.edu
Public; founded 1876
Affiliation: Undenominational
Freshman admissions: selective; 2017-2018: 5,494 applied, 4,441 accepted. Either SAT or ACT required. ACT 25/75 percentile: 21-26. High school rank: 17% in top tenth, 46% in top quarter, 82% in top half
Early decision deadline: N/A, notification date: N/A
Early action deadline: N/A, notification date: N/A
Application deadline (fall): 8/15
Undergraduate student body: 9,100 full time, 905 part time; 43% male, 57% female; 0% American Indian, 1% Asian, 3% black, 4% Hispanic, 2% multiracial, 0% Pacific Islander, 82% white, 3% international; 91% from in state; 37% live on campus; 4% of students in fraternities, 7% in sororities
Most popular majors: 21% Business, Management, Marketing, and Related Support Services, 18% Education, 7% Social Sciences, 6% Parks, Recreation, Leisure, and Fitness Studies, 5% Communication, Journalism, and Related Programs
Expenses: 2018-2019: $8,938 in state, $19,480 out of state; room/board: $8,948
Financial aid: (319) 273-2722; 60% of undergrads determined to have financial need; average aid package $8,499

Upper Iowa University[1]

Fayette IA
(563) 425-5281
U.S. News ranking: Reg. U. (Mid. W), second tier
Website: www.uiu.edu
Admissions email: admission@uiu.edu
Private; founded 1857
Application deadline (fall): rolling
Undergraduate student body: N/A full time, N/A part time
Expenses: 2017-2018: $29,600; room/board: $9,760
Financial aid: (563) 425-5276

Waldorf University[1]

Forest City IA
(641) 585-8112
U.S. News ranking: Reg. Coll. (Mid. W), second tier
Website: www.waldorf.edu
Admissions email: admissions@waldorf.edu
For-profit
Application deadline (fall): N/A
Undergraduate student body: N/A full time, N/A part time
Expenses: 2017-2018: $21,664; room/board: $7,384
Financial aid: N/A

Wartburg College

Waverly IA
(319) 352-8264
U.S. News ranking: Nat. Lib. Arts, No. 143
Website: www.wartburg.edu
Admissions email: admissions@wartburg.edu
Private; founded 1852
Affiliation: Evangelical Lutheran Church
Freshman admissions: selective; 2017-2018: 4,342 applied, 3,339 accepted. Either SAT or ACT required. ACT 25/75 percentile: 21-27. High school rank: 27% in top tenth, 53% in top quarter, 82% in top half
Early decision deadline: N/A, notification date: N/A
Early action deadline: 12/1, notification date: N/A
Application deadline (fall): rolling
Undergraduate student body: 1,474 full time, 53 part time; 47% male, 53% female; 0% American Indian, 1% Asian, 5% black, 5% Hispanic, 3% multiracial, 0% Pacific Islander, 76% white, 7% international; 67% from in state; 87% live on campus; N/A of students in fraternities, N/A in sororities
Most popular majors: 18% Business/Commerce, General, 15% Biology/Biological Sciences, General, 7% Elementary Education and Teaching, 6% Mass Communication/Media Studies, 6% Sport and Fitness Administration/Management
Expenses: 2018-2019: $41,280; room/board: $9,995
Financial aid: (319) 352-8262; 76% of undergrads determined to have financial need; average aid package $32,262

William Penn University[1]

Oskaloosa IA
(641) 673-1012
U.S. News ranking: Reg. U. (Mid. W), second tier
Website: www.wmpenn.edu
Admissions email: admissions@wmpenn.edu
Private
Application deadline (fall): N/A
Undergraduate student body: N/A full time, N/A part time
Expenses: 2017-2018: $25,000; room/board: $6,952
Financial aid: N/A

KANSAS

Baker University

Baldwin City KS
(800) 873-4282
U.S. News ranking: Reg. U. (Mid. W), No. 50
Website: www.bakeru.edu
Admissions email: admission@bakeru.edu
Private; founded 1858
Affiliation: United Methodist
Freshman admissions: selective; 2017-2018: 799 applied, 688 accepted. Either SAT or ACT required. ACT 25/75 percentile: 21-25. High school rank: 18% in top tenth, 48% in top quarter, 79% in top half
Early decision deadline: N/A, notification date: N/A
Early action deadline: N/A, notification date: N/A
Application deadline (fall): rolling
Undergraduate student body: 850 full time, 309 part time; 48% male, 52% female; 1% American Indian, 0% Asian, 10% black, 8% Hispanic, 5% multiracial, 0% Pacific Islander, 69% white, 3% international; 68% from in state; 83% live on campus; 44% of students in fraternities, 47% in sororities
Most popular majors: 17% Business Administration and Management, General, 10% Kinesiology and Exercise Science, 9% Sport and Fitness Administration/Management, 8% Sociology, 5% Psychology, General
Expenses: 2018-2019: $29,750; room/board: $8,410
Financial aid: (785) 594-4595; 79% of undergrads determined to have financial need; average aid package $25,714

Benedictine College

Atchison KS
(800) 467-5340
U.S. News ranking: Reg. Coll. (Mid. W), No. 13
Website: www.benedictine.edu
Admissions email: bcadmiss@benedictine.edu
Private; founded 1859
Affiliation: Roman Catholic
Freshman admissions: selective; 2017-2018: 2,367 applied, 2,307 accepted. Either SAT or ACT required. ACT 25/75 percentile: 22-28. High school rank: 26% in top tenth, 48% in top quarter, 76% in top half
Early decision deadline: N/A, notification date: N/A
Early action deadline: N/A, notification date: N/A
Application deadline (fall): rolling
Undergraduate student body: 1,809 full time, 265 part time; 45% male, 55% female; 1% American Indian, 1% Asian, 3% black, 7% Hispanic, 0% multiracial, 0% Pacific Islander, 79% white, 2% international; 24% from in state; 82% live on campus; 0% of students in fraternities, 0% in sororities
Most popular majors: 17% Business, Management, Marketing, and Related Support Services, 11% Education, 11% Theology and Religious Vocations, 8% Social Sciences, 7% Psychology
Expenses: 2018-2019: $29,530; room/board: $10,300
Financial aid: (913) 360-7484; 68% of undergrads determined to have financial need; average aid package $23,698

Bethany College

Lindsborg KS
(800) 826-2281
U.S. News ranking: Reg. Coll. (Mid. W), No. 48
Website: www.bethanylb.edu
Admissions email: admissions@bethanylb.edu
Private; founded 1881
Affiliation: Evangelical Lutheran Church
Freshman admissions: selective; 2017-2018: 1,358 applied, 952 accepted. Either SAT or ACT required. ACT 25/75 percentile: 18-23. High school rank: 7% in top tenth, 25% in top quarter, 56% in top half
Early decision deadline: N/A, notification date: N/A
Early action deadline: N/A, notification date: N/A
Application deadline (fall): rolling
Undergraduate student body: 710 full time, 65 part time; 58% male, 42% female; 1% American Indian, 1% Asian, 16% black, 18% Hispanic, 3% multiracial, 1% Pacific Islander, 55% white, 6% international
Most popular majors: Information not available
Expenses: 2018-2019: $28,475; room/board: $10,605
Financial aid: (785) 227-3380; 85% of undergrads determined to have financial need; average aid package $22,713

Bethel College

North Newton KS
(800) 522-1887
U.S. News ranking: Nat. Lib. Arts, second tier
Website: www.bethelks.edu
Admissions email: admissions@bethelks.edu
Private; founded 1887
Affiliation: Other
Freshman admissions: selective; 2017-2018: 886 applied, 493 accepted. Either SAT or ACT required. ACT 25/75 percentile: 18-24. High school rank: 16% in top tenth, 39% in top quarter, 76% in top half
Early decision deadline: N/A, notification date: N/A
Early action deadline: N/A, notification date: N/A
Application deadline (fall): N/A
Undergraduate student body: 489 full time, 14 part time; 47% male, 53% female; 0% American Indian, 2% Asian, 16% black, 9% Hispanic, 4% multiracial, 0% Pacific Islander, 67% white, 1% international; 65% from in state; 68% live on campus; 0% of students in fraternities, 0% in sororities
Most popular majors: 33% Health Professions and Related Programs, 19% Business, Management, Marketing, and Related Support Services, 10% Visual and Performing Arts, 7% Biological and Biomedical Sciences, 7% Education
Expenses: 2018-2019: $28,540; room/board: $9,400
Financial aid: (316) 284-5232; 85% of undergrads determined to have financial need; average aid package $27,012

Central Christian College

McPherson KS
(620) 241-0723
U.S. News ranking: Reg. Coll. (Mid. W), second tier
Website: www.centralchristian.edu/
Admissions email: admissions@centralchristian.edu
Private; founded 1884
Affiliation: Free Methodist
Freshman admissions: selective; 2017-2018: 824 applied, 291 accepted. Neither SAT nor ACT required. ACT 25/75 percentile: 17-22. High school rank: N/A
Early decision deadline: N/A, notification date: N/A
Early action deadline: 11/30, notification date: 12/1
Application deadline (fall): rolling
Undergraduate student body: 730 full time, 135 part time; 52% male, 48% female; 2% American Indian, 1% Asian, 22% black, 14% Hispanic, 3% multiracial, 0% Pacific Islander, 53% white, 2% international; 23% from in state; 90% live on campus; 0% of students in fraternities, 0% in sororities
Most popular majors: 28% Business, Management, Marketing, and Related Support Services, 27% Homeland Security, Law Enforcement, Firefighting and Related Protective Services, 26% Parks, Recreation, Leisure, and Fitness Studies, 5% Theology and Religious Vocations, 4% Health Professions and Related Programs
Expenses: 2018-2019: $26,652; room/board: $8,308
Financial aid: (620) 241-0723; 69% of undergrads determined to have financial need; average aid package $20,708

Donnelly College

Kansas City KS
(913) 621-8700
U.S. News ranking: Reg. Coll. (Mid. W), unranked
Website: donnelly.edu
Admissions email: admissions@donnelly.edu
Private; founded 1949
Affiliation: Roman Catholic
Freshman admissions: least selective; 2017-2018: 463 applied, 463 accepted. Neither SAT nor ACT required. SAT 25/75 percentile: N/A. High school rank: N/A
Early decision deadline: N/A, notification date: N/A
Early action deadline: N/A, notification date: N/A
Application deadline (fall): rolling
Undergraduate student body: 220 full time, 140 part time; 29% male, 71% female; 2% American Indian, 6% Asian, 33% black, 39% Hispanic, 4% multiracial, 1% Pacific Islander, 13% white, 1% international
Most popular majors: 39% Licensed Practical/Vocational Nurse Training, 34% Liberal Arts and Sciences/Liberal Studies, 16% Non-Profit/Public/Organizational Management, 8% Elementary Education and Teaching, 3% Information Technology
Expenses: 2017-2018: $7,140; room/board: N/A
Financial aid: N/A

Emporia State University

Emporia KS
(620) 341-5465
U.S. News ranking: Reg. U. (Mid. W), No. 106
Website: www.emporia.edu
Admissions email: go2esu@emporia.edu
Public; founded 1863
Freshman admissions: selective; 2017-2018: 1,693 applied, 1,401 accepted. Neither SAT nor ACT required. ACT 25/75 percentile: 19-25. High school rank: 14% in top tenth, 38% in top quarter, 73% in top half
Early decision deadline: N/A, notification date: N/A
Early action deadline: N/A, notification date: N/A
Application deadline (fall): rolling
Undergraduate student body: 3,340 full time, 265 part time; 38% male, 62% female; 0% American Indian, 1% Asian, 5% black, 7% Hispanic, 8% multiracial, 0% Pacific Islander, 71% white, 7% international; 82% from in state; 24% live on campus; 11% of students in fraternities, 11% in sororities
Most popular majors: 27% Education, 17% Business, Management, Marketing, and Related Support Services, 11% Health Professions and Related Programs, 6% Psychology, 6% Social Sciences
Expenses: 2018-2019: $6,758 in state, $20,675 out of state; room/board: $8,912
Financial aid: (620) 341-5457; 63% of undergrads determined to have financial need; average aid package $9,540

Fort Hays State University

Hays KS
(800) 628-3478
U.S. News ranking: Reg. U. (Mid. W), second tier
Website: www.fhsu.edu
Admissions email: tigers@fhsu.edu
Public; founded 1902
Freshman admissions: selective; 2017-2018: 2,294 applied, 2,033 accepted. Neither SAT nor ACT required. ACT 25/75 percentile: 18-24. High school rank: 13% in top tenth, 31% in top quarter, 63% in top half
Early decision deadline: N/A, notification date: N/A
Early action deadline: N/A, notification date: N/A
Application deadline (fall): rolling
Undergraduate student body: 5,889 full time, 6,605 part time; 40% male, 60% female; 0% American Indian, 1% Asian, 4% black, 8% Hispanic, 2% multiracial, 0% Pacific Islander, 54% white, 30% international; 69% from in state; 12% live on campus; 1% of students in fraternities, 1% in sororities
Most popular majors: 40% Business, Management, Marketing, and Related Support Services, 11% Education, 10% Liberal Arts and Sciences, General Studies and Humanities, 9% Health Professions and Related Programs, 5% Psychology
Expenses: 2017-2018: $5,009 in state, $14,832 out of state; room/board: $7,669
Financial aid: (785) 628-4408; 70% of undergrads determined to have financial need; average aid package $7,612

Friends University

Wichita KS
(316) 295-5100
U.S. News ranking: Reg. U. (Mid. W), No. 124
Website: www.friends.edu
Admissions email: learn@friends.edu
Private; founded 1898
Freshman admissions: selective; 2017-2018: 881 applied, 423 accepted. Either SAT or ACT required. ACT 25/75 percentile: 19-25. High school rank: 22% in top tenth, 48% in top quarter, 80% in top half
Early decision deadline: N/A, notification date: N/A
Early action deadline: N/A, notification date: N/A
Application deadline (fall): rolling
Undergraduate student body: 906 full time, 240 part time; 44% male, 56% female; 2% American Indian, 1% Asian, 9% black, 11% Hispanic, 1% multiracial, 0% Pacific Islander, 59% white, 0% international; 80% from in state; 25% live on campus; 0% of students in fraternities, 0% in sororities
Most popular majors: 45% Business, Management, Marketing, and Related Support Services, 9% Biological and Biomedical Sciences, 7% Computer and Information Sciences and Support Services, 6% Education, 6% Visual and Performing Arts
Expenses: 2018-2019: $28,415; room/board: $7,972
Financial aid: (316) 295-5200; 88% of undergrads determined to have financial need; average aid package $17,135

Kansas State University

Manhattan KS
(785) 532-6250
U.S. News ranking: Nat. U., No. 147
Website: www.k-state.edu
Admissions email: k-state@k-state.edu
Public; founded 1863
Freshman admissions: selective; 2017-2018: 8,310 applied, 7,864 accepted. Either SAT or ACT required. ACT 25/75 percentile: 22-28. High school

rank: 25% in top tenth, 51% in top quarter, 80% in top half
Early decision deadline: N/A, notification date: N/A
Early action deadline: N/A, notification date: N/A
Application deadline (fall): rolling
Undergraduate student body: 16,770 full time, 1,718 part time; 53% male, 47% female; 0% American Indian, 1% Asian, 3% black, 7% Hispanic, 4% multiracial, 0% Pacific Islander, 78% white, 5% international; 82% from in state; 24% live on campus; N/A of students in fraternities, N/A in sororities
Most popular majors: 18% Business, Management, Marketing, and Related Support Services, 13% Agriculture, Agriculture Operations, and Related Sciences, 11% Engineering, 8% Family and Consumer Sciences/Human Sciences, 8% Social Sciences
Expenses: 2017-2018: $10,135 in state, $25,492 out of state; room/board: $9,430
Financial aid: (785) 532-7626; 50% of undergrads determined to have financial need; average aid package $13,182

Kansas Wesleyan University

Salina KS
(785) 833-4305
U.S. News ranking: Reg. Coll. (Mid. W), No. 52
Website: www.kwu.edu
Admissions email: admissions@kwu.edu
Private; founded 1886
Affiliation: United Methodist
Freshman admissions: selective; 2017-2018: 825 applied, 441 accepted. Either SAT or ACT required. ACT 25/75 percentile: 19-24. High school rank: 11% in top tenth, 34% in top quarter, 65% in top half
Early decision deadline: N/A, notification date: N/A
Early action deadline: N/A, notification date: N/A
Application deadline (fall): rolling
Undergraduate student body: 631 full time, 62 part time; 59% male, 41% female; 0% American Indian, 0% Asian, 14% black, 16% Hispanic, 4% multiracial, 0% Pacific Islander, 62% white, 2% international; 45% from in state; 68% live on campus; 0% of students in fraternities, 0% in sororities
Most popular majors: 27% Business, Management, Marketing, and Related Support Services, 14% Homeland Security, Law Enforcement, Firefighting and Related Protective Services, 13% Parks, Recreation, Leisure, and Fitness Studies, 8% Education, 6% Communication, Journalism, and Related Programs
Expenses: 2018-2019: $29,700; room/board: $9,500
Financial aid: (785) 833-4315; 86% of undergrads determined to have financial need; average aid package $22,353

McPherson College

McPherson KS
(800) 365-7402
U.S. News ranking: Reg. Coll. (Mid. W), No. 36
Website: www.mcpherson.edu
Admissions email: admissions@mcpherson.edu
Private; founded 1887
Affiliation: Church of Brethren
Freshman admissions: selective; 2017-2018: 759 applied, 522 accepted. Neither SAT nor ACT required. ACT 25/75 percentile: 19-22. High school rank: 10% in top tenth, 21% in top quarter, 63% in top half
Early decision deadline: N/A, notification date: N/A
Early action deadline: N/A, notification date: N/A
Application deadline (fall): rolling
Undergraduate student body: 673 full time, 52 part time; 64% male, 36% female; 2% American Indian, 1% Asian, 12% black, 14% Hispanic, 1% multiracial, 0% Pacific Islander, 64% white, 1% international; 47% from in state; 75% live on campus; 0% of students in fraternities, 0% in sororities
Most popular majors: 37% Business Administration and Management, General, 20% Mechanical Engineering Related Technologies/Technicians, Other, 8% Biology/Biological Sciences, General, 8% Health and Physical Education/Fitness, General, 7% Drama and Dramatics/Theatre Arts, General
Expenses: 2018-2019: $28,951; room/board: $8,411
Financial aid: (620) 242-0400; 90% of undergrads determined to have financial need; average aid package $25,406

MidAmerica Nazarene University

Olathe KS
(913) 971-3380
U.S. News ranking: Reg. U. (Mid. W), No. 88
Website: www.mnu.edu
Admissions email: admissions@mnu.edu
Private; founded 1966
Affiliation: Church of the Nazarene
Freshman admissions: selective; 2017-2018: 957 applied, 628 accepted. Neither SAT nor ACT required. ACT 25/75 percentile: 18-24. High school rank: 16% in top tenth, 36% in top quarter, 64% in top half
Early decision deadline: N/A, notification date: N/A
Early action deadline: N/A, notification date: N/A
Application deadline (fall): N/A
Undergraduate student body: 998 full time, 310 part time; 41% male, 59% female; 1% American Indian, 2% Asian, 13% black, 8% Hispanic, 4% multiracial, 1% Pacific Islander, 60% white, 0% international; 60% from in state; 43% live on campus; N/A of students in fraternities, N/A in sororities
Most popular majors: 48% Health Professions and Related Programs, 24% Business, Management, Marketing, and Related Support Services
Expenses: 2018-2019: $30,736; room/board: $8,708
Financial aid: (913) 971-3298; 80% of undergrads determined to have financial need; average aid package $25,027

Newman University

Wichita KS
(877) 639-6268
U.S. News ranking: Reg. U. (Mid. W), second tier
Website: www.newmanu.edu
Admissions email: admissions@newmanu.edu
Private; founded 1933
Affiliation: Roman Catholic
Freshman admissions: selective; 2017-2018: 1,084 applied, 692 accepted. Neither SAT nor ACT required. ACT 25/75 percentile: 19-25. High school rank: 23% in top tenth, 48% in top quarter, 76% in top half
Early decision deadline: N/A, notification date: N/A
Early action deadline: N/A, notification date: N/A
Application deadline (fall): rolling
Undergraduate student body: 1,013 full time, 1,797 part time; 38% male, 62% female; 1% American Indian, 5% Asian, 6% black, 15% Hispanic, 2% multiracial, 0% Pacific Islander, 62% white, 7% international; 83% from in state; 23% live on campus; N/A of students in fraternities, N/A in sororities
Most popular majors: 21% Education, 20% Health Professions and Related Programs, 18% Biological and Biomedical Sciences, 14% Business, Management, Marketing, and Related Support Services, 6% Communication, Journalism, and Related Programs
Expenses: 2018-2019: $30,564; room/board: $8,326
Financial aid: (316) 942-4291; 65% of undergrads determined to have financial need; average aid package $13,253

Ottawa University

Ottawa KS
(785) 242-5200
U.S. News ranking: Reg. Coll. (Mid. W), No. 44
Website: www.ottawa.edu
Admissions email: admiss@ottawa.edu
Private; founded 1865
Affiliation: American Baptist
Freshman admissions: selective; 2017-2018: 1,118 applied, 248 accepted. Neither SAT nor ACT required. ACT 25/75 percentile: 18-22. High school rank: 27% in top tenth, 30% in top quarter, 52% in top half
Early decision deadline: N/A, notification date: N/A
Early action deadline: N/A, notification date: N/A
Application deadline (fall): 8/15
Undergraduate student body: 646 full time, 25 part time; 59% male, 41% female; 3% American Indian, 0% Asian, 12% black, 10% Hispanic, 6% multiracial, 0% Pacific Islander, 60% white, 0% international; 51% from in state; 68% live on campus; 0% of students in fraternities, 0% in sororities
Most popular majors: 16% Business Administration and Management, General, 14% Kinesiology and Exercise Science, 10% Accounting, 10% Sports Studies, 7% Speech Communication and Rhetoric
Expenses: 2018-2019: $29,690; room/board: $10,236
Financial aid: (602) 749-5120; 86% of undergrads determined to have financial need; average aid package $12,712

Pittsburg State University

Pittsburg KS
(800) 854-7488
U.S. News ranking: Reg. U. (Mid. W), No. 101
Website: www.pittstate.edu
Admissions email: psuadmit@pittstate.edu
Public; founded 1903
Freshman admissions: selective; 2017-2018: 2,486 applied, 2,168 accepted. ACT required. ACT 25/75 percentile: 19-25. High school rank: 40% in top tenth, 55% in top quarter, 79% in top half
Early decision deadline: N/A, notification date: N/A
Early action deadline: N/A, notification date: N/A
Application deadline (fall): N/A
Undergraduate student body: 5,109 full time, 597 part time; 52% male, 48% female; 1% American Indian, 1% Asian, 4% black, 6% Hispanic, 6% multiracial, 0% Pacific Islander, 79% white, 3% international; 69% from in state; 19% live on campus; N/A of students in fraternities, N/A in sororities
Most popular majors: 20% Business, Management, Marketing, and Related Support Services, 15% Engineering Technologies and Engineering-Related Fields, 14% Education, 8% Health Professions and Related Programs, 5% Psychology
Expenses: 2017-2018: $7,100 in state, $18,152 out of state; room/board: $7,700
Financial aid: (620) 235-4240; 100% of undergrads determined to have financial need; average aid package $7,092

Southwestern College

Winfield KS
(620) 229-6236
U.S. News ranking: Reg. U. (Mid. W), No. 124
Website: www.sckans.edu
Admissions email: scadmit@sckans.edu
Private; founded 1885
Affiliation: United Methodist
Freshman admissions: selective; 2017-2018: 512 applied, 496 accepted. Either SAT or ACT required. ACT 25/75 percentile: 18-23. High school rank: 11% in top tenth, 33% in top quarter, 65% in top half
Early decision deadline: N/A, notification date: N/A
Early action deadline: N/A, notification date: N/A
Application deadline (fall): 8/25
Undergraduate student body: 577 full time, 570 part time; 63% male, 37% female; 1% American Indian, 1% Asian, 11% black, 9% Hispanic, 4% multiracial, 0% Pacific Islander, 42% white, 5% international; 39% from in state; 37% live on campus; N/A of students in fraternities, N/A in sororities
Most popular majors: 45% Business, Management, Marketing, and Related Support Services, 11% Computer and Information Sciences and Support Services, 11% Health Professions and Related Programs, 10% Homeland Security, Law Enforcement, Firefighting and Related Protective Services, 5% Education
Expenses: 2018-2019: $30,150; room/board: $7,760
Financial aid: (620) 229-6215; 82% of undergrads determined to have financial need; average aid package $26,094

Sterling College[1]

Sterling KS
(800) 346-1017
U.S. News ranking: Reg. Coll. (Mid. W), second tier
Website: www.sterling.edu
Admissions email: admissions@sterling.edu
Private; founded 1887
Application deadline (fall): rolling
Undergraduate student body: N/A full time, N/A part time
Expenses: 2018-2019: $26,300; room/board: $7,426
Financial aid: (620) 278-4226; 87% of undergrads determined to have financial need; average aid package $23,110

Tabor College

Hillsboro KS
(620) 947-3121
U.S. News ranking: Reg. Coll. (Mid. W), No. 51
Website: www.tabor.edu
Admissions email: admissions@tabor.edu
Private; founded 1908
Affiliation: Mennonite Brethren Church
Freshman admissions: selective; 2017-2018: 1,017 applied, 526 accepted. Either SAT or ACT required. ACT 25/75 percentile: 18-24. High school rank: 13% in top tenth, 33% in top quarter, 70% in top half
Early decision deadline: N/A, notification date: N/A
Early action deadline: N/A, notification date: N/A
Application deadline (fall): rolling
Undergraduate student body: 554 full time, 157 part time; 54% male, 46% female; 1% American Indian, 0% Asian, 13% black, 17% Hispanic, 4% multiracial, 1% Pacific Islander, 60% white, 3% international; 51% from in state; 92% live on campus; 0% of students in fraternities, 0% in sororities

Most popular majors: 19% Business, Management, Marketing, and Related Support Services, 19% Health Professions and Related Programs, 14% Education, 13% Parks, Recreation, Leisure, and Fitness Studies, 7% Psychology
Expenses: 2018-2019: $27,220; room/board: $9,577
Financial aid: (620) 947-3121

University of Kansas
Lawrence KS
(785) 864-3911
U.S. News ranking: Nat. U., No. 129
Website: www.ku.edu/
Admissions email: adm@ku.edu
Public; founded 1865
Freshman admissions: more selective; 2017-2018: 14,538 applied, 13,576 accepted. Either SAT or ACT required. ACT 25/75 percentile: 23-28. High school rank: 26% in top tenth, 57% in top quarter, 88% in top half
Early decision deadline: N/A, notification date: N/A
Early action deadline: N/A, notification date: N/A
Application deadline (fall): 8/13
Undergraduate student body: 17,151 full time, 2,187 part time; 49% male, 51% female; 0% American Indian, 5% Asian, 4% black, 8% Hispanic, 5% multiracial, 0% Pacific Islander, 71% white, 6% international; 72% from in state; 26% live on campus; 20% of students in fraternities, 28% in sororities
Most popular majors: 18% Business, Management, Marketing, and Related Support Services, 11% Health Professions and Related Programs, 10% Communication, Journalism, and Related Programs, 9% Engineering, 6% Biological and Biomedical Sciences
Expenses: 2018-2019: $11,148 in state, $27,358 out of state; room/board: $10,350
Financial aid: (785) 864-4700; 47% of undergrads determined to have financial need; average aid package $16,185

University of St. Mary
Leavenworth KS
(913) 758-5151
U.S. News ranking: Reg. U. (Mid. W), second tier
Website: www.stmary.edu
Admissions email: admiss@stmary.edu
Private; founded 1923
Affiliation: Roman Catholic
Freshman admissions: selective; 2017-2018: 1,001 applied, 492 accepted. Either SAT or ACT required. ACT 25/75 percentile: 19-24. High school rank: 1% in top tenth, 8% in top quarter, 36% in top half
Early decision deadline: N/A, notification date: N/A
Early action deadline: N/A, notification date: N/A
Application deadline (fall): rolling
Undergraduate student body: 641 full time, 107 part time; 48% male, 52% female; 1% American Indian, 2% Asian, 12% black, 14% Hispanic, 1% multiracial, 1% Pacific Islander, 55% white, 1% international; 50% from in state; 37% live on campus; N/A of students in fraternities, N/A in sororities
Most popular majors: 50% Health Professions and Related Programs, 11% Psychology, 9% Business, Management, Marketing, and Related Support Services, 7% Biological and Biomedical Sciences, 4% Social Sciences
Expenses: 2018-2019: $28,690; room/board: $8,140
Financial aid: (913) 758-4303; 81% of undergrads determined to have financial need; average aid package $25,498

Washburn University
Topeka KS
(785) 670-1030
U.S. News ranking: Reg. U. (Mid. W), No. 106
Website: www.washburn.edu
Admissions email: admissions@washburn.edu
Public; founded 1865
Freshman admissions: selective; 2017-2018: 1,770 applied, 1,770 accepted. ACT required. ACT 25/75 percentile: 18-25. High school rank: 14% in top tenth, 34% in top quarter, 64% in top half
Early decision deadline: N/A, notification date: N/A
Early action deadline: N/A, notification date: N/A
Application deadline (fall): 8/1
Undergraduate student body: 3,944 full time, 1,929 part time; 40% male, 60% female; 1% American Indian, 1% Asian, 6% black, 11% Hispanic, 5% multiracial, 0% Pacific Islander, 65% white, 4% international
Most popular majors: Information not available
Expenses: 2017-2018: $8,540 in state, $19,190 out of state; room/board: $7,890
Financial aid: (785) 670-2770; 64% of undergrads determined to have financial need; average aid package $9,584

Wichita State University
Wichita KS
(316) 978-3085
U.S. News ranking: Nat. U., second tier
Website: www.wichita.edu
Admissions email: admissions@wichita.edu
Public; founded 1895
Freshman admissions: selective; 2017-2018: 5,075 applied, 4,944 accepted. Neither SAT nor ACT required. ACT 25/75 percentile: 20-27. High school rank: 20% in top tenth, 44% in top quarter, 80% in top half
Early decision deadline: N/A, notification date: N/A
Early action deadline: N/A, notification date: N/A
Application deadline (fall): rolling
Undergraduate student body: 8,749 full time, 3,649 part time; 46% male, 54% female; 1% American Indian, 7% Asian, 6% black, 12% Hispanic, 5% multiracial, 0% Pacific Islander, 60% white, 7% international; 91% from in state; 11% live on campus; 4% of students in fraternities, 5% in sororities
Most popular majors: 20% Business, Management, Marketing, and Related Support Services, 17% Health Professions and Related Programs, 14% Engineering, 9% Education, 7% Parks, Recreation, Leisure, and Fitness Studies
Expenses: 2018-2019: $8,271 in state, $17,452 out of state; room/board: $11,252
Financial aid: (316) 978-3430; 60% of undergrads determined to have financial need; average aid package $7,808

KENTUCKY

Alice Lloyd College
Pippa Passes KY
(888) 280-4252
U.S. News ranking: Reg. Coll. (S), No. 16
Website: www.alc.edu
Admissions email: admissions@alc.edu
Private; founded 1923
Freshman admissions: selective; 2017-2018: 5,599 applied, 1,437 accepted. Either SAT or ACT required. ACT 25/75 percentile: 18-23. High school rank: 12% in top tenth, 40% in top quarter, 73% in top half
Early decision deadline: N/A, notification date: N/A
Early action deadline: N/A, notification date: N/A
Application deadline (fall): 7/1
Undergraduate student body: 578 full time, 20 part time; 47% male, 53% female; 0% American Indian, 0% Asian, 2% black, 1% Hispanic, 0% multiracial, 0% Pacific Islander, 94% white, 1% international; N/A from in state; 81% live on campus; N/A of students in fraternities, N/A in sororities
Most popular majors: 28% Biological and Biomedical Sciences, 13% Social Sciences, 10% Parks, Recreation, Leisure, and Fitness Studies, 9% Parks, Recreation, Leisure, and Fitness Studies, 8% History
Expenses: 2018-2019: $12,150; room/board: $6,880
Financial aid: (606) 368-6058; 93% of undergrads determined to have financial need; average aid package $13,842

Asbury University
Wilmore KY
(800) 888-1818
U.S. News ranking: Reg. U. (S), No. 14
Website: www.asbury.edu
Admissions email: admissions@asbury.edu
Private; founded 1890
Affiliation: Other Protestant
Freshman admissions: more selective; 2017-2018: 1,101 applied, 768 accepted. Either SAT or ACT required. ACT 25/75 percentile: 21-28. High school rank: 29% in top tenth, 66% in top quarter, 89% in top half
Early decision deadline: N/A, notification date: N/A
Early action deadline: N/A, notification date: N/A
Application deadline (fall): rolling
Undergraduate student body: 1,323 full time, 394 part time; 40% male, 60% female; 1% American Indian, 2% Asian, 4% black, 6% Hispanic, 3% multiracial, 0% Pacific Islander, 78% white, 4% international
Most popular majors: 21% Radio, Television, and Digital Communication, Other, 7% Elementary Education and Teaching, 6% Business/Commerce, General, 5% Equestrian/Equine Studies, 5% Psychology, General
Expenses: 2018-2019: $30,198; room/board: $7,160
Financial aid: (859) 858-3511; 79% of undergrads determined to have financial need; average aid package $21,452

Bellarmine University
Louisville KY
(502) 272-7100
U.S. News ranking: Reg. U. (S), No. 17
Website: www.bellarmine.edu
Admissions email: admissions@bellarmine.edu
Private; founded 1950
Affiliation: Roman Catholic
Freshman admissions: selective; 2017-2018: 5,692 applied, 5,080 accepted. Either SAT or ACT required. ACT 25/75 percentile: 22-27. High school rank: N/A
Early decision deadline: N/A, notification date: N/A
Early action deadline: 11/1, notification date: 11/15
Application deadline (fall): 8/15
Undergraduate student body: 2,410 full time, 134 part time; 36% male, 64% female; 0% American Indian, 2% Asian, 5% black, 4% Hispanic, 3% multiracial, 0% Pacific Islander, 81% white, 1% international; 70% from in state; 38% live on campus; 1% of students in fraternities, 1% in sororities
Most popular majors: 24% Health Professions and Related Programs, 13% Business, Management, Marketing, and Related Support Services, 10% Education, 9% Psychology, 7% Parks, Recreation, Leisure, and Fitness Studies
Expenses: 2018-2019: $41,800; room/board: $12,250
Financial aid: (502) 272-7300; 80% of undergrads determined to have financial need; average aid package $33,094

Berea College
Berea KY
(859) 985-3500
U.S. News ranking: Nat. Lib. Arts, No. 61
Website: www.berea.edu
Admissions email: admissions@berea.edu
Private; founded 1855
Freshman admissions: more selective; 2017-2018: 1,710 applied, 600 accepted. Either SAT or ACT required. ACT 25/75 percentile: 22-27. High school rank: 24% in top tenth, 64% in top quarter, 93% in top half
Early decision deadline: N/A, notification date: N/A
Early action deadline: N/A, notification date: N/A
Application deadline (fall): 4/30
Undergraduate student body: 1,615 full time, 55 part time; 42% male, 58% female; 0% American Indian, 2% Asian, 15% black, 11% Hispanic, 7% multiracial, 0% Pacific Islander, 56% white, 8% international; 48% from in state; 89% live on campus; N/A of students in fraternities, N/A in sororities
Most popular majors: 10% Biological and Biomedical Sciences, 9% Computer and Information Sciences and Support Services, 8% Biological and Biomedical Sciences, 7% Social Sciences, 7% Visual and Performing Arts
Expenses: 2018-2019: $590; room/board: $6,764
Financial aid: (859) 985-3313; 100% of undergrads determined to have financial need; average aid package $34,714

Brescia University
Owensboro KY
(270) 686-4241
U.S. News ranking: Reg. Coll. (S), No. 30
Website: www.brescia.edu
Admissions email: admissions@brescia.edu
Private; founded 1950
Affiliation: Roman Catholic
Freshman admissions: selective; 2017-2018: 3,988 applied, 1,698 accepted. Either SAT or ACT required. ACT 25/75 percentile: 19-23. High school rank: N/A
Early decision deadline: N/A, notification date: N/A
Early action deadline: N/A, notification date: N/A
Application deadline (fall): rolling
Undergraduate student body: 715 full time, 460 part time; 29% male, 71% female; 0% American Indian, 1% Asian, 15% black, 7% Hispanic, 3% multiracial, 0% Pacific Islander, 61% white, 1% international
Most popular majors: 55% Social Work, 8% Accounting, 8% Liberal Arts and Sciences/Liberal Studies, 8% Psychology, General, 6% Audiology/Audiologist and Speech-Language Pathology/Pathologist
Expenses: 2018-2019: $22,100; room/board: $9,350
Financial aid: (270) 686-4253; 91% of undergrads determined to have financial need; average aid package $15,825

Campbellsville University
Campbellsville KY
(270) 789-5220
U.S. News ranking: Reg. U. (S), second tier
Website: www.campbellsville.edu
Admissions email: admissions@campbellsville.edu
Private; founded 1906

Freshman admissions: selective; 2017-2018: 2,770 applied, 1,900 accepted. Either SAT or ACT required. ACT 25/75 percentile: 18-24. High school rank: 12% in top tenth, 33% in top quarter, 67% in top half
Early decision deadline: N/A, notification date: N/A
Early action deadline: N/A, notification date: N/A
Application deadline (fall): rolling
Undergraduate student body: 2,120 full time, 1,979 part time; 41% male, 59% female; 0% American Indian, 0% Asian, 13% black, 3% Hispanic, 2% multiracial, 0% Pacific Islander, 71% white, 7% international; 84% from in state; 36% live on campus; N/A of students in fraternities, N/A in sororities
Most popular majors: 15% Business/Commerce, General, 9% Criminal Justice/Law Enforcement Administration, 9% Registered Nursing/Registered Nurse, 8% Social Work, 6% Sport and Fitness Administration/Management
Expenses: 2018-2019: $25,400; room/board: $9,000
Financial aid: (270) 789-5013; 87% of undergrads determined to have financial need; average aid package $19,583

Centre College

Danville KY
(859) 238-5350
U.S. News ranking: Nat. Lib. Arts, No. 46
Website: www.centre.edu
Admissions email: admission@centre.edu
Private; founded 1819
Affiliation: Presbyterian
Freshman admissions: more selective; 2017-2018: 2,454 applied, 1,873 accepted. Either SAT or ACT required. ACT 25/75 percentile: 26-31. High school rank: 64% in top tenth, 86% in top quarter, 99% in top half
Early decision deadline: 11/15, notification date: 12/15
Early action deadline: 12/1, notification date: 1/15
Application deadline (fall): 1/15
Undergraduate student body: 1,449 full time, 1 part time; 49% male, 51% female; 0% American Indian, 5% Asian, 5% black, 5% Hispanic, 3% multiracial, 0% Pacific Islander, 73% white, 7% international; 56% from in state; 98% live on campus; 36% of students in fraternities, 40% in sororities
Most popular majors: 16% Economics, Other, 9% Physiological Psychology/Psychobiology, 8% International/Global Studies, 7% English Language and Literature, General, 7% Political Science and Government, General
Expenses: 2018-2019: $41,700; room/board: $10,480
Financial aid: (859) 238-5365; 59% of undergrads determined to have financial need; average aid package $33,516

Eastern Kentucky University

Richmond KY
(800) 465-9191
U.S. News ranking: Reg. U. (S), No. 76
Website: www.eku.edu
Admissions email: admissions@eku.edu
Public; founded 1906
Freshman admissions: selective; 2017-2018: 9,187 applied, 8,027 accepted. Either SAT or ACT required. ACT 25/75 percentile: 20-25. High school rank: 17% in top tenth, 42% in top quarter, 71% in top half
Early decision deadline: N/A, notification date: N/A
Early action deadline: N/A, notification date: N/A
Application deadline (fall): 8/1
Undergraduate student body: 10,744 full time, 3,399 part time; 43% male, 57% female; 0% American Indian, 1% Asian, 6% black, 3% Hispanic, 3% multiracial, 0% Pacific Islander, 85% white, 1% international
Most popular majors: 19% Health Professions and Related Programs, 16% Homeland Security, Law Enforcement, Firefighting and Related Protective Services, 10% Business, Management, Marketing, and Related Support Services, 8% Liberal Arts and Sciences, General Studies and Humanities, 7% Education
Expenses: 2018-2019: $9,296 in state, $19,074 out of state; room/board: $9,624
Financial aid: (859) 622-2361; 72% of undergrads determined to have financial need; average aid package $11,620

Georgetown College

Georgetown KY
(502) 863-8009
U.S. News ranking: Nat. Lib. Arts, second tier
Website: www.georgetowncollege.edu
Admissions email: admissions@georgetowncollege.edu
Private; founded 1829
Freshman admissions: selective; 2017-2018: 2,498 applied, 1,682 accepted. Either SAT or ACT required. ACT 25/75 percentile: 20-25. High school rank: 23% in top tenth, 50% in top quarter, N/A in top half
Early decision deadline: N/A, notification date: N/A
Early action deadline: N/A, notification date: N/A
Application deadline (fall): 8/15
Undergraduate student body: 976 full time, 85 part time; 46% male, 54% female; 0% American Indian, 1% Asian, 9% black, 0% Hispanic, 5% multiracial, 0% Pacific Islander, 79% white, 1% international; 26% from in state; 90% live on campus; 17% of students in fraternities, 24% in sororities
Most popular majors: 22% Psychology, General, 13% Kinesiology and Exercise Science, 6% Communication and Media Studies, Other, 5% Biology/Biological Sciences, General, 5% Elementary Education and Teaching
Expenses: 2018-2019: $38,650; room/board: $9,780
Financial aid: (502) 863-8027; 77% of undergrads determined to have financial need; average aid package $36,918

Kentucky Christian University[1]

Grayson KY
(800) 522-3181
U.S. News ranking: Reg. Coll. (S), No. 60
Website: www.kcu.edu
Admissions email: knights@kcu.edu
Private; founded 1919
Application deadline (fall): 8/1
Undergraduate student body: N/A full time, N/A part time
Expenses: 2017-2018: $19,256; room/board: $8,080
Financial aid: (606) 474-3226

Kentucky State University

Frankfort KY
(877) 367-5978
U.S. News ranking: Reg. Coll. (S), No. 30
Website: www.kysu.edu
Admissions email: admissions@kysu.edu
Public; founded 1886
Freshman admissions: selective; 2017-2018: 2,078 applied, 941 accepted. Either SAT or ACT required. ACT 25/75 percentile: 16-21. High school rank: N/A
Early decision deadline: N/A, notification date: N/A
Early action deadline: N/A, notification date: N/A
Application deadline (fall): 7/31
Undergraduate student body: 1,122 full time, 635 part time; 40% male, 60% female; 1% American Indian, 1% Asian, 63% black, 3% Hispanic, 4% multiracial, 0% Pacific Islander, 24% white, 1% international; 69% from in state; N/A live on campus; 2% of students in fraternities, 3% in sororities
Most popular majors: 12% Liberal Arts and Sciences/Liberal Studies, 11% Business Administration and Management, General, 10% Criminal Justice/Police Science, 8% Psychology, General, 8% Registered Nursing/Registered Nurse
Expenses: 2018-2019: $7,796 in state, $18,704 out of state; room/board: $6,690
Financial aid: (502) 597-5759; 87% of undergrads determined to have financial need; average aid package $12,829

Kentucky Wesleyan College

Owensboro KY
(800) 999-0592
U.S. News ranking: Reg. Coll. (S), No. 13
Website: kwc.edu/
Admissions email: admissions@kwc.edu
Private; founded 1858
Affiliation: United Methodist
Freshman admissions: selective; 2017-2018: 1,365 applied, 798 accepted. Either SAT or ACT required. ACT 25/75 percentile: 19-26. High school rank: N/A
Early decision deadline: N/A, notification date: N/A
Early action deadline: N/A, notification date: N/A
Application deadline (fall): 9/4
Undergraduate student body: 673 full time, 41 part time; 52% male, 48% female; 0% American Indian, 1% Asian, 17% black, 2% Hispanic, 1% multiracial, 0% Pacific Islander, 72% white, 0% international; 22% from in state; 56% live on campus; 16% of students in fraternities, 30% in sororities
Most popular majors: 14% Business/Commerce, General, 14% Kinesiology and Exercise Science, 10% Speech Communication and Rhetoric, 9% Criminal Justice/Safety Studies, 7% Biology/Biological Sciences, General
Expenses: 2018-2019: $26,440; room/board: $9,764
Financial aid: (270) 852-3130

Lindsey Wilson College

Columbia KY
(270) 384-8100
U.S. News ranking: Reg. U. (S), second tier
Website: www.lindsey.edu
Admissions email: admissions@lindsey.edu
Private; founded 1903
Affiliation: United Methodist
Freshman admissions: selective; 2017-2018: 1,980 applied, 1,863 accepted. Neither SAT nor ACT required. ACT 25/75 percentile: 19-24. High school rank: 15% in top tenth, 36% in top quarter, 71% in top half
Early decision deadline: N/A, notification date: N/A
Early action deadline: N/A, notification date: N/A
Application deadline (fall): rolling
Undergraduate student body: 1,919 full time, 149 part time; 39% male, 61% female; 0% American Indian, 0% Asian, 8% black, 1% Hispanic, 2% multiracial, 0% Pacific Islander, 62% white, 0% international; 81% from in state; 48% live on campus; N/A of students in fraternities, N/A in sororities
Most popular majors: 49% Public Administration and Social Service Professions, 10% Business Administration and Management, General, 7% Criminal Justice/Safety Studies, 4% Registered Nursing/Registered Nurse, 4% Speech Communication and Rhetoric
Expenses: 2018-2019: $24,850; room/board: $9,385
Financial aid: (270) 384-8022; 94% of undergrads determined to have financial need; average aid package $20,660

Midway University[1]

Midway KY
(800) 755-0031
U.S. News ranking: Reg. U. (S), second tier
Website: www.midway.edu
Admissions email: admissions@midway.edu
Private; founded 1847
Affiliation: Christian Church (Disciples of Christ)
Application deadline (fall): rolling
Undergraduate student body: N/A full time, N/A part time
Expenses: 2017-2018: $23,950; room/board: $8,480
Financial aid: (859) 846-5304

Morehead State University

Morehead KY
(606) 783-2000
U.S. News ranking: Reg. U. (S), No. 65
Website: www.moreheadstate.edu
Admissions email: admissions@moreheadstate.edu
Public; founded 1887
Freshman admissions: selective; 2017-2018: 5,392 applied, 4,293 accepted. Either SAT or ACT required. ACT 25/75 percentile: 20-26. High school rank: 23% in top tenth, 51% in top quarter, 83% in top half
Early decision deadline: N/A, notification date: N/A
Early action deadline: N/A, notification date: N/A
Application deadline (fall): rolling
Undergraduate student body: 5,835 full time, 3,830 part time; 40% male, 60% female; 0% American Indian, 0% Asian, 4% black, 2% Hispanic, 2% multiracial, 0% Pacific Islander, 88% white, 3% international; 87% from in state; 42% live on campus; 6% of students in fraternities, 7% in sororities
Most popular majors: 14% Business, Management, Marketing, and Related Support Services, 12% Liberal Arts and Sciences, General Studies and Humanities, 10% Education, 9% Health Professions and Related Programs, 7% Public Administration and Social Service Professions
Expenses: 2018-2019: $9,070 in state, $13,546 out of state; room/board: $9,730
Financial aid: (606) 783-2011; 76% of undergrads determined to have financial need; average aid package $11,532

Murray State University

Murray KY
(270) 809-3741
U.S. News ranking: Reg. U. (S), No. 34
Website: www.murraystate.edu
Admissions email: msu.admissions@murraystate.edu
Public; founded 1922
Freshman admissions: selective; 2017-2018: 6,884 applied, 5,968 accepted. Either SAT or ACT required. ACT 25/75 percentile: 21-27. High school rank: 25% in top tenth, 52% in top quarter, 80% in top half
Early decision deadline: N/A, notification date: N/A
Early action deadline: N/A, notification date: N/A
Undergraduate student body: 6,611 full time, 2,025 part time; 40% male, 60% female; 0% American Indian, 1% Asian, 6% black,

2% Hispanic, 3% multiracial, 0% Pacific Islander, 82% white, 3% international; 67% from in state; 33% live on campus; 17% of students in fraternities, 16% in sororities
Most popular majors: 15% Health Professions and Related Programs, 12% Business, Management, Marketing, and Related Support Services, 9% Education, 9% Engineering Technologies and Engineering-Related Fields, 7% Liberal Arts and Sciences, General Studies and Humanities
Expenses: 2018-2019: $9,084 in state, $24,540 out of state; room/board: $9,190
Financial aid: (270) 809-2546; 66% of undergrads determined to have financial need; average aid package $11,833

Northern Kentucky University

Highland Heights KY
(859) 572-5220
U.S. News ranking: Reg. U. (S), No. 84
Website: www.nku.edu/
Admissions email: beanorse@nku.edu
Public; founded 1968
Freshman admissions: selective; 2017-2018: 5,852 applied, 5,289 accepted. Either SAT or ACT required. ACT 25/75 percentile: 20-26. High school rank: 12% in top tenth, 34% in top quarter, 68% in top half
Early decision deadline: N/A, notification date: N/A
Early action deadline: N/A, notification date: N/A
Application deadline (fall): 8/22
Undergraduate student body: 8,980 full time, 3,367 part time; 44% male, 56% female; 0% American Indian, 1% Asian, 7% black, 3% Hispanic, 3% multiracial, 0% Pacific Islander, 81% white, 3% international; 68% from in state; 15% live on campus; 9% of students in fraternities, 13% in sororities
Most popular majors: 7% Organizational Behavior Studies, 6% Registered Nursing/Registered Nurse, 4% Biology/Biological Sciences, General, 4% Information Technology, 4% Social Work
Expenses: 2018-2019: $10,032 in state, $19,680 out of state; room/board: $10,022
Financial aid: (859) 572-5143; 65% of undergrads determined to have financial need; average aid package $12,065

Spalding University[1]

Louisville KY
(502) 585-7111
U.S. News ranking: Nat. U., second tier
Website: www.spalding.edu
Admissions email: admissions@spalding.edu
Private; founded 1814
Application deadline (fall): rolling
Undergraduate student body: N/A full time, N/A part time
Expenses: 2017-2018: $24,000; room/board: $7,900
Financial aid: N/A

Sullivan University[1]

Louisville KY
(502) 456-6504
U.S. News ranking: Reg. U. (S), unranked
Website: www.sullivan.edu
Admissions email: admissions@sullivan.edu
Private
Application deadline (fall): N/A
Undergraduate student body: N/A full time, N/A part time
Expenses: 2017-2018: $25,950; room/board: $10,485
Financial aid: N/A

Thomas More College

Crestview Hills KY
(800) 825-4557
U.S. News ranking: Reg. U. (S), No. 87
Website: www.thomasmore.edu
Admissions email: admissions@thomasmore.edu
Private; founded 1921
Affiliation: Roman Catholic
Freshman admissions: selective; 2017-2018: 2,416 applied, 2,204 accepted. Either SAT or ACT required. ACT 25/75 percentile: 19-24. High school rank: N/A
Early decision deadline: N/A, notification date: N/A
Early action deadline: N/A, notification date: N/A
Application deadline (fall): rolling
Undergraduate student body: 1,356 full time, 525 part time; 49% male, 51% female; 0% American Indian, 1% Asian, 8% black, 2% Hispanic, 5% multiracial, 0% Pacific Islander, 76% white, 1% international; 55% from in state; 29% live on campus; 0% of students in fraternities, 0% in sororities
Most popular majors: 32% Business Administration and Management, General, 23% Biology/Biological Sciences, General, 17% Registered Nursing/Registered Nurse, 6% Education, 4% Communication and Media Studies
Expenses: 2018-2019: $31,200; room/board: $8,650
Financial aid: (859) 344-3506; 79% of undergrads determined to have financial need; average aid package $20,845

Transylvania University

Lexington KY
(859) 233-8242
U.S. News ranking: Nat. Lib. Arts, No. 76
Website: www.transy.edu
Admissions email: admissions@transy.edu
Private; founded 1780
Affiliation: Christian Church (Disciples of Christ)
Freshman admissions: more selective; 2017-2018: 1,567 applied, 1,496 accepted. Neither SAT nor ACT required. ACT 25/75 percentile: 25-30. High school rank: 34% in top tenth, 65% in top quarter, 87% in top half
Early decision deadline: N/A, notification date: N/A
Early action deadline: 10/15, notification date: 11/1
Application deadline (fall): rolling
Undergraduate student body: 959 full time, 4 part time; 40% male, 60% female; 0% American Indian, 1% Asian, 4% black, 5% Hispanic, 4% multiracial, 0% Pacific Islander, 80% white, 3% international; 76% from in state; 74% live on campus; 57% of students in fraternities, 56% in sororities
Most popular majors: 17% Business, Management, Marketing, and Related Support Services, 12% Biological and Biomedical Sciences, 11% Parks, Recreation, Leisure, and Fitness Studies, 10% Psychology, 7% Foreign Languages, Literatures, and Linguistics
Expenses: 2018-2019: $38,750; room/board: $10,820
Financial aid: (859) 233-8239; 69% of undergrads determined to have financial need; average aid package $28,380

Union College[1]

Barbourville KY
(606) 546-4151
U.S. News ranking: Reg. U. (S), second tier
Website: www.unionky.edu
Admissions email: enroll@unionky.edu
Private
Application deadline (fall): N/A
Undergraduate student body: N/A full time, N/A part time
Expenses: 2017-2018: $26,080; room/board: $7,400
Financial aid: (606) 546-1223

University of Kentucky

Lexington KY
(859) 257-2000
U.S. News ranking: Nat. U., No. 147
Website: www.uky.edu
Admissions email: admissions@uky.edu
Public; founded 1865
Freshman admissions: more selective; 2017-2018: 18,925 applied, 18,125 accepted. Either SAT or ACT required. ACT 25/75 percentile: 22-28. High school rank: 29% in top tenth, 58% in top quarter, 86% in top half
Early decision deadline: N/A, notification date: N/A
Early action deadline: 12/1, notification date: N/A
Application deadline (fall): 2/15
Undergraduate student body: 20,657 full time, 1,768 part time; 45% male, 55% female; 0% American Indian, 3% Asian, 8% black, 5% Hispanic, 4% multiracial, 0% Pacific Islander, 76% white, 2% international; 69% from in state; 33% live on campus; 19% of students in fraternities, 31% in sororities
Most popular majors: 19% Business, Management, Marketing, and Related Support Services, 11% Engineering, 10% Communication, Journalism, and Related Programs, 9% Education, 9% Health Professions and Related Programs
Expenses: 2018-2019: $12,180 in state, $29,168 out of state; room/board: $12,814
Financial aid: (859) 257-3172; 53% of undergrads determined to have financial need; average aid package $13,195

University of Louisville

Louisville KY
(502) 852-6531
U.S. News ranking: Nat. U., No. 171
Website: www.louisville.edu
Admissions email: admitme@louisville.edu
Public; founded 1798
Freshman admissions: selective; 2017-2018: 10,767 applied, 8,139 accepted. Either SAT or ACT required. ACT 25/75 percentile: 22-29. High school rank: 28% in top tenth, 56% in top quarter, 86% in top half
Early decision deadline: N/A, notification date: N/A
Early action deadline: N/A, notification date: N/A
Application deadline (fall): 8/1
Undergraduate student body: 12,025 full time, 3,522 part time; 49% male, 51% female; 0% American Indian, 4% Asian, 11% black, 5% Hispanic, 5% multiracial, 0% Pacific Islander, 73% white, 1% international; 83% from in state; 22% live on campus; 15% of students in fraternities, 16% in sororities
Most popular majors: 15% Business, Management, Marketing, and Related Support Services, 12% Engineering, 10% Health Professions and Related Programs, 9% Parks, Recreation, Leisure, and Fitness Studies, 8% Education
Expenses: 2018-2019: $11,264 in state, $26,286 out of state; room/board: $9,226
Financial aid: (502) 852-5511; 62% of undergrads determined to have financial need; average aid package $12,382

University of Pikeville

Pikeville KY
(606) 218-5251
U.S. News ranking: Nat. Lib. Arts, second tier
Website: www.upike.edu/
Admissions email: wewantyou@upike.edu
Private; founded 1889
Affiliation: Presbyterian Church (USA)
Freshman admissions: selective; 2017-2018: 2,299 applied, 2,299 accepted. Either SAT or ACT required. ACT 25/75 percentile: 18-23. High school rank: 15% in top tenth, 35% in top quarter, 59% in top half
Early decision deadline: N/A, notification date: N/A
Early action deadline: N/A, notification date: N/A
Application deadline (fall): rolling
Undergraduate student body: 1,049 full time, 510 part time; 45% male, 55% female; 1% American Indian, 1% Asian, 9% black, 1% Hispanic, 0% multiracial, 0% Pacific Islander, 86% white, 2% international; 80% from in state; 50% live on campus; 4% of students in fraternities, 1% in sororities
Most popular majors: 22% Business, Management, Marketing, and Related Support Services, 15% Biological and Biomedical Sciences, 13% Psychology, 8% Homeland Security, Law Enforcement, Firefighting and Related Protective Services, 6% Communication, Journalism, and Related Programs
Expenses: 2018-2019: $20,950; room/board: $7,800
Financial aid: (606) 218-5254; 99% of undergrads determined to have financial need; average aid package $20,102

University of the Cumberlands

Williamsburg KY
(800) 343-1609
U.S. News ranking: Nat. U., second tier
Website: www.ucumberlands.edu
Admissions email: admiss@ucumberlands.edu
Private; founded 1888
Affiliation: Baptist
Freshman admissions: selective; 2017-2018: 2,305 applied, 1,713 accepted. Either SAT or ACT required. ACT 25/75 percentile: 19-25. High school rank: 11% in top tenth, 29% in top quarter, 49% in top half
Early decision deadline: N/A, notification date: N/A
Early action deadline: N/A, notification date: N/A
Application deadline (fall): 8/31
Undergraduate student body: 1,828 full time, 1,487 part time; 43% male, 57% female; 0% American Indian, 0% Asian, 3% black, 1% Hispanic, 1% multiracial, 0% Pacific Islander, 52% white, 3% international
Most popular majors: Information not available
Expenses: 2017-2018: $23,000; room/board: $9,000
Financial aid: (606) 539-4239

Western Kentucky University

Bowling Green KY
(270) 745-2551
U.S. News ranking: Reg. U. (S), No. 34
Website: www.wku.edu
Admissions email: admission@wku.edu
Public; founded 1906
Freshman admissions: selective; 2017-2018: 9,804 applied, 9,358 accepted. Either SAT or ACT required. ACT 25/75 percentile: 19-27. High school rank: 22% in top tenth, 46% in top quarter, 72% in top half
Early decision deadline: N/A, notification date: N/A
Early action deadline: N/A, notification date: N/A
Application deadline (fall): 8/1
Undergraduate student body: 12,919 full time, 4,737 part time; 41% male, 59% female; 0% American Indian, 1% Asian, 10% black, 3% Hispanic, 3% multiracial, 0% Pacific Islander, 77% white, 4% international;

79% from in state; 33% live on campus; 14% of students in fraternities, 18% in sororities
Most popular majors: 10% General Studies, 8% Registered Nursing/Registered Nurse, 4% Business Administration and Management, General, 4% Elementary Education and Teaching, 4% Psychology, General
Expenses: 2018-2019: $10,602 in state, $26,496 out of state; room/board: $8,343
Financial aid: (270) 745-2755; 55% of undergrads determined to have financial need; average aid package $14,435

LOUISIANA

Centenary College of Louisiana

Shreveport LA
(800) 234-4448
U.S. News ranking: Nat. Lib. Arts, No. 168
Website: www.centenary.edu
Admissions email: admission@centenary.edu
Private; founded 1825
Affiliation: United Methodist
Freshman admissions: more selective; 2017-2018: 848 applied, 524 accepted. Either SAT or ACT required. ACT 25/75 percentile: 22-28. High school rank: 29% in top tenth, 54% in top quarter, 80% in top half
Early decision deadline: N/A, notification date: N/A
Early action deadline: 12/15, notification date: 1/15
Application deadline (fall): rolling
Undergraduate student body: 524 full time, 9 part time; 44% male, 56% female; 1% American Indian, 3% Asian, 16% black, 10% Hispanic, 5% multiracial, 0% Pacific Islander, 63% white, 2% international
Most popular majors: 19% Business Administration and Management, General, 18% Biology/Biological Sciences, General, 10% Psychology, General, 6% English Language and Literature, General, 6% Geology/Earth Science, General
Expenses: 2018-2019: $36,580; room/board: $13,400
Financial aid: (318) 869-5137; 78% of undergrads determined to have financial need; average aid package $30,528

Dillard University

New Orleans LA
(800) 216-6637
U.S. News ranking: Nat. Lib. Arts, second tier
Website: www.dillard.edu
Admissions email: admissions@dillard.edu
Private; founded 1869
Affiliation: United Methodist
Freshman admissions: selective; 2017-2018: 6,445 applied, 2,630 accepted. Either SAT or ACT required. ACT 25/75 percentile: 18-21. High school rank: 12% in top tenth, 38% in top quarter, 73% in top half
Early decision deadline: N/A, notification date: N/A
Early action deadline: N/A, notification date: N/A
Application deadline (fall): 8/1
Undergraduate student body: 1,200 full time, 91 part time; 25% male, 75% female; 1% American Indian, 0% Asian, 91% black, 0% Hispanic, 0% multiracial, 0% Pacific Islander, 0% white, 1% international; 59% from in state; 59% live on campus; 5% of students in fraternities, 5% in sororities
Most popular majors: 23% Public Health, General, 16% Biology/Biological Sciences, General, 11% Registered Nursing/Registered Nurse, 8% Psychology, General, 7% Speech Communication and Rhetoric
Expenses: 2017-2018: $18,711; room/board: $9,985
Financial aid: (504) 816-4864

Grambling State University

Grambling LA
(318) 274-6183
U.S. News ranking: Reg. U. (S), second tier
Website: www.gram.edu/
Admissions email: admissions@gram.edu
Public; founded 1901
Freshman admissions: less selective; 2017-2018: 7,060 applied, 3,044 accepted. Either SAT or ACT required. ACT 25/75 percentile: 16-20. High school rank: 6% in top tenth, 15% in top quarter, 52% in top half
Early decision deadline: N/A, notification date: N/A
Early action deadline: N/A, notification date: N/A
Application deadline (fall): rolling
Undergraduate student body: 3,731 full time, 345 part time; 42% male, 58% female; 0% American Indian, 0% Asian, 89% black, 1% Hispanic, 2% multiracial, 0% Pacific Islander, 1% white, 5% international; 71% from in state; 53% live on campus; 22% of students in fraternities, N/A in sororities
Most popular majors: 19% Criminal Justice/Safety Studies, 13% Social Work, 8% Business Administration and Management, General, 7% Physical Education Teaching and Coaching, 6% Mass Communication/Media Studies
Expenses: 2018-2019: $7,435 in state, $7,435 out of state; room/board: $10,054
Financial aid: (318) 274-6328; 81% of undergrads determined to have financial need; average aid package $4,045

Louisiana College

Pineville LA
(318) 487-7259
U.S. News ranking: Reg. U. (S), No. 91
Website: www.lacollege.edu
Admissions email: admissions@lacollege.edu
Private; founded 1906
Affiliation: Southern Baptist
Freshman admissions: selective; 2017-2018: 780 applied, 561 accepted. Either SAT or ACT required. ACT 25/75 percentile: 19-24. High school rank: 13% in top tenth, 30% in top quarter, 61% in top half
Early decision deadline: N/A, notification date: N/A
Early action deadline: N/A, notification date: N/A
Application deadline (fall): rolling
Undergraduate student body: 872 full time, 117 part time; 54% male, 46% female; N/A American Indian, N/A Asian, N/A black, N/A Hispanic, N/A multiracial, N/A Pacific Islander, N/A white, N/A international; 90% from in state; 54% live on campus; 0% of students in fraternities, 0% in sororities
Most popular majors: 21% Registered Nursing/Registered Nurse, 6% Business Administration and Management, General, 4% Criminal Justice/Safety Studies, 4% English Language and Literature, General, 4% Health and Physical Education/Fitness, General
Expenses: 2017-2018: $16,000; room/board: $5,274
Financial aid: (318) 487-7387

Louisiana State University–Alexandria

Alexandria LA
(318) 473-6417
U.S. News ranking: Nat. Lib. Arts, second tier
Website: www.lsua.edu
Admissions email: admissions@lsua.edu
Public; founded 1960
Freshman admissions: selective; 2017-2018: 2,068 applied, 648 accepted. Either SAT or ACT required. ACT 25/75 percentile: 18-22. High school rank: 8% in top tenth, 28% in top quarter, 60% in top half
Early decision deadline: N/A, notification date: N/A
Early action deadline: N/A, notification date: N/A
Application deadline (fall): 8/1
Undergraduate student body: 1,844 full time, 1,528 part time; 34% male, 66% female; 7% American Indian, 2% Asian, 17% black, 2% Hispanic, 2% multiracial, 0% Pacific Islander, 65% white, 3% international; 96% from in state; 7% live on campus; N/A of students in fraternities, N/A in sororities
Most popular majors: Information not available
Expenses: 2017-2018: $6,669 in state, $14,024 out of state; room/board: $7,950
Financial aid: (318) 473-6477

Louisiana State University–Baton Rouge

Baton Rouge LA
(225) 578-1175
U.S. News ranking: Nat. U., No. 140
Website: www.lsu.edu
Admissions email: admissions@lsu.edu
Public; founded 1860
Freshman admissions: more selective; 2017-2018: 17,907 applied, 13,236 accepted. Either SAT or ACT required. ACT 25/75 percentile: 23-28. High school rank: 23% in top tenth, 48% in top quarter, 77% in top half
Early decision deadline: N/A, notification date: N/A
Early action deadline: N/A, notification date: N/A
Application deadline (fall): 4/15
Undergraduate student body: 22,060 full time, 3,384 part time; 48% male, 52% female; 0% American Indian, 4% Asian, 12% black, 6% Hispanic, 2% multiracial, 0% Pacific Islander, 72% white, 2% international; 83% from in state; 23% live on campus; 16% of students in fraternities, 28% in sororities
Most popular majors: 23% Business, Management, Marketing, and Related Support Services, 15% Engineering, 11% Education, 7% Biological and Biomedical Sciences, 6% Communication, Journalism, and Related Programs
Expenses: 2018-2019: $11,950 in state, $28,627 out of state; room/board: $11,830
Financial aid: (225) 578-3103; 51% of undergrads determined to have financial need; average aid package $18,412

Louisiana State University–Shreveport[1]

Shreveport LA
(318) 797-5061
U.S. News ranking: Reg. U. (S), second tier
Website: www.lsus.edu
Admissions email: admissions@pilot.lsus.edu
Public; founded 1967
Application deadline (fall): rolling
Undergraduate student body: N/A full time, N/A part time
Expenses: 2017-2018: $7,166 in state, $20,320 out of state; room/board: N/A
Financial aid: N/A

Louisiana Tech University

Ruston LA
(318) 257-3036
U.S. News ranking: Nat. U., second tier
Website: www.latech.edu
Admissions email: bulldog@latech.edu
Public; founded 1894
Freshman admissions: more selective; 2017-2018: 6,952 applied, 4,508 accepted. Either SAT or ACT required. ACT 25/75 percentile: 22-27. High school rank: 20% in top tenth, 49% in top quarter, 79% in top half
Early decision deadline: N/A, notification date: N/A
Early action deadline: N/A, notification date: N/A
Application deadline (fall): rolling
Undergraduate student body: 8,112 full time, 2,697 part time; 52% male, 48% female; 0% American Indian, 1% Asian, 13% black, 4% Hispanic, 3% multiracial, 0% Pacific Islander, 71% white, 2% international; 84% from in state; 4% live on campus; N/A of students in fraternities, N/A in sororities
Most popular majors: 6% Biological and Biomedical Sciences, 5% Engineering, 4% Business, Management, Marketing, and Related Support Services, 4% Education, 4% Psychology
Expenses: 2018-2019: $9,645 in state, $18,558 out of state; room/board: $8,529
Financial aid: (318) 257-2641; 59% of undergrads determined to have financial need; average aid package $11,304

Loyola University New Orleans

New Orleans LA
(800) 456-9652
U.S. News ranking: Reg. U. (S), No. 12
Website: www.loyno.edu
Admissions email: admit@loyno.edu
Private; founded 1912
Affiliation: Roman Catholic
Freshman admissions: more selective; 2017-2018: 5,112 applied, 3,533 accepted. Either SAT or ACT required. ACT 25/75 percentile: 22-28. High school rank: 31% in top tenth, 60% in top quarter, 87% in top half
Early decision deadline: N/A, notification date: N/A
Early action deadline: N/A, notification date: N/A
Application deadline (fall): rolling
Undergraduate student body: 2,446 full time, 156 part time; 38% male, 62% female; 0% American Indian, 3% Asian, 15% black, 16% Hispanic, 5% multiracial, 0% Pacific Islander, 51% white, 2% international; 43% from in state; 54% live on campus; 4% of students in fraternities, 13% in sororities
Most popular majors: 14% Psychology, General, 8% Music Management, 6% Business Administration and Management, General, 6% Marketing/Marketing Management, General, 4% Creative Writing
Expenses: 2018-2019: $39,692; room/board: $13,380
Financial aid: (504) 865-3231; 75% of undergrads determined to have financial need; average aid package $33,676

McNeese State University

Lake Charles LA
(337) 475-5504
U.S. News ranking: Reg. U. (S), second tier
Website: www.mcneese.edu
Admissions email: admissions@mcneese.edu
Public; founded 1939
Freshman admissions: selective; 2017-2018: 3,300 applied, 2,054 accepted. Either SAT or ACT required. ACT 25/75 percentile: 20-25. High school rank: 20% in top tenth, 45% in top quarter, 79% in top half
Early decision deadline: N/A, notification date: N/A
Early action deadline: N/A, notification date: N/A
Application deadline (fall): 8/13

Undergraduate student body: 5,567 full time, 1,398 part time; 40% male, 60% female; 0% American Indian, 2% Asian, 18% black, 3% Hispanic, 3% multiracial, 0% Pacific Islander, 67% white, 7% international; 92% from in state; 11% live on campus; N/A of students in fraternities, N/A in sororities
Most popular majors: 10% General Studies, 10% Registered Nursing/Registered Nurse, 9% Business Administration and Management, General, 8% Engineering, General, 6% Psychology, General
Expenses: 2017-2018: $7,920 in state, $15,958 out of state; room/board: $8,188
Financial aid: (337) 475-5065

Nicholls State University

Thibodaux LA
(985) 448-4507
U.S. News ranking: Reg. U. (S), No. 100
Website: www.nicholls.edu
Admissions email: nicholls@nicholls.edu
Public; founded 1948
Freshman admissions: selective; 2017-2018: 2,571 applied, 2,410 accepted. Either SAT or ACT required. ACT 25/75 percentile: 20-24. High school rank: 16% in top tenth, 40% in top quarter, 71% in top half
Early decision deadline: N/A, notification date: N/A
Early action deadline: N/A, notification date: N/A
Application deadline (fall): rolling
Undergraduate student body: 4,665 full time, 1,052 part time; 36% male, 64% female; 2% American Indian, 1% Asian, 20% black, 3% Hispanic, 3% multiracial, 0% Pacific Islander, 68% white, 2% international; 94% from in state; 17% live on campus; 14% of students in fraternities, 15% in sororities
Most popular majors: 23% Business, Management, Marketing, and Related Support Services, 19% Health Professions and Related Programs, 13% Multi/Interdisciplinary Studies, 7% Education, 7% Engineering Technologies and Engineering-Related Fields
Expenses: 2018-2019: $7,346 in state, $8,394 out of state; room/board: $7,200
Financial aid: (985) 448-4047; 65% of undergrads determined to have financial need; average aid package $9,900

Northwestern State University of Louisiana

Natchitoches LA
(800) 426-3754
U.S. News ranking: Reg. U. (S), second tier
Website: www.nsula.edu
Admissions email: applications@nsula.edu
Public; founded 1884
Freshman admissions: selective; 2017-2018: 4,409 applied, 3,540 accepted. Either SAT or ACT required. ACT 25/75 percentile: 19-24. High school rank: 14% in top tenth, 40% in top quarter, 71% in top half
Early decision deadline: N/A, notification date: N/A
Early action deadline: N/A, notification date: N/A
Application deadline (fall): 10/15
Undergraduate student body: 5,471 full time, 3,981 part time; 31% male, 69% female; 1% American Indian, 1% Asian, 32% black, 6% Hispanic, 4% multiracial, 0% Pacific Islander, 53% white, 1% international; 92% from in state; 19% live on campus; N/A of students in fraternities, N/A in sororities
Most popular majors: 27% Health Professions and Related Programs, 17% Liberal Arts and Sciences, General Studies and Humanities, 15% Education, 9% Business, Management, Marketing, and Related Support Services, 5% Psychology
Expenses: 2018-2019: $8,580 in state, $19,368 out of state; room/board: $8,684
Financial aid: (318) 357-5961; 74% of undergrads determined to have financial need; average aid package $14,383

Southeastern Louisiana University

Hammond LA
(985) 549-5637
U.S. News ranking: Reg. U. (S), second tier
Website: www.southeastern.edu
Admissions email: admissions@southeastern.edu
Public; founded 1925
Freshman admissions: selective; 2017-2018: 4,402 applied, 3,892 accepted. Either SAT or ACT required. ACT 25/75 percentile: 20-24. High school rank: 14% in top tenth, 37% in top quarter, 69% in top half
Early decision deadline: N/A, notification date: N/A
Early action deadline: N/A, notification date: N/A
Application deadline (fall): 8/1
Undergraduate student body: 8,998 full time, 4,342 part time; 38% male, 62% female; 0% American Indian, 1% Asian, 20% black, 8% Hispanic, 5% multiracial, 0% Pacific Islander, 62% white, 2% international; 95% from in state; 21% live on campus; 7% of students in fraternities, 8% in sororities
Most popular majors: 19% Business, Management, Marketing, and Related Support Services, 12% Liberal Arts and Sciences, General Studies and Humanities, 11% Health Professions and Related Programs, 8% Education, 7% Parks, Recreation, Leisure, and Fitness Studies
Expenses: 2018-2019: $8,165 in state, $20,643 out of state; room/board: $8,420
Financial aid: (985) 549-2244; 65% of undergrads determined to have financial need; average aid package $10,255

Southern University and A&M College

Baton Rouge LA
(225) 771-2430
U.S. News ranking: Reg. U. (S), second tier
Website: www.subr.edu/
Admissions email: admit@subr.edu
Public; founded 1880
Freshman admissions: less selective; 2017-2018: 8,291 applied, 2,785 accepted. Either SAT or ACT required. ACT 25/75 percentile: 16-20. High school rank: N/A
Early decision deadline: N/A, notification date: N/A
Early action deadline: N/A, notification date: N/A
Application deadline (fall): 7/1
Undergraduate student body: 4,582 full time, 765 part time; 35% male, 65% female; 0% American Indian, 0% Asian, 94% black, 1% Hispanic, 1% multiracial, 0% Pacific Islander, 2% white, 1% international; 5% from in state; N/A live on campus; N/A of students in fraternities, N/A in sororities
Most popular majors: 19% Health Professions and Related Programs, 12% Homeland Security, Law Enforcement, Firefighting and Related Protective Services, 10% Communication, Journalism, and Related Programs, 8% Psychology, 7% Engineering
Expenses: 2017-2018: $8,666 in state, $18,080 out of state; room/board: $9,440
Financial aid: N/A

Southern University–New Orleans

New Orleans LA
(504) 286-5314
U.S. News ranking: Reg. U. (S), second tier
Website: www.suno.edu
Admissions email: N/A
Public; founded 1956
Freshman admissions: less selective; 2017-2018: 1,650 applied, 407 accepted. Either SAT or ACT required. ACT 25/75 percentile: 15-18. High school rank: 10% in top tenth, 24% in top quarter, 52% in top half
Early decision deadline: N/A, notification date: N/A
Early action deadline: N/A, notification date: N/A
Application deadline (fall): N/A
Undergraduate student body: 1,520 full time, 588 part time; 28% male, 72% female; 0% American Indian, 0% Asian, 77% black, 1% Hispanic, 0% multiracial, 0% Pacific Islander, 2% white, 1% international
Most popular majors: 16% Business Administration and Management, General, 14% Psychology, General, 13% Criminal Justice/Safety Studies, 12% Social Work, 9% General Studies
Expenses: 2017-2018: $6,421 in state, $15,322 out of state; room/board: $8,980
Financial aid: (504) 286-5263; 78% of undergrads determined to have financial need; average aid package $2,301

Tulane University

New Orleans LA
(504) 865-5731
U.S. News ranking: Nat. U., No. 44
Website: www.tulane.edu
Admissions email: undergrad.admission@tulane.edu
Private; founded 1834
Freshman admissions: most selective; 2017-2018: 35,622 applied, 7,657 accepted. Either SAT or ACT required. ACT 25/75 percentile: 30-33. High school rank: 62% in top tenth, 88% in top quarter, 96% in top half
Early decision deadline: 11/1, notification date: 12/15
Early action deadline: 11/15, notification date: 1/15
Application deadline (fall): 11/15
Undergraduate student body: 6,540 full time, 31 part time; 41% male, 59% female; 0% American Indian, 5% Asian, 4% black, 7% Hispanic, 4% multiracial, 0% Pacific Islander, 75% white, 4% international; 23% from in state; 48% live on campus; 29% of students in fraternities, 50% in sororities
Most popular majors: 26% Business, Management, Marketing, and Related Support Services, 16% Social Sciences, 10% Health Professions and Related Programs, 9% Biological and Biomedical Sciences, 7% Psychology
Expenses: 2018-2019: $54,820; room/board: $15,190
Financial aid: (504) 865-5723; 32% of undergrads determined to have financial need; average aid package $47,540

University of Holy Cross

New Orleans LA
(504) 398-2175
U.S. News ranking: Reg. Coll. (S), No. 22
Website: www.uhcno.edu/
Admissions email: admissions@UHCNO.edu
Private; founded 1916
Affiliation: Roman Catholic
Freshman admissions: selective; 2017-2018: 1,747 applied, 811 accepted. Neither SAT nor ACT required. ACT 25/75 percentile: 18-23. High school rank: N/A
Early decision deadline: N/A, notification date: N/A
Early action deadline: N/A, notification date: N/A
Application deadline (fall): rolling
Undergraduate student body: 457 full time, 455 part time; 14% male, 86% female; 1% American Indian, 4% Asian, 28% black, 10% Hispanic, 1% multiracial, 0% Pacific Islander, 47% white, 1% international; N/A from in state; 0% live on campus; N/A of students in fraternities, N/A in sororities
Most popular majors: 32% Registered Nursing/Registered Nurse, 11% Allied Health Diagnostic, Intervention, and Treatment Professions, Other, 10% Business Administration and Management, General, 9% Psychology, General, 7% Electroneurodiagnostic/Electroencephalographic Technology/Technologist
Expenses: 2018-2019: $14,372; room/board: $12,400
Financial aid: (504) 398-2133; 85% of undergrads determined to have financial need; average aid package $8,626

University of Louisiana–Lafayette

Lafayette LA
(337) 482-6553
U.S. News ranking: Nat. U., second tier
Website: www.louisiana.edu
Admissions email: enroll@louisiana.edu
Public; founded 1898
Freshman admissions: more selective; 2017-2018: 10,436 applied, 5,309 accepted. Either SAT or ACT required. ACT 25/75 percentile: 21-26. High school rank: 21% in top tenth, 46% in top quarter, 77% in top half
Early decision deadline: N/A, notification date: N/A
Early action deadline: N/A, notification date: N/A
Application deadline (fall): rolling
Undergraduate student body: 12,767 full time, 2,899 part time; 43% male, 57% female; 0% American Indian, 2% Asian, 20% black, 6% Hispanic, 2% multiracial, 0% Pacific Islander, 65% white, 2% international; 92% from in state; 18% live on campus; 9% of students in fraternities, 12% in sororities
Most popular majors: 24% Health Professions and Related Programs, 15% Business, Management, Marketing, and Related Support Services, 10% Education, 10% Engineering, 8% Liberal Arts and Sciences, General Studies and Humanities
Expenses: 2017-2018: $9,888 in state, $23,616 out of state; room/board: $10,294
Financial aid: (337) 482-6506; 63% of undergrads determined to have financial need; average aid package $76

University of Louisiana–Monroe

Monroe LA
(318) 342-7777
U.S. News ranking: Nat. U., second tier
Website: www.ulm.edu
Admissions email: admissions@ulm.edu
Public; founded 1931
Freshman admissions: selective; 2017-2018: 3,969 applied, 2,840 accepted. Either SAT or ACT required. ACT 25/75 percentile: 20-25. High school rank: 20% in top tenth, 49% in top quarter, 79% in top half
Early decision deadline: N/A, notification date: N/A
Early action deadline: N/A, notification date: N/A
Application deadline (fall): rolling
Undergraduate student body: 5,212 full time, 2,736 part time; 37% male, 63% female; 0% American Indian, 2% Asian,

5% black, 2% Hispanic, ?% multiracial, 0% Pacific Islander, 61% white, 4% international; 91% from in state; ?0% live on campus; 11% of students in fraternities, 11% in sororities
Most popular majors: 10% General Studies, 10% Psychology, General, 9% Kinesiology and Exercise Science, 8% Business Administration and Management, General, 8% Pharmacy, Pharmaceutical Sciences, and Administration, Other
Expenses: 2017-2018: $8,470 in state, $20,570 out of state; room/board: $7,850
Financial aid: (318) 342-5329; ?6% of undergrads determined to have financial need; average aid package $7,821

University of New Orleans

New Orleans LA
(504) 280-6595
U.S. News ranking: Nat. U., second tier
Website: www.uno.edu
Admissions email: admissions@uno.edu
Public; founded 1958
Freshman admissions: selective; 2017-2018: 3,736 applied, ?,115 accepted. Either SAT or ACT required. ACT 25/75 percentile: 20-25. High school rank: 15% in top tenth, 34% in top quarter, 64% in top half
Early decision deadline: N/A, notification date: N/A
Early action deadline: N/A, notification date: N/A
Application deadline (fall): 8/10
Undergraduate student body: 4,737 full time, 1,735 part time; 50% male, 50% female; 0% American Indian, 9% Asian, 15% black, ?3% Hispanic, 4% multiracial, 0% Pacific Islander, 52% white, ?% international; 94% from in state; N/A live on campus; 3% of students in fraternities, 5% in sororities
Most popular majors: 31% Business, Management, Marketing, and Related Support Services, 11% Multi/Interdisciplinary Studies, 10% Engineering, 10% Visual and Performing Arts, 9% Psychology
Expenses: 2018-2019: $9,054 in state, $13,890 out of state; room/board: $10,712
Financial aid: (504) 280-6603; ?7% of undergrads determined to have financial need; average aid package $9,594

Xavier University of Louisiana

New Orleans LA
(504) 520-7388
U.S. News ranking: Reg. U. (S), No. 28
Website: www.xula.edu
Admissions email: apply@xula.edu
Private; founded 1915
Affiliation: Roman Catholic
Freshman admissions: selective; 2017-2018: 7,164 applied, 4,589 accepted. Either SAT or ACT required. ACT 25/75 percentile: 20-25. High school rank: 28% in top tenth, 54% in top quarter, 78% in top half
Early decision deadline: N/A, notification date: N/A
Early action deadline: N/A, notification date: N/A
Application deadline (fall): 7/1
Undergraduate student body: 2,155 full time, 138 part time; 27% male, 73% female; 0% American Indian, 7% Asian, 78% black, 3% Hispanic, 4% multiracial, 0% Pacific Islander, 3% white, 2% international; 54% from in state; 48% live on campus; 1% of students in fraternities, 2% in sororities
Most popular majors: 39% Biological and Biomedical Sciences, 14% Physical Sciences, 12% Psychology, 9% Health Professions and Related Programs, 8% Business, Management, Marketing, and Related Support Services
Expenses: 2018-2019: $24,348; room/board: $9,047
Financial aid: (504) 520-7835

MAINE

Bates College

Lewiston ME
(855) 228-3755
U.S. News ranking: Nat. Lib. Arts, No. 22
Website: www.bates.edu
Admissions email: admission@bates.edu
Private; founded 1855
Freshman admissions: most selective; 2017-2018: 5,316 applied, 1,166 accepted. Neither SAT nor ACT required. SAT 25/75 percentile: 1270-1450. High school rank: 63% in top tenth, 86% in top quarter, 97% in top half
Early decision deadline: 11/15, notification date: 12/20
Early action deadline: N/A, notification date: N/A
Application deadline (fall): 1/1
Undergraduate student body: 1,787 full time, 0 part time; 49% male, 51% female; 0% American Indian, 4% Asian, 5% black, 9% Hispanic, 5% multiracial, 0% Pacific Islander, 70% white, 7% international
Most popular majors: 30% Social Sciences, 10% Biological and Biomedical Sciences, 10% Psychology, 8% English Language and Literature/Letters, 7% Visual and Performing Arts
Expenses: 2018-2019: $53,794; room/board: $15,224
Financial aid: (207) 786-6096; 43% of undergrads determined to have financial need; average aid package $46,794

Bowdoin College

Brunswick ME
(207) 725-3100
U.S. News ranking: Nat. Lib. Arts, No. 5
Website: www.bowdoin.edu
Admissions email: admissions@bowdoin.edu
Private; founded 1794
Affiliation: Other
Freshman admissions: most selective; 2017-2018: 7,251 applied, 988 accepted. Neither SAT nor ACT required. SAT 25/75 percentile: 1290-1510. High school rank: 86% in top tenth, 96% in top quarter, 100% in top half
Early decision deadline: 11/15, notification date: 12/15
Early action deadline: N/A, notification date: N/A
Application deadline (fall): 1/1
Undergraduate student body: 1,813 full time, 3 part time; 50% male, 50% female; 0% American Indian, 7% Asian, 6% black, 11% Hispanic, 7% multiracial, 0% Pacific Islander, 62% white, 5% international; 11% from in state; 90% live on campus; N/A of students in fraternities, N/A in sororities
Most popular majors: 20% Political Science and Government, General, 14% Economics, General, 8% Mathematics, General, 7% Biology/Biological Sciences, General, 7% English Language and Literature, General
Expenses: 2018-2019: $53,922; room/board: $14,698
Financial aid: (207) 725-3146; 46% of undergrads determined to have financial need; average aid package $46,562

Colby College

Waterville ME
(800) 723-3032
U.S. News ranking: Nat. Lib. Arts, No. 18
Website: www.colby.edu
Admissions email: admissions@colby.edu
Private; founded 1813
Freshman admissions: most selective; 2017-2018: 11,190 applied, 1,767 accepted. Neither SAT nor ACT required. ACT 25/75 percentile: 31-33. High school rank: 78% in top tenth, 94% in top quarter, 100% in top half
Early decision deadline: 11/15, notification date: 12/15
Early action deadline: N/A, notification date: N/A
Application deadline (fall): 1/1
Undergraduate student body: 1,917 full time, 0 part time; 48% male, 52% female; 0% American Indian, 7% Asian, 4% black, 7% Hispanic, 5% multiracial, 0% Pacific Islander, 64% white, 10% international; 11% from in state; 95% live on campus; 0% of students in fraternities, 0% in sororities
Most popular majors: 31% Social Sciences, 13% Biological and Biomedical Sciences, 9% Multi/Interdisciplinary Studies, 8% Natural Resources and Conservation, 7% Psychology
Expenses: 2018-2019: $55,210; room/board: $14,190
Financial aid: (800) 723-4033; 42% of undergrads determined to have financial need; average aid package $48,467

College of the Atlantic

Bar Harbor ME
(800) 528-0025
U.S. News ranking: Nat. Lib. Arts, No. 95
Website: www.coa.edu/
Admissions email: inquiry@coa.edu
Private; founded 1969
Freshman admissions: selective; 2017-2018: 474 applied, 322 accepted. Neither SAT nor ACT required. SAT 25/75 percentile: 1190-1350. High school rank: 22% in top tenth, 50% in top quarter, 97% in top half
Early decision deadline: 12/1, notification date: 12/15
Early action deadline: N/A, notification date: N/A
Application deadline (fall): 2/1
Undergraduate student body: 330 full time, 19 part time; 25% male, 75% female; 0% American Indian, 3% Asian, 1% black, 5% Hispanic, 2% multiracial, 0% Pacific Islander, 65% white, 22% international; 22% from in state; 46% live on campus; 0% of students in fraternities, 0% in sororities
Most popular majors: Information not available
Expenses: 2018-2019: $43,542; room/board: $9,747
Financial aid: (207) 801-5645; 83% of undergrads determined to have financial need; average aid package $42,122

Husson University

Bangor ME
(207) 941-7100
U.S. News ranking: Reg. U. (N), second tier
Website: www.husson.edu
Admissions email: admit@husson.edu
Private; founded 1898
Freshman admissions: selective; 2017-2018: 2,476 applied, 2,136 accepted. Either SAT or ACT required. SAT 25/75 percentile: 950-1130. High school rank: 11% in top tenth, 37% in top quarter, 69% in top half
Early decision deadline: N/A, notification date: N/A
Early action deadline: N/A, notification date: N/A
Application deadline (fall): 8/15
Undergraduate student body: 2,298 full time, 465 part time; 44% male, 56% female; 0% American Indian, 1% Asian, 4% black, 2% Hispanic, 2% multiracial, 0% Pacific Islander, 86% white, 4% international; 76% from in state; 39% live on campus; 3% of students in fraternities, 6% in sororities
Most popular majors: 29% Health Professions and Related Programs, 25% Business, Management, Marketing, and Related Support Services, 15% Communications Technologies/Technicians and Support Services, 13% Homeland Security, Law Enforcement, Firefighting and Related Protective Services, 8% Psychology
Expenses: 2018-2019: $17,610; room/board: $9,830
Financial aid: (207) 941-7156; 83% of undergrads determined to have financial need; average aid package $15,074

Maine College of Art[1]

Portland ME
(800) 699-1509
U.S. News ranking: Arts, unranked
Website: www.meca.edu
Admissions email: admissions@meca.edu
Private; founded 1882
Application deadline (fall): rolling
Undergraduate student body: N/A full time, N/A part time
Expenses: N/A
Financial aid: (207) 699-5073

Maine Maritime Academy

Castine ME
(207) 326-2206
U.S. News ranking: Reg. Coll. (N), No. 4
Website: www.mainemaritime.edu
Admissions email: admissions@mma.edu
Public; founded 1941
Freshman admissions: selective; 2017-2018: 760 applied, 605 accepted. Either SAT or ACT required. SAT 25/75 percentile: 990-1180. High school rank: 10% in top tenth, 57% in top quarter, 76% in top half
Early decision deadline: N/A, notification date: N/A
Early action deadline: 11/30, notification date: 2/1
Application deadline (fall): 3/1
Undergraduate student body: 989 full time, 33 part time; 85% male, 15% female; 1% American Indian, 1% Asian, 1% black, 2% Hispanic, 0% multiracial, 0% Pacific Islander, 87% white, 0% international; 71% from in state; 64% live on campus; 0% of students in fraternities, 0% in sororities
Most popular majors: 35% Engineering Technologies and Engineering-Related Fields, Other, 24% Naval Architecture and Marine Engineering, 20% Marine Science/Merchant Marine Officer, 13% International Business/Trade/Commerce, 5% Biological and Biomedical Sciences, Other
Expenses: 2018-2019: $13,478 in state, $27,098 out of state; room/board: $10,310
Financial aid: (207) 326-2339; 82% of undergrads determined to have financial need; average aid package $9,981

St. Joseph's College[1]

Standish ME
(207) 893-7746
U.S. News ranking: Reg. U. (N), second tier
Website: www.sjcme.edu
Admissions email: admission@sjcme.edu
Private
Application deadline (fall): N/A
Undergraduate student body: N/A full time, N/A part time
Expenses: 2017-2018: $34,610; room/board: $13,280
Financial aid: N/A

Thomas College[1]

Waterville ME
(800) 339-7001
U.S. News ranking: Reg. U. (N), second tier
Website: www.thomas.edu
Admissions email: admiss@thomas.edu
Private; founded 1894
Application deadline (fall): rolling
Undergraduate student body: N/A full time, N/A part time
Expenses: 2018-2019: $26,900; room/board: $11,250
Financial aid: (207) 859-1105; 86% of undergrads determined to have financial need; average aid package $20,266

Unity College

Unity ME
(800) 624-1024
U.S. News ranking: Reg. Coll. (N), No. 16
Website: www.unity.edu
Admissions email: admissions@unity.edu
Private; founded 1965
Freshman admissions: selective; 2017-2018: 915 applied, 812 accepted. Neither SAT nor ACT required. SAT 25/75 percentile: 990-1240. High school rank: 5% in top tenth, 35% in top quarter, 68% in top half
Early decision deadline: N/A, notification date: N/A
Early action deadline: 12/15, notification date: 9/1
Application deadline (fall): rolling
Undergraduate student body: 694 full time, 10 part time; 49% male, 51% female; 2% American Indian, 1% Asian, 1% black, 1% Hispanic, 3% multiracial, 0% Pacific Islander, 86% white, 0% international; 26% from in state; 70% live on campus; 0% of students in fraternities, 0% in sororities
Most popular majors: 31% Wildlife, Fish and Wildlands Science and Management, 18% Natural Resources Law Enforcement and Protective Services, 15% Biology/Biological Sciences, General, 6% Environmental Science, 6% Marine Biology and Biological Oceanography
Expenses: 2018-2019: $28,660; room/board: $10,710
Financial aid: (207) 509-7235; 84% of undergrads determined to have financial need; average aid package $20,848

University of Maine

Orono ME
(877) 486-2364
U.S. News ranking: Nat. U., No. 177
Website: www.umaine.edu
Admissions email: umaineadmissions@maine.edu
Public; founded 1865
Freshman admissions: selective; 2017-2018: 13,231 applied, 12,207 accepted. Either SAT or ACT required. SAT 25/75 percentile: 1050-1250. High school rank: 18% in top tenth, 44% in top quarter, 76% in top half
Early decision deadline: N/A, notification date: N/A
Early action deadline: 12/1, notification date: 1/15
Application deadline (fall): 2/1
Undergraduate student body: 8,204 full time, 1,075 part time; 53% male, 47% female; 1% American Indian, 2% Asian, 2% black, 4% Hispanic, 3% multiracial, 0% Pacific Islander, 84% white, 2% international; 65% from in state; 40% live on campus; N/A of students in fraternities, N/A in sororities
Most popular majors: 16% Business, Management, Marketing, and Related Support Services, 15% Engineering, 10% Education, 7% Biological and Biomedical Sciences, 6% Social Sciences
Expenses: 2018-2019: $11,170 in state, $30,970 out of state; room/board: $10,418
Financial aid: (207) 581-1324; 69% of undergrads determined to have financial need; average aid package $13,589

University of Maine–Augusta

Augusta ME
(207) 621-3465
U.S. News ranking: Reg. Coll. (N), second tier
Website: www.uma.edu
Admissions email: umaadm@maine.edu
Public; founded 1965
Freshman admissions: less selective; 2017-2018: 574 applied, 554 accepted. Neither SAT nor ACT required. SAT 25/75 percentile: N/A. High school rank: N/A
Early decision deadline: N/A, notification date: N/A
Early action deadline: N/A, notification date: N/A
Application deadline (fall): 9/1
Undergraduate student body: 1,317 full time, 2,697 part time; 29% male, 71% female; 2% American Indian, 1% Asian, 1% black, 2% Hispanic, 4% multiracial, 0% Pacific Islander, 86% white, 0% international
Most popular majors: 30% Liberal Arts and Sciences/Liberal Studies, 21% Psychiatric/Mental Health Services Technician, 9% Business Administration and Management, General, 6% Clinical Nurse Leader, 5% Library and Information Science
Expenses: 2018-2019: $7,988 in state, $17,918 out of state; room/board: N/A
Financial aid: (207) 621-3141; 85% of undergrads determined to have financial need; average aid package $9,599

University of Maine–Farmington

Farmington ME
(207) 778-7050
U.S. News ranking: Reg. Coll. (N), No. 9
Website: www.farmington.edu
Admissions email: umfadmit@maine.edu
Public; founded 1864
Freshman admissions: selective; 2017-2018: 1,939 applied, 1,601 accepted. Neither SAT nor ACT required. SAT 25/75 percentile: 970-1075. High school rank: 14% in top tenth, 42% in top quarter, 84% in top half
Early decision deadline: N/A, notification date: N/A
Early action deadline: 11/15, notification date: 12/15
Application deadline (fall): rolling
Undergraduate student body: 1,673 full time, 138 part time; 34% male, 66% female; 0% American Indian, 1% Asian, 2% black, 2% Hispanic, 2% multiracial, 0% Pacific Islander, 89% white, 0% international; 84% from in state; 53% live on campus; 0% of students in fraternities, 0% in sororities
Most popular majors: 36% Education, 14% Health Professions and Related Programs, 11% Psychology, 8% Business, Management, Marketing, and Related Support Services, 8% English Language and Literature/Letters
Expenses: 2018-2019: $9,616 in state, $19,728 out of state; room/board: $9,726
Financial aid: (207) 778-7100; 79% of undergrads determined to have financial need; average aid package $14,535

University of Maine–Fort Kent

Fort Kent ME
(207) 834-7600
U.S. News ranking: Reg. Coll. (N), No. 34
Website: www.umfk.maine.edu
Admissions email: umfkadm@maine.edu
Public; founded 1878
Freshman admissions: less selective; 2017-2018: 572 applied, 556 accepted. Neither SAT nor ACT required. SAT 25/75 percentile: 860-1110. High school rank: 3% in top tenth, 11% in top quarter, 38% in top half
Early decision deadline: N/A, notification date: N/A
Early action deadline: N/A, notification date: N/A
Application deadline (fall): rolling
Undergraduate student body: 582 full time, 1,178 part time; 29% male, 71% female; 1% American Indian, 1% Asian, 3% black, 3% Hispanic, 3% multiracial, 0% Pacific Islander, 79% white, 7% international
Most popular majors: 71% Health Professions and Related Programs, 12% Business, Management, Marketing, and Related Support Services, 3% Biological and Biomedical Sciences, 3% Public Administration and Social Service Professions, 3% Social Sciences
Expenses: 2018-2019: $8,115 in state, $12,315 out of state; room/board: $8,220
Financial aid: (207) 834-7607; 68% of undergrads determined to have financial need; average aid package $11,094

University of Maine–Machias[1]

Machias ME
(888) 468-6866
U.S. News ranking: Nat. Lib. Arts, second tier
Website: machias.edu/
Admissions email: ummadmissions@maine.edu
Public; founded 1909
Application deadline (fall): 8/15
Undergraduate student body: N/A full time, N/A part time
Expenses: 2017-2018: $7,680 in state, $19,320 out of state; room/board: $8,486
Financial aid: N/A

University of Maine–Presque Isle

Presque Isle ME
(207) 768-9532
U.S. News ranking: Reg. Coll. (N), No. 31
Website: www.umpi.edu
Admissions email: admissions@umpi.edu
Public; founded 1903
Freshman admissions: less selective; 2017-2018: 1,424 applied, 1,359 accepted. Neither SAT nor ACT required. SAT 25/75 percentile: 910-1130. High school rank: 1% in top tenth, 25% in top quarter, 52% in top half
Early decision deadline: N/A, notification date: N/A
Early action deadline: N/A, notification date: N/A
Application deadline (fall): rolling
Undergraduate student body: 710 full time, 698 part time; 38% male, 62% female; 2% American Indian, 0% Asian, 4% black, 3% Hispanic, 4% multiracial, 0% Pacific Islander, 79% white, 6% international; 84% from in state; 33% live on campus; N/A of students in fraternities, N/A in sororities
Most popular majors: 18% Liberal Arts and Sciences/Liberal Studies, 15% Multicultural Education, 14% Business Administration and Management, General, 11% Psychology, General, 10% Social Work
Expenses: 2018-2019: $8,034 in state, $12,234 out of state; room/board: $8,406
Financial aid: (207) 768-9511; 74% of undergrads determined to have financial need; average aid package $11,451

University of New England

Biddeford ME
(800) 477-4863
U.S. News ranking: Reg. U. (N), No. 74
Website: www.une.edu
Admissions email: admissions@une.edu
Private; founded 1831
Freshman admissions: selective; 2017-2018: 5,087 applied, 4,107 accepted. Either SAT or ACT required. SAT 25/75 percentile: 1030-1210. High school rank: N/A
Early decision deadline: N/A, notification date: N/A
Early action deadline: 12/1, notification date: 12/15
Application deadline (fall): 2/15
Undergraduate student body: 2,361 full time, 2,062 part time; 25% male, 75% female; 0% American Indian, 3% Asian, 1% black, 0% Hispanic, 2% multiracial, 0% Pacific Islander, 88% white, 0% international; 30% from in state; 65% live on campus; N/A of students in fraternities, N/A in sororities
Most popular majors: 45% Health Professions and Related Programs, 22% Biological and Biomedical Sciences, 12% Parks, Recreation, Leisure, and Fitness Studies, 6% Psychology, 5% Business, Management, Marketing, and Related Support Services
Expenses: 2018-2019: $37,620; room/board: $13,990
Financial aid: (207) 602-2342; 84% of undergrads determined to have financial need; average aid package $23,554

University of Southern Maine

Portland ME
(207) 780-5670
U.S. News ranking: Reg. U. (N), second tier
Website: www.usm.maine.edu
Admissions email: admitusm@maine.edu
Public; founded 1878
Freshman admissions: less selective; 2017-2018: 4,339 applied, 3,622 accepted. Either SAT or ACT required. SAT 25/75 percentile: 950-1160. High school rank: 10% in top tenth, 37% in top quarter, 74% in top half
Early decision deadline: N/A, notification date: N/A
Early action deadline: N/A, notification date: N/A
Application deadline (fall): rolling
Undergraduate student body: 3,901 full time, 2,209 part time; 43% male, 57% female; 1% American Indian, 2% Asian, 6% black, 3% Hispanic, 3% multiracial, 0% Pacific Islander, 80% white, 2% international; 86% from in state; 23% live on campus; N/A of students in fraternities, N/A in sororities
Most popular majors: 23% Business, Management, Marketing, and Related Support Services, 18% Health Professions and Related Programs, 12% Social Sciences, 6% Communication, Journalism, and Related Programs 5% Psychology
Expenses: 2017-2018: $9,220 in state, $22,030 out of state; room/board: $9,200
Financial aid: (207) 780-5250; 72% of undergrads determined to have financial need; average aid package $14,493

More @ usnews.com/bestcolleges

MARYLAND

Bowie State University

Bowie MD
(301) 860-3415
U.S. News ranking: Reg. U. (N), second tier
Website: www.bowiestate.edu
Admissions email: ugradadmissions@bowiestate.edu
Public
Freshman admissions: less selective; 2017-2018: N/A applied, N/A accepted. Either SAT or ACT required. SAT 25/75 percentile: 860-1040. High school rank: N/A
Early decision deadline: N/A, notification date: N/A
Early action deadline: N/A, notification date: N/A
Application deadline (fall): rolling
Undergraduate student body: 4,390 full time, 798 part time; 58% male, 42% female; 0% American Indian, 1% Asian, 84% black, 4% Hispanic, 4% multiracial, 0% Pacific Islander, 2% white, 2% international; 91% from in state; 45% live on campus; 22% of students in fraternities, 35% in sororities
Most popular majors: Information not available
Expenses: 2018-2019: $8,234 in state, $18,874 out of state; room/board: $10,904
Financial aid: N/A; 87% of undergrads determined to have financial need; average aid package $8,736

Capitol Technology University[1]

Laurel MD
(301) 369-2800
U.S. News ranking: Engineering, unranked
Website: www.captechu.edu/
Admissions email: N/A
Private
Application deadline (fall): N/A
Undergraduate student body: N/A full time, N/A part time
Expenses: N/A
Financial aid: (301) 369-2324

Coppin State University

Baltimore MD
(410) 951-3600
U.S. News ranking: Reg. U. (N), second tier
Website: www.coppin.edu
Admissions email: admissions@coppin.edu
Public; founded 1900
Freshman admissions: least selective; 2017-2018: 383 applied, N/A accepted. Either SAT or ACT required. SAT 25/75 percentile: 850-1010. High school rank: N/A
Early decision deadline: N/A, notification date: N/A
Early action deadline: N/A, notification date: N/A
Application deadline (fall): rolling
Undergraduate student body: 1,854 full time, 653 part time; 24% male, 76% female; 0% American Indian, 1% Asian, 80% black, 3% Hispanic, 1% multiracial, 0% Pacific Islander, 2% white, 12% international
Most popular majors: Information not available
Expenses: 2018-2019: $7,563 in state, $13,834 out of state; room/board: $10,101
Financial aid: N/A

Frostburg State University

Frostburg MD
(301) 687-4201
U.S. News ranking: Reg. U. (N), No. 126
Website: www.frostburg.edu
Admissions email: fsuadmissions@frostburg.edu
Public; founded 1898
Freshman admissions: selective; 2017-2018: 3,436 applied, 2,484 accepted. Either SAT or ACT required. SAT 25/75 percentile: 920-1110. High school rank: 10% in top tenth, 29% in top quarter, 65% in top half
Early decision deadline: 12/15, notification date: N/A
Early action deadline: N/A, notification date: N/A
Application deadline (fall): rolling
Undergraduate student body: 3,849 full time, 876 part time; 48% male, 52% female; 0% American Indian, 2% Asian, 33% black, 6% Hispanic, 4% multiracial, 0% Pacific Islander, 52% white, 1% international; 93% from in state; 28% live on campus; N/A of students in fraternities, N/A in sororities
Most popular majors: 15% Registered Nursing/Registered Nurse, 9% Business Administration and Management, General, 8% Liberal Arts and Sciences/Liberal Studies, 7% Psychology, General, 4% Criminal Justice/Safety Studies
Expenses: 2018-2019: $9,172 in state, $22,892 out of state; room/board: $10,328
Financial aid: (301) 687-4301; 67% of undergrads determined to have financial need; average aid package $9,993

Goucher College

Baltimore MD
(410) 337-6100
U.S. News ranking: Nat. Lib. Arts, No. 116
Website: www.goucher.edu
Admissions email: admissions@goucher.edu
Private; founded 1885
Freshman admissions: selective; 2017-2018: 3,474 applied, 2,739 accepted. Neither SAT nor ACT required. SAT 25/75 percentile: 1050-1260. High school rank: 28% in top tenth, 54% in top quarter, 78% in top half
Early decision deadline: 11/15, notification date: 12/15
Early action deadline: 12/1, notification date: 2/1
Application deadline (fall): 1/15
Undergraduate student body: 1,434 full time, 21 part time; 31% male, 69% female; 0% American Indian, 4% Asian, 14% black, 9% Hispanic, 5% multiracial, 0% Pacific Islander, 59% white, 3% international; 35% from in state; 93% live on campus; N/A of students in fraternities, N/A in sororities
Most popular majors: 17% Social Sciences, 13% Psychology, 13% Visual and Performing Arts, 8% English Language and Literature/Letters, 7% Biological and Biomedical Sciences
Expenses: 2018-2019: $44,300; room/board: $14,506
Financial aid: (410) 337-6141; 67% of undergrads determined to have financial need; average aid package $36,918

Hood College

Frederick MD
(800) 922-1599
U.S. News ranking: Reg. U. (N), No. 43
Website: www.hood.edu
Admissions email: admission@hood.edu
Private; founded 1893
Affiliation: United Church of Christ
Freshman admissions: less selective; 2017-2018: 1,431 applied, 1,161 accepted. Neither SAT nor ACT required. SAT 25/75 percentile: 980-1220. High school rank: 15% in top tenth, 34% in top quarter, 76% in top half
Early decision deadline: N/A, notification date: N/A
Early action deadline: N/A, notification date: N/A
Application deadline (fall): rolling
Undergraduate student body: 1,048 full time, 80 part time; 38% male, 62% female; 0% American Indian, 3% Asian, 17% black, 11% Hispanic, 6% multiracial, 0% Pacific Islander, 58% white, 2% international; 76% from in state; 52% live on campus; 0% of students in fraternities, 0% in sororities
Most popular majors: 17% Business, Management, Marketing, and Related Support Services, 11% Communication, Journalism, and Related Programs, 10% Social Sciences, 9% Education, 7% Psychology
Expenses: 2018-2019: $39,492; room/board: $12,700
Financial aid: (301) 696-3411; 83% of undergrads determined to have financial need; average aid package $30,919

Johns Hopkins University

Baltimore MD
(410) 516-8171
U.S. News ranking: Nat. U., No. 10
Website: www.jhu.edu
Admissions email: gotojhu@jhu.edu
Private; founded 1876
Freshman admissions: most selective; 2017-2018: 26,578 applied, 3,115 accepted. Either SAT or ACT required. ACT 25/75 percentile: 33-35. High school rank: 94% in top tenth, 99% in top quarter, 100% in top half
Early decision deadline: 11/1, notification date: 12/15
Early action deadline: N/A, notification date: N/A
Application deadline (fall): 1/2
Undergraduate student body: 5,565 full time, 544 part time; 48% male, 52% female; 0% American Indian, 26% Asian, 6% black, 14% Hispanic, 5% multiracial, 0% Pacific Islander, 34% white, 10% international; 11% from in state; 48% live on campus; 18% of students in fraternities, 31% in sororities
Most popular majors: 12% Public Health, General, 8% Bioengineering and Biomedical Engineering, 8% International Relations and Affairs, 7% Economics, General, 7% Neuroscience
Expenses: 2018-2019: $53,740; room/board: $15,836
Financial aid: (410) 516-8028; 51% of undergrads determined to have financial need; average aid package $41,611

Loyola University Maryland

Baltimore MD
(410) 617-5012
U.S. News ranking: Reg. U. (N), No. 5
Website: www.loyola.edu
Admissions email: admissions@loyola.edu
Private; founded 1852
Affiliation: Roman Catholic
Freshman admissions: more selective; 2017-2018: 11,600 applied, 8,733 accepted. Neither SAT nor ACT required. SAT 25/75 percentile: 1140-1310. High school rank: 29% in top tenth, 68% in top quarter, 95% in top half
Early decision deadline: 11/1, notification date: 12/15
Early action deadline: 11/15, notification date: 1/15
Application deadline (fall): 1/15
Undergraduate student body: 3,886 full time, 38 part time; 42% male, 58% female; 0% American Indian, 4% Asian, 5% black, 10% Hispanic, 3% multiracial, 0% Pacific Islander, 78% white, 1% international; 18% from in state; 81% live on campus; 0% of students in fraternities, 0% in sororities
Most popular majors: 39% Business, Management, Marketing, and Related Support Services, 11% Communication, Journalism, and Related Programs, 10% Social Sciences, 6% Psychology, 5% Multi/Interdisciplinary Studies
Expenses: 2018-2019: $49,085; room/board: $14,430
Financial aid: (410) 617-2576; 53% of undergrads determined to have financial need; average aid package $34,269

Maryland Institute College of Art

Baltimore MD
(410) 225-2222
U.S. News ranking: Arts, unranked
Website: www.mica.edu
Admissions email: admissions@mica.edu
Private; founded 1826
Freshman admissions: selective; 2017-2018: 3,636 applied, 2,240 accepted. Either SAT or ACT required. SAT 25/75 percentile: 1060-1290. High school rank: N/A
Early decision deadline: 11/1, notification date: 12/1
Early action deadline: 12/1, notification date: 1/15
Application deadline (fall): 2/1
Undergraduate student body: 1,674 full time, 20 part time; 25% male, 75% female; 0% American Indian, 11% Asian, 7% black, 3% Hispanic, 12% multiracial, 0% Pacific Islander, 41% white, 24% international; 26% from in state; 88% live on campus; N/A of students in fraternities, N/A in sororities
Most popular majors: 20% Graphic Design, 19% Illustration, 12% Painting, 11% Intermedia/Multimedia, 8% Fiber, Textile and Weaving Arts
Expenses: 2018-2019: $48,630; room/board: $13,280
Financial aid: (410) 225-2285

McDaniel College

Westminster MD
(800) 638-5005
U.S. News ranking: Nat. Lib. Arts, No. 124
Website: www.mcdaniel.edu
Admissions email: admissions@mcdaniel.edu
Private; founded 1867
Freshman admissions: selective; 2017-2018: 2,814 applied, 2,392 accepted. Either SAT or ACT required. SAT 25/75 percentile: 1060-1230. High school rank: 26% in top tenth, 51% in top quarter, 84% in top half
Early decision deadline: 11/1, notification date: 12/1
Early action deadline: 12/15, notification date: 1/15
Application deadline (fall): 4/1
Undergraduate student body: 1,536 full time, 41 part time; 49% male, 51% female; 0% American Indian, 3% Asian, 14% black, 6% Hispanic, 4% multiracial, 0% Pacific Islander, 65% white, 4% international; 66% from in state; 82% live on campus; 15% of students in fraternities, 19% in sororities
Most popular majors: 14% Parks, Recreation, Leisure, and Fitness Studies, 13% Social Sciences, 11% Business, Management, Marketing, and Related Support Services, 11% Psychology, 7% Communication, Journalism, and Related Programs
Expenses: 2018-2019: $43,260; room/board: $11,430
Financial aid: (410) 857-2233; 79% of undergrads determined to have financial need; average aid package $36,984

Morgan State University

Baltimore MD
(800) 332-6674
U.S. News ranking: Nat. U., second tier
Website: www.morgan.edu
Admissions email: admissions@morgan.edu

Public; founded 1867
Freshman admissions: less selective; 2017-2018: 7,247 applied, 4,618 accepted. Either SAT or ACT required. SAT 25/75 percentile: 900-1070. High school rank: 7% in top tenth, 25% in top quarter, 56% in top half
Early decision deadline: 11/15, notification date: 2/15
Early action deadline: 11/15, notification date: 2/15
Application deadline (fall): 2/15
Undergraduate student body: 5,825 full time, 615 part time; 47% male, 53% female; 0% American Indian, 1% Asian, 77% black, 3% Hispanic, 3% multiracial, 0% Pacific Islander, 2% white, 12% international; 77% from in state; N/A live on campus; N/A of students in fraternities, N/A in sororities
Most popular majors: 20% Business, Management, Marketing, and Related Support Services, 13% Engineering, 11% Communication, Journalism, and Related Programs, 10% Education, 9% Social Sciences
Expenses: 2018-2019: $7,900 in state, $18,167 out of state; room/board: $10,862
Financial aid: (443) 885-3170; 81% of undergrads determined to have financial need; average aid package $11,374

Mount St. Mary's University

Emmitsburg MD
(800) 448-4347
U.S. News ranking: Reg. U. (N), No. 41
Website: www.msmary.edu
Admissions email: admissions@msmary.edu
Private; founded 1808
Affiliation: Roman Catholic
Freshman admissions: selective; 2017-2018: 6,130 applied, 3,937 accepted. Either SAT or ACT required. SAT 25/75 percentile: 970-1190. High school rank: 8% in top tenth, 30% in top quarter, 64% in top half
Early decision deadline: N/A, notification date: N/A
Early action deadline: 12/1, notification date: 12/25
Application deadline (fall): 3/1
Undergraduate student body: 1,696 full time, 121 part time; 48% male, 52% female; 1% American Indian, 3% Asian, 17% black, 11% Hispanic, 4% multiracial, 0% Pacific Islander, 63% white, 1% international; 57% from in state; 80% live on campus; 0% of students in fraternities, 0% in sororities
Most popular majors: 29% Business/Commerce, General, 13% Criminology, 9% Biology/Biological Sciences, General, 7% Education, General, 6% Speech Communication and Rhetoric
Expenses: 2018-2019: $41,350; room/board: $13,075
Financial aid: (301) 447-8364; 73% of undergrads determined to have financial need; average aid package $29,515

Notre Dame of Maryland University

Baltimore MD
(410) 532-5330
U.S. News ranking: Reg. U. (N), No. 81
Website: www.ndm.edu
Admissions email: admiss@ndm.edu
Private; founded 1895
Affiliation: Roman Catholic
Freshman admissions: less selective; 2017-2018: 895 applied, 639 accepted. Neither SAT nor ACT required. SAT 25/75 percentile: 870-1110. High school rank: N/A
Early decision deadline: N/A, notification date: N/A
Early action deadline: N/A, notification date: N/A
Application deadline (fall): rolling
Undergraduate student body: 528 full time, 288 part time; 5% male, 95% female; 0% American Indian, 7% Asian, 31% black, 10% Hispanic, 5% multiracial, 0% Pacific Islander, 44% white, 1% international; 91% from in state; 0% live on campus; 0% of students in fraternities, 0% in sororities
Most popular majors: 61% Registered Nursing/Registered Nurse, 10% Liberal Arts and Sciences, General Studies and Humanities, Other, 7% Multi-/Interdisciplinary Studies, Other, 4% Biology/Biological Sciences, General, 4% Business Administration and Management, General
Expenses: 2018-2019: $36,900; room/board: $11,850
Financial aid: (410) 532-5369; 80% of undergrads determined to have financial need

Salisbury University

Salisbury MD
(410) 543-6161
U.S. News ranking: Reg. U. (N), No. 87
Website: www.salisbury.edu/
Admissions email: admissions@salisbury.edu
Public; founded 1925
Freshman admissions: selective; 2017-2018: 8,171 applied, 5,313 accepted. Neither SAT nor ACT required. SAT 25/75 percentile: 1100-1260. High school rank: 16% in top tenth, 50% in top quarter, 84% in top half
Early decision deadline: 11/15, notification date: 12/15
Early action deadline: 12/1, notification date: 1/15
Application deadline (fall): 1/15
Undergraduate student body: 7,191 full time, 591 part time; 44% male, 56% female; 1% American Indian, 4% Asian, 14% black, 4% Hispanic, 3% multiracial, 0% Pacific Islander, 71% white, 1% international; 87% from in state; 31% live on campus; N/A of students in fraternities, N/A in sororities
Most popular majors: 17% Business, Management, Marketing, and Related Support Services, 12% Education, 8% Communication, Journalism, and Related Programs, 8% Parks, Recreation, Leisure, and Fitness Studies, 7% Psychology
Expenses: 2018-2019: $9,824 in state, $19,526 out of state; room/board: $11,950
Financial aid: (410) 543-6165; 55% of undergrads determined to have financial need; average aid package $8,186

Stevenson University

Stevenson MD
(877) 468-6852
U.S. News ranking: Reg. U. (N), No. 81
Website: www.stevenson.edu/
Admissions email: admissions@stevenson.edu
Private; founded 1947
Freshman admissions: selective; 2017-2018: 5,533 applied, 3,368 accepted. Either SAT or ACT required. SAT 25/75 percentile: 1010-1190. High school rank: 20% in top tenth, 45% in top quarter, 81% in top half
Early decision deadline: N/A, notification date: N/A
Early action deadline: N/A, notification date: N/A
Application deadline (fall): rolling
Undergraduate student body: 2,926 full time, 471 part time; 34% male, 66% female; 0% American Indian, 4% Asian, 27% black, 6% Hispanic, 5% multiracial, 0% Pacific Islander, 55% white, 0% international; 77% from in state; 52% live on campus; N/A of students in fraternities, N/A in sororities
Most popular majors: 24% Business, Management, Marketing, and Related Support Services, 24% Health Professions and Related Programs, 7% Computer and Information Sciences and Support Services, 7% Education, 6% Homeland Security, Law Enforcement, Firefighting and Related Protective Services
Expenses: 2018-2019: $36,182; room/board: $13,130
Financial aid: (443) 334-3200; 80% of undergrads determined to have financial need; average aid package $23,636

St. John's College

Annapolis MD
(410) 626-2522
U.S. News ranking: Nat. Lib. Arts, No. 61
Website: www.sjc.edu
Admissions email: annapolis.admissions@sjc.edu
Private; founded 1696
Freshman admissions: more selective; 2017-2018: 753 applied, 411 accepted. Neither SAT nor ACT required. SAT 25/75 percentile: 1220-1430. High school rank: 36% in top tenth, 59% in top quarter, 87% in top half
Early decision deadline: N/A, notification date: N/A
Early action deadline: 11/15, notification date: 12/15
Application deadline (fall): rolling
Undergraduate student body: 458 full time, 0 part time; 53% male, 47% female; 0% American Indian, 4% Asian, 2% black, 6% Hispanic, 3% multiracial, 0% Pacific Islander, 64% white, 22% international; 38% from in state; 70% live on campus; 0% of students in fraternities, 0% in sororities
Most popular majors: 100% Liberal Arts and Sciences/Liberal Studies
Expenses: 2018-2019: $53,218; room/board: $12,602
Financial aid: (410) 626-2502; 78% of undergrads determined to have financial need; average aid package $44,590

St. Mary's College of Maryland

St. Marys City MD
(800) 492-7181
U.S. News ranking: Nat. Lib. Arts, No. 95
Website: www.smcm.edu
Admissions email: admissions@smcm.edu
Public; founded 1840
Freshman admissions: selective; 2017-2018: 1,655 applied, 1,364 accepted. Either SAT or ACT required. SAT 25/75 percentile: 1070-1280. High school rank: 8% in top tenth, 23% in top quarter, N/A in top half
Early decision deadline: N/A, notification date: N/A
Early action deadline: 11/15, notification date: 12/20
Application deadline (fall): 2/15
Undergraduate student body: 1,516 full time, 54 part time; 42% male, 58% female; 0% American Indian, 4% Asian, 9% black, 8% Hispanic, 5% multiracial, 0% Pacific Islander, 71% white, 0% international; 93% from in state; 82% live on campus; 0% of students in fraternities, 0% in sororities
Most popular majors: 26% Political Science and Government, General, 14% Psychology, General, 11% Biology/Biological Sciences, General, 7% English Language and Literature, General, 6% Mathematics, General
Expenses: 2018-2019: $14,806 in state, $30,568 out of state; room/board: $13,202
Financial aid: (240) 895-3000; 54% of undergrads determined to have financial need; average aid package $14,061

Towson University

Towson MD
(410) 704-2113
U.S. News ranking: Reg. U. (N), No. 50
Website: www.towson.edu
Admissions email: admissions@towson.edu
Public; founded 1866
Freshman admissions: selective; 2017-2018: 12,747 applied, 9,854 accepted. Either SAT or ACT required. SAT 25/75 percentile: 1055-1210. High school rank: 15% in top tenth, 41% in top quarter, 81% in top half
Early decision deadline: N/A, notification date: N/A
Early action deadline: 12/1, notification date: 12/31
Application deadline (fall): 1/17
Undergraduate student body: 17,106 full time, 2,490 part time; 40% male, 60% female; 0% American Indian, 6% Asian, 21% black, 8% Hispanic, 5% multiracial, 0% Pacific Islander, 57% white, 1% international; 87% from in state; 26% live on campus; 10% of students in fraternities, 12% in sororities
Most popular majors: 15% Business, Management, Marketing, and Related Support Services, 13% Health Professions and Related Programs, 10% Communication, Journalism, and Related Programs, 10% Social Sciences, 9% Education
Expenses: 2018-2019: $9,940 in state, $23,208 out of state; room/board: $12,464
Financial aid: (410) 704-4236; 58% of undergrads determined to have financial need; average aid package $10,468

United States Naval Academy

Annapolis MD
(410) 293-1858
U.S. News ranking: Nat. Lib. Arts, No. 22
Website: www.usna.edu
Admissions email: inquire@usna.edu
Public; founded 1845
Freshman admissions: more selective; 2017-2018: 16,299 applied, 1,376 accepted. Either SAT or ACT required. SAT 25/75 percentile: 1150-1370. High school rank: 57% in top tenth, 83% in top quarter, 97% in top half
Early decision deadline: N/A, notification date: N/A
Early action deadline: N/A, notification date: N/A
Application deadline (fall): 1/31
Undergraduate student body: 4,495 full time, 0 part time; 73% male, 27% female; 0% American Indian, 7% Asian, 7% black, 12% Hispanic, 9% multiracial, 1% Pacific Islander, 63% white, 1% international; 6% from in state; 100% live on campus; 0% of students in fraternities, 0% in sororities
Most popular majors: 40% Engineering, 26% Social Sciences, 12% Physical Sciences, 5% History, 4% English Language and Literature/Letters
Expenses: 2017-2018: $0 in state, $0 out of state; room/board: N/A
Financial aid: N/A

University of Baltimore

Baltimore MD
(410) 837-4777
U.S. News ranking: Reg. U. (N), second tier
Website: www.ubalt.edu
Admissions email: admissions@ubalt.edu
Public; founded 1925
Freshman admissions: less selective; 2017-2018: 426 applied, 345 accepted. Either

More @ usnews.com/bestcolleges

AT or ACT required. SAT 25/75 ercentile: 900-1110. High :hool rank: N/A
arly decision deadline: N/A, otification date: N/A
arly action deadline: N/A, otification date: N/A
pplication deadline (fall): rolling
ndergraduate student body: 1,716 ll time, 1,233 part time; 42% ale, 58% female; 1% American dian, 5% Asian, 48% black, % Hispanic, 4% multiracial, % Pacific Islander, 32% white, % international; 95% from in ate; N/A live on campus; N/A students in fraternities, N/A in orities
ost popular majors: 34% usiness/Commerce, General, 2% Criminal Justice/Police cience, 9% Health Services dministration, 5% Animation, teractive Technology, Video raphics and Special Effects, 5% sychology, General
xpenses: 2018-2019: $9,090 in ate, $21,208 out of state; room/ oard: N/A
inancial aid: (410) 837-4763; 3% of undergrads determined to ave financial need; average aid ackage $4,500

Jniversity of Maryland– Baltimore County

altimore MD
410) 455-2292
.S. News ranking: Nat. U., o. 165
Vebsite: www.umbc.edu
dmissions email: dmissions@umbc.edu
ublic; founded 1966
reshman admissions: more elective; 2017-2018: 11,201 pplied, 6,744 accepted. Either SAT or ACT required. SAT 25/75 ercentile: 1140-1360. High chool rank: 25% in top tenth, 56% in top quarter, 85% in op half
arly decision deadline: N/A, otification date: N/A
arly action deadline: 11/1, otification date: 12/15
Application deadline (fall): 2/1
Jndergraduate student body: 9,543 ull time, 1,691 part time; 55% nale, 45% female; 0% American ndian, 22% Asian, 18% black, 7% Hispanic, 4% multiracial, 0% Pacific Islander, 41% white, 4% international; 95% from in state; 35% live on campus; 2% of students in fraternities, 3% in sororities
Most popular majors: 17% Biological and Biomedical Sciences, 17% Computer and nformation Sciences and Support Services, 13% Psychology, 11% Social Sciences, 8% Engineering
Expenses: 2018-2019: $11,798 n state, $26,892 out of state; room/board: $12,046
Financial aid: (410) 455-1517; 55% of undergrads determined to have financial need; average aid package $11,533

University of Maryland– College Park

College Park MD
(301) 314-8385
U.S. News ranking: Nat. U., No. 63
Website: www.maryland.edu
Admissions email: ApplyMaryland@umd.edu
Public; founded 1856
Freshman admissions: more selective; 2017-2018: 33,907 applied, 15,081 accepted. Either SAT or ACT required. SAT 25/75 percentile: 1290-1470. High school rank: 72% in top tenth, 90% in top quarter, 99% in top half
Early decision deadline: N/A, notification date: N/A
Early action deadline: 11/1, notification date: 1/31
Application deadline (fall): 1/20
Undergraduate student body: 27,708 full time, 2,160 part time; 53% male, 47% female; 0% American Indian, 17% Asian, 12% black, 10% Hispanic, 4% multiracial, 0% Pacific Islander, 50% white, 5% international; 78% from in state; 41% live on campus; 15% of students in fraternities, 20% in sororities
Most popular majors: 7% Biology/ Biological Sciences, General, 5% Computer Engineering, General, 5% Computer and Information Sciences, General, 5% Finance, General, 4% Kinesiology and Exercise Science
Expenses: 2018-2019: $10,595 in state, $35,216 out of state; room/board: $12,429
Financial aid: (301) 314-9000; 42% of undergrads determined to have financial need; average aid package $12,153

University of Maryland– Eastern Shore

Princess Anne MD
(410) 651-6410
U.S. News ranking: Nat. U., second tier
Website: www.umes.edu
Admissions email: umesadmissions@umes.edu
Public; founded 1886
Freshman admissions: less selective; 2017-2018: 7,827 applied, 3,053 accepted. Either SAT or ACT required. SAT 25/75 percentile: 860-1040. High school rank: N/A
Early decision deadline: N/A, notification date: N/A
Early action deadline: N/A, notification date: N/A
Application deadline (fall): 6/30
Undergraduate student body: 2,573 full time, 289 part time; 45% male, 55% female; 0% American Indian, 1% Asian, 76% black, 4% Hispanic, 5% multiracial, 0% Pacific Islander, 10% white, 3% international; 82% from in state; 68% live on campus; N/A of students in fraternities, N/A in sororities
Most popular majors: 13% Criminal Justice/Police Science, 9% Kinesiology and Exercise Science, 8% Rehabilitation and Therapeutic Professions, Other, 8% Sociology, 7% Biology/ Biological Sciences, General
Expenses: 2017-2018: $8,042 in state, $18,048 out of state; room/ board: $9,623
Financial aid: (410) 651-6172

University of Maryland University College

Adelphi MD
(800) 888-8682
U.S. News ranking: Reg. U. (N), unranked
Website: www.umuc.edu/
Admissions email: enroll@umuc.edu
Public; founded 1947
Freshman admissions: least selective; 2017-2018: 2,496 applied, 2,496 accepted. Neither SAT nor ACT required. SAT 25/75 percentile: N/A. High school rank: N/A
Early decision deadline: N/A, notification date: N/A
Early action deadline: N/A, notification date: N/A
Application deadline (fall): rolling
Undergraduate student body: 9,714 full time, 35,890 part time; 56% male, 44% female; 0% American Indian, 5% Asian, 27% black, 13% Hispanic, 5% multiracial, 1% Pacific Islander, 40% white, 1% international; 41% from in state; N/A live on campus; N/A of students in fraternities, N/A in sororities
Most popular majors: 36% Business, Management, Marketing, and Related Support Services, 30% Computer and Information Sciences and Support Services, 7% Psychology, 6% Homeland Security, Law Enforcement, Firefighting and Related Protective Services, 4% Social Sciences
Expenses: 2018-2019: $7,296 in state, $12,336 out of state; room/ board: N/A
Financial aid: (301) 985-7510; 60% of undergrads determined to have financial need; average aid package $6,959

Washington Adventist University

Takoma Park MD
(301) 891-4000
U.S. News ranking: Reg. U. (N), second tier
Website: www.wau.edu
Admissions email: enroll@wau.edu
Private; founded 1904
Affiliation: Seventh Day Adventist
Freshman admissions: less selective; 2017-2018: 726 applied, 449 accepted. Neither SAT nor ACT required. SAT 25/75 percentile: 800-1000. High school rank: N/A
Early decision deadline: N/A, notification date: N/A
Early action deadline: N/A, notification date: N/A
Application deadline (fall): 8/1
Undergraduate student body: 760 full time, 113 part time; 39% male, 61% female; 0% American Indian, 5% Asian, 47% black, 15% Hispanic, 2% multiracial, 0% Pacific Islander, 10% white, 10% international
Most popular majors: Information not available
Expenses: 2018-2019: $23,900; room/board: $9,370
Financial aid: (301) 891-4005; 96% of undergrads determined to have financial need; average aid package $10,500

Washington College

Chestertown MD
(410) 778-7700
U.S. News ranking: Nat. Lib. Arts, No. 108
Website: www.washcoll.edu
Admissions email: wc_admissions@washcoll.edu
Private; founded 1782
Freshman admissions: more selective; 2017-2018: 5,515 applied, 2,626 accepted. Either SAT or ACT required. SAT 25/75 percentile: 1090-1300. High school rank: 38% in top tenth, 70% in top quarter, 91% in top half
Early decision deadline: 11/15, notification date: 12/15
Early action deadline: 12/1, notification date: 1/15
Application deadline (fall): 2/15
Undergraduate student body: 1,456 full time, 28 part time; 42% male, 58% female; 1% American Indian, 3% Asian, 8% black, 6% Hispanic, 1% multiracial, 0% Pacific Islander, 69% white, 9% international; 45% from in state; 85% live on campus; 15% of students in fraternities, 17% in sororities
Most popular majors: 22% Social Sciences, 16% Business, Management, Marketing, and Related Support Services, 11% Biological and Biomedical Sciences, 9% Psychology, 8% Natural Resources and Conservation
Expenses: 2018-2019: $47,006; room/board: $12,190
Financial aid: (410) 778-7214; 67% of undergrads determined to have financial need; average aid package $32,393

MASSACHUSETTS

American International College

Springfield MA
(413) 205-3201
U.S. News ranking: Nat. U., second tier
Website: www.aic.edu
Admissions email: admissions@aic.edu
Private; founded 1885
Freshman admissions: less selective; 2017-2018: 1,988 applied, 1,428 accepted. Neither SAT nor ACT required. SAT 25/75 percentile: 902-1090. High school rank: N/A
Early decision deadline: N/A, notification date: N/A
Early action deadline: N/A, notification date: N/A
Application deadline (fall): 9/7
Undergraduate student body: 1,254 full time, 118 part time; 41% male, 59% female; 1% American Indian, 1% Asian, 25% black, 20% Hispanic, 3% multiracial, 0% Pacific Islander, 38% white, 3% international; 38% from in state; 49% live on campus; 1% of students in fraternities, 0% in sororities
Most popular majors: 44% Health Professions and Related Programs, 13% Business, Management, Marketing, and Related Support Services, 9% Social Sciences, 8% Homeland Security, Law Enforcement, Firefighting and Related Protective Services, 8% Psychology
Expenses: 2018-2019: $35,680; room/board: $14,300
Financial aid: (413) 205-3521

Amherst College

Amherst MA
(413) 542-2328
U.S. News ranking: Nat. Lib. Arts, No. 2
Website: www.amherst.edu
Admissions email: admission@amherst.edu
Private; founded 1821
Freshman admissions: most selective; 2017-2018: 9,285 applied, 1,198 accepted. Either SAT or ACT required. ACT 25/75 percentile: 32-34. High school rank: 83% in top tenth, 94% in top quarter, 100% in top half
Early decision deadline: 11/15, notification date: 12/15
Early action deadline: N/A, notification date: N/A
Application deadline (fall): 1/1
Undergraduate student body: 1,836 full time, 0 part time; 51% male, 49% female; 1% American Indian, 14% Asian, 11% black, 13% Hispanic, 5% multiracial, 0% Pacific Islander, 44% white, 9% international; 14% from in state; 97% live on campus; 0% of students in fraternities, 0% in sororities
Most popular majors: 16% Economics, General, 12% Research and Experimental Psychology, Other, 11% Mathematics, General, 9% English Language and Literature, General, 9% Political Science and Government, General
Expenses: 2018-2019: $56,426; room/board: $14,740
Financial aid: (413) 542-2296; 57% of undergrads determined to have financial need; average aid package $53,052

Anna Maria College

Paxton MA
(508) 849-3360
U.S. News ranking: Reg. U. (N), second tier
Website: www.annamaria.edu
Admissions email: admissions@annamaria.edu
Private; founded 1946
Affiliation: Roman Catholic
Freshman admissions: less selective; 2017-2018: 2,089 applied, 1,654 accepted. Neither SAT nor ACT required. SAT 25/75 percentile: 910-1110. High

school rank: 7% in top tenth, 16% in top quarter, 46% in top half
Early decision deadline: N/A, notification date: N/A
Early action deadline: N/A, notification date: N/A
Application deadline (fall): rolling
Undergraduate student body: 865 full time, 255 part time; 44% male, 56% female; 1% American Indian, 2% Asian, 13% black, 11% Hispanic, 1% multiracial, 0% Pacific Islander, 64% white, 0% international; 75% from in state; 62% live on campus; N/A of students in fraternities, N/A in sororities
Most popular majors: 42% Health Professions and Related Programs, 33% Homeland Security, Law Enforcement, Firefighting and Related Protective Services, 11% Public Administration and Social Service Professions
Expenses: 2018-2019: $37,860; room/board: $14,230
Financial aid: (508) 849-3363; 88% of undergrads determined to have financial need; average aid package $30,003

Assumption College
Worcester MA
(866) 477-7776
U.S. News ranking: Reg. U. (N), No. 28
Website: www.assumption.edu
Admissions email: admiss@assumption.edu
Private; founded 1904
Affiliation: Roman Catholic
Freshman admissions: selective; 2017-2018: 4,508 applied, 3,561 accepted. Neither SAT nor ACT required. SAT 25/75 percentile: 1070-1250. High school rank: 12% in top tenth, 41% in top quarter, 80% in top half
Early decision deadline: 11/1, notification date: 12/1
Early action deadline: 11/1, notification date: 12/15
Application deadline (fall): 2/15
Undergraduate student body: 1,925 full time, 15 part time; 42% male, 58% female; 0% American Indian, 3% Asian, 5% black, 7% Hispanic, 2% multiracial, 0% Pacific Islander, 77% white, 2% international; 65% from in state; 85% live on campus; N/A of students in fraternities, N/A in sororities
Most popular majors: 25% Business, Management, Marketing, and Related Support Services, 13% Health Professions and Related Programs, 13% Social Sciences, 9% Biological and Biomedical Sciences, 8% Psychology
Expenses: 2018-2019: $39,600; room/board: $12,684
Financial aid: (508) 767-7158; 75% of undergrads determined to have financial need; average aid package $27,681

Babson College
Babson Park MA
(781) 239-5522
U.S. News ranking: Business, unranked
Website: www.babson.edu
Admissions email: ugradadmission@babson.edu
Private; founded 1919
Freshman admissions: more selective; 2017-2018: 7,122 applied, 1,722 accepted. Either SAT or ACT required. SAT 25/75 percentile: 1230-1400. High school rank: N/A
Early decision deadline: 11/1, notification date: 12/15
Early action deadline: 11/1, notification date: 1/1
Application deadline (fall): 1/2
Undergraduate student body: 2,342 full time, 0 part time; 52% male, 48% female; 0% American Indian, 12% Asian, 5% black, 11% Hispanic, 2% multiracial, 0% Pacific Islander, 37% white, 28% international; 27% from in state; 79% live on campus; 13% of students in fraternities, 26% in sororities
Most popular majors: Economics, General, Entrepreneurship/ Entrepreneurial Studies, Finance, General, Management Sciences and Quantitative Methods, Marketing/Marketing Management, General
Expenses: 2018-2019: $51,104; room/board: $16,312
Financial aid: (781) 239-4015; 40% of undergrads determined to have financial need; average aid package $42,671

Bard College at Simon's Rock
Great Barrington MA
(800) 234-7186
U.S. News ranking: Nat. Lib. Arts, second tier
Website: www.simons-rock.edu
Admissions email: admit@simons-rock.edu
Private; founded 1966
Freshman admissions: more selective; 2017-2018: 373 applied, 206 accepted. Neither SAT nor ACT required. SAT 25/75 percentile: 1240-1440. High school rank: 56% in top tenth, 72% in top quarter, 96% in top half
Early decision deadline: N/A, notification date: N/A
Early action deadline: N/A, notification date: N/A
Application deadline (fall): rolling
Undergraduate student body: 400 full time, 0 part time; 43% male, 57% female; 1% American Indian, 7% Asian, 6% black, 2% Hispanic, 3% multiracial, 0% Pacific Islander, 56% white, 15% international; 12% from in state; 94% live on campus; N/A of students in fraternities, N/A in sororities
Most popular majors: Computer Science, Environmental Studies, Pre-Engineering, Psychology, General, Visual and Performing Arts, General
Expenses: 2018-2019: $55,732; room/board: $14,916
Financial aid: (413) 528-7297; 91% of undergrads determined to have financial need; average aid package $31,816

Bay Path University
Longmeadow MA
(413) 565-1331
U.S. News ranking: Reg. U. (N), No. 105
Website: www.baypath.edu
Admissions email: admiss@baypath.edu
Private; founded 1897
Freshman admissions: selective; 2017-2018: 1,470 applied, 924 accepted. Neither SAT nor ACT required. SAT 25/75 percentile: 970-1190. High school rank: 19% in top tenth, 47% in top quarter, 76% in top half
Early decision deadline: N/A, notification date: N/A
Early action deadline: 12/15, notification date: 1/2
Application deadline (fall): 8/1
Undergraduate student body: 1,367 full time, 580 part time; 0% male, 100% female; 0% American Indian, 2% Asian, 13% black, 19% Hispanic, 3% multiracial, 0% Pacific Islander, 57% white, 1% international; 58% from in state; 44% live on campus; 0% of students in fraternities, 0% in sororities
Most popular majors: 22% Business, Management, Marketing, and Related Support Services, 21% Psychology, 17% Health Professions and Related Programs, 11% Education, 9% Liberal Arts and Sciences, General Studies and Humanities
Expenses: 2018-2019: $34,225; room/board: $12,799
Financial aid: (413) 565-1256; 92% of undergrads determined to have financial need; average aid package $27,333

Bay State College
Boston MA
(617) 217-9000
U.S. News ranking: Reg. Coll. (N), second tier
Website: www.baystate.edu
Admissions email: admissions@baystate.edu
For-profit; founded 1946
Affiliation: Undenominational
Freshman admissions: less selective; 2017-2018: 620 applied, 274 accepted. Neither SAT nor ACT required. SAT 25/75 percentile: N/A. High school rank: N/A
Early decision deadline: N/A, notification date: N/A
Early action deadline: N/A, notification date: N/A
Application deadline (fall): rolling
Undergraduate student body: 430 full time, 287 part time; 29% male, 71% female; 0% American Indian, 4% Asian, 22% black, 15% Hispanic, 6% multiracial, 0% Pacific Islander, 43% white, 3% international
Most popular majors: Information not available
Expenses: 2017-2018: $22,320; room/board: $13,000
Financial aid: (617) 217-9003

Becker College[1]
Worcester MA
(877) 523-2537
U.S. News ranking: Reg. Coll. (N), second tier
Website: www.beckercollege.edu
Admissions email: admissions@beckercollege.edu
Private; founded 1784
Application deadline (fall): rolling
Undergraduate student body: N/A full time, N/A part time
Expenses: 2017-2018: $38,250; room/board: $13,300
Financial aid: (508) 373-9430

Bentley University
Waltham MA
(781) 891-2244
U.S. News ranking: Reg. U. (N), No. 3
Website: www.bentley.edu
Admissions email: ugadmission@bentley.edu
Private; founded 1917
Freshman admissions: more selective; 2017-2018: 8,867 applied, 3,915 accepted. Either SAT or ACT required. SAT 25/75 percentile: 1210-1380. High school rank: 34% in top tenth, 74% in top quarter, 94% in top half
Early decision deadline: 11/15, notification date: 12/31
Early action deadline: N/A, notification date: N/A
Application deadline (fall): 1/7
Undergraduate student body: 4,171 full time, 101 part time; 59% male, 41% female; 0% American Indian, 8% Asian, 3% black, 7% Hispanic, 2% multiracial, 0% Pacific Islander, 61% white, 14% international; 42% from in state; 78% live on campus; 16% of students in fraternities, 19% in sororities
Most popular majors: 20% Finance, General, 16% Business, Management, Marketing, and Related Support Services, Other, 15% Marketing/Marketing Management, General, 11% Accounting and Finance, 11% Business Administration and Management, General
Expenses: 2018-2019: $49,880; room/board: $16,320
Financial aid: (781) 891-3441; 44% of undergrads determined to have financial need; average aid package $37,680

Berklee College of Music
Boston MA
(800) 237-5533
U.S. News ranking: Arts, unranked
Website: www.berklee.edu
Admissions email: admissions@berklee.edu
Private; founded 1945
Freshman admissions: least selective; 2017-2018: 6,222 applied, 3,268 accepted. Neither SAT nor ACT required. SAT 25/75 percentile: N/A. High school rank: N/A
Early decision deadline: N/A, notification date: N/A
Early action deadline: 11/1, notification date: 1/31
Application deadline (fall): 1/15
Undergraduate student body: 4,88 full time, 1,401 part time; 62% male, 38% female; 0% American Indian, 4% Asian, 7% black, 10% Hispanic, 4% multiracial, 0% Pacific Islander, 43% white, 28% international; 11% from in state; 28% live on campus; 0% of students in fraternities, 0% in sororities
Most popular majors: 96% Visual and Performing Arts, 3% Health Professions and Related Program 1% Education
Expenses: 2018-2019: $44,140; room/board: $18,360
Financial aid: (617) 747-2274; 40% of undergrads determined t have financial need; average aid package $20,315

Boston Architectural College
Boston MA
(617) 585-0123
U.S. News ranking: Arts, unranked
Website: www.the-bac.edu
Admissions email: admissions@the-bac.edu
Private; founded 1889
Freshman admissions: least selective; 2017-2018: 60 applie 60 accepted. Neither SAT nor AC required. SAT 25/75 percentile: N/A. High school rank: N/A
Early decision deadline: N/A, notification date: N/A
Early action deadline: N/A, notification date: N/A
Application deadline (fall): rolling
Undergraduate student body: 306 full time, 37 part time; 55% male, 45% female; 0% American Indian, 7% Asian, 9% black, 13% Hispanic, 4% multiracial, 0% Pacific Islander, 38% white, 21% international
Most popular majors: 54% Architecture, 33% Environmental Design/Architecture, 9% Interior Architecture, 4% Landscape Architecture
Expenses: 2018-2019: $21,894; room/board: $13,280
Financial aid: (617) 585-0183; 76% of undergrads determined to have financial need; average aid package $12,985

Boston College
Chestnut Hill MA
(617) 552-3100
U.S. News ranking: Nat. U., No. 38
Website: www.bc.edu
Admissions email: N/A
Private; founded 1863
Affiliation: Roman Catholic
Freshman admissions: most selective; 2017-2018: 28,454 applied, 9,223 accepted. Either SAT or ACT required. SAT 25/75 percentile: 1320-1490. High school rank: 78% in top tenth, 95% in top quarter, 99% in top half
Early decision deadline: N/A, notification date: N/A

arly action deadline: 11/1, otification date: 12/25
pplication deadline (fall): 1/1
ndergraduate student body: ,358 full time, 0 part time; 47% nale, 53% female; 0% American ndian, 10% Asian, 4% black, 1% Hispanic, 3% multiracial, % Pacific Islander, 62% white, % international; 26% from in tate; 84% live on campus; 0% f students in fraternities, 0% in ororities
lost popular majors: 13% conomics, General, 13% inance, General, 8% Biology/ iological Sciences, General, % Speech Communication and hetoric, 6% Psychology, General
xpenses: 2018-2019: $55,464; oom/board: $14,478
inancial aid: (617) 552-3300; 1% of undergrads determined to ave financial need; average aid ackage $44,157

Boston Conservatory[1]

Boston MA
617) 536-6340
.S. News ranking: Arts, unranked
Vebsite: www.bostonconservatory.edu
dmissions email: admissions@ bostonconservatory.edu
rivate
pplication deadline (fall): N/A
ndergraduate student body: N/A ull time, N/A part time
xpenses: 2017-2018: $44,735; oom/board: $11,820
inancial aid: N/A

Boston University

Boston MA
617) 353-2300
.S. News ranking: Nat. U., No. 42
Website: www.bu.edu
Admissions email: admissions@bu.edu
Private; founded 1839
reshman admissions: most selective; 2017-2018: 60,825 applied, 15,273 accepted. Neither SAT nor ACT required. SAT 25/75 percentile: 1300-1480. High school rank: 62% in top tenth, 92% in top quarter, 99% n top half
Early decision deadline: 11/1, notification date: 12/15
Early action deadline: N/A, notification date: N/A
Application deadline (fall): 1/2
Undergraduate student body: 16,839 full time, 1,241 part time; 40% male, 60% female; 0% American Indian, 15% Asian, 4% black, 12% Hispanic, 4% multiracial, 0% Pacific Islander, 40% white, 22% international; 20% from in state; 75% live on campus; 5% of students in fraternities, 15% in sororities
Most popular majors: 34% Business, Management, Marketing, and Related Support Services, 16% Biological and Biomedical Sciences, 16% Public Administration and Social Service Professions, 12% Social Sciences, 9% Computer and Information Sciences and Support Services
Expenses: 2018-2019: $53,948; room/board: $15,720
Financial aid: (617) 353-2965; 39% of undergrads determined to have financial need; average aid package $42,180

Brandeis University

Waltham MA
(781) 736-3500
U.S. News ranking: Nat. U., No. 35
Website: www.brandeis.edu
Admissions email: admissions@brandeis.edu
Private; founded 1948
Freshman admissions: most selective; 2017-2018: 11,721 applied, 4,011 accepted. Either SAT or ACT required. ACT 25/75 percentile: 29-33. High school rank: 65% in top tenth, 90% in top quarter, 99% in top half
Early decision deadline: 11/1, notification date: 12/15
Early action deadline: N/A, notification date: N/A
Application deadline (fall): 1/1
Undergraduate student body: 3,620 full time, 15 part time; 41% male, 59% female; 0% American Indian, 13% Asian, 5% black, 7% Hispanic, 3% multiracial, 0% Pacific Islander, 47% white, 21% international; 29% from in state; 75% live on campus; 0% of students in fraternities, 0% in sororities
Most popular majors: 11% Economics, General, 10% Biology/ Biological Sciences, General, 9% Business/Commerce, General, 8% Health Policy Analysis, 8% Psychology, General
Expenses: 2018-2019: $55,395; room/board: $15,440
Financial aid: (781) 736-3700; 47% of undergrads determined to have financial need; average aid package $44,868

Bridgewater State University

Bridgewater MA
(508) 531-1237
U.S. News ranking: Reg. U. (N), No. 117
Website: www.bridgew.edu/ admissions
Admissions email: admission@bridgew.edu
Public; founded 1840
Freshman admissions: selective; 2017-2018: 6,343 applied, 5,097 accepted. Neither SAT nor ACT required. SAT 25/75 percentile: 980-1160. High school rank: N/A
Early decision deadline: N/A, notification date: N/A
Early action deadline: 11/15, notification date: 12/15
Application deadline (fall): rolling
Undergraduate student body: 7,858 full time, 1,700 part time; 41% male, 59% female; 0% American Indian, 2% Asian, 11% black, 7% Hispanic, 4% multiracial, 0% Pacific Islander, 74% white, 0% international; 96% from in state; 42% live on campus; 4% of students in fraternities, 6% in sororities
Most popular majors: 18% Education, 17% Business, Management, Marketing, and Related Support Services, 13% Psychology, 11% Homeland Security, Law Enforcement, Firefighting and Related Protective Services, 7% Communication, Journalism, and Related Programs
Expenses: 2018-2019: $10,312 in state, $16,452 out of state; room/board: $13,000
Financial aid: (508) 531-2685; 73% of undergrads determined to have financial need; average aid package $8,482

Cambridge College[1]

Cambridge MA
(617) 868-1000
U.S. News ranking: Reg. U. (N), unranked
Website: www.cambridgecollege.edu
Admissions email: N/A
Private; founded 1971
Application deadline (fall): N/A
Undergraduate student body: N/A full time, N/A part time
Expenses: 2017-2018: $14,940; room/board: N/A
Financial aid: (617) 873-0440

Clark University

Worcester MA
(508) 793-7431
U.S. News ranking: Nat. U., No. 66
Website: www.clarku.edu
Admissions email: admissions@clarku.edu
Private; founded 1887
Freshman admissions: more selective; 2017-2018: 8,355 applied, 4,701 accepted. Neither SAT nor ACT required. SAT 25/75 percentile: 1180-1380. High school rank: 37% in top tenth, 75% in top quarter, 96% in top half
Early decision deadline: 11/1, notification date: 12/15
Early action deadline: 11/1, notification date: 12/15
Application deadline (fall): 1/15
Undergraduate student body: 2,199 full time, 41 part time; 39% male, 61% female; 0% American Indian, 8% Asian, 4% black, 8% Hispanic, 2% multiracial, 0% Pacific Islander, 58% white, 14% international; 38% from in state; 67% live on campus; 0% of students in fraternities, 0% in sororities
Most popular majors: 28% Social Sciences, 16% Psychology, 11% Biological and Biomedical Sciences, 6% Business, Management, Marketing, and Related Support Services, 6% Visual and Performing Arts
Expenses: 2018-2019: $45,730; room/board: $9,170
Financial aid: (508) 793-7478; 56% of undergrads determined to have financial need; average aid package $32,098

College of Our Lady of the Elms

Chicopee MA
(800) 255-3567
U.S. News ranking: Reg. U. (N), No. 99
Website: www.elms.edu
Admissions email: admissions@elms.edu
Private; founded 1928
Affiliation: Roman Catholic
Freshman admissions: less selective; 2017-2018: 868 applied, 690 accepted. Either SAT or ACT required. SAT 25/75 percentile: 930-1130. High school rank: N/A
Early decision deadline: N/A, notification date: N/A
Early action deadline: N/A, notification date: N/A
Application deadline (fall): rolling
Undergraduate student body: 973 full time, 201 part time; 26% male, 74% female; 0% American Indian, 2% Asian, 9% black, 14% Hispanic, 0% multiracial, 0% Pacific Islander, 56% white, 1% international; 77% from in state; 32% live on campus; 0% of students in fraternities, 0% in sororities
Most popular majors: 42% Health Professions and Related Programs, 12% Business, Management, Marketing, and Related Support Services, 12% Public Administration and Social Service Professions, 8% Education, 5% Psychology
Expenses: 2018-2019: $35,788; room/board: $13,106
Financial aid: (413) 265-2303; 90% of undergrads determined to have financial need; average aid package $22,746

College of the Holy Cross

Worcester MA
(508) 793-2443
U.S. News ranking: Nat. Lib. Arts, No. 35
Website: www.holycross.edu
Admissions email: admissions@holycross.edu
Private; founded 1843
Affiliation: Roman Catholic
Freshman admissions: more selective; 2017-2018: 6,622 applied, 2,622 accepted. Neither SAT nor ACT required. SAT 25/75 percentile: 1270-1410. High school rank: 57% in top tenth, 90% in top quarter, 100% in top half
Early decision deadline: 12/15, notification date: N/A
Early action deadline: N/A, notification date: N/A
Application deadline (fall): 1/15
Undergraduate student body: 3,020 full time, 31 part time; 48% male, 52% female; 0% American Indian, 5% Asian, 4% black, 10% Hispanic, 3% multiracial, 0% Pacific Islander, 70% white, 3% international; 41% from in state; 91% live on campus; N/A of students in fraternities, N/A in sororities
Most popular majors: 32% Social Sciences, 13% Psychology, 9% Mathematics and Statistics, 8% English Language and Literature/ Letters, 8% Foreign Languages, Literatures, and Linguistics
Expenses: 2018-2019: $52,770; room/board: $14,520
Financial aid: (508) 793-2265; 53% of undergrads determined to have financial need; average aid package $40,304

Curry College

Milton MA
(800) 669-0686
U.S. News ranking: Reg. U. (N), second tier
Website: www.curry.edu
Admissions email: adm@curry.edu
Private; founded 1879
Freshman admissions: less selective; 2017-2018: 6,031 applied, 5,431 accepted. Neither SAT nor ACT required. SAT 25/75 percentile: 930-1100. High school rank: 3% in top tenth, 16% in top quarter, 47% in top half
Early decision deadline: N/A, notification date: N/A
Early action deadline: 12/1, notification date: 12/15
Application deadline (fall): rolling
Undergraduate student body: 2,059 full time, 506 part time; 40% male, 60% female; 0% American Indian, 3% Asian, 11% black, 7% Hispanic, 2% multiracial, 0% Pacific Islander, 67% white, 2% international; 75% from in state; 58% live on campus; 0% of students in fraternities, 0% in sororities
Most popular majors: 38% Health Professions and Related Programs, 16% Homeland Security, Law Enforcement, Firefighting and Related Protective Services, 12% Business, Management, Marketing, and Related Support Services, 10% Communication, Journalism, and Related Programs, 9% Psychology
Expenses: 2018-2019: $39,720; room/board: $15,885
Financial aid: (617) 333-2354; 77% of undergrads determined to have financial need; average aid package $28,668

Dean College

Franklin MA
(508) 541-1508
U.S. News ranking: Reg. Coll. (N), No. 23
Website: www.dean.edu
Admissions email: admissions@dean.edu
Private; founded 1865
Freshman admissions: less selective; 2017-2018: 6,045 applied, 4,000 accepted. Neither SAT nor ACT required. SAT 25/75 percentile: 880-1080. High school rank: N/A
Early decision deadline: N/A, notification date: N/A
Early action deadline: 12/1, notification date: 1/15
Application deadline (fall): rolling
Undergraduate student body: 1,101 full time, 200 part time; 46% male, 54% female; 1% American

Indian, 2% Asian, 14% black, 8% Hispanic, 4% multiracial, 0% Pacific Islander, 54% white, 5% international; 43% from in state; 88% live on campus; 0% of students in fraternities, 0% in sororities
Most popular majors: 28% Dance, General, 25% Business, Management, Marketing, and Related Support Services, Other, 15% Arts, Entertainment,and Media Management, General, 11% Theatre/Theatre Arts Management, 9% Psychology, General
Expenses: 2018-2019: $39,434; room/board: $16,836
Financial aid: (508) 541-1518; 77% of undergrads determined to have financial need; average aid package $27,979

Eastern Nazarene College

Quincy MA
(617) 745-3711
U.S. News ranking: Reg. U. (N), second tier
Website: www.enc.edu
Admissions email: admissions@enc.edu
Private; founded 1918
Affiliation: Church of the Nazarene
Freshman admissions: selective; 2017-2018: 1,157 applied, 784 accepted. Either SAT or ACT required. SAT 25/75 percentile: 940-1160. High school rank: N/A
Early decision deadline: N/A, notification date: N/A
Early action deadline: N/A, notification date: N/A
Application deadline (fall): rolling
Undergraduate student body: 571 full time, 123 part time; 43% male, 57% female; 0% American Indian, 2% Asian, 21% black, 13% Hispanic, 4% multiracial, 0% Pacific Islander, 54% white, 4% international
Most popular majors: 35% Elementary Education and Teaching, 25% Business Administration and Management, General, 6% Psychology, General, 4% Biology/Biological Sciences, General, 4% Electrical, Electronic and Communications Engineering Technology/Technician
Expenses: 2018-2019: $25,598; room/board: $9,624
Financial aid: (617) 745-3712; 82% of undergrads determined to have financial need

Emerson College

Boston MA
(617) 824-8600
U.S. News ranking: Reg. U. (N), No. 6
Website: www.emerson.edu
Admissions email: admission@emerson.edu
Private; founded 1880
Freshman admissions: more selective; 2017-2018: 10,360 applied, 4,772 accepted. Neither SAT nor ACT required. SAT 25/75 percentile: 1200-1360. High school rank: 28% in top tenth, 71% in top quarter, 95% in top half
Early decision deadline: N/A, notification date: N/A
Early action deadline: 11/1, notification date: 12/15
Application deadline (fall): 1/15
Undergraduate student body: 3,748 full time, 65 part time; 41% male, 59% female; 0% American Indian, 5% Asian, 3% black, 12% Hispanic, 4% multiracial, 0% Pacific Islander, 65% white, 9% international; 21% from in state; 52% live on campus; 2% of students in fraternities, 3% in sororities
Most popular majors: 29% Cinematography and Film/ Video Production, 15% Radio and Television, 14% Creative Writing, 11% Marketing/Marketing Management, General, 9% Journalism
Expenses: 2018-2019: $46,852; room/board: $17,690
Financial aid: (617) 824-8655; 55% of undergrads determined to have financial need; average aid package $22,432

Emmanuel College

Boston MA
(617) 735-9715
U.S. News ranking: Nat. Lib. Arts, second tier
Website: www.emmanuel.edu
Admissions email: enroll@emmanuel.edu
Private; founded 1919
Affiliation: Roman Catholic
Freshman admissions: selective; 2017-2018: 5,965 applied, 4,354 accepted. Neither SAT nor ACT required. SAT 25/75 percentile: 1090-1250. High school rank: 13% in top tenth, 24% in top quarter, 76% in top half
Early decision deadline: N/A, notification date: N/A
Early action deadline: 11/1, notification date: 12/15
Application deadline (fall): 2/15
Undergraduate student body: 1,804 full time, 143 part time; 27% male, 73% female; 0% American Indian, 4% Asian, 5% black, 10% Hispanic, 4% multiracial, 0% Pacific Islander, 71% white, 1% international; 58% from in state; 68% live on campus; N/A of students in fraternities, N/A in sororities
Most popular majors: 17% Biological and Biomedical Sciences, 14% Psychology, 12% Business, Management, Marketing, and Related Support Services, 8% Communication, Journalism, and Related Programs, 8% Education
Expenses: 2018-2019: $39,804; room/board: $14,994
Financial aid: (617) 735-9938; 80% of undergrads determined to have financial need; average aid package $29,174

Endicott College

Beverly MA
(978) 921-1000
U.S. News ranking: Reg. U. (N), No. 25
Website: www.endicott.edu
Admissions email: admission@endicott.edu
Private; founded 1939
Freshman admissions: selective; 2017-2018: 3,623 applied, 2,949 accepted. Neither SAT nor ACT required. SAT 25/75 percentile: 1050-1210. High school rank: 16% in top tenth, 44% in top quarter, 77% in top half
Early decision deadline: N/A, notification date: N/A
Early action deadline: N/A, notification date: N/A
Application deadline (fall): 2/15
Undergraduate student body: 3,075 full time, 406 part time; 39% male, 61% female; 0% American Indian, 1% Asian, 2% black, 4% Hispanic, 2% multiracial, 0% Pacific Islander, 83% white, 2% international; 49% from in state; 91% live on campus; N/A of students in fraternities, N/A in sororities
Most popular majors: 13% Registered Nursing/Registered Nurse, 11% Business Administration and Management, General, 7% Hospitality Administration/Management, General, 6% Psychology, General, 6% Sport and Fitness Administration/Management
Expenses: 2018-2019: $33,050; room/board: $15,276
Financial aid: (978) 232-2060; 66% of undergrads determined to have financial need; average aid package $20,831

Fisher College

Boston MA
(617) 236-8818
U.S. News ranking: Reg. Coll. (N), No. 21
Website: www.fisher.edu
Admissions email: admissions@fisher.edu
Private; founded 1903
Freshman admissions: least selective; 2017-2018: 2,792 applied, 1,838 accepted. Neither SAT nor ACT required. SAT 25/75 percentile: 800-1040. High school rank: N/A
Early decision deadline: N/A, notification date: N/A
Early action deadline: N/A, notification date: N/A
Application deadline (fall): rolling
Undergraduate student body: 748 full time, 1,134 part time; 27% male, 73% female; 0% American Indian, 1% Asian, 11% black, 10% Hispanic, 2% multiracial, 0% Pacific Islander, 28% white, 9% international; 79% from in state; 22% live on campus; 0% of students in fraternities, 0% in sororities
Most popular majors: 21% Public Administration and Social Service Professions, 16% Business, Management, Marketing, and Related Support Services, 12% Homeland Security, Law Enforcement, Firefighting and Related Protective Services, 9% Health Professions and Related Programs, 8% Communication, Journalism, and Related Programs
Expenses: 2018-2019: $31,384; room/board: $15,926
Financial aid: (617) 236-8821; 92% of undergrads determined to have financial need; average aid package $21,050

Fitchburg State University

Fitchburg MA
(978) 665-3144
U.S. News ranking: Reg. U. (N), No. 137
Website: www.fitchburgstate.edu
Admissions email: admissions@fitchburgstate.edu
Public; founded 1894
Freshman admissions: selective; 2017-2018: 3,608 applied, 2,888 accepted. Neither SAT nor ACT required. SAT 25/75 percentile: 970-1140. High school rank: N/A
Early decision deadline: N/A, notification date: N/A
Early action deadline: N/A, notification date: N/A
Application deadline (fall): rolling
Undergraduate student body: 3,386 full time, 731 part time; 47% male, 53% female; 0% American Indian, 3% Asian, 10% black, 13% Hispanic, 3% multiracial, 0% Pacific Islander, 70% white, 0% international; 92% from in state; 42% live on campus; 1% of students in fraternities, 3% in sororities
Most popular majors: 15% Visual and Performing Arts, 13% Biological and Biomedical Sciences, 13% Business, Management, Marketing, and Related Support Services, 10% Health Professions and Related Programs, 7% Multi/ Interdisciplinary Studies
Expenses: 2018-2019: $10,410 in state, $16,490 out of state; room/board: $10,780
Financial aid: (978) 665-3302; 71% of undergrads determined to have financial need; average aid package $9,889

Framingham State University

Framingham MA
(508) 626-4500
U.S. News ranking: Reg. U. (N), No. 123
Website: www.framingham.edu
Admissions email: admissions@framingham.edu
Public; founded 1839
Freshman admissions: selective; 2017-2018: 6,039 applied, 4,113 accepted. Either SAT or ACT required. SAT 25/75 percentile: 950-1130. High school rank: 6% in top tenth, 21% in top quarter, 58% in top half
Early decision deadline: N/A, notification date: N/A
Early action deadline: 11/15, notification date: 12/15
Application deadline (fall): rolling
Undergraduate student body: 3,558 full time, 568 part time; 41% male, 59% female; 0% American Indian, 3% Asian, 11% black, 14% Hispanic, 4% multiracial, 0% Pacific Islander, 65% white, 1% international; 94% from in state; 46% live on campus; N/A of students in fraternities, N/A in sororities
Most popular majors: 19% Business, Management, Marketing, and Related Support Services, 16% Social Sciences, 14% Family and Consumer Sciences/Human Sciences, 9% Psychology, 6% Education
Expenses: 2017-2018: $9,920 in state, $16,000 out of state; room/board: $11,820
Financial aid: N/A

Franklin W. Olin College of Engineering

Needham MA
(781) 292-2222
U.S. News ranking: Engineering, unranked
Website: www.olin.edu/
Admissions email: info@olin.edu
Private; founded 1997
Freshman admissions: more selective; 2017-2018: 1,062 applied, 142 accepted. Either SAT or ACT required. SAT 25/75 percentile: 1450-1570. High school rank: N/A
Early decision deadline: N/A, notification date: N/A
Early action deadline: N/A, notification date: N/A
Application deadline (fall): 1/1
Undergraduate student body: 351 full time, 29 part time; 52% male, 48% female; 0% American Indian, 12% Asian, 3% black, 9% Hispanic, 8% multiracial, 0% Pacific Islander, 53% white, 8% international; 12% from in state; 100% live on campus; 0% of students in fraternities, 0% in sororities
Most popular majors: 54% Engineering, General, 29% Electrical and Electronics Engineering, 17% Mechanical Engineering
Expenses: 2018-2019: $51,080; room/board: $16,300
Financial aid: (781) 292-2215; 47% of undergrads determined to have financial need; average aid package $47,140

Gordon College

Wenham MA
(866) 464-6736
U.S. News ranking: Nat. Lib. Arts, No. 162
Website: www.gordon.edu
Admissions email: admissions@gordon.edu
Private; founded 1889
Affiliation: Other
Freshman admissions: selective; 2017-2018: 2,924 applied, 2,599 accepted. Either SAT or ACT required. SAT 25/75 percentile: 1050-1290. High school rank: 28% in top tenth, 53% in top quarter, 82% in top half
Early decision deadline: N/A, notification date: N/A
Early action deadline: 12/1, notification date: 12/15
Application deadline (fall): 8/1
Undergraduate student body: 1,528 full time, 63 part time; 37% male, 63% female; 0% American Indian, 5% Asian, 6% black, 8% Hispanic, 3% multiracial, 0% Pacific Islander, 68% white, 9% international; 35% from in state; 88% live on campus; N/A of students in fraternities, N/A in sororities

More @ usnews.com/bestcolleges

Most popular majors: 8% Psychology, General, 7% Business Administration and Management, General, 5% Biology/Biological Sciences, General, 5% English Language and Literature, General, 4% Speech Communication and Rhetoric
Expenses: 2018-2019: $37,400; room/board: $11,070
Financial aid: (800) 343-1379; 67% of undergrads determined to have financial need; average aid package $26,133

Hampshire College[1]
Amherst MA
(413) 549-4600
U.S. News ranking: Nat. Lib. Arts, unranked
Website: www.hampshire.edu
Admissions email: admissions@hampshire.edu
Private; founded 1965
Application deadline (fall): N/A
Undergraduate student body: N/A full time, N/A part time
Expenses: 2017-2018: $51,608; room/board: $13,606
Financial aid: (413) 559-5739

Harvard University
Cambridge MA
(617) 495-1551
U.S. News ranking: Nat. U., No. 2
Website: www.harvard.edu/
Admissions email: college@fas.harvard.edu
Private; founded 1636
Freshman admissions: most selective; 2017-2018: 39,506 applied, 2,037 accepted. Either SAT or ACT required. SAT 25/75 percentile: 1460-1590. High school rank: 95% in top tenth, 99% in top quarter, 100% in top half
Early decision deadline: N/A, notification date: N/A
Early action deadline: 11/1, notification date: 12/15
Application deadline (fall): 1/1
Undergraduate student body: 6,764 full time, 2 part time; 52% male, 48% female; 0% American Indian, 21% Asian, 8% black, 12% Hispanic, 7% multiracial, 0% Pacific Islander, 40% white, 11% international; 16% from in state; 98% live on campus; N/A of students in fraternities, N/A in sororities
Most popular majors: 27% Social Sciences, General, 14% Biology/Biological Sciences, General, 10% Mathematics, General, 9% History, General, 8% Physical Sciences
Expenses: 2018-2019: $50,420; room/board: $17,160
Financial aid: (617) 495-1581; 55% of undergrads determined to have financial need; average aid package $56,654

Lasell College
Newton MA
(617) 243-2225
U.S. News ranking: Reg. U. (N), No. 126
Website: www.lasell.edu
Admissions email: info@lasell.edu
Private; founded 1851
Freshman admissions: less selective; 2017-2018: 3,466 applied, 2,824 accepted. Neither SAT nor ACT required. SAT 25/75 percentile: 980-1160. High school rank: 2% in top tenth, 17% in top quarter, 54% in top half
Early decision deadline: N/A, notification date: N/A
Early action deadline: 11/15, notification date: 12/1
Application deadline (fall): rolling
Undergraduate student body: 1,669 full time, 62 part time; 36% male, 64% female; 0% American Indian, 2% Asian, 7% black, 9% Hispanic, 2% multiracial, 0% Pacific Islander, 69% white, 7% international; 58% from in state; 74% live on campus; 0% of students in fraternities, 0% in sororities
Most popular majors: 12% Speech Communication and Rhetoric, 9% Fashion Merchandising, 8% Communication and Media Studies, Other, 7% Sport and Fitness Administration/Management, 6% Psychology, General
Expenses: 2018-2019: $36,000; room/board: $15,400
Financial aid: (617) 243-2227; 78% of undergrads determined to have financial need; average aid package $28,275

Lesley University
Cambridge MA
(617) 349-8800
U.S. News ranking: Nat. U., No. 183
Website: www.lesley.edu
Admissions email: admissions@lesley.edu
Private; founded 1909
Freshman admissions: selective; 2017-2018: 3,165 applied, 2,298 accepted. Either SAT or ACT required. SAT 25/75 percentile: 1020-1210. High school rank: N/A
Early decision deadline: N/A, notification date: N/A
Early action deadline: 12/1, notification date: 12/23
Application deadline (fall): 7/15
Undergraduate student body: 1,653 full time, 443 part time; 23% male, 77% female; 0% American Indian, 5% Asian, 8% black, 13% Hispanic, 4% multiracial, 0% Pacific Islander, 63% white, 3% international; 67% from in state; 43% live on campus; N/A of students in fraternities, N/A in sororities
Most popular majors: 24% Psychology, 19% Visual and Performing Arts, 14% Liberal Arts and Sciences, General Studies and Humanities, 9% Business, Management, Marketing, and Related Support Services, 9% Health Professions and Related Programs
Expenses: 2018-2019: $27,850; room/board: $16,200
Financial aid: (617) 349-8760; 70% of undergrads determined to have financial need; average aid package $17,580

Massachusetts College of Art and Design
Boston MA
(617) 879-7222
U.S. News ranking: Arts, unranked
Website: www.massart.edu
Admissions email: admissions@massart.edu
Public; founded 1873
Freshman admissions: least selective; 2017-2018: 2,386 applied, 1,686 accepted. Neither SAT nor ACT required. SAT 25/75 percentile: N/A. High school rank: N/A
Early decision deadline: N/A, notification date: N/A
Early action deadline: 12/1, notification date: 1/5
Application deadline (fall): 2/1
Undergraduate student body: 1,662 full time, 269 part time; 30% male, 70% female; 0% American Indian, 8% Asian, 5% black, 11% Hispanic, 2% multiracial, 0% Pacific Islander, 62% white, 4% international; 67% from in state; 41% live on campus; N/A of students in fraternities, N/A in sororities
Most popular majors: 16% Illustration, 11% Graphic Design, 10% Film/Video and Photographic Arts, Other, 8% Fashion/Apparel Design, 8% Photography
Expenses: 2018-2019: $13,200 in state, $36,400 out of state; room/board: $13,500
Financial aid: (617) 879-7849; 91% of undergrads determined to have financial need; average aid package $10,436

Massachusetts College of Liberal Arts
North Adams MA
(413) 662-5410
U.S. News ranking: Nat. Lib. Arts, No. 162
Website: www.mcla.edu
Admissions email: admissions@mcla.edu
Public; founded 1894
Freshman admissions: selective; 2017-2018: 1,947 applied, 1,492 accepted. Either SAT or ACT required. SAT 25/75 percentile: 970-1190. High school rank: 10% in top tenth, 35% in top quarter, 73% in top half
Early decision deadline: N/A, notification date: N/A
Early action deadline: 12/1, notification date: 12/15
Application deadline (fall): rolling
Undergraduate student body: 1,201 full time, 206 part time; 38% male, 62% female; 0% American Indian, 2% Asian, 9% black, 8% Hispanic, 3% multiracial, 0% Pacific Islander, 73% white, 1% international; 76% from in state; 58% live on campus; N/A of students in fraternities, N/A in sororities
Most popular majors: 14% Business, Management, Marketing, and Related Support Services, 14% Multi/Interdisciplinary Studies, 12% English Language and Literature/Letters, 12% Psychology, 12% Visual and Performing Arts
Expenses: 2018-2019: $10,075 in state, $19,020 out of state; room/board: N/A
Financial aid: (413) 662-5219; 79% of undergrads determined to have financial need; average aid package $15,345

Massachusetts Institute of Technology
Cambridge MA
(617) 253-3400
U.S. News ranking: Nat. U., No. 3
Website: web.mit.edu/
Admissions email: admissions@mit.edu
Private; founded 1861
Freshman admissions: most selective; 2017-2018: 20,247 applied, 1,452 accepted. Either SAT or ACT required. SAT 25/75 percentile: 1490-1570. High school rank: 98% in top tenth, 100% in top quarter, 100% in top half
Early decision deadline: N/A, notification date: N/A
Early action deadline: 11/1, notification date: 12/20
Application deadline (fall): 1/1
Undergraduate student body: 4,510 full time, 37 part time; 54% male, 46% female; 0% American Indian, 27% Asian, 6% black, 14% Hispanic, 7% multiracial, 0% Pacific Islander, 34% white, 10% international; 10% from in state; 89% live on campus; 48% of students in fraternities, 30% in sororities
Most popular majors: 36% Engineering, 29% Computer and Information Sciences and Support Services, 9% Mathematics and Statistics, 7% Biological and Biomedical Sciences, 7% Physical Sciences
Expenses: 2018-2019: $51,832; room/board: $15,510
Financial aid: (617) 258-8600; 61% of undergrads determined to have financial need; average aid package $50,080

Massachusetts Maritime Academy
Buzzards Bay MA
(800) 544-3411
U.S. News ranking: Reg. U. (N), No. 19
Website: www.maritime.edu
Admissions email: admissions@maritime.edu
Public; founded 1891
Freshman admissions: selective; 2017-2018: 838 applied, 697 accepted. Either SAT or ACT required. SAT 25/75 percentile: 1040-1200. High school rank: N/A
Early decision deadline: N/A, notification date: N/A
Early action deadline: 11/1, notification date: 12/31
Application deadline (fall): rolling
Undergraduate student body: 1,607 full time, 81 part time; 87% male, 13% female; 0% American Indian, 1% Asian, 1% black, 3% Hispanic, 3% multiracial, 0% Pacific Islander, 88% white, 1% international; 80% from in state; 97% live on campus; 0% of students in fraternities, 0% in sororities
Most popular majors: 55% Engineering, 21% Transportation and Materials Moving, 10% Business, Management, Marketing, and Related Support Services, 9% Natural Resources and Conservation
Expenses: 2017-2018: $8,381 in state, $25,807 out of state; room/board: $12,306
Financial aid: (508) 830-5087; 59% of undergrads determined to have financial need; average aid package $12,762

Merrimack College
North Andover MA
(978) 837-5100
U.S. News ranking: Reg. U. (N), No. 50
Website: www.merrimack.edu
Admissions email: Admission@Merrimack.edu
Private; founded 1947
Affiliation: Roman Catholic
Freshman admissions: selective; 2017-2018: 8,656 applied, 7,058 accepted. Neither SAT nor ACT required. SAT 25/75 percentile: 1020-1190. High school rank: 6% in top tenth, 24% in top quarter, 54% in top half
Early decision deadline: 11/15, notification date: 12/15
Early action deadline: 1/15, notification date: 2/15
Application deadline (fall): 2/15
Undergraduate student body: 3,346 full time, 169 part time; 49% male, 51% female; 0% American Indian, 1% Asian, 4% black, 7% Hispanic, 1% multiracial, 0% Pacific Islander, 77% white, 2% international; 71% from in state; 69% live on campus; N/A of students in fraternities, N/A in sororities
Most popular majors: 29% Business, Management, Marketing, and Related Support Services, 13% Family and Consumer Sciences/Human Sciences, 9% Health Professions and Related Programs, 8% Engineering, 5% Homeland Security, Law Enforcement, Firefighting and Related Protective Services
Expenses: 2018-2019: $41,760; room/board: $15,845
Financial aid: (978) 837-5186; 71% of undergrads determined to have financial need; average aid package $23,808

Montserrat College of Art[1]
Beverly MA
(978) 922-8222
U.S. News ranking: Arts, unranked
Website: www.montserrat.edu
Admissions email: admissions@montserrrat.edu
Private; founded 1970
Application deadline (fall): N/A
Undergraduate student body: N/A full time, N/A part time
Expenses: N/A
Financial aid: (978) 921-4242

Mount Holyoke College

South Hadley MA
(413) 538-2023
U.S. News ranking: Nat. Lib. Arts, No. 30
Website: www.mtholyoke.edu
Admissions email: admission@mtholyoke.edu
Private; founded 1837
Freshman admissions: more selective; 2017-2018: 3,446 applied, 1,752 accepted. Neither SAT nor ACT required. SAT 25/75 percentile: 1270-1463. High school rank: 54% in top tenth, 91% in top quarter, 98% in top half
Early decision deadline: 11/15, notification date: 1/1
Early action deadline: N/A, notification date: N/A
Application deadline (fall): 1/15
Undergraduate student body: 2,161 full time, 49 part time; 0% male, 100% female; 0% American Indian, 10% Asian, 5% black, 7% Hispanic, 4% multiracial, 0% Pacific Islander, 45% white, 27% international; 47% from in state; 95% live on campus; 0% of students in fraternities, 0% in sororities
Most popular majors: 10% Biology/Biological Sciences, General, 10% Psychology, General, 9% Economics, General, 8% English Language and Literature, General, 8% International Relations and Affairs
Expenses: 2018-2019: $49,998; room/board: $14,660
Financial aid: (413) 538-2291; 65% of undergrads determined to have financial need; average aid package $40,769

National Graduate School of Quality Management[1]

Falmouth MA
(800) 838-2580
U.S. News ranking: Business, unranked
Website: www.ngs.edu
Admissions email: N/A
Private; founded 1993
Application deadline (fall): N/A
Undergraduate student body: N/A full time, N/A part time
Expenses: N/A
Financial aid: N/A

Newbury College

Brookline MA
(617) 730-7007
U.S. News ranking: Reg. Coll. (N), No. 31
Website: www.newbury.edu/
Admissions email: admissions@newbury.edu
Private; founded 1962
Freshman admissions: less selective; 2017-2018: 2,821 applied, 2,122 accepted. Neither SAT nor ACT required. SAT 25/75 percentile: 870-1110. High school rank: N/A
Early decision deadline: N/A, notification date: N/A
Early action deadline: N/A, notification date: N/A
Application deadline (fall): 8/1
Undergraduate student body: 545 full time, 75 part time; 44% male, 56% female; 0% American Indian, 6% Asian, 34% black, 17% Hispanic, 0% multiracial, 0% Pacific Islander, 39% white, 4% international; N/A from in state; N/A live on campus; 0% of students in fraternities, 0% in sororities
Most popular majors: 14% Psychology, General, 10% Sport and Fitness Administration/Management, 9% Business Administration and Management, General, 9% Corrections and Criminal Justice, Other, 7% Graphic Design
Expenses: 2018-2019: $35,540; room/board: $14,900
Financial aid: (617) 730-7102; 90% of undergrads determined to have financial need; average aid package $28,211

New England College of Business and Finance[1]

Boston MA
(617) 951-2350
U.S. News ranking: Business, unranked
Website: www.necb.edu/
Admissions email: N/A
For-profit; founded 1909
Application deadline (fall): N/A
Undergraduate student body: N/A full time, N/A part time
Expenses: N/A
Financial aid: N/A

New England Conservatory of Music

Boston MA
(617) 585-1101
U.S. News ranking: Arts, unranked
Website: www.newenglandconservatory.edu
Admissions email: admission@newenglandconservatory.edu
Private; founded 1867
Freshman admissions: least selective; 2017-2018: N/A applied, N/A accepted. Neither SAT nor ACT required. SAT 25/75 percentile: N/A. High school rank: N/A
Early decision deadline: N/A, notification date: N/A
Early action deadline: N/A, notification date: N/A
Application deadline (fall): 12/1
Undergraduate student body: 407 full time, 29 part time; 53% male, 47% female; N/A American Indian, N/A Asian, N/A black, N/A Hispanic, N/A multiracial, N/A Pacific Islander, N/A white, N/A international
Most popular majors: Information not available
Expenses: 2018-2019: $48,750; room/board: $15,900
Financial aid: (617) 585-1110; 41% of undergrads determined to have financial need; average aid package $28,249

New England Institute of Art[1]

Brookline MA
(800) 903-4425
U.S. News ranking: Arts, unranked
Website: www.artinstitutes.edu/boston/
Admissions email: N/A
For-profit
Application deadline (fall): N/A
Undergraduate student body: N/A full time, N/A part time
Expenses: N/A
Financial aid: N/A

Nichols College

Dudley MA
(800) 470-3379
U.S. News ranking: Business, unranked
Website: www.nichols.edu/
Admissions email: admissions@nichols.edu
Private; founded 1815
Freshman admissions: less selective; 2017-2018: 2,161 applied, 1,999 accepted. Neither SAT nor ACT required. SAT 25/75 percentile: 916-1110. High school rank: 3% in top tenth, 17% in top quarter, 47% in top half
Early decision deadline: N/A, notification date: N/A
Early action deadline: 12/1, notification date: N/A
Application deadline (fall): rolling
Undergraduate student body: 1,211 full time, 90 part time; 63% male, 37% female; 0% American Indian, 1% Asian, 8% black, 9% Hispanic, 4% multiracial, 0% Pacific Islander, 77% white, 1% international; 60% from in state; 77% live on campus; N/A of students in fraternities, N/A in sororities
Most popular majors: 24% Business/Commerce, General, 13% Criminal Justice/Law Enforcement Administration, 12% Sport and Fitness Administration/Management, 10% Accounting, 8% Marketing/Marketing Management, General
Expenses: 2018-2019: $34,800; room/board: $13,950
Financial aid: (508) 213-2118; 75% of undergrads determined to have financial need; average aid package $30,653

Northeastern University

Boston MA
(617) 373-2200
U.S. News ranking: Nat. U., No. 44
Website: www.northeastern.edu/
Admissions email: admissions@northeastern.edu
Private; founded 1898
Freshman admissions: most selective; 2017-2018: 54,209 applied, 14,876 accepted. Either SAT or ACT required. ACT 25/75 percentile: 32-34. High school rank: 75% in top tenth, 93% in top quarter, 99% in top half
Early decision deadline: 11/1, notification date: 12/15
Early action deadline: 11/1, notification date: 2/1
Application deadline (fall): 1/1
Undergraduate student body: 13,786 full time, 39 part time; 49% male, 51% female; 0% American Indian, 13% Asian, 4% black, 8% Hispanic, 4% multiracial, 0% Pacific Islander, 46% white, 19% international; 27% from in state; 49% live on campus; 10% of students in fraternities, 16% in sororities
Most popular majors: 25% Business, Management, Marketing, and Related Support Services, 15% Engineering, 12% Health Professions and Related Programs, 12% Social Sciences, 8% Biological and Biomedical Sciences
Expenses: 2018-2019: $51,387; room/board: $16,880
Financial aid: (617) 373-3190; 34% of undergrads determined to have financial need; average aid package $34,461

Pine Manor College

Chestnut Hill MA
(617) 731-7111
U.S. News ranking: Nat. Lib. Arts, second tier
Website: www.pmc.edu
Admissions email: admission@pmc.edu
Private; founded 1911
Freshman admissions: least selective; 2017-2018: 679 applied, 95 accepted. Neither SAT nor ACT required. SAT 25/75 percentile: 740-915. High school rank: N/A
Early decision deadline: N/A, notification date: N/A
Early action deadline: 12/1, notification date: 12/31
Application deadline (fall): rolling
Undergraduate student body: 417 full time, 2 part time; 52% male, 48% female; 2% American Indian, 3% Asian, 40% black, 24% Hispanic, 9% multiracial, 0% Pacific Islander, 9% white, 1% international
Most popular majors: 27% Biology/Biological Sciences, General, 20% Psychology, General, 15% Business Administration and Management, General, 15% Early Childhood Education and Teaching, 12% Social Sciences, General
Expenses: 2018-2019: $31,580; room/board: $13,830
Financial aid: (617) 731-7628; 92% of undergrads determined to have financial need; average aid package $28,353

Salem State University

Salem MA
(978) 542-6200
U.S. News ranking: Reg. U. (N), second tier
Website: www.salemstate.edu
Admissions email: admissions@salemstate.edu
Public; founded 1854
Freshman admissions: selective; 2017-2018: 6,185 applied, 5,066 accepted. Neither SAT nor ACT required. SAT 25/75 percentile: 980-1150. High school rank: N/A
Early decision deadline: N/A, notification date: N/A
Early action deadline: 11/15, notification date: 1/1
Application deadline (fall): rolling
Undergraduate student body: 5,792 full time, 1,318 part time; 38% male, 62% female; 0% American Indian, 3% Asian, 10% black, 16% Hispanic, 3% multiracial, 0% Pacific Islander, 63% white, 3% international; 97% from in state; 33% live on campus; N/A of students in fraternities, N/A in sororities
Most popular majors: 22% Business, Management, Marketing, and Related Support Services, 12% Health Professions and Related Programs, 9% Education, 9% Psychology, 8% Homeland Security, Law Enforcement, Firefighting and Related Protective Services
Expenses: 2017-2018: $10,278 in state, $16,706 out of state; room/board: $13,000
Financial aid: N/A

Simmons College

Boston MA
(617) 521-2051
U.S. News ranking: Reg. U. (N), No. 11
Website: www.simmons.edu
Admissions email: ugadm@simmons.edu
Private; founded 1899
Freshman admissions: more selective; 2017-2018: 3,483 applied, 2,105 accepted. Either SAT or ACT required. SAT 25/75 percentile: 1130-1310. High school rank: 36% in top tenth, 70% in top quarter, 94% in top half
Early decision deadline: 11/1, notification date: 12/15
Early action deadline: N/A, notification date: N/A
Application deadline (fall): 2/1
Undergraduate student body: 1,55 full time, 210 part time; 1% male, 99% female; 0% American Indian, 10% Asian, 6% black, 6% Hispanic, 5% multiracial, 0% Pacific Islander, 65% white, 5% international; 60% from in state; 63% live on campus; 0% of students in fraternities, 0% in sororities
Most popular majors: 38% Health Professions and Related Program 9% Business, Management, Marketing, and Related Support Services, 9% Social Sciences, 6% Biological and Biomedical Sciences, 5% Parks, Recreation, Leisure, and Fitness Studies
Expenses: 2018-2019: $40,800 room/board: $15,200
Financial aid: (617) 521-2037; 76% of undergrads determined t have financial need; average aid package $31,887

Smith College

Northampton MA
(413) 585-2500
U.S. News ranking: Nat. Lib. Arts, No. 11
Website: www.smith.edu
Admissions email: admission@smith.edu
Private; founded 1871

eshman admissions: most ective; 2017-2018: 5,432 plied, 1,731 accepted. Neither AT nor ACT required. SAT 25/75 rcentile: 1290-1490. High hool rank: 72% in top tenth, % in top quarter, 100% in half
rly decision deadline: 11/15, tification date: 12/15
rly action deadline: N/A, tification date: N/A
plication deadline (fall): 1/15
dergraduate student body: 2,505 l time, 16 part time; 0% male, 0% female; 0% American dian, 11% Asian, 7% black, % Hispanic, 4% multiracial, Pacific Islander, 48% white, % international; 21% from in te; 95% live on campus; 0% students in fraternities, 0% in orities
st popular majors: 10% search and Experimental ychology, Other, 9% Economics, neral, 8% Political Science and vernment, General, 6% Biology/ ological Sciences, General, 4% glish Language and Literature, neral
penses: 2018-2019: $52,404; m/board: $17,520
ancial aid: (413) 585-2530; % of undergrads determined to ve financial need; average aid ckage $51,046

pringfield College

ringfield MA
13) 748-3136
S. News ranking: Reg. U. (N), . 28
bsite: springfield.edu/
missions email: admissions@ ringfieldcollege.edu
vate; founded 1885
shman admissions: selective; 17-2018: 3,770 applied, 535 accepted. Either SAT ACT required. SAT 25/75 centile: 1020-1220. High ool rank: 13% in top tenth, % in top quarter, 76% in half
ly decision deadline: 12/1, ification date: 2/1
ly action deadline: N/A, ification date: N/A
plication deadline (fall): 8/1
dergraduate student body: 2,188 time, 35 part time; 51% le, 49% female; 0% American ian, 2% Asian, 6% black, Hispanic, 2% multiracial, Pacific Islander, 76% white, international; 39% from in te; 87% live on campus; N/A students in fraternities, N/A in orities
st popular majors: 9% Physical erapy/Therapist, 8% Kinesiology d Exercise Science, 8% ysical Education Teaching and aching, 6% Sport and Fitness ministration/Management, 5% ychology, General
enses: 2018-2019: $37,445; m/board: $12,550
ancial aid: (413) 748-3108; % of undergrads determined to e financial need; average aid ckage $28,115

Stonehill College

Easton MA
(508) 565-1373
U.S. News ranking: Nat. Lib. Arts, No. 124
Website: www.stonehill.edu
Admissions email: admission@stonehill.edu
Private; founded 1948
Affiliation: Roman Catholic
Freshman admissions: selective; 2017-2018: 6,260 applied, 4,515 accepted. Neither SAT nor ACT required. SAT 25/75 percentile: 1080-1270. High school rank: 22% in top tenth, 51% in top quarter, 88% in top half
Early decision deadline: 12/1, notification date: 12/31
Early action deadline: 11/1, notification date: 12/31
Application deadline (fall): 1/15
Undergraduate student body: 2,482 full time, 16 part time; 41% male, 59% female; 0% American Indian, 2% Asian, 4% black, 4% Hispanic, 2% multiracial, 0% Pacific Islander, 85% white, 1% international; 62% from in state; 89% live on campus; 0% of students in fraternities, 0% in sororities
Most popular majors: 23% Business, Management, Marketing, and Related Support Services, 17% Social Sciences, 13% Biological and Biomedical Sciences, 11% Psychology, 7% Communication, Journalism, and Related Programs
Expenses: 2018-2019: $42,746; room/board: $16,000
Financial aid: (508) 565-1088; 66% of undergrads determined to have financial need; average aid package $30,891

Suffolk University

Boston MA
(617) 573-8460
U.S. News ranking: Nat. U., No. 177
Website: www.suffolk.edu
Admissions email: admission@suffolk.edu
Private; founded 1906
Freshman admissions: selective; 2017-2018: 8,237 applied, 6,867 accepted. Either SAT or ACT required. SAT 25/75 percentile: 1000-1180. High school rank: 12% in top tenth, 39% in top quarter, 69% in top half
Early decision deadline: N/A, notification date: N/A
Early action deadline: 11/15, notification date: 12/15
Application deadline (fall): 2/15
Undergraduate student body: 4,849 full time, 268 part time; 46% male, 54% female; 0% American Indian, 8% Asian, 5% black, 12% Hispanic, 2% multiracial, 0% Pacific Islander, 47% white, 22% international; 68% from in state; 25% live on campus; N/A of students in fraternities, N/A in sororities
Most popular majors: 45% Business, Management, Marketing, and Related Support Services, 14% Communication, Journalism, and Related Programs, 14% Social Sciences, 6% Psychology, 5% Biological and Biomedical Sciences
Expenses: 2018-2019: $38,566; room/board: $17,846
Financial aid: (617) 573-8470; 62% of undergrads determined to have financial need; average aid package $31,688

Tufts University

Medford MA
(617) 627-3170
U.S. News ranking: Nat. U., No. 27
Website: www.tufts.edu
Admissions email: undergraduate.admissions@tufts.edu
Private; founded 1852
Freshman admissions: most selective; 2017-2018: 21,101 applied, 3,127 accepted. Either SAT or ACT required. ACT 25/75 percentile: 31-34. High school rank: 80% in top tenth, 94% in top quarter, 100% in top half
Early decision deadline: 11/1, notification date: 12/15
Early action deadline: N/A, notification date: N/A
Application deadline (fall): 1/1
Undergraduate student body: 5,483 full time, 58 part time; 49% male, 51% female; 0% American Indian, 12% Asian, 4% black, 7% Hispanic, 5% multiracial, 0% Pacific Islander, 57% white, 10% international; 25% from in state; 63% live on campus; 10% of students in fraternities, 9% in sororities
Most popular majors: 28% Social Sciences, 9% Computer and Information Sciences and Support Services, 9% Engineering, 8% Biological and Biomedical Sciences, 8% Multi/Interdisciplinary Studies
Expenses: 2018-2019: $56,382; room/board: $14,560
Financial aid: (617) 627-2000; 38% of undergrads determined to have financial need; average aid package $45,107

University of Massachusetts–Amherst

Amherst MA
(413) 545-0222
U.S. News ranking: Nat. U., No. 70
Website: www.umass.edu
Admissions email: mail@admissions.umass.edu
Public; founded 1863
Freshman admissions: more selective; 2017-2018: 41,922 applied, 24,102 accepted. Either SAT or ACT required. SAT 25/75 percentile: 1180-1360. High school rank: 34% in top tenth, 73% in top quarter, 97% in top half
Early decision deadline: N/A, notification date: N/A
Early action deadline: 11/1, notification date: 12/31
Application deadline (fall): 1/15
Undergraduate student body: 21,577 full time, 1,811 part time; 50% male, 50% female; 0% American Indian, 10% Asian, 4% black, 6% Hispanic, 3% multiracial, 0% Pacific Islander, 64% white, 6% international; 82% from in state; 61% live on campus; 9% of students in fraternities, 9% in sororities
Most popular majors: 15% Business, Management, Marketing, and Related Support Services, 13% Social Sciences, 10% Biological and Biomedical Sciences, 9% Health Professions and Related Programs, 7% Psychology
Expenses: 2018-2019: $15,887 in state, $34,570 out of state; room/board: $13,202
Financial aid: (413) 545-0801; 57% of undergrads determined to have financial need; average aid package $17,717

University of Massachusetts–Boston

Boston MA
(617) 287-6100
U.S. News ranking: Nat. U., No. 191
Website: www.umb.edu
Admissions email: undergrad.admissions@umb.edu
Public; founded 1964
Freshman admissions: selective; 2017-2018: 10,507 applied, 7,896 accepted. Neither SAT nor ACT required. SAT 25/75 percentile: 1000-1200. High school rank: 15% in top tenth, 43% in top quarter, 80% in top half
Early decision deadline: N/A, notification date: N/A
Early action deadline: 11/1, notification date: 12/31
Application deadline (fall): 3/1
Undergraduate student body: 9,574 full time, 3,086 part time; 47% male, 53% female; 0% American Indian, 13% Asian, 17% black, 16% Hispanic, 3% multiracial, 0% Pacific Islander, 34% white, 12% international; 95% from in state; N/A live on campus; N/A of students in fraternities, N/A in sororities
Most popular majors: 17% Business, Management, Marketing, and Related Support Services, 14% Health Professions and Related Programs, 12% Psychology, 12% Social Sciences, 8% Biological and Biomedical Sciences
Expenses: 2018-2019: $14,167 in state, $33,966 out of state; room/board: $16,290
Financial aid: (617) 297-6300; 66% of undergrads determined to have financial need; average aid package $15,935

University of Massachusetts–Dartmouth

North Dartmouth MA
(508) 999-8605
U.S. News ranking: Nat. U., No. 215
Website: www.umassd.edu
Admissions email: admissions@umassd.edu
Public; founded 1895
Freshman admissions: selective; 2017-2018: 7,959 applied, 6,707 accepted. Either SAT or ACT required. SAT 25/75 percentile: 1000-1190. High school rank: N/A
Early decision deadline: N/A, notification date: N/A
Early action deadline: 11/11, notification date: 12/15
Application deadline (fall): rolling
Undergraduate student body: 5,790 full time, 973 part time; 51% male, 49% female; 0% American Indian, 4% Asian, 16% black, 10% Hispanic, 4% multiracial, 0% Pacific Islander, 61% white, 2% international; 93% from in state; 52% live on campus; 1% of students in fraternities, 1% in sororities
Most popular majors: 28% Business, Management, Marketing, and Related Support Services, 14% Health Professions and Related Programs, 13% Engineering, 10% Social Sciences, 8% Psychology
Expenses: 2018-2019: $13,921 in state, $29,141 out of state; room/board: $13,582
Financial aid: (508) 999-8643; 73% of undergrads determined to have financial need; average aid package $17,361

University of Massachusetts–Lowell

Lowell MA
(978) 934-3931
U.S. News ranking: Nat. U., No. 157
Website: www.uml.edu
Admissions email: admissions@uml.edu
Public; founded 1894
Freshman admissions: more selective; 2017-2018: 11,113 applied, 7,636 accepted. Neither SAT nor ACT required. SAT 25/75 percentile: 1130-1310. High school rank: 21% in top tenth, 52% in top quarter, 87% in top half
Early decision deadline: N/A, notification date: N/A
Early action deadline: 11/1, notification date: 12/10
Application deadline (fall): 2/1
Undergraduate student body: 10,495 full time, 3,518 part time; 62% male, 38% female; 0% American Indian, 10% Asian, 6% black, 11% Hispanic, 3% multiracial, 0% Pacific Islander, 62% white, 4% international; 91% from in state; 32% live on campus; N/A of students in fraternities, N/A in sororities
Most popular majors: 19% Business, Management, Marketing, and Related Support Services, 18% Engineering, 11% Computer and Information Sciences and Support Services, 11% Health Professions and Related Programs, 9% Homeland Security, Law Enforcement, Firefighting and Related Protective Services
Expenses: 2017-2018: $14,800 in state, $31,865 out of state; room/board: N/A
Financial aid: (978) 934-4220; 62% of undergrads determined to have financial need; average aid package $16,194

Wellesley College

Wellesley MA
(781) 283-2270
U.S. News ranking: Nat. Lib. Arts, No. 3
Website: www.wellesley.edu
Admissions email: admission@wellesley.edu
Private; founded 1870
Freshman admissions: most selective; 2017-2018: 5,666 applied, 1,251 accepted. Either SAT or ACT required. ACT 25/75 percentile: 30-33. High school rank: 81% in top tenth, 96% in top quarter, 99% in top half
Early decision deadline: 11/1, notification date: 12/15
Early action deadline: N/A, notification date: N/A
Application deadline (fall): 1/15
Undergraduate student body: 2,374 full time, 134 part time; 2% male, 98% female; 0% American Indian, 23% Asian, 6% black, 12% Hispanic, 6% multiracial, 0% Pacific Islander, 39% white, 13% international; 13% from in state; 98% live on campus; 0% of students in fraternities, 0% in sororities
Most popular majors: 24% Construction Trades, 15% Biological and Biomedical Sciences, 9% Area, Ethnic, Cultural, Gender, and Group Studies, 8% Foreign Languages, Literatures, and Linguistics, 8% Psychology
Expenses: 2018-2019: $53,732; room/board: $16,468
Financial aid: (781) 283-2360; 59% of undergrads determined to have financial need; average aid package $49,713

Wentworth Institute of Technology

Boston MA
(617) 989-4000
U.S. News ranking: Reg. U. (N), No. 62
Website: www.wit.edu
Admissions email: admissions@wit.edu
Private; founded 1904
Freshman admissions: selective; 2017-2018: 6,172 applied, 5,670 accepted. Either SAT or ACT required. SAT 25/75 percentile: 1080-1270. High school rank: 13% in top tenth, 41% in top quarter, 79% in top half
Early decision deadline: N/A, notification date: N/A
Early action deadline: N/A, notification date: N/A
Application deadline (fall): rolling
Undergraduate student body: 3,904 full time, 361 part time; 79% male, 21% female; 0% American Indian, 7% Asian, 4% black, 10% Hispanic, 2% multiracial, 0% Pacific Islander, 62% white, 8% international; 66% from in state; 49% live on campus; 0% of students in fraternities, 0% in sororities
Most popular majors: 31% Engineering, 22% Business, Management, Marketing, and Related Support Services, 13% Computer and Information Sciences and Support Services, 12% Architecture and Related Services, 12% Engineering Technologies and Engineering-Related Fields
Expenses: 2018-2019: $35,973; room/board: $14,190
Financial aid: (617) 989-4020; 71% of undergrads determined to have financial need; average aid package $20,181

Western New England University

Springfield MA
(413) 782-1321
U.S. News ranking: Reg. U. (N), No. 68
Website: www.wne.edu
Admissions email: learn@wne.edu
Private; founded 1919
Freshman admissions: selective; 2017-2018: 6,645 applied, 5,363 accepted. Neither SAT nor ACT required. SAT 25/75 percentile: 980-1180. High school rank: 14% in top tenth, 40% in top quarter, 76% in top half
Early decision deadline: N/A, notification date: N/A
Early action deadline: N/A, notification date: N/A
Application deadline (fall): rolling
Undergraduate student body: 2,613 full time, 123 part time; 63% male, 37% female; 0% American Indian, 3% Asian, 6% black, 9% Hispanic, 2% multiracial, 0% Pacific Islander, 74% white, 3% international; 51% from in state; 61% live on campus; N/A of students in fraternities, N/A in sororities
Most popular majors: 25% Engineering, 23% Business, Management, Marketing, and Related Support Services, 11% Health Professions and Related Programs, 6% Homeland Security, Law Enforcement, Firefighting and Related Protective Services, 6% Psychology
Expenses: 2018-2019: $36,804; room/board: $13,590
Financial aid: (413) 796-2080; 79% of undergrads determined to have financial need; average aid package $26,004

Westfield State University

Westfield MA
(413) 572-5218
U.S. News ranking: Reg. U. (N), No. 112
Website: www.westfield.ma.edu
Admissions email: admissions@westfield.ma.edu
Public; founded 1839
Freshman admissions: selective; 2017-2018: 4,381 applied, 3,735 accepted. Either SAT or ACT required. SAT 25/75 percentile: 970-1150. High school rank: 5% in top tenth, 20% in top quarter, 55% in top half
Early decision deadline: N/A, notification date: N/A
Early action deadline: N/A, notification date: N/A
Application deadline (fall): 4/1
Undergraduate student body: 4,791 full time, 761 part time; 47% male, 53% female; 0% American Indian, 2% Asian, 5% black, 10% Hispanic, 5% multiracial, 0% Pacific Islander, 75% white, 0% international; 93% from in state; 51% live on campus; 0% of students in fraternities, 0% in sororities
Most popular majors: 16% Homeland Security, Law Enforcement, Firefighting and Related Protective Services, 14% Liberal Arts and Sciences, General Studies and Humanities, 13% Business, Management, Marketing, and Related Support Services, 10% Education, 7% Psychology
Expenses: 2018-2019: $10,155 in state, $16,235 out of state; room/board: $10,968
Financial aid: (413) 572-8530; 62% of undergrads determined to have financial need; average aid package $8,746

Wheaton College

Norton MA
(508) 286-8251
U.S. News ranking: Nat. Lib. Arts, No. 86
Website: www.wheatoncollege.edu
Admissions email: admission@wheatoncollege.edu
Private; founded 1834
Freshman admissions: more selective; 2017-2018: 6,089 applied, 2,916 accepted. Neither SAT nor ACT required. SAT 25/75 percentile: 1150-1350. High school rank: 26% in top tenth, 55% in top quarter, 85% in top half
Early decision deadline: 11/1, notification date: 12/15
Early action deadline: 11/1, notification date: 1/15
Application deadline (fall): 1/1
Undergraduate student body: 1,675 full time, 13 part time; 39% male, 61% female; 0% American Indian, 5% Asian, 6% black, 8% Hispanic, 3% multiracial, 0% Pacific Islander, 65% white, 10% international; 37% from in state; 96% live on campus; 0% of students in fraternities, 0% in sororities
Most popular majors: 19% Social Sciences, 14% Biological and Biomedical Sciences, 13% Psychology, 8% Business, Management, Marketing, and Related Support Services, 8% Visual and Performing Arts
Expenses: 2018-2019: $52,626; room/board: $13,424
Financial aid: (508) 286-8232; 69% of undergrads determined to have financial need; average aid package $41,564

Wheelock College[1]

Boston MA
(617) 879-2206
U.S. News ranking: Reg. U. (N), No. 105
Website: www.wheelock.edu
Admissions email: undergrad@wheelock.edu
Private; founded 1888
Application deadline (fall): 5/1
Undergraduate student body: N/A full time, N/A part time
Expenses: 2017-2018: $36,200; room/board: $14,975
Financial aid: N/A

Williams College

Williamstown MA
(413) 597-2211
U.S. News ranking: Nat. Lib. Arts, No. 1
Website: www.williams.edu
Admissions email: admission@williams.edu
Private; founded 1793
Freshman admissions: most selective; 2017-2018: 8,593 applied, 1,253 accepted. Either SAT or ACT required. ACT 25/75 percentile: 31-35. High school rank: 88% in top tenth, 98% in top quarter, 99% in top half
Early decision deadline: 11/15, notification date: 12/15
Early action deadline: N/A, notification date: N/A
Application deadline (fall): 1/1
Undergraduate student body: 2,018 full time, 43 part time; 53% male, 47% female; 0% American Indian, 13% Asian, 8% black, 13% Hispanic, 6% multiracial, 0% Pacific Islander, 51% white, 8% international; 14% from in state; 93% live on campus; N/A of students in fraternities, N/A in sororities
Most popular majors: 20% Economics, General, 13% Mathematics, General, 12% English Language and Literature, General, 11% Biology/Biological Sciences, General, 11% Psychology, General
Expenses: 2018-2019: $55,450; room/board: $14,500
Financial aid: (413) 597-4181; 51% of undergrads determined to have financial need; average aid package $54,932

Worcester Polytechnic Institute

Worcester MA
(508) 831-5286
U.S. News ranking: Nat. U., No. 59
Website: www.wpi.edu/admissions/undergraduate
Admissions email: admissions@wpi.edu
Private; founded 1865
Freshman admissions: more selective; 2017-2018: 10,331 applied, 5,009 accepted. Neither SAT nor ACT required. SAT 25/75 percentile: 1280-1440. High school rank: 68% in top tenth, 92% in top quarter, 100% in top half
Early decision deadline: N/A, notification date: N/A
Early action deadline: 11/11, notification date: 12/20
Application deadline (fall): 2/1
Undergraduate student body: 4,301 full time, 134 part time; 64% male, 36% female; 0% American Indian, 3% Asian, 3% black, 9% Hispanic, 2% multiracial, 0% Pacific Islander, 64% white, 11% international; 43% from in state; 59% live on campus; 27% of students in fraternities, 45% in sororities
Most popular majors: 19% Mechanical Engineering, 12% Computer Science, 10% Electrical and Electronics Engineering, 9% Bioengineering and Biomedical Engineering, 8% Chemical Engineering
Expenses: 2018-2019: $50,530; room/board: $14,774
Financial aid: (508) 831-5469; 61% of undergrads determined tc have financial need; average aid package $36,710

Worcester State University

Worcester MA
(508) 929-8040
U.S. News ranking: Reg. U. (N), No. 117
Website: www.worcester.edu
Admissions email: admissions@worcester.edu
Public; founded 1874
Freshman admissions: selective; 2017-2018: 3,747 applied, 2,860 accepted. Neither SAT nor ACT required. SAT 25/75 percentile: 980-1170. High school rank: N/A
Early decision deadline: N/A, notification date: N/A
Early action deadline: 11/15, notification date: 12/15
Application deadline (fall): 5/1
Undergraduate student body: 4,15 full time, 1,342 part time; 41% male, 59% female; 0% American Indian, 5% Asian, 9% black, 12% Hispanic, 3% multiracial, 0% Pacific Islander, 66% white, 1% international; 96% from in state; 30% live on campus; N/A of students in fraternities, N/A in sororities
Most popular majors: 19% Health Professions and Related Program 16% Business, Management, Marketing, and Related Support Services, 14% Psychology, 8% Biological and Biomedical Sciences, 7% Social Sciences
Expenses: 2018-2019: $10,161 in state, $16,241 out of state; room/board: $12,262
Financial aid: (508) 929-8056; 62% of undergrads determined t have financial need; average aid package $18,395

MICHIGAN

Adrian College

Adrian MI
(800) 877-2246
U.S. News ranking: Reg. Coll. (Mid. W), No. 19
Website: www.adrian.edu
Admissions email: admissions@adrian.edu
Private; founded 1859
Affiliation: United Methodist
Freshman admissions: selective; 2017-2018: 5,004 applied, 2,989 accepted. Either SAT or ACT required. SAT 25/75 percentile: 950-1148. High sch rank: 28% in top tenth, 52% in top quarter, 86% in top half
Early decision deadline: N/A, notification date: N/A
Early action deadline: N/A, notification date: N/A
Application deadline (fall): rolling
Undergraduate student body: 1,6C full time, 65 part time; 50% male, 50% female; 0% American Indian, 0% Asian, 7% black, 5% Hispanic,

3% multiracial, 0% Pacific Islander, 71% white, 0% international; 78% from in state; 84% live on campus; 20% of students in fraternities, 21% in sororities
Most popular majors: 25% Business, Management, Marketing, and Related Support Services, 20% Parks, Recreation, Leisure, and Fitness Studies, 9% Biological and Biomedical Sciences, 9% Visual and Performing Arts, 7% Education
Expenses: 2018-2019: $37,087; room/board: $11,318
Financial aid: (888) 876-0194; 84% of undergrads determined to have financial need; average aid package $29,525

Albion College

Albion MI
(800) 858-6770
U.S. News ranking: Nat. Lib. Arts, No. 152
Website: www.albion.edu/
Admissions email: admission@albion.edu
Private; founded 1835
Affiliation: United Methodist
Freshman admissions: selective; 2017-2018: 3,884 applied, 2,742 accepted. Either SAT or ACT required. SAT 25/75 percentile: 1010-1200. High school rank: N/A
Early decision deadline: N/A, notification date: N/A
Early action deadline: 12/1, notification date: N/A
Application deadline (fall): rolling
Undergraduate student body: 1,554 full time, 14 part time; 47% male, 53% female; 0% American Indian, 3% Asian, 13% black, 9% Hispanic, 3% multiracial, 0% Pacific Islander, 65% white, 2% international; 77% from in state; 95% live on campus; 26% of students in fraternities, 23% in sororities
Most popular majors: 13% Biology/Biological Sciences, General, 13% Economics, General, 11% Psychology, General, 7% Business Administration and Management, General, 7% Communication and Media Studies
Expenses: 2018-2019: $45,590; room/board: $12,380
Financial aid: (517) 629-0440; 79% of undergrads determined to have financial need; average aid package $40,402

Alma College

Alma MI
(800) 321-2562
U.S. News ranking: Nat. Lib. Arts, No. 143
Website: www.alma.edu
Admissions email: admissions@alma.edu
Private; founded 1886
Affiliation: Presbyterian Church (USA)
Freshman admissions: selective; 2017-2018: 4,728 applied, 3,026 accepted. Either SAT or ACT required. SAT 25/75 percentile: 1030-1230. High school rank: 18% in top tenth, 25% in top quarter, 84% in top half
Early decision deadline: N/A, notification date: N/A
Early action deadline: N/A, notification date: N/A
Application deadline (fall): rolling
Undergraduate student body: 1,376 full time, 50 part time; 43% male, 57% female; 0% American Indian, 1% Asian, 3% black, 5% Hispanic, 3% multiracial, 0% Pacific Islander, 78% white, 2% international; 91% from in state; 88% live on campus; 22% of students in fraternities, 18% in sororities
Most popular majors: 21% Health Professions and Related Programs, 14% Business, Management, Marketing, and Related Support Services, 10% Education, 9% Biological and Biomedical Sciences, 7% Psychology
Expenses: 2018-2019: $40,258; room/board: $10,998
Financial aid: (989) 463-7347; 84% of undergrads determined to have financial need; average aid package $28,542

Andrews University

Berrien Springs MI
(800) 253-2874
U.S. News ranking: Nat. U., No. 194
Website: www.andrews.edu
Admissions email: enroll@andrews.edu
Private; founded 1874
Affiliation: Seventh Day Adventist
Freshman admissions: more selective; 2017-2018: 1,554 applied, 896 accepted. Either SAT or ACT required. ACT 25/75 percentile: 21-29. High school rank: 19% in top tenth, 42% in top quarter, 69% in top half
Early decision deadline: N/A, notification date: N/A
Early action deadline: N/A, notification date: N/A
Application deadline (fall): rolling
Undergraduate student body: 1,344 full time, 360 part time; 45% male, 55% female; 0% American Indian, 14% Asian, 19% black, 14% Hispanic, 4% multiracial, 0% Pacific Islander, 27% white, 18% international; 36% from in state; 57% live on campus; 0% of students in fraternities, 0% in sororities
Most popular majors: 12% Visual and Performing Arts, 10% Business, Management, Marketing, and Related Support Services, 7% Agriculture, Agriculture Operations, and Related Sciences, 7% Biological and Biomedical Sciences, 7% Health Professions and Related Programs
Expenses: 2018-2019: $29,288; room/board: $9,078
Financial aid: (269) 471-3334; 59% of undergrads determined to have financial need; average aid package $31,058

Aquinas College

Grand Rapids MI
(616) 632-2900
U.S. News ranking: Reg. U. (Mid. W), No. 38
Website: www.aquinas.edu
Admissions email: admissions@aquinas.edu
Private; founded 1886
Affiliation: Roman Catholic
Freshman admissions: selective; 2017-2018: 1,875 applied, 1,397 accepted. Either SAT or ACT required. SAT 25/75 percentile: 1020-1220. High school rank: N/A
Early decision deadline: N/A, notification date: N/A
Early action deadline: N/A, notification date: N/A
Application deadline (fall): rolling
Undergraduate student body: 1,317 full time, 234 part time; 39% male, 61% female; 0% American Indian, 1% Asian, 4% black, 7% Hispanic, 3% multiracial, 0% Pacific Islander, 76% white, 2% international; 94% from in state; 50% live on campus; N/A of students in fraternities, N/A in sororities
Most popular majors: 21% Business, Management, Marketing, and Related Support Services, 9% Biological and Biomedical Sciences, 9% Social Sciences, 7% Foreign Languages, Literatures, and Linguistics, 6% Psychology
Expenses: 2018-2019: $32,574; room/board: $9,332
Financial aid: (616) 632-2893; 77% of undergrads determined to have financial need; average aid package $24,384

Baker College of Flint[1]

Flint MI
(810) 767-7600
U.S. News ranking: Reg. Coll. (Mid. W), unranked
Website: www.baker.edu
Admissions email: troy.crowe@baker.edu
Private
Application deadline (fall): N/A
Undergraduate student body: N/A full time, N/A part time
Expenses: 2017-2018: $9,360; room/board: $5,400
Financial aid: N/A

Calvin College

Grand Rapids MI
(800) 688-0122
U.S. News ranking: Reg. Coll. (Mid. W), No. 1
Website: calvin.edu
Admissions email: admissions@calvin.edu
Private; founded 1876
Affiliation: Christian Reformed Church
Freshman admissions: more selective; 2017-2018: 3,221 applied, 2,689 accepted. Neither SAT nor ACT required. ACT 25/75 percentile: 23-30. High school rank: 28% in top tenth, 57% in top quarter, 85% in top half
Early decision deadline: N/A, notification date: N/A
Early action deadline: N/A, notification date: N/A
Application deadline (fall): 8/15
Undergraduate student body: 3,524 full time, 222 part time; 46% male, 54% female; 0% American Indian, 5% Asian, 3% black, 5% Hispanic, 3% multiracial, 0% Pacific Islander, 70% white, 12% international; 58% from in state; 58% live on campus; 0% of students in fraternities, 0% in sororities
Most popular majors: 13% Business Administration and Management, General, 10% Education, 10% Engineering, General, 10% Registered Nursing/Registered Nurse, 8% Biology/Biological Sciences, General
Expenses: 2018-2019: $34,600; room/board: $10,200
Financial aid: (616) 526-6134; 60% of undergrads determined to have financial need; average aid package $23,940

Central Michigan University

Mount Pleasant MI
(989) 774-3076
U.S. News ranking: Nat. U., No. 205
Website: www.cmich.edu
Admissions email: cmuadmit@cmich.edu
Public; founded 1892
Freshman admissions: selective; 2017-2018: 19,021 applied, 12,887 accepted. Either SAT or ACT required. SAT 25/75 percentile: 1010-1200. High school rank: 17% in top tenth, 39% in top quarter, 72% in top half
Early decision deadline: N/A, notification date: N/A
Early action deadline: 5/1, notification date: N/A
Application deadline (fall): 7/1
Undergraduate student body: 15,590 full time, 2,255 part time; 43% male, 57% female; 1% American Indian, 1% Asian, 9% black, 5% Hispanic, 4% multiracial, 0% Pacific Islander, 78% white, 2% international; 92% from in state; 37% live on campus; 9% of students in fraternities, 11% in sororities
Most popular majors: 28% Business, Management, Marketing, and Related Support Services, 8% Communication, Journalism, and Related Programs, 8% Parks, Recreation, Leisure, and Fitness Studies, 7% Education, 7% Health Professions and Related Programs
Expenses: 2018-2019: $12,510 in state, $12,510 out of state; room/board: $9,736
Financial aid: (989) 774-3674; 60% of undergrads determined to have financial need; average aid package $13,496

Cleary University[1]

Howell MI
(800) 686-1883
U.S. News ranking: Business, unranked
Website: www.cleary.edu
Admissions email: admissions@cleary.edu
Private; founded 1883
Application deadline (fall): 8/24
Undergraduate student body: N/A full time, N/A part time
Expenses: 2017-2018: $19,600; room/board: $9,600
Financial aid: (517) 338-3015

College for Creative Studies[1]

Detroit MI
(313) 664-7425
U.S. News ranking: Arts, unranked
Website: www.collegeforcreativestudies.edu
Admissions email: admissions@collegeforcreativestudies.edu
Private; founded 1906
Application deadline (fall): N/A
Undergraduate student body: N/A full time, N/A part time
Expenses: N/A
Financial aid: (313) 664-7495

Cornerstone University

Grand Rapids MI
(616) 222-1426
U.S. News ranking: Reg. U. (Mid. W), No. 106
Website: www.cornerstone.edu
Admissions email: admissions@cornerstone.edu
Private; founded 1941
Affiliation: Interdenominational
Freshman admissions: selective; 2017-2018: 2,737 applied, 1,844 accepted. Either SAT or ACT required. SAT 25/75 percentile: 920-1160. High school rank: 19% in top tenth, 43% in top quarter, 80% in top half
Early decision deadline: N/A, notification date: N/A
Early action deadline: N/A, notification date: N/A
Application deadline (fall): rolling
Undergraduate student body: 1,259 full time, 422 part time; 38% male, 62% female; 0% American Indian, 2% Asian, 12% black, 5% Hispanic, 1% multiracial, 0% Pacific Islander, 77% white, 4% international; 81% from in state; 63% live on campus; 0% of students in fraternities, 0% in sororities
Most popular majors: 35% Business, Management, Marketing, and Related Support Services, 13% Theology and Religious Vocations, 10% Psychology, 9% Parks, Recreation, Leisure, and Fitness Studies, 8% Communication, Journalism, and Related Programs
Expenses: 2018-2019: $24,500; room/board: $9,300
Financial aid: (616) 222-1424; 80% of undergrads determined to have financial need; average aid package $21,975

Davenport University

Grand Rapids MI
(866) 925-3884
U.S. News ranking: Reg. U. (Mid. W), second tier
Website: www.davenport.edu
Admissions email: Davenport.Admissions@davenport.edu
Private; founded 1866
Freshman admissions: less selective; 2017-2018: 2,412 applied, 1,976 accepted. Neither SAT nor ACT required. SAT 25/75 percentile: 950-1160. High school rank: N/A
Early decision deadline: N/A, notification date: N/A

Early action deadline: N/A, notification date: N/A
Application deadline (fall): rolling
Undergraduate student body: 2,621 full time, 2,976 part time; 44% male, 56% female; 1% American Indian, 3% Asian, 12% black, 4% Hispanic, 3% multiracial, 0% Pacific Islander, 69% white, 3% international; 96% from in state; 15% live on campus; 0% of students in fraternities, 0% in sororities
Most popular majors: 24% Business Administration and Management, General, 12% Business/Commerce, General, 10% Health/Health Care Administration/Management, 9% Registered Nursing/Registered Nurse, 7% Accounting
Expenses: 2017-2018: $21,662; room/board: $9,902
Financial aid: (616) 732-1132

Eastern Michigan University

Ypsilanti MI
(734) 487-3060
U.S. News ranking: Nat. U., second tier
Website: www.emich.edu/
Admissions email: admissions@emich.edu
Public; founded 1849
Freshman admissions: selective; 2017-2018: 16,012 applied, 11,675 accepted. Either SAT or ACT required. SAT 25/75 percentile: 840-1310. High school rank: 14% in top tenth, 38% in top quarter, 74% in top half
Early decision deadline: N/A, notification date: N/A
Early action deadline: N/A, notification date: N/A
Application deadline (fall): rolling
Undergraduate student body: 12,395 full time, 4,602 part time; 46% male, 54% female; 0% American Indian, 2% Asian, 18% black, 5% Hispanic, 4% multiracial, 0% Pacific Islander, 64% white, 2% international
Most popular majors: 20% Business, Management, Marketing, and Related Support Services, 15% Health Professions and Related Programs, 8% Education, 7% Public Administration and Social Service Professions, 7% Social Sciences
Expenses: 2018-2019: $12,430 in state, $12,430 out of state; room/board: $10,167
Financial aid: (734) 487-1048; 68% of undergrads determined to have financial need; average aid package $10,030

Ferris State University

Big Rapids MI
(231) 591-2100
U.S. News ranking: Reg. U. (Mid. W), No. 94
Website: www.ferris.edu
Admissions email: admissions@ferris.edu
Public; founded 1884
Freshman admissions: less selective; 2017-2018: 9,926 applied, 7,361 accepted. Neither SAT nor ACT required. SAT 25/75 percentile: 940-1170. High school rank: N/A
Early decision deadline: N/A, notification date: N/A
Early action deadline: N/A, notification date: N/A
Application deadline (fall): rolling
Undergraduate student body: 8,469 full time, 4,035 part time; 47% male, 53% female; 1% American Indian, 2% Asian, 8% black, 5% Hispanic, 4% multiracial, 0% Pacific Islander, 78% white, 2% international; 94% from in state; 26% live on campus; 1% of students in fraternities, 1% in sororities
Most popular majors: 4% Criminal Justice/Law Enforcement Administration, 2% Business Administration and Management, General, 2% Registered Nursing/Registered Nurse, 1% Pharmacy
Expenses: 2018-2019: $13,018 in state, $19,461 out of state; room/board: $9,894
Financial aid: (231) 591-2110; 71% of undergrads determined to have financial need; average aid package $11,610

Finlandia University[1]

Hancock MI
(906) 487-7274
U.S. News ranking: Reg. Coll. (Mid. W), second tier
Website: www.finlandia.edu
Admissions email: admissions@finlandia.edu
Private; founded 1896
Affiliation: Evangelical Lutheran Church
Application deadline (fall): N/A
Undergraduate student body: N/A full time, N/A part time
Expenses: 2017-2018: $22,758; room/board: $8,800
Financial aid: N/A

Grace Christian University

Grand Rapids MI
(616) 538-2330
U.S. News ranking: Reg. Coll. (Mid. W), No. 58
Website: www.gbcol.edu
Admissions email: enrollment@gbcol.edu
Private; founded 1939
Affiliation: Other
Freshman admissions: selective; 2017-2018: 291 applied, 160 accepted. Neither SAT nor ACT required. ACT 25/75 percentile: 17-23. High school rank: 2% in top tenth, 25% in top quarter, 43% in top half
Early decision deadline: N/A, notification date: N/A
Early action deadline: N/A, notification date: N/A
Application deadline (fall): rolling
Undergraduate student body: 977 full time, 52 part time; 44% male, 56% female; N/A American Indian, N/A Asian, N/A black, N/A Hispanic, N/A multiracial, N/A Pacific Islander, N/A white, N/A international
Most popular majors: 47% Lay Ministry, 24% Public Administration and Social Service Professions, 12% Business/Commerce, General, 9% Bible/Biblical Studies, 6% Music, Other
Expenses: 2018-2019: $19,950; room/board: $7,700
Financial aid: (616) 538-2330; 82% of undergrads determined to have financial need; average aid package $7,909

Grand Valley State University

Allendale MI
(800) 748-0246
U.S. News ranking: Reg. U. (Mid. W), No. 29
Website: www.gvsu.edu
Admissions email: admissions@gvsu.edu
Public; founded 1960
Freshman admissions: selective; 2017-2018: 17,509 applied, 14,168 accepted. Either SAT or ACT required. SAT 25/75 percentile: 1060-1230. High school rank: 16% in top tenth, 45% in top quarter, 84% in top half
Early decision deadline: N/A, notification date: N/A
Early action deadline: N/A, notification date: N/A
Application deadline (fall): 5/1
Undergraduate student body: 19,373 full time, 2,564 part time; 41% male, 59% female; 0% American Indian, 3% Asian, 5% black, 5% Hispanic, 4% multiracial, 0% Pacific Islander, 82% white, 1% international; 93% from in state; 27% live on campus; N/A of students in fraternities, N/A in sororities
Most popular majors: 21% Business, Management, Marketing, and Related Support Services, 17% Health Professions and Related Programs, 7% Communication, Journalism, and Related Programs, 6% Psychology, 5% Social Sciences
Expenses: 2018-2019: $12,484 in state, $17,762 out of state; room/board: $8,690
Financial aid: (616) 331-3234; 60% of undergrads determined to have financial need; average aid package $10,093

Hillsdale College

Hillsdale MI
(517) 607-2327
U.S. News ranking: Nat. Lib. Arts, No. 76
Website: www.hillsdale.edu
Admissions email: admissions@hillsdale.edu
Private; founded 1844
Affiliation: Undenominational
Freshman admissions: more selective; 2017-2018: 2,080 applied, 863 accepted. Either SAT or ACT required. ACT 25/75 percentile: 28-32. High school rank: N/A
Early decision deadline: 11/1, notification date: 12/1
Early action deadline: N/A, notification date: N/A
Application deadline (fall): 4/1
Undergraduate student body: 1,463 full time, 49 part time; 51% male, 49% female; N/A American Indian, N/A Asian, N/A black, N/A Hispanic, N/A multiracial, N/A Pacific Islander, N/A white, N/A international; 35% from in state; 69% live on campus; 24% of students in fraternities, 34% in sororities
Most popular majors: 13% Economics, General, 12% History, General, 9% English Language and Literature, General, 8% Finance, General, 7% Biology/Biological Sciences, General
Expenses: 2018-2019: $27,577; room/board: $11,000
Financial aid: (517) 607-2350; 53% of undergrads determined to have financial need; average aid package $19,939

Hope College

Holland MI
(616) 395-7850
U.S. News ranking: Nat. Lib. Arts, No. 103
Website: www.hope.edu
Admissions email: admissions@hope.edu
Private; founded 1866
Affiliation: Christian Reformed Church
Freshman admissions: more selective; 2017-2018: 4,377 applied, 3,223 accepted. Either SAT or ACT required. ACT 25/75 percentile: 24-29. High school rank: 32% in top tenth, 66% in top quarter, 93% in top half
Early decision deadline: N/A, notification date: N/A
Early action deadline: 11/2, notification date: 11/23
Application deadline (fall): rolling
Undergraduate student body: 3,018 full time, 132 part time; 39% male, 61% female; 0% American Indian, 2% Asian, 3% black, 8% Hispanic, 2% multiracial, 0% Pacific Islander, 83% white, 2% international; 72% from in state; 79% live on campus; 14% of students in fraternities, 18% in sororities
Most popular majors: 17% Business Administration and Management, General, 10% Education/Teaching of Individuals with Specific Learning Disabilities, 9% Social Work, 7% Speech Communication and Rhetoric, 6% Registered Nursing/Registered Nurse
Expenses: 2018-2019: $34,010; room/board: $10,310
Financial aid: (616) 395-7765; 57% of undergrads determined to have financial need; average aid package $26,952

Jackson College[1]

Jackson MI
U.S. News ranking: Reg. Coll. (Mid. W), unranked
Admissions email: N/A
Public
Application deadline (fall): N/A
Undergraduate student body: N/A full time, N/A part time
Expenses: 2017-2018: $8,288 in state, $10,624 out of state; room/board: $7,960
Financial aid: N/A

Kalamazoo College

Kalamazoo MI
(800) 253-3602
U.S. News ranking: Nat. Lib. Arts, No. 65
Website: www.kzoo.edu
Admissions email: admission@kzoo.edu
Private; founded 1833
Freshman admissions: more selective; 2017-2018: 3,434 applied, 2,520 accepted. Neither SAT nor ACT required. ACT 25/75 percentile: 26-30. High school rank: 50% in top tenth, 87% in top quarter, 99% in top half
Early decision deadline: 11/1, notification date: 12/1
Early action deadline: 11/1, notification date: 12/20
Application deadline (fall): 1/15
Undergraduate student body: 1,427 full time, 9 part time; 43% male, 57% female; 0% American Indian, 8% Asian, 8% black, 13% Hispanic, 4% multiracial, 0% Pacific Islander, 57% white, 6% international; 67% from in state; 60% live on campus; 0% of students in fraternities, 0% in sororities
Most popular majors: 18% Social Sciences, 12% Physical Sciences, 12% Psychology, 9% Biological and Biomedical Sciences, 8% Visual and Performing Arts
Expenses: 2018-2019: $48,516; room/board: $9,756
Financial aid: (269) 337-7192; 71% of undergrads determined to have financial need; average aid package $40,877

Kettering University

Flint MI
(800) 955-4464
U.S. News ranking: Reg. U. (Mid. W), No. 25
Website: www.kettering.edu
Admissions email: admissions@kettering.edu
Private; founded 1919
Freshman admissions: more selective; 2017-2018: 1,931 applied, 1,358 accepted. Either SAT or ACT required. SAT 25/75 percentile: 1190-1350. High school rank: 32% in top tenth, 60% in top quarter, 91% in top half
Early decision deadline: N/A, notification date: N/A
Early action deadline: 11/15, notification date: 12/15
Application deadline (fall): rolling
Undergraduate student body: 1,807 full time, 82 part time; 81% male, 19% female; 0% American Indian, 4% Asian, 3% black, 5% Hispanic, 3% multiracial, 0% Pacific Islander, 76% white, 4% international; 85% from in state; 9% live on campus; 15% of students in fraternities, 9% in sororities
Most popular majors: 86% Engineering, 5% Computer and Information Sciences and Support Services, 4% Business, Management, Marketing, and Related Support Services, 2% Biological and Biomedical Sciences, 2% Mathematics and Statistics

Expenses: 2017-2018: $42,490; room/board: $8,040
Financial aid: N/A; average aid package $22,564

Kuyper College[1]

Grand Rapids MI
(800) 511-3749
U.S. News ranking: Reg. Coll. (Mid. W), No. 54
Website: www.kuyper.edu
Admissions email: admissions@kuyper.edu
Private
Application deadline (fall): N/A
Undergraduate student body: N/A full time, N/A part time
Expenses: 2017-2018: $21,090; room/board: $7,254
Financial aid: N/A

Lake Superior State University

Sault Ste. Marie MI
(906) 635-2231
U.S. News ranking: Reg. Coll. (Mid. W), No. 44
Website: www.lssu.edu
Admissions email: admissions@lssu.edu
Public; founded 1946
Freshman admissions: selective; 2017-2018: 1,184 applied, 665 accepted. Neither SAT nor ACT required. SAT 25/75 percentile: 990-1180. High school rank: 15% in top tenth, 37% in top quarter, 73% in top half
Early decision deadline: N/A, notification date: N/A
Early action deadline: N/A, notification date: N/A
Application deadline (fall): rolling
Undergraduate student body: 1,706 full time, 257 part time; 48% male, 52% female; 8% American Indian, 0% Asian, 1% black, 2% Hispanic, 0% multiracial, 0% Pacific Islander, 80% white, 7% international; 94% from in state; N/A live on campus; N/A of students in fraternities, N/A in sororities
Most popular majors: 16% Health Professions and Related Programs, 12% Homeland Security, Law Enforcement, Firefighting and Related Protective Services, 6% Natural Resources and Conservation, 4% Business, Management, Marketing, and Related Support Services, 4% Education
Expenses: 2018-2019: $11,830 in state, $11,830 out of state; room/board: $9,882
Financial aid: (906) 635-2678; 65% of undergrads determined to have financial need; average aid package $11,557

Lawrence Technological University

Southfield MI
(248) 204-3160
U.S. News ranking: Reg. U. (Mid. W), No. 62
Website: www.ltu.edu
Admissions email: admissions@ltu.edu
Private; founded 1932
Freshman admissions: selective; 2017-2018: 2,173 applied, 1,296 accepted. Either SAT or ACT required. SAT 25/75 percentile: 1060-1280. High school rank: 39% in top tenth, 54% in top quarter, 100% in top half
Early decision deadline: N/A, notification date: N/A
Early action deadline: N/A, notification date: N/A
Application deadline (fall): rolling
Undergraduate student body: 1,672 full time, 519 part time; 74% male, 26% female; 0% American Indian, 3% Asian, 6% black, 3% Hispanic, 2% multiracial, 0% Pacific Islander, 65% white, 15% international; 92% from in state; 36% live on campus; 9% of students in fraternities, 20% in sororities
Most popular majors: 20% Mechanical Engineering, 11% Architectural and Building Sciences/Technology, 8% Electrical and Electronics Engineering, 6% Civil Engineering, General, 5% Computer Science
Expenses: 2018-2019: $33,570; room/board: $9,950
Financial aid: (248) 204-2280; 62% of undergrads determined to have financial need; average aid package $27,588

Madonna University

Livonia MI
(734) 432-5339
U.S. News ranking: Reg. U. (Mid. W), No. 65
Website: www.madonna.edu
Admissions email: admissions@madonna.edu
Private; founded 1937
Affiliation: Roman Catholic
Freshman admissions: selective; 2017-2018: 1,009 applied, 750 accepted. Either SAT or ACT required. ACT 25/75 percentile: 19-24. High school rank: 9% in top tenth, 30% in top quarter, 62% in top half
Early decision deadline: 12/1, notification date: 1/15
Early action deadline: N/A, notification date: N/A
Application deadline (fall): rolling
Undergraduate student body: 1,358 full time, 1,098 part time; 35% male, 65% female; 0% American Indian, 1% Asian, 12% black, 4% Hispanic, 3% multiracial, 0% Pacific Islander, 64% white, 13% international; 98% from in state; 13% live on campus; N/A of students in fraternities, N/A in sororities
Most popular majors: 29% Business, Management, Marketing, and Related Support Services, 22% Health Professions and Related Programs, 15% Homeland Security, Law Enforcement, Firefighting and Related Protective Services, 4% Biological and Biomedical Sciences, 4% Public Administration and Social Service Professions
Expenses: 2018-2019: $21,900; room/board: $9,950
Financial aid: (734) 432-5662; 78% of undergrads determined to have financial need; average aid package $14,137

Marygrove College[1]

Detroit MI
(313) 927-1240
U.S. News ranking: Reg. U. (Mid. W), second tier
Website: www.marygrove.edu
Admissions email: info@marygrove.edu
Private
Application deadline (fall): rolling
Undergraduate student body: N/A full time, N/A part time
Expenses: 2017-2018: $22,750; room/board: $7,800
Financial aid: N/A

Michigan State University

East Lansing MI
(517) 355-8332
U.S. News ranking: Nat. U., No. 85
Website: www.msu.edu/
Admissions email: admis@msu.edu
Public; founded 1855
Freshman admissions: more selective; 2017-2018: 36,143 applied, 25,860 accepted. Either SAT or ACT required. SAT 25/75 percentile: 1100-1320. High school rank: 30% in top tenth, 67% in top quarter, 95% in top half
Early decision deadline: N/A, notification date: N/A
Early action deadline: N/A, notification date: N/A
Application deadline (fall): rolling
Undergraduate student body: 35,404 full time, 3,592 part time; 49% male, 51% female; 0% American Indian, 5% Asian, 7% black, 4% Hispanic, 3% multiracial, 0% Pacific Islander, 67% white, 12% international; 87% from in state; 40% live on campus; 12% of students in fraternities, 11% in sororities
Most popular majors: 17% Business, Management, Marketing, and Related Support Services, 12% Communication, Journalism, and Related Programs, 12% Social Sciences, 10% Biological and Biomedical Sciences, 8% Engineering
Expenses: 2018-2019: $14,460 in state, $39,750 out of state; room/board: $10,272
Financial aid: (517) 353-5940; 48% of undergrads determined to have financial need; average aid package $13,466

Michigan Technological University

Houghton MI
(906) 487-2335
U.S. News ranking: Nat. U., No. 136
Website: www.mtu.edu
Admissions email: mtu4u@mtu.edu
Public; founded 1885
Freshman admissions: more selective; 2017-2018: 5,469 applied, 4,074 accepted. Either SAT or ACT required. SAT 25/75 percentile: 1160-1340. High school rank: 32% in top tenth, 65% in top quarter, 91% in top half
Early decision deadline: N/A, notification date: N/A
Early action deadline: N/A, notification date: N/A
Application deadline (fall): rolling
Undergraduate student body: 5,517 full time, 400 part time; 73% male, 27% female; 0% American Indian, 1% Asian, 1% black, 2% Hispanic, 3% multiracial, 0% Pacific Islander, 88% white, 3% international; 78% from in state; 45% live on campus; 11% of students in fraternities, 15% in sororities
Most popular majors: 60% Engineering, 9% Business, Management, Marketing, and Related Support Services, 7% Computer and Information Sciences and Support Services, 5% Biological and Biomedical Sciences, 4% Engineering Technologies and Engineering-Related Fields
Expenses: 2018-2019: $15,646 in state, $33,726 out of state; room/board: $10,756
Financial aid: (906) 487-2622; 66% of undergrads determined to have financial need; average aid package $15,463

Northern Michigan University

Marquette MI
(906) 227-2650
U.S. News ranking: Reg. U. (Mid. W), No. 81
Website: www.nmu.edu
Admissions email: admissions@nmu.edu
Public; founded 1899
Freshman admissions: less selective; 2017-2018: 6,173 applied, 4,591 accepted. Either SAT or ACT required. SAT 25/75 percentile: 940-1150. High school rank: N/A
Early decision deadline: N/A, notification date: N/A
Early action deadline: N/A, notification date: N/A
Application deadline (fall): rolling
Undergraduate student body: 6,207 full time, 811 part time; 46% male, 54% female; 1% American Indian, 1% Asian, 2% black, 3% Hispanic, 5% multiracial, 0% Pacific Islander, 86% white, 1% international; 81% from in state; 42% live on campus; N/A of students in fraternities, N/A in sororities
Most popular majors: 16% Business, Management, Marketing, and Related Support Services, 13% Health Professions and Related Programs, 12% Biological and Biomedical Sciences, 8% Visual and Performing Arts, 6% Homeland Security, Law Enforcement, Firefighting and Related Protective Services
Expenses: 2018-2019: $10,730 in state, $16,226 out of state; room/board: $10,666
Financial aid: (906) 227-2327; 66% of undergrads determined to have financial need; average aid package $9,747

Northwestern Michigan College[1]

Traverse City MI
U.S. News ranking: Reg. Coll. (Mid. W), unranked
Admissions email: N/A
Public
Application deadline (fall): N/A
Undergraduate student body: N/A full time, N/A part time
Expenses: 2017-2018: $7,463 in state, $9,425 out of state; room/board: $9,475
Financial aid: N/A

Northwood University

Midland MI
(989) 837-4273
U.S. News ranking: Business, unranked
Website: www.northwood.edu
Admissions email: miadmit@northwood.edu
Private; founded 1959
Freshman admissions: selective; 2017-2018: 1,819 applied, 1,260 accepted. Either SAT or ACT required. SAT 25/75 percentile: 1000-1160. High school rank: 8% in top tenth, 30% in top quarter, 67% in top half
Early decision deadline: N/A, notification date: N/A
Early action deadline: N/A, notification date: N/A
Application deadline (fall): rolling
Undergraduate student body: 1,282 full time, 69 part time; 66% male, 34% female; 0% American Indian, 1% Asian, 1% black, 3% Hispanic, 9% multiracial, 0% Pacific Islander, 66% white, 6% international; 88% from in state; 43% live on campus; 12% of students in fraternities, 13% in sororities
Most popular majors: 21% Business Administration and Management, General, 15% Marketing/Marketing Management, General, 14% Accounting, 10% Finance, General, 9% Vehicle and Vehicle Parts and Accessories Marketing Operations
Expenses: 2018-2019: $27,060; room/board: $10,480
Financial aid: (989) 837-4230; 65% of undergrads determined to have financial need; average aid package $18,932

Oakland University

Rochester MI
(248) 370-3360
U.S. News ranking: Nat. U., second tier
Website: www.oakland.edu
Admissions email: visit@oakland.edu
Public; founded 1957
Freshman admissions: selective; 2017-2018: 10,296 applied, 8,691 accepted. Either SAT or ACT required. SAT 25/75 percentile: 1010-1230. High school rank: 20% in top tenth, 46% in top quarter, 78% in top half
Early decision deadline: N/A, notification date: N/A
Early action deadline: N/A, notification date: N/A
Application deadline (fall): 8/1

Undergraduate student body: 12,549 full time, 3,352 part time; 44% male, 56% female; 0% American Indian, 5% Asian, 7% black, 4% Hispanic, 3% multiracial, 0% Pacific Islander, 75% white, 2% international; 99% from in state; 16% live on campus; N/A of students in fraternities, N/A in sororities
Most popular majors: 23% Health Professions and Related Programs, 17% Business, Management, Marketing, and Related Support Services, 8% Engineering, 6% Biological and Biomedical Sciences, 6% Communication, Journalism, and Related Programs
Expenses: 2018-2019: $12,893 in state, $23,873 out of state; room/board: $9,910
Financial aid: (248) 370-2550; 64% of undergrads determined to have financial need; average aid package $14,046

Olivet College

Olivet MI
(800) 456-7189
U.S. News ranking: Reg. Coll. (Mid. W), No. 48
Website: www.olivetcollege.edu
Admissions email: admissions@olivetcollege.edu
Private; founded 1844
Affiliation: United Church of Christ
Freshman admissions: selective; 2017-2018: 1,292 applied, 906 accepted. Either SAT or ACT required. ACT 25/75 percentile: 18-23. High school rank: N/A
Early decision deadline: N/A, notification date: N/A
Early action deadline: N/A, notification date: N/A
Application deadline (fall): 8/31
Undergraduate student body: 1,032 full time, 145 part time; 58% male, 42% female; 0% American Indian, 0% Asian, 19% black, 6% Hispanic, 6% multiracial, 0% Pacific Islander, 65% white, 1% international
Most popular majors: 32% Insurance, 31% Criminal Justice/ Safety Studies, 26% Marketing/ Marketing Management, General
Expenses: 2018-2019: $27,700; room/board: $9,590
Financial aid: (269) 749-7645; 93% of undergrads determined to have financial need; average aid package $19,750

Rochester College

Rochester Hills MI
(248) 218-2222
U.S. News ranking: Reg. Coll. (Mid. W), No. 59
Website: www.rc.edu
Admissions email: admissions@rc.edu
Private; founded 1959
Affiliation: Churches of Christ
Freshman admissions: less selective; 2017-2018: 404 applied, 404 accepted. Either SAT or ACT required. ACT 25/75 percentile: 16-23. High school rank: N/A
Early decision deadline: N/A, notification date: N/A
Early action deadline: N/A, notification date: N/A
Application deadline (fall): rolling
Undergraduate student body: 762 full time, 391 part time; 37% male, 63% female; 0% American Indian, 1% Asian, 18% black, 2% Hispanic, 3% multiracial, 0% Pacific Islander, 72% white, 2% international; 97% from in state; 24% live on campus; N/A of students in fraternities, N/A in sororities
Most popular majors: 23% Business, Management, Marketing, and Related Support Services, 18% Communication, Journalism, and Related Programs, 16% Education, 16% Psychology, 11% Health Professions and Related Programs
Expenses: 2017-2018: $22,312; room/board: $7,160
Financial aid: (248) 218-2038

Saginaw Valley State University

University Center MI
(989) 964-4200
U.S. News ranking: Reg. U. (Mid. W), second tier
Website: www.svsu.edu
Admissions email: admissions@svsu.edu
Public; founded 1963
Freshman admissions: selective; 2017-2018: 6,457 applied, 4,768 accepted. Either SAT or ACT required. SAT 25/75 percentile: 990-1190. High school rank: 20% in top tenth, 45% in top quarter, 77% in top half
Early decision deadline: N/A, notification date: N/A
Early action deadline: N/A, notification date: N/A
Application deadline (fall): rolling
Undergraduate student body: 6,601 full time, 1,292 part time; 41% male, 59% female; 0% American Indian, 1% Asian, 8% black, 4% Hispanic, 3% multiracial, 0% Pacific Islander, 73% white, 6% international; 98% from in state; 30% live on campus; 3% of students in fraternities, 3% in sororities
Most popular majors: 22% Health Professions and Related Programs, 21% Business, Management, Marketing, and Related Support Services, 7% Public Administration and Social Service Professions, 6% Education, 6% Homeland Security, Law Enforcement, Firefighting and Related Protective Services
Expenses: 2018-2019: $10,308 in state, $24,215 out of state; room/board: $10,186
Financial aid: (989) 964-4900; 67% of undergrads determined to have financial need

Siena Heights University[1]

Adrian MI
(517) 264-7180
U.S. News ranking: Reg. U. (Mid. W), No. 115
Website: www.sienaheights.edu
Admissions email: admissions@sienaheights.edu
Private; founded 1919
Affiliation: Roman Catholic
Application deadline (fall): 8/1
Undergraduate student body: N/A full time, N/A part time
Expenses: 2017-2018: $25,932; room/board: $10,390
Financial aid: (517) 264-7110

Spring Arbor University

Spring Arbor MI
(800) 968-0011
U.S. News ranking: Reg. U. (Mid. W), No. 53
Website: www.arbor.edu/
Admissions email: admissions@arbor.edu
Private; founded 1873
Affiliation: Free Methodist
Freshman admissions: selective; 2017-2018: 1,688 applied, 1,131 accepted. Either SAT or ACT required. SAT 25/75 percentile: 1000-1205. High school rank: 22% in top tenth, 48% in top quarter, 73% in top half
Early decision deadline: N/A, notification date: N/A
Early action deadline: N/A, notification date: N/A
Application deadline (fall): 8/1
Undergraduate student body: 1,380 full time, 577 part time; 34% male, 66% female; 0% American Indian, 1% Asian, 11% black, 4% Hispanic, 3% multiracial, 0% Pacific Islander, 75% white, 0% international; 87% from in state; 78% live on campus; 0% of students in fraternities, 0% in sororities
Most popular majors: 12% Business Administration and Management, General, 10% Religion/Religious Studies, 10% Social Work, 9% Psychology, General, 8% Teacher Education and Professional Development, Specific Subject Areas
Expenses: 2018-2019: $28,810; room/board: $10,010
Financial aid: (517) 750-6463; 83% of undergrads determined to have financial need; average aid package $24,045

University of Detroit Mercy

Detroit MI
(313) 993-1245
U.S. News ranking: Reg. U. (Mid. W), No. 25
Website: www.udmercy.edu
Admissions email: admissions@udmercy.edu
Private; founded 1877
Affiliation: Roman Catholic
Freshman admissions: selective; 2017-2018: 4,301 applied, 2,783 accepted. Either SAT or ACT required. SAT 25/75 percentile: 1040-1230. High school rank: 24% in top tenth, 54% in top quarter, 85% in top half
Early decision deadline: 11/1, notification date: 12/1
Early action deadline: N/A, notification date: N/A
Application deadline (fall): 3/1
Undergraduate student body: 2,338 full time, 505 part time; 37% male, 63% female; 0% American Indian, 6% Asian, 13% black, 5% Hispanic, 3% multiracial, 0% Pacific Islander, 61% white, 8% international; 96% from in state; 29% live on campus; 3% of students in fraternities, 4% in sororities
Most popular majors: 51% Registered Nursing/Registered Nurse, 11% Biology/Biological Sciences, General, 4% Business Administration and Management, General, 4% Dental Hygiene/ Hygienist, 3% Architecture
Expenses: 2018-2019: $28,000; room/board: $9,736
Financial aid: (313) 993-3354; 69% of undergrads determined to have financial need; average aid package $34,929

University of Michigan–Ann Arbor

Ann Arbor MI
(734) 764-7433
U.S. News ranking: Nat. U., No. 27
Website: umich.edu
Admissions email: N/A
Public; founded 1817
Freshman admissions: more selective; 2017-2018: 59,886 applied, 15,871 accepted. Either SAT or ACT required. ACT 25/75 percentile: 30-33. High school rank: 77% in top tenth, 95% in top quarter, 99% in top half
Early decision deadline: N/A, notification date: N/A
Early action deadline: 11/1, notification date: 12/24
Application deadline (fall): 2/1
Undergraduate student body: 28,702 full time, 1,119 part time; 50% male, 50% female; 0% American Indian, 14% Asian, 4% black, 6% Hispanic, 4% multiracial, 0% Pacific Islander, 61% white, 7% international; 59% from in state; 32% live on campus; 17% of students in fraternities, 25% in sororities
Most popular majors: 7% Computer and Information Sciences, General, 6% Business Administration and Management, General, 6% Economics, General, 6% Experimental Psychology, 4% Political Science and Government, General
Expenses: 2018-2019: $15,262 in state, $49,350 out of state; room/board: $11,534
Financial aid: (734) 763-6600; 38% of undergrads determined to have financial need; average aid package $26,477

University of Michigan–Dearborn

Dearborn MI
(313) 593-5100
U.S. News ranking: Reg. U. (Mid. W), No. 38
Website: umdearborn.edu/
Admissions email: umd-admissions@umich.edu
Public; founded 1959
Freshman admissions: selective; 2017-2018: 5,731 applied, 3,684 accepted. Either SAT or ACT required. SAT 25/75 percentile: 1060-1290. High school rank: 24% in top tenth, 55% in top quarter, 88% in top half
Early decision deadline: N/A, notification date: N/A
Early action deadline: N/A, notification date: N/A
Application deadline (fall): 9/5
Undergraduate student body: 5,137 full time, 2,004 part time; 53% male, 47% female; 0% American Indian, 8% Asian, 9% black, 6% Hispanic, 3% multiracial, 0% Pacific Islander, 69% white, 2% international; 96% from in state; 0% live on campus; N/A of students in fraternities, N/A in sororities
Most popular majors: 22% Business, Management, Marketing, and Related Support Services, 16% Engineering, 11% Psychology, 8% Biological and Biomedical Sciences, 7% Social Sciences
Expenses: 2018-2019: $12,930 in state, $25,182 out of state; room/board: N/A
Financial aid: (313) 593-5300; 68% of undergrads determined to have financial need; average aid package $13,659

University of Michigan–Flint

Flint MI
(810) 762-3300
U.S. News ranking: Reg. U. (Mid. W), No. 115
Website: www.umflint.edu
Admissions email: admissions@umflint.edu
Public; founded 1956
Freshman admissions: selective; 2017-2018: 4,558 applied, 2,968 accepted. Either SAT or ACT required. SAT 25/75 percentile: 950-1200. High school rank: 18% in top tenth, 43% in top quarter, 80% in top half
Early decision deadline: N/A, notification date: N/A
Early action deadline: N/A, notification date: N/A
Application deadline (fall): 8/22
Undergraduate student body: 3,809 full time, 2,625 part time; 39% male, 61% female; 1% American Indian, 2% Asian, 13% black, 4% Hispanic, 3% multiracial, 0% Pacific Islander, 70% white, 4% international; 98% from in state; 6% live on campus; 2% of students in fraternities, 3% in sororities
Most popular majors: 7% Business Administration and Management, General, 6% Osteopathic Medicine/Osteopathy, 2% Computer Science, 2% Mechanical Engineering, 0% Engineering Science
Expenses: 2018-2019: $11,820 in state, $22,578 out of state; room/board: $8,769
Financial aid: (810) 762-3444

Walsh College of Accountancy and Business Administration

Troy MI
(248) 823-1600
U.S. News ranking: Business, unranked
Website: www.walshcollege.edu
Admissions email: admissions@walshcollege.edu

Private; founded 1922
Freshman admissions: least selective; 2017-2018: N/A applied, N/A accepted. Neither SAT nor ACT required. SAT 25/75 percentile: N/A. High school rank: N/A
Early decision deadline: N/A, notification date: N/A
Early action deadline: N/A, notification date: N/A
Application deadline (fall): rolling
Undergraduate student body: 78 full time, 815 part time; 52% male, 48% female; 0% American Indian, 5% Asian, 5% black, 2% Hispanic, 2% multiracial, 0% Pacific Islander, 82% white, 2% international
Most popular majors: 28% Accounting, 20% Business/Commerce, General, 18% Business Administration and Management, General, 16% Finance, General, 12% Marketing/Marketing Management, General
Expenses: 2018-2019: $14,625; room/board: N/A
Financial aid: (248) 823-1665; 71% of undergrads determined to have financial need

Wayne State University
Detroit MI
(313) 577-2100
U.S. News ranking: Nat. U., No. 205
Website: wayne.edu/
Admissions email: studentservice@wayne.edu
Public; founded 1868
Freshman admissions: selective; 2017-2018: 15,331 applied, 10,334 accepted. Either SAT or ACT required. SAT 25/75 percentile: 1000-1210. High school rank: 19% in top tenth, 47% in top quarter, 79% in top half
Early decision deadline: N/A, notification date: N/A
Early action deadline: N/A, notification date: N/A
Application deadline (fall): 8/1
Undergraduate student body: 12,409 full time, 4,913 part time; 44% male, 56% female; 0% American Indian, 10% Asian, 17% black, 5% Hispanic, 4% multiracial, 0% Pacific Islander, 59% white, 2% international; 98% from in state; 13% live on campus; N/A of students in fraternities, N/A in sororities
Most popular majors: 11% Psychology, General, 6% Biology/Biological Sciences, General, 5% Social Work, 4% International Business/Trade/Commerce, 3% Health Professions and Related Clinical Sciences, Other
Expenses: 2017-2018: $13,776 in state, $29,663 out of state; room/board: $10,106
Financial aid: (313) 577-2100; 72% of undergrads determined to have financial need; average aid package $11,695

Western Michigan University
Kalamazoo MI
(269) 387-2000
U.S. News ranking: Nat. U., No. 205
Website: wmich.edu/
Admissions email: ask-wmu@wmich.edu
Public; founded 1903
Freshman admissions: selective; 2017-2018: 14,263 applied, 11,741 accepted. Either SAT or ACT required. SAT 25/75 percentile: 960-1190. High school rank: 11% in top tenth, 33% in top quarter, 70% in top half
Early decision deadline: N/A, notification date: N/A
Early action deadline: N/A, notification date: N/A
Application deadline (fall): rolling
Undergraduate student body: 15,063 full time, 2,873 part time; 50% male, 50% female; 0% American Indian, 2% Asian, 12% black, 6% Hispanic, 4% multiracial, 0% Pacific Islander, 71% white, 4% international; 90% from in state; 28% live on campus; 6% of students in fraternities, 8% in sororities
Most popular majors: 20% Business, Management, Marketing, and Related Support Services, 12% Health Professions and Related Programs, 8% Multi/Interdisciplinary Studies, 7% Engineering, 6% Visual and Performing Arts
Expenses: 2018-2019: $12,483 in state, $15,373 out of state; room/board: $10,143
Financial aid: (269) 387-6000; 45% of undergrads determined to have financial need; average aid package $13,776

MINNESOTA

Augsburg University
Minneapolis MN
(612) 330-1001
U.S. News ranking: Reg. U. (Mid. W), No. 20
Website: www.augsburg.edu
Admissions email: admissions@augsburg.edu
Private; founded 1869
Affiliation: Evangelical Lutheran Church
Freshman admissions: selective; 2017-2018: 3,163 applied, 1,423 accepted. Either SAT or ACT required. ACT 25/75 percentile: 19-24. High school rank: N/A
Early decision deadline: N/A, notification date: N/A
Early action deadline: N/A, notification date: N/A
Application deadline (fall): 8/1
Undergraduate student body: 2,033 full time, 394 part time; 46% male, 54% female; 1% American Indian, 9% Asian, 13% black, 8% Hispanic, 4% multiracial, 0% Pacific Islander, 46% white, 3% international; 89% from in state; 36% live on campus; N/A of students in fraternities, N/A in sororities
Most popular majors: 21% Business, Management, Marketing, and Related Support Services, 12% Health Professions and Related Programs, 10% Education, 8% Social Sciences, 5% Psychology
Expenses: 2018-2019: $38,800; room/board: $10,280
Financial aid: (612) 330-1046; 81% of undergrads determined to have financial need; average aid package $32,019

Bemidji State University
Bemidji MN
(218) 755-2040
U.S. News ranking: Reg. U. (Mid. W), No. 94
Website: www.bemidjistate.edu
Admissions email: admissions@bemidjistate.edu
Public; founded 1919
Freshman admissions: selective; 2017-2018: 4,033 applied, 2,670 accepted. Either SAT or ACT required. ACT 25/75 percentile: 20-24. High school rank: 11% in top tenth, 30% in top quarter, 73% in top half
Early decision deadline: N/A, notification date: N/A
Early action deadline: N/A, notification date: N/A
Application deadline (fall): rolling
Undergraduate student body: 3,351 full time, 1,482 part time; 42% male, 58% female; 3% American Indian, 1% Asian, 2% black, 2% Hispanic, 3% multiracial, 0% Pacific Islander, 84% white, 2% international; 88% from in state; 28% live on campus; N/A of students in fraternities, N/A in sororities
Most popular majors: 23% Business, Management, Marketing, and Related Support Services, 19% Health Professions and Related Programs, 14% Education, 6% Homeland Security, Law Enforcement, Firefighting and Related Protective Services, 5% Biological and Biomedical Sciences
Expenses: 2018-2019: $8,690 in state, $8,690 out of state; room/board: $8,408
Financial aid: (218) 755-2034; 64% of undergrads determined to have financial need; average aid package $10,192

Bethany Lutheran College
Mankato MN
(507) 344-7331
U.S. News ranking: Nat. Lib. Arts, second tier
Website: www.blc.edu
Admissions email: admiss@blc.edu
Private; founded 1927
Affiliation: Evangelical Lutheran Church
Freshman admissions: selective; 2017-2018: 388 applied, 307 accepted. Either SAT or ACT required. ACT 25/75 percentile: 20-25. High school rank: 17% in top tenth, 34% in top quarter, 56% in top half
Early decision deadline: N/A, notification date: N/A
Early action deadline: N/A, notification date: N/A
Application deadline (fall): 7/1
Undergraduate student body: 523 full time, 129 part time; 46% male, 54% female; 0% American Indian, 0% Asian, 3% black, 4% Hispanic, 3% multiracial, 0% Pacific Islander, 84% white, 5% international; 76% from in state; 64% live on campus; 0% of students in fraternities, 0% in sororities
Most popular majors: 21% Business, Management, Marketing, and Related Support Services, 17% Communication, Journalism, and Related Programs, 16% Biological and Biomedical Sciences, 9% Education, 7% Visual and Performing Arts
Expenses: 2018-2019: $27,780; room/board: $8,100
Financial aid: (507) 344-7328; 80% of undergrads determined to have financial need; average aid package $22,773

Bethel University
St. Paul MN
(800) 255-8706
U.S. News ranking: Reg. U. (Mid. W), No. 17
Website: www.bethel.edu
Admissions email: undergrad-admissions@bethel.edu
Private; founded 1871
Affiliation: Baptist
Freshman admissions: selective; 2017-2018: 1,812 applied, 1,513 accepted. Either SAT or ACT required. ACT 25/75 percentile: 21-27. High school rank: 25% in top tenth, 52% in top quarter, 81% in top half
Early decision deadline: N/A, notification date: N/A
Early action deadline: N/A, notification date: N/A
Application deadline (fall): rolling
Undergraduate student body: 2,407 full time, 497 part time; 38% male, 62% female; 0% American Indian, 3% Asian, 4% black, 5% Hispanic, 4% multiracial, 0% Pacific Islander, 76% white, 0% international; 81% from in state; 63% live on campus; N/A of students in fraternities, N/A in sororities
Most popular majors: 16% Business, Management, Marketing, and Related Support Services, 16% Health Professions and Related Programs, 13% Education, 8% Biological and Biomedical Sciences, 7% Communication, Journalism, and Related Programs
Expenses: 2018-2019: $37,300; room/board: $10,520
Financial aid: (651) 638-6241; 75% of undergrads determined to have financial need; average aid package $28,736

Capella University[1]
Minneapolis MN
(866) 283-7921
U.S. News ranking: Nat. U., unranked
Website: www.capella.edu
Admissions email: admissionsoffice@capella.edu
For-profit
Application deadline (fall): N/A
Undergraduate student body: N/A full time, N/A part time
Expenses: 2017-2018: $14,250; room/board: N/A
Financial aid: N/A

Carleton College
Northfield MN
(507) 222-4190
U.S. News ranking: Nat. Lib. Arts, No. 5
Website: www.carleton.edu
Admissions email: admissions@carleton.edu
Private; founded 1866
Freshman admissions: most selective; 2017-2018: 6,499 applied, 1,378 accepted. Either SAT or ACT required. ACT 25/75 percentile: 31-34. High school rank: 86% in top tenth, 98% in top quarter, 100% in top half
Early decision deadline: 11/15, notification date: 12/15
Early action deadline: N/A, notification date: N/A
Application deadline (fall): 1/15
Undergraduate student body: 2,055 full time, 23 part time; 49% male, 51% female; 0% American Indian, 8% Asian, 5% black, 8% Hispanic, 6% multiracial, 0% Pacific Islander, 61% white, 10% international; 15% from in state; 96% live on campus; 0% of students in fraternities, 0% in sororities
Most popular majors: 19% Social Sciences, 14% Physical Sciences, 12% Computer and Information Sciences and Support Services, 10% Biological and Biomedical Sciences, 10% Mathematics and Statistics
Expenses: 2018-2019: $54,759; room/board: $14,085
Financial aid: (507) 222-4138; 55% of undergrads determined to have financial need; average aid package $48,110

College of St. Benedict
St. Joseph MN
(320) 363-5060
U.S. News ranking: Nat. Lib. Arts, No. 86
Website: www.csbsju.edu
Admissions email: admissions@csbsju.edu
Private; founded 1913
Affiliation: Roman Catholic
Freshman admissions: more selective; 2017-2018: 2,003 applied, 1,615 accepted. Either SAT or ACT required. ACT 25/75 percentile: 22-28. High school rank: 32% in top tenth, 66% in top quarter, 93% in top half
Early decision deadline: N/A, notification date: N/A
Early action deadline: 11/15, notification date: 12/15
Application deadline (fall): N/A
Undergraduate student body: 1,916 full time, 21 part time; 0% male, 100% female; 1% American Indian, 6% Asian, 3% black, 7% Hispanic, 0% multiracial, 0% Pacific Islander, 80% white, 4% international; 84% from in

state; 91% live on campus; 0% of students in fraternities, 0% in sororities
Most popular majors: 11% Biology/Biological Sciences, General, 11% Rhetoric and Composition, 10% Registered Nursing/Registered Nurse, 9% Elementary Education and Teaching, 9% Psychology, General
Expenses: 2018-2019: $45,264; room/board: $10,904
Financial aid: (320) 363-5388; 75% of undergrads determined to have financial need; average aid package $36,390

College of St. Scholastica

Duluth MN
(218) 723-6046
U.S. News ranking: Reg. U. (Mid. W), No. 47
Website: www.css.edu
Admissions email: admissions@css.edu
Private; founded 1912
Affiliation: Roman Catholic
Freshman admissions: selective; 2017-2018: 3,834 applied, 2,617 accepted. Either SAT or ACT required. ACT 25/75 percentile: 19-27. High school rank: 25% in top tenth, 55% in top quarter, 85% in top half
Early decision deadline: N/A, notification date: N/A
Early action deadline: N/A, notification date: N/A
Application deadline (fall): rolling
Undergraduate student body: 2,179 full time, 540 part time; 29% male, 71% female; 1% American Indian, 2% Asian, 3% black, 4% Hispanic, 3% multiracial, 0% Pacific Islander, 84% white, 2% international; 86% from in state; 52% live on campus; 0% of students in fraternities, 0% in sororities
Most popular majors: 48% Health Professions and Related Programs, 14% Business, Management, Marketing, and Related Support Services, 12% Biological and Biomedical Sciences, 8% Public Administration and Social Service Professions, 5% Psychology
Expenses: 2018-2019: $37,212; room/board: $9,710
Financial aid: (218) 723-7027; 80% of undergrads determined to have financial need; average aid package $26,120

Concordia College–Moorhead

Moorhead MN
(800) 699-9897
U.S. News ranking: Nat. Lib. Arts, No. 127
Website: www.concordiacollege.edu
Admissions email: admissions@cord.edu
Private; founded 1891
Affiliation: Evangelical Lutheran Church
Freshman admissions: more selective; 2017-2018: 4,539 applied, 2,796 accepted. Either SAT or ACT required. ACT 25/75 percentile: 22-28. High school rank: 27% in top tenth, 55% in top quarter, 85% in top half
Early decision deadline: N/A, notification date: N/A
Early action deadline: N/A, notification date: N/A
Application deadline (fall): 9/10
Undergraduate student body: 1,997 full time, 37 part time; 42% male, 58% female; 1% American Indian, 2% Asian, 2% black, 2% Hispanic, 2% multiracial, 0% Pacific Islander, 84% white, 4% international; 71% from in state; 61% live on campus; 0% of students in fraternities, 0% in sororities
Most popular majors: 16% Business, Management, Marketing, and Related Support Services, 12% Biological and Biomedical Sciences, 12% Education, 8% Communication, Journalism, and Related Programs, 7% Psychology
Expenses: 2018-2019: $40,042; room/board: $8,230
Financial aid: (218) 299-3010; 74% of undergrads determined to have financial need; average aid package $30,890

Concordia University–St. Paul

St. Paul MN
(651) 641-8230
U.S. News ranking: Reg. U. (Mid. W), No. 94
Website: www.csp.edu
Admissions email: admissions@csp.edu
Private; founded 1893
Affiliation: Lutheran Church–Missouri Synod
Freshman admissions: selective; 2017-2018: 1,500 applied, 823 accepted. Either SAT or ACT required. ACT 25/75 percentile: 18-24. High school rank: N/A
Early decision deadline: N/A, notification date: N/A
Early action deadline: N/A, notification date: N/A
Application deadline (fall): 8/1
Undergraduate student body: 1,444 full time, 1,407 part time; 41% male, 59% female; 0% American Indian, 8% Asian, 12% black, 5% Hispanic, 4% multiracial, 0% Pacific Islander, 64% white, 4% international; 74% from in state; 18% live on campus; N/A of students in fraternities, N/A in sororities
Most popular majors: 15% Business Administration and Management, General, 13% Kinesiology and Exercise Science, 7% Psychology, General, 6% Criminal Justice/Safety Studies, 5% Marketing/Marketing Management, General
Expenses: 2018-2019: $22,775; room/board: $9,000
Financial aid: (651) 603-6300; 76% of undergrads determined to have financial need; average aid package $14,920

Crown College

St. Bonifacius MN
(952) 446-4142
U.S. News ranking: Reg. Coll. (Mid. W), No. 46
Website: www.crown.edu
Admissions email: admissions@crown.edu
Private; founded 1916
Affiliation: Christ and Missionary Alliance Church
Freshman admissions: selective; 2017-2018: 873 applied, 447 accepted. Either SAT or ACT required. ACT 25/75 percentile: 18-25. High school rank: 61% in top tenth, 17% in top quarter, N/A in top half
Early decision deadline: N/A, notification date: N/A
Early action deadline: N/A, notification date: N/A
Application deadline (fall): 8/20
Undergraduate student body: 698 full time, 361 part time; 46% male, 54% female; 1% American Indian, 7% Asian, 8% black, 7% Hispanic, 2% multiracial, 0% Pacific Islander, 72% white, 2% international
Most popular majors: Information not available
Expenses: 2018-2019: $26,200; room/board: $8,660
Financial aid: (952) 446-4177; 87% of undergrads determined to have financial need; average aid package $17,709

Dunwoody College of Technology

Minneapolis MN
(800) 292-4625
U.S. News ranking: Reg. Coll. (Mid. W), No. 30
Website: www.dunwoody.edu
Admissions email: admissions@dunwoody.edu
Private; founded 1914
Freshman admissions: less selective; 2017-2018: 929 applied, 752 accepted. Neither SAT nor ACT required. SAT 25/75 percentile: N/A. High school rank: 10% in top tenth, 30% in top quarter, 72% in top half
Early decision deadline: N/A, notification date: N/A
Early action deadline: N/A, notification date: N/A
Application deadline (fall): rolling
Undergraduate student body: 1,073 full time, 229 part time; 83% male, 17% female; 0% American Indian, 8% Asian, 4% black, 3% Hispanic, 5% multiracial, 0% Pacific Islander, 74% white, 0% international; 98% from in state; 0% live on campus; 0% of students in fraternities, 0% in sororities
Most popular majors: 43% Manufacturing Engineering, 37% Business Administration and Management, General, 12% Construction Management, 4% Computer Science, 4% Interior Design
Expenses: 2018-2019: $21,974; room/board: N/A
Financial aid: (612) 381-3347; 74% of undergrads determined to have financial need; average aid package $11,266

Gustavus Adolphus College

St. Peter MN
(507) 933-7676
U.S. News ranking: Nat. Lib. Arts, No. 90
Website: gustavus.edu
Admissions email: admission@gustavus.edu
Private; founded 1862
Affiliation: Evangelical Lutheran Church
Freshman admissions: more selective; 2017-2018: 4,834 applied, 3,279 accepted. Neither SAT nor ACT required. ACT 25/75 percentile: 24-30. High school rank: 33% in top tenth, 65% in top quarter, 93% in top half
Early decision deadline: N/A, notification date: N/A
Early action deadline: 11/1, notification date: 11/15
Application deadline (fall): 4/1
Undergraduate student body: 2,170 full time, 31 part time; 44% male, 56% female; 0% American Indian, 5% Asian, 2% black, 5% Hispanic, 4% multiracial, 0% Pacific Islander, 78% white, 5% international; 83% from in state; 95% live on campus; 13% of students in fraternities, 15% in sororities
Most popular majors: 14% Business, Management, Marketing, and Related Support Services, 11% Social Sciences, 10% Biological and Biomedical Sciences, 9% Physical Sciences, 9% Psychology
Expenses: 2018-2019: $45,100; room/board: $9,910
Financial aid: (507) 933-7527; 70% of undergrads determined to have financial need; average aid package $37,892

Hamline University

St. Paul MN
(651) 523-2207
U.S. News ranking: Reg. U. (Mid. W), No. 13
Website: www.hamline.edu
Admissions email: admission@hamline.edu
Private; founded 1854
Affiliation: United Methodist
Freshman admissions: selective; 2017-2018: 4,250 applied, 2,937 accepted. Either SAT or ACT required. ACT 25/75 percentile: 20-26. High school rank: 19% in top tenth, 43% in top quarter, 81% in top half
Early decision deadline: 11/1, notification date: 11/15
Early action deadline: 12/1, notification date: N/A
Application deadline (fall): rolling
Undergraduate student body: 2,082 full time, 86 part time; 39% male, 61% female; 0% American Indian, 7% Asian, 9% black, 9% Hispanic, 6% multiracial, 0% Pacific Islander, 66% white, 1% international; 81% from in state; 38% live on campus; N/A of students in fraternities, N/A in sororities
Most popular majors: 17% Social Sciences, 15% Business, Management, Marketing, and Related Support Services, 8% English Language and Literature/Letters, 8% Multi/Interdisciplinary Studies, 8% Psychology
Expenses: 2018-2019: $41,473; room/board: $10,358
Financial aid: (651) 523-2933; 85% of undergrads determined to have financial need; average aid package $30,738

Macalester College

St. Paul MN
(651) 696-6357
U.S. News ranking: Nat. Lib. Arts, No. 27
Website: www.macalester.edu
Admissions email: admissions@macalester.edu
Private; founded 1874
Freshman admissions: most selective; 2017-2018: 5,900 applied, 2,394 accepted. Either SAT or ACT required. ACT 25/75 percentile: 29-32. High school rank: 67% in top tenth, 91% in top quarter, 100% in top half
Early decision deadline: 11/15, notification date: 12/15
Early action deadline: N/A, notification date: N/A
Application deadline (fall): 1/15
Undergraduate student body: 2,093 full time, 43 part time; 39% male, 61% female; 0% American Indian, 7% Asian, 3% black, 8% Hispanic, 6% multiracial, 0% Pacific Islander, 61% white, 15% international; 17% from in state; 60% live on campus; 0% of students in fraternities, 0% in sororities
Most popular majors: 27% Social Sciences, 14% Biological and Biomedical Sciences, 8% Multi/Interdisciplinary Studies, 7% Foreign Languages, Literatures, and Linguistics, 6% Mathematics and Statistics
Expenses: 2018-2019: $54,348; room/board: $12,156
Financial aid: (651) 696-6214; 70% of undergrads determined to have financial need; average aid package $45,680

Metropolitan State University[1]

St. Paul MN
(651) 772-7600
U.S. News ranking: Reg. U. (Mid. W), second tier
Website: www.metrostate.edu
Admissions email: admissions@metrostate.edu
Public
Application deadline (fall): N/A
Undergraduate student body: N/A full time, N/A part time
Expenses: 2017-2018: $7,859 in state, $14,960 out of state; room/board: N/A
Financial aid: N/A

Minneapolis College of Art and Design

Minneapolis MN
(612) 874-3800
U.S. News ranking: Arts, unranked
Website: www.mcad.edu
Admissions email: admissions@mcad.edu
Private; founded 1886
Freshman admissions: selective; 2017-2018: 692 applied, 405 accepted. Either SAT or ACT required. ACT 25/75 percentile: 20-26. High school rank: N/A
Early decision deadline: N/A, notification date: N/A
Early action deadline: 12/1, notification date: 12/15
Application deadline (fall): 4/1

Undergraduate student body: 668 full time, 20 part time; 31% male, 69% female; 2% American Indian, 8% Asian, 6% black, 7% Hispanic, 2% multiracial, 0% Pacific Islander, 67% white, 2% international; 53% from in state; 42% live on campus; 0% of students in fraternities, 0% in sororities
Most popular majors: 68% Visual and Performing Arts, 16% Communications Technologies/Technicians and Support Services, 9% Business, Management, Marketing, and Related Support Services, 4% Precision Production, 3% Communication, Journalism, and Related Programs
Expenses: 2018-2019: $39,210; room/board: N/A
Financial aid: (612) 874-3733

Minnesota State University–Mankato

Mankato MN
(507) 389-1822
U.S. News ranking: Reg. U. (Mid. W), No. 111
Website: www.mnsu.edu
Admissions email: admissions@mnsu.edu
Public; founded 1868
Freshman admissions: selective; 2017-2018: 11,689 applied, 7,126 accepted. ACT required. ACT 25/75 percentile: 20-24. High school rank: 7% in top tenth, 27% in top quarter, 69% in top half
Early decision deadline: N/A, notification date: N/A
Early action deadline: N/A, notification date: N/A
Application deadline (fall): rolling
Undergraduate student body: 10,832 full time, 1,950 part time; 47% male, 53% female; 0% American Indian, 4% Asian, 6% black, 4% Hispanic, 3% multiracial, 0% Pacific Islander, 73% white, 9% international; 86% from in state; 22% live on campus; N/A of students in fraternities, N/A in sororities
Most popular majors: 8% Health Professions and Related Programs, 6% Psychology, 5% Business, Management, Marketing, and Related Support Services, 4% Communication, Journalism, and Related Programs, 4% Homeland Security, Law Enforcement, Firefighting and Related Protective Services
Expenses: 2017-2018: $8,164 in state, $16,216 out of state; room/board: $9,096
Financial aid: (507) 389-1419

Minnesota State University–Moorhead

Moorhead MN
(800) 593-7246
U.S. News ranking: Reg. U. (Mid. W), No. 101
Website: www.mnstate.edu
Admissions email: admissions@mnstate.edu
Public; founded 1887
Freshman admissions: selective; 2017-2018: 4,400 applied, 2,657 accepted. Either SAT or ACT required. ACT 25/75 percentile: 20-25. High school rank: 11% in top tenth, 30% in top quarter, 65% in top half
Early decision deadline: N/A, notification date: N/A
Early action deadline: N/A, notification date: N/A
Application deadline (fall): rolling
Undergraduate student body: 4,165 full time, 982 part time; 39% male, 61% female; 1% American Indian, 1% Asian, 3% black, 3% Hispanic, 4% multiracial, 0% Pacific Islander, 79% white, 7% international; 68% from in state; 25% live on campus; 1% of students in fraternities, 2% in sororities
Most popular majors: 16% Business, Management, Marketing, and Related Support Services, 16% Education, 11% Health Professions and Related Programs, 11% Visual and Performing Arts, 6% Communication, Journalism, and Related Programs
Expenses: 2018-2019: $8,496 in state, $15,906 out of state; room/board: $9,280
Financial aid: (218) 477-2251; 61% of undergrads determined to have financial need; average aid package $3,211

North Central University

Minneapolis MN
(800) 289-6222
U.S. News ranking: Reg. Coll. (Mid. W), No. 57
Website: www.northcentral.edu
Admissions email: admissions@northcentral.edu
Private; founded 1930
Affiliation: Assemblies of God Church
Freshman admissions: selective; 2017-2018: 739 applied, 480 accepted. Either SAT or ACT required. ACT 25/75 percentile: 18-25. High school rank: 16% in top tenth, 45% in top quarter, 71% in top half
Early decision deadline: N/A, notification date: N/A
Early action deadline: 12/1, notification date: 8/1
Application deadline (fall): rolling
Undergraduate student body: 860 full time, 24 part time; 44% male, 56% female; 0% American Indian, 3% Asian, 5% black, 6% Hispanic, 4% multiracial, 0% Pacific Islander, 73% white, 1% international; 49% from in state; 82% live on campus; 0% of students in fraternities, 0% in sororities
Most popular majors: 23% Human Development and Family Studies, General, 19% Pastoral Studies/Counseling, 17% Youth Ministry, 16% Elementary Education and Teaching, 15% Religious/Sacred Music
Expenses: 2018-2019: $24,240; room/board: $7,400
Financial aid: (612) 343-4485; 85% of undergrads determined to have financial need; average aid package $18,460

Southwest Minnesota State University

Marshall MN
(507) 537-6286
U.S. News ranking: Reg. U. (Mid. W), second tier
Website: www.smsu.edu
Admissions email: smsu.admissions@smsu.edu
Public
Freshman admissions: selective; 2017-2018: 2,051 applied, 1,264 accepted. Either SAT or ACT required. ACT 25/75 percentile: 18-24. High school rank: 5% in top tenth, 20% in top quarter, 50% in top half
Early decision deadline: N/A, notification date: N/A
Early action deadline: N/A, notification date: N/A
Application deadline (fall): 9/1
Undergraduate student body: 1,900 full time, 4,626 part time; 41% male, 59% female; 1% American Indian, 3% Asian, 7% black, 3% Hispanic, 0% multiracial, 0% Pacific Islander, 78% white, 6% international
Most popular majors: Business, Management, Marketing, and Related Support Services, Education, Parks, Recreation, Leisure, and Fitness Studies, Psychology
Expenses: 2018-2019: $8,612 in state, $8,612 out of state; room/board: $8,502
Financial aid: (507) 537-6281; 67% of undergrads determined to have financial need; average aid package $9,396

St. Catherine University

St. Paul MN
(800) 945-4599
U.S. News ranking: Reg. U. (Mid. W), No. 13
Website: www.stkate.edu
Admissions email: admissions@stkate.edu
Private; founded 1905
Affiliation: Roman Catholic
Freshman admissions: selective; 2017-2018: 2,682 applied, 1,881 accepted. Either SAT or ACT required. ACT 25/75 percentile: 21-26. High school rank: 24% in top tenth, 62% in top quarter, 94% in top half
Early decision deadline: N/A, notification date: N/A
Early action deadline: N/A, notification date: N/A
Application deadline (fall): rolling
Undergraduate student body: 2,124 full time, 1,034 part time; 4% male, 96% female; 0% American Indian, 11% Asian, 10% black, 9% Hispanic, 4% multiracial, 0% Pacific Islander, 62% white, 1% international; 87% from in state; 38% live on campus; N/A of students in fraternities, N/A in sororities
Most popular majors: 32% Registered Nursing/Registered Nurse, 7% Public Health, General, 7% Social Work, 4% Accounting, 4% Psychology, General
Expenses: 2018-2019: $39,669; room/board: $9,260
Financial aid: (651) 690-6061; 85% of undergrads determined to have financial need; average aid package $36,000

St. Cloud State University

St. Cloud MN
(320) 308-2244
U.S. News ranking: Reg. U. (Mid. W), No. 118
Website: www.stcloudstate.edu
Admissions email: scsu4u@stcloudstate.edu
Public; founded 1869
Freshman admissions: selective; 2017-2018: 6,387 applied, 5,479 accepted. Either SAT or ACT required. ACT 25/75 percentile: 18-24. High school rank: 7% in top tenth, 27% in top quarter, 62% in top half
Early decision deadline: N/A, notification date: N/A
Early action deadline: N/A, notification date: N/A
Application deadline (fall): 8/11
Undergraduate student body: 8,364 full time, 4,424 part time; 47% male, 53% female; 0% American Indian, 7% Asian, 8% black, 4% Hispanic, 4% multiracial, 0% Pacific Islander, 67% white, 10% international; 89% from in state; 17% live on campus; 2% of students in fraternities, 3% in sororities
Most popular majors: 23% Business, Management, Marketing, and Related Support Services, 9% Education, 9% Health Professions and Related Programs, 8% Communication, Journalism, and Related Programs, 8% Psychology
Expenses: 2017-2018: $8,184 in state, $16,418 out of state; room/board: $8,230
Financial aid: (320) 308-2047; 59% of undergrads determined to have financial need; average aid package $11,989

St. John's University

Collegeville MN
(320) 363-5060
U.S. News ranking: Nat. Lib. Arts, No. 95
Website: www.csbsju.edu
Admissions email: admissions@csbsju.edu
Private; founded 1857
Affiliation: Roman Catholic
Freshman admissions: selective; 2017-2018: 1,639 applied, 1,315 accepted. Either SAT or ACT required. ACT 25/75 percentile: 22-27. High school rank: 15% in top tenth, 43% in top quarter, 80% in top half
Early decision deadline: N/A, notification date: N/A
Early action deadline: 11/15, notification date: 12/15
Application deadline (fall): N/A
Undergraduate student body: 1,703 full time, 17 part time; 100% male, 0% female; 1% American Indian, 3% Asian, 5% black, 8% Hispanic, 0% multiracial, 0% Pacific Islander, 78% white, 5% international; 80% from in state; 91% live on campus; 0% of students in fraternities, 0% in sororities
Most popular majors: 20% Business Administration and Management, General, 12% Accounting, 10% Biology/Biological Sciences, General, 6% Economics, General, 6% Rhetoric and Composition
Expenses: 2018-2019: $44,990; room/board: $10,319
Financial aid: (320) 363-3664; 69% of undergrads determined to have financial need; average aid package $33,379

St. Mary's University of Minnesota

Winona MN
(507) 457-1700
U.S. News ranking: Reg. U. (Mid. W), No. 50
Website: www.smumn.edu
Admissions email: admission@smumn.edu
Private; founded 1912
Affiliation: Roman Catholic
Freshman admissions: selective; 2017-2018: 2,417 applied, 1,556 accepted. Either SAT or ACT required. ACT 25/75 percentile: 20-25. High school rank: N/A
Early decision deadline: N/A, notification date: N/A
Early action deadline: N/A, notification date: N/A
Application deadline (fall): 5/1
Undergraduate student body: 1,129 full time, 374 part time; 47% male, 53% female; 1% American Indian, 3% Asian, 8% black, 8% Hispanic, 1% multiracial, 0% Pacific Islander, 66% white, 3% international; 55% from in state; 85% live on campus; 4% of students in fraternities, 3% in sororities
Most popular majors: 12% Business Administration and Management, General, 10% Health/Health Care Administration/Management, 7% Psychology, General, 6% Accounting, 5% Criminal Justice/Police Science
Expenses: 2018-2019: $35,110; room/board: $9,080
Financial aid: (612) 238-4552; 74% of undergrads determined to have financial need; average aid package $27,927

St. Olaf College

Northfield MN
(507) 786-3025
U.S. News ranking: Nat. Lib. Arts, No. 61
Website: wp.stolaf.edu/
Admissions email: admissions@stolaf.edu
Private; founded 1874
Freshman admissions: more selective; 2017-2018: 5,949 applied, 2,571 accepted. Either SAT or ACT required. ACT 25/75 percentile: 25-31. High school rank: 45% in top tenth, 76% in top quarter, 94% in top half
Early decision deadline: 11/15, notification date: 12/15
Early action deadline: N/A, notification date: N/A
Application deadline (fall): 1/15
Undergraduate student body: 3,003 full time, 32 part time; 42% male, 58% female; 0% American Indian, 7% Asian, 3% black, 6% Hispanic, 3% multiracial,

0% Pacific Islander, 71% white, 10% international; 47% from in state; 94% live on campus; N/A of students in fraternities, N/A in sororities
Most popular majors: 17% Social Sciences, 11% Biological and Biomedical Sciences, 10% Visual and Performing Arts, 8% Physical Sciences, 7% Psychology
Expenses: 2018-2019: $47,840; room/board: $10,850
Financial aid: (507) 786-3019; 74% of undergrads determined to have financial need; average aid package $40,769

University of Minnesota–Crookston

Crookston MN
(800) 232-6466
U.S. News ranking: Reg. Coll. (Mid. W), No. 36
Website: www.crk.umn.edu
Admissions email: UMCinfo@umn.edu
Public; founded 1966
Freshman admissions: selective; 2017-2018: 1,377 applied, 946 accepted. Either SAT or ACT required. ACT 25/75 percentile: 19-24. High school rank: 16% in top tenth, 34% in top quarter, 66% in top half
Early decision deadline: N/A, notification date: N/A
Early action deadline: N/A, notification date: N/A
Application deadline (fall): rolling
Undergraduate student body: 1,195 full time, 1,639 part time; 46% male, 54% female; 1% American Indian, 3% Asian, 6% black, 4% Hispanic, 2% multiracial, 0% Pacific Islander, 76% white, 5% international; 69% from in state; N/A live on campus; N/A of students in fraternities, N/A in sororities
Most popular majors: 43% Business, Management, Marketing, and Related Support Services, 14% Agriculture, Agriculture Operations, and Related Sciences, 13% Health Professions and Related Programs, 7% Natural Resources and Conservation, 5% Multi/Interdisciplinary Studies
Expenses: 2017-2018: $12,202 in state, $12,202 out of state; room/board: $7,658
Financial aid: (218) 281-6510

University of Minnesota–Duluth

Duluth MN
(218) 726-7171
U.S. News ranking: Reg. U. (Mid. W), No. 45
Website: www.d.umn.edu
Admissions email: umdadmis@d.umn.edu
Public; founded 1947
Freshman admissions: selective; 2017-2018: 8,689 applied, 6,660 accepted. Either SAT or ACT required. ACT 25/75 percentile: 22-26. High school rank: 18% in top tenth, 48% in top quarter, 88% in top half
Early decision deadline: N/A, notification date: N/A
Early action deadline: N/A, notification date: N/A
Application deadline (fall): 6/15
Undergraduate student body: 8,906 full time, 1,212 part time; 53% male, 47% female; 0% American Indian, 4% Asian, 2% black, 3% Hispanic, 3% multiracial, 0% Pacific Islander, 85% white, 2% international; 88% from in state; 32% live on campus; N/A of students in fraternities, N/A in sororities
Most popular majors: 20% Business, Management, Marketing, and Related Support Services, 12% Engineering, 10% Biological and Biomedical Sciences, 9% Social Sciences, 7% Education
Expenses: 2018-2019: $13,367 in state, $18,485 out of state; room/board: $7,760
Financial aid: (218) 726-8000; 58% of undergrads determined to have financial need; average aid package $12,884

University of Minnesota–Morris

Morris MN
(888) 866-3382
U.S. News ranking: Nat. Lib. Arts, No. 155
Website: www.morris.umn.edu
Admissions email: admissions@morris.umn.edu
Public; founded 1959
Freshman admissions: more selective; 2017-2018: 3,211 applied, 2,048 accepted. Either SAT or ACT required. ACT 25/75 percentile: 22-28. High school rank: 24% in top tenth, 49% in top quarter, 84% in top half
Early decision deadline: N/A, notification date: N/A
Early action deadline: N/A, notification date: N/A
Application deadline (fall): 3/15
Undergraduate student body: 1,526 full time, 101 part time; 44% male, 56% female; 8% American Indian, 3% Asian, 2% black, 5% Hispanic, 13% multiracial, 0% Pacific Islander, 58% white, 11% international; 83% from in state; 52% live on campus; N/A of students in fraternities, N/A in sororities
Most popular majors: 11% Psychology, General, 8% Biology/Biological Sciences, General, 8% English Language and Literature, General, 6% Business Administration and Management, General, 5% Economics, General
Expenses: 2018-2019: $24,352 in state, $26,392 out of state; room/board: N/A
Financial aid: (320) 589-6046; 64% of undergrads determined to have financial need; average aid package $13,123

University of Minnesota–Twin Cities

Minneapolis MN
(800) 752-1000
U.S. News ranking: Nat. U., No. 76
Website: twin-cities.umn.edu/
Admissions email: N/A
Public; founded 1851
Freshman admissions: more selective; 2017-2018: 43,720 applied, 21,681 accepted. Either SAT or ACT required. ACT 25/75 percentile: 26-31. High school rank: 50% in top tenth, 84% in top quarter, 99% in top half
Early decision deadline: N/A, notification date: N/A
Early action deadline: N/A, notification date: N/A
Application deadline (fall): rolling
Undergraduate student body: 29,991 full time, 5,442 part time; 47% male, 53% female; 0% American Indian, 10% Asian, 5% black, 4% Hispanic, 4% multiracial, 0% Pacific Islander, 68% white, 9% international; 73% from in state; 23% live on campus; N/A of students in fraternities, N/A in sororities
Most popular majors: 12% Biological and Biomedical Sciences, 12% Engineering, 12% Social Sciences, 9% Business, Management, Marketing, and Related Support Services, 7% Psychology
Expenses: 2018-2019: $14,693 in state, $30,371 out of state; room/board: $10,312
Financial aid: (800) 400-8636; 49% of undergrads determined to have financial need; average aid package $13,381

University of Northwestern–St. Paul

St. Paul MN
(800) 692-4020
U.S. News ranking: Reg. U. (Mid. W), No. 58
Website: www.unwsp.edu
Admissions email: reerickson@unwsp.edu
Private; founded 1902
Affiliation: Undenominational
Freshman admissions: selective; 2017-2018: 1,213 applied, 1,133 accepted. Either SAT or ACT required. ACT 25/75 percentile: 21-27. High school rank: 27% in top tenth, 50% in top quarter, 81% in top half
Early decision deadline: N/A, notification date: N/A
Early action deadline: N/A, notification date: N/A
Application deadline (fall): 8/1
Undergraduate student body: 2,030 full time, 1,305 part time; 39% male, 61% female; 0% American Indian, 3% Asian, 4% black, 4% Hispanic, 4% multiracial, 0% Pacific Islander, 83% white, 1% international
Most popular majors: 10% Psychology, General, 8% Business Administration and Management, General, 7% Biology/Biological Sciences, General, 6% Registered Nursing/Registered Nurse, 5% Kinesiology and Exercise Science
Expenses: 2017-2018: $30,794; room/board: $9,270
Financial aid: (651) 631-5321

University of St. Thomas

St. Paul MN
(651) 962-6150
U.S. News ranking: Nat. U., No. 124
Website: www.stthomas.edu
Admissions email: admissions@stthomas.edu
Private; founded 1885
Affiliation: Roman Catholic
Freshman admissions: more selective; 2017-2018: 6,439 applied, 5,419 accepted. Either SAT or ACT required. ACT 25/75 percentile: 24-29. High school rank: 23% in top tenth, 55% in top quarter, 88% in top half
Early decision deadline: N/A, notification date: N/A
Early action deadline: 11/1, notification date: 12/15
Application deadline (fall): rolling
Undergraduate student body: 5,945 full time, 254 part time; 54% male, 46% female; 0% American Indian, 4% Asian, 3% black, 5% Hispanic, 3% multiracial, 0% Pacific Islander, 80% white, 3% international; 80% from in state; 41% live on campus; 0% of students in fraternities, 0% in sororities
Most popular majors: 42% Business, Management, Marketing, and Related Support Services, 8% Engineering, 6% Biological and Biomedical Sciences, 6% Philosophy and Religious Studies, 5% Social Sciences
Expenses: 2017-2018: $41,133; room/board: $10,054
Financial aid: (651) 962-6168; 54% of undergrads determined to have financial need; average aid package $28,746

Walden University[1]

Minneapolis MN
(866) 492-5336
U.S. News ranking: Nat. U., unranked
Website: www.waldenu.edu/
Admissions email: N/A
For-profit; founded 1970
Application deadline (fall): N/A
Undergraduate student body: N/A full time, N/A part time
Expenses: 2017-2018: $12,465; room/board: N/A
Financial aid: (443) 537-1719

Winona State University

Winona MN
(507) 457-5100
U.S. News ranking: Reg. U. (Mid. W), No. 72
Website: www.winona.edu
Admissions email: admissions@winona.edu
Public; founded 1858
Freshman admissions: selective; 2017-2018: 7,468 applied, 4,966 accepted. Either SAT or ACT required. ACT 25/75 percentile: 20-25. High school rank: 10% in top tenth, 31% in top quarter, 70% in top half
Early decision deadline: N/A, notification date: N/A
Early action deadline: N/A, notification date: N/A
Application deadline (fall): 7/16
Undergraduate student body: 6,501 full time, 935 part time; 37% male, 63% female; 0% American Indian, 2% Asian, 3% black, 3% Hispanic, 3% multiracial, 0% Pacific Islander, 85% white, 2% international; 72% from in state; 29% live on campus; N/A of students in fraternities, N/A in sororities
Most popular majors: 21% Business, Management, Marketing, and Related Support Services, 18% Health Professions and Related Programs, 15% Education, 7% Parks, Recreation, Leisure, and Fitness Studies, 6% Communication, Journalism, and Related Programs
Expenses: 2017-2018: $9,379 in state, $15,302 out of state; room/board: $8,730
Financial aid: (507) 457-2800

MISSISSIPPI

Alcorn State University

Lorman MS
(601) 877-6147
U.S. News ranking: Reg. U. (S), No. 89
Website: www.alcorn.edu
Admissions email: ksampson@alcorn.edu
Public; founded 1871
Freshman admissions: less selective; 2017-2018: 2,544 applied, 2,111 accepted. Either SAT or ACT required. ACT 25/75 percentile: 16-21. High school rank: 0% in top tenth, 0% in top quarter, 79% in top half
Early decision deadline: N/A, notification date: N/A
Early action deadline: N/A, notification date: N/A
Application deadline (fall): rolling
Undergraduate student body: 2,893 full time, 279 part time; 36% male, 64% female; 0% American Indian, 0% Asian, 91% black, 0% Hispanic, 2% multiracial, 0% Pacific Islander, 3% white, 3% international; 76% from in state; 64% live on campus; N/A of students in fraternities, N/A in sororities
Most popular majors: 17% Liberal Arts and Sciences, General Studies and Humanities, 16% Biological and Biomedical Sciences, 8% Health Professions and Related Programs, 7% Business, Management, Marketing, and Related Support Services, 5% Public Administration and Social Service Professions
Expenses: 2018-2019: $6,938 in state, $6,938 out of state; room/board: $9,238
Financial aid: (601) 877-6672; 42% of undergrads determined to have financial need; average aid package $7,517

Belhaven University

Jackson MS
(601) 968-5940
U.S. News ranking: Reg. U. (S), No. 65
Website: www.belhaven.edu
Admissions email: admission@belhaven.edu
Private; founded 1883
Affiliation: Presbyterian
Freshman admissions: selective; 2017-2018: 2,324 applied, 1,374 accepted. Either SAT or ACT required. ACT 25/75 percentile: 22-25. High school rank: 4% in top tenth, 27% in top quarter, 67% in top half
Early decision deadline: N/A, notification date: N/A
Early action deadline: N/A, notification date: N/A
Application deadline (fall): rolling
Undergraduate student body: 1,248 full time, 1,237 part time; 34% male, 66% female; 0% American Indian, 1% Asian, 45% black, 5% Hispanic, 3% multiracial, 0% Pacific Islander, 38% white, 2% international; 67% from in state; 22% live on campus; 0% of students in fraternities, 0% in sororities
Most popular majors: 32% Business Administration and Management, General, 9% Social Sciences, General, 8% Health/Health Care Administration/Management, 5% Bible/Biblical Studies, 5% Multi-/Interdisciplinary Studies, Other
Expenses: 2018-2019: $25,300; room/board: $8,500
Financial aid: (601) 968-5933; 78% of undergrads determined to have financial need; average aid package $17,835

Blue Mountain College

Blue Mountain MS
(662) 685-4161
U.S. News ranking: Reg. Coll. (S), No. 8
Website: www.bmc.edu
Admissions email: admissions@bmc.edu
Private; founded 1873
Affiliation: Southern Baptist
Freshman admissions: selective; 2017-2018: 207 applied, 206 accepted. Either SAT or ACT required. ACT 25/75 percentile: 18-24. High school rank: 13% in top tenth, 40% in top quarter, 70% in top half
Early decision deadline: N/A, notification date: N/A
Early action deadline: N/A, notification date: N/A
Application deadline (fall): rolling
Undergraduate student body: 531 full time, 57 part time; 45% male, 55% female; 1% American Indian, 0% Asian, 12% black, 2% Hispanic, 1% multiracial, 0% Pacific Islander, 82% white, 2% international; 81% from in state; 60% live on campus; 0% of students in fraternities, 0% in sororities
Most popular majors: 17% Bible/Biblical Studies, 16% Business Administration and Management, General, 16% Elementary Education and Teaching, 13% Psychology, General, 8% Biology/Biological Sciences, General
Expenses: 2018-2019: $12,584; room/board: $6,554
Financial aid: (662) 685-4771; 85% of undergrads determined to have financial need; average aid package $11,919

Delta State University[1]

Cleveland MS
(662) 846-4018
U.S. News ranking: Reg. U. (S), second tier
Website: www.deltastate.edu
Admissions email: admissions@deltastate.edu
Public; founded 1924
Application deadline (fall): 8/1
Undergraduate student body: N/A full time, N/A part time
Expenses: 2017-2018: $6,859 in state, $6,859 out of state; room/board: $7,584
Financial aid: (662) 846-4670

Jackson State University

Jackson MS
(601) 979-2100
U.S. News ranking: Nat. U., second tier
Website: www.jsums.edu
Admissions email: admappl@jsums.edu
Public; founded 1877
Freshman admissions: less selective; 2017-2018: 6,282 applied, 4,506 accepted. Either SAT or ACT required. ACT 25/75 percentile: 17-21. High school rank: N/A
Early decision deadline: N/A, notification date: N/A
Early action deadline: N/A, notification date: N/A
Application deadline (fall): 8/1
Undergraduate student body: 5,935 full time, 565 part time; 37% male, 63% female; 0% American Indian, 0% Asian, 91% black, 1% Hispanic, 1% multiracial, 0% Pacific Islander, 4% white, 2% international; N/A from in state; 1% live on campus; 1% of students in fraternities, 1% in sororities
Most popular majors: 14% Business, Management, Marketing, and Related Support Services, 12% Education, 12% Public Administration and Social Service Professions, 11% Biological and Biomedical Sciences, 9% Multi/Interdisciplinary Studies
Expenses: 2017-2018: $7,621 in state, $7,621 out of state; room/board: $8,952
Financial aid: (601) 979-2227; 85% of undergrads determined to have financial need; average aid package $11,283

Millsaps College

Jackson MS
(601) 974-1050
U.S. News ranking: Nat. Lib. Arts, No. 108
Website: www.millsaps.edu
Admissions email: admissions@millsaps.edu
Private; founded 1890
Affiliation: United Methodist
Freshman admissions: more selective; 2017-2018: 4,276 applied, 2,093 accepted. Either SAT or ACT required. ACT 25/75 percentile: 22-28. High school rank: 100% in top tenth, 100% in top quarter, 100% in top half
Early decision deadline: N/A, notification date: N/A
Early action deadline: 11/15, notification date: 1/15
Application deadline (fall): 7/1
Undergraduate student body: 796 full time, 11 part time; 51% male, 49% female; 1% American Indian, 3% Asian, 17% black, 5% Hispanic, 0% multiracial, 0% Pacific Islander, 66% white, 5% international; 44% from in state; 89% live on campus; 56% of students in fraternities, 55% in sororities
Most popular majors: 51% Business, Management, Marketing, and Related Support Services, 18% Biological and Biomedical Sciences, 8% Psychology, 5% Social Sciences, 4% Physical Sciences
Expenses: 2018-2019: $39,910; room/board: $13,730
Financial aid: (601) 974-1220; 65% of undergrads determined to have financial need; average aid package $34,823

Mississippi College

Clinton MS
(601) 925-3800
U.S. News ranking: Reg. U. (S), No. 32
Website: www.mc.edu
Admissions email: admissions@mc.edu
Private; founded 1826
Affiliation: Southern Baptist
Freshman admissions: more selective; 2017-2018: 2,918 applied, 1,139 accepted. Either SAT or ACT required. ACT 25/75 percentile: 22-29. High school rank: 40% in top tenth, 63% in top quarter, 86% in top half
Early decision deadline: N/A, notification date: N/A
Early action deadline: N/A, notification date: N/A
Application deadline (fall): rolling
Undergraduate student body: 2,793 full time, 449 part time; 38% male, 62% female; 1% American Indian, 2% Asian, 19% black, 3% Hispanic, 0% multiracial, 0% Pacific Islander, 70% white, 4% international; 72% from in state; 63% live on campus; 22% of students in fraternities, 32% in sororities
Most popular majors: 11% Kinesiology and Exercise Science, 11% Registered Nursing/Registered Nurse, 9% Business Administration and Management, General, 6% Biomedical Sciences, General, 6% Elementary Education and Teaching
Expenses: 2018-2019: $18,026; room/board: $10,300
Financial aid: (601) 925-3212; 52% of undergrads determined to have financial need; average aid package $16,941

Mississippi State University

Mississippi State MS
(662) 325-2224
U.S. News ranking: Nat. U., No. 177
Website: www.msstate.edu
Admissions email: admit@admissions.msstate.edu
Public; founded 1878
Freshman admissions: more selective; 2017-2018: 13,817 applied, 10,144 accepted. Either SAT or ACT required. ACT 25/75 percentile: 21-28. High school rank: 25% in top tenth, 54% in top quarter, 82% in top half
Early decision deadline: N/A, notification date: N/A
Early action deadline: N/A, notification date: N/A
Application deadline (fall): rolling
Undergraduate student body: 16,803 full time, 1,509 part time; 50% male, 50% female; 0% American Indian, 1% Asian, 20% black, 3% Hispanic, 2% multiracial, 0% Pacific Islander, 72% white, 1% international; 70% from in state; 27% live on campus; 14% of students in fraternities, 17% in sororities
Most popular majors: 18% Business, Management, Marketing, and Related Support Services, 14% Engineering, 8% Multi/Interdisciplinary Studies, 8% Parks, Recreation, Leisure, and Fitness Studies, 7% Education
Expenses: 2018-2019: $8,650 in state, $23,250 out of state; room/board: $10,090
Financial aid: (662) 325-2450; 65% of undergrads determined to have financial need; average aid package $13,849

Mississippi University for Women

Columbus MS
(662) 329-7106
U.S. News ranking: Reg. U. (S), No. 58
Website: www.muw.edu
Admissions email: admissions@muw.edu
Public; founded 1884
Freshman admissions: selective; 2017-2018: 708 applied, 694 accepted. Either SAT or ACT required. ACT 25/75 percentile: 18-23. High school rank: 20% in top tenth, 48% in top quarter, 73% in top half
Early decision deadline: N/A, notification date: N/A
Early action deadline: N/A, notification date: N/A
Application deadline (fall): rolling
Undergraduate student body: 2,113 full time, 464 part time; 20% male, 80% female; 1% American Indian, 1% Asian, 38% black, 0% Hispanic, 0% multiracial, 0% Pacific Islander, 56% white, 3% international; 87% from in state; 25% live on campus; 8% of students in fraternities, 13% in sororities
Most popular majors: 55% Registered Nursing/Registered Nurse, 10% Business Administration and Management, General, 6% Public Health Education and Promotion, 3% Health and Physical Education/Fitness, General, 3% Liberal Arts and Sciences/Liberal Studies
Expenses: 2018-2019: $6,940 in state, $6,940 out of state; room/board: $7,424
Financial aid: (662) 329-7114; 77% of undergrads determined to have financial need; average aid package $9,765

Mississippi Valley State University

Itta Bena MS
(662) 254-3344
U.S. News ranking: Reg. U. (S), second tier
Website: www.mvsu.edu
Admissions email: admsn@mvsu.edu
Public; founded 1950
Freshman admissions: less selective; 2017-2018: 2,310 applied, 1,993 accepted. Either SAT or ACT required. ACT 25/75 percentile: 16-19. High school rank: N/A
Early decision deadline: N/A, notification date: N/A
Early action deadline: N/A, notification date: N/A
Application deadline (fall): 8/17
Undergraduate student body: 1,667 full time, 310 part time; 39% male, 61% female; 0% American Indian, 0% Asian, 89% black, 1% Hispanic, 1% multiracial, 0% Pacific Islander, 3% white, 0% international; 85% from in state; 47% live on campus; 12% of students in fraternities, 14% in sororities
Most popular majors: 20% Public Administration and Social Service Professions, 11% Education, 10% Parks, Recreation, Leisure, and Fitness Studies, 9% Business, Management, Marketing, and Related Support Services, 8% Biological and Biomedical Sciences
Expenses: 2017-2018: $6,422 in state, $6,422 out of state; room/board: $7,764
Financial aid: N/A

Rust College[1]

Holly Springs MS
(662) 252-8000
U.S. News ranking: Reg. Coll. (S), second tier
Website: www.rustcollege.edu
Admissions email: admissions@rustcollege.edu
Private; founded 1866
Affiliation: United Methodist
Application deadline (fall): rolling
Undergraduate student body: N/A full time, N/A part time
Expenses: 2017-2018: $9,700; room/board: $4,300
Financial aid: (662) 252-8000

Tougaloo College

Tougaloo MS
(601) 977-7768
U.S. News ranking: Nat. Lib. Arts, second tier
Website: www.tougaloo.edu
Admissions email: admission@tougaloo.edu
Private; founded 1869
Affiliation: United Church of Christ
Freshman admissions: selective; 2017-2018: 2,227 applied, 1,670 accepted. Either SAT

or ACT required. ACT 25/75 percentile: 16-24. High school rank: 25% in top tenth, 51% in top quarter, 77% in top half
Early decision deadline: N/A, notification date: N/A
Early action deadline: N/A, notification date: N/A
Application deadline (fall): 7/1
Undergraduate student body: 766 full time, 27 part time; 34% male, 66% female; 0% American Indian, 0% Asian, 98% black, 1% Hispanic, 0% multiracial, 0% Pacific Islander, 0% white, 2% international; 73% from in state; 76% live on campus; 4% of students in fraternities, 6% in sororities
Most popular majors: 20% Sociology, 12% Psychology, General, 10% Biology/Biological Sciences, General, 8% Health and Physical Education/Fitness, Other, 7% English Language and Literature/Letters, Other
Expenses: 2018-2019: $10,600; room/board: $6,330
Financial aid: (601) 977-7769; 94% of undergrads determined to have financial need; average aid package $12,500

University of Mississippi

University MS
(662) 915-7226
U.S. News ranking: Nat. U., No. 152
Website: www.olemiss.edu
Admissions email: admissions@olemiss.edu
Public; founded 1848
Freshman admissions: more selective; 2017-2018: 17,416 applied, 14,614 accepted. Neither SAT nor ACT required. ACT 25/75 percentile: 22-29. High school rank: 26% in top tenth, 52% in top quarter, 80% in top half
Early decision deadline: N/A, notification date: N/A
Early action deadline: N/A, notification date: N/A
Application deadline (fall): rolling
Undergraduate student body: 17,511 full time, 1,226 part time; 44% male, 56% female; 0% American Indian, 2% Asian, 13% black, 3% Hispanic, 2% multiracial, 0% Pacific Islander, 78% white, 2% international; 56% from in state; 25% live on campus; 35% of students in fraternities, 44% in sororities
Most popular majors: 7% General Studies, 6% Accounting, 5% Elementary Education and Teaching, 5% Marketing/Marketing Management, General, 5% Psychology, General
Expenses: 2018-2019: $8,290 in state, $23,554 out of state; room/board: $10,502
Financial aid: (662) 915-5788; 49% of undergrads determined to have financial need; average aid package $10,630

University of Southern Mississippi

Hattiesburg MS
(601) 266-5000
U.S. News ranking: Nat. U., second tier
Website: www.usm.edu/admissions
Admissions email: admissions@usm.edu
Public; founded 1910
Freshman admissions: selective; 2017-2018: 6,405 applied, 6,306 accepted. Either SAT or ACT required. ACT 25/75 percentile: 19-26. High school rank: N/A
Early decision deadline: N/A, notification date: N/A
Early action deadline: N/A, notification date: N/A
Application deadline (fall): rolling
Undergraduate student body: 10,384 full time, 1,431 part time; 37% male, 63% female; 0% American Indian, 1% Asian, 28% black, 3% Hispanic, 3% multiracial, 0% Pacific Islander, 61% white, 2% international; 82% from in state; 28% live on campus; 10% of students in fraternities, 14% in sororities
Most popular majors: 18% Business Administration and Management, General, 13% Registered Nursing/Registered Nurse, 7% Elementary Education and Teaching, 7% Psychology, General, 6% Kinesiology and Exercise Science
Expenses: 2018-2019: $8,514 in state, $10,514 out of state; room/board: $9,557
Financial aid: (601) 266-4774; 75% of undergrads determined to have financial need; average aid package $10,251

William Carey University

Hattiesburg MS
(601) 318-6103
U.S. News ranking: Reg. U. (S), No. 39
Website: www.wmcarey.edu
Admissions email: admissions@wmcarey.edu
Private; founded 1892
Affiliation: Southern Baptist
Freshman admissions: selective; 2017-2018: 891 applied, 435 accepted. Either SAT or ACT required. ACT 25/75 percentile: 21-28. High school rank: 28% in top tenth, 54% in top quarter, 78% in top half
Early decision deadline: N/A, notification date: N/A
Early action deadline: N/A, notification date: N/A
Application deadline (fall): rolling
Undergraduate student body: 1,676 full time, 1,421 part time; 39% male, 61% female; 0% American Indian, 1% Asian, 30% black, 2% Hispanic, 0% multiracial, 0% Pacific Islander, 60% white, 4% international; 83% from in state; 15% live on campus; 0% of students in fraternities, 2% in sororities
Most popular majors: 17% Registered Nursing/Registered Nurse, 14% Business Administration and Management, General, 14% Psychology, General, 12% Elementary Education and Teaching, 9% Biology/Biological Sciences, General
Expenses: 2018-2019: $12,600; room/board: $4,320
Financial aid: (601) 318-6153; 95% of undergrads determined to have financial need; average aid package $17,100

MISSOURI

Avila University[1]

Kansas City MO
(816) 501-2400
U.S. News ranking: Reg. U. (Mid. W), second tier
Website: www.Avila.edu
Admissions email: admissions@mail.avila.edu
Private
Application deadline (fall): N/A
Undergraduate student body: N/A full time, N/A part time
Expenses: 2017-2018: $28,020; room/board: $8,546
Financial aid: N/A

Central Methodist University

Fayette MO
(660) 248-6251
U.S. News ranking: Reg. Coll. (Mid. W), No. 24
Website: www.centralmethodist.edu
Admissions email: admissions@centralmethodist.edu
Private; founded 1854
Affiliation: United Methodist
Freshman admissions: selective; 2017-2018: 1,357 applied, 850 accepted. Either SAT or ACT required. ACT 25/75 percentile: 20-25. High school rank: 17% in top tenth, 42% in top quarter, 73% in top half
Early decision deadline: N/A, notification date: N/A
Early action deadline: N/A, notification date: N/A
Application deadline (fall): 8/15
Undergraduate student body: 1,034 full time, 26 part time; 47% male, 53% female; 0% American Indian, 0% Asian, 8% black, 4% Hispanic, 4% multiracial, 0% Pacific Islander, 75% white, 6% international; 85% from in state; 58% live on campus; 22% of students in fraternities, 25% in sororities
Most popular majors: 24% Health Professions and Related Programs, 14% Education, 12% Business, Management, Marketing, and Related Support Services, 8% Biological and Biomedical Sciences, 8% Homeland Security, Law Enforcement, Firefighting and Related Protective Services
Expenses: 2018-2019: $24,420; room/board: $7,940
Financial aid: (660) 248-6245; 81% of undergrads determined to have financial need; average aid package $20,911

College of the Ozarks

Point Lookout MO
(800) 222-0525
U.S. News ranking: Reg. Coll. (Mid. W), No. 3
Website: www.cofo.edu
Admissions email: admissions@cofo.edu
Private; founded 1906
Affiliation: Interdenominational
Freshman admissions: selective; 2017-2018: 2,879 applied, 447 accepted. Either SAT or ACT required. ACT 25/75 percentile: 21-26. High school rank: 25% in top tenth, 62% in top quarter, 96% in top half
Early decision deadline: N/A, notification date: N/A
Early action deadline: N/A, notification date: N/A
Application deadline (fall): rolling
Undergraduate student body: 1,477 full time, 31 part time; 45% male, 55% female; 0% American Indian, 1% Asian, 1% black, 2% Hispanic, 2% multiracial, 0% Pacific Islander, 90% white, 1% international; 76% from in state; 90% live on campus; N/A of students in fraternities, N/A in sororities
Most popular majors: 16% Business, Management, Marketing, and Related Support Services, 12% Education, 11% Computer and Information Sciences and Support Services, 9% Health Professions and Related Programs, 5% Homeland Security, Law Enforcement, Firefighting and Related Protective Services
Expenses: 2018-2019: $19,360; room/board: $7,400
Financial aid: (417) 690-3292; 90% of undergrads determined to have financial need; average aid package $15,914

Columbia College[1]

Columbia MO
(573) 875-7352
U.S. News ranking: Reg. U. (Mid. W), unranked
Website: www.ccis.edu
Admissions email: admissions@ccis.edu
Private; founded 1851
Application deadline (fall): rolling
Undergraduate student body: N/A full time, N/A part time
Expenses: 2017-2018: $21,936; room/board: $7,094
Financial aid: (573) 875-7390

Cottey College

Nevada MO
(888) 526-8839
U.S. News ranking: Reg. Coll. (Mid. W), No. 9
Website: www.cottey.edu
Admissions email: admit@cottey.edu
Private; founded 1884
Freshman admissions: selective; 2017-2018: 361 applied, 272 accepted. Either SAT or ACT required. ACT 25/75 percentile: 19-23. High school rank: 18% in top tenth, 39% in top quarter, 75% in top half
Early decision deadline: N/A, notification date: N/A
Early action deadline: N/A, notification date: N/A
Application deadline (fall): rolling
Undergraduate student body: 260 full time, 10 part time; 0% male, 100% female; 2% American Indian, 0% Asian, 5% black, 8% Hispanic, 5% multiracial, 0% Pacific Islander, 65% white, 15% international; 21% from in state; 88% live on campus; 0% of students in fraternities, 0% in sororities
Most popular majors: 44% Business, Management, Marketing, and Related Support Services, 19% English Language and Literature/Letters, 13% Social Sciences, 7% Liberal Arts and Sciences, General Studies and Humanities, 7% Psychology
Expenses: 2018-2019: $21,150; room/board: $7,700
Financial aid: (417) 667-8181; 72% of undergrads determined to have financial need; average aid package $20,620

Culver-Stockton College

Canton MO
(800) 537-1883
U.S. News ranking: Reg. Coll. (Mid. W), No. 39
Website: www.culver.edu
Admissions email: admission@culver.edu
Private; founded 1853
Affiliation: Christian Church (Disciples of Christ)
Freshman admissions: selective; 2017-2018: 3,308 applied, 1,808 accepted. Either SAT or ACT required. ACT 25/75 percentile: 18-23. High school rank: 9% in top tenth, 28% in top quarter, 64% in top half
Early decision deadline: N/A, notification date: N/A
Early action deadline: N/A, notification date: N/A
Application deadline (fall): rolling
Undergraduate student body: 969 full time, 124 part time; 50% male, 50% female; 0% American Indian, 0% Asian, 12% black, 6% Hispanic, 3% multiracial, 0% Pacific Islander, 71% white, 7% international; 54% from in state; 76% live on campus; 38% of students in fraternities, 37% in sororities
Most popular majors: 19% Business Administration and Management, General, 11% Criminal Justice/Law Enforcement Administration, 8% Psychology, General, 7% Biology/Biological Sciences, General, 6% Elementary Education and Teaching
Expenses: 2018-2019: $26,680; room/board: $8,520
Financial aid: (573) 288-6307; 82% of undergrads determined to have financial need; average aid package $21,033

Drury University

Springfield MO
(417) 873-7205
U.S. News ranking: Reg. U. (Mid. W), No. 29
Website: www.drury.edu
Admissions email: druryad@drury.edu
Private; founded 1873
Freshman admissions: more selective; 2017-2018: 1,474 applied, 1,067 accepted. Either SAT or ACT required. ACT 25/75 percentile: 23-28. High school rank: 34% in top tenth, 66% in top quarter, 87% in top half

Early decision deadline: N/A, notification date: N/A
Early action deadline: N/A, notification date: N/A
Application deadline (fall): 8/30
Undergraduate student body: 2,483 full time, 801 part time; 39% male, 61% female; 1% American Indian, 2% Asian, 3% black, 3% Hispanic, 4% multiracial, 0% Pacific Islander, 79% white, 9% international; 75% from in state; 55% live on campus; 21% of students in fraternities, 26% in sororities
Most popular majors: 9% Biological and Biomedical Sciences, 8% Business, Management, Marketing, and Related Support Services, 3% Architecture and Related Services, 2% Education, 2% Psychology
Expenses: 2018-2019: $28,515; room/board: $9,040
Financial aid: (417) 873-7312; 67% of undergrads determined to have financial need; average aid package $20,254

Evangel University

Springfield MO
(800) 382-6435
U.S. News ranking: Reg. U. (Mid. W), second tier
Website: www.evangel.edu
Admissions email: admissions@evangel.edu
Private; founded 1955
Affiliation: Assemblies of God Church
Freshman admissions: less selective; 2017-2018: 918 applied, 863 accepted. Either SAT or ACT required. ACT 25/75 percentile: 19-25. High school rank: N/A
Early decision deadline: N/A, notification date: N/A
Early action deadline: N/A, notification date: N/A
Application deadline (fall): rolling
Undergraduate student body: 1,461 full time, 170 part time; 45% male, 55% female; N/A American Indian, N/A Asian, N/A black, N/A Hispanic, N/A multiracial, N/A Pacific Islander, N/A white, N/A international
Most popular majors: 18% Business, Management, Marketing, and Related Support Services, 14% Education, 14% Theology and Religious Vocations, 10% Communication, Journalism, and Related Programs, 9% Psychology
Expenses: 2018-2019: $23,296; room/board: $8,522
Financial aid: (417) 865-2811; 85% of undergrads determined to have financial need; average aid package $18,255

Fontbonne University

St. Louis MO
(314) 889-1400
U.S. News ranking: Reg. U. (Mid. W), No. 72
Website: www.fontbonne.edu
Admissions email: admissions@fontbonne.edu
Private; founded 1923
Affiliation: Roman Catholic
Freshman admissions: selective; 2017-2018: 550 applied, 508 accepted. Either SAT or ACT required. ACT 25/75 percentile: 20-26. High school rank: N/A
Early decision deadline: N/A, notification date: N/A
Early action deadline: N/A, notification date: N/A
Application deadline (fall): rolling
Undergraduate student body: 765 full time, 128 part time; 38% male, 62% female; 0% American Indian, 2% Asian, 11% black, 2% Hispanic, 3% multiracial, 0% Pacific Islander, 74% white, 6% international; 76% from in state; 34% live on campus; N/A of students in fraternities, N/A in sororities
Most popular majors: 12% Business Administration and Management, General, 8% Special Education and Teaching, General, 8% Speech-Language Pathology/Pathologist, 5% Psychology, General, 5% Social Work
Expenses: 2018-2019: $26,340; room/board: $9,989
Financial aid: (314) 889-1414; 83% of undergrads determined to have financial need; average aid package $17,994

Hannibal-LaGrange University

Hannibal MO
(800) 454-1119
U.S. News ranking: Reg. Coll. (Mid. W), second tier
Website: www.hlg.edu
Admissions email: admissions@hlg.edu
Private; founded 1858
Affiliation: Southern Baptist
Freshman admissions: less selective; 2017-2018: 682 applied, 372 accepted. Either SAT or ACT required. SAT 25/75 percentile: N/A. High school rank: N/A
Early decision deadline: N/A, notification date: N/A
Early action deadline: N/A, notification date: N/A
Application deadline (fall): 8/27
Undergraduate student body: 705 full time, 193 part time; 41% male, 59% female; 0% American Indian, 0% Asian, 5% black, 3% Hispanic, 3% multiracial, 0% Pacific Islander, 81% white, 8% international; 78% from in state; 41% live on campus; N/A of students in fraternities, N/A in sororities
Most popular majors: 23% Registered Nursing/Registered Nurse, 21% Education, 16% Business, Management, Marketing, and Related Support Services, 8% Parks, Recreation, Leisure, and Fitness Studies, 6% Homeland Security, Law Enforcement, Firefighting and Related Protective Services
Expenses: 2017-2018: $21,810; room/board: $8,108
Financial aid: N/A

Harris-Stowe State University

St. Louis MO
(314) 340-3300
U.S. News ranking: Reg. Coll. (Mid. W), second tier
Website: www.hssu.edu
Admissions email: admissions@hssu.edu
Public; founded 1857
Freshman admissions: less selective; 2017-2018: 4,414 applied, 1,749 accepted. Either SAT or ACT required. ACT 25/75 percentile: 16-19. High school rank: N/A
Early decision deadline: N/A, notification date: N/A
Early action deadline: N/A, notification date: N/A
Application deadline (fall): rolling
Undergraduate student body: 1,163 full time, 279 part time; 34% male, 66% female; 0% American Indian, 0% Asian, 80% black, 3% Hispanic, 3% multiracial, 0% Pacific Islander, 6% white, 1% international; 76% from in state; 29% live on campus; N/A of students in fraternities, N/A in sororities
Most popular majors: 33% Business, Management, Marketing, and Related Support Services, 31% Education, 17% Homeland Security, Law Enforcement, Firefighting and Related Protective Services, 8% Social Sciences, 5% Biological and Biomedical Sciences
Expenses: 2018-2019: $5,340 in state, $9,973 out of state; room/board: $9,250
Financial aid: (314) 340-3502

Kansas City Art Institute[1]

Kansas City MO
(816) 472-4852
U.S. News ranking: Arts, unranked
Website: www.kcai.edu
Admissions email: admiss@kcai.edu
Private; founded 1885
Application deadline (fall): N/A
Undergraduate student body: N/A full time, N/A part time
Expenses: N/A
Financial aid: (816) 802-3448

Lincoln University

Jefferson City MO
(573) 681-5102
U.S. News ranking: Reg. U. (Mid. W), second tier
Website: www.lincolnu.edu
Admissions email: a dmissions@lincolnu.edu
Public; founded 1866
Freshman admissions: less selective; 2017-2018: 3,423 applied, 1,796 accepted. Either SAT or ACT required. ACT 25/75 percentile: 14-19. High school rank: 5% in top tenth, 15% in top quarter, 39% in top half
Early decision deadline: N/A, notification date: N/A
Early action deadline: N/A, notification date: N/A
Application deadline (fall): rolling
Undergraduate student body: 1,804 full time, 708 part time; 42% male, 58% female; 0% American Indian, 1% Asian, 57% black, 2% Hispanic, 3% multiracial, 0% Pacific Islander, 29% white, 2% international; 70% from in state; 48% live on campus; N/A of students in fraternities, N/A in sororities
Most popular majors: 21% Registered Nursing/Registered Nurse, 11% Criminal Justice/Law Enforcement Administration, 11% Liberal Arts and Sciences/Liberal Studies, 7% Elementary Education and Teaching, 6% Business Administration and Management, General
Expenses: 2018-2019: $7,632 in state, $14,172 out of state; room/board: $7,068
Financial aid: (573) 681-5032; 81% of undergrads determined to have financial need; average aid package $14,660

Lindenwood University

St. Charles MO
(636) 949-4949
U.S. News ranking: Nat. U., second tier
Website: www.lindenwood.edu
Admissions email: admissions@lindenwood.edu
Private; founded 1827
Freshman admissions: selective; 2017-2018: 2,895 applied, 2,135 accepted. Neither SAT nor ACT required. ACT 25/75 percentile: 20-25. High school rank: 18% in top tenth, 46% in top quarter, 79% in top half
Early decision deadline: N/A, notification date: N/A
Early action deadline: N/A, notification date: N/A
Application deadline (fall): rolling
Undergraduate student body: 6,235 full time, 713 part time; 46% male, 54% female; 0% American Indian, 1% Asian, 12% black, 4% Hispanic, 2% multiracial, 0% Pacific Islander, 50% white, 12% international; 61% from in state; 61% live on campus; 1% of students in fraternities, 3% in sororities
Most popular majors: 16% Business/Commerce, General, 6% Educational Leadership and Administration, General, 5% Criminal Justice/Safety Studies, 5% Human Resources Management/Personnel Administration, General, 4% Mental Health Counseling/Counselor
Expenses: 2018-2019: $17,600; room/board: $9,000
Financial aid: (636) 949-4923; 61% of undergrads determined to have financial need; average aid package $12,478

Maryville University of St. Louis

St Louis MO
(800) 627-9855
U.S. News ranking: Nat. U., No. 177
Website: www.maryville.edu
Admissions email: admissions@maryville.edu
Private; founded 1872
Freshman admissions: selective; 2017-2018: 2,241 applied, 2,059 accepted. Neither SAT nor ACT required. ACT 25/75 percentile: 21-27. High school rank: 21% in top tenth, 56% in top quarter, 86% in top half
Early decision deadline: N/A, notification date: N/A
Early action deadline: N/A, notification date: N/A
Application deadline (fall): 8/15
Undergraduate student body: 2,375 full time, 808 part time; 34% male, 66% female; 0% American Indian, 3% Asian, 8% black, 4% Hispanic, 3% multiracial, 0% Pacific Islander, 72% white, 4% international; 74% from in state; 11% live on campus; 0% of students in fraternities, 0% in sororities
Most popular majors: 36% Health Professions and Related Programs, 25% Business, Management, Marketing, and Related Support Services, 9% Psychology, 7% Biological and Biomedical Sciences, 4% Visual and Performing Arts
Expenses: 2018-2019: $28,470; room/board: $10,088
Financial aid: (314) 529-9361; 84% of undergrads determined to have financial need; average aid package $15,811

Missouri Baptist University[1]

St. Louis MO
(314) 434-2290
U.S. News ranking: Reg. U. (Mid. W), second tier
Website: www.mobap.edu
Admissions email: admissions@mobap.edu
Private; founded 1964
Application deadline (fall): rolling
Undergraduate student body: N/A full time, N/A part time
Expenses: 2017-2018: $26,020; room/board: $11,105
Financial aid: (314) 744-7639

Missouri Southern State University

Joplin MO
(417) 781-6778
U.S. News ranking: Reg. Coll. (Mid. W), second tier
Website: www.mssu.edu
Admissions email: admissions@mssu.edu
Public; founded 1937
Freshman admissions: selective; 2017-2018: 2,682 applied, 2,550 accepted. Either SAT or ACT required. ACT 25/75 percentile: 19-24. High school rank: N/A
Early decision deadline: N/A, notification date: N/A
Early action deadline: N/A, notification date: N/A
Application deadline (fall): rolling
Undergraduate student body: 4,358 full time, 1,663 part time; 40% male, 60% female; 3% American Indian, 2% Asian, 7% black, 7% Hispanic, 2% multiracial, 0% Pacific Islander, 74% white, 2% international
Most popular majors: 22% Business/Commerce, General, 9% Criminal Justice/Law Enforcement Administration, 9% Health Professions and Related Clinical Sciences, Other, 9% Liberal Arts and Sciences, General Studies and Humanities, Other, 8% Elementary Education and Teaching

Expenses: 2017-2018: $6,067 in state, $11,568 out of state; room/board: $6,901
Financial aid: (417) 659-5422

Missouri State University

Springfield MO
(800) 492-7900
U.S. News ranking: Reg. U. (Mid. W), No. 111
Website: www.missouristate.edu
Admissions email: info@missouristate.edu
Public; founded 1906
Freshman admissions: selective; 2017-2018: 9,453 applied, 7,944 accepted. Either SAT or ACT required. ACT 25/75 percentile: 21-26. High school rank: 21% in top tenth, 49% in top quarter, 83% in top half
Early decision deadline: N/A, notification date: N/A
Early action deadline: N/A, notification date: N/A
Undergraduate student body: 15,363 full time, 5,001 part time; 42% male, 58% female; 0% American Indian, 1% Asian, 5% black, 4% Hispanic, 4% multiracial, 0% Pacific Islander, 81% white, 4% international; 89% from in state; 23% live on campus; 43% of students in fraternities, 39% in sororities
Most popular majors: 27% Business, Management, Marketing, and Related Support Services, 13% Education, 7% Health Professions and Related Programs, 7% Psychology, 6% Biological and Biomedical Sciences
Expenses: 2018-2019: $7,452 in state, $15,342 out of state; room/board: $8,755
Financial aid: (417) 836-5262; 61% of undergrads determined to have financial need; average aid package $9,224

Missouri University of Science & Technology

Rolla MO
(573) 341-4165
U.S. News ranking: Nat. U., No. 157
Website: www.mst.edu
Admissions email: admissions@mst.edu
Public; founded 1870
Freshman admissions: more selective; 2017-2018: 3,876 applied, 3,237 accepted. Either SAT or ACT required. ACT 25/75 percentile: 25-31. High school rank: 39% in top tenth, 72% in top quarter, 94% in top half
Early decision deadline: N/A, notification date: N/A
Early action deadline: N/A, notification date: N/A
Application deadline (fall): 7/1
Undergraduate student body: 6,128 full time, 792 part time; 76% male, 24% female; 0% American Indian, 4% Asian, 3% black, 4% Hispanic, 3% multiracial, 0% Pacific Islander, 81% white, 3% international; 83% from in state; 30% live on campus; N/A of students in fraternities, N/A in sororities
Most popular majors: 65% Engineering, 10% Computer and Information Sciences and Support Services, 7% Engineering Technologies and Engineering-Related Fields, 4% Physical Sciences, 3% Biological and Biomedical Sciences
Expenses: 2017-2018: $9,839 in state, $27,701 out of state; room/board: $9,980
Financial aid: (573) 341-4282

Missouri Valley College[1]

Marshall MO
(660) 831-4114
U.S. News ranking: Reg. Coll. (Mid. W), second tier
Website: www.moval.edu
Admissions email: admissions@moval.edu
Private; founded 1889
Affiliation: Presbyterian
Application deadline (fall): rolling
Undergraduate student body: N/A full time, N/A part time
Expenses: 2017-2018: $20,200; room/board: $8,750
Financial aid: N/A

Missouri Western State University[1]

St. Joseph MO
(816) 271-4266
U.S. News ranking: Reg. Coll. (Mid. W), second tier
Website: www.missouriwestern.edu
Admissions email: admission@missouriwestern.edu
Public; founded 1969
Application deadline (fall): rolling
Undergraduate student body: N/A full time, N/A part time
Expenses: 2017-2018: $7,570 in state, $13,465 out of state; room/board: $8,730
Financial aid: (816) 271-4361

Northwest Missouri State University

Maryville MO
(800) 633-1175
U.S. News ranking: Reg. U. (Mid. W), No. 86
Website: www.nwmissouri.edu
Admissions email: admissions@nwmissouri.edu
Public; founded 1905
Freshman admissions: selective; 2017-2018: 5,129 applied, 3,801 accepted. Either SAT or ACT required. ACT 25/75 percentile: 18-25. High school rank: 16% in top tenth, 41% in top quarter, 76% in top half
Early decision deadline: N/A, notification date: N/A
Early action deadline: N/A, notification date: N/A
Application deadline (fall): rolling
Undergraduate student body: 4,806 full time, 668 part time; 43% male, 57% female; 0% American Indian, 1% Asian, 6% black, 4% Hispanic, 3% multiracial, 0% Pacific Islander, 80% white, 4% international; 70% from in state; 33% live on campus; 15% of students in fraternities, 17% in sororities
Most popular majors: 20% Business, Management, Marketing, and Related Support Services, 16% Education, 14% Agriculture, Agriculture Operations, and Related Sciences, 10% Psychology, 7% Communication, Journalism, and Related Programs
Expenses: 2018-2019: $9,805 in state, $16,458 out of state; room/board: $8,932
Financial aid: (660) 562-1138; 67% of undergrads determined to have financial need; average aid package $9,727

Park University

Parkville MO
(877) 505-1059
U.S. News ranking: Reg. U. (Mid. W), second tier
Website: www.park.edu
Admissions email: enrollmentservices@park.edu
Private; founded 1875
Freshman admissions: less selective; 2017-2018: 1,910 applied, 1,289 accepted. Neither SAT nor ACT required. ACT 25/75 percentile: 17-22. High school rank: N/A
Early decision deadline: N/A, notification date: N/A
Early action deadline: N/A, notification date: N/A
Application deadline (fall): rolling
Undergraduate student body: 4,134 full time, 5,727 part time; 52% male, 48% female; 1% American Indian, 2% Asian, 19% black, 19% Hispanic, 3% multiracial, 1% Pacific Islander, 47% white, 2% international; 20% from in state; 2% live on campus; 0% of students in fraternities, 0% in sororities
Most popular majors: 50% Business, Management, Marketing, and Related Support Services, 16% Psychology, 10% Homeland Security, Law Enforcement, Firefighting and Related Protective Services, 9% Computer and Information Sciences and Support Services, 5% Health Professions and Related Programs
Expenses: 2018-2019: $12,650; room/board: $8,200
Financial aid: (816) 584-6250; 72% of undergrads determined to have financial need; average aid package $8,972

Ranken Technical College[1]

Saint Louis MO
(314) 371-0236
U.S. News ranking: Reg. Coll. (Mid. W), unranked
Website: www.ranken.edu
Admissions email: N/A
Private
Application deadline (fall): N/A
Undergraduate student body: N/A full time, N/A part time
Expenses: 2017-2018: $14,457; room/board: $5,200
Financial aid: N/A

Rockhurst University

Kansas City MO
(816) 501-4100
U.S. News ranking: Reg. U. (Mid. W), No. 23
Website: www.rockhurst.edu
Admissions email: admissions@rockhurst.edu
Private; founded 1910
Affiliation: Roman Catholic
Freshman admissions: more selective; 2017-2018: 3,115 applied, 2,257 accepted. Either SAT or ACT required. ACT 25/75 percentile: 22-27. High school rank: 25% in top tenth, 56% in top quarter, 84% in top half
Early decision deadline: N/A, notification date: N/A
Early action deadline: N/A, notification date: N/A
Application deadline (fall): rolling
Undergraduate student body: 1,445 full time, 763 part time; 39% male, 61% female; 1% American Indian, 3% Asian, 5% black, 9% Hispanic, 3% multiracial, 0% Pacific Islander, 72% white, 1% international; 67% from in state; 49% live on campus; 37% of students in fraternities, 47% in sororities
Most popular majors: 24% Health Professions and Related Programs, 20% Business, Management, Marketing, and Related Support Services, 10% Biological and Biomedical Sciences, 10% Psychology, 7% Parks, Recreation, Leisure, and Fitness Studies
Expenses: 2018-2019: $37,590; room/board: $9,570
Financial aid: (816) 501-4600; 71% of undergrads determined to have financial need; average aid package $30,198

Saint Louis University

St. Louis MO
(314) 977-2500
U.S. News ranking: Nat. U., No. 106
Website: www.slu.edu
Admissions email: admission@slu.edu
Private; founded 1818
Affiliation: Roman Catholic
Freshman admissions: more selective; 2017-2018: 13,431 applied, 8,653 accepted. Either SAT or ACT required. ACT 25/75 percentile: 25-31. High school rank: 50% in top tenth, 76% in top quarter, 94% in top half
Early decision deadline: N/A, notification date: N/A
Early action deadline: N/A, notification date: N/A
Application deadline (fall): 8/15
Undergraduate student body: 6,725 full time, 686 part time; 40% male, 60% female; 0% American Indian, 10% Asian, 6% black, 6% Hispanic, 3% multiracial, 0% Pacific Islander, 69% white, 5% international; 41% from in state; 51% live on campus; 4% of students in fraternities, 7% in sororities
Most popular majors: 29% Health Professions and Related Programs, 21% Business, Management, Marketing, and Related Support Services, 9% Engineering, 5% Biological and Biomedical Sciences, 5% Parks, Recreation, Leisure, and Fitness Studies
Expenses: 2018-2019: $43,996; room/board: $12,290
Financial aid: (314) 977-2350; 55% of undergrads determined to have financial need; average aid package $31,030

Southeast Missouri State University

Cape Girardeau MO
(573) 651-2590
U.S. News ranking: Reg. U. (Mid. W), No. 90
Website: www.semo.edu
Admissions email: admissions@semo.edu
Public; founded 1873
Freshman admissions: selective; 2017-2018: 4,977 applied, 4,208 accepted. Either SAT or ACT required. ACT 25/75 percentile: 20-26. High school rank: 16% in top tenth, 42% in top quarter, 75% in top half
Early decision deadline: N/A, notification date: N/A
Early action deadline: N/A, notification date: N/A
Application deadline (fall): 7/1
Undergraduate student body: 7,779 full time, 2,679 part time; 42% male, 58% female; 0% American Indian, 1% Asian, 10% black, 2% Hispanic, 1% multiracial, 0% Pacific Islander, 79% white, 5% international; 80% from in state; 34% live on campus; 17% of students in fraternities, 18% in sororities
Most popular majors: 14% Business, Management, Marketing, and Related Support Services, 10% Education, 10% Health Professions and Related Programs, 10% Liberal Arts and Sciences, General Studies and Humanities, 8% Communication, Journalism, and Related Programs
Expenses: 2018-2019: $7,425 in state, $13,080 out of state; room/board: $8,935
Financial aid: (573) 651-2253; 65% of undergrads determined to have financial need; average aid package $9,611

Southwest Baptist University

Bolivar MO
(417) 328-1810
U.S. News ranking: Reg. U. (Mid. W), No. 124
Website: www.sbuniv.edu
Admissions email: admissions@sbuniv.edu
Private; founded 1878
Affiliation: Southern Baptist
Freshman admissions: selective; 2017-2018: 1,884 applied, 1,379 accepted. Either SAT or ACT required. ACT 25/75 percentile: 20-26. High school rank: 24% in top tenth, 49% in top quarter, 77% in top half
Early decision deadline: N/A, notification date: N/A
Early action deadline: N/A, notification date: N/A
Application deadline (fall): rolling
Undergraduate student body: 1,835 full time, 987 part time; 36% male, 64% female; 1% American Indian, 1% Asian, 6% black, 3% Hispanic, 1% multiracial,

0% Pacific Islander, 83% white, 2% international; 80% from in state; 41% live on campus; 0% of students in fraternities, 0% in sororities
Most popular majors: 22% Education, General, 19% Registered Nursing/Registered Nurse, 11% Elementary Education and Teaching, 7% Business Administration and Management, General, 6% Psychology, General
Expenses: 2018-2019: $24,010; room/board: $7,720
Financial aid: (417) 328-1823; 82% of undergrads determined to have financial need; average aid package $19,846

Stephens College

Columbia MO
(800) 876-7207
U.S. News ranking: Reg. U. (Mid. W), No. 72
Website: www.stephens.edu
Admissions email: apply@stephens.edu
Private; founded 1833
Freshman admissions: selective; 2017-2018: 1,269 applied, 676 accepted. Either SAT or ACT required. ACT 25/75 percentile: 19-25. High school rank: 16% in top tenth, 40% in top quarter, 80% in top half
Early decision deadline: 12/31, notification date: 11/1
Early action deadline: 12/31, notification date: 12/31
Application deadline (fall): rolling
Undergraduate student body: 543 full time, 105 part time; 1% male, 99% female; 1% American Indian, 1% Asian, 14% black, 6% Hispanic, 10% multiracial, 0% Pacific Islander, 66% white, 0% international
Most popular majors: 13% Fashion Merchandising, 13% Health Information/Medical Records Administration/Administrator, 9% Acting, 9% Biology/Biological Sciences, General, 7% Marketing, Other
Expenses: 2018-2019: $30,950; room/board: $10,632
Financial aid: (573) 876-7106; 83% of undergrads determined to have financial need; average aid package $10,000

Truman State University

Kirksville MO
(660) 785-4114
U.S. News ranking: Reg. U. (Mid. W), No. 9
Website: www.truman.edu
Admissions email: admissions@truman.edu
Public; founded 1867
Freshman admissions: more selective; 2017-2018: 5,263 applied, 3,552 accepted. Either SAT or ACT required. ACT 25/75 percentile: 24-30. High school rank: 51% in top tenth, 83% in top quarter, 98% in top half
Early decision deadline: N/A, notification date: N/A
Early action deadline: N/A, notification date: N/A
Application deadline (fall): rolling
Undergraduate student body: 5,134 full time, 764 part time; 41% male, 59% female; 0% American Indian, 3% Asian, 4% black, 3% Hispanic, 3% multiracial, 0% Pacific Islander, 79% white, 7% international; 71% from in state; 42% live on campus; 9% of students in fraternities, 9% in sororities
Most popular majors: 11% Business Administration and Management, General, 9% Biology/Biological Sciences, General, 9% Psychology, General, 6% Accounting, 6% Kinesiology and Exercise Science
Expenses: 2017-2018: $7,656 in state, $14,440 out of state; room/board: $8,630
Financial aid: (660) 785-4130; 53% of undergrads determined to have financial need; average aid package $12,445

University of Central Missouri

Warrensburg MO
(660) 543-4290
U.S. News ranking: Reg. U. (Mid. W), No. 81
Website: www.ucmo.edu
Admissions email: admit@ucmo.edu
Public; founded 1871
Freshman admissions: selective; 2017-2018: 4,748 applied, 3,982 accepted. Neither SAT nor ACT required. ACT 25/75 percentile: 19-25. High school rank: 11% in top tenth, 34% in top quarter, 71% in top half
Early decision deadline: N/A, notification date: N/A
Early action deadline: N/A, notification date: N/A
Application deadline (fall): rolling
Undergraduate student body: 7,701 full time, 2,100 part time; 44% male, 56% female; 0% American Indian, 1% Asian, 11% black, 5% Hispanic, 5% multiracial, 0% Pacific Islander, 75% white, 2% international; 89% from in state; 33% live on campus; 11% of students in fraternities, 14% in sororities
Most popular majors: 16% Education, 15% Health Professions and Related Programs, 13% Business, Management, Marketing, and Related Support Services, 9% Engineering Technologies and Engineering-Related Fields, 8% Homeland Security, Law Enforcement, Firefighting and Related Protective Services
Expenses: 2018-2019: $7,673 in state, $14,442 out of state; room/board: $8,766
Financial aid: (660) 543-8266; 62% of undergrads determined to have financial need; average aid package $8,707

University of Missouri

Columbia MO
(573) 882-7786
U.S. News ranking: Nat. U., No. 129
Website: www.missouri.edu
Admissions email: mu4u@missouri.edu
Public; founded 1839
Freshman admissions: more selective; 2017-2018: 16,373 applied, 12,787 accepted. Either SAT or ACT required. ACT 25/75 percentile: 23-29. High school rank: 29% in top tenth, 60% in top quarter, 89% in top half
Early decision deadline: N/A, notification date: N/A
Early action deadline: N/A, notification date: N/A
Application deadline (fall): rolling
Undergraduate student body: 22,197 full time, 1,620 part time; 48% male, 52% female; 0% American Indian, 3% Asian, 7% black, 4% Hispanic, 3% multiracial, 0% Pacific Islander, 78% white, 3% international; 79% from in state; 21% live on campus; 25% of students in fraternities, 34% in sororities
Most popular majors: 17% Business, Management, Marketing, and Related Support Services, 15% Health Professions and Related Programs, 11% Communication, Journalism, and Related Programs, 8% Engineering, 6% Biological and Biomedical Sciences
Expenses: 2018-2019: $9,879 in state, $26,949 out of state; room/board: $10,676
Financial aid: (573) 882-7506; 48% of undergrads determined to have financial need; average aid package $12,070

University of Missouri–Kansas City[1]

Kansas City MO
(816) 235-1111
U.S. News ranking: Nat. U., second tier
Website: www.umkc.edu
Admissions email: admit@umkc.edu
Public; founded 1929
Application deadline (fall): rolling
Undergraduate student body: N/A full time, N/A part time
Expenses: 2017-2018: $9,734 in state, $25,999 out of state; room/board: $10,150
Financial aid: (816) 235-5511

University of Missouri–St. Louis

St. Louis MO
(314) 516-5451
U.S. News ranking: Nat. U., No. 226
Website: www.umsl.edu
Admissions email: admissions@umsl.edu
Public; founded 1963
Freshman admissions: more selective; 2017-2018: 1,970 applied, 1,496 accepted. Either SAT or ACT required. ACT 25/75 percentile: 22-27. High school rank: 27% in top tenth, 58% in top quarter, 88% in top half
Early decision deadline: N/A, notification date: N/A
Early action deadline: N/A, notification date: N/A
Application deadline (fall): 8/20
Undergraduate student body: 5,492 full time, 8,320 part time; 43% male, 57% female; 0% American Indian, 5% Asian, 17% black, 3% Hispanic, 3% multiracial, 0% Pacific Islander, 64% white, 3% international; 89% from in state; 11% live on campus; 1% of students in fraternities, 1% in sororities
Most popular majors: 25% Business, Management, Marketing, and Related Support Services, 12% Health Professions and Related Programs, 10% Education, 9% Social Sciences, 7% Psychology
Expenses: 2017-2018: $10,275 in state, $27,327 out of state; room/board: $9,363
Financial aid: (314) 516-5526; 70% of undergrads determined to have financial need; average aid package $11,989

Washington University in St. Louis

St. Louis MO
(800) 638-0700
U.S. News ranking: Nat. U., No. 19
Website: www.wustl.edu
Admissions email: admissions@wustl.edu
Private; founded 1853
Freshman admissions: most selective; 2017-2018: 30,463 applied, 4,863 accepted. Either SAT or ACT required. ACT 25/75 percentile: 32-34. High school rank: 87% in top tenth, 98% in top quarter, 100% in top half
Early decision deadline: 11/1, notification date: 12/15
Early action deadline: N/A, notification date: N/A
Application deadline (fall): 1/2
Undergraduate student body: 7,074 full time, 601 part time; 46% male, 54% female; 0% American Indian, 17% Asian, 8% black, 9% Hispanic, 5% multiracial, 0% Pacific Islander, 52% white, 7% international; 9% from in state; 74% live on campus; 25% of students in fraternities, 44% in sororities
Most popular majors: 17% Business, Management, Marketing, and Related Support Services, 16% Engineering, 12% Biological and Biomedical Sciences, 10% Social Sciences, 7% Multi/Interdisciplinary Studies
Expenses: 2018-2019: $53,399; room/board: $16,440
Financial aid: (888) 547-6670; 42% of undergrads determined to have financial need; average aid package $46,638

Webster University

St. Louis MO
(314) 246-7800
U.S. News ranking: Reg. U. (Mid. W), No. 23
Website: www.webster.edu
Admissions email: admit@webster.edu
Private; founded 1915
Freshman admissions: selective; 2017-2018: 2,585 applied, 1,205 accepted. Either SAT or ACT required. ACT 25/75 percentile: 21-26. High school rank: 12% in top tenth, 37% in top quarter, 75% in top half
Early decision deadline: N/A, notification date: N/A
Early action deadline: N/A, notification date: N/A
Application deadline (fall): 8/1
Undergraduate student body: 2,212 full time, 332 part time; 45% male, 55% female; 0% American Indian, 2% Asian, 12% black, 6% Hispanic, 4% multiracial, 0% Pacific Islander, 66% white, 3% international; 73% from in state; N/A live on campus; 0% of students in fraternities, 3% in sororities
Most popular majors: 24% Business, Management, Marketing, and Related Support Services, 21% Visual and Performing Arts, 12% Communication, Journalism, and Related Programs, 7% Computer and Information Sciences and Support Services, 5% Communications Technologies/Technicians and Support Services
Expenses: 2018-2019: $27,900; room/board: $11,050
Financial aid: (800) 983-4623; 68% of undergrads determined to have financial need; average aid package $23,727

Westminster College

Fulton MO
(800) 475-3361
U.S. News ranking: Nat. Lib. Arts, No. 155
Website: www.westminster-mo.edu
Admissions email: admissions@westminster-mo.edu
Private; founded 1851
Freshman admissions: selective; 2017-2018: 1,035 applied, 933 accepted. Either SAT or ACT required. ACT 25/75 percentile: 21-26. High school rank: 13% in top tenth, 26% in top quarter, 70% in top half
Early decision deadline: N/A, notification date: N/A
Early action deadline: N/A, notification date: N/A
Application deadline (fall): rolling
Undergraduate student body: 760 full time, 7 part time; 56% male, 44% female; 2% American Indian, 2% Asian, 7% black, 4% Hispanic, 0% multiracial, 0% Pacific Islander, 70% white, 6% international; 81% from in state; 84% live on campus; 56% of students in fraternities, 40% in sororities
Most popular majors: 26% Business, Management, Marketing, and Related Support Services, 13% Biological and Biomedical Sciences, 13% Social Sciences, 8% Education, 5% Psychology
Expenses: 2017-2018: $25,940; room/board: $9,810
Financial aid: (573) 592-5364

William Jewell College

Liberty MO
(888) 253-9355
U.S. News ranking: Nat. Lib. Arts, No. 155
Website: www.jewell.edu
Admissions email: admission@william.jewell.edu
Private; founded 1849
Freshman admissions: more selective; 2017-2018: 1,684 applied, 783 accepted. Neither SAT nor ACT required. ACT 25/75

percentile: 23-28. High school rank: 26% in top tenth, 57% in top quarter, 88% in top half
Early decision deadline: N/A, notification date: N/A
Early action deadline: N/A, notification date: N/A
Application deadline (fall): 8/15
Undergraduate student body: 909 full time, 19 part time; 41% male, 59% female; 0% American Indian, 1% Asian, 5% black, 4% Hispanic, 5% multiracial, 0% Pacific Islander, 79% white, 4% international; 58% from in state; 85% live on campus; 38% of students in fraternities, 44% in sororities
Most popular majors: 34% Health Professions and Related Programs, 18% Business, Management, Marketing, and Related Support Services, 8% Education, 7% Psychology, 5% Biological and Biomedical Sciences
Expenses: 2018-2019: $34,400; room/board: $9,930
Financial aid: (816) 415-5977; 68% of undergrads determined to have financial need; average aid package $30,556

William Woods University

Fulton MO
(573) 592-4221
U.S. News ranking: Reg. U. (Mid. W), No. 90
Website: www.williamwoods.edu
Admissions email: admissions@williamwoods.edu
Private; founded 1870
Affiliation: Other
Freshman admissions: selective; 2017-2018: 892 applied, 668 accepted. Either SAT or ACT required. ACT 25/75 percentile: 20-26. High school rank: 10% in top tenth, 37% in top quarter, 82% in top half
Early decision deadline: N/A, notification date: N/A
Early action deadline: N/A, notification date: N/A
Application deadline (fall): rolling
Undergraduate student body: 796 full time, 162 part time; 27% male, 73% female; 1% American Indian, 1% Asian, 5% black, 3% Hispanic, 2% multiracial, 0% Pacific Islander, 81% white, 5% international; 61% from in state; 63% live on campus; 33% of students in fraternities, 31% in sororities
Most popular majors: 26% Foreign Languages, Literatures, and Linguistics, 18% Business, Management, Marketing, and Related Support Services, 11% Agriculture, Agriculture Operations, and Related Sciences, 11% Education, 7% Biological and Biomedical Sciences
Expenses: 2018-2019: $24,110; room/board: $9,700
Financial aid: (573) 592-4255; 97% of undergrads determined to have financial need; average aid package $16,149

MONTANA

Carroll College

Helena MT
(406) 447-4384
U.S. News ranking: Reg. Coll. (W), No. 1
Website: www.carroll.edu
Admissions email: admission@carroll.edu
Private; founded 1909
Affiliation: Roman Catholic
Freshman admissions: more selective; 2017-2018: 2,686 applied, 2,090 accepted. Either SAT or ACT required. ACT 25/75 percentile: 22-28. High school rank: 32% in top tenth, 64% in top quarter, 93% in top half
Early decision deadline: N/A, notification date: N/A
Early action deadline: 12/1, notification date: 1/1
Application deadline (fall): 5/1
Undergraduate student body: 1,287 full time, 65 part time; 41% male, 59% female; 1% American Indian, 1% Asian, 1% black, 5% Hispanic, 3% multiracial, 0% Pacific Islander, 81% white, 1% international; 44% from in state; 55% live on campus; N/A of students in fraternities, N/A in sororities
Most popular majors: 35% Health Professions and Related Programs, 13% Business, Management, Marketing, and Related Support Services, 12% Biological and Biomedical Sciences, 7% Social Sciences, 5% Psychology
Expenses: 2018-2019: $35,786; room/board: $9,980
Financial aid: (406) 447-5425; 65% of undergrads determined to have financial need; average aid package $26,744

Montana State University

Bozeman MT
(406) 994-2452
U.S. News ranking: Nat. U., No. 205
Website: www.montana.edu
Admissions email: admissions@montana.edu
Public; founded 1893
Freshman admissions: selective; 2017-2018: 16,769 applied, 13,937 accepted. Either SAT or ACT required. ACT 25/75 percentile: 21-28. High school rank: 20% in top tenth, 44% in top quarter, 76% in top half
Early decision deadline: N/A, notification date: N/A
Early action deadline: N/A, notification date: N/A
Application deadline (fall): rolling
Undergraduate student body: 12,403 full time, 2,322 part time; 54% male, 46% female; 1% American Indian, 1% Asian, 0% black, 4% Hispanic, 4% multiracial, 0% Pacific Islander, 84% white, 3% international; 62% from in state; 25% live on campus; 2% of students in fraternities, 2% in sororities
Most popular majors: 19% Engineering, 10% Business, Management, Marketing, and Related Support Services, 9% Health Professions and Related Programs, 8% Biological and Biomedical Sciences, 8% Family and Consumer Sciences/Human Sciences
Expenses: 2018-2019: $7,421 in state, $24,849 out of state; room/board: $10,100
Financial aid: (406) 994-2845; 45% of undergrads determined to have financial need; average aid package $11,308

Montana State University–Billings

Billings MT
(406) 657-2158
U.S. News ranking: Reg. U. (W), second tier
Website: www.msubillings.edu
Admissions email: admissions@msubillings.edu
Public; founded 1927
Freshman admissions: less selective; 2017-2018: 1,423 applied, 1,421 accepted. Neither SAT nor ACT required. ACT 25/75 percentile: 18-23. High school rank: 7% in top tenth, 26% in top quarter, 61% in top half
Early decision deadline: N/A, notification date: N/A
Early action deadline: N/A, notification date: N/A
Application deadline (fall): rolling
Undergraduate student body: 2,400 full time, 1,621 part time; 37% male, 63% female; 5% American Indian, 1% Asian, 1% black, 6% Hispanic, 4% multiracial, 0% Pacific Islander, 81% white, 2% international; 95% from in state; 10% live on campus; N/A of students in fraternities, N/A in sororities
Most popular majors: 26% Business, Management, Marketing, and Related Support Services, 19% Education, 9% Psychology, 7% Health Professions and Related Programs, 7% Liberal Arts and Sciences, General Studies and Humanities
Expenses: 2018-2019: $5,833 in state, $18,098 out of state; room/board: $7,600
Financial aid: (406) 657-2188; 70% of undergrads determined to have financial need; average aid package $10,006

Montana State University–Northern[1]

Havre MT
(406) 265-3704
U.S. News ranking: Reg. Coll. (W), second tier
Website: www.msun.edu
Admissions email: admissions@msun.edu
Public
Application deadline (fall): N/A
Undergraduate student body: N/A full time, N/A part time
Expenses: 2017-2018: $5,861 in state, $18,171 out of state; room/board: $6,470
Financial aid: N/A

Montana Tech of the University of Montana

Butte MT
(406) 496-4256
U.S. News ranking: Reg. Coll. (W), No. 5
Website: www.mtech.edu/
Admissions email: enrollment@mtech.edu
Public; founded 1893
Freshman admissions: selective; 2017-2018: 981 applied, 898 accepted. Either SAT or ACT required. ACT 25/75 percentile: 22-27. High school rank: 25% in top tenth, 56% in top quarter, 87% in top half
Early decision deadline: N/A, notification date: N/A
Early action deadline: N/A, notification date: N/A
Application deadline (fall): rolling
Undergraduate student body: 1,924 full time, 504 part time; 62% male, 38% female; 2% American Indian, 1% Asian, 1% black, 2% Hispanic, 0% multiracial, 0% Pacific Islander, 78% white, 10% international; 86% from in state; 12% live on campus; N/A of students in fraternities, N/A in sororities
Most popular majors: 25% Petroleum Engineering, 13% Engineering, General, 12% Business/Commerce, General, 10% Occupational Health and Industrial Hygiene, 6% Mechanical Engineering
Expenses: 2018-2019: $7,411 in state, $22,574 out of state; room/board: $9,828
Financial aid: (406) 496-4256; 54% of undergrads determined to have financial need; average aid package $11,025

Rocky Mountain College

Billings MT
(406) 657-1026
U.S. News ranking: Reg. Coll. (W), No. 8
Website: www.rocky.edu
Admissions email: admissions@rocky.edu
Private; founded 1878
Affiliation: Presbyterian Church (USA)
Freshman admissions: selective; 2017-2018: 1,238 applied, 797 accepted. Either SAT or ACT required. ACT 25/75 percentile: 20-25. High school rank: 15% in top tenth, 43% in top quarter, 77% in top half
Early decision deadline: N/A, notification date: N/A
Early action deadline: N/A, notification date: N/A
Application deadline (fall): rolling
Undergraduate student body: 869 full time, 30 part time; 51% male, 49% female; 2% American Indian, 1% Asian, 3% black, 5% Hispanic, 6% multiracial, 1% Pacific Islander, 78% white, 4% international; 52% from in state; 49% live on campus; N/A of students in fraternities, N/A in sororities
Most popular majors: 28% Business, Management, Marketing, and Related Support Services, 11% Education, 11% Parks, Recreation, Leisure, and Fitness Studies, 8% Transportation and Materials Moving, 7% Biological and Biomedical Sciences
Expenses: 2018-2019: $28,512; room/board: $8,330
Financial aid: (406) 657-1031; 76% of undergrads determined to have financial need; average aid package $24,480

University of Montana

Missoula MT
(800) 462-8636
U.S. News ranking: Nat. U., No. 201
Website: www.umt.edu
Admissions email: admiss@umontana.edu
Public; founded 1893
Freshman admissions: selective; 2017-2018: 6,182 applied, 5,727 accepted. Either SAT or ACT required. ACT 25/75 percentile: 21-26. High school rank: 14% in top tenth, 42% in top quarter, 73% in top half
Early decision deadline: N/A, notification date: N/A
Early action deadline: N/A, notification date: N/A
Application deadline (fall): rolling
Undergraduate student body: 7,444 full time, 1,879 part time; 45% male, 55% female; 3% American Indian, 1% Asian, 1% black, 5% Hispanic, 4% multiracial, 0% Pacific Islander, 79% white, 1% international; 72% from in state; 35% live on campus; 6% of students in fraternities, 6% in sororities
Most popular majors: 18% Business, Management, Marketing, and Related Support Services, 11% Social Sciences, 10% Education, 10% Natural Resources and Conservation, 8% Visual and Performing Arts
Expenses: 2018-2019: $7,244 in state, $24,959 out of state; room/board: $9,178
Financial aid: (406) 243-5504; 60% of undergrads determined to have financial need; average aid package $11,594

University of Montana–Western

Dillon MT
(877) 683-7331
U.S. News ranking: Reg. Coll. (W), No. 9
Website: w.umwestern.edu/
Admissions email: admissions@umwestern.edu
Public; founded 1893
Freshman admissions: less selective; 2017-2018: 815 applied, 495 accepted. Either SAT or ACT required. ACT 25/75 percentile: 16-22. High school rank: 6% in top tenth, 18% in top quarter, 51% in top half
Early decision deadline: N/A, notification date: N/A
Early action deadline: N/A, notification date: N/A
Application deadline (fall): rolling
Undergraduate student body: 1,217 full time, 361 part time; 36% male, 64% female; 4% American Indian, 1% Asian, 1% black,

3% Hispanic, 2% multiracial, 1% Pacific Islander, 85% white, 0% international; 79% from in state; 21% live on campus; N/A of students in fraternities, N/A in sororities
Most popular majors: 30% Education, 25% Business, Management, Marketing, and Related Support Services, 12% Agriculture, Agriculture Operations, and Related Sciences, 9% Parks, Recreation, Leisure, and Fitness Studies, 7% Biological and Biomedical Sciences
Expenses: 2017-2018: $5,502 in state, $16,644 out of state; room/board: $7,744
Financial aid: (406) 683-7893

University of Providence

Great Falls MT
(406) 791-5210
U.S. News ranking: Reg. Coll. (W), No. 20
Website: www.uprovidence.edu
Admissions email: melanie.houge@uprovidence.edu
Private; founded 1932
Freshman admissions: less selective; 2017-2018: 805 applied, 610 accepted. Either SAT or ACT required. ACT 25/75 percentile: 17-24. High school rank: N/A
Early decision deadline: N/A, notification date: N/A
Early action deadline: N/A, notification date: N/A
Application deadline (fall): 9/1
Undergraduate student body: 469 full time, 458 part time; 30% male, 70% female; 1% American Indian, 4% Asian, 3% black, 6% Hispanic, 0% multiracial, 1% Pacific Islander, 76% white, 0% international; 30% from in state; 38% live on campus; 0% of students in fraternities, 0% in sororities
Most popular majors: 53% Health Professions and Related Programs, 11% Biological and Biomedical Sciences, 10% Business, Management, Marketing, and Related Support Services, 6% Education, 6% Psychology
Expenses: 2018-2019: $25,318; room/board: $9,200
Financial aid: (406) 791-5235; 76% of undergrads determined to have financial need; average aid package $20,968

NEBRASKA

Bellevue University[1]

Bellevue NE
(402) 293-2000
U.S. News ranking: Reg. U. (Mid. W), unranked
Website: www.bellevue.edu
Admissions email: info@bellevue.edu
Private
Application deadline (fall): N/A
Undergraduate student body: N/A full time, N/A part time
Expenses: 2017-2018: $7,752; room/board: $8,532
Financial aid: (402) 557-7095

Chadron State College[1]

Chadron NE
(308) 432-6000
U.S. News ranking: Reg. U. (Mid. W), unranked
Website: www.csc.edu
Admissions email: inquire@csc.edu
Public; founded 1911
Application deadline (fall): N/A
Undergraduate student body: N/A full time, N/A part time
Expenses: 2017-2018: $7,122 in state, $7,152 out of state; room/board: $7,072
Financial aid: N/A

College of St. Mary

Omaha NE
(402) 399-2407
U.S. News ranking: Reg. U. (Mid. W), No. 72
Website: www.csm.edu
Admissions email: enroll@csm.edu
Private; founded 1923
Affiliation: Roman Catholic
Freshman admissions: selective; 2017-2018: 378 applied, 212 accepted. Either SAT or ACT required. ACT 25/75 percentile: 18-24. High school rank: 15% in top tenth, 40% in top quarter, 72% in top half
Early decision deadline: N/A, notification date: N/A
Early action deadline: N/A, notification date: N/A
Application deadline (fall): rolling
Undergraduate student body: 761 full time, 71 part time; 1% male, 99% female; 1% American Indian, 3% Asian, 8% black, 14% Hispanic, 3% multiracial, 0% Pacific Islander, 70% white, 1% international; 76% from in state; 36% live on campus; 0% of students in fraternities, 0% in sororities
Most popular majors: 33% Rehabilitation Science, 19% Biology/Biological Sciences, General, 14% Registered Nursing/Registered Nurse, 9% Elementary Education and Teaching, 9% General Studies
Expenses: 2018-2019: $20,350; room/board: $7,700
Financial aid: (402) 399-2362; 81% of undergrads determined to have financial need; average aid package $15,056

Concordia University

Seward NE
(800) 535-5494
U.S. News ranking: Reg. U. (Mid. W), No. 35
Website: www.cune.edu
Admissions email: admiss@cune.edu
Private; founded 1894
Affiliation: Lutheran Church–Missouri Synod
Freshman admissions: selective; 2017-2018: 1,537 applied, 1,152 accepted. Either SAT or ACT required. ACT 25/75 percentile: 21-26. High school rank: 18% in top tenth, 43% in top quarter, 72% in top half
Early decision deadline: N/A, notification date: N/A
Early action deadline: N/A, notification date: N/A
Application deadline (fall): 8/1
Undergraduate student body: 1,231 full time, 453 part time; 46% male, 54% female; 0% American Indian, 1% Asian, 4% black, 6% Hispanic, 1% multiracial, 0% Pacific Islander, 78% white, 2% international; 48% from in state; 57% live on campus; N/A of students in fraternities, N/A in sororities
Most popular majors: 22% Education, 18% Business, Management, Marketing, and Related Support Services, 11% Biological and Biomedical Sciences, 10% Theology and Religious Vocations, 8% Psychology
Expenses: 2018-2019: $32,220; room/board: $8,470
Financial aid: (402) 643-7270; 77% of undergrads determined to have financial need; average aid package $25,229

Creighton University

Omaha NE
(800) 282-5835
U.S. News ranking: Reg. U. (Mid. W), No. 1
Website: www.creighton.edu
Admissions email: admissions@creighton.edu
Private; founded 1878
Affiliation: Roman Catholic
Freshman admissions: more selective; 2017-2018: 9,727 applied, 7,004 accepted. Either SAT or ACT required. ACT 25/75 percentile: 25-30. High school rank: 33% in top tenth, 69% in top quarter, 93% in top half
Early decision deadline: N/A, notification date: N/A
Early action deadline: 11/1, notification date: N/A
Application deadline (fall): 2/15
Undergraduate student body: 4,011 full time, 244 part time; 44% male, 56% female; 0% American Indian, 9% Asian, 3% black, 8% Hispanic, 5% multiracial, 0% Pacific Islander, 71% white, 3% international; 23% from in state; 57% live on campus; 32% of students in fraternities, 51% in sororities
Most popular majors: 22% Business, Management, Marketing, and Related Support Services, 21% Health Professions and Related Programs, 9% Biological and Biomedical Sciences, 7% Psychology, 7% Social Sciences
Expenses: 2018-2019: $39,916; room/board: $11,036
Financial aid: (402) 280-2731; 54% of undergrads determined to have financial need; average aid package $28,732

Doane University

Crete NE
(402) 826-8222
U.S. News ranking: Nat. Lib. Arts, No. 155
Website: www.doane.edu
Admissions email: admissions@doane.edu
Private; founded 1872
Freshman admissions: selective; 2017-2018: 2,392 applied, 1,559 accepted. Either SAT or ACT required. ACT 25/75 percentile: 20-25. High school rank: 15% in top tenth, 36% in top quarter, 89% in top half
Early decision deadline: N/A, notification date: N/A
Early action deadline: N/A, notification date: N/A
Application deadline (fall): rolling
Undergraduate student body: 1,062 full time, 7 part time; 53% male, 47% female; 0% American Indian, 1% Asian, 2% black, 7% Hispanic, 4% multiracial, 0% Pacific Islander, 82% white, 2% international; 77% from in state; 78% live on campus; 26% of students in fraternities, 35% in sororities
Most popular majors: 19% Education, 14% Business, Management, Marketing, and Related Support Services, 13% Biological and Biomedical Sciences, 11% Visual and Performing Arts, 9% Social Sciences
Expenses: 2018-2019: $33,800; room/board: $9,400
Financial aid: (402) 826-8260; 76% of undergrads determined to have financial need; average aid package $25,179

Hastings College

Hastings NE
(800) 532-7642
U.S. News ranking: Reg. Coll. (Mid. W), No. 23
Website: www.hastings.edu
Admissions email: hcadmissions@hastings.edu
Private; founded 1882
Affiliation: Presbyterian
Freshman admissions: selective; 2017-2018: 1,945 applied, 1,329 accepted. Either SAT or ACT required. ACT 25/75 percentile: 20-25. High school rank: 18% in top tenth, 45% in top quarter, 71% in top half
Early decision deadline: N/A, notification date: N/A
Early action deadline: N/A, notification date: N/A
Application deadline (fall): rolling
Undergraduate student body: 1,072 full time, 82 part time; 51% male, 49% female; 0% American Indian, 1% Asian, 4% black, 7% Hispanic, 5% multiracial, 1% Pacific Islander, 80% white, 0% international
Most popular majors: 29% Business, Management, Marketing, and Related Support Services, 23% Education, 11% Social Sciences, 10% Biological and Biomedical Sciences, 9% Communication, Journalism, and Related Programs
Expenses: 2018-2019: $30,050; room/board: $9,700
Financial aid: (402) 461-7431; 75% of undergrads determined to have financial need; average aid package $24,151

Midland University[1]

Fremont NE
(402) 941-6501
U.S. News ranking: Reg. Coll. (Mid. W), No. 56
Website: www.midlandu.edu/
Admissions email: admissions@midlandu.edu
Private; founded 1883
Application deadline (fall): rolling
Undergraduate student body: N/A full time, N/A part time
Expenses: 2017-2018: $31,630; room/board: $8,274
Financial aid: N/A

Nebraska Wesleyan University

Lincoln NE
(402) 465-2218
U.S. News ranking: Reg. U. (Mid. W), No. 17
Website: www.nebrwesleyan.edu/undergraduate/how-apply
Admissions email: admissions@nebrwesleyan.edu
Private; founded 1887
Affiliation: United Methodist
Freshman admissions: more selective; 2017-2018: 1,910 applied, 1,361 accepted. Either SAT or ACT required. ACT 25/75 percentile: 22-28. High school rank: 21% in top tenth, 51% in top quarter, 85% in top half
Early decision deadline: 12/1, notification date: N/A
Early action deadline: N/A, notification date: N/A
Application deadline (fall): 8/15
Undergraduate student body: 1,566 full time, 213 part time; 40% male, 60% female; 0% American Indian, 1% Asian, 4% black, 6% Hispanic, 3% multiracial, 0% Pacific Islander, 82% white, 1% international; 87% from in state; 60% live on campus; 25% of students in fraternities, 26% in sororities
Most popular majors: 16% Business, Management, Marketing, and Related Support Services, 15% Health Professions and Related Programs, 10% Parks, Recreation, Leisure, and Fitness Studies, 9% Education, 9% Visual and Performing Arts
Expenses: 2017-2018: $32,894; room/board: $9,150
Financial aid: (402) 465-2167

Peru State College[1]

Peru NE
(402) 872-3815
U.S. News ranking: Reg. U. (Mid. W), unranked
Website: www.peru.edu
Admissions email: admissions@peru.edu
Public
Application deadline (fall): N/A
Undergraduate student body: N/A full time, N/A part time
Expenses: 2017-2018: $7,260 in state, $7,260 out of state; room/board: $7,808
Financial aid: N/A

Union College

Lincoln NE
(800) 228-4600
U.S. News ranking: Reg. Coll. (Mid. W), No. 27
Website: www.ucollege.edu
Admissions email: ucenroll@ucollege.edu
Private; founded 1891
Affiliation: Seventh Day Adventist
Freshman admissions: selective; 2017-2018: 1,573 applied, 943 accepted. Either SAT or ACT required. ACT 25/75 percentile: 19-26. High school rank: N/A

Early decision deadline: N/A, notification date: N/A
Early action deadline: N/A, notification date: N/A
Application deadline (fall): 8/20
Undergraduate student body: 707 full time, 74 part time; 42% male, 58% female; 0% American Indian, 5% Asian, 8% black, 22% Hispanic, 3% multiracial, 1% Pacific Islander, 52% white, 8% international; 20% from in state; 75% live on campus; 0% of students in fraternities, 0% in sororities
Most popular majors: Information not available
Expenses: 2018-2019: $23,780; room/board: $7,070
Financial aid: (402) 486-2505; 75% of undergrads determined to have financial need; average aid package $18,097

University of Nebraska–Kearney

Kearney NE
(800) 532-7639
U.S. News ranking: Reg. U. (Mid. W), No. 53
Website: www.unk.edu
Admissions email: admissionsug@unk.edu
Public; founded 1903
Freshman admissions: selective; 2017-2018: 5,911 applied, 4,832 accepted. Either SAT or ACT required. ACT 25/75 percentile: 19-25. High school rank: 20% in top tenth, 44% in top quarter, 79% in top half
Early decision deadline: N/A, notification date: N/A
Early action deadline: N/A, notification date: N/A
Application deadline (fall): 9/1
Undergraduate student body: 4,063 full time, 780 part time; 43% male, 57% female; 0% American Indian, 1% Asian, 2% black, 11% Hispanic, 2% multiracial, 0% Pacific Islander, 78% white, 5% international; 92% from in state; 35% live on campus; 16% of students in fraternities, 21% in sororities
Most popular majors: 15% Business Administration and Management, General, 13% Elementary Education and Teaching, 7% Operations Management and Supervision, 7% Parks, Recreation and Leisure Studies, 6% Psychology, General
Expenses: 2018-2019: $7,513 in state, $14,503 out of state; room/board: $9,878
Financial aid: (308) 865-8520; 67% of undergrads determined to have financial need; average aid package $11,147

University of Nebraska–Lincoln

Lincoln NE
(800) 742-8800
U.S. News ranking: Nat. U., No. 129
Website: www.unl.edu
Admissions email: Admissions@unl.edu
Public; founded 1869
Freshman admissions: more selective; 2017-2018: 14,947 applied, 9,623 accepted. Either SAT or ACT required. ACT 25/75 percentile: 22-29. High school rank: 26% in top tenth, 53% in top quarter, 85% in top half
Early decision deadline: N/A, notification date: N/A
Early action deadline: N/A, notification date: N/A
Application deadline (fall): 5/1
Undergraduate student body: 19,534 full time, 1,420 part time; 52% male, 48% female; 0% American Indian, 3% Asian, 3% black, 6% Hispanic, 3% multiracial, 0% Pacific Islander, 75% white, 9% international; 77% from in state; 37% live on campus; 17% of students in fraternities, 24% in sororities
Most popular majors: 23% Business, Management, Marketing, and Related Support Services, 10% Engineering, 9% Agriculture, Agriculture Operations, and Related Sciences, 8% Communication, Journalism, and Related Programs, 8% Family and Consumer Sciences/Human Sciences
Expenses: 2018-2019: $9,242 in state, $25,038 out of state; room/board: $11,430
Financial aid: (402) 472-2030; 45% of undergrads determined to have financial need; average aid package $14,021

University of Nebraska–Omaha

Omaha NE
(402) 554-2393
U.S. News ranking: Nat. U., second tier
Website: www.unomaha.edu
Admissions email: unoadmissions@unomaha.edu
Public; founded 1908
Freshman admissions: selective; 2017-2018: 9,158 applied, 7,924 accepted. Either SAT or ACT required. ACT 25/75 percentile: 19-26. High school rank: 14% in top tenth, 37% in top quarter, 71% in top half
Early decision deadline: N/A, notification date: N/A
Early action deadline: N/A, notification date: N/A
Application deadline (fall): 8/1
Undergraduate student body: 9,820 full time, 2,804 part time; 48% male, 52% female; 0% American Indian, 4% Asian, 6% black, 13% Hispanic, 5% multiracial, 0% Pacific Islander, 67% white, 4% international; 91% from in state; 16% live on campus; 2% of students in fraternities, 2% in sororities
Most popular majors: 10% Criminal Justice/Safety Studies, 6% Business Administration and Management, General, 5% Finance, General, 5% Marketing/Marketing Management, General, 5% Psychology, General
Expenses: 2018-2019: $8,930 in state, $21,904 out of state; room/board: $9,690
Financial aid: (402) 554-3408; 59% of undergrads determined to have financial need; average aid package $9,779

Wayne State College

Wayne NE
(800) 228-9972
U.S. News ranking: Reg. U. (Mid. W), No. 90
Website: www.wsc.edu/
Admissions email: admit1@wsc.edu
Public; founded 1909
Freshman admissions: selective; 2017-2018: 1,706 applied, 1,706 accepted. Neither SAT nor ACT required. ACT 25/75 percentile: 18-25. High school rank: 12% in top tenth, 30% in top quarter, 59% in top half
Early decision deadline: N/A, notification date: N/A
Early action deadline: N/A, notification date: N/A
Application deadline (fall): 8/20
Undergraduate student body: 2,404 full time, 353 part time; 42% male, 58% female; 1% American Indian, 1% Asian, 3% black, 9% Hispanic, 3% multiracial, 0% Pacific Islander, 81% white, 1% international; 85% from in state; 40% live on campus; N/A of students in fraternities, N/A in sororities
Most popular majors: 30% Education, 15% Business, Management, Marketing, and Related Support Services, 10% Homeland Security, Law Enforcement, Firefighting and Related Protective Services, 7% Psychology, 5% Parks, Recreation, Leisure, and Fitness Studies
Expenses: 2018-2019: $6,989 in state, $12,299 out of state; room/board: $7,668
Financial aid: (402) 375-7230; 71% of undergrads determined to have financial need; average aid package $9,494

York College

York NE
(800) 950-9675
U.S. News ranking: Reg. Coll. (Mid. W), No. 54
Website: www.york.edu
Admissions email: enroll@york.edu
Private; founded 1890
Freshman admissions: selective; 2017-2018: 530 applied, 133 accepted. Either SAT or ACT required. ACT 25/75 percentile: 18-23. High school rank: 8% in top tenth, 20% in top quarter, 55% in top half
Early decision deadline: N/A, notification date: N/A
Early action deadline: N/A, notification date: N/A
Application deadline (fall): 8/31
Undergraduate student body: 401 full time, 33 part time; 55% male, 45% female; 1% American Indian, 1% Asian, 16% black, 18% Hispanic, 0% multiracial, 1% Pacific Islander, 58% white, 2% international; 32% from in state; 85% live on campus; 80% of students in fraternities, 80% in sororities
Most popular majors: 23% Business Administration and Management, General, 14% General Studies, 7% Biology/Biological Sciences, General, 7% Elementary Education and Teaching, 7% Psychology, General
Expenses: 2018-2019: $19,310; room/board: $7,220
Financial aid: (402) 363-5624; 81% of undergrads determined to have financial need; average aid package $15,058

NEVADA

College of Southern Nevada[1]

Las Vegas NV
(702) 651-5000
U.S. News ranking: Reg. Coll. (W), unranked
Website: www.csn.edu
Admissions email: N/A
Public; founded 1971
Application deadline (fall): N/A
Undergraduate student body: N/A full time, N/A part time
Expenses: 2017-2018: $3,285 in state, $10,063 out of state; room/board: N/A
Financial aid: N/A

Great Basin College[1]

Elko NV
(775) 738-8493
U.S. News ranking: Reg. Coll. (W), unranked
Website: www.gbcnv.edu
Admissions email: N/A
Public
Application deadline (fall): N/A
Undergraduate student body: N/A full time, N/A part time
Expenses: 2017-2018: $3,015 in state, $9,793 out of state; room/board: $6,800
Financial aid: N/A

Nevada State College[1]

Henderson NV
(702) 992-2130
U.S. News ranking: Reg. Coll. (W), second tier
Website: nsc.nevada.edu
Admissions email: N/A
Public; founded 2002
Application deadline (fall): rolling
Undergraduate student body: N/A full time, N/A part time
Expenses: 2017-2018: $5,131 in state, $16,688 out of state; room/board: N/A
Financial aid: N/A

Sierra Nevada College

Incline Village NV
(866) 412-4636
U.S. News ranking: Reg. U. (W), second tier
Website: www.sierranevada.edu
Admissions email: admissions@sierranevada.edu
Private; founded 1969
Freshman admissions: least selective; 2017-2018: 735 applied, 507 accepted. Either SAT or ACT required. SAT 25/75 percentile: 910-1140. High school rank: 10% in top tenth, 20% in top quarter, 45% in top half
Early decision deadline: N/A, notification date: N/A
Early action deadline: N/A, notification date: N/A
Application deadline (fall): 8/26
Undergraduate student body: 410 full time, 25 part time; 57% male, 43% female; 3% American Indian, 3% Asian, 3% black, 4% Hispanic, 0% multiracial, 2% Pacific Islander, 80% white, 0% international
Most popular majors: Information not available
Expenses: 2017-2018: $32,639; room/board: $12,764
Financial aid: (775) 831-1314

University of Nevada–Las Vegas

Las Vegas NV
(702) 774-8658
U.S. News ranking: Nat. U., second tier
Website: www.unlv.edu
Admissions email: admissions@unlv.edu
Public; founded 1957
Freshman admissions: selective; 2017-2018: 9,872 applied, 8,003 accepted. Either SAT or ACT required. ACT 25/75 percentile: 18-25. High school rank: 23% in top tenth, 54% in top quarter, 84% in top half
Early decision deadline: N/A, notification date: N/A
Early action deadline: N/A, notification date: N/A
Application deadline (fall): 7/1
Undergraduate student body: 18,958 full time, 6,321 part time; 43% male, 57% female; 0% American Indian, 16% Asian, 8% black, 29% Hispanic, 10% multiracial, 1% Pacific Islander, 32% white, 4% international; 89% from in state; 7% live on campus; 8% of students in fraternities, 8% in sororities
Most popular majors: 27% Business, Management, Marketing, and Related Support Services, 8% Psychology, 6% Health Professions and Related Programs, 6% Homeland Security, Law Enforcement, Firefighting and Related Protective Services, 6% Social Sciences
Expenses: 2018-2019: $7,308 in state, $21,774 out of state; room/board: $10,488
Financial aid: (702) 895-3424; 62% of undergrads determined to have financial need; average aid package $8,852

University of Nevada–Reno

Reno NV
(775) 784-4700
U.S. News ranking: Nat. U., No. 201
Website: www.unr.edu
Admissions email: asknevada@unr.edu
Public; founded 1874
Freshman admissions: selective; 2017-2018: 9,721 applied, 8,557 accepted. Either SAT or ACT required. ACT 25/75 percentile: 21-26. High school rank: 25% in top tenth, 54% in top quarter, 86% in top half
Early decision deadline: N/A, notification date: N/A
Early action deadline: 11/1, notification date: 11/15
Application deadline (fall): 4/7

More @ usnews.com/bestcolleges

Undergraduate student body: 15,572 full time, 2,776 part time; 47% male, 53% female; 1% American Indian, 8% Asian, 3% black, 21% Hispanic, 7% multiracial, 1% Pacific Islander, 58% white, 1% international; 72% from in state; 16% live on campus; N/A of students in fraternities, N/A in sororities
Most popular majors: 17% Business, Management, Marketing, and Related Support Services, 14% Health Professions and Related Programs, 11% Engineering, 10% Social Sciences, 9% Biological and Biomedical Sciences
Expenses: 2018-2019: $7,925 in state, $22,397 out of state; room/board: $10,868
Financial aid: (775) 784-4666; 50% of undergrads determined to have financial need; average aid package $9,000

Western Nevada College[1]

Carson City NV
(775) 445-3000
U.S. News ranking: Reg. Coll. (W), unranked
Website: www.wnc.edu
Admissions email: N/A
Public; founded 1971
Application deadline (fall): N/A
Undergraduate student body: N/A full time, N/A part time
Expenses: 2017-2018: $3,045 in state, $9,823 out of state; room/board: N/A
Financial aid: N/A

NEW HAMPSHIRE

Colby-Sawyer College

New London NH
(800) 272-1015
U.S. News ranking: Reg. Coll. (N), No. 7
Website: colby-sawyer.edu/
Admissions email: admissions@colby-sawyer.edu
Private; founded 1837
Freshman admissions: selective; 2017-2018: 2,559 applied, 2,235 accepted. Neither SAT nor ACT required. SAT 25/75 percentile: 1030-1210. High school rank: N/A
Early decision deadline: N/A, notification date: N/A
Early action deadline: 12/1, notification date: 12/15
Application deadline (fall): rolling
Undergraduate student body: 920 full time, 62 part time; 30% male, 70% female; 1% American Indian, 3% Asian, 6% black, 2% Hispanic, 0% multiracial, 0% Pacific Islander, 73% white, 5% international; N/A from in state; N/A live on campus; 0% of students in fraternities, 0% in sororities
Most popular majors: 14% Registered Nursing/Registered Nurse, 13% Business Administration and Management, General, 11% Biology/Biological Sciences, General, 9% Kinesiology and Exercise Science, 7% Psychology, General
Expenses: 2018-2019: $42,398; room/board: $14,264
Financial aid: (603) 526-3717; 79% of undergrads determined to have financial need; average aid package $33,742

Dartmouth College

Hanover NH
(603) 646-2875
U.S. News ranking: Nat. U., No. 12
Website: www.dartmouth.edu
Admissions email: admissions.office@dartmouth.edu
Private; founded 1769
Freshman admissions: most selective; 2017-2018: 20,035 applied, 2,093 accepted. Either SAT or ACT required. SAT 25/75 percentile: 1430-1560. High school rank: 93% in top tenth, 98% in top quarter, 100% in top half
Early decision deadline: 11/1, notification date: 12/15
Early action deadline: N/A, notification date: N/A
Application deadline (fall): 1/1
Undergraduate student body: 4,360 full time, 50 part time; 51% male, 49% female; 2% American Indian, 15% Asian, 7% black, 10% Hispanic, 5% multiracial, 0% Pacific Islander, 50% white, 9% international; 3% from in state; 88% live on campus; 44% of students in fraternities, 46% in sororities
Most popular majors: 37% Social Sciences, 9% Biological and Biomedical Sciences, 8% Computer and Information Sciences and Support Services, 8% Engineering, 6% History
Expenses: 2018-2019: $55,035; room/board: $15,756
Financial aid: (800) 443-3605; 51% of undergrads determined to have financial need; average aid package $50,665

Franklin Pierce University

Rindge NH
(800) 437-0048
U.S. News ranking: Reg. U. (N), second tier
Website: www.franklinpierce.edu/
Admissions email: admissions@franklinpierce.edu
Private; founded 1962
Freshman admissions: less selective; 2017-2018: 5,642 applied, 4,312 accepted. Neither SAT nor ACT required. SAT 25/75 percentile: 940-1160. High school rank: 3% in top tenth, 20% in top quarter, 46% in top half
Early decision deadline: N/A, notification date: N/A
Early action deadline: N/A, notification date: N/A
Application deadline (fall): rolling
Undergraduate student body: 1,520 full time, 192 part time; 44% male, 56% female; 0% American Indian, 1% Asian, 6% black, 3% Hispanic, 5% multiracial, 0% Pacific Islander, 68% white, 3% international; 18% from in state; 90% live on campus; 0% of students in fraternities, 0% in sororities
Most popular majors: 33% Health Professions and Related Programs, 22% Business, Management, Marketing, and Related Support Services, 7% Parks, Recreation, Leisure, and Fitness Studies, 6% Homeland Security, Law Enforcement, Firefighting and Related Protective Services, 5% Biological and Biomedical Sciences
Expenses: 2018-2019: $36,900; room/board: $13,345
Financial aid: (603) 899-4186; 85% of undergrads determined to have financial need; average aid package $26,243

Granite State College

Concord NH
(603) 513-1391
U.S. News ranking: Reg. Coll. (N), unranked
Website: www.granite.edu
Admissions email: gsc.admissions@granite.edu
Public; founded 1972
Freshman admissions: least selective; 2017-2018: 271 applied, 271 accepted. Neither SAT nor ACT required. SAT 25/75 percentile: N/A. High school rank: N/A
Early decision deadline: N/A, notification date: N/A
Early action deadline: N/A, notification date: N/A
Application deadline (fall): rolling
Undergraduate student body: 807 full time, 951 part time; 27% male, 73% female; 0% American Indian, 1% Asian, 3% black, 4% Hispanic, 2% multiracial, 0% Pacific Islander, 84% white, 0% international
Most popular majors: 31% Business, Management, Marketing, and Related Support Services, 16% Psychology, 15% Multi/Interdisciplinary Studies, 11% Health Professions and Related Programs, 8% Education
Expenses: 2018-2019: $7,761 in state, $8,745 out of state; room/board: N/A
Financial aid: (603) 513-1392; 73% of undergrads determined to have financial need; average aid package $6,637

Keene State College

Keene NH
(603) 358-2276
U.S. News ranking: Reg. U. (N), No. 81
Website: www.keene.edu
Admissions email: admissions@keene.edu
Public; founded 1909
Freshman admissions: less selective; 2017-2018: 5,580 applied, 4,613 accepted. Neither SAT nor ACT required. SAT 25/75 percentile: 930-1140. High school rank: 6% in top tenth, 21% in top quarter, 55% in top half
Early decision deadline: N/A, notification date: N/A
Early action deadline: N/A, notification date: N/A
Application deadline (fall): 4/1
Undergraduate student body: 3,624 full time, 156 part time; 45% male, 55% female; 0% American Indian, 2% Asian, 2% black, 4% Hispanic, 2% multiracial, 0% Pacific Islander, 86% white, 0% international; 43% from in state; 55% live on campus; 6% of students in fraternities, 7% in sororities
Most popular majors: 18% Engineering Technologies and Engineering-Related Fields, 13% Health Professions and Related Programs, 10% Education, 8% Psychology, 8% Visual and Performing Arts
Expenses: 2018-2019: $14,212 in state, $23,176 out of state; room/board: $11,008
Financial aid: (603) 358-2280; 66% of undergrads determined to have financial need; average aid package $12,701

New England College

Henniker NH
(603) 428-2223
U.S. News ranking: Reg. U. (N), second tier
Website: www.nec.edu
Admissions email: admission@nec.edu
Private; founded 1946
Freshman admissions: least selective; 2017-2018: 9,206 applied, 9,170 accepted. Neither SAT nor ACT required. SAT 25/75 percentile: 870-1080. High school rank: 8% in top tenth, 30% in top quarter, 67% in top half
Early decision deadline: N/A, notification date: N/A
Early action deadline: N/A, notification date: N/A
Application deadline (fall): rolling
Undergraduate student body: 1,794 full time, 33 part time; 40% male, 60% female; 1% American Indian, 2% Asian, 24% black, 10% Hispanic, 2% multiracial, 0% Pacific Islander, 52% white, 3% international; 18% from in state; 38% live on campus; 0% of students in fraternities, 0% in sororities
Most popular majors: 17% Business, Management, Marketing, and Related Support Services, 17% Education, 11% Parks, Recreation, Leisure, and Fitness Studies, 6% Social Sciences, 6% Visual and Performing Arts
Expenses: 2018-2019: $37,914; room/board: $14,222
Financial aid: (603) 428-2436; 88% of undergrads determined to have financial need; average aid package $23,463

New Hampshire Institute of Art[1]

Manchester NH
U.S. News ranking: Arts, unranked
Admissions email: N/A
Private
Application deadline (fall): N/A
Undergraduate student body: N/A full time, N/A part time
Expenses: N/A
Financial aid: N/A

Plymouth State University

Plymouth NH
(603) 535-2237
U.S. News ranking: Reg. U. (N), No. 132
Website: www.plymouth.edu
Admissions email: admissions@plymouth.edu
Public; founded 1871
Freshman admissions: less selective; 2017-2018: 6,715 applied, 5,291 accepted. Neither SAT nor ACT required. SAT 25/75 percentile: 890-1130. High school rank: 6% in top tenth, 18% in top quarter, 51% in top half
Early decision deadline: N/A, notification date: N/A
Early action deadline: N/A, notification date: N/A
Application deadline (fall): 4/1
Undergraduate student body: 3,971 full time, 177 part time; 50% male, 50% female; 1% American Indian, 2% Asian, 2% black, 2% Hispanic, 2% multiracial, 0% Pacific Islander, 83% white, 1% international; 55% from in state; 54% live on campus; 0% of students in fraternities, 2% in sororities
Most popular majors: 27% Education, 26% Business, Management, Marketing, and Related Support Services, 9% Health Professions and Related Programs, 4% Homeland Security, Law Enforcement, Firefighting and Related Protective Services, 4% Psychology
Expenses: 2018-2019: $14,099 in state, $22,769 out of state; room/board: $11,100
Financial aid: (603) 535-2338; 70% of undergrads determined to have financial need; average aid package $12,183

Rivier University[1]

Nashua NH
(603) 888-1311
U.S. News ranking: Reg. U. (N), second tier
Website: rivier.edu
Admissions email: admissions@rivier.edu
Private
Application deadline (fall): rolling
Undergraduate student body: N/A full time, N/A part time
Expenses: 2017-2018: $31,090; room/board: $12,768
Financial aid: N/A

Southern New Hampshire University

Manchester NH
(603) 645-9611
U.S. News ranking: Reg. U. (N), No. 112
Website: www.snhu.edu
Admissions email: admission@snhu.edu
Private; founded 1932
Freshman admissions: less selective; 2017-2018: 3,899 applied, 3,686 accepted. Neither SAT nor ACT required. SAT 25/75 percentile: 990-1160. High school rank: 7% in top tenth, 27% in top quarter, 63% in top half

Early decision deadline: N/A, notification date: N/A
Early action deadline: 11/15, notification date: 12/15
Application deadline (fall): rolling
Undergraduate student body: 2,917 full time, 116 part time; 50% male, 50% female; 0% American Indian, 2% Asian, 3% black, 4% Hispanic, 2% multiracial, 0% Pacific Islander, 74% white, 7% international; 51% from in state; 59% live on campus; 3% of students in fraternities, 4% in sororities
Most popular majors: 43% Business, Management, Marketing, and Related Support Services, 10% Education, 9% Psychology, 8% Homeland Security, Law Enforcement, Firefighting and Related Protective Services, 7% Computer and Information Sciences and Support Services
Expenses: 2018-2019: $31,136; room/board: $13,120
Financial aid: (877) 455-7648; 73% of undergrads determined to have financial need; average aid package $22,638

St. Anselm College

Manchester NH
(603) 641-7500
U.S. News ranking: Nat. Lib. Arts, No. 95
Website: www.anselm.edu
Admissions email: admission@anselm.edu
Private; founded 1889
Affiliation: Roman Catholic
Freshman admissions: more selective; 2017-2018: 3,892 applied, 2,960 accepted. Neither SAT nor ACT required. SAT 25/75 percentile: 1140-1300. High school rank: 24% in top tenth, 55% in top quarter, 88% in top half
Early decision deadline: 12/1, notification date: 1/1
Early action deadline: 11/15, notification date: 1/15
Application deadline (fall): 2/1
Undergraduate student body: 1,926 full time, 38 part time; 39% male, 61% female; 0% American Indian, 1% Asian, 2% black, 4% Hispanic, 2% multiracial, 0% Pacific Islander, 88% white, 1% international; 22% from in state; 92% live on campus; 0% of students in fraternities, 0% in sororities
Most popular majors: 15% Registered Nursing/Registered Nurse, 12% Business/Commerce, General, 9% Criminology, 7% Speech Communication and Rhetoric, 5% Elementary Education and Teaching
Expenses: 2018-2019: $41,500; room/board: $14,500
Financial aid: (603) 641-7110; 73% of undergrads determined to have financial need; average aid package $28,108

Thomas More College of Liberal Arts[1]

Merrimack NH
(800) 880-8308
U.S. News ranking: Nat. Lib. Arts, second tier
Website: www.thomasmorecollege.edu
Admissions email: admissions@thomasmorecollege.edu
Private
Application deadline (fall): N/A
Undergraduate student body: N/A full time, N/A part time
Expenses: 2017-2018: $21,000; room/board: $9,700
Financial aid: (603) 880-8308

University of New Hampshire

Durham NH
(603) 862-1360
U.S. News ranking: Nat. U., No. 106
Website: www.unh.edu
Admissions email: admissions@unh.edu
Public; founded 1866
Freshman admissions: selective; 2017-2018: 19,966 applied, 15,275 accepted. Either SAT or ACT required. SAT 25/75 percentile: 1080-1260. High school rank: 20% in top tenth, 49% in top quarter, 86% in top half
Early decision deadline: N/A, notification date: N/A
Early action deadline: 11/15, notification date: 1/1
Application deadline (fall): 2/1
Undergraduate student body: 12,646 full time, 321 part time; 45% male, 55% female; 0% American Indian, 3% Asian, 1% black, 3% Hispanic, 2% multiracial, 0% Pacific Islander, 83% white, 4% international; 47% from in state; 54% live on campus; 14% of students in fraternities, 14% in sororities
Most popular majors: 20% Business Administration and Management, General, 6% Psychology, General, 6% Speech Communication and Rhetoric, 5% Biomedical Sciences, General, 4% Mechanical Engineering
Expenses: 2018-2019: $18,499 in state, $33,879 out of state; room/board: $11,580
Financial aid: (603) 862-3600; 66% of undergrads determined to have financial need; average aid package $23,953

NEW JERSEY

Berkeley College

Woodland Park NJ
(800) 446-5400
U.S. News ranking: Business, unranked
Website: www.berkeleycollege.edu
Admissions email: admissions@berkeleycollege.edu
For-profit; founded 1931
Freshman admissions: least selective; 2017-2018: N/A applied, N/A accepted. Neither SAT nor ACT required. SAT 25/75 percentile: N/A. High school rank: N/A
Early decision deadline: N/A, notification date: N/A
Early action deadline: N/A, notification date: N/A
Application deadline (fall): 8/28
Undergraduate student body: 2,414 full time, 939 part time; 28% male, 72% female; 0% American Indian, 2% Asian, 20% black, 39% Hispanic, 0% multiracial, 0% Pacific Islander, 12% white, 1% international; 97% from in state; N/A live on campus; N/A of students in fraternities, N/A in sororities
Most popular majors: 26% Business Administration and Management, General, 23% Criminal Justice/Law Enforcement Administration, 13% Accounting, 11% Fashion Merchandising, 11% Health/Health Care Administration/ Management
Expenses: 2018-2019: $25,900; room/board: N/A
Financial aid: (973) 278-5400

Bloomfield College

Bloomfield NJ
(973) 748-9000
U.S. News ranking: Nat. Lib. Arts, second tier
Website: www.bloomfield.edu
Admissions email: admission@bloomfield.edu
Private; founded 1868
Affiliation: Presbyterian Church (USA)
Freshman admissions: less selective; 2017-2018: 3,340 applied, 2,137 accepted. Neither SAT nor ACT required. SAT 25/75 percentile: 840-1040. High school rank: 10% in top tenth, 26% in top quarter, 57% in top half
Early decision deadline: N/A, notification date: N/A
Early action deadline: 11/30, notification date: 12/20
Application deadline (fall): 8/1
Undergraduate student body: 1,691 full time, 133 part time; 37% male, 63% female; 0% American Indian, 2% Asian, 51% black, 28% Hispanic, 1% multiracial, 0% Pacific Islander, 9% white, 5% international; 95% from in state; 34% live on campus; 4% of students in fraternities, 2% in sororities
Most popular majors: 17% Social Sciences, 16% Business, Management, Marketing, and Related Support Services, 16% Psychology, 14% Visual and Performing Arts, 10% Biological and Biomedical Sciences
Expenses: 2018-2019: $29,550; room/board: $11,950
Financial aid: (973) 748-9000; 94% of undergrads determined to have financial need; average aid package $28,087

Caldwell University

Caldwell NJ
(973) 618-3600
U.S. News ranking: Reg. U. (N), No. 74
Website: www.caldwell.edu
Admissions email: admissions@caldwell.edu
Private; founded 1939
Affiliation: Roman Catholic
Freshman admissions: less selective; 2017-2018: 4,004 applied, 2,552 accepted. Either SAT or ACT required. SAT 25/75 percentile: 930-1150. High school rank: 11% in top tenth, 32% in top quarter, 63% in top half
Early decision deadline: N/A, notification date: N/A
Early action deadline: 12/1, notification date: 12/31
Application deadline (fall): 4/1
Undergraduate student body: 1,440 full time, 163 part time; 32% male, 68% female; 0% American Indian, 3% Asian, 13% black, 23% Hispanic, 1% multiracial, 0% Pacific Islander, 36% white, 12% international; 92% from in state; 40% live on campus; 1% of students in fraternities, 4% in sororities
Most popular majors: 22% Psychology, 20% Business, Management, Marketing, and Related Support Services, 15% Health Professions and Related Programs, 10% Communication, Journalism, and Related Programs, 6% Social Sciences
Expenses: 2018-2019: $34,715; room/board: $12,025
Financial aid: (973) 618-3221; 75% of undergrads determined to have financial need; average aid package $28,449

Centenary University[1]

Hackettstown NJ
(800) 236-8679
U.S. News ranking: Reg. U. (N), second tier
Website: www.centenaryuniversity.edu
Admissions email: admissions@centenaryuniversity.edu
Private; founded 1867
Affiliation: United Methodist
Application deadline (fall): 8/15
Undergraduate student body: N/A full time, N/A part time
Expenses: 2017-2018: $32,580; room/board: $11,110
Financial aid: (908) 852-1400

College of New Jersey

Ewing NJ
(609) 771-2131
U.S. News ranking: Reg. U. (N), No. 4
Website: www.tcnj.edu
Admissions email: admiss@tcnj.edu
Public; founded 1855
Freshman admissions: more selective; 2017-2018: 12,898 applied, 6,130 accepted. Either SAT or ACT required. SAT 25/75 percentile: 1170-1330. High school rank: 36% in top tenth, 73% in top quarter, 98% in top half
Early decision deadline: 11/1, notification date: 12/1
Early action deadline: N/A, notification date: N/A
Application deadline (fall): 2/1
Undergraduate student body: 6,728 full time, 227 part time; 42% male, 58% female; 0% American Indian, 12% Asian, 6% black, 13% Hispanic, 0% multiracial, 0% Pacific Islander, 66% white, 0% international; 94% from in state; 55% live on campus; 15% of students in fraternities, 13% in sororities
Most popular majors: 19% Business Administration, Management and Operations, 16% Teacher Education and Professional Development, Specific Levels and Methods, 8% Communication and Media Studies, 7% Psychology, General, 6% Biology, General
Expenses: 2018-2019: $16,551 in state, $28,266 out of state; room/board: $13,617
Financial aid: (609) 771-2211; 53% of undergrads determined to have financial need; average aid package $11,455

College of St. Elizabeth

Morristown NJ
(973) 290-4700
U.S. News ranking: Reg. U. (N), second tier
Website: www.cse.edu
Admissions email: apply@cse.edu
Private; founded 1899
Affiliation: Roman Catholic
Freshman admissions: least selective; 2017-2018: 1,964 applied, 1,261 accepted. Either SAT or ACT required. SAT 25/75 percentile: 800-1000. High school rank: N/A
Early decision deadline: N/A, notification date: N/A
Early action deadline: N/A, notification date: N/A
Application deadline (fall): rolling
Undergraduate student body: 587 full time, 178 part time; 21% male, 79% female; 0% American Indian, 4% Asian, 33% black, 25% Hispanic, 2% multiracial, 0% Pacific Islander, 25% white, 3% international
Most popular majors: Business Administration and Management, General, Dietetics/Dietitian, Psychology, General, Registered Nursing/Registered Nurse
Expenses: 2018-2019: $33,613; room/board: $12,744
Financial aid: (973) 290-4393

Drew University

Madison NJ
(973) 408-3739
U.S. News ranking: Nat. Lib. Arts, No. 116
Website: www.drew.edu
Admissions email: cadm@drew.edu
Private; founded 1867
Affiliation: United Methodist
Freshman admissions: more selective; 2017-2018: 3,205 applied, 2,033 accepted. Neither SAT nor ACT required. SAT 25/75 percentile: 1100-1300. High school rank: 24% in top tenth, 60% in top quarter, 84% in top half
Early decision deadline: 11/15, notification date: 12/15
Early action deadline: 12/15, notification date: 1/25
Application deadline (fall): 2/1
Undergraduate student body: 1,507 full time, 30 part time; 43% male, 57% female; 0% American Indian, 5% Asian, 7% black, 13% Hispanic, 5% multiracial, 0% Pacific Islander, 55% white, 10% international; 65% from in state; 79% live on campus; N/A of students in fraternities, N/A in sororities

More @ usnews.com/bestcolleges

Most popular majors: 11% Psychology, General, 9% English Language and Literature, General, 7% Biology/Biological Sciences, General, 7% Business Administration and Management, General, 7% Economics, General
Expenses: 2018-2019: $39,500; room/board: $14,108
Financial aid: (973) 408-3112; 71% of undergrads determined to have financial need; average aid package $44,512

Fairleigh Dickinson University

Teaneck NJ
(800) 338-8803
U.S. News ranking: Reg. U. (N), No. 62
Website: www.fdu.edu
Admissions email: admissions@fdu.edu
Private; founded 1942
Freshman admissions: selective; 2017-2018: 7,952 applied, 6,809 accepted. Either SAT or ACT required. SAT 25/75 percentile: 1020-1210. High school rank: 19% in top tenth, 49% in top quarter, 80% in top half
Early decision deadline: N/A, notification date: N/A
Early action deadline: N/A, notification date: N/A
Application deadline (fall): rolling
Undergraduate student body: 5,014 full time, 3,200 part time; 43% male, 57% female; 0% American Indian, 5% Asian, 9% black, 30% Hispanic, 2% multiracial, 0% Pacific Islander, 39% white, 3% international; 86% from in state; 40% live on campus; N/A of students in fraternities, N/A in sororities
Most popular majors: 33% Liberal Arts and Sciences, General Studies and Humanities, 16% Business, Management, Marketing, and Related Support Services, 9% Psychology, 6% Health Professions and Related Programs, 6% Visual and Performing Arts
Expenses: 2018-2019: $41,427; room/board: $13,370
Financial aid: (973) 443-8700; 82% of undergrads determined to have financial need; average aid package $38,485

Felician University

Lodi NJ
(201) 355-1457
U.S. News ranking: Reg. U. (N), second tier
Website: www.felician.edu
Admissions email: admissions@felician.edu
Private; founded 1942
Affiliation: Roman Catholic
Freshman admissions: less selective; 2017-2018: 2,249 applied, 1,786 accepted. Either SAT or ACT required. SAT 25/75 percentile: 900-1080. High school rank: 7% in top tenth, 23% in top quarter, 56% in top half
Early decision deadline: N/A, notification date: N/A
Early action deadline: 11/15, notification date: 12/23
Application deadline (fall): rolling
Undergraduate student body: 1,430 full time, 196 part time; 29% male, 71% female; 0% American Indian, 5% Asian, 24% black, 29% Hispanic, 1% multiracial, 0% Pacific Islander, 30% white, 2% international; 92% from in state; 30% live on campus; 3% of students in fraternities, 1% in sororities
Most popular majors: 41% Health Professions and Related Programs, 11% Business, Management, Marketing, and Related Support Services, 10% Biological and Biomedical Sciences, 9% Multi/Interdisciplinary Studies, 8% Psychology
Expenses: 2018-2019: $34,315; room/board: $12,880
Financial aid: (201) 559-6040; 90% of undergrads determined to have financial need; average aid package $28,680

Georgian Court University

Lakewood NJ
(800) 458-8422
U.S. News ranking: Reg. U. (N), No. 139
Website: georgian.edu
Admissions email: admissions@georgian.edu
Private; founded 1908
Affiliation: Roman Catholic
Freshman admissions: less selective; 2017-2018: 1,946 applied, 1,340 accepted. Either SAT or ACT required. SAT 25/75 percentile: 910-1120. High school rank: 7% in top tenth, 28% in top quarter, 57% in top half
Early decision deadline: N/A, notification date: N/A
Early action deadline: 12/1, notification date: N/A
Application deadline (fall): 8/1
Undergraduate student body: 1,343 full time, 270 part time; 29% male, 71% female; 0% American Indian, 3% Asian, 12% black, 13% Hispanic, 2% multiracial, 0% Pacific Islander, 60% white, 1% international; 94% from in state; 27% live on campus; N/A of students in fraternities, N/A in sororities
Most popular majors: 19% Psychology, General, 18% Registered Nursing/Registered Nurse, 12% Business Administration and Management, General, 9% English Language and Literature, General, 7% Biology/Biological Sciences, General
Expenses: 2018-2019: $32,876; room/board: $10,808
Financial aid: (732) 987-2254; 84% of undergrads determined to have financial need; average aid package $28,824

Kean University

Union NJ
(908) 737-7100
U.S. News ranking: Reg. U. (N), No. 139
Website: www.kean.edu
Admissions email: admitme@kean.edu
Public; founded 1855
Freshman admissions: less selective; 2017-2018: 8,788 applied, 7,277 accepted. Either SAT or ACT required. SAT 25/75 percentile: 880-1070. High school rank: N/A
Early decision deadline: N/A, notification date: N/A
Early action deadline: 12/1, notification date: 1/1
Application deadline (fall): 8/15
Undergraduate student body: 9,516 full time, 2,468 part time; 40% male, 60% female; 0% American Indian, 5% Asian, 20% black, 28% Hispanic, 2% multiracial, 0% Pacific Islander, 33% white, 3% international; 98% from in state; 16% live on campus; N/A of students in fraternities, N/A in sororities
Most popular majors: 17% Psychology, General, 8% Business Administration and Management, General, 6% Biology/Biological Sciences, General, 6% Criminal Justice/Law Enforcement Administration, 6% Speech Communication and Rhetoric
Expenses: 2018-2019: $12,348 in state, $19,383 out of state; room/board: $14,470
Financial aid: (908) 737-3190; 74% of undergrads determined to have financial need; average aid package $11,052

Monmouth University

West Long Branch NJ
(800) 543-9671
U.S. News ranking: Reg. U. (N), No. 28
Website: www.monmouth.edu
Admissions email: admission@monmouth.edu
Private; founded 1933
Freshman admissions: selective; 2017-2018: 9,261 applied, 6,848 accepted. Either SAT or ACT required. SAT 25/75 percentile: 970-1190. High school rank: 12% in top tenth, 37% in top quarter, 76% in top half
Early decision deadline: N/A, notification date: N/A
Early action deadline: 12/1, notification date: 1/15
Application deadline (fall): 3/1
Undergraduate student body: 4,502 full time, 204 part time; 42% male, 58% female; 0% American Indian, 3% Asian, 5% black, 13% Hispanic, 2% multiracial, 0% Pacific Islander, 71% white, 1% international; 83% from in state; 41% live on campus; 14% of students in fraternities, 18% in sororities
Most popular majors: 26% Business, Management, Marketing, and Related Support Services, 10% Communication, Journalism, and Related Programs, 8% Education, 6% Health Professions and Related Programs, 6% Social Sciences
Expenses: 2018-2019: $38,138; room/board: $13,981
Financial aid: (732) 571-3463; 72% of undergrads determined to have financial need; average aid package $27,389

Montclair State University

Montclair NJ
(973) 655-4444
U.S. News ranking: Nat. U., No. 169
Website: www.montclair.edu
Admissions email: undergraduate.admissions@montclair.edu
Public; founded 1908
Freshman admissions: less selective; 2017-2018: 13,384 applied, 9,457 accepted. Neither SAT nor ACT required. SAT 25/75 percentile: 990-1150. High school rank: 10% in top tenth, 34% in top quarter, 76% in top half
Early decision deadline: N/A, notification date: N/A
Early action deadline: N/A, notification date: N/A
Application deadline (fall): 3/1
Undergraduate student body: 14,944 full time, 1,908 part time; 39% male, 61% female; 0% American Indian, 6% Asian, 13% black, 28% Hispanic, 3% multiracial, 0% Pacific Islander, 41% white, 1% international; 97% from in state; 30% live on campus; N/A of students in fraternities, N/A in sororities
Most popular majors: 16% Business Administration and Management, General, 12% Psychology, General, 8% Family and Consumer Sciences/Human Sciences, General, 6% Multi-/Interdisciplinary Studies, Other, 5% Biology/Biological Sciences, General
Expenses: 2018-2019: $12,970 in state, $20,578 out of state; room/board: N/A
Financial aid: (973) 655-7020; 64% of undergrads determined to have financial need; average aid package $9,633

New Jersey City University

Jersey City NJ
(888) 441-6528
U.S. News ranking: Reg. U. (N), second tier
Website: www.njcu.edu/
Admissions email: admissions@njcu.edu
Public; founded 1927
Freshman admissions: least selective; 2017-2018: 4,381 applied, 3,988 accepted. Either SAT or ACT required. SAT 25/75 percentile: 870-1080. High school rank: 11% in top tenth, 28% in top quarter, 61% in top half
Early decision deadline: N/A, notification date: N/A
Early action deadline: N/A, notification date: N/A
Undergraduate student body: 5,210 full time, 1,298 part time; 41% male, 59% female; 0% American Indian, 8% Asian, 23% black, 40% Hispanic, 2% multiracial, 1% Pacific Islander, 21% white, 1% international; 91% from in state; 9% live on campus; N/A of students in fraternities, N/A in sororities
Most popular majors: 15% Registered Nursing/Registered Nurse, 12% Psychology, General, 10% Corrections and Criminal Justice, Other, 6% Accounting, 6% Homeland Security, Other
Expenses: 2017-2018: $11,761 in state, $21,051 out of state; room/board: $12,805
Financial aid: (201) 200-3171; 87% of undergrads determined to have financial need; average aid package $10,636

New Jersey Institute of Technology

Newark NJ
(973) 596-3300
U.S. News ranking: Nat. U., No. 106
Website: www.njit.edu
Admissions email: admissions@njit.edu
Public; founded 1881
Freshman admissions: more selective; 2017-2018: 7,254 applied, 4,453 accepted. Either SAT or ACT required. SAT 25/75 percentile: 1190-1370. High school rank: 37% in top tenth, 66% in top quarter, 89% in top half
Early decision deadline: N/A, notification date: N/A
Early action deadline: 11/10, notification date: 12/15
Application deadline (fall): 3/1
Undergraduate student body: 6,380 full time, 2,103 part time; 74% male, 26% female; 0% American Indian, 22% Asian, 8% black, 21% Hispanic, 3% multiracial, 0% Pacific Islander, 35% white, 5% international; 97% from in state; 22% live on campus; 6% of students in fraternities, 6% in sororities
Most popular majors: 40% Engineering, 18% Computer and Information Sciences and Support Services, 13% Engineering Technologies and Engineering-Related Fields, 9% Architecture and Related Services, 7% Biological and Biomedical Sciences
Expenses: 2018-2019: $16,898 in state, $31,918 out of state; room/board: $13,808
Financial aid: (973) 596-3476; 71% of undergrads determined to have financial need; average aid package $13,104

Princeton University

Princeton NJ
(609) 258-3060
U.S. News ranking: Nat. U., No. 1
Website: www.princeton.edu
Admissions email: uaoffice@princeton.edu
Private; founded 1746
Freshman admissions: most selective; 2017-2018: 31,056 applied, 1,990 accepted. Either SAT or ACT required. SAT 25/75 percentile: 1430-1570. High school rank: 91% in top tenth, 98% in top quarter, 100% in top half
Early decision deadline: N/A, notification date: N/A
Early action deadline: 11/1, notification date: 12/15
Application deadline (fall): 1/1
Undergraduate student body: 5,260 full time, 134 part time; 51% male, 49% female; 0% American Indian, 21% Asian, 8% black, 10% Hispanic, 4% multiracial, 0% Pacific Islander, 43% white, 12% international; 18% from in state; 96% live on campus; 0% of students in fraternities, 0% in sororities
Most popular majors: 27% Engineering, 20% Social Sciences, 9% Biological and Biomedical Sciences, 8% Public

Administration and Social Service Professions, 7% History
Expenses: 2018-2019: $47,140; room/board: $15,610
Financial aid: (609) 258-3330; 60% of undergrads determined to have financial need; average aid package $53,415

Ramapo College of New Jersey

Mahwah NJ
(201) 684-7300
U.S. News ranking: Reg. U. (N), No. 28
Website: www.ramapo.edu
Admissions email: admissions@ramapo.edu
Public; founded 1969
Freshman admissions: selective; 2017-2018: 6,695 applied, 3,840 accepted. Either SAT or ACT required. SAT 25/75 percentile: 1050-1230. High school rank: 16% in top tenth, 41% in top quarter, 79% in top half
Early decision deadline: 11/1, notification date: 12/5
Early action deadline: N/A, notification date: N/A
Application deadline (fall): 2/1
Undergraduate student body: 4,910 full time, 708 part time; 45% male, 55% female; 1% American Indian, 8% Asian, 5% black, 16% Hispanic, 1% multiracial, 0% Pacific Islander, 64% white, 2% international; 95% from in state; 46% live on campus; 5% of students in fraternities, 7% in sororities
Most popular majors: 16% Business Administration and Management, General, 10% Psychology, General, 10% Speech Communication and Rhetoric, 8% Nursing Science, 7% Biology/Biological Sciences, General
Expenses: 2018-2019: $14,108 in state, $23,261 out of state; room/board: $12,204
Financial aid: (201) 684-7549; 55% of undergrads determined to have financial need; average aid package $10,830

Rider University

Lawrenceville NJ
(609) 896-5042
U.S. News ranking: Reg. U. (N), No. 35
Website: www.rider.edu
Admissions email: admissions@rider.edu
Private; founded 1865
Freshman admissions: selective; 2017-2018: 9,519 applied, 6,389 accepted. Either SAT or ACT required. SAT 25/75 percentile: 990-1190. High school rank: 14% in top tenth, 43% in top quarter, 74% in top half
Early decision deadline: N/A, notification date: N/A
Early action deadline: 11/15, notification date: 12/15
Application deadline (fall): rolling
Undergraduate student body: 3,711 full time, 383 part time; 42% male, 58% female; 0% American Indian, 5% Asian, 13% black, 15% Hispanic, 3% multiracial, 0% Pacific Islander, 59% white, 3% international; 77% from in state; 54% live on campus; 6% of students in fraternities, 11% in sororities
Most popular majors: 12% Accounting, 9% Psychology, General, 6% Finance, General, 5% Business Administration and Management, General, 5% Elementary Education and Teaching
Expenses: 2018-2019: $42,860; room/board: $15,280
Financial aid: (609) 896-5000; 76% of undergrads determined to have financial need; average aid package $30,642

Rowan University

Glassboro NJ
(856) 256-4200
U.S. News ranking: Nat. U., No. 171
Website: www.rowan.edu
Admissions email: admissions@rowan.edu
Public; founded 1923
Freshman admissions: selective; 2017-2018: 13,900 applied, 8,159 accepted. Either SAT or ACT required. SAT 25/75 percentile: 1040-1250. High school rank: N/A
Early decision deadline: N/A, notification date: N/A
Early action deadline: N/A, notification date: N/A
Application deadline (fall): 3/1
Undergraduate student body: 13,635 full time, 1,766 part time; 54% male, 46% female; 0% American Indian, 5% Asian, 10% black, 10% Hispanic, 3% multiracial, 0% Pacific Islander, 66% white, 1% international; 94% from in state; 37% live on campus; 6% of students in fraternities, 8% in sororities
Most popular majors: 18% Business, Management, Marketing, and Related Support Services, 11% Education, 9% Psychology, 8% Biological and Biomedical Sciences, 8% Communication, Journalism, and Related Programs
Expenses: 2018-2019: $13,422 in state, $21,890 out of state; room/board: $12,236
Financial aid: (856) 256-4281; 68% of undergrads determined to have financial need; average aid package $10,253

Rutgers University–Camden

Camden NJ
(856) 225-6104
U.S. News ranking: Reg. U. (N), No. 28
Website: www.camden.rutgers.edu/
Admissions email: admissions@camden.rutgers.edu
Public; founded 1926
Freshman admissions: selective; 2017-2018: 11,338 applied, 7,861 accepted. Either SAT or ACT required. SAT 25/75 percentile: 1000-1180. High school rank: 12% in top tenth, 37% in top quarter, 76% in top half
Early decision deadline: N/A, notification date: N/A
Early action deadline: 11/1, notification date: 1/31
Application deadline (fall): rolling
Undergraduate student body: 4,493 full time, 996 part time; 41% male, 59% female; 0% American Indian, 10% Asian, 18% black, 15% Hispanic, 4% multiracial, 0% Pacific Islander, 49% white, 2% international; 98% from in state; 15% live on campus; N/A of students in fraternities, N/A in sororities
Most popular majors: 20% Registered Nursing/Registered Nurse, 12% Business Administration and Management, General, 9% Psychology, General, 7% Criminal Justice/Safety Studies, 5% Biology/Biological Sciences, General
Expenses: 2018-2019: $14,835 in state, $30,613 out of state; room/board: $12,336
Financial aid: (856) 225-6039; 82% of undergrads determined to have financial need; average aid package $14,247

Rutgers University–Newark

Newark NJ
(973) 353-5205
U.S. News ranking: Nat. U., No. 115
Website: www.newark.rutgers.edu/
Admissions email: newark@admissions.rutgers.edu
Public; founded 1908
Freshman admissions: selective; 2017-2018: 13,435 applied, 8,631 accepted. Either SAT or ACT required. SAT 25/75 percentile: 1010-1170. High school rank: 22% in top tenth, 54% in top quarter, 88% in top half
Early decision deadline: N/A, notification date: N/A
Early action deadline: 11/1, notification date: 1/31
Application deadline (fall): rolling
Undergraduate student body: 7,162 full time, 1,389 part time; 45% male, 55% female; 0% American Indian, 18% Asian, 20% black, 29% Hispanic, 3% multiracial, 0% Pacific Islander, 23% white, 5% international; 99% from in state; 21% live on campus; N/A of students in fraternities, N/A in sororities
Most popular majors: 16% Accounting, 12% Psychology, General, 11% Criminal Justice/Safety Studies, 9% Finance, General, 7% Biology/Biological Sciences, General
Expenses: 2018-2019: $14,409 in state, $30,717 out of state; room/board: $13,536
Financial aid: (848) 932-7507; 79% of undergrads determined to have financial need; average aid package $15,215

Rutgers University–New Brunswick

Piscataway NJ
(732) 932-4636
U.S. News ranking: Nat. U., No. 56
Website: newbrunswick.rutgers.edu
Admissions email: admissions@ugadm.rutgers.edu
Public; founded 1766
Freshman admissions: more selective; 2017-2018: 38,384 applied, 22,186 accepted. Either SAT or ACT required. SAT 25/75 percentile: 1190-1400. High school rank: 40% in top tenth, 75% in top quarter, 96% in top half
Early decision deadline: N/A, notification date: N/A
Early action deadline: 11/1, notification date: 1/31
Application deadline (fall): rolling
Undergraduate student body: 33,677 full time, 1,964 part time; 50% male, 50% female; 0% American Indian, 27% Asian, 7% black, 13% Hispanic, 3% multiracial, 0% Pacific Islander, 39% white, 9% international; 94% from in state; 43% live on campus; N/A of students in fraternities, N/A in sororities
Most popular majors: 7% Psychology, General, 5% Kinesiology and Exercise Science, 5% Registered Nursing/Registered Nurse, 4% Biology/Biological Sciences, General, 4% Speech Communication and Rhetoric
Expenses: 2018-2019: $14,974 in state, $31,282 out of state; room/board: $12,706
Financial aid: (848) 932-7057; 53% of undergrads determined to have financial need; average aid package $14,847

Saint Peter's University

Jersey City NJ
(201) 761-7100
U.S. News ranking: Reg. U. (N), No. 81
Website: www.saintpeters.edu
Admissions email: admissions@saintpeters.edu
Private; founded 1872
Affiliation: Roman Catholic
Freshman admissions: selective; 2017-2018: 4,650 applied, 3,310 accepted. Neither SAT nor ACT required. SAT 25/75 percentile: 930-1110. High school rank: 17% in top tenth, 43% in top quarter, 76% in top half
Early decision deadline: N/A, notification date: N/A
Early action deadline: 12/15, notification date: 1/30
Application deadline (fall): rolling
Undergraduate student body: 2,387 full time, 250 part time; 36% male, 64% female; 0% American Indian, 7% Asian, 22% black, 45% Hispanic, 2% multiracial, 1% Pacific Islander, 15% white, 2% international; 91% from in state; 30% live on campus; N/A of students in fraternities, N/A in sororities
Most popular majors: 23% Business, Management, Marketing, and Related Support Services, 12% Biological and Biomedical Sciences, 12% Health Professions and Related Programs, 12% Homeland Security, Law Enforcement, Firefighting and Related Protective Services, 6% Psychology
Expenses: 2018-2019: $37,486; room/board: $15,414
Financial aid: (201) 761-6060; 92% of undergrads determined to have financial need; average aid package $32,097

Seton Hall University

South Orange NJ
(800) 843-4255
U.S. News ranking: Nat. U., No. 119
Website: www.shu.edu
Admissions email: thehall@shu.edu
Private; founded 1856
Affiliation: Roman Catholic
Freshman admissions: more selective; 2017-2018: 16,719 applied, 12,232 accepted. Either SAT or ACT required. SAT 25/75 percentile: 1140-1280. High school rank: 32% in top tenth, 61% in top quarter, 88% in top half
Early decision deadline: N/A, notification date: N/A
Early action deadline: 12/15, notification date: 1/31
Application deadline (fall): rolling
Undergraduate student body: 5,554 full time, 415 part time; 46% male, 54% female; 0% American Indian, 10% Asian, 9% black, 18% Hispanic, 4% multiracial, 0% Pacific Islander, 49% white, 4% international
Most popular majors: 15% Registered Nursing/Registered Nurse, 10% Biology/Biological Sciences, General, 10% Humanities/Humanistic Studies, 6% Finance, General, 6% International Relations and Affairs
Expenses: 2018-2019: $42,170; room/board: $15,800
Financial aid: (973) 761-9350

Stevens Institute of Technology

Hoboken NJ
(201) 216-5194
U.S. News ranking: Nat. U., No. 70
Website: www.stevens.edu
Admissions email: admissions@stevens.edu
Private; founded 1870
Freshman admissions: most selective; 2017-2018: 8,335 applied, 3,657 accepted. Neither SAT nor ACT required. SAT 25/75 percentile: 1320-1470. High school rank: 72% in top tenth, 91% in top quarter, 99% in top half
Early decision deadline: 11/15, notification date: 12/15
Early action deadline: N/A, notification date: N/A
Application deadline (fall): 1/15
Undergraduate student body: 2,864 full time, 114 part time; 70% male, 30% female; 0% American Indian, 12% Asian, 2% black, 10% Hispanic, 0% multiracial, 0% Pacific Islander, 67% white, 4% international; 61% from in state; 64% live on campus; 31% of students in fraternities, 49% in sororities
Most popular majors: 27% Mechanical Engineering, 15% Business Administration and Management, General, 9% Electrical and Electronics Engineering, 8% Civil Engineering, General, 7% Chemical Engineering
Expenses: 2018-2019: $52,202; room/board: $15,244
Financial aid: (201) 216-3400; 65% of undergrads determined to have financial need; average aid package $29,681

More @ usnews.com/bestcolleges

Stockton University

Galloway NJ
(609) 652-4261
U.S. News ranking: Reg. U. (N), No. 35
Website: www.stockton.edu
Admissions email: admissions@stockton.edu
Public; founded 1969
Affiliation: Other
Freshman admissions: selective; 2017-2018: 5,706 applied, 4,652 accepted. Either SAT or ACT required. SAT 25/75 percentile: 1010-1200. High school rank: 20% in top tenth, 47% in top quarter, 82% in top half
Early decision deadline: N/A, notification date: N/A
Early action deadline: N/A, notification date: N/A
Application deadline (fall): 5/1
Undergraduate student body: 7,809 full time, 466 part time; 41% male, 59% female; 0% American Indian, 6% Asian, 8% black, 13% Hispanic, 2% multiracial, 0% Pacific Islander, 68% white, 1% international; 98% from in state; 37% live on campus; 8% of students in fraternities, 8% in sororities
Most popular majors: 16% Business Administration and Management, General, 16% Health Professions and Related Programs, 9% Psychology, General, 8% Biology/Biological Sciences, General, 8% Criminology
Expenses: 2018-2019: $13,739 in state, $20,866 out of state; room/board: $12,282
Financial aid: (609) 652-4203; 73% of undergrads determined to have financial need; average aid package $16,756

Thomas Edison State University

Trenton NJ
(888) 442-8372
U.S. News ranking: Reg. U. (N), unranked
Website: www.tesu.edu
Admissions email: admissions@tesu.edu
Public; founded 1972
Freshman admissions: least selective; 2017-2018: N/A applied, N/A accepted. Neither SAT nor ACT required. SAT 25/75 percentile: N/A. High school rank: N/A
Early decision deadline: N/A, notification date: N/A
Early action deadline: N/A, notification date: N/A
Application deadline (fall): rolling
Undergraduate student body: 49 full time, 15,189 part time; 57% male, 43% female; 1% American Indian, 4% Asian, 15% black, 10% Hispanic, 2% multiracial, 1% Pacific Islander, 51% white, 1% international
Most popular majors: Information not available
Expenses: 2018-2019: $7,591 in state, $9,967 out of state; room/board: N/A
Financial aid: (609) 633-9658

William Paterson University of New Jersey

Wayne NJ
(973) 720-2125
U.S. News ranking: Reg. U. (N), No. 93
Website: www.wpunj.edu/
Admissions email: admissions@wpunj.edu
Public; founded 1855
Freshman admissions: less selective; 2017-2018: 7,935 applied, 7,331 accepted. Either SAT or ACT required. SAT 25/75 percentile: 930-1120. High school rank: N/A
Early decision deadline: N/A, notification date: N/A
Early action deadline: N/A, notification date: N/A
Application deadline (fall): 6/1
Undergraduate student body: 7,285 full time, 1,553 part time; 46% male, 54% female; 0% American Indian, 7% Asian, 17% black, 32% Hispanic, 3% multiracial, 0% Pacific Islander, 39% white, 1% international; 98% from in state; 24% live on campus; 3% of students in fraternities, 3% in sororities
Most popular majors: 20% Business, Management, Marketing, and Related Support Services, 10% Communication, Journalism, and Related Programs, 10% Psychology, 8% Health Professions and Related Programs, 8% Social Sciences
Expenses: 2018-2019: $13,060 in state, $21,260 out of state; room/board: $11,445
Financial aid: (973) 720-3945; 76% of undergrads determined to have financial need; average aid package $11,535

NEW MEXICO

Eastern New Mexico University

Portales NM
(575) 562-2178
U.S. News ranking: Reg. U. (W), second tier
Website: www.enmu.edu
Admissions email: admissions.office@enmu.edu
Public; founded 1934
Freshman admissions: less selective; 2017-2018: 2,647 applied, 1,600 accepted. Either SAT or ACT required. ACT 25/75 percentile: 16-22. High school rank: 13% in top tenth, 30% in top quarter, 58% in top half
Early decision deadline: N/A, notification date: N/A
Early action deadline: N/A, notification date: N/A
Application deadline (fall): rolling
Undergraduate student body: 2,588 full time, 2,009 part time; 44% male, 56% female; N/A American Indian, N/A Asian, N/A black, N/A Hispanic, N/A multiracial, N/A Pacific Islander, N/A white, N/A international; 76% from in state; 20% live on campus; N/A of students in fraternities, N/A in sororities
Most popular majors: Information not available
Expenses: 2018-2019: $6,206 in state, $8,128 out of state; room/board: $7,162
Financial aid: N/A; 70% of undergrads determined to have financial need; average aid package $11,017

New Mexico Highlands University[1]

Las Vegas NM
(505) 454-3439
U.S. News ranking: Reg. U. (W), second tier
Website: www.nmhu.edu
Admissions email: admissions@nmhu.edu
Public; founded 1893
Application deadline (fall): rolling
Undergraduate student body: N/A full time, N/A part time
Expenses: 2017-2018: $6,150 in state, $10,302 out of state; room/board: $7,872
Financial aid: (505) 454-3430

New Mexico Institute of Mining and Technology

Socorro NM
(575) 835-5424
U.S. News ranking: Reg. U. (W), No. 35
Website: www.nmt.edu
Admissions email: Admission@nmt.edu
Public; founded 1889
Freshman admissions: more selective; 2017-2018: 1,513 applied, 328 accepted. Either SAT or ACT required. ACT 25/75 percentile: 23-29. High school rank: 35% in top tenth, 68% in top quarter, 87% in top half
Early decision deadline: N/A, notification date: N/A
Early action deadline: N/A, notification date: N/A
Application deadline (fall): 8/1
Undergraduate student body: 1,294 full time, 177 part time; 70% male, 30% female; 4% American Indian, 4% Asian, 2% black, 30% Hispanic, 5% multiracial, 0% Pacific Islander, 52% white, 2% international; 90% from in state; 45% live on campus; 0% of students in fraternities, 0% in sororities
Most popular majors: 18% Mechanical Engineering, 15% Petroleum Engineering, 10% Electrical and Electronics Engineering, 9% Chemical Engineering, 8% Biology/Biological Sciences, General
Expenses: 2018-2019: $7,570 in state, $22,068 out of state; room/board: N/A
Financial aid: (575) 835-5333; 53% of undergrads determined to have financial need; average aid package $12,524

New Mexico State University

Las Cruces NM
(575) 646-3121
U.S. News ranking: Nat. U., No. 221
Website: www.nmsu.edu
Admissions email: admissions@nmsu.edu
Public; founded 1888
Freshman admissions: selective; 2017-2018: 8,192 applied, 5,230 accepted. Either SAT or ACT required. ACT 25/75 percentile: 18-23. High school rank: 22% in top tenth, 51% in top quarter, 83% in top half
Early decision deadline: N/A, notification date: N/A
Early action deadline: N/A, notification date: N/A
Application deadline (fall): rolling
Undergraduate student body: 9,703 full time, 2,010 part time; 45% male, 55% female; 2% American Indian, 1% Asian, 3% black, 59% Hispanic, 2% multiracial, 0% Pacific Islander, 27% white, 4% international; 74% from in state; 20% live on campus; 5% of students in fraternities, 4% in sororities
Most popular majors: 17% Business, Management, Marketing, and Related Support Services, 12% Engineering, 9% Health Professions and Related Programs, 7% Homeland Security, Law Enforcement, Firefighting and Related Protective Services, 7% Liberal Arts and Sciences, General Studies and Humanities
Expenses: 2018-2019: $7,368 in state, $23,508 out of state; room/board: $9,252
Financial aid: (575) 646-4105; 69% of undergrads determined to have financial need; average aid package $13,803

Northern New Mexico University[1]

Espanola NM
(505) 747-2100
U.S. News ranking: Reg. Coll. (W), unranked
Website: www.nnmc.edu
Admissions email: N/A
Public
Application deadline (fall): N/A
Undergraduate student body: N/A full time, N/A part time
Expenses: 2017-2018: $4,765 in state, $13,619 out of state; room/board: $8,506
Financial aid: N/A

Santa Fe University of Art and Design[1]

Santa Fe NM
(505) 473-6937
U.S. News ranking: Arts, unranked
Website: www.santafeuniversity.edu
Admissions email: admissions@santafeuniversity.edu
For-profit; founded 1859
Application deadline (fall): rolling
Undergraduate student body: N/A full time, N/A part time
Expenses: N/A
Financial aid: (505) 473-6454

St. John's College

Santa Fe NM
(505) 984-6060
U.S. News ranking: Nat. Lib. Arts, No. 72
Website: www.sjc.edu/admissions-and-aid
Admissions email: santafe.admissions@sjc.edu
Private; founded 1696
Freshman admissions: more selective; 2017-2018: 342 applied, 216 accepted. Neither SAT nor ACT required. SAT 25/75 percentile: 1120-1410. High school rank: 47% in top tenth, 56% in top quarter, 78% in top half
Early decision deadline: N/A, notification date: N/A
Early action deadline: 11/15, notification date: 12/15
Application deadline (fall): rolling
Undergraduate student body: 309 full time, 13 part time; 56% male, 44% female; 0% American Indian, 2% Asian, 1% black, 9% Hispanic, 6% multiracial, 0% Pacific Islander, 55% white, 26% international
Most popular majors: 100% Liberal Arts and Sciences/Liberal Studies
Expenses: 2018-2019: $53,218; room/board: $12,148
Financial aid: (505) 984-6058; 89% of undergrads determined to have financial need; average aid package $42,100

University of New Mexico

Albuquerque NM
(505) 277-8900
U.S. News ranking: Nat. U., No. 187
Website: www.unm.edu
Admissions email: apply@unm.edu
Public; founded 1889
Freshman admissions: selective; 2017-2018: 11,347 applied, 5,604 accepted. Either SAT or ACT required. ACT 25/75 percentile: 19-25. High school rank: N/A
Early decision deadline: N/A, notification date: N/A
Early action deadline: N/A, notification date: N/A
Application deadline (fall): rolling
Undergraduate student body: 15,060 full time, 4,456 part time; 44% male, 56% female; 6% American Indian, 4% Asian, 2% black, 49% Hispanic, 4% multiracial, 0% Pacific Islander, 32% white, 2% international; 87% from in state; 6% live on campus; 5% of students in fraternities, 6% in sororities
Most popular majors: 15% Business, Management, Marketing, and Related Support Services, 12% Psychology, 9% Health Professions and Related Programs, 8% Biological and Biomedical Sciences, 8% Education
Expenses: 2018-2019: $7,322 in state, $22,966 out of state; room/board: $9,864
Financial aid: (505) 277-8900; 74% of undergrads determined to have financial need

University of the Southwest[1]

Hobbs NM
(575) 392-6563
U.S. News ranking: Reg. U. (W), second tier
Website: www.usw.edu
Admissions email: admissions@usw.edu
Private; founded 1962
Application deadline (fall): rolling
Undergraduate student body: N/A full time, N/A part time
Expenses: 2017-2018: $16,200; room/board: $7,526
Financial aid: N/A

Western New Mexico University[1]

Silver City NM
(575) 538-6011
U.S. News ranking: Reg. U. (W), unranked
Website: www.wnmu.edu
Admissions email: admissions@wnmu.edu
Public; founded 1893
Application deadline (fall): N/A
Undergraduate student body: N/A full time, N/A part time
Expenses: 2017-2018: $6,066 in state, $13,539 out of state; room/board: $10,500
Financial aid: N/A

NEW YORK

Adelphi University

Garden City NY
(800) 233-5744
U.S. News ranking: Nat. U., No. 147
Website: www.adelphi.edu
Admissions email: admissions@adelphi.edu
Private; founded 1896
Freshman admissions: selective; 2017-2018: 11,851 applied, 8,666 accepted. Neither SAT nor ACT required. SAT 25/75 percentile: 1060-1240. High school rank: 26% in top tenth, 58% in top quarter, 89% in top half
Early decision deadline: N/A, notification date: N/A
Early action deadline: 12/1, notification date: 12/31
Application deadline (fall): rolling
Undergraduate student body: 4,874 full time, 392 part time; 32% male, 68% female; 0% American Indian, 11% Asian, 9% black, 17% Hispanic, 2% multiracial, 0% Pacific Islander, 51% white, 3% international; 94% from in state; 22% live on campus; 9% of students in fraternities, 2% in sororities
Most popular majors: 30% Registered Nursing/Registered Nurse, 6% Business Administration and Management, General, 5% Biology/Biological Sciences, General, 5% Psychology, General, 5% Social Sciences, General
Expenses: 2018-2019: $38,660; room/board: $16,030
Financial aid: (516) 877-3080; 70% of undergrads determined to have financial need; average aid package $21,500

Alfred University

Alfred NY
(800) 541-9229
U.S. News ranking: Reg. U. (N), No. 62
Website: www.alfred.edu
Admissions email: admissions@alfred.edu
Private; founded 1836
Freshman admissions: selective; 2017-2018: 3,566 applied, 2,237 accepted. Either SAT or ACT required. SAT 25/75 percentile: 990-1210. High school rank: 14% in top tenth, 41% in top quarter, 72% in top half
Early decision deadline: 12/1, notification date: 12/15
Early action deadline: N/A, notification date: N/A
Application deadline (fall): 8/1
Undergraduate student body: 1,600 full time, 107 part time; 52% male, 48% female; 0% American Indian, 2% Asian, 10% black, 8% Hispanic, 3% multiracial, 0% Pacific Islander, 66% white, 1% international; 81% from in state; 73% live on campus; 0% of students in fraternities, 0% in sororities
Most popular majors: 23% Ceramic Arts and Ceramics, 22% Mechanical Engineering, 16% Business Administration and Management, General, 8% Psychology, General, 5% Electroneurodiagnostic/Electroencephalographic Technology/Technologist
Expenses: 2018-2019: $33,484; room/board: $12,516
Financial aid: (607) 871-2150; 84% of undergrads determined to have financial need; average aid package $27,889

Bard College

Annandale on Hudson NY
(845) 758-7472
U.S. News ranking: Nat. Lib. Arts, No. 56
Website: www.bard.edu
Admissions email: admissions@bard.edu
Private; founded 1860
Freshman admissions: more selective; 2017-2018: 4,922 applied, 2,865 accepted. Neither SAT nor ACT required. SAT 25/75 percentile: 1220-1400. High school rank: 41% in top tenth, 66% in top quarter, 96% in top half
Early decision deadline: N/A, notification date: 11/1
Early action deadline: 11/1, notification date: 1/1
Application deadline (fall): 1/1
Undergraduate student body: 1,855 full time, 75 part time; 41% male, 59% female; 0% American Indian, 4% Asian, 7% black, 7% Hispanic, 5% multiracial, 0% Pacific Islander, 60% white, 10% international; 34% from in state; 75% live on campus; N/A of students in fraternities, N/A in sororities
Most popular majors: 32% Visual and Performing Arts, 27% Social Sciences, 22% English Language and Literature/Letters, 18% Multi/Interdisciplinary Studies
Expenses: 2018-2019: $54,680; room/board: $15,488
Financial aid: (845) 758-7526; 66% of undergrads determined to have financial need; average aid package $46,810

Barnard College

New York NY
(212) 854-2014
U.S. News ranking: Nat. Lib. Arts, No. 25
Website: www.barnard.edu
Admissions email: admissions@barnard.edu
Private; founded 1889
Freshman admissions: most selective; 2017-2018: 7,716 applied, 1,190 accepted. Either SAT or ACT required. ACT 25/75 percentile: 30-33. High school rank: 84% in top tenth, 93% in top quarter, 100% in top half
Early decision deadline: 11/1, notification date: 12/15
Early action deadline: N/A, notification date: N/A
Application deadline (fall): 1/1
Undergraduate student body: 2,574 full time, 30 part time; 0% male, 100% female; 0% American Indian, 15% Asian, 6% black, 12% Hispanic, 6% multiracial, 0% Pacific Islander, 52% white, 9% international; 27% from in state; 91% live on campus; N/A of students in fraternities, N/A in sororities
Most popular majors: 30% Social Sciences, 12% Psychology, 9% Biological and Biomedical Sciences, 9% Visual and Performing Arts, 8% English Language and Literature/Letters
Expenses: 2018-2019: $55,032; room/board: $17,225
Financial aid: (212) 854-2154; 39% of undergrads determined to have financial need; average aid package $50,194

Berkeley College

New York NY
(800) 446-5400
U.S. News ranking: Business, unranked
Website: www.berkeleycollege.edu
Admissions email: admissions@berkeleycollege.edu
For-profit; founded 1931
Freshman admissions: least selective; 2017-2018: N/A applied, N/A accepted. Neither SAT nor ACT required. SAT 25/75 percentile: N/A. High school rank: N/A
Early decision deadline: N/A, notification date: N/A
Early action deadline: N/A, notification date: N/A
Application deadline (fall): 8/28
Undergraduate student body: 2,759 full time, 876 part time; 35% male, 65% female; 1% American Indian, 2% Asian, 24% black, 22% Hispanic, 0% multiracial, 0% Pacific Islander, 7% white, 11% international; 88% from in state; 5% live on campus; N/A of students in fraternities, N/A in sororities
Most popular majors: 23% Business Administration and Management, General, 17% Criminal Justice/Law Enforcement Administration, 17% Fashion Merchandising, 11% Health/Health Care Administration/Management, 9% Accounting
Expenses: 2018-2019: $25,900; room/board: $11,400
Financial aid: (212) 986-4343

Binghamton University–SUNY

Binghamton NY
(607) 777-2171
U.S. News ranking: Nat. U., No. 80
Website: www.binghamton.edu
Admissions email: admit@binghamton.edu
Public; founded 1946
Freshman admissions: more selective; 2017-2018: 33,467 applied, 13,507 accepted. Either SAT or ACT required. SAT 25/75 percentile: 1290-1431. High school rank: 49% in top tenth, 81% in top quarter, 97% in top half
Early decision deadline: N/A, notification date: N/A
Early action deadline: 11/1, notification date: 1/15
Application deadline (fall): rolling
Undergraduate student body: 13,336 full time, 392 part time; 51% male, 49% female; 0% American Indian, 14% Asian, 5% black, 11% Hispanic, 2% multiracial, 0% Pacific Islander, 57% white, 8% international; 94% from in state; 51% live on campus; N/A of students in fraternities, N/A in sororities
Most popular majors: 15% Business Administration and Management, General, 14% Biology/Biological Sciences, General, 10% Engineering, General, 9% Psychology, General, 6% Chiropractic
Expenses: 2018-2019: $9,808 in state, $24,488 out of state; room/board: $15,058
Financial aid: (607) 777-6358; 52% of undergrads determined to have financial need; average aid package $13,677

Boricua College

New York NY
(212) 694-1000
U.S. News ranking: Reg. Coll. (N), unranked
Website: www.boricuacollege.edu/
Admissions email: isanchez@boricuacollege.edu
Private; founded 1973
Freshman admissions: least selective; 2017-2018: 198 applied, 144 accepted. Neither SAT nor ACT required. SAT 25/75 percentile: N/A. High school rank: N/A
Early decision deadline: N/A, notification date: N/A
Early action deadline: N/A, notification date: N/A
Application deadline (fall): rolling
Undergraduate student body: 769 full time, 0 part time; 25% male, 75% female; 0% American Indian, 0% Asian, 13% black, 83% Hispanic, 0% multiracial, 0% Pacific Islander, 1% white, 0% international
Most popular majors: Information not available
Expenses: 2017-2018: $11,025; room/board: N/A
Financial aid: N/A

Canisius College

Buffalo NY
(800) 843-1517
U.S. News ranking: Reg. U. (N), No. 23
Website: www.canisius.edu
Admissions email: admissions@canisius.edu
Private; founded 1870
Affiliation: Roman Catholic
Freshman admissions: selective; 2017-2018: 4,488 applied, 3,509 accepted. Either SAT or ACT required. SAT 25/75 percentile: 1040-1260. High school rank: 23% in top tenth, 49% in top quarter, 81% in top half
Early decision deadline: N/A, notification date: N/A
Early action deadline: 11/1, notification date: 12/15
Application deadline (fall): rolling
Undergraduate student body: 2,303 full time, 95 part time; 50% male, 50% female; 0% American Indian, 3% Asian, 8% black, 6% Hispanic, 2% multiracial, 0% Pacific Islander, 73% white, 4% international; 89% from in state; 46% live on campus; 1% of students in fraternities, 1% in sororities
Most popular majors: 27% Business, Management, Marketing, and Related Support Services, 17% Biological and Biomedical Sciences, 9% Psychology, 9% Social Sciences, 8% Communication, Journalism, and Related Programs
Expenses: 2018-2019: $28,488; room/board: $11,300
Financial aid: (716) 888-2300; 76% of undergrads determined to have financial need; average aid package $30,770

Cazenovia College

Cazenovia NY
(800) 654-3210
U.S. News ranking: Reg. Coll. (N), No. 11
Website: www.cazenovia.edu
Admissions email: admission@cazenovia.edu
Private; founded 1824
Freshman admissions: less selective; 2017-2018: 1,802 applied, 1,665 accepted. Neither SAT nor ACT required. SAT 25/75 percentile: 923-1098. High school rank: 5% in top tenth, 23% in top quarter, 64% in top half
Early decision deadline: N/A, notification date: N/A
Early action deadline: N/A, notification date: N/A
Application deadline (fall): rolling
Undergraduate student body: 713 full time, 180 part time; 28% male, 72% female; 1% American Indian, 2% Asian, 9% black, 6% Hispanic, 4% multiracial, 0% Pacific Islander, 66% white, 1% international; 90% from in state; N/A live on campus; N/A of students in fraternities, N/A in sororities

ɔst popular majors: 29% Busi-
ss, Management, Marketing,
d Related Support Services,
% Visual and Performing
s, 14% Public Administration
d Social Service Professions,
% Psychology, 7% Homeland
curity, Law Enforcement,
efighting and Related Protective
rvices
penses: 2018-2019: $34,630;
m/board: $14,596
ancial aid: (315) 655-7000;
% of undergrads determined to
ve financial need; average aid
ckage $33,543

larkson University

tsdam NY
00) 527-6577
S. News ranking: Nat. U.,
. 102
ebsite: www.clarkson.edu
missions email:
missions@clarkson.edu
ivate; founded 1896
eshman admissions: more
lective; 2017-2018: 7,000
plied, 4,600 accepted. Either
T or ACT required. SAT 25/75
rcentile: 1143-1330. High
hool rank: 37% in top tenth,
% in top quarter, 96% in
half
rly decision deadline: 12/1,
tification date: 1/1
rly action deadline: N/A,
tification date: N/A
plication deadline (fall): 1/15
dergraduate student body: 3,021
l time, 69 part time; 70%
ale, 30% female; 0% American
dian, 4% Asian, 2% black, 5%
spanic, 3% multiracial, 0%
cific Islander, 81% white, 3%
ernational; 73% from in state;
% live on campus; 14% of
udents in fraternities, 12% in
rorities
ɔst popular majors: 60%
gineering, General, 20%
siness Administration and
anagement, General, 6%
ology/Biological Sciences,
eneral, 2% Computer Science,
% Psychology, General
penses: 2018-2019: $49,444;
om/board: $15,222
ancial aid: (315) 268-6413;
% of undergrads determined to
ve financial need; average aid
ckage $43,666

olgate University

amilton NY
15) 228-7401
S. News ranking: Nat. Lib. Arts,
. 16
ebsite: www.colgate.edu
missions email:
mission@colgate.edu
ivate; founded 1819
eshman admissions: most
lective; 2017-2018: 8,542
plied, 2,404 accepted. Either
AT or ACT required. ACT 25/75
rcentile: 31-33. High school
nk: 77% in top tenth, 94% in
p quarter, 99% in top half
rly decision deadline: 11/15,
tification date: 12/15
rly action deadline: N/A,
tification date: N/A
plication deadline (fall): 1/15
Undergraduate student body: 2,854 full time, 19 part time; 45% male, 55% female; 0% American Indian, 4% Asian, 5% black, 9% Hispanic, 4% multiracial, 0% Pacific Islander, 65% white, 9% international; 26% from in state; 90% live on campus; N/A of students in fraternities, N/A in sororities
Most popular majors: 10% Economics, General, 8% Political Science and Government, General, 6% History, General, 5% International Relations and Affairs, 5% Psychology, General
Expenses: 2018-2019: $55,870; room/board: $13,995
Financial aid: (315) 228-7431; 36% of undergrads determined to have financial need; average aid package $52,488

College at Brockport–SUNY

Brockport NY
(585) 395-2751
U.S. News ranking: Reg. U. (N), No. 90
Website: www.brockport.edu
Admissions email: admit@brockport.edu
Public; founded 1835
Freshman admissions: selective; 2017-2018: 9,628 applied, 5,120 accepted. Either SAT or ACT required. SAT 25/75 percentile: 1000-1180. High school rank: 12% in top tenth, 34% in top quarter, 74% in top half
Early decision deadline: N/A, notification date: N/A
Early action deadline: N/A, notification date: N/A
Application deadline (fall): 8/1
Undergraduate student body: 6,419 full time, 761 part time; 43% male, 57% female; 0% American Indian, 2% Asian, 11% black, 7% Hispanic, 3% multiracial, 0% Pacific Islander, 70% white, 1% international; 98% from in state; 37% live on campus; 1% of students in fraternities, 1% in sororities
Most popular majors: 23% Health Professions and Related Programs, 16% Business, Management, Marketing, and Related Support Services, 13% Parks, Recreation, Leisure, and Fitness Studies, 7% Homeland Security, Law Enforcement, Firefighting and Related Protective Services, 7% Psychology
Expenses: 2018-2019: $7,980 in state, $17,830 out of state; room/board: $13,410
Financial aid: (585) 395-2501; 75% of undergrads determined to have financial need; average aid package $11,568

College of Mount St. Vincent

Bronx NY
(718) 405-3267
U.S. News ranking: Reg. U. (N), No. 112
Website: www.mountsaintvincent.edu
Admissions email: admissions.office@mountsaintvincent.edu
Private; founded 1847
Affiliation: Roman Catholic
Freshman admissions: less selective; 2017-2018: 2,740 applied, 2,496 accepted. Either SAT or ACT required. SAT 25/75 percentile: 880-1060. High school rank: 3% in top tenth, 17% in top quarter, 43% in top half
Early decision deadline: N/A, notification date: N/A
Early action deadline: 11/15, notification date: 12/15
Application deadline (fall): rolling
Undergraduate student body: 1,585 full time, 110 part time; 31% male, 69% female; 0% American Indian, 9% Asian, 15% black, 42% Hispanic, 4% multiracial, 0% Pacific Islander, 25% white, 1% international; 88% from in state; 49% live on campus; 0% of students in fraternities, 0% in sororities
Most popular majors: 47% Health Professions and Related Programs, 12% Business, Management, Marketing, and Related Support Services, 12% Psychology, 6% Communication, Journalism, and Related Programs, 5% Biological and Biomedical Sciences
Expenses: 2018-2019: $38,180; room/board: $10,500
Financial aid: (718) 405-3289; 77% of undergrads determined to have financial need; average aid package $25,119

College of New Rochelle[1]

New Rochelle NY
(800) 933-5923
U.S. News ranking: Reg. U. (N), second tier
Website: www.cnr.edu
Admissions email: admission@cnr.edu
Private; founded 1904
Application deadline (fall): rolling
Undergraduate student body: N/A full time, N/A part time
Expenses: 2017-2018: $36,618; room/board: $14,136
Financial aid: (914) 654-5225

College of Saint Rose

Albany NY
(518) 454-5150
U.S. News ranking: Reg. U. (N), No. 99
Website: www.strose.edu
Admissions email: admit@strose.edu
Private; founded 1920
Freshman admissions: less selective; 2017-2018: 6,727 applied, 5,565 accepted. Neither SAT nor ACT required. SAT 25/75 percentile: 970-1142. High school rank: 8% in top tenth, 24% in top quarter, 63% in top half
Early decision deadline: N/A, notification date: N/A
Early action deadline: 12/1, notification date: 12/15
Application deadline (fall): 5/1
Undergraduate student body: 2,426 full time, 97 part time; 33% male, 67% female; 0% American Indian, 3% Asian, 15% black, 8% Hispanic, 10% multiracial, 0% Pacific Islander, 59% white, 2% international; 88% from in state; 48% live on campus; 0% of students in fraternities, 0% in sororities
Most popular majors: 19% Business, Management, Marketing, and Related Support Services, 17% Education, 10% Communication, Journalism, and Related Programs, 9% Psychology, 9% Visual and Performing Arts
Expenses: 2018-2019: $32,574; room/board: $12,714
Financial aid: (518) 337-4915; 84% of undergrads determined to have financial need; average aid package $21,805

The College of Westchester[1]

White Plains NY
U.S. News ranking: Reg. Coll. (N), unranked
Admissions email: N/A
For-profit
Application deadline (fall): N/A
Undergraduate student body: N/A full time, N/A part time
Expenses: 2017-2018: $21,015; room/board: N/A
Financial aid: N/A

Columbia University

New York NY
(212) 854-2522
U.S. News ranking: Nat. U., No. 3
Website: www.columbia.edu
Admissions email: ugrad-ask@columbia.edu
Private; founded 1754
Freshman admissions: most selective; 2017-2018: 37,389 applied, 2,263 accepted. Either SAT or ACT required. ACT 25/75 percentile: 32-35. High school rank: 96% in top tenth, 98% in top quarter, 100% in top half
Early decision deadline: 11/1, notification date: 12/15
Early action deadline: N/A, notification date: N/A
Application deadline (fall): 1/1
Undergraduate student body: 6,162 full time, 0 part time; 52% male, 48% female; N/A American Indian, N/A Asian, N/A black, N/A Hispanic, N/A multiracial, N/A Pacific Islander, N/A white, N/A international; 22% from in state; 93% live on campus; 24% of students in fraternities, 16% in sororities
Most popular majors: 22% Social Sciences, 20% Engineering, 9% Biological and Biomedical Sciences, 8% Computer and Information Sciences and Support Services, 6% Mathematics and Statistics
Expenses: 2018-2019: $59,430; room/board: $14,016
Financial aid: (212) 854-3711; 50% of undergrads determined to have financial need; average aid package $58,630

Concordia College

Bronxville NY
(800) 937-2655
U.S. News ranking: Reg. Coll. (N), No. 22
Website: www.concordia-ny.edu
Admissions email: admission@concordia-ny.edu
Private; founded 1881
Affiliation: Lutheran Church–Missouri Synod
Freshman admissions: selective; 2017-2018: 1,086 applied, 821 accepted. Neither SAT nor ACT required. SAT 25/75 percentile: 930-1140. High school rank: 8% in top tenth, 38% in top quarter, 70% in top half
Early decision deadline: N/A, notification date: N/A
Early action deadline: 11/15, notification date: 12/15
Application deadline (fall): 8/15
Undergraduate student body: 1,024 full time, 105 part time; 26% male, 74% female; 0% American Indian, 3% Asian, 18% black, 21% Hispanic, 2% multiracial, 0% Pacific Islander, 43% white, 11% international; 82% from in state; N/A live on campus; N/A of students in fraternities, N/A in sororities
Most popular majors: Business Administration and Management, General, Education/Teaching of Individuals in Early Childhood Special Education Programs, Registered Nursing/Registered Nurse, Social Sciences, General
Expenses: 2018-2019: $32,900; room/board: $12,690
Financial aid: (914) 337-9300; 65% of undergrads determined to have financial need; average aid package $19,218

Cooper Union

New York NY
(212) 353-4120
U.S. News ranking: Reg. Coll. (N), No. 1
Website: cooper.edu
Admissions email: admissions@cooper.edu
Private; founded 1859
Freshman admissions: most selective; 2017-2018: 2,574 applied, 336 accepted. Either SAT or ACT required. SAT 25/75 percentile: 1310-1530. High school rank: 51% in top tenth, 85% in top quarter, 99% in top half
Early decision deadline: 12/1, notification date: 12/22
Early action deadline: N/A, notification date: N/A
Application deadline (fall): 1/1
Undergraduate student body: 859 full time, 8 part time; 65% male, 35% female; 0% American Indian, 20% Asian, 3% black, 10% Hispanic, 8% multiracial, 0% Pacific Islander, 31% white, 19% international; 50% from in state; 20% live on campus; 2% of students in fraternities, N/A in sororities
Most popular majors: 34% Fine/Studio Arts, General, 15% Mechanical Engineering, 14% Architecture, 14% Electrical and Electronics Engineering, 12% Chemical Engineering
Expenses: 2018-2019: $46,700; room/board: $16,638
Financial aid: (212) 353-4113; 54% of undergrads determined to have financial need; average aid package $45,715

Cornell University

Ithaca NY
(607) 255-5241
U.S. News ranking: Nat. U., No. 16
Website: www.cornell.edu
Admissions email: admissions@cornell.edu
Private; founded 1865
Freshman admissions: most selective; 2017-2018: 47,039 applied, 5,962 accepted. Either SAT or ACT required. SAT 25/75 percentile: 1390-1550. High school rank: 86% in top tenth, 98% in top quarter, 100% in top half
Early decision deadline: 11/1, notification date: 12/15
Early action deadline: N/A, notification date: N/A
Application deadline (fall): 1/2
Undergraduate student body: 14,907 full time, 0 part time; 48% male, 52% female; 0% American Indian, 19% Asian, 7% black, 13% Hispanic, 5% multiracial, 0% Pacific Islander, 38% white, 10% international; 41% from in state; 54% live on campus; 32% of students in fraternities, 31% in sororities
Most popular majors: 17% Engineering, 14% Biological and Biomedical Sciences, 14% Business, Management, Marketing, and Related Support Services, 12% Agriculture, Agriculture Operations, and Related Sciences, 10% Computer and Information Sciences and Support Services
Expenses: 2018-2019: $55,188; room/board: $14,816
Financial aid: (607) 255-5142; 47% of undergrads determined to have financial need; average aid package $47,202

CUNY–Baruch College

New York NY
(646) 312-1400
U.S. News ranking: Reg. U. (N), No. 20
Website: www.baruch.cuny.edu
Admissions email: admissions@baruch.cuny.edu
Public; founded 1919
Freshman admissions: more selective; 2017-2018: 21,432 applied, 6,268 accepted. Either SAT or ACT required. SAT 25/75 percentile: 1190-1350. High school rank: 48% in top tenth, 75% in top quarter, 92% in top half
Early decision deadline: 12/13, notification date: 1/7
Early action deadline: N/A, notification date: N/A
Application deadline (fall): 2/1
Undergraduate student body: 11,598 full time, 3,655 part time; 51% male, 49% female; 0% American Indian, 31% Asian, 9% black, 26% Hispanic, 1% multiracial, 0% Pacific Islander, 20% white, 11% international; 97% from in state; 2% live on campus; 0% of students in fraternities, 0% in sororities
Most popular majors: 25% Finance, General, 17% Accounting, 11% Sales, Distribution, and Marketing Operations, General, 9% Business/Corporate Communications, 7% Business Administration and Management, General
Expenses: 2018-2019: $7,921 in state, $18,371 out of state; room/board: $15,178
Financial aid: (646) 312-1399; 67% of undergrads determined to have financial need; average aid package $5,836

CUNY–Brooklyn College

Brooklyn NY
(718) 951-5001
U.S. News ranking: Reg. U. (N), No. 74
Website: www.brooklyn.cuny.edu
Admissions email: adminqry@brooklyn.cuny.edu
Public; founded 1930
Freshman admissions: selective; 2017-2018: 20,642 applied, 8,345 accepted. Either SAT or ACT required. SAT 25/75 percentile: 1030-1190. High school rank: N/A
Early decision deadline: N/A, notification date: N/A
Early action deadline: N/A, notification date: N/A
Application deadline (fall): 2/1
Undergraduate student body: 10,786 full time, 3,903 part time; 42% male, 58% female; 0% American Indian, 20% Asian, 21% black, 23% Hispanic, 2% multiracial, 0% Pacific Islander, 30% white, 3% international
Most popular majors: 19% Business Administration and Management, General, 17% Psychology, General, 9% Accounting, 3% Biology/Biological Sciences, General, 3% Computer and Information Sciences, General
Expenses: 2018-2019: $7,240 in state, $18,510 out of state; room/board: N/A
Financial aid: (718) 951-5051; 81% of undergrads determined to have financial need; average aid package $8,717

CUNY–City College

New York NY
(212) 650-6977
U.S. News ranking: Reg. U. (N), No. 55
Website: www.ccny.cuny.edu
Admissions email: admissions@ccny.cuny.edu
Public; founded 1847
Freshman admissions: selective; 2017-2018: 25,373 applied, 10,340 accepted. SAT required. SAT 25/75 percentile: 980-1190. High school rank: N/A
Early decision deadline: N/A, notification date: N/A
Early action deadline: N/A, notification date: N/A
Application deadline (fall): 1/15
Undergraduate student body: 10,167 full time, 3,443 part time; 49% male, 51% female; 0% American Indian, 24% Asian, 16% black, 38% Hispanic, 2% multiracial, 0% Pacific Islander, 13% white, 6% international; 99% from in state; N/A live on campus; N/A of students in fraternities, N/A in sororities
Most popular majors: 16% Engineering, 14% Psychology, 10% Biological and Biomedical Sciences, 10% Social Sciences, 8% Visual and Performing Arts
Expenses: 2018-2019: $7,048 in state, $17,759 out of state; room/board: N/A
Financial aid: (212) 650-5824; 89% of undergrads determined to have financial need; average aid package $9,340

CUNY–College of Staten Island

Staten Island NY
(718) 982-2010
U.S. News ranking: Reg. U. (N), second tier
Website: www.csi.cuny.edu
Admissions email: admissions@csi.cuny.edu
Public; founded 1976
Freshman admissions: selective; 2017-2018: 14,684 applied, 14,684 accepted. Either SAT or ACT required. SAT 25/75 percentile: 990-1160. High school rank: N/A
Early decision deadline: N/A, notification date: N/A
Early action deadline: N/A, notification date: N/A
Application deadline (fall): rolling
Undergraduate student body: 9,710 full time, 2,799 part time; 45% male, 55% female; 0% American Indian, 12% Asian, 16% black, 18% Hispanic, 0% multiracial, 0% Pacific Islander, 50% white, 3% international; 99% from in state; 3% live on campus; 0% of students in fraternities, 0% in sororities
Most popular majors: 18% Psychology, 17% Business, Management, Marketing, and Related Support Services, 10% Health Professions and Related Programs, 10% Social Sciences, 6% English Language and Literature/Letters
Expenses: 2018-2019: $7,289 in state, $18,559 out of state; room/board: N/A
Financial aid: (718) 982-2030; 75% of undergrads determined to have financial need; average aid package $8,307

CUNY–Hunter College

New York NY
(212) 772-4490
U.S. News ranking: Reg. U. (N), No. 25
Website: www.hunter.cuny.edu
Admissions email: admissions@hunter.cuny.edu
Public; founded 1870
Freshman admissions: more selective; 2017-2018: 29,326 applied, 11,782 accepted. Either SAT or ACT required. SAT 25/75 percentile: 1070-1260. High school rank: 24% in top tenth, 57% in top quarter, 87% in top half
Early decision deadline: N/A, notification date: N/A
Early action deadline: N/A, notification date: N/A
Application deadline (fall): 3/15
Undergraduate student body: 12,612 full time, 4,232 part time; 35% male, 65% female; 0% American Indian, 30% Asian, 12% black, 22% Hispanic, 0% multiracial, 0% Pacific Islander, 30% white, 6% international; 97% from in state; N/A live on campus; N/A of students in fraternities, N/A in sororities
Most popular majors: 26% Psychology, 16% Social Sciences, 9% English Language and Literature/Letters, 8% Health Professions and Related Programs, 7% Visual and Performing Arts
Expenses: 2018-2019: $6,980 in state, $17,850 out of state; room/board: $10,573
Financial aid: (212) 772-4820; 76% of undergrads determined to have financial need; average aid package $8,126

CUNY–John Jay College of Criminal Justice

New York NY
(212) 237-8866
U.S. News ranking: Reg. U. (N), No. 139
Website: www.jjay.cuny.edu/
Admissions email: admissions@jjay.cuny.edu
Public; founded 1965
Freshman admissions: less selective; 2017-2018: N/A applied, N/A accepted. Either SAT or ACT required. SAT 25/75 percentile: 920-1060. High school rank: N/A
Early decision deadline: N/A, notification date: N/A
Early action deadline: N/A, notification date: N/A
Application deadline (fall): rolling
Undergraduate student body: 10,276 full time, 2,640 part time; 44% male, 56% female; 0% American Indian, 12% Asian, 20% black, 44% Hispanic, 0% multiracial, 0% Pacific Islander, 21% white, 3% international; 97% from in state; 1% live on campus; N/A of students in fraternities, N/A in sororities
Most popular majors: 54% Criminal Justice/Law Enforcement Administration, 17% Forensic Psychology, 16% Social Sciences, 4% Legal Professions and Studies, 3% Public Administration
Expenses: 2017-2018: $7,070 in state, $17,940 out of state; room/board: $10,386
Financial aid: (212) 237-8897

CUNY–Lehman College

Bronx NY
(718) 960-8700
U.S. News ranking: Reg. U. (N), No. 120
Website: www.lehman.cuny.edu
Admissions email: undergraduate.admissions@lehman.cuny.edu
Public; founded 1968
Freshman admissions: less selective; 2017-2018: 15,138 applied, 5,298 accepted. Either SAT or ACT required. SAT 25/75 percentile: 970-1100. High school rank: N/A
Early decision deadline: N/A, notification date: N/A
Early action deadline: N/A, notification date: N/A
Undergraduate student body: 7,21[illegible] full time, 4,762 part time; 32% male, 68% female; 0% American Indian, 7% Asian, 30% black, 53% Hispanic, 0% multiracial, 0% Pacific Islander, 7% white, 3% international; 100% from in state; N/A live on campus; N/A of students in fraternities, N/A in sororities
Most popular majors: 28% Health Professions and Related Programs, 19% Business, Management, Marketing, and Related Support Services, 12% Social Sciences, 10% Public Administration and Social Service Professions, 9% Computer and Information Sciences and Support Services
Expenses: 2018-2019: $7,210 in state, $14,400 out of state; room/board: N/A
Financial aid: (718) 960-8545; 89% of undergrads determined to have financial need; average aid package $9,448

CUNY–Medgar Evers College

Brooklyn NY
(718) 270-6024
U.S. News ranking: Reg. Coll. (N), second tier
Website: ares.mec.cuny.edu/admissions/admissions/
Admissions email: mecadmissions@mec.cuny.edu
Public; founded 1970
Freshman admissions: least selective; 2017-2018: 10,834 applied, 10,834 accepted. Neither SAT nor ACT required. SAT 25/75 percentile: 730-910. High school rank: N/A
Early decision deadline: N/A, notification date: N/A
Early action deadline: N/A, notification date: N/A
Application deadline (fall): rolling
Undergraduate student body: 4,80[illegible] full time, 1,846 part time; 28% male, 72% female; 0% American Indian, 2% Asian, 62% black, 15% Hispanic, 0% multiracial, 0% Pacific Islander, 1% white, 1% international; 99% from in state; 0% live on campus; 0% of students in fraternities, 0% in sororities
Most popular majors: 24% Biological and Biomedical Sciences, 24% Business, Management, Marketing, and Related Support Services, 15% Psychology, 14% Public Administration and Social Service Professions, 7% Health Professions and Related Programs
Expenses: 2018-2019: $6,655 in state, $17,525 out of state; room/board: N/A
Financial aid: (718) 270-6038; 93% of undergrads determined to have financial need; average aid package $9,209

CUNY–New York City College of Technology

Brooklyn NY
(718) 260-5500
U.S. News ranking: Reg. Coll. (N), second tier
Website: www.citytech.cuny.edu
Admissions email: admissions@citytech.cuny.edu
Public; founded 1946
Freshman admissions: least selective; 2017-2018: 18,163 applied, 14,021 accepted. Neither SAT nor ACT required. SAT 25/75 percentile: 740-940. High school rank: N/A
Early decision deadline: N/A, notification date: N/A
Early action deadline: N/A, notification date: N/A
Application deadline (fall): 2/1
Undergraduate student body: 11,030 full time, 6,249 part time; 56% male, 44% female; 0% American Indian, 20% Asian, 28% black, 34% Hispanic, 1% multiracial, 0% Pacific Islander, 11% white, 5% international
Most popular majors: 17% Engineering Technologies and Engineering-Related Fields, 16% Computer and Information Sciences and Support Services, 16% Health Professions and Related Programs, 12% Business, Management, Marketing, and Related Support Services, 12% Visual and Performing Arts
Expenses: 2017-2018: $6,920 in state, $14,310 out of state; room/board: N/A
Financial aid: N/A

CUNY–Queens College

Queens NY
(718) 997-5600
U.S. News ranking: Reg. U. (N), No. 55
Website: www.qc.cuny.edu/
Admissions email: admissions@qc.cuny.edu
Public; founded 1937
Freshman admissions: selective; 2017-2018: 18,180 applied, 7,769 accepted. Either SAT or ACT required. SAT 25/75 percentile: 1060-1220. High school rank: N/A
Early decision deadline: N/A, notification date: N/A
Early action deadline: N/A, notification date: N/A
Application deadline (fall): 2/1
Undergraduate student body: 12,149 full time, 4,531 part time; 45% male, 55% female; 0% American Indian, 28% Asian, 9% black, 29% Hispanic, 1% multiracial, 0% Pacific Islander, 26% white, 5% international; 99% from in state; N/A live on campus; 1% of students in fraternities, 1% in sororities
Most popular majors: 20% Psychology, General, 12% Accounting, 8% Economics, General, 7% Sociology, 5% English Language and Literature, General
Expenses: 2018-2019: $7,138 in state, $18,008 out of state; room/board: $15,998
Financial aid: (718) 997-5102; 72% of undergrads determined to have financial need; average aid package $6,856

CUNY–York College

Jamaica NY
(718) 262-2165
U.S. News ranking: Reg. Coll. (N), No. 34
Website: www.york.cuny.edu
Admissions email: admissions@york.cuny.edu
Public; founded 1966
Freshman admissions: less selective; 2017-2018: 13,167 applied, 8,620 accepted. Either SAT or ACT required. SAT 25/75 percentile: 860-1020. High school rank: N/A
Early decision deadline: N/A, notification date: N/A
Early action deadline: N/A, notification date: N/A
Application deadline (fall): 6/1
Undergraduate student body: 5,056 full time, 3,337 part time; 37% male, 63% female; 1% American Indian, 24% Asian, 37% black, 26% Hispanic, 2% multiracial, 1% Pacific Islander, 5% white, 4% international; 99% from in state; 0% live on campus; 0% of students in fraternities, 0% in sororities
Most popular majors: 23% Health Professions and Related Programs, 19% Psychology, 16% Business, Management, Marketing, and Related Support Services, 10% Public Administration and Social Service Professions, 6% Social Sciences
Expenses: 2018-2019: $6,957 in state, $17,827 out of state; room/board: N/A
Financial aid: (718) 262-2240

Daemen College

Amherst NY
(716) 839-8225
U.S. News ranking: Reg. U. (N), No. 132
Website: www.daemen.edu
Admissions email: admissions@daemen.edu
Private; founded 1947
Freshman admissions: selective; 2017-2018: 3,529 applied, 1,744 accepted. Neither SAT nor ACT required. SAT 25/75 percentile: 1040-1220. High school rank: 24% in top tenth, 58% in top quarter, 88% in top half
Early decision deadline: N/A, notification date: N/A
Early action deadline: N/A, notification date: N/A
Application deadline (fall): rolling
Undergraduate student body: 1,559 full time, 243 part time; 29% male, 71% female; 0% American Indian, 3% Asian, 11% black, 7% Hispanic, 1% multiracial, 0% Pacific Islander, 75% white, 2% international; N/A from in state; 36% live on campus; 2% of students in fraternities, 5% in sororities
Most popular majors: 36% Registered Nursing/Registered Nurse, 26% Natural Sciences, 5% Business Administration and Management, General, 5% Health and Wellness, General, 3% Social Work
Expenses: 2018-2019: $28,580; room/board: $12,915
Financial aid: (716) 839-8254; 61% of undergrads determined to have financial need; average aid package $28,324

Dominican College

Orangeburg NY
(845) 848-7901
U.S. News ranking: Reg. U. (N), second tier
Website: www.dc.edu
Admissions email: admissions@dc.edu
Private; founded 1952
Freshman admissions: less selective; 2017-2018: 2,865 applied, 1,321 accepted. Neither SAT nor ACT required. SAT 25/75 percentile: 880-1080. High school rank: N/A
Early decision deadline: N/A, notification date: N/A
Early action deadline: N/A, notification date: N/A
Application deadline (fall): rolling
Undergraduate student body: 1,271 full time, 154 part time; 33% male, 67% female; 0% American Indian, 6% Asian, 15% black, 31% Hispanic, 3% multiracial, 1% Pacific Islander, 35% white, 1% international; 81% from in state; 48% live on campus; N/A of students in fraternities, N/A in sororities
Most popular majors: 27% Physical Therapy/Therapist, 16% Social Sciences, General, 8% Management Science, 6% Criminal Justice/Law Enforcement Administration, 5% Biology/Biological Sciences, General
Expenses: 2018-2019: $29,000; room/board: $13,150
Financial aid: (845) 848-7818; 84% of undergrads determined to have financial need; average aid package $23,168

D'Youville College

Buffalo NY
(716) 829-7600
U.S. News ranking: Reg. U. (N), second tier
Website: www.dyc.edu
Admissions email: admissions@dyc.edu
Private; founded 1908
Freshman admissions: less selective; 2017-2018: 1,541 applied, 1,491 accepted. Either SAT or ACT required. SAT 25/75 percentile: 710-930. High school rank: 17% in top tenth, 50% in top quarter, 84% in top half
Early decision deadline: N/A, notification date: N/A
Early action deadline: N/A, notification date: N/A
Application deadline (fall): rolling
Undergraduate student body: 1,295 full time, 440 part time; 26% male, 74% female; 0% American Indian, 5% Asian, 9% black, 5% Hispanic, 2% multiracial, 0% Pacific Islander, 73% white, 1% international; 91% from in state; 18% live on campus; N/A of students in fraternities, N/A in sororities
Most popular majors: 64% Health Professions and Related Programs, 11% Multi/Interdisciplinary Studies, 9% Business, Management, Marketing, and Related Support Services, 8% Biological and Biomedical Sciences, 3% Psychology
Expenses: 2018-2019: $26,780; room/board: $12,224
Financial aid: (716) 829-7500; 91% of undergrads determined to have financial need; average aid package $16,671

Elmira College

Elmira NY
(800) 935-6472
U.S. News ranking: Nat. Lib. Arts, No. 155
Website: www.elmira.edu
Admissions email: admissions@elmira.edu
Private; founded 1855
Freshman admissions: selective; 2017-2018: 2,210 applied, 1,880 accepted. Neither SAT nor ACT required. SAT 25/75 percentile: 1040-1200. High school rank: N/A
Early decision deadline: N/A, notification date: N/A
Early action deadline: 10/15, notification date: 10/31
Application deadline (fall): rolling
Undergraduate student body: 833 full time, 105 part time; 29% male, 71% female; 1% American Indian, 2% Asian, 5% black, 3% Hispanic, 2% multiracial, 0% Pacific Islander, 78% white, 4% international
Most popular majors: Information not available
Expenses: 2018-2019: $41,900; room/board: $12,000
Financial aid: (607) 735-1728; 83% of undergrads determined to have financial need; average aid package $32,512

Excelsior College[1]

Albany NY
(518) 464-8500
U.S. News ranking: Reg. U. (N), unranked
Website: www.excelsior.edu
Admissions email: admissions@excelsior.edu
Private; founded 1971
Application deadline (fall): N/A
Undergraduate student body: N/A full time, N/A part time
Expenses: N/A
Financial aid: N/A

Farmingdale State College–SUNY

Farmingdale NY
(631) 420-2200
U.S. News ranking: Reg. Coll. (N), No. 19
Website: www.farmingdale.edu
Admissions email: admissions@farmingdale.edu
Public; founded 1912
Freshman admissions: selective; 2017-2018: 6,063 applied, 3,579 accepted. Either SAT or ACT required. SAT 25/75 percentile: 980-1140. High school rank: 8% in top tenth, 30% in top quarter, 69% in top half
Early decision deadline: N/A, notification date: N/A
Early action deadline: N/A, notification date: N/A
Application deadline (fall): 5/1
Undergraduate student body: 7,407 full time, 2,145 part time; 57% male, 43% female; 0% American Indian, 8% Asian, 10% black, 21% Hispanic, 2% multiracial, 0% Pacific Islander, 57% white, 1% international; 100% from in state; 7% live on campus; 3% of students in fraternities, 4% in sororities
Most popular majors: 24% Business, Management, Marketing, and Related Support Services, 12% Engineering Technologies and Engineering-Related Fields, 12% Multi/Interdisciplinary Studies, 11% Homeland Security, Law Enforcement, Firefighting and Related Protective Services, 9% Health Professions and Related Programs
Expenses: 2018-2019: $8,306 in state, $18,086 out of state; room/board: N/A
Financial aid: (631) 420-2578; 55% of undergrads determined to have financial need; average aid package $7,950

Fashion Institute of Technology

New York NY
(212) 217-3760
U.S. News ranking: Reg. U. (N), unranked
Website: www.fitnyc.edu
Admissions email: FITinfo@fitnyc.edu
Public; founded 1944
Freshman admissions: least selective; 2017-2018: 4,739 applied, 2,229 accepted. Neither SAT nor ACT required. SAT 25/75 percentile: N/A. High school rank: N/A
Early decision deadline: N/A, notification date: N/A
Early action deadline: N/A, notification date: N/A
Application deadline (fall): 1/1
Undergraduate student body: 7,210 full time, 1,451 part time; 15% male, 85% female; 0% American Indian, 11% Asian, 9% black, 19% Hispanic, 3% multiracial, 0% Pacific Islander, 45% white, 12% international; 69% from in state; 21% live on campus; 0% of students in fraternities, 0% in sororities
Most popular majors: 42% Business, Management, Marketing, and Related Support Services, 35% Visual and Performing Arts, 18% Communication, Journalism, and Related Programs, 4% Family and Consumer Sciences/Human Sciences
Expenses: 2018-2019: $5,740 in state, $15,520 out of state; room/board: $14,480
Financial aid: (212) 217-3560; 50% of undergrads determined to have financial need; average aid package $11,880

Five Towns College[1]

Dix Hills NY
(631) 424-7000
U.S. News ranking: Reg. Coll. (N), second tier
Website: www.ftc.edu
Admissions email: admissions@ftc.edu
For-profit; founded 1972
Application deadline (fall): rolling
Undergraduate student body: N/A full time, N/A part time
Expenses: 2017-2018: $19,590; room/board: $12,300
Financial aid: (631) 656-2168

Fordham University

New York NY
(800) 367-3426
U.S. News ranking: Nat. U., No. 70
Website: www.fordham.edu
Admissions email: enroll@fordham.edu
Private; founded 1841
Affiliation: Roman Catholic
Freshman admissions: more selective; 2017-2018: 45,147 applied, 20,966 accepted. Either SAT or ACT required. SAT 25/75 percentile: 1230-1410. High school rank: 48% in top tenth, 78% in top quarter, 97% in top half
Early decision deadline: 11/1, notification date: 12/20
Early action deadline: 11/1, notification date: 12/20
Application deadline (fall): 1/1
Undergraduate student body: 9,132 full time, 467 part time; 42% male, 58% female; 0% American Indian, 10% Asian, 4% black, 14% Hispanic, 3% multiracial, 0% Pacific Islander, 58% white, 8% international; 43% from in state; 50% live on campus; N/A of students in fraternities, N/A in sororities
Most popular majors: 12% Speech Communication and Rhetoric, 10% Business Administration and Management, General, 8% Finance, General, 8% Psychology, General, 7% Economics, General
Expenses: 2018-2019: $52,248; room/board: $17,969
Financial aid: N/A

Hamilton College

Clinton NY
(800) 843-2655
U.S. News ranking: Nat. Lib. Arts, No. 16
Website: www.hamilton.edu
Admissions email: admission@hamilton.edu
Private; founded 1812
Freshman admissions: most selective; 2017-2018: 5,678 applied, 1,375 accepted. Either SAT or ACT required. ACT 25/75 percentile: 31-33. High school rank: 77% in top tenth, 96% in top quarter, 100% in top half
Early decision deadline: 11/15, notification date: 12/15
Early action deadline: N/A, notification date: N/A
Application deadline (fall): 1/1
Undergraduate student body: 1,886 full time, 11 part time; 47% male, 53% female; 0% American Indian, 7% Asian, 4% black, 9% Hispanic, 4% multiracial, 0% Pacific Islander, 64% white, 6% international; 30% from in state; 100% live on campus; 26% of students in fraternities, 16% in sororities
Most popular majors: 17% Economics, General, 8% Mathematics, General, 7% Political Science and Government, General, 6% Research and Experimental Psychology, Other, 5% Hispanic and Latin American Languages, Literatures, and Linguistics, General
Expenses: 2018-2019: $54,620; room/board: $13,870
Financial aid: (800) 859-4413; 51% of undergrads determined to have financial need; average aid package $47,372

Hartwick College

Oneonta NY
(607) 431-4150
U.S. News ranking: Nat. Lib. Arts, second tier
Website: www.hartwick.edu
Admissions email: admissions@hartwick.edu
Private; founded 1797
Freshman admissions: less selective; 2017-2018: 3,019 applied, 2,674 accepted. Neither SAT nor ACT required. SAT 25/75 percentile: 920-1100. High school rank: 8% in top tenth, 32% in top quarter, 69% in top half
Early decision deadline: 11/1, notification date: 11/15
Early action deadline: N/A, notification date: N/A
Application deadline (fall): rolling
Undergraduate student body: 1,180 full time, 21 part time; 41% male, 59% female; 1% American Indian, 3% Asian, 9% black, 9% Hispanic, 0% multiracial, 0% Pacific Islander, 62% white, 3% international; 80% from in state; 80% live on campus; 4% of students in fraternities, 7% in sororities
Most popular majors: 22% Social Sciences, 20% Business, Management, Marketing, and Related Support Services, 20% Health Professions and Related Programs, 15% Biological and Biomedical Sciences, 9% Psychology
Expenses: 2018-2019: $45,510; room/board: $12,460
Financial aid: (607) 431-4130; 84% of undergrads determined to have financial need; average aid package $36,253

Hilbert College[1]

Hamburg NY
(716) 649-7900
U.S. News ranking: Reg. Coll. (N), unranked
Website: www.hilbert.edu/
Admissions email: admissions@hilbert.edu
Private
Application deadline (fall): N/A
Undergraduate student body: N/A full time, N/A part time
Expenses: 2017-2018: $21,800; room/board: $9,000
Financial aid: N/A

Hobart and William Smith Colleges

Geneva NY
(315) 781-3622
U.S. News ranking: Nat. Lib. Arts, No. 68
Website: www.hws.edu
Admissions email: admissions@hws.edu
Private; founded 1822
Freshman admissions: more selective; 2017-2018: 4,409 applied, 2,696 accepted. Neither SAT nor ACT required. SAT 25/75 percentile: 1210-1360. High school rank: 33% in top tenth, 59% in top quarter, 83% in top half
Early decision deadline: 11/15, notification date: 12/15
Early action deadline: N/A, notification date: N/A
Application deadline (fall): 2/1
Undergraduate student body: 2,220 full time, 17 part time; 49% male, 51% female; 0% American Indian, 3% Asian, 6% black, 5% Hispanic, 0% multiracial, 0% Pacific Islander, 75% white, 6% international; 40% from in state; 90% live on campus; 15% of students in fraternities, 4% in sororities
Most popular majors: 12% Economics, General, 9% Mass Communication/Media Studies, 8% Social Sciences, General, 7% Biology/Biological Sciences, General, 7% Political Science and Government, General
Expenses: 2018-2019: $55,255; room/board: $14,035
Financial aid: (315) 781-3315; 64% of undergrads determined to have financial need; average aid package $39,732

Hofstra University

Hempstead NY
(516) 463-6700
U.S. News ranking: Nat. U., No. 140
Website: www.hofstra.edu
Admissions email: admission@hofstra.edu
Private; founded 1935
Freshman admissions: more selective; 2017-2018: 26,808 applied, 17,143 accepted. Neither SAT nor ACT required. SAT 25/75 percentile: 1130-1310. High school rank: 28% in top tenth, 62% in top quarter, 90% in top half
Early decision deadline: N/A, notification date: N/A
Early action deadline: 11/15, notification date: 12/15
Application deadline (fall): rolling
Undergraduate student body: 6,494 full time, 367 part time; 45% male, 55% female; 0% American Indian, 10% Asian, 9% black, 13% Hispanic, 3% multiracial, 1% Pacific Islander, 56% white, 6% international; 62% from in state; 45% live on campus; 9% of students in fraternities, 11% in sororities
Most popular majors: 7% Marketing/Marketing Management, General, 6% Accounting, 6% Psychology, General, 5% Finance, General, 4% Public Relations/Image Management
Expenses: 2018-2019: $45,700; room/board: $15,708
Financial aid: (516) 463-8000; 65% of undergrads determined to have financial need; average aid package $31,000

Houghton College

Houghton NY
(800) 777-2556
U.S. News ranking: Nat. Lib. Arts, No. 143
Website: www.houghton.edu
Admissions email: admission@houghton.edu
Private; founded 1883
Affiliation: Wesleyan
Freshman admissions: selective; 2017-2018: 821 applied, 750 accepted. Neither SAT nor ACT required. SAT 25/75 percentile: 1060-1320. High school rank: 26% in top tenth, 54% in top quarter, 80% in top half
Early decision deadline: N/A, notification date: N/A
Early action deadline: N/A, notification date: N/A
Application deadline (fall): rolling
Undergraduate student body: 967 full time, 64 part time; 38% male, 62% female; 0% American Indian, 4% Asian, 4% black, 2% Hispanic, 4% multiracial, 0% Pacific Islander, 73% white, 10% international; 65% from in state; 75% live on campus; N/A of students in fraternities, N/A in sororities
Most popular majors: Information not available
Expenses: 2018-2019: $32,488; room/board: $9,288
Financial aid: (585) 567-9328; 89% of undergrads determined to have financial need; average aid package $18,498

Iona College

New Rochelle NY
(914) 633-2502
U.S. News ranking: Reg. U. (N), No. 68
Website: www.iona.edu
Admissions email: admissions@iona.edu
Private; founded 1940
Affiliation: Roman Catholic
Freshman admissions: selective; 2017-2018: 10,304 applied, 9,501 accepted. Either SAT or ACT required. SAT 25/75 percentile: 980-1180. High school rank: 7% in top tenth, 21% in top quarter, 51% in top half
Early decision deadline: N/A, notification date: N/A
Early action deadline: 12/1, notification date: 12/15
Application deadline (fall): 2/15
Undergraduate student body: 2,949 full time, 229 part time; 49% male, 51% female; 0% American Indian, 2% Asian, 10% black, 24% Hispanic, 2% multiracial, 0% Pacific Islander, 56% white, 3% international; 76% from in state; 46% live on campus; 6% of students in fraternities, 8% in sororities
Most popular majors: 35% Business, Management, Marketing, and Related Support Services, 17% Communication, Journalism, and Related Programs, 10% Homeland Security, Law Enforcement, Firefighting and Related Protective Services, 9% Psychology, 7% Health Professions and Related Programs
Expenses: 2018-2019: $38,812; room/board: $15,278
Financial aid: (914) 633-2497; 86% of undergrads determined to have financial need; average aid package $26,300

Ithaca College

Ithaca NY
(800) 429-4274
U.S. News ranking: Reg. U. (N), No. 9
Website: www.ithaca.edu
Admissions email: admission@ithaca.edu
Private; founded 1892
Freshman admissions: more selective; 2017-2018: 14,152 applied, 9,980 accepted. Neither SAT nor ACT required. SAT 25/75 percentile: 1150-1330. High school rank: 21% in top tenth, 55% in top quarter, 88% in top half
Early decision deadline: 11/1, notification date: 12/15
Early action deadline: 12/1, notification date: 2/1
Application deadline (fall): 2/1
Undergraduate student body: 5,936 full time, 123 part time; 42% male, 58% female; 0% American Indian, 4% Asian, 6% black, 8% Hispanic, 3% multiracial, 0% Pacific Islander, 73% white, 2% international; 45% from in state; 70% live on campus; 2% of students in fraternities, 1% in sororities
Most popular majors: 24% Communication, Journalism, and Related Programs, 16% Health Professions and Related Programs, 16% Visual and Performing Arts, 10% Business, Management, Marketing, and Related Support Services, 5% Psychology
Expenses: 2018-2019: $43,978; room/board: $15,562
Financial aid: (607) 274-3131; 68% of undergrads determined to have financial need; average aid package $37,506

Jamestown Business College[1]

Jamestown NY
U.S. News ranking: Business, unranked
Admissions email: N/A
For-profit
Application deadline (fall): N/A
Undergraduate student body: N/A full time, N/A part time
Expenses: N/A
Financial aid: N/A

Juilliard School

New York NY
(212) 799-5000
U.S. News ranking: Arts, unranked
Website: www.juilliard.edu
Admissions email: admissions@juilliard.edu
Private; founded 1905
Freshman admissions: least selective; 2017-2018: 2,753 applied, 163 accepted. Neither SAT nor ACT required. SAT 25/75 percentile: N/A. High school rank: N/A

More @ usnews.com/bestcolleges

Early decision deadline: N/A, notification date: N/A
Early action deadline: N/A, notification date: N/A
Application deadline (fall): 12/1
Undergraduate student body: 486 full time, 80 part time; 54% male, 46% female; 0% American Indian, 12% Asian, 7% black, 9% Hispanic, 6% multiracial, 0% Pacific Islander, 38% white, 27% international; 21% from in state; N/A live on campus; N/A of students in fraternities, N/A in sororities
Most popular majors: Information not available
Expenses: 2018-2019: $45,210; room/board: $16,950
Financial aid: (212) 799-5000; 73% of undergrads determined to have financial need; average aid package $35,281

Keuka College

Keuka Park NY
(315) 279-5254
U.S. News ranking: Reg. U. (N), No. 112
Website: www.keuka.edu
Admissions email: admissions@keuka.edu
Private; founded 1890
Affiliation: American Baptist
Freshman admissions: less selective; 2017-2018: 2,396 applied, 2,089 accepted. Neither SAT nor ACT required. SAT 25/75 percentile: 980-1140. High school rank: N/A
Early decision deadline: N/A, notification date: N/A
Early action deadline: N/A, notification date: N/A
Application deadline (fall): rolling
Undergraduate student body: 1,314 full time, 329 part time; 27% male, 73% female; N/A American Indian, N/A Asian, N/A black, N/A Hispanic, N/A multiracial, N/A Pacific Islander, N/A white, N/A international
Most popular majors: Information not available
Expenses: 2018-2019: $32,093; room/board: $11,906
Financial aid: (315) 279-5232; 95% of undergrads determined to have financial need; average aid package $32,000

The King's College

New York NY
(212) 659-3610
U.S. News ranking: Nat. Lib. Arts, second tier
Website: www.tkc.edu/
Admissions email: admissions@tkc.edu
Private; founded 1938
Affiliation: Undenominational
Freshman admissions: more selective; 2017-2018: 2,098 applied, 858 accepted. Either SAT or ACT required. ACT 25/75 percentile: 24-29. High school rank: N/A
Early decision deadline: N/A, notification date: N/A
Early action deadline: 11/15, notification date: 12/15
Application deadline (fall): rolling
Undergraduate student body: 542 full time, 13 part time; 36% male, 64% female; 0% American Indian, 4% Asian, 6% black, 7% Hispanic, 0% multiracial, 0% Pacific Islander, 66% white, 3% international
Most popular majors: 39% Humanities/Humanistic Studies, 32% Liberal Arts and Sciences, General Studies and Humanities, Other, 28% Business Administration and Management, General, 1% Finance, General
Expenses: 2018-2019: $36,450; room/board: $16,840
Financial aid: (646) 237-8902; 69% of undergrads determined to have financial need; average aid package $27,649

Le Moyne College

Syracuse NY
(315) 445-4300
U.S. News ranking: Reg. U. (N), No. 17
Website: www.lemoyne.edu
Admissions email: admission@lemoyne.edu
Private; founded 1946
Affiliation: Roman Catholic
Freshman admissions: selective; 2017-2018: 7,429 applied, 4,751 accepted. Neither SAT nor ACT required. SAT 25/75 percentile: 1080-1240. High school rank: 23% in top tenth, 51% in top quarter, 88% in top half
Early decision deadline: N/A, notification date: N/A
Early action deadline: 11/15, notification date: 12/15
Application deadline (fall): rolling
Undergraduate student body: 2,410 full time, 378 part time; 40% male, 60% female; 0% American Indian, 3% Asian, 6% black, 5% Hispanic, 2% multiracial, 0% Pacific Islander, 78% white, 1% international; 94% from in state; 58% live on campus; 0% of students in fraternities, 0% in sororities
Most popular majors: 19% Biology/Biological Sciences, General, 14% Psychology, General, 12% Registered Nursing/Registered Nurse, 7% Accounting, 7% Communication and Media Studies
Expenses: 2018-2019: $34,625; room/board: $13,780
Financial aid: (315) 445-4400; 83% of undergrads determined to have financial need; average aid package $27,162

LIM College

New York NY
(800) 677-1323
U.S. News ranking: Business, unranked
Website: www.limcollege.edu
Admissions email: admissions@limcollege.edu
For-profit; founded 1939
Freshman admissions: less selective; 2017-2018: 1,340 applied, 1,050 accepted. Neither SAT nor ACT required. SAT 25/75 percentile: 860-1180. High school rank: N/A
Early decision deadline: N/A, notification date: N/A
Early action deadline: 11/15, notification date: 12/15
Application deadline (fall): rolling
Undergraduate student body: 1,300 full time, 102 part time; 9% male, 91% female; 1% American Indian, 8% Asian, 15% black, 8% Hispanic, 0% multiracial, 0% Pacific Islander, 53% white, 6% international; 35% from in state; 26% live on campus; N/A of students in fraternities, N/A in sororities
Most popular majors: 94% Business, Management, Marketing, and Related Support Services, 6% Visual and Performing Arts
Expenses: 2018-2019: $27,030; room/board: $20,350
Financial aid: (212) 310-0689

LIU Post

Brookville NY
(516) 299-2900
U.S. News ranking: Reg. U. (N), No. 120
Website: www.liu.edu/post
Admissions email: post-enroll@liu.edu
Private; founded 1954
Freshman admissions: selective; 2017-2018: 6,951 applied, 5,748 accepted. Either SAT or ACT required. SAT 25/75 percentile: 1055-1240. High school rank: 10% in top tenth, 33% in top quarter, 65% in top half
Early decision deadline: N/A, notification date: N/A
Early action deadline: 12/1, notification date: 12/31
Application deadline (fall): rolling
Undergraduate student body: 2,845 full time, 3,471 part time; 41% male, 59% female; 0% American Indian, 4% Asian, 11% black, 15% Hispanic, 2% multiracial, 0% Pacific Islander, 48% white, 6% international; 91% from in state; 30% live on campus; 8% of students in fraternities, 11% in sororities
Most popular majors: 13% Business Administration and Management, General, 9% Psychology, General, 7% Criminal Justice/Law Enforcement Administration, 6% Clinical Nutrition/Nutritionist, 5% Health Professions and Related Clinical Sciences, Other
Expenses: 2017-2018: $36,978; room/board: $13,720
Financial aid: (516) 299-2553; 74% of undergrads determined to have financial need; average aid package $24,166

Manhattan College

Riverdale NY
(718) 862-7200
U.S. News ranking: Reg. U. (N), No. 15
Website: www.manhattan.edu
Admissions email: admit@manhattan.edu
Private; founded 1853
Affiliation: Roman Catholic
Freshman admissions: selective; 2017-2018: 7,622 applied, 5,746 accepted. Either SAT or ACT required. SAT 25/75 percentile: 1050-1243. High school rank: 23% in top tenth, 54% in top quarter, 79% in top half
Early decision deadline: 11/15, notification date: 12/15
Early action deadline: N/A, notification date: N/A
Application deadline (fall): rolling
Undergraduate student body: 3,479 full time, 185 part time; 55% male, 45% female; 0% American Indian, 5% Asian, 5% black, 22% Hispanic, 2% multiracial, 0% Pacific Islander, 55% white, 3% international
Most popular majors: 29% Engineering, 21% Business, Management, Marketing, and Related Support Services, 13% Communications Technologies/Technicians and Support Services, 7% Education, 6% Psychology
Expenses: 2018-2019: $42,608; room/board: $16,220
Financial aid: (718) 862-7178; 74% of undergrads determined to have financial need; average aid package $16,846

Manhattan School of Music[1]

New York NY
(917) 493-4436
U.S. News ranking: Arts, unranked
Website: msmnyc.edu/
Admissions email: admission@msmnyc.edu
Private; founded 1917
Application deadline (fall): N/A
Undergraduate student body: N/A full time, N/A part time
Expenses: N/A
Financial aid: (917) 493-4809

Manhattanville College

Purchase NY
(914) 323-5464
U.S. News ranking: Reg. U. (N), No. 99
Website: www.mville.edu
Admissions email: admissions@mville.edu
Private; founded 1841
Freshman admissions: less selective; 2017-2018: 3,841 applied, 3,152 accepted. Neither SAT nor ACT required. SAT 25/75 percentile: 940-1160. High school rank: 5% in top tenth, 27% in top quarter, 63% in top half
Early decision deadline: N/A, notification date: N/A
Early action deadline: 12/1, notification date: 12/20
Application deadline (fall): 9/4
Undergraduate student body: 1,633 full time, 92 part time; 37% male, 63% female; 0% American Indian, 2% Asian, 9% black, 25% Hispanic, 2% multiracial, 0% Pacific Islander, 47% white, 7% international; 73% from in state; 60% live on campus; 0% of students in fraternities, 0% in sororities
Most popular majors: 14% Business Administration and Management, General, 13% Psychology, General, 9% Speech Communication and Rhetoric, 7% Finance, General, 7% Sports Studies
Expenses: 2018-2019: $38,820; room/board: $14,520
Financial aid: (914) 323-5357; 75% of undergrads determined to have financial need; average aid package $28,326

Marist College

Poughkeepsie NY
(845) 575-3226
U.S. News ranking: Reg. U. (N), No. 8
Website: www.marist.edu
Admissions email: admissions@marist.edu
Private; founded 1929
Freshman admissions: more selective; 2017-2018: 11,376 applied, 4,849 accepted. Neither SAT nor ACT required. SAT 25/75 percentile: 1120-1320. High school rank: 24% in top tenth, 53% in top quarter, 87% in top half
Early decision deadline: 11/15, notification date: 12/15
Early action deadline: 11/15, notification date: 1/15
Application deadline (fall): 2/1
Undergraduate student body: 5,085 full time, 614 part time; 42% male, 58% female; 0% American Indian, 3% Asian, 4% black, 10% Hispanic, 2% multiracial, 0% Pacific Islander, 77% white, 2% international; 53% from in state; 66% live on campus; 3% of students in fraternities, 3% in sororities
Most popular majors: 33% Business, Management, Marketing, and Related Support Services, 19% Communication, Journalism, and Related Programs, 11% Psychology, 5% Biological and Biomedical Sciences, 5% Computer and Information Sciences and Support Services
Expenses: 2018-2019: $39,600; room/board: $15,550
Financial aid: (845) 575-3230; 58% of undergrads determined to have financial need; average aid package $26,750

Marymount Manhattan College

New York NY
(212) 517-0430
U.S. News ranking: Nat. Lib. Arts, second tier
Website: www.mmm.edu
Admissions email: admissions@mmm.edu
Private; founded 1936
Freshman admissions: selective; 2017-2018: 5,532 applied, 4,363 accepted. Either SAT or ACT required. SAT 25/75 percentile: 980-1200. High school rank: N/A
Early decision deadline: N/A, notification date: N/A
Early action deadline: N/A, notification date: N/A
Application deadline (fall): rolling
Undergraduate student body: 1,915 full time, 235 part time; 23% male, 77% female; 0% American Indian, 3% Asian, 8% black, 16% Hispanic, 4% multiracial, 0% Pacific Islander, 58% white, 4% international; 38% from in state; 35% live on campus; N/A of students in fraternities, N/A in sororities
Most popular majors: 48% Visual and Performing Arts, 17% Communication, Journalism, and Related Programs, 14% Business, Management, Marketing, and Related Support Services, 6% History, 6% Psychology

Expenses: 2018-2019: $33,778; room/board: $16,832
Financial aid: (212) 517-0500; 67% of undergrads determined to have financial need; average aid package $17,829

Medaille College[1]

Buffalo NY
(716) 880-2200
U.S. News ranking: Reg. U. (N), second tier
Website: www.medaille.edu
Admissions email: admissionsug@medaille.edu
Private; founded 1937
Application deadline (fall): rolling
Undergraduate student body: N/A full time, N/A part time
Expenses: 2017-2018: $28,360; room/board: $13,340
Financial aid: (716) 880-2256

Mercy College

Dobbs Ferry NY
(877) 637-2946
U.S. News ranking: Reg. U. (N), unranked
Website: www.mercy.edu
Admissions email: admissions@mercy.edu
Private; founded 1950
Freshman admissions: least selective; 2017-2018: 6,901 applied, 5,433 accepted. Neither SAT nor ACT required. SAT 25/75 percentile: N/A. High school rank: N/A
Early decision deadline: N/A, notification date: N/A
Early action deadline: N/A, notification date: N/A
Application deadline (fall): rolling
Undergraduate student body: 5,055 full time, 1,809 part time; 34% male, 66% female; 0% American Indian, 4% Asian, 23% black, 40% Hispanic, 1% multiracial, 0% Pacific Islander, 23% white, 1% international; 92% from in state; 11% live on campus; N/A of students in fraternities, N/A in sororities
Most popular majors: 27% Social Sciences, 22% Health Professions and Related Programs, 18% Business, Management, Marketing, and Related Support Services, 11% Psychology, 6% Homeland Security, Law Enforcement, Firefighting and Related Protective Services
Expenses: 2018-2019: $19,042; room/board: $14,400
Financial aid: (888) 464-6737; 87% of undergrads determined to have financial need; average aid package $14,084

Metropolitan College of New York

New York NY
(212) 343-1234
U.S. News ranking: Reg. U. (N), second tier
Website: www.mcny.edu
Admissions email: admissions@mcny.edu
Private; founded 1964
Freshman admissions: less selective; 2017-2018: 126 applied, 115 accepted. Neither SAT nor ACT required. SAT 25/75 percentile: N/A. High school rank: N/A
Early decision deadline: N/A, notification date: N/A
Early action deadline: N/A, notification date: N/A
Application deadline (fall): rolling
Undergraduate student body: 681 full time, 96 part time; 30% male, 70% female; 1% American Indian, 3% Asian, 55% black, 29% Hispanic, 3% multiracial, 0% Pacific Islander, 3% white, 1% international; 96% from in state; 0% live on campus; 0% of students in fraternities, 0% in sororities
Most popular majors: 38% Public Administration and Social Service Professions, 37% Health Professions and Related Programs, 22% Business, Management, Marketing, and Related Support Services, 2% Social Sciences
Expenses: 2018-2019: $19,454; room/board: N/A
Financial aid: (212) 343-1234; 93% of undergrads determined to have financial need; average aid package $17,286

Molloy College

Rockville Centre NY
(516) 323-4000
U.S. News ranking: Reg. U. (N), No. 25
Website: www.molloy.edu
Admissions email: admissions@molloy.edu
Private; founded 1955
Freshman admissions: selective; 2017-2018: 4,188 applied, 3,184 accepted. Either SAT or ACT required. SAT 25/75 percentile: 1020-1200. High school rank: 19% in top tenth, 54% in top quarter, 89% in top half
Early decision deadline: N/A, notification date: N/A
Early action deadline: 12/1, notification date: 12/15
Application deadline (fall): rolling
Undergraduate student body: 2,800 full time, 734 part time; 25% male, 75% female; 0% American Indian, 8% Asian, 11% black, 17% Hispanic, 2% multiracial, 0% Pacific Islander, 60% white, 0% international; 96% from in state; 8% live on campus; N/A of students in fraternities, N/A in sororities
Most popular majors: 48% Health Professions and Related Programs, 13% Business, Management, Marketing, and Related Support Services, 8% Education, 6% Psychology, 5% Communication, Journalism, and Related Programs
Expenses: 2018-2019: $31,490; room/board: $15,032
Financial aid: (516) 323-4200; 81% of undergrads determined to have financial need; average aid package $16,690

Monroe College

Bronx NY
(800) 556-6676
U.S. News ranking: Reg. U. (N), No. 90
Website: www.monroecollege.edu
Admissions email: admissions@monroecollege.edu
For-profit; founded 1933
Freshman admissions: least selective; 2017-2018: 5,046 applied, 2,635 accepted. Neither SAT nor ACT required. SAT 25/75 percentile: 744-1053. High school rank: N/A
Early decision deadline: N/A, notification date: N/A
Early action deadline: 12/15, notification date: 1/31
Application deadline (fall): rolling
Undergraduate student body: 4,126 full time, 1,388 part time; 38% male, 62% female; 0% American Indian, 2% Asian, 43% black, 40% Hispanic, 0% multiracial, 0% Pacific Islander, 2% white, 10% international; 99% from in state; 18% live on campus; N/A of students in fraternities, N/A in sororities
Most popular majors: 38% Health Professions and Related Programs, 32% Business, Management, Marketing, and Related Support Services, 19% Homeland Security, Law Enforcement, Firefighting and Related Protective Services, 11% Computer and Information Sciences and Support Services
Expenses: 2018-2019: $15,428; room/board: $10,850
Financial aid: (718) 933-6700; 88% of undergrads determined to have financial need; average aid package $12,860

Mount St. Mary College

Newburgh NY
(845) 569-3488
U.S. News ranking: Reg. U. (N), No. 123
Website: www.msmc.edu
Admissions email: admissions@msmc.edu
Private; founded 1959
Freshman admissions: selective; 2017-2018: 3,824 applied, 3,571 accepted. Either SAT or ACT required. SAT 25/75 percentile: 1000-1160. High school rank: 9% in top tenth, 29% in top quarter, 69% in top half
Early decision deadline: N/A, notification date: N/A
Early action deadline: N/A, notification date: N/A
Application deadline (fall): 8/15
Undergraduate student body: 1,737 full time, 299 part time; 30% male, 70% female; 1% American Indian, 2% Asian, 7% black, 17% Hispanic, 1% multiracial, 0% Pacific Islander, 61% white, 1% international; 88% from in state; 48% live on campus; 0% of students in fraternities, 0% in sororities
Most popular majors: 28% Health Professions and Related Programs, 20% Business, Management, Marketing, and Related Support Services, 12% Psychology, 7% Mathematics and Statistics, 6% Public Administration and Social Service Professions
Expenses: 2018-2019: $31,118; room/board: $15,108
Financial aid: (845) 569-3394; 79% of undergrads determined to have financial need; average aid package $20,126

Nazareth College

Rochester NY
(585) 389-2860
U.S. News ranking: Reg. U. (N), No. 35
Website: www.naz.edu
Admissions email: admissions@naz.edu
Private; founded 1924
Freshman admissions: more selective; 2017-2018: 4,494 applied, 2,815 accepted. Neither SAT nor ACT required. SAT 25/75 percentile: 1070-1250. High school rank: 26% in top tenth, 60% in top quarter, 89% in top half
Early decision deadline: 11/15, notification date: 12/15
Early action deadline: N/A, notification date: N/A
Application deadline (fall): 2/1
Undergraduate student body: 2,099 full time, 95 part time; 26% male, 74% female; 0% American Indian, 3% Asian, 6% black, 6% Hispanic, 2% multiracial, 0% Pacific Islander, 79% white, 1% international; 90% from in state; 57% live on campus; 0% of students in fraternities, 0% in sororities
Most popular majors: 30% Health Professions and Related Programs, 12% Business, Management, Marketing, and Related Support Services, 10% Education, 10% Visual and Performing Arts, 7% Public Administration and Social Service Professions
Expenses: 2018-2019: $34,280; room/board: $13,730
Financial aid: (585) 389-2310; 84% of undergrads determined to have financial need; average aid package $27,685

The New School

New York NY
(800) 292-3040
U.S. News ranking: Nat. U., No. 147
Website: www.newschool.edu
Admissions email: admission@newschool.edu
Private
Freshman admissions: selective; 2017-2018: 9,056 applied, 6,355 accepted. Neither SAT nor ACT required. SAT 25/75 percentile: 1100-1310. High school rank: 17% in top tenth, 47% in top quarter, 79% in top half
Early decision deadline: N/A, notification date: N/A
Early action deadline: 11/1, notification date: 12/20
Application deadline (fall): rolling
Undergraduate student body: 6,351 full time, 852 part time; 26% male, 74% female; 0% American Indian, 10% Asian, 6% black, 12% Hispanic, 4% multiracial, 0% Pacific Islander, 33% white, 32% international; 33% from in state; 28% live on campus; N/A of students in fraternities, N/A in sororities
Most popular majors: 21% Fashion/Apparel Design, 12% Fine and Studio Arts Management, 8% Web Page, Digital/Multimedia and Information Resources Design, 7% Liberal Arts and Sciences/Liberal Studies, 5% Jazz/Jazz Studies
Expenses: 2018-2019: $48,631; room/board: $18,000
Financial aid: (212) 229-8930; 39% of undergrads determined to have financial need; average aid package $24,206

New York Institute of Technology

Old Westbury NY
(800) 345-6948
U.S. News ranking: Reg. U. (N), No. 50
Website: www.nyit.edu
Admissions email: admissions@nyit.edu
Private; founded 1955
Freshman admissions: selective; 2017-2018: 9,945 applied, 7,651 accepted. Either SAT or ACT required. SAT 25/75 percentile: 1040-1230. High school rank: N/A
Early decision deadline: N/A, notification date: N/A
Early action deadline: N/A, notification date: N/A
Application deadline (fall): rolling
Undergraduate student body: 3,239 full time, 425 part time; 64% male, 36% female; 0% American Indian, 18% Asian, 9% black, 16% Hispanic, 4% multiracial, 0% Pacific Islander, 25% white, 16% international; 85% from in state; 15% live on campus; 3% of students in fraternities, 4% in sororities
Most popular majors: 16% Engineering, 15% Business, Management, Marketing, and Related Support Services, 15% Health Professions and Related Programs, 13% Architecture and Related Services, 10% Communication, Journalism, and Related Programs
Expenses: 2018-2019: $36,890; room/board: $14,290
Financial aid: (516) 686-7680; 74% of undergrads determined to have financial need; average aid package $26,036

New York University

New York NY
(212) 998-4500
U.S. News ranking: Nat. U., No. 30
Website: www.nyu.edu
Admissions email: admissions@nyu.edu
Private; founded 1831
Freshman admissions: most selective; 2017-2018: 64,007 applied, 17,707 accepted. Neither SAT nor ACT required. SAT 25/75 percentile: 1290-1490. High school rank: 72% in top tenth, 100% in top quarter, 100% in top half
Early decision deadline: 11/1, notification date: 12/15
Early action deadline: N/A, notification date: N/A
Application deadline (fall): 1/1
Undergraduate student body: 25,347 full time, 1,070 part time; 43% male, 57% female; 0% American Indian, 20% Asian, 6% black, 14% Hispanic, 5% multiracial, 0% Pacific Islander, 31% white, 19% international; 34% from in state; 43% live on campus; 5% of students in fraternities, 7% in sororities

More @ usnews.com/bestcolleges

Most popular majors: 18% Visual and Performing Arts, 14% Business, Management, Marketing, and Related Support Services, 14% Social Sciences, 9% Health Professions and Related Programs, 9% Liberal Arts and Sciences, General Studies and Humanities
Expenses: 2018-2019: $51,828; room/board: $18,156
Financial aid: (212) 998-4444; 52% of undergrads determined to have financial need; average aid package $34,950

Niagara University

Niagara University NY
(716) 286-8700
U.S. News ranking: Reg. U. (N), No. 43
Website: www.niagara.edu
Admissions email: admissions@niagara.edu
Private; founded 1856
Affiliation: Roman Catholic
Freshman admissions: selective; 2017-2018: 3,101 applied, ,611 accepted. Either SAT or ACT required. SAT 25/75 percentile: 1020-1200. High school rank: 16% in top tenth, 7% in top quarter, 76% in top half
Early decision deadline: N/A, notification date: N/A
Early action deadline: 12/15, notification date: 1/3
Application deadline (fall): 8/30
Undergraduate student body: 2,827 full time, 167 part time; 38% male, 62% female; 1% American Indian, 2% Asian, 5% black, % Hispanic, 3% multiracial, % Pacific Islander, 71% white, 3% international; 92% from in state; 40% live on campus; 1% of students in fraternities, 3% in sororities
Most popular majors: 29% Business, Management, Marketing, and Related Support Services, 20% Education, 11% Health Professions and Related Programs, 10% Social Sciences, % Biological and Biomedical Sciences
Expenses: 2018-2019: $33,180; room/board: $13,200
Financial aid: (716) 286-8686; 1% of undergrads determined to have financial need; average aid package $26,503

Nyack College

Nyack NY
845) 675-4401
U.S. News ranking: Reg. U. (N), second tier
Website: www.nyack.edu
Admissions email: admissions@nyack.edu
Private; founded 1882
Affiliation: Christ and Missionary Alliance Church
Freshman admissions: less selective; 2017-2018: 435 applied, 428 accepted. Neither SAT nor ACT required. SAT 25/75 percentile: 860-1110. High school rank: 5% in top tenth, 16% in top quarter, 38% in top half
Early decision deadline: N/A, notification date: N/A
Early action deadline: N/A, notification date: N/A
Application deadline (fall): rolling
Undergraduate student body: 1,131 full time, 267 part time; 42% male, 58% female; 1% American Indian, 8% Asian, 30% black, 29% Hispanic, 2% multiracial, 1% Pacific Islander, 21% white, 6% international; 65% from in state; N/A live on campus; N/A of students in fraternities, N/A in sororities
Most popular majors: 38% Business, Management, Marketing, and Related Support Services, 14% Theology and Religious Vocations, 11% Multi/Interdisciplinary Studies, 8% Psychology, 6% Public Administration and Social Service Professions
Expenses: 2018-2019: $25,350; room/board: $9,450
Financial aid: (845) 675-4737

Pace University

New York NY
(212) 346-1323
U.S. News ranking: Nat. U., No. 177
Website: www.pace.edu
Admissions email: undergradadmission@pace.edu
Private; founded 1906
Freshman admissions: selective; 2017-2018: 20,944 applied, 16,662 accepted. Neither SAT nor ACT required. SAT 25/75 percentile: 1040-1220. High school rank: 16% in top tenth, 42% in top quarter, 75% in top half
Early decision deadline: 11/1, notification date: 12/1
Early action deadline: 11/1, notification date: 12/1
Application deadline (fall): 2/15
Undergraduate student body: 7,878 full time, 1,122 part time; 39% male, 61% female; 0% American Indian, 8% Asian, 11% black, 13% Hispanic, 4% multiracial, 0% Pacific Islander, 51% white, 10% international; 59% from in state; 42% live on campus; 4% of students in fraternities, 5% in sororities
Most popular majors: 32% Business, Management, Marketing, and Related Support Services, 14% Communication, Journalism, and Related Programs, 13% Visual and Performing Arts, 10% Health Professions and Related Programs, 7% Psychology
Expenses: 2018-2019: $45,330; room/board: $19,053
Financial aid: (877) 672-1830; 69% of undergrads determined to have financial need; average aid package $33,152

Paul Smith's College

Paul Smiths NY
(888) 873-6570
U.S. News ranking: Reg. Coll. (N), No. 14
Website: www.paulsmiths.edu
Admissions email: admissions@paulsmiths.edu
Private; founded 1946
Freshman admissions: less selective; 2017-2018: 924 applied, 751 accepted. Neither SAT nor ACT required. SAT 25/75 percentile: 860-1100. High school rank: 5% in top tenth, 14% in top quarter, 47% in top half
Early decision deadline: N/A, notification date: N/A
Early action deadline: N/A, notification date: N/A
Application deadline (fall): rolling
Undergraduate student body: 760 full time, 11 part time; 65% male, 35% female; 1% American Indian, 1% Asian, 3% black, 4% Hispanic, 1% multiracial, 0% Pacific Islander, 87% white, 0% international; 67% from in state; 78% live on campus; 0% of students in fraternities, 0% in sororities
Most popular majors: 51% Natural Resources and Conservation, 13% Parks, Recreation, Leisure, and Fitness Studies, 10% Business, Management, Marketing, and Related Support Services, 10% Personal and Culinary Services, 7% Multi/Interdisciplinary Studies
Expenses: 2018-2019: $28,452; room/board: $12,240
Financial aid: (518) 327-6119; 90% of undergrads determined to have financial need; average aid package $24,134

Plaza College[1]

Forest Hills NY
(718) 779-1430
U.S. News ranking: Reg. Coll. (N), unranked
Website: www.plazacollege.edu
Admissions email: N/A
For-profit; founded 1916
Application deadline (fall): N/A
Undergraduate student body: N/A full time, N/A part time
Expenses: 2017-2018: $12,450; room/board: N/A
Financial aid: N/A

Pratt Institute

Brooklyn NY
(718) 636-3514
U.S. News ranking: Arts, unranked
Website: www.pratt.edu
Admissions email: admissions@pratt.edu
Private; founded 1887
Freshman admissions: selective; 2017-2018: 6,044 applied, 3,018 accepted. Neither SAT nor ACT required. SAT 25/75 percentile: 1090-1310. High school rank: N/A
Early decision deadline: N/A, notification date: N/A
Early action deadline: 11/1, notification date: 12/22
Application deadline (fall): 1/5
Undergraduate student body: 3,331 full time, 108 part time; 30% male, 70% female; 0% American Indian, 13% Asian, 4% black, 10% Hispanic, 4% multiracial, 0% Pacific Islander, 39% white, 30% international
Most popular majors: 21% Architecture, 13% Graphic Design, 10% Industrial and Product Design, 10% Interior Design, 8% Fashion/Apparel Design
Expenses: 2018-2019: $51,870; room/board: $12,622
Financial aid: (718) 636-3599; 46% of undergrads determined to have financial need; average aid package $30,560

Purchase College–SUNY

Purchase NY
(914) 251-6300
U.S. News ranking: Nat. Lib. Arts, No. 172
Website: www.purchase.edu
Admissions email: admissions@purchase.edu
Public; founded 1967
Freshman admissions: selective; 2017-2018: 4,056 applied, 3,002 accepted. Neither SAT nor ACT required. SAT 25/75 percentile: 1020-1200. High school rank: N/A
Early decision deadline: N/A, notification date: N/A
Early action deadline: 11/15, notification date: 12/15
Application deadline (fall): 7/15
Undergraduate student body: 3,762 full time, 340 part time; 43% male, 57% female; 0% American Indian, 4% Asian, 12% black, 22% Hispanic, 5% multiracial, 0% Pacific Islander, 53% white, 3% international; 85% from in state; 67% live on campus; 0% of students in fraternities, 0% in sororities
Most popular majors: 44% Visual and Performing Arts, 17% Liberal Arts and Sciences, General Studies and Humanities, 10% Social Sciences, 8% Communication, Journalism, and Related Programs, 6% Psychology
Expenses: 2018-2019: $8,498 in state, $18,148 out of state; room/board: $13,334
Financial aid: (914) 251-6354; 65% of undergrads determined to have financial need; average aid package $10,660

Rensselaer Polytechnic Institute

Troy NY
(518) 276-6216
U.S. News ranking: Nat. U., No. 49
Website: www.rpi.edu
Admissions email: admissions@rpi.edu
Private; founded 1824
Freshman admissions: more selective; 2017-2018: 19,505 applied, 8,420 accepted. Either SAT or ACT required. SAT 25/75 percentile: 1320-1500. High school rank: 63% in top tenth, 91% in top quarter, 98% in top half
Early decision deadline: 11/1, notification date: 12/10
Early action deadline: N/A, notification date: N/A
Application deadline (fall): 2/1
Undergraduate student body: 6,340 full time, 26 part time; 68% male, 32% female; 0% American Indian, 12% Asian, 4% black, 9% Hispanic, 7% multiracial, 0% Pacific Islander, 53% white, 14% international; 33% from in state; 57% live on campus; 30% of students in fraternities, 16% in sororities
Most popular majors: 55% Engineering, 13% Computer and Information Sciences and Support Services, 5% Business, Management, Marketing, and Related Support Services, 5% Engineering Technologies and Engineering-Related Fields, 5% Mathematics and Statistics
Expenses: 2018-2019: $53,880; room/board: $15,260
Financial aid: (518) 276-6813; 58% of undergrads determined to have financial need; average aid package $40,405

Roberts Wesleyan College

Rochester NY
(585) 594-6400
U.S. News ranking: Reg. U. (N), No. 93
Website: www.roberts.edu
Admissions email: admissions@roberts.edu
Private; founded 1866
Affiliation: Free Methodist
Freshman admissions: selective; 2017-2018: 1,330 applied, 916 accepted. Either SAT or ACT required. SAT 25/75 percentile: 1040-1230. High school rank: 20% in top tenth, 48% in top quarter, 83% in top half
Early decision deadline: N/A, notification date: N/A
Early action deadline: N/A, notification date: N/A
Application deadline (fall): 8/20
Undergraduate student body: 1,248 full time, 73 part time; 31% male, 69% female; 0% American Indian, 2% Asian, 9% black, 6% Hispanic, 3% multiracial, 0% Pacific Islander, 74% white, 4% international; 91% from in state; 61% live on campus; 0% of students in fraternities, 0% in sororities
Most popular majors: 38% Health Professions and Related Programs, 21% Business, Management, Marketing, and Related Support Services, 9% Education, 7% Public Administration and Social Service Professions, 5% Psychology
Expenses: 2018-2019: $31,568; room/board: $10,628
Financial aid: (585) 594-6150; 83% of undergrads determined to have financial need; average aid package $22,500

Rochester Institute of Technology

Rochester NY
(585) 475-6631
U.S. News ranking: Nat. U., No. 102
Website: www.rit.edu
Admissions email: admissions@rit.edu
Private; founded 1829
Freshman admissions: more selective; 2017-2018: 20,451 applied, 11,599 accepted. Either SAT or ACT required. SAT 25/75 percentile: 1190-1380. High school rank: 40% in top tenth, 74% in top quarter, 95% in top half
Early decision deadline: 11/15, notification date: 12/15
Early action deadline: N/A, notification date: N/A
Application deadline (fall): rolling
Undergraduate student body: 11,361 full time, 1,068 part time; 67% male, 33% female; 0% American Indian, 9% Asian, 5% black, 8% Hispanic, 4% multiracial, 0% Pacific Islander,

66% white, 7% international; 52% from in state; 52% live on campus; 4% of students in fraternities, 2% in sororities
Most popular majors: 22% Engineering, 16% Computer and Information Sciences and Support Services, 13% Visual and Performing Arts, 11% Engineering Technologies and Engineering-Related Fields, 10% Business, Management, Marketing, and Related Support Services
Expenses: 2018-2019: $44,130; room/board: $13,046
Financial aid: (585) 475-2186; 74% of undergrads determined to have financial need; average aid package $26,000

The Sage Colleges

Troy NY
(888) 837-9724
U.S. News ranking: Reg. U. (N), No. 93
Website: www.sage.edu
Admissions email: tscadm@sage.edu
Private; founded 1916
Freshman admissions: selective; 2017-2018: 1,813 applied, 1,008 accepted. Neither SAT nor ACT required. SAT 25/75 percentile: 980-1170. High school rank: 15% in top tenth, 50% in top quarter, 87% in top half
Early decision deadline: N/A, notification date: N/A
Early action deadline: N/A, notification date: N/A
Application deadline (fall): rolling
Undergraduate student body: 1,159 full time, 161 part time; 21% male, 79% female; 0% American Indian, 3% Asian, 13% black, 9% Hispanic, 3% multiracial, 0% Pacific Islander, 64% white, 0% international; 92% from in state; 52% live on campus; N/A of students in fraternities, N/A in sororities
Most popular majors: 28% Health Professions and Related Programs, 11% Biological and Biomedical Sciences, 11% Business, Management, Marketing, and Related Support Services, 10% Social Sciences, 9% Visual and Performing Arts
Expenses: 2018-2019: $30,857; room/board: $12,618
Financial aid: (518) 244-4525; 89% of undergrads determined to have financial need

Sarah Lawrence College

Bronxville NY
(914) 395-2510
U.S. News ranking: Nat. Lib. Arts, No. 65
Website: www.slc.edu
Admissions email: slcadmit@sarahlawrence.edu
Private; founded 1926
Freshman admissions: more selective; 2017-2018: 3,463 applied, 1,842 accepted. Neither SAT nor ACT required. SAT 25/75 percentile: 1240-1410. High school rank: 25% in top tenth, 67% in top quarter, 89% in top half
Early decision deadline: 11/1, notification date: 12/15
Early action deadline: 11/1, notification date: 12/15
Application deadline (fall): 1/15
Undergraduate student body: 1,384 full time, 15 part time; 29% male, 71% female; 0% American Indian, 5% Asian, 4% black, 9% Hispanic, 7% multiracial, 0% Pacific Islander, 56% white, 13% international; 22% from in state; 84% live on campus; 0% of students in fraternities, 0% in sororities
Most popular majors: 100% Liberal Arts and Sciences, General Studies and Humanities
Expenses: 2018-2019: $55,900; room/board: $15,370
Financial aid: (914) 395-2570; 61% of undergrads determined to have financial need; average aid package $38,437

School of Visual Arts

New York NY
(212) 592-2100
U.S. News ranking: Arts, unranked
Website: www.sva.edu/admissions/undergraduate
Admissions email: admissions@sva.edu
For-profit; founded 1947
Freshman admissions: selective; 2017-2018: 3,708 applied, 2,683 accepted. Neither SAT nor ACT required. SAT 25/75 percentile: 1020-1230. High school rank: N/A
Early decision deadline: N/A, notification date: N/A
Early action deadline: N/A, notification date: N/A
Application deadline (fall): N/A
Undergraduate student body: 3,506 full time, 246 part time; 31% male, 69% female; 0% American Indian, 14% Asian, 4% black, 11% Hispanic, 1% multiracial, 0% Pacific Islander, 24% white, 43% international; 47% from in state; 31% live on campus; 0% of students in fraternities, 0% in sororities
Most popular majors: Information not available
Expenses: 2018-2019: $39,900; room/board: $20,400
Financial aid: (212) 592-2043; 40% of undergrads determined to have financial need; average aid package $19,523

Siena College

Loudonville NY
(888) 287-4362
U.S. News ranking: Nat. Lib. Arts, No. 135
Website: www.siena.edu
Admissions email: admissions@siena.edu
Private; founded 1937
Affiliation: Roman Catholic
Freshman admissions: selective; 2017-2018: 9,146 applied, 5,937 accepted. Neither SAT nor ACT required. SAT 25/75 percentile: 1060-1250. High school rank: 22% in top tenth, 49% in top quarter, 85% in top half
Early decision deadline: 12/1, notification date: 1/1
Early action deadline: 2/15, notification date: 3/15
Application deadline (fall): 2/15
Undergraduate student body: 3,039 full time, 135 part time; 47% male, 53% female; 0% American Indian, 4% Asian, 3% black, 8% Hispanic, 2% multiracial, 0% Pacific Islander, 79% white, 2% international; 82% from in state; 77% live on campus; 0% of students in fraternities, 0% in sororities
Most popular majors: 15% Biology Technician/Biotechnology Laboratory Technician, 14% Accounting, 11% Marketing/Marketing Management, General, 9% Management Science, 7% Finance, General
Expenses: 2018-2019: $36,975; room/board: $15,000
Financial aid: (518) 783-2427; 75% of undergrads determined to have financial need; average aid package $30,553

Skidmore College

Saratoga Springs NY
(518) 580-5570
U.S. News ranking: Nat. Lib. Arts, No. 41
Website: www.skidmore.edu
Admissions email: admissions@skidmore.edu
Private; founded 1903
Freshman admissions: more selective; 2017-2018: 10,053 applied, 2,465 accepted. Neither SAT nor ACT required. SAT 25/75 percentile: 1205-1400. High school rank: 29% in top tenth, 73% in top quarter, 92% in top half
Early decision deadline: 11/15, notification date: 12/15
Early action deadline: N/A, notification date: N/A
Application deadline (fall): 1/15
Undergraduate student body: 2,636 full time, 44 part time; 40% male, 60% female; 0% American Indian, 5% Asian, 5% black, 9% Hispanic, 4% multiracial, 0% Pacific Islander, 63% white, 11% international; 34% from in state; 89% live on campus; 0% of students in fraternities, 0% in sororities
Most popular majors: 18% Social Sciences, 14% Business, Management, Marketing, and Related Support Services, 13% Visual and Performing Arts, 10% Biological and Biomedical Sciences, 9% Psychology
Expenses: 2018-2019: $54,270; room/board: $14,494
Financial aid: (518) 580-5750; 42% of undergrads determined to have financial need; average aid package $49,300

St. Bonaventure University

St. Bonaventure NY
(800) 462-5050
U.S. News ranking: Reg. U. (N), No. 22
Website: www.sbu.edu
Admissions email: admissions@sbu.edu
Private; founded 1858
Affiliation: Roman Catholic
Freshman admissions: selective; 2017-2018: 2,986 applied, 2,106 accepted. Either SAT or ACT required. SAT 25/75 percentile: 1020-1220. High school rank: 21% in top tenth, 47% in top quarter, 76% in top half
Early decision deadline: N/A, notification date: N/A
Early action deadline: N/A, notification date: N/A
Application deadline (fall): 7/1
Undergraduate student body: 1,591 full time, 36 part time; 52% male, 48% female; 0% American Indian, 4% Asian, 6% black, 8% Hispanic, 2% multiracial, 0% Pacific Islander, 70% white, 3% international; 68% from in state; 80% live on campus; 0% of students in fraternities, 0% in sororities
Most popular majors: 15% Journalism, 12% Biology/Biological Sciences, General, 9% Psychology, General, 8% Business/Commerce, General, 7% Digital Communication and Media/Multimedia
Expenses: 2018-2019: $34,301; room/board: $12,170
Financial aid: (716) 375-2020; 74% of undergrads determined to have financial need; average aid package $27,746

St. Francis College

Brooklyn Heights NY
(718) 489-5200
U.S. News ranking: Reg. Coll. (N), No. 10
Website: www.sfc.edu
Admissions email: admissions@sfc.edu
Private; founded 1884
Freshman admissions: selective; 2017-2018: 3,447 applied, 2,179 accepted. Either SAT or ACT required. SAT 25/75 percentile: 950-1120. High school rank: N/A
Early decision deadline: N/A, notification date: N/A
Early action deadline: N/A, notification date: N/A
Application deadline (fall): rolling
Undergraduate student body: 2,098 full time, 191 part time; 41% male, 59% female; 1% American Indian, 4% Asian, 19% black, 22% Hispanic, 3% multiracial, 1% Pacific Islander, 39% white, 6% international; 97% from in state; 4% live on campus; 2% of students in fraternities, 2% in sororities
Most popular majors: 13% Communication and Media Studies, 12% Accounting and Related Services, 12% Business Administration, Management and Operations, 8% Psychology, General, 6% Criminal Justice and Corrections
Expenses: 2018-2019: $26,188; room/board: $15,200
Financial aid: (718) 489-5259; 74% of undergrads determined to have financial need; average aid package $16,961

St. John Fisher College

Rochester NY
(585) 385-8064
U.S. News ranking: Nat. U., No. 152
Website: www.sjfc.edu
Admissions email: admissions@sjfc.edu
Private; founded 1948
Affiliation: Roman Catholic
Freshman admissions: selective; 2017-2018: 4,432 applied, 2,860 accepted. Either SAT or ACT required. SAT 25/75 percentile: 1060-1230. High school rank: 16% in top tenth, 52% in top quarter, 86% in top half
Early decision deadline: 12/1, notification date: 1/15
Early action deadline: N/A, notification date: N/A
Application deadline (fall): rolling
Undergraduate student body: 2,63[illegible] full time, 129 part time; 40% male, 60% female; 0% American Indian, 3% Asian, 4% black, 5% Hispanic, 2% multiracial, 0% Pacific Islander, 84% white, 0% international; 97% from in state; 51% live on campus; 0% of students in fraternities, 0% in sororities
Most popular majors: 33% Business, Management, Marketing, and Related Support Services, 29% Health Professions and Related Programs, 8% Biological and Biomedical Sciences, 5% Psychology, 5% Social Sciences
Expenses: 2018-2019: $34,310; room/board: $12,400
Financial aid: (585) 385-8042; 82% of undergrads determined to have financial need; average aid package $23,140

St. John's University

Queens NY
(718) 990-2000
U.S. News ranking: Nat. U., No. 152
Website: www.stjohns.edu/
Admissions email: admhelp@stjohns.edu
Private; founded 1870
Affiliation: Roman Catholic
Freshman admissions: selective; 2017-2018: 27,179 applied, 18,408 accepted. Neither SAT nor ACT required. SAT 25/75 percentile: 1060-1250. High school rank: 16% in top tenth, 43% in top quarter, 77% in top half
Early decision deadline: 11/15, notification date: 12/15
Early action deadline: 12/15, notification date: 1/15
Application deadline (fall): rolling
Undergraduate student body: 11,531 full time, 5,235 part time; 42% male, 58% female; 1% American Indian, 16% Asian, 17% black, 8% Hispanic, 5% multiracial, 0% Pacific Islander, 40% white, 5% international; 75% from in state; 26% live on campus; 10% of students in fraternities, 9% in sororities
Most popular majors: 23% Business, Management, Marketing, and Related Support Services, 11% Communication, Journalism, and Related Programs, 11% Health Professions and Related Programs, 8% Biological and Biomedical Sciences, 7% Homeland Security, Law Enforcement, Firefighting and Related Protective Services
Expenses: 2018-2019: $41,76[illegible]; room/board: $17,280

nancial aid: (718) 990-2000; 8% of undergrads determined to ave financial need; average aid ackage $28,656

St. Joseph's College New York

rooklyn NY
718) 940-5800
.S. News ranking: Reg. U. (N), o. 62
ebsite: www.sjcny.edu
dmissions email: ngislandas@sjcny.edu
rivate; founded 1916
eshman admissions: selective; 017-2018: 3,959 applied, ,737 accepted. Either SAT ACT required. SAT 25/75 ercentile: 1000-1170. High chool rank: N/A
arly decision deadline: N/A, otification date: N/A
arly action deadline: N/A, otification date: N/A
pplication deadline (fall): rolling
ndergraduate student body: 3,411 ll time, 577 part time; 33% ale, 67% female; 0% American dian, 3% Asian, 9% black, 5% Hispanic, 2% multiracial, % Pacific Islander, 59% white, % international; 98% from in ate; 5% live on campus; N/A students in fraternities, N/A in rorities
ost popular majors: 14% usiness Administration and anagement, General, 14% pecial Education and Teaching, eneral, 7% Criminal Justice/Law nforcement Administration, 7% sychology, General, 7% Rhetoric d Composition
penses: 2018-2019: $27,845; om/board: N/A
nancial aid: (631) 687-2600;)% of undergrads determined to ve financial need; average aid ckage $15,196

t. Lawrence niversity

nton NY
15) 229-5261
S. News ranking: Nat. Lib. Arts,). 56
ebsite: www.stlawu.edu
missions email: lmissions@stlawu.edu
ivate; founded 1856
eshman admissions: more lective; 2017-2018: 5,866 plied, 2,835 accepted. Neither T nor ACT required. SAT /75 percentile: 1170-1355. gh school rank: 46% in top nth, 79% in top quarter, 95% top half
rly decision deadline: 11/1, tification date: N/A
rly action deadline: N/A, tification date: N/A
plication deadline (fall): 2/1
dergraduate student body: 2,372 l time, 42 part time; 44% ale, 56% female; 0% American dian, 1% Asian, 3% black, 5% spanic, 2% multiracial, 0% cific Islander, 78% white, 9% ernational; 40% from in state; % live on campus; 12% of dents in fraternities, 16% in orities

Most popular majors: 30% Social Sciences, 14% Business, Management, Marketing, and Related Support Services, 10% Biological and Biomedical Sciences, 8% Psychology, 6% Mathematics and Statistics
Expenses: 2018-2019: $54,846; room/board: $14,134
Financial aid: (315) 229-5265; 64% of undergrads determined to have financial need; average aid package $44,793

Stony Brook University–SUNY

Stony Brook NY
(631) 632-6868
U.S. News ranking: Nat. U., No. 80
Website: www.stonybrook.edu
Admissions email: enroll@stonybrook.edu
Public; founded 1957
Freshman admissions: more selective; 2017-2018: 35,313 applied, 14,899 accepted. Either SAT or ACT required. SAT 25/75 percentile: 1210-1410. High school rank: 48% in top tenth, 81% in top quarter, 95% in top half
Early decision deadline: N/A, notification date: N/A
Early action deadline: N/A, notification date: N/A
Application deadline (fall): 1/15
Undergraduate student body: 16,212 full time, 1,152 part time; 53% male, 47% female; 0% American Indian, 24% Asian, 7% black, 12% Hispanic, 3% multiracial, 0% Pacific Islander, 33% white, 14% international; 94% from in state; 53% live on campus; 2% of students in fraternities, 2% in sororities
Most popular majors: 20% Health Professions and Related Programs, 14% Biological and Biomedical Sciences, 10% Engineering, 10% Psychology, 9% Business, Management, Marketing, and Related Support Services
Expenses: 2018-2019: $9,624 in state, $26,934 out of state; room/board: $13,698
Financial aid: (631) 632-6840; 56% of undergrads determined to have financial need; average aid package $13,600

St. Thomas Aquinas College

Sparkill NY
(845) 398-4100
U.S. News ranking: Reg. U. (N), No. 126
Website: www.stac.edu
Admissions email: admissions@stac.edu
Private; founded 1952
Affiliation: Roman Catholic
Freshman admissions: less selective; 2017-2018: 1,926 applied, 1,502 accepted. Either SAT or ACT required. SAT 25/75 percentile: 880-1110. High school rank: 7% in top tenth, 23% in top quarter, 67% in top half
Early decision deadline: N/A, notification date: N/A
Early action deadline: N/A, notification date: N/A
Application deadline (fall): rolling
Undergraduate student body: 1,091 full time, 687 part time; 46% male, 54% female; 0% American Indian, 2% Asian, 12% black, 23% Hispanic, 1% multiracial, 0% Pacific Islander, 51% white, 5% international; 79% from in state; 52% live on campus; 0% of students in fraternities, 0% in sororities
Most popular majors: 17% Business Administration and Management, General, 11% Psychology, General, 10% Criminal Justice/Law Enforcement Administration, 7% Special Education and Teaching, General, 6% Sport and Fitness Administration/Management
Expenses: 2018-2019: $31,950; room/board: $13,250
Financial aid: (845) 398-4097; 76% of undergrads determined to have financial need; average aid package $18,100

SUNY Buffalo State

Buffalo NY
(716) 878-4017
U.S. News ranking: Reg. U. (N), No. 103
Website: www.buffalostate.edu
Admissions email: admissions@buffalostate.edu
Public
Freshman admissions: less selective; 2017-2018: 14,663 applied, 8,440 accepted. Either SAT or ACT required. SAT 25/75 percentile: 870-1070. High school rank: N/A
Early decision deadline: N/A, notification date: N/A
Early action deadline: N/A, notification date: N/A
Application deadline (fall): rolling
Undergraduate student body: 7,665 full time, 862 part time; 44% male, 56% female; 0% American Indian, 3% Asian, 34% black, 13% Hispanic, 3% multiracial, 0% Pacific Islander, 45% white, 1% international; 98% from in state; 29% live on campus; 1% of students in fraternities, 1% in sororities
Most popular majors: 15% Business, Management, Marketing, and Related Support Services, 10% Homeland Security, Law Enforcement, Firefighting and Related Protective Services, 9% Education, 8% Social Sciences, 7% Liberal Arts and Sciences, General Studies and Humanities
Expenses: 2018-2019: $8,210 in state, $17,990 out of state; room/board: $14,130
Financial aid: (716) 878-4902; 93% of undergrads determined to have financial need; average aid package $12,945

SUNY College–Cortland

Cortland NY
(607) 753-4711
U.S. News ranking: Reg. U. (N), No. 68
Website: www2.cortland.edu/home/
Admissions email: admissions@cortland.edu
Public; founded 1868
Freshman admissions: selective; 2017-2018: 11,909 applied, 5,708 accepted. Neither SAT nor ACT required. SAT 25/75 percentile: 1050-1200. High school rank: 11% in top tenth, 42% in top quarter, 89% in top half
Early decision deadline: N/A, notification date: N/A
Early action deadline: 11/15, notification date: 1/1
Application deadline (fall): rolling
Undergraduate student body: 6,196 full time, 150 part time; 44% male, 56% female; 0% American Indian, 1% Asian, 6% black, 13% Hispanic, 2% multiracial, 0% Pacific Islander, 73% white, 1% international
Most popular majors: 21% Education, 20% Parks, Recreation, Leisure, and Fitness Studies, 11% Health Professions and Related Programs, 10% Social Sciences, 9% Business, Management, Marketing, and Related Support Services
Expenses: 2018-2019: $8,300 in state, $17,950 out of state; room/board: $12,810
Financial aid: (607) 753-4717

SUNY College of Agriculture and Technology–Cobleskill

Cobleskill NY
(518) 255-5525
U.S. News ranking: Reg. Coll. (N), No. 14
Website: www.cobleskill.edu
Admissions email: admissionsoffice@cobleskill.edu
Public; founded 1911
Freshman admissions: less selective; 2017-2018: 3,089 applied, 2,912 accepted. Neither SAT nor ACT required. ACT 25/75 percentile: 17-22. High school rank: 4% in top tenth, 21% in top quarter, 51% in top half
Early decision deadline: N/A, notification date: N/A
Early action deadline: N/A, notification date: N/A
Application deadline (fall): rolling
Undergraduate student body: 2,190 full time, 108 part time; 48% male, 52% female; 1% American Indian, 2% Asian, 13% black, 4% Hispanic, 0% multiracial, 0% Pacific Islander, 67% white, 1% international; 90% from in state; 58% live on campus; 0% of students in fraternities, 0% in sororities
Most popular majors: 19% Business, Management, Marketing, and Related Support Services, Other, 18% Agricultural Animal Breeding, 11% Agribusiness/Agricultural Business Operations, 6% Business, Management, Marketing, and Related Support Services, Other, 6% Wildlife, Fish and Wildlands Science and Management
Expenses: 2018-2019: $8,162 in state, $17,812 out of state; room/board: $13,862
Financial aid: (518) 255-5637; 79% of undergrads determined to have financial need; average aid package $7,472

SUNY College of Environmental Science and Forestry

Syracuse NY
(315) 470-6600
U.S. News ranking: Nat. U., No. 106
Website: www.esf.edu
Admissions email: esfinfo@esf.edu
Public; founded 1911
Freshman admissions: more selective; 2017-2018: 1,815 applied, 948 accepted. Either SAT or ACT required. SAT 25/75 percentile: 1150-1300. High school rank: 32% in top tenth, 62% in top quarter, 95% in top half
Early decision deadline: 12/1, notification date: 1/15
Early action deadline: N/A, notification date: N/A
Application deadline (fall): rolling
Undergraduate student body: 1,737 full time, 55 part time; 53% male, 47% female; 0% American Indian, 4% Asian, 2% black, 6% Hispanic, 3% multiracial, 0% Pacific Islander, 80% white, 2% international; 85% from in state; 35% live on campus; 2% of students in fraternities, 2% in sororities
Most popular majors: 43% Natural Resources and Conservation, 38% Biological and Biomedical Sciences, 9% Engineering, 6% Business, Management, Marketing, and Related Support Services, 4% Natural Resources and Conservation
Expenses: 2018-2019: $8,568 in state, $18,218 out of state; room/board: $16,140
Financial aid: (315) 470-6670; 60% of undergrads determined to have financial need; average aid package $10,160

SUNY College of Technology–Alfred

Alfred NY
(800) 425-3733
U.S. News ranking: Reg. Coll. (N), No. 12
Website: www.alfredstate.edu
Admissions email: admissions@alfredstate.edu
Public; founded 1908
Freshman admissions: selective; 2017-2018: 5,395 applied, 3,650 accepted. Neither SAT nor ACT required. SAT 25/75 percentile: 940-1130. High school rank: N/A
Early decision deadline: N/A, notification date: N/A
Early action deadline: N/A, notification date: N/A
Application deadline (fall): rolling
Undergraduate student body: 3,396 full time, 290 part time; 64% male, 36% female; 0% American Indian, 1% Asian, 12% black, 9% Hispanic, 3% multiracial, 0% Pacific Islander, 72% white, 1% international; 96% from in state; 65% live on campus; 5% of students in fraternities, 9% in sororities
Most popular majors: 41% Business, Management, Marketing, and Related Support Services, 26% Engineering Technologies and Engineering-Related Fields, 11% Health Professions and

Related Programs, 8% Computer and Information Sciences and Support Services, 6% Homeland Security, Law Enforcement, Firefighting and Related Protective Services
Expenses: 2018-2019: $8,327 in state, $11,397 out of state; room/board: $12,250
Financial aid: (607) 587-4253; 80% of undergrads determined to have financial need; average aid package $10,778

SUNY College of Technology–Canton

Canton NY
(800) 388-7123
U.S. News ranking: Reg. Coll. (N), No. 26
Website: www.canton.edu/
Admissions email: admissions@canton.edu
Public; founded 1906
Freshman admissions: less selective; 2017-2018: 3,672 applied, 2,886 accepted. Neither SAT nor ACT required. SAT 25/75 percentile: 880-1080. High school rank: 5% in top tenth, 20% in top quarter, 51% in top half
Early decision deadline: N/A, notification date: N/A
Early action deadline: N/A, notification date: N/A
Application deadline (fall): rolling
Undergraduate student body: 2,657 full time, 523 part time; 41% male, 59% female; 1% American Indian, 1% Asian, 15% black, 11% Hispanic, 3% multiracial, 0% Pacific Islander, 65% white, 2% international; 97% from in state; 39% live on campus; 1% of students in fraternities, 2% in sororities
Most popular majors: 14% Corrections and Criminal Justice, Other, 10% Business Administration and Management, General, 9% Registered Nursing/Registered Nurse, 7% Business, Management, Marketing, and Related Support Services, Other, 7% Health/Health Care Administration/Management
Expenses: 2018-2019: $8,389 in state, $18,169 out of state; room/board: $12,900
Financial aid: (315) 386-7616; 86% of undergrads determined to have financial need; average aid package $11,131

SUNY College of Technology–Delhi

Delhi NY
(607) 746-4550
U.S. News ranking: Reg. Coll. (N), No. 18
Website: www.delhi.edu/
Admissions email: enroll@delhi.edu
Public; founded 1913
Freshman admissions: less selective; 2017-2018: 6,206 applied, 3,889 accepted. Either SAT or ACT required. SAT 25/75 percentile: 900-1120. High school rank: 4% in top tenth, 17% in top quarter, 49% in top half
Early decision deadline: N/A, notification date: N/A
Early action deadline: 12/1, notification date: 12/15
Application deadline (fall): rolling
Undergraduate student body: 2,704 full time, 765 part time; 44% male, 56% female; 0% American Indian, 3% Asian, 17% black, 14% Hispanic, 1% multiracial, 0% Pacific Islander, 60% white, 1% international; 97% from in state; 52% live on campus; 10% of students in fraternities, 7% in sororities
Most popular majors: 46% Health Professions and Related Programs, 37% Business, Management, Marketing, and Related Support Services, 6% Construction Trades, 5% Personal and Culinary Services, 4% Architecture and Related Services
Expenses: 2018-2019: $8,360 in state, $12,330 out of state; room/board: $12,360
Financial aid: (607) 746-4570; 79% of undergrads determined to have financial need; average aid package $10,458

SUNY College–Old Westbury

Old Westbury NY
(516) 876-3073
U.S. News ranking: Reg. U. (N), second tier
Website: www.oldwestbury.edu
Admissions email: enroll@oldwestbury.edu
Public; founded 1965
Freshman admissions: less selective; 2017-2018: 3,752 applied, 2,935 accepted. Either SAT or ACT required. SAT 25/75 percentile: 950-1100. High school rank: N/A
Early decision deadline: N/A, notification date: N/A
Early action deadline: N/A, notification date: N/A
Application deadline (fall): rolling
Undergraduate student body: 4,058 full time, 577 part time; 41% male, 59% female; 1% American Indian, 11% Asian, 29% black, 26% Hispanic, 0% multiracial, 0% Pacific Islander, 29% white, 1% international; 98% from in state; 19% live on campus; 5% of students in fraternities, 5% in sororities
Most popular majors: 14% Sociology, 11% Accounting, 10% Business Administration and Management, General, 9% Speech Communication and Rhetoric, 7% Social Sciences, Other
Expenses: 2017-2018: $7,883 in state, $17,533 out of state; room/board: $11,020
Financial aid: N/A

SUNY College–Oneonta

Oneonta NY
(607) 436-2524
U.S. News ranking: Reg. U. (N), No. 55
Website: suny.oneonta.edu/
Admissions email: admissions@oneonta.edu
Public; founded 1889
Freshman admissions: selective; 2017-2018: 11,100 applied, 6,607 accepted. Either SAT or ACT required. SAT 25/75 percentile: 1040-1190. High school rank: 11% in top tenth, 39% in top quarter, 83% in top half
Early decision deadline: N/A, notification date: N/A
Early action deadline: 11/15, notification date: 12/1
Application deadline (fall): rolling
Undergraduate student body: 5,828 full time, 112 part time; 40% male, 60% female; 0% American Indian, 2% Asian, 4% black, 14% Hispanic, 2% multiracial, 0% Pacific Islander, 75% white, 1% international; 99% from in state; 59% live on campus; N/A of students in fraternities, N/A in sororities
Most popular majors: 12% Business, Management, Marketing, and Related Support Services, 12% Communication, Journalism, and Related Programs, 11% Family and Consumer Sciences/Human Sciences, 11% Psychology, 10% Education
Expenses: 2018-2019: $8,421 in state, $17,871 out of state; room/board: $13,205
Financial aid: N/A; 61% of undergrads determined to have financial need; average aid package $15,505

SUNY College–Potsdam

Potsdam NY
(315) 267-2180
U.S. News ranking: Reg. U. (N), No. 87
Website: www.potsdam.edu
Admissions email: admissions@potsdam.edu
Public; founded 1816
Freshman admissions: selective; 2017-2018: 5,581 applied, 3,717 accepted. Neither SAT nor ACT required. SAT 25/75 percentile: 1000-1190. High school rank: 6% in top tenth, 35% in top quarter, 59% in top half
Early decision deadline: N/A, notification date: N/A
Early action deadline: N/A, notification date: N/A
Application deadline (fall): rolling
Undergraduate student body: 3,196 full time, 125 part time; 42% male, 58% female; 2% American Indian, 2% Asian, 13% black, 15% Hispanic, 2% multiracial, 0% Pacific Islander, 61% white, 1% international; 96% from in state; 58% live on campus; 4% of students in fraternities, 5% in sororities
Most popular majors: 15% Visual and Performing Arts, 12% Education, 10% Psychology, 9% Business, Management, Marketing, and Related Support Services, 9% Social Sciences
Expenses: 2017-2018: $8,221 in state, $17,871 out of state; room/board: $12,830
Financial aid: (315) 267-2162; 78% of undergrads determined to have financial need; average aid package $16,750

SUNY Empire State College

Saratoga Springs NY
(518) 587-2100
U.S. News ranking: Reg. U. (N), unranked
Website: www.esc.edu
Admissions email: admissions@esc.edu
Public; founded 1971
Freshman admissions: least selective; 2017-2018: 1,081 applied, 907 accepted. Neither SAT nor ACT required. SAT 25/75 percentile: N/A. High school rank: N/A
Early decision deadline: N/A, notification date: N/A
Early action deadline: N/A, notification date: N/A
Application deadline (fall): rolling
Undergraduate student body: 3,773 full time, 6,066 part time; 38% male, 62% female; 0% American Indian, 3% Asian, 16% black, 14% Hispanic, 2% multiracial, 0% Pacific Islander, 62% white, 0% international; 95% from in state; N/A live on campus; N/A of students in fraternities, N/A in sororities
Most popular majors: 35% Business, Management, Marketing, and Related Support Services, 26% Public Administration and Social Service Professions, 8% Health Professions and Related Programs, 8% Psychology, 6% Physical Sciences
Expenses: 2017-2018: $7,185 in state, $16,835 out of state; room/board: N/A
Financial aid: N/A

SUNY–Fredonia

Fredonia NY
(800) 252-1212
U.S. News ranking: Reg. U. (N), No. 50
Website: www.fredonia.edu
Admissions email: admissions@fredonia.edu
Public; founded 1826
Freshman admissions: selective; 2017-2018: 5,474 applied, 3,553 accepted. Either SAT or ACT required. SAT 25/75 percentile: 980-1190. High school rank: 15% in top tenth, 35% in top quarter, 68% in top half
Early decision deadline: N/A, notification date: N/A
Early action deadline: N/A, notification date: N/A
Application deadline (fall): rolling
Undergraduate student body: 4,279 full time, 113 part time; 42% male, 58% female; 1% American Indian, 2% Asian, 8% black, 9% Hispanic, 3% multiracial, 0% Pacific Islander, 74% white, 2% international; 97% from in state; 50% live on campus; 86% of students in fraternities, 4% in sororities
Most popular majors: 18% Business, Management, Marketing, and Related Support Services, 14% Education, 13% Visual and Performing Arts, 11% Communication, Journalism, and Related Programs, 5% Multi/Interdisciplinary Studies
Expenses: 2018-2019: $8,286 in state, $17,936 out of state; room/board: $12,590
Financial aid: (716) 673-3253; 73% of undergrads determined to have financial need; average aid package $11,791

SUNY–Geneseo

Geneseo NY
(585) 245-5571
U.S. News ranking: Reg. U. (N), No. 14
Website: www.geneseo.edu
Admissions email: admissions@geneseo.edu
Public; founded 1871
Freshman admissions: more selective; 2017-2018: 8,789 applied, 6,360 accepted. Either SAT or ACT required. SAT 25/75 percentile: 1120-1300. High school rank: 28% in top tenth, 64% in top quarter, 93% in top half
Early decision deadline: 11/15, notification date: 12/15
Early action deadline: N/A, notification date: N/A
Application deadline (fall): 1/1
Undergraduate student body: 5,391 full time, 104 part time; 40% male, 60% female; 0% American Indian, 6% Asian, 3% black, 8% Hispanic, 3% multiracial, 0% Pacific Islander, 76% white, 2% international; 98% from in state; 54% live on campus; 23% of students in fraternities, 33% in sororities
Most popular majors: 19% Social Sciences, 14% Business, Management, Marketing, and Related Support Services, 14% Psychology, 11% Biological and Biomedical Sciences, 10% Education
Expenses: 2018-2019: $8,651 in state, $18,431 out of state; room/board: $13,610
Financial aid: (585) 245-5731; 52% of undergrads determined to have financial need; average aid package $9,946

SUNY Maritime College

Throggs Neck NY
(718) 409-7221
U.S. News ranking: Reg. U. (N), No. 74
Website: www.sunymaritime.edu
Admissions email: admissions@sunymaritime.edu
Public; founded 1874
Freshman admissions: selective; 2017-2018: 1,272 applied, 884 accepted. Either SAT or ACT required. SAT 25/75 percentile: 1100-1253. High school rank: 33% in top tenth, 33% in top quarter, 67% in top half
Early decision deadline: 11/1, notification date: 12/15
Early action deadline: N/A, notification date: N/A
Application deadline (fall): 1/31
Undergraduate student body: 1,581 full time, 60 part time; 88% male, 12% female; 0% American Indian, 5% Asian, 4% black, 13% Hispanic, 3% multiracial, 0% Pacific Islander, 71% white, 2% international; 76% from in state; 83% live on campus; N/A of students in fraternities, N/A in sororities
Most popular majors: 41% Marine Science/Merchant Marine Officer, 16% Business, Management, Marketing, and Related Support Services, Other, 14% Mechanical Engineering, 13% Naval Architecture and Marine

More @ usnews.com/bestcollege

Engineering, 6% Electrical and Electronics Engineering
Expenses: 2018-2019: $8,283 in state, $17,733 out of state; room/board: $12,522
Financial aid: (718) 409-7400; 53% of undergrads determined to have financial need; average aid package $4,667

SUNY–Morrisville

Morrisville NY
(315) 684-6046
U.S. News ranking: Reg. Coll. (N), No. 26
Website: www.morrisville.edu
Admissions email: admissions@morrisville.edu
Public; founded 1908
Freshman admissions: less selective; 2017-2018: 4,766 applied, 3,409 accepted. Neither SAT nor ACT required. SAT 25/75 percentile: 910-1100. High school rank: 4% in top tenth, 16% in top quarter, 46% in top half
Early decision deadline: N/A, notification date: N/A
Early action deadline: N/A, notification date: N/A
Application deadline (fall): 8/17
Undergraduate student body: 2,614 full time, 449 part time; 50% male, 50% female; 0% American Indian, 1% Asian, 18% black, 9% Hispanic, 2% multiracial, 0% Pacific Islander, 67% white, 1% international; 94% from in state; 54% live on campus; 0% of students in fraternities, 0% in sororities
Most popular majors: 25% Agriculture, Agriculture Operations, and Related Sciences, 23% Homeland Security, Law Enforcement, Firefighting and Related Protective Services, 13% Business, Management, Marketing, and Related Support Services, 11% Computer and Information Sciences and Support Services, 8% Mechanic and Repair Technologies/Technicians
Expenses: 2018-2019: $8,270 in state, $13,340 out of state; room/board: $15,600
Financial aid: (315) 684-6289; 85% of undergrads determined to have financial need; average aid package $10,161

SUNY–New Paltz

New Paltz NY
(845) 257-3200
U.S. News ranking: Reg. U. (N), No. 41
Website: www.newpaltz.edu
Admissions email: admissions@newpaltz.edu
Public; founded 1828
Freshman admissions: more selective; 2017-2018: 13,753 applied, 6,092 accepted. Either SAT or ACT required. SAT 25/75 percentile: 1100-1260. High school rank: 31% in top tenth, 69% in top quarter, 93% in top half
Early decision deadline: N/A, notification date: N/A
Early action deadline: 11/15, notification date: 12/15
Application deadline (fall): 4/1
Undergraduate student body: 6,235 full time, 498 part time; 39% male, 61% female; 0% American Indian, 5% Asian, 6% black, 20% Hispanic, 3% multiracial, 0% Pacific Islander, 62% white, 2% international; 97% from in state; 46% live on campus; 5% of students in fraternities, 5% in sororities
Most popular majors: 19% Education, 15% Business, Management, Marketing, and Related Support Services, 11% Communication, Journalism, and Related Programs, 10% Social Sciences, 10% Visual and Performing Arts
Expenses: 2018-2019: $8,254 in state, $18,034 out of state; room/board: $13,462
Financial aid: (845) 257-3256; 61% of undergrads determined to have financial need; average aid package $11,568

SUNY–Oswego

Oswego NY
(315) 312-2250
U.S. News ranking: Reg. U. (N), No. 48
Website: www.oswego.edu
Admissions email: admiss@oswego.edu
Public; founded 1861
Freshman admissions: selective; 2017-2018: 11,727 applied, 6,292 accepted. Either SAT or ACT required. SAT 25/75 percentile: 1075-1225. High school rank: 12% in top tenth, 52% in top quarter, 86% in top half
Early decision deadline: N/A, notification date: N/A
Early action deadline: 11/15, notification date: 12/15
Application deadline (fall): rolling
Undergraduate student body: 6,836 full time, 289 part time; 51% male, 49% female; 0% American Indian, 3% Asian, 9% black, 12% Hispanic, 3% multiracial, 0% Pacific Islander, 71% white, 3% international; 97% from in state; 55% live on campus; 5% of students in fraternities, 4% in sororities
Most popular majors: 10% Business Administration and Management, General, 10% Psychology, General, 7% Mass Communication/Media Studies, 5% Health and Wellness, General, 4% Marketing/Marketing Management, General
Expenses: 2018-2019: $8,440 in state, $18,220 out of state; room/board: $14,140
Financial aid: (315) 312-2248; 69% of undergrads determined to have financial need; average aid package $11,345

SUNY–Plattsburgh

Plattsburgh NY
(888) 673-0012
U.S. News ranking: Reg. U. (N), No. 87
Website: www.plattsburgh.edu
Admissions email: admissions@plattsburgh.edu
Public; founded 1889
Freshman admissions: selective; 2017-2018: 9,643 applied, 5,101 accepted. Either SAT or ACT required. SAT 25/75 percentile: 1050-1190. High school rank: 18% in top tenth, 47% in top quarter, 82% in top half
Early decision deadline: N/A, notification date: N/A
Early action deadline: N/A, notification date: N/A
Application deadline (fall): rolling
Undergraduate student body: 4,894 full time, 457 part time; 43% male, 57% female; 0% American Indian, 3% Asian, 9% black, 12% Hispanic, 2% multiracial, 0% Pacific Islander, 64% white, 6% international; 96% from in state; 48% live on campus; 19% of students in fraternities, 15% in sororities
Most popular majors: 22% Business, Management, Marketing, and Related Support Services, 14% Health Professions and Related Programs, 9% Communication, Journalism, and Related Programs, 9% Psychology, 6% Biological and Biomedical Sciences
Expenses: 2018-2019: $8,164 in state, $17,814 out of state; room/board: $12,988
Financial aid: (518) 564-2072; 67% of undergrads determined to have financial need; average aid package $14,076

SUNY Polytechnic Institute–Albany/Utica

Utica NY
(315) 792-7500
U.S. News ranking: Reg. U. (N), No. 18
Website: www.sunypoly.edu
Admissions email: admissions@sunypoly.edu
Public; founded 1966
Freshman admissions: selective; 2017-2018: 2,984 applied, 1,863 accepted. Either SAT or ACT required. SAT 25/75 percentile: 1000-1290. High school rank: 45% in top tenth, 66% in top quarter, 95% in top half
Early decision deadline: N/A, notification date: N/A
Early action deadline: 11/15, notification date: 12/15
Application deadline (fall): 7/1
Undergraduate student body: 1,860 full time, 324 part time; 66% male, 34% female; 0% American Indian, 6% Asian, 6% black, 9% Hispanic, 3% multiracial, 0% Pacific Islander, 73% white, 1% international; 98% from in state; 44% live on campus; N/A of students in fraternities, N/A in sororities
Most popular majors: 21% Business, Management, Marketing, and Related Support Services, 20% Computer and Information Sciences and Support Services, 20% Engineering Technologies and Engineering-Related Fields, 7% Engineering, 7% Social Sciences
Expenses: 2018-2019: $8,332 in state, $17,782 out of state; room/board: $13,886
Financial aid: (315) 792-7210; 74% of undergrads determined to have financial need; average aid package $11,381

Syracuse University

Syracuse NY
(315) 443-3611
U.S. News ranking: Nat. U., No. 53
Website: www.syracuse.edu
Admissions email: orange@syr.edu
Private; founded 1870
Freshman admissions: more selective; 2017-2018: 33,099 applied, 15,517 accepted. Either SAT or ACT required. SAT 25/75 percentile: 1160-1350. High school rank: 36% in top tenth, 69% in top quarter, 94% in top half
Early decision deadline: 11/15, notification date: 12/15
Early action deadline: N/A, notification date: N/A
Application deadline (fall): 1/1
Undergraduate student body: 14,675 full time, 577 part time; 46% male, 54% female; 1% American Indian, 7% Asian, 7% black, 10% Hispanic, 3% multiracial, 0% Pacific Islander, 57% white, 13% international; 40% from in state; 53% live on campus; 27% of students in fraternities, 40% in sororities
Most popular majors: 14% Communication, Journalism, and Related Programs, 13% Social Sciences, 12% Business, Management, Marketing, and Related Support Services, 11% Visual and Performing Arts, 9% Engineering
Expenses: 2018-2019: $51,853; room/board: $15,550
Financial aid: (315) 443-1513; 47% of undergrads determined to have financial need; average aid package $38,870

Touro College

New York NY
(718) 253-9455
U.S. News ranking: Reg. U. (N), second tier
Website: www.touro.edu/
Admissions email: lasadmit@touro.edu
Private; founded 1971
Freshman admissions: selective; 2017-2018: 2,259 applied, 1,680 accepted. Neither SAT nor ACT required. SAT 25/75 percentile: 1010-1300. High school rank: N/A
Early decision deadline: N/A, notification date: N/A
Early action deadline: N/A, notification date: N/A
Application deadline (fall): rolling
Undergraduate student body: 4,232 full time, 2,194 part time; 29% male, 71% female; 0% American Indian, 3% Asian, 14% black, 10% Hispanic, 1% multiracial, 0% Pacific Islander, 61% white, 5% international; 93% from in state; N/A live on campus; N/A of students in fraternities, N/A in sororities
Most popular majors: 23% Health Professions and Related Programs, 20% Psychology, 14% Business, Management, Marketing, and Related Support Services, 14% Multi/Interdisciplinary Studies, 8% Biological and Biomedical Sciences
Expenses: 2018-2019: $16,953; room/board: $11,200
Financial aid: (646) 565-6000; 91% of undergrads determined to have financial need; average aid package $11,966

Union College

Schenectady NY
(888) 843-6688
U.S. News ranking: Nat. Lib. Arts, No. 39
Website: www.union.edu
Admissions email: admissions@union.edu
Private; founded 1795
Freshman admissions: more selective; 2017-2018: 6,676 applied, 2,495 accepted. Neither SAT nor ACT required. SAT 25/75 percentile: 1270-1430. High school rank: 63% in top tenth, 88% in top quarter, 99% in top half
Early decision deadline: 11/15, notification date: 12/15
Early action deadline: N/A, notification date: N/A
Application deadline (fall): 1/15
Undergraduate student body: 2,176 full time, 91 part time; 54% male, 46% female; 0% American Indian, 6% Asian, 4% black, 7% Hispanic, 3% multiracial, 0% Pacific Islander, 72% white, 7% international; 38% from in state; 90% live on campus; 32% of students in fraternities, 41% in sororities
Most popular majors: 12% Economics, General, 9% Mechanical Engineering, 8% Political Science and Government, General, 8% Psychology, General, 6% Neuroscience
Expenses: 2018-2019: $55,290; room/board: $13,563
Financial aid: (518) 388-6123; 49% of undergrads determined to have financial need; average aid package $44,649

United States Merchant Marine Academy

Kings Point NY
(866) 546-4778
U.S. News ranking: Reg. Coll. (N), No. 3
Website: www.usmma.edu
Admissions email: admissions@usmma.edu
Public; founded 1943
Freshman admissions: more selective; 2017-2018: 1,850 applied, 279 accepted. Either SAT or ACT required. ACT 25/75 percentile: 25-29. High school rank: 22% in top tenth, 64% in top quarter, 96% in top half
Early decision deadline: N/A, notification date: N/A
Early action deadline: N/A, notification date: N/A
Application deadline (fall): 2/1
Undergraduate student body: 954 full time, 0 part time; 83% male, 17% female; 1% American Indian, 8% Asian, 3% black, 10% Hispanic, 0% multiracial, 0% Pacific Islander, 75% white, 1% international
Most popular majors: Information not available
Expenses: 2018-2019: $1,080 in state, $1,080 out of state; room/board: N/A

Financial aid: (516) 726-5638; 11% of undergrads determined to have financial need; average aid package $4,229

United States Military Academy

West Point NY
(845) 938-4041
U.S. News ranking: Nat. Lib. Arts, No. 18
Website: www.usma.edu/SitePages/Home.aspx
Admissions email: admissions-info@usma.edu
Public; founded 1802
Freshman admissions: more selective; 2017-2018: 12,972 applied, 1,240 accepted. Either SAT or ACT required. SAT 25/75 percentile: 1185-1400. High school rank: 46% in top tenth, 74% in top quarter, 94% in top half
Early decision deadline: N/A, notification date: N/A
Early action deadline: N/A, notification date: N/A
Application deadline (fall): 2/28
Undergraduate student body: 4,491 full time, 0 part time; 78% male, 22% female; 1% American Indian, 8% Asian, 12% black, 10% Hispanic, 3% multiracial, 0% Pacific Islander, 62% white, 1% international; 6% from in state; 100% live on campus; 0% of students in fraternities, 0% in sororities
Most popular majors: 26% Engineering, 15% Social Sciences, 10% Business, Management, Marketing, and Related Support Services, 8% Foreign Languages, Literatures, and Linguistics, 5% Engineering Technologies and Engineering-Related Fields
Expenses: 2018-2019: $0 in state, $0 out of state; room/board: $0
Financial aid: N/A; 0% of undergrads determined to have financial need

University at Albany–SUNY

Albany NY
(518) 442-5435
U.S. News ranking: Nat. U., No. 140
Website: www.albany.edu
Admissions email: ugadmissions@albany.edu
Public; founded 1844
Freshman admissions: selective; 2017-2018: 24,887 applied, 13,442 accepted. Either SAT or ACT required. SAT 25/75 percentile: 1000-1190. High school rank: 16% in top tenth, 48% in top quarter, 82% in top half
Early decision deadline: N/A, notification date: N/A
Early action deadline: 11/1, notification date: 1/15
Application deadline (fall): 3/1
Undergraduate student body: 12,740 full time, 768 part time; 49% male, 51% female; 0% American Indian, 8% Asian, 19% black, 17% Hispanic, 3% multiracial, 0% Pacific Islander, 45% white, 5% international; 95% from in state; 56% live on campus; 3% of students in fraternities, 3% in sororities
Most popular majors: 26% Social Sciences, 14% Business, Management, Marketing, and Related Support Services, 12% Biological and Biomedical Sciences, 11% English Language and Literature/Letters, 11% Psychology
Expenses: 2018-2019: $9,756 in state, $24,436 out of state; room/board: $13,882
Financial aid: (518) 442-3202; 68% of undergrads determined to have financial need; average aid package $11,415

University at Buffalo–SUNY

Buffalo NY
(716) 645-6900
U.S. News ranking: Nat. U., No. 89
Website: www.buffalo.edu
Admissions email: ub-admissions@buffalo.edu
Public; founded 1846
Freshman admissions: more selective; 2017-2018: 28,088 applied, 16,128 accepted. Either SAT or ACT required. SAT 25/75 percentile: 1140-1310. High school rank: 38% in top tenth, 73% in top quarter, 94% in top half
Early decision deadline: N/A, notification date: N/A
Early action deadline: 11/15, notification date: N/A
Application deadline (fall): rolling
Undergraduate student body: 19,453 full time, 1,567 part time; 57% male, 43% female; 0% American Indian, 15% Asian, 8% black, 7% Hispanic, 2% multiracial, 0% Pacific Islander, 48% white, 16% international; 98% from in state; 35% live on campus; 2% of students in fraternities, 2% in sororities
Most popular majors: 19% Business, Management, Marketing, and Related Support Services, 17% Social Sciences, 16% Engineering, 11% Psychology, 9% Biological and Biomedical Sciences
Expenses: 2018-2019: $10,028 in state, $27,758 out of state; room/board: $13,723
Financial aid: (716) 645-8232; 55% of undergrads determined to have financial need; average aid package $10,235

University of Rochester

Rochester NY
(585) 275-3221
U.S. News ranking: Nat. U., No. 33
Website: www.rochester.edu
Admissions email: admit@admissions.rochester.edu
Private; founded 1850
Freshman admissions: more selective; 2017-2018: 19,058 applied, 6,520 accepted. Neither SAT nor ACT required. SAT 25/75 percentile: 1300-1490. High school rank: 66% in top tenth, 91% in top quarter, 100% in top half
Early decision deadline: 11/1, notification date: 12/15
Early action deadline: N/A, notification date: N/A
Application deadline (fall): 1/5
Undergraduate student body: 6,250 full time, 296 part time; 50% male, 50% female; 0% American Indian, 11% Asian, 5% black, 7% Hispanic, 3% multiracial, 0% Pacific Islander, 45% white, 24% international; 42% from in state; 76% live on campus; 18% of students in fraternities, 18% in sororities
Most popular majors: 15% Engineering, 14% Social Sciences, 12% Health Professions and Related Programs, 11% Biological and Biomedical Sciences, 9% Visual and Performing Arts
Expenses: 2018-2019: $53,926; room/board: $15,938
Financial aid: (585) 275-3226; 53% of undergrads determined to have financial need; average aid package $47,340

Utica College

Utica NY
(315) 792-3006
U.S. News ranking: Reg. U. (N), No. 120
Website: www.utica.edu
Admissions email: admiss@utica.edu
Private; founded 1946
Freshman admissions: selective; 2017-2018: 5,656 applied, 4,732 accepted. Neither SAT nor ACT required. SAT 25/75 percentile: 980-1180. High school rank: 10% in top tenth, 33% in top quarter, 65% in top half
Early decision deadline: 11/1, notification date: 12/15
Early action deadline: 11/15, notification date: 12/15
Application deadline (fall): rolling
Undergraduate student body: 2,901 full time, 784 part time; 40% male, 60% female; 0% American Indian, 3% Asian, 12% black, 9% Hispanic, 3% multiracial, 0% Pacific Islander, 67% white, 1% international; 81% from in state; 31% live on campus; 2% of students in fraternities, 2% in sororities
Most popular majors: 53% Health Professions and Related Programs, 17% Homeland Security, Law Enforcement, Firefighting and Related Protective Services, 10% Business, Management, Marketing, and Related Support Services, 5% Psychology, 4% Communication, Journalism, and Related Programs
Expenses: 2018-2019: $21,382; room/board: $11,248
Financial aid: (315) 792-3215; 83% of undergrads determined to have financial need; average aid package $13,958

Vassar College

Poughkeepsie NY
(845) 437-7300
U.S. News ranking: Nat. Lib. Arts, No. 11
Website: www.vassar.edu
Admissions email: admissions@vassar.edu
Private; founded 1861
Freshman admissions: most selective; 2017-2018: 7,746 applied, 1,842 accepted. Either SAT or ACT required. SAT 25/75 percentile: 1370-1510. High school rank: 65% in top tenth, 93% in top quarter, 99% in top half
Early decision deadline: 11/15, notification date: 12/15
Early action deadline: N/A, notification date: N/A
Application deadline (fall): 1/1
Undergraduate student body: 2,334 full time, 19 part time; 41% male, 59% female; 0% American Indian, 13% Asian, 4% black, 11% Hispanic, 7% multiracial, 0% Pacific Islander, 57% white, 7% international; 25% from in state; 95% live on campus; 0% of students in fraternities, 0% in sororities
Most popular majors: 27% Social Sciences, 11% Biological and Biomedical Sciences, 11% Visual and Performing Arts, 9% Foreign Languages, Literatures, and Linguistics, 7% Multi/Interdisciplinary Studies
Expenses: 2018-2019: $56,960; room/board: $13,550
Financial aid: (845) 437-5320; 62% of undergrads determined to have financial need; average aid package $53,642

Vaughn College of Aeronautics and Technology

Flushing NY
(718) 429-6600
U.S. News ranking: Reg. Coll. (N), No. 8
Website: www.vaughn.edu
Admissions email: admitme@vaughn.edu
Private; founded 1932
Freshman admissions: less selective; 2017-2018: 711 applied, 643 accepted. Either SAT or ACT required. SAT 25/75 percentile: 921-1100. High school rank: N/A
Early decision deadline: N/A, notification date: N/A
Early action deadline: N/A, notification date: N/A
Application deadline (fall): rolling
Undergraduate student body: 1,228 full time, 268 part time; 87% male, 13% female; 0% American Indian, 11% Asian, 18% black, 33% Hispanic, 2% multiracial, 1% Pacific Islander, 13% white, 5% international; 88% from in state; 11% live on campus; 3% of students in fraternities, 0% in sororities
Most popular majors: 50% Transportation and Materials Moving, 30% Engineering Technologies and Engineering-Related Fields, 10% Engineering, 6% Mechanic and Repair Technologies/Technicians, 4% Business, Management, Marketing, and Related Support Services
Expenses: 2018-2019: $25,550; room/board: $14,550
Financial aid: (718) 429-6600; 78% of undergrads determined to have financial need; average aid package $8,329

Villa Maria College[1]

Buffalo NY
U.S. News ranking: Reg. Coll. (N), unranked
Admissions email: N/A
Private
Application deadline (fall): N/A
Undergraduate student body: N/A full time, N/A part time
Expenses: 2017-2018: $22,080; room/board: $1,150
Financial aid: N/A

Wagner College

Staten Island NY
(718) 390-3411
U.S. News ranking: Reg. U. (N), No. 43
Website: www.wagner.edu
Admissions email: admissions@wagner.edu
Private; founded 1883
Freshman admissions: selective; 2017-2018: 2,834 applied, 1,975 accepted. Neither SAT nor ACT required. SAT 25/75 percentile: 1070-1250. High school rank: 25% in top tenth, 50% in top quarter, 88% in top half
Early decision deadline: N/A, notification date: N/A
Early action deadline: 12/1, notification date: 1/5
Application deadline (fall): 2/15
Undergraduate student body: 1,745 full time, 67 part time; 36% male, 64% female; 0% American Indian, 4% Asian, 8% black, 12% Hispanic, 3% multiracial, 0% Pacific Islander, 64% white, 4% international; 46% from in state; 68% live on campus; 10% of students in fraternities, 7% in sororities
Most popular majors: 33% Health Professions and Related Programs, 17% Business, Management, Marketing, and Related Support Services, 13% Visual and Performing Arts, 9% Multi/Interdisciplinary Studies, 6% Psychology
Expenses: 2018-2019: $47,090; room/board: $14,124
Financial aid: (718) 390-3122; 65% of undergrads determined to have financial need; average aid package $31,526

Webb Institute

Glen Cove NY
(516) 671-8355
U.S. News ranking: Engineering, unranked
Website: www.webb.edu
Admissions email: admissions@webb.edu
Private; founded 1889
Freshman admissions: more selective; 2017-2018: 106 applied, 37 accepted. Either SAT or ACT required. SAT 25/75 percentile: 1440-1540. High school rank: 44% in top tenth, 56% in top quarter, 100% in top half
Early decision deadline: 10/15, notification date: 12/15
Early action deadline: N/A, notification date: N/A
Application deadline (fall): 2/1
Undergraduate student body: 98 full time, 0 part time; 80% male, 20% female; 1% American Indian, 11% Asian, 0% black,

2% Hispanic, 5% multiracial, 0% Pacific Islander, 79% white, 0% international; 22% from in state; 100% live on campus; 0% of students in fraternities, 0% in sororities
Most popular majors: 100% Naval Architecture and Marine Engineering
Expenses: 2018-2019: $50,175; room/board: $15,050
Financial aid: (516) 403-5928; 31% of undergrads determined to have financial need; average aid package $53,590

Wells College
Aurora NY
(800) 952-9355
U.S. News ranking: Nat. Lib. Arts, second tier
Website: www.wells.edu/
Admissions email: admissions@wells.edu
Private; founded 1868
Freshman admissions: selective; 2017-2018: 1,693 applied, 1,350 accepted. Neither SAT nor ACT required. ACT 25/75 percentile: 17-27. High school rank: 14% in top tenth, 45% in top quarter, 76% in top half
Early decision deadline: 12/15, notification date: 1/15
Early action deadline: 12/15, notification date: 1/15
Application deadline (fall): 3/1
Undergraduate student body: 481 full time, 7 part time; 36% male, 64% female; 1% American Indian, 2% Asian, 13% black, 14% Hispanic, 2% multiracial, 0% Pacific Islander, 61% white, 0% international; N/A from in state; 91% live on campus; N/A of students in fraternities, N/A in sororities
Most popular majors: 21% Psychology, 14% Social Sciences, 13% Biological and Biomedical Sciences, 11% English Language and Literature/Letters, 6% Business, Management, Marketing, and Related Support Services
Expenses: 2018-2019: $40,700; room/board: $14,100
Financial aid: (315) 364-3289; 94% of undergrads determined to have financial need; average aid package $38,070

Yeshiva University
New York NY
(212) 960-5277
U.S. News ranking: Nat. U., No. 80
Website: www.yu.edu
Admissions email: yuadmit@ymail.yu.edu
Private; founded 1886
Freshman admissions: more selective; 2017-2018: 1,861 applied, 1,169 accepted. Either SAT or ACT required. SAT 25/75 percentile: 1160-1420. High school rank: N/A
Early decision deadline: 11/1, notification date: 12/15
Early action deadline: N/A, notification date: N/A
Application deadline (fall): 2/1
Undergraduate student body: 2,636 full time, 92 part time; 53% male, 47% female; 0% American Indian, 0% Asian, 0% black, 0% Hispanic, 0% multiracial, 0% Pacific Islander, 93% white, 5% international; 36% from in state; 67% live on campus; N/A of students in fraternities, N/A in sororities
Most popular majors: 16% Biology/Biological Sciences, General, 14% Accounting, 13% Psychology, General, 8% Business Administration and Management, General, 7% Finance, General
Expenses: 2018-2019: $43,500; room/board: $12,250
Financial aid: (212) 960-5399; 56% of undergrads determined to have financial need; average aid package $38,226

NORTH CAROLINA

Appalachian State University
Boone NC
(828) 262-2120
U.S. News ranking: Reg. U. (S), No. 8
Website: www.appstate.edu
Admissions email: admissions@appstate.edu
Public; founded 1899
Freshman admissions: more selective; 2017-2018: 14,049 applied, 9,826 accepted. Either SAT or ACT required. ACT 25/75 percentile: 24-27. High school rank: 19% in top tenth, 57% in top quarter, 92% in top half
Early decision deadline: N/A, notification date: N/A
Early action deadline: 11/15, notification date: 1/25
Application deadline (fall): 3/15
Undergraduate student body: 16,071 full time, 946 part time; 45% male, 55% female; 0% American Indian, 2% Asian, 4% black, 6% Hispanic, 4% multiracial, 0% Pacific Islander, 83% white, 0% international; 92% from in state; 33% live on campus; 9% of students in fraternities, 12% in sororities
Most popular majors: 20% Business, Management, Marketing, and Related Support Services, 11% Education, 11% Health Professions and Related Programs, 7% Communication, Journalism, and Related Programs, 7% Parks, Recreation, Leisure, and Fitness Studies
Expenses: 2018-2019: $7,303 in state, $22,110 out of state; room/board: $8,174
Financial aid: (828) 262-2190; 54% of undergrads determined to have financial need; average aid package $9,569

Barton College
Wilson NC
(800) 345-4973
U.S. News ranking: Reg. Coll. (S), No. 5
Website: www.barton.edu
Admissions email: enroll@barton.edu
Private; founded 1902
Affiliation: Christian Church (Disciples of Christ)
Freshman admissions: selective; 2017-2018: 2,632 applied, 1,024 accepted. Either SAT or ACT required. SAT 25/75 percentile: 950-1140. High school rank: 13% in top tenth, 39% in top quarter, 75% in top half
Early decision deadline: N/A, notification date: N/A
Early action deadline: N/A, notification date: N/A
Application deadline (fall): rolling
Undergraduate student body: 830 full time, 57 part time; 31% male, 69% female; 1% American Indian, 1% Asian, 22% black, 8% Hispanic, 3% multiracial, 0% Pacific Islander, 55% white, 5% international; 82% from in state; 45% live on campus; 11% of students in fraternities, 11% in sororities
Most popular majors: 26% Health Professions and Related Programs, 16% Business, Management, Marketing, and Related Support Services, 9% Public Administration and Social Service Professions, 8% Education
Expenses: 2018-2019: $30,880; room/board: $10,120
Financial aid: (252) 399-6371; 87% of undergrads determined to have financial need; average aid package $22,703

Belmont Abbey College
Belmont NC
(888) 222-0110
U.S. News ranking: Reg. Coll. (S), No. 18
Website: www.belmontabbeycollege.edu
Admissions email: admissions@bac.edu
Private; founded 1876
Affiliation: Roman Catholic
Freshman admissions: selective; 2017-2018: 1,488 applied, 1,476 accepted. Neither SAT nor ACT required. SAT 25/75 percentile: 980-1120. High school rank: N/A
Early decision deadline: N/A, notification date: N/A
Early action deadline: N/A, notification date: N/A
Application deadline (fall): 8/1
Undergraduate student body: 1,381 full time, 174 part time; 49% male, 51% female; N/A American Indian, N/A Asian, N/A black, N/A Hispanic, N/A multiracial, N/A Pacific Islander, N/A white, N/A international
Most popular majors: Information not available
Expenses: 2018-2019: $18,500; room/board: $10,354
Financial aid: (704) 461-6719; 72% of undergrads determined to have financial need; average aid package $13,551

Bennett College
Greensboro NC
(336) 370-8624
U.S. News ranking: Reg. Coll. (S), No. 34
Website: www.bennett.edu
Admissions email: admiss@bennett.edu
Private; founded 1873
Affiliation: United Methodist
Freshman admissions: least selective; 2017-2018: 2,150 applied, 1,912 accepted. Either SAT or ACT required. SAT 25/75 percentile: 780-930. High school rank: 3% in top tenth, 18% in top quarter, 36% in top half
Early decision deadline: N/A, notification date: N/A
Early action deadline: N/A, notification date: N/A
Application deadline (fall): rolling
Undergraduate student body: 400 full time, 93 part time; 0% male, 100% female; 0% American Indian, 0% Asian, 85% black, 2% Hispanic, 4% multiracial, 0% Pacific Islander, 0% white, 0% international; N/A from in state; N/A live on campus; 0% of students in fraternities, N/A in sororities
Most popular majors: 19% Biology/Biological Sciences, General, 12% Multi-/Interdisciplinary Studies, Other, 12% Social Work, 6% Business Administration and Management, General, 6% Journalism, Other
Expenses: 2018-2019: $18,513; room/board: $8,114
Financial aid: (336) 517-2209; 97% of undergrads determined to have financial need

Brevard College[1]
Brevard NC
(828) 884-8300
U.S. News ranking: Reg. Coll. (S), No. 40
Website: www.brevard.edu
Admissions email: admissions@brevard.edu
Private; founded 1853
Application deadline (fall): rolling
Undergraduate student body: N/A full time, N/A part time
Expenses: 2017-2018: $28,640; room/board: $10,365
Financial aid: (828) 884-8287

Campbell University
Buies Creek NC
(910) 893-1200
U.S. News ranking: Reg. U. (S), No. 30
Website: www.campbell.edu
Admissions email: admissions@campbell.edu
Private; founded 1887
Freshman admissions: selective; 2017-2018: 5,495 applied, 4,428 accepted. Either SAT or ACT required. ACT 25/75 percentile: 20-25. High school rank: 27% in top tenth, 60% in top quarter, 86% in top half
Early decision deadline: N/A, notification date: N/A
Early action deadline: N/A, notification date: N/A
Application deadline (fall): rolling
Undergraduate student body: 3,634 full time, 750 part time; 48% male, 52% female; 1% American Indian, 2% Asian, 16% black, 9% Hispanic, 4% multiracial, 0% Pacific Islander, 58% white, 2% international; 84% from in state; 41% live on campus; 3% of students in fraternities, 5% in sororities
Most popular majors: 12% Business Administration and Management, General, 9% Science Technologies/Technicians, Other, 8% Psychology, General, 6% Biology/Biological Sciences, General, 5% Kinesiology and Exercise Science
Expenses: 2018-2019: $32,500; room/board: $11,430
Financial aid: (910) 893-1232; 66% of undergrads determined to have financial need; average aid package $25,720

Catawba College
Salisbury NC
(800) 228-2922
U.S. News ranking: Reg. Coll. (S), No. 4
Website: www.catawba.edu
Admissions email: admission@catawba.edu
Private; founded 1851
Affiliation: United Church of Christ
Freshman admissions: selective; 2017-2018: 3,125 applied, 1,325 accepted. Neither SAT nor ACT required. ACT 25/75 percentile: 18-23. High school rank: 13% in top tenth, 44% in top quarter, 77% in top half
Early decision deadline: N/A, notification date: N/A
Early action deadline: N/A, notification date: N/A
Application deadline (fall): rolling
Undergraduate student body: 1,267 full time, 58 part time; 47% male, 53% female; 0% American Indian, 1% Asian, 19% black, 7% Hispanic, 3% multiracial, 0% Pacific Islander, 65% white, 4% international; 81% from in state; 57% live on campus; 0% of students in fraternities, 0% in sororities
Most popular majors: 30% Business, Management, Marketing, and Related Support Services, 12% Education, 12% Visual and Performing Arts, 11% Parks, Recreation, Leisure, and Fitness Studies, 8% Biological and Biomedical Sciences
Expenses: 2018-2019: $30,520; room/board: $10,488
Financial aid: (704) 637-4416; 83% of undergrads determined to have financial need; average aid package $25,556

Chowan University
Murfreesboro NC
(252) 398-1236
U.S. News ranking: Reg. Coll. (S), No. 50
Website: chowan.edu/
Admissions email: admissions@chowan.edu
Private; founded 1848
Affiliation: Baptist
Freshman admissions: least selective; 2017-2018: 3,899 applied, 2,460 accepted. Either SAT or ACT required. SAT 25/75 percentile: 780-950. High school rank: 5% in top tenth, 25% in top quarter, 61% in top half
Early decision deadline: N/A, notification date: N/A
Early action deadline: N/A, notification date: N/A
Application deadline (fall): rolling
Undergraduate student body: 1,440 full time, 58 part time; 47% male, 53% female; 1% American Indian, 0% Asian, 70% black, 4% Hispanic, 2% multiracial, 0% Pacific Islander, 17% white, 3% international; 59% from in state; 86% live on campus; 1% of students in fraternities, 1% in sororities

Most popular majors: 22% Multi/Interdisciplinary Studies, 12% Homeland Security, Law Enforcement, Firefighting and Related Protective Services, 11% Psychology, 8% Business, Management, Marketing, and Related Support Services, 7% Parks, Recreation, Leisure, and Fitness Studies
Expenses: 2018-2019: $24,980; room/board: $9,400
Financial aid: (252) 398-6269; 94% of undergrads determined to have financial need; average aid package $23,216

Davidson College

Davidson NC
(800) 768-0380
U.S. News ranking: Nat. Lib. Arts, No. 10
Website: www.davidson.edu
Admissions email: admission@davidson.edu
Private; founded 1837
Freshman admissions: most selective; 2017-2018: 5,673 applied, 1,148 accepted. Either SAT or ACT required. ACT 25/75 percentile: 30-33. High school rank: 76% in top tenth, 95% in top quarter, 99% in top half
Early decision deadline: 11/15, notification date: 12/15
Early action deadline: N/A, notification date: N/A
Application deadline (fall): 1/2
Undergraduate student body: 1,810 full time, 0 part time; 51% male, 49% female; 0% American Indian, 6% Asian, 7% black, 8% Hispanic, 5% multiracial, 0% Pacific Islander, 67% white, 7% international; 23% from in state; 98% live on campus; 39% of students in fraternities, 70% in sororities
Most popular majors: 15% Biology/Biological Sciences, General, 14% Political Science and Government, General, 11% Economics, General, 11% Psychology, General, 9% English Language and Literature, General
Expenses: 2018-2019: $51,447; room/board: $14,372
Financial aid: (800) 768-0380; 50% of undergrads determined to have financial need; average aid package $47,803

Duke University

Durham NC
(919) 684-3214
U.S. News ranking: Nat. U., No. 8
Website: www.duke.edu/
Admissions email: undergrad-admissions@duke.edu
Private; founded 1838
Freshman admissions: most selective; 2017-2018: 33,077 applied, 3,261 accepted. Either SAT or ACT required. ACT 25/75 percentile: 31-35. High school rank: 90% in top tenth, 97% in top quarter, 99% in top half
Early decision deadline: 11/1, notification date: 12/15
Early action deadline: N/A, notification date: N/A
Application deadline (fall): 1/3
Undergraduate student body: 6,665 full time, 27 part time; 50% male, 50% female; 1% American Indian, 21% Asian, 10% black, 9% Hispanic, 2% multiracial, 0% Pacific Islander, 44% white, 10% international
Most popular majors: 10% Computer Science, 10% Economics, General, 10% Public Policy Analysis, General, 8% Biology/Biological Sciences, General, 6% Bioengineering and Biomedical Engineering
Expenses: 2018-2019: $55,960; room/board: $15,944
Financial aid: (919) 684-6225; 43% of undergrads determined to have financial need; average aid package $52,745

East Carolina University

Greenville NC
(252) 328-6640
U.S. News ranking: Nat. U., No. 194
Website: www.ecu.edu
Admissions email: admis@ecu.edu
Public; founded 1907
Freshman admissions: selective; 2017-2018: 16,007 applied, 12,615 accepted. Either SAT or ACT required. ACT 25/75 percentile: 20-24. High school rank: 13% in top tenth, 39% in top quarter, 78% in top half
Early decision deadline: N/A, notification date: N/A
Early action deadline: N/A, notification date: N/A
Application deadline (fall): 3/1
Undergraduate student body: 19,999 full time, 3,266 part time; 43% male, 57% female; 1% American Indian, 3% Asian, 16% black, 7% Hispanic, 4% multiracial, 0% Pacific Islander, 67% white, 1% international; 90% from in state; 20% live on campus; 9% of students in fraternities, 6% in sororities
Most popular majors: 19% Business, Management, Marketing, and Related Support Services, 17% Health Professions and Related Programs, 8% Engineering, 7% Biological and Biomedical Sciences, 6% Communication, Journalism, and Related Programs
Expenses: 2018-2019: $7,188 in state, $23,465 out of state; room/board: $10,354
Financial aid: (252) 328-6610; 62% of undergrads determined to have financial need; average aid package $10,383

Elizabeth City State University

Elizabeth City NC
(252) 335-3305
U.S. News ranking: Reg. U. (S), No. 71
Website: www.ecsu.edu
Admissions email: admissions@mail.ecsu.edu
Public; founded 1891
Freshman admissions: least selective; 2017-2018: 2,677 applied, 1,601 accepted. Either SAT or ACT required. SAT 25/75 percentile: 860-990. High school rank: 1% in top tenth, 3% in top quarter, 36% in top half
Early decision deadline: N/A, notification date: N/A
Early action deadline: N/A, notification date: N/A
Application deadline (fall): 8/1
Undergraduate student body: 1,181 full time, 190 part time; 44% male, 56% female; 0% American Indian, 1% Asian, 71% black, 3% Hispanic, 2% multiracial, 0% Pacific Islander, 17% white, 0% international
Most popular majors: Information not available
Expenses: 2018-2019: $3,673 in state, $7,673 out of state; room/board: $8,124
Financial aid: (252) 335-4850; 94% of undergrads determined to have financial need; average aid package $8,554

Elon University

Elon NC
(800) 334-8448
U.S. News ranking: Reg. U. (S), No. 1
Website: www.elon.edu
Admissions email: admissions@elon.edu
Private; founded 1889
Freshman admissions: more selective; 2017-2018: 9,623 applied, 6,402 accepted. Either SAT or ACT required. SAT 25/75 percentile: 1140-1330. High school rank: 21% in top tenth, 54% in top quarter, 89% in top half
Early decision deadline: 11/1, notification date: 12/1
Early action deadline: 11/10, notification date: 12/20
Application deadline (fall): 1/10
Undergraduate student body: 5,885 full time, 160 part time; 40% male, 60% female; 0% American Indian, 2% Asian, 5% black, 6% Hispanic, 3% multiracial, 0% Pacific Islander, 80% white, 2% international; 18% from in state; 64% live on campus; 20% of students in fraternities, 39% in sororities
Most popular majors: 29% Business/Commerce, General, 18% Communication and Media Studies, 5% Health and Physical Education/Fitness, 5% Psychology, General, 3% Biology, General
Expenses: 2018-2019: $35,319; room/board: $12,230
Financial aid: (336) 278-7640; 33% of undergrads determined to have financial need; average aid package $20,060

Fayetteville State University

Fayetteville NC
(910) 672-1371
U.S. News ranking: Reg. U. (S), No. 95
Website: www.uncfsu.edu
Admissions email: admissions@uncfsu.edu
Public; founded 1867
Freshman admissions: less selective; 2017-2018: 3,859 applied, 2,607 accepted. Either SAT or ACT required. SAT 25/75 percentile: 870-1020. High school rank: 5% in top tenth, 24% in top quarter, 59% in top half
Early decision deadline: N/A, notification date: N/A
Early action deadline: N/A, notification date: N/A
Application deadline (fall): 6/30
Undergraduate student body: 3,905 full time, 1,488 part time; 40% male, 60% female; 3% American Indian, 2% Asian, 63% black, 7% Hispanic, 2% multiracial, 0% Pacific Islander, 18% white, 0% international; 93% from in state; 28% live on campus; 1% of students in fraternities, 1% in sororities
Most popular majors: 20% Registered Nursing/Registered Nurse, 13% Psychology, General, 10% Business Administration and Management, General, 10% Criminal Justice/Safety Studies, 6% Biology/Biological Sciences, General
Expenses: 2018-2019: $4,915 in state, $16,523 out of state; room/board: $8,236
Financial aid: (910) 672-1325; 85% of undergrads determined to have financial need; average aid package $10,879

Gardner-Webb University

Boiling Springs NC
(800) 253-6472
U.S. News ranking: Nat. U., second tier
Website: www.gardner-webb.edu
Admissions email: admissions@gardner-webb.edu
Private; founded 1905
Freshman admissions: selective; 2017-2018: 2,969 applied, 1,566 accepted. Either SAT or ACT required. SAT 25/75 percentile: 1000-1200. High school rank: 22% in top tenth, 54% in top quarter, 84% in top half
Early decision deadline: N/A, notification date: N/A
Early action deadline: N/A, notification date: N/A
Application deadline (fall): rolling
Undergraduate student body: 1,781 full time, 426 part time; 35% male, 65% female; 1% American Indian, 1% Asian, 14% black, 4% Hispanic, 1% multiracial, 0% Pacific Islander, 67% white, 0% international
Most popular majors: 25% Health Professions and Related Programs, 23% Business, Management, Marketing, and Related Support Services, 13% Psychology, 6% Biological and Biomedical Sciences, 6% Homeland Security, Law Enforcement, Firefighting and Related Protective Services
Expenses: 2018-2019: $31,460; room/board: $10,390
Financial aid: (704) 406-4247; 75% of undergrads determined to have financial need; average aid package $25,228

Greensboro College

Greensboro NC
(336) 272-7102
U.S. News ranking: Reg. Coll. (S), No. 19
Website: www.gborocollege.edu
Admissions email: admissions@gborocollege.edu
Private; founded 1838
Affiliation: United Methodist
Freshman admissions: selective; 2017-2018: 2,192 applied, 892 accepted. Either SAT or ACT required. ACT 25/75 percentile: 17-22. High school rank: 6% in top tenth, 24% in top quarter, 57% in top half
Early decision deadline: N/A, notification date: N/A
Early action deadline: N/A, notification date: N/A
Application deadline (fall): 8/28
Undergraduate student body: 769 full time, 125 part time; 51% male, 49% female; 0% American Indian, 1% Asian, 30% black, 3% Hispanic, 5% multiracial, 0% Pacific Islander, 55% white, 0% international; 95% from in state; 21% live on campus; 0% of students in fraternities, 21% in sororities
Most popular majors: 13% Business, Management, Marketing, and Related Support Services, 12% Liberal Arts and Sciences, General Studies and Humanities, 11% Social Sciences, 10% Health Professions and Related Programs, 7% Biological and Biomedical Sciences
Expenses: 2018-2019: $29,140; room/board: $10,800
Financial aid: (336) 272-7102; 89% of undergrads determined to have financial need; average aid package $12,095

Guilford College

Greensboro NC
(800) 992-7759
U.S. News ranking: Nat. Lib. Arts, No. 168
Website: www.guilford.edu
Admissions email: admission@guilford.edu
Private; founded 1837
Affiliation: Friends
Freshman admissions: selective; 2017-2018: 1,865 applied, 1,692 accepted. Neither SAT nor ACT required. ACT 25/75 percentile: 19-25. High school rank: 13% in top tenth, 32% in top quarter, 66% in top half
Early decision deadline: N/A, notification date: N/A
Early action deadline: 12/1, notification date: 12/15
Application deadline (fall): 8/10
Undergraduate student body: 1,429 full time, 245 part time; 47% male, 53% female; N/A American Indian, N/A Asian, N/A black, N/A Hispanic, N/A multiracial, N/A Pacific Islander, N/A white, N/A international; 71% from in state; 74% live on campus; 0% of students in fraternities, 0% in sororities
Most popular majors: 17% Business, Management, Marketing, and Related Support Services, 10% Biological and Biomedical Sciences, 10% Parks, Recreation, Leisure, and Fitness Studies, 10% Psychology, 8% Homeland Security, Law Enforcement, Firefighting and Related Protective Services
Expenses: 2018-2019: $36,965; room/board: $11,200
Financial aid: (336) 316-2354; 74% of undergrads determined to have financial need; average aid package $25,481

High Point University

High Point NC
(800) 345-6993
U.S. News ranking: Reg. Coll. (S), No. 1
Website: www.highpoint.edu
Admissions email: admiss@highpoint.edu
Private; founded 1924
Affiliation: United Methodist
Freshman admissions: selective; 2017-2018: 8,936 applied, 7,208 accepted. Neither SAT nor ACT required. SAT 25/75 percentile: 1050-1240. High school rank: 18% in top tenth, 47% in top quarter, 78% in top half
Early decision deadline: 11/1, notification date: 11/27
Early action deadline: 11/15, notification date: 12/15
Application deadline (fall): 7/1
Undergraduate student body: 4,418 full time, 49 part time; 41% male, 59% female; 0% American Indian, 2% Asian, 5% black, 5% Hispanic, 7% multiracial, 0% Pacific Islander, 77% white, 2% international; 22% from in state; 94% live on campus; 7% of students in fraternities, 22% in sororities
Most popular majors: 37% Business, Management, Marketing, and Related Support Services, 14% Communication, Journalism, and Related Programs, 9% Visual and Performing Arts, 7% Biological and Biomedical Sciences, 6% Parks, Recreation, Leisure, and Fitness Studies
Expenses: 2018-2019: $35,118; room/board: $14,130
Financial aid: (336) 841-9128; 43% of undergrads determined to have financial need; average aid package $16,146

Johnson C. Smith University

Charlotte NC
(704) 378-1010
U.S. News ranking: Nat. Lib. Arts, second tier
Website: www.jcsu.edu
Admissions email: admissions@jcsu.edu
Private; founded 1867
Freshman admissions: least selective; 2017-2018: 6,657 applied, 2,536 accepted. Either SAT or ACT required. SAT 25/75 percentile: 748-960. High school rank: N/A
Early decision deadline: N/A, notification date: N/A
Early action deadline: N/A, notification date: N/A
Application deadline (fall): rolling
Undergraduate student body: 1,329 full time, 65 part time; 39% male, 61% female; 0% American Indian, 0% Asian, 84% black, 4% Hispanic, 1% multiracial, 0% Pacific Islander, 1% white, 1% international; 60% from in state; 66% live on campus; 8% of students in fraternities, 8% in sororities
Most popular majors: 29% Social Work, 14% Business Administration and Management, General, 11% Mass Communication/Media Studies, 9% Biology/Biological Sciences, General, 9% Sport and Fitness Administration/Management
Expenses: 2018-2019: $18,236; room/board: $7,100
Financial aid: (704) 378-1035; 92% of undergrads determined to have financial need; average aid package $15,658

Lees-McRae College

Banner Elk NC
(828) 898-5241
U.S. News ranking: Reg. Coll. (S), No. 27
Website: www.lmc.edu
Admissions email: admissions@lmc.edu
Private; founded 1900
Affiliation: Presbyterian Church (USA)
Freshman admissions: less selective; 2017-2018: 1,190 applied, 842 accepted. Neither SAT nor ACT required. ACT 25/75 percentile: 18-23. High school rank: N/A
Early decision deadline: N/A, notification date: N/A
Early action deadline: N/A, notification date: N/A
Application deadline (fall): rolling
Undergraduate student body: 891 full time, 30 part time; 33% male, 67% female; 1% American Indian, 0% Asian, 6% black, 6% Hispanic, 1% multiracial, 0% Pacific Islander, 72% white, 2% international; 66% from in state; 62% live on campus; 7% of students in fraternities, 3% in sororities
Most popular majors: 31% Health Professions and Related Programs, 17% Homeland Security, Law Enforcement, Firefighting and Related Protective Services, 14% Biological and Biomedical Sciences, 12% Education, 7% Business, Management, Marketing, and Related Support Services
Expenses: 2018-2019: $26,198; room/board: $11,078
Financial aid: (828) 898-8740; 76% of undergrads determined to have financial need; average aid package $25,260

Lenoir-Rhyne University

Hickory NC
(828) 328-7300
U.S. News ranking: Reg. U. (S), No. 71
Website: www.lr.edu
Admissions email: admission@lr.edu
Private; founded 1891
Affiliation: Evangelical Lutheran Church
Freshman admissions: less selective; 2017-2018: 5,356 applied, 3,958 accepted. Neither SAT nor ACT required. SAT 25/75 percentile: 870-1090. High school rank: N/A
Early decision deadline: N/A, notification date: N/A
Early action deadline: 11/7, notification date: 11/21
Application deadline (fall): rolling
Undergraduate student body: 1,441 full time, 258 part time; 41% male, 59% female; 0% American Indian, 2% Asian, 13% black, 7% Hispanic, 4% multiracial, 0% Pacific Islander, 67% white, 3% international; 81% from in state; 51% live on campus; 9% of students in fraternities, 13% in sororities
Most popular majors: 23% Health Professions and Related Programs, 19% Parks, Recreation, Leisure, and Fitness Studies, 18% Business, Management, Marketing, and Related Support Services, 8% Biological and Biomedical Sciences, 5% Psychology
Expenses: 2018-2019: $36,400; room/board: $12,510
Financial aid: (828) 328-7300; 86% of undergrads determined to have financial need; average aid package $30,121

Livingstone College

Salisbury NC
(704) 216-6001
U.S. News ranking: Reg. Coll. (S), second tier
Website: www.livingstone.edu/
Admissions email: admissions@livingstone.edu
Private; founded 1879
Affiliation: African Methodist Episcopal Zion Church
Freshman admissions: least selective; 2017-2018: 7,295 applied, 2,717 accepted. Either SAT or ACT required. SAT 25/75 percentile: 755-920. High school rank: 3% in top tenth, 8% in top quarter, 25% in top half
Early decision deadline: N/A, notification date: N/A
Early action deadline: N/A, notification date: N/A
Application deadline (fall): rolling
Undergraduate student body: 1,140 full time, 10 part time; 51% male, 49% female; 0% American Indian, 0% Asian, 80% black, 0% Hispanic, 3% multiracial, 0% Pacific Islander, 1% white, 1% international; 99% from in state; 85% live on campus; 30% of students in fraternities, 35% in sororities
Most popular majors: Information not available
Expenses: 2018-2019: $17,763; room/board: $6,596
Financial aid: (704) 216-6069; 97% of undergrads determined to have financial need; average aid package $14,455

Mars Hill University

Mars Hill NC
(866) 642-4968
U.S. News ranking: Reg. Coll. (S), No. 22
Website: www.mhu.edu
Admissions email: admissions@mhu.edu
Private; founded 1856
Freshman admissions: selective; 2017-2018: 2,257 applied, 1,347 accepted. Either SAT or ACT required. ACT 25/75 percentile: 17-22. High school rank: 7% in top tenth, 26% in top quarter, 66% in top half
Early decision deadline: N/A, notification date: N/A
Early action deadline: N/A, notification date: N/A
Application deadline (fall): rolling
Undergraduate student body: 1,199 full time, 64 part time; 45% male, 55% female; 2% American Indian, 2% Asian, 18% black, 4% Hispanic, 4% multiracial, 0% Pacific Islander, 62% white, 5% international; 78% from in state; 70% live on campus; 7% of students in fraternities, 11% in sororities
Most popular majors: 21% Business, Management, Marketing, and Related Support Services, 15% Education, 14% Public Administration and Social Service Professions, 11% Biological and Biomedical Sciences, 7% Health Professions and Related Programs
Expenses: 2018-2019: $32,968; room/board: $9,592
Financial aid: (828) 689-1103; 89% of undergrads determined to have financial need; average aid package $21,917

Meredith College

Raleigh NC
(919) 760-8581
U.S. News ranking: Nat. Lib. Arts, No. 162
Website: www.meredith.edu
Admissions email: admissions@meredith.edu
Private; founded 1891
Freshman admissions: selective; 2017-2018: 1,737 applied, 1,197 accepted. Either SAT or ACT required. ACT 25/75 percentile: 20-25. High school rank: 17% in top tenth, 45% in top quarter, 85% in top half
Early decision deadline: 10/30, notification date: 11/1
Early action deadline: N/A, notification date: N/A
Application deadline (fall): rolling
Undergraduate student body: 1,600 full time, 82 part time; 0% male, 100% female; 1% American Indian, 3% Asian, 8% black, 8% Hispanic, 4% multiracial, 0% Pacific Islander, 71% white, 2% international
Most popular majors: 10% Biology/Biological Sciences, General, 10% Psychology, General, 7% Business Administration and Management, General, 6% Child Development, 4% Social Work
Expenses: 2018-2019: $37,176; room/board: $10,930
Financial aid: (919) 760-8565; 74% of undergrads determined to have financial need; average aid package $27,707

Methodist University

Fayetteville NC
(910) 630-7027
U.S. News ranking: Reg. U. (S), No. 87
Website: www.methodist.edu
Admissions email: admissions@methodist.edu
Private; founded 1956
Affiliation: United Methodist
Freshman admissions: selective; 2017-2018: 3,762 applied, 2,152 accepted. Either SAT or ACT required. ACT 25/75 percentile: 18-23. High school rank: 14% in top tenth, 37% in top quarter, 74% in top half
Early decision deadline: N/A, notification date: N/A
Early action deadline: N/A, notification date: N/A
Application deadline (fall): rolling
Undergraduate student body: 1,755 full time, 178 part time; 52% male, 48% female; 1% American Indian, 1% Asian, 17% black, 8% Hispanic, 3% multiracial, 0% Pacific Islander, 43% white, 10% international
Most popular majors: Information not available
Expenses: 2018-2019: $33,846; room/board: $12,576
Financial aid: (910) 630-7000; 76% of undergrads determined to have financial need; average aid package $22,474

Montreat College

Montreat NC
(800) 622-6968
U.S. News ranking: Reg. U. (S), No. 95
Website: www.montreat.edu
Admissions email: admissions@montreat.edu
Private; founded 1916
Freshman admissions: selective; 2017-2018: 942 applied, 615 accepted. Either SAT or ACT required. SAT 25/75 percentile: 920-1150. High school rank: 8% in top tenth, 28% in top quarter, 69% in top half
Early decision deadline: N/A, notification date: N/A
Early action deadline: N/A, notification date: N/A
Application deadline (fall): rolling
Undergraduate student body: 543 full time, 152 part time; 51% male, 49% female; N/A American Indian, N/A Asian, N/A black, N/A Hispanic, N/A multiracial, N/A Pacific Islander, N/A white, N/A international
Most popular majors: 30% Business Administration and Management, General, 25% Psychology, Other, 10% Business Administration, Management and Operations, Other, 4% Outdoor Education, 4% Theology/Theological Studies
Expenses: 2018-2019: $26,920; room/board: $8,857
Financial aid: (828) 669-8012; 83% of undergrads determined to have financial need; average aid package $20,427

North Carolina A&T State University

Greensboro NC
(336) 334-7946
U.S. News ranking: Nat. U., second tier
Website: www.ncat.edu
Admissions email: uadmit@ncat.edu
Public; founded 1891
Freshman admissions: less selective; 2017-2018: 10,745 applied, 6,699 accepted. Either SAT or ACT required. SAT 25/75 percentile: 930-1090. High school rank: 10% in top tenth, 33% in top quarter, 73% in top half
Early decision deadline: N/A, notification date: N/A
Early action deadline: N/A, notification date: N/A
Application deadline (fall): 6/30

Undergraduate student body: 9,304 full time, 1,037 part time; 43% male, 57% female; 0% American Indian, 1% Asian, 82% black, 4% Hispanic, 4% multiracial, 0% Pacific Islander, 5% white, 1% international; 78% from in state; 42% live on campus; N/A of students in fraternities, N/A in sororities
Most popular majors: 13% Engineering, 10% Business, Management, Marketing, and Related Support Services, 10% Communication, Journalism, and Related Programs, 8% Parks, Recreation, Leisure, and Fitness Studies, 6% Liberal Arts and Sciences, General Studies and Humanities
Expenses: 2018-2019: $6,612 in state, $19,822 out of state; room/board: $7,624
Financial aid: (336) 334-7973; 86% of undergrads determined to have financial need; average aid package $11,426

North Carolina Central University

Durham NC
(919) 530-6298
U.S. News ranking: Reg. U. (S), No. 64
Website: www.nccu.edu
Admissions email: admissions@nccu.edu
Public; founded 1910
Freshman admissions: less selective; 2017-2018: 6,671 applied, 5,524 accepted. Either SAT or ACT required. SAT 25/75 percentile: 890-1030. High school rank: 6% in top tenth, 22% in top quarter, 60% in top half
Early decision deadline: N/A, notification date: N/A
Early action deadline: N/A, notification date: N/A
Application deadline (fall): rolling
Undergraduate student body: 5,363 full time, 992 part time; 33% male, 67% female; 0% American Indian, 1% Asian, 82% black, 5% Hispanic, 5% multiracial, 0% Pacific Islander, 6% white, 0% international
Most popular majors: 12% Criminal Justice/Safety Studies, 10% Business Administration and Management, General, 10% Family and Consumer Sciences/Human Sciences, General, 8% Psychology, General, 7% Registered Nursing/Registered Nurse
Expenses: 2018-2019: $6,684 in state, $19,391 out of state; room/board: $8,552
Financial aid: (919) 530-6180; 92% of undergrads determined to have financial need; average aid package $12,212

North Carolina State University–Raleigh

Raleigh NC
(919) 515-2434
U.S. News ranking: Nat. U., No. 80
Website: admissions.ncsu.edu
Admissions email: undergrad-admissions@ncsu.edu
Public; founded 1887
Freshman admissions: more selective; 2017-2018: 26,859 applied, 13,690 accepted. Either SAT or ACT required. ACT 25/75 percentile: 27-31. High school rank: 46% in top tenth, 88% in top quarter, 99% in top half
Early decision deadline: N/A, notification date: N/A
Early action deadline: 10/15, notification date: 1/30
Application deadline (fall): 1/15
Undergraduate student body: 21,384 full time, 2,766 part time; 55% male, 45% female; 0% American Indian, 6% Asian, 6% black, 5% Hispanic, 4% multiracial, 0% Pacific Islander, 71% white, 5% international; 90% from in state; 39% live on campus; 12% of students in fraternities, 17% in sororities
Most popular majors: 27% Engineering, 15% Business, Management, Marketing, and Related Support Services, 9% Biological and Biomedical Sciences, 7% Agriculture, Agriculture Operations, and Related Sciences, 4% Communication, Journalism, and Related Programs
Expenses: 2018-2019: $9,101 in state, $28,444 out of state; room/board: $11,078
Financial aid: N/A; 49% of undergrads determined to have financial need; average aid package $13,108

North Carolina Wesleyan College

Rocky Mount NC
(800) 488-6292
U.S. News ranking: Reg. Coll. (S), No. 37
Website: www.ncwc.edu
Admissions email: adm@ncwc.edu
Private; founded 1956
Affiliation: United Methodist
Freshman admissions: less selective; 2017-2018: 3,068 applied, 1,625 accepted. Neither SAT nor ACT required. SAT 25/75 percentile: 870-1060. High school rank: 8% in top tenth, 23% in top quarter, 52% in top half
Early decision deadline: N/A, notification date: N/A
Early action deadline: N/A, notification date: N/A
Application deadline (fall): rolling
Undergraduate student body: 1,754 full time, 339 part time; 42% male, 58% female; 1% American Indian, 1% Asian, 42% black, 3% Hispanic, 3% multiracial, 0% Pacific Islander, 32% white, 5% international; 87% from in state; 72% live on campus; 1% of students in fraternities, 2% in sororities
Most popular majors: 22% Business Administration and Management, General, 17% Criminal Justice/Law Enforcement Administration, 16% Organizational Leadership, 15% Psychology, General, 8% Accounting
Expenses: 2018-2019: $31,000; room/board: $10,800
Financial aid: (252) 985-5200; 76% of undergrads determined to have financial need; average aid package $20,427

Pfeiffer University

Misenheimer NC
(800) 338-2060
U.S. News ranking: Reg. U. (S), No. 78
Website: www.pfeiffer.edu
Admissions email: admissions@pfeiffer.edu
Private; founded 1885
Affiliation: United Methodist
Freshman admissions: less selective; 2017-2018: 1,860 applied, 1,228 accepted. Neither SAT nor ACT required. ACT 25/75 percentile: 16-22. High school rank: 10% in top tenth, 28% in top quarter, 63% in top half
Early decision deadline: N/A, notification date: N/A
Early action deadline: N/A, notification date: N/A
Application deadline (fall): rolling
Undergraduate student body: 732 full time, 81 part time; 48% male, 52% female; 0% American Indian, 1% Asian, 23% black, 7% Hispanic, 3% multiracial, 0% Pacific Islander, 63% white, 2% international; 81% from in state; 59% live on campus; 0% of students in fraternities, 30% in sororities
Most popular majors: 24% Business, Management, Marketing, and Related Support Services, 20% Health Professions and Related Programs, 12% Parks, Recreation, Leisure, and Fitness Studies, 8% Education, 8% Homeland Security, Law Enforcement, Firefighting and Related Protective Services
Expenses: 2018-2019: $30,234; room/board: $11,226
Financial aid: (704) 463-3060; 79% of undergrads determined to have financial need; average aid package $24,928

Queens University of Charlotte

Charlotte NC
(800) 849-0202
U.S. News ranking: Reg. U. (S), No. 18
Website: www.queens.edu
Admissions email: admissions@queens.edu
Private; founded 1857
Affiliation: Presbyterian
Freshman admissions: selective; 2017-2018: 2,155 applied, 1,706 accepted. Either SAT or ACT required. SAT 25/75 percentile: 1010-1198. High school rank: 18% in top tenth, 42% in top quarter, 82% in top half
Early decision deadline: N/A, notification date: N/A
Early action deadline: 12/1, notification date: 12/31
Application deadline (fall): 9/5
Undergraduate student body: 1,449 full time, 270 part time; 33% male, 67% female; 1% American Indian, 2% Asian, 16% black, 10% Hispanic, 1% multiracial, 0% Pacific Islander, 58% white, 8% international
Most popular majors: 29% Health Professions and Related Programs, 13% Business, Management, Marketing, and Related Support Services, 12% Biological and Biomedical Sciences, 10% Communication, Journalism, and Related Programs
Expenses: 2018-2019: $34,684; room/board: $10,860
Financial aid: (704) 337-2225; 72% of undergrads determined to have financial need; average aid package $26,578

Salem College[1]

Winston-Salem NC
(336) 721-2621
U.S. News ranking: Nat. Lib. Arts, No. 131
Website: www.salem.edu
Admissions email: admissions@salem.edu
Private; founded 1772
Affiliation: Moravian Church
Application deadline (fall): rolling
Undergraduate student body: N/A full time, N/A part time
Expenses: 2018-2019: $29,416; room/board: $11,850
Financial aid: (336) 721-2808; 86% of undergrads determined to have financial need; average aid package $33,358

Shaw University

Raleigh NC
(800) 214-6683
U.S. News ranking: Reg. Coll. (S), second tier
Website: www.shawu.edu
Admissions email: admissions@shawu.edu
Private; founded 1865
Affiliation: Baptist
Freshman admissions: least selective; 2017-2018: 12,060 applied, 6,375 accepted. Either SAT or ACT required. SAT 25/75 percentile: 763-935. High school rank: 2% in top tenth, 5% in top quarter, 30% in top half
Early decision deadline: N/A, notification date: N/A
Early action deadline: N/A, notification date: N/A
Application deadline (fall): 7/30
Undergraduate student body: 1,466 full time, 80 part time; 42% male, 58% female; 0% American Indian, 1% Asian, 74% black, 0% Hispanic, 3% multiracial, 1% Pacific Islander, 2% white, 4% international; 63% from in state; 56% live on campus; N/A of students in fraternities, N/A in sororities
Most popular majors: 15% Business/Commerce, General, 13% Social Work, 10% Mass Communication/Media Studies, 10% Psychology, General, 9% Parks, Recreation and Leisure Studies
Expenses: 2017-2018: $16,480; room/board: $8,158
Financial aid: (919) 546-8565

Southeastern Baptist Theological Seminary[1]

Wake Forest NC
(919) 761-2246
U.S. News ranking: Reg. U. (S), unranked
Website: www.sebts.edu/
Admissions email: admissions@sebts.edu
Private; founded 1950
Affiliation: Southern Baptist
Application deadline (fall): 8/1
Undergraduate student body: N/A full time, N/A part time
Expenses: 2017-2018: $10,730; room/board: $2,196
Financial aid: N/A

St. Augustine's University

Raleigh NC
(919) 516-4012
U.S. News ranking: Reg. Coll. (S), No. 61
Website: www.st-aug.edu
Admissions email: admissions@st-aug.edu
Private; founded 1867
Affiliation: Episcopal Church, Reformed
Freshman admissions: least selective; 2017-2018: 3,684 applied, 2,807 accepted. Either SAT or ACT required. SAT 25/75 percentile: 760-950. High school rank: N/A
Early decision deadline: N/A, notification date: N/A
Early action deadline: N/A, notification date: N/A
Application deadline (fall): rolling
Undergraduate student body: 961 full time, 13 part time; 55% male, 45% female; 0% American Indian, 0% Asian, 84% black, 1% Hispanic, 0% multiracial, 0% Pacific Islander, 2% white, 2% international
Most popular majors: 23% Criminalistics and Criminal Science, 10% Sociology, 9% Non-Profit/Public/Organizational Management, 8% Business Administration and Management, General, 7% Communication, Journalism, and Related Programs, Other
Expenses: 2018-2019: $17,890; room/board: $8,746
Financial aid: N/A

University of Mount Olive

Mount Olive NC
(919) 658-2502
U.S. News ranking: Reg. Coll. (S), No. 25
Website: www.umo.edu/
Admissions email: admissions@umo.edu
Private; founded 1951
Affiliation: Original Free Will Baptist
Freshman admissions: less selective; 2017-2018: 3,067 applied, 1,506 accepted. Neither SAT nor ACT required. SAT 25/75 percentile: 870-1066. High school rank: N/A
Early decision deadline: N/A, notification date: N/A
Early action deadline: N/A, notification date: N/A
Application deadline (fall): rolling
Undergraduate student body: 1,472 full time, 1,727 part time; 34% male, 66% female; 1% American Indian, 1% Asian, 28% black, 3% Hispanic, 7% multiracial, 0% Pacific Islander, 52% white, 3% international
Most popular majors: Information not available
Expenses: 2017-2018: $19,700; room/board: $8,150
Financial aid: (919) 658-2502

More @ usnews.com/bestcolleges

University of North Carolina–Asheville

Asheville NC
(828) 251-6481
U.S. News ranking: Nat. Lib. Arts, No. 143
Website: www.unca.edu
Admissions email: admissions@unca.edu
Public; founded 1927
Freshman admissions: selective; 2017-2018: 3,358 applied, 2,730 accepted. Either SAT or ACT required. ACT 25/75 percentile: 22-27. High school rank: 15% in top tenth, 44% in top quarter, 88% in top half
Early decision deadline: N/A, notification date: N/A
Early action deadline: 11/15, notification date: 12/15
Application deadline (fall): 2/15
Undergraduate student body: 3,285 full time, 541 part time; 43% male, 57% female; 1% American Indian, 2% Asian, 5% black, 6% Hispanic, 4% multiracial, 0% Pacific Islander, 78% white, 1% international; 89% from in state; 38% live on campus; 3% of students in fraternities, 3% in sororities
Most popular majors: 10% Psychology, General, 7% Business Administration and Management, General, 7% Environmental Studies, 6% Digital Arts, 6% Public Health Education and Promotion
Expenses: 2018-2019: $7,145 in state, $23,868 out of state; room/board: $9,106
Financial aid: (828) 251-6535; 58% of undergrads determined to have financial need; average aid package $13,098

University of North Carolina–Chapel Hill

Chapel Hill NC
(919) 966-3621
U.S. News ranking: Nat. U., No. 30
Website: www.unc.edu
Admissions email: unchelp@admissions.unc.edu
Public; founded 1789
Freshman admissions: most selective; 2017-2018: 40,918 applied, 9,709 accepted. Either SAT or ACT required. ACT 25/75 percentile: 27-32. High school rank: 78% in top tenth, 96% in top quarter, 99% in top half
Early decision deadline: N/A, notification date: N/A
Early action deadline: 10/15, notification date: 1/31
Application deadline (fall): 1/15
Undergraduate student body: 18,303 full time, 559 part time; 41% male, 59% female; 0% American Indian, 11% Asian, 8% black, 8% Hispanic, 4% multiracial, 0% Pacific Islander, 62% white, 3% international; 84% from in state; 51% live on campus; 18% of students in fraternities, 18% in sororities
Most popular majors: 16% Social Sciences, 10% Communication, Journalism, and Related Programs, 9% Biological and Biomedical Sciences, 8% Business, Management, Marketing, and Related Support Services, 8% Psychology
Expenses: 2018-2019: $8,986 in state, $35,169 out of state; room/board: $11,190
Financial aid: (919) 962-8396; 46% of undergrads determined to have financial need; average aid package $19,994

University of North Carolina–Charlotte

Charlotte NC
(704) 687-5507
U.S. News ranking: Nat. U., No. 194
Website: www.uncc.edu/
Admissions email: admissions@uncc.edu
Public; founded 1946
Freshman admissions: selective; 2017-2018: 16,743 applied, 11,061 accepted. Either SAT or ACT required. ACT 25/75 percentile: 22-26. High school rank: 17% in top tenth, 50% in top quarter, 83% in top half
Early decision deadline: N/A, notification date: N/A
Early action deadline: 11/1, notification date: 1/30
Application deadline (fall): 6/1
Undergraduate student body: 20,597 full time, 3,317 part time; 53% male, 47% female; 0% American Indian, 7% Asian, 16% black, 10% Hispanic, 5% multiracial, 0% Pacific Islander, 58% white, 3% international; 96% from in state; 24% live on campus; 7% of students in fraternities, 11% in sororities
Most popular majors: 19% Business, Management, Marketing, and Related Support Services, 9% Engineering, 8% Health Professions and Related Programs, 8% Psychology, 8% Social Sciences
Expenses: 2018-2019: $6,854 in state, $20,813 out of state; room/board: $12,822
Financial aid: (704) 687-5504; 63% of undergrads determined to have financial need; average aid package $9,297

University of North Carolina–Greensboro

Greensboro NC
(336) 334-5243
U.S. News ranking: Nat. U., No. 201
Website: www.uncg.edu/
Admissions email: admissions@uncg.edu
Public; founded 1891
Freshman admissions: selective; 2017-2018: 8,524 applied, 6,645 accepted. Either SAT or ACT required. SAT 25/75 percentile: 1030-1180. High school rank: 13% in top tenth, 39% in top quarter, 77% in top half
Early decision deadline: N/A, notification date: N/A
Early action deadline: N/A, notification date: N/A
Application deadline (fall): 3/1
Undergraduate student body: 14,136 full time, 2,303 part time; 34% male, 66% female; 0% American Indian, 5% Asian, 29% black, 9% Hispanic, 5% multiracial, 0% Pacific Islander, 49% white, 2% international; 95% from in state; 32% live on campus; 2% of students in fraternities, 4% in sororities
Most popular majors: 13% Business Administration and Management, General, 6% Biology/Biological Sciences, General, 6% Kinesiology and Exercise Science, 6% Registered Nursing/Registered Nurse, 4% Psychology, General
Expenses: 2018-2019: $7,248 in state, $22,494 out of state; room/board: $9,038
Financial aid: (336) 334-5702; 85% of undergrads determined to have financial need; average aid package $11,508

University of North Carolina–Pembroke

Pembroke NC
(910) 521-6262
U.S. News ranking: Reg. U. (S), No. 102
Website: www.uncp.edu
Admissions email: admissions@uncp.edu
Public; founded 1887
Freshman admissions: less selective; 2017-2018: 4,549 applied, 3,666 accepted. Either SAT or ACT required. ACT 25/75 percentile: 18-21. High school rank: 10% in top tenth, 32% in top quarter, 70% in top half
Early decision deadline: N/A, notification date: N/A
Early action deadline: N/A, notification date: N/A
Application deadline (fall): 6/30
Undergraduate student body: 4,483 full time, 998 part time; 39% male, 61% female; 16% American Indian, 2% Asian, 35% black, 5% Hispanic, 3% multiracial, 0% Pacific Islander, 37% white, 1% international; 97% from in state; 37% live on campus; 6% of students in fraternities, 5% in sororities
Most popular majors: 14% Criminal Justice/Safety Studies, 13% Parks, Recreation, Leisure, and Fitness Studies, Other, 11% Biology/Biological Sciences, General, 10% Sociology, 9% Business Administration and Management, General
Expenses: 2018-2019: $3,418 in state, $7,418 out of state; room/board: $9,116
Financial aid: (910) 521-6255; 82% of undergrads determined to have financial need; average aid package $10,050

University of North Carolina School of the Arts

Winston-Salem NC
(336) 770-3291
U.S. News ranking: Arts, unranked
Website: www.uncsa.edu
Admissions email: admissions@uncsa.edu
Public; founded 1963
Freshman admissions: selective; 2017-2018: 956 applied, 312 accepted. Either SAT or ACT required. SAT 25/75 percentile: 1080-1290. High school rank: 18% in top tenth, 47% in top quarter, 77% in top half
Early decision deadline: N/A, notification date: N/A
Early action deadline: N/A, notification date: N/A
Application deadline (fall): 3/15
Undergraduate student body: 847 full time, 26 part time; 47% male, 53% female; 1% American Indian, 2% Asian, 10% black, 6% Hispanic, 5% multiracial, 0% Pacific Islander, 71% white, 2% international; 52% from in state; 58% live on campus; N/A of students in fraternities, N/A in sororities
Most popular majors: 100% Visual and Performing Arts
Expenses: 2018-2019: $9,358 in state, $25,628 out of state; room/board: $9,021
Financial aid: (336) 770-3297; 56% of undergrads determined to have financial need; average aid package $14,145

University of North Carolina–Wilmington

Wilmington NC
(910) 962-3243
U.S. News ranking: Reg. U. (S), No. 15
Website: www.uncw.edu
Admissions email: admissions@uncw.edu
Public; founded 1947
Freshman admissions: more selective; 2017-2018: 11,677 applied, 7,767 accepted. Either SAT or ACT required. ACT 25/75 percentile: 23-27. High school rank: 25% in top tenth, 62% in top quarter, 93% in top half
Early decision deadline: N/A, notification date: N/A
Early action deadline: 11/1, notification date: 1/20
Application deadline (fall): 2/1
Undergraduate student body: 12,346 full time, 2,156 part time; 38% male, 62% female; 0% American Indian, 2% Asian, 4% black, 7% Hispanic, 4% multiracial, 0% Pacific Islander, 78% white, 1% international; 88% from in state; 22% live on campus; 10% of students in fraternities, 10% in sororities
Most popular majors: 20% Business Administration and Management, General, 13% Registered Nursing/Registered Nurse, 7% Psychology, General, 5% Biology/Biological Sciences, General, 5% Speech Communication and Rhetoric
Expenses: 2018-2019: $7,000 in state, $21,065 out of state; room/board: $10,686
Financial aid: (910) 962-3177; 54% of undergrads determined to have financial need; average aid package $9,398

Wake Forest University

Winston-Salem NC
(336) 758-5201
U.S. News ranking: Nat. U., No. 27
Website: www.wfu.edu
Admissions email: admissions@wfu.edu
Private; founded 1834
Freshman admissions: most selective; 2017-2018: 13,071 applied, 3,604 accepted. Neither SAT nor ACT required. ACT 25/75 percentile: 28-32. High school rank: 77% in top tenth, 93% in top quarter, 98% in top half
Early decision deadline: 11/15, notification date: N/A
Early action deadline: N/A, notification date: N/A
Application deadline (fall): 1/1
Undergraduate student body: 5,046 full time, 56 part time; 46% male, 54% female; 0% American Indian, 4% Asian, 7% black, 7% Hispanic, 3% multiracial, 0% Pacific Islander, 70% white, 10% international; 22% from in state; 75% live on campus; 35% of students in fraternities, 60% in sororities
Most popular majors: 21% Social Sciences, 20% Business, Management, Marketing, and Related Support Services, 10% Communication, Journalism, and Related Programs, 9% Psychology, 8% Biological and Biomedical Sciences
Expenses: 2018-2019: $53,322; room/board: $16,032
Financial aid: (336) 758-5154; 31% of undergrads determined to have financial need; average aid package $49,309

Warren Wilson College

Asheville NC
(800) 934-3536
U.S. News ranking: Nat. Lib. Arts, No. 143
Website: www.warren-wilson.edu/
Admissions email: admit@warren-wilson.edu
Private; founded 1894
Freshman admissions: more selective; 2017-2018: 1,003 applied, 796 accepted. Neither SAT nor ACT required. ACT 25/75 percentile: 25-29. High school rank: 15% in top tenth, 39% in top quarter, 70% in top half
Early decision deadline: 11/1, notification date: 12/1
Early action deadline: 11/15, notification date: 12/1
Application deadline (fall): rolling
Undergraduate student body: 579 full time, 10 part time; 38% male, 62% female; 1% American Indian, 1% Asian, 5% black, 7% Hispanic, 3% multiracial, 0% Pacific Islander, 78% white, 2% international; 75% from in state; 80% live on campus; 0% of students in fraternities, 0% in sororities
Most popular majors: 21% Environmental Studies, 12% Biology/Biological Sciences, General, 11% Psychology, General, 9% Creative Writing, 7% Visual and Performing Arts, General

Expenses: 2018-2019: $36,280; room/board: $10,980
Financial aid: (828) 771-2082; 73% of undergrads determined to have financial need; average aid package $27,000

Western Carolina University

Cullowhee NC
(828) 227-7317
U.S. News ranking: Reg. U. (S), No. 34
Website: www.wcu.edu
Admissions email: admiss@email.wcu.edu
Public; founded 1889
Freshman admissions: selective; 2017-2018: 19,477 applied, 7,554 accepted. Either SAT or ACT required. ACT 25/75 percentile: 20-24. High school rank: 13% in top tenth, 38% in top quarter, 78% in top half
Early decision deadline: N/A, notification date: N/A
Early action deadline: 11/15, notification date: 12/15
Application deadline (fall): 3/1
Undergraduate student body: 8,040 full time, 1,366 part time; 45% male, 55% female; 1% American Indian, 1% Asian, 6% black, 7% Hispanic, 4% multiracial, 0% Pacific Islander, 79% white, 1% international; 93% from in state; N/A live on campus; N/A of students in fraternities, N/A in sororities
Most popular majors: 19% Business, Management, Marketing, and Related Support Services, 17% Health Professions and Related Programs, 10% Education, 7% Homeland Security, Law Enforcement, Firefighting and Related Protective Services, 6% Psychology
Expenses: 2018-2019: $4,220 in state, $8,220 out of state; room/board: $9,682
Financial aid: (828) 227-7290

William Peace University[1]

Raleigh NC
(919) 508-2214
U.S. News ranking: Nat. Lib. Arts, second tier
Website: www.peace.edu
Admissions email: admissions@peace.edu
Private; founded 1857
Application deadline (fall): rolling
Undergraduate student body: N/A full time, N/A part time
Expenses: 2017-2018: $28,700; room/board: $10,800
Financial aid: N/A

Wingate University

Wingate NC
(800) 755-5550
U.S. News ranking: Reg. U. (S), No. 52
Website: www.wingate.edu
Admissions email: admit@wingate.edu
Private; founded 1896
Freshman admissions: selective; 2017-2018: 15,198 applied, 14,170 accepted. Either SAT or ACT required. ACT 25/75 percentile: 18-23. High school rank: 10% in top tenth, 32% in top quarter, 72% in top half
Early decision deadline: N/A, notification date: N/A
Early action deadline: N/A, notification date: N/A
Application deadline (fall): rolling
Undergraduate student body: 2,537 full time, 55 part time; 39% male, 61% female; 0% American Indian, 2% Asian, 17% black, 4% Hispanic, 9% multiracial, 0% Pacific Islander, 58% white, 4% international; 73% from in state; 73% live on campus; 4% of students in fraternities, 10% in sororities
Most popular majors: 19% Business, Management, Marketing, and Related Support Services, 13% Communication, Journalism, and Related Programs, 10% Public Administration and Social Service Professions, 8% Biological and Biomedical Sciences, 8% Psychology
Expenses: 2018-2019: $33,166; room/board: $10,780
Financial aid: (704) 233-8010; 78% of undergrads determined to have financial need; average aid package $28,922

Winston-Salem State University[1]

Winston-Salem NC
(336) 750-2070
U.S. News ranking: Reg. U. (S), second tier
Website: www.wssu.edu
Admissions email: admissions@wssu.edu
Public; founded 1892
Application deadline (fall): 3/15
Undergraduate student body: N/A full time, N/A part time
Expenses: 2017-2018: $5,941 in state, $16,188 out of state; room/board: $10,029
Financial aid: N/A

NORTH DAKOTA

Bismarck State College[1]

Bismarck ND
(701) 224-2459
U.S. News ranking: Reg. Coll. (Mid. W), second tier
Website: bismarckstate.edu/
Admissions email: bsc.admissions@bismarckstate.edu
Public; founded 1939
Application deadline (fall): rolling
Undergraduate student body: N/A full time, N/A part time
Expenses: 2017-2018: $4,591 in state, $10,921 out of state; room/board: $6,992
Financial aid: (701) 224-5441

Dickinson State University

Dickinson ND
(701) 483-2175
U.S. News ranking: Reg. Coll. (Mid. W), No. 52
Website: www.dickinsonstate.edu/
Admissions email: dsu.hawks@dsu.nodak.edu
Public; founded 1918
Freshman admissions: less selective; 2017-2018: 388 applied, 384 accepted. Neither SAT nor ACT required. ACT 25/75 percentile: 18-23. High school rank: N/A
Early decision deadline: N/A, notification date: N/A
Early action deadline: N/A, notification date: N/A
Application deadline (fall): 8/15
Undergraduate student body: 922 full time, 503 part time; 39% male, 61% female; 1% American Indian, 1% Asian, 5% black, 6% Hispanic, 3% multiracial, 0% Pacific Islander, 77% white, 5% international; 71% from in state; N/A live on campus; N/A of students in fraternities, N/A in sororities
Most popular majors: 43% Business, Management, Marketing, and Related Support Services, 12% Multi/Interdisciplinary Studies, 8% Agriculture, Agriculture Operations, and Related Sciences, 7% Education, 6% Parks, Recreation, Leisure, and Fitness Studies
Expenses: 2018-2019: $6,765 in state, $9,544 out of state; room/board: $6,898
Financial aid: (701) 483-2371; 53% of undergrads determined to have financial need; average aid package $11,366

Mayville State University

Mayville ND
(701) 788-4667
U.S. News ranking: Reg. Coll. (Mid. W), No. 43
Website: www.mayvillestate.edu
Admissions email: masuadmissions@mayvillestate.edu
Public; founded 1889
Freshman admissions: selective; 2017-2018: 368 applied, 177 accepted. Either SAT or ACT required. ACT 25/75 percentile: 18-23. High school rank: N/A
Early decision deadline: N/A, notification date: N/A
Early action deadline: N/A, notification date: N/A
Application deadline (fall): rolling
Undergraduate student body: 600 full time, 497 part time; 39% male, 61% female; 2% American Indian, 0% Asian, 6% black, 7% Hispanic, 3% multiracial, 1% Pacific Islander, 78% white, 3% international; 51% from in state; 8% live on campus; N/A of students in fraternities, N/A in sororities
Most popular majors: Information not available
Expenses: 2018-2019: $6,666 in state, $8,033 out of state; room/board: $5,285
Financial aid: (701) 788-4767; 66% of undergrads determined to have financial need; average aid package $10,839

Minot State University

Minot ND
(701) 858-3350
U.S. News ranking: Reg. U. (Mid. W), second tier
Website: www.minotstateu.edu
Admissions email: askmsu@minotstateu.edu
Public; founded 1913
Freshman admissions: selective; 2017-2018: 709 applied, 489 accepted. Either SAT or ACT required. ACT 25/75 percentile: 19-24. High school rank: 9% in top tenth, 20% in top quarter, 64% in top half
Early decision deadline: N/A, notification date: N/A
Early action deadline: N/A, notification date: N/A
Application deadline (fall): rolling
Undergraduate student body: 1,952 full time, 1,004 part time; 40% male, 60% female; 2% American Indian, 2% Asian, 5% black, 7% Hispanic, 5% multiracial, 0% Pacific Islander, 69% white, 9% international; 81% from in state; 15% live on campus; N/A of students in fraternities, N/A in sororities
Most popular majors: Information not available
Expenses: 2018-2019: $7,064 in state, $7,064 out of state; room/board: $6,610
Financial aid: (701) 858-3375; 47% of undergrads determined to have financial need; average aid package $10,552

North Dakota State University

Fargo ND
(701) 231-8643
U.S. News ranking: Nat. U., No. 215
Website: www.ndsu.edu
Admissions email: NDSU.Admission@ndsu.edu
Public; founded 1890
Freshman admissions: selective; 2017-2018: 6,424 applied, 5,884 accepted. Either SAT or ACT required. ACT 25/75 percentile: 21-26. High school rank: 16% in top tenth, 41% in top quarter, 76% in top half
Early decision deadline: N/A, notification date: N/A
Early action deadline: N/A, notification date: N/A
Application deadline (fall): 8/1
Undergraduate student body: 10,782 full time, 1,202 part time; 54% male, 46% female; 1% American Indian, 1% Asian, 3% black, 2% Hispanic, 3% multiracial, 0% Pacific Islander, 87% white, 2% international; 42% from in state; 39% live on campus; 8% of students in fraternities, 8% in sororities
Most popular majors: 15% Engineering, 14% Business, Management, Marketing, and Related Support Services, 12% Agriculture, Agriculture Operations, and Related Sciences, 12% Health Professions and Related Programs, 7% Family and Consumer Sciences/Human Sciences
Expenses: 2018-2019: $10,176 in state, $15,144 out of state; room/board: $8,822
Financial aid: (701) 231-6221; 52% of undergrads determined to have financial need; average aid package $11,968

University of Jamestown

Jamestown ND
(701) 252-3467
U.S. News ranking: Reg. Coll. (Mid. W), No. 29
Website: www.uj.edu
Admissions email: admissions@uj.edu
Private; founded 1883
Affiliation: Presbyterian Church (USA)
Freshman admissions: selective; 2017-2018: 1,154 applied, 753 accepted. Either SAT or ACT required. ACT 25/75 percentile: 19-24. High school rank: 15% in top tenth, 37% in top quarter, 73% in top half
Early decision deadline: N/A, notification date: N/A
Early action deadline: N/A, notification date: N/A
Application deadline (fall): 9/10
Undergraduate student body: 869 full time, 46 part time; 50% male, 50% female; 1% American Indian, 1% Asian, 4% black, 7% Hispanic, 0% multiracial, 1% Pacific Islander, 75% white, 10% international; 51% from in state; 76% live on campus; N/A of students in fraternities, N/A in sororities
Most popular majors: 24% Registered Nursing/Registered Nurse, 14% Business Administration and Management, General, 8% Elementary Education and Teaching, 8% Kinesiology and Exercise Science, 6% Psychology, General
Expenses: 2018-2019: $21,976; room/board: $7,886
Financial aid: (701) 252-3467; 63% of undergrads determined to have financial need; average aid package $16,626

University of Mary[1]

Bismarck ND
(701) 355-8030
U.S. News ranking: Reg. U. (Mid. W), No. 111
Website: www.umary.edu
Admissions email: marauder@umary.edu
Private; founded 1959
Affiliation: Roman Catholic
Application deadline (fall): rolling
Undergraduate student body: N/A full time, N/A part time
Expenses: 2017-2018: $18,150; room/board: $6,970
Financial aid: (701) 355-8226

University of North Dakota

Grand Forks ND
(800) 225-5863
U.S. News ranking: Nat. U., No. 205
Website: und.edu
Admissions email: admissions@und.edu
Public; founded 1883
Freshman admissions: selective; 2017-2018: 5,230 applied, 4,366 accepted. Either SAT or ACT required. ACT 25/75 percentile: 21-26. High school rank: 17% in top tenth, 43% in top quarter, 75% in top half

Early decision deadline: N/A, notification date: N/A
Early action deadline: N/A, notification date: N/A
Application deadline (fall): rolling
Undergraduate student body: 8,525 full time, 2,475 part time; 56% male, 44% female; 1% American Indian, 2% Asian, 2% black, 3% Hispanic, 3% multiracial, 0% Pacific Islander, 81% white, 5% international; 39% from in state; 28% live on campus; 10% of students in fraternities, 13% in sororities
Most popular majors: 6% General Studies, 6% Psychology, General, 6% Registered Nursing/Registered Nurse, 5% Airline/Commercial/ Professional Pilot and Flight Crew, 5% Speech Communication and Rhetoric
Expenses: 2018-2019: $8,827 in state, $20,891 out of state; room/ board: $8,974
Financial aid: (701) 777-3121; 50% of undergrads determined to have financial need; average aid package $13,946

Valley City State University

Valley City ND
(701) 845-7101
U.S. News ranking: Reg. Coll. (Mid. W), No. 42
Website: www.vcsu.edu
Admissions email: enrollment.services@vcsu.edu
Public; founded 1890
Freshman admissions: selective; 2017-2018: 384 applied, 380 accepted. Either SAT or ACT required. ACT 25/75 percentile: 18-23. High school rank: N/A
Early decision deadline: N/A, notification date: N/A
Early action deadline: N/A, notification date: N/A
Application deadline (fall): rolling
Undergraduate student body: 834 full time, 538 part time; 43% male, 57% female; 1% American Indian, 1% Asian, 3% black, 7% Hispanic, 4% multiracial, 0% Pacific Islander, 81% white, 2% international; 62% from in state; 32% live on campus; 1% of students in fraternities, 1% in sororities
Most popular majors: 55% Education, 9% Business, Management, Marketing, and Related Support Services, 7% Natural Resources and Conservation, 6% Psychology, 5% Health Professions and Related Programs
Expenses: 2018-2019: $7,626 in state, $17,166 out of state; room/ board: $6,388
Financial aid: (701) 845-7541; 58% of undergrads determined to have financial need; average aid package $12,648

OHIO

Antioch University

Yellow Springs OH
(937) 769-1818
U.S. News ranking: Reg. U. (Mid. W), unranked
Website: midwest.antioch.edu
Admissions email: admission.aum@antioch.edu
Private; founded 1852
Freshman admissions: least selective; 2017-2018: N/A applied, N/A accepted. Neither SAT nor ACT required. SAT 25/75 percentile: N/A. High school rank: N/A
Early decision deadline: N/A, notification date: N/A
Early action deadline: N/A, notification date: N/A
Application deadline (fall): rolling
Undergraduate student body: 20 full time, 21 part time; 27% male, 73% female; 0% American Indian, 0% Asian, 12% black, 7% Hispanic, 0% multiracial, 0% Pacific Islander, 78% white, 0% international
Most popular majors: Information not available
Expenses: N/A
Financial aid: N/A

Art Academy of Cincinnati[1]

Cincinnati OH
(513) 562-6262
U.S. News ranking: Arts, unranked
Website: www.artacademy.edu
Admissions email: admissions@artacademy.edu
Private; founded 1869
Application deadline (fall): N/A
Undergraduate student body: N/A full time, N/A part time
Expenses: N/A
Financial aid: N/A

Ashland University

Ashland OH
(419) 289-5052
U.S. News ranking: Nat. U., second tier
Website: www.ashland.edu/ admissions
Admissions email: enrollme@ashland.edu
Private; founded 1878
Freshman admissions: selective; 2017-2018: 3,118 applied, 2,292 accepted. Either SAT or ACT required. ACT 25/75 percentile: 20-25. High school rank: N/A
Early decision deadline: N/A, notification date: N/A
Early action deadline: N/A, notification date: N/A
Application deadline (fall): rolling
Undergraduate student body: 2,610 full time, 749 part time; 37% male, 63% female; 0% American Indian, 1% Asian, 6% black, 3% Hispanic, 2% multiracial, 0% Pacific Islander, 83% white, 2% international; 78% from in state; 44% live on campus; 8% of students in fraternities, 14% in sororities
Most popular majors: 24% Health Professions and Related Programs, 20% Education, 18% Business, Management, Marketing, and Related Support Services, 8% Biological and Biomedical Sciences, 7% Homeland Security, Law Enforcement, Firefighting and Related Protective Services
Expenses: 2018-2019: $21,342; room/board: $9,942
Financial aid: (419) 289-5944; 73% of undergrads determined to have financial need; average aid package $17,734

Baldwin Wallace University

Berea OH
(440) 826-2222
U.S. News ranking: Reg. U. (Mid. W), No. 13
Website: www.bw.edu
Admissions email: admission@bw.edu
Private; founded 1845
Affiliation: United Methodist
Freshman admissions: selective; 2017-2018: 3,576 applied, 2,791 accepted. Neither SAT nor ACT required. ACT 25/75 percentile: 21-27. High school rank: 22% in top tenth, 48% in top quarter, 81% in top half
Early decision deadline: N/A, notification date: N/A
Early action deadline: N/A, notification date: N/A
Application deadline (fall): rolling
Undergraduate student body: 2,979 full time, 225 part time; 45% male, 55% female; 0% American Indian, 2% Asian, 9% black, 5% Hispanic, 5% multiracial, 0% Pacific Islander, 78% white, 1% international; 76% from in state; 61% live on campus; 13% of students in fraternities, 20% in sororities
Most popular majors: 24% Business, Management, Marketing, and Related Support Services, 12% Visual and Performing Arts, 11% Biological and Biomedical Sciences, 10% Health Professions and Related Programs, 7% Psychology
Expenses: 2018-2019: $32,586; room/board: $9,554
Financial aid: (440) 826-2108; 79% of undergrads determined to have financial need; average aid package $26,990

Bluffton University

Bluffton OH
(800) 488-3257
U.S. News ranking: Reg. Coll. (Mid. W), No. 30
Website: www.bluffton.edu
Admissions email: admissions@bluffton.edu
Private; founded 1899
Affiliation: Mennonite Church
Freshman admissions: selective; 2017-2018: 1,767 applied, 863 accepted. Either SAT or ACT required. ACT 25/75 percentile: 18-24. High school rank: 11% in top tenth, 34% in top quarter, 64% in top half
Early decision deadline: N/A, notification date: N/A
Early action deadline: N/A, notification date: N/A
Application deadline (fall): rolling
Undergraduate student body: 665 full time, 92 part time; 50% male, 50% female; 0% American Indian, 1% Asian, 9% black, 4% Hispanic, 4% multiracial, 0% Pacific Islander, 79% white, 1% international; 88% from in state; 80% live on campus; N/A of students in fraternities, N/A in sororities
Most popular majors: 32% Business, Management, Marketing, and Related Support Services, 16% Education, 11% Parks, Recreation, Leisure, and Fitness Studies, 7% Family and Consumer Sciences/ Human Sciences, 7% Public Administration and Social Service Professions
Expenses: 2018-2019: $32,766; room/board: $10,800
Financial aid: (419) 358-3266; 86% of undergrads determined to have financial need; average aid package $27,173

Bowling Green State University

Bowling Green OH
(419) 372-2478
U.S. News ranking: Nat. U., No. 215
Website: www.bgsu.edu
Admissions email: choosebgsu@bgsu.edu
Public; founded 1910
Freshman admissions: selective; 2017-2018: 16,739 applied, 11,438 accepted. Either SAT or ACT required. ACT 25/75 percentile: 20-25. High school rank: 12% in top tenth, 36% in top quarter, 70% in top half
Early decision deadline: N/A, notification date: N/A
Early action deadline: N/A, notification date: N/A
Application deadline (fall): 7/15
Undergraduate student body: 13,104 full time, 1,576 part time; 44% male, 56% female; 0% American Indian, 1% Asian, 9% black, 4% Hispanic, 3% multiracial, 0% Pacific Islander, 78% white, 2% international; 88% from in state; 42% live on campus; 13% of students in fraternities, 12% in sororities
Most popular majors: 4% Biology/ Biological Sciences, General, 4% Education, Other, 4% Education/ Teaching of Individuals in Early Childhood Special Education Programs, 4% Psychology, General, 4% Rhetoric and Composition
Expenses: 2018-2019: $11,105 in state, $19,093 out of state; room/board: $9,168
Financial aid: (419) 372-2651; 66% of undergrads determined to have financial need; average aid package $14,097

Capital University

Columbus OH
(866) 544-6175
U.S. News ranking: Reg. U. (Mid. W), No. 35
Website: www.capital.edu
Admissions email: admission@capital.edu
Private; founded 1830
Affiliation: Evangelical Lutheran Church
Freshman admissions: selective; 2017-2018: 4,208 applied, 2,889 accepted. Either SAT or ACT required. ACT 25/75 percentile: 22-27. High school rank: 18% in top tenth, 48% in top quarter, 80% in top half
Early decision deadline: N/A, notification date: N/A
Early action deadline: N/A, notification date: N/A
Application deadline (fall): 5/1
Undergraduate student body: 2,493 full time, 206 part time; 39% male, 61% female; 0% American Indian, 1% Asian, 10% black, 4% Hispanic, 5% multiracial, 0% Pacific Islander, 74% white, 2% international; 91% from in state; 58% live on campus; 2% of students in fraternities, 3% in sororities
Most popular majors: 20% Health Professions and Related Programs, 13% Business, Management, Marketing, and Related Support Services, 11% Education, 8% Visual and Performing Arts, 7% Biological and Biomedical Sciences
Expenses: 2018-2019: $35,466; room/board: $10,842
Financial aid: (614) 236-6771; 81% of undergrads determined to have financial need; average aid package $28,702

Case Western Reserve University

Cleveland OH
(216) 368-4450
U.S. News ranking: Nat. U., No. 42
Website: www.case.edu
Admissions email: admission@case.edu
Private; founded 1826
Freshman admissions: most selective; 2017-2018: 25,380 applied, 8,405 accepted. Either SAT or ACT required. ACT 25/75 percentile: 30-33. High school rank: 70% in top tenth, 95% in top quarter, 100% in top half
Early decision deadline: 11/1, notification date: 12/17
Early action deadline: 11/1, notification date: 12/15
Application deadline (fall): 1/15
Undergraduate student body: 4,978 full time, 172 part time; 55% male, 45% female; 0% American Indian, 21% Asian, 4% black, 7% Hispanic, 5% multiracial, 0% Pacific Islander, 49% white, 13% international; 28% from in state; 80% live on campus; 27% of students in fraternities, 26% in sororities
Most popular majors: 10% Bioengineering and Biomedical Engineering, 8% Mechanical Engineering, 7% Psychology, General, 6% Biology/Biological Sciences, General, 6% Registered Nursing/Registered Nurse
Expenses: 2018-2019: $49,042; room/board: $15,190
Financial aid: (216) 368-4530; 50% of undergrads determined to have financial need; average aid package $44,122

Cedarville University

Cedarville OH
(800) 233-2784
U.S. News ranking: Reg. Coll. (Mid. W), No. 12
Website: www.cedarville.edu
Admissions email: admissions@cedarville.edu
Private; founded 1887
Affiliation: Baptist

Freshman admissions: more selective; 2017-2018: 4,039 applied, 2,885 accepted. Either SAT or ACT required. ACT 25/75 percentile: 23-29. High school rank: 33% in top tenth, 62% in top quarter, 88% in top half
Early decision deadline: N/A, notification date: N/A
Early action deadline: N/A, notification date: N/A
Application deadline (fall): 8/1
Undergraduate student body: 3,109 full time, 426 part time; 47% male, 53% female; 0% American Indian, 2% Asian, 1% black, 3% Hispanic, 3% multiracial, 0% Pacific Islander, 87% white, 2% international; 43% from in state; 73% live on campus; 0% of students in fraternities, 0% in sororities
Most popular majors: 19% Health Professions and Related Programs, 10% Business, Management, Marketing, and Related Support Services, 10% Education, 10% Engineering, 10% Theology and Religious Vocations
Expenses: 2018-2019: $30,270; room/board: $7,360
Financial aid: (937) 766-7866; 70% of undergrads determined to have financial need; average aid package $21,864

Central State University

Wilberforce OH
(937) 376-6348
U.S. News ranking: Reg. Coll. (Mid. W), second tier
Website: www.centralstate.edu
Admissions email: admissions@centralstate.edu
Public; founded 1887
Freshman admissions: least selective; 2017-2018: 12,517 applied, 6,010 accepted. Neither SAT nor ACT required. ACT 25/75 percentile: 15-18. High school rank: 10% in top tenth, 26% in top quarter, 51% in top half
Early decision deadline: N/A, notification date: N/A
Early action deadline: N/A, notification date: N/A
Application deadline (fall): rolling
Undergraduate student body: 1,710 full time, 74 part time; 41% male, 59% female; 0% American Indian, 0% Asian, 92% black, 1% Hispanic, 2% multiracial, 0% Pacific Islander, 1% white, 2% international; 62% from in state; 36% live on campus; 1% of students in fraternities, 1% in sororities
Most popular majors: 19% Business, Management, Marketing, and Related Support Services, 14% Psychology, 12% Homeland Security, Law Enforcement, Firefighting and Related Protective Services, 7% Biological and Biomedical Sciences, 6% Public Administration and Social Service Professions
Expenses: 2018-2019: $6,346 in state, $8,346 out of state; room/board: $10,232
Financial aid: (937) 376-6574; 99% of undergrads determined to have financial need; average aid package $9,695

Cleveland Institute of Art

Cleveland OH
(216) 421-7418
U.S. News ranking: Arts, unranked
Website: www.cia.edu
Admissions email: admissions@cia.edu
Private; founded 1882
Freshman admissions: selective; 2017-2018: 957 applied, 519 accepted. Neither SAT nor ACT required. ACT 25/75 percentile: 20-26. High school rank: 13% in top tenth, 38% in top quarter, 68% in top half
Early decision deadline: N/A, notification date: N/A
Early action deadline: 12/1, notification date: 12/15
Application deadline (fall): rolling
Undergraduate student body: 620 full time, 17 part time; 37% male, 63% female; 0% American Indian, 3% Asian, 9% black, 8% Hispanic, 4% multiracial, 0% Pacific Islander, 66% white, 9% international; N/A from in state; 32% live on campus; 1% of students in fraternities, 1% in sororities
Most popular majors: 15% Industrial and Product Design, 14% Illustration, 11% Animation, Interactive Technology, Video Graphics and Special Effects, 11% Medical Illustration/Medical Illustrator, 7% Painting
Expenses: 2018-2019: $42,055; room/board: $11,070
Financial aid: (216) 421-7425; 82% of undergrads determined to have financial need; average aid package $28,600

Cleveland Institute of Music

Cleveland OH
(216) 795-3107
U.S. News ranking: Arts, unranked
Website: www.cim.edu/
Admissions email: admission@cim.edu
Private; founded 1920
Freshman admissions: least selective; 2017-2018: 490 applied, 211 accepted. Neither SAT nor ACT required. SAT 25/75 percentile: N/A. High school rank: N/A
Early decision deadline: N/A, notification date: N/A
Early action deadline: N/A, notification date: N/A
Application deadline (fall): 12/1
Undergraduate student body: 216 full time, 5 part time; 52% male, 48% female; 0% American Indian, 9% Asian, 2% black, 0% Hispanic, 0% multiracial, 0% Pacific Islander, 32% white, 26% international
Most popular majors: 100% Music
Expenses: 2018-2019: $41,487; room/board: $15,048
Financial aid: (216) 795-3192; 50% of undergrads determined to have financial need; average aid package $34,169

Cleveland State University

Cleveland OH
(216) 687-2100
U.S. News ranking: Nat. U., second tier
Website: www.csuohio.edu
Admissions email: admissions@csuohio.edu
Public; founded 1964
Freshman admissions: selective; 2017-2018: 7,537 applied, 6,788 accepted. Either SAT or ACT required. ACT 25/75 percentile: 19-25. High school rank: 16% in top tenth, 40% in top quarter, 72% in top half
Early decision deadline: N/A, notification date: N/A
Early action deadline: 5/1, notification date: N/A
Application deadline (fall): 8/16
Undergraduate student body: 9,268 full time, 3,038 part time; 46% male, 54% female; 0% American Indian, 3% Asian, 16% black, 6% Hispanic, 4% multiracial, 0% Pacific Islander, 64% white, 5% international; 97% from in state; 8% live on campus; 1% of students in fraternities, 1% in sororities
Most popular majors: 8% Psychology, General, 6% Clinical/Medical Laboratory Science and Allied Professions, Other, 4% Business Administration and Management, General, 4% Mechanical Engineering, 4% Social Work
Expenses: 2018-2019: $10,112 in state, $14,164 out of state; room/board: $11,358
Financial aid: (216) 687-5594; 72% of undergrads determined to have financial need; average aid package $8,932

College of Wooster

Wooster OH
(330) 263-2322
U.S. News ranking: Nat. Lib. Arts, No. 67
Website: www.wooster.edu/
Admissions email: admissions@wooster.edu
Private; founded 1866
Freshman admissions: more selective; 2017-2018: 5,615 applied, 3,169 accepted. Either SAT or ACT required. ACT 25/75 percentile: 24-30. High school rank: 45% in top tenth, 75% in top quarter, 92% in top half
Early decision deadline: 11/1, notification date: 11/15
Early action deadline: 11/15, notification date: 12/31
Application deadline (fall): 2/15
Undergraduate student body: 1,962 full time, 18 part time; 45% male, 55% female; 1% American Indian, 5% Asian, 9% black, 5% Hispanic, 0% multiracial, 0% Pacific Islander, 66% white, 13% international; 37% from in state; 99% live on campus; 14% of students in fraternities, 17% in sororities
Most popular majors: 24% Social Sciences, 15% Biological and Biomedical Sciences, 11% Physical Sciences, 8% Psychology, 7% English Language and Literature/Letters
Expenses: 2018-2019: $50,250; room/board: $11,850
Financial aid: (330) 263-2317; 56% of undergrads determined to have financial need; average aid package $43,407

Columbus College of Art and Design

Columbus OH
(614) 222-3261
U.S. News ranking: Arts, unranked
Website: www.ccad.edu
Admissions email: admissions@ccad.edu
Private; founded 1879
Freshman admissions: selective; 2017-2018: 856 applied, 749 accepted. Neither SAT nor ACT required. ACT 25/75 percentile: 19-26. High school rank: N/A
Early decision deadline: N/A, notification date: N/A
Early action deadline: N/A, notification date: N/A
Application deadline (fall): 8/1
Undergraduate student body: 1,001 full time, 24 part time; 30% male, 70% female; 0% American Indian, 4% Asian, 10% black, 7% Hispanic, 5% multiracial, 0% Pacific Islander, 65% white, 7% international
Most popular majors: 22% Commercial and Advertising Art, 20% Illustration, 12% Animation, Interactive Technology, Video Graphics and Special Effects, 11% Fine Arts and Art Studies, Other, 7% Photography
Expenses: 2018-2019: $36,020; room/board: $9,570
Financial aid: (614) 222-3274; 79% of undergrads determined to have financial need; average aid package $23,109

Defiance College

Defiance OH
(419) 783-2359
U.S. News ranking: Reg. Coll. (Mid. W), No. 33
Website: www.defiance.edu
Admissions email: admissions@defiance.edu
Private; founded 1850
Affiliation: United Church of Christ
Freshman admissions: less selective; 2017-2018: 1,393 applied, 777 accepted. Either SAT or ACT required. ACT 25/75 percentile: 18-22. High school rank: 13% in top tenth, 23% in top quarter, 79% in top half
Early decision deadline: N/A, notification date: N/A
Early action deadline: N/A, notification date: N/A
Application deadline (fall): rolling
Undergraduate student body: 525 full time, 59 part time; 56% male, 44% female; 0% American Indian, 1% Asian, 13% black, 7% Hispanic, 3% multiracial, 0% Pacific Islander, 74% white, 2% international; 29% from in state; 50% live on campus; 9% of students in fraternities, 9% in sororities
Most popular majors: 10% Athletic Training/Trainer, 10% Business Administration, Management and Operations, 9% Criminal Justice and Corrections, 9% Social Work, 9% Sport and Fitness Administration/Management
Expenses: 2018-2019: $32,730; room/board: $10,220
Financial aid: (419) 783-2376; 90% of undergrads determined to have financial need; average aid package $23,951

Denison University

Granville OH
(740) 587-6276
U.S. News ranking: Nat. Lib. Arts, No. 43
Website: www.denison.edu
Admissions email: admission@denison.edu
Private; founded 1831
Freshman admissions: more selective; 2017-2018: 7,540 applied, 2,808 accepted. Neither SAT nor ACT required. ACT 25/75 percentile: 28-31. High school rank: 65% in top tenth, 87% in top quarter, 100% in top half
Early decision deadline: 11/15, notification date: 12/15
Early action deadline: N/A, notification date: N/A
Application deadline (fall): 1/15
Undergraduate student body: 2,319 full time, 22 part time; 45% male, 55% female; 0% American Indian, 4% Asian, 7% black, 9% Hispanic, 3% multiracial, 0% Pacific Islander, 65% white, 10% international; 26% from in state; 99% live on campus; 30% of students in fraternities, 49% in sororities
Most popular majors: 26% Social Sciences, 14% Communication, Journalism, and Related Programs 10% Biological and Biomedical Sciences, 9% Psychology, 6% Visual and Performing Arts
Expenses: 2018-2019: $51,960; room/board: $12,710
Financial aid: (740) 587-6276; 54% of undergrads determined to have financial need; average aid package $44,138

Franciscan University of Steubenville

Steubenville OH
(740) 283-6226
U.S. News ranking: Reg. U. (Mid. W), No. 11
Website: www.franciscan.edu
Admissions email: admissions@franciscan.edu
Private; founded 1946
Affiliation: Roman Catholic
Freshman admissions: more selective; 2017-2018: 1,653 applied, 1,385 accepted. Either SAT or ACT required. ACT 25/75 percentile: 23-28. High school rank: 28% in top tenth, 55% in top quarter, 82% in top half
Early decision deadline: N/A, notification date: N/A
Early action deadline: N/A, notification date: N/A
Application deadline (fall): rolling
Undergraduate student body: 2,011 full time, 189 part time; 41% male, 59% female; 0% American Indian, 2% Asian, 1% black, 11% Hispanic, 2% multiracial, 0% Pacific Islander, 81% white, 1% international; 22% from in state; 75% live on campus; 0% of students in fraternities, 0% in sororities

More @ usnews.com/bestcolleges

Most popular majors: 25% Theology/Theological Studies, 13% Business Administration and Management, General, 9% Registered Nursing/Registered Nurse, 8% Multicultural Education, 7% Psychology, General
Expenses: 2018-2019: $27,630; room/board: $8,500
Financial aid: (740) 284-5216; 54% of undergrads determined to have financial need; average aid package $17,301

Franklin University[1]

Columbus OH
(888) 341-6237
U.S. News ranking: Business, unranked
Website: www.franklin.edu
Admissions email: info@franklin.edu
Private; founded 1902
Application deadline (fall): N/A
Undergraduate student body: N/A full time, N/A part time
Expenses: N/A
Financial aid: N/A

Heidelberg University

Tiffin OH
(419) 448-2330
U.S. News ranking: Reg. U. (Mid. W), No. 58
Website: www.heidelberg.edu
Admissions email: adminfo@heidelberg.edu
Private; founded 1850
Affiliation: United Church of Christ
Freshman admissions: selective; 2017-2018: 1,715 applied, 1,303 accepted. Either SAT or ACT required. ACT 25/75 percentile: 20-26. High school rank: N/A
Early decision deadline: N/A, notification date: N/A
Early action deadline: N/A, notification date: N/A
Application deadline (fall): 8/1
Undergraduate student body: 1,043 full time, 23 part time; 54% male, 46% female; 0% American Indian, 1% Asian, 10% black, 3% Hispanic, 3% multiracial, 0% Pacific Islander, 78% white, 0% international; 81% from in state; 79% live on campus; 11% of students in fraternities, 23% in sororities
Most popular majors: 15% Business, Management, Marketing, and Related Support Services, 13% Health Professions and Related Programs, 10% Homeland Security, Law Enforcement, Firefighting and Related Protective Services, 10% Psychology, 8% Education
Expenses: 2018-2019: $31,000; room/board: $10,400
Financial aid: (419) 448-2293; 87% of undergrads determined to have financial need; average aid package $25,112

Hiram College

Hiram OH
(330) 569-5169
U.S. News ranking: Nat. Lib. Arts, No. 155
Website: www.hiram.edu
Admissions email: admission@hiram.edu
Private; founded 1850
Freshman admissions: selective; 2017-2018: 2,761 applied, 1,754 accepted. Neither SAT nor ACT required. ACT 25/75 percentile: 18-24. High school rank: 11% in top tenth, 30% in top quarter, 70% in top half
Early decision deadline: N/A, notification date: N/A
Early action deadline: N/A, notification date: N/A
Application deadline (fall): rolling
Undergraduate student body: 853 full time, 357 part time; 46% male, 54% female; 0% American Indian, 1% Asian, 16% black, 4% Hispanic, 3% multiracial, 0% Pacific Islander, 64% white, 1% international; 82% from in state; 84% live on campus; 0% of students in fraternities, 2% in sororities
Most popular majors: 33% Business, Management, Marketing, and Related Support Services, 12% Social Sciences, 10% Biological and Biomedical Sciences, 9% Health Professions and Related Programs, 5% Psychology
Expenses: 2018-2019: $36,358; room/board: $10,290
Financial aid: (330) 569-5441

John Carroll University

University Heights OH
(216) 397-4294
U.S. News ranking: Reg. U. (Mid. W), No. 4
Website: www.jcu.edu
Admissions email: admission@jcu.edu
Private; founded 1886
Affiliation: Roman Catholic
Freshman admissions: selective; 2017-2018: 3,840 applied, 3,265 accepted. Either SAT or ACT required. ACT 25/75 percentile: 22-27. High school rank: 29% in top tenth, 57% in top quarter, 93% in top half
Early decision deadline: N/A, notification date: N/A
Early action deadline: 12/1, notification date: 12/15
Application deadline (fall): rolling
Undergraduate student body: 2,959 full time, 93 part time; 51% male, 49% female; 0% American Indian, 2% Asian, 4% black, 4% Hispanic, 2% multiracial, 0% Pacific Islander, 84% white, 3% international; 67% from in state; 53% live on campus; 9% of students in fraternities, 21% in sororities
Most popular majors: 30% Business, Management, Marketing, and Related Support Services, 12% Communication, Journalism, and Related Programs, 11% Psychology, 10% Biological and Biomedical Sciences, 10% Social Sciences
Expenses: 2018-2019: $39,990; room/board: $11,430
Financial aid: (216) 397-4248; 71% of undergrads determined to have financial need; average aid package $31,771

Kent State University

Kent OH
(330) 672-2444
U.S. News ranking: Nat. U., No. 191
Website: www.kent.edu
Admissions email: kentadm@kent.edu
Public; founded 1910
Freshman admissions: selective; 2017-2018: 15,538 applied, 13,598 accepted. Either SAT or ACT required. ACT 25/75 percentile: 21-25. High school rank: 15% in top tenth, 39% in top quarter, 78% in top half
Early decision deadline: N/A, notification date: N/A
Early action deadline: N/A, notification date: N/A
Application deadline (fall): 5/1
Undergraduate student body: 20,509 full time, 2,669 part time; 39% male, 61% female; 0% American Indian, 2% Asian, 9% black, 4% Hispanic, 4% multiracial, 0% Pacific Islander, 75% white, 5% international; 85% from in state; 29% live on campus; N/A of students in fraternities, N/A in sororities
Most popular majors: 22% Business, Management, Marketing, and Related Support Services, 17% Health Professions and Related Programs, 9% Communication, Journalism, and Related Programs, 8% Education, 6% Visual and Performing Arts
Expenses: 2018-2019: $10,756 in state, $19,456 out of state; room/board: $11,362
Financial aid: (330) 672-2972; 63% of undergrads determined to have financial need; average aid package $10,715

Kenyon College

Gambier OH
(740) 427-5776
U.S. News ranking: Nat. Lib. Arts, No. 30
Website: www.kenyon.edu
Admissions email: admissions@kenyon.edu
Private; founded 1824
Freshman admissions: more selective; 2017-2018: 5,603 applied, 1,896 accepted. Either SAT or ACT required. ACT 25/75 percentile: 29-33. High school rank: 63% in top tenth, 86% in top quarter, 100% in top half
Early decision deadline: 11/15, notification date: 12/18
Early action deadline: N/A, notification date: N/A
Application deadline (fall): 1/15
Undergraduate student body: 1,661 full time, 16 part time; 44% male, 56% female; 0% American Indian, 3% Asian, 3% black, 6% Hispanic, 7% multiracial, 0% Pacific Islander, 72% white, 6% international; 15% from in state; 100% live on campus; 27% of students in fraternities, 32% in sororities
Most popular majors: 14% English Language and Literature, General, 10% Economics, General, 9% Political Science and Government, General, 8% Psychology, General, 5% History, General
Expenses: 2018-2019: $55,930; room/board: $12,510
Financial aid: (740) 427-5430; 41% of undergrads determined to have financial need; average aid package $46,458

Lake Erie College

Painesville OH
(855) 467-8676
U.S. News ranking: Reg. U. (Mid. W), second tier
Website: www.lec.edu
Admissions email: admissions@lec.edu
Private; founded 1856
Freshman admissions: selective; 2017-2018: 1,656 applied, 1,000 accepted. Neither SAT nor ACT required. ACT 25/75 percentile: 18-23. High school rank: 13% in top tenth, 29% in top quarter, 58% in top half
Early decision deadline: N/A, notification date: N/A
Early action deadline: 12/1, notification date: 12/14
Application deadline (fall): 8/1
Undergraduate student body: 724 full time, 231 part time; 46% male, 54% female; 0% American Indian, 1% Asian, 15% black, 3% Hispanic, 4% multiracial, 0% Pacific Islander, 70% white, 3% international
Most popular majors: Information not available
Expenses: 2018-2019: $31,422; room/board: $9,908
Financial aid: (440) 375-7100; 85% of undergrads determined to have financial need; average aid package $25,144

Lourdes University

Sylvania OH
(419) 885-5291
U.S. News ranking: Reg. U. (Mid. W), second tier
Website: www.lourdes.edu
Admissions email: luadmits@lourdes.edu
Private; founded 1958
Affiliation: Roman Catholic
Freshman admissions: selective; 2017-2018: 991 applied, 958 accepted. Either SAT or ACT required. ACT 25/75 percentile: 18-24. High school rank: 11% in top tenth, 28% in top quarter, 60% in top half
Early decision deadline: N/A, notification date: N/A
Early action deadline: N/A, notification date: N/A
Application deadline (fall): rolling
Undergraduate student body: 827 full time, 217 part time; 35% male, 65% female; N/A American Indian, N/A Asian, N/A black, N/A Hispanic, N/A multiracial, N/A Pacific Islander, N/A white, N/A international; 70% from in state; 41% live on campus; N/A of students in fraternities, N/A in sororities
Most popular majors: 37% Registered Nursing/Registered Nurse, 8% Multi-/Interdisciplinary Studies, Other, 5% Business Administration and Management, General, 5% Criminal Justice/ Safety Studies, 5% Marketing, Other
Expenses: 2018-2019: $22,480; room/board: $10,100
Financial aid: (419) 824-3504

Malone University

Canton OH
(330) 471-8145
U.S. News ranking: Reg. U. (Mid. W), No. 81
Website: www.malone.edu
Admissions email: admissions@malone.edu
Private; founded 1892
Affiliation: Friends
Freshman admissions: selective; 2017-2018: 1,864 applied, 1,230 accepted. Either SAT or ACT required. ACT 25/75 percentile: 19-24. High school rank: 15% in top tenth, 33% in top quarter, 67% in top half
Early decision deadline: N/A, notification date: N/A
Early action deadline: N/A, notification date: N/A
Application deadline (fall): rolling
Undergraduate student body: 1,099 full time, 234 part time; 42% male, 58% female; 0% American Indian, 1% Asian, 11% black, 3% Hispanic, 4% multiracial, 0% Pacific Islander, 80% white, 1% international; 88% from in state; 63% live on campus; 0% of students in fraternities, 0% in sororities
Most popular majors: 12% Registered Nursing/Registered Nurse, 10% Business Administration and Management, General, 5% Social Work, 4% Kinesiology and Exercise Science, 3% Education/Teaching of Individuals with Specific Learning Disabilities
Expenses: 2018-2019: $30,860; room/board: $9,500
Financial aid: (330) 471-8161; 86% of undergrads determined to have financial need; average aid package $25,724

Marietta College

Marietta OH
(800) 331-7896
U.S. News ranking: Reg. Coll. (Mid. W), No. 13
Website: www.marietta.edu
Admissions email: admit@marietta.edu
Private; founded 1797
Freshman admissions: selective; 2017-2018: 1,644 applied, 1,122 accepted. Either SAT or ACT required. ACT 25/75 percentile: 20-25. High school rank: 19% in top tenth, 41% in top quarter, 74% in top half
Early decision deadline: N/A, notification date: N/A
Early action deadline: 11/1, notification date: 11/15
Application deadline (fall): 4/15
Undergraduate student body: 960 full time, 105 part time; 61% male, 39% female; 0% American Indian, 1% Asian, 5% black, 2% Hispanic, 4% multiracial, 0% Pacific Islander, 65% white, 18% international; 67% from in state; 70% live on campus; 15% of students in fraternities, 18% in sororities
Most popular majors: 37% Petroleum Engineering, 4% Geological and Earth Sciences/ Geosciences, Other, 4% Land Use Planning and Management/ Development, 3% Psychology, General, 3% Sport and Fitness Administration/Management

Expenses: 2018-2019: $36,040; room/board: $11,320
Financial aid: (740) 376-4712; 69% of undergrads determined to have financial need; average aid package $37,327

Miami University–Oxford

Oxford OH
(513) 529-2531
U.S. News ranking: Nat. U., No. 96
Website: www.MiamiOH.edu
Admissions email: admission@MiamiOH.edu
Public; founded 1809
Freshman admissions: more selective; 2017-2018: 30,255 applied, 20,635 accepted. Either SAT or ACT required. ACT 25/75 percentile: 26-31. High school rank: 34% in top tenth, 66% in top quarter, 94% in top half
Early decision deadline: 11/15, notification date: 12/15
Early action deadline: 12/1, notification date: 2/1
Application deadline (fall): 2/1
Undergraduate student body: 16,619 full time, 528 part time; 50% male, 50% female; 0% American Indian, 2% Asian, 3% black, 5% Hispanic, 3% multiracial, 0% Pacific Islander, 72% white, 14% international; 64% from in state; 45% live on campus; 19% of students in fraternities, 31% in sororities
Most popular majors: 25% Business, Management, Marketing, and Related Support Services, 9% Communication, Journalism, and Related Programs, 8% Health Professions and Related Programs, 8% Social Sciences, 7% Education
Expenses: 2018-2019: $14,825 in state, $33,577 out of state; room/board: $13,031
Financial aid: (513) 529-8734; 34% of undergrads determined to have financial need; average aid package $15,056

Mount St. Joseph University

Cincinnati OH
(513) 244-4531
U.S. News ranking: Reg. U. (Mid. W), No. 84
Website: www.msj.edu
Admissions email: admission@mail.msj.edu
Private; founded 1920
Affiliation: Roman Catholic
Freshman admissions: selective; 2017-2018: 1,647 applied, 945 accepted. Either SAT or ACT required. ACT 25/75 percentile: 20-24. High school rank: 13% in top tenth, 36% in top quarter, 79% in top half
Early decision deadline: N/A, notification date: N/A
Early action deadline: N/A, notification date: N/A
Application deadline (fall): 8/18
Undergraduate student body: 1,000 full time, 318 part time; 39% male, 61% female; 0% American Indian, 1% Asian, 13% black, 1% Hispanic, 5% multiracial, 0% Pacific Islander, 78% white, 0% international; 81% from in state; 29% live on campus; 0% of students in fraternities, 0% in sororities
Most popular majors: 26% Health Professions and Related Programs, 16% Business, Management, Marketing, and Related Support Services, 10% Parks, Recreation, Leisure, and Fitness Studies, 8% Biological and Biomedical Sciences, 6% Visual and Performing Arts
Expenses: 2018-2019: $30,100; room/board: $9,442
Financial aid: (513) 244-4418; 83% of undergrads determined to have financial need; average aid package $22,394

Mount Vernon Nazarene University

Mount Vernon OH
(866) 462-6868
U.S. News ranking: Reg. U. (Mid. W), No. 84
Website: www.mvnu.edu/
Admissions email: admoffice@mvnu.edu
Private; founded 1968
Affiliation: Church of the Nazarene
Freshman admissions: selective; 2017-2018: 1,187 applied, 910 accepted. Either SAT or ACT required. ACT 25/75 percentile: 19-28. High school rank: 22% in top tenth, 44% in top quarter, 79% in top half
Early decision deadline: N/A, notification date: N/A
Early action deadline: N/A, notification date: N/A
Application deadline (fall): 7/15
Undergraduate student body: 1,439 full time, 389 part time; 37% male, 63% female; 0% American Indian, 0% Asian, 3% black, 3% Hispanic, 3% multiracial, 0% Pacific Islander, 87% white, 0% international; 93% from in state; 77% live on campus; 0% of students in fraternities, 0% in sororities
Most popular majors: 23% Business Administration and Management, General, 16% Social Work, 12% Registered Nursing/Registered Nurse, 5% Biology/Biological Sciences, General, 4% Early Childhood Education and Teaching
Expenses: 2017-2018: $28,090; room/board: $7,854
Financial aid: (740) 397-9000

Muskingum University

New Concord OH
(740) 826-8137
U.S. News ranking: Reg. U. (Mid. W), No. 62
Website: www.muskingum.edu
Admissions email: adminfo@muskingum.edu
Private; founded 1837
Affiliation: Presbyterian Church (USA)
Freshman admissions: selective; 2017-2018: 1,850 applied, 1,376 accepted. Either SAT or ACT required. ACT 25/75 percentile: 18-24. High school rank: 20% in top tenth, 40% in top quarter, 70% in top half
Early decision deadline: N/A, notification date: N/A
Early action deadline: N/A, notification date: N/A
Application deadline (fall): 8/1
Undergraduate student body: 1,363 full time, 194 part time; 45% male, 55% female; 0% American Indian, 1% Asian, 5% black, 3% Hispanic, 4% multiracial, 0% Pacific Islander, 79% white, 4% international; 92% from in state; 68% live on campus; 30% of students in fraternities, 39% in sororities
Most popular majors: 24% Health Professions and Related Programs, 16% Business, Management, Marketing, and Related Support Services, 14% Education, 8% Homeland Security, Law Enforcement, Firefighting and Related Protective Services, 7% Psychology
Expenses: 2018-2019: $28,516; room/board: $11,310
Financial aid: (740) 826-8139; 85% of undergrads determined to have financial need; average aid package $25,673

Notre Dame College of Ohio[1]

Cleveland OH
(216) 373-5355
U.S. News ranking: Reg. U. (Mid. W), second tier
Website: www.notredamecollege.edu
Admissions email: admissions@ndc.edu
Private; founded 1922
Application deadline (fall): rolling
Undergraduate student body: N/A full time, N/A part time
Expenses: 2017-2018: $29,300; room/board: $10,500
Financial aid: (216) 373-5263

Oberlin College

Oberlin OH
(440) 775-8411
U.S. News ranking: Nat. Lib. Arts, No. 30
Website: www.oberlin.edu
Admissions email: college.admissions@oberlin.edu
Private; founded 1833
Freshman admissions: more selective; 2017-2018: 7,762 applied, 2,617 accepted. Either SAT or ACT required. ACT 25/75 percentile: 28-33. High school rank: 58% in top tenth, 79% in top quarter, 97% in top half
Early decision deadline: 11/15, notification date: 12/10
Early action deadline: N/A, notification date: N/A
Application deadline (fall): 1/15
Undergraduate student body: 2,793 full time, 34 part time; 42% male, 58% female; 0% American Indian, 4% Asian, 5% black, 8% Hispanic, 8% multiracial, 0% Pacific Islander, 64% white, 10% international; 6% from in state; 93% live on campus; 0% of students in fraternities, 0% in sororities
Most popular majors: Information not available
Expenses: 2018-2019: $55,052; room/board: $16,338
Financial aid: (440) 775-8142; 51% of undergrads determined to have financial need; average aid package $43,251

Ohio Christian University

Circleville OH
(877) 762-8669
U.S. News ranking: Reg. Coll. (Mid. W), second tier
Website: www.ohiochristian.edu/
Admissions email: enroll@ohiochristian.edu
Private; founded 1948
Affiliation: Churches of Christ
Freshman admissions: less selective; 2017-2018: N/A applied, N/A accepted. Neither SAT nor ACT required. SAT 25/75 percentile: N/A. High school rank: N/A
Early decision deadline: N/A, notification date: N/A
Early action deadline: N/A, notification date: N/A
Application deadline (fall): N/A
Undergraduate student body: 2,434 full time, 1,620 part time; 35% male, 65% female; 0% American Indian, 1% Asian, 29% black, 3% Hispanic, 3% multiracial, 0% Pacific Islander, 49% white, 0% international
Most popular majors: 29% Theology/Theological Studies, 24% Marketing/Marketing Management, General, 24% Psychology, General, 7% Public Administration, 6% Marine Sciences
Expenses: 2017-2018: $20,240; room/board: $7,996
Financial aid: N/A

Ohio Dominican University

Columbus OH
(614) 251-4500
U.S. News ranking: Reg. U. (Mid. W), No. 90
Website: www.ohiodominican.edu
Admissions email: admissions@ohiodominican.edu
Private; founded 1911
Affiliation: Roman Catholic
Freshman admissions: selective; 2017-2018: 1,238 applied, 956 accepted. Neither SAT nor ACT required. ACT 25/75 percentile: 19-24. High school rank: 15% in top tenth, 43% in top quarter, 76% in top half
Early decision deadline: N/A, notification date: N/A
Early action deadline: N/A, notification date: N/A
Application deadline (fall): rolling
Undergraduate student body: 957 full time, 220 part time; 45% male, 55% female; 0% American Indian, 1% Asian, 22% black, 4% Hispanic, 5% multiracial, 0% Pacific Islander, 56% white, 2% international; 95% from in state; 43% live on campus; 0% of students in fraternities, 0% in sororities
Most popular majors: 24% Business Administration and Management, General, 8% Accounting, 6% Biology/Biological Sciences, General, 6% Kinesiology and Exercise Science, 4% Criminology
Expenses: 2018-2019: $31,080; room/board: $10,948
Financial aid: (614) 251-4778; 83% of undergrads determined to have financial need; average aid package $23,989

Ohio Northern University

Ada OH
(888) 408-4668
U.S. News ranking: Reg. Coll. (Mid. W), No. 4
Website: www.onu.edu
Admissions email: admissions-ug@onu.edu
Private; founded 1871
Affiliation: United Methodist
Freshman admissions: more selective; 2017-2018: 4,159 applied, 2,749 accepted. Either SAT or ACT required. ACT 25/75 percentile: 22-28. High school rank: 25% in top tenth, 55% in top quarter, 89% in top half
Early decision deadline: N/A, notification date: N/A
Early action deadline: N/A, notification date: N/A
Application deadline (fall): 8/15
Undergraduate student body: 2,092 full time, 220 part time; 56% male, 44% female; 0% American Indian, 2% Asian, 4% black, 1% Hispanic, 2% multiracial, 0% Pacific Islander, 77% white, 3% international; 83% from in state; 75% live on campus; 18% of students in fraternities, 24% in sororities
Most popular majors: 20% Engineering, 17% Business, Management, Marketing, and Related Support Services, 13% Health Professions and Related Programs, 8% Biological and Biomedical Sciences, 7% Parks, Recreation, Leisure, and Fitness Studies
Expenses: 2018-2019: $32,260; room/board: $11,650
Financial aid: (419) 772-2271; 81% of undergrads determined to have financial need; average aid package $27,756

Ohio State University–Columbus

Columbus OH
(614) 292-3980
U.S. News ranking: Nat. U., No. 56
Website: www.osu.edu
Admissions email: askabuckeye@osu.edu
Public; founded 1870
Freshman admissions: more selective; 2017-2018: 47,782 applied, 22,964 accepted. Either SAT or ACT required. ACT 25/75 percentile: 27-31. High school rank: 64% in top tenth, 95% in top quarter, 99% in top half
Early decision deadline: N/A, notification date: N/A
Early action deadline: 11/1, notification date: 1/15
Application deadline (fall): 2/1
Undergraduate student body: 42,003 full time, 3,943 part time; 52% male, 48% female; 0% American Indian, 7% Asian, 6% black, 4% Hispanic, 3% multiracial, 0% Pacific Islander, 69% white, 8% international; 81% from in state; 32% live on campus; 13% of students in fraternities, 14% in sororities
Most popular majors: 5% Psychology, General, 5% Speech Communication and Rhetoric, 4% Biology/Biological Sciences, General, 4% Finance, General,

More @ usnews.com/bestcolleges

4% Marketing/Marketing Management, General
Expenses: 2018-2019: $10,726 in state, $30,742 out of state; room/board: $12,434
Financial aid: (614) 292-8595; 48% of undergrads determined to have financial need; average aid package $13,960

Ohio University

Athens OH
(740) 593-4100
U.S. News ranking: Nat. U., No. 171
Website: www.ohio.edu
Admissions email: admissions@ohio.edu
Public; founded 1804
Freshman admissions: selective; 2017-2018: 26,263 applied, 19,416 accepted. Either SAT or ACT required. ACT 25/75 percentile: 22-26. High school rank: 18% in top tenth, 46% in top quarter, 82% in top half
Early decision deadline: N/A, notification date: N/A
Early action deadline: 12/1, notification date: N/A
Application deadline (fall): 2/1
Undergraduate student body: 17,802 full time, 5,521 part time; 40% male, 60% female; 0% American Indian, 1% Asian, 6% black, 3% Hispanic, 4% multiracial, 0% Pacific Islander, 83% white, 2% international; 85% from in state; 43% live on campus; 12% of students in fraternities, 16% in sororities
Most popular majors: 38% Registered Nursing/Registered Nurse, 4% Business Administration and Management, General, 4% Liberal Arts and Sciences, General Studies and Humanities, Other, 4% Speech Communication and Rhetoric, 3% Journalism
Expenses: 2018-2019: $12,192 in state, $21,656 out of state; room/board: $12,966
Financial aid: (740) 593-4141; 57% of undergrads determined to have financial need; average aid package $8,870

Ohio Wesleyan University

Delaware OH
(740) 368-3020
U.S. News ranking: Nat. Lib. Arts, No. 95
Website: www.owu.edu
Admissions email: owuadmit@owu.edu
Private; founded 1842
Freshman admissions: selective; 2017-2018: 4,160 applied, 2,970 accepted. Neither SAT nor ACT required. ACT 25/75 percentile: 22-28. High school rank: 22% in top tenth, 47% in top quarter, 78% in top half
Early decision deadline: 11/15, notification date: 11/30
Early action deadline: 12/15, notification date: 1/15
Application deadline (fall): 3/1
Undergraduate student body: 1,550 full time, 15 part time; 47% male, 53% female; 0% American Indian, 3% Asian, 10% black, 6% Hispanic, 5% multiracial, 0% Pacific Islander, 69% white, 5% international; 46% from in state; 86% live on campus; 36% of students in fraternities, 33% in sororities
Most popular majors: 15% Biological and Biomedical Sciences, 12% Business, Management, Marketing, and Related Support Services, 11% Psychology, 11% Social Sciences, 8% Parks, Recreation, Leisure, and Fitness Studies
Expenses: 2018-2019: $45,760; room/board: $12,430
Financial aid: (740) 368-3052; 73% of undergrads determined to have financial need; average aid package $37,804

Otterbein University

Westerville OH
(614) 823-1500
U.S. News ranking: Reg. U. (Mid. W), No. 17
Website: www.otterbein.edu
Admissions email: UOtterB@Otterbein.edu
Private; founded 1847
Affiliation: United Methodist
Freshman admissions: selective; 2017-2018: 3,119 applied, 2,383 accepted. Either SAT or ACT required. ACT 25/75 percentile: 21-27. High school rank: 26% in top tenth, 55% in top quarter, 87% in top half
Early decision deadline: N/A, notification date: N/A
Early action deadline: N/A, notification date: N/A
Application deadline (fall): rolling
Undergraduate student body: 2,294 full time, 186 part time; 38% male, 62% female; 0% American Indian, 2% Asian, 7% black, 3% Hispanic, 5% multiracial, 0% Pacific Islander, 78% white, 1% international; 88% from in state; 52% live on campus; 10% of students in fraternities, 16% in sororities
Most popular majors: 16% Business, Management, Marketing, and Related Support Services, 16% Health Professions and Related Programs, 10% Education, 10% Visual and Performing Arts, 9% Communication, Journalism, and Related Programs
Expenses: 2018-2019: $31,874; room/board: $10,958
Financial aid: (614) 823-1502; 74% of undergrads determined to have financial need; average aid package $22,706

Shawnee State University

Portsmouth OH
(800) 959-2778
U.S. News ranking: Reg. Coll. (Mid. W), second tier
Website: www.shawnee.edu
Admissions email: To_SSU@shawnee.edu
Public; founded 1986
Freshman admissions: selective; 2017-2018: 2,815 applied, 1,961 accepted. Neither SAT nor ACT required. ACT 25/75 percentile: 19-24. High school rank: 2% in top tenth, 8% in top quarter, 25% in top half
Early decision deadline: N/A, notification date: N/A
Early action deadline: N/A, notification date: N/A
Application deadline (fall): rolling
Undergraduate student body: 2,832 full time, 574 part time; 46% male, 54% female; 1% American Indian, 1% Asian, 5% black, 1% Hispanic, 3% multiracial, 0% Pacific Islander, 86% white, 1% international; 88% from in state; 12% live on campus; 2% of students in fraternities, 2% in sororities
Most popular majors: 9% Psychology, General, 8% Art/Art Studies, General, 7% Business Administration and Management, General, 6% Sociology, 6% Sport and Fitness Administration/ Management
Expenses: 2018-2019: $7,439 in state, $13,247 out of state; room/ board: $9,559
Financial aid: (740) 351-4243; 75% of undergrads determined to have financial need

Tiffin University

Tiffin OH
(419) 448-3423
U.S. News ranking: Reg. U. (Mid. W), second tier
Website: www.tiffin.edu
Admissions email: admiss@tiffin.edu
Private; founded 1888
Freshman admissions: selective; 2017-2018: 3,808 applied, 2,621 accepted. Neither SAT nor ACT required. ACT 25/75 percentile: 17-22. High school rank: 5% in top tenth, 42% in top quarter, 74% in top half
Early decision deadline: N/A, notification date: N/A
Early action deadline: N/A, notification date: N/A
Application deadline (fall): rolling
Undergraduate student body: 1,772 full time, 471 part time; 54% male, 46% female; 0% American Indian, 0% Asian, 11% black, 3% Hispanic, 2% multiracial, 0% Pacific Islander, 40% white, 14% international
Most popular majors: 38% Business, Management, Marketing, and Related Support Services, 33% Homeland Security, Law Enforcement, Firefighting and Related Protective Services, 10% Psychology, 5% Health Professions and Related Programs, 5% Parks, Recreation, Leisure, and Fitness Studies
Expenses: 2018-2019: $25,000; room/board: $11,200
Financial aid: (419) 448-3279; 73% of undergrads determined to have financial need; average aid package $18,067

Union Institute and University

Cincinnati OH
(800) 861-6400
U.S. News ranking: Nat. U., unranked
Website: www.myunion.edu
Admissions email: admissions@myunion.edu
Private; founded 1964
Affiliation: Other
Freshman admissions: least selective; 2017-2018: 10 applied, 10 accepted. Neither SAT nor ACT required. SAT 25/75 percentile: N/A. High school rank: N/A
Early decision deadline: N/A, notification date: N/A
Early action deadline: N/A, notification date: N/A
Application deadline (fall): rolling
Undergraduate student body: 434 full time, 379 part time; 47% male, 53% female; 0% American Indian, 2% Asian, 19% black, 24% Hispanic, 3% multiracial, 0% Pacific Islander, 35% white, 0% international; N/A from in state; 0% live on campus; 0% of students in fraternities, 0% in sororities
Most popular majors: 62% Criminal Justice/Law Enforcement Administration, 18% Child Development, 4% Child Care and Support Services Management, 4% Crisis/Emergency/Disaster Management, 3% Maternal and Child Health
Expenses: 2018-2019: $16,526; room/board: N/A
Financial aid: (513) 487-1126; average aid package $9,000

University of Akron

Akron OH
(330) 972-7077
U.S. News ranking: Nat. U., second tier
Website: www.uakron.edu
Admissions email: admissions@uakron.edu
Public; founded 1870
Freshman admissions: selective; 2017-2018: 15,109 applied, 13,983 accepted. Either SAT or ACT required. ACT 25/75 percentile: 19-26. High school rank: 24% in top tenth, 50% in top quarter, 77% in top half
Early decision deadline: N/A, notification date: N/A
Early action deadline: 11/1, notification date: 12/15
Application deadline (fall): 7/1
Undergraduate student body: 13,562 full time, 3,309 part time; 53% male, 47% female; 0% American Indian, 3% Asian, 12% black, 3% Hispanic, 5% multiracial, 0% Pacific Islander, 73% white, 2% international; 94% from in state; 16% live on campus; N/A of students in fraternities, N/A in sororities
Most popular majors: 22% Marketing, Other, 15% Business/ Commerce, General, 13% Engineering, General, 8% Education, General, 4% Speech Communication and Rhetoric
Expenses: 2018-2019: $11,463 in state, $17,750 out of state; room/board: $12,200
Financial aid: (330) 972-5860; 68% of undergrads determined to have financial need; average aid package $7,960

University of Cincinnati

Cincinnati OH
(513) 556-1100
U.S. News ranking: Nat. U., No. 147
Website: www.uc.edu
Admissions email: admissions@uc.edu
Public; founded 1819
Freshman admissions: more selective; 2017-2018: 21,593 applied, 16,517 accepted. Either SAT or ACT required. ACT 25/75 percentile: 23-28. High school rank: 22% in top tenth, 48% in top quarter, 81% in top half
Early decision deadline: N/A, notification date: N/A
Early action deadline: 12/1, notification date: N/A
Application deadline (fall): 3/1
Undergraduate student body: 22,671 full time, 3,937 part time; 51% male, 49% female; 0% American Indian, 4% Asian, 7% black, 3% Hispanic, 4% multiracial, 0% Pacific Islander, 74% white, 4% international; 84% from in state; 23% live on campus; N/A of students in fraternities, N/A in sororities
Most popular majors: 20% Business, Management, Marketing, and Related Support Services, 17% Health Professions and Related Programs, 9% Engineering, 8% Visual and Performing Arts, 6% Communication, Journalism, and Related Programs
Expenses: 2018-2019: $11,000 in state, $26,334 out of state; room/board: $11,340
Financial aid: (513) 556-6982; 54% of undergrads determined to have financial need; average aid package $8,797

University of Cincinnati–UC Blue Ash College[1]

Cincinnati OH
(513) 745-5600
U.S. News ranking: Reg. Coll. (Mid. W), unranked
Website: www.rwc.uc.edu/
Admissions email: N/A
Public
Application deadline (fall): N/A
Undergraduate student body: N/A full time, N/A part time
Expenses: 2017-2018: $6,010 in state, $14,808 out of state; room/ board: N/A
Financial aid: N/A

University of Dayton

Dayton OH
(937) 229-4411
U.S. News ranking: Nat. U., No. 127
Website: www.udayton.edu
Admissions email: admission@udayton.edu
Private; founded 1850
Freshman admissions: selective; 2017-2018: 15,942 applied, 11,427 accepted. Either SAT or ACT required. ACT 25/75 percentile: 24-29. High school rank: 29% in top tenth, 61% in top quarter, 87% in top half
Early decision deadline: N/A, notification date: N/A
Early action deadline: 12/15, notification date: 2/1
Application deadline (fall): 3/1
Undergraduate student body: 8,079 full time, 420 part time; 52% male, 48% female; 0% American Indian, 1% Asian, 3% black, 5% Hispanic, 3% multiracial, 0% Pacific Islander, 79% white,

7% international; 48% from in state; 75% live on campus; 12% of students in fraternities, 21% in sororities
Most popular majors: 32% Business, Management, Marketing, and Related Support Services, 21% Engineering, 7% Education, 6% Communication, Journalism, and Related Programs, 6% Health Professions and Related Programs
Expenses: 2018-2019: $42,900; room/board: $13,580
Financial aid: (800) 427-5029; 60% of undergrads determined to have financial need; average aid package $31,029

University of Findlay

Findlay OH
(419) 434-4732
U.S. News ranking: Reg. U. (Mid. W), No. 37
Website: www.findlay.edu
Admissions email: admissions@findlay.edu
Private; founded 1882
Affiliation: Church of God
Freshman admissions: more selective; 2017-2018: 3,611 applied, 2,711 accepted. Either SAT or ACT required. ACT 25/75 percentile: 21-27. High school rank: 24% in top tenth, 56% in top quarter, 83% in top half
Early decision deadline: N/A, notification date: N/A
Early action deadline: N/A, notification date: N/A
Application deadline (fall): rolling
Undergraduate student body: 2,499 full time, 1,063 part time; 35% male, 65% female; 0% American Indian, 1% Asian, 4% black, 3% Hispanic, 3% multiracial, 0% Pacific Islander, 82% white, 7% international; N/A from in state; 45% live on campus; 1% of students in fraternities, 2% in sororities
Most popular majors: 30% Health/Medical Preparatory Programs, 23% Business Administration, Management and Operations, 11% Agricultural and Domestic Animal Services, 7% Education, 6% Health and Physical Education/Fitness
Expenses: 2018-2019: $34,360; room/board: $10,000
Financial aid: (419) 434-4791; 64% of undergrads determined to have financial need; average aid package $21,000

University of Mount Union

Alliance OH
(330) 823-2590
U.S. News ranking: Reg. Coll. (Mid. W), No. 7
Website: www.mountunion.edu/
Admissions email: admission@mountunion.edu
Private; founded 1846
Affiliation: United Methodist
Freshman admissions: selective; 2017-2018: 2,020 applied, 1,638 accepted. Either SAT or ACT required. ACT 25/75 percentile: 20-25. High school rank: 18% in top tenth, 45% in top quarter, 78% in top half
Early decision deadline: N/A, notification date: N/A
Early action deadline: N/A, notification date: N/A
Application deadline (fall): rolling
Undergraduate student body: 2,046 full time, 49 part time; 52% male, 48% female; 1% American Indian, 1% Asian, 6% black, 3% Hispanic, 4% multiracial, 0% Pacific Islander, 81% white, 0% international; 83% from in state; 66% live on campus; 18% of students in fraternities, 35% in sororities
Most popular majors: 22% Business, Management, Marketing, and Related Support Services, 16% Parks, Recreation, Leisure, and Fitness Studies, 10% Biological and Biomedical Sciences, 9% Education, 7% Health Professions and Related Programs
Expenses: 2018-2019: $30,860; room/board: $10,200
Financial aid: (330) 823-2674; 79% of undergrads determined to have financial need; average aid package $22,766

University of Northwestern Ohio[1]

Lima OH
(419) 998-3120
U.S. News ranking: Reg. Coll. (Mid. W), unranked
Website: www.unoh.edu/
Admissions email: info@unoh.edu
Private
Application deadline (fall): N/A
Undergraduate student body: N/A full time, N/A part time
Expenses: 2017-2018: $11,050; room/board: $6,850
Financial aid: N/A

University of Rio Grande[1]

Rio Grande OH
(740) 245-7208
U.S. News ranking: Reg. Coll. (Mid. W), unranked
Website: www.rio.edu
Admissions email: admissions@rio.edu
Private; founded 1876
Application deadline (fall): rolling
Undergraduate student body: N/A full time, N/A part time
Expenses: 2017-2018: $26,175; room/board: $10,630
Financial aid: (740) 245-7285

University of Toledo

Toledo OH
(419) 530-8888
U.S. News ranking: Nat. U., second tier
Website: www.utoledo.edu
Admissions email: enroll@utoledo.edu
Public; founded 1872
Freshman admissions: selective; 2017-2018: 10,946 applied, 10,328 accepted. Either SAT or ACT required. ACT 25/75 percentile: 20-26. High school rank: 17% in top tenth, 41% in top quarter, 71% in top half
Early decision deadline: N/A, notification date: N/A
Early action deadline: N/A, notification date: N/A
Application deadline (fall): rolling
Undergraduate student body: 13,056 full time, 3,138 part time; 51% male, 49% female; 0% American Indian, 2% Asian, 11% black, 5% Hispanic, 3% multiracial, 0% Pacific Islander, 68% white, 6% international; 80% from in state; 21% live on campus; N/A of students in fraternities, N/A in sororities
Most popular majors: 23% Business, Management, Marketing, and Related Support Services, 17% Health Professions and Related Programs, 14% Engineering, 6% Multi/Interdisciplinary Studies, 5% Engineering Technologies and Engineering-Related Fields
Expenses: 2018-2019: $9,795 in state, $19,133 out of state; room/board: $11,434
Financial aid: (419) 530-5833; 64% of undergrads determined to have financial need; average aid package $10,938

Urbana University[1]

Urbana OH
(937) 484-1400
U.S. News ranking: Reg. Coll. (Mid. W), second tier
Website: www.urbana.edu
Admissions email: admiss@urbana.edu
Private
Application deadline (fall): N/A
Undergraduate student body: N/A full time, N/A part time
Expenses: 2017-2018: $22,452; room/board: $9,706
Financial aid: N/A

Ursuline College

Pepper Pike OH
(440) 449-4203
U.S. News ranking: Reg. U. (Mid. W), No. 45
Website: www.ursuline.edu
Admissions email: admission@ursuline.edu
Private; founded 1871
Affiliation: Roman Catholic
Freshman admissions: selective; 2017-2018: 525 applied, 490 accepted. Either SAT or ACT required. ACT 25/75 percentile: 18-24. High school rank: 17% in top tenth, 50% in top quarter, 76% in top half
Early decision deadline: N/A, notification date: N/A
Early action deadline: N/A, notification date: N/A
Application deadline (fall): rolling
Undergraduate student body: 455 full time, 166 part time; 8% male, 92% female; 0% American Indian, 2% Asian, 22% black, 2% Hispanic, 4% multiracial, 0% Pacific Islander, 62% white, 2% international; 93% from in state; 25% live on campus; N/A of students in fraternities, N/A in sororities
Most popular majors: 55% Health Professions and Related Programs, 16% Business, Management, Marketing, and Related Support Services, 6% Psychology, 5% Biological and Biomedical Sciences, 5% Communication, Journalism, and Related Programs
Expenses: 2018-2019: $32,390; room/board: $10,776
Financial aid: (440) 646-8309; 83% of undergrads determined to have financial need; average aid package $24,765

Walsh University

North Canton OH
(800) 362-9846
U.S. News ranking: Reg. U. (Mid. W), No. 58
Website: www.walsh.edu
Admissions email: admissions@walsh.edu
Private; founded 1958
Affiliation: Roman Catholic
Freshman admissions: selective; 2017-2018: 1,666 applied, 1,320 accepted. Neither SAT nor ACT required. ACT 25/75 percentile: 20-26. High school rank: N/A
Early decision deadline: N/A, notification date: N/A
Early action deadline: N/A, notification date: N/A
Application deadline (fall): rolling
Undergraduate student body: 1,744 full time, 265 part time; 41% male, 59% female; 0% American Indian, 1% Asian, 7% black, 4% Hispanic, 3% multiracial, 0% Pacific Islander, 68% white, 4% international
Most popular majors: 32% Business, Management, Marketing, and Related Support Services, 18% Health Professions and Related Programs, 13% Education, 10% Biological and Biomedical Sciences, 9% Psychology
Expenses: 2018-2019: $29,980; room/board: $10,680
Financial aid: (330) 490-7146; 71% of undergrads determined to have financial need; average aid package $23,888

Wilberforce University[1]

Wilberforce OH
(800) 367-8568
U.S. News ranking: Reg. Coll. (Mid. W), second tier
Website: www.wilberforce.edu
Admissions email: admissions@wilberforce.edu
Private
Application deadline (fall): N/A
Undergraduate student body: N/A full time, N/A part time
Expenses: 2017-2018: $13,250; room/board: $7,000
Financial aid: N/A

Wilmington College[1]

Wilmington OH
(937) 382-6661
U.S. News ranking: Reg. Coll. (Mid. W), No. 46
Website: www.wilmington.edu/
Admissions email: admission@wilmington.edu
Private; founded 1870
Undergraduate student body: N/A full time, N/A part time
Expenses: 2017-2018: $25,000; room/board: $9,600
Financial aid: N/A

Wittenberg University

Springfield OH
(937) 327-6314
U.S. News ranking: Nat. Lib. Arts, No. 168
Website: www.wittenberg.edu/
Admissions email: admission@wittenberg.edu
Private; founded 1845
Affiliation: Evangelical Lutheran Church
Freshman admissions: selective; 2017-2018: 7,249 applied, 5,232 accepted. Neither SAT nor ACT required. ACT 25/75 percentile: 22-28. High school rank: 14% in top tenth, 39% in top quarter, 72% in top half
Early decision deadline: 11/15, notification date: 12/1
Early action deadline: 12/1, notification date: 1/1
Application deadline (fall): rolling
Undergraduate student body: 1,775 full time, 82 part time; 46% male, 54% female; 0% American Indian, 1% Asian, 10% black, 4% Hispanic, 6% multiracial, 0% Pacific Islander, 76% white, 1% international; 76% from in state; 85% live on campus; 29% of students in fraternities, 32% in sororities
Most popular majors: 18% Business, Management, Marketing, and Related Support Services, 15% Social Sciences, 14% Biological and Biomedical Sciences, 8% Education, 7% English Language and Literature/Letters
Expenses: 2018-2019: $39,500; room/board: $10,356
Financial aid: (937) 327-7321; 81% of undergrads determined to have financial need; average aid package $32,409

Wright State University

Dayton OH
(937) 775-5700
U.S. News ranking: Nat. U., second tier
Website: www.wright.edu
Admissions email: admissions@wright.edu
Public; founded 1967
Freshman admissions: selective; 2017-2018: 5,826 applied, 5,638 accepted. Either SAT or ACT required. ACT 25/75 percentile: 19-25. High school rank: 18% in top tenth, 40% in top quarter, 68% in top half
Early decision deadline: N/A, notification date: N/A
Early action deadline: N/A, notification date: N/A
Application deadline (fall): 8/20
Undergraduate student body: 9,423 full time, 2,692 part time; 48% male, 52% female; 0% American Indian, 3% Asian, 11% black, 4% Hispanic, 4% multiracial, 0% Pacific Islander, 75% white, 3% international; 95% from in state; 19% live on campus; N/A of students in fraternities, N/A in sororities
Most popular majors: 27% Business, Management, Marketing, and Related Support Services, 15% Engineering, 11% Health Professions and Related Programs, 7% Psychology, 6% Social Sciences

More @ usnews.com/bestcolleges

Expenses: 2018-2019: $8,730 in state, $17,874 out of state; room/board: $11,832
Financial aid: (937) 775-4000; 64% of undergrads determined to have financial need; average aid package $10,526

Xavier University

Cincinnati OH
(877) 982-3648
U.S. News ranking: Reg. U. (Mid. W), No. 8
Website: www.xavier.edu
Admissions email: xuadmit@xavier.edu
Private; founded 1831
Affiliation: Roman Catholic
Freshman admissions: selective; 2017-2018: 13,006 applied, 9,613 accepted. Either SAT or ACT required. ACT 25/75 percentile: 22-28. High school rank: 16% in top tenth, 45% in top quarter, 80% in top half
Early decision deadline: N/A, notification date: N/A
Early action deadline: N/A, notification date: N/A
Application deadline (fall): rolling
Undergraduate student body: 4,370 full time, 275 part time; 46% male, 54% female; 0% American Indian, 3% Asian, 9% black, 6% Hispanic, 4% multiracial, 0% Pacific Islander, 75% white, 2% international; 47% from in state; 51% live on campus; N/A of students in fraternities, N/A in sororities
Most popular majors: 29% Business, Management, Marketing, and Related Support Services, 14% Health Professions and Related Programs, 8% Liberal Arts and Sciences, General Studies and Humanities, 7% Biological and Biomedical Sciences, 6% Social Sciences
Expenses: 2018-2019: $38,530; room/board: $12,780
Financial aid: (513) 745-3142; 57% of undergrads determined to have financial need; average aid package $25,406

Youngstown State University

Youngstown OH
(877) 468-6978
U.S. News ranking: Reg. U. (Mid. W), second tier
Website: www.ysu.edu
Admissions email: enroll@ysu.edu
Public; founded 1908
Freshman admissions: selective; 2017-2018: 9,765 applied, 6,379 accepted. Either SAT or ACT required. ACT 25/75 percentile: 19-25. High school rank: 13% in top tenth, 34% in top quarter, 67% in top half
Early decision deadline: N/A, notification date: N/A
Early action deadline: N/A, notification date: N/A
Application deadline (fall): 8/1
Undergraduate student body: 8,880 full time, 2,506 part time; 48% male, 52% female; 0% American Indian, 1% Asian, 9% black, 4% Hispanic, 3% multiracial, 0% Pacific Islander, 75% white, 4% international; 85% from in state; 13% live on campus; 2% of students in fraternities, 2% in sororities
Most popular majors: 7% Criminal Justice/Safety Studies, 6% Biology/Biological Sciences, General, 6% Registered Nursing/Registered Nurse, 6% Social Work, 4% General Studies
Expenses: 2018-2019: $9,259 in state, $14,899 out of state; room/board: $9,400
Financial aid: (330) 941-3505; 69% of undergrads determined to have financial need; average aid package $9,460

OKLAHOMA

Bacone College[1]

Muskogee OK
(888) 682-5514
U.S. News ranking: Reg. Coll. (W), second tier
Website: www.bacone.edu/
Admissions email: admissions@bacone.edu
Private
Application deadline (fall): rolling
Undergraduate student body: N/A full time, N/A part time
Expenses: 2017-2018: $17,700; room/board: $7,200
Financial aid: N/A

Cameron University

Lawton OK
(580) 581-2289
U.S. News ranking: Reg. U. (W), second tier
Website: www.cameron.edu
Admissions email: admissions@cameron.edu
Public; founded 1908
Freshman admissions: less selective; 2017-2018: 1,063 applied, 1,063 accepted. Neither SAT nor ACT required. ACT 25/75 percentile: 16-21. High school rank: 4% in top tenth, 14% in top quarter, 43% in top half
Early decision deadline: N/A, notification date: N/A
Early action deadline: N/A, notification date: N/A
Application deadline (fall): rolling
Undergraduate student body: 2,814 full time, 1,336 part time; 40% male, 60% female; 5% American Indian, 2% Asian, 13% black, 13% Hispanic, 9% multiracial, 1% Pacific Islander, 50% white, 4% international; 88% from in state; 8% live on campus; 1% of students in fraternities, 1% in sororities
Most popular majors: 15% Business Administration and Management, General, 15% Elementary Education and Teaching, 11% Psychology, General, 10% Corrections and Criminal Justice, Other, 7% Health and Physical Education/Fitness, General
Expenses: 2018-2019: $6,180 in state, $15,510 out of state; room/board: $5,452
Financial aid: (580) 581-2293; 66% of undergrads determined to have financial need; average aid package $9,202

East Central University

Ada OK
(580) 559-5628
U.S. News ranking: Reg. U. (W), second tier
Website: www.ecok.edu
Admissions email: admissions@ecok.edu
Public; founded 1909
Freshman admissions: selective; 2017-2018: 1,847 applied, 470 accepted. ACT required. ACT 25/75 percentile: 18-23. High school rank: N/A
Early decision deadline: N/A, notification date: N/A
Early action deadline: N/A, notification date: N/A
Application deadline (fall): rolling
Undergraduate student body: 2,551 full time, 530 part time; 40% male, 60% female; 15% American Indian, 0% Asian, 4% black, 6% Hispanic, 8% multiracial, 0% Pacific Islander, 57% white, 8% international; 93% from in state; 31% live on campus; 3% of students in fraternities, 3% in sororities
Most popular majors: 17% Health Professions and Related Programs, 14% Business, Management, Marketing, and Related Support Services, 11% Public Administration and Social Service Professions, 7% Biological and Biomedical Sciences, 7% Education
Expenses: 2018-2019: $6,600 in state, $15,720 out of state; room/board: $5,350
Financial aid: (580) 559-5243; 77% of undergrads determined to have financial need; average aid package $6,226

Langston University

Langston OK
(405) 466-3231
U.S. News ranking: Reg. U. (W), second tier
Website: www.langston.edu/
Admissions email: admissions@langston.edu
Public; founded 1897
Freshman admissions: least selective; 2017-2018: 12,083 applied, 5,239 accepted. Either SAT or ACT required. ACT 25/75 percentile: 17-26. High school rank: N/A
Early decision deadline: N/A, notification date: N/A
Early action deadline: N/A, notification date: N/A
Application deadline (fall): rolling
Undergraduate student body: 1,822 full time, 211 part time; 36% male, 64% female; 1% American Indian, 0% Asian, 70% black, 2% Hispanic, 9% multiracial, 0% Pacific Islander, 6% white, 10% international
Most popular majors: 21% Registered Nursing/Registered Nurse, 15% Business Administration and Management, General, 10% Psychology, General, 6% Agriculture, Agriculture Operations, and Related Sciences, 6% Corrections
Expenses: 2018-2019: $6,232 in state, $13,950 out of state; room/board: $10,597
Financial aid: (405) 466-3357

Mid-America Christian University[1]

Oklahoma City OK
(405) 691-3800
U.S. News ranking: Reg. U. (W), unranked
Website: www.macu.edu
Admissions email: info@macu.edu
Private
Application deadline (fall): N/A
Undergraduate student body: N/A full time, N/A part time
Expenses: 2017-2018: $17,830; room/board: $8,096
Financial aid: N/A

Northeastern State University

Tahlequah OK
(918) 444-2200
U.S. News ranking: Reg. U. (W), second tier
Website: www.nsuok.edu
Admissions email: nsuinfo@nsuok.edu
Public; founded 1846
Freshman admissions: selective; 2017-2018: 1,767 applied, 1,598 accepted. ACT required. ACT 25/75 percentile: 19-24. High school rank: 24% in top tenth, 51% in top quarter, 82% in top half
Early decision deadline: N/A, notification date: N/A
Early action deadline: N/A, notification date: N/A
Application deadline (fall): rolling
Undergraduate student body: 4,787 full time, 2,031 part time; 40% male, 60% female; 18% American Indian, 2% Asian, 4% black, 6% Hispanic, 21% multiracial, 0% Pacific Islander, 46% white, 3% international; 94% from in state; 18% live on campus; N/A of students in fraternities, N/A in sororities
Most popular majors: 9% Research and Experimental Psychology, Other, 7% Criminal Justice/Law Enforcement Administration, 6% Accounting, 6% Biology/Biological Sciences, General, 6% Elementary Education and Teaching
Expenses: 2018-2019: $6,702 in state, $14,814 out of state; room/board: $7,638
Financial aid: (918) 444-3410; 68% of undergrads determined to have financial need; average aid package $12,937

Northwestern Oklahoma State University

Alva OK
(580) 327-8545
U.S. News ranking: Reg. U. (W), second tier
Website: www.nwosu.edu
Admissions email: recruit@nwosu.edu
Public; founded 1897
Freshman admissions: selective; 2017-2018: 1,014 applied, 842 accepted. Either SAT or ACT required. ACT 25/75 percentile: 17-23. High school rank: 13% in top tenth, 29% in top quarter, 58% in top half
Early decision deadline: N/A, notification date: N/A
Early action deadline: N/A, notification date: N/A
Application deadline (fall): rolling
Undergraduate student body: 1,359 full time, 519 part time; 41% male, 59% female; 7% American Indian, 0% Asian, 8% black, 9% Hispanic, 2% multiracial, 0% Pacific Islander, 65% white, 3% international; 79% from in state; 50% live on campus; N/A of students in fraternities, N/A in sororities
Most popular majors: 13% Registered Nursing/Registered Nurse, 11% Parks, Recreation, Leisure, and Fitness Studies, Other, 6% Agribusiness/Agricultural Business Operations, 6% Biology/Biological Sciences, General, 6% Business Administration and Management, General
Expenses: 2017-2018: $7,066 in state, $14,183 out of state; room/board: $4,480
Financial aid: N/A

Oklahoma Baptist University

Shawnee OK
(405) 585-5000
U.S. News ranking: Reg. Coll. (W), No. 7
Website: www.okbu.edu
Admissions email: admissions@okbu.edu
Private; founded 1910
Affiliation: Southern Baptist
Freshman admissions: selective; 2017-2018: 4,070 applied, 2,634 accepted. Either SAT or ACT required. ACT 25/75 percentile: 20-26. High school rank: 28% in top tenth, 56% in top quarter, 81% in top half
Early decision deadline: N/A, notification date: N/A
Early action deadline: N/A, notification date: N/A
Application deadline (fall): 8/1
Undergraduate student body: 1,835 full time, 130 part time; 41% male, 59% female; 5% American Indian, 1% Asian, 5% black, 2% Hispanic, 13% multiracial, 0% Pacific Islander, 69% white, 3% international
Most popular majors: Information not available
Expenses: 2018-2019: $28,258; room/board: $7,618
Financial aid: (405) 585-5020; 74% of undergrads determined to have financial need; average aid package $23,506

Oklahoma Christian University

Oklahoma City OK
(405) 425-5050
U.S. News ranking: Reg. U. (W), No. 64
Website: www.oc.edu/
Admissions email: admissions@oc.edu
Private; founded 1950
Affiliation: Churches of Christ
Freshman admissions: selective; 2017-2018: 2,530 applied, 1,589 accepted. Either SAT or ACT required. ACT 25/75 percentile: 20-27. High school rank: 26% in top tenth, 52% in top quarter, 79% in top half
Early decision deadline: N/A, notification date: N/A

Early action deadline: N/A, notification date: N/A
Application deadline (fall): rolling
Undergraduate student body: 1,870 full time, 116 part time; 51% male, 49% female; 2% American Indian, 1% Asian, 5% black, 6% Hispanic, 7% multiracial, 0% Pacific Islander, 72% white, 6% international; 45% from in state; 80% live on campus; 30% of students in fraternities, 36% in sororities
Most popular majors: 18% Business, Management, Marketing, and Related Support Services, 14% Engineering, 11% Health Professions and Related Programs, 9% Education, 9% Visual and Performing Arts
Expenses: 2018-2019: $22,760; room/board: $8,190
Financial aid: (405) 425-5190; 67% of undergrads determined to have financial need; average aid package $24,150

Oklahoma City University

Oklahoma City OK
(405) 208-5050
U.S. News ranking: Reg. U. (W), No. 28
Website: www.okcu.edu
Admissions email: uadmissions@okcu.edu
Private; founded 1904
Affiliation: United Methodist
Freshman admissions: selective; 2017-2018: 1,820 applied, 1,305 accepted. Either SAT or ACT required. ACT 25/75 percentile: 23-28. High school rank: 31% in top tenth, 61% in top quarter, 82% in top half
Early decision deadline: N/A, notification date: N/A
Early action deadline: N/A, notification date: N/A
Application deadline (fall): rolling
Undergraduate student body: 1,542 full time, 150 part time; 32% male, 68% female; 2% American Indian, 2% Asian, 5% black, 9% Hispanic, 8% multiracial, 0% Pacific Islander, 63% white, 11% international; 50% from in state; 53% live on campus; 24% of students in fraternities, 11% in sororities
Most popular majors: 34% Adult Health Nurse/Nursing, 11% General Studies, 8% Music Performance, General, 6% Acting, 6% Dance, General
Expenses: 2018-2019: $31,026; room/board: $10,796
Financial aid: (405) 208-5211; 41% of undergrads determined to have financial need; average aid package $22,380

Oklahoma Panhandle State University

Goodwell OK
(580) 349-1370
U.S. News ranking: Reg. Coll. (W), second tier
Website: www.opsu.edu
Admissions email: opsu.admissions@opsu.edu
Public; founded 1909
Freshman admissions: less selective; 2017-2018: N/A applied, N/A accepted. Neither SAT nor ACT required. SAT 25/75 percentile: N/A. High school rank: N/A
Early decision deadline: N/A, notification date: N/A
Early action deadline: N/A, notification date: N/A
Application deadline (fall): rolling
Undergraduate student body: 852 full time, 286 part time; 49% male, 51% female; 2% American Indian, 1% Asian, 8% black, 23% Hispanic, 5% multiracial, 0% Pacific Islander, 54% white, 4% international
Most popular majors: Information not available
Expenses: 2017-2018: $6,196 in state, $6,196 out of state; room/board: $4,695
Financial aid: N/A

Oklahoma State University

Stillwater OK
(405) 744-5358
U.S. News ranking: Nat. U., No. 157
Website: go.okstate.edu
Admissions email: admissions@okstate.edu
Public; founded 1890
Freshman admissions: more selective; 2017-2018: 13,635 applied, 10,128 accepted. Either SAT or ACT required. ACT 25/75 percentile: 22-28. High school rank: 27% in top tenth, 54% in top quarter, 85% in top half
Early decision deadline: N/A, notification date: N/A
Early action deadline: N/A, notification date: N/A
Application deadline (fall): rolling
Undergraduate student body: 18,167 full time, 2,811 part time; 51% male, 49% female; 5% American Indian, 2% Asian, 5% black, 8% Hispanic, 10% multiracial, 0% Pacific Islander, 68% white, 4% international; 73% from in state; 45% live on campus; 18% of students in fraternities, 25% in sororities
Most popular majors: 27% Business, Management, Marketing, and Related Support Services, 11% Engineering, 9% Agriculture, Agriculture Operations, and Related Sciences, 7% Family and Consumer Sciences/Human Sciences, 6% Biological and Biomedical Sciences
Expenses: 2018-2019: $9,019 in state, $24,539 out of state; room/board: $8,558
Financial aid: (405) 744-6604; 51% of undergrads determined to have financial need; average aid package $14,534

Oklahoma State University Institute of Technology–Okmulgee

Okmulgee OK
(918) 293-4680
U.S. News ranking: Reg. Coll. (W), No. 27
Website: www.osuit.edu/admissions
Admissions email: osuit.admissions@okstate.edu
Public; founded 1946
Freshman admissions: less selective; 2017-2018: 2,925 applied, 856 accepted. Either SAT or ACT required. ACT 25/75 percentile: 16-21. High school rank: 6% in top tenth, 22% in top quarter, 54% in top half
Early decision deadline: N/A, notification date: N/A
Early action deadline: N/A, notification date: N/A
Application deadline (fall): rolling
Undergraduate student body: 1,744 full time, 758 part time; 64% male, 36% female; 12% American Indian, 1% Asian, 5% black, 6% Hispanic, 11% multiracial, 0% Pacific Islander, 52% white, 1% international; 93% from in state; 25% live on campus; 0% of students in fraternities, 0% in sororities
Most popular majors: 56% Computer and Information Systems Security/Information Assurance, 29% Civil Engineering Technology/Technician, 15% Instrumentation Technology/Technician
Expenses: 2018-2019: $5,250 in state, $10,860 out of state; room/board: $6,178
Financial aid: (918) 293-5222; 76% of undergrads determined to have financial need; average aid package $8,193

Oklahoma State University–Oklahoma City

Oklahoma City OK
(405) 945-3224
U.S. News ranking: Reg. Coll. (W), unranked
Website: www.osuokc.edu/
Admissions email: admissions@osuokc.edu
Public; founded 1961
Freshman admissions: least selective; 2017-2018: 6,545 applied, 3,489 accepted. Neither SAT nor ACT required. SAT 25/75 percentile: N/A. High school rank: N/A
Early decision deadline: N/A, notification date: N/A
Early action deadline: N/A, notification date: N/A
Application deadline (fall): rolling
Undergraduate student body: 1,728 full time, 4,111 part time; 38% male, 62% female; 4% American Indian, 3% Asian, 12% black, 16% Hispanic, 7% multiracial, 0% Pacific Islander, 52% white, 2% international; 95% from in state; 0% live on campus; 0% of students in fraternities, 0% in sororities
Most popular majors: 29% Multi-/Interdisciplinary Studies, Other, 11% Registered Nursing, Nursing Administration, Nursing Research and Clinical Nursing, Other, 6% Child Care and Support Services Management, 6% Criminal Justice/Police Science, 5% Health/Health Care Administration/Management
Expenses: 2018-2019: $781 in state, $11,558 out of state; room/board: N/A
Financial aid: (405) 945-3211; 65% of undergrads determined to have financial need; average aid package $1,757

Oklahoma Wesleyan University

Bartlesville OK
(866) 222-8226
U.S. News ranking: Reg. U. (W), No. 85
Website: www.okwu.edu
Admissions email: admissions@okwu.edu
Private; founded 1972
Affiliation: Wesleyan
Freshman admissions: selective; 2017-2018: 2,790 applied, 1,723 accepted. Either SAT or ACT required. ACT 25/75 percentile: 18-24. High school rank: 2% in top tenth, 4% in top quarter, 19% in top half
Early decision deadline: N/A, notification date: N/A
Early action deadline: N/A, notification date: N/A
Application deadline (fall): rolling
Undergraduate student body: 609 full time, 397 part time; 42% male, 58% female; 6% American Indian, 0% Asian, 9% black, 4% Hispanic, 9% multiracial, 0% Pacific Islander, 64% white, 4% international; N/A from in state; 73% live on campus; N/A of students in fraternities, N/A in sororities
Most popular majors: 23% Nursing Science, 18% Business, Management, Marketing, and Related Support Services, Other, 8% General Studies, 5% Theological and Ministerial Studies, Other, 4% Business, Management, Marketing, and Related Support Services, Other
Expenses: 2018-2019: $26,956; room/board: $8,344
Financial aid: (918) 335-6282; 79% of undergrads determined to have financial need; average aid package $17,677

Oral Roberts University

Tulsa OK
(800) 678-8876
U.S. News ranking: Reg. U. (W), No. 41
Website: www.oru.edu
Admissions email: admissions@oru.edu
Private; founded 1963
Affiliation: Interdenominational
Freshman admissions: selective; 2017-2018: 2,433 applied, 2,271 accepted. Either SAT or ACT required. ACT 25/75 percentile: 20-26. High school rank: 22% in top tenth, 46% in top quarter, 80% in top half
Early decision deadline: N/A, notification date: N/A
Early action deadline: N/A, notification date: N/A
Application deadline (fall): rolling
Undergraduate student body: 2,866 full time, 515 part time; 41% male, 59% female; 3% American Indian, 2% Asian, 13% black, 13% Hispanic, 5% multiracial, 0% Pacific Islander, 44% white, 10% international; 44% from in state; 61% live on campus; 0% of students in fraternities, 0% in sororities
Most popular majors: 27% Business, Management, Marketing, and Related Support Services, 15% Theology and Religious Vocations, 11% Health Professions and Related Programs 9% Education, 7% Communication, Journalism, and Related Programs
Expenses: 2018-2019: $27,728; room/board: $9,450
Financial aid: (918) 495-6510; 72% of undergrads determined to have financial need; average aid package $25,595

Rogers State University

Claremore OK
(918) 343-7545
U.S. News ranking: Reg. Coll. (W), second tier
Website: www.rsu.edu/
Admissions email: admissions@rsu.edu
Public; founded 1909
Freshman admissions: less selective; 2017-2018: 1,241 applied, 1,032 accepted. Either SAT or ACT required. ACT 25/75 percentile: 18-19. High school rank: 13% in top tenth, 19% in top quarter, 63% in top half
Early decision deadline: N/A, notification date: N/A
Early action deadline: N/A, notification date: N/A
Application deadline (fall): rolling
Undergraduate student body: 2,182 full time, 1,514 part time; 40% male, 60% female; 8% American Indian, 2% Asian, 4% black, 6% Hispanic, 21% multiracial, 0% Pacific Islander, 58% white, 0% international; 95% from in state; 22% live on campus; 5% of students in fraternities, 5% in sororities
Most popular majors: 30% Business Administration and Management, General, 10% Biology/Biological Sciences, General, 9% Registered Nursing/Registered Nurse, 9% Social Sciences, General, 8% Multi-/Interdisciplinary Studies, Other
Expenses: 2017-2018: $6,870 in state, $15,210 out of state; room/board: $9,814
Financial aid: (918) 343-7553

Southeastern Oklahoma State University

Durant OK
(580) 745-2060
U.S. News ranking: Reg. U. (W), second tier
Website: www.se.edu
Admissions email: admissions@se.edu
Public; founded 1909
Affiliation: Other
Freshman admissions: selective; 2017-2018: 1,174 applied, 851 accepted. Either SAT or ACT required. ACT 25/75 percentile: 18-23. High school rank: 19% in top tenth, 45% in top quarter, 75% in top half
Early decision deadline: N/A, notification date: N/A
Early action deadline: N/A, notification date: N/A
Application deadline (fall): rolling
Undergraduate student body: 2,368 full time, 702 part time; 47% male, 53% female; 30% American Indian, 1% Asian, 6% black,

More @ usnews.com/bestcolleges

% Hispanic, 0% multiracial, % Pacific Islander, 54% white, % international; 65% from in tate; 10% live on campus; 2% f students in fraternities, 2% in ororities
ost popular majors: 20% ngineering Technologies and ngineering-Related Fields, 4% Business, Management, Marketing, and Related Support ervices, 10% Education, 8% iberal Arts and Sciences, General tudies and Humanities, 6% sychology
xpenses: 2017-2018: $9,149 in tate, $18,929 out of state; room/ oard: $6,973
inancial aid: (580) 745-2186; 1% of undergrads determined to ave financial need; average aid ackage $11,735

outhern Nazarene Jniversity[1]

ethany OK
405) 491-6324
.S. News ranking: Reg. U. (W), econd tier
Vebsite: www.snu.edu
dmissions email: dmissions@snu.edu
rivate; founded 1899
pplication deadline (fall): 8/6
ndergraduate student body: N/A ull time, N/A part time
xpenses: 2017-2018: $25,178; oom/board: $9,884
inancial aid: (405) 491-6310

outhwestern hristian University

ethany OK
405) 789-7661
.S. News ranking: Reg. Coll. (W), o. 24
Vebsite: www.swcu.edu/
dmissions email: dmissions@swcu.edu
rivate; founded 1946
ffiliation: Pentecostal Holiness hurch
reshman admissions: least elective; 2017-2018: 597 pplied, 282 accepted. Either AT or ACT required. ACT 25/75 ercentile: 6-22. High school ank: N/A
arly decision deadline: N/A, otification date: N/A
arly action deadline: N/A, otification date: N/A
pplication deadline (fall): rolling
ndergraduate student body: 539 ull time, 81 part time; 54% nale, 46% female; 5% American ndian, 1% Asian, 18% black, % Hispanic, 4% multiracial, 1% acific Islander, 46% white, 12% nternational
ost popular majors: 49% usiness Administration and Management, General, 18% port and Fitness Administration/ Management, 17% Theology and eligious Vocations, Other, 15% sychology, General
xpenses: 2018-2019: $17,630; oom/board: $8,000
inancial aid: (405) 789-7661

Southwestern Oklahoma State University

Weatherford OK
(580) 774-3782
U.S. News ranking: Reg. U. (W), second tier
Website: www.swosu.edu
Admissions email: admissions@swosu.edu
Public; founded 1901
Freshman admissions: selective; 2017-2018: 2,541 applied, 2,337 accepted. Neither SAT nor ACT required. ACT 25/75 percentile: 18-24. High school rank: 27% in top tenth, 48% in top quarter, 78% in top half
Early decision deadline: N/A, notification date: N/A
Early action deadline: N/A, notification date: N/A
Application deadline (fall): rolling
Undergraduate student body: 3,713 full time, 910 part time; 41% male, 59% female; 4% American Indian, 2% Asian, 4% black, 11% Hispanic, 8% multiracial, 0% Pacific Islander, 62% white, 6% international; 91% from in state; 27% live on campus; 4% of students in fraternities, 5% in sororities
Most popular majors: 24% Registered Nursing/Registered Nurse, 13% Business Administration and Management, General, 7% Elementary Education and Teaching, 7% Parks, Recreation and Leisure Facilities Management, General, 5% Health Professions and Related Clinical Sciences, Other
Expenses: 2017-2018: $6,690 in state, $13,440 out of state; room/ board: $5,400
Financial aid: (580) 774-3786

University of Central Oklahoma

Edmond OK
(405) 974-2727
U.S. News ranking: Reg. U. (W), No. 77
Website: www.uco.edu/em/ become-a-broncho/index.asp
Admissions email: onestop@uco.edu
Public; founded 1890
Freshman admissions: selective; 2017-2018: 4,722 applied, 3,831 accepted. Either SAT or ACT required. ACT 25/75 percentile: 19-24. High school rank: 14% in top tenth, 37% in top quarter, 72% in top half
Early decision deadline: N/A, notification date: N/A
Early action deadline: N/A, notification date: N/A
Application deadline (fall): rolling
Undergraduate student body: 10,449 full time, 3,888 part time; 41% male, 59% female; 4% American Indian, 4% Asian, 9% black, 10% Hispanic, 10% multiracial, 0% Pacific Islander, 56% white, 6% international; 97% from in state; 11% live on campus; 1% of students in fraternities, 2% in sororities
Most popular majors: 12% General Studies, 6% Business Administration and Management, General, 5% Psychology, General, 4% Forensic Science and Technology, 4% Registered Nursing/Registered Nurse
Expenses: 2018-2019: $7,489 in state, $18,376 out of state; room/ board: $7,970
Financial aid: (405) 974-2727; 53% of undergrads determined to have financial need; average aid package $9,879

University of Oklahoma

Norman OK
(405) 325-2252
U.S. News ranking: Nat. U., No. 124
Website: www.ou.edu
Admissions email: admrec@ou.edu
Public; founded 1890
Freshman admissions: more selective; 2017-2018: 16,777 applied, 11,552 accepted. Either SAT or ACT required. ACT 25/75 percentile: 23-29. High school rank: 36% in top tenth, 65% in top quarter, 92% in top half
Early decision deadline: N/A, notification date: N/A
Early action deadline: N/A, notification date: N/A
Application deadline (fall): 2/1
Undergraduate student body: 19,793 full time, 3,026 part time; 49% male, 51% female; 4% American Indian, 6% Asian, 5% black, 10% Hispanic, 8% multiracial, 0% Pacific Islander, 61% white, 4% international; 67% from in state; 31% live on campus; 25% of students in fraternities, 31% in sororities
Most popular majors: 20% Business, Management, Marketing, and Related Support Services, 13% Engineering, 10% Health Professions and Related Programs, 9% Communication, Journalism, and Related Programs, 7% Liberal Arts and Sciences, General Studies and Humanities
Expenses: 2018-2019: $9,062 in state, $24,443 out of state; room/ board: $10,994
Financial aid: (405) 325-4521; 48% of undergrads determined to have financial need; average aid package $13,595

University of Science and Arts of Oklahoma

Chickasha OK
(405) 574-1357
U.S. News ranking: Nat. Lib. Arts, second tier
Website: www.usao.edu
Admissions email: usao-admissions@usao.edu
Public; founded 1908
Freshman admissions: selective; 2017-2018: 1,052 applied, 508 accepted. Neither SAT nor ACT required. ACT 25/75 percentile: 19-24. High school rank: 17% in top tenth, 51% in top quarter, 100% in top half
Early decision deadline: N/A, notification date: N/A
Early action deadline: N/A, notification date: N/A
Application deadline (fall): 8/30
Undergraduate student body: 786 full time, 97 part time; 35% male, 65% female; N/A American Indian, N/A Asian, N/A black, N/A Hispanic, N/A multiracial, N/A Pacific Islander, N/A white, N/A international
Most popular majors: Information not available
Expenses: 2018-2019: $7,680 in state, $18,030 out of state; room/ board: $6,150
Financial aid: (405) 574-1350; 68% of undergrads determined to have financial need; average aid package $11,420

University of Tulsa

Tulsa OK
(918) 631-2307
U.S. News ranking: Nat. U., No. 106
Website: utulsa.edu
Admissions email: admission@utulsa.edu
Private; founded 1894
Affiliation: Presbyterian Church (USA)
Freshman admissions: more selective; 2017-2018: 7,869 applied, 3,065 accepted. Either SAT or ACT required. ACT 25/75 percentile: 25-32. High school rank: 70% in top tenth, 85% in top quarter, 97% in top half
Early decision deadline: N/A, notification date: N/A
Early action deadline: 11/1, notification date: 12/15
Application deadline (fall): rolling
Undergraduate student body: 3,203 full time, 140 part time; 56% male, 44% female; 3% American Indian, 5% Asian, 5% black, 6% Hispanic, 3% multiracial, 0% Pacific Islander, 57% white, 19% international; 59% from in state; 65% live on campus; 18% of students in fraternities, 20% in sororities
Most popular majors: 27% Engineering, 24% Business, Management, Marketing, and Related Support Services, 6% Health Professions and Related Programs, 6% Visual and Performing Arts, 5% Biological and Biomedical Sciences
Expenses: 2018-2019: $39,552; room/board: $11,116
Financial aid: (918) 631-2526; 47% of undergrads determined to have financial need; average aid package $31,580

OREGON

Art Institute of Portland[1]

Portland OR
(503) 228-6528
U.S. News ranking: Arts, unranked
Website: www.artinstitutes.edu/ portland/
Admissions email: N/A
For-profit
Application deadline (fall): N/A
Undergraduate student body: N/A full time, N/A part time
Expenses: N/A
Financial aid: N/A

Corban University

Salem OR
(800) 845-3005
U.S. News ranking: Reg. U. (W), No. 64
Website: www.corban.edu
Admissions email: admissions@corban.edu
Private; founded 1935
Affiliation: Evangelical Christian
Freshman admissions: selective; 2017-2018: 1,943 applied, 641 accepted. Either SAT or ACT required. SAT 25/75 percentile: 1040-1230. High school rank: 25% in top tenth, 60% in top quarter, 91% in top half
Early decision deadline: N/A, notification date: N/A
Early action deadline: N/A, notification date: N/A
Application deadline (fall): 8/1
Undergraduate student body: 936 full time, 85 part time; 39% male, 61% female; 1% American Indian, 2% Asian, 1% black, 2% Hispanic, 8% multiracial, 1% Pacific Islander, 75% white, 6% international; 54% from in state; 49% live on campus; 0% of students in fraternities, 0% in sororities
Most popular majors: 23% Education, General, 18% Business Administration and Management, General, 18% Psychology, General, 8% Health/Medical Preparatory Programs, Other, 6% Theology/Theological Studies
Expenses: 2018-2019: $33,040; room/board: $10,228
Financial aid: (503) 375-7106; 82% of undergrads determined to have financial need; average aid package $22,273

Eastern Oregon University

La Grande OR
(541) 962-3393
U.S. News ranking: Reg. U. (W), second tier
Website: www.eou.edu
Admissions email: admissions@eou.edu
Public; founded 1929
Freshman admissions: selective; 2017-2018: 1,011 applied, 988 accepted. Either SAT or ACT required. ACT 25/75 percentile: 18-23. High school rank: 15% in top tenth, 39% in top quarter, 79% in top half
Early decision deadline: N/A, notification date: N/A
Early action deadline: 2/1, notification date: N/A
Application deadline (fall): 9/1
Undergraduate student body: 1,668 full time, 1,069 part time; 39% male, 61% female; 2% American Indian, 2% Asian, 2% black, 10% Hispanic, 5% multiracial, 2% Pacific Islander, 72% white, 1% international; 69% from in state; 15% live on campus; N/A of students in fraternities, N/A in sororities
Most popular majors: 32% Business, Management, Marketing, and Related Support Services, 17% Liberal Arts and Sciences, General Studies and Humanities, 12% Education, 7% Parks, Recreation, Leisure, and Fitness Studies, 7% Social Sciences
Expenses: 2018-2019: $8,679 in state, $20,739 out of state; room/ board: $10,040

Financial aid: (800) 452-8639; 75% of undergrads determined to have financial need; average aid package $10,087

George Fox University

Newberg OR
(800) 765-4369
U.S. News ranking: Reg. U. (W), No. 24
Website: www.georgefox.edu
Admissions email: admissions@georgefox.edu
Private; founded 1891
Affiliation: Friends
Freshman admissions: selective; 2017-2018: 2,877 applied, 2,356 accepted. Either SAT or ACT required. SAT 25/75 percentile: 1030-1240. High school rank: 29% in top tenth, 60% in top quarter, 88% in top half
Early decision deadline: N/A, notification date: N/A
Early action deadline: 11/1, notification date: 12/9
Application deadline (fall): rolling
Undergraduate student body: 2,494 full time, 204 part time; 43% male, 57% female; 1% American Indian, 4% Asian, 2% black, 12% Hispanic, 8% multiracial, 1% Pacific Islander, 70% white, 2% international; 60% from in state; 55% live on campus; 0% of students in fraternities, 0% in sororities
Most popular majors: 18% Business Administration and Management, General, 7% Registered Nursing/Registered Nurse, 6% Elementary Education and Teaching, 6% Engineering, General, 6% Social Work
Expenses: 2018-2019: $36,020; room/board: $11,250
Financial aid: (503) 554-2302; 74% of undergrads determined to have financial need; average aid package $22,230

Lewis & Clark College

Portland OR
(800) 444-4111
U.S. News ranking: Nat. Lib. Arts, No. 68
Website: www.lclark.edu
Admissions email: admissions@lclark.edu
Private; founded 1867
Freshman admissions: more selective; 2017-2018: 6,305 applied, 4,500 accepted. Neither SAT nor ACT required. ACT 25/75 percentile: 27-31. High school rank: 35% in top tenth, 71% in top quarter, 98% in top half
Early decision deadline: 11/1, notification date: 12/15
Early action deadline: 11/1, notification date: 12/31
Application deadline (fall): 1/15
Undergraduate student body: 2,068 full time, 38 part time; 42% male, 58% female; 1% American Indian, 6% Asian, 3% black, 12% Hispanic, 5% multiracial, 0% Pacific Islander, 64% white, 5% international; 12% from in state; 66% live on campus; N/A of students in fraternities, N/A in sororities
Most popular majors: 23% Social Sciences, 12% Biological and Biomedical Sciences, 12% Psychology, 8% Foreign Languages, Literatures, and Linguistics, 6% Visual and Performing Arts
Expenses: 2018-2019: $50,934; room/board: $12,490
Financial aid: (503) 768-7090; 60% of undergrads determined to have financial need; average aid package $40,854

Linfield College

McMinnville OR
(800) 640-2287
U.S. News ranking: Nat. Lib. Arts, No. 108
Website: www.linfield.edu
Admissions email: admission@linfield.edu
Private; founded 1858
Affiliation: American Baptist
Freshman admissions: selective; 2017-2018: 2,325 applied, 1,878 accepted. Either SAT or ACT required. SAT 25/75 percentile: 1020-1210. High school rank: 30% in top tenth, 67% in top quarter, 93% in top half
Early decision deadline: N/A, notification date: N/A
Early action deadline: 11/1, notification date: 12/1
Application deadline (fall): rolling
Undergraduate student body: 1,505 full time, 30 part time; 40% male, 60% female; 1% American Indian, 5% Asian, 2% black, 17% Hispanic, 10% multiracial, 1% Pacific Islander, 59% white, 3% international; 58% from in state; 74% live on campus; 23% of students in fraternities, 24% in sororities
Most popular majors: 22% Business, Management, Marketing, and Related Support Services, 12% Education, 11% Social Sciences, 10% Psychology, 6% Biological and Biomedical Sciences
Expenses: 2018-2019: $43,232; room/board: $13,055
Financial aid: (503) 883-2225; 78% of undergrads determined to have financial need; average aid package $34,716

Northwest Christian University

Eugene OR
(541) 684-7201
U.S. News ranking: Reg. U. (W), No. 75
Website: www.nwcu.edu
Admissions email: admissions@nwcu.edu
Private; founded 1895
Affiliation: Christian Church (Disciples of Christ)
Freshman admissions: selective; 2017-2018: 407 applied, 280 accepted. Either SAT or ACT required. SAT 25/75 percentile: 943-1118. High school rank: 10% in top tenth, 16% in top quarter, 19% in top half
Early decision deadline: N/A, notification date: N/A
Early action deadline: N/A, notification date: N/A
Application deadline (fall): rolling
Undergraduate student body: 443 full time, 162 part time; 39% male, 61% female; 4% American Indian, 2% Asian, 5% black, 7% Hispanic, 6% multiracial, 1% Pacific Islander, 73% white, 0% international; 77% from in state; 32% live on campus; 0% of students in fraternities, 0% in sororities
Most popular majors: 32% Business, Management, Marketing, and Related Support Services, 15% Education, 13% Multi/Interdisciplinary Studies, 11% Health Professions and Related Programs, 10% Biological and Biomedical Sciences
Expenses: 2018-2019: $30,050; room/board: $9,300
Financial aid: (541) 684-7201; 80% of undergrads determined to have financial need; average aid package $21,511

Oregon College of Art and Craft[1]

Portland OR
(971) 255-4192
U.S. News ranking: Arts, unranked
Website: www.ocac.edu/
Admissions email: admissions@ocac.edu
Private; founded 1907
Application deadline (fall): rolling
Undergraduate student body: N/A full time, N/A part time
Expenses: 2017-2018: $33,160; room/board: $9,900
Financial aid: N/A

Oregon Institute of Technology

Klamath Falls OR
(541) 885-1150
U.S. News ranking: Reg. Coll. (W), No. 5
Website: www.oit.edu
Admissions email: oit@oit.edu
Public; founded 1947
Freshman admissions: selective; 2017-2018: 1,314 applied, 807 accepted. Either SAT or ACT required. SAT 25/75 percentile: 1040-1230. High school rank: 25% in top tenth, 57% in top quarter, 86% in top half
Early decision deadline: N/A, notification date: N/A
Early action deadline: N/A, notification date: N/A
Application deadline (fall): 9/4
Undergraduate student body: 2,284 full time, 3,100 part time; 51% male, 49% female; 1% American Indian, 6% Asian, 2% black, 11% Hispanic, 5% multiracial, 1% Pacific Islander, 70% white, 2% international; 72% from in state; 15% live on campus; 0% of students in fraternities, 0% in sororities
Most popular majors: 43% Health Professions and Related Programs, 20% Engineering, 16% Engineering Technologies and Engineering-Related Fields, 8% Business, Management, Marketing, and Related Support Services, 4% Psychology
Expenses: 2018-2019: $9,987 in state, $28,055 out of state; room/board: $9,640
Financial aid: N/A; 68% of undergrads determined to have financial need; average aid package $11,152

Oregon State University

Corvallis OR
(541) 737-4411
U.S. News ranking: Nat. U., No. 140
Website: oregonstate.edu
Admissions email: osuadmit@oregonstate.edu
Public; founded 1868
Freshman admissions: more selective; 2017-2018: 14,888 applied, 11,738 accepted. Either SAT or ACT required. SAT 25/75 percentile: 1070-1300. High school rank: 26% in top tenth, 58% in top quarter, 91% in top half
Early decision deadline: N/A, notification date: N/A
Early action deadline: 11/1, notification date: 12/15
Application deadline (fall): 9/1
Undergraduate student body: 18,829 full time, 7,009 part time; 54% male, 46% female; 1% American Indian, 8% Asian, 1% black, 10% Hispanic, 7% multiracial, 0% Pacific Islander, 64% white, 7% international; 68% from in state; 17% live on campus; 10% of students in fraternities, 16% in sororities
Most popular majors: 9% Computer Science, 6% Human Development, Family Studies, and Related Services, 4% Psychology, General, 4% Public Health, 3% Mechanical Engineering
Expenses: 2018-2019: $11,166 in state, $30,141 out of state; room/board: $12,855
Financial aid: (541) 737-2241; 52% of undergrads determined to have financial need; average aid package $12,946

Pacific Northwest College of Art[1]

Portland OR
(503) 226-4391
U.S. News ranking: Arts, unranked
Website: www.pnca.edu
Admissions email: admissions@pnca.edu
Private
Application deadline (fall): N/A
Undergraduate student body: N/A full time, N/A part time
Expenses: N/A
Financial aid: N/A

Pacific University

Forest Grove OR
(800) 677-6712
U.S. News ranking: Reg. U. (W), No. 21
Website: www.pacificu.edu
Admissions email: admissions@pacificu.edu
Private; founded 1849
Freshman admissions: selective; 2017-2018: 2,586 applied, 2,185 accepted. Either SAT or ACT required. SAT 25/75 percentile: 1070-1260. High school rank: N/A
Early decision deadline: N/A, notification date: N/A
Early action deadline: N/A, notification date: N/A
Application deadline (fall): 8/15
Undergraduate student body: 1,818 full time, 58 part time; 40% male, 60% female; 1% American Indian, 12% Asian, 2% black, 14% Hispanic, 13% multiracial, 2% Pacific Islander, 51% white, 1% international; 43% from in state; 58% live on campus; N/A of students in fraternities, N/A in sororities
Most popular majors: 19% Health Professions and Related Programs 10% Business, Management, Marketing, and Related Support Services, 10% Parks, Recreation, Leisure, and Fitness Studies, 9% Biological and Biomedical Sciences, 8% Social Sciences
Expenses: 2018-2019: $44,298; room/board: $12,528
Financial aid: (503) 352-2871; 81% of undergrads determined to have financial need; average aid package $31,952

Portland State University

Portland OR
(800) 547-8887
U.S. News ranking: Nat. U., second tier
Website: www.pdx.edu
Admissions email: admissions@pdx.edu
Public; founded 1946
Freshman admissions: selective; 2017-2018: 6,815 applied, 6,300 accepted. Neither SAT nor ACT required. ACT 25/75 percentile: 19-25. High school rank: 15% in top tenth, 48% in top quarter, 85% in top half
Early decision deadline: N/A, notification date: N/A
Early action deadline: N/A, notification date: N/A
Application deadline (fall): rolling
Undergraduate student body: 13,991 full time, 7,734 part time; 46% male, 54% female; 1% American Indian, 9% Asian, 4% black, 14% Hispanic, 7% multiracial, 1% Pacific Islander, 55% white, 6% international; 85% from in state; 9% live on campus; 1% of students in fraternities, 1% in sororities
Most popular majors: Education, General, Liberal Arts and Sciences/Liberal Studies, Psychology, General, Social Sciences, General, Teacher Education and Professional Development, Specific Levels and Methods, Other
Expenses: 2018-2019: $9,105 in state, $27,060 out of state; room/board: $10,428
Financial aid: (503) 725-5442; 66% of undergrads determined to have financial need; average aid package $10,562

Reed College[1]

Portland OR
(503) 777-7511
U.S. News ranking: Nat. Lib. Arts, No. 90
Website: www.reed.edu/
Admissions email: admission@reed.edu
Private
Application deadline (fall): N/A
Undergraduate student body: N/A full time, N/A part time
Expenses: 2017-2018: $54,200; room/board: $13,670
Financial aid: N/A

More @ usnews.com/bestcolleges

;outhern Oregon Jniversity

.shland OR
541) 552-6411
.S. News ranking: Reg. U. (W), **l**o. 88
/ebsite: www.sou.edu
dmissions email: dmissions@sou.edu
ublic; founded 1926
'eshman admissions: less elective; 2017-2018: 2,779 pplied, 2,181 accepted. Either AT or ACT required. SAT 25/75 ercentile: 870-1120. High chool rank: N/A
arly decision deadline: N/A, otification date: N/A
arly action deadline: N/A, otification date: N/A
pplication deadline (fall): rolling
ndergraduate student body: 3,646 ıll time, 1,829 part time; 41% ıale, 59% female; 1% American ıdian, 2% Asian, 2% black, 2% Hispanic, 9% multiracial, % Pacific Islander, 60% white, % international; 59% from in tate; 17% live on campus; N/A f students in fraternities, N/A in ɔrorities
lost popular majors: 17% usiness, Management, **l**arketing, and Related Support ervices, 13% Visual and erforming Arts, 10% Education, 0% Psychology, 8% Social ciences
xpenses: 2017-2018: $8,523 in ate, $23,170 out of state; room/ ɔard: $12,756
inancial aid: N/A; 64% of ndergrads determined to have nancial need; average aid ackage $10,995

Iniversity of Oregon

ugene OR
300) 232-3825
.S. News ranking: Nat. U., o. 102
'ebsite: www.uoregon.edu
dmissions email: ɔadmit@uoregon.edu
ıblic; founded 1876
eshman admissions: selective; 017-2018: 20,317 applied, 6,824 accepted. Either SAT ACT required. SAT 25/75 ercentile: 1080-1270. High chool rank: 20% in top tenth, 5% in top quarter, 88% in p half
arly decision deadline: N/A, otification date: N/A
arly action deadline: 11/1, otification date: 12/15
pplication deadline (fall): 1/15
ndergraduate student body: 7,801 full time, 1,539 part me; 46% male, 54% female; % American Indian, 6% Asian, % black, 12% Hispanic, 8% ultiracial, 0% Pacific Islander, 3% white, 12% international; 7% from in state; 21% live ı campus; 16% of students in aternities, 21% in sororities
ost popular majors: 16% usiness/Commerce, General, 1% Journalism, 9% Social ciences, General, 8% sychology, General, 7% conomics, General
xpenses: 2018-2019: $11,898 state, $35,478 out of state; om/board: $12,963
Financial aid: (800) 760-6953; 45% of undergrads determined to have financial need; average aid package $11,187

University of Portland

Portland OR
(888) 627-5601
U.S. News ranking: Reg. U. (W), No. 6
Website: www.up.edu
Admissions email: admissions@up.edu
Private; founded 1901
Affiliation: Roman Catholic
Freshman admissions: more selective; 2017-2018: 11,137 applied, 7,745 accepted. Either SAT or ACT required. SAT 25/75 percentile: 1140-1320. High school rank: 54% in top tenth, 83% in top quarter, 96% in top half
Early decision deadline: N/A, notification date: N/A
Early action deadline: N/A, notification date: N/A
Application deadline (fall): 1/15
Undergraduate student body: 3,792 full time, 91 part time; 40% male, 60% female; 0% American Indian, 13% Asian, 1% black, 13% Hispanic, 8% multiracial, 2% Pacific Islander, 58% white, 3% international; 26% from in state; 56% live on campus; N/A of students in fraternities, N/A in sororities
Most popular majors: 21% Health Professions and Related Programs, 13% Business, Management, Marketing, and Related Support Services, 10% Engineering, 9% Biological and Biomedical Sciences, 7% Mathematics and Statistics
Expenses: 2018-2019: $45,904; room/board: $13,174
Financial aid: (503) 943-7311; 58% of undergrads determined to have financial need; average aid package $31,632

Warner Pacific College

Portland OR
(503) 517-1020
U.S. News ranking: Reg. Coll. (W), No. 10
Website: www.warnerpacific.edu
Admissions email: admissions@warnerpacific.edu
Private; founded 1937
Freshman admissions: less selective; 2017-2018: 556 applied, 530 accepted. Either SAT or ACT required. SAT 25/75 percentile: 880-1100. High school rank: 11% in top tenth, 34% in top quarter, 72% in top half
Early decision deadline: N/A, notification date: N/A
Early action deadline: N/A, notification date: N/A
Application deadline (fall): rolling
Undergraduate student body: 396 full time, 4 part time; 41% male, 60% female; 1% American Indian, 5% Asian, 9% black, 34% Hispanic, 10% multiracial, 2% Pacific Islander, 36% white, 1% international
Most popular majors: Information not available
Expenses: 2018-2019: $18,660; room/board: $9,670
Financial aid: (503) 517-1091; 85% of undergrads determined to have financial need; average aid package $21,056

Western Oregon University

Monmouth OR
(503) 838-8211
U.S. News ranking: Reg. U. (W), No. 63
Website: www.wou.edu
Admissions email: wolfgram@wou.edu
Public; founded 1856
Freshman admissions: less selective; 2017-2018: 2,942 applied, 2,371 accepted. Neither SAT nor ACT required. ACT 25/75 percentile: 16-25. High school rank: N/A
Early decision deadline: N/A, notification date: N/A
Early action deadline: N/A, notification date: N/A
Application deadline (fall): rolling
Undergraduate student body: 4,042 full time, 734 part time; 38% male, 62% female; 2% American Indian, 5% Asian, 4% black, 16% Hispanic, 0% multiracial, 3% Pacific Islander, 61% white, 6% international; 79% from in state; 24% live on campus; N/A of students in fraternities, N/A in sororities
Most popular majors: 14% Business, Management, Marketing, and Related Support Services, 14% Parks, Recreation, Leisure, and Fitness Studies, 14% Psychology, 10% Education, 8% Social Sciences
Expenses: 2018-2019: $9,198 in state, $25,653 out of state; room/board: $10,203
Financial aid: (503) 838-8475; 80% of undergrads determined to have financial need; average aid package $9,865

Willamette University[1]

Salem OR
(877) 542-2787
U.S. News ranking: Nat. Lib. Arts, No. 76
Website: www.willamette.edu
Admissions email: bearcat@willamette.edu
Private; founded 1842
Application deadline (fall): 1/15
Undergraduate student body: 1,786 full time, 164 part time
Expenses: 2018-2019: $50,074; room/board: $12,440
Financial aid: (503) 370-6273; 63% of undergrads determined to have financial need; average aid package $36,235

PENNSYLVANIA

Albright College

Reading PA
(800) 252-1856
U.S. News ranking: Nat. Lib. Arts, second tier
Website: www.albright.edu
Admissions email: admission@albright.edu
Private; founded 1856
Affiliation: United Methodist
Freshman admissions: selective; 2017-2018: 8,332 applied, 4,169 accepted. Neither SAT nor ACT required. SAT 25/75 percentile: 990-1170. High school rank: 15% in top tenth, 37% in top quarter, 73% in top half
Early decision deadline: N/A, notification date: N/A
Early action deadline: N/A, notification date: N/A
Application deadline (fall): rolling
Undergraduate student body: 1,993 full time, 22 part time; 41% male, 59% female; 1% American Indian, 3% Asian, 21% black, 12% Hispanic, 2% multiracial, 0% Pacific Islander, 51% white, 2% international; 60% from in state; 68% live on campus; 16% of students in fraternities, 21% in sororities
Most popular majors: 30% Business, Management, Marketing, and Related Support Services, 18% Psychology, 11% Visual and Performing Arts, 10% Social Sciences, 6% Biological and Biomedical Sciences
Expenses: 2018-2019: $45,306; room/board: $12,070
Financial aid: (610) 921-7515; 92% of undergrads determined to have financial need; average aid package $38,880

Allegheny College

Meadville PA
(800) 521-5293
U.S. News ranking: Nat. Lib. Arts, No. 76
Website: allegheny.edu
Admissions email: admissions@allegheny.edu
Private; founded 1815
Affiliation: United Methodist
Freshman admissions: more selective; 2017-2018: 5,114 applied, 3,472 accepted. Neither SAT nor ACT required. SAT 25/75 percentile: 1140-1320. High school rank: 33% in top tenth, 65% in top quarter, 88% in top half
Early decision deadline: 11/1, notification date: 11/15
Early action deadline: 12/1, notification date: 1/1
Application deadline (fall): 2/15
Undergraduate student body: 1,752 full time, 50 part time; 46% male, 54% female; 0% American Indian, 3% Asian, 9% black, 9% Hispanic, 4% multiracial, 0% Pacific Islander, 70% white, 3% international; 50% from in state; 95% live on campus; 26% of students in fraternities, 24% in sororities
Most popular majors: 13% Biology/Biological Sciences, General, 11% Economics, General, 11% Psychology, General, 9% Speech Communication and Rhetoric, 7% Environmental Science
Expenses: 2018-2019: $47,540; room/board: $12,140
Financial aid: (800) 835-7780; 78% of undergrads determined to have financial need; average aid package $41,669

Alvernia University

Reading PA
(610) 796-8220
U.S. News ranking: Reg. U. (N), No. 105
Website: www.alvernia.edu
Admissions email: admissions@alvernia.edu
Private; founded 1958
Affiliation: Roman Catholic
Freshman admissions: selective; 2017-2018: 2,179 applied, 1,543 accepted. Either SAT or ACT required. SAT 25/75 percentile: 950-1148. High school rank: N/A
Early decision deadline: N/A, notification date: N/A
Early action deadline: N/A, notification date: N/A
Application deadline (fall): rolling
Undergraduate student body: 1,670 full time, 581 part time; 27% male, 73% female; 0% American Indian, 2% Asian, 10% black, 10% Hispanic, 2% multiracial, 0% Pacific Islander, 67% white, 0% international; 75% from in state; 62% live on campus; 0% of students in fraternities, 0% in sororities
Most popular majors: 44% Health Professions and Related Programs, 16% Business, Management, Marketing, and Related Support Services, 10% Homeland Security, Law Enforcement, Firefighting and Related Protective Services, 6% Education, 6% Public Administration and Social Service Professions
Expenses: 2017-2018: $33,640; room/board: $11,690
Financial aid: (610) 796-8356

Arcadia University

Glenside PA
(215) 572-2910
U.S. News ranking: Reg. U. (N), No. 55
Website: www.arcadia.edu
Admissions email: admiss@arcadia.edu
Private; founded 1853
Freshman admissions: more selective; 2017-2018: 8,931 applied, 5,563 accepted. Either SAT or ACT required. SAT 25/75 percentile: 1060-1240. High school rank: 24% in top tenth, 55% in top quarter, 89% in top half
Early decision deadline: N/A, notification date: N/A
Early action deadline: N/A, notification date: N/A
Application deadline (fall): rolling
Undergraduate student body: 2,163 full time, 227 part time; 31% male, 69% female; 0% American Indian, 5% Asian, 9% black, 9% Hispanic, 4% multiracial, 0% Pacific Islander, 68% white, 3% international; 62% from in state; 49% live on campus; 0% of students in fraternities, 0% in sororities
Most popular majors: 14% Biology/Biological Sciences, General, 11% Psychology, General, 6% International Business/Trade/Commerce, 5% Health/Health Care Administration/Management, 5% Speech Communication and Rhetoric
Expenses: 2018-2019: $43,580; room/board: $13,800
Financial aid: (215) 572-2980; 84% of undergrads determined to have financial need; average aid package $30,047

The Art Institute of Philadelphia[1]

Philadelphia PA
U.S. News ranking: Arts, unranked
Admissions email: N/A
Private
Application deadline (fall): N/A
Undergraduate student body: N/A full time, N/A part time
Expenses: N/A
Financial aid: N/A

Art Institute of Pittsburgh[1]

Pittsburgh PA
(412) 263-6600
U.S. News ranking: Arts, unranked
Website: www.artinstitutes.edu/pittsburgh/Admissions
Admissions email: aip@aii.edu
For-profit
Application deadline (fall): N/A
Undergraduate student body: N/A full time, N/A part time
Expenses: N/A
Financial aid: N/A

Bloomsburg University of Pennsylvania

Bloomsburg PA
(570) 389-4316
U.S. News ranking: Reg. U. (N), No. 117
Website: www.bloomu.edu
Admissions email: buadmiss@bloomu.edu
Public; founded 1839
Freshman admissions: selective; 2017-2018: 9,683 applied, 7,093 accepted. Either SAT or ACT required. SAT 25/75 percentile: 970-1150. High school rank: 8% in top tenth, 29% in top quarter, 63% in top half
Early decision deadline: N/A, notification date: N/A
Early action deadline: N/A, notification date: 5/1
Application deadline (fall): rolling
Undergraduate student body: 7,863 full time, 743 part time; 43% male, 57% female; 0% American Indian, 1% Asian, 9% black, 7% Hispanic, 3% multiracial, 0% Pacific Islander, 78% white, 0% international; 91% from in state; 41% live on campus; N/A of students in fraternities, N/A in sororities
Most popular majors: 19% Business Administration and Management, General, 6% Organizational Communication, General, 6% Registered Nursing/Registered Nurse, 5% Mass Communication/Media Studies, 5% Psychology, General
Expenses: 2018-2019: $10,958 in state, $22,532 out of state; room/board: $9,686
Financial aid: (570) 389-4297; 68% of undergrads determined to have financial need; average aid package $9,310

Bryn Athyn College of the New Church[1]

Bryn Athyn PA
(267) 502-6000
U.S. News ranking: Nat. Lib. Arts, second tier
Website: www.brynathyn.edu
Admissions email: admissions@brynathyn.edu
Private; founded 1877
Affiliation: Other
Application deadline (fall): rolling
Undergraduate student body: N/A full time, N/A part time
Expenses: 2017-2018: $21,071; room/board: $11,538
Financial aid: (267) 502-6034

Bryn Mawr College

Bryn Mawr PA
(610) 526-5152
U.S. News ranking: Nat. Lib. Arts, No. 27
Website: www.brynmawr.edu
Admissions email: admissions@brynmawr.edu
Private; founded 1885
Freshman admissions: most selective; 2017-2018: 2,936 applied, 1,116 accepted. Neither SAT nor ACT required. SAT 25/75 percentile: 1310-1500. High school rank: 68% in top tenth, 91% in top quarter, 97% in top half
Early decision deadline: 11/15, notification date: 12/15
Early action deadline: N/A, notification date: N/A
Application deadline (fall): 1/15
Undergraduate student body: 1,325 full time, 9 part time; 0% male, 100% female; 0% American Indian, 12% Asian, 6% black, 9% Hispanic, 6% multiracial, 0% Pacific Islander, 37% white, 23% international; 18% from in state; 91% live on campus; N/A of students in fraternities, N/A in sororities
Most popular majors: 24% Social Sciences, 10% Mathematics and Statistics, 9% Biological and Biomedical Sciences, 9% Foreign Languages, Literatures, and Linguistics, 9% Psychology
Expenses: 2018-2019: $52,360; room/board: $16,500
Financial aid: (610) 526-5245; 53% of undergrads determined to have financial need; average aid package $47,906

Bucknell University

Lewisburg PA
(570) 577-3000
U.S. News ranking: Nat. Lib. Arts, No. 36
Website: www.bucknell.edu
Admissions email: admissions@bucknell.edu
Private; founded 1846
Freshman admissions: more selective; 2017-2018: 10,253 applied, 3,187 accepted. Either SAT or ACT required. SAT 25/75 percentile: 1250-1420. High school rank: 60% in top tenth, 89% in top quarter, 100% in top half
Early decision deadline: 11/15, notification date: 12/15
Early action deadline: N/A, notification date: N/A
Application deadline (fall): 1/15
Undergraduate student body: 3,585 full time, 26 part time; 49% male, 51% female; 0% American Indian, 5% Asian, 4% black, 7% Hispanic, 4% multiracial, 0% Pacific Islander, 74% white, 6% international; 22% from in state; 91% live on campus; 32% of students in fraternities, 48% in sororities
Most popular majors: 11% Economics, General, 7% Accounting and Finance, 7% Psychology, General, 6% Biology/Biological Sciences, General, 4% Mechanical Engineering
Expenses: 2018-2019: $56,092; room/board: $13,662
Financial aid: (570) 577-1331; 36% of undergrads determined to have financial need; average aid package $33,500

Cabrini University

Radnor PA
(610) 902-8552
U.S. News ranking: Reg. U. (N), No. 132
Website: www.cabrini.edu
Admissions email: admit@cabrini.edu
Private; founded 1957
Affiliation: Roman Catholic
Freshman admissions: less selective; 2017-2018: 3,524 applied, 2,580 accepted. Neither SAT nor ACT required. SAT 25/75 percentile: 990-1160. High school rank: N/A
Early decision deadline: N/A, notification date: N/A
Early action deadline: N/A, notification date: N/A
Application deadline (fall): 9/5
Undergraduate student body: 1,479 full time, 71 part time; 40% male, 60% female; 0% American Indian, 2% Asian, 21% black, 12% Hispanic, 4% multiracial, 0% Pacific Islander, 56% white, 1% international; 71% from in state; 32% live on campus; N/A of students in fraternities, N/A in sororities
Most popular majors: Information not available
Expenses: 2017-2018: $31,350; room/board: $12,340
Financial aid: (610) 902-8424

Cairn University

Langhorne PA
(215) 702-4235
U.S. News ranking: Reg. U. (N), No. 126
Website: cairn.edu/
Admissions email: admissions@cairn.edu
Private; founded 1913
Freshman admissions: selective; 2017-2018: 345 applied, 340 accepted. Either SAT or ACT required. SAT 25/75 percentile: 880-1125. High school rank: 19% in top tenth, 36% in top quarter, 58% in top half
Early decision deadline: N/A, notification date: N/A
Early action deadline: N/A, notification date: N/A
Application deadline (fall): rolling
Undergraduate student body: 726 full time, 36 part time; 44% male, 56% female; 0% American Indian, 4% Asian, 13% black, 6% Hispanic, 2% multiracial, 0% Pacific Islander, 72% white, 3% international; 54% from in state; 62% live on campus; 0% of students in fraternities, 0% in sororities
Most popular majors: 42% Philosophy and Religious Studies, 23% Education, 12% Public Administration and Social Service Professions, 5% Psychology, 4% Business, Management, Marketing, and Related Support Services
Expenses: 2018-2019: $27,279; room/board: $10,294
Financial aid: (215) 702-4243; 81% of undergrads determined to have financial need; average aid package $21,885

California University of Pennsylvania

California PA
(724) 938-4404
U.S. News ranking: Reg. U. (N), second tier
Website: www.calu.edu/
Admissions email: inquiry@calu.edu
Public; founded 1852
Affiliation: Episcopal Church, Reformed
Freshman admissions: less selective; 2017-2018: 3,324 applied, 3,133 accepted. Either SAT or ACT required. SAT 25/75 percentile: 930-1140. High school rank: 7% in top tenth, 23% in top quarter, 55% in top half
Early decision deadline: N/A, notification date: N/A
Early action deadline: N/A, notification date: N/A
Application deadline (fall): 8/21
Undergraduate student body: 4,534 full time, 1,023 part time; 47% male, 53% female; 0% American Indian, 1% Asian, 13% black, 3% Hispanic, 4% multiracial, 0% Pacific Islander, 76% white, 1% international; 89% from in state; 33% live on campus; 6% of students in fraternities, 7% in sororities
Most popular majors: 18% Health Professions and Related Programs, 14% Business, Management, Marketing, and Related Support Services, 10% Parks, Recreation, Leisure, and Fitness Studies, 9% Homeland Security, Law Enforcement, Firefighting and Related Protective Services, 7% Social Sciences
Expenses: 2018-2019: $10,840 in state, $14,586 out of state; room/board: $10,344
Financial aid: (724) 938-4415; 79% of undergrads determined to have financial need; average aid package $9,213

Carlow University

Pittsburgh PA
(412) 578-6059
U.S. News ranking: Reg. U. (N), No. 105
Website: www.carlow.edu
Admissions email: admissions@carlow.edu
Private; founded 1929
Affiliation: Roman Catholic
Freshman admissions: less selective; 2017-2018: 873 applied, 800 accepted. Either SAT or ACT required. SAT 25/75 percentile: 900-1070. High school rank: 16% in top tenth, 41% in top quarter, 78% in top half
Early decision deadline: N/A, notification date: N/A
Early action deadline: N/A, notification date: N/A
Application deadline (fall): rolling
Undergraduate student body: 1,075 full time, 290 part time; 16% male, 84% female; 0% American Indian, 2% Asian, 18% black, 2% Hispanic, 4% multiracial, 0% Pacific Islander, 67% white, 0% international; 95% from in state; 32% live on campus; 0% of students in fraternities, 5% in sororities
Most popular majors: 28% Registered Nursing/Registered Nurse, 10% Psychology, General, 9% Business Administration and Management, General, 6% Biology/Biological Sciences, General, 4% Health/Health Care Administration/Management
Expenses: 2018-2019: $29,454; room/board: $11,442
Financial aid: (412) 578-6171; 88% of undergrads determined to have financial need; average aid package $20,316

Carnegie Mellon University

Pittsburgh PA
(412) 268-2082
U.S. News ranking: Nat. U., No. 25
Website: www.cmu.edu
Admissions email: admission@andrew.cmu.edu
Private; founded 1900
Freshman admissions: most selective; 2017-2018: 20,497 applied, 4,550 accepted. Either SAT or ACT required. SAT 25/75 percentile: 1430-1560. High school rank: 74% in top tenth, 94% in top quarter, 99% in top half
Early decision deadline: 11/1, notification date: 12/15
Early action deadline: N/A, notification date: N/A
Application deadline (fall): 1/1
Undergraduate student body: 6,664 full time, 232 part time; 51% male, 49% female; 0% American Indian, 29% Asian, 4% black, 9% Hispanic, 4% multiracial, 0% Pacific Islander, 26% white, 22% international; 15% from in state; 60% live on campus; 16% of students in fraternities, 11% in sororities
Most popular majors: 24% Engineering, 13% Computer and Information Sciences and Support Services, 10% Business, Management, Marketing, and Related Support Services, 10% Multi/Interdisciplinary Studies, 9% Mathematics and Statistics
Expenses: 2018-2019: $55,465; room/board: $14,418
Financial aid: (412) 268-8981; 39% of undergrads determined to have financial need; average aid package $43,182

Cedar Crest College

Allentown PA
(800) 360-1222
U.S. News ranking: Reg. Coll. (N), No. 6
Website: www.cedarcrest.edu
Admissions email: admissions@cedarcrest.edu
Private; founded 1867
Freshman admissions: selective; 2017-2018: 1,208 applied, 765 accepted. Either SAT or ACT

required. SAT 25/75 percentile: 940-1170. High school rank: 20% in top tenth, 44% in top quarter, 80% in top half
Early decision deadline: N/A, notification date: N/A
Early action deadline: N/A, notification date: N/A
Application deadline (fall): rolling
Undergraduate student body: 931 full time, 502 part time; 12% male, 88% female; 0% American Indian, 3% Asian, 9% black, 15% Hispanic, 1% multiracial, 0% Pacific Islander, 59% white, 9% international; 85% from in state; 32% live on campus; N/A of students in fraternities, N/A in sororities
Most popular majors: 42% Health Professions and Related Programs, 12% Business, Management, Marketing, and Related Support Services, 8% Psychology, 8% Public Administration and Social Service Professions, 6% Biological and Biomedical Sciences
Expenses: 2018-2019: $39,216; room/board: $11,544
Financial aid: (610) 606-4666; 94% of undergrads determined to have financial need; average aid package $29,602

Central Penn College

Summerdale PA
(717) 728-2401
U.S. News ranking: Reg. Coll. (N), second tier
Website: www.centralpenn.edu
Admissions email: admissions@centralpenn.edu
For-profit; founded 1881
Freshman admissions: least selective; 2017-2018: 436 applied, 344 accepted. Neither SAT nor ACT required. SAT 25/75 percentile: 660-910. High school rank: N/A
Early decision deadline: N/A, notification date: N/A
Early action deadline: N/A, notification date: N/A
Application deadline (fall): rolling
Undergraduate student body: 316 full time, 872 part time; 35% male, 65% female; 3% American Indian, 3% Asian, 21% black, 4% Hispanic, 3% multiracial, 0% Pacific Islander, 61% white, 1% international; 96% from in state; 13% live on campus; 0% of students in fraternities, 0% in sororities
Most popular majors: 42% Business Administration and Management, General, 17% Criminal Justice/Safety Studies, 14% Computer Science, 11% Accounting, 6% Legal Professions and Studies, Other
Expenses: 2018-2019: $18,714; room/board: $8,094
Financial aid: (717) 728-2261; 82% of undergrads determined to have financial need

Chatham University

Pittsburgh PA
(800) 837-1290
U.S. News ranking: Reg. U. (N), No. 62
Website: www.chatham.edu
Admissions email: admissions@chatham.edu
Private; founded 1869
Freshman admissions: selective; 2017-2018: 2,231 applied, 1,217 accepted. Neither SAT nor ACT required. SAT 25/75 percentile: 1050-1240. High school rank: 24% in top tenth, 51% in top quarter, 79% in top half
Early decision deadline: N/A, notification date: N/A
Early action deadline: N/A, notification date: N/A
Application deadline (fall): 8/1
Undergraduate student body: 951 full time, 257 part time; 24% male, 76% female; 1% American Indian, 3% Asian, 6% black, 4% Hispanic, 2% multiracial, 0% Pacific Islander, 77% white, 3% international; 79% from in state; 60% live on campus; N/A of students in fraternities, N/A in sororities
Most popular majors: 32% Health Professions and Related Programs, 14% Biological and Biomedical Sciences, 9% Business, Management, Marketing, and Related Support Services, 7% Psychology, 6% English Language and Literature/Letters
Expenses: 2018-2019: $37,611; room/board: $12,090
Financial aid: (412) 365-1849; 89% of undergrads determined to have financial need; average aid package $26,138

Chestnut Hill College

Philadelphia PA
(215) 248-7001
U.S. News ranking: Reg. U. (N), No. 105
Website: www.chc.edu
Admissions email: admissions@chc.edu
Private; founded 1924
Affiliation: Roman Catholic
Freshman admissions: selective; 2017-2018: 1,286 applied, 1,231 accepted. Either SAT or ACT required. SAT 25/75 percentile: 960-1150. High school rank: 6% in top tenth, 21% in top quarter, 60% in top half
Early decision deadline: N/A, notification date: N/A
Early action deadline: N/A, notification date: N/A
Application deadline (fall): rolling
Undergraduate student body: 1,118 full time, 246 part time; 37% male, 63% female; 0% American Indian, 2% Asian, 35% black, 9% Hispanic, 4% multiracial, 0% Pacific Islander, 40% white, 2% international; 78% from in state; 51% live on campus; 0% of students in fraternities, 0% in sororities
Most popular majors: 22% Business, Management, Marketing, and Related Support Services, 21% Public Administration and Social Service Professions, 11% Psychology, 10% Education, 10% Homeland Security, Law Enforcement, Firefighting and Related Protective Services
Expenses: 2018-2019: $36,180; room/board: $11,000
Financial aid: (215) 248-7182; 81% of undergrads determined to have financial need; average aid package $24,523

Cheyney University of Pennsylvania

Cheyney PA
(610) 399-2275
U.S. News ranking: Nat. Lib. Arts, second tier
Website: www.cheyney.edu
Admissions email: admissions@cheyney.edu
Public; founded 1837
Freshman admissions: least selective; 2017-2018: 3,205 applied, 1,239 accepted. Either SAT or ACT required. SAT 25/75 percentile: 650-860. High school rank: N/A
Early decision deadline: N/A, notification date: N/A
Early action deadline: N/A, notification date: N/A
Application deadline (fall): N/A
Undergraduate student body: 670 full time, 52 part time; 52% male, 48% female; 0% American Indian, 1% Asian, 78% black, 5% Hispanic, 4% multiracial, 0% Pacific Islander, 2% white, 0% international
Most popular majors: Information not available
Expenses: 2017-2018: $12,104 in state, $18,386 out of state; room/board: $10,766
Financial aid: N/A

Clarion University of Pennsylvania

Clarion PA
(814) 393-2306
U.S. News ranking: Reg. U. (N), second tier
Website: www.clarion.edu
Admissions email: admissions@clarion.edu
Public; founded 1867
Freshman admissions: less selective; 2017-2018: 2,726 applied, 2,603 accepted. Either SAT or ACT required. SAT 25/75 percentile: 920-1120. High school rank: 9% in top tenth, 27% in top quarter, 62% in top half
Early decision deadline: N/A, notification date: N/A
Early action deadline: N/A, notification date: N/A
Application deadline (fall): rolling
Undergraduate student body: 3,481 full time, 840 part time; 36% male, 64% female; 0% American Indian, 1% Asian, 8% black, 3% Hispanic, 3% multiracial, 0% Pacific Islander, 83% white, 0% international; 92% from in state; 42% live on campus; 6% of students in fraternities, 12% in sororities
Most popular majors: 31% Legal Professions and Studies, 23% Education, 15% Communication, Journalism, and Related Programs, 15% Health Professions and Related Programs, 8% Library Science
Expenses: 2018-2019: $11,175 in state, $15,033 out of state; room/board: $12,670
Financial aid: (814) 393-2315; 82% of undergrads determined to have financial need; average aid package $9,478

Curtis Institute of Music[1]

Philadelphia PA
(215) 893-5252
U.S. News ranking: Arts, unranked
Website: www.curtis.edu
Admissions email: admissions@curtis.edu
Private; founded 1924
Application deadline (fall): N/A
Undergraduate student body: N/A full time, N/A part time
Expenses: N/A
Financial aid: (215) 717-3188

Delaware Valley University

Doylestown PA
(215) 489-2211
U.S. News ranking: Reg. U. (N), No. 132
Website: www.delval.edu
Admissions email: admitme@delval.edu
Private; founded 1896
Freshman admissions: selective; 2017-2018: 2,405 applied, 1,597 accepted. Either SAT or ACT required. SAT 25/75 percentile: 960-1165. High school rank: 6% in top tenth, 23% in top quarter, 59% in top half
Early decision deadline: N/A, notification date: N/A
Early action deadline: N/A, notification date: N/A
Application deadline (fall): rolling
Undergraduate student body: 1,756 full time, 236 part time; 40% male, 60% female; 1% American Indian, 1% Asian, 9% black, 8% Hispanic, 1% multiracial, 0% Pacific Islander, 69% white, 0% international; 62% from in state; 51% live on campus; 0% of students in fraternities, 1% in sororities
Most popular majors: 36% Agriculture, Agriculture Operations, and Related Sciences, 17% Natural Resources and Conservation, 16% Biological and Biomedical Sciences, 16% Business, Management, Marketing, and Related Support Services, 4% Homeland Security, Law Enforcement, Firefighting and Related Protective Services
Expenses: 2018-2019: $39,440; room/board: $14,340
Financial aid: (215) 489-2975; 80% of undergrads determined to have financial need; average aid package $27,782

DeSales University

Center Valley PA
(610) 282-4443
U.S. News ranking: Reg. U. (N), No. 55
Website: www.desales.edu
Admissions email: admiss@desales.edu
Private; founded 1964
Affiliation: Roman Catholic
Freshman admissions: selective; 2017-2018: 3,033 applied, 2,238 accepted. Either SAT or ACT required. SAT 25/75 percentile: 1010-1230. High school rank: 34% in top tenth, 52% in top quarter, 79% in top half
Early decision deadline: N/A, notification date: N/A
Early action deadline: N/A, notification date: N/A
Application deadline (fall): 8/1
Undergraduate student body: 1,811 full time, 534 part time; 39% male, 61% female; 0% American Indian, 3% Asian, 5% black, 14% Hispanic, 3% multiracial, 0% Pacific Islander, 71% white, 0% international; 76% from in state; 46% live on campus; 0% of students in fraternities, 0% in sororities
Most popular majors: 26% Business, Management, Marketing, and Related Support Services, 22% Health Professions and Related Programs, 10% Visual and Performing Arts, 8% Biological and Biomedical Sciences, 7% Parks, Recreation, Leisure, and Fitness Studies
Expenses: 2018-2019: $37,400; room/board: $12,800
Financial aid: (610) 282-1100; 77% of undergrads determined to have financial need; average aid package $25,821

Dickinson College

Carlisle PA
(800) 644-1773
U.S. News ranking: Nat. Lib. Arts, No. 51
Website: www.dickinson.edu
Admissions email: admissions@dickinson.edu
Private; founded 1783
Freshman admissions: more selective; 2017-2018: 5,941 applied, 2,894 accepted. Neither SAT nor ACT required. SAT 25/75 percentile: 1230-1420. High school rank: 48% in top tenth, 77% in top quarter, 96% in top half
Early decision deadline: 11/15, notification date: 12/15
Early action deadline: 12/1, notification date: 2/15
Application deadline (fall): 1/15
Undergraduate student body: 2,346 full time, 36 part time; 42% male, 58% female; 0% American Indian, 4% Asian, 5% black, 8% Hispanic, 4% multiracial, 0% Pacific Islander, 66% white, 13% international; 21% from in state; 95% live on campus; 16% of students in fraternities, 27% in sororities
Most popular majors: 9% Economics, General, 8% International Business/Trade/Commerce, 7% Biology/Biological Sciences, General, 7% Psychology, General, 6% Political Science and Government, General
Expenses: 2018-2019: $54,636; room/board: $13,698
Financial aid: (717) 245-1308; 57% of undergrads determined to have financial need; average aid package $45,710

Drexel University

Philadelphia PA
(800) 237-3935
U.S. News ranking: Nat. U., No. 102
Website: www.drexel.edu
Admissions email: enroll@drexel.edu
Private; founded 1891
Freshman admissions: more selective; 2017-2018: 28,454

applied, 22,489 accepted. Either SAT or ACT required. SAT 25/75 percentile: 1155-1360. High school rank: 36% in top tenth, 65% in top quarter, 91% in top half
Early decision deadline: 11/1, notification date: N/A
Early action deadline: 11/1, notification date: 12/15
Application deadline (fall): 1/15
Undergraduate student body: 11,357 full time, 1,915 part time; 50% male, 50% female; 0% American Indian, 15% Asian, 8% black, 7% Hispanic, 4% multiracial, 0% Pacific Islander, 52% white, 12% international; 49% from in state; 22% live on campus; 14% of students in fraternities, 13% in sororities
Most popular majors: 24% Business, Management, Marketing, and Related Support Services, 22% Engineering, 21% Health Professions and Related Programs, 8% Visual and Performing Arts, 4% Biological and Biomedical Sciences
Expenses: 2018-2019: $52,002; room/board: $13,890
Financial aid: (215) 895-1600; 63% of undergrads determined to have financial need; average aid package $37,744

Duquesne University

Pittsburgh PA
(412) 396-6222
U.S. News ranking: Nat. U., No. 119
Website: www.duq.edu
Admissions email: admissions@duq.edu
Private; founded 1878
Affiliation: Roman Catholic
Freshman admissions: more selective; 2017-2018: 7,336 applied, 5,260 accepted. Neither SAT nor ACT required. SAT 25/75 percentile: 1120-1270. High school rank: 25% in top tenth, 56% in top quarter, 86% in top half
Early decision deadline: 11/1, notification date: 11/15
Early action deadline: 12/1, notification date: 1/15
Application deadline (fall): 7/1
Undergraduate student body: 5,826 full time, 116 part time; 36% male, 64% female; 0% American Indian, 3% Asian, 5% black, 4% Hispanic, 3% multiracial, 0% Pacific Islander, 80% white, 4% international; 72% from in state; 59% live on campus; 17% of students in fraternities, 24% in sororities
Most popular majors: 17% Nursing Science, 7% Biology/Biological Sciences, General, 5% Psychology, General, 4% Early Childhood Education and Teaching, 4% Finance, General
Expenses: 2018-2019: $38,178; room/board: $12,586
Financial aid: (412) 396-6607; 68% of undergrads determined to have financial need; average aid package $25,125

Eastern University

St. Davids PA
(800) 452-0996
U.S. News ranking: Reg. U. (N), No. 74
Website: www.eastern.edu
Admissions email: ugadm@eastern.edu
Private; founded 1952
Affiliation: American Baptist
Freshman admissions: selective; 2017-2018: 1,759 applied, 1,154 accepted. Neither SAT nor ACT required. SAT 25/75 percentile: 1000-1200. High school rank: N/A
Early decision deadline: N/A, notification date: N/A
Early action deadline: N/A, notification date: N/A
Application deadline (fall): rolling
Undergraduate student body: 1,462 full time, 425 part time; 31% male, 69% female; 0% American Indian, 2% Asian, 20% black, 19% Hispanic, 2% multiracial, 0% Pacific Islander, 50% white, 2% international; 57% from in state; 80% live on campus; N/A of students in fraternities, N/A in sororities
Most popular majors: 17% Early Childhood Education and Teaching, 13% Registered Nursing/Registered Nurse, 12% Business Administration and Management, General, 6% Psychology, General, 5% Social Work
Expenses: 2018-2019: $32,882; room/board: $11,254
Financial aid: (610) 225-5102; 81% of undergrads determined to have financial need; average aid package $25,037

East Stroudsburg University of Pennsylvania

East Stroudsburg PA
(570) 422-3542
U.S. News ranking: Reg. U. (N), second tier
Website: www.esu.edu/admissions/index.cfm
Admissions email: admission@esu.edu
Public; founded 1893
Freshman admissions: less selective; 2017-2018: 9,997 applied, 7,849 accepted. Neither SAT nor ACT required. SAT 25/75 percentile: 910-1090. High school rank: 7% in top tenth, 23% in top quarter, 60% in top half
Early decision deadline: N/A, notification date: N/A
Early action deadline: N/A, notification date: N/A
Application deadline (fall): 5/1
Undergraduate student body: 5,552 full time, 499 part time; 44% male, 56% female; 0% American Indian, 2% Asian, 18% black, 13% Hispanic, 4% multiracial, 0% Pacific Islander, 61% white, 0% international; 80% from in state; 43% live on campus; 0% of students in fraternities, 0% in sororities
Most popular majors: 16% Athletic Training/Trainer, 15% Business Administration and Management, General, 12% Parks, Recreation and Leisure Facilities Management, General, 9% Biology/Biological Sciences, General, 8% Psychology, General
Expenses: 2018-2019: $10,228 in state, $22,153 out of state; room/board: $10,492
Financial aid: (570) 422-2800; 54% of undergrads determined to have financial need; average aid package $8,857

Edinboro University of Pennsylvania[1]

Edinboro PA
(888) 846-2676
U.S. News ranking: Reg. U. (N), second tier
Website: www.edinboro.edu
Admissions email: eup_admissions@edinboro.edu
Public; founded 1857
Application deadline (fall): rolling
Undergraduate student body: N/A full time, N/A part time
Expenses: 2017-2018: $10,282 in state, $14,668 out of state; room/board: $11,219
Financial aid: (814) 732-3500

Elizabethtown College

Elizabethtown PA
(717) 361-1400
U.S. News ranking: Nat. Lib. Arts, No. 113
Website: www.etown.edu
Admissions email: admissions@etown.edu
Private; founded 1899
Freshman admissions: selective; 2017-2018: 3,030 applied, 2,243 accepted. Either SAT or ACT required. SAT 25/75 percentile: 1070-1280. High school rank: 30% in top tenth, 60% in top quarter, 88% in top half
Early decision deadline: N/A, notification date: N/A
Early action deadline: N/A, notification date: N/A
Application deadline (fall): rolling
Undergraduate student body: 1,636 full time, 35 part time; 38% male, 62% female; 0% American Indian, 3% Asian, 3% black, 4% Hispanic, 2% multiracial, 0% Pacific Islander, 85% white, 2% international; 68% from in state; 84% live on campus; 0% of students in fraternities, 0% in sororities
Most popular majors: 16% Business, Management, Marketing, and Related Support Services, 13% Health Professions and Related Programs, 9% Biological and Biomedical Sciences, 9% Engineering, 8% Education
Expenses: 2018-2019: $46,940; room/board: $11,370
Financial aid: N/A; 77% of undergrads determined to have financial need; average aid package $33,166

Franklin and Marshall College

Lancaster PA
(717) 358-3953
U.S. News ranking: Nat. Lib. Arts, No. 36
Website: www.fandm.edu
Admissions email: admission@fandm.edu
Private; founded 1787
Freshman admissions: more selective; 2017-2018: 6,720 applied, 2,292 accepted. Neither SAT nor ACT required. SAT 25/75 percentile: 1260-1420. High school rank: 68% in top tenth, 90% in top quarter, 100% in top half
Early decision deadline: 11/15, notification date: 12/15
Early action deadline: N/A, notification date: N/A
Application deadline (fall): 1/15
Undergraduate student body: 2,263 full time, 20 part time; 46% male, 54% female; 0% American Indian, 5% Asian, 6% black, 10% Hispanic, 3% multiracial, 0% Pacific Islander, 57% white, 16% international
Most popular majors: Information not available
Expenses: 2018-2019: $56,550; room/board: $14,050
Financial aid: (717) 358-3991; 55% of undergrads determined to have financial need; average aid package $50,865

Gannon University

Erie PA
(814) 871-7240
U.S. News ranking: Reg. U. (N), No. 48
Website: www.gannon.edu
Admissions email: admissions@gannon.edu
Private; founded 1925
Affiliation: Roman Catholic
Freshman admissions: selective; 2017-2018: 4,642 applied, 3,709 accepted. Either SAT or ACT required. SAT 25/75 percentile: 990-1220. High school rank: 22% in top tenth, 53% in top quarter, 78% in top half
Early decision deadline: N/A, notification date: N/A
Early action deadline: N/A, notification date: N/A
Application deadline (fall): rolling
Undergraduate student body: 2,530 full time, 546 part time; 43% male, 57% female; 0% American Indian, 1% Asian, 5% black, 3% Hispanic, 3% multiracial, 0% Pacific Islander, 73% white, 9% international; 71% from in state; 46% live on campus; 13% of students in fraternities, 13% in sororities
Most popular majors: 30% Health Professions and Related Programs, 14% Business, Management, Marketing, and Related Support Services, 11% Parks, Recreation, Leisure, and Fitness Studies, 10% Engineering, 8% Biological and Biomedical Sciences
Expenses: 2018-2019: $32,136; room/board: $12,650
Financial aid: (814) 871-7337; 77% of undergrads determined to have financial need; average aid package $25,829

Geneva College

Beaver Falls PA
(724) 847-6500
U.S. News ranking: Reg. U. (N), No. 67
Website: www.geneva.edu
Admissions email: admissions@geneva.edu
Private; founded 1848
Affiliation: Reformed Presbyterian Church
Freshman admissions: selective; 2017-2018: 1,691 applied, 1,167 accepted. Either SAT or ACT required. SAT 25/75 percentile: 950-1210. High school rank: 15% in top tenth, 42% in top quarter, 78% in top half
Early decision deadline: N/A, notification date: N/A
Early action deadline: N/A, notification date: N/A
Application deadline (fall): rolling
Undergraduate student body: 1,248 full time, 170 part time; 50% male, 50% female; 0% American Indian, 1% Asian, 8% black, 1% Hispanic, 3% multiracial, 0% Pacific Islander, 82% white, 2% international
Most popular majors: 12% Engineering, General, 12% Public Administration and Social Service Professions, 10% Business Administration and Management, General, 8% Human Resources Management/Personnel Administration, General, 6% Accounting
Expenses: 2018-2019: $27,230; room/board: $10,170
Financial aid: (724) 847-6532; 83% of undergrads determined to have financial need; average aid package $21,287

Gettysburg College

Gettysburg PA
(800) 431-0803
U.S. News ranking: Nat. Lib. Arts, No. 49
Website: www.gettysburg.edu
Admissions email: admiss@gettysburg.edu
Private; founded 1832
Freshman admissions: more selective; 2017-2018: 6,384 applied, 2,924 accepted. Either SAT or ACT required. SAT 25/75 percentile: 1270-1410. High school rank: 65% in top tenth, 84% in top quarter, 99% in top half
Early decision deadline: 11/15, notification date: 12/15
Early action deadline: N/A, notification date: N/A
Application deadline (fall): 1/15
Undergraduate student body: 2,400 full time, 9 part time; 47% male, 53% female; N/A American Indian, N/A Asian, N/A black, N/A Hispanic, N/A multiracial, N/A Pacific Islander, N/A white, N/A international; 26% from in state; 94% live on campus; 32% of students in fraternities, 35% in sororities
Most popular majors: 25% Social Sciences, 14% Biological and Biomedical Sciences, 10% Business, Management, Marketing, and Related Support Services, 7% Psychology, 6% History
Expenses: 2018-2019: $54,480; room/board: $13,010
Financial aid: (717) 337-6611; 63% of undergrads determined to have financial need; average aid package $40,700

More @ usnews.com/bestcolleges

irove City College

rove City PA
'24) 458-2100
.S. News ranking: Nat. Lib. Arts, o. 120
/ebsite: www.gcc.edu
dmissions email: dmissions@gcc.edu
rivate; founded 1876
ffiliation: Undenominational
reshman admissions: more elective; 2017-2018: 1,783 pplied, 1,424 accepted. Either AT or ACT required. SAT 25/75 ercentile: 1071-1349. High chool rank: 35% in top tenth, 4% in top quarter, 90% in op half
arly decision deadline: 11/1, otification date: 12/1
arly action deadline: N/A, otification date: N/A
pplication deadline (fall): 1/20
ndergraduate student body: 2,315 ıll time, 58 part time; 51% ale, 49% female; 0% American ndian, 2% Asian, 1% black, 1% ispanic, 3% multiracial, 0% acific Islander, 92% white, 1% ternational; 56% from in state; 5% live on campus; 14% of udents in fraternities, 20% in ororities
lost popular majors: 8% Biology/ iological Sciences, General, % Speech Communication nd Rhetoric, 7% Mechanical ngineering, 5% Business dministration and Management, eneral, 5% Psychology, General
xpenses: 2018-2019: $17,930; oom/board: $9,770
inancial aid: (724) 458-3300; 6% of undergrads determined to ave financial need; average aid ackage $7,424

iwynedd Mercy Jniversity

wynedd Valley PA
215) 641-5510
.S. News ranking: Reg. U. (N), econd tier
/ebsite: www.gmercyu.edu/
dmissions email: dmissions@gmercyu.edu
rivate; founded 1948
ffiliation: Roman Catholic
reshman admissions: less elective; 2017-2018: 1,043 pplied, 978 accepted. Either AT or ACT required. SAT 25/75 ercentile: 930-1110. High chool rank: 6% in top tenth, 21% top quarter, 58% in top half
arly decision deadline: N/A, otification date: N/A
arly action deadline: N/A, otification date: N/A
pplication deadline (fall): 8/20
ndergraduate student body: 1,934 ıll time, 147 part time; 22% ıale, 78% female; 0% American ndian, 6% Asian, 23% black, % Hispanic, 1% multiracial, % Pacific Islander, 59% white, % international; 87% from in tate; 20% live on campus; N/A f students in fraternities, N/A in ororities
lost popular majors: 57% Health rofessions and Related Programs, 9% Business, Management, arketing, and Related Support ervices, 8% Education, % Homeland Security, Law nforcement, Firefighting and Related Protective Services, 3% Psychology
Expenses: 2018-2019: $33,520; room/board: $11,980
Financial aid: (215) 646-7300; 83% of undergrads determined to have financial need; average aid package $22,116

Harrisburg University of Science and Technology

Harrisburg PA
(717) 901-5150
U.S. News ranking: Reg. U. (N), second tier
Website: www.harrisburgu.edu
Admissions email: admissions@harrisburgu.edu
Private; founded 2001
Freshman admissions: less selective; 2017-2018: N/A applied, N/A accepted. Neither SAT nor ACT required. SAT 25/75 percentile: N/A. High school rank: N/A
Early decision deadline: N/A, notification date: N/A
Early action deadline: N/A, notification date: N/A
Application deadline (fall): rolling
Undergraduate student body: 463 full time, 46 part time; 51% male, 49% female; 1% American Indian, 3% Asian, 40% black, 13% Hispanic, 4% multiracial, 0% Pacific Islander, 36% white, 1% international
Most popular majors: 24% Computer and Information Sciences, General, 24% Natural Sciences, 19% Game and Interactive Media Design, 15% Geological and Earth Sciences/ Geosciences, Other, 9% Biotechnology
Expenses: 2018-2019: $23,900; room/board: $6,800
Financial aid: (717) 901-5115; 93% of undergrads determined to have financial need; average aid package $21,651

Haverford College

Haverford PA
(610) 896-1350
U.S. News ranking: Nat. Lib. Arts, No. 11
Website: www.haverford.edu
Admissions email: admission@haverford.edu
Private; founded 1833
Freshman admissions: most selective; 2017-2018: 4,408 applied, 884 accepted. Either SAT or ACT required. SAT 25/75 percentile: 1390-1530. High school rank: 96% in top tenth, 99% in top quarter, 100% in top half
Early decision deadline: 11/15, notification date: 12/15
Early action deadline: N/A, notification date: N/A
Application deadline (fall): 1/15
Undergraduate student body: 1,294 full time, 2 part time; 48% male, 52% female; 0% American Indian, 12% Asian, 7% black, 10% Hispanic, 3% multiracial, 0% Pacific Islander, 57% white, 9% international; 14% from in state; 98% live on campus; 0% of students in fraternities, 0% in sororities
Most popular majors: 25% Social Sciences, General, 14% Physical Sciences, 11% Biology/Biological Sciences, General, 10% English Language and Literature, General, 7% Psychology, General
Expenses: 2018-2019: $54,592; room/board: $16,402
Financial aid: (610) 896-1350; 47% of undergrads determined to have financial need; average aid package $51,271

Holy Family University

Philadelphia PA
(215) 637-3050
U.S. News ranking: Reg. U. (N), second tier
Website: www.holyfamily.edu
Admissions email: admissions@holyfamily.edu
Private; founded 1954
Affiliation: Roman Catholic
Freshman admissions: less selective; 2017-2018: 1,429 applied, 1,011 accepted. Either SAT or ACT required. SAT 25/75 percentile: 920-1090. High school rank: 9% in top tenth, 28% in top quarter, 58% in top half
Early decision deadline: N/A, notification date: N/A
Early action deadline: N/A, notification date: N/A
Application deadline (fall): rolling
Undergraduate student body: 1,621 full time, 472 part time; 26% male, 74% female; 0% American Indian, 6% Asian, 13% black, 5% Hispanic, 0% multiracial, 0% Pacific Islander, 63% white, 0% international; 86% from in state; 15% live on campus; 0% of students in fraternities, 0% in sororities
Most popular majors: 44% Health Professions and Related Programs, 18% Business, Management, Marketing, and Related Support Services, 11% Psychology, 9% Education, 6% Homeland Security, Law Enforcement, Firefighting and Related Protective Services
Expenses: 2018-2019: $30,346; room/board: $13,576
Financial aid: (267) 341-3234; 85% of undergrads determined to have financial need; average aid package $21,883

Immaculata University

Immaculata PA
(610) 647-4400
U.S. News ranking: Nat. U., No. 183
Website: www.immaculata.edu
Admissions email: admiss@immaculata.edu
Private; founded 1920
Affiliation: Roman Catholic
Freshman admissions: selective; 2017-2018: 1,550 applied, 1,293 accepted. Neither SAT nor ACT required. SAT 25/75 percentile: 950-1170. High school rank: 13% in top tenth, 32% in top quarter, 60% in top half
Early decision deadline: N/A, notification date: N/A
Early action deadline: N/A, notification date: N/A
Application deadline (fall): rolling
Undergraduate student body: 885 full time, 597 part time; 25% male, 75% female; 0% American Indian, 2% Asian, 16% black, 7% Hispanic, 2% multiracial, 0% Pacific Islander, 71% white, 1% international; 73% from in state; 32% live on campus; 1% of students in fraternities, 3% in sororities
Most popular majors: 45% Health Professions and Related Programs, 21% Business, Management, Marketing, and Related Support Services, 7% Parks, Recreation, Leisure, and Fitness Studies, 7% Psychology, 6% Education
Expenses: 2018-2019: $27,350; room/board: $12,620
Financial aid: (610) 647-4400; 78% of undergrads determined to have financial need; average aid package $20,271

Indiana University of Pennsylvania

Indiana PA
(724) 357-2230
U.S. News ranking: Nat. U., second tier
Website: www.iup.edu
Admissions email: admissions-inquiry@iup.edu
Public; founded 1875
Freshman admissions: less selective; 2017-2018: 9,880 applied, 8,973 accepted. Either SAT or ACT required. SAT 25/75 percentile: 910-1100. High school rank: 8% in top tenth, 27% in top quarter, 59% in top half
Early decision deadline: N/A, notification date: N/A
Early action deadline: N/A, notification date: N/A
Application deadline (fall): rolling
Undergraduate student body: 9,350 full time, 793 part time; 43% male, 57% female; 0% American Indian, 1% Asian, 12% black, 4% Hispanic, 4% multiracial, 0% Pacific Islander, 74% white, 3% international; 95% from in state; 32% live on campus; 8% of students in fraternities, 8% in sororities
Most popular majors: 27% Business, Management, Marketing, and Related Support Services, 15% Social Sciences, 10% Health Professions and Related Programs, 6% Communication, Journalism, and Related Programs, 6% Visual and Performing Arts
Expenses: 2018-2019: $12,979 in state, $17,299 out of state; room/board: $12,592
Financial aid: (724) 357-2218; 73% of undergrads determined to have financial need; average aid package $10,237

Juniata College

Huntingdon PA
(877) 586-4282
U.S. News ranking: Nat. Lib. Arts, No. 86
Website: www.juniata.edu
Admissions email: admissions@juniata.edu
Private; founded 1876
Freshman admissions: more selective; 2017-2018: 2,289 applied, 1,620 accepted. Neither SAT nor ACT required. SAT 25/75 percentile: 1080-1290. High school rank: 31% in top tenth, 64% in top quarter, 92% in top half
Early decision deadline: 11/15, notification date: 12/1
Early action deadline: 1/5, notification date: 2/15
Application deadline (fall): 3/15
Undergraduate student body: 1,400 full time, 85 part time; 44% male, 56% female; 0% American Indian, 4% Asian, 3% black, 5% Hispanic, 3% multiracial, 0% Pacific Islander, 75% white, 8% international; 66% from in state; 82% live on campus; 0% of students in fraternities, 0% in sororities
Most popular majors: 17% Business, Management, Marketing, and Related Support Services, 13% Biological and Biomedical Sciences, 8% Natural Resources and Conservation, 7% Education, 6% Psychology
Expenses: 2018-2019: $45,597; room/board: $12,521
Financial aid: (814) 641-3144; 75% of undergrads determined to have financial need; average aid package $36,787

Keystone College

La Plume PA
(570) 945-8000
U.S. News ranking: Reg. Coll. (N), No. 29
Website: www.keystone.edu
Admissions email: admissions@keystone.edu
Private; founded 1868
Freshman admissions: least selective; 2017-2018: 2,338 applied, 2,207 accepted. Neither SAT nor ACT required. SAT 25/75 percentile: 780-970. High school rank: N/A
Early decision deadline: N/A, notification date: N/A
Early action deadline: N/A, notification date: N/A
Application deadline (fall): 7/1
Undergraduate student body: 1,065 full time, 391 part time; 36% male, 64% female; 0% American Indian, 1% Asian, 10% black, 7% Hispanic, 2% multiracial, 0% Pacific Islander, 71% white, 0% international; 84% from in state; 31% live on campus; 0% of students in fraternities, 0% in sororities
Most popular majors: 21% Business, Management, Marketing, and Related Support Services, 12% Education, 12% Homeland Security, Law Enforcement, Firefighting and Related Protective Services, 9% Parks, Recreation, Leisure, and Fitness Studies, 8% Psychology
Expenses: 2017-2018: $26,670; room/board: $10,700
Financial aid: N/A

King's College

Wilkes-Barre PA
(888) 546-4772
U.S. News ranking: Reg. U. (N), No. 55
Website: www.kings.edu
Admissions email: admissions@kings.edu
Private; founded 1946
Affiliation: Roman Catholic

Freshman admissions: selective; 2017-2018: 4,354 applied, 3,080 accepted. Neither SAT nor ACT required. SAT 25/75 percentile: 980-1190. High school rank: 18% in top tenth, 42% in top quarter, 72% in top half
Early decision deadline: N/A, notification date: N/A
Early action deadline: 12/1, notification date: 12/15
Application deadline (fall): rolling
Undergraduate student body: 2,025 full time, 172 part time; 54% male, 46% female; 0% American Indian, 2% Asian, 4% black, 7% Hispanic, 3% multiracial, 0% Pacific Islander, 73% white, 8% international; 70% from in state; 53% live on campus; 0% of students in fraternities, 0% in sororities
Most popular majors: 14% Accounting, 14% Health Professions and Related Clinical Sciences, Other, 7% Elementary Education and Teaching, 7% Neuroscience, 6% Criminal Justice/Safety Studies
Expenses: 2018-2019: $37,226; room/board: $12,940
Financial aid: (570) 208-5900; 79% of undergrads determined to have financial need; average aid package $25,469

Kutztown University of Pennsylvania

Kutztown PA
(610) 683-4060
U.S. News ranking: Reg. U. (N), No. 137
Website: www.kutztown.edu
Admissions email: admissions@kutztown.edu
Public; founded 1866
Freshman admissions: selective; 2017-2018: 8,073 applied, 5,965 accepted. Either SAT or ACT required. SAT 25/75 percentile: 970-1140. High school rank: 7% in top tenth, 24% in top quarter, 55% in top half
Early decision deadline: N/A, notification date: N/A
Early action deadline: N/A, notification date: N/A
Application deadline (fall): rolling
Undergraduate student body: 7,053 full time, 436 part time; 47% male, 53% female; 0% American Indian, 1% Asian, 7% black, 9% Hispanic, 3% multiracial, 0% Pacific Islander, 76% white, 1% international; 88% from in state; 45% live on campus; 5% of students in fraternities, 11% in sororities
Most popular majors: 21% Business Administration and Management, General, 8% Criminal Justice/Safety Studies, 8% Psychology, General, 7% Speech Communication and Rhetoric, 6% Parks, Recreation and Leisure Studies
Expenses: 2018-2019: $10,802 in state, $14,660 out of state; room/board: $10,334
Financial aid: (610) 683-4077; 72% of undergrads determined to have financial need; average aid package $8,860

Lafayette College

Easton PA
(610) 330-5100
U.S. News ranking: Nat. Lib. Arts, No. 36
Website: www.lafayette.edu
Admissions email: admissions@lafayette.edu
Private; founded 1826
Freshman admissions: more selective; 2017-2018: 8,469 applied, 2,609 accepted. Either SAT or ACT required. ACT 25/75 percentile: 28-31. High school rank: 58% in top tenth, 82% in top quarter, 95% in top half
Early decision deadline: 11/15, notification date: 12/15
Early action deadline: N/A, notification date: N/A
Application deadline (fall): 1/15
Undergraduate student body: 2,551 full time, 43 part time; 48% male, 52% female; 0% American Indian, 4% Asian, 5% black, 7% Hispanic, 3% multiracial, 0% Pacific Islander, 66% white, 10% international; 19% from in state; 93% live on campus; 22% of students in fraternities, 34% in sororities
Most popular majors: 34% Social Sciences, 22% Engineering, 11% Biological and Biomedical Sciences, 6% Visual and Performing Arts, 4% Psychology
Expenses: 2018-2019: $52,880; room/board: $15,640
Financial aid: (610) 330-5055; 30% of undergrads determined to have financial need; average aid package $49,361

La Roche College

Pittsburgh PA
(800) 838-4572
U.S. News ranking: Reg. Coll. (N), No. 23
Website: www.laroche.edu
Admissions email: admissions@laroche.edu
Private; founded 1963
Affiliation: Roman Catholic
Freshman admissions: less selective; 2017-2018: 1,197 applied, 1,156 accepted. Either SAT or ACT required. SAT 25/75 percentile: 950-1140. High school rank: 8% in top tenth, 17% in top quarter, 71% in top half
Early decision deadline: N/A, notification date: N/A
Early action deadline: N/A, notification date: N/A
Application deadline (fall): rolling
Undergraduate student body: 1,163 full time, 215 part time; 45% male, 55% female; 0% American Indian, 1% Asian, 10% black, 4% Hispanic, 2% multiracial, 0% Pacific Islander, 63% white, 16% international; 90% from in state; 37% live on campus; N/A of students in fraternities, N/A in sororities
Most popular majors: 10% Registered Nursing/Registered Nurse, 8% Medical Radiologic Technology/Science - Radiation Therapist, 7% Accounting, 7% Management Science, 7% Psychology, General
Expenses: 2018-2019: $28,564; room/board: $11,556
Financial aid: (412) 536-1120; 69% of undergrads determined to have financial need; average aid package $30,310

La Salle University

Philadelphia PA
(215) 951-1500
U.S. News ranking: Reg. U. (N), No. 35
Website: www.lasalle.edu
Admissions email: admiss@lasalle.edu
Private; founded 1863
Affiliation: Roman Catholic
Freshman admissions: selective; 2017-2018: 6,562 applied, 5,205 accepted. Either SAT or ACT required. SAT 25/75 percentile: 970-1160. High school rank: 14% in top tenth, 36% in top quarter, 64% in top half
Early decision deadline: N/A, notification date: N/A
Early action deadline: 11/15, notification date: 12/15
Application deadline (fall): rolling
Undergraduate student body: 3,322 full time, 499 part time; 39% male, 61% female; 0% American Indian, 5% Asian, 20% black, 18% Hispanic, 3% multiracial, 0% Pacific Islander, 50% white, 2% international; 69% from in state; 46% live on campus; 16% of students in fraternities, 17% in sororities
Most popular majors: 15% Registered Nursing/Registered Nurse, 10% Accounting, 8% Marketing/Marketing Management, General, 8% Psychology, General, 7% Communication and Media Studies, Other
Expenses: 2018-2019: $30,710; room/board: $15,080
Financial aid: (215) 951-1070; 79% of undergrads determined to have financial need; average aid package $22,177

Lebanon Valley College

Annville PA
(717) 867-6181
U.S. News ranking: Reg. U. (N), No. 24
Website: www.lvc.edu
Admissions email: admission@lvc.edu
Private; founded 1866
Affiliation: United Methodist
Freshman admissions: selective; 2017-2018: 2,833 applied, 2,068 accepted. Neither SAT nor ACT required. SAT 25/75 percentile: 1063-1250. High school rank: 28% in top tenth, 55% in top quarter, 85% in top half
Early decision deadline: 11/1, notification date: 12/1
Early action deadline: N/A, notification date: N/A
Application deadline (fall): rolling
Undergraduate student body: 1,624 full time, 132 part time; 45% male, 55% female; 0% American Indian, 2% Asian, 3% black, 6% Hispanic, 3% multiracial, 0% Pacific Islander, 83% white, 1% international; 80% from in state; 80% live on campus; 6% of students in fraternities, 9% in sororities
Most popular majors: 19% Education, 17% Business, Management, Marketing, and Related Support Services, 13% Social Sciences, 10% Biological and Biomedical Sciences, 9% Health Professions and Related Programs
Expenses: 2018-2019: $43,650; room/board: $11,860
Financial aid: (717) 867-6126; 86% of undergrads determined to have financial need; average aid package $33,826

Lehigh University

Bethlehem PA
(610) 758-3100
U.S. News ranking: Nat. U., No. 53
Website: www1.lehigh.edu
Admissions email: admissions@lehigh.edu
Private; founded 1865
Freshman admissions: most selective; 2017-2018: 13,871 applied, 3,489 accepted. Either SAT or ACT required. SAT 25/75 percentile: 1270-1430. High school rank: 63% in top tenth, 89% in top quarter, 99% in top half
Early decision deadline: 11/15, notification date: 12/15
Early action deadline: N/A, notification date: N/A
Application deadline (fall): 1/1
Undergraduate student body: 5,013 full time, 62 part time; 55% male, 45% female; 0% American Indian, 8% Asian, 4% black, 9% Hispanic, 3% multiracial, 0% Pacific Islander, 64% white, 9% international; 27% from in state; 65% live on campus; 38% of students in fraternities, 45% in sororities
Most popular majors: 13% Finance, General, 10% Mechanical Engineering, 6% Accounting, 5% Marketing/Marketing Management, General, 4% Chemical Engineering
Expenses: 2018-2019: $52,930; room/board: $13,600
Financial aid: (610) 758-3181; 42% of undergrads determined to have financial need; average aid package $46,861

Lincoln University

Lincoln University PA
(800) 790-0191
U.S. News ranking: Reg. U. (N), second tier
Website: www.lincoln.edu
Admissions email: admissions@lincoln.edu
Public; founded 1854
Freshman admissions: least selective; 2017-2018: 3,587 applied, 2,858 accepted. Either SAT or ACT required. SAT 25/75 percentile: 870-1070. High school rank: 15% in top tenth, 34% in top quarter, 60% in top half
Early decision deadline: N/A, notification date: N/A
Early action deadline: N/A, notification date: N/A
Application deadline (fall): 5/1
Undergraduate student body: 1,826 full time, 176 part time; 34% male, 66% female; 0% American Indian, 0% Asian, 84% black, 3% Hispanic, 2% multiracial, 0% Pacific Islander, 1% white, 3% international; 46% from in state; 87% live on campus; 2% of students in fraternities, 1% in sororities
Most popular majors: 16% Health Professions and Related Programs, 14% Public Administration and Social Service Professions, 12% Business, Management, Marketing, and Related Support Services, 9% Communication, Journalism, and Related Programs, 9% Social Sciences
Expenses: 2018-2019: $11,666 in state, $16,802 out of state; room/board: $9,588
Financial aid: (484) 365-7564; 91% of undergrads determined to have financial need; average aid package $13,745

Lock Haven University of Pennsylvania

Lock Haven PA
(570) 484-2011
U.S. News ranking: Reg. U. (N), No. 126
Website: www.lockhaven.edu
Admissions email: admissions@lockhaven.edu
Public; founded 1870
Freshman admissions: less selective; 2017-2018: 3,020 applied, 2,689 accepted. Either SAT or ACT required. SAT 25/75 percentile: 910-1110. High school rank: 8% in top tenth, 27% in top quarter, 58% in top half
Early decision deadline: N/A, notification date: N/A
Early action deadline: N/A, notification date: N/A
Application deadline (fall): rolling
Undergraduate student body: 3,176 full time, 296 part time; 42% male, 58% female; 1% American Indian, 1% Asian, 10% black, 2% Hispanic, 1% multiracial, 0% Pacific Islander, 81% white, 1% international; 95% from in state; 34% live on campus; 3% of students in fraternities, 4% in sororities
Most popular majors: 14% Health Professions and Related Clinical Sciences, Other, 10% Business Administration and Management, General, 10% Criminal Justice/Law Enforcement Administration, 7% Sport and Fitness Administration/Management, 6% Psychology, General
Expenses: 2018-2019: $10,878 in state, $20,452 out of state; room/board: $10,368
Financial aid: (570) 484-2452; 80% of undergrads determined to have financial need; average aid package $9,662

Lycoming College

Williamsport PA
(800) 345-3920
U.S. News ranking: Nat. Lib. Arts, No. 131
Website: www.lycoming.edu
Admissions email: admissions@lycoming.edu
Private; founded 1812
Freshman admissions: selective; 2017-2018: 1,924 applied, 1,232 accepted. Neither SAT nor ACT required. SAT 25/75 percentile: 988-1200. High school rank: 14% in top tenth, 33% in top quarter, 69% in top half

Early decision deadline: 11/15, notification date: 12/1
Early action deadline: 12/1, notification date: 12/15
Application deadline (fall): rolling
Undergraduate student body: 1,199 full time, 24 part time; 50% male, 50% female; 0% American Indian, 1% Asian, 12% black, 10% Hispanic, 3% multiracial, 0% Pacific Islander, 63% white, 5% international; 59% from in state; 87% live on campus; 11% of students in fraternities, 23% in sororities
Most popular majors: 21% Business, Management, Marketing, and Related Support Services, 15% Social Sciences, 12% Psychology, 9% Biological and Biomedical Sciences, 8% Visual and Performing Arts
Expenses: 2018-2019: $40,090; room/board: $12,568
Financial aid: (570) 321-4140; 85% of undergrads determined to have financial need; average aid package $37,279

Mansfield University of Pennsylvania

Mansfield PA
(800) 577-6826
U.S. News ranking: Reg. U. (N), No. 123
Website: www.mansfield.edu
Admissions email: admissns@mansfield.edu
Public; founded 1857
Freshman admissions: less selective; 2017-2018: 2,501 applied, 1,703 accepted. Neither SAT nor ACT required. SAT 25/75 percentile: 950-1130. High school rank: 8% in top tenth, 29% in top quarter, 70% in top half
Early decision deadline: N/A, notification date: N/A
Early action deadline: N/A, notification date: N/A
Application deadline (fall): rolling
Undergraduate student body: 1,655 full time, 181 part time; 41% male, 59% female; 0% American Indian, 1% Asian, 10% black, 4% Hispanic, 2% multiracial, 0% Pacific Islander, 81% white, 1% international; 83% from in state; 49% live on campus; N/A of students in fraternities, N/A in sororities
Most popular majors: 15% Health Professions and Related Programs, 10% Homeland Security, Law Enforcement, Firefighting and Related Protective Services, 10% Psychology, 9% Visual and Performing Arts, 8% Business, Management, Marketing, and Related Support Services
Expenses: 2017-2018: $12,316 in state, $21,766 out of state; room/board: $11,928
Financial aid: (570) 662-8231; 60% of undergrads determined to have financial need; average aid package $10,205

Marywood University

Scranton PA
(866) 279-9663
U.S. News ranking: Reg. U. (N), No. 43
Website: www.marywood.edu
Admissions email: YourFuture@marywood.edu
Private; founded 1915
Affiliation: Roman Catholic
Freshman admissions: selective; 2017-2018: 2,263 applied, 1,700 accepted. Either SAT or ACT required. SAT 25/75 percentile: 1000-1190. High school rank: 19% in top tenth, 47% in top quarter, 81% in top half
Early decision deadline: N/A, notification date: N/A
Early action deadline: N/A, notification date: N/A
Application deadline (fall): rolling
Undergraduate student body: 1,756 full time, 208 part time; 31% male, 69% female; 0% American Indian, 2% Asian, 3% black, 7% Hispanic, 2% multiracial, 0% Pacific Islander, 78% white, 1% international; 69% from in state; 38% live on campus; N/A of students in fraternities, N/A in sororities
Most popular majors: 29% Health Professions and Related Programs, 13% Business, Management, Marketing, and Related Support Services, 10% Visual and Performing Arts, 8% Architecture and Related Services, 8% Psychology
Expenses: 2018-2019: $34,910; room/board: $13,900
Financial aid: (570) 348-4500; 84% of undergrads determined to have financial need; average aid package $26,010

Mercyhurst University

Erie PA
(814) 824-2202
U.S. News ranking: Reg. U. (N), No. 68
Website: www.mercyhurst.edu
Admissions email: admug@mercyhurst.edu
Private; founded 1926
Affiliation: Roman Catholic
Freshman admissions: selective; 2017-2018: 3,673 applied, 2,568 accepted. Neither SAT nor ACT required. SAT 25/75 percentile: 1000-1190. High school rank: N/A
Early decision deadline: N/A, notification date: N/A
Early action deadline: N/A, notification date: N/A
Application deadline (fall): rolling
Undergraduate student body: 2,383 full time, 87 part time; 42% male, 58% female; 1% American Indian, 2% Asian, 6% black, 4% Hispanic, 0% multiracial, 0% Pacific Islander, 71% white, 9% international; 52% from in state; 68% live on campus; 0% of students in fraternities, 0% in sororities
Most popular majors: 24% Business, Management, Marketing, and Related Support Services, 13% Health Professions and Related Programs, 11% Military Technologies and Applied Sciences, 9% Homeland Security, Law Enforcement, Firefighting and Related Protective Services, 7% Biological and Biomedical Sciences
Expenses: 2018-2019: $38,070; room/board: $12,880
Financial aid: (814) 824-2288; 78% of undergrads determined to have financial need; average aid package $27,744

Messiah College

Mechanicsburg PA
(717) 691-6000
U.S. News ranking: Reg. Coll. (N), No. 5
Website: www.messiah.edu
Admissions email: admissions@messiah.edu
Private; founded 1909
Affiliation: Interdenominational
Freshman admissions: more selective; 2017-2018: 2,558 applied, 1,970 accepted. Either SAT or ACT required. SAT 25/75 percentile: 1100-1310. High school rank: 33% in top tenth, 63% in top quarter, 90% in top half
Early decision deadline: N/A, notification date: N/A
Early action deadline: N/A, notification date: N/A
Application deadline (fall): rolling
Undergraduate student body: 2,637 full time, 122 part time; 40% male, 60% female; 0% American Indian, 2% Asian, 2% black, 5% Hispanic, 4% multiracial, 0% Pacific Islander, 81% white, 5% international; 64% from in state; 87% live on campus; N/A of students in fraternities, N/A in sororities
Most popular majors: 11% Engineering, General, 6% Business Administration and Management, General, 6% Health Professions and Related Programs, 6% Registered Nursing/Registered Nurse, 5% Family and Community Services
Expenses: 2018-2019: $35,160; room/board: $10,520
Financial aid: (717) 691-6007; 73% of undergrads determined to have financial need; average aid package $24,287

Millersville University of Pennsylvania

Millersville PA
(717) 871-4625
U.S. News ranking: Reg. U. (N), No. 103
Website: www.millersville.edu
Admissions email: Admissions@millersville.edu
Public; founded 1855
Freshman admissions: selective; 2017-2018: 6,717 applied, 5,340 accepted. Either SAT or ACT required. SAT 25/75 percentile: 970-1160. High school rank: 10% in top tenth, 28% in top quarter, 65% in top half
Early decision deadline: N/A, notification date: N/A
Early action deadline: N/A, notification date: N/A
Application deadline (fall): rolling
Undergraduate student body: 5,666 full time, 1,092 part time; 43% male, 57% female; 0% American Indian, 3% Asian, 9% black, 11% Hispanic, 2% multiracial, 0% Pacific Islander, 74% white, 1% international; 94% from in state; 32% live on campus; 4% of students in fraternities, 4% in sororities
Most popular majors: 12% Business, Management, Marketing, and Related Support Services, 11% Social Sciences, 10% Education, 9% Communication, Journalism, and Related Programs, 8% Psychology
Expenses: 2017-2018: $11,858 in state, $21,318 out of state; room/board: $13,440
Financial aid: (717) 871-5100; 69% of undergrads determined to have financial need; average aid package $8,892

Misericordia University

Dallas PA
(570) 674-6264
U.S. News ranking: Reg. U. (N), No. 35
Website: www.misericordia.edu/
Admissions email: admiss@misericordia.edu
Private; founded 1924
Affiliation: Roman Catholic
Freshman admissions: selective; 2017-2018: 1,740 applied, 1,371 accepted. Either SAT or ACT required. SAT 25/75 percentile: 1030-1205. High school rank: 21% in top tenth, 51% in top quarter, 80% in top half
Early decision deadline: N/A, notification date: N/A
Early action deadline: N/A, notification date: N/A
Application deadline (fall): rolling
Undergraduate student body: 1,660 full time, 486 part time; 33% male, 67% female; 0% American Indian, 1% Asian, 3% black, 3% Hispanic, 3% multiracial, 0% Pacific Islander, 87% white, 0% international; 73% from in state; 45% live on campus; N/A of students in fraternities, N/A in sororities
Most popular majors: 46% Health Professions and Related Programs, 18% Business, Management, Marketing, and Related Support Services, 8% Social Sciences, 4% Liberal Arts and Sciences, General Studies and Humanities, 4% Psychology
Expenses: 2018-2019: $33,240; room/board: $13,960
Financial aid: (570) 674-6222; 82% of undergrads determined to have financial need; average aid package $24,313

Moore College of Art & Design[1]

Philadelphia PA
(215) 965-4015
U.S. News ranking: Arts, unranked
Website: www.moore.edu
Admissions email: admiss@moore.edu
Private; founded 1848
Application deadline (fall): rolling
Undergraduate student body: N/A full time, N/A part time
Expenses: N/A
Financial aid: N/A

Moravian College

Bethlehem PA
(610) 861-1320
U.S. News ranking: Nat. Lib. Arts, No. 155
Website: www.moravian.edu
Admissions email: admission@moravian.edu
Private; founded 1742
Affiliation: Moravian Church
Freshman admissions: selective; 2017-2018: 3,059 applied, 2,324 accepted. Either SAT or ACT required. SAT 25/75 percentile: 1010-1210. High school rank: 18% in top tenth, 48% in top quarter, 85% in top half
Early decision deadline: N/A, notification date: N/A
Early action deadline: N/A, notification date: N/A
Application deadline (fall): 3/1
Undergraduate student body: 1,840 full time, 193 part time; 41% male, 59% female; 0% American Indian, 2% Asian, 5% black, 11% Hispanic, 2% multiracial, 0% Pacific Islander, 72% white, 6% international; 69% from in state; 65% live on campus; 11% of students in fraternities, 13% in sororities
Most popular majors: 25% Health Professions and Related Programs, 19% Business, Management, Marketing, and Related Support Services, 15% Social Sciences, 10% Biological and Biomedical Sciences, 9% Visual and Performing Arts
Expenses: 2018-2019: $43,636; room/board: $13,378
Financial aid: (610) 861-1330; 80% of undergrads determined to have financial need; average aid package $30,834

Mount Aloysius College[1]

Cresson PA
(814) 886-6383
U.S. News ranking: Reg. Coll. (N), No. 33
Website: www.mtaloy.edu
Admissions email: admissions@mtaloy.edu
Private; founded 1853
Application deadline (fall): rolling
Undergraduate student body: N/A full time, N/A part time
Expenses: 2017-2018: $22,430; room/board: $11,378
Financial aid: (814) 886-6357

Muhlenberg College

Allentown PA
(484) 664-3200
U.S. News ranking: Nat. Lib. Arts, No. 81
Website: www.muhlenberg.edu
Admissions email: admissions@muhlenberg.edu
Private; founded 1848
Affiliation: Lutheran Church in America
Freshman admissions: more selective; 2017-2018: 4,636 applied, 2,242 accepted. Neither SAT nor ACT required. SAT 25/75 percentile: 1140-1340. High school rank: 31% in top tenth, 61% in top quarter, 90% in top half

Early decision deadline: 11/15, notification date: 12/15
Early action deadline: N/A, notification date: N/A
Application deadline (fall): 2/1
Undergraduate student body: 2,279 full time, 88 part time; 40% male, 60% female; 0% American Indian, 3% Asian, 4% black, 7% Hispanic, 2% multiracial, 0% Pacific Islander, 75% white, 4% international; 29% from in state; 91% live on campus; 17% of students in fraternities, 21% in sororities
Most popular majors: 13% Business Administration and Management, General, 11% Psychology, General, 10% Drama and Dramatics/Theatre Arts, General, 8% Speech Communication and Rhetoric, 6% Finance, General
Expenses: 2018-2019: $52,595; room/board: $11,765
Financial aid: (484) 664-3175; 57% of undergrads determined to have financial need; average aid package $36,168

Neumann University

Aston PA
(610) 558-5616
U.S. News ranking: Reg. U. (N), second tier
Website: www.neumann.edu
Admissions email: neumann@neumann.edu
Private; founded 1965
Affiliation: Roman Catholic
Freshman admissions: less selective; 2017-2018: 1,505 applied, 1,449 accepted. Either SAT or ACT required. SAT 25/75 percentile: 890-1080. High school rank: N/A
Early decision deadline: N/A, notification date: N/A
Early action deadline: N/A, notification date: N/A
Application deadline (fall): rolling
Undergraduate student body: 1,462 full time, 623 part time; 34% male, 66% female; 0% American Indian, 1% Asian, 24% black, 6% Hispanic, 2% multiracial, 0% Pacific Islander, 53% white, 1% international; 69% from in state; 35% live on campus; 0% of students in fraternities, 0% in sororities
Most popular majors: 17% Registered Nursing, Nursing Administration, Nursing Research and Clinical Nursing, Other, 14% Liberal Arts and Sciences/Liberal Studies, 10% Homeland Security, Law Enforcement, Firefighting and Related Protective Services, Other, 10% Psychology, General, 8% Education/Teaching of Individuals in Elementary Special Education Programs
Expenses: 2018-2019: $31,400; room/board: $13,020
Financial aid: (610) 558-5521

Peirce College

Philadelphia PA
(888) 467-3472
U.S. News ranking: Reg. Coll. (N), unranked
Website: www.peirce.edu
Admissions email: info@peirce.edu
Private; founded 1865
Freshman admissions: least selective; 2017-2018: N/A applied, N/A accepted. Neither SAT nor ACT required. SAT 25/75 percentile: N/A. High school rank: N/A
Early decision deadline: N/A, notification date: N/A
Early action deadline: N/A, notification date: N/A
Application deadline (fall): rolling
Undergraduate student body: 315 full time, 1,074 part time; 28% male, 72% female; 0% American Indian, 2% Asian, 65% black, 8% Hispanic, 1% multiracial, 0% Pacific Islander, 18% white, 0% international; 91% from in state; N/A live on campus; N/A of students in fraternities, N/A in sororities
Most popular majors: 49% Business, Management, Marketing, and Related Support Services, 17% Computer and Information Sciences and Support Services, 16% Legal Professions and Studies, 13% Health Professions and Related Programs, 4% Homeland Security, Law Enforcement, Firefighting and Related Protective Services
Expenses: 2017-2018: $15,060; room/board: N/A
Financial aid: N/A

Pennsylvania Academy of the Fine Arts

Philadelphia PA
(215) 972-7625
U.S. News ranking: Arts, unranked
Website: www.pafa.edu
Admissions email: admissions@pafa.edu
Private; founded 1805
Freshman admissions: least selective; 2017-2018: 216 applied, 202 accepted. Neither SAT nor ACT required. SAT 25/75 percentile: N/A. High school rank: N/A
Early decision deadline: 11/15, notification date: 12/22
Early action deadline: 12/1, notification date: 12/22
Application deadline (fall): 8/29
Undergraduate student body: 184 full time, 6 part time; 32% male, 68% female; 0% American Indian, 3% Asian, 6% black, 8% Hispanic, 8% multiracial, 0% Pacific Islander, 63% white, 6% international; 46% from in state; 57% live on campus; 0% of students in fraternities, 0% in sororities
Most popular majors: 100% Fine and Studio Arts
Expenses: 2018-2019: $38,878; room/board: $11,658
Financial aid: N/A; 100% of undergrads determined to have financial need

Pennsylvania College of Art and Design[1]

Lancaster PA
(717) 396-7833
U.S. News ranking: Arts, unranked
Website: www.pcad.edu
Admissions email: N/A
Private; founded 1982
Application deadline (fall): N/A
Undergraduate student body: N/A full time, N/A part time
Expenses: N/A
Financial aid: N/A

Pennsylvania College of Technology

Williamsport PA
(570) 327-4761
U.S. News ranking: Reg. Coll. (N), No. 12
Website: www.pct.edu
Admissions email: admissions@pct.edu
Public; founded 1914
Freshman admissions: less selective; 2017-2018: 6,115 applied, 3,591 accepted. Neither SAT nor ACT required. SAT 25/75 percentile: 950-1140. High school rank: 7% in top tenth, 25% in top quarter, 57% in top half
Early decision deadline: N/A, notification date: N/A
Early action deadline: N/A, notification date: N/A
Application deadline (fall): 7/1
Undergraduate student body: 4,577 full time, 805 part time; 64% male, 36% female; 0% American Indian, 1% Asian, 3% black, 4% Hispanic, 2% multiracial, 0% Pacific Islander, 88% white, 1% international; 90% from in state; 27% live on campus; N/A of students in fraternities, 0% in sororities
Most popular majors: 26% Health Professions and Related Programs, 24% Engineering Technologies and Engineering-Related Fields, 16% Mechanic and Repair Technologies/Technicians, 7% Construction Trades, 6% Business, Management, Marketing, and Related Support Services
Expenses: 2018-2019: $16,830 in state, $23,970 out of state; room/board: $10,702
Financial aid: (570) 327-4766; 79% of undergrads determined to have financial need

Pennsylvania State University–University Park

University Park PA
(814) 865-5471
U.S. News ranking: Nat. U., No. 59
Website: www.psu.edu
Admissions email: admissions@psu.edu
Public; founded 1855
Freshman admissions: more selective; 2017-2018: 56,114 applied, 28,233 accepted. Either SAT or ACT required. SAT 25/75 percentile: 1160-1340. High school rank: 35% in top tenth, 73% in top quarter, 96% in top half
Early decision deadline: N/A, notification date: N/A
Early action deadline: N/A, notification date: N/A
Application deadline (fall): rolling
Undergraduate student body: 39,785 full time, 1,050 part time; 53% male, 47% female; 0% American Indian, 6% Asian, 4% black, 7% Hispanic, 3% multiracial, 0% Pacific Islander, 66% white, 12% international; 66% from in state; 35% live on campus; 17% of students in fraternities, 20% in sororities
Most popular majors: 17% Business, Management, Marketing, and Related Support Services, 17% Engineering, 9% Computer and Information Sciences and Support Services, 8% Social Sciences, 7% Communication, Journalism, and Related Programs
Expenses: 2018-2019: $18,454 in state, $34,858 out of state; room/board: $11,570
Financial aid: (814) 865-6301; 49% of undergrads determined to have financial need; average aid package $10,282

Point Park University

Pittsburgh PA
(800) 321-0129
U.S. News ranking: Reg. U. (N), No. 105
Website: www.pointpark.edu
Admissions email: enroll@pointpark.edu
Private; founded 1960
Freshman admissions: selective; 2017-2018: 4,860 applied, 3,152 accepted. Either SAT or ACT required. SAT 25/75 percentile: 980-1190. High school rank: 11% in top tenth, 38% in top quarter, 71% in top half
Early decision deadline: N/A, notification date: N/A
Early action deadline: N/A, notification date: N/A
Application deadline (fall): rolling
Undergraduate student body: 2,758 full time, 523 part time; 41% male, 59% female; 0% American Indian, 2% Asian, 14% black, 2% Hispanic, 5% multiracial, 0% Pacific Islander, 72% white, 4% international; 76% from in state; 32% live on campus; N/A of students in fraternities, N/A in sororities
Most popular majors: 12% Business, Management, Marketing, and Related Support Services, Other, 8% Dance, General, 8% Drama and Dramatics/Theatre Arts, General, 7% Cinematography and Film/Video Production, 6% Business Administration and Management, General
Expenses: 2018-2019: $31,450; room/board: $12,200
Financial aid: (412) 392-3930; 93% of undergrads determined to have financial need; average aid package $25,353

Robert Morris University

Moon Township PA
(412) 397-5200
U.S. News ranking: Nat. U., No. 183
Website: www.rmu.edu
Admissions email: admissions@rmu.edu
Private; founded 1921
Freshman admissions: selective; 2017-2018: 6,407 applied, 5,338 accepted. Either SAT or ACT required. SAT 25/75 percentile: 1020-1200. High school rank: 18% in top tenth, 42% in top quarter, 76% in top half
Early decision deadline: N/A, notification date: N/A
Early action deadline: N/A, notification date: N/A
Application deadline (fall): rolling
Undergraduate student body: 3,840 full time, 403 part time; 57% male, 43% female; 0% American Indian, 1% Asian, 6% black, 2% Hispanic, 3% multiracial, 0% Pacific Islander, 73% white, 12% international; 87% from in state; 46% live on campus; 10% of students in fraternities, 13% in sororities
Most popular majors: 14% Engineering, Other, 12% Registered Nursing/Registered Nurse, 8% Accounting, 6% Business Administration and Management, General, 6% Marketing/Marketing Management, General
Expenses: 2018-2019: $30,300; room/board: $11,400
Financial aid: (412) 397-6250; 69% of undergrads determined to have financial need; average aid package $22,897

Rosemont College

Rosemont PA
(610) 526-2966
U.S. News ranking: Reg. U. (N), No. 126
Website: www.rosemont.edu
Admissions email: admissions@rosemont.edu
Private; founded 1921
Affiliation: Roman Catholic
Freshman admissions: less selective; 2017-2018: 1,313 applied, 914 accepted. Either SAT or ACT required. SAT 25/75 percentile: 910-1110. High school rank: N/A
Early decision deadline: N/A, notification date: N/A
Early action deadline: N/A, notification date: N/A
Application deadline (fall): 8/27
Undergraduate student body: 520 full time, 115 part time; 37% male, 63% female; 0% American Indian, 2% Asian, 41% black, 6% Hispanic, 3% multiracial, 0% Pacific Islander, 35% white, 2% international; 75% from in state; 67% live on campus; N/A of students in fraternities, N/A in sororities
Most popular majors: 38% Business, Management, Marketing, and Related Support Services, 17% Social Sciences, 11% Biological and Biomedical Sciences, 7% English Language and Literature/Letters, 3% Visual and Performing Arts
Expenses: 2017-2018: $19,486; room/board: $11,960
Financial aid: (610) 527-0200

Saint Vincent College

Latrobe PA
(800) 782-5549
U.S. News ranking: Nat. Lib. Arts, No. 152
Website: www.stvincent.edu
Admissions email: admission@stvincent.edu
Private; founded 1846
Freshman admissions: selective; 2017-2018: 2,490 applied, 1,542 accepted. Either SAT or ACT required. SAT 25/75

More @ usnews.com/bestcolleges

percentile: 1020-1210. High school rank: 13% in top tenth, 38% in top quarter, 72% in top half
Early decision deadline: N/A, notification date: N/A
Early action deadline: N/A, notification date: N/A
Application deadline (fall): 5/1
Undergraduate student body: 1,616 full time, 50 part time; 55% male, 45% female; 0% American Indian, 1% Asian, 6% black, 4% Hispanic, 2% multiracial, 0% Pacific Islander, 84% white, 0% international; 78% from in state; 75% live on campus; N/A of students in fraternities, N/A in sororities
Most popular majors: 24% Business, Management, Marketing, and Related Support Services, 16% Biological and Biomedical Sciences, 10% Psychology, 10% Social Sciences, 7% Communication, Journalism, and Related Programs
Expenses: 2018-2019: $35,874; room/board: $11,470
Financial aid: (724) 805-2627; 86% of undergrads determined to have financial need; average aid package $29,423

Seton Hill University

Greensburg PA
(724) 838-4255
U.S. News ranking: Reg. U. (N), No. 50
Website: www.setonhill.edu
Admissions email: admit@setonhill.edu
Private; founded 1883
Affiliation: Roman Catholic
Freshman admissions: selective; 2017-2018: 2,573 applied, 1,902 accepted. Neither SAT nor ACT required. SAT 25/75 percentile: 1020-1220. High school rank: 20% in top tenth, 47% in top quarter, 81% in top half
Early decision deadline: N/A, notification date: N/A
Early action deadline: N/A, notification date: N/A
Application deadline (fall): 8/15
Undergraduate student body: 1,548 full time, 128 part time; 36% male, 64% female; 0% American Indian, 1% Asian, 8% black, 4% Hispanic, 3% multiracial, 0% Pacific Islander, 82% white, 2% international; 77% from in state; 43% live on campus; N/A of students in fraternities, N/A in sororities
Most popular majors: 23% Business, Management, Marketing, and Related Support Services, 12% Health Professions and Related Programs, 10% Visual and Performing Arts, 9% Parks, Recreation, Leisure, and Fitness Studies, 8% Education
Expenses: 2018-2019: $35,748; room/board: $14,368
Financial aid: (724) 830-1010; 83% of undergrads determined to have financial need; average aid package $26,786

Shippensburg University of Pennsylvania

Shippensburg PA
(717) 477-1231
U.S. News ranking: Reg. U. (N), No. 112
Website: www.ship.edu
Admissions email: admiss@ship.edu
Public; founded 1871
Freshman admissions: selective; 2017-2018: 5,247 applied, 4,384 accepted. Either SAT or ACT required. SAT 25/75 percentile: 960-1140. High school rank: 9% in top tenth, 25% in top quarter, 59% in top half
Early decision deadline: N/A, notification date: N/A
Early action deadline: N/A, notification date: N/A
Application deadline (fall): rolling
Undergraduate student body: 5,160 full time, 425 part time; 50% male, 50% female; 0% American Indian, 2% Asian, 10% black, 6% Hispanic, 4% multiracial, 0% Pacific Islander, 77% white, 1% international; 93% from in state; 30% live on campus; 10% of students in fraternities, 10% in sororities
Most popular majors: 9% Psychology, General, 8% Business Administration and Management, General, 8% Criminal Justice/Safety Studies, 7% Biology/Biological Sciences, General, 6% Journalism
Expenses: 2018-2019: $12,718 in state, $20,510 out of state; room/board: $12,268
Financial aid: (717) 477-1131; 71% of undergrads determined to have financial need; average aid package $9,429

Slippery Rock University of Pennsylvania

Slippery Rock PA
(800) 929-4778
U.S. News ranking: Reg. U. (N), No. 90
Website: www.sru.edu/admissions
Admissions email: asktherock@sru.edu
Public; founded 1889
Freshman admissions: selective; 2017-2018: 5,836 applied, 4,172 accepted. Either SAT or ACT required. SAT 25/75 percentile: 1000-1160. High school rank: 13% in top tenth, 36% in top quarter, 72% in top half
Early decision deadline: N/A, notification date: N/A
Early action deadline: N/A, notification date: N/A
Application deadline (fall): rolling
Undergraduate student body: 7,125 full time, 513 part time; 43% male, 57% female; 0% American Indian, 1% Asian, 5% black, 2% Hispanic, 4% multiracial, 0% Pacific Islander, 86% white, 1% international; 90% from in state; 36% live on campus; 6% of students in fraternities, 7% in sororities
Most popular majors: 24% Health Professions and Related Programs, 12% Business, Management, Marketing, and Related Support Services, 9% Education, 8% Engineering Technologies and Engineering-Related Fields, 7% Parks, Recreation, Leisure, and Fitness Studies
Expenses: 2018-2019: $10,205 in state, $13,951 out of state; room/board: $10,312
Financial aid: (724) 738-2044; 70% of undergrads determined to have financial need; average aid package $9,352

St. Francis University

Loretto PA
(814) 472-3100
U.S. News ranking: Reg. U. (N), No. 28
Website: www.francis.edu/undergraduate_admissions
Admissions email: admissions@francis.edu
Private; founded 1847
Affiliation: Roman Catholic
Freshman admissions: selective; 2017-2018: 1,715 applied, 1,299 accepted. Either SAT or ACT required. SAT 25/75 percentile: 1030-1230. High school rank: 25% in top tenth, 57% in top quarter, 81% in top half
Early decision deadline: N/A, notification date: N/A
Early action deadline: N/A, notification date: N/A
Application deadline (fall): 7/30
Undergraduate student body: 1,526 full time, 591 part time; 37% male, 63% female; 0% American Indian, 2% Asian, 6% black, 1% Hispanic, 1% multiracial, 0% Pacific Islander, 82% white, 1% international; 75% from in state; 76% live on campus; 6% of students in fraternities, 14% in sororities
Most popular majors: 12% Physician Assistant, 8% Occupational Therapy/Therapist, 6% Accounting, 6% Business Administration and Management, General, 6% Physical Therapy/Therapist
Expenses: 2017-2018: $35,066; room/board: $11,928
Financial aid: (814) 472-3010

St. Joseph's University

Philadelphia PA
(610) 660-1300
U.S. News ranking: Reg. U. (N), No. 12
Website: www.sju.edu
Admissions email: admit@sju.edu
Private; founded 1851
Affiliation: Roman Catholic
Freshman admissions: more selective; 2017-2018: 8,972 applied, 6,925 accepted. Neither SAT nor ACT required. SAT 25/75 percentile: 1110-1290. High school rank: 21% in top tenth, 51% in top quarter, 87% in top half
Early decision deadline: 11/1, notification date: 12/20
Early action deadline: 11/1, notification date: 12/20
Application deadline (fall): rolling
Undergraduate student body: 4,481 full time, 663 part time; 46% male, 54% female; 0% American Indian, 2% Asian, 6% black, 7% Hispanic, 2% multiracial, 0% Pacific Islander, 78% white, 2% international; 47% from in state; 54% live on campus; 11% of students in fraternities, 25% in sororities
Most popular majors: 55% Business, Management, Marketing, and Related Support Services, 7% Social Sciences, 6% Education, 5% Biological and Biomedical Sciences, 5% Communication, Journalism, and Related Programs
Expenses: 2018-2019: $44,974; room/board: $14,840
Financial aid: (610) 660-1346; 59% of undergrads determined to have financial need; average aid package $29,634

Susquehanna University

Selinsgrove PA
(800) 326-9762
U.S. News ranking: Nat. Lib. Arts, No. 135
Website: www.susqu.edu
Admissions email: suadmiss@susqu.edu
Private; founded 1858
Affiliation: Evangelical Lutheran Church
Freshman admissions: selective; 2017-2018: 6,033 applied, 4,121 accepted. Neither SAT nor ACT required. SAT 25/75 percentile: 1070-1240. High school rank: 26% in top tenth, 57% in top quarter, 88% in top half
Early decision deadline: 11/15, notification date: 12/1
Early action deadline: 11/1, notification date: 12/1
Application deadline (fall): rolling
Undergraduate student body: 2,198 full time, 68 part time; 44% male, 56% female; 0% American Indian, 2% Asian, 6% black, 7% Hispanic, 3% multiracial, 0% Pacific Islander, 80% white, 2% international; 56% from in state; 93% live on campus; 20% of students in fraternities, 19% in sororities
Most popular majors: 25% Business, Management, Marketing, and Related Support Services, 16% Communication, Journalism, and Related Programs, 12% Biological and Biomedical Sciences, 8% English Language and Literature/Letters, 8% Visual and Performing Arts
Expenses: 2018-2019: $47,290; room/board: $12,630
Financial aid: (570) 372-4450; 82% of undergrads determined to have financial need; average aid package $36,552

Swarthmore College

Swarthmore PA
(610) 328-8300
U.S. News ranking: Nat. Lib. Arts, No. 3
Website: www.swarthmore.edu
Admissions email: admissions@swarthmore.edu
Private; founded 1864
Freshman admissions: most selective; 2017-2018: 9,382 applied, 1,004 accepted. Either SAT or ACT required. ACT 25/75 percentile: 31-34. High school rank: 91% in top tenth, 99% in top quarter, 100% in top half
Early decision deadline: 11/15, notification date: 12/15
Early action deadline: N/A, notification date: N/A
Application deadline (fall): 1/1
Undergraduate student body: 1,573 full time, 4 part time; 50% male, 50% female; 0% American Indian, 17% Asian, 7% black, 12% Hispanic, 7% multiracial, 0% Pacific Islander, 40% white, 13% international; 13% from in state; 96% live on campus; 9% of students in fraternities, 4% in sororities
Most popular majors: 23% Social Sciences, 13% Biological and Biomedical Sciences, 10% Computer and Information Sciences and Support Services, 8% Mathematics and Statistics, 8% Psychology
Expenses: 2018-2019: $52,588; room/board: $15,474
Financial aid: (610) 328-8358; 56% of undergrads determined to have financial need; average aid package $50,361

Temple University

Philadelphia PA
(215) 204-7200
U.S. News ranking: Nat. U., No. 106
Website: www.temple.edu
Admissions email: tuadm@temple.edu
Public; founded 1884
Freshman admissions: more selective; 2017-2018: 35,880 applied, 20,332 accepted. Neither SAT nor ACT required. SAT 25/75 percentile: 1130-1310. High school rank: 21% in top tenth, 55% in top quarter, 90% in top half
Early decision deadline: N/A, notification date: N/A
Early action deadline: 11/1, notification date: 1/10
Application deadline (fall): 2/1
Undergraduate student body: 26,613 full time, 2,937 part time; 47% male, 53% female; 0% American Indian, 12% Asian, 13% black, 7% Hispanic, 3% multiracial, 0% Pacific Islander, 56% white, 7% international; 79% from in state; 6% live on campus; 4% of students in fraternities, 7% in sororities
Most popular majors: 25% Business, Management, Marketing, and Related Support Services, 13% Communication, Journalism, and Related Programs, 7% Parks, Recreation, Leisure, and Fitness Studies, 7% Visual and Performing Arts, 6% Psychology
Expenses: 2018-2019: $16,666 in state, $28,426 out of state; room/board: $11,566
Financial aid: (215) 204-2244; 68% of undergrads determined to have financial need; average aid package $18,627

Thiel College

Greenville PA
(800) 248-4435
U.S. News ranking: Nat. Lib. Arts, second tier
Website: www.thiel.edu
Admissions email: admission@thiel.edu

Private; founded 1866
Affiliation: Evangelical Lutheran Church
Freshman admissions: less selective; 2017-2018: N/A applied, N/A accepted. Either SAT or ACT required. SAT 25/75 percentile: 860-1110. High school rank: 5% in top tenth, 23% in top quarter, 59% in top half
Early decision deadline: N/A, notification date: N/A
Early action deadline: 12/15, notification date: 12/23
Application deadline (fall): rolling
Undergraduate student body: 751 full time, 3 part time; 57% male, 43% female; N/A American Indian, N/A Asian, N/A black, N/A Hispanic, N/A multiracial, N/A Pacific Islander, N/A white, N/A international
Most popular majors: Information not available
Expenses: 2017-2018: $30,830; room/board: $12,120
Financial aid: (724) 589-2178

Thomas Jefferson University

Philadelphia PA
(800) 951-7287
U.S. News ranking: Reg. U. (N), No. 15
Website: www.jefferson.edu/
Admissions email: admissions@PhilaU.edu
Private; founded 1824
Freshman admissions: selective; 2017-2018: 3,746 applied, 2,235 accepted. Either SAT or ACT required. SAT 25/75 percentile: 1030-1210. High school rank: 10% in top tenth, 42% in top quarter, 77% in top half
Early decision deadline: N/A, notification date: N/A
Early action deadline: N/A, notification date: 11/15
Application deadline (fall): rolling
Undergraduate student body: 2,953 full time, 529 part time; 28% male, 72% female; 0% American Indian, 7% Asian, 16% black, 7% Hispanic, 2% multiracial, 0% Pacific Islander, 57% white, 3% international; 63% from in state; 38% live on campus; 1% of students in fraternities, 1% in sororities
Most popular majors: 28% Family Practice Nurse/Nursing, 9% Fashion Merchandising, 8% Business Administration and Management, General, 7% Diagnostic Medical Sonography/Sonographer and Ultrasound Technician, 4% Architecture
Expenses: 2018-2019: $40,501; room/board: $13,465
Financial aid: N/A; 79% of undergrads determined to have financial need; average aid package $26,346

University of Pennsylvania

Philadelphia PA
(215) 898-7507
U.S. News ranking: Nat. U., No. 8
Website: www.upenn.edu
Admissions email: info@admissions.upenn.edu
Private; founded 1740
Freshman admissions: most selective; 2017-2018: 40,413 applied, 3,757 accepted. Either SAT or ACT required. ACT 25/75 percentile: 32-35. High school rank: 96% in top tenth, 100% in top quarter, 100% in top half
Early decision deadline: 11/1, notification date: 12/15
Early action deadline: N/A, notification date: N/A
Application deadline (fall): 1/5
Undergraduate student body: 9,782 full time, 251 part time; 49% male, 51% female; 0% American Indian, 21% Asian, 7% black, 10% Hispanic, 5% multiracial, 0% Pacific Islander, 43% white, 13% international; 19% from in state; 52% live on campus; 30% of students in fraternities, 29% in sororities
Most popular majors: 11% Finance, General, 7% Registered Nursing/Registered Nurse, 5% Biology/Biological Sciences, General, 5% Economics, General, 5% Political Science and Government, General
Expenses: 2018-2019: $55,584; room/board: $15,616
Financial aid: (215) 898-1988; 46% of undergrads determined to have financial need; average aid package $48,971

University of Pittsburgh

Pittsburgh PA
(412) 624-7488
U.S. News ranking: Nat. U., No. 70
Website: www.oafa.pitt.edu/
Admissions email: oafa@pitt.edu
Public; founded 1787
Freshman admissions: more selective; 2017-2018: 27,679 applied, 16,528 accepted. Either SAT or ACT required. SAT 25/75 percentile: 1240-1420. High school rank: 53% in top tenth, 87% in top quarter, 99% in top half
Early decision deadline: N/A, notification date: N/A
Early action deadline: N/A, notification date: N/A
Application deadline (fall): rolling
Undergraduate student body: 18,390 full time, 936 part time; 49% male, 51% female; 0% American Indian, 10% Asian, 5% black, 4% Hispanic, 4% multiracial, 0% Pacific Islander, 72% white, 4% international; 72% from in state; 43% live on campus; 10% of students in fraternities, 12% in sororities
Most popular majors: 17% Business, Management, Marketing, and Related Support Services, 13% Engineering, 12% Health Professions and Related Programs, 10% Biological and Biomedical Sciences, 10% Social Sciences
Expenses: 2018-2019: $19,080 in state, $32,052 out of state; room/board: $11,050
Financial aid: (412) 624-7180; 52% of undergrads determined to have financial need; average aid package $12,159

University of Scranton

Scranton PA
(570) 941-7540
U.S. News ranking: Reg. U. (N), No. 6
Website: www.scranton.edu
Admissions email: admissions@scranton.edu
Private; founded 1888
Affiliation: Roman Catholic
Freshman admissions: more selective; 2017-2018: 10,002 applied, 7,480 accepted. Either SAT or ACT required. SAT 25/75 percentile: 1080-1280. High school rank: 32% in top tenth, 63% in top quarter, 89% in top half
Early decision deadline: N/A, notification date: N/A
Early action deadline: 11/15, notification date: 12/15
Application deadline (fall): 3/1
Undergraduate student body: 3,630 full time, 180 part time; 42% male, 58% female; 0% American Indian, 2% Asian, 2% black, 9% Hispanic, 2% multiracial, 0% Pacific Islander, 80% white, 1% international; 39% from in state; 65% live on campus; 0% of students in fraternities, 0% in sororities
Most popular majors: 9% Registered Nursing/Registered Nurse, 7% Biology/Biological Sciences, General, 7% Kinesiology and Exercise Science, 6% Accounting, 6% Health Professions and Related Clinical Sciences, Other
Expenses: 2018-2019: $44,532; room/board: $15,182
Financial aid: (570) 941-7701; 69% of undergrads determined to have financial need; average aid package $27,055

University of the Arts[1]

Philadelphia PA
(215) 717-6049
U.S. News ranking: Arts, unranked
Website: www.uarts.edu
Admissions email: admissions@uarts.edu
Private; founded 1876
Application deadline (fall): rolling
Undergraduate student body: N/A full time, N/A part time
Expenses: 2017-2018: $43,100; room/board: $15,710
Financial aid: (215) 717-6170

University of Valley Forge

Phoenixville PA
(800) 432-8322
U.S. News ranking: Reg. Coll. (N), No. 26
Website: www.valleyforge.edu/
Admissions email: admissions@valleyforge.edu
Private; founded 1939
Affiliation: Assemblies of God Church
Freshman admissions: selective; 2017-2018: 498 applied, 265 accepted. Neither SAT nor ACT required. SAT 25/75 percentile: 918-1150. High school rank: 13% in top tenth, 11% in top quarter, 24% in top half
Early decision deadline: N/A, notification date: N/A
Early action deadline: N/A, notification date: N/A
Application deadline (fall): 8/1
Undergraduate student body: 589 full time, 115 part time; 47% male, 53% female; 0% American Indian, 1% Asian, 16% black, 16% Hispanic, 5% multiracial, 0% Pacific Islander, 56% white, 1% international; 45% from in state; 0% live on campus; 0% of students in fraternities, 0% in sororities
Most popular majors: 19% Digital Communication and Media/Multimedia, 11% Youth Ministry, 10% Divinity/Ministry, 10% Psychology, General, 9% Early Childhood Education and Teaching
Expenses: 2018-2019: $21,438; room/board: $8,806
Financial aid: (610) 917-1475; 88% of undergrads determined to have financial need; average aid package $15,016

Ursinus College

Collegeville PA
(610) 409-3200
U.S. News ranking: Nat. Lib. Arts, No. 90
Website: www.ursinus.edu
Admissions email: admission@ursinus.edu
Private; founded 1869
Freshman admissions: more selective; 2017-2018: 3,488 applied, 2,728 accepted. Neither SAT nor ACT required. SAT 25/75 percentile: 1110-1310. High school rank: 25% in top tenth, 53% in top quarter, 81% in top half
Early decision deadline: 12/1, notification date: 12/15
Early action deadline: 11/1, notification date: 12/15
Application deadline (fall): rolling
Undergraduate student body: 1,489 full time, 18 part time; 47% male, 53% female; 0% American Indian, 4% Asian, 7% black, 7% Hispanic, 3% multiracial, 0% Pacific Islander, 74% white, 2% international; 60% from in state; 94% live on campus; 18% of students in fraternities, 32% in sororities
Most popular majors: 18% Biology/Biological Sciences, General, 13% Applied Economics, 13% Psychology, General, 10% Mass Communication/Media Studies, 9% Exercise Physiology
Expenses: 2018-2019: $52,050; room/board: $12,750
Financial aid: (610) 409-3600; 75% of undergrads determined to have financial need; average aid package $40,845

Villanova University

Villanova PA
(610) 519-4000
U.S. News ranking: Nat. U., No. 49
Website: www.villanova.edu
Admissions email: gotovu@villanova.edu
Private; founded 1842
Affiliation: Roman Catholic
Freshman admissions: most selective; 2017-2018: 21,123 applied, 7,605 accepted. Either SAT or ACT required. ACT 25/75 percentile: 30-33. High school rank: 65% in top tenth, 95% in top quarter, 98% in top half
Early decision deadline: N/A, notification date: N/A
Early action deadline: 11/1, notification date: 12/20
Application deadline (fall): 1/15
Undergraduate student body: 6,525 full time, 441 part time; 47% male, 53% female; 0% American Indian, 6% Asian, 5% black, 8% Hispanic, 3% multiracial, 0% Pacific Islander, 74% white, 2% international; 21% from in state; 66% live on campus; 17% of students in fraternities, 32% in sororities
Most popular majors: 31% Business, Management, Marketing, and Related Support Services, 13% Engineering, 12% Health Professions and Related Programs, 11% Social Sciences, 7% Communication, Journalism, and Related Programs
Expenses: 2018-2019: $53,458; room/board: $14,020
Financial aid: (610) 519-4010; 49% of undergrads determined to have financial need; average aid package $37,455

Washington and Jefferson College

Washington PA
(724) 223-6025
U.S. News ranking: Nat. Lib. Arts, No. 103
Website: www.washjeff.edu
Admissions email: admission@washjeff.edu
Private; founded 1781
Freshman admissions: more selective; 2017-2018: 5,358 applied, 2,564 accepted. Neither SAT nor ACT required. SAT 25/75 percentile: 1120-1290. High school rank: 34% in top tenth, 62% in top quarter, 88% in top half
Early decision deadline: 12/1, notification date: 12/15
Early action deadline: 1/15, notification date: 2/15
Application deadline (fall): 3/1
Undergraduate student body: 1,398 full time, 7 part time; 52% male, 48% female; 0% American Indian, 2% Asian, 5% black, 5% Hispanic, 4% multiracial, 0% Pacific Islander, 75% white, 4% international; 77% from in state; 94% live on campus; 33% of students in fraternities, 30% in sororities
Most popular majors: 19% Business/Commerce, General, 13% Economics, General, 11% Biology/Biological Sciences, General, 9% Foreign Languages, Literatures, and Linguistics, 5% English Language and Literature, General
Expenses: 2018-2019: $47,964; room/board: $12,676
Financial aid: (724) 223-6019; 77% of undergrads determined to have financial need; average aid package $37,503

Waynesburg University

Waynesburg PA
(800) 225-7393
U.S. News ranking: Reg. U. (N), No. 81
Website: www.waynesburg.edu/
Admissions email: admissions@waynesburg.edu
Private; founded 1849
Affiliation: Presbyterian Church (USA)
Freshman admissions: selective; 2017-2018: 1,608 applied, 1,533 accepted. Either SAT or ACT required. SAT 25/75 percentile: 980-1160. High school rank: 15% in top tenth, 36% in top quarter, 74% in top half
Early decision deadline: N/A, notification date: N/A
Early action deadline: N/A, notification date: N/A
Application deadline (fall): rolling
Undergraduate student body: 1,330 full time, 46 part time; 41% male, 59% female; 0% American Indian, 1% Asian, 4% black, 2% Hispanic, 3% multiracial, 0% Pacific Islander, 86% white, 0% international; 79% from in state; 80% live on campus; N/A of students in fraternities, N/A in sororities
Most popular majors: 29% Registered Nursing/Registered Nurse, 14% Business Administration and Management, General, 10% Criminal Justice/Law Enforcement Administration, 9% Speech Communication and Rhetoric, 7% Psychology, General
Expenses: 2018-2019: $24,820; room/board: $10,160
Financial aid: (724) 852-3208; 81% of undergrads determined to have financial need; average aid package $19,800

West Chester University of Pennsylvania

West Chester PA
(610) 436-3414
U.S. News ranking: Reg. U. (N), No. 68
Website: www.wcupa.edu/
Admissions email: ugadmiss@wcupa.edu
Public; founded 1871
Freshman admissions: selective; 2017-2018: 12,667 applied, 8,677 accepted. Either SAT or ACT required. SAT 25/75 percentile: 1040-1210. High school rank: 10% in top tenth, 32% in top quarter, 69% in top half
Early decision deadline: N/A, notification date: N/A
Early action deadline: N/A, notification date: N/A
Application deadline (fall): rolling
Undergraduate student body: 13,020 full time, 1,431 part time; 41% male, 59% female; 0% American Indian, 2% Asian, 11% black, 6% Hispanic, 3% multiracial, 0% Pacific Islander, 75% white, 0% international; 89% from in state; 36% live on campus; 12% of students in fraternities, 18% in sororities
Most popular majors: 23% Business, Management, Marketing, and Related Support Services, 15% Health Professions and Related Programs, 10% Education, 8% English Language and Literature/Letters, 6% Psychology
Expenses: 2018-2019: $10,308 in state, $21,882 out of state; room/board: $8,494
Financial aid: (610) 436-2627; 59% of undergrads determined to have financial need; average aid package $8,296

Westminster College

New Wilmington PA
(724) 946-7100
U.S. News ranking: Nat. Lib. Arts, No. 120
Website: www.westminster.edu
Admissions email: admis@westminster.edu
Private; founded 1852
Affiliation: Presbyterian Church (USA)
Freshman admissions: selective; 2017-2018: 2,874 applied, 2,083 accepted. Either SAT or ACT required. SAT 25/75 percentile: 940-1200. High school rank: 22% in top tenth, 42% in top quarter, 75% in top half
Early decision deadline: N/A, notification date: N/A
Early action deadline: 11/15, notification date: 12/1
Application deadline (fall): 5/1
Undergraduate student body: 1,171 full time, 21 part time; 47% male, 53% female; 0% American Indian, 1% Asian, 5% black, 2% Hispanic, 1% multiracial, 0% Pacific Islander, 70% white, 1% international; 78% from in state; 75% live on campus; 33% of students in fraternities, 49% in sororities
Most popular majors: 20% Business, Management, Marketing, and Related Support Services, 14% Education, 11% Biological and Biomedical Sciences, 10% Social Sciences, 8% Visual and Performing Arts
Expenses: 2018-2019: $36,806; room/board: $11,130
Financial aid: (724) 946-7102; 84% of undergrads determined to have financial need; average aid package $29,959

Widener University

Chester PA
(610) 499-4126
U.S. News ranking: Nat. U., No. 194
Website: www.widener.edu
Admissions email: admissions.office@widener.edu
Private; founded 1821
Freshman admissions: selective; 2017-2018: 6,045 applied, 3,955 accepted. Either SAT or ACT required. SAT 25/75 percentile: 1020-1180. High school rank: N/A
Early decision deadline: N/A, notification date: N/A
Early action deadline: N/A, notification date: N/A
Application deadline (fall): rolling
Undergraduate student body: 2,919 full time, 508 part time; 43% male, 57% female; 0% American Indian, 4% Asian, 13% black, 5% Hispanic, 3% multiracial, 0% Pacific Islander, 71% white, 2% international; 60% from in state; 45% live on campus; 10% of students in fraternities, 9% in sororities
Most popular majors: 30% Health Professions and Related Programs, 19% Business, Management, Marketing, and Related Support Services, 16% Engineering, 9% Psychology, 3% Education
Expenses: 2018-2019: $45,948; room/board: $14,446
Financial aid: (610) 499-4161; 80% of undergrads determined to have financial need; average aid package $33,521

Wilkes University

Wilkes-Barre PA
(570) 408-4400
U.S. News ranking: Reg. U. (N), No. 68
Website: www.wilkes.edu
Admissions email: admissions@wilkes.edu
Private; founded 1933
Freshman admissions: selective; 2017-2018: 4,067 applied, 3,063 accepted. Either SAT or ACT required. SAT 25/75 percentile: 1040-1220. High school rank: 23% in top tenth, 51% in top quarter, 84% in top half
Early decision deadline: N/A, notification date: N/A
Early action deadline: N/A, notification date: N/A
Application deadline (fall): rolling
Undergraduate student body: 2,233 full time, 258 part time; 53% male, 47% female; 0% American Indian, 2% Asian, 5% black, 6% Hispanic, 3% multiracial, 0% Pacific Islander, 71% white, 9% international; 81% from in state; 41% live on campus; 0% of students in fraternities, 0% in sororities
Most popular majors: 20% Business, Management, Marketing, and Related Support Services, 16% Health Professions and Related Programs, 14% Engineering, 7% Biological and Biomedical Sciences, 7% Psychology
Expenses: 2018-2019: $36,194; room/board: $14,682
Financial aid: (570) 408-4512; 80% of undergrads determined to have financial need; average aid package $25,457

Wilson College

Chambersburg PA
(800) 421-8402
U.S. News ranking: Reg. Coll. (N), No. 16
Website: www.wilson.edu
Admissions email: admissions@wilson.edu
Private; founded 1869
Affiliation: Presbyterian Church (USA)
Freshman admissions: less selective; 2017-2018: 1,201 applied, 707 accepted. Neither SAT nor ACT required. SAT 25/75 percentile: 940-1120. High school rank: 12% in top tenth, 38% in top quarter, 80% in top half
Early decision deadline: N/A, notification date: N/A
Early action deadline: N/A, notification date: N/A
Application deadline (fall): rolling
Undergraduate student body: 565 full time, 262 part time; 19% male, 81% female; 0% American Indian, 1% Asian, 6% black, 5% Hispanic, 3% multiracial, 0% Pacific Islander, 71% white, 5% international; 78% from in state; 47% live on campus; 0% of students in fraternities, 0% in sororities
Most popular majors: 27% Veterinary/Animal Health Technology/Technician and Veterinary Assistant, 11% Animal-Assisted Therapy, 11% Business Administration and Management, General, 9% Equestrian/Equine Studies, 5% Registered Nursing/Registered Nurse
Expenses: 2018-2019: $24,595; room/board: $11,594
Financial aid: (717) 264-3787; 94% of undergrads determined to have financial need; average aid package $21,720

York College of Pennsylvania

York PA
(717) 849-1600
U.S. News ranking: Reg. U. (N), No. 93
Website: www.ycp.edu
Admissions email: admissions@ycp.edu
Private; founded 1787
Freshman admissions: selective; 2017-2018: 5,209 applied, 3,637 accepted. Either SAT or ACT required. SAT 25/75 percentile: 1000-1190. High school rank: 8% in top tenth, 34% in top quarter, 70% in top half
Early decision deadline: N/A, notification date: N/A
Early action deadline: N/A, notification date: N/A
Application deadline (fall): 9/6
Undergraduate student body: 3,814 full time, 357 part time; 46% male, 54% female; 0% American Indian, 2% Asian, 5% black, 7% Hispanic, 3% multiracial, 0% Pacific Islander, 80% white, 1% international; 60% from in state; 58% live on campus; 4% of students in fraternities, 7% in sororities
Most popular majors: 20% Business, Management, Marketing, and Related Support Services, 14% Health Professions and Related Programs, 9% Homeland Security, Law Enforcement, Firefighting and Related Protective Services, 8% Communication, Journalism, and Related Programs, 7% Parks, Recreation, Leisure, and Fitness Studies
Expenses: 2018-2019: $20,100; room/board: $11,200
Financial aid: (717) 849-6539; 69% of undergrads determined to have financial need; average aid package $12,845

RHODE ISLAND

Brown University

Providence RI
(401) 863-2378
U.S. News ranking: Nat. U., No. 14
Website: www.brown.edu/admission/undergraduate/
Admissions email: admission@brown.edu
Private; founded 1764
Freshman admissions: most selective; 2017-2018: 32,723 applied, 2,799 accepted. Either SAT or ACT required. ACT 25/75 percentile: 31-35. High school rank: 94% in top tenth, 99% in top quarter, 100% in top half
Early decision deadline: 11/1, notification date: 12/15
Early action deadline: N/A, notification date: N/A
Application deadline (fall): 1/1
Undergraduate student body: 6,666 full time, 322 part time; 46% male, 54% female; 0% American Indian, 15% Asian, 6% black, 12% Hispanic, 6% multiracial, 0% Pacific Islander, 44% white, 11% international; 6% from in state; 74% live on campus; 10% of students in fraternities, 9% in sororities
Most popular majors: 9% Computer Science, 9% Econometrics and Quantitative Economics, 8% Applied Mathematics, General, 6% Biology/Biological Sciences, General, 6% Engineering, General
Expenses: 2018-2019: $55,656; room/board: $14,670
Financial aid: (401) 863-2721; 44% of undergrads determined to have financial need; average aid package $49,269

Bryant University

Smithfield RI
(800) 622-7001
U.S. News ranking: Reg. U. (N), No. 10
Website: www.bryant.edu
Admissions email: admission@bryant.edu
Private; founded 1863
Freshman admissions: more selective; 2017-2018: 7,242 applied, 5,285 accepted. Neither SAT nor ACT required. SAT 25/75 percentile: 1120-1280. High school rank: 22% in top tenth, 52% in top quarter, 88% in top half
Early decision deadline: 11/1, notification date: 12/1
Early action deadline: 11/15, notification date: 1/15
Application deadline (fall): 2/1
Undergraduate student body: 3,418 full time, 59 part time; 61% male, 39% female; 0% American Indian, 4% Asian, 4% black, 7% Hispanic, 1% multiracial, 0% Pacific Islander, 75% white, 8% international; 14% from in state; 76% live on campus; 4% of students in fraternities, 16% in sororities
Most popular majors: 76% Business, Management, Marketing, and Related Support Services, 5% Communication, Journalism, and Related Programs, 5% Mathematics and Statistics,

3% Computer and Information Sciences and Support Services, 3% Social Sciences
Expenses: 2018-2019: $43,973; room/board: $15,702
Financial aid: (401) 232-6020; 61% of undergrads determined to have financial need; average aid package $25,319

Johnson & Wales University

Providence RI
(800) 342-5598
U.S. News ranking: Reg. U. (N), No. 74
Website: www.jwu.edu/
Admissions email: pvd@admissions.jwu.edu
Private; founded 1914
Freshman admissions: less selective; 2017-2018: 14,372 applied, 12,580 accepted. Neither SAT nor ACT required. SAT 25/75 percentile: 980-1170. High school rank: N/A
Early decision deadline: N/A, notification date: N/A
Early action deadline: 11/1, notification date: 11/15
Application deadline (fall): rolling
Undergraduate student body: 7,267 full time, 443 part time; 40% male, 60% female; 0% American Indian, 2% Asian, 13% black, 12% Hispanic, 5% multiracial, 0% Pacific Islander, 55% white, 8% international; 20% from in state; 38% live on campus; 1% of students in fraternities, 1% in sororities
Most popular majors: 37% Business, Management, Marketing, and Related Support Services, 22% Family and Consumer Sciences/Human Sciences, 11% Parks, Recreation, Leisure, and Fitness Studies, 10% Personal and Culinary Services, 6% Homeland Security, Law Enforcement, Firefighting and Related Protective Services
Expenses: 2018-2019: $32,441; room/board: $12,267
Financial aid: (401) 598-1857; 76% of undergrads determined to have financial need; average aid package $23,561

New England Institute of Technology[1]

East Greenwich RI
(800) 736-7744
U.S. News ranking: Reg. Coll. (N), second tier
Website: www.neit.edu/
Admissions email: NEITAdmissions@neit.edu
Private; founded 1940
Affiliation: Other
Application deadline (fall): rolling
Undergraduate student body: N/A full time, N/A part time
Expenses: 2017-2018: $28,740; room/board: $11,640
Financial aid: (401) 739-5000

Providence College

Providence RI
(401) 865-2535
U.S. News ranking: Reg. U. (N), No. 2
Website: www.providence.edu
Admissions email: pcadmiss@providence.edu
Private; founded 1917
Affiliation: Roman Catholic
Freshman admissions: more selective; 2017-2018: 11,251 applied, 5,797 accepted. Neither SAT nor ACT required. SAT 25/75 percentile: 1160-1330. High school rank: 36% in top tenth, 65% in top quarter, 92% in top half
Early decision deadline: 11/15, notification date: 1/1
Early action deadline: 11/1, notification date: 1/1
Application deadline (fall): 1/15
Undergraduate student body: 4,049 full time, 257 part time; 45% male, 55% female; 0% American Indian, 1% Asian, 4% black, 9% Hispanic, 2% multiracial, 0% Pacific Islander, 78% white, 2% international; 9% from in state; 80% live on campus; 0% of students in fraternities, 0% in sororities
Most popular majors: 44% Business, Management, Marketing, and Related Support Services, 14% Social Sciences, 9% Biological and Biomedical Sciences, 7% Health Professions and Related Programs, 7% Psychology
Expenses: 2018-2019: $50,390; room/board: $14,700
Financial aid: (401) 865-2286; 47% of undergrads determined to have financial need; average aid package $31,565

Rhode Island College

Providence RI
(800) 669-5760
U.S. News ranking: Reg. U. (N), second tier
Website: www.ric.edu
Admissions email: admissions@ric.edu
Public; founded 1854
Freshman admissions: less selective; 2017-2018: 4,846 applied, 3,566 accepted. Either SAT or ACT required. SAT 25/75 percentile: 880-1090. High school rank: 12% in top tenth, 39% in top quarter, 74% in top half
Early decision deadline: N/A, notification date: N/A
Early action deadline: N/A, notification date: N/A
Application deadline (fall): 3/15
Undergraduate student body: 5,464 full time, 1,616 part time; 32% male, 68% female; 1% American Indian, 3% Asian, 10% black, 20% Hispanic, 2% multiracial, 0% Pacific Islander, 58% white, 0% international; 86% from in state; 15% live on campus; N/A of students in fraternities, N/A in sororities
Most popular majors: 22% Health Professions and Related Programs, 14% Business, Management, Marketing, and Related Support Services, 11% Education, 9% Psychology, 7% Public Administration and Social Service Professions
Expenses: 2018-2019: $8,929 in state, $21,692 out of state; room/board: $11,829
Financial aid: (401) 456-8033; 71% of undergrads determined to have financial need; average aid package $9,745

Rhode Island School of Design

Providence RI
(401) 454-6300
U.S. News ranking: Arts, unranked
Website: www.risd.edu
Admissions email: admissions@risd.edu
Private; founded 1877
Freshman admissions: more selective; 2017-2018: 3,420 applied, 985 accepted. Either SAT or ACT required. SAT 25/75 percentile: 1130-1370. High school rank: N/A
Early decision deadline: 11/1, notification date: 12/7
Early action deadline: N/A, notification date: N/A
Application deadline (fall): 2/1
Undergraduate student body: 1,976 full time, 0 part time; 32% male, 68% female; 0% American Indian, 19% Asian, 3% black, 8% Hispanic, 5% multiracial, 0% Pacific Islander, 31% white, 30% international; 5% from in state; 60% live on campus; N/A of students in fraternities, N/A in sororities
Most popular majors: 16% Illustration, 16% Industrial and Product Design, 12% Graphic Design, 8% Film/Video and Photographic Arts, Other, 8% Painting
Expenses: 2018-2019: $50,960; room/board: $13,400
Financial aid: (401) 454-6661; 40% of undergrads determined to have financial need; average aid package $31,349

Roger Williams University

Bristol RI
(401) 254-3500
U.S. News ranking: Reg. U. (N), No. 43
Website: www.rwu.edu
Admissions email: admit@rwu.edu
Private; founded 1956
Freshman admissions: selective; 2017-2018: 9,515 applied, 7,830 accepted. Neither SAT nor ACT required. SAT 25/75 percentile: 1090-1250. High school rank: N/A
Early decision deadline: N/A, notification date: N/A
Early action deadline: 11/15, notification date: 12/1
Application deadline (fall): 2/1
Undergraduate student body: 4,042 full time, 661 part time; 47% male, 53% female; 0% American Indian, 2% Asian, 2% black, 6% Hispanic, 2% multiracial, 0% Pacific Islander, 77% white, 3% international; 21% from in state; 76% live on campus; N/A of students in fraternities, N/A in sororities
Most popular majors: 28% Business, Management, Marketing, and Related Support Services, 10% Homeland Security, Law Enforcement, Firefighting and Related Protective Services, 9% Architecture and Related Services, 8% Psychology, 7% Biological and Biomedical Sciences
Expenses: 2018-2019: $34,512; room/board: $15,516
Financial aid: (401) 254-3100; 64% of undergrads determined to have financial need; average aid package $22,130

Salve Regina University

Newport RI
(888) 467-2583
U.S. News ranking: Reg. U. (N), No. 28
Website: www.salve.edu
Admissions email: admissions@salve.edu
Private; founded 1934
Affiliation: Roman Catholic
Freshman admissions: selective; 2017-2018: 4,991 applied, 3,588 accepted. Neither SAT nor ACT required. SAT 25/75 percentile: 1080-1230. High school rank: 11% in top tenth, 42% in top quarter, 78% in top half
Early decision deadline: N/A, notification date: N/A
Early action deadline: 11/1, notification date: 1/1
Application deadline (fall): rolling
Undergraduate student body: 2,087 full time, 93 part time; 33% male, 67% female; 0% American Indian, 1% Asian, 2% black, 7% Hispanic, 3% multiracial, 0% Pacific Islander, 81% white, 2% international; 21% from in state; 59% live on campus; 0% of students in fraternities, 0% in sororities
Most popular majors: 21% Registered Nursing/Registered Nurse, 10% Psychology, General, 9% Biology/Biological Sciences, General, 9% Business Administration and Management, General, 9% Criminal Justice/Law Enforcement Administration
Expenses: 2018-2019: $40,150; room/board: $14,500
Financial aid: (401) 341-2901; 73% of undergrads determined to have financial need; average aid package $27,756

University of Rhode Island

Kingston RI
(401) 874-7100
U.S. News ranking: Nat. U., No. 157
Website: www.uri.edu
Admissions email: admission@uri.edu
Public; founded 1892
Freshman admissions: selective; 2017-2018: 22,667 applied, 15,618 accepted. Either SAT or ACT required. SAT 25/75 percentile: 1080-1250. High school rank: 17% in top tenth, 48% in top quarter, 85% in top half
Early decision deadline: N/A, notification date: N/A
Early action deadline: 12/1, notification date: 1/31
Application deadline (fall): 2/1
Undergraduate student body: 12,615 full time, 2,477 part time; 44% male, 56% female; 0% American Indian, 3% Asian, 5% black, 10% Hispanic, 3% multiracial, 0% Pacific Islander, 73% white, 1% international; 54% from in state; 41% live on campus; 16% of students in fraternities, 22% in sororities
Most popular majors: 7% Registered Nursing/Registered Nurse, 6% Psychology, General, 6% Speech Communication and Rhetoric, 5% Human Developmer and Family Studies, General, 5% Kinesiology and Exercise Science
Expenses: 2018-2019: $14,138 in state, $30,862 out of state; room/board: $12,350
Financial aid: (401) 874-9500; 83% of undergrads determined to have financial need; average aid package $16,362

SOUTH CAROLINA

Allen University[1]

Columbia SC
(803) 376-5735
U.S. News ranking: Nat. Lib. Arts, second tier
Website: www.allenuniversity.edu
Admissions email: admissions@allenuniversity.edu
Private; founded 1870
Application deadline (fall): rolling
Undergraduate student body: N/A full time, N/A part time
Expenses: 2017-2018: $13,140; room/board: $6,880
Financial aid: (803) 376-5930

Anderson University

Anderson SC
(864) 231-5607
U.S. News ranking: Reg. U. (S), No. 65
Website: www.andersonuniversity.edu
Admissions email: admission@andersonuniversity.ed
Private; founded 1911
Freshman admissions: selective; 2017-2018: 2,322 applied, 1,836 accepted. Either SAT or ACT required. SAT 25/75 percentile: 1000-1190. High school rank: 37% in top tenth, 58% in top quarter, 85% in top half
Early decision deadline: N/A, notification date: N/A
Early action deadline: N/A, notification date: N/A
Application deadline (fall): rolling
Undergraduate student body: 2,55C full time, 433 part time; 31% male, 69% female; 0% American Indian, 1% Asian, 6% black, 3% Hispanic, 3% multiracial, 0% Pacific Islander, 84% white, 1% international; 81% from in state; 46% live on campus; N/A of students in fraternities, N/A in sororities
Most popular majors: 24% Health Professions and Related Programs 17% Business, Management, Marketing, and Related Support Services, 14% Education, 9% Visual and Performing Arts, 7% Homeland Security, Law Enforcement, Firefighting and Related Protective Services
Expenses: 2018-2019: $28,000; room/board: $9,830
Financial aid: (864) 231-2181; 80% of undergrads determined to have financial need; average aid package $19,354

More @ usnews.com/bestcollege

Benedict College[1]

Columbia SC
(803) 253-5143
U.S. News ranking: Reg. Coll. (S), second tier
Website: www.benedict.edu
Admissions email: admissions@benedict.edu
Private; founded 1870
Application deadline (fall): rolling
Undergraduate student body: N/A full time, N/A part time
Expenses: 2017-2018: $19,958; room/board: $8,924
Financial aid: N/A

Bob Jones University

Greenville SC
(800) 252-6363
U.S. News ranking: Reg. U. (S), No. 34
Website: www.bju.edu/admission
Admissions email: admission@bju.edu
Private; founded 1927
Affiliation: Evangelical Christian
Freshman admissions: selective; 2017-2018: 1,065 applied, 915 accepted. ACT required. ACT 25/75 percentile: 24-27. High school rank: 13% in top tenth, 35% in top quarter, 62% in top half
Early decision deadline: N/A, notification date: N/A
Early action deadline: N/A, notification date: N/A
Application deadline (fall): rolling
Undergraduate student body: 2,306 full time, 300 part time; 45% male, 55% female; 0% American Indian, 2% Asian, 2% black, 6% Hispanic, 3% multiracial, 1% Pacific Islander, 76% white, 6% international; 32% from in state; 77% live on campus; N/A of students in fraternities, N/A in sororities
Most popular majors: 14% Business Administration and Management, General, 8% Registered Nursing/Registered Nurse, 7% Accounting, 4% Biology/Biological Sciences, General, 4% Engineering, General
Expenses: 2018-2019: $18,150; room/board: $6,976
Financial aid: (864) 242-5100; 73% of undergrads determined to have financial need; average aid package $12,341

Charleston Southern University

Charleston SC
(843) 863-7050
U.S. News ranking: Reg. U. (S), No. 89
Website: www.csuniv.edu
Admissions email: enroll@csuniv.edu
Private; founded 1964
Affiliation: Baptist
Freshman admissions: selective; 2017-2018: 4,125 applied, 2,323 accepted. Either SAT or ACT required. ACT 25/75 percentile: 20-22. High school rank: 21% in top tenth, 52% in top quarter, 77% in top half
Early decision deadline: N/A, notification date: N/A
Early action deadline: N/A, notification date: N/A
Application deadline (fall): rolling
Undergraduate student body: 2,804 full time, 258 part time; 38% male, 62% female; 1% American Indian, 2% Asian, 24% black, 4% Hispanic, 3% multiracial, 0% Pacific Islander, 62% white, 1% international
Most popular majors: 12% Registered Nursing/Registered Nurse, 9% Kinesiology and Exercise Science, 8% Criminal Justice/Law Enforcement Administration, 7% Biology/Biological Sciences, General, 6% Psychology, General
Expenses: 2018-2019: $25,540; room/board: $10,200
Financial aid: (843) 863-7050

The Citadel

Charleston SC
(843) 953-5230
U.S. News ranking: Reg. U. (S), No. 3
Website: www.citadel.edu
Admissions email: admission@citadel.edu
Public; founded 1842
Freshman admissions: selective; 2017-2018: 2,642 applied, 2,142 accepted. Either SAT or ACT required. ACT 25/75 percentile: 20-25. High school rank: 9% in top tenth, 30% in top quarter, 64% in top half
Early decision deadline: N/A, notification date: N/A
Early action deadline: N/A, notification date: N/A
Application deadline (fall): rolling
Undergraduate student body: 2,559 full time, 278 part time; 89% male, 11% female; 0% American Indian, 2% Asian, 10% black, 7% Hispanic, 5% multiracial, 0% Pacific Islander, 75% white, 1% international; 67% from in state; 100% live on campus; 0% of students in fraternities, 0% in sororities
Most popular majors: 30% Business Administration and Management, General, 19% Engineering, General, 17% Criminal Justice/Law Enforcement Administration, 9% Social Sciences, General, 6% Kinesiology and Exercise Science
Expenses: 2018-2019: $12,516 in state, $33,869 out of state; room/board: $6,904
Financial aid: (843) 953-5187; 59% of undergrads determined to have financial need; average aid package $17,136

Claflin University

Orangeburg SC
(800) 922-1276
U.S. News ranking: Nat. Lib. Arts, No. 162
Website: www.claflin.edu
Admissions email: admissions@claflin.edu
Private
Affiliation: United Methodist
Freshman admissions: less selective; 2017-2018: 9,767 applied, 4,021 accepted. Either SAT or ACT required. ACT 25/75 percentile: 18-20. High school rank: 11% in top tenth, 30% in top quarter, 71% in top half
Early decision deadline: N/A, notification date: N/A
Early action deadline: N/A, notification date: N/A
Application deadline (fall): 8/1
Undergraduate student body: 1,955 full time, 83 part time; 32% male, 68% female; 2% American Indian, 1% Asian, 92% black, 2% Hispanic, 0% multiracial, 0% Pacific Islander, 1% white, 1% international; 86% from in state; 74% live on campus; N/A of students in fraternities, N/A in sororities
Most popular majors: 10% Criminal Justice/Law Enforcement Administration, 9% Business Administration and Management, General, 9% Sociology, 8% Management Information Systems, General, 7% Biology/Biological Sciences, General
Expenses: 2018-2019: $16,722; room/board: $9,294
Financial aid: (803) 535-5720; 93% of undergrads determined to have financial need; average aid package $15,962

Clemson University

Clemson SC
(864) 656-2287
U.S. News ranking: Nat. U., No. 66
Website: www.clemson.edu
Admissions email: cuadmissions@clemson.edu
Public; founded 1889
Freshman admissions: more selective; 2017-2018: 26,241 applied, 12,380 accepted. Either SAT or ACT required. ACT 25/75 percentile: 27-31. High school rank: 62% in top tenth, 91% in top quarter, 99% in top half
Early decision deadline: N/A, notification date: N/A
Early action deadline: N/A, notification date: N/A
Application deadline (fall): 5/1
Undergraduate student body: 18,642 full time, 760 part time; 51% male, 49% female; 0% American Indian, 2% Asian, 7% black, 4% Hispanic, 3% multiracial, 0% Pacific Islander, 83% white, 1% international; 66% from in state; 41% live on campus; 10% of students in fraternities, 15% in sororities
Most popular majors: 21% Engineering, 19% Business, Management, Marketing, and Related Support Services, 10% Biological and Biomedical Sciences, 7% Health Professions and Related Programs, 6% Psychology
Expenses: 2018-2019: $14,970 in state, $36,724 out of state; room/board: $10,832
Financial aid: (864) 656-2280; 46% of undergrads determined to have financial need; average aid package $11,582

Coastal Carolina University

Conway SC
(843) 349-2170
U.S. News ranking: Reg. U. (S), No. 52
Website: www.coastal.edu
Admissions email: admissions@coastal.edu
Public; founded 1954
Freshman admissions: selective; 2017-2018: 18,563 applied, 11,359 accepted. Either SAT or ACT required. ACT 25/75 percentile: 19-24. High school rank: 11% in top tenth, 36% in top quarter, 71% in top half
Early decision deadline: N/A, notification date: N/A
Early action deadline: N/A, notification date: N/A
Application deadline (fall): 8/1
Undergraduate student body: 9,021 full time, 877 part time; 46% male, 54% female; 0% American Indian, 1% Asian, 20% black, 4% Hispanic, 5% multiracial, 0% Pacific Islander, 67% white, 2% international; 49% from in state; 44% live on campus; 3% of students in fraternities, 7% in sororities
Most popular majors: 10% Business Administration and Management, General, 9% Speech Communication and Rhetoric, 8% Kinesiology and Exercise Science, 7% Marine Biology and Biological Oceanography, 6% Marketing/Marketing Management, General
Expenses: 2018-2019: $11,536 in state, $26,648 out of state; room/board: $9,190
Financial aid: (843) 349-2313; 70% of undergrads determined to have financial need; average aid package $10,802

Coker College

Hartsville SC
(843) 383-8050
U.S. News ranking: Reg. Coll. (S), No. 5
Website: www.coker.edu
Admissions email: admissions@coker.edu
Private; founded 1908
Freshman admissions: selective; 2017-2018: 1,389 applied, 857 accepted. Either SAT or ACT required. ACT 25/75 percentile: 17-21. High school rank: 9% in top tenth, 22% in top quarter, 55% in top half
Early decision deadline: N/A, notification date: N/A
Early action deadline: 12/1, notification date: 12/15
Application deadline (fall): 8/1
Undergraduate student body: 908 full time, 115 part time; 40% male, 60% female; 1% American Indian, 0% Asian, 34% black, 3% Hispanic, 6% multiracial, 0% Pacific Islander, 53% white, 3% international; 80% from in state; 56% live on campus; 0% of students in fraternities, 0% in sororities
Most popular majors: 14% Business/Commerce, General, 14% Sport and Fitness Administration/Management, 11% Business Administration and Management, General, 11% Health and Physical Education/Fitness, General, 11% Sociology
Expenses: 2018-2019: $29,550; room/board: $9,090
Financial aid: (843) 383-8050

College of Charleston

Charleston SC
(843) 953-5670
U.S. News ranking: Reg. U. (S), No. 11
Website: www.cofc.edu
Admissions email: admissions@cofc.edu
Public; founded 1770
Freshman admissions: selective; 2017-2018: 11,900 applied, 9,574 accepted. Either SAT or ACT required. ACT 25/75 percentile: 22-27. High school rank: 22% in top tenth, 53% in top quarter, 89% in top half
Early decision deadline: 11/1, notification date: 12/1
Early action deadline: 12/1, notification date: 1/15
Application deadline (fall): 2/15
Undergraduate student body: 9,083 full time, 812 part time; 37% male, 63% female; 0% American Indian, 2% Asian, 8% black, 5% Hispanic, 4% multiracial, 0% Pacific Islander, 78% white, 1% international; 67% from in state; 31% live on campus; 18% of students in fraternities, 35% in sororities
Most popular majors: 25% Business, Management, Marketing, and Related Support Services, 13% Biological and Biomedical Sciences, 10% Social Sciences, 9% Visual and Performing Arts, 7% Psychology
Expenses: 2018-2019: $12,738 in state, $31,920 out of state; room/board: N/A
Financial aid: (843) 953-5540; 51% of undergrads determined to have financial need; average aid package $13,716

Columbia College

Columbia SC
(800) 277-1301
U.S. News ranking: Reg. U. (S), No. 52
Website: www.columbiasc.edu
Admissions email: admissions@columbiasc.edu
Private; founded 1854
Affiliation: United Methodist
Freshman admissions: less selective; 2017-2018: 880 applied, 764 accepted. Neither SAT nor ACT required. ACT 25/75 percentile: 17-21. High school rank: 9% in top tenth, 34% in top quarter, 72% in top half
Early decision deadline: N/A, notification date: N/A
Early action deadline: N/A, notification date: N/A
Application deadline (fall): rolling
Undergraduate student body: 802 full time, 577 part time; 26% male, 74% female; 1% American Indian, 1% Asian, 33% black, 4% Hispanic, 3% multiracial, 0% Pacific Islander, 54% white, 3% international; 89% from in state; 29% live on campus; 0% of students in fraternities, 0% in sororities
Most popular majors: 26% Criminal Justice/Safety Studies, 10% Speech Communication and Rhetoric, 9% Community Organization and Advocacy, 7% Psychology, General, 6% Crisis/Emergency/Disaster Management
Expenses: 2018-2019: $19,500; room/board: $7,900

Financial aid: (803) 786-3612; 82% of undergrads determined to have financial need; average aid package $16,066

Columbia International University

Columbia SC
(800) 777-2227
U.S. News ranking: Reg. U. (S), No. 47
Website: www.ciu.edu
Admissions email: yesciu@ciu.edu
Private; founded 1923
Affiliation: Multiple Protestant Denomination
Freshman admissions: selective; 2017-2018: 584 applied, 165 accepted. Either SAT or ACT required. SAT 25/75 percentile: 840-1070. High school rank: 5% in top tenth, 25% in top quarter, 58% in top half
Early decision deadline: N/A, notification date: N/A
Early action deadline: N/A, notification date: N/A
Application deadline (fall): 8/1
Undergraduate student body: 446 full time, 40 part time; 50% male, 50% female; 0% American Indian, 1% Asian, 13% black, 6% Hispanic, 2% multiracial, 0% Pacific Islander, 68% white, 5% international; 60% from in state; 73% live on campus; 0% of students in fraternities, 0% in sororities
Most popular majors: 58% Theology and Religious Vocations, 14% Liberal Arts and Sciences, General Studies and Humanities, 8% Business, Management, Marketing, and Related Support Services, 6% Education, 4% Psychology
Expenses: 2018-2019: $23,690; room/board: $8,150
Financial aid: (803) 807-5036; 83% of undergrads determined to have financial need; average aid package $19,096

Converse College

Spartanburg SC
(864) 596-9040
U.S. News ranking: Reg. U. (S), No. 23
Website: www.converse.edu
Admissions email: admissions@converse.edu
Private; founded 1889
Freshman admissions: selective; 2017-2018: 1,496 applied, 1,066 accepted. Either SAT or ACT required. ACT 25/75 percentile: 20-26. High school rank: 16% in top tenth, 50% in top quarter, 82% in top half
Early decision deadline: N/A, notification date: N/A
Early action deadline: N/A, notification date: N/A
Application deadline (fall): 8/1
Undergraduate student body: 860 full time, 58 part time; 0% male, 100% female; 0% American Indian, 1% Asian, 10% black, 5% Hispanic, 5% multiracial, 0% Pacific Islander, 66% white, 3% international; 79% from in state; 62% live on campus; N/A of students in fraternities, N/A in sororities
Most popular majors: Information not available
Expenses: 2018-2019: $18,690; room/board: $10,930
Financial aid: N/A; 87% of undergrads determined to have financial need; average aid package $15,701

Erskine College

Due West SC
(864) 379-8838
U.S. News ranking: Nat. Lib. Arts, second tier
Website: www.erskine.edu
Admissions email: admissions@erskine.edu
Private; founded 1839
Affiliation: Presbyterian
Freshman admissions: selective; 2017-2018: 1,227 applied, 669 accepted. Either SAT or ACT required. ACT 25/75 percentile: 19-24. High school rank: 17% in top tenth, 29% in top quarter, 72% in top half
Early decision deadline: N/A, notification date: N/A
Early action deadline: N/A, notification date: N/A
Application deadline (fall): rolling
Undergraduate student body: 568 full time, 7 part time; 51% male, 49% female; 2% American Indian, 2% Asian, 10% black, 3% Hispanic, 0% multiracial, 1% Pacific Islander, 57% white, 0% international; 48% from in state; 92% live on campus; 0% of students in fraternities, 0% in sororities
Most popular majors: 21% Business, Management, Marketing, and Related Support Services, 18% Biological and Biomedical Sciences, 11% English Language and Literature/Letters, 10% Parks, Recreation, Leisure, and Fitness Studies, 8% Physical Sciences
Expenses: 2018-2019: $36,150; room/board: $11,350
Financial aid: (864) 379-8886; 100% of undergrads determined to have financial need; average aid package $24,595

Francis Marion University

Florence SC
(843) 661-1231
U.S. News ranking: Reg. U. (S), No. 78
Website: www.fmarion.edu
Admissions email: admissions@fmarion.edu
Public; founded 1970
Freshman admissions: selective; 2017-2018: 3,787 applied, 2,274 accepted. Either SAT or ACT required. ACT 25/75 percentile: 17-22. High school rank: 15% in top tenth, 46% in top quarter, 82% in top half
Early decision deadline: N/A, notification date: N/A
Early action deadline: N/A, notification date: N/A
Application deadline (fall): 8/10
Undergraduate student body: 3,006 full time, 454 part time; 32% male, 68% female; 0% American Indian, 1% Asian, 42% black, 2% Hispanic, 3% multiracial, 0% Pacific Islander, 49% white, 2% international; 96% from in state; 38% live on campus; 2% of students in fraternities, 6% in sororities
Most popular majors: 22% Health Professions and Related Programs, 16% Biological and Biomedical Sciences, 16% Business, Management, Marketing, and Related Support Services, 11% Psychology, 9% Social Sciences
Expenses: 2018-2019: $11,160 in state, $21,544 out of state; room/board: $7,948
Financial aid: (843) 661-1190; 79% of undergrads determined to have financial need; average aid package $12,437

Furman University

Greenville SC
(864) 294-2034
U.S. News ranking: Nat. Lib. Arts, No. 51
Website: www.furman.edu/
Admissions email: admissions@furman.edu
Private; founded 1826
Freshman admissions: more selective; 2017-2018: 5,002 applied, 3,060 accepted. Neither SAT nor ACT required. ACT 25/75 percentile: 26-31. High school rank: 38% in top tenth, 71% in top quarter, 94% in top half
Early decision deadline: 11/1, notification date: 11/15
Early action deadline: 11/1, notification date: 12/20
Application deadline (fall): 1/15
Undergraduate student body: 2,658 full time, 88 part time; 41% male, 59% female; 0% American Indian, 2% Asian, 6% black, 5% Hispanic, 3% multiracial, 0% Pacific Islander, 76% white, 5% international; 31% from in state; 89% live on campus; 30% of students in fraternities, 58% in sororities
Most popular majors: 10% Business Administration and Management, General, 9% Health Professions and Related Clinical Sciences, Other, 9% Speech Communication and Rhetoric, 8% Political Science and Government, General, 5% Biology/Biological Sciences, General
Expenses: 2018-2019: $49,532; room/board: $12,712
Financial aid: (864) 294-2030; 47% of undergrads determined to have financial need; average aid package $39,679

Lander University

Greenwood SC
(864) 388-8307
U.S. News ranking: Reg. Coll. (S), No. 21
Website: www.lander.edu
Admissions email: admissions@lander.edu
Public; founded 1872
Freshman admissions: selective; 2017-2018: 4,367 applied, 2,078 accepted. Either SAT or ACT required. SAT 25/75 percentile: 940-1120. High school rank: 11% in top tenth, 35% in top quarter, 73% in top half
Early decision deadline: N/A, notification date: N/A
Early action deadline: N/A, notification date: N/A
Application deadline (fall): rolling
Undergraduate student body: 2,600 full time, 187 part time; 31% male, 69% female; 0% American Indian, 2% Asian, 27% black, 2% Hispanic, 3% multiracial, 0% Pacific Islander, 62% white, 2% international
Most popular majors: 22% Business Administration and Management, General, 8% Humanities/Humanistic Studies, 8% Registered Nursing/Registered Nurse, 7% Kinesiology and Exercise Science, 7% Sociology
Expenses: 2017-2018: $11,700 in state, $21,300 out of state; room/board: $8,900
Financial aid: (864) 388-8340

Limestone College

Gaffney SC
(864) 488-4554
U.S. News ranking: Reg. Coll. (S), No. 45
Website: www.limestone.edu
Admissions email: admiss@limestone.edu
Private; founded 1845
Affiliation: Undenominational
Freshman admissions: selective; 2017-2018: N/A applied, N/A accepted. Neither SAT nor ACT required. ACT 25/75 percentile: 17-22. High school rank: N/A
Early decision deadline: N/A, notification date: N/A
Early action deadline: N/A, notification date: N/A
Application deadline (fall): 8/22
Undergraduate student body: 1,943 full time, 654 part time; 45% male, 55% female; 0% American Indian, 1% Asian, 43% black, 3% Hispanic, 0% multiracial, 0% Pacific Islander, 46% white, 5% international
Most popular majors: 23% Parks, Recreation, Leisure, and Fitness Studies, 20% Business, Management, Marketing, and Related Support Services, 10% Biological and Biomedical Sciences, 10% Education, 9% Public Administration and Social Service Professions
Expenses: 2017-2018: $25,150; room/board: N/A
Financial aid: (864) 488-8251

Morris College

Sumter SC
(803) 934-3225
U.S. News ranking: Reg. Coll. (S), second tier
Website: www.morris.edu
Admissions email: admissions@morris.edu
Private; founded 1908
Affiliation: Baptist
Freshman admissions: less selective; 2017-2018: 2,616 applied, 2,076 accepted. Either SAT or ACT required. SAT 25/75 percentile: N/A. High school rank: N/A
Early decision deadline: N/A, notification date: N/A
Early action deadline: N/A, notification date: N/A
Application deadline (fall): rolling
Undergraduate student body: 731 full time, 16 part time; 45% male, 55% female; 0% American Indian, 0% Asian, 98% black, 1% Hispanic, 1% multiracial, 0% Pacific Islander, 0% white, 0% international
Most popular majors: Information not available
Expenses: 2018-2019: $13,886; room/board: $6,033
Financial aid: N/A; 98% of undergrads determined to have financial need; average aid package $15,585

Newberry College

Newberry SC
(800) 845-4955
U.S. News ranking: Reg. Coll. (S), No. 12
Website: www.newberry.edu/
Admissions email: admissions@newberry.edu
Private; founded 1856
Affiliation: Lutheran Church in America
Freshman admissions: less selective; 2017-2018: 1,807 applied, 1,054 accepted. Either SAT or ACT required. ACT 25/75 percentile: 17-22. High school rank: 8% in top tenth, 30% in top quarter, 60% in top half
Early decision deadline: N/A, notification date: N/A
Early action deadline: N/A, notification date: N/A
Application deadline (fall): rolling
Undergraduate student body: 1,159 full time, 22 part time; 56% male, 44% female; 1% American Indian, 0% Asian, 25% black, 4% Hispanic, 4% multiracial, 0% Pacific Islander, 55% white, 5% international; 79% from in state; 77% live on campus; 15% of students in fraternities, 27% in sororities
Most popular majors: 19% Business Administration and Management, General, 12% Biology/Biological Sciences, General, 11% Education, General, 10% Parks, Recreation and Leisure Studies, 8% Registered Nursing/Registered Nurse
Expenses: 2018-2019: $26,424; room/board: $10,666
Financial aid: (803) 321-5127; 92% of undergrads determined to have financial need; average aid package $22,707

North Greenville University

Tigerville SC
(864) 977-7001
U.S. News ranking: Reg. U. (S), No. 78
Website: www.ngu.edu
Admissions email: admissions@ngu.edu
Private; founded 1892
Affiliation: Southern Baptist
Freshman admissions: selective; 2017-2018: 1,701 applied, 1,019 accepted. Either SAT or ACT required. ACT 25/75 percentile: 19-28. High school rank: 20% in top tenth, 38% in top quarter, 72% in top half
Early decision deadline: N/A, notification date: N/A
Early action deadline: N/A, notification date: N/A
Application deadline (fall): rolling
Undergraduate student body: 2,083 full time, 280 part time; 48% male, 52% female; 0% American Indian, 1% Asian, 8% black,

More @ usnews.com/bestcolleges

% Hispanic, 3% multiracial, % Pacific Islander, 78% white, % international; 80% from in tate; 64% live on campus; % of students in fraternities, % in sororities
lost popular majors: 17% usiness Administration and lanagement, General, 16% iberal Arts and Sciences/Liberal tudies, 15% Early Childhood ducation and Teaching, 9% ible/Biblical Studies, 9% Sport nd Fitness Administration/ lanagement
xpenses: 2018-2019: $19,750; oom/board: $10,240
inancial aid: (864) 977-7057; 1% of undergrads determined to ave financial need; average aid ackage $6,110

Presbyterian College
linton SC
864) 833-8230
.S. News ranking: Nat. Lib. Arts, lo. 127
Vebsite: www.presby.edu
dmissions email: dmissions@presby.edu
rivate; founded 1880
ffiliation: Presbyterian Church USA)
reshman admissions: selective; 017-2018: 2,277 applied, ,434 accepted. Neither SAT or ACT required. ACT 25/75 ercentile: 21-27. High school ank: 25% in top tenth, 62% in op quarter, 88% in top half
arly decision deadline: 11/1, otification date: 12/1
arly action deadline: 11/15, otification date: 12/15
pplication deadline (fall): 6/30
ndergraduate student body: 976 ull time, 40 part time; 49% nale, 51% female; 0% American ndian, 1% Asian, 12% black, % Hispanic, 3% multiracial, % Pacific Islander, 75% white, % international; 66% from in tate; 99% live on campus; 33% f students in fraternities, 50% n sororities
lost popular majors: 28% usiness, Management, larketing, and Related Support ervices, 12% Psychology, 11% nglish Language and Literature/ etters, 10% Biological and iomedical Sciences, 9% History
xpenses: 2018-2019: $38,660; oom/board: $10,480
inancial aid: (864) 833-8287; 5% of undergrads determined to ave financial need; average aid ackage $36,465

South Carolina State University
rangeburg SC
303) 536-7185
.S. News ranking: Reg. U. (S), econd tier
Vebsite: www.scsu.edu
dmissions email: dmissions@scsu.edu
ublic; founded 1896
reshman admissions: least elective; 2017-2018: 2,521 pplied, 1,973 accepted. Either AT or ACT required. ACT 25/75 ercentile: 15-18. High school ank: 11% in top tenth, 27% in op quarter, 43% in top half
Early decision deadline: N/A, notification date: N/A
Early action deadline: N/A, notification date: N/A
Application deadline (fall): 7/31
Undergraduate student body: 2,281 full time, 243 part time; 52% male, 48% female; 0% American Indian, 0% Asian, 95% black, 0% Hispanic, 1% multiracial, 0% Pacific Islander, 2% white, 0% international; 85% from in state; 61% live on campus; 3% of students in fraternities, 1% in sororities
Most popular majors: 11% Biological and Biomedical Sciences, 9% Homeland Security, Law Enforcement, Firefighting and Related Protective Services, 8% Family and Consumer Sciences/Human Sciences, 7% Communication, Journalism, and Related Programs, 6% Public Administration and Social Service Professions
Expenses: 2017-2018: $10,740 in state, $21,120 out of state; room/board: $9,000
Financial aid: (803) 536-7067

Southern Wesleyan University[1]
Central SC
(864) 644-5550
U.S. News ranking: Reg. U. (S), No. 102
Website: www.swu.edu
Admissions email: admissions@swu.edu
Private
Application deadline (fall): N/A
Undergraduate student body: N/A full time, N/A part time
Expenses: 2017-2018: $24,700; room/board: $8,970
Financial aid: N/A

University of South Carolina
Columbia SC
(803) 777-7700
U.S. News ranking: Nat. U., No. 106
Website: www.sc.edu
Admissions email: admissions-ugrad@sc.edu
Public; founded 1801
Freshman admissions: more selective; 2017-2018: 26,019 applied, 18,811 accepted. Either SAT or ACT required. ACT 25/75 percentile: 25-30. High school rank: 29% in top tenth, 61% in top quarter, 91% in top half
Early decision deadline: N/A, notification date: N/A
Early action deadline: 10/15, notification date: 12/20
Application deadline (fall): 12/1
Undergraduate student body: 25,243 full time, 1,119 part time; 46% male, 54% female; 0% American Indian, 3% Asian, 9% black, 5% Hispanic, 4% multiracial, 0% Pacific Islander, 76% white, 2% international; 62% from in state; 28% live on campus; 20% of students in fraternities, 33% in sororities
Most popular majors: 5% Business Administration, Management and Operations, 5% Social Work, 4% Finance and Financial Management Services, 4% Physiology, Pathology and Related Sciences, 4% Public Health
Expenses: 2017-2018: $12,262 in state, $32,362 out of state; room/board: $10,008
Financial aid: (803) 777-8134; 51% of undergrads determined to have financial need; average aid package $9,482

University of South Carolina–Aiken
Aiken SC
(803) 641-3366
U.S. News ranking: Reg. Coll. (S), No. 8
Website: www.usca.edu/
Admissions email: admit@sc.edu
Public; founded 1961
Freshman admissions: selective; 2017-2018: 3,075 applied, 1,628 accepted. Either SAT or ACT required. ACT 25/75 percentile: 18-23. High school rank: 16% in top tenth, 42% in top quarter, 78% in top half
Early decision deadline: N/A, notification date: N/A
Early action deadline: N/A, notification date: N/A
Application deadline (fall): 7/1
Undergraduate student body: 2,718 full time, 636 part time; 36% male, 64% female; 0% American Indian, 1% Asian, 28% black, 4% Hispanic, 4% multiracial, 0% Pacific Islander, 57% white, 3% international; 90% from in state; 27% live on campus; 8% of students in fraternities, 9% in sororities
Most popular majors: 25% Business, Management, Marketing, and Related Support Services, 18% Health Professions and Related Programs, 11% Education, 10% Parks, Recreation, Leisure, and Fitness Studies, 9% Communication, Journalism, and Related Programs
Expenses: 2018-2019: $10,760 in state, $21,218 out of state; room/board: $7,766
Financial aid: (803) 641-3476; 70% of undergrads determined to have financial need; average aid package $11,155

University of South Carolina–Beaufort
Bluffton SC
(843) 208-8000
U.S. News ranking: Reg. Coll. (S), No. 49
Website: www.uscb.edu
Admissions email: admissions@uscb.edu
Public; founded 1959
Freshman admissions: less selective; 2017-2018: 2,211 applied, 1,425 accepted. Either SAT or ACT required. SAT 25/75 percentile: 930-1090. High school rank: 11% in top tenth, 34% in top quarter, 67% in top half
Early decision deadline: N/A, notification date: N/A
Early action deadline: N/A, notification date: N/A
Application deadline (fall): 7/1
Undergraduate student body: 1,797 full time, 280 part time; 32% male, 68% female; 1% American Indian, 1% Asian, 23% black, 7% Hispanic, 5% multiracial, 0% Pacific Islander, 58% white, 1% international; 83% from in state; N/A live on campus; N/A of students in fraternities, N/A in sororities
Most popular majors: 20% Business Administration and Management, General, 12% Hospitality Administration/ Management, General, 11% Psychology, General, 10% Social Sciences, General, 7% Biology/ Biological Sciences, General
Expenses: 2017-2018: $10,454 in state, $21,230 out of state; room/board: $9,650
Financial aid: (843) 521-4117

University of South Carolina–Upstate
Spartanburg SC
(864) 503-5283
U.S. News ranking: Reg. Coll. (S), No. 10
Website: www.uscupstate.edu/
Admissions email: admissions@uscupstate.edu
Public; founded 1967
Freshman admissions: selective; 2017-2018: 3,437 applied, 1,774 accepted. Either SAT or ACT required. ACT 25/75 percentile: 17-22. High school rank: 9% in top tenth, 32% in top quarter, 70% in top half
Early decision deadline: N/A, notification date: N/A
Early action deadline: N/A, notification date: N/A
Application deadline (fall): rolling
Undergraduate student body: 4,345 full time, 1,375 part time; 35% male, 65% female; 0% American Indian, 3% Asian, 31% black, 6% Hispanic, 4% multiracial, 0% Pacific Islander, 53% white, 1% international; 95% from in state; 16% live on campus; 1% of students in fraternities, 4% in sororities
Most popular majors: 25% Registered Nursing/Registered Nurse, 16% Business Administration and Management, General, 10% Liberal Arts and Sciences/Liberal Studies, 7% Criminal Justice/Law Enforcement Administration, 6% Psychology, General
Expenses: 2018-2019: $11,688 in state, $23,190 out of state; room/board: $9,480
Financial aid: (864) 503-5340; 76% of undergrads determined to have financial need; average aid package $9,733

Voorhees College
Denmark SC
(803) 780-1030
U.S. News ranking: Reg. Coll. (S), No. 61
Website: www,voorhees.edu
Admissions email: admissions@voorhees.edu
Private; founded 1897
Affiliation: Protestant Episcopal
Freshman admissions: least selective; 2017-2018: 7,668 applied, 4,098 accepted. Neither SAT nor ACT required. SAT 25/75 percentile: 800-940. High school rank: 1% in top tenth, 8% in top quarter, 22% in top half
Early decision deadline: N/A, notification date: N/A
Early action deadline: N/A, notification date: N/A
Application deadline (fall): N/A
Undergraduate student body: 464 full time, 11 part time; 41% male, 59% female; 0% American Indian, 0% Asian, 96% black, 1% Hispanic, 0% multiracial, 0% Pacific Islander, 1% white, 0% international
Most popular majors: 14% Biology/ Biological Sciences, General, 14% Sociology, 13% Sport and Fitness Administration/Management, 12% Criminal Justice/Law Enforcement Administration, 10% Business Administration and Management, General
Expenses: 2018-2019: $12,630; room/board: $7,346
Financial aid: (803) 780-1234; 97% of undergrads determined to have financial need; average aid package $13,565

Winthrop University
Rock Hill SC
(803) 323-2191
U.S. News ranking: Reg. U. (S), No. 25
Website: www.winthrop.edu
Admissions email: admissions@winthrop.edu
Public; founded 1886
Affiliation: Other
Freshman admissions: selective; 2017-2018: 4,573 applied, 3,356 accepted. Either SAT or ACT required. ACT 25/75 percentile: 19-25. High school rank: 19% in top tenth, 51% in top quarter, 84% in top half
Early decision deadline: N/A, notification date: N/A
Early action deadline: N/A, notification date: N/A
Application deadline (fall): rolling
Undergraduate student body: 4,488 full time, 526 part time; 30% male, 70% female; N/A American Indian, N/A Asian, N/A black, N/A Hispanic, N/A multiracial, N/A Pacific Islander, N/A white, N/A international; 91% from in state; 48% live on campus; 1% of students in fraternities, 2% in sororities
Most popular majors: 19% Business, Management, Marketing, and Related Support Services, 16% Education, 9% Parks, Recreation, Leisure, and Fitness Studies, 9% Visual and Performing Arts, 7% Psychology
Expenses: 2018-2019: $15,590 in state, $29,846 out of state; room/board: N/A
Financial aid: (803) 323-2189; 75% of undergrads determined to have financial need; average aid package $13,080

Wofford College
Spartanburg SC
(864) 597-4130
U.S. News ranking: Nat. Lib. Arts, No. 72
Website: www.wofford.edu
Admissions email: admissions@wofford.edu
Private; founded 1854
Affiliation: United Methodist

Freshman admissions: more selective; 2017-2018: 3,092 applied, 2,142 accepted. Neither SAT nor ACT required. ACT 25/75 percentile: 24-30. High school rank: 43% in top tenth, 76% in top quarter, 95% in top half
Early decision deadline: 11/1, notification date: 12/1
Early action deadline: 11/15, notification date: 2/1
Application deadline (fall): 1/15
Undergraduate student body: 1,572 full time, 20 part time; 47% male, 53% female; 0% American Indian, 2% Asian, 8% black, 4% Hispanic, 4% multiracial, 0% Pacific Islander, 79% white, 2% international; 54% from in state; 93% live on campus; 50% of students in fraternities, 55% in sororities
Most popular majors: 15% Biology/Biological Sciences, General, 12% Finance, General, 8% Business/Managerial Economics, 5% Accounting, 5% Chemistry, General
Expenses: 2018-2019: $43,845; room/board: $12,685
Financial aid: (864) 597-4160; 63% of undergrads determined to have financial need; average aid package $36,140

SOUTH DAKOTA

Augustana University
Sioux Falls SD
(605) 274-5516
U.S. News ranking: Reg. Coll. (Mid. W), No. 4
Website: www.augie.edu
Admissions email: admission@augie.edu
Private; founded 1860
Affiliation: Evangelical Lutheran Church
Freshman admissions: more selective; 2017-2018: 1,975 applied, 1,339 accepted. Either SAT or ACT required. ACT 25/75 percentile: 23-29. High school rank: 35% in top tenth, 64% in top quarter, 89% in top half
Early decision deadline: N/A, notification date: N/A
Early action deadline: N/A, notification date: N/A
Application deadline (fall): rolling
Undergraduate student body: 1,679 full time, 70 part time; 38% male, 62% female; 0% American Indian, 1% Asian, 2% black, 3% Hispanic, 2% multiracial, 0% Pacific Islander, 85% white, 7% international; 50% from in state; 70% live on campus; 0% of students in fraternities, 0% in sororities
Most popular majors: 16% Business, Management, Marketing, and Related Support Services, 16% Education, 12% Biological and Biomedical Sciences, 10% Social Sciences, 9% Foreign Languages, Literatures, and Linguistics
Expenses: 2018-2019: $33,018; room/board: $8,248
Financial aid: (605) 274-5216; 63% of undergrads determined to have financial need; average aid package $26,851

Black Hills State University
Spearfish SD
(800) 255-2478
U.S. News ranking: Reg. U. (Mid. W), second tier
Website: www.bhsu.edu
Admissions email: admissions@bhsu.edu
Public; founded 1883
Freshman admissions: selective; 2017-2018: 1,696 applied, 1,475 accepted. Either SAT or ACT required. ACT 25/75 percentile: 19-24. High school rank: N/A
Early decision deadline: N/A, notification date: N/A
Early action deadline: N/A, notification date: N/A
Application deadline (fall): rolling
Undergraduate student body: 2,195 full time, 1,752 part time; 37% male, 63% female; 4% American Indian, 1% Asian, 2% black, 6% Hispanic, 5% multiracial, 0% Pacific Islander, 81% white, 1% international
Most popular majors: Information not available
Expenses: 2018-2019: $8,733 in state, $11,778 out of state; room/board: N/A
Financial aid: (605) 642-6145

Dakota State University
Madison SD
(888) 378-9988
U.S. News ranking: Reg. U. (Mid. W), No. 118
Website: www.dsu.edu
Admissions email: admissions@dsu.edu
Public; founded 1881
Freshman admissions: selective; 2017-2018: 972 applied, 820 accepted. Either SAT or ACT required. ACT 25/75 percentile: 19-26. High school rank: 7% in top tenth, 25% in top quarter, 60% in top half
Early decision deadline: N/A, notification date: N/A
Early action deadline: N/A, notification date: N/A
Application deadline (fall): rolling
Undergraduate student body: 1,397 full time, 1,565 part time; 58% male, 42% female; 1% American Indian, 2% Asian, 4% black, 4% Hispanic, 4% multiracial, 0% Pacific Islander, 84% white, 1% international; 61% from in state; N/A live on campus; N/A of students in fraternities, N/A in sororities
Most popular majors: 43% Computer and Information Sciences and Support Services, 16% Business, Management, Marketing, and Related Support Services, 16% Education, 8% Parks, Recreation, Leisure, and Fitness Studies, 5% Health Professions and Related Programs
Expenses: 2018-2019: $9,276 in state, $12,249 out of state; room/board: $6,872
Financial aid: (605) 256-5152; 69% of undergrads determined to have financial need; average aid package $8,325

Dakota Wesleyan University
Mitchell SD
(800) 333-8506
U.S. News ranking: Reg. Coll. (Mid. W), No. 28
Website: www.dwu.edu
Admissions email: admissions@dwu.edu
Private; founded 1885
Affiliation: United Methodist
Freshman admissions: selective; 2017-2018: 676 applied, 514 accepted. Either SAT or ACT required. ACT 25/75 percentile: 20-24. High school rank: 14% in top tenth, 36% in top quarter, 69% in top half
Early decision deadline: N/A, notification date: N/A
Early action deadline: N/A, notification date: N/A
Application deadline (fall): rolling
Undergraduate student body: 668 full time, 124 part time; 42% male, 58% female; 1% American Indian, 1% Asian, 2% black, 2% Hispanic, 1% multiracial, 0% Pacific Islander, 92% white, 2% international
Most popular majors: 30% Registered Nursing/Registered Nurse, 9% Business Administration and Management, General, 6% Biology/Biological Sciences, General, 5% Sport and Fitness Administration/Management, 4% Criminal Justice/Safety Studies
Expenses: 2018-2019: $27,640; room/board: $6,950
Financial aid: (605) 995-2663; 68% of undergrads determined to have financial need; average aid package $14,633

Mount Marty College
Yankton SD
(855) 686-2789
U.S. News ranking: Reg. U. (Mid. W), No. 101
Website: www.mtmc.edu
Admissions email: mmcadmit@mtmc.edu
Private; founded 1936
Freshman admissions: selective; 2017-2018: 466 applied, 310 accepted. Either SAT or ACT required. ACT 25/75 percentile: 19-24. High school rank: N/A
Early decision deadline: N/A, notification date: N/A
Early action deadline: N/A, notification date: N/A
Application deadline (fall): 8/30
Undergraduate student body: 457 full time, 419 part time; 42% male, 58% female; 3% American Indian, 1% Asian, 4% black, 9% Hispanic, 1% multiracial, 0% Pacific Islander, 80% white, 0% international; 53% from in state; 72% live on campus; 0% of students in fraternities, 0% in sororities
Most popular majors: 24% Registered Nursing/Registered Nurse, 16% Education, General, 7% Business Administration and Management, General, 7% Radiologic Technology/Science - Radiographer, 6% Accounting
Expenses: 2018-2019: $27,276; room/board: $7,986
Financial aid: (605) 668-1589; 83% of undergrads determined to have financial need; average aid package $27,350

National American University[1]
Rapid City SD
(605) 394-4827
U.S. News ranking: Reg. Coll. (Mid. W), unranked
Website: www.national.edu/rc
Admissions email: N/A
For-profit
Application deadline (fall): N/A
Undergraduate student body: N/A full time, N/A part time
Expenses: 2017-2018: $15,000; room/board: N/A
Financial aid: N/A

Northern State University
Aberdeen SD
(800) 678-5330
U.S. News ranking: Reg. U. (Mid. W), No. 101
Website: www.northern.edu
Admissions email: admissions@northern.edu
Public; founded 1901
Freshman admissions: selective; 2017-2018: 994 applied, 873 accepted. Either SAT or ACT required. ACT 25/75 percentile: 19-24. High school rank: 7% in top tenth, 24% in top quarter, 61% in top half
Early decision deadline: N/A, notification date: N/A
Early action deadline: N/A, notification date: N/A
Application deadline (fall): rolling
Undergraduate student body: 1,346 full time, 1,816 part time; 43% male, 57% female; 2% American Indian, 2% Asian, 2% black, 4% Hispanic, 3% multiracial, 0% Pacific Islander, 81% white, 5% international; 71% from in state; 35% live on campus; 0% of students in fraternities, 0% in sororities
Most popular majors: 30% Business, Management, Marketing, and Related Support Services, 20% Education, 11% Parks, Recreation, Leisure, and Fitness Studies, 7% Psychology, 7% Visual and Performing Arts
Expenses: 2018-2019: $8,497 in state, $11,470 out of state; room/board: $8,924
Financial aid: (605) 626-2640; 63% of undergrads determined to have financial need; average aid package $10,864

South Dakota School of Mines and Technology[1]
Rapid City SD
(605) 394-2414
U.S. News ranking: Engineering, unranked
Website: www.sdsmt.edu
Admissions email: admissions@sdsmt.edu
Public; founded 1885
Application deadline (fall): rolling
Undergraduate student body: N/A full time, N/A part time
Expenses: 2017-2018: $10,400 in state, $14,580 out of state; room/board: $8,170
Financial aid: (605) 394-2274

South Dakota State University
Brookings SD
(800) 952-3541
U.S. News ranking: Nat. U., No. 226
Website: www.sdstate.edu
Admissions email: SDSU_Admissions@sdstate.edu
Public; founded 1881
Freshman admissions: selective; 2017-2018: 5,551 applied, 5,072 accepted. Either SAT or ACT required. ACT 25/75 percentile: 20-26. High school rank: 14% in top tenth, 36% in top quarter, 68% in top half
Early decision deadline: N/A, notification date: N/A
Early action deadline: N/A, notification date: N/A
Undergraduate student body: 8,425 full time, 2,471 part time; 47% male, 53% female; 1% American Indian, 1% Asian, 2% black, 2% Hispanic, 2% multiracial, 0% Pacific Islander, 87% white, 4% international
Most popular majors: 24% Health Professions and Related Programs, 17% Agriculture, Agriculture Operations, and Related Sciences, 8% Engineering, 7% Social Sciences, 6% Education
Expenses: 2018-2019: $8,764 in state, $12,128 out of state; room/board: N/A
Financial aid: (605) 688-4695

University of Sioux Falls
Sioux Falls SD
(605) 331-6600
U.S. News ranking: Reg. U. (Mid. W), No. 94
Website: www.usiouxfalls.edu
Admissions email: admissions@usiouxfalls.edu
Private; founded 1883
Affiliation: American Baptist
Freshman admissions: selective; 2017-2018: 1,602 applied, 1,474 accepted. Either SAT or ACT required. ACT 25/75 percentile: 20-25. High school rank: 10% in top tenth, 35% in top quarter, 74% in top half
Early decision deadline: N/A, notification date: N/A
Early action deadline: N/A, notification date: N/A
Application deadline (fall): rolling
Undergraduate student body: 1,036 full time, 179 part time; 37% male, 63% female; 1% American Indian, 1% Asian, 5% black, 1% Hispanic, 4% multiracial, 0% Pacific Islander, 85% white, 1% international; 57% from in state; 53% live on campus; N/A of students in fraternities, N/A in sororities
Most popular majors: 28% Business, Management, Marketing, and Related Support Services, 16% Health Professions and Related Programs, 9% Psychology, 8% Parks, Recreation, Leisure, and Fitness Studies, 7% Education

More @ usnews.com/bestcolleges

Expenses: 2018-2019: $18,280; room/board: $7,350
Financial aid: (605) 331-6623; 74% of undergrads determined to have financial need; average aid package $21,132

University of South Dakota

Vermillion SD
(605) 658-6200
U.S. News ranking: Nat. U., No. 226
Website: www.usd.edu
Admissions email: admissions@usd.edu
Public; founded 1862
Freshman admissions: selective; 2017-2018: 3,865 applied, 3,359 accepted. Either SAT or ACT required. ACT 25/75 percentile: 20-25. High school rank: 14% in top tenth, 36% in top quarter, 69% in top half
Early decision deadline: N/A, notification date: N/A
Early action deadline: N/A, notification date: N/A
Application deadline (fall): N/A
Undergraduate student body: 4,908 full time, 2,740 part time; 38% male, 62% female; N/A American Indian, N/A Asian, N/A black, N/A Hispanic, N/A multiracial, N/A Pacific Islander, N/A white, N/A international
Most popular majors: Information not available
Expenses: 2018-2019: $9,061 in state, $12,425 out of state; room/board: $8,216
Financial aid: N/A

TENNESSEE

Austin Peay State University

Clarksville TN
(931) 221-7661
U.S. News ranking: Reg. U. (S), No. 85
Website: www.apsu.edu
Admissions email: admissions@apsu.edu
Public; founded 1927
Freshman admissions: selective; 2017-2018: 7,180 applied, 5,473 accepted. Neither SAT nor ACT required. ACT 25/75 percentile: 19-24. High school rank: 11% in top tenth, 35% in top quarter, 70% in top half
Early decision deadline: N/A, notification date: N/A
Early action deadline: N/A, notification date: N/A
Application deadline (fall): 8/8
Undergraduate student body: 7,065 full time, 2,526 part time; 41% male, 59% female; 0% American Indian, 2% Asian, 22% black, 7% Hispanic, 6% multiracial, 0% Pacific Islander, 60% white, 0% international; 89% from in state; 17% live on campus; 7% of students in fraternities, 9% in sororities
Most popular majors: 14% Business, Management, Marketing, and Related Support Services, 12% Health Professions and Related Programs, 11% Parks, Recreation, Leisure, and Fitness Studies, 7% Homeland Security, Law Enforcement, Firefighting and Related Protective Services, 6% Communication, Journalism, and Related Programs
Expenses: 2017-2018: $8,225 in state, $24,221 out of state; room/board: $9,170
Financial aid: (931) 221-7907; 82% of undergrads determined to have financial need; average aid package $11,135

Belmont University

Nashville TN
(615) 460-6785
U.S. News ranking: Reg. U. (S), No. 6
Website: www.Belmont.edu
Admissions email: buadmission@belmont.edu
Private; founded 1890
Affiliation: Interdenominational
Freshman admissions: more selective; 2017-2018: 7,737 applied, 6,282 accepted. Either SAT or ACT required. ACT 25/75 percentile: 24-29. High school rank: 27% in top tenth, 56% in top quarter, 86% in top half
Early decision deadline: N/A, notification date: N/A
Early action deadline: N/A, notification date: N/A
Application deadline (fall): 8/1
Undergraduate student body: 6,161 full time, 336 part time; 35% male, 65% female; 0% American Indian, 2% Asian, 5% black, 5% Hispanic, 4% multiracial, 0% Pacific Islander, 81% white, 1% international; 30% from in state; 52% live on campus; N/A of students in fraternities, N/A in sororities
Most popular majors: Business, Management, Marketing, and Related Support Services, Communication, Journalism, and Related Programs, Communications Technologies/Technicians and Support Services, Health Professions and Related Programs, Visual and Performing Arts
Expenses: 2018-2019: $34,310; room/board: $12,120
Financial aid: (615) 460-6403; 52% of undergrads determined to have financial need; average aid package $19,176

Bethel University

McKenzie TN
(731) 352-4030
U.S. News ranking: Reg. U. (S), second tier
Website: www.bethelu.edu
Admissions email: N/A
Private; founded 1842
Affiliation: Cumberland Presbyterian
Freshman admissions: less selective; 2017-2018: 1,388 applied, 1,299 accepted. Neither SAT nor ACT required. ACT 25/75 percentile: 16-21. High school rank: 6% in top tenth, 23% in top quarter, 53% in top half
Early decision deadline: N/A, notification date: N/A
Early action deadline: N/A, notification date: N/A
Application deadline (fall): rolling
Undergraduate student body: 3,454 full time, 1,375 part time; 44% male, 56% female; 0% American Indian, 1% Asian, 40% black, 2% Hispanic, 2% multiracial, 0% Pacific Islander, 51% white, 2% international
Most popular majors: 28% Organizational Leadership, 18% Criminal Justice/Safety Studies, 3% Crisis/Emergency/Disaster Management, 2% Registered Nursing/Registered Nurse, 1% Elementary Education and Teaching
Expenses: 2018-2019: $16,552; room/board: $9,198
Financial aid: (731) 352-6418; 85% of undergrads determined to have financial need; average aid package $11,878

Bryan College

Dayton TN
(800) 277-9522
U.S. News ranking: Reg. U. (S), No. 71
Website: www.bryan.edu
Admissions email: admissions@bryan.edu
Private; founded 1930
Affiliation: Evangelical Christian
Freshman admissions: selective; 2017-2018: 679 applied, 369 accepted. Neither SAT nor ACT required. ACT 25/75 percentile: 20-26. High school rank: 22% in top tenth, 44% in top quarter, 89% in top half
Early decision deadline: N/A, notification date: N/A
Early action deadline: N/A, notification date: N/A
Application deadline (fall): rolling
Undergraduate student body: 802 full time, 599 part time; 46% male, 54% female; 0% American Indian, 1% Asian, 4% black, 3% Hispanic, 2% multiracial, 0% Pacific Islander, 55% white, 4% international; 32% from in state; 72% live on campus; N/A of students in fraternities, N/A in sororities
Most popular majors: 51% Business, Management, Marketing, and Related Support Services, 8% Education, 8% Parks, Recreation, Leisure, and Fitness Studies, 8% Psychology, 4% Theology and Religious Vocations
Expenses: 2018-2019: $26,800; room/board: $7,500
Financial aid: (423) 775-7339; 77% of undergrads determined to have financial need; average aid package $21,946

Carson-Newman University

Jefferson City TN
(800) 678-9061
U.S. News ranking: Reg. U. (S), No. 76
Website: www.cn.edu
Admissions email: admitme@cn.edu
Private; founded 1851
Affiliation: Baptist
Freshman admissions: selective; 2017-2018: 3,294 applied, 2,219 accepted. Either SAT or ACT required. ACT 25/75 percentile: 20-26. High school rank: N/A
Early decision deadline: N/A, notification date: N/A
Early action deadline: N/A, notification date: N/A
Application deadline (fall): rolling
Undergraduate student body: 1,608 full time, 82 part time; 42% male, 58% female; 0% American Indian, 1% Asian, 8% black, 4% Hispanic, 3% multiracial, 0% Pacific Islander, 78% white, 4% international; 80% from in state; 52% live on campus; N/A of students in fraternities, N/A in sororities
Most popular majors: 17% Business, Management, Marketing, and Related Support Services, 17% Health Professions and Related Programs, 16% Education, 10% Psychology, 6% Visual and Performing Arts
Expenses: 2018-2019: $27,900; room/board: $8,810
Financial aid: (865) 471-3247; 83% of undergrads determined to have financial need; average aid package $24,656

Christian Brothers University

Memphis TN
(901) 321-3205
U.S. News ranking: Reg. U. (S), No. 39
Website: www.cbu.edu
Admissions email: admissions@cbu.edu
Private; founded 1871
Affiliation: Roman Catholic
Freshman admissions: more selective; 2017-2018: 2,757 applied, 1,451 accepted. Either SAT or ACT required. ACT 25/75 percentile: 21-27. High school rank: 27% in top tenth, 56% in top quarter, 85% in top half
Early decision deadline: N/A, notification date: N/A
Early action deadline: N/A, notification date: N/A
Application deadline (fall): rolling
Undergraduate student body: 1,402 full time, 124 part time; 47% male, 53% female; 1% American Indian, 5% Asian, 27% black, 9% Hispanic, 3% multiracial, 0% Pacific Islander, 40% white, 3% international; 79% from in state; 40% live on campus; N/A of students in fraternities, N/A in sororities
Most popular majors: 20% Business Administration and Management, General, 11% Psychology, General, 8% Mechanical Engineering, 8% Nursing Practice, 7% Natural Sciences
Expenses: 2018-2019: $32,820; room/board: $7,400
Financial aid: (901) 321-3305; 69% of undergrads determined to have financial need; average aid package $24,970

Cumberland University

Lebanon TN
(615) 444-2562
U.S. News ranking: Reg. U. (S), second tier
Website: www.cumberland.edu
Admissions email: admissions@cumberland.edu
Private; founded 1842
Freshman admissions: selective; 2017-2018: 2,230 applied, 1,159 accepted. Either SAT or ACT required. ACT 25/75 percentile: 19-23. High school rank: 0% in top tenth, 8% in top quarter, 46% in top half
Early decision deadline: N/A, notification date: N/A
Early action deadline: N/A, notification date: N/A
Application deadline (fall): rolling
Undergraduate student body: 1,578 full time, 393 part time; 42% male, 58% female; 1% American Indian, 1% Asian, 13% black, 3% Hispanic, 0% multiracial, 0% Pacific Islander, 58% white, 3% international
Most popular majors: 44% Registered Nursing/Registered Nurse, 8% Physical Education Teaching and Coaching, 7% Business Administration and Management, General, 5% Criminal Justice/Law Enforcement Administration, 5% Management Science
Expenses: 2018-2019: $22,890; room/board: $9,290
Financial aid: (615) 547-1399; 85% of undergrads determined to have financial need; average aid package $14,897

East Tennessee State University

Johnson City TN
(423) 439-4213
U.S. News ranking: Nat. U., second tier
Website: www.etsu.edu
Admissions email: go2etsu@etsu.edu
Public; founded 1911
Freshman admissions: selective; 2017-2018: 8,158 applied, 6,972 accepted. Either SAT or ACT required. ACT 25/75 percentile: 19-26. High school rank: N/A
Early decision deadline: N/A, notification date: N/A
Early action deadline: N/A, notification date: N/A
Application deadline (fall): 8/15
Undergraduate student body: 9,641 full time, 1,682 part time; 44% male, 56% female; 0% American Indian, 1% Asian, 7% black, 3% Hispanic, 3% multiracial, 0% Pacific Islander, 81% white, 3% international
Most popular majors: 25% Health Professions and Related Programs, 12% Business, Management, Marketing, and Related Support Services, 7% Liberal Arts and Sciences, General Studies and Humanities, 7% Parks, Recreation, Leisure, and Fitness Studies, 5% Psychology
Expenses: 2017-2018: $8,679 in state, $26,463 out of state; room/board: $12,640
Financial aid: (423) 439-4300

Fisk University

Nashville TN
(888) 702-0022
U.S. News ranking: Nat. Lib. Arts, No. 152
Website: www.fisk.edu
Admissions email: admissions@fisk.edu
Private; founded 1866
Freshman admissions: selective; 2017-2018: 2,801 applied, 1,272 accepted. Either SAT or ACT required. ACT 25/75

percentile: 16-22. High school rank: 11% in top tenth, 26% in top quarter, 54% in top half
Early decision deadline: N/A, notification date: N/A
Early action deadline: 11/1, notification date: 12/31
Application deadline (fall): rolling
Undergraduate student body: 639 full time, 25 part time; 32% male, 68% female; 0% American Indian, 0% Asian, 85% black, 1% Hispanic, 2% multiracial, 0% Pacific Islander, 1% white, 3% international
Most popular majors: 25% Business Administration and Management, General, 19% Biology/Biological Sciences, General, 14% Psychology, General, 8% Political Science and Government, General, 7% English Language and Literature, General
Expenses: 2017-2018: $21,480; room/board: $10,790
Financial aid: (615) 329-8585

Freed-Hardeman University

Henderson TN
(731) 348-3481
U.S. News ranking: Reg. U. (S), No. 39
Website: www.fhu.edu
Admissions email: admissions@fhu.edu
Private; founded 1869
Affiliation: Churches of Christ
Freshman admissions: more selective; 2017-2018: 919 applied, 876 accepted. Either SAT or ACT required. ACT 25/75 percentile: 22-28. High school rank: 31% in top tenth, 58% in top quarter, 84% in top half
Early decision deadline: N/A, notification date: N/A
Early action deadline: N/A, notification date: N/A
Application deadline (fall): rolling
Undergraduate student body: 1,261 full time, 210 part time; 41% male, 59% female; 1% American Indian, 1% Asian, 4% black, 1% Hispanic, 1% multiracial, 0% Pacific Islander, 85% white, 2% international; 64% from in state; 83% live on campus; 0% of students in fraternities, 0% in sororities
Most popular majors: 19% Business, Management, Marketing, and Related Support Services, 10% Education, 8% Health Professions and Related Programs, 7% Theology and Religious Vocations, 7% Visual and Performing Arts
Expenses: 2018-2019: $21,950; room/board: $7,950
Financial aid: (731) 989-6662; 79% of undergrads determined to have financial need; average aid package $19,065

King University

Bristol TN
(423) 652-4861
U.S. News ranking: Reg. U. (S), No. 71
Website: www.king.edu
Admissions email: admissions@king.edu
Private; founded 1867
Affiliation: Presbyterian
Freshman admissions: selective; 2017-2018: 1,152 applied, 683 accepted. Neither SAT nor ACT required. ACT 25/75 percentile: 18-28. High school rank: 23% in top tenth, 50% in top quarter, 80% in top half
Early decision deadline: N/A, notification date: N/A
Early action deadline: N/A, notification date: N/A
Application deadline (fall): rolling
Undergraduate student body: 1,608 full time, 191 part time; 39% male, 61% female; 0% American Indian, 1% Asian, 7% black, 4% Hispanic, 2% multiracial, 0% Pacific Islander, 80% white, 3% international; 60% from in state; 19% live on campus; N/A of students in fraternities, N/A in sororities
Most popular majors: 35% Health Professions and Related Programs, 30% Business, Management, Marketing, and Related Support Services, 9% Computer and Information Sciences and Support Services, 8% Psychology, 5% Homeland Security, Law Enforcement, Firefighting and Related Protective Services
Expenses: 2018-2019: $29,714; room/board: $8,762
Financial aid: (423) 652-4726; 85% of undergrads determined to have financial need; average aid package $16,036

Lane College[1]

Jackson TN
(731) 426-7533
U.S. News ranking: Reg. Coll. (S), second tier
Website: www.lanecollege.edu
Admissions email: admissions@lanecollege.edu
Private; founded 1882
Application deadline (fall): 7/1
Undergraduate student body: N/A full time, N/A part time
Expenses: 2017-2018: $10,690; room/board: $7,270
Financial aid: N/A

Lee University

Cleveland TN
(423) 614-8500
U.S. News ranking: Reg. U. (S), No. 47
Website: www.leeuniversity.edu
Admissions email: admissions@leeuniversity.edu
Private; founded 1918
Affiliation: Church of God
Freshman admissions: selective; 2017-2018: 2,387 applied, 2,030 accepted. Either SAT or ACT required. ACT 25/75 percentile: 21-28. High school rank: 24% in top tenth, 50% in top quarter, 79% in top half
Early decision deadline: N/A, notification date: N/A
Early action deadline: N/A, notification date: N/A
Application deadline (fall): rolling
Undergraduate student body: 3,854 full time, 1,006 part time; 38% male, 62% female; 1% American Indian, 1% Asian, 5% black, 2% Hispanic, 3% multiracial, 0% Pacific Islander, 81% white, 3% international; 45% from in state; 48% live on campus; 9% of students in fraternities, 8% in sororities
Most popular majors: 20% Theology and Religious Vocations, 16% Education, 11% Communication, Journalism, and Related Programs, 9% Business, Management, Marketing, and Related Support Services, 9% Health Professions and Related Programs
Expenses: 2018-2019: $17,690; room/board: $7,410
Financial aid: (423) 614-8300; 72% of undergrads determined to have financial need; average aid package $12,666

LeMoyne-Owen College

Memphis TN
(901) 435-1500
U.S. News ranking: Reg. Coll. (S), second tier
Website: www.loc.edu/
Admissions email: admission@loc.edu
Private; founded 1862
Affiliation: United Church of Christ
Freshman admissions: least selective; 2017-2018: 467 applied, 467 accepted. ACT required. ACT 25/75 percentile: 14-17. High school rank: N/A
Early decision deadline: N/A, notification date: N/A
Early action deadline: N/A, notification date: N/A
Application deadline (fall): 8/1
Undergraduate student body: 770 full time, 93 part time; 33% male, 67% female; 0% American Indian, 0% Asian, 98% black, 1% Hispanic, 0% multiracial, 0% Pacific Islander, 0% white, 2% international
Most popular majors: 48% Business Administration and Management, General, 12% Criminal Justice/Safety Studies, 10% Education, General, 6% Social Work, 4% Biology/Biological Sciences, General
Expenses: 2017-2018: $11,196; room/board: $6,100
Financial aid: (901) 435-1550

Lincoln Memorial University

Harrogate TN
(423) 869-6280
U.S. News ranking: Reg. U. (S), No. 58
Website: www.lmunet.edu
Admissions email: admissions@lmunet.edu
Private; founded 1897
Freshman admissions: selective; 2017-2018: 1,676 applied, 1,029 accepted. Neither SAT nor ACT required. ACT 25/75 percentile: 19-25. High school rank: N/A
Early decision deadline: N/A, notification date: N/A
Early action deadline: N/A, notification date: N/A
Application deadline (fall): rolling
Undergraduate student body: 1,355 full time, 564 part time; 30% male, 70% female; 1% American Indian, 1% Asian, 6% black, 0% Hispanic, 0% multiracial, 0% Pacific Islander, 85% white, 0% international; N/A from in state; 56% live on campus; 2% of students in fraternities, 3% in sororities
Most popular majors: 59% Registered Nursing/Registered Nurse, 7% Veterinary/Animal Health Technology/Technician and Veterinary Assistant, 5% Kinesiology and Exercise Science, 4% Biology/Biological Sciences, General, 2% Business Administration, Management and Operations, Other
Expenses: 2018-2019: $22,010; room/board: $10,196
Financial aid: (423) 869-6336; 85% of undergrads determined to have financial need; average aid package $21,955

Lipscomb University

Nashville TN
(615) 966-1776
U.S. News ranking: Nat. U., No. 194
Website: www.lipscomb.edu
Admissions email: admissions@lipscomb.edu
Private; founded 1891
Affiliation: Churches of Christ
Freshman admissions: more selective; 2017-2018: 3,581 applied, 2,164 accepted. Either SAT or ACT required. ACT 25/75 percentile: 23-29. High school rank: 29% in top tenth, 54% in top quarter, 80% in top half
Early decision deadline: N/A, notification date: N/A
Early action deadline: N/A, notification date: N/A
Application deadline (fall): rolling
Undergraduate student body: 2,723 full time, 264 part time; 39% male, 61% female; 0% American Indian, 3% Asian, 7% black, 7% Hispanic, 3% multiracial, 0% Pacific Islander, 76% white, 3% international; 66% from in state; 53% live on campus; 23% of students in fraternities, 24% in sororities
Most popular majors: 22% Business, Management, Marketing, and Related Support Services, 15% Health Professions and Related Programs, 8% Education, 7% Biological and Biomedical Sciences, 7% Psychology
Expenses: 2018-2019: $32,144; room/board: $12,652
Financial aid: (615) 966-6205; 64% of undergrads determined to have financial need; average aid package $26,236

Martin Methodist College

Pulaski TN
(931) 363-9800
U.S. News ranking: Reg. Coll. (S), No. 37
Website: www.martinmethodist.edu
Admissions email: info@martinmethodist.edu
Private; founded 1870
Affiliation: United Methodist
Freshman admissions: less selective; 2017-2018: 690 applied, 681 accepted. Either SAT or ACT required. ACT 25/75 percentile: 18-23. High school rank: N/A
Early decision deadline: N/A, notification date: N/A
Early action deadline: N/A, notification date: N/A
Application deadline (fall): rolling
Undergraduate student body: 810 full time, 167 part time; 38% male, 62% female; 0% American Indian, 0% Asian, 11% black, 3% Hispanic, 2% multiracial, 0% Pacific Islander, 72% white, 3% international; 82% from in state; 39% live on campus; 0% of students in fraternities, 0% in sororities
Most popular majors: 20% Business Administration and Management, General, 19% Registered Nursing/Registered Nurse, 9% Psychology, General, 8% Sport and Fitness Administration/Management, 7% Criminal Justice/Law Enforcement Administration
Expenses: 2018-2019: $23,496; room/board: $8,400
Financial aid: (931) 424-7366

Maryville College

Maryville TN
(865) 981-8092
U.S. News ranking: Nat. Lib. Arts, second tier
Website: www.maryvillecollege.edu
Admissions email: admissions@maryvillecollege.edu
Private; founded 1819
Affiliation: Presbyterian Church (USA)
Freshman admissions: selective; 2017-2018: 2,778 applied, 1,371 accepted. Either SAT or ACT required. ACT 25/75 percentile: 20-27. High school rank: 21% in top tenth, 43% in top quarter, 72% in top half
Early decision deadline: N/A, notification date: N/A
Early action deadline: N/A, notification date: N/A
Application deadline (fall): 5/1
Undergraduate student body: 1,158 full time, 23 part time; 46% male, 54% female; 1% American Indian, 1% Asian, 13% black, 4% Hispanic, 5% multiracial, 0% Pacific Islander, 74% white, 2% international; 68% from in state; 72% live on campus; 0% of students in fraternities, 0% in sororities
Most popular majors: 23% Business, Management, Marketing, and Related Support Services, 13% Social Sciences, 12% Psychology, 11% Education, 10% Biological and Biomedical Sciences
Expenses: 2018-2019: $34,880; room/board: $11,424
Financial aid: (865) 981-8100; 85% of undergrads determined to have financial need; average aid package $32,881

Memphis College of Art[1]

Memphis TN
(800) 727-1088
U.S. News ranking: Arts, unranked
Website: www.mca.edu
Admissions email: info@mca.edu
Private; founded 1936
Application deadline (fall): rolling
Undergraduate student body: N/A full time, N/A part time

Expenses: N/A
Financial aid: (901) 272-5138

Middle Tennessee State University

Murfreesboro TN
(615) 898-2233
U.S. News ranking: Nat. U., second tier
Website: www.mtsu.edu
Admissions email: admissions@mtsu.edu
Public; founded 1911
Freshman admissions: selective; 2017-2018: 9,938 applied, 5,898 accepted. Either SAT or ACT required. ACT 25/75 percentile: 20-25. High school rank: 18% in top tenth, 27% in top quarter, 33% in top half
Early decision deadline: N/A, notification date: N/A
Early action deadline: N/A, notification date: N/A
Application deadline (fall): rolling
Undergraduate student body: 15,812 full time, 3,711 part time; 46% male, 54% female; 0% American Indian, 3% Asian, 21% black, 5% Hispanic, 3% multiracial, 0% Pacific Islander, 63% white, 4% international; 97% from in state; 17% live on campus; 4% of students in fraternities, 5% in sororities
Most popular majors: 15% Business, Management, Marketing, and Related Support Services, 12% Liberal Arts and Sciences, General Studies and Humanities, 8% Visual and Performing Arts, 7% Communication, Journalism, and Related Programs, 6% Health Professions and Related Programs
Expenses: 2018-2019: $9,216 in state, $28,364 out of state; room/board: $9,590
Financial aid: N/A; 69% of undergrads determined to have financial need; average aid package $9,866

Milligan College

Milligan College TN
(423) 461-8730
U.S. News ranking: Reg. U. (S), No. 23
Website: www.milligan.edu
Admissions email: admissions@milligan.edu
Private; founded 1866
Affiliation: Christian Churches and Churches of Christ
Freshman admissions: more selective; 2017-2018: 621 applied, 417 accepted. Either SAT or ACT required. ACT 25/75 percentile: 23-27. High school rank: N/A
Early decision deadline: N/A, notification date: N/A
Early action deadline: N/A, notification date: N/A
Application deadline (fall): rolling
Undergraduate student body: 764 full time, 95 part time; 43% male, 57% female; 0% American Indian, 2% Asian, 4% black, 5% Hispanic, 2% multiracial, 0% Pacific Islander, 83% white, 3% international; 64% from in state; 79% live on campus; N/A of students in fraternities, N/A in sororities
Most popular majors: 22% Business Administration and Management, General, 18% Registered Nursing/Registered Nurse, 10% Psychology, General, 7% Early Childhood Education and Teaching, 7% Health and Physical Education/Fitness, General
Expenses: 2018-2019: $33,700; room/board: $7,100
Financial aid: (423) 461-8968; 83% of undergrads determined to have financial need; average aid package $24,755

Rhodes College

Memphis TN
(800) 844-5969
U.S. News ranking: Nat. Lib. Arts, No. 51
Website: www.rhodes.edu
Admissions email: adminfo@rhodes.edu
Private; founded 1848
Affiliation: Presbyterian
Freshman admissions: more selective; 2017-2018: 4,733 applied, 2,416 accepted. Either SAT or ACT required. ACT 25/75 percentile: 27-32. High school rank: 50% in top tenth, 79% in top quarter, 98% in top half
Early decision deadline: 11/1, notification date: 9/15
Early action deadline: 11/15, notification date: 1/1
Application deadline (fall): 1/15
Undergraduate student body: 1,979 full time, 9 part time; 44% male, 56% female; 0% American Indian, 6% Asian, 8% black, 6% Hispanic, 4% multiracial, 0% Pacific Islander, 70% white, 4% international; 28% from in state; 70% live on campus; 45% of students in fraternities, 54% in sororities
Most popular majors: 21% Social Sciences, 18% Business, Management, Marketing, and Related Support Services, 16% Biological and Biomedical Sciences, 7% Psychology, 5% Visual and Performing Arts
Expenses: 2018-2019: $47,890; room/board: $11,403
Financial aid: (800) 844-5969; 49% of undergrads determined to have financial need; average aid package $38,952

Sewanee–University of the South

Sewanee TN
(800) 522-2234
U.S. News ranking: Nat. Lib. Arts, No. 49
Website: www.sewanee.edu
Admissions email: admiss@sewanee.edu
Private; founded 1857
Affiliation: Protestant Episcopal
Freshman admissions: more selective; 2017-2018: 4,218 applied, 1,971 accepted. Neither SAT nor ACT required. ACT 25/75 percentile: 27-30. High school rank: 36% in top tenth, 61% in top quarter, 88% in top half
Early decision deadline: 11/15, notification date: 12/15
Early action deadline: 12/1, notification date: 2/15
Application deadline (fall): 2/1
Undergraduate student body: 1,687 full time, 15 part time; 47% male, 53% female; 0% American Indian, 1% Asian, 5% black, 6% Hispanic, 3% multiracial, 0% Pacific Islander, 82% white, 3% international; 22% from in state; 98% live on campus; 70% of students in fraternities, 80% in sororities
Most popular majors: 15% Economics, General, 12% Psychology, General, 9% English Language and Literature, General, 8% International/Global Studies, 7% Political Science and Government, General
Expenses: 2018-2019: $45,120; room/board: $12,880
Financial aid: (931) 598-1312; 48% of undergrads determined to have financial need; average aid package $34,316

South College[1]

Knoxville TN
(865) 251-1800
U.S. News ranking: Reg. U. (S), unranked
Website: www.southcollegetn.edu/
Admissions email: N/A
For-profit
Application deadline (fall): N/A
Undergraduate student body: N/A full time, N/A part time
Expenses: 2017-2018: $18,000; room/board: N/A
Financial aid: N/A

Southern Adventist University

Collegedale TN
(423) 236-2835
U.S. News ranking: Reg. U. (S), No. 65
Website: www.southern.edu
Admissions email: admissions@southern.edu
Private; founded 1892
Affiliation: Seventh Day Adventist
Freshman admissions: selective; 2017-2018: 1,423 applied, 1,349 accepted. Either SAT or ACT required. ACT 25/75 percentile: 20-27. High school rank: N/A
Early decision deadline: N/A, notification date: N/A
Early action deadline: N/A, notification date: N/A
Application deadline (fall): rolling
Undergraduate student body: 2,160 full time, 404 part time; 42% male, 58% female; 0% American Indian, 9% Asian, 10% black, 21% Hispanic, 6% multiracial, 1% Pacific Islander, 45% white, 9% international
Most popular majors: 26% Health Professions and Related Programs, 14% Business, Management, Marketing, and Related Support Services, 12% Biological and Biomedical Sciences, 8% Education, 8% Visual and Performing Arts
Expenses: 2018-2019: $21,950; room/board: $6,940
Financial aid: (423) 236-2535; 68% of undergrads determined to have financial need; average aid package $16,299

Tennessee State University

Nashville TN
(615) 963-5101
U.S. News ranking: Nat. U., second tier
Website: www.tnstate.edu
Admissions email: jcade@tnstate.edu
Public; founded 1912
Freshman admissions: less selective; 2017-2018: 9,404 applied, 4,523 accepted. Either SAT or ACT required. ACT 25/75 percentile: 16-20. High school rank: N/A
Early decision deadline: N/A, notification date: N/A
Early action deadline: N/A, notification date: N/A
Application deadline (fall): 7/1
Undergraduate student body: 5,429 full time, 1,074 part time; 38% male, 62% female; 0% American Indian, 1% Asian, 74% black, 1% Hispanic, 2% multiracial, 0% Pacific Islander, 11% white, 9% international
Most popular majors: 14% Basic Skills and Developmental/Remedial Education, 14% Parks, Recreation, Leisure, and Fitness Studies, 13% Area, Ethnic, Cultural, Gender, and Group Studies, 11% Mathematics and Statistics
Expenses: 2017-2018: $7,458 in state, $20,178 out of state; room/board: $5,580
Financial aid: (615) 963-5701

Tennessee Technological University

Cookeville TN
(800) 255-8881
U.S. News ranking: Nat. U., second tier
Website: www.tntech.edu
Admissions email: admissions@tntech.edu
Public; founded 1915
Freshman admissions: more selective; 2017-2018: 6,788 applied, 4,457 accepted. Either SAT or ACT required. ACT 25/75 percentile: 21-28. High school rank: 25% in top tenth, 53% in top quarter, 83% in top half
Early decision deadline: N/A, notification date: N/A
Early action deadline: N/A, notification date: N/A
Application deadline (fall): rolling
Undergraduate student body: 8,259 full time, 1,106 part time; 55% male, 45% female; 0% American Indian, 1% Asian, 4% black, 3% Hispanic, 3% multiracial, 0% Pacific Islander, 83% white, 4% international; 97% from in state; 25% live on campus; 10% of students in fraternities, 13% in sororities
Most popular majors: 8% Teacher Education, Multiple Levels, 7% Business Administration and Management, General, 6% Health and Physical Education/Fitness, General, 6% Mechanical Engineering, 5% Registered Nursing/Registered Nurse
Expenses: 2018-2019: $8,700 in state, $17,081 out of state; room/board: $9,416
Financial aid: (931) 372-3073; 75% of undergrads determined to have financial need; average aid package $10,151

Tennessee Wesleyan University

Athens TN
(423) 746-5286
U.S. News ranking: Reg. Coll. (S), No. 16
Website: www.tnwesleyan.edu
Admissions email: admissions@tnwesleyan.edu
Private; founded 1857
Affiliation: United Methodist
Freshman admissions: selective; 2017-2018: 878 applied, 526 accepted. Either SAT or ACT required. ACT 25/75 percentile: 19-25. High school rank: 10% in top tenth, 36% in top quarter, 74% in top half
Early decision deadline: N/A, notification date: N/A
Early action deadline: N/A, notification date: N/A
Application deadline (fall): rolling
Undergraduate student body: 863 full time, 72 part time; 37% male, 63% female; 0% American Indian, 1% Asian, 9% black, 5% Hispanic, 4% multiracial, 0% Pacific Islander, 76% white, 4% international; 87% from in state; 30% live on campus; 6% of students in fraternities, 7% in sororities
Most popular majors: 34% Business, Management, Marketing, and Related Support Services, 26% Health Professions and Related Programs, 9% Parks, Recreation, Leisure, and Fitness Studies, 8% Education, 5% Multi/Interdisciplinary Studies
Expenses: 2018-2019: $24,300; room/board: $7,880
Financial aid: (423) 746-5209; 88% of undergrads determined to have financial need; average aid package $19,855

Trevecca Nazarene University

Nashville TN
(615) 248-1320
U.S. News ranking: Nat. U., second tier
Website: www.trevecca.edu
Admissions email: admissions_und@trevecca.edu
Private; founded 1901
Affiliation: Church of the Nazarene
Freshman admissions: selective; 2017-2018: 1,489 applied, 1,048 accepted. Either SAT or ACT required. ACT 25/75 percentile: 19-26. High school rank: N/A
Early decision deadline: N/A, notification date: N/A
Early action deadline: N/A, notification date: N/A
Application deadline (fall): 8/1
Undergraduate student body: 1,317 full time, 902 part time; 38% male, 62% female; 0% American Indian, 1% Asian, 12% black, 9% Hispanic, 3% multiracial, 0% Pacific Islander, 61% white, 6% international; 67% from in state; 39% live on campus; N/A of students in fraternities, N/A in sororities

Most popular majors: 39% Business, Management, Marketing, and Related Support Services, 8% Health Professions and Related Programs, 7% Psychology, 7% Theology and Religious Vocations, 6% Visual and Performing Arts
Expenses: 2018-2019: $25,598; room/board: $8,400
Financial aid: (615) 248-1242

Tusculum University

Greeneville TN
(800) 729-0256
U.S. News ranking: Reg. U. (S), No. 102
Website: www.tusculum.edu
Admissions email: admissions@tusculum.edu
Private; founded 1794
Affiliation: Presbyterian
Freshman admissions: less selective; 2017-2018: 2,139 applied, 1,896 accepted. Either SAT or ACT required. ACT 25/75 percentile: 17-24. High school rank: N/A
Early decision deadline: N/A, notification date: N/A
Early action deadline: N/A, notification date: N/A
Application deadline (fall): rolling
Undergraduate student body: 1,376 full time, 112 part time; 49% male, 51% female; 0% American Indian, 0% Asian, 17% black, 4% Hispanic, 2% multiracial, 0% Pacific Islander, 70% white, 5% international; 67% from in state; 44% live on campus; N/A of students in fraternities, N/A in sororities
Most popular majors: 45% Business, Management, Marketing, and Related Support Services, 13% Education, 13% Psychology, 9% Parks, Recreation, Leisure, and Fitness Studies, 4% Health Professions and Related Programs
Expenses: 2017-2018: $23,700; room/board: $8,700
Financial aid: (423) 636-5377

Union University

Jackson TN
(800) 338-6466
U.S. News ranking: Nat. U., No. 152
Website: www.uu.edu
Admissions email: admissions@uu.edu
Private; founded 1823
Affiliation: Southern Baptist
Freshman admissions: more selective; 2017-2018: 2,634 applied, 1,580 accepted. Either SAT or ACT required. ACT 25/75 percentile: 23-29. High school rank: 35% in top tenth, 62% in top quarter, 89% in top half
Early decision deadline: N/A, notification date: N/A
Early action deadline: N/A, notification date: N/A
Application deadline (fall): rolling
Undergraduate student body: 1,892 full time, 261 part time; 33% male, 67% female; 1% American Indian, 2% Asian, 16% black, 3% Hispanic, 0% multiracial, 0% Pacific Islander, 77% white, 0% international; 97% from in state; 66% live on campus; 29% of students in fraternities, 30% in sororities
Most popular majors: 27% Health Professions and Related Programs, 22% Business, Management, Marketing, and Related Support Services, 12% Education, 5% Biological and Biomedical Sciences, 5% Public Administration and Social Service Professions
Expenses: 2018-2019: $32,610; room/board: $10,570
Financial aid: (731) 661-5015; 78% of undergrads determined to have financial need; average aid package $26,805

University of Memphis

Memphis TN
(901) 678-2111
U.S. News ranking: Nat. U., second tier
Website: www.memphis.edu
Admissions email: recruitment@memphis.edu
Public; founded 1912
Freshman admissions: selective; 2017-2018: 13,727 applied, 11,647 accepted. Either SAT or ACT required. ACT 25/75 percentile: 19-25. High school rank: 15% in top tenth, 38% in top quarter, 71% in top half
Early decision deadline: N/A, notification date: N/A
Early action deadline: N/A, notification date: N/A
Application deadline (fall): 8/1
Undergraduate student body: 12,400 full time, 4,994 part time; 42% male, 58% female; 0% American Indian, 3% Asian, 37% black, 5% Hispanic, 4% multiracial, 0% Pacific Islander, 48% white, 2% international; 88% from in state; 14% live on campus; 8% of students in fraternities, 7% in sororities
Most popular majors: 20% Business, Management, Marketing, and Related Support Services, 10% Multi/Interdisciplinary Studies, 9% Health Professions and Related Programs, 7% Parks, Recreation, Leisure, and Fitness Studies, 6% Education
Expenses: 2018-2019: $9,701 in state, $21,413 out of state; room/board: $9,590
Financial aid: (901) 678-4825; 77% of undergrads determined to have financial need; average aid package $10,477

University of Tennessee

Knoxville TN
(865) 974-1111
U.S. News ranking: Nat. U., No. 115
Website: utk.edu
Admissions email: admissions@utk.edu
Public; founded 1794
Freshman admissions: more selective; 2017-2018: 18,872 applied, 14,526 accepted. Either SAT or ACT required. ACT 25/75 percentile: 24-30. High school rank: N/A
Early decision deadline: N/A, notification date: N/A
Early action deadline: N/A, notification date: N/A
Application deadline (fall): rolling
Undergraduate student body: 20,965 full time, 1,352 part time; 50% male, 50% female; 0% American Indian, 4% Asian, 7% black, 4% Hispanic, 3% multiracial, 0% Pacific Islander, 78% white, 1% international; 87% from in state; 33% live on campus; 14% of students in fraternities, 25% in sororities
Most popular majors: 22% Business, Management, Marketing, and Related Support Services, 11% Engineering, 8% Parks, Recreation, Leisure, and Fitness Studies, 7% Communication, Journalism, and Related Programs, 7% Social Sciences
Expenses: 2018-2019: $13,006 in state, $31,196 out of state; room/board: $11,240
Financial aid: (865) 974-1111; 59% of undergrads determined to have financial need; average aid package $13,351

University of Tennessee–Chattanooga

Chattanooga TN
(423) 425-4662
U.S. News ranking: Reg. U. (S), No. 65
Website: www.utc.edu
Admissions email: utcmocs@utc.edu
Public; founded 1886
Freshman admissions: selective; 2017-2018: 7,235 applied, 5,990 accepted. Either SAT or ACT required. ACT 25/75 percentile: 21-26. High school rank: N/A
Early decision deadline: N/A, notification date: N/A
Early action deadline: N/A, notification date: N/A
Application deadline (fall): 5/1
Undergraduate student body: 8,962 full time, 1,214 part time; 44% male, 56% female; 0% American Indian, 2% Asian, 10% black, 4% Hispanic, 4% multiracial, 0% Pacific Islander, 76% white, 1% international; 94% from in state; 31% live on campus; 12% of students in fraternities, 18% in sororities
Most popular majors: 18% Business, Management, Marketing, and Related Support Services, 9% Education, 9% Parks, Recreation, Leisure, and Fitness Studies, 8% Psychology, 7% Biological and Biomedical Sciences
Expenses: 2018-2019: $8,664 in state, $24,782 out of state; room/board: $9,050
Financial aid: (423) 425-4677; 62% of undergrads determined to have financial need; average aid package $10,084

University of Tennessee–Martin

Martin TN
(800) 829-8861
U.S. News ranking: Reg. U. (S), No. 42
Website: www.utm.edu
Admissions email: admitme@utm.edu
Public; founded 1900
Freshman admissions: selective; 2017-2018: 4,884 applied, 3,004 accepted. Either SAT or ACT required. ACT 25/75 percentile: 20-25. High school rank: 16% in top tenth, 44% in top quarter, 78% in top half
Early decision deadline: N/A, notification date: N/A
Early action deadline: N/A, notification date: N/A
Application deadline (fall): rolling
Undergraduate student body: 4,950 full time, 1,408 part time; 41% male, 59% female; 0% American Indian, 1% Asian, 14% black, 3% Hispanic, 2% multiracial, 0% Pacific Islander, 78% white, 2% international; 92% from in state; 29% live on campus; 12% of students in fraternities, 15% in sororities
Most popular majors: 17% Business, Management, Marketing, and Related Support Services, 14% Agriculture, Agriculture Operations, and Related Sciences, 11% Multi/Interdisciplinary Studies, 9% Parks, Recreation, Leisure, and Fitness Studies, 8% Education
Expenses: 2018-2019: $9,512 in state, $15,552 out of state; room/board: $6,164
Financial aid: (731) 881-7040; 76% of undergrads determined to have financial need; average aid package $11,501

Vanderbilt University

Nashville TN
(800) 288-0432
U.S. News ranking: Nat. U., No. 14
Website: www.vanderbilt.edu
Admissions email: admissions@vanderbilt.edu
Private; founded 1873
Freshman admissions: most selective; 2017-2018: 31,462 applied, 3,415 accepted. Either SAT or ACT required. ACT 25/75 percentile: 32-35. High school rank: 90% in top tenth, 96% in top quarter, 98% in top half
Early decision deadline: 11/1, notification date: 12/15
Early action deadline: N/A, notification date: N/A
Application deadline (fall): 1/1
Undergraduate student body: 6,805 full time, 80 part time; 49% male, 51% female; 1% American Indian, 13% Asian, 10% black, 10% Hispanic, 5% multiracial, 0% Pacific Islander, 48% white, 8% international; 10% from in state; 90% live on campus; 34% of students in fraternities, 50% in sororities
Most popular majors: 13% Economics, General, 10% Social Sciences, General, 9% Multi-/Interdisciplinary Studies, Other, 5% Neuroscience, 5% Political Science and Government, General
Expenses: 2018-2019: $49,816; room/board: $16,234
Financial aid: (615) 322-3591; 50% of undergrads determined to have financial need; average aid package $49,242

Watkins College of Art, Design & Film[1]

Nashville TN
(615) 383-4848
U.S. News ranking: Arts, unranked
Website: www.watkins.edu
Admissions email: admission@watkins.edu
Private
Application deadline (fall): N/A
Undergraduate student body: N/A full time, N/A part time
Expenses: N/A
Financial aid: N/A

Welch College

Gallatin TN
(615) 675-5255
U.S. News ranking: Reg. Coll. (S), No. 13
Website: www.welch.edu
Admissions email: Recruit@welch.edu
Private; founded 1942
Affiliation: Free Will Baptist Church
Freshman admissions: selective; 2017-2018: 178 applied, 81 accepted. Either SAT or ACT required. ACT 25/75 percentile: 21-26. High school rank: 31% in top tenth, 66% in top quarter, 84% in top half
Early decision deadline: N/A, notification date: N/A
Early action deadline: N/A, notification date: N/A
Application deadline (fall): rolling
Undergraduate student body: 224 full time, 126 part time; 47% male, 53% female; 1% American Indian, 1% Asian, 6% black, 2% Hispanic, 1% multiracial, 0% Pacific Islander, 88% white, 0% international; 56% from in state; 55% live on campus; 95% of students in fraternities, 95% in sororities
Most popular majors: 36% Theology and Religious Vocations, 12% Education, 7% English Language and Literature/Letters, 7% Psychology, 4% Business, Management, Marketing, and Related Support Services
Expenses: 2018-2019: $19,012; room/board: $7,704
Financial aid: (615) 675-5278; 83% of undergrads determined to have financial need; average aid package $13,374

TEXAS

Abilene Christian University

Abilene TX
(800) 460-6228
U.S. News ranking: Reg. U. (W), No. 21
Website: www.acu.edu
Admissions email: info@admissions.acu.edu
Private; founded 1906
Affiliation: Churches of Christ
Freshman admissions: selective; 2017-2018: 9,827 applied, 5,952 accepted. Either SAT or ACT required. ACT 25/75 percentile: 21-26. High school rank: 22% in top tenth, 54% in top quarter, 84% in top half
Early decision deadline: N/A, notification date: N/A
Early action deadline: 11/1, notification date: 11/15

Application deadline (fall): 2/15
Undergraduate student body: 3,512 full time, 158 part time; 42% male, 58% female; 0% American Indian, 1% Asian, 9% black, 17% Hispanic, 5% multiracial, 0% Pacific Islander, 64% white, 4% international; 89% from in state; 47% live on campus; 28% of students in fraternities, 35% in sororities
Most popular majors: 7% Business Administration and Management, General, 7% Psychology, General, 5% Registered Nursing/Registered Nurse, 6% Sport and Fitness Administration/Management, 5% Accounting
Expenses: 2018-2019: $34,850; room/board: $10,350
Financial aid: (325) 674-2300; 58% of undergrads determined to have financial need; average aid package $23,433

Amberton University

Garland TX
(972) 279-6511
U.S. News ranking: Reg. U. (W), unranked
Website: www.amberton.edu
Admissions email: advisor@amberton.edu
Private; founded 1981
Affiliation: Other
Freshman admissions: least selective; 2017-2018: N/A applied, N/A accepted. Neither SAT nor ACT required. SAT 25/75 percentile: N/A. High school rank: N/A
Early decision deadline: N/A, notification date: N/A
Early action deadline: N/A, notification date: N/A
Application deadline (fall): rolling
Undergraduate student body: 26 full time, 191 part time; 38% male, 62% female; N/A American Indian, N/A Asian, N/A black, N/A Hispanic, N/A multiracial, N/A Pacific Islander, N/A white, N/A international
Most popular majors: Information not available
Expenses: N/A
Financial aid: N/A

Angelo State University

San Angelo TX
(325) 942-2041
U.S. News ranking: Reg. U. (W), second tier
Website: www.angelo.edu
Admissions email: admissions@angelo.edu
Public; founded 1928
Freshman admissions: less selective; 2017-2018: 4,316 applied, 3,174 accepted. Either SAT or ACT required. ACT 25/75 percentile: 17-22. High school rank: 10% in top tenth, 33% in top quarter, 69% in top half
Early decision deadline: N/A, notification date: N/A
Early action deadline: N/A, notification date: N/A
Application deadline (fall): 8/27
Undergraduate student body: 5,377 full time, 3,421 part time; 44% male, 56% female; 0% American Indian, 1% Asian, 7% black, 36% Hispanic, 3% multiracial, 0% Pacific Islander, 49% white, 4% international; 97% from in state; 35% live on campus; 5% of students in fraternities, 5% in sororities
Most popular majors: 17% Business, Management, Marketing, and Related Support Services, 13% Multi/Interdisciplinary Studies, 9% Health Professions and Related Programs, 8% Parks, Recreation, Leisure, and Fitness Studies, 7% Agriculture, Agriculture Operations, and Related Sciences
Expenses: 2018-2019: $8,489 in state, $20,939 out of state; room/board: $9,130
Financial aid: (325) 942-2246

Art Institute of Houston[1]

Houston TX
(713) 623-2040
U.S. News ranking: Arts, unranked
Website: www.artinstitute.edu/houston/
Admissions email: N/A
For-profit
Application deadline (fall): N/A
Undergraduate student body: N/A full time, N/A part time
Expenses: N/A
Financial aid: N/A

Austin College

Sherman TX
(800) 526-4276
U.S. News ranking: Nat. Lib. Arts, No. 103
Website: www.austincollege.edu
Admissions email: admission@austincollege.edu
Private; founded 1849
Affiliation: Presbyterian
Freshman admissions: more selective; 2017-2018: 3,545 applied, 1,849 accepted. Neither SAT nor ACT required. SAT 25/75 percentile: 1160-1360. High school rank: 41% in top tenth, 76% in top quarter, 96% in top half
Early decision deadline: 11/1, notification date: 12/4
Early action deadline: 1/5, notification date: 1/15
Application deadline (fall): 3/1
Undergraduate student body: 1,215 full time, 8 part time; 49% male, 51% female; 1% American Indian, 13% Asian, 9% black, 21% Hispanic, 4% multiracial, 0% Pacific Islander, 49% white, 3% international; 92% from in state; 86% live on campus; 15% of students in fraternities, 15% in sororities
Most popular majors: 20% Business, Management, Marketing, and Related Support Services, 16% Biological and Biomedical Sciences, 12% Psychology, 11% Social Sciences, 6% Health Professions and Related Programs
Expenses: 2018-2019: $39,985; room/board: $12,527
Financial aid: (903) 813-2900; 67% of undergrads determined to have financial need; average aid package $34,957

Baylor University

Waco TX
(800) 229-5678
U.S. News ranking: Nat. U., No. 78
Website: www.baylor.edu
Admissions email: Admissions@Baylor.edu
Private; founded 1845
Affiliation: Baptist
Freshman admissions: more selective; 2017-2018: 37,083 applied, 14,442 accepted. Either SAT or ACT required. ACT 25/75 percentile: 26-31. High school rank: 44% in top tenth, 77% in top quarter, 96% in top half
Early decision deadline: N/A, notification date: N/A
Early action deadline: 11/1, notification date: 1/15
Application deadline (fall): 2/1
Undergraduate student body: 14,100 full time, 216 part time; 41% male, 59% female; 0% American Indian, 6% Asian, 6% black, 15% Hispanic, 5% multiracial, 0% Pacific Islander, 63% white, 3% international; 70% from in state; 35% live on campus; 18% of students in fraternities, 33% in sororities
Most popular majors: 7% Biology/Biological Sciences, General, 7% Registered Nursing/Registered Nurse, 5% Accounting, 4% Marketing/Marketing Management, General, 4% Psychology, General
Expenses: 2018-2019: $45,542; room/board: $7,800
Financial aid: (254) 710-2611; 56% of undergrads determined to have financial need; average aid package $30,498

Brazosport College[1]

Lake Jackson TX
(979) 230-3000
U.S. News ranking: Reg. Coll. (W), unranked
Website: www.brazosport.edu
Admissions email: N/A
Public
Application deadline (fall): N/A
Undergraduate student body: N/A full time, N/A part time
Expenses: 2017-2018: $3,735 in state, $5,355 out of state; room/board: N/A
Financial aid: N/A

Concordia University Texas[1]

Austin TX
(800) 865-4282
U.S. News ranking: Reg. U. (W), second tier
Website: www.concordia.edu
Admissions email: admissions@concordia.edu
Private; founded 1926
Application deadline (fall): 8/1
Undergraduate student body: N/A full time, N/A part time
Expenses: 2017-2018: $30,600; room/board: $10,406
Financial aid: (512) 313-4672

Dallas Baptist University

Dallas TX
(214) 333-5360
U.S. News ranking: Nat. U., No. 221
Website: www.dbu.edu
Admissions email: admiss@dbu.edu
Private; founded 1898
Affiliation: Baptist
Freshman admissions: selective; 2017-2018: 3,770 applied, 1,486 accepted. Either SAT or ACT required. ACT 25/75 percentile: 19-24. High school rank: 21% in top tenth, 48% in top quarter, 79% in top half
Early decision deadline: N/A, notification date: N/A
Early action deadline: N/A, notification date: N/A
Application deadline (fall): rolling
Undergraduate student body: 2,423 full time, 738 part time; 41% male, 59% female; 1% American Indian, 2% Asian, 13% black, 17% Hispanic, 0% multiracial, 0% Pacific Islander, 61% white, 7% international; 92% from in state; 62% live on campus; 14% of students in fraternities, 21% in sororities
Most popular majors: 15% Multi-/Interdisciplinary Studies, Other, 14% Business Administration and Management, General, 9% Psychology, General, 7% Religious Education, 6% Speech Communication and Rhetoric
Expenses: 2018-2019: $28,870; room/board: $7,992
Financial aid: (214) 333-5363; 64% of undergrads determined to have financial need; average aid package $16,211

East Texas Baptist University

Marshall TX
(800) 804-3828
U.S. News ranking: Reg. Coll. (W), No. 17
Website: www.etbu.edu
Admissions email: admissions@etbu.edu
Private; founded 1912
Affiliation: Baptist
Freshman admissions: selective; 2017-2018: 1,839 applied, 999 accepted. Either SAT or ACT required. ACT 25/75 percentile: 18-23. High school rank: 13% in top tenth, 38% in top quarter, 74% in top half
Early decision deadline: N/A, notification date: N/A
Early action deadline: N/A, notification date: N/A
Application deadline (fall): 8/31
Undergraduate student body: 1,216 full time, 205 part time; 46% male, 54% female; 0% American Indian, 0% Asian, 16% black, 10% Hispanic, 4% multiracial, 0% Pacific Islander, 68% white, 1% international; 89% from in state; 82% live on campus; 0% of students in fraternities, 0% in sororities
Most popular majors: 17% Business, Management, Marketing, and Related Support Services, 15% Education, 12% Health Professions and Related Programs, 11% Multi/Interdisciplinary Studies, 11% Psychology
Expenses: 2018-2019: $26,370; room/board: $9,079
Financial aid: (903) 923-2137; 85% of undergrads determined to have financial need; average aid package $20,993

Hardin-Simmons University

Abilene TX
(325) 670-1206
U.S. News ranking: Reg. U. (W), No. 41
Website: www.hsutx.edu/
Admissions email: enroll@hsutx.edu
Private; founded 1891
Affiliation: Baptist
Freshman admissions: selective; 2017-2018: 1,673 applied, 1,368 accepted. Either SAT or ACT required. ACT 25/75 percentile: 18-24. High school rank: 18% in top tenth, 44% in top quarter, 76% in top half
Early decision deadline: N/A, notification date: N/A
Early action deadline: N/A, notification date: N/A
Application deadline (fall): rolling
Undergraduate student body: 1,585 full time, 164 part time; 48% male, 52% female; 0% American Indian, 1% Asian, 8% black, 19% Hispanic, 5% multiracial, 0% Pacific Islander, 64% white, 2% international; 94% from in state; 39% live on campus; 6% of students in fraternities, 10% in sororities
Most popular majors: 15% Business, Management, Marketing, and Related Support Services, 13% Health Professions and Related Programs, 12% Education, 10% Biological and Biomedical Sciences, 9% Parks, Recreation, Leisure, and Fitness Studies
Expenses: 2018-2019: $28,990; room/board: $8,080
Financial aid: (325) 670-1482; 75% of undergrads determined to have financial need; average aid package $24,855

Houston Baptist University

Houston TX
(281) 649-3211
U.S. News ranking: Reg. U. (W), No. 69
Website: www.hbu.edu
Admissions email: admissions@hbu.edu
Private; founded 1960
Affiliation: Baptist
Freshman admissions: selective; 2017-2018: 6,461 applied, 4,459 accepted. Either SAT or ACT required. SAT 25/75 percentile: 1030-1190. High school rank: 22% in top tenth, 51% in top quarter, 78% in top half
Early decision deadline: N/A, notification date: N/A
Early action deadline: N/A, notification date: N/A
Application deadline (fall): N/A
Undergraduate student body: 2,098 full time, 218 part time; 36% male, 64% female; 0% American Indian, 9% Asian, 19% black,

35% Hispanic, 4% multiracial, 0% Pacific Islander, 24% white, 3% international; 97% from in state; 36% live on campus; 5% of students in fraternities, 9% in sororities
Most popular majors: 26% Business, Management, Marketing, and Related Support Services, 20% Education, 13% Health Professions and Related Programs, 10% Psychology, 6% Biological and Biomedical Sciences
Expenses: 2018-2019: $32,530; room/board: $8,814
Financial aid: (281) 649-3749; 72% of undergrads determined to have financial need; average aid package $27,234

Howard Payne University

Brownwood TX
(325) 649-8020
U.S. News ranking: Reg. Coll. (W), No. 14
Website: www.hputx.edu
Admissions email: enroll@hputx.edu
Private; founded 1889
Affiliation: Baptist
Freshman admissions: less selective; 2017-2018: 1,396 applied, 826 accepted. Either SAT or ACT required. ACT 25/75 percentile: 19-22. High school rank: 10% in top tenth, 28% in top quarter, 64% in top half
Early decision deadline: N/A, notification date: N/A
Early action deadline: N/A, notification date: N/A
Application deadline (fall): rolling
Undergraduate student body: 860 full time, 121 part time; 52% male, 48% female; 1% American Indian, 1% Asian, 11% black, 22% Hispanic, 2% multiracial, 0% Pacific Islander, 55% white, 0% international
Most popular majors: 11% Education, 11% Parks, Recreation, Leisure, and Fitness Studies, 10% Business, Management, Marketing, and Related Support Services, 7% Social Sciences, 5% Psychology
Expenses: 2018-2019: $28,090; room/board: $8,580
Financial aid: (325) 649-8014; 85% of undergrads determined to have financial need; average aid package $21,576

Huston-Tillotson University[1]

Austin TX
(512) 505-3029
U.S. News ranking: Reg. Coll. (W), second tier
Website: htu.edu/
Admissions email: admission@htu.edu
Private
Application deadline (fall): 5/1
Undergraduate student body: N/A full time, N/A part time
Expenses: 2017-2018: $14,346; room/board: $7,568
Financial aid: N/A

Jarvis Christian College

Hawkins TX
(903) 730-4890
U.S. News ranking: Reg. Coll. (W), second tier
Website: www.jarvis.edu
Admissions email: Recruitment@jarvis.edu
Private; founded 1912
Affiliation: Christian Church (Disciples of Christ)
Freshman admissions: least selective; 2017-2018: 3,650 applied, 417 accepted. Either SAT or ACT required. SAT 25/75 percentile: 750-930. High school rank: N/A
Early decision deadline: N/A, notification date: N/A
Early action deadline: N/A, notification date: N/A
Application deadline (fall): 8/1
Undergraduate student body: 835 full time, 74 part time; 46% male, 54% female; 0% American Indian, 0% Asian, 79% black, 9% Hispanic, 0% multiracial, 0% Pacific Islander, 4% white, 0% international; 55% from in state; 92% live on campus; 5% of students in fraternities, 7% in sororities
Most popular majors: 32% Business, Management, Marketing, and Related Support Services, Other, 29% Kinesiology and Exercise Science, 10% Criminal Justice/Safety Studies, 10% General Studies, 6% Social Sciences, Other
Expenses: 2018-2019: $11,720; room/board: $8,440
Financial aid: (903) 730-4890; 93% of undergrads determined to have financial need; average aid package $12,841

Lamar University

Beaumont TX
(409) 880-8888
U.S. News ranking: Nat. U., second tier
Website: www.lamar.edu
Admissions email: admissions@lamar.edu
Public; founded 1923
Freshman admissions: less selective; 2017-2018: 5,445 applied, 4,446 accepted. Either SAT or ACT required. SAT 25/75 percentile: 950-1140. High school rank: 15% in top tenth, 39% in top quarter, 72% in top half
Early decision deadline: N/A, notification date: N/A
Early action deadline: N/A, notification date: N/A
Undergraduate student body: 5,965 full time, 3,269 part time; 42% male, 58% female; 1% American Indian, 5% Asian, 28% black, 17% Hispanic, 1% multiracial, 0% Pacific Islander, 46% white, 1% international; 97% from in state; 25% live on campus; N/A of students in fraternities, N/A in sororities
Most popular majors: 20% Health Professions and Related Programs, 14% Multi-/Interdisciplinary Studies, Other, 12% Engineering, 11% Business, Management, Marketing, and Related Support Services, 8% Liberal Arts and Sciences, General Studies and Humanities
Expenses: 2018-2019: $10,192 in state, $22,642 out of state; room/board: $8,920
Financial aid: (409) 880-7011; 63% of undergrads determined to have financial need; average aid package $5,125

LeTourneau University

Longview TX
(903) 233-4300
U.S. News ranking: Reg. U. (W), No. 28
Website: www.letu.edu
Admissions email: admissions@letu.edu
Private; founded 1946
Freshman admissions: more selective; 2017-2018: 1,780 applied, 838 accepted. Neither SAT nor ACT required. SAT 25/75 percentile: 1060-1310. High school rank: 25% in top tenth, 52% in top quarter, 84% in top half
Early decision deadline: N/A, notification date: N/A
Early action deadline: N/A, notification date: N/A
Application deadline (fall): rolling
Undergraduate student body: 1,302 full time, 1,309 part time; 54% male, 46% female; 0% American Indian, 1% Asian, 10% black, 8% Hispanic, 6% multiracial, 0% Pacific Islander, 64% white, 3% international; 65% from in state; 70% live on campus; N/A of students in fraternities, N/A in sororities
Most popular majors: 24% Business, Management, Marketing, and Related Support Services, 23% Engineering, 12% Education, 7% Parks, Recreation, Leisure, and Fitness Studies, 7% Transportation and Materials Moving
Expenses: 2018-2019: $30,210; room/board: $9,970
Financial aid: (903) 233-4356; 71% of undergrads determined to have financial need; average aid package $23,366

Lubbock Christian University

Lubbock TX
(806) 720-7151
U.S. News ranking: Reg. U. (W), No. 85
Website: www.lcu.edu
Admissions email: admissions@lcu.edu
Private; founded 1957
Affiliation: Churches of Christ
Freshman admissions: selective; 2017-2018: 810 applied, 762 accepted. Either SAT or ACT required. ACT 25/75 percentile: 19-25. High school rank: 16% in top tenth, 39% in top quarter, 70% in top half
Early decision deadline: 10/31, notification date: 12/15
Early action deadline: 6/15, notification date: 7/15
Application deadline (fall): 6/1
Undergraduate student body: 1,276 full time, 208 part time; 42% male, 58% female; 1% American Indian, 1% Asian, 5% black, 24% Hispanic, 0% multiracial, 1% Pacific Islander, 67% white, 1% international; 91% from in state; 36% live on campus; 18% of students in fraternities, 31% in sororities
Most popular majors: 25% Registered Nursing/Registered Nurse, 8% Early Childhood Education and Teaching, 5% Psychology, General, 4% Design and Visual Communications, General, 4% Health and Physical Education/Fitness, Other
Expenses: 2018-2019: $22,440; room/board: $6,650
Financial aid: (806) 720-7176; 75% of undergrads determined to have financial need; average aid package $15,731

McMurry University

Abilene TX
(325) 793-4700
U.S. News ranking: Reg. Coll. (W), No. 16
Website: ww2.mcm.edu/
Admissions email: admissions@mcm.edu
Private; founded 1923
Affiliation: United Methodist
Freshman admissions: selective; 2017-2018: 1,843 applied, 799 accepted. Either SAT or ACT required. ACT 25/75 percentile: 17-22. High school rank: 12% in top tenth, 33% in top quarter, 73% in top half
Early decision deadline: N/A, notification date: N/A
Early action deadline: N/A, notification date: N/A
Application deadline (fall): 8/15
Undergraduate student body: 956 full time, 149 part time; 52% male, 48% female; 1% American Indian, 1% Asian, 15% black, 26% Hispanic, 3% multiracial, 0% Pacific Islander, 47% white, 6% international; 95% from in state; 54% live on campus; 15% of students in fraternities, 18% in sororities
Most popular majors: 20% Education, 19% Business, Management, Marketing, and Related Support Services, 10% Multi/Interdisciplinary Studies, 9% Visual and Performing Arts, 8% Social Sciences
Expenses: 2018-2019: $27,244; room/board: $8,602
Financial aid: (325) 793-4978; 82% of undergrads determined to have financial need; average aid package $21,941

Midland College[1]

Midland TX
(432) 685-4500
U.S. News ranking: Reg. Coll. (W), unranked
Website: www.midland.edu/
Admissions email: pebensberger@midland.edu
Public
Application deadline (fall): N/A
Undergraduate student body: N/A full time, N/A part time
Expenses: 2017-2018: $4,230 in state, $5,490 out of state; room/board: $4,900
Financial aid: N/A

Midwestern State University

Wichita Falls TX
(800) 842-1922
U.S. News ranking: Reg. U. (W), No. 94
Website: www.mwsu.edu
Admissions email: admissions@mwsu.edu
Public; founded 1922
Freshman admissions: selective; 2017-2018: 3,354 applied, 2,730 accepted. Either SAT or ACT required. SAT 25/75 percentile: 930-1120. High school rank: 11% in top tenth, 35% in top quarter, 72% in top half
Early decision deadline: N/A, notification date: N/A
Early action deadline: N/A, notification date: N/A
Application deadline (fall): 8/1
Undergraduate student body: 4,199 full time, 1,131 part time; 42% male, 58% female; 1% American Indian, 3% Asian, 15% black, 19% Hispanic, 4% multiracial, 0% Pacific Islander, 49% white, 9% international; 91% from in state; 29% live on campus; 8% of students in fraternities, 10% in sororities
Most popular majors: 38% Health Professions and Related Programs, 14% Business, Management, Marketing, and Related Support Services, 13% Multi/Interdisciplinary Studies, 5% Biological and Biomedical Sciences, 5% Engineering
Expenses: 2018-2019: $9,233 in state, $11,183 out of state; room/board: $8,877
Financial aid: (940) 397-4214; 62% of undergrads determined to have financial need; average aid package $10,091

Our Lady of the Lake University

San Antonio TX
(800) 436-6558
U.S. News ranking: Reg. U. (W), No. 69
Website: www.ollusa.edu
Admissions email: admission@lake.ollusa.edu
Private; founded 1895
Affiliation: Roman Catholic
Freshman admissions: less selective; 2017-2018: 3,389 applied, 3,094 accepted. Either SAT or ACT required. SAT 25/75 percentile: 930-1080. High school rank: 13% in top tenth, 36% in top quarter, 75% in top half
Early decision deadline: N/A, notification date: N/A
Early action deadline: N/A, notification date: N/A
Application deadline (fall): 8/1
Undergraduate student body: 1,221 full time, 121 part time; 31% male, 69% female; 0% American Indian, 1% Asian, 8% black, 76% Hispanic, 2% multiracial, 0% Pacific Islander, 10% white, 2% international; 98% from in state; 39% live on campus; 5% of students in fraternities, 5% in sororities
Most popular majors: 16% Social Work, 13% Psychology, General, 10% Communication Sciences and Disorders, General,

More @ usnews.com/bestcolleges

9% Business Administration and Management, General, 7% Kinesiology and Exercise Science
Expenses: 2018-2019: $28,740; room/board: $9,602
Financial aid: (210) 434-6711; 37% of undergrads determined to have financial need; average aid package $23,305

Prairie View A&M University

Prairie View TX
(936) 261-1000
U.S. News ranking: Nat. U., second tier
Website: www.pvamu.edu
Admissions email: admission@pvamu.edu
Public; founded 1876
Freshman admissions: less selective; 2017-2018: 6,422 applied, 5,069 accepted. Either SAT or ACT required. SAT 25/75 percentile: 870-1050. High school rank: 6% in top tenth, 19% in top quarter, 65% in top half
Early decision deadline: N/A, notification date: N/A
Early action deadline: N/A, notification date: N/A
Application deadline (fall): 6/1
Undergraduate student body: 7,341 full time, 645 part time; 39% male, 61% female; 0% American Indian, 2% Asian, 83% black, 9% Hispanic, 1% multiracial, 0% Pacific Islander, 2% white, 1% international; 93% from in state; N/A live on campus; 8% of students in fraternities, 4% in sororities
Most popular majors: 18% Health Professions and Related Programs, 16% Engineering, 11% Business, Management, Marketing, and Related Support Services, 9% Homeland Security, Law Enforcement, Firefighting and Related Protective Services, 6% Education
Expenses: 2017-2018: $10,533 in state, $24,843 out of state; room/board: $8,743
Financial aid: (936) 261-1000; 36% of undergrads determined to have financial need; average aid package $15,507

Rice University

Houston TX
(713) 348-7423
U.S. News ranking: Nat. U., No. 16
Website: www.rice.edu
Admissions email: admission@rice.edu
Private; founded 1912
Freshman admissions: most selective; 2017-2018: 18,063 applied, 2,864 accepted. Either SAT or ACT required. ACT 25/75 percentile: 33-35. High school rank: 89% in top tenth, 97% in top quarter, 99% in top half
Early decision deadline: 11/1, notification date: 12/15
Early action deadline: N/A, notification date: N/A
Application deadline (fall): 1/1
Undergraduate student body: 3,916 full time, 85 part time; 53% male, 47% female; 0% American Indian, 26% Asian, 7% black, 15% Hispanic, 4% multiracial, 0% Pacific Islander, 35% white, 12% international; 48% from in state; 72% live on campus; 0% of students in fraternities, 0% in sororities
Most popular majors: 7% Computer and Information Sciences, General, 6% Biochemistry, 6% Chemical Engineering, 6% Mechanical Engineering, 5% Kinesiology and Exercise Science
Expenses: 2018-2019: $47,350; room/board: $14,000
Financial aid: (713) 348-4958; 38% of undergrads determined to have financial need; average aid package $44,799

Sam Houston State University

Huntsville TX
(936) 294-1828
U.S. News ranking: Nat. U., second tier
Website: www.shsu.edu
Admissions email: admissions@shsu.edu
Public; founded 1879
Freshman admissions: selective; 2017-2018: 12,365 applied, 9,212 accepted. Either SAT or ACT required. SAT 25/75 percentile: 1000-1140. High school rank: 19% in top tenth, 46% in top quarter, 78% in top half
Early decision deadline: N/A, notification date: N/A
Early action deadline: N/A, notification date: N/A
Application deadline (fall): 8/1
Undergraduate student body: 14,808 full time, 3,608 part time; 38% male, 62% female; 1% American Indian, 2% Asian, 18% black, 23% Hispanic, 3% multiracial, 0% Pacific Islander, 51% white, 1% international; 99% from in state; 21% live on campus; 7% of students in fraternities, 5% in sororities
Most popular majors: 23% Business, Management, Marketing, and Related Support Services, 20% Homeland Security, Law Enforcement, Firefighting and Related Protective Services, 10% Multi/Interdisciplinary Studies, 6% Health Professions and Related Programs, 5% Psychology
Expenses: 2018-2019: $10,183 in state, $22,633 out of state; room/board: $9,386
Financial aid: (936) 294-1774; 65% of undergrads determined to have financial need; average aid package $10,849

Schreiner University

Kerrville TX
(800) 343-4919
U.S. News ranking: Nat. Lib. Arts, second tier
Website: www.schreiner.edu
Admissions email: admissions@schreiner.edu
Private; founded 1923
Affiliation: Presbyterian Church (USA)
Freshman admissions: selective; 2017-2018: 1,178 applied, 1,088 accepted. Either SAT or ACT required. SAT 25/75 percentile: 960-1140. High school rank: 14% in top tenth, 37% in top quarter, 74% in top half
Early decision deadline: N/A, notification date: N/A
Early action deadline: N/A, notification date: N/A
Application deadline (fall): 8/1
Undergraduate student body: 1,137 full time, 112 part time; 42% male, 58% female; 0% American Indian, 1% Asian, 4% black, 40% Hispanic, 2% multiracial, 0% Pacific Islander, 53% white, 1% international; 99% from in state; 61% live on campus; N/A of students in fraternities, N/A in sororities
Most popular majors: 36% Health Professions and Related Programs, 17% Business, Management, Marketing, and Related Support Services, 12% Biological and Biomedical Sciences, 9% Parks, Recreation, Leisure, and Fitness Studies, 5% Education
Expenses: 2018-2019: $27,960; room/board: $10,508
Financial aid: (830) 792-7229; 88% of undergrads determined to have financial need; average aid package $20,822

Southern Methodist University

Dallas TX
(800) 323-0672
U.S. News ranking: Nat. U., No. 59
Website: www.smu.edu
Admissions email: ugadmission@smu.edu
Private; founded 1911
Affiliation: United Methodist
Freshman admissions: more selective; 2017-2018: 13,128 applied, 6,402 accepted. Either SAT or ACT required. ACT 25/75 percentile: 28-32. High school rank: 52% in top tenth, 79% in top quarter, 95% in top half
Early decision deadline: 11/1, notification date: 12/31
Early action deadline: 11/1, notification date: 12/31
Application deadline (fall): 1/15
Undergraduate student body: 6,240 full time, 212 part time; 50% male, 50% female; 0% American Indian, 6% Asian, 5% black, 11% Hispanic, 4% multiracial, 0% Pacific Islander, 65% white, 9% international; 45% from in state; 54% live on campus; 28% of students in fraternities, 35% in sororities
Most popular majors: 24% Business, Management, Marketing, and Related Support Services, 14% Social Sciences, 11% Communication, Journalism, and Related Programs, 9% Engineering, 7% Visual and Performing Arts
Expenses: 2018-2019: $54,493; room/board: $16,845
Financial aid: (214) 768-3417; 32% of undergrads determined to have financial need; average aid package $44,049

South Texas College[1]

McAllen TX
(956) 872-8311
U.S. News ranking: Reg. Coll. (W), unranked
Website: www.southtexascollege.edu/
Admissions email: N/A
Public
Application deadline (fall): N/A
Undergraduate student body: N/A full time, N/A part time
Expenses: 2017-2018: $4,020 in state, $7,620 out of state; room/board: N/A
Financial aid: N/A

Southwestern Adventist University

Keene TX
(817) 202-6749
U.S. News ranking: Reg. Coll. (W), No. 13
Website: www.swau.edu
Admissions email: admissions@swau.edu
Private; founded 1893
Affiliation: Seventh Day Adventist
Freshman admissions: selective; 2017-2018: 1,350 applied, 842 accepted. Either SAT or ACT required. SAT 25/75 percentile: 900-1140. High school rank: 10% in top tenth, 30% in top quarter, 58% in top half
Early decision deadline: N/A, notification date: N/A
Early action deadline: N/A, notification date: N/A
Application deadline (fall): rolling
Undergraduate student body: 653 full time, 146 part time; 43% male, 57% female; 0% American Indian, 4% Asian, 14% black, 45% Hispanic, 4% multiracial, 2% Pacific Islander, 22% white, 7% international; 69% from in state; 45% live on campus; N/A of students in fraternities, 0% in sororities
Most popular majors: 28% Registered Nursing/Registered Nurse, 10% Elementary Education and Teaching, 10% Psychology, General, 10% Religion/Religious Studies, 9% Biology/Biological Sciences, General
Expenses: 2018-2019: $21,564; room/board: $7,500
Financial aid: (817) 202-6262; 77% of undergrads determined to have financial need; average aid package $18,111

Southwestern Assemblies of God University[1]

Waxahachie TX
(888) 937-7248
U.S. News ranking: Reg. U. (W), second tier
Website: www.sagu.edu/
Admissions email: admissions@sagu.edu
Private; founded 1927
Application deadline (fall): rolling
Undergraduate student body: N/A full time, N/A part time
Expenses: 2017-2018: $19,994; room/board: $7,352
Financial aid: (972) 825-4730

Southwestern Christian College[1]

Terrell TX
(972) 524-3341
U.S. News ranking: Reg. Coll. (W), unranked
Website: www.swcc.edu
Admissions email: N/A
Private
Application deadline (fall): N/A
Undergraduate student body: N/A full time, N/A part time
Expenses: 2017-2018: $8,136; room/board: $5,600
Financial aid: N/A

Southwestern University

Georgetown TX
(512) 863-1200
U.S. News ranking: Nat. Lib. Arts, No. 90
Website: www.southwestern.edu
Admissions email: admission@southwestern.edu
Private; founded 1840
Affiliation: United Methodist
Freshman admissions: more selective; 2017-2018: 4,133 applied, 1,783 accepted. Either SAT or ACT required. SAT 25/75 percentile: 1110-1320. High school rank: 37% in top tenth, 73% in top quarter, 96% in top half
Early decision deadline: 11/1, notification date: 12/1
Early action deadline: 12/1, notification date: 3/1
Application deadline (fall): 2/1
Undergraduate student body: 1,367 full time, 20 part time; 43% male, 57% female; 0% American Indian, 3% Asian, 5% black, 24% Hispanic, 5% multiracial, 0% Pacific Islander, 61% white, 1% international; 90% from in state; 77% live on campus; 28% of students in fraternities, 23% in sororities
Most popular majors: 16% Business, Management, Marketing, and Related Support Services, 11% Social Sciences, 10% Biological and Biomedical Sciences, 9% Psychology, 8% Communication, Journalism, and Related Programs
Expenses: 2018-2019: $42,000; room/board: $12,000
Financial aid: (512) 863-1259; 65% of undergrads determined to have financial need; average aid package $36,217

St. Edward's University

Austin TX
(512) 448-8500
U.S. News ranking: Reg. U. (W), No. 12
Website: www.stedwards.edu
Admissions email: seu.admit@stedwards.edu
Private; founded 1885
Affiliation: Roman Catholic
Freshman admissions: selective; 2017-2018: 5,519 applied, 4,646 accepted. Either SAT or ACT required. SAT 25/75 percentile: 1080-1250. High school rank: 24% in top tenth, 58% in top quarter, 88% in top half
Early decision deadline: N/A, notification date: N/A
Early action deadline: N/A, notification date: N/A
Application deadline (fall): 5/1
Undergraduate student body: 3,528 full time, 413 part time; 39% male, 61% female; 1% American Indian, 3% Asian, 4% black, 43% Hispanic, 3% multiracial, 0% Pacific Islander, 36% white,

8% international; 87% from in state; 35% live on campus; 0% of students in fraternities, 0% in sororities
Most popular majors: 8% Communication and Media Studies, 8% Psychology, General, 6% Business Administration and Management, General, 5% Biology/Biological Sciences, General, 5% International/Global Studies
Expenses: 2018-2019: $45,178; room/board: $13,650
Financial aid: (512) 448-8516; 70% of undergrads determined to have financial need; average aid package $34,850

Stephen F. Austin State University

Nacogdoches TX
(936) 468-2504
U.S. News ranking: Reg. U. (W), No. 75
Website: www.sfasu.edu
Admissions email: admissions@sfasu.edu
Public; founded 1923
Freshman admissions: selective; 2017-2018: 11,081 applied, 7,250 accepted. Either SAT or ACT required. SAT 25/75 percentile: 990-1180. High school rank: 13% in top tenth, 43% in top quarter, 77% in top half
Early decision deadline: N/A, notification date: N/A
Early action deadline: N/A, notification date: N/A
Application deadline (fall): rolling
Undergraduate student body: 9,567 full time, 1,418 part time; 37% male, 63% female; 0% American Indian, 1% Asian, 18% black, 19% Hispanic, 4% multiracial, 0% Pacific Islander, 57% white, 1% international; 98% from in state; 43% live on campus; 12% of students in fraternities, 10% in sororities
Most popular majors: Information not available
Expenses: 2018-2019: $10,287 in state, $22,737 out of state; room/board: $8,964
Financial aid: (936) 468-2230; 65% of undergrads determined to have financial need; average aid package $12,338

St. Mary's University of San Antonio

San Antonio TX
(210) 436-3126
U.S. News ranking: Reg. U. (W), No. 15
Website: www.stmarytx.edu
Admissions email: uadm@stmarytx.edu
Private; founded 1852
Affiliation: Roman Catholic
Freshman admissions: selective; 2017-2018: 4,468 applied, 3,570 accepted. Either SAT or ACT required. SAT 25/75 percentile: 1040-1230. High school rank: 32% in top tenth, 58% in top quarter, 85% in top half
Early decision deadline: N/A, notification date: N/A
Early action deadline: N/A, notification date: N/A
Application deadline (fall): rolling
Undergraduate student body: 2,228 full time, 99 part time; 46% male, 54% female; 0% American Indian, 2% Asian, 3% black, 67% Hispanic, 1% multiracial, 0% Pacific Islander, 15% white, 9% international; 92% from in state; 56% live on campus; 7% of students in fraternities, 5% in sororities
Most popular majors: 21% Business, Management, Marketing, and Related Support Services, 16% Social Sciences, 10% Biological and Biomedical Sciences, 8% Parks, Recreation, Leisure, and Fitness Studies, 8% Psychology
Expenses: 2018-2019: $30,650; room/board: $10,270
Financial aid: (210) 436-3141; 76% of undergrads determined to have financial need; average aid package $27,098

Sul Ross State University[1]

Alpine TX
(432) 837-8050
U.S. News ranking: Reg. U. (W), second tier
Website: www.sulross.edu
Admissions email: admissions@sulross.edu
Public; founded 1917
Application deadline (fall): rolling
Undergraduate student body: N/A full time, N/A part time
Expenses: 2017-2018: $8,072 in state, $20,522 out of state; room/board: $8,802
Financial aid: (432) 837-8059

Tarleton State University

Stephenville TX
(800) 687-8236
U.S. News ranking: Reg. U. (W), No. 91
Website: www.tarleton.edu
Admissions email: uadm@tarleton.edu
Public; founded 1899
Freshman admissions: selective; 2017-2018: 7,158 applied, 5,324 accepted. Either SAT or ACT required. SAT 25/75 percentile: 960-1130. High school rank: 10% in top tenth, 29% in top quarter, 88% in top half
Early decision deadline: N/A, notification date: N/A
Early action deadline: 3/1, notification date: N/A
Application deadline (fall): 6/1
Undergraduate student body: 8,428 full time, 2,860 part time; 39% male, 61% female; 1% American Indian, 1% Asian, 8% black, 20% Hispanic, 3% multiracial, 0% Pacific Islander, 66% white, 0% international; 98% from in state; 25% live on campus; N/A of students in fraternities, N/A in sororities
Most popular majors: 19% Business, Management, Marketing, and Related Support Services, 15% Multi/Interdisciplinary Studies, 9% Agriculture, Agriculture Operations, and Related Sciences, 8% Health Professions and Related Programs, 7% Parks, Recreation, Leisure, and Fitness Studies
Expenses: 2018-2019: $8,679 in state, $21,412 out of state; room/board: $11,800
Financial aid: (254) 968-9070; 65% of undergrads determined to have financial need; average aid package $9,445

Texas A&M International University

Laredo TX
(956) 326-2200
U.S. News ranking: Reg. U. (W), No. 59
Website: www.tamiu.edu
Admissions email: enroll@tamiu.edu
Public; founded 1970
Freshman admissions: selective; 2017-2018: 7,976 applied, 4,037 accepted. Either SAT or ACT required. SAT 25/75 percentile: 930-1100. High school rank: 23% in top tenth, 52% in top quarter, 83% in top half
Early decision deadline: N/A, notification date: N/A
Early action deadline: N/A, notification date: N/A
Application deadline (fall): 8/1
Undergraduate student body: 5,191 full time, 1,608 part time; 40% male, 60% female; 0% American Indian, 0% Asian, 0% black, 95% Hispanic, 0% multiracial, 0% Pacific Islander, 2% white, 2% international; 99% from in state; 29% live on campus; 2% of students in fraternities, 2% in sororities
Most popular majors: 20% Business, Management, Marketing, and Related Support Services, 15% Homeland Security, Law Enforcement, Firefighting and Related Protective Services, 13% Health Professions and Related Programs, 12% Psychology, 9% Multi/Interdisciplinary Studies
Expenses: 2018-2019: $8,637 in state, $21,087 out of state; room/board: $8,416
Financial aid: (956) 326-2225; 84% of undergrads determined to have financial need; average aid package $9,533

Texas A&M University–College Station

College Station TX
(979) 845-3741
U.S. News ranking: Nat. U., No. 66
Website: www.tamu.edu
Admissions email: admissions@tamu.edu
Public; founded 1876
Freshman admissions: more selective; 2017-2018: 37,191 applied, 26,064 accepted. Either SAT or ACT required. SAT 25/75 percentile: 1140-1360. High school rank: 60% in top tenth, 88% in top quarter, 98% in top half
Early decision deadline: N/A, notification date: N/A
Early action deadline: N/A, notification date: N/A
Application deadline (fall): 12/1
Undergraduate student body: 46,724 full time, 6,341 part time; 52% male, 48% female; 0% American Indian, 7% Asian, 3% black, 23% Hispanic, 3% multiracial, 0% Pacific Islander, 62% white, 1% international; 96% from in state; 23% live on campus; 8% of students in fraternities, 17% in sororities
Most popular majors: 15% Business, Management, Marketing, and Related Support Services, 15% Engineering, 10% Multi/Interdisciplinary Studies, 9% Agriculture, Agriculture Operations, and Related Sciences, 8% Social Sciences
Expenses: 2018-2019: $10,968 in state, $36,636 out of state; room/board: $10,436
Financial aid: (979) 845-3236; 46% of undergrads determined to have financial need; average aid package $16,695

Texas A&M University–Commerce

Commerce TX
(903) 886-5000
U.S. News ranking: Nat. U., second tier
Website: www.tamuc.edu/
Admissions email: Admissions@tamuc.edu
Public; founded 1889
Freshman admissions: selective; 2017-2018: 9,757 applied, 3,362 accepted. Either SAT or ACT required. SAT 25/75 percentile: 960-1150. High school rank: 15% in top tenth, 43% in top quarter, 77% in top half
Early decision deadline: N/A, notification date: N/A
Early action deadline: N/A, notification date: N/A
Application deadline (fall): 8/15
Undergraduate student body: 5,650 full time, 2,381 part time; 40% male, 60% female; 1% American Indian, 1% Asian, 23% black, 21% Hispanic, 7% multiracial, 0% Pacific Islander, 45% white, 2% international; 97% from in state; 31% live on campus; 5% of students in fraternities, 5% in sororities
Most popular majors: 36% Multi/Interdisciplinary Studies, 8% Business, Management, Marketing, and Related Support Services, 6% Parks, Recreation, Leisure, and Fitness Studies, 5% Homeland Security, Law Enforcement, Firefighting and Related Protective Services, 4% Visual and Performing Arts
Expenses: 2018-2019: $8,748 in state, $21,198 out of state; room/board: $8,326
Financial aid: (903) 886-5091; 75% of undergrads determined to have financial need; average aid package $9,553

Texas A&M University–Corpus Christi

Corpus Christi TX
(361) 825-2624
U.S. News ranking: Nat. U., second tier
Website: www.tamucc.edu/
Admissions email: admiss@tamucc.edu
Public; founded 1947
Freshman admissions: less selective; 2017-2018: 8,812 applied, 7,563 accepted. Either SAT or ACT required. SAT 25/75 percentile: 870-1080. High school rank: 7% in top tenth, 27% in top quarter, 73% in top half
Early decision deadline: N/A, notification date: N/A
Early action deadline: N/A, notification date: N/A
Application deadline (fall): 7/1
Undergraduate student body: 8,357 full time, 1,817 part time; 42% male, 58% female; 0% American Indian, 3% Asian, 6% black, 50% Hispanic, 1% multiracial, 0% Pacific Islander, 36% white, 2% international; 97% from in state; 25% live on campus; N/A of students in fraternities, N/A in sororities
Most popular majors: 19% Health Professions and Related Programs, 18% Business, Management, Marketing, and Related Support Services, 11% Parks, Recreation, Leisure, and Fitness Studies, 10% Multi/Interdisciplinary Studies, 7% Psychology
Expenses: 2018-2019: $9,308 in state, $4,316 out of state; room/board: $10,220
Financial aid: (361) 825-2332; 86% of undergrads determined to have financial need; average aid package $11,451

Texas A&M University–Kingsville

Kingsville TX
(361) 593-2315
U.S. News ranking: Nat. U., second tier
Website: www.tamuk.edu
Admissions email: admissions@tamuk.edu
Public; founded 1925
Freshman admissions: selective; 2017-2018: 6,717 applied, 5,651 accepted. Either SAT or ACT required. ACT 25/75 percentile: 17-22. High school rank: 15% in top tenth, 41% in top quarter, 77% in top half
Early decision deadline: N/A, notification date: N/A
Early action deadline: N/A, notification date: N/A
Application deadline (fall): 8/17
Undergraduate student body: 5,020 full time, 1,755 part time; 51% male, 49% female; 0% American Indian, 1% Asian, 6% black, 71% Hispanic, 0% multiracial, 0% Pacific Islander, 17% white, 4% international; 99% from in state; 27% live on campus; N/A of students in fraternities, N/A in sororities
Most popular majors: 23% Engineering, 10% Multi/Interdisciplinary Studies, 9% Business, Management, Marketing, and Related Support Services, 8% Biological and Biomedical Sciences, 8% Health Professions and Related Programs
Expenses: 2018-2019: $8,462 in state, $20,912 out of state; room/board: $8,760
Financial aid: (361) 593-3911; 77% of undergrads determined to have financial need; average aid package $10,278

Texas A&M University–Texarkana

Texarkana TX
(903) 223-3069
U.S. News ranking: Reg. U. (W), second tier
Website: www.tamut.edu
Admissions email: admissions@tamut.edu
Public; founded 1971
Freshman admissions: selective; 2017-2018: 3,764 applied, 3,515 accepted. Neither SAT nor ACT required. ACT 25/75 percentile: 19-23. High school rank: 7% in top tenth, 30% in top quarter, 70% in top half
Early decision deadline: N/A, notification date: N/A
Early action deadline: N/A, notification date: N/A
Application deadline (fall): rolling
Undergraduate student body: 1,191 full time, 453 part time; 39% male, 61% female; 1% American Indian, 1% Asian, 14% black, 15% Hispanic, 4% multiracial, 0% Pacific Islander, 60% white, 2% international; 80% from in state; 18% live on campus; N/A of students in fraternities, N/A in sororities
Most popular majors: 30% Multi/Interdisciplinary Studies, 21% Business, Management, Marketing, and Related Support Services, 10% Psychology, 8% Liberal Arts and Sciences, General Studies and Humanities, 5% Biological and Biomedical Sciences
Expenses: 2018-2019: $7,023 in state, $8,120 out of state; room/board: $8,732
Financial aid: (903) 334-6601; 71% of undergrads determined to have financial need; average aid package $10,368

Texas Christian University

Fort Worth TX
(800) 828-3764
U.S. News ranking: Nat. U., No. 80
Website: www.tcu.edu
Admissions email: frogmail@tcu.edu
Private; founded 1873
Affiliation: Christian Church (Disciples of Christ)
Freshman admissions: more selective; 2017-2018: 19,740 applied, 8,110 accepted. Either SAT or ACT required. ACT 25/75 percentile: 25-30. High school rank: 48% in top tenth, 77% in top quarter, 95% in top half
Early decision deadline: 11/1, notification date: 12/5
Early action deadline: 11/1, notification date: 12/15
Application deadline (fall): 2/1
Undergraduate student body: 8,738 full time, 273 part time; 41% male, 59% female; 1% American Indian, 3% Asian, 5% black, 13% Hispanic, 0% multiracial, 0% Pacific Islander, 71% white, 5% international; 54% from in state; 48% live on campus; 41% of students in fraternities, 58% in sororities
Most popular majors: 26% Business, Management, Marketing, and Related Support Services, 14% Communication, Journalism, and Related Programs, 13% Health Professions and Related Programs, 10% Social Sciences, 6% Visual and Performing Arts
Expenses: 2018-2019: $46,950; room/board: $12,804
Financial aid: (817) 257-7858; 39% of undergrads determined to have financial need; average aid package $30,763

Texas College[1]

Tyler TX
(903) 593-8311
U.S. News ranking: Reg. Coll. (W), unranked
Website: www.texascollege.edu
Admissions email: cmarshall-biggins@texascollege.edu
Private
Application deadline (fall): N/A
Undergraduate student body: N/A full time, N/A part time
Expenses: 2017-2018: $10,008; room/board: $7,200
Financial aid: N/A

Texas Lutheran University

Seguin TX
(800) 771-8521
U.S. News ranking: Reg. Coll. (W), No. 4
Website: www.tlu.edu
Admissions email: admissions@tlu.edu
Private; founded 1891
Affiliation: Evangelical Lutheran Church
Freshman admissions: selective; 2017-2018: 2,250 applied, 1,092 accepted. Either SAT or ACT required. SAT 25/75 percentile: 970-1150. High school rank: 17% in top tenth, 44% in top quarter, 78% in top half
Early decision deadline: N/A, notification date: N/A
Early action deadline: 12/15, notification date: 2/15
Application deadline (fall): 2/1
Undergraduate student body: 1,305 full time, 54 part time; 48% male, 52% female; 0% American Indian, 1% Asian, 11% black, 34% Hispanic, 1% multiracial, 0% Pacific Islander, 51% white, 0% international; 99% from in state; 60% live on campus; 7% of students in fraternities, 11% in sororities
Most popular majors: 26% Business, Management, Marketing, and Related Support Services, 11% Parks, Recreation, Leisure, and Fitness Studies, 10% Education, 8% Social Sciences, 6% Biological and Biomedical Sciences
Expenses: 2018-2019: $29,960; room/board: $10,150
Financial aid: (830) 372-8075; 82% of undergrads determined to have financial need; average aid package $25,526

Texas Southern University

Houston TX
(713) 313-7071
U.S. News ranking: Nat. U., second tier
Website: www.tsu.edu
Admissions email: admissions@tsu.edu
Public; founded 1947
Freshman admissions: least selective; 2017-2018: 12,995 applied, 8,663 accepted. Either SAT or ACT required. SAT 25/75 percentile: 717-912. High school rank: 4% in top tenth, 16% in top quarter, 47% in top half
Early decision deadline: 12/1, notification date: N/A
Early action deadline: N/A, notification date: N/A
Application deadline (fall): 8/1
Undergraduate student body: 6,695 full time, 1,272 part time; 44% male, 56% female; 1% American Indian, 2% Asian, 79% black, 7% Hispanic, 2% multiracial, 0% Pacific Islander, 1% white, 9% international; 90% from in state; 27% live on campus; N/A of students in fraternities, N/A in sororities
Most popular majors: 8% Biology/Biological Sciences, General, 8% Business Administration and Management, General, 7% Health/Health Care Administration/Management, 5% Banking and Financial Support Services, 5% Criminal Justice/Law Enforcement Administration
Expenses: 2017-2018: $9,173 in state, $21,623 out of state; room/board: $9,664
Financial aid: (713) 313-7071

Texas State University

San Marcos TX
(512) 245-2364
U.S. News ranking: Nat. U., second tier
Website: www.txstate.edu
Admissions email: admissions@txstate.edu
Public; founded 1899
Freshman admissions: selective; 2017-2018: 24,277 applied, 17,717 accepted. Either SAT or ACT required. SAT 25/75 percentile: 1020-1200. High school rank: 14% in top tenth, 51% in top quarter, 94% in top half
Early decision deadline: N/A, notification date: N/A
Early action deadline: N/A, notification date: N/A
Application deadline (fall): 5/1
Undergraduate student body: 28,019 full time, 6,161 part time; 43% male, 57% female; 0% American Indian, 2% Asian, 10% black, 37% Hispanic, 4% multiracial, 0% Pacific Islander, 46% white, 1% international; 98% from in state; 20% live on campus; 5% of students in fraternities, 5% in sororities
Most popular majors: 6% Business Administration and Management, General, 6% Psychology, General, 5% Kinesiology and Exercise Science, 5% Multi-/Interdisciplinary Studies, Other, 4% Marketing/Marketing Management, General
Expenses: 2018-2019: $10,935 in state, $23,385 out of state; room/board: $9,374
Financial aid: (512) 245-2315; 61% of undergrads determined to have financial need; average aid package $11,383

Texas Tech University

Lubbock TX
(806) 742-1480
U.S. News ranking: Nat. U., No. 187
Website: www.ttu.edu
Admissions email: admissions@ttu.edu
Public; founded 1923
Freshman admissions: selective; 2017-2018: 25,207 applied, 17,438 accepted. Either SAT or ACT required. SAT 25/75 percentile: 1070-1240. High school rank: 19% in top tenth, 50% in top quarter, 85% in top half
Early decision deadline: N/A, notification date: N/A
Early action deadline: N/A, notification date: N/A
Application deadline (fall): 8/1
Undergraduate student body: 27,318 full time, 3,419 part time; 54% male, 46% female; 0% American Indian, 2% Asian, 6% black, 28% Hispanic, 2% multiracial, 0% Pacific Islander, 56% white, 5% international; 94% from in state; 26% live on campus; 5% of students in fraternities, 8% in sororities
Most popular majors: 20% Business, Management, Marketing, and Related Support Services, 13% Engineering, 10% Multi/Interdisciplinary Studies, 7% Communication, Journalism, and Related Programs, 7% Parks, Recreation, Leisure, and Fitness Studies
Expenses: 2018-2019: $11,045 in state, $23,495 out of state; room/board: $9,772
Financial aid: (806) 834-1780; 49% of undergrads determined to have financial need; average aid package $10,293

Texas Wesleyan University

Fort Worth TX
(817) 531-4422
U.S. News ranking: Reg. U. (W), No. 64
Website: www.txwes.edu
Admissions email: admission@txwes.edu
Private; founded 1890
Affiliation: United Methodist
Freshman admissions: selective; 2017-2018: 4,097 applied, 1,404 accepted. Either SAT or ACT required. SAT 25/75 percentile: 930-1100. High school rank: 17% in top tenth, 38% in top quarter, 68% in top half
Early decision deadline: N/A, notification date: N/A
Early action deadline: N/A, notification date: N/A
Application deadline (fall): rolling
Undergraduate student body: 1,509 full time, 319 part time; 47% male, 53% female; 1% American Indian, 1% Asian, 16% black, 31% Hispanic, 7% multiracial, 0% Pacific Islander, 29% white, 13% international; 85% from in state; 32% live on campus; 5% of students in fraternities, 4% in sororities
Most popular majors: 16% Multi-/Interdisciplinary Studies, Other, 9% Business Administration and Management, General, 9% Management Science, 9% Psychology, General, 8% Finance, General
Expenses: 2018-2019: $30,300; room/board: N/A
Financial aid: (817) 531-4420; 74% of undergrads determined to have financial need; average aid package $23,340

Texas Woman's University

Denton TX
(940) 898-3188
U.S. News ranking: Nat. U., second tier
Website: www.twu.edu
Admissions email: admissions@twu.edu
Public; founded 1901
Freshman admissions: less selective; 2017-2018: 5,502 applied, 4,716 accepted. Neither SAT nor ACT required. SAT 25/75 percentile: 890-1080. High school rank: 15% in top tenth, 47% in top quarter, 81% in top half
Early decision deadline: N/A, notification date: N/A
Early action deadline: N/A, notification date: N/A
Application deadline (fall): 8/25
Undergraduate student body: 6,968 full time, 3,341 part time; 12% male, 88% female; 0% American Indian, 8% Asian, 17% black, 30% Hispanic, 4% multiracial, 0% Pacific Islander, 38% white, 1% international; 99% from in state; 13% live on campus; 3% of students in fraternities, 4% in sororities
Most popular majors: 30% Health Professions and Related Programs, 12% Liberal Arts and Sciences, General Studies and Humanities, 11% Business, Management, Marketing, and Related Support Services, 11% Multi/Interdisciplinary Studies, 6% Family and Consumer Sciences/Human Sciences
Expenses: 2018-2019: $9,360 in state, $21,540 out of state; room/board: $8,181
Financial aid: (940) 898-3064; 69% of undergrads determined to have financial need; average aid package $13,916

Trinity University

San Antonio TX
(800) 874-6489
U.S. News ranking: Reg. U. (W), No. 2
Website: www.trinity.edu
Admissions email: admissions@trinity.edu
Private; founded 1869
Affiliation: Presbyterian
Freshman admissions: more selective; 2017-2018: 7,663 applied, 2,946 accepted. Either SAT or ACT required. ACT 25/75 percentile: 27-32. High school rank: 44% in top tenth, 76% in top quarter, 97% in top half

Early decision deadline: 11/1, notification date: 12/15
Early action deadline: 1/1, notification date: 2/15
Application deadline (fall): 2/1
Undergraduate student body: 2,383 full time, 45 part time; 47% male, 53% female; 0% American Indian, 7% Asian, 4% black, 21% Hispanic, 5% multiracial, 0% Pacific Islander, 56% white, 6% international; 78% from in state; 80% live on campus; 17% of students in fraternities, 32% in sororities
Most popular majors: 18% Business, Management, Marketing, and Related Support Services, 14% Social Sciences, 10% Biological and Biomedical Sciences, 8% Communication, Journalism, and Related Programs, 7% Physical Sciences
Expenses: 2018-2019: $42,976; room/board: $13,464
Financial aid: (210) 999-8005; 46% of undergrads determined to have financial need; average aid package $38,968

University of Dallas

Irving TX
(800) 628-6999
U.S. News ranking: Reg. U. (W), No. 14
Website: www.udallas.edu
Admissions email: ugadmis@udallas.edu
Private; founded 1956
Affiliation: Roman Catholic
Freshman admissions: more selective; 2017-2018: 3,857 applied, 1,830 accepted. Either SAT or ACT required. SAT 25/75 percentile: 1140-1370. High school rank: 37% in top tenth, 71% in top quarter, 95% in top half
Early decision deadline: N/A, notification date: N/A
Early action deadline: 12/1, notification date: 1/15
Application deadline (fall): 8/1
Undergraduate student body: 1,425 full time, 25 part time; 46% male, 54% female; 1% American Indian, 6% Asian, 2% black, 23% Hispanic, 3% multiracial, 0% Pacific Islander, 61% white, 4% international; 52% from in state; 43% live on campus; 0% of students in fraternities, 0% in sororities
Most popular majors: 18% Biological and Biomedical Sciences, 14% Social Sciences, 13% Business, Management, Marketing, and Related Support Services, 11% Theology and Religious Vocations, 10% English Language and Literature/Letters
Expenses: 2018-2019: $40,652; room/board: $12,400
Financial aid: (972) 721-5266; 64% of undergrads determined to have financial need; average aid package $32,804

University of Houston

Houston TX
(713) 743-1010
U.S. News ranking: Nat. U., No. 171
Website: www.uh.edu
Admissions email: admissions@uh.edu
Public; founded 1927
Freshman admissions: more selective; 2017-2018: 20,768 applied, 12,691 accepted. Either SAT or ACT required. SAT 25/75 percentile: 1110-1280. High school rank: 32% in top tenth, 65% in top quarter, 88% in top half
Early decision deadline: N/A, notification date: N/A
Early action deadline: N/A, notification date: N/A
Application deadline (fall): 6/15
Undergraduate student body: 27,159 full time, 10,056 part time; 50% male, 50% female; 0% American Indian, 22% Asian, 10% black, 35% Hispanic, 3% multiracial, 0% Pacific Islander, 24% white, 4% international; 99% from in state; 17% live on campus; 4% of students in fraternities, 5% in sororities
Most popular majors: 29% Business, Management, Marketing, and Related Support Services, 9% Engineering, 6% Biological and Biomedical Sciences, 6% Communication, Journalism, and Related Programs, 6% Psychology
Expenses: 2018-2019: $10,890 in state, $26,340 out of state; room/board: $9,104
Financial aid: (713) 743-1010; 63% of undergrads determined to have financial need; average aid package $12,374

University of Houston–Clear Lake

Houston TX
(281) 283-2500
U.S. News ranking: Reg. U. (W), No. 61
Website: www.uhcl.edu
Admissions email: admissions@uhcl.edu
Public; founded 1974
Freshman admissions: selective; 2017-2018: 1,037 applied, 752 accepted. Either SAT or ACT required. SAT 25/75 percentile: 1020-1190. High school rank: 15% in top tenth, 43% in top quarter, 79% in top half
Early decision deadline: N/A, notification date: N/A
Early action deadline: N/A, notification date: N/A
Application deadline (fall): 6/1
Undergraduate student body: 2,946 full time, 2,852 part time; 36% male, 64% female; 0% American Indian, 6% Asian, 8% black, 39% Hispanic, 3% multiracial, 0% Pacific Islander, 41% white, 2% international; N/A from in state; 3% live on campus; N/A of students in fraternities, N/A in sororities
Most popular majors: 26% Business, Management, Marketing, and Related Support Services, 22% Multi/Interdisciplinary Studies, 10% Psychology, 5% Health Professions and Related Programs, 5% Social Sciences
Expenses: 2018-2019: $8,500 in state, $24,731 out of state; room/board: $8,620
Financial aid: (281) 283-2480; 67% of undergrads determined to have financial need; average aid package $9,059

University of Houston–Downtown

Houston TX
(713) 221-8522
U.S. News ranking: Reg. U. (W), second tier
Website: www.uhd.edu
Admissions email: uhdadmit@uhd.edu
Public; founded 1974
Freshman admissions: least selective; 2017-2018: 3,931 applied, 3,305 accepted. Either SAT or ACT required. SAT 25/75 percentile: 920-1078. High school rank: 6% in top tenth, 32% in top quarter, 76% in top half
Early decision deadline: N/A, notification date: N/A
Early action deadline: N/A, notification date: N/A
Application deadline (fall): 6/1
Undergraduate student body: 6,320 full time, 6,087 part time; 39% male, 61% female; 0% American Indian, 9% Asian, 20% black, 48% Hispanic, 1% multiracial, 0% Pacific Islander, 16% white, 5% international; 99% from in state; 0% live on campus; 1% of students in fraternities, 1% in sororities
Most popular majors: 34% Business, Management, Marketing, and Related Support Services, 26% Multi/Interdisciplinary Studies, 9% Homeland Security, Law Enforcement, Firefighting and Related Protective Services, 9% Psychology, 4% Communication, Journalism, and Related Programs
Expenses: 2018-2019: $7,832 in state, $20,282 out of state; room/board: N/A
Financial aid: (713) 221-8041; 74% of undergrads determined to have financial need; average aid package $9,634

University of Houston–Victoria[1]

Victoria TX
(877) 970-4848
U.S. News ranking: Reg. U. (W), second tier
Website: www.uhv.edu/
Admissions email: admissions@uhv.edu
Public; founded 1973
Application deadline (fall): 8/1
Undergraduate student body: N/A full time, N/A part time
Expenses: 2017-2018: $7,468 in state, $21,075 out of state; room/board: $7,663
Financial aid: N/A

University of Mary Hardin-Baylor

Belton TX
(254) 295-4520
U.S. News ranking: Reg. U. (W), No. 54
Website: www.umhb.edu
Admissions email: admission@umhb.edu
Private; founded 1845
Affiliation: Baptist
Freshman admissions: selective; 2017-2018: 8,289 applied, 6,535 accepted. Either SAT or ACT required. SAT 25/75 percentile: 1020-1200. High school rank: 17% in top tenth, 45% in top quarter, 75% in top half
Early decision deadline: N/A, notification date: N/A
Early action deadline: N/A, notification date: N/A
Application deadline (fall): rolling
Undergraduate student body: 3,045 full time, 288 part time; 36% male, 64% female; 1% American Indian, 2% Asian, 15% black, 21% Hispanic, 3% multiracial, 0% Pacific Islander, 56% white, 1% international; 97% from in state; 56% live on campus; N/A of students in fraternities, N/A in sororities
Most popular majors: 26% Health Professions and Related Programs, 16% Business, Management, Marketing, and Related Support Services, 12% Education, 7% Parks, Recreation, Leisure, and Fitness Studies, 6% Biological and Biomedical Sciences
Expenses: 2018-2019: $28,750; room/board: $8,446
Financial aid: (254) 295-4517; 80% of undergrads determined to have financial need; average aid package $17,854

University of North Texas

Denton TX
(940) 565-2681
U.S. News ranking: Nat. U., second tier
Website: www.unt.edu
Admissions email: unt.freshmen@unt.edu
Public; founded 1890
Freshman admissions: selective; 2017-2018: 18,508 applied, 13,385 accepted. Either SAT or ACT required. SAT 25/75 percentile: 1060-1260. High school rank: 20% in top tenth, 53% in top quarter, 90% in top half
Early decision deadline: N/A, notification date: N/A
Early action deadline: N/A, notification date: N/A
Application deadline (fall): 8/1
Undergraduate student body: 25,618 full time, 5,787 part time; 48% male, 52% female; 0% American Indian, 6% Asian, 14% black, 25% Hispanic, 4% multiracial, 0% Pacific Islander, 46% white, 3% international; 97% from in state; 19% live on campus; 6% of students in fraternities, 6% in sororities
Most popular majors: 20% Business, Management, Marketing, and Related Support Services, 11% Multi/Interdisciplinary Studies, 9% Liberal Arts and Sciences, General Studies and Humanities, 8% Visual and Performing Arts, 7% Communication, Journalism, and Related Programs
Expenses: 2018-2019: $10,906 in state, $23,716 out of state; room/board: $9,610
Financial aid: (940) 565-3901; 62% of undergrads determined to have financial need; average aid package $11,882

University of North Texas at Dallas

Dallas TX
U.S. News ranking: Reg. U. (W), second tier
Admissions email: N/A
Public; founded 2010
Freshman admissions: less selective; 2017-2018: 1,483 applied, 1,097 accepted. Either SAT or ACT required. SAT 25/75 percentile: 820-990. High school rank: 16% in top tenth, 33% in top quarter, 65% in top half
Early decision deadline: N/A, notification date: N/A
Early action deadline: N/A, notification date: N/A
Application deadline (fall): 8/10
Undergraduate student body: 1,705 full time, 1,022 part time; 32% male, 68% female; 0% American Indian, 2% Asian, 31% black, 53% Hispanic, 2% multiracial, 0% Pacific Islander, 10% white, 1% international; 99% from in state; 3% live on campus; N/A of students in fraternities, N/A in sororities
Most popular majors: 36% Multi/Interdisciplinary Studies, 27% Business, Management, Marketing, and Related Support Services, 12% Social Sciences, 10% Homeland Security, Law Enforcement, Firefighting and Related Protective Services, 8% Psychology
Expenses: 2017-2018: $7,848 in state, $20,088 out of state; room/board: $8,398
Financial aid: N/A

University of St. Thomas

Houston TX
(713) 525-3500
U.S. News ranking: Reg. U. (W), No. 28
Website: www.stthom.edu
Admissions email: admissions@stthom.edu
Private; founded 1947
Affiliation: Roman Catholic
Freshman admissions: selective; 2017-2018: 1,060 applied, 858 accepted. Either SAT or ACT required. SAT 25/75 percentile: 1070-1235. High school rank: 23% in top tenth, 29% in top quarter, 84% in top half
Early decision deadline: N/A, notification date: N/A
Early action deadline: 12/1, notification date: 12/15
Application deadline (fall): 5/1
Undergraduate student body: 1,436 full time, 428 part time; 38% male, 62% female; 0% American Indian, 11% Asian, 6% black, 45% Hispanic, 3% multiracial, 0% Pacific Islander, 23% white, 9% international; 97% from in state; 24% live on campus; N/A of students in fraternities, N/A in sororities
Most popular majors: 24% Business, Management, Marketing, and Related Support Services, 13% Biological and Biomedical Sciences, 13% Liberal Arts and Sciences, General Studies and Humanities, 10% Health Professions and Related Programs, 9% Social Sciences

More @ usnews.com/bestcolleges

Expenses: 2018-2019: $33,580; room/board: $9,070
Financial aid: (713) 525-2151; 69% of undergrads determined to have financial need; average aid package $24,587

University of Texas–Arlington

Arlington TX
(817) 272-6287
U.S. News ranking: Nat. U., No. 221
Website: www.uta.edu
Admissions email: admissions@uta.edu
Public; founded 1895
Freshman admissions: selective; 2017-2018: 12,333 applied, 8,784 accepted. Either SAT or ACT required. SAT 25/75 percentile: 1060-1270. High school rank: 31% in top tenth, 75% in top quarter, 96% in top half
Early decision deadline: N/A, notification date: N/A
Early action deadline: N/A, notification date: N/A
Application deadline (fall): N/A
Undergraduate student body: 17,819 full time, 15,488 part time; 39% male, 61% female; 0% American Indian, 11% Asian, 15% black, 27% Hispanic, 4% multiracial, 0% Pacific Islander, 36% white, 4% international; 86% from in state; 5% live on campus; 7% of students in fraternities, 5% in sororities
Most popular majors: 44% Health Professions and Related Programs, 12% Business, Management, Marketing, and Related Support Services, 6% Engineering, 6% Liberal Arts and Sciences, General Studies and Humanities, 4% Biological and Biomedical Sciences
Expenses: 2018-2019: $10,496 in state, $26,533 out of state; room/board: $10,302
Financial aid: (817) 272-3568; 78% of undergrads determined to have financial need; average aid package $11,344

University of Texas–Austin

Austin TX
(512) 475-7399
U.S. News ranking: Nat. U., No. 49
Website: www.utexas.edu
Admissions email: N/A
Public; founded 1883
Freshman admissions: more selective; 2017-2018: 51,033 applied, 18,620 accepted. Either SAT or ACT required. SAT 25/75 percentile: 1230-1460. High school rank: 74% in top tenth, 95% in top quarter, 99% in top half
Early decision deadline: N/A, notification date: N/A
Early action deadline: N/A, notification date: N/A
Application deadline (fall): 12/1
Undergraduate student body: 37,740 full time, 2,752 part time; 47% male, 53% female; 0% American Indian, 21% Asian, 4% black, 23% Hispanic, 4% multiracial, 0% Pacific Islander, 41% white, 5% international; 94% from in state; 18% live on campus; 15% of students in fraternities, 18% in sororities
Most popular majors: 12% Business, Management, Marketing, and Related Support Services, 12% Engineering, 11% Biological and Biomedical Sciences, 11% Communication, Journalism, and Related Programs, 11% Social Sciences
Expenses: 2018-2019: $10,606 in state, $37,480 out of state; room/board: $10,804
Financial aid: (512) 475-6282; 40% of undergrads determined to have financial need; average aid package $12,154

University of Texas–Dallas

Richardson TX
(972) 883-2270
U.S. News ranking: Nat. U., No. 129
Website: www.utdallas.edu
Admissions email: interest@utdallas.edu
Public; founded 1969
Freshman admissions: more selective; 2017-2018: 11,791 applied, 8,965 accepted. Either SAT or ACT required. SAT 25/75 percentile: 1220-1430. High school rank: 36% in top tenth, 64% in top quarter, 89% in top half
Early decision deadline: N/A, notification date: N/A
Early action deadline: N/A, notification date: N/A
Application deadline (fall): 5/1
Undergraduate student body: 15,294 full time, 3,094 part time; 57% male, 43% female; 0% American Indian, 31% Asian, 6% black, 18% Hispanic, 4% multiracial, 0% Pacific Islander, 34% white, 4% international; 96% from in state; 26% live on campus; 5% of students in fraternities, 7% in sororities
Most popular majors: 24% Business, Management, Marketing, and Related Support Services, 14% Biological and Biomedical Sciences, 12% Engineering, 10% Computer and Information Sciences and Support Services, 9% Health Professions and Related Programs
Expenses: 2018-2019: $13,034 in state, $36,876 out of state; room/board: $11,532
Financial aid: (972) 883-4020; 53% of undergrads determined to have financial need; average aid package $13,489

University of Texas–El Paso

El Paso TX
(915) 747-5890
U.S. News ranking: Nat. U., second tier
Website: www.utep.edu
Admissions email: futureminer@utep.edu
Public; founded 1914
Freshman admissions: less selective; 2017-2018: 9,382 applied, 9,382 accepted. Neither SAT nor ACT required. SAT 25/75 percentile: 920-1130. High school rank: 17% in top tenth, 40% in top quarter, 68% in top half
Early decision deadline: N/A, notification date: N/A
Early action deadline: N/A, notification date: N/A
Application deadline (fall): 9/5
Undergraduate student body: 14,025 full time, 7,316 part time; 47% male, 53% female; 0% American Indian, 1% Asian, 2% black, 84% Hispanic, 1% multiracial, 0% Pacific Islander, 6% white, 6% international; 96% from in state; N/A live on campus; N/A of students in fraternities, N/A in sororities
Most popular majors: 18% Business, Management, Marketing, and Related Support Services, 11% Engineering, 11% Health Professions and Related Programs, 9% Biological and Biomedical Sciences, 8% Multi/Interdisciplinary Studies
Expenses: 2017-2018: $7,651 in state, $21,396 out of state; room/board: $9,495
Financial aid: (915) 747-5204; 78% of undergrads determined to have financial need; average aid package $11,820

University of Texas of the Permian Basin

Odessa TX
(432) 552-2605
U.S. News ranking: Reg. U. (W), No. 88
Website: www.utpb.edu
Admissions email: admissions@utpb.edu
Public; founded 1973
Freshman admissions: selective; 2017-2018: 940 applied, 768 accepted. Either SAT or ACT required. SAT 25/75 percentile: 900-1120. High school rank: 23% in top tenth, 56% in top quarter, 86% in top half
Early decision deadline: N/A, notification date: N/A
Early action deadline: N/A, notification date: N/A
Application deadline (fall): 8/26
Undergraduate student body: 2,192 full time, 3,873 part time; 43% male, 57% female; 0% American Indian, 2% Asian, 6% black, 53% Hispanic, 2% multiracial, 0% Pacific Islander, 33% white, 3% international; 97% from in state; 19% live on campus; 0% of students in fraternities, 0% in sororities
Most popular majors: 23% Business Administration and Management, General, 12% Psychology, General, 10% Petroleum Engineering, 7% Registered Nursing/Registered Nurse, 6% Multi-/Interdisciplinary Studies, Other
Expenses: 2018-2019: $7,124 in state, $8,274 out of state; room/board: $10,944
Financial aid: (432) 552-2620; 83% of undergrads determined to have financial need; average aid package $8,486

University of Texas–Rio Grande Valley

Edinburg TX
(888) 882-4026
U.S. News ranking: Nat. U., second tier
Website: www.utrgv.edu/en-us/index.htm
Admissions email: admissions@utrgv.edu
Public; founded 2013
Freshman admissions: selective; 2017-2018: 10,540 applied, 8,483 accepted. Either SAT or ACT required. ACT 25/75 percentile: 17-22. High school rank: 21% in top tenth, 53% in top quarter, 85% in top half
Early decision deadline: N/A, notification date: N/A
Early action deadline: N/A, notification date: N/A
Application deadline (fall): 7/1
Undergraduate student body: 18,754 full time, 5,880 part time; 44% male, 56% female; 0% American Indian, 1% Asian, 0% black, 92% Hispanic, 0% multiracial, 0% Pacific Islander, 3% white, 2% international
Most popular majors: 10% Criminal Justice/Law Enforcement Administration, 9% Biology/Biological Sciences, General, 8% Psychology, General, 6% Multi-/Interdisciplinary Studies, Other, 6% Rehabilitation Science
Expenses: 2017-2018: $7,587 in state, $17,547 out of state; room/board: $7,986
Financial aid: N/A

University of Texas–San Antonio

San Antonio TX
(210) 458-8000
U.S. News ranking: Nat. U., second tier
Website: www.utsa.edu
Admissions email: prospects@utsa.edu
Public; founded 1969
Freshman admissions: selective; 2017-2018: 15,973 applied, 12,692 accepted. Either SAT or ACT required. SAT 25/75 percentile: 1030-1210. High school rank: 17% in top tenth, 58% in top quarter, 90% in top half
Early decision deadline: N/A, notification date: N/A
Early action deadline: N/A, notification date: N/A
Application deadline (fall): 6/1
Undergraduate student body: 21,510 full time, 4,934 part time; 50% male, 50% female; 0% American Indian, 6% Asian, 9% black, 55% Hispanic, 3% multiracial, 0% Pacific Islander, 23% white, 2% international; 98% from in state; 12% live on campus; 3% of students in fraternities, 5% in sororities
Most popular majors: 21% Business, Management, Marketing, and Related Support Services, 10% Engineering, 8% Psychology, 7% Biological and Biomedical Sciences, 6% Education
Expenses: 2018-2019: $9,468 in state, $23,830 out of state; room/board: $7,143
Financial aid: (210) 458-8000; 68% of undergrads determined to have financial need; average aid package $9,937

University of Texas–Tyler

Tyler TX
(903) 566-7203
U.S. News ranking: Reg. U. (W), No. 81
Website: www.uttyler.edu
Admissions email: admissions@uttyler.edu
Public; founded 1971
Freshman admissions: selective; 2017-2018: 2,511 applied, 1,632 accepted. Either SAT or ACT required. SAT 25/75 percentile: 1070-1240. High school rank: 17% in top tenth, 47% in top quarter, 77% in top half
Early decision deadline: N/A, notification date: N/A
Early action deadline: N/A, notification date: N/A
Application deadline (fall): 8/28
Undergraduate student body: 4,845 full time, 2,595 part time; 45% male, 55% female; 0% American Indian, 4% Asian, 10% black, 20% Hispanic, 4% multiracial, 0% Pacific Islander, 58% white, 2% international; 99% from in state; 19% live on campus; 1% of students in fraternities, 2% in sororities
Most popular majors: Information not available
Expenses: 2018-2019: $8,292 in state, $21,530 out of state; room/board: $9,502
Financial aid: (903) 566-7180; 73% of undergrads determined to have financial need; average aid package $7,828

University of the Incarnate Word

San Antonio TX
(210) 829-6005
U.S. News ranking: Reg. U. (W), No. 39
Website: www.uiw.edu
Admissions email: admis@uiwtx.edu
Private; founded 1881
Affiliation: Roman Catholic
Freshman admissions: selective; 2017-2018: 4,149 applied, 3,894 accepted. Either SAT or ACT required. SAT 25/75 percentile: 940-1120. High school rank: 16% in top tenth, 40% in top quarter, 70% in top half
Early decision deadline: N/A, notification date: N/A
Early action deadline: N/A, notification date: N/A
Application deadline (fall): rolling
Undergraduate student body: 4,461 full time, 1,533 part time; 40% male, 60% female; 0% American Indian, 2% Asian, 7% black, 56% Hispanic, 2% multiracial, 0% Pacific Islander, 19% white, 5% international; 92% from in state; 17% live on campus; N/A of students in fraternities, N/A in sororities
Most popular majors: 12% Business Administration and Management, General, 8% Biology/Biological Sciences, General, 7% Psychology, General,

6% Business Administration, Management and Operations, Other, 6% Registered Nursing/ Registered Nurse
Expenses: 2018-2019: $31,484; room/board: $12,716
Financial aid: (210) 829-6008; 76% of undergrads determined to have financial need; average aid package $18,750

Wade College[1]

Dallas TX
U.S. News ranking: Reg. Coll. (W), unranked
Admissions email: N/A
For-profit
Application deadline (fall): N/A
Undergraduate student body: N/A full time, N/A part time
Expenses: 2017-2018: $13,654; room/board: N/A
Financial aid: N/A

Wayland Baptist University

Plainview TX
(806) 291-3500
U.S. News ranking: Reg. U. (W), second tier
Website: www.wbu.edu
Admissions email: admitme@wbu.edu
Private; founded 1908
Affiliation: Baptist
Freshman admissions: less selective; 2017-2018: 652 applied, 642 accepted. Either SAT or ACT required. ACT 25/75 percentile: 17-23. High school rank: 10% in top tenth, 21% in top quarter, 57% in top half
Early decision deadline: N/A, notification date: N/A
Early action deadline: N/A, notification date: N/A
Application deadline (fall): rolling
Undergraduate student body: 978 full time, 2,565 part time; 50% male, 50% female; 1% American Indian, 2% Asian, 18% black, 32% Hispanic, 4% multiracial, 1% Pacific Islander, 37% white, 1% international; 70% from in state; 18% live on campus; 1% of students in fraternities, 2% in sororities
Most popular majors: 39% Business Administration and Management, General, 26% Liberal Arts and Sciences, General Studies and Humanities, Other, 10% Criminal Justice/Law Enforcement Administration, 8% Public Administration and Social Service Professions, 4% Christian Studies
Expenses: 2018-2019: $20,070; room/board: $7,864
Financial aid: (806) 291-3520; 100% of undergrads determined to have financial need; average aid package $11,880

West Texas A&M University

Canyon TX
(806) 651-2020
U.S. News ranking: Reg. U. (W), No. 81
Website: www.wtamu.edu
Admissions email: admissions@wtamu.edu
Public; founded 1910
Freshman admissions: selective; 2017-2018: 6,116 applied, 3,753 accepted. Either SAT or ACT required. ACT 25/75 percentile: 19-23. High school rank: 15% in top tenth, 43% in top quarter, 80% in top half
Early decision deadline: N/A, notification date: N/A
Early action deadline: N/A, notification date: N/A
Application deadline (fall): 8/1
Undergraduate student body: 5,615 full time, 1,779 part time; 43% male, 57% female; 0% American Indian, 2% Asian, 5% black, 28% Hispanic, 3% multiracial, 0% Pacific Islander, 58% white, 2% international; 86% from in state; 26% live on campus; 4% of students in fraternities, 5% in sororities
Most popular majors: 25% Business, Management, Marketing, and Related Support Services, 14% Health Professions and Related Programs, 8% Liberal Arts and Sciences, General Studies and Humanities, 7% Agriculture, Agriculture Operations, and Related Sciences, 7% Multi/Interdisciplinary Studies
Expenses: 2018-2019: $8,849 in state, $10,476 out of state; room/ board: $7,196
Financial aid: (806) 651-2055; 62% of undergrads determined to have financial need; average aid package $8,975

Wiley College[1]

Marshall TX
(800) 658-6889
U.S. News ranking: Reg. Coll. (W), second tier
Website: www.wileyc.edu
Admissions email: admissions@wileyc.edu
Private; founded 1873
Application deadline (fall): rolling
Undergraduate student body: N/A full time, N/A part time
Expenses: 2017-2018: $12,306; room/board: $7,338
Financial aid: (903) 927-3216

UTAH

Brigham Young University–Provo

Provo UT
(801) 422-2507
U.S. News ranking: Nat. U., No. 66
Website: www.byu.edu
Admissions email: admissions@byu.edu
Private; founded 1875
Affiliation: Latter Day Saints (Mormon Church)
Freshman admissions: more selective; 2017-2018: 12,858 applied, 6,738 accepted. Either SAT or ACT required. ACT 25/75 percentile: 27-32. High school rank: 54% in top tenth, 85% in top quarter, 98% in top half
Early decision deadline: N/A, notification date: N/A
Early action deadline: N/A, notification date: N/A
Application deadline (fall): 12/15
Undergraduate student body: 28,156 full time, 3,077 part time; 51% male, 49% female; 0% American Indian, 2% Asian, 1% black, 6% Hispanic, 4% multiracial, 1% Pacific Islander, 82% white, 3% international; 36% from in state; 19% live on campus; N/A of students in fraternities, N/A in sororities
Most popular majors: 14% Business, Management, Marketing, and Related Support Services, 12% Biological and Biomedical Sciences, 8% Education, 8% Health Professions and Related Programs, 8% Social Sciences
Expenses: 2018-2019: $5,620; room/board: $7,628
Financial aid: (801) 422-4104; 49% of undergrads determined to have financial need; average aid package $7,637

Dixie State University

Saint George UT
(435) 652-7702
U.S. News ranking: Reg. Coll. (W), No. 26
Website: www.dixie.edu
Admissions email: admissions@dixie.edu
Public; founded 1911
Freshman admissions: less selective; 2017-2018: 14,619 applied, 14,619 accepted. Neither SAT nor ACT required. ACT 25/75 percentile: 17-23. High school rank: 9% in top tenth, 29% in top quarter, 61% in top half
Early decision deadline: N/A, notification date: N/A
Early action deadline: N/A, notification date: N/A
Application deadline (fall): 8/15
Undergraduate student body: 6,778 full time, 2,895 part time; 37% male, 63% female; 1% American Indian, 1% Asian, 3% black, 12% Hispanic, 4% multiracial, 2% Pacific Islander, 75% white, 2% international; 76% from in state; 9% live on campus; N/A of students in fraternities, N/A in sororities
Most popular majors: 19% Business, Management, Marketing, and Related Support Services, 15% Communication, Journalism, and Related Programs, 13% Education, 11% Multi/ Interdisciplinary Studies, 8% Science Technologies/Technicians
Expenses: 2018-2019: $6,048 in state, $15,051 out of state; room/ board: $5,615
Financial aid: (435) 652-7575; 67% of undergrads determined to have financial need; average aid package $10,544

Snow College

Ephraim UT
(435) 283-7159
U.S. News ranking: Reg. Coll. (W), unranked
Website: www.snow.edu/admissions/
Admissions email: admissions@snow.edu
Public; founded 1888
Freshman admissions: selective; 2017-2018: 9,109 applied, 9,109 accepted. Neither SAT nor ACT required. ACT 25/75 percentile: 17-24. High school rank: N/A
Early decision deadline: N/A, notification date: N/A
Early action deadline: N/A, notification date: N/A
Application deadline (fall): rolling
Undergraduate student body: 4,052 full time, 1,511 part time; 32% male, 68% female; 2% American Indian, 1% Asian, 2% black, 5% Hispanic, 0% multiracial, 2% Pacific Islander, 85% white, 3% international; 98% from in state; 10% live on campus; N/A of students in fraternities, N/A in sororities
Most popular majors: 56% General Studies, 6% Registered Nursing/ Registered Nurse, 5% Business Administration, Management and Operations, Other, 4% Music, General, 3% Licensed Practical/ Vocational Nurse Training
Expenses: 2017-2018: $3,692 in state, $12,382 out of state; room/ board: $4,200
Financial aid: N/A

Southern Utah University

Cedar City UT
(435) 586-7740
U.S. News ranking: Reg. U. (W), No. 81
Website: www.suu.edu
Admissions email: adminfo@suu.edu
Public; founded 1897
Freshman admissions: selective; 2017-2018: 11,693 applied, 8,863 accepted. Either SAT or ACT required. ACT 25/75 percentile: 20-27. High school rank: 18% in top tenth, 44% in top quarter, 73% in top half
Early decision deadline: N/A, notification date: N/A
Early action deadline: N/A, notification date: N/A
Application deadline (fall): 5/1
Undergraduate student body: 6,279 full time, 2,271 part time; 44% male, 56% female; 1% American Indian, 1% Asian, 2% black, 6% Hispanic, 0% multiracial, 1% Pacific Islander, 75% white, 6% international; 83% from in state; 8% live on campus; N/A of students in fraternities, N/A in sororities
Most popular majors: 13% Business, Management, Marketing, and Related Support Services, 12% Education, 8% Family and Consumer Sciences/ Human Sciences, 7% Health Professions and Related Programs, 7% Visual and Performing Arts
Expenses: 2018-2019: $6,770 in state, $20,586 out of state; room/ board: $7,250
Financial aid: (435) 586-7735; 62% of undergrads determined to have financial need; average aid package $9,436

University of Utah

Salt Lake City UT
(801) 581-8761
U.S. News ranking: Nat. U., No. 119
Website: www.utah.edu
Admissions email: admissions@utah.edu
Public
Freshman admissions: more selective; 2017-2018: 22,400 applied, 14,818 accepted. Either SAT or ACT required. ACT 25/75 percentile: 22-29. High school rank: 39% in top tenth, 71% in top quarter, 95% in top half
Early decision deadline: N/A, notification date: N/A
Early action deadline: 12/1, notification date: 1/15
Application deadline (fall): 4/1
Undergraduate student body: 18,066 full time, 6,569 part time; 53% male, 47% female; 0% American Indian, 6% Asian, 1% black, 13% Hispanic, 5% multiracial, 0% Pacific Islander, 69% white, 5% international; 81% from in state; 14% live on campus; 6% of students in fraternities, 7% in sororities
Most popular majors: 7% Communication and Media Studies, 5% Economics, General, 5% Psychology, General, 4% Biology/Biological Sciences, General, 4% Registered Nursing/ Registered Nurse
Expenses: 2018-2019: $9,222 in state, $29,215 out of state; room/ board: $10,262
Financial aid: (801) 581-6211; 48% of undergrads determined to have financial need; average aid package $21,290

Utah State University

Logan UT
(435) 797-1079
U.S. News ranking: Nat. U., No. 205
Website: www.usu.edu
Admissions email: admit@usu.edu
Public; founded 1888
Freshman admissions: selective; 2017-2018: 15,555 applied, 13,857 accepted. Either SAT or ACT required. ACT 25/75 percentile: 21-27. High school rank: 20% in top tenth, 44% in top quarter, 74% in top half
Early decision deadline: N/A, notification date: N/A
Early action deadline: N/A, notification date: N/A
Application deadline (fall): rolling
Undergraduate student body: 17,188 full time, 7,430 part time; 47% male, 53% female; 2% American Indian, 1% Asian, 1% black, 6% Hispanic, 2% multiracial, 0% Pacific Islander, 82% white, 1% international; 73% from in state; N/A live on campus; 2% of students in fraternities, 3% in sororities
Most popular majors: 10% Economics, General, 7% Communication Sciences and Disorders, General, 5% Business Administration and Management, General, 4% Physical Education Teaching and Coaching, 4% Psychology, General
Expenses: 2018-2019: $7,424 in state, $21,505 out of state; room/ board: $6,400
Financial aid: (435) 797-0173; 56% of undergrads determined to have financial need; average aid package $10,263

Utah Valley University
Orem UT
(801) 863-8706
U.S. News ranking: Reg. U. (W), second tier
Website: www.uvu.edu/
Admissions email: admissions@uvu.edu
Public; founded 1941
Freshman admissions: selective; 2017-2018: 11,735 applied, 10,374 accepted. Neither SAT nor ACT required. ACT 25/75 percentile: 18-25. High school rank: 9% in top tenth, 27% in top quarter, 59% in top half
Early decision deadline: N/A, notification date: N/A
Early action deadline: N/A, notification date: N/A
Application deadline (fall): 8/1
Undergraduate student body: 18,404 full time, 18,464 part time; 53% male, 47% female; 1% American Indian, 1% Asian, 1% black, 11% Hispanic, 3% multiracial, 1% Pacific Islander, 78% white, 2% international; 89% from in state; 0% live on campus; 0% of students in fraternities, 0% in sororities
Most popular majors: 20% Business, Management, Marketing, and Related Support Services, 10% Psychology, 8% Education, 7% Computer and Information Sciences and Support Services, 7% Transportation and Materials Moving
Expenses: 2018-2019: $5,726 in state, $16,296 out of state; room/board: N/A
Financial aid: (801) 863-6746; 58% of undergrads determined to have financial need; average aid package $8,129

Weber State University
Ogden UT
(801) 626-6744
U.S. News ranking: Reg. U. (W), second tier
Website: weber.edu
Admissions email: admissions@weber.edu
Public; founded 1889
Freshman admissions: selective; 2017-2018: 6,255 applied, 6,255 accepted. Neither SAT nor ACT required. ACT 25/75 percentile: 18-24. High school rank: 10% in top tenth, 26% in top quarter, 60% in top half
Early decision deadline: N/A, notification date: N/A
Early action deadline: N/A, notification date: N/A
Application deadline (fall): 8/31
Undergraduate student body: 11,311 full time, 15,800 part time; 46% male, 54% female; 1% American Indian, 2% Asian, 2% black, 12% Hispanic, 3% multiracial, 1% Pacific Islander, 74% white, 2% international
Most popular majors: 14% Registered Nursing/Registered Nurse, 5% Selling Skills and Sales Operations, 4% Criminal Justice/Safety Studies, 3% Accounting, 3% Speech Communication and Rhetoric
Expenses: 2018-2019: $5,850 in state, $15,637 out of state; room/board: $8,400
Financial aid: (801) 626-7569; 60% of undergrads determined to have financial need; average aid package $6,004

Western Governors University[1]
Salt Lake City UT
(801) 274-3280
U.S. News ranking: Reg. U. (W), unranked
Website: www.wgu.edu/
Admissions email: info@wgu.edu
Private; founded 1996
Application deadline (fall): N/A
Undergraduate student body: N/A full time, N/A part time
Expenses: 2017-2018: $6,070; room/board: N/A
Financial aid: (877) 435-7948

Westminster College
Salt Lake City UT
(801) 832-2200
U.S. News ranking: Reg. U. (W), No. 20
Website: www.westminstercollege.edu
Admissions email: admission@westminstercollege.edu
Private; founded 1875
Affiliation: Undenominational
Freshman admissions: selective; 2017-2018: 1,702 applied, 1,578 accepted. Either SAT or ACT required. ACT 25/75 percentile: 21-28. High school rank: 28% in top tenth, 53% in top quarter, 88% in top half
Early decision deadline: N/A, notification date: N/A
Early action deadline: N/A, notification date: N/A
Application deadline (fall): rolling
Undergraduate student body: 1,906 full time, 124 part time; 41% male, 59% female; 1% American Indian, 3% Asian, 2% black, 11% Hispanic, 5% multiracial, 0% Pacific Islander, 71% white, 5% international; 61% from in state; 30% live on campus; N/A of students in fraternities, N/A in sororities
Most popular majors: 25% Business, Management, Marketing, and Related Support Services, 23% Health Professions and Related Programs, 7% Biological and Biomedical Sciences, 7% Social Sciences, 5% Visual and Performing Arts
Expenses: 2018-2019: $34,000; room/board: $9,524
Financial aid: (801) 832-2500; 61% of undergrads determined to have financial need; average aid package $25,833

VERMONT

Bennington College
Bennington VT
(800) 833-6845
U.S. News ranking: Nat. Lib. Arts, No. 95
Website: www.bennington.edu
Admissions email: admissions@bennington.edu
Private; founded 1932
Freshman admissions: selective; 2017-2018: 1,465 applied, 829 accepted. Neither SAT nor ACT required. SAT 25/75 percentile: 1210-1390. High school rank: N/A
Early decision deadline: 11/15, notification date: 12/14
Early action deadline: 12/1, notification date: 2/1
Application deadline (fall): 1/15
Undergraduate student body: 724 full time, 51 part time; 35% male, 65% female; 0% American Indian, 2% Asian, 4% black, 10% Hispanic, 4% multiracial, 0% Pacific Islander, 58% white, 17% international; 2% from in state; 98% live on campus; 0% of students in fraternities, 0% in sororities
Most popular majors: 39% Visual and Performing Arts, 15% English Language and Literature/Letters, 11% Social Sciences, 10% Foreign Languages, Literatures, and Linguistics, 4% Psychology
Expenses: 2018-2019: $53,860; room/board: $15,610
Financial aid: (802) 440-4325; 78% of undergrads determined to have financial need; average aid package $45,537

Castleton University[1]
Castleton VT
(800) 639-8521
U.S. News ranking: Reg. Coll. (N), No. 30
Website: www.castleton.edu
Admissions email: info@castleton.edu
Public; founded 1787
Application deadline (fall): rolling
Undergraduate student body: N/A full time, N/A part time
Expenses: 2017-2018: $11,970 in state, $27,522 out of state; room/board: $10,290
Financial aid: N/A

Champlain College
Burlington VT
(800) 570-5858
U.S. News ranking: Reg. U. (N), No. 81
Website: www.champlain.edu
Admissions email: admission@champlain.edu
Private; founded 1878
Freshman admissions: selective; 2017-2018: 5,197 applied, 3,900 accepted. Neither SAT nor ACT required. SAT 25/75 percentile: 1090-1300. High school rank: 15% in top tenth, 42% in top quarter, 66% in top half
Early decision deadline: 11/15, notification date: 12/15
Early action deadline: N/A, notification date: N/A
Application deadline (fall): 1/15
Undergraduate student body: 2,170 full time, 52 part time; 62% male, 38% female; 0% American Indian, 3% Asian, 2% black, 6% Hispanic, 3% multiracial, 0% Pacific Islander, 75% white, 1% international; 21% from in state; 68% live on campus; 0% of students in fraternities, 0% in sororities
Most popular majors: 9% Business Administration and Management, General, 6% Computer Graphics, 6% Digital Arts, 6% Game and Interactive Media Design, 6% Speech Communication and Rhetoric
Expenses: 2018-2019: $41,010; room/board: $15,354
Financial aid: (802) 865-5435; 70% of undergrads determined to have financial need; average aid package $27,736

College of St. Joseph[1]
Rutland VT
(802) 773-5286
U.S. News ranking: Reg. Coll. (N), second tier
Website: www.csj.edu
Admissions email: admissions@csj.edu
Private; founded 1956
Application deadline (fall): 8/15
Undergraduate student body: N/A full time, N/A part time
Expenses: 2017-2018: $24,000; room/board: $11,900
Financial aid: (802) 776-5262

Goddard College[1]
Plainfield VT
(800) 906-8312
U.S. News ranking: Reg. U. (N), unranked
Website: www.goddard.edu
Admissions email: admissions@goddard.edu
Private; founded 1863
Application deadline (fall): N/A
Undergraduate student body: N/A full time, N/A part time
Expenses: 2017-2018: $16,260; room/board: $1,648
Financial aid: (800) 468-4888

Green Mountain College
Poultney VT
(802) 287-8207
U.S. News ranking: Reg. U. (N), second tier
Website: www.greenmtn.edu
Admissions email: admiss@greenmtn.edu
Private; founded 1834
Affiliation: United Methodist
Freshman admissions: less selective; 2017-2018: 677 applied, 530 accepted. Neither SAT nor ACT required. SAT 25/75 percentile: 925-1175. High school rank: N/A
Early decision deadline: N/A, notification date: N/A
Early action deadline: 11/1, notification date: 12/14
Application deadline (fall): rolling
Undergraduate student body: 447 full time, 21 part time; 43% male, 57% female; 1% American Indian, 1% Asian, 6% black, 4% Hispanic, 2% multiracial, 0% Pacific Islander, 65% white, 1% international; 18% from in state; 82% live on campus; 0% of students in fraternities, 0% in sororities
Most popular majors: 11% Environmental Studies, 9% Parks, Recreation and Leisure Studies, 8% Agroecology and Sustainable Agriculture, 7% Business Administration and Management, General, 7% Psychology, General
Expenses: 2017-2018: $37,002; room/board: $11,722
Financial aid: (802) 287-8285

Johnson State College[1]
Johnson VT
(800) 635-2356
U.S. News ranking: Reg. U. (N), second tier
Website: www.jsc.edu
Admissions email: JSCAdmissions@jsc.edu
Public; founded 1828
Application deadline (fall): rolling
Undergraduate student body: N/A full time, N/A part time
Expenses: 2017-2018: $11,730 in state, $24,690 out of state; room/board: $10,290
Financial aid: N/A

Landmark College[1]
Putney VT
U.S. News ranking: Reg. Coll. (N), unranked
Admissions email: N/A
Private
Application deadline (fall): N/A
Undergraduate student body: N/A full time, N/A part time
Expenses: 2018-2019: $56,800; room/board: $11,840
Financial aid: (802) 781-6178; 60% of undergrads determined to have financial need; average aid package $28,764

Lyndon State College[1]
Lyndonville VT
(802) 626-6413
U.S. News ranking: Reg. Coll. (N), second tier
Website: www.lyndonstate.edu
Admissions email: admissions@lyndonstate.edu
Public; founded 1911
Application deadline (fall): rolling
Undergraduate student body: N/A full time, N/A part time
Expenses: 2017-2018: $11,730 in state, $23,898 out of state; room/board: $10,290
Financial aid: N/A

Marlboro College
Marlboro VT
(800) 343-0049
U.S. News ranking: Nat. Lib. Arts, No. 116
Website: www.marlboro.edu
Admissions email: admissions@marlboro.edu
Private; founded 1946
Freshman admissions: selective; 2017-2018: 120 applied, 116 accepted. Neither SAT nor ACT required. SAT 25/75 percentile: 1150-1340. High school rank: N/A
Early decision deadline: 11/15, notification date: 12/1
Early action deadline: 1/15, notification date: 2/1
Application deadline (fall): rolling
Undergraduate student body: 177 full time, 6 part time; 46% male, 54% female; 1% American Indian, 1% Asian, 4% black, 3% Hispanic, 5% multiracial, 0% Pacific Islander, 78% white, 2% international; 11% from in state; 66% live on campus; 0% of students in fraternities, 0% in sororities
Most popular majors: 33% Visual and Performing Arts, 13% English Language and Literature/Letters,

11% Social Sciences, 8% Natural Resources and Conservation, 6% Philosophy and Religious Studies
Expenses: 2018-2019: $40,840; room/board: $12,348
Financial aid: (802) 258-9237; 81% of undergrads determined to have financial need; average aid package $39,880

Middlebury College

Middlebury VT
(802) 443-3000
U.S. News ranking: Nat. Lib. Arts, No. 5
Website: www.middlebury.edu
Admissions email: admissions@middlebury.edu
Private; founded 1800
Freshman admissions: most selective; 2017-2018: 8,909 applied, 1,523 accepted. Either SAT or ACT required. ACT 25/75 percentile: 30-34. High school rank: 85% in top tenth, 95% in top quarter, 99% in top half
Early decision deadline: 11/1, notification date: 12/15
Early action deadline: N/A, notification date: N/A
Application deadline (fall): 1/1
Undergraduate student body: 2,531 full time, 30 part time; 48% male, 52% female; 0% American Indian, 6% Asian, 4% black, 10% Hispanic, 5% multiracial, 0% Pacific Islander, 64% white, 10% international; 6% from in state; 95% live on campus; 0% of students in fraternities, 0% in sororities
Most popular majors: 16% Economics, General, 7% Political Science and Government, General, 6% Environmental Studies, 5% Neuroscience, 5% Psychology, General
Expenses: 2018-2019: $54,450; room/board: $15,530
Financial aid: (802) 443-5228; 45% of undergrads determined to have financial need; average aid package $50,792

Norwich University

Northfield VT
(800) 468-6679
U.S. News ranking: Reg. U. (N), No. 74
Website: www.norwich.edu
Admissions email: nuadm@norwich.edu
Private; founded 1819
Freshman admissions: selective; 2017-2018: 4,280 applied, 2,762 accepted. Neither SAT nor ACT required. ACT 25/75 percentile: 20-26. High school rank: 14% in top tenth, 34% in top quarter, 68% in top half
Early decision deadline: N/A, notification date: N/A
Early action deadline: N/A, notification date: N/A
Application deadline (fall): rolling
Undergraduate student body: 2,542 full time, 683 part time; 77% male, 23% female; 1% American Indian, 3% Asian, 4% black, 8% Hispanic, 5% multiracial, 0% Pacific Islander, 71% white, 3% international
Most popular majors: 22% Military Science, Leadership and Operational Art, 18% Homeland Security, Law Enforcement, Firefighting and Related Protective Services, 13% Business, Management, Marketing, and Related Support Services, 8% Engineering, 8% Health Professions and Related Programs
Expenses: 2018-2019: $40,016; room/board: $13,840
Financial aid: (802) 485-3015; 75% of undergrads determined to have financial need; average aid package $37,468

Southern Vermont College

Bennington VT
(802) 447-6300
U.S. News ranking: Reg. Coll. (N), No. 25
Website: svc.edu/
Admissions email: admissions@svc.edu
Private; founded 1974
Freshman admissions: less selective; 2017-2018: 353 applied, 318 accepted. Neither SAT nor ACT required. SAT 25/75 percentile: 920-1080. High school rank: 11% in top tenth, 24% in top quarter, 65% in top half
Early decision deadline: N/A, notification date: N/A
Early action deadline: N/A, notification date: N/A
Application deadline (fall): rolling
Undergraduate student body: 339 full time, 22 part time; 42% male, 58% female; 0% American Indian, 1% Asian, 9% black, 10% Hispanic, 2% multiracial, 0% Pacific Islander, 56% white, 0% international; 23% from in state; 55% live on campus; 0% of students in fraternities, 0% in sororities
Most popular majors: 34% Health Professions and Related Programs, 18% Psychology, 17% Biological and Biomedical Sciences, 10% Business, Management, Marketing, and Related Support Services, 9% Homeland Security, Law Enforcement, Firefighting and Related Protective Services
Expenses: 2018-2019: $25,356; room/board: $11,000
Financial aid: (802) 447-6339; 84% of undergrads determined to have financial need; average aid package $16,000

Sterling College[1]

Craftsbury Common VT
(802) 586-7711
U.S. News ranking: Nat. Lib. Arts, unranked
Website: www.sterlingcollege.edu
Admissions email: admissions@sterlingcollege.edu
Private; founded 1958
Application deadline (fall): N/A
Undergraduate student body: N/A full time, N/A part time
Expenses: 2017-2018: $37,588; room/board: $9,846
Financial aid: N/A

St. Michael's College

Colchester VT
(800) 762-8000
U.S. News ranking: Nat. Lib. Arts, No. 116
Website: www.smcvt.edu
Admissions email: admission@smcvt.edu
Private; founded 1904
Affiliation: Roman Catholic
Freshman admissions: selective; 2017-2018: 3,094 applied, 2,633 accepted. Neither SAT nor ACT required. SAT 25/75 percentile: 1150-1310. High school rank: 25% in top tenth, 48% in top quarter, 76% in top half
Early decision deadline: N/A, notification date: N/A
Early action deadline: 11/1, notification date: 12/21
Application deadline (fall): 2/1
Undergraduate student body: 1,766 full time, 26 part time; 44% male, 56% female; 0% American Indian, 1% Asian, 2% black, 5% Hispanic, 2% multiracial, 0% Pacific Islander, 83% white, 4% international; 15% from in state; 92% live on campus; N/A of students in fraternities, N/A in sororities
Most popular majors: 17% Business, Management, Marketing, and Related Support Services, 14% Social Sciences, 10% Biological and Biomedical Sciences, 10% Psychology, 7% Natural Resources and Conservation
Expenses: 2018-2019: $45,375; room/board: $12,220
Financial aid: (802) 654-3243; 65% of undergrads determined to have financial need; average aid package $32,102

University of Vermont

Burlington VT
(802) 656-3370
U.S. News ranking: Nat. U., No. 96
Website: www.uvm.edu
Admissions email: admissions@uvm.edu
Public; founded 1791
Freshman admissions: more selective; 2017-2018: 21,991 applied, 14,777 accepted. Either SAT or ACT required. SAT 25/75 percentile: 1180-1350. High school rank: 38% in top tenth, 76% in top quarter, 98% in top half
Early decision deadline: N/A, notification date: N/A
Early action deadline: 11/1, notification date: 12/15
Application deadline (fall): 1/15
Undergraduate student body: 10,395 full time, 944 part time; 42% male, 58% female; 0% American Indian, 3% Asian, 1% black, 4% Hispanic, 3% multiracial, 0% Pacific Islander, 81% white, 6% international; 29% from in state; 51% live on campus; 8% of students in fraternities, 7% in sororities
Most popular majors: 9% Business Administration and Management, General, 5% Environmental Studies, 5% Psychology, General, 4% Mechanical Engineering, 4% Registered Nursing/Registered Nurse
Expenses: 2018-2019: $18,276 in state, $42,516 out of state; room/board: $12,462
Financial aid: (802) 656-5700; 55% of undergrads determined to have financial need; average aid package $26,256

Vermont Technical College

Randolph Center VT
(802) 728-1244
U.S. News ranking: Reg. Coll. (N), No. 19
Website: www.vtc.edu
Admissions email: admissions@vtc.edu
Public; founded 1866
Freshman admissions: less selective; 2017-2018: 684 applied, 433 accepted. Neither SAT nor ACT required. ACT 25/75 percentile: 20-23. High school rank: 7% in top tenth, 25% in top quarter, 59% in top half
Early decision deadline: N/A, notification date: N/A
Early action deadline: N/A, notification date: N/A
Application deadline (fall): rolling
Undergraduate student body: 1,052 full time, 563 part time; 52% male, 48% female; 1% American Indian, 2% Asian, 2% black, 3% Hispanic, 5% multiracial, 0% Pacific Islander, 82% white, 2% international; 86% from in state; 26% live on campus; N/A of students in fraternities, N/A in sororities
Most popular majors: Information not available
Expenses: 2018-2019: $15,510 in state, $28,182 out of state; room/board: $10,598
Financial aid: (802) 728-1248; 74% of undergrads determined to have financial need; average aid package $14,736

VIRGINIA

Averett University

Danville VA
(800) 283-7388
U.S. News ranking: Reg. Coll. (S), No. 13
Website: www.averett.edu
Admissions email: admit@averett.edu
Private; founded 1859
Affiliation: Other
Freshman admissions: less selective; 2017-2018: 2,721 applied, 1,684 accepted. Either SAT or ACT required. SAT 25/75 percentile: 830-1020. High school rank: 7% in top tenth, 24% in top quarter, 48% in top half
Early decision deadline: N/A, notification date: N/A
Early action deadline: N/A, notification date: N/A
Application deadline (fall): rolling
Undergraduate student body: 892 full time, 37 part time; 55% male, 45% female; 0% American Indian, 1% Asian, 30% black, 5% Hispanic, 2% multiracial, 0% Pacific Islander, 56% white, 6% international; 61% from in state; 57% live on campus; 8% of students in fraternities, 6% in sororities
Most popular majors: 24% Health Professions and Related Programs, 10% Business, Management, Marketing, and Related Support Services, 9% Homeland Security, Law Enforcement, Firefighting and Related Protective Services, 9% Parks, Recreation, Leisure, and Fitness Studies, 8% Psychology
Expenses: 2018-2019: $34,520; room/board: $9,976
Financial aid: (434) 791-5646; 86% of undergrads determined to have financial need; average aid package $26,742

Bluefield College

Bluefield VA
(276) 326-4231
U.S. News ranking: Reg. Coll. (S), No. 43
Website: www.bluefield.edu
Admissions email: admissions@bluefield.edu
Private; founded 1922
Affiliation: Baptist
Freshman admissions: less selective; 2017-2018: 1,521 applied, 1,386 accepted. Either SAT or ACT required. SAT 25/75 percentile: 870-1085. High school rank: 7% in top tenth, 25% in top quarter, 59% in top half
Early decision deadline: N/A, notification date: N/A
Early action deadline: N/A, notification date: N/A
Application deadline (fall): rolling
Undergraduate student body: 829 full time, 119 part time; 47% male, 53% female; 0% American Indian, 0% Asian, 23% black, 5% Hispanic, 4% multiracial, 0% Pacific Islander, 61% white, 4% international; 64% from in state; 61% live on campus; 2% of students in fraternities, 2% in sororities
Most popular majors: 18% Organizational Leadership, 17% Public Administration and Social Service Professions, 16% Public Health/Community Nurse/Nursing, 15% Criminal Justice/Safety Studies, 9% Kinesiology and Exercise Science
Expenses: 2018-2019: $25,290; room/board: $9,024
Financial aid: (276) 326-4280; 88% of undergrads determined to have financial need; average aid package $16,746

Bridgewater College

Bridgewater VA
(800) 759-8328
U.S. News ranking: Nat. Lib. Arts, second tier
Website: www.bridgewater.edu
Admissions email: admissions@bridgewater.edu
Private; founded 1880
Affiliation: Church of Brethren
Freshman admissions: selective; 2017-2018: 7,241 applied, 3,764 accepted. Either SAT or ACT required. SAT 25/75 percentile: 970-1170. High school rank: 15% in top tenth, 36% in top quarter, 72% in top half
Early decision deadline: N/A, notification date: N/A
Early action deadline: N/A, notification date: N/A
Application deadline (fall): 5/1
Undergraduate student body: 1,876 full time, 6 part time; 46% male, 54% female; 0% American Indian, 1% Asian, 16% black, 7% Hispanic, 5% multiracial, 0% Pacific Islander, 66% white, 1% international; 74% from in state; 81% live on campus; N/A of students in fraternities, N/A in sororities

Most popular majors: 19% Business, Management, Marketing, and Related Support Services, 13% Parks, Recreation, Leisure, and Fitness Studies, 11% Biological and Biomedical Sciences, 8% Psychology, 8% Social Sciences
Expenses: 2018-2019: $35,160; room/board: $12,720
Financial aid: (540) 828-5376; 82% of undergrads determined to have financial need; average aid package $31,101

Christopher Newport University

Newport News VA
(757) 594-7015
U.S. News ranking: Reg. U. (S), No. 10
Website: www.cnu.edu
Admissions email: admit@cnu.edu
Public; founded 1960
Freshman admissions: selective; 2017-2018: 6,948 applied, 5,030 accepted. Neither SAT nor ACT required. SAT 25/75 percentile: 1110-1270. High school rank: 18% in top tenth, 50% in top quarter, 84% in top half
Early decision deadline: 11/15, notification date: 12/15
Early action deadline: 12/1, notification date: 1/15
Application deadline (fall): 2/1
Undergraduate student body: 4,867 full time, 87 part time; 44% male, 56% female; 0% American Indian, 3% Asian, 7% black, 5% Hispanic, 5% multiracial, 0% Pacific Islander, 75% white, 0% international; 92% from in state; 78% live on campus; 22% of students in fraternities, 34% in sororities
Most popular majors: 15% Biology/Biological Sciences, General, 15% Business Administration and Management, General, 12% Psychology, General, 9% Speech Communication and Rhetoric, 6% Political Science and Government, General
Expenses: 2018-2019: $14,754 in state, $27,220 out of state; room/board: $11,460
Financial aid: (757) 594-7170; 45% of undergrads determined to have financial need; average aid package $9,669

College of William and Mary

Williamsburg VA
(757) 221-4223
U.S. News ranking: Nat. U., No. 38
Website: www.wm.edu
Admissions email: admission@wm.edu
Public; founded 1693
Freshman admissions: most selective; 2017-2018: 14,921 applied, 5,359 accepted. Either SAT or ACT required. SAT 25/75 percentile: 1300-1480. High school rank: 81% in top tenth, 97% in top quarter, 100% in top half
Early decision deadline: 11/1, notification date: 12/1
Early action deadline: N/A, notification date: N/A
Application deadline (fall): 1/1
Undergraduate student body: 6,199 full time, 86 part time; 42% male, 58% female; 0% American Indian, 8% Asian, 7% black, 9% Hispanic, 5% multiracial, 0% Pacific Islander, 59% white, 6% international; 70% from in state; 72% live on campus; 27% of students in fraternities, 31% in sororities
Most popular majors: 20% Social Sciences, 10% Biological and Biomedical Sciences, 10% Multi/Interdisciplinary Studies, 9% Business, Management, Marketing, and Related Support Services, 7% Parks, Recreation, Leisure, and Fitness Studies
Expenses: 2018-2019: $21,830 in state, $44,701 out of state; room/board: $12,236
Financial aid: (757) 221-2420; 38% of undergrads determined to have financial need; average aid package $24,089

Eastern Mennonite University

Harrisonburg VA
(800) 368-2665
U.S. News ranking: Reg. U. (S), No. 47
Website: www.emu.edu
Admissions email: admiss@emu.edu
Private; founded 1917
Affiliation: Mennonite Church
Freshman admissions: selective; 2017-2018: 1,232 applied, 662 accepted. Either SAT or ACT required. SAT 25/75 percentile: 990-1170. High school rank: N/A
Early decision deadline: N/A, notification date: N/A
Early action deadline: N/A, notification date: N/A
Application deadline (fall): rolling
Undergraduate student body: 942 full time, 156 part time; 37% male, 63% female; 0% American Indian, 2% Asian, 9% black, 7% Hispanic, 3% multiracial, 0% Pacific Islander, 69% white, 4% international; 66% from in state; 59% live on campus; 0% of students in fraternities, 0% in sororities
Most popular majors: 48% Health Professions and Related Programs, 8% Business, Management, Marketing, and Related Support Services, 6% Liberal Arts and Sciences, General Studies and Humanities, 5% Biological and Biomedical Sciences, 4% Visual and Performing Arts
Expenses: 2018-2019: $37,110; room/board: $11,160
Financial aid: (540) 432-4137

ECPI University

Virginia Beach VA
(866) 499-0336
U.S. News ranking: Reg. Coll. (S), second tier
Website: www.ecpi.edu/
Admissions email: request@ecpi.edu
For-profit; founded 1966
Freshman admissions: less selective; 2017-2018: 5,298 applied, 3,777 accepted. Neither SAT nor ACT required. SAT 25/75 percentile: N/A. High school rank: N/A
Early decision deadline: N/A, notification date: N/A
Early action deadline: N/A, notification date: N/A
Application deadline (fall): rolling
Undergraduate student body: 11,512 full time, 233 part time; 44% male, 56% female; 1% American Indian, 3% Asian, 42% black, 9% Hispanic, 3% multiracial, 1% Pacific Islander, 41% white, 0% international
Most popular majors: 16% Medical/Clinical Assistant, 15% Licensed Practical/Vocational Nurse Training, 12% Registered Nursing/Registered Nurse, 9% Computer and Information Systems Security/Information Assurance, 8% Network and System Administration/Administrator
Expenses: 2018-2019: $15,051; room/board: N/A
Financial aid: N/A; 93% of undergrads determined to have financial need; average aid package $11,941

Emory and Henry College

Emory VA
(800) 848-5493
U.S. News ranking: Nat. Lib. Arts, No. 162
Website: www.ehc.edu
Admissions email: ehadmiss@ehc.edu
Private; founded 1836
Affiliation: United Methodist
Freshman admissions: selective; 2017-2018: 1,426 applied, 1,030 accepted. Either SAT or ACT required. SAT 25/75 percentile: 988-1170. High school rank: 20% in top tenth, 49% in top quarter, 78% in top half
Early decision deadline: 11/15, notification date: 12/15
Early action deadline: N/A, notification date: N/A
Application deadline (fall): rolling
Undergraduate student body: 966 full time, 34 part time; 49% male, 51% female; 0% American Indian, 1% Asian, 9% black, 4% Hispanic, 2% multiracial, 0% Pacific Islander, 78% white, 0% international; 66% from in state; 77% live on campus; N/A of students in fraternities, N/A in sororities
Most popular majors: 17% Education, 12% Social Sciences, 10% Business, Management, Marketing, and Related Support Services, 7% History, 7% Parks, Recreation, Leisure, and Fitness Studies
Expenses: 2018-2019: $35,135; room/board: $12,533
Financial aid: (276) 944-6105; 85% of undergrads determined to have financial need; average aid package $32,567

Ferrum College

Ferrum VA
(800) 868-9797
U.S. News ranking: Reg. Coll. (S), No. 36
Website: www.ferrum.edu
Admissions email: admissions@ferrum.edu
Private; founded 1913
Freshman admissions: least selective; 2017-2018: 3,228 applied, 2,321 accepted. Neither SAT nor ACT required. SAT 25/75 percentile: 850-1078. High school rank: 3% in top tenth, 12% in top quarter, 15% in top half
Early decision deadline: N/A, notification date: N/A
Early action deadline: N/A, notification date: N/A
Application deadline (fall): rolling
Undergraduate student body: 1,118 full time, 19 part time; 56% male, 44% female; 1% American Indian, 1% Asian, 33% black, 5% Hispanic, 7% multiracial, 0% Pacific Islander, 49% white, 1% international; 78% from in state; 90% live on campus; 4% of students in fraternities, 14% in sororities
Most popular majors: 13% Business Administration and Management, General, 13% Criminal Justice/Safety Studies, 10% Physical Education Teaching and Coaching, 8% Environmental Studies, 6% Liberal Arts and Sciences/Liberal Studies
Expenses: 2018-2019: $34,175; room/board: $11,570
Financial aid: N/A; 94% of undergrads determined to have financial need; average aid package $28,940

George Mason University

Fairfax VA
(703) 993-2400
U.S. News ranking: Nat. U., No. 136
Website: www2.gmu.edu
Admissions email: admissions@gmu.edu
Public; founded 1972
Freshman admissions: selective; 2017-2018: 18,993 applied, 15,446 accepted. Neither SAT nor ACT required. SAT 25/75 percentile: 1100-1290. High school rank: 17% in top tenth, 51% in top quarter, 87% in top half
Early decision deadline: N/A, notification date: N/A
Early action deadline: 11/1, notification date: 12/15
Application deadline (fall): 1/15
Undergraduate student body: 20,199 full time, 4,788 part time; 50% male, 50% female; 0% American Indian, 20% Asian, 11% black, 14% Hispanic, 5% multiracial, 0% Pacific Islander, 41% white, 5% international; 90% from in state; 24% live on campus; 7% of students in fraternities, 9% in sororities
Most popular majors: 6% Criminal Justice/Police Science, 6% Psychology, General, 5% Accounting, 5% Biology/Biological Sciences, General, 5% Information Technology
Expenses: 2018-2019: $12,462 in state, $35,922 out of state; room/board: $11,460
Financial aid: (703) 993-2353; 58% of undergrads determined to have financial need; average aid package $13,702

Hampden-Sydney College

Hampden-Sydney VA
(800) 755-0733
U.S. News ranking: Nat. Lib. Arts, No. 113
Website: www.hsc.edu
Admissions email: hsapp@hsc.edu
Private; founded 1775
Affiliation: Presbyterian
Freshman admissions: selective; 2017-2018: 3,573 applied, 1,967 accepted. Either SAT or ACT required. SAT 25/75 percentile: 1050-1265. High school rank: 13% in top tenth, 30% in top quarter, 66% in top half
Early decision deadline: 11/1, notification date: 12/1
Early action deadline: 1/15, notification date: 2/15
Application deadline (fall): 3/1
Undergraduate student body: 1,046 full time, 0 part time; 100% male, 0% female; 1% American Indian, 0% Asian, 4% black, 4% Hispanic, 3% multiracial, 0% Pacific Islander, 86% white, 0% international; 68% from in state; 98% live on campus; 30% of students in fraternities, N/A in sororities
Most popular majors: 29% Business/Managerial Economics, 14% Economics, General, 13% Biology/Biological Sciences, General, 12% History, General, 8% English Language and Literature, General
Expenses: 2018-2019: $45,396; room/board: $13,558
Financial aid: (434) 223-6265; 66% of undergrads determined to have financial need; average aid package $33,875

Hampton University

Hampton VA
(757) 727-5328
U.S. News ranking: Reg. U. (S), No. 27
Website: www.hamptonu.edu
Admissions email: admissions@hamptonu.edu
Private; founded 1868
Freshman admissions: selective; 2017-2018: 12,130 applied, 4,391 accepted. Neither SAT nor ACT required. ACT 25/75 percentile: 20-24. High school rank: 13% in top tenth, 35% in top quarter, 72% in top half
Early decision deadline: N/A, notification date: N/A
Early action deadline: 11/1, notification date: 12/31
Application deadline (fall): 3/1
Undergraduate student body: 3,651 full time, 148 part time; 33% male, 67% female; 0% American Indian, 0% Asian, 96% black, 1% Hispanic, 0% multiracial, 0% Pacific Islander, 1% white, 1% international; 27% from in state; 64% live on campus; 5% of students in fraternities, 4% in sororities
Most popular majors: 19% Psychology, General, 18% Organizational Communication, General, 17% Broadcast Journalism, 10% Liberal Arts and Sciences/Liberal Studies, 6% Political Science and Government, General

Expenses: 2018-2019: $26,702; room/board: $11,778
Financial aid: (757) 727-5635; 64% of undergrads determined to have financial need; average aid package $5,931

Hollins University

Roanoke VA
(800) 456-9595
U.S. News ranking: Nat. Lib. Arts, No. 103
Website: www.hollins.edu
Admissions email: huadm@hollins.edu
Private; founded 1842
Freshman admissions: more selective; 2017-2018: 2,842 applied, 1,375 accepted. Either SAT or ACT required. SAT 25/75 percentile: 1110-1300. High school rank: 29% in top tenth, 66% in top quarter, 89% in top half
Early decision deadline: 11/1, notification date: 11/15
Early action deadline: 11/15, notification date: 12/1
Application deadline (fall): N/A
Undergraduate student body: 632 full time, 13 part time; 1% male, 99% female; 1% American Indian, 2% Asian, 12% black, 6% Hispanic, 6% multiracial, 0% Pacific Islander, 66% white, 5% international; 53% from in state; 87% live on campus; N/A of students in fraternities, N/A in sororities
Most popular majors: 21% English Language and Literature/Letters, 17% Visual and Performing Arts, 12% Biological and Biomedical Sciences, 12% Business, Management, Marketing, and Related Support Services, 11% Psychology
Expenses: 2018-2019: $39,035; room/board: $13,520
Financial aid: (540) 362-6332; 80% of undergrads determined to have financial need; average aid package $36,843

James Madison University

Harrisonburg VA
(540) 568-5681
U.S. News ranking: Reg. U. (S), No. 6
Website: www.jmu.edu
Admissions email: admissions@jmu.edu
Public; founded 1908
Freshman admissions: selective; 2017-2018: 21,099 applied, 15,866 accepted. Neither SAT nor ACT required. SAT 25/75 percentile: 1100-1260. High school rank: 16% in top tenth, 51% in top quarter, 94% in top half
Early decision deadline: N/A, notification date: N/A
Early action deadline: 11/1, notification date: 1/15
Application deadline (fall): 1/15
Undergraduate student body: 18,905 full time, 1,069 part time; 41% male, 59% female; 0% American Indian, 5% Asian, 5% black, 7% Hispanic, 4% multiracial, 0% Pacific Islander, 75% white, 2% international; 77% from in state; 30% live on campus; 4% of students in fraternities, 9% in sororities
Most popular majors: 18% Health Professions and Related Programs, 16% Business, Management, Marketing, and Related Support Services, 8% Communication, Journalism, and Related Programs, 8% Social Sciences, 6% Liberal Arts and Sciences, General Studies and Humanities
Expenses: 2018-2019: $11,386 in state, $28,100 out of state; room/board: $10,092
Financial aid: (540) 568-7820; 43% of undergrads determined to have financial need; average aid package $8,945

Liberty University

Lynchburg VA
(800) 543-5317
U.S. News ranking: Nat. U., second tier
Website: www.liberty.edu
Admissions email: admissions@liberty.edu
Private; founded 1971
Affiliation: Evangelical Christian
Freshman admissions: selective; 2017-2018: 32,873 applied, 9,795 accepted. Either SAT or ACT required. SAT 25/75 percentile: 1040-1240. High school rank: 20% in top tenth, 44% in top quarter, 78% in top half
Early decision deadline: N/A, notification date: N/A
Early action deadline: N/A, notification date: N/A
Application deadline (fall): rolling
Undergraduate student body: 26,892 full time, 18,862 part time; 42% male, 58% female; 0% American Indian, 1% Asian, 11% black, 5% Hispanic, 2% multiracial, 0% Pacific Islander, 50% white, 1% international; 27% from in state; 18% live on campus; N/A of students in fraternities, N/A in sororities
Most popular majors: 17% Business, Management, Marketing, and Related Support Services, 11% Health Professions and Related Programs, 8% Visual and Performing Arts, 7% Parks, Recreation, Leisure, and Fitness Studies, 7% Psychology
Expenses: 2018-2019: $25,276; room/board: $10,478
Financial aid: (434) 582-2270; 74% of undergrads determined to have financial need; average aid package $15,024

Longwood University

Farmville VA
(434) 395-2060
U.S. News ranking: Reg. U. (S), No. 25
Website: www.longwood.edu/
Admissions email: admissions@longwood.edu
Public; founded 1839
Freshman admissions: selective; 2017-2018: 4,873 applied, 4,475 accepted. Either SAT or ACT required. SAT 25/75 percentile: 960-1140. High school rank: 9% in top tenth, 29% in top quarter, 63% in top half
Early decision deadline: N/A, notification date: N/A
Early action deadline: 12/1, notification date: 1/15
Application deadline (fall): rolling
Undergraduate student body: 3,959 full time, 511 part time; 33% male, 67% female; 0% American Indian, 1% Asian, 10% black, 5% Hispanic, 4% multiracial, 0% Pacific Islander, 74% white, 2% international; 96% from in state; 66% live on campus; 14% of students in fraternities, 14% in sororities
Most popular majors: 14% Business, Management, Marketing, and Related Support Services, 14% Liberal Arts and Sciences, General Studies and Humanities, 10% Health Professions and Related Programs, 8% Parks, Recreation, Leisure, and Fitness Studies, 7% Social Sciences
Expenses: 2018-2019: $13,340 in state, $29,300 out of state; room/board: $11,026
Financial aid: (434) 395-2077

Mary Baldwin University

Staunton VA
(800) 468-2262
U.S. News ranking: Reg. U. (S), No. 31
Website: www.marybaldwin.edu
Admissions email: admit@marybaldwin.edu
Private; founded 1842
Freshman admissions: selective; 2017-2018: 1,397 applied, 1,323 accepted. Either SAT or ACT required. SAT 25/75 percentile: 950-1200. High school rank: 18% in top tenth, 55% in top quarter, 77% in top half
Early decision deadline: N/A, notification date: N/A
Early action deadline: N/A, notification date: N/A
Application deadline (fall): rolling
Undergraduate student body: 720 full time, 417 part time; 7% male, 93% female; 1% American Indian, 2% Asian, 21% black, 7% Hispanic, 4% multiracial, 0% Pacific Islander, 58% white, 1% international; 77% from in state; 42% live on campus; N/A of students in fraternities, N/A in sororities
Most popular majors: 14% Business Administration and Management, General, 11% Psychology, General, 10% Liberal Arts and Sciences/Liberal Studies, 9% Social Work, 8% Registered Nursing/Registered Nurse
Expenses: 2018-2019: $31,355; room/board: $9,410
Financial aid: (540) 887-7025; 94% of undergrads determined to have financial need; average aid package $26,009

Marymount University

Arlington VA
(703) 284-1500
U.S. News ranking: Reg. U. (S), No. 58
Website: www.marymount.edu
Admissions email: admissions@marymount.edu
Private; founded 1950
Affiliation: Roman Catholic
Freshman admissions: less selective; 2017-2018: 2,416 applied, 2,229 accepted. Neither SAT nor ACT required. SAT 25/75 percentile: 960-1140. High school rank: 12% in top tenth, 26% in top quarter, 62% in top half
Early decision deadline: N/A, notification date: N/A
Early action deadline: N/A, notification date: N/A
Application deadline (fall): rolling
Undergraduate student body: 2,069 full time, 236 part time; 35% male, 65% female; 0% American Indian, 7% Asian, 15% black, 17% Hispanic, 4% multiracial, 0% Pacific Islander, 35% white, 17% international; 60% from in state; 31% live on campus; N/A of students in fraternities, N/A in sororities
Most popular majors: 24% Registered Nursing/Registered Nurse, 16% Business Administration and Management, General, 8% Information Technology, 7% Criminal Justice/ Law Enforcement Administration, 7% Health Professions and Related Programs
Expenses: 2018-2019: $31,466; room/board: $13,190
Financial aid: (703) 284-1530; 61% of undergrads determined to have financial need; average aid package $20,543

Norfolk State University

Norfolk VA
(757) 823-8396
U.S. News ranking: Reg. U. (S), No. 91
Website: www.nsu.edu
Admissions email: admissions@nsu.edu
Public; founded 1935
Freshman admissions: least selective; 2017-2018: 6,008 applied, 5,415 accepted. Either SAT or ACT required. SAT 25/75 percentile: 840-1040. High school rank: 5% in top tenth, 15% in top quarter, 43% in top half
Early decision deadline: N/A, notification date: N/A
Early action deadline: N/A, notification date: N/A
Undergraduate student body: 4,013 full time, 676 part time; 35% male, 65% female; 0% American Indian, 0% Asian, 85% black, 4% Hispanic, 5% multiracial, 0% Pacific Islander, 4% white, 0% international; 80% from in state; 51% live on campus; N/A of students in fraternities, N/A in sororities
Most popular majors: 9% Business/ Commerce, General, 9% Psychology, General, 9% Social Work, 8% Biology/Biological Sciences, General, 7% Multi-/ Interdisciplinary Studies, Other
Expenses: 2018-2019: $9,490 in state, $20,658 out of state; room/ board: $10,360
Financial aid: (757) 823-8381; 75% of undergrads determined to have financial need

Old Dominion University

Norfolk VA
(757) 683-3685
U.S. News ranking: Nat. U., No. 215
Website: www.odu.edu
Admissions email: admissions@odu.edu
Public; founded 1930
Freshman admissions: selective; 2017-2018: 11,159 applied, 9,566 accepted. Neither SAT nor ACT required. SAT 25/75 percentile: 980-1200. High school rank: 9% in top tenth, 31% in top quarter, 69% in top half
Early decision deadline: N/A, notification date: N/A
Early action deadline: 12/1, notification date: 1/15
Application deadline (fall): 8/1
Undergraduate student body: 15,036 full time, 4,504 part time; 45% male, 55% female; 0% American Indian, 5% Asian, 31% black, 9% Hispanic, 7% multiracial, 0% Pacific Islander, 45% white, 2% international; 92% from in state; 24% live on campus; 9% of students in fraternities, 6% in sororities
Most popular majors: 20% Health Professions and Related Programs, 15% Business, Management, Marketing, and Related Support Services, 12% Social Sciences, 7% Education, 7% Psychology
Expenses: 2018-2019: $11,140 in state, $29,680 out of state; room/board: $12,318
Financial aid: (757) 683-3683; 69% of undergrads determined to have financial need; average aid package $11,059

Radford University

Radford VA
(540) 831-5371
U.S. News ranking: Reg. U. (S), No. 46
Website: www.radford.edu
Admissions email: admissions@radford.edu
Public; founded 1910
Freshman admissions: less selective; 2017-2018: 14,620 applied, 10,866 accepted. Neither SAT nor ACT required. SAT 25/75 percentile: 940-1120. High school rank: 6% in top tenth, 21% in top quarter, 58% in top half
Early decision deadline: N/A, notification date: N/A
Early action deadline: 12/1, notification date: 1/15
Application deadline (fall): rolling
Undergraduate student body: 8,049 full time, 369 part time; 43% male, 57% female; 0% American Indian, 1% Asian, 17% black, 7% Hispanic, 5% multiracial, 0% Pacific Islander, 67% white, 1% international; 94% from in state; 41% live on campus; 11% of students in fraternities, 10% in sororities
Most popular majors: 10% Multi-/Interdisciplinary Studies, Other, 8% Physical Education Teaching and Coaching, 8% Psychology, General, 7% Business Administration and Management, General, 7% Criminal Justice/ Safety Studies

More @ usnews.com/bestcolleges

Expenses: 2018-2019: $11,210 in state, $22,845 out of state; room/board: $9,406
Financial aid: (540) 831-5408; 64% of undergrads determined to have financial need; average aid package $10,054

Randolph College

Lynchburg VA
(800) 745-7692
U.S. News ranking: Nat. Lib. Arts, No. 141
Website: www.randolphcollege.edu/
Admissions email: admissions@randolphcollege.edu
Private; founded 1891
Affiliation: United Methodist
Freshman admissions: selective; 2017-2018: 1,696 applied, 1,466 accepted. Either SAT or ACT required. SAT 25/75 percentile: 950-1190. High school rank: 15% in top tenth, 38% in top quarter, 75% in top half
Early decision deadline: N/A, notification date: N/A
Early action deadline: 11/15, notification date: N/A
Application deadline (fall): rolling
Undergraduate student body: 645 full time, 18 part time; 37% male, 63% female; 0% American Indian, 3% Asian, 15% black, 6% Hispanic, 6% multiracial, 0% Pacific Islander, 65% white, 4% international; 71% from in state; 76% live on campus; 0% of students in fraternities, 0% in sororities
Most popular majors: 17% Biology/Biological Sciences, General, 11% Health and Physical Education/Fitness, General, 8% History, General, 8% Physics, General, 8% Psychology, General
Expenses: 2018-2019: $39,695; room/board: $13,580
Financial aid: (434) 947-8128; 79% of undergrads determined to have financial need; average aid package $32,962

Randolph-Macon College

Ashland VA
(800) 888-1762
U.S. News ranking: Nat. Lib. Arts, No. 120
Website: www.rmc.edu
Admissions email: admissions@rmc.edu
Private; founded 1830
Affiliation: United Methodist
Freshman admissions: selective; 2017-2018: 2,820 applied, 1,755 accepted. Either SAT or ACT required. SAT 25/75 percentile: 1050-1233. High school rank: 19% in top tenth, 56% in top quarter, 84% in top half
Early decision deadline: N/A, notification date: N/A
Early action deadline: 11/15, notification date: 1/1
Application deadline (fall): 3/1
Undergraduate student body: 1,428 full time, 25 part time; 46% male, 54% female; 1% American Indian, 2% Asian, 9% black, 4% Hispanic, 4% multiracial, 0% Pacific Islander, 77% white, 1% international; 75% from in state; 80% live on campus; 29% of students in fraternities, 25% in sororities
Most popular majors: 16% Accounting, 13% Communication and Media Studies, 10% Biology/Biological Sciences, General, 8% Political Science and Government, General, 6% Psychology, General
Expenses: 2018-2019: $41,300; room/board: $11,860
Financial aid: (804) 752-7259; 74% of undergrads determined to have financial need; average aid package $29,069

Regent University

Virginia Beach VA
(888) 718-1222
U.S. News ranking: Nat. U., No. 201
Website: www.regent.edu/
Admissions email: admissions@regent.edu
Private; founded 1978
Affiliation: Undenominational
Freshman admissions: selective; 2017-2018: 1,887 applied, 1,530 accepted. Either SAT or ACT required. SAT 25/75 percentile: 960-1180. High school rank: 13% in top tenth, 32% in top quarter, 58% in top half
Early decision deadline: N/A, notification date: N/A
Early action deadline: N/A, notification date: N/A
Application deadline (fall): 8/1
Undergraduate student body: 2,364 full time, 2,296 part time; 37% male, 63% female; 1% American Indian, 1% Asian, 29% black, 9% Hispanic, 5% multiracial, 0% Pacific Islander, 52% white, 1% international; 43% from in state; 14% live on campus; N/A of students in fraternities, N/A in sororities
Most popular majors: 22% Business Administration, Management and Operations, 18% Psychology, General, 15% Communication and Media Studies, 13% Theological and Ministerial Studies, 10% Public Administration
Expenses: 2018-2019: $18,108; room/board: $7,080
Financial aid: (757) 352-4125; 79% of undergrads determined to have financial need; average aid package $10,819

Roanoke College

Salem VA
(540) 375-2270
U.S. News ranking: Nat. Lib. Arts, No. 135
Website: www.roanoke.edu
Admissions email: admissions@roanoke.edu
Private; founded 1842
Affiliation: Evangelical Lutheran Church
Freshman admissions: selective; 2017-2018: 5,117 applied, 3,438 accepted. Either SAT or ACT required. SAT 25/75 percentile: 1040-1230. High school rank: 16% in top tenth, 39% in top quarter, 77% in top half
Early decision deadline: 11/15, notification date: 12/15
Early action deadline: N/A, notification date: N/A
Application deadline (fall): 3/15
Undergraduate student body: 1,973 full time, 64 part time; 42% male, 58% female; 0% American Indian, 1% Asian, 6% black, 5% Hispanic, 5% multiracial, 0% Pacific Islander, 80% white, 3% international; 52% from in state; 76% live on campus; 22% of students in fraternities, 22% in sororities
Most popular majors: 18% Business Administration and Management, General, 11% Psychology, General, 7% Biology/Biological Sciences, General, 7% Communication and Media Studies, 6% Kinesiology and Exercise Science
Expenses: 2018-2019: $43,780; room/board: $13,690
Financial aid: (540) 375-2235; 75% of undergrads determined to have financial need; average aid package $34,319

Shenandoah University

Winchester VA
(540) 665-4581
U.S. News ranking: Nat. U., No. 215
Website: www.su.edu
Admissions email: admit@su.edu
Private; founded 1875
Affiliation: United Methodist
Freshman admissions: selective; 2017-2018: 1,737 applied, 1,446 accepted. Either SAT or ACT required. SAT 25/75 percentile: 1010-1200. High school rank: 16% in top tenth, 39% in top quarter, N/A in top half
Early decision deadline: N/A, notification date: N/A
Early action deadline: N/A, notification date: N/A
Application deadline (fall): rolling
Undergraduate student body: 1,991 full time, 72 part time; 40% male, 60% female; 1% American Indian, 3% Asian, 11% black, 7% Hispanic, 2% multiracial, 0% Pacific Islander, 57% white, 3% international; 60% from in state; 48% live on campus; 0% of students in fraternities, 0% in sororities
Most popular majors: 25% Registered Nursing/Registered Nurse, 12% Business Administration and Management, General, 8% Exercise Physiology, 5% Biology/Biological Sciences, General, 5% Criminal Justice/Law Enforcement Administration
Expenses: 2018-2019: $32,530; room/board: $10,370
Financial aid: (540) 665-4538; 84% of undergrads determined to have financial need; average aid package $18,768

Southern Virginia University[1]

Buena Vista VA
U.S. News ranking: Nat. Lib. Arts, second tier
Admissions email: N/A
Private
Application deadline (fall): N/A
Undergraduate student body: N/A full time, N/A part time
Expenses: 2017-2018: $15,900; room/board: $6,310
Financial aid: N/A

Sweet Briar College

Sweet Briar VA
(800) 381-6142
U.S. News ranking: Nat. Lib. Arts, No. 127
Website: www.sbc.edu
Admissions email: admissions@sbc.edu
Private; founded 1901
Freshman admissions: selective; 2017-2018: 361 applied, 335 accepted. Neither SAT nor ACT required. SAT 25/75 percentile: 993-1180. High school rank: 17% in top tenth, 32% in top quarter, 69% in top half
Early decision deadline: N/A, notification date: N/A
Early action deadline: N/A, notification date: N/A
Application deadline (fall): rolling
Undergraduate student body: 314 full time, 5 part time; 2% male, 98% female; 0% American Indian, 2% Asian, 9% black, 10% Hispanic, 4% multiracial, 0% Pacific Islander, 73% white, 0% international; 53% from in state; 93% live on campus; N/A of students in fraternities, N/A in sororities
Most popular majors: 13% Business/Commerce, General, 12% Psychology, General, 9% Biology/Biological Sciences, General, 7% History, General, 6% Engineering Science
Expenses: 2018-2019: $21,000; room/board: $13,000
Financial aid: (434) 381-6156; 79% of undergrads determined to have financial need; average aid package $35,363

University of Lynchburg

Lynchburg VA
(434) 544-8300
U.S. News ranking: Reg. U. (S), No. 32
Website: www.lynchburg.edu
Admissions email: admissions@lynchburg.edu
Private; founded 1903
Affiliation: Christian Church (Disciples of Christ)
Freshman admissions: selective; 2017-2018: 4,880 applied, 3,638 accepted. Either SAT or ACT required. SAT 25/75 percentile: 1000-1180. High school rank: 9% in top tenth, 17% in top quarter, N/A in top half
Early decision deadline: 11/15, notification date: 12/15
Early action deadline: N/A, notification date: N/A
Application deadline (fall): rolling
Undergraduate student body: 1,928 full time, 122 part time; 39% male, 61% female; 0% American Indian, 1% Asian, 10% black, 4% Hispanic, 4% multiracial, 0% Pacific Islander, 76% white, 2% international; 71% from in state; 72% live on campus; 12% of students in fraternities, 12% in sororities
Most popular majors: 18% Health Professions and Related Programs, 14% Business, Management, Marketing, and Related Support Services, 13% Social Sciences, 11% Biological and Biomedical Sciences, 9% Communication, Journalism, and Related Programs
Expenses: 2018-2019: $37,690; room/board: $10,680
Financial aid: (800) 426-8101; 78% of undergrads determined to have financial need; average aid package $28,781

University of Mary Washington

Fredericksburg VA
(540) 654-2000
U.S. News ranking: Reg. U. (S), No. 19
Website: www.umw.edu
Admissions email: admit@umw.edu
Public; founded 1908
Freshman admissions: selective; 2017-2018: 5,977 applied, 4,393 accepted. Neither SAT nor ACT required. SAT 25/75 percentile: 1080-1260. High school rank: 16% in top tenth, 46% in top quarter, 85% in top half
Early decision deadline: 11/1, notification date: 12/10
Early action deadline: 11/15, notification date: 1/31
Application deadline (fall): 2/1
Undergraduate student body: 3,905 full time, 493 part time; 36% male, 64% female; 0% American Indian, 4% Asian, 8% black, 9% Hispanic, 6% multiracial, 0% Pacific Islander, 69% white, 1% international; 92% from in state; 0% live on campus; 0% of students in fraternities, 0% in sororities
Most popular majors: 16% Business, Management, Marketing, and Related Support Services, 15% Social Sciences, 10% Liberal Arts and Sciences, General Studies and Humanities, 10% Psychology, 9% English Language and Literature/Letters
Expenses: 2018-2019: $11,630 in state, $26,220 out of state; room/board: $11,118
Financial aid: (540) 654-2468; 47% of undergrads determined to have financial need; average aid package $9,932

University of Richmond

Univ. of Richmond VA
(804) 289-8640
U.S. News ranking: Nat. Lib. Arts, No. 25
Website: www.richmond.edu
Admissions email: admission@richmond.edu
Private; founded 1830
Freshman admissions: most selective; 2017-2018: 10,013 applied, 3,301 accepted. Either SAT or ACT required. ACT 25/75 percentile: 29-32. High school rank: 62% in top tenth, 92% in top quarter, 98% in top half
Early decision deadline: 11/1, notification date: 12/15
Early action deadline: 11/1, notification date: 1/20
Application deadline (fall): 1/15
Undergraduate student body: 3,004 full time, 190 part time; 47% male, 53% female; 0% American Indian, 8% Asian, 8% black, 9% Hispanic, 4% multiracial, 0% Pacific Islander, 57% white, 9% international; 20% from in state; 92% live on campus; 21% of

students in fraternities, 28% in sororities
Most popular majors: 39% Business, Management, Marketing, and Related Support Services, 11% Social Sciences, 9% Biological and Biomedical Sciences, 8% Multi/Interdisciplinary Studies, 4% Psychology
Expenses: 2018-2019: $52,610; room/board: $12,250
Financial aid: (804) 289-8438; 42% of undergrads determined to have financial need; average aid package $47,968

University of Virginia

Charlottesville VA
(434) 982-3200
U.S. News ranking: Nat. U., No. 25
Website: www.virginia.edu
Admissions email: undergradadmission@virginia.edu
Public; founded 1819
Freshman admissions: most selective; 2017-2018: 36,779 applied, 10,058 accepted. Either SAT or ACT required. SAT 25/75 percentile: 1310-1500. High school rank: 89% in top tenth, 99% in top quarter, 100% in top half
Early decision deadline: N/A, notification date: N/A
Early action deadline: 11/1, notification date: 1/31
Application deadline (fall): 1/1
Undergraduate student body: 15,774 full time, 881 part time; 45% male, 55% female; 0% American Indian, 14% Asian, 7% black, 7% Hispanic, 4% multiracial, 0% Pacific Islander, 58% white, 4% international; 73% from in state; 39% live on campus; 24% of students in fraternities, 28% in sororities
Most popular majors: 10% Economics, General, 8% Biology/Biological Sciences, General, 8% Business/Commerce, General, 6% International Relations and Affairs, 6% Psychology, General
Expenses: 2018-2019: $17,350 in state, $48,891 out of state; room/board: $11,590
Financial aid: (434) 982-6000; 34% of undergrads determined to have financial need; average aid package $27,799

University of Virginia–Wise

Wise VA
(888) 282-9324
U.S. News ranking: Nat. Lib. Arts, second tier
Website: www.uvawise.edu
Admissions email: admissions@uvawise.edu
Public; founded 1954
Freshman admissions: selective; 2017-2018: 845 applied, 655 accepted. Either SAT or ACT required. SAT 25/75 percentile: 940-1118. High school rank: 18% in top tenth, 44% in top quarter, 74% in top half
Early decision deadline: N/A, notification date: N/A
Early action deadline: 12/1, notification date: 12/15
Application deadline (fall): 8/15
Undergraduate student body: 1,210 full time, 885 part time; 39% male, 61% female; 0% American Indian, 1% Asian, 12% black, 1% Hispanic, 0% multiracial, 0% Pacific Islander, 76% white, 0% international; 94% from in state; 37% live on campus; 2% of students in fraternities, 4% in sororities
Most popular majors: 16% Education, 14% Business, Management, Marketing, and Related Support Services, 14% Social Sciences, 10% Basic Skills and Developmental/Remedial Education, 9% Biological and Biomedical Sciences
Expenses: 2018-2019: $10,119 in state, $27,176 out of state; room/board: $10,438
Financial aid: (276) 376-7130; 80% of undergrads determined to have financial need; average aid package $13,971

Virginia Commonwealth University

Richmond VA
(800) 841-3638
U.S. News ranking: Nat. U., No. 157
Website: www.vcu.edu
Admissions email: ugrad@vcu.edu
Public; founded 1838
Freshman admissions: selective; 2017-2018: 16,847 applied, 12,901 accepted. Neither SAT nor ACT required. SAT 25/75 percentile: 1076-1292. High school rank: 17% in top tenth, 46% in top quarter, 82% in top half
Early decision deadline: N/A, notification date: N/A
Early action deadline: N/A, notification date: N/A
Application deadline (fall): 1/16
Undergraduate student body: 20,338 full time, 3,672 part time; 41% male, 59% female; 0% American Indian, 13% Asian, 19% black, 9% Hispanic, 6% multiracial, 0% Pacific Islander, 46% white, 3% international; 93% from in state; 16% live on campus; N/A of students in fraternities, N/A in sororities
Most popular majors: 14% Business, Management, Marketing, and Related Support Services, 11% Visual and Performing Arts, 10% Psychology, 7% Biological and Biomedical Sciences, 6% Homeland Security, Law Enforcement, Firefighting and Related Protective Services
Expenses: 2018-2019: $14,490 in state, $35,138 out of state; room/board: $10,428
Financial aid: (804) 828-6181; 65% of undergrads determined to have financial need; average aid package $11,717

Virginia Military Institute

Lexington VA
(800) 767-4207
U.S. News ranking: Nat. Lib. Arts, No. 81
Website: www.vmi.edu
Admissions email: admissions@vmi.edu
Public; founded 1839
Freshman admissions: selective; 2017-2018: 1,718 applied, 913 accepted. Either SAT or ACT required. SAT 25/75 percentile: 1100-1280. High school rank: 15% in top tenth, 45% in top quarter, 81% in top half
Early decision deadline: 11/15, notification date: 12/15
Early action deadline: N/A, notification date: N/A
Application deadline (fall): 2/1
Undergraduate student body: 1,722 full time, 0 part time; 88% male, 12% female; 1% American Indian, 4% Asian, 6% black, 7% Hispanic, 1% multiracial, 0% Pacific Islander, 79% white, 2% international; 64% from in state; 100% live on campus; N/A of students in fraternities, N/A in sororities
Most popular majors: 18% Economics, General, 16% Civil Engineering, General, 15% International Relations and Affairs, 10% Biology/Biological Sciences, General, 8% Psychology, General
Expenses: 2018-2019: $18,862 in state, $45,706 out of state; room/board: $9,482
Financial aid: (540) 464-7208

Virginia State University

Petersburg VA
(804) 524-5902
U.S. News ranking: Reg. U. (S), No. 78
Website: www.vsu.edu
Admissions email: admiss@vsu.edu
Public; founded 1882
Freshman admissions: least selective; 2017-2018: 6,307 applied, 5,746 accepted. Either SAT or ACT required. SAT 25/75 percentile: 820-1010. High school rank: 7% in top tenth, 18% in top quarter, 49% in top half
Early decision deadline: N/A, notification date: N/A
Early action deadline: N/A, notification date: N/A
Application deadline (fall): 5/1
Undergraduate student body: 3,976 full time, 326 part time; 43% male, 57% female; 0% American Indian, 0% Asian, 40% black, 1% Hispanic, 0% multiracial, 0% Pacific Islander, 1% white, 1% international; 73% from in state; N/A live on campus; N/A of students in fraternities, N/A in sororities
Most popular majors: 12% Mass Communication/Media Studies, 11% Criminal Justice/Safety Studies, 10% Physical Education Teaching and Coaching, 6% Business Administration and Management, General, 6% Social Work
Expenses: 2017-2018: $8,726 in state, $18,841 out of state; room/board: $10,880
Financial aid: (800) 823-7214; 92% of undergrads determined to have financial need; average aid package $11,600

Virginia Tech

Blacksburg VA
(540) 231-6267
U.S. News ranking: Nat. U., No. 76
Website: www.vt.edu
Admissions email: admissions@vt.edu
Public; founded 1872
Freshman admissions: more selective; 2017-2018: 27,423 applied, 19,212 accepted. Either SAT or ACT required. SAT 25/75 percentile: 1180-1360. High school rank: 38% in top tenth, 77% in top quarter, 98% in top half
Early decision deadline: 11/1, notification date: 12/15
Early action deadline: 12/1, notification date: 12/7
Application deadline (fall): 1/15
Undergraduate student body: 26,603 full time, 590 part time; 57% male, 43% female; 0% American Indian, 10% Asian, 4% black, 6% Hispanic, 4% multiracial, 0% Pacific Islander, 66% white, 6% international; 76% from in state; 35% live on campus; 13% of students in fraternities, 19% in sororities
Most popular majors: 26% Engineering, 20% Business, Management, Marketing, and Related Support Services, 9% Family and Consumer Sciences/Human Sciences, 8% Social Sciences, 7% Biological and Biomedical Sciences
Expenses: 2018-2019: $13,620 in state, $31,304 out of state; room/board: $8,408
Financial aid: (540) 231-5179; 43% of undergrads determined to have financial need; average aid package $17,772

Virginia Union University

Richmond VA
(804) 257-5600
U.S. News ranking: Nat. Lib. Arts, second tier
Website: www.vuu.edu/
Admissions email: admissions@vuu.edu
Private; founded 1865
Affiliation: Baptist
Freshman admissions: least selective; 2017-2018: 7,156 applied, 3,549 accepted. Neither SAT nor ACT required. SAT 25/75 percentile: 780-980. High school rank: 2% in top tenth, 12% in top quarter, 39% in top half
Early decision deadline: N/A, notification date: N/A
Early action deadline: N/A, notification date: N/A
Application deadline (fall): 6/30
Undergraduate student body: 1,201 full time, 94 part time; 46% male, 54% female; 0% American Indian, 0% Asian, 95% black, 1% Hispanic, 0% multiracial, 0% Pacific Islander, 1% white, 0% international
Most popular majors: Information not available
Expenses: 2018-2019: $17,723; room/board: $8,414
Financial aid: (804) 257-5882; 96% of undergrads determined to have financial need; average aid package $14,339

Virginia Wesleyan University

Norfolk VA
(800) 737-8684
U.S. News ranking: Nat. Lib. Arts, second tier
Website: www.vwu.edu
Admissions email: admissions@vwc.edu
Private; founded 1961
Affiliation: United Methodist
Freshman admissions: selective; 2017-2018: 2,200 applied, 1,559 accepted. Either SAT or ACT required. SAT 25/75 percentile: 952-1160. High school rank: 15% in top tenth, 33% in top quarter, 63% in top half
Early decision deadline: N/A, notification date: N/A
Early action deadline: N/A, notification date: N/A
Application deadline (fall): rolling
Undergraduate student body: 1,354 full time, 82 part time; 40% male, 60% female; 1% American Indian, 1% Asian, 27% black, 9% Hispanic, 7% multiracial, 0% Pacific Islander, 49% white, 1% international; 75% from in state; 66% live on campus; N/A of students in fraternities, N/A in sororities
Most popular majors: 15% Business, Management, Marketing, and Related Support Services, 11% Homeland Security, Law Enforcement, Firefighting and Related Protective Services, 10% Psychology, 9% Multi/Interdisciplinary Studies, 8% Biological and Biomedical Sciences
Expenses: 2018-2019: $36,660; room/board: $9,255
Financial aid: (757) 455-3345; 84% of undergrads determined to have financial need; average aid package $25,303

Washington and Lee University

Lexington VA
(540) 458-8710
U.S. News ranking: Nat. Lib. Arts, No. 11
Website: www.wlu.edu
Admissions email: admissions@wlu.edu
Private; founded 1749
Freshman admissions: most selective; 2017-2018: 5,455 applied, 1,200 accepted. Either SAT or ACT required. ACT 25/75 percentile: 31-33. High school rank: 81% in top tenth, 96% in top quarter, 100% in top half
Early decision deadline: 11/1, notification date: 12/15
Early action deadline: N/A, notification date: N/A
Application deadline (fall): 1/1
Undergraduate student body: 1,823 full time, 4 part time; 52% male, 48% female; 0% American Indian, 3% Asian, 2% black, 5% Hispanic, 3% multiracial, 0% Pacific Islander, 83% white, 4% international; 16% from in state; 75% live on campus; 73% of students in fraternities, 77% in sororities
Most popular majors: 17% Business Administration and Management, General, 9% Accounting and Business/Management,

9% Economics, General, 9% Political Science and Government, General, 5% English Language and Literature, General
Expenses: 2018-2019: $52,455; room/board: $13,925
Financial aid: (540) 458-8717; 43% of undergrads determined to have financial need; average aid package $50,827

WASHINGTON

Art Institute of Seattle[1]

Seattle WA
(206) 448-0900
U.S. News ranking: Arts, unranked
Website: www.ais.edu
Admissions email: N/A
For-profit
Application deadline (fall): N/A
Undergraduate student body: N/A full time, N/A part time
Expenses: N/A
Financial aid: N/A

Bellevue College[1]

Bellevue WA
(425) 564-1000
U.S. News ranking: Reg. Coll. (W), unranked
Website: www.bellevuecollege.edu
Admissions email: N/A
Public
Application deadline (fall): N/A
Undergraduate student body: N/A full time, N/A part time
Expenses: 2017-2018: $3,699 in state, $9,052 out of state; room/board: N/A
Financial aid: N/A

Centralia College[1]

Centralia WA
U.S. News ranking: Reg. Coll. (W), unranked
Admissions email: N/A
Public
Application deadline (fall): N/A
Undergraduate student body: N/A full time, N/A part time
Expenses: 2017-2018: $4,343 in state, $4,766 out of state; room/board: $10,260
Financial aid: N/A

Central Washington University

Ellensburg WA
(509) 963-1211
U.S. News ranking: Reg. U. (W), No. 48
Website: www.cwu.edu
Admissions email: admissions@cwu.edu
Public; founded 1891
Freshman admissions: less selective; 2017-2018: 8,600 applied, 7,428 accepted. Either SAT or ACT required. SAT 25/75 percentile: 960-1160. High school rank: N/A
Early decision deadline: N/A, notification date: N/A
Early action deadline: N/A, notification date: N/A
Application deadline (fall): rolling
Undergraduate student body: 9,926 full time, 1,709 part time; 48% male, 52% female; 1% American Indian, 4% Asian, 4% black, 16% Hispanic, 8% multiracial, 1% Pacific Islander, 53% white, 3% international; 95% from in state; 32% live on campus; 0% of students in fraternities, 0% in sororities
Most popular majors: 19% Business, Management, Marketing, and Related Support Services, 12% Education, 10% Social Sciences, 8% Computer and Information Sciences and Support Services, 7% Homeland Security, Law Enforcement, Firefighting and Related Protective Services
Expenses: 2018-2019: $7,153 in state, $21,260 out of state; room/board: $10,684
Financial aid: (509) 963-1611; 66% of undergrads determined to have financial need; average aid package $10,340

City University of Seattle[1]

Seattle WA
(888) 422-4898
U.S. News ranking: Reg. U. (W), unranked
Website: www.cityu.edu
Admissions email: info@cityu.edu
Private; founded 1973
Application deadline (fall): N/A
Undergraduate student body: N/A full time, N/A part time
Expenses: 2017-2018: $16,920; room/board: $10,050
Financial aid: N/A

Columbia Basin College[1]

Pasco WA
U.S. News ranking: Reg. Coll. (W), unranked
Admissions email: N/A
Public
Application deadline (fall): N/A
Undergraduate student body: N/A full time, N/A part time
Expenses: 2017-2018: $4,554 in state, $6,530 out of state; room/board: $9,680
Financial aid: N/A

Cornish College of the Arts

Seattle WA
(800) 726-2787
U.S. News ranking: Arts, unranked
Website: www.cornish.edu
Admissions email: admission@cornish.edu
Private; founded 1914
Freshman admissions: least selective; 2017-2018: 1,118 applied, 953 accepted. Neither SAT nor ACT required. SAT 25/75 percentile: N/A. High school rank: N/A
Early decision deadline: N/A, notification date: N/A
Early action deadline: 12/1, notification date: 12/15
Application deadline (fall): N/A
Undergraduate student body: 650 full time, 8 part time; 34% male, 66% female; 1% American Indian, 4% Asian, 3% black, 14% Hispanic, 10% multiracial, 1% Pacific Islander, 62% white, 1% international; 43% from in state; 33% live on campus; N/A of students in fraternities, N/A in sororities
Most popular majors: 26% Drama and Dramatics/Theatre Arts, General, 18% Dance, General, 18% Design and Visual Communications, General, 15% Fine/Studio Arts, General, 12% Music Performance, General
Expenses: 2018-2019: $41,642; room/board: $12,400
Financial aid: (206) 726-5063; 78% of undergrads determined to have financial need; average aid package $23,677

Eastern Washington University

Cheney WA
(509) 359-2397
U.S. News ranking: Reg. U. (W), No. 77
Website: www.ewu.edu
Admissions email: admissions@ewu.edu
Public; founded 1882
Freshman admissions: less selective; 2017-2018: 4,444 applied, 4,276 accepted. Either SAT or ACT required. SAT 25/75 percentile: 870-1090. High school rank: N/A
Early decision deadline: N/A, notification date: N/A
Early action deadline: N/A, notification date: N/A
Application deadline (fall): 5/15
Undergraduate student body: 10,060 full time, 1,413 part time; 46% male, 54% female; 1% American Indian, 3% Asian, 3% black, 16% Hispanic, 7% multiracial, 0% Pacific Islander, 63% white, 5% international; 95% from in state; 16% live on campus; N/A of students in fraternities, N/A in sororities
Most popular majors: 19% Business, Management, Marketing, and Related Support Services, 10% Health Professions and Related Programs, 9% Biological and Biomedical Sciences, 8% Education, 8% Social Sciences
Expenses: 2018-2019: $7,333 in state, $24,455 out of state; room/board: $12,058
Financial aid: (509) 359-2314; 61% of undergrads determined to have financial need; average aid package $13,055

Evergreen State College

Olympia WA
(360) 867-6170
U.S. News ranking: Reg. U. (W), No. 35
Website: www.evergreen.edu
Admissions email: admissions@evergreen.edu
Public; founded 1967
Freshman admissions: selective; 2017-2018: 1,772 applied, 1,706 accepted. Either SAT or ACT required. SAT 25/75 percentile: 960-1190. High school rank: 9% in top tenth, 32% in top quarter, 59% in top half
Early decision deadline: N/A, notification date: N/A
Early action deadline: N/A, notification date: N/A
Application deadline (fall): rolling
Undergraduate student body: 3,330 full time, 280 part time; 42% male, 58% female; 2% American Indian, 3% Asian, 5% black, 11% Hispanic, 8% multiracial, 0% Pacific Islander, 66% white, 1% international; 80% from in state; 24% live on campus; 0% of students in fraternities, 0% in sororities
Most popular majors: 82% Liberal Arts and Sciences/Liberal Studies, 18% Biological and Physical Sciences
Expenses: 2018-2019: $7,944 in state, $26,460 out of state; room/board: $11,346
Financial aid: (360) 867-6205; 67% of undergrads determined to have financial need; average aid package $12,210

Gonzaga University

Spokane WA
(800) 322-2584
U.S. News ranking: Reg. U. (W), No. 4
Website: www.gonzaga.edu
Admissions email: admissions@gonzaga.edu
Private; founded 1887
Affiliation: Roman Catholic
Freshman admissions: more selective; 2017-2018: 7,613 applied, 4,937 accepted. Either SAT or ACT required. SAT 25/75 percentile: 1180-1350. High school rank: 42% in top tenth, 75% in top quarter, 96% in top half
Early decision deadline: N/A, notification date: N/A
Early action deadline: 11/15, notification date: 1/15
Application deadline (fall): 2/1
Undergraduate student body: 5,110 full time, 99 part time; 48% male, 52% female; 1% American Indian, 5% Asian, 1% black, 11% Hispanic, 6% multiracial, 0% Pacific Islander, 72% white, 1% international; 49% from in state; 55% live on campus; N/A of students in fraternities, N/A in sororities
Most popular majors: 24% Business, Management, Marketing, and Related Support Services, 15% Engineering, 12% Social Sciences, 10% Biological and Biomedical Sciences, 8% Psychology
Expenses: 2018-2019: $43,210; room/board: $11,944
Financial aid: (509) 313-6562; 53% of undergrads determined to have financial need; average aid package $32,280

Heritage University[1]

Toppenish WA
(509) 865-8500
U.S. News ranking: Reg. U. (W), unranked
Website: www.heritage.edu
Admissions email: admissions@heritage.edu
Private
Application deadline (fall): N/A
Undergraduate student body: N/A full time, N/A part time
Expenses: 2017-2018: $17,914; room/board: N/A
Financial aid: N/A

Lake Washington Institute of Technology

Kirkland WA
(425) 739-8104
U.S. News ranking: Reg. Coll. (W), unranked
Website: www.lwtech.edu/
Admissions email: admissions@lwtech.edu
Public; founded 1949
Freshman admissions: least selective; 2017-2018: 354 applied, 354 accepted. Neither SAT nor ACT required. SAT 25/75 percentile: N/A. High school rank: N/A
Early decision deadline: N/A, notification date: N/A
Early action deadline: N/A, notification date: N/A
Application deadline (fall): N/A
Undergraduate student body: 2,177 full time, 2,294 part time; 40% male, 60% female; N/A American Indian, N/A Asian, N/A black, N/A Hispanic, N/A multiracial, N/A Pacific Islander, N/A white, N/A international
Most popular majors: Information not available
Expenses: 2018-2019: $7,539 in state, $19,084 out of state; room/board: N/A
Financial aid: (425) 739-8106

North Seattle College[1]

Seattle WA
U.S. News ranking: Reg. Coll. (W), unranked
Admissions email: N/A
Public
Application deadline (fall): N/A
Undergraduate student body: N/A full time, N/A part time
Expenses: 2017-2018: $4,302 in state, $4,302 out of state; room/board: N/A
Financial aid: N/A

Northwest University

Kirkland WA
(425) 889-5231
U.S. News ranking: Reg. U. (W), No. 46
Website: www.northwestu.edu
Admissions email: admissions@northwestu.edu
Private; founded 1934
Affiliation: Assemblies of God Church
Freshman admissions: selective; 2017-2018: 473 applied, 459 accepted. Either SAT or ACT required. SAT 25/75 percentile: 1005-1240. High school rank: N/A
Early decision deadline: N/A, notification date: N/A
Early action deadline: 11/15, notification date: 12/15
Application deadline (fall): rolling
Undergraduate student body: 929 full time, 21 part time; 36% male, 64% female; 2% American Indian, 5% Asian, 4% black, 9% Hispanic, 5% multiracial, 2% Pacific Islander, 67% white, 5% international; 82% from in state; 54% live on campus; 0% of students in fraternities, 0% in sororities
Most popular majors: 14% Registered Nursing/Registered Nurse, 8% Business Adminis-

tration and Management, General, 6% Psychology, General, 4% Organizational Communication, General, 2% Music, Other
Expenses: 2018-2019: $31,540; room/board: $8,620
Financial aid: (425) 889-5210; 80% of undergrads determined to have financial need; average aid package $18,812

Olympic College[1]

Bremerton WA
(360) 792-6050
U.S. News ranking: Reg. Coll. (W), unranked
Website: www.olympic.edu
Admissions email: N/A
Public
Application deadline (fall): N/A
Undergraduate student body: N/A full time, N/A part time
Expenses: 2017-2018: $3,693 in state, $4,147 out of state; room/board: $9,855
Financial aid: N/A

Pacific Lutheran University

Tacoma WA
(800) 274-6758
U.S. News ranking: Reg. U. (W), No. 23
Website: www.plu.edu
Admissions email: admission@plu.edu
Private; founded 1890
Affiliation: Lutheran Church in America
Freshman admissions: selective; 2017-2018: 3,629 applied, 2,736 accepted. Either SAT or ACT required. SAT 25/75 percentile: 1040-1270. High school rank: N/A
Early decision deadline: N/A, notification date: N/A
Early action deadline: N/A, notification date: N/A
Application deadline (fall): N/A
Undergraduate student body: 2,638 full time, 71 part time; 37% male, 63% female; 1% American Indian, 10% Asian, 3% black, 9% Hispanic, 9% multiracial, 1% Pacific Islander, 63% white, 3% international; 78% from in state; 49% live on campus; N/A of students in fraternities, N/A in sororities
Most popular majors: 13% Business, Management, Marketing, and Related Support Services, 12% Health Professions and Related Programs, 9% Biological and Biomedical Sciences, 9% Social Sciences, 7% Physical Sciences
Expenses: 2018-2019: $42,066; room/board: $10,790
Financial aid: (253) 535-7161; 75% of undergrads determined to have financial need; average aid package $37,858

Peninsula College[1]

Port Angeles WA
(360) 452-9277
U.S. News ranking: Reg. Coll. (W), unranked
Website: www.pencol.edu
Admissions email: N/A
Public
Application deadline (fall): N/A
Undergraduate student body: N/A full time, N/A part time
Expenses: 2017-2018: $4,347 in state, $4,752 out of state; room/board: N/A
Financial aid: N/A

Saint Martin's University

Lacey WA
(800) 368-8803
U.S. News ranking: Reg. U. (W), No. 37
Website: www.stmartin.edu
Admissions email: admissions@stmartin.edu
Private; founded 1895
Affiliation: Roman Catholic
Freshman admissions: selective; 2017-2018: 1,367 applied, 1,333 accepted. Neither SAT nor ACT required. SAT 25/75 percentile: 980-1190. High school rank: 24% in top tenth, 52% in top quarter, 76% in top half
Early decision deadline: N/A, notification date: N/A
Early action deadline: N/A, notification date: N/A
Application deadline (fall): 7/31
Undergraduate student body: 1,119 full time, 191 part time; 52% male, 48% female; 1% American Indian, 8% Asian, 6% black, 15% Hispanic, 7% multiracial, 5% Pacific Islander, 49% white, 5% international; 72% from in state; 41% live on campus; 0% of students in fraternities, 0% in sororities
Most popular majors: 20% Business, Management, Marketing, and Related Support Services, 16% Engineering, 12% Education, 9% Psychology, 8% Biological and Biomedical Sciences
Expenses: 2018-2019: $37,356; room/board: $11,445
Financial aid: (360) 486-8868; 84% of undergrads determined to have financial need; average aid package $27,128

Seattle Central College[1]

Seattle WA
(206) 934-5450
U.S. News ranking: Reg. Coll. (W), unranked
Website: www.seattlecentral.edu/
Admissions email: Admissions.Central@seattlecolleges.edu
Public; founded 1966
Application deadline (fall): rolling
Undergraduate student body: N/A full time, N/A part time
Expenses: 2017-2018: $3,795 in state, $3,795 out of state; room/board: N/A
Financial aid: N/A

Seattle Pacific University

Seattle WA
(800) 366-3344
U.S. News ranking: Nat. U., No. 169
Website: www.spu.edu
Admissions email: admissions@spu.edu
Private; founded 1891
Freshman admissions: selective; 2017-2018: 3,692 applied, 3,355 accepted. Either SAT or ACT required. SAT 25/75 percentile: 990-1230. High school rank: N/A
Early decision deadline: N/A, notification date: N/A
Early action deadline: 11/15, notification date: 1/5
Application deadline (fall): 2/1
Undergraduate student body: 2,783 full time, 128 part time; 33% male, 67% female; 0% American Indian, 12% Asian, 4% black, 12% Hispanic, 9% multiracial, 1% Pacific Islander, 55% white, 5% international; 63% from in state; 52% live on campus; 0% of students in fraternities, 0% in sororities
Most popular majors: Information not available
Expenses: 2018-2019: $42,939; room/board: $11,796
Financial aid: (206) 281-2061; 70% of undergrads determined to have financial need; average aid package $35,839

Seattle University

Seattle WA
(206) 296-2000
U.S. News ranking: Reg. U. (W), No. 8
Website: www.seattleu.edu
Admissions email: admissions@seattleu.edu
Private; founded 1891
Affiliation: Roman Catholic
Freshman admissions: more selective; 2017-2018: 8,576 applied, 6,329 accepted. Either SAT or ACT required. SAT 25/75 percentile: 1130-1330. High school rank: 33% in top tenth, 68% in top quarter, 94% in top half
Early decision deadline: N/A, notification date: N/A
Early action deadline: 11/15, notification date: 12/23
Application deadline (fall): rolling
Undergraduate student body: 4,383 full time, 264 part time; 38% male, 62% female; 0% American Indian, 16% Asian, 3% black, 12% Hispanic, 8% multiracial, 1% Pacific Islander, 44% white, 10% international; 41% from in state; 45% live on campus; 0% of students in fraternities, 0% in sororities
Most popular majors: 23% Business, Management, Marketing, and Related Support Services, 14% Health Professions and Related Programs, 8% Engineering, 5% Biological and Biomedical Sciences, 5% Psychology
Expenses: 2018-2019: $44,610; room/board: $12,288
Financial aid: (206) 296-5852; 58% of undergrads determined to have financial need; average aid package $36,167

South Seattle College[1]

Seattle WA
(206) 764-5300
U.S. News ranking: Reg. Coll. (W), unranked
Website: www.southseattle.edu
Admissions email: N/A
Public
Application deadline (fall): N/A
Undergraduate student body: N/A full time, N/A part time
Expenses: 2017-2018: $4,515 in state, $4,515 out of state; room/board: N/A
Financial aid: N/A

University of Puget Sound

Tacoma WA
(253) 879-3211
U.S. News ranking: Nat. Lib. Arts, No. 72
Website: www.pugetsound.edu
Admissions email: admission@pugetsound.edu
Private; founded 1888
Freshman admissions: more selective; 2017-2018: 5,958 applied, 4,997 accepted. Neither SAT nor ACT required. ACT 25/75 percentile: 25-31. High school rank: 34% in top tenth, 66% in top quarter, 91% in top half
Early decision deadline: 11/15, notification date: 12/15
Early action deadline: 11/15, notification date: 1/15
Application deadline (fall): 1/15
Undergraduate student body: 2,390 full time, 23 part time; 40% male, 60% female; 0% American Indian, 6% Asian, 1% black, 8% Hispanic, 9% multiracial, 0% Pacific Islander, 71% white, 1% international; 21% from in state; 65% live on campus; 28% of students in fraternities, 27% in sororities
Most popular majors: 17% Social Sciences, 12% Business, Management, Marketing, and Related Support Services, 11% Biological and Biomedical Sciences, 10% Psychology, 7% Foreign Languages, Literatures, and Linguistics
Expenses: 2018-2019: $49,776; room/board: $12,540
Financial aid: (253) 879-3214; 52% of undergrads determined to have financial need; average aid package $34,720

University of Washington

Seattle WA
(206) 543-9686
U.S. News ranking: Nat. U., No. 59
Website: www.washington.edu
Admissions email: pseegert@uw.edu
Public; founded 1861
Freshman admissions: more selective; 2017-2018: 44,877 applied, 20,833 accepted. Either SAT or ACT required. SAT 25/75 percentile: 1190-1420. High school rank: 63% in top tenth, 93% in top quarter, 100% in top half
Early decision deadline: N/A, notification date: N/A
Early action deadline: N/A, notification date: N/A
Application deadline (fall): 11/15
Undergraduate student body: 28,759 full time, 2,572 part time; 47% male, 53% female; 0% American Indian, 24% Asian, 3% black, 8% Hispanic, 7% multiracial, 0% Pacific Islander, 40% white, 15% international; 82% from in state; 27% live on campus; 16% of students in fraternities, 15% in sororities
Most popular majors: 14% Social Sciences, 13% Biological and Biomedical Sciences, 11% Business, Management, Marketing, and Related Support Services, 10% Engineering, 6% Health Professions and Related Programs
Expenses: 2018-2019: $11,517 in state, $36,898 out of state; room/board: $12,798
Financial aid: (206) 543-6101; 43% of undergrads determined to have financial need; average aid package $17,380

Walla Walla University

College Place WA
(509) 527-2327
U.S. News ranking: Reg. U. (W), No. 44
Website: www.wallawalla.edu
Admissions email: info@wallawalla.edu
Private; founded 1892
Affiliation: Seventh Day Adventist
Freshman admissions: selective; 2017-2018: 1,846 applied, 1,194 accepted. Either SAT or ACT required. SAT 25/75 percentile: 1020-1240. High school rank: N/A
Early decision deadline: N/A, notification date: N/A
Early action deadline: N/A, notification date: N/A
Application deadline (fall): rolling
Undergraduate student body: 1,580 full time, 69 part time; 50% male, 50% female; 1% American Indian, 6% Asian, 4% black, 15% Hispanic, 0% multiracial, 4% Pacific Islander, 63% white, 5% international; 37% from in state; 77% live on campus; N/A of students in fraternities, N/A in sororities
Most popular majors: 26% Health Professions and Related Programs, 15% Engineering, 10% Business, Management, Marketing, and Related Support Services, 8% Biological and Biomedical Sciences, 6% Visual and Performing Arts
Expenses: 2018-2019: $28,035; room/board: $7,845
Financial aid: (509) 527-2815; 64% of undergrads determined to have financial need; average aid package $22,645

Washington State University

Pullman WA
(888) 468-6978
U.S. News ranking: Nat. U., No. 140
Website: www.wsu.edu
Admissions email: admissions@wsu.edu
Public; founded 1890
Freshman admissions: selective; 2017-2018: 22,565 applied, 16,487 accepted. Either SAT or ACT required. SAT 25/75 percentile: 1020-1220. High school rank: 38% in top tenth, 61% in top quarter, 89% in top half
Early decision deadline: N/A, notification date: N/A
Early action deadline: N/A, notification date: N/A
Application deadline (fall): rolling

More @ usnews.com/bestcolleges

Undergraduate student body: 22,166 full time, 3,111 part time; 48% male, 52% female; 1% American Indian, 6% Asian, 3% black, 15% Hispanic, 7% multiracial, 0% Pacific Islander, 61% white, 4% international; 87% from in state; 24% live on campus; 23% of students in fraternities, 25% in sororities
Most popular majors: 21% Business, Management, Marketing, and Related Support Services, 11% Engineering, 10% Social Sciences, 8% Communication, Journalism, and Related Programs, 8% Health Professions and Related Programs
Expenses: 2018-2019: $11,584 in state, $25,820 out of state; room/board: $11,398
Financial aid: (509) 335-9711; 59% of undergrads determined to have financial need; average aid package $12,992

Western Washington University

Bellingham WA
(360) 650-3440
U.S. News ranking: Reg. U. (W), No. 19
Website: www.wwu.edu
Admissions email: admit@wwu.edu
Public; founded 1893
Freshman admissions: selective; 2017-2018: 11,244 applied, 9,534 accepted. Either SAT or ACT required. SAT 25/75 percentile: 1080-1280. High school rank: 22% in top tenth, 53% in top quarter, 88% in top half
Early decision deadline: N/A, notification date: N/A
Early action deadline: 11/1, notification date: 12/31
Application deadline (fall): 1/31
Undergraduate student body: 13,728 full time, 1,240 part time; 44% male, 56% female; 0% American Indian, 6% Asian, 2% black, 9% Hispanic, 9% multiracial, 0% Pacific Islander, 72% white, 1% international; 89% from in state; 27% live on campus; 0% of students in fraternities, 0% in sororities
Most popular majors: 13% Business, Management, Marketing, and Related Support Services, 13% Social Sciences, 7% Multi/Interdisciplinary Studies, 6% Education, 6% English Language and Literature/Letters
Expenses: 2018-2019: $8,055 in state, $22,440 out of state; room/board: $11,466
Financial aid: (360) 650-2422; 50% of undergrads determined to have financial need; average aid package $15,563

Whitman College

Walla Walla WA
(509) 527-5176
U.S. News ranking: Nat. Lib. Arts, No. 43
Website: www.whitman.edu
Admissions email: admission@whitman.edu
Private; founded 1883
Freshman admissions: more selective; 2017-2018: 4,081 applied, 2,111 accepted. Neither SAT nor ACT required. ACT 25/75 percentile: 26-31. High school rank: 59% in top tenth, 88% in top quarter, 98% in top half
Early decision deadline: 11/15, notification date: 12/20
Early action deadline: N/A, notification date: N/A
Application deadline (fall): 1/15
Undergraduate student body: 1,455 full time, 55 part time; 43% male, 57% female; 1% American Indian, 5% Asian, 2% black, 7% Hispanic, 7% multiracial, 0% Pacific Islander, 69% white, 7% international; 34% from in state; 64% live on campus; 33% of students in fraternities, 41% in sororities
Most popular majors: 11% Biology/Biological Sciences, General, 9% Psychology, General, 7% Economics, General, 6% Social Sciences, General, 5% Fine/Studio Arts, General
Expenses: 2018-2019: $51,764; room/board: $13,174
Financial aid: (509) 527-5178; 44% of undergrads determined to have financial need; average aid package $41,281

Whitworth University

Spokane WA
(800) 533-4668
U.S. News ranking: Reg. U. (W), No. 8
Website: www.whitworth.edu
Admissions email: admissions@whitworth.edu
Private; founded 1890
Affiliation: Presbyterian Church (USA)
Freshman admissions: more selective; 2017-2018: 3,166 applied, 2,818 accepted. Neither SAT nor ACT required. SAT 25/75 percentile: 1090-1310. High school rank: 36% in top tenth, 70% in top quarter, 94% in top half
Early decision deadline: N/A, notification date: N/A
Early action deadline: 11/15, notification date: 12/6
Application deadline (fall): 8/1
Undergraduate student body: 2,211 full time, 40 part time; 40% male, 60% female; 1% American Indian, 5% Asian, 2% black, 9% Hispanic, 7% multiracial, 1% Pacific Islander, 70% white, 4% international; 67% from in state; 51% live on campus; 0% of students in fraternities, 0% in sororities
Most popular majors: 13% Business, Management, Marketing, and Related Support Services, 10% Education, 10% Multi/Interdisciplinary Studies, 8% Psychology, 7% Social Sciences
Expenses: 2018-2019: $43,640; room/board: $11,496
Financial aid: (509) 777-3215; 70% of undergrads determined to have financial need; average aid package $36,320

WEST VIRGINIA

Alderson Broaddus University

Philippi WV
(800) 263-1549
U.S. News ranking: Reg. Coll. (S), No. 30
Website: www.ab.edu
Admissions email: admissions@ab.edu
Private; founded 1871
Affiliation: American Baptist
Freshman admissions: selective; 2017-2018: 4,329 applied, 1,759 accepted. Either SAT or ACT required. ACT 25/75 percentile: 18-23. High school rank: 7% in top tenth, 24% in top quarter, 62% in top half
Early decision deadline: N/A, notification date: N/A
Early action deadline: N/A, notification date: N/A
Application deadline (fall): 8/25
Undergraduate student body: 903 full time, 49 part time; 55% male, 45% female; 1% American Indian, 1% Asian, 24% black, 5% Hispanic, 1% multiracial, 0% Pacific Islander, 63% white, 6% international; 39% from in state; 82% live on campus; 4% of students in fraternities, 5% in sororities
Most popular majors: 14% Registered Nursing/Registered Nurse, 9% Biology/Biological Sciences, General, 9% Business Administration and Management, General, 7% Criminology, 7% Sport and Fitness Administration/Management
Expenses: 2018-2019: $27,910; room/board: $8,960
Financial aid: (304) 457-6354; 88% of undergrads determined to have financial need; average aid package $23,198

American Public University System

Charles Town WV
(877) 777-9081
U.S. News ranking: Reg. U. (S), unranked
Website: www.apus.edu
Admissions email: N/A
For-profit; founded 1991
Freshman admissions: least selective; 2017-2018: N/A applied, N/A accepted. Neither SAT nor ACT required. SAT 25/75 percentile: N/A. High school rank: N/A
Early decision deadline: N/A, notification date: N/A
Early action deadline: N/A, notification date: N/A
Application deadline (fall): rolling
Undergraduate student body: 2,914 full time, 34,996 part time; 64% male, 36% female; 1% American Indian, 2% Asian, 16% black, 12% Hispanic, 4% multiracial, 1% Pacific Islander, 56% white, 1% international
Most popular majors: 16% Business Administration and Management, General, 11% General Studies, 7% International/Global Studies, 6% Criminal Justice/Safety Studies, 4% Homeland Security
Expenses: 2017-2018: $8,100; room/board: N/A
Financial aid: (855) 731-9218

Bethany College

Bethany WV
(304) 829-7611
U.S. News ranking: Nat. Lib. Arts, second tier
Website: www.bethanywv.edu
Admissions email: enrollment@bethanywv.edu
Private; founded 1840
Affiliation: Christian Church (Disciples of Christ)
Freshman admissions: less selective; 2017-2018: 855 applied, 804 accepted. Either SAT or ACT required. SAT 25/75 percentile: 850-1110. High school rank: 10% in top tenth, 15% in top quarter, 55% in top half
Early decision deadline: N/A, notification date: N/A
Early action deadline: N/A, notification date: N/A
Application deadline (fall): rolling
Undergraduate student body: 599 full time, 4 part time; 60% male, 40% female; 2% American Indian, 1% Asian, 20% black, 4% Hispanic, 0% multiracial, 0% Pacific Islander, 54% white, 2% international
Most popular majors: 15% Communication and Media Studies, 15% Social Work, 12% Psychology, General, 10% Physical Education Teaching and Coaching, 7% Business Administration and Management, General
Expenses: 2018-2019: $29,773; room/board: $10,270
Financial aid: (304) 829-7601; 87% of undergrads determined to have financial need; average aid package $25,215

Bluefield State College

Bluefield WV
(304) 327-4065
U.S. News ranking: Reg. Coll. (S), No. 58
Website: www.bluefieldstate.edu
Admissions email: bscadmit@bluefieldstate.edu
Public; founded 1895
Freshman admissions: selective; 2017-2018: 489 applied, 445 accepted. Either SAT or ACT required. ACT 25/75 percentile: 17-21. High school rank: 18% in top tenth, 56% in top quarter, 82% in top half
Early decision deadline: N/A, notification date: N/A
Early action deadline: N/A, notification date: N/A
Application deadline (fall): rolling
Undergraduate student body: 1,099 full time, 280 part time; 37% male, 63% female; 0% American Indian, 1% Asian, 8% black, 1% Hispanic, 3% multiracial, 0% Pacific Islander, 84% white, 2% international; 98% from in state; 0% live on campus; N/A of students in fraternities, N/A in sororities
Most popular majors: 19% Engineering Technologies and Engineering-Related Fields, 17% Business, Management, Marketing, and Related Support Services, 16% Liberal Arts and Sciences, General Studies and Humanities, 13% Education, 11% Health Professions and Related Programs
Expenses: 2018-2019: $10,038 in state, $13,683 out of state; room/board: N/A
Financial aid: N/A; 82% of undergrads determined to have financial need; average aid package $3,200

Concord University

Athens WV
(888) 384-5249
U.S. News ranking: Reg. U. (S), second tier
Website: www.concord.edu
Admissions email: admissions@concord.edu
Public; founded 1872
Freshman admissions: selective; 2017-2018: 2,507 applied, 2,261 accepted. Either SAT or ACT required. ACT 25/75 percentile: 18-23. High school rank: 15% in top tenth, 42% in top quarter, 73% in top half
Early decision deadline: N/A, notification date: N/A
Early action deadline: N/A, notification date: N/A
Application deadline (fall): rolling
Undergraduate student body: 1,696 full time, 157 part time; 42% male, 58% female; 0% American Indian, 1% Asian, 6% black, 1% Hispanic, 2% multiracial, 0% Pacific Islander, 83% white, 6% international; 86% from in state; 40% live on campus; N/A of students in fraternities, N/A in sororities
Most popular majors: 23% Liberal Arts and Sciences, General Studies and Humanities, 21% Business, Management, Marketing, and Related Support Services, 13% Education, 7% Social Sciences, 6% Biological and Biomedical Sciences
Expenses: 2018-2019: $8,026 in state, $17,470 out of state; room/board: $8,988
Financial aid: (304) 384-5358; 77% of undergrads determined to have financial need; average aid package $8,471

Davis and Elkins College[1]

Elkins WV
(304) 637-1230
U.S. News ranking: Nat. Lib. Arts, second tier
Website: www.davisandelkins.edu
Admissions email: admiss@davisandelkins.edu
Private
Application deadline (fall): N/A
Undergraduate student body: N/A full time, N/A part time
Expenses: 2017-2018: $28,992; room/board: $9,250
Financial aid: N/A

Fairmont State University

Fairmont WV
(304) 367-4010
U.S. News ranking: Reg. U. (S), second tier
Website: www.fairmontstate.edu
Admissions email: admit@fairmontstate.edu
Public; founded 1865
Freshman admissions: selective; 2017-2018: 2,630 applied, 1,856 accepted. Either SAT or ACT required. ACT 25/75 percentile: 18-23. High school rank: 10% in top tenth, 33% in top quarter, 69% in top half
Early decision deadline: N/A, notification date: N/A
Early action deadline: N/A, notification date: N/A

Application deadline (fall): 8/1
Undergraduate student body: 3,106 full time, 421 part time; 44% male, 56% female; 0% American Indian, 1% Asian, 6% black, 2% Hispanic, 4% multiracial, 0% Pacific Islander, 85% white, 2% international; 91% from in state; 28% live on campus; N/A of students in fraternities, N/A in sororities
Most popular majors: 15% Business, Management, Marketing, and Related Support Services, 14% Homeland Security, Law Enforcement, Firefighting and Related Protective Services, 12% Health Professions and Related Programs, 10% Family and Consumer Sciences/ Human Sciences, 10% Foreign Languages, Literatures, and Linguistics
Expenses: 2018-2019: $7,514 in state, $16,324 out of state; room/ board: $9,174
Financial aid: (304) 367-4826; 71% of undergrads determined to have financial need; average aid package $9,342

Glenville State College

Glenville WV
(304) 462-4128
U.S. News ranking: Reg. Coll. (S), No. 52
Website: www.glenville.edu
Admissions email: admissions@glenville.edu
Public; founded 1872
Freshman admissions: less selective; 2017-2018: 2,463 applied, 1,326 accepted. Either SAT or ACT required. ACT 25/75 percentile: 16-21. High school rank: 4% in top tenth, 23% in top quarter, 56% in top half
Early decision deadline: N/A, notification date: N/A
Early action deadline: N/A, notification date: N/A
Application deadline (fall): rolling
Undergraduate student body: 1,045 full time, 627 part time; 57% male, 43% female; N/A American Indian, N/A Asian, N/A black, N/A Hispanic, N/A multiracial, N/A Pacific Islander, N/A white, N/A international; 87% from in state; 55% live on campus; 3% of students in fraternities, 6% in sororities
Most popular majors: 24% Liberal Arts and Sciences, General Studies and Humanities, 17% Homeland Security, Law Enforcement, Firefighting and Related Protective Services, 15% Natural Resources and Conservation, 13% Business, Management, Marketing, and Related Support Services, 12% Education
Expenses: 2018-2019: $7,308 in state, $14,872 out of state; room/ board: $9,942
Financial aid: (304) 462-6171; 85% of undergrads determined to have financial need; average aid package $14,539

Marshall University

Huntington WV
(800) 642-3499
U.S. News ranking: Reg. U. (S), No. 42
Website: www.marshall.edu
Admissions email: admissions@marshall.edu
Public; founded 1837
Freshman admissions: selective; 2017-2018: 5,026 applied, 4,533 accepted. Either SAT or ACT required. ACT 25/75 percentile: 19-25. High school rank: N/A
Early decision deadline: N/A, notification date: N/A
Early action deadline: N/A, notification date: N/A
Undergraduate student body: 7,846 full time, 1,643 part time; 42% male, 58% female; 0% American Indian, 1% Asian, 6% black, 2% Hispanic, 3% multiracial, 0% Pacific Islander, 84% white, 1% international; 80% from in state; N/A live on campus; N/A of students in fraternities, N/A in sororities
Most popular majors: 19% Health Professions and Related Programs, 16% Business, Management, Marketing, and Related Support Services, 12% Liberal Arts and Sciences, General Studies and Humanities, 10% Education, 5% Psychology
Expenses: 2018-2019: $8,128 in state, $18,614 out of state; room/ board: $9,470
Financial aid: (304) 696-3162; 72% of undergrads determined to have financial need; average aid package $11,101

Ohio Valley University

Vienna WV
(877) 446-8668
U.S. News ranking: Reg. Coll. (S), No. 43
Website: www.ovu.edu
Admissions email: admissions@ovu.edu
Private; founded 1958
Affiliation: Churches of Christ
Freshman admissions: selective; 2017-2018: 788 applied, 386 accepted. Neither SAT nor ACT required. ACT 25/75 percentile: 18-23. High school rank: 7% in top tenth, 26% in top quarter, 71% in top half
Early decision deadline: N/A, notification date: N/A
Early action deadline: N/A, notification date: N/A
Application deadline (fall): 8/15
Undergraduate student body: 439 full time, 96 part time; 49% male, 51% female; 0% American Indian, 1% Asian, 8% black, 5% Hispanic, 3% multiracial, 0% Pacific Islander, 61% white, 11% international; 49% from in state; 48% live on campus; 36% of students in fraternities, 54% in sororities
Most popular majors: 34% Business, Management, Marketing, and Related Support Services, 17% Education, 9% Health Professions and Related Programs, 9% Homeland Security, Law Enforcement, Firefighting and Related Protective Services, 9% Psychology
Expenses: 2018-2019: $21,900; room/board: $7,980
Financial aid: (304) 865-6077; 76% of undergrads determined to have financial need; average aid package $16,134

Salem University[1]

Salem WV
(304) 326-1109
U.S. News ranking: Reg. U. (S), unranked
Website: www.salemu.edu
Admissions email: admissions@salemu.edu
For-profit
Application deadline (fall): N/A
Undergraduate student body: N/A full time, N/A part time
Expenses: 2017-2018: $16,700; room/board: $7,480
Financial aid: N/A

Shepherd University

Shepherdstown WV
(304) 876-5212
U.S. News ranking: Nat. Lib. Arts, second tier
Website: www.shepherd.edu
Admissions email: admission@shepherd.edu
Public; founded 1871
Freshman admissions: selective; 2017-2018: 1,573 applied, 1,402 accepted. Either SAT or ACT required. ACT 25/75 percentile: 19-24. High school rank: N/A
Early decision deadline: N/A, notification date: N/A
Early action deadline: 11/15, notification date: 12/1
Application deadline (fall): rolling
Undergraduate student body: 2,614 full time, 807 part time; 43% male, 57% female; 0% American Indian, 2% Asian, 9% black, 4% Hispanic, 3% multiracial, 0% Pacific Islander, 79% white, 1% international; 67% from in state; 32% live on campus; 3% of students in fraternities, 4% in sororities
Most popular majors: 16% General Studies, 10% Registered Nursing/ Registered Nurse, 7% Business Administration and Management, General, 6% Biology/Biological Sciences, General, 6% Parks, Recreation and Leisure Studies
Expenses: 2018-2019: $7,548 in state, $18,048 out of state; room/ board: $10,628
Financial aid: (304) 876-5470; 66% of undergrads determined to have financial need; average aid package $12,802

University of Charleston

Charleston WV
(800) 995-4682
U.S. News ranking: Reg. U. (S), No. 91
Website: www.ucwv.edu
Admissions email: admissions@ucwv.edu
Private; founded 1888
Freshman admissions: less selective; 2017-2018: 2,737 applied, 1,765 accepted. Either SAT or ACT required. ACT 25/75 percentile: 18-22. High school rank: N/A
Early decision deadline: N/A, notification date: N/A
Early action deadline: N/A, notification date: N/A
Application deadline (fall): rolling
Undergraduate student body: 1,220 full time, 611 part time; 55% male, 45% female; 1% American Indian, 1% Asian, 9% black, 2% Hispanic, 0% multiracial, 0% Pacific Islander, 48% white, 7% international
Most popular majors: Information not available
Expenses: 2018-2019: $30,100; room/board: $9,300
Financial aid: (304) 357-4944; 76% of undergrads determined to have financial need; average aid package $23,812

West Liberty University

West Liberty WV
(304) 336-8076
U.S. News ranking: Reg. Coll. (S), No. 37
Website: www.westliberty.edu
Admissions email: admissions@westliberty.edu
Public; founded 1837
Freshman admissions: selective; 2017-2018: 1,831 applied, 1,314 accepted. Either SAT or ACT required. ACT 25/75 percentile: 17-23. High school rank: 12% in top tenth, 34% in top quarter, 67% in top half
Early decision deadline: N/A, notification date: N/A
Early action deadline: N/A, notification date: N/A
Application deadline (fall): rolling
Undergraduate student body: 1,869 full time, 307 part time; 38% male, 62% female; 0% American Indian, 0% Asian, 3% black, 1% Hispanic, 5% multiracial, 0% Pacific Islander, 71% white, 2% international; 70% from in state; 37% live on campus; 3% of students in fraternities, 4% in sororities
Most popular majors: 20% Business Administration and Management, General, 13% General Studies, 7% Dental Hygiene/Hygienist, 6% Elementary Education and Teaching, 6% Kinesiology and Exercise Science
Expenses: 2018-2019: $7,730 in state, $15,670 out of state; room/ board: $9,406
Financial aid: (304) 336-8016

West Virginia State University

Institute WV
(304) 766-4345
U.S. News ranking: Nat. Lib. Arts, second tier
Website: www.wvstateu.edu
Admissions email: admissions@wvstateu.edu
Public; founded 1891
Freshman admissions: less selective; 2017-2018: 3,182 applied, 3,105 accepted. Either SAT or ACT required. ACT 25/75 percentile: 17-22. High school rank: N/A
Early decision deadline: N/A, notification date: N/A
Early action deadline: N/A, notification date: N/A
Application deadline (fall): 8/17
Undergraduate student body: 1,786 full time, 1,969 part time; 42% male, 58% female; 6% American Indian, 0% Asian, 16% black, 2% Hispanic, 11% multiracial, 0% Pacific Islander, 60% white, 1% international; 85% from in state; 17% live on campus; N/A of students in fraternities, N/A in sororities
Most popular majors: 15% Liberal Arts and Sciences, General Studies and Humanities, 14% Business, Management, Marketing, and Related Support Services, 10% Homeland Security, Law Enforcement, Firefighting and Related Protective Services, 6% Communication, Journalism, and Related Programs, 6% Public Administration and Social Service Professions
Expenses: 2018-2019: $8,212 in state, $17,666 out of state; room/ board: $12,366
Financial aid: (304) 204-4361; 79% of undergrads determined to have financial need; average aid package $15,550

West Virginia University

Morgantown WV
(304) 442-3146
U.S. News ranking: Nat. U., No. 205
Website: www.wvu.edu
Admissions email: go2wvu@mail.wvu.edu
Public; founded 1867
Freshman admissions: selective; 2017-2018: 20,594 applied, 14,807 accepted. Either SAT or ACT required. ACT 25/75 percentile: 21-27. High school rank: 20% in top tenth, 44% in top quarter, 75% in top half
Early decision deadline: N/A, notification date: N/A
Early action deadline: N/A, notification date: N/A
Application deadline (fall): 8/1
Undergraduate student body: 20,713 full time, 1,791 part time; 53% male, 47% female; 0% American Indian, 1% Asian, 4% black, 4% Hispanic, 4% multiracial, 0% Pacific Islander, 79% white, 7% international; 57% from in state; 15% live on campus; 6% of students in fraternities, 5% in sororities
Most popular majors: 15% Engineering, 13% Business, Management, Marketing, and Related Support Services, 8% Communication, Journalism, and Related Programs, 8% Social Sciences, 6% Biological and Biomedical Sciences
Expenses: 2018-2019: $8,856 in state, $24,950 out of state; room/ board: $10,918
Financial aid: (304) 293-8571; 51% of undergrads determined to have financial need; average aid package $7,292

West Virginia University–Parkersburg[1]

Parkersburg WV
(304) 424-8000
U.S. News ranking: Reg. Coll. (S), unranked
Website: www.wvup.edu
Admissions email: info@mail.wvup.edu

Public
Application deadline (fall): N/A
Undergraduate student body: N/A full time, N/A part time
Expenses: 2017-2018: $3,552 in state, $7,920 out of state; room/board: N/A
Financial aid: N/A

West Virginia Wesleyan College

Buckhannon WV
(800) 722-9933
U.S. News ranking: Reg. U. (S), No. 58
Website: www.wvwc.edu
Admissions email: admissions@wvwc.edu
Private; founded 1890
Affiliation: United Methodist
Freshman admissions: selective; 2017-2018: 2,272 applied, 1,605 accepted. Either SAT or ACT required. ACT 25/75 percentile: 19-25. High school rank: 20% in top tenth, 49% in top quarter, 83% in top half
Early decision deadline: N/A, notification date: N/A
Early action deadline: N/A, notification date: N/A
Application deadline (fall): 8/15
Undergraduate student body: 1,289 full time, 40 part time; 44% male, 56% female; 0% American Indian, 0% Asian, 9% black, 3% Hispanic, 4% multiracial, 0% Pacific Islander, 78% white, 6% international; 62% from in state; 76% live on campus; 25% of students in fraternities, 25% in sororities
Most popular majors: 15% Physical Sciences, 12% Business, Management, Marketing, and Related Support Services, 10% Education, 9% Health Professions and Related Programs, 9% Parks, Recreation, Leisure, and Fitness Studies
Expenses: 2018-2019: $31,640; room/board: $8,856
Financial aid: (304) 473-8080; 80% of undergrads determined to have financial need; average aid package $28,136

Wheeling Jesuit University

Wheeling WV
(800) 624-6992
U.S. News ranking: Reg. U. (S), No. 38
Website: www.wju.edu
Admissions email: admiss@wju.edu
Private; founded 1954
Affiliation: Roman Catholic
Freshman admissions: selective; 2017-2018: 2,150 applied, 1,105 accepted. Either SAT or ACT required. ACT 25/75 percentile: 19-24. High school rank: 13% in top tenth, 38% in top quarter, 68% in top half
Early decision deadline: N/A, notification date: N/A
Early action deadline: N/A, notification date: N/A
Application deadline (fall): rolling
Undergraduate student body: 673 full time, 120 part time; 49% male, 51% female; 1% American Indian, 1% Asian, 10% black, 3% Hispanic, 3% multiracial, 2% Pacific Islander, 71% white, 4% international; 46% from in state; 79% live on campus; 0% of students in fraternities, 0% in sororities
Most popular majors: 30% Business, Management, Marketing, and Related Support Services, 23% Health Professions and Related Programs, 5% History, 5% Homeland Security, Law Enforcement, Firefighting and Related Protective Services, 5% Social Sciences
Expenses: 2018-2019: $29,290; room/board: $9,900
Financial aid: (304) 243-2304; 77% of undergrads determined to have financial need; average aid package $27,281

WISCONSIN

Alverno College

Milwaukee WI
(414) 382-6100
U.S. News ranking: Reg. U. (Mid. W), No. 47
Website: www.alverno.edu
Admissions email: admissions@alverno.edu
Private; founded 1887
Affiliation: Roman Catholic
Freshman admissions: selective; 2017-2018: 610 applied, 475 accepted. Either SAT or ACT required. ACT 25/75 percentile: 17-22. High school rank: N/A
Early decision deadline: N/A, notification date: N/A
Early action deadline: N/A, notification date: N/A
Application deadline (fall): rolling
Undergraduate student body: 1,036 full time, 276 part time; 0% male, 100% female; 1% American Indian, 6% Asian, 13% black, 27% Hispanic, 4% multiracial, 0% Pacific Islander, 49% white, 0% international; 93% from in state; 16% live on campus; 0% of students in fraternities, 0% in sororities
Most popular majors: 36% Health Professions and Related Programs, 16% Business, Management, Marketing, and Related Support Services, 16% Liberal Arts and Sciences, General Studies and Humanities, 6% Biological and Biomedical Sciences, 6% Psychology
Expenses: 2018-2019: $28,302; room/board: $8,546
Financial aid: (414) 382-6040; 91% of undergrads determined to have financial need; average aid package $21,312

Beloit College

Beloit WI
(608) 363-2500
U.S. News ranking: Nat. Lib. Arts, No. 68
Website: www.beloit.edu
Admissions email: admiss@beloit.edu
Private; founded 1846
Freshman admissions: more selective; 2017-2018: 5,400 applied, 2,915 accepted. Neither SAT nor ACT required. ACT 25/75 percentile: 24-30. High school rank: 30% in top tenth, 57% in top quarter, 92% in top half
Early decision deadline: 11/1, notification date: 12/1
Early action deadline: 12/1, notification date: 1/1
Application deadline (fall): rolling
Undergraduate student body: 1,346 full time, 56 part time; 47% male, 53% female; 0% American Indian, 3% Asian, 7% black, 10% Hispanic, 4% multiracial, 0% Pacific Islander, 56% white, 15% international; 15% from in state; 88% live on campus; N/A of students in fraternities, N/A in sororities
Most popular majors: 23% Social Sciences, 11% Physical Sciences, 10% Multi/Interdisciplinary Studies, 8% English Language and Literature/Letters, 8% Visual and Performing Arts
Expenses: 2018-2019: $50,040; room/board: $8,830
Financial aid: (608) 363-2696; 61% of undergrads determined to have financial need; average aid package $43,088

Cardinal Stritch University

Milwaukee WI
(414) 410-4040
U.S. News ranking: Nat. U., second tier
Website: www.stritch.edu
Admissions email: admissions@stritch.edu
Private; founded 1937
Affiliation: Roman Catholic
Freshman admissions: selective; 2017-2018: 642 applied, 503 accepted. Neither SAT nor ACT required. ACT 25/75 percentile: 18-23. High school rank: 21% in top tenth, 52% in top quarter, 79% in top half
Early decision deadline: N/A, notification date: N/A
Early action deadline: N/A, notification date: N/A
Application deadline (fall): rolling
Undergraduate student body: 901 full time, 642 part time; 32% male, 68% female; 1% American Indian, 3% Asian, 20% black, 17% Hispanic, 2% multiracial, 0% Pacific Islander, 43% white, 13% international; 87% from in state; 10% live on campus; 2% of students in fraternities, 0% in sororities
Most popular majors: 50% Business, Management, Marketing, and Related Support Services, 15% Health Professions and Related Programs, 7% Education, 4% Public Administration and Social Service Professions
Expenses: 2018-2019: $29,998; room/board: $8,440
Financial aid: (414) 410-4016; 67% of undergrads determined to have financial need; average aid package $23,056

Carroll University

Waukesha WI
(262) 524-7220
U.S. News ranking: Reg. U. (Mid. W), No. 53
Website: www.carrollu.edu/
Admissions email: info@carrollu.edu
Private; founded 1846
Affiliation: Presbyterian
Freshman admissions: selective; 2017-2018: 3,688 applied, 2,612 accepted. Either SAT or ACT required. ACT 25/75 percentile: 21-26. High school rank: 19% in top tenth, 47% in top quarter, N/A in top half
Early decision deadline: N/A, notification date: N/A
Early action deadline: N/A, notification date: N/A
Application deadline (fall): rolling
Undergraduate student body: 2,737 full time, 245 part time; 36% male, 64% female; 0% American Indian, 4% Asian, 2% black, 8% Hispanic, 3% multiracial, 0% Pacific Islander, 80% white, 3% international
Most popular majors: 20% Parks, Recreation, Leisure, and Fitness Studies, 19% Health Professions and Related Programs, 13% Business, Management, Marketing, and Related Support Services, 10% Biological and Biomedical Sciences, 9% Psychology
Expenses: 2018-2019: $31,918; room/board: $9,484
Financial aid: (262) 524-7296; 78% of undergrads determined to have financial need; average aid package $24,794

Carthage College

Kenosha WI
(262) 551-6000
U.S. News ranking: Nat. Lib. Arts, second tier
Website: www.carthage.edu
Admissions email: admissions@carthage.edu
Private; founded 1847
Freshman admissions: selective; 2017-2018: 7,649 applied, 5,186 accepted. Neither SAT nor ACT required. ACT 25/75 percentile: 21-27. High school rank: 22% in top tenth, 45% in top quarter, 73% in top half
Early decision deadline: N/A, notification date: N/A
Early action deadline: N/A, notification date: N/A
Application deadline (fall): rolling
Undergraduate student body: 2,596 full time, 152 part time; 44% male, 56% female; 1% American Indian, 2% Asian, 6% black, 8% Hispanic, 4% multiracial, 0% Pacific Islander, 73% white, 1% international; 35% from in state; 66% live on campus; 8% of students in fraternities, 10% in sororities
Most popular majors: 27% Business, Management, Marketing, and Related Support Services, 8% Biological and Biomedical Sciences, 8% Education, 7% Communication, Journalism, and Related Programs, 7% Psychology
Expenses: 2018-2019: $43,550; room/board: $11,990
Financial aid: (262) 551-6001; 81% of undergrads determined to have financial need; average aid package $34,356

Concordia University Wisconsin

Mequon WI
(262) 243-4300
U.S. News ranking: Reg. U. (Mid. W), No. 70
Website: www.cuw.edu
Admissions email: admissions@cuw.edu
Private; founded 1881
Affiliation: Lutheran Church–Missouri Synod
Freshman admissions: selective; 2017-2018: 3,621 applied, 2,288 accepted. Either SAT or ACT required. ACT 25/75 percentile: 20-26. High school rank: 19% in top tenth, 51% in top quarter, 88% in top half
Early decision deadline: N/A, notification date: N/A
Early action deadline: N/A, notification date: N/A
Application deadline (fall): N/A
Undergraduate student body: 2,616 full time, 1,093 part time; 34% male, 66% female; 1% American Indian, 2% Asian, 12% black, 1% Hispanic, 4% multiracial, 0% Pacific Islander, 74% white, 3% international; 75% from in state; 46% live on campus; N/A of students in fraternities, N/A in sororities
Most popular majors: 29% Health Professions and Related Programs, 28% Business, Management, Marketing, and Related Support Services, 7% Biological and Biomedical Sciences, 6% Education, 6% Homeland Security, Law Enforcement, Firefighting and Related Protective Services
Expenses: 2018-2019: $29,450; room/board: $10,850
Financial aid: (262) 243-2025; 80% of undergrads determined to have financial need; average aid package $21,208

Edgewood College

Madison WI
(608) 663-2294
U.S. News ranking: Nat. U., No. 165
Website: www.edgewood.edu
Admissions email: admissions@edgewood.edu
Private; founded 1927
Affiliation: Roman Catholic
Freshman admissions: selective; 2017-2018: 1,447 applied, 1,029 accepted. Either SAT or ACT required. ACT 25/75 percentile: 21-25. High school rank: 17% in top tenth, 46% in top quarter, 81% in top half
Early decision deadline: N/A, notification date: N/A
Early action deadline: N/A, notification date: N/A
Application deadline (fall): 8/15
Undergraduate student body: 1,361 full time, 203 part time; 27% male, 73% female; 0% American Indian, 3% Asian, 3% black, 6% Hispanic, 3% multiracial, 0% Pacific Islander, 79% white, 3% international; 92% from in state; 35% live on campus; N/A of students in fraternities, N/A in sororities
Most popular majors: 27% Registered Nursing/Registered Nurse, 10% Business/Commerce, General, 9% Psychology, General, 7% Education, Other, 5% Speech Communication and Rhetoric
Expenses: 2018-2019: $29,500; room/board: $11,020
Financial aid: (608) 663-4300; 76% of undergrads determined to have financial need; average aid package $22,072

Herzing University[1]

Madison WI
(800) 596-0724
U.S. News ranking: Reg. U. (Mid. W), second tier
Website: www.herzing.edu/
Admissions email: info@msn.herzing.edu
For-profit; founded 1965
Affiliation: Other
Application deadline (fall): N/A
Undergraduate student body: N/A full time, N/A part time
Expenses: 2017-2018: $13,850; room/board: N/A
Financial aid: N/A

Lakeland University[1]

Plymouth WI
(920) 565-1226
U.S. News ranking: Reg. U. (Mid. W), second tier
Website: www.lakeland.edu
Admissions email: admissions@lakeland.edu
Private; founded 1862
Application deadline (fall): rolling
Undergraduate student body: N/A full time, N/A part time
Expenses: 2017-2018: $27,760; room/board: $8,600
Financial aid: N/A

Lawrence University

Appleton WI
(800) 227-0982
U.S. News ranking: Nat. Lib. Arts, No. 56
Website: www.lawrence.edu
Admissions email: admissions@lawrence.edu
Private; founded 1847
Freshman admissions: more selective; 2017-2018: 3,612 applied, 2,216 accepted. Neither SAT nor ACT required. ACT 25/75 percentile: 25-32. High school rank: 38% in top tenth, 68% in top quarter, 94% in top half
Early decision deadline: 10/31, notification date: 12/1
Early action deadline: 11/1, notification date: 12/15
Application deadline (fall): 1/15
Undergraduate student body: 1,434 full time, 39 part time; 47% male, 53% female; 0% American Indian, 5% Asian, 5% black, 9% Hispanic, 4% multiracial, 0% Pacific Islander, 65% white, 12% international; 29% from in state; 94% live on campus; 10% of students in fraternities, 14% in sororities
Most popular majors: 23% Visual and Performing Arts, 14% Biological and Biomedical Sciences, 14% Social Sciences, 8% Psychology, 7% Foreign Languages, Literatures, and Linguistics
Expenses: 2018-2019: $47,475; room/board: $10,341
Financial aid: (920) 832-6583; 62% of undergrads determined to have financial need; average aid package $39,869

Maranatha Baptist University

Watertown WI
(920) 206-2327
U.S. News ranking: Reg. Coll. (Mid. W), No. 48
Website: www.mbu.edu
Admissions email: admissions@mbu.edu
Private; founded 1968
Freshman admissions: selective; 2017-2018: 279 applied, 204 accepted. Either SAT or ACT required. ACT 25/75 percentile: 20-25. High school rank: 13% in top tenth, 37% in top quarter, 70% in top half
Early decision deadline: N/A, notification date: N/A
Early action deadline: N/A, notification date: N/A
Application deadline (fall): rolling
Undergraduate student body: 591 full time, 335 part time; 44% male, 56% female; 0% American Indian, 1% Asian, 1% black, 3% Hispanic, 4% multiracial, 0% Pacific Islander, 88% white, 1% international
Most popular majors: 20% Education, 17% Theology and Religious Vocations, 16% Business, Management, Marketing, and Related Support Services, 12% Liberal Arts and Sciences, General Studies and Humanities, 7% Health Professions and Related Programs
Expenses: 2017-2018: $14,910; room/board: $7,000
Financial aid: (920) 206-2318

Marian University

Fond du Lac WI
(920) 923-7650
U.S. News ranking: Reg. U. (Mid. W), No. 118
Website: www.marianuniversity.edu/
Admissions email: admissions@marianuniversity.edu
Private; founded 1936
Affiliation: Roman Catholic
Freshman admissions: selective; 2017-2018: 1,684 applied, 1,138 accepted. Either SAT or ACT required. ACT 25/75 percentile: 17-22. High school rank: 9% in top tenth, 25% in top quarter, 59% in top half
Early decision deadline: N/A, notification date: N/A
Early action deadline: N/A, notification date: N/A
Application deadline (fall): rolling
Undergraduate student body: 1,249 full time, 212 part time; 31% male, 69% female; N/A American Indian, N/A Asian, N/A black, N/A Hispanic, N/A multiracial, N/A Pacific Islander, N/A white, N/A international
Most popular majors: Information not available
Expenses: 2018-2019: $27,400; room/board: $7,222
Financial aid: (920) 923-8737; 80% of undergrads determined to have financial need; average aid package $17,459

Marquette University

Milwaukee WI
(800) 222-6544
U.S. News ranking: Nat. U., No. 89
Website: www.marquette.edu
Admissions email: admissions@marquette.edu
Private; founded 1881
Affiliation: Roman Catholic
Freshman admissions: more selective; 2017-2018: 12,957 applied, 11,574 accepted. Either SAT or ACT required. ACT 25/75 percentile: 24-29. High school rank: 34% in top tenth, 64% in top quarter, 93% in top half
Early decision deadline: N/A, notification date: N/A
Early action deadline: N/A, notification date: N/A
Application deadline (fall): 12/1
Undergraduate student body: 8,026 full time, 309 part time; 47% male, 53% female; 0% American Indian, 7% Asian, 4% black, 12% Hispanic, 4% multiracial, 0% Pacific Islander, 70% white, 3% international; 31% from in state; 54% live on campus; N/A of students in fraternities, N/A in sororities
Most popular majors: 28% Business, Management, Marketing, and Related Support Services, 12% Biological and Biomedical Sciences, 10% Engineering, 9% Communication, Journalism, and Related Programs, 8% Social Sciences
Expenses: 2018-2019: $41,870; room/board: $12,720
Financial aid: (414) 288-4000; 58% of undergrads determined to have financial need; average aid package $29,472

Milwaukee Institute of Art and Design

Milwaukee WI
(414) 291-8070
U.S. News ranking: Arts, unranked
Website: www.miad.edu
Admissions email: admissions@miad.edu
Private; founded 1974
Freshman admissions: least selective; 2017-2018: 1,150 applied, 360 accepted. Neither SAT nor ACT required. SAT 25/75 percentile: N/A. High school rank: 10% in top tenth, 33% in top quarter, 69% in top half
Early decision deadline: N/A, notification date: N/A
Early action deadline: 12/1, notification date: 12/15
Application deadline (fall): 8/15
Undergraduate student body: 649 full time, 13 part time; 31% male, 69% female; N/A American Indian, N/A Asian, N/A black, N/A Hispanic, N/A multiracial, N/A Pacific Islander, N/A white, N/A international; 56% from in state; 47% live on campus; N/A of students in fraternities, N/A in sororities
Most popular majors: 100% Visual and Performing Arts
Expenses: 2018-2019: $37,360; room/board: $9,300
Financial aid: (414) 847-3270

Milwaukee School of Engineering

Milwaukee WI
(800) 332-6763
U.S. News ranking: Reg. U. (Mid. W), No. 10
Website: www.msoe.edu
Admissions email: explore@msoe.edu
Private; founded 1903
Freshman admissions: more selective; 2017-2018: 2,893 applied, 1,818 accepted. Either SAT or ACT required. ACT 25/75 percentile: 25-30. High school rank: N/A
Early decision deadline: N/A, notification date: N/A
Early action deadline: N/A, notification date: N/A
Application deadline (fall): rolling
Undergraduate student body: 2,508 full time, 102 part time; 73% male, 27% female; 0% American Indian, 4% Asian, 2% black, 6% Hispanic, 3% multiracial, 0% Pacific Islander, 67% white, 10% international; 66% from in state; 42% live on campus; 3% of students in fraternities, 11% in sororities
Most popular majors: 74% Engineering, 12% Health Professions and Related Programs, 11% Business, Management, Marketing, and Related Support Services, 2% Engineering Technologies and Engineering-Related Fields, 1% Communication, Journalism, and Related Programs
Expenses: 2018-2019: $40,749; room/board: $10,389
Financial aid: (414) 277-7224; 77% of undergrads determined to have financial need; average aid package $28,577

Mount Mary University

Milwaukee WI
(414) 930-3024
U.S. News ranking: Reg. U. (Mid. W), No. 122
Website: www.mtmary.edu
Admissions email: mmu-admiss@mtmary.edu
Private; founded 1913
Affiliation: Roman Catholic
Freshman admissions: selective; 2017-2018: 709 applied, 397 accepted. Either SAT or ACT required. ACT 25/75 percentile: 17-21. High school rank: 19% in top tenth, 44% in top quarter, 72% in top half
Early decision deadline: N/A, notification date: N/A
Early action deadline: N/A, notification date: N/A
Application deadline (fall): rolling
Undergraduate student body: 652 full time, 83 part time; 0% male, 100% female; 0% American Indian, 8% Asian, 17% black, 20% Hispanic, 4% multiracial, 0% Pacific Islander, 48% white, 1% international; 98% from in state; 31% live on campus; N/A of students in fraternities, N/A in sororities
Most popular majors: 21% Visual and Performing Arts, 20% Health Professions and Related Programs, 13% Business, Management, Marketing, and Related Support Services, 8% Public Administration and Social Service Professions, 7% Homeland Security, Law Enforcement, Firefighting and Related Protective Services
Expenses: 2018-2019: $30,100; room/board: $8,870
Financial aid: (414) 930-3163; 86% of undergrads determined to have financial need; average aid package $25,707

Northland College

Ashland WI
(715) 682-1224
U.S. News ranking: Nat. Lib. Arts, No. 162
Website: www.northland.edu
Admissions email: admit@northland.edu
Private; founded 1892
Affiliation: United Church of Christ
Freshman admissions: selective; 2017-2018: 1,625 applied, 994 accepted. Neither SAT nor ACT required. ACT 25/75 percentile: 20-26. High school rank: 16% in top tenth, 41% in top quarter, 75% in top half
Early decision deadline: N/A, notification date: N/A
Early action deadline: N/A, notification date: N/A
Application deadline (fall): rolling
Undergraduate student body: 594 full time, 41 part time; 46% male, 54% female; 2% American Indian, 1% Asian, 3% black, 5% Hispanic, 3% multiracial, 0% Pacific Islander, 80% white, 4% international; 50% from in state; 73% live on campus; 0% of students in fraternities, 0% in sororities
Most popular majors: 18% Natural Resources and Conservation, 17% Biological and Biomedical Sciences, 15% Business, Management, Marketing, and Related Support Services, 15% Education
Expenses: 2018-2019: $36,183; room/board: $9,176
Financial aid: (715) 682-1255; 86% of undergrads determined to have financial need; average aid package $30,526

Ripon College

Ripon WI
(800) 947-4766
U.S. News ranking: Nat. Lib. Arts, No. 120
Website: www.ripon.edu
Admissions email: adminfo@ripon.edu
Private; founded 1851
Freshman admissions: selective; 2017-2018: 2,504 applied, 1,691 accepted. Neither SAT nor ACT required. ACT 25/75 percentile: 20-26. High school rank: 16% in top tenth, 43% in top quarter, 79% in top half
Early decision deadline: N/A, notification date: N/A
Early action deadline: N/A, notification date: N/A
Application deadline (fall): rolling
Undergraduate student body: 740 full time, 16 part time; 46% male, 54% female; 0% American Indian, 1% Asian, 4% black, 9% Hispanic, 3% multiracial, 0% Pacific Islander, 80% white, 4% international; 76% from in state; 95% live on campus; 40% of students in fraternities, 26% in sororities
Most popular majors: 12% Business/Commerce, General, 12% Psychology, General, 11% Biology/Biological Sciences, General, 11% English Language and Literature, General, 8% Health and Physical Education/Fitness, General
Expenses: 2018-2019: $43,808; room/board: $8,400

More @ usnews.com/bestcolleges

Financial aid: (920) 748-8301; 86% of undergrads determined to have financial need; average aid package $35,453

Silver Lake College[1]

Manitowoc WI
(920) 686-6175
U.S. News ranking: Reg. U. (Mid. W), second tier
Website: www.sl.edu
Admissions email: admissions@sl.edu
Private; founded 1935
Affiliation: Roman Catholic
Application deadline (fall): rolling
Undergraduate student body: N/A full time, N/A part time
Expenses: 2017-2018: $27,360; room/board: $7,200
Financial aid: (920) 686-6175

St. Norbert College

De Pere WI
(800) 236-4878
U.S. News ranking: Nat. Lib. Arts, No. 127
Website: www.snc.edu
Admissions email: admit@snc.edu
Private; founded 1898
Affiliation: Roman Catholic
Freshman admissions: more selective; 2017-2018: 3,860 applied, 3,058 accepted. Either SAT or ACT required. ACT 25/75 percentile: 22-27. High school rank: 20% in top tenth, 51% in top quarter, 85% in top half
Early decision deadline: N/A, notification date: N/A
Early action deadline: N/A, notification date: N/A
Application deadline (fall): rolling
Undergraduate student body: 2,021 full time, 46 part time; 43% male, 57% female; 1% American Indian, 2% Asian, 1% black, 4% Hispanic, 1% multiracial, 0% Pacific Islander, 87% white, 3% international; 78% from in state; 85% live on campus; 10% of students in fraternities, 10% in sororities
Most popular majors: 20% Business/Commerce, General, 11% Elementary Education and Teaching, 10% Speech Communication and Rhetoric, 9% Biology/Biological Sciences, General, 7% Psychology, General
Expenses: 2018-2019: $38,129; room/board: $9,954
Financial aid: (920) 403-3071; 72% of undergrads determined to have financial need; average aid package $26,921

University of Wisconsin–Eau Claire

Eau Claire WI
(715) 836-5415
U.S. News ranking: Reg. U. (Mid. W), No. 38
Website: www.uwec.edu
Admissions email: admissions@uwec.edu
Public; founded 1916
Freshman admissions: selective; 2017-2018: 5,990 applied, 5,133 accepted. Either SAT or ACT required. ACT 25/75 percentile: 21-26. High school rank: 16% in top tenth, 48% in top quarter, 91% in top half
Early decision deadline: N/A, notification date: N/A
Early action deadline: N/A, notification date: N/A
Application deadline (fall): 8/20
Undergraduate student body: 9,347 full time, 675 part time; 39% male, 61% female; 0% American Indian, 3% Asian, 1% black, 3% Hispanic, 2% multiracial, 0% Pacific Islander, 88% white, 2% international; 70% from in state; 38% live on campus; N/A of students in fraternities, N/A in sororities
Most popular majors: 22% Business, Management, Marketing, and Related Support Services, 16% Health Professions and Related Programs, 8% Education, 6% Biological and Biomedical Sciences, 6% Parks, Recreation, Leisure, and Fitness Studies
Expenses: 2018-2019: $8,820 in state, $17,096 out of state; room/ board: $7,813
Financial aid: (715) 836-3000; 52% of undergrads determined to have financial need; average aid package $9,864

University of Wisconsin–Green Bay

Green Bay WI
(920) 465-2111
U.S. News ranking: Reg. U. (Mid. W), No. 94
Website: www.uwgb.edu
Admissions email: uwgb@uwgb.edu
Public; founded 1965
Freshman admissions: selective; 2017-2018: 2,151 applied, 2,036 accepted. Either SAT or ACT required. ACT 25/75 percentile: 20-25. High school rank: N/A
Early decision deadline: N/A, notification date: N/A
Early action deadline: N/A, notification date: N/A
Application deadline (fall): rolling
Undergraduate student body: 4,020 full time, 2,795 part time; 34% male, 66% female; 1% American Indian, 3% Asian, 2% black, 5% Hispanic, 3% multiracial, 0% Pacific Islander, 84% white, 1% international; 91% from in state; 36% live on campus; 1% of students in fraternities, 1% in sororities
Most popular majors: 17% Business Administration and Management, General, 14% Human Biology, 13% Liberal Arts and Sciences/Liberal Studies, 10% Registered Nursing, Nursing Administration, Nursing Research and Clinical Nursing, Other, 8% Psychology, General
Expenses: 2018-2019: $7,878 in state, $15,728 out of state; room/ board: $7,306
Financial aid: (920) 465-2111; 65% of undergrads determined to have financial need; average aid package $9,497

University of Wisconsin–La Crosse

La Crosse WI
(608) 785-8939
U.S. News ranking: Reg. U. (Mid. W), No. 32
Website: www.uwlax.edu
Admissions email: admissions@uwlax.edu
Public; founded 1909
Freshman admissions: more selective; 2017-2018: 5,879 applied, 4,783 accepted. Either SAT or ACT required. ACT 25/75 percentile: 22-26. High school rank: 21% in top tenth, 58% in top quarter, 95% in top half
Early decision deadline: N/A, notification date: N/A
Early action deadline: N/A, notification date: N/A
Application deadline (fall): rolling
Undergraduate student body: 9,064 full time, 591 part time; 44% male, 56% female; 0% American Indian, 2% Asian, 1% black, 3% Hispanic, 3% multiracial, 0% Pacific Islander, 90% white, 1% international; 82% from in state; 36% live on campus; 1% of students in fraternities, 1% in sororities
Most popular majors: 21% Business, Management, Marketing, and Related Support Services, 15% Biological and Biomedical Sciences, 12% Health Professions and Related Programs, 10% Parks, Recreation, Leisure, and Fitness Studies, 9% Psychology
Expenses: 2017-2018: $8,922 in state, $17,591 out of state; room/ board: $6,206
Financial aid: (608) 785-8604; 52% of undergrads determined to have financial need; average aid package $8,016

University of Wisconsin–Madison

Madison WI
(608) 262-3961
U.S. News ranking: Nat. U., No. 49
Website: www.wisc.edu
Admissions email: onwisconsin@admissions.wisc.edu
Public; founded 1848
Freshman admissions: more selective; 2017-2018: 35,615 applied, 19,150 accepted. Either SAT or ACT required. ACT 25/75 percentile: 27-31. High school rank: 52% in top tenth, 89% in top quarter, 99% in top half
Early decision deadline: N/A, notification date: N/A
Early action deadline: 11/1, notification date: 1/31
Application deadline (fall): 2/1
Undergraduate student body: 29,016 full time, 3,180 part time; 49% male, 51% female; 0% American Indian, 6% Asian, 2% black, 5% Hispanic, 3% multiracial, 0% Pacific Islander, 73% white, 9% international; 66% from in state; 25% live on campus; 9% of students in fraternities, 8% in sororities
Most popular majors: 7% Biology/ Biological Sciences, General, 7% Economics, General, 5% Computer and Information Sciences, General, 5% Finance, General, 5% Psychology, General
Expenses: 2018-2019: $10,555 in state, $36,805 out of state; room/board: $11,114
Financial aid: (608) 262-3060; 38% of undergrads determined to have financial need; average aid package $16,308

University of Wisconsin–Milwaukee

Milwaukee WI
(414) 229-2222
U.S. News ranking: Nat. U., second tier
Website: www.uwm.edu
Admissions email: uwmlook@uwm.edu
Public; founded 1956
Freshman admissions: selective; 2017-2018: 10,000 applied, 7,227 accepted. Neither SAT nor ACT required. ACT 25/75 percentile: 20-25. High school rank: 10% in top tenth, 21% in top quarter, 68% in top half
Early decision deadline: N/A, notification date: N/A
Early action deadline: N/A, notification date: N/A
Application deadline (fall): 8/11
Undergraduate student body: 17,055 full time, 3,695 part time; 48% male, 52% female; 0% American Indian, 7% Asian, 8% black, 11% Hispanic, 4% multiracial, 0% Pacific Islander, 66% white, 4% international; 89% from in state; 8% live on campus; N/A of students in fraternities, N/A in sororities
Most popular majors: 22% Business, Management, Marketing, and Related Support Services, 13% Health Professions and Related Programs, 7% Engineering, 7% Visual and Performing Arts, 6% Communication, Journalism, and Related Programs
Expenses: 2017-2018: $9,565 in state, $20,844 out of state; room/ board: $10,560
Financial aid: N/A

University of Wisconsin–Oshkosh

Oshkosh WI
(920) 424-0202
U.S. News ranking: Reg. U. (Mid. W), No. 94
Website: www.uwosh.edu
Admissions email: admissions@uwosh.edu
Public; founded 1871
Freshman admissions: selective; 2017-2018: 6,436 applied, 4,101 accepted. Either SAT or ACT required. ACT 25/75 percentile: 20-24. High school rank: 11% in top tenth, 33% in top quarter, 77% in top half
Early decision deadline: N/A, notification date: N/A
Early action deadline: N/A, notification date: N/A
Application deadline (fall): rolling
Undergraduate student body: 8,005 full time, 4,135 part time; 39% male, 61% female; 0% American Indian, 4% Asian, 3% black, 5% Hispanic, 3% multiracial, 0% Pacific Islander, 85% white, 1% international; 94% from in state; 31% live on campus; 3% of students in fraternities, 3% in sororities
Most popular majors: 18% Business, Management, Marketing, and Related Support Services, 12% Health Professions and Related Programs, 11% Education, 8% Public Administration and Social Service Professions, 7% Biological and Biomedical Sciences
Expenses: 2017-2018: $7,600 in state, $15,174 out of state; room/ board: $7,792
Financial aid: (920) 424-3377

University of Wisconsin–Parkside

Kenosha WI
(262) 595-2355
U.S. News ranking: Nat. Lib. Arts, second tier
Website: www.uwp.edu
Admissions email: admissions@uwp.edu
Public; founded 1968
Freshman admissions: selective; 2017-2018: 1,743 applied, 1,399 accepted. Neither SAT nor ACT required. ACT 25/75 percentile: 18-23. High school rank: 14% in top tenth, 36% in top quarter, 73% in top half
Early decision deadline: N/A, notification date: N/A
Early action deadline: N/A, notification date: N/A
Application deadline (fall): rolling
Undergraduate student body: 3,275 full time, 893 part time; 47% male, 53% female; 0% American Indian, 4% Asian, 9% black, 16% Hispanic, 4% multiracial, 0% Pacific Islander, 65% white, 2% international; 82% from in state; 19% live on campus; 1% of students in fraternities, 1% in sororities
Most popular majors: 27% Business, Management, Marketing, and Related Support Services, 11% Homeland Security, Law Enforcement, Firefighting and Related Protective Services, 8% Biological and Biomedical Sciences, 8% Psychology, 6% Parks, Recreation, Leisure, and Fitness Studies
Expenses: 2017-2018: $7,389 in state, $15,378 out of state; room/ board: $7,924
Financial aid: (262) 595-2574; 64% of undergrads determined to have financial need; average aid package $9,703

University of Wisconsin–Platteville

Platteville WI
(608) 342-1125
U.S. News ranking: Reg. U. (Mid. W), No. 111
Website: www.uwplatt.edu
Admissions email: admit@uwplatt.edu
Public; founded 1866
Freshman admissions: selective; 2017-2018: 3,711 applied, 2,937 accepted. Either SAT or ACT required. ACT 25/75 percentile: 20-25. High school rank: 10% in top tenth, 28% in top quarter, 59% in top half
Early decision deadline: N/A, notification date: N/A
Early action deadline: N/A, notification date: N/A
Application deadline (fall): rolling
Undergraduate student body: 6,751 full time, 769 part time; 66% male, 34% female; 0% American Indian, 1% Asian, 1% black, 3% Hispanic, 3% multiracial, 0% Pacific Islander, 89% white, 1% international; 76% from in

state; 86% live on campus; 1% of students in fraternities, 1% in sororities
Most popular majors: 29% Engineering, 12% Agriculture, Agriculture Operations, and Related Sciences, 12% Homeland Security, Law Enforcement, Firefighting and Related Protective Services, 11% Business, Management, Marketing, and Related Support Services, 9% Engineering Technologies and Engineering-Related Fields
Expenses: 2017-2018: $7,543 in state, $15,393 out of state; room/board: $7,160
Financial aid: (608) 342-6188; 67% of undergrads determined to have financial need; average aid package $4,166

University of Wisconsin–River Falls

River Falls WI
(715) 425-3500
U.S. News ranking: Reg. U. (Mid. W), No. 106
Website: www.uwrf.edu
Admissions email: admit@uwrf.edu
Public; founded 1874
Freshman admissions: selective; 2017-2018: 3,450 applied, 2,571 accepted. Either SAT or ACT required. ACT 25/75 percentile: 20-25. High school rank: 11% in top tenth, 34% in top quarter, 73% in top half
Early decision deadline: N/A, notification date: N/A
Early action deadline: N/A, notification date: N/A
Application deadline (fall): rolling
Undergraduate student body: 4,988 full time, 690 part time; 39% male, 61% female; 0% American Indian, 3% Asian, 2% black, 4% Hispanic, 2% multiracial, 0% Pacific Islander, 88% white, 1% international; 51% from in state; 41% live on campus; N/A of students in fraternities, N/A in sororities
Most popular majors: 19% Agriculture, Agriculture Operations, and Related Sciences, 15% Education, 14% Business, Management, Marketing, and Related Support Services, 9% Biological and Biomedical Sciences, 8% Communication, Journalism, and Related Programs
Expenses: 2018-2019: $8,020 in state, $15,593 out of state; room/board: $7,760
Financial aid: (715) 425-3141; 66% of undergrads determined to have financial need; average aid package $6,820

University of Wisconsin–Stevens Point

Stevens Point WI
(715) 346-2441
U.S. News ranking: Reg. U. (Mid. W), No. 65
Website: www.uwsp.edu
Admissions email: admiss@uwsp.edu
Public; founded 1894
Freshman admissions: selective; 2017-2018: 3,368 applied, 3,062 accepted. Neither SAT nor ACT required. ACT 25/75 percentile: 20-25. High school rank: 11% in top tenth, 33% in top quarter, 69% in top half
Early decision deadline: N/A, notification date: N/A
Early action deadline: N/A, notification date: N/A
Application deadline (fall): rolling
Undergraduate student body: 7,166 full time, 664 part time; 47% male, 53% female; 0% American Indian, 3% Asian, 2% black, 4% Hispanic, 2% multiracial, 0% Pacific Islander, 86% white, 2% international; 88% from in state; 29% live on campus; 5% of students in fraternities, 5% in sororities
Most popular majors: 16% Wildlife, Fish and Wildlands Science and Management, 10% Business Administration and Management, General, 9% Health Professions and Related Clinical Sciences, Other, 8% Biology/Biological Sciences, General, 8% Elementary Education and Teaching
Expenses: 2018-2019: $8,209 in state, $16,476 out of state; room/board: $7,422
Financial aid: (715) 346-4771; 63% of undergrads determined to have financial need; average aid package $8,715

University of Wisconsin–Stout

Menomonie WI
(715) 232-1232
U.S. News ranking: Reg. U. (Mid. W), No. 80
Website: www.uwstout.edu
Admissions email: admissions@uwstout.edu
Public; founded 1891
Freshman admissions: selective; 2017-2018: 3,267 applied, 2,809 accepted. Either SAT or ACT required. ACT 25/75 percentile: 19-25. High school rank: 9% in top tenth, 31% in top quarter, 64% in top half
Early decision deadline: N/A, notification date: N/A
Early action deadline: N/A, notification date: N/A
Application deadline (fall): rolling
Undergraduate student body: 6,585 full time, 1,531 part time; 56% male, 44% female; 0% American Indian, 3% Asian, 2% black, 1% Hispanic, 4% multiracial, 0% Pacific Islander, 87% white, 2% international; 67% from in state; 40% live on campus; 2% of students in fraternities, 3% in sororities
Most popular majors: 35% Business, Management, Marketing, and Related Support Services, 9% Engineering Technologies and Engineering-Related Fields, 9% Visual and Performing Arts, 8% Family and Consumer Sciences/Human Sciences, 7% Computer and Information Sciences and Support Services
Expenses: 2018-2019: $9,456 in state, $17,423 out of state; room/board: $6,924
Financial aid: (715) 232-1363; 57% of undergrads determined to have financial need; average aid package $11,237

University of Wisconsin–Superior

Superior WI
(715) 394-8230
U.S. News ranking: Reg. Coll. (Mid. W), No. 35
Website: www.uwsuper.edu
Admissions email: admissions@uwsuper.edu
Public; founded 1893
Freshman admissions: selective; 2017-2018: 1,002 applied, 718 accepted. Either SAT or ACT required. ACT 25/75 percentile: 19-23. High school rank: 6% in top tenth, 26% in top quarter, 57% in top half
Early decision deadline: N/A, notification date: N/A
Early action deadline: N/A, notification date: N/A
Application deadline (fall): 8/1
Undergraduate student body: 1,828 full time, 540 part time; 38% male, 62% female; 2% American Indian, 1% Asian, 2% black, 3% Hispanic, 3% multiracial, 0% Pacific Islander, 80% white, 9% international; 51% from in state; 32% live on campus; 0% of students in fraternities, 0% in sororities
Most popular majors: 14% Biological and Biomedical Sciences, 13% Business, Management, Marketing, and Related Support Services, 13% Multi/Interdisciplinary Studies, 11% Education, 7% Public Administration and Social Service Professions
Expenses: 2018-2019: $15,682 in state, $15,682 out of state; room/board: $6,730
Financial aid: (715) 394-8200; 64% of undergrads determined to have financial need; average aid package $11,252

University of Wisconsin–Whitewater

Whitewater WI
(262) 472-1440
U.S. News ranking: Reg. U. (Mid. W), No. 65
Website: www.uww.edu
Admissions email: uwwadmit@mail.uww.edu
Public; founded 1868
Freshman admissions: selective; 2017-2018: 5,706 applied, 4,745 accepted. Either SAT or ACT required. ACT 25/75 percentile: 20-24. High school rank: 9% in top tenth, 30% in top quarter, 71% in top half
Early decision deadline: N/A, notification date: N/A
Early action deadline: N/A, notification date: N/A
Application deadline (fall): 5/1
Undergraduate student body: 9,806 full time, 1,322 part time; 51% male, 49% female; 0% American Indian, 2% Asian, 4% black, 6% Hispanic, 5% multiracial, 0% Pacific Islander, 82% white, 1% international; 84% from in state; 40% live on campus; 7% of students in fraternities, 6% in sororities
Most popular majors: 32% Business, Management, Marketing, and Related Support Services, 14% Education, 8% Communication, Journalism, and Related Programs, 8% Social Sciences, 6% Public Administration and Social Service Professions
Expenses: 2018-2019: $7,692 in state, $16,265 out of state; room/board: $6,786
Financial aid: (262) 472-1130; 58% of undergrads determined to have financial need; average aid package $8,582

Viterbo University[1]

La Crosse WI
(608) 796-3010
U.S. News ranking: Reg. U. (Mid. W), No. 124
Website: www.viterbo.edu
Admissions email: admission@viterbo.edu
Private
Application deadline (fall): N/A
Undergraduate student body: N/A full time, N/A part time
Expenses: 2017-2018: $27,150; room/board: $8,760
Financial aid: N/A

Wisconsin Lutheran College

Milwaukee WI
(414) 443-8811
U.S. News ranking: Reg. Coll. (Mid. W), No. 16
Website: www.wlc.edu
Admissions email: admissions@wlc.edu
Private; founded 1973
Affiliation: Wisconsin Evangelical Lutheran Synod
Freshman admissions: selective; 2017-2018: 708 applied, 639 accepted. Either SAT or ACT required. ACT 25/75 percentile: 20-26. High school rank: 12% in top tenth, 35% in top quarter, 71% in top half
Early decision deadline: N/A, notification date: N/A
Early action deadline: N/A, notification date: N/A
Application deadline (fall): rolling
Undergraduate student body: 921 full time, 71 part time; 45% male, 55% female; 1% American Indian, 2% Asian, 5% black, 6% Hispanic, 3% multiracial, 0% Pacific Islander, 82% white, 1% international; 76% from in state; 63% live on campus; N/A of students in fraternities, N/A in sororities
Most popular majors: 18% Business Administration, Management and Operations, Other, 13% Business Administration and Management, General, 7% Biology/Biological Sciences, General, 7% Kinesiology and Exercise Science, 7% Registered Nursing/Registered Nurse
Expenses: 2018-2019: $29,725; room/board: $10,190
Financial aid: (414) 443-8856; 82% of undergrads determined to have financial need; average aid package $22,824

WYOMING

University of Wyoming

Laramie WY
(307) 766-5160
U.S. News ranking: Nat. U., No. 183
Website: www.uwyo.edu
Admissions email: admissions@uwyo.edu
Public; founded 1886
Freshman admissions: selective; 2017-2018: 4,290 applied, 4,158 accepted. Either SAT or ACT required. ACT 25/75 percentile: 22-27. High school rank: 24% in top tenth, 51% in top quarter, 82% in top half
Early decision deadline: N/A, notification date: N/A
Early action deadline: N/A, notification date: N/A
Application deadline (fall): 8/10
Undergraduate student body: 8,281 full time, 1,510 part time; 50% male, 50% female; 0% American Indian, 1% Asian, 1% black, 7% Hispanic, 4% multiracial, 0% Pacific Islander, 71% white, 4% international; 67% from in state; 24% live on campus; 5% of students in fraternities, 5% in sororities
Most popular majors: 7% Registered Nursing/Registered Nurse, 6% Psychology, General, 5% Elementary Education and Teaching, 4% Criminal Justice/Safety Studies, 3% Petroleum Engineering
Expenses: 2018-2019: $5,400 in state, $17,490 out of state; room/board: $10,320
Financial aid: (307) 766-2116; 45% of undergrads determined to have financial need; average aid package $9,904

More @ usnews.com/bestcolleges

A

B

C

D

E

F

T

U

V

W

X, Y